The Quran
English Translation with Original Arabic Text

English Translation by:
Abdullah Yusuf Ali

Published by
Tahrike Tarsile Qur'an, Inc.
Publishers and Distributors of the Holy Qur'an
80-08 51st Avenue
Elmhurst, New York 11373-4141
Email: read@koranusa.org
http://www.koranusa.org

بسم الله الرحمن الرحيم

In the name of God, Most Gracious, Most Merciful

28th US Edition 2016

ISBN: 978-0-940368-08-8
Library of Congress Catalog Number: 2016936306
British Library Cataloguing in Publication Data

Published by
Tahrike Tarsile Qur'an, Inc.
Publishers and Distributors of the Holy Qur'an
80-08 51st Avenue
Elmhurst, New York 11373-4141
Email: read@koranusa.org
www.koranusa.org

Printed in India

FROM THE PREFACE TO FIRST EDITION,

1934

... It may be asked: Is there any need for a fresh English translation? To those who ask this question I commend a careful consideration of the facts which I have set out in my Note on Translation. After they have read it, I would invite them to take any particular passage, say 2: 74 or 2: 102, or 2:164 and compare it with any previous version they choose. If they find that I have helped them even the least bit further in understanding its meanings, or appreciating its beauty or catching something of the grandeur of the original, I would claim that my humble attempt is justified.

It is the duty of every Muslim, man, woman, or child, to read the Qur'ân and understand it according to his own capacity. If any one of us attains to some knowledge or understanding of it by study, contemplation, and the test of life, both outward and inward, it his duty, according to his capacity, to instruct others, and share with them the joy and peace which result from contact with the spiritual world. The Qur'ân-indeed every religious book-has to be read, not only with the tongue and voice and eyes, but with the best light that our intellect can supply, and even more, with the truest and purest light which our heart and conscience can give us. It is in this spirit that I would have my readers approach the Qur'ân.

It was between the age of four and five that I first learned to read its Arabic words, to revel in its rhythm and music and wonder at its meaning. I have a dim recollection of the *Khatm* ceremony which closed that stage. It was called "completion": it really just *began* a spiritual awakening that has gone on ever since. My revered father taught me Arabic, but I must have imbibed from him into my innermost being something more-something which told me that all the world's thoughts, all the world's most beautiful languages and literatures, are but vehicles for that ineffable message which comes to the heart in rare moments of ecstasy. The soul of mysticism and ecstasy is in the Qur'ân, as well as that plain guidance for the plain man which a world in a hurry affects to consider as sufficient. It is good to make this personal confession, to an age in which it is in the highest degree unfashionable to speak of religion or spiritual peace or consolation, an age in which words like these draw forth only derision, pity, or contempt.

I have explored Western lands, Western manners, and the depths of Western thought and Western learning to an extent which has rarely fallen to the lot of an Eastern mortal. But I have never lost touch with my Eastern heritage. Through all my successes and failures I have learned to rely more and more upon the one true thing in all life-the voice that speaks in a tongue above that of mortal man. For me the embodiment of that voice has been in the noble words of the Arabic Qur'ân, which I have tried to translate for myself and apply to my experience again and again. The service of the Qur'ân has been the pride and the privilege of many Muslims. I felt that with such life-experience as has fallen to my lot, my service to the Qur'ân should be to present it in a fitting garb in English. That ambition I have cherished in my mind for more than forty years. I have collected books and materials for it. I have visited places, undertaken journeys, taken notes, sought the society of men, and tried to explore their thoughts and hearts, in order to equip myself for the task. Sometimes I have considered it too stupendous for me-the double task of understanding the original, and reproducing its nobility, its beauty, its poetry, its grandeur, and its sweet, practical, reasonable application to everyday experience. Then I have blamed myself for lack of courage,- the spiritual courage of men who dared all in the Cause which was so dear to them.

Two sets of apparently accidental circumstances at last decided me. A man's life i s subj ect to inner storms far more devastating than those in the physical world around him. In such a storm, in the bitter anguish of a personal sorrow which nearly unseated my reason and made life seem meaningless, a new hope was born out of a systematic pursuit of my long-cherished project. Watered by tears, my manuscript began to grow in depth and earnestness if not in bulk. I guarded it like a secret treasure. Wanderer that I am, I carried it about, thousands of miles, to all sorts of countries and among all sorts of people. At length, in the city of Lahore, I happened to mention the matter to some young people who help me in respect and affection. They showed an enthusiasm and an eagerness which surprised me. They almost took the matter out of my hands. They asked for immediate publication, I had various bits ready, but not even one complete *Sipâra.* They made me promise to complete at least one *Sipâra* before I left Lahore. As it by magic, a publisher, a *kâtib* (calligraphist, to write the Arabic Text), an engraver of blocks for such text, and a printer were found, all equally anxious to push forward the scheme. Blessed be youth, for its energy and determination! "Where others flinch, rash youth will dare!"

Gentle and discerning reader! what I wish to present to you is an English Interpretation, side by side with the Arabic Text. The English shall be, not a mere substitution of one word for another, but the best expression I can give to the fullest meaning which I can understand from the Arabic Text. The rhythm, music, and exalted tone of the original should be reflected in the English Interpretation. It may be but a faint reflection, but such beauty and power as my pen commands shall be brought to its service. I want to make English itself an Islamic language, if such a person as I can do it. And I must give you all the necessary aid which I can....

The Text in English is printed... in parallel columns with the Arabic Text. Each *Sûra* and the verse of each *Sûra* is separately numbered, and the numbers are shown page by page. The system of numbering the verses has not been uniform in previous translations. European editors and translators have allowed their numbering to diverge considerably from that accepted in the East. This causes confusion in giving and verifying references. The different *Qirâats* sometimes differ as to the punctuation stops and the numbering of the verses. This is not a vital matter, but it causes confusion in references. It is important that at least in Islamic countries one system of numbering should be adopted. I have adopted mainly that of the Egyptian edition published under the authority of the King of Egypt. This will probably be accepted in Egypt and in Arabic-speaking countries, as those countries generally look up to Egypt in matters of literature. I am glad to see that the text ... published by the Anjuman-i-Himayat-i-Islam of Lahore is following the same system of numbering. I recommend to other publishers ... the same good example. If once this is done, we shall have a uniform system of numbering. I have retained the numbering of Sections as it is universally used in the Arabic copies, and marks a logical division of the *Sûras*. I have supplied a further aid to the reader in indicating sub-division of the Sections in to paragraphs. They are not numbered, but are distinguished by the use of a flowery initial letter....

... Every earnest and reverent student of the Qur'ân, as he proceeds with his study, will find, with an inward joy difficult to describe, how this general meaning also enlarges as his own capacity for understanding increases. It is like a traveler climbing a mountain; the higher he goes, the farther he sees. From a literary point of view the poet Keats has described his feeling when he discovered Chapman's Homer:

Then felt I like some watcher of the skies
When a new planet swims into his ken,
Or like stout Cortez when with eagle eyes.
He stared at the Pacific,-and all his men
Looked at each other with a wild surmise,-
Silent, upon a peak in Darien.

How much greater is the joy and sense of wonder and miracle when the Qur'ân opens our spiritual eyes! The meaning which we thought we had grasped expands. New words are opened out.-As we progress, still newer, and again newer worlds "swim into our ken". The miracle deepens and deepens, and almost completely absorbs us. And yet we know that the "face of God"-our final goal-has not yet been reached. We are in the *mulk* of Sulaiman (Q. 2: 102), which the evil ones denied, belied, and even turned into blasphemy. But we can ignore blasphemy, ridicule and contempt, for we are in the threshold of Realities and a little perfume from the garden of the Holy One has already gladdened our nostrils...

The Arabic Text I have had printed from photographic blocks, made for me by Master Muhammad Sharif. The calligraphy is from the pen of Pir Abdul Hamid, with whom I have been in touch and who has complied with my desire for a bold round hand, with the words clearly separated, the vowel points accurately placed over or under the letter to which they relate, and the verses duly numbered and placed in juxtaposition with their English equivalents. Calligraphy occupies an important place in Muslim Art, and it is my desire that my version should not in any way be deficient in this respect.

I have been fortunate in securing the co-operation of Professor Zafar Iqbal in looking over the proofs of the Arabic Text. In connection with the Anjuman's edition of the Arabic Qur'ân he has devoted much time and thought to the correct punctuation of the Text, and he has also investigated its history and problems. I hope he will some day publish these valuable notes. I have been privileged to see the Anjuman's Text before its formal Publication. I consider it the most carefully prepared Text of any produced in India and I have generally followed it in punctuation and the numbering of verses,-the only points on which my difficulties are likely to arise on the Qur'anic Text....

One final word to my readers. Read, study and digest the Holy Book. Read slowly, and let it sink into your heart and soul. Such study will, like virtue, be its own reward. If you find anything in this volume to criticise, please let it not spoil your enjoyment of the rest. If you write to me, quoting chapter and verse, I shall be glad to consider your criticism, but let it not vex you if I exercise my own judgment in deciding for myself. Any corrections accepted will be gratefully acknowledged. On the other hand, if there is something that specially pleases you or helps you, please do not hesitate to write to me. I have given up other interests to help you. It will be a pleasure to know that my labour has not been in vain. If you address me care of my Publisher at his Lahore address, he will always forward the letters to me.

A. YUSUF ALI

LAHORE
4th April, 1934
= 18th of the month of Pilgrimage 1352 H.

VIII
Index of Sûras – Chapters
(Showing The Makki and The Madani ones)

Arabic Words Explained

A comprehensive list of names, places and topics appears as an index at the end of the book. Here some oft-repeated Arabic words occurring in the translation are given with brief explanation.

ALLAH: The proper name of God in Arabic.

HAJJ: The pilgrimage to Makkah which takes place in the last month of the Islamic calendar.

IBLIS: Satan.

ISLAM: Literally, to submit.
The Religion of all the Prophets of Allah confirmed finally by the mission of the Prophet Muhammad ﷺ.

JINN: Invisible beings constituting a whole race like mankind.

MUHAJIR: Literally, the emigrant.
One who leaves the home town to join a Muslim community

MUSLIM: One who professes the faith of Islam or born to a Muslim family.

QIBLA: The Ka'ba. The direction for the daily prayers of a Muslim.

QUR'ÂN: Literally, the recital.
The final revelation given to the Prophet Muhammad ﷺ in Arabic.

RAMADAN: The ninth month of the Islamic calendar during which the Muslims fast.

SÛRAH: A chapter of the Qur'ân.

TAGUT: Literally, a tyrant, oppresser, false god, temper to error.
Tagut is applied to any object which is worshipped besides Allah.

UMRAH: A minor form of pilgrimage to Makkah.

UMMAH: Literally, a nation but is usually applied to the Muslim Brotherhood.

YATHRIB: The name by which Madinah was known before the Prophet's migration to that city.

ZAKAT: Literally, to grow, to purify.
The third pillar of Islam.
It is a definite portion of wealth which is given to needy at the turn of the year.

TRANSLITERATION OF ARABIC WORDS AND NAMES

Arabic	Translit.		Arabic	Translit.
ا ء	{ consonantal sound } a		ط	.... ṭ
أ	Long vowel ˙ â		ظ	.... ẓ
ب	.... b		ع	.... (inverted apostrophe)
ت	.... t		غ	.... g
ث	.... th		ف	.... f
ج	.... j		ق	.... q
ح	.... ḥ		ك	.... k
خ	.... kh		ل	 l
د	.... d		م	.... m
ذ	.... ẓ		ن	.... n
ر	.... r		ه ه	.... h
ز	.... z		و consonant	w
س	.... s		و long vowel ˙	û
ش	.... sh		و diphthong	au
ص	.... ṣ		ي consonant	y
ض	.... dh		ي long vowel ˙	î
			ي diphthong	ai

Short vowels: ــَ (*fatḥa*) a
ــِ (*kasra*) i
ــُ (*dhamma*) u

1. For the hamzâ (٠) I have used no distinctive sign. An apostrophe for it and an inverted apostrophe for the *'ain* (ع), or *vice versa*, is confusing to English readers. As a moved consonant, it is sufficiently <u>shown</u> in <u>English</u> by the long or short vowel which moves it, e.g. ab, Raûf.

˙ Where it is really pronounced long. Hence *Khalaqnâ-kum* but *khalaqnal-insân; Abû Sufyân* but *Abul-Qâsim; fin-nâr* but *fî-hi*.

Where it is a hiatus preceded by a *fatha,* 1 have shown it by a second a; thus, Iqraa, the cave of Hiraa. In other cases it has not been possible to show it without using a distinctive sign. The name of the Holy Book is usually written Qur'ân; but I prefer to write Qur'ân. However a few words like juz have an apostrophe indicating Hamza.

2. The final h preceded by the short a is scarcely pronounced, and I have left it out. Hence Sura, Fatiḥa, Hijrah, etc., where the Arabic spelling would require Surah, Fatiḥa, Hijrah, etc.

3. In internationalised word and names I have used the spelling ordinarily current in English; e.g. Mecca, Medina, Maulvi, Urud, Islam, Israel, Abraham, Jacob. Here the boundary is thin and rather ill-defined, and possibly my practice and that of my proof-readers have not been absolutely uniform. But in place of Mecca and Madina, the more accurate form of Makkah and Madinah is adopted.

**In the name of Allah,
Most Gracious, Most Merciful.**

SÛRAH-1
AL-FÂTIHA
(INTRODUCTION)

First comes this beautiful Sûrah, The Opening Chapter of Seven Verses, rightly called the Essence of the Book. It teaches us the perfect Prayer. For if we can pray aright, it means that we have some knowledge of Allah and His attributes, of His relations to us and His creation, which includes ourselves; that we glimpse the source from which we come, and that final goal which is our spiritual destiny under Allah's true judgement: then we offer ourselves to Allah and seek His light.

Prayer is the heart of Religion and Faith: but how shall we pray? What words shall convey the yearnings of our miserable, ignorant hearts to the Knower of all? Is it worth of Him or of our spiritual nature to ask for vanities, or even for such physical needs as our daily bread? The Inspired One taught us a Prayer that sums up our faith, our hope, and our aspiration in things that matter. We think in devotion of Allah's name and His Nature; we praise Him for His creation and His cherishing care; we call to mind the Realities, seen and unseen; we offer Him worship and ask for His guidance; and we know the straight from the crooked path by the light of His grace that illumines the righteous.

1. The Opening
In the name of Allah. Most Gracious, Most Merciful.

(١) سُوْرَةُ الْفَاتِحَةِ مَكِّيَّةٌ (٥)

بِسْمِ اللهِ الرَّحْمٰنِ الرَّحِيْمِ

1. Praise be to Allah, the Cherisher and Sustainer of the Worlds:

اَلْحَمْدُ لِلّٰهِ رَبِّ الْعٰلَمِيْنَ ۙ

الرَّحْمٰنِ الرَّحِيْمِ ۙ

2. Most Gracious, Most Merciful.

مٰلِكِ يَوْمِ الدِّيْنِ ؕ

3. Master of the Day of Judgment.

اِيَّاكَ نَعْبُدُ وَاِيَّاكَ نَسْتَعِيْنُ ؕ

4. You do we worship, and Your aid do we seek.

اِهْدِنَا الصِّرَاطَ الْمُسْتَقِيْمَ ۙ

5. Show us the straight way.

صِرَاطَ الَّذِيْنَ اَنْعَمْتَ عَلَيْهِمْ ۙ

6. The way of those on whom You have bestowed your Grace, those whose (portion) is not wrath, and who do not go astray.

غَيْرِ الْمَغْضُوْبِ عَلَيْهِمْ

وَلَا الضَّآلِّيْنَ ۧ

SÛRAH-2
AL-BAQARAH
(INTRODUCTION)

As the Opening Sûrah sums up in seven beautiful verses the essence of the Qur'ân, so this Sûrah sums up in 286 verses the whole teaching of the Qur'ân. It is a closely reasoned argument.

This is the longest Sûrah of the Qur'ân and in it occurs the longest verse (2:282). The name of the Sûrah is from the Parable of the Heifer in 2:67-71, which illustrates the insufficiency of carping obedience. When faith is lost, people put off obedience with various excuses: even when at last they obey in the letter, they fail in the spirit, which means that they get fossilised, and their self-sufficiency prevents them from seeing that spiritually they are not alive but dead. For life is movement, activity, striving, fighting, against baser things. And this is the burden of the Sûrah.

This is in the main an early Madinah Sûrah.

2. The Cow

In the name of Allah. Most Gracious, Most Merciful.

1. *Alif-Lam-Meem*

2. This is the Book; in it is guidance sure, without doubt, to those who fear Allah;

3. Who believe in the Unseen, are steadfast in prayer, and spend out of what We have provided for them;

4. And who believe in the Revelation sent to you, and sent before your time, and (in their hearts) have the assurance of the Hereafter.

5. They are on (true) guidance, from their Lord, and it is these who will prosper.

6. As to those who reject Faith, it is the same to them whether you warn them or do not warn them; they will not believe.

7. Allah has set a seal on their hearts and on their hearing. And on their eyes is a veil; great is the chastisement they (incur).

8. Of the people there are some who say: "We believe in Allah and the Last Day;" but they do not (really) believe.

9. Fain would they deceive Allah and those who believe, but they only deceive themselves, and realize (it) not!

10. In their hearts is a disease; and Allah has increased their disease: and grievous is the chastisement they (incur), because they are false (to themselves).

11. When it is said to them: "Make not mischief on the earth," they say: "Why, we only want to make peace!"

12. Of a surety, they are the ones who make mischief, but they realize (it) not.

أَلَا إِنَّهُمْ هُمُ الْمُفْسِدُونَ وَلٰكِنْ لَّا يَشْعُرُونَ ۝

13. When it is said to them: "Believe as the others believe:" They say: "Shall we believe as the fools believe?" Nay, of a surety they are the fools, but they do not know.

وَإِذَا قِيلَ لَهُمْ اٰمِنُوا كَمَا اٰمَنَ النَّاسُ قَالُوٓا أَنُؤْمِنُ كَمَا اٰمَنَ السُّفَهَآءُ أَلَا إِنَّهُمْ هُمُ السُّفَهَآءُ وَلٰكِنْ لَّا يَعْلَمُونَ ۝

14. When they meet those who believe, they say: "We believe;" but when they are alone with their evil ones, they say: "We are really with you: we (were) only jesting."

وَإِذَا لَقُوا الَّذِينَ اٰمَنُوا قَالُوٓا اٰمَنَّا وَإِذَا خَلَوْا إِلٰى شَيٰطِينِهِمْ قَالُوٓا إِنَّا مَعَكُمْ إِنَّمَا نَحْنُ مُسْتَهْزِءُونَ ۝

15. Allah will throw back their mockery on them, and give them rope in their trespasses; so they will wander like blind ones (to and fro).

اللهُ يَسْتَهْزِئُ بِهِمْ وَيَمُدُّهُمْ فِيْ طُغْيَانِهِمْ يَعْمَهُونَ ۝

16. These are they who have bartered guidance for error: but their traffic is profitless, and they have lost true direction.

أُولٰئِكَ الَّذِينَ اشْتَرَوُا الضَّلٰلَةَ بِالْهُدٰى فَمَا رَبِحَتْ تِجَارَتُهُمْ وَمَا كَانُوا مُهْتَدِينَ ۝

17. Their similitude is that of a man who kindled a fire; when it lighted all around him, Allah took away their light and left them in utter darkness, so they could not see.

مَثَلُهُمْ كَمَثَلِ الَّذِي اسْتَوْقَدَ نَارًا فَلَمَّا أَضَآءَتْ مَا حَوْلَهُ ذَهَبَ اللهُ بِنُورِهِمْ وَتَرَكَهُمْ فِيْ ظُلُمَاتٍ لَّا يُبْصِرُونَ ۝

18. Deaf, dumb, and blind, they will not return (to the path).

صُمٌّ بُكْمٌ عُمْيٌ فَهُمْ لَا يَرْجِعُونَ ۝

19. Or (another similitude) is that of a rain-laden cloud from the sky: In it are zones of darkness, and thunder and lightning: they press their fingers in their ears to keep out the stunning thunder-clap, the while they are in terror of death. But Allah is ever round the rejecters of Faith!

أَوْ كَصَيِّبٍ مِّنَ السَّمَآءِ فِيهِ ظُلُمَاتٌ وَّرَعْدٌ وَّبَرْقٌ يَجْعَلُونَ أَصَابِعَهُمْ فِيْ اٰذَانِهِمْ مِّنَ الصَّوَاعِقِ حَذَرَ الْمَوْتِ وَاللهُ مُحِيطٌ بِالْكَافِرِينَ ۝

20. The lightning all but snatches away their sight; every time the light (helps) them, they walk therein, and when the darkness grows on them, they stand still. And if Allah willed,

يَكَادُ الْبَرْقُ يَخْطَفُ أَبْصَارَهُمْ كُلَّمَا أَضَآءَ لَهُمْ مَّشَوْا فِيهِ وَإِذَا أَظْلَمَ عَلَيْهِمْ قَامُوا وَلَوْ شَآءَ اللهُ

He could take away their faculty of hearing and seeing; for Allah has power over all things.

21. O you people! Worship your Guardian-Lord, Who created you and those who came before you, that you my become righteous.

22. Who has made the earth your couch, and the heavens your canopy; and sent down rain from the heavens; and brought forth therewith fruits for your sustenance; then do not set up rivals unto Allah when you know (the truth).

23. And if you are in doubt as to what We have revealed from time to time to Our servant, then produce a Sura like thereof; and call your witnesses or helpers (if there are any) besides Allah, if you are truthful-

24. But if you cannot- and of a surety you cannot- then fear the Fire whose fuel is men and stones,- which is prepared for those who reject Faith.

25. But give glad tidings to those who believe and work righteous-ness, that their portion is Gardens beneath which rivers flow. Every time they are fed with fruits therefrom, they say: "Why, this is what we were fed with before," for they are given things in similitude; and they have therein spouses purified; and they abide therein (for ever).

26. Allah disdains not to use the similitude of things, lowest as well as highest. Those who

believe know that it is Truth from their Lord; but those who reject Faith say: "What means Allah by this similitude?" By it He causes many to stray, and many He leads into the right path; but He causes not to stray, except those who forsake (the path),-

27. Those who break Allah's Covenant after it is ratified, and who sunder what Allah has ordered to be joined, and do mischief on earth: these cause loss (only) to themselves.

28. How can you reject the Faith in Allah?- seeing that you were without life, and He gave you life; then will He cause you to die, and will again bring you to life; and again to Him will you return.

29. It is He Who has created for you all things that are on earth; moreover His design comprehends the heavens, for He gave order and perfection to the seven firmaments; and of all things He has perfect knowledge.

30. Behold, your Lord said to the angels: "I will create a vicegerent on earth." They said: "Will You place therein one who will make mischief therein and shed blood?- while we do celebrate Your praises and glorify Your holy (name)?" He said: "I know what you know not."

31. And He taught Adam the nature of all things; then He placed them before the angels, and said: "Tell Me the nature of these if you are right."

32. They said: "Glory to You, of knowledge we have none, save what You have taught us: in truth it is You Who are perfect in knowledge and wisdom."

33. He said: "O Adam! tell them their natures." When

he had told them, Allah said: "Did I not tell you that I know the secrets of heaven and earth, and I know what you reveal and what you conceal?"

34. And behold, We said to the angels: "Bow down to Adam" and they bowed down: not so Iblis: he refused and was haughty: he was of those who reject Faith.

35. We said: "O Adam! dwell you and your wife in the Garden; and eat of the bountiful things therein as (where and when) you will; but approach not this tree, or you run into harm and transgression."

36. Then did Satan make them slip from the (Garden), and get them out of the state (of felicity) in which they had been. We said: "Get you down, all (you people), with enmity between yourselves. On earth will be your dwelling-place and your means of livelihood for a time."

37. Then learnt Adam from his Lord words of inspiration, and his Lord turned towards him; for He is Oft-Returning, Most Merciful.

38. We said: "Get you down all from here; and if, as is sure, there comes to you Guidance from Me, whosoever follows My Guidance, on them shall be no fear, nor shall they grieve.

39. "But those who reject Faith and belie Our Signs, they shall be companions of the Fire; they shall abide therein."

40. O Children of Israel! call to mind the (special) favour which I bestowed upon you, and fulfil your Covenant with Me as I fulfil My Covenant with you, and fear none but Me.

41. And believe in what I reveal, confirming the revelation which is

with you, and be not the first to reject Faith therein, nor sell My Signs for a small price; and fear Me, and Me alone.

مَعَكُمْ وَلَا تَكُوْنُوْا أَوَّلَ كَافِرٍ بِهٖ وَلَا تَشْتَرُوْا بِاٰيٰتِيْ ثَمَنًا قَلِيْلًا وَّإِيَّايَ فَاتَّقُوْنِ ۞

42. And cover not Truth with falsehood, nor conceal the Truth when you know (what it is).

وَلَا تَلْبِسُوا الْحَقَّ بِالْبَاطِلِ وَتَكْتُمُوا الْحَقَّ وَأَنْتُمْ تَعْلَمُوْنَ ۞

43. And be steadfast in prayer; practise regular charity; and bow down your heads with those who bow down (in worship).

وَأَقِيْمُوا الصَّلٰوةَ وَاٰتُوا الزَّكٰوةَ وَارْكَعُوْا مَعَ الرّٰكِعِيْنَ ۞

44. Do you enjoin right conduct on the people, and forget (to practise it) yourselves, and yet you study the Scripture? Will you not understand?

أَتَأْمُرُوْنَ النَّاسَ بِالْبِرِّ وَتَنْسَوْنَ أَنْفُسَكُمْ وَأَنْتُمْ تَتْلُوْنَ الْكِتٰبَ ۚ أَفَلَا تَعْقِلُوْنَ ۞

45. Nay, seek (Allah's) help with patient perseverance and prayer: it is indeed hard, except to those who bring a lowly spirit,-

وَاسْتَعِيْنُوْا بِالصَّبْرِ وَالصَّلٰوةِ ۚ وَإِنَّهَا لَكَبِيْرَةٌ إِلَّا عَلَى الْخٰشِعِيْنَ ۞

46. Who bear in mind the certainty that they are to meet their Lord, and that they are to return to Him.

الَّذِيْنَ يَظُنُّوْنَ أَنَّهُمْ مُّلٰقُوْا رَبِّهِمْ وَأَنَّهُمْ إِلَيْهِ رٰجِعُوْنَ ۞

47. O Children of Israel! call to mind the (special) favour which I bestowed upon you, and that I preferred you to all others (for My Message).

يٰبَنِيْ إِسْرَآءِيْلَ اذْكُرُوْا نِعْمَتِيَ الَّتِيْ أَنْعَمْتُ عَلَيْكُمْ وَأَنِّيْ فَضَّلْتُكُمْ عَلَى الْعٰلَمِيْنَ ۞

48. Then guard yourselves against a day when one soul shall not avail another nor shall intercession be accepted for her, nor shall compensation be taken from her, nor shall anyone be helped (from outside).

وَاتَّقُوْا يَوْمًا لَّا تَجْزِيْ نَفْسٌ عَنْ نَّفْسٍ شَيْئًا وَّلَا يُقْبَلُ مِنْهَا شَفَاعَةٌ وَّلَا يُؤْخَذُ مِنْهَا عَدْلٌ وَّلَا هُمْ يُنْصَرُوْنَ ۞

49. And remember, We delivered you from the people of Pharaoh. They set you hard tasks and punishments, slaughtered your sons and let your women-folk live; therein was a tremendous trial from your Lord.

وَإِذْ نَجَّيْنٰكُمْ مِّنْ اٰلِ فِرْعَوْنَ يَسُوْمُوْنَكُمْ سُوْٓءَ الْعَذَابِ يُذَبِّحُوْنَ أَبْنَآءَكُمْ وَيَسْتَحْيُوْنَ نِسَآءَكُمْ ۚ وَفِيْ ذٰلِكُمْ بَلَآءٌ مِّنْ رَّبِّكُمْ عَظِيْمٌ ۞

50. And remember, We divided the sea for you and saved you and drowned Pharaoh's people within your very sight.

51. And remember We appointed forty nights for Moses, and in his absence, you took the calf (for worship), and you did grievous wrong.

52. Even then We did forgive you; there was a chance for you to be grateful.

53. And remember We gave Moses the Scripture and the Criterion (between right and wrong): there was a chance for you to be guided aright.

54. And remember, Moses said to his people: "O my people! you have indeed wronged yourselves by your worship of the calf: So turn (in repentance) to your Maker, and slay yourselves (the wrong-doers); that will be better for you in the sight of your Maker." Then He turned towards you (in forgiveness): for He is Oft-Returning, Most Merciful.

55. And remember, you said: "O Moses! we shall never believe in you until we see Allah manifestly," but you were dazed with thunder and lightning even as you looked on.

56. Then We raised you up after your death: you had the chance to be grateful.

57. And We gave you the shade of clouds and sent down to you manna and quails, saying: "Eat of the good things We have provided for you:" (But they rebelled); to Us they did no harm, but they harmed their own souls.

58. And remember, We said: "Enter this town, and eat of the plenty therein as you wish;

وَإِذْ فَرَقْنَا بِكُمُ الْبَحْرَ فَأَنْجَيْنَاكُمْ وَأَغْرَقْنَا آلَ فِرْعَوْنَ وَأَنْتُمْ تَنْظُرُوْنَ ۝

وَإِذْ وَاعَدْنَا مُوْسٰى أَرْبَعِيْنَ لَيْلَةً ثُمَّ اتَّخَذْتُمُ الْعِجْلَ مِنْ بَعْدِهٖ وَأَنْتُمْ ظٰلِمُوْنَ ۝

ثُمَّ عَفَوْنَا عَنْكُمْ مِّنْ بَعْدِ ذٰلِكَ لَعَلَّكُمْ تَشْكُرُوْنَ ۝

وَإِذْ اٰتَيْنَا مُوْسَى الْكِتٰبَ وَ الْفُرْقَانَ لَعَلَّكُمْ تَهْتَدُوْنَ ۝

وَإِذْ قَالَ مُوْسٰى لِقَوْمِهٖ يٰقَوْمِ إِنَّكُمْ ظَلَمْتُمْ أَنْفُسَكُمْ بِاتِّخَاذِكُمُ الْعِجْلَ فَتُوْبُوا إِلٰى بَارِئِكُمْ فَاقْتُلُوا أَنْفُسَكُمْ ذٰلِكُمْ خَيْرٌ لَّكُمْ عِنْدَ بَارِئِكُمْ فَتَابَ عَلَيْكُمْ إِنَّهٗ هُوَ التَّوَّابُ الرَّحِيْمُ ۝

وَإِذْ قُلْتُمْ يٰمُوْسٰى لَنْ نُّؤْمِنَ لَكَ حَتّٰى نَرَى اللّٰهَ جَهْرَةً فَأَخَذَتْكُمُ الصّٰعِقَةُ وَأَنْتُمْ تَنْظُرُوْنَ ۝

ثُمَّ بَعَثْنٰكُمْ مِّنْ بَعْدِ مَوْتِكُمْ لَعَلَّكُمْ تَشْكُرُوْنَ ۝

وَظَلَّلْنَا عَلَيْكُمُ الْغَمَامَ وَأَنْزَلْنَا عَلَيْكُمُ الْمَنَّ وَالسَّلْوٰى كُلُوْا مِنْ طَيِّبٰتِ مَا رَزَقْنٰكُمْ ۖ وَمَا ظَلَمُوْنَا وَلٰكِنْ كَانُوْا أَنْفُسَهُمْ يَظْلِمُوْنَ ۝

وَإِذْ قُلْنَا ادْخُلُوْا هٰذِهِ الْقَرْيَةَ فَكُلُوْا مِنْهَا حَيْثُ شِئْتُمْ رَغَدًا

but enter the gate with humility, in posture and in words, and We shall forgive you your faults and increase (the portion of) those who do good."

وَادْخُلُوا الْبَابَ سُجَّدًا وَّقُولُوا
حِطَّةٌ نَّغْفِرْ لَكُمْ خَطٰيٰكُمْ ۚ وَسَنَزِيْدُ
الْمُحْسِنِيْنَ ۟

59. But the transgressors changed the word from that which had been given them; so We sent on the transgressors a plague from heaven, for that they infringed (Our command) repeatedly.

فَبَدَّلَ الَّذِيْنَ ظَلَمُوا قَوْلًا غَيْرَ
الَّذِيْ قِيْلَ لَهُمْ فَاَنْزَلْنَا عَلَى الَّذِيْنَ
ظَلَمُوا رِجْزًا مِّنَ السَّمَآءِ بِمَا
كَانُوْا يَفْسُقُوْنَ ۟

60. And remember, Moses prayed for water for his people; We said: "Strike the rock with your staff." Then gushed forth therefrom twelve springs. Each group knew its own place for water. So eat and drink of the sustenance provided by Allah, and do no evil nor mischief on the (face of the) earth.

وَاِذِ اسْتَسْقٰى مُوْسٰى لِقَوْمِهٖ
فَقُلْنَا اضْرِبْ بِّعَصَاكَ الْحَجَرَ ۚ
فَانْفَجَرَتْ مِنْهُ اثْنَتَا عَشْرَةَ عَيْنًا ۚ
قَدْ عَلِمَ كُلُّ اُنَاسٍ مَّشْرَبَهُمْ ۚ كُلُوْا
وَاشْرَبُوْا مِنْ رِّزْقِ اللّٰهِ وَلَا تَعْثَوْا
فِى الْاَرْضِ مُفْسِدِيْنَ ۟

61. And remember, you said: "O Moses! we cannot endure one kind of food (always); so beseech your Lord for us to produce for us of what the earth grows, - its pot-herbs, and cucumbers, its garlic, lentils, and onions." He said: "Will you exchange the better for the worse? You go down to any town, and you shall find what you want!" They were covered with humiliation and misery; they drew on themselves the wrath of Allah. This because they went on rejecting the Signs of Allah and slaying His Messengers without just cause. This because they rebelled and went on transgressing.

وَاِذْ قُلْتُمْ يٰمُوْسٰى لَنْ نَّصْبِرَ عَلٰى
طَعَامٍ وَّاحِدٍ فَادْعُ لَنَا رَبَّكَ يُخْرِجْ
لَنَا مِمَّا تُنْبِتُ الْاَرْضُ مِنْ بَقْلِهَا
وَقِثَّآئِهَا وَفُوْمِهَا وَعَدَسِهَا وَبَصَلِهَا ۚ
قَالَ اَتَسْتَبْدِلُوْنَ الَّذِيْ هُوَ اَدْنٰى
بِالَّذِيْ هُوَ خَيْرٌ ۚ اِهْبِطُوْا مِصْرًا فَاِنَّ
لَكُمْ مَّا سَاَلْتُمْ ۗ وَضُرِبَتْ عَلَيْهِمُ
الذِّلَّةُ وَالْمَسْكَنَةُ ۗ وَبَآءُوْ بِغَضَبٍ
مِّنَ اللّٰهِ ۚ ذٰلِكَ بِاَنَّهُمْ كَانُوْا يَكْفُرُوْنَ
بِاٰيٰتِ اللّٰهِ وَيَقْتُلُوْنَ النَّبِيّٖنَ بِغَيْرِ
الْحَقِّ ۗ ذٰلِكَ بِمَا عَصَوْا وَّكَانُوْا
يَعْتَدُوْنَ ۟

62. Those who believe (in the Qur'an), and those who follow the Jewish (scriptures),

اِنَّ الَّذِيْنَ اٰمَنُوْا وَالَّذِيْنَ هَادُوْا

and the Christians and the Sabians, - and who believe in Allah and the Last Day, and work righteousness, shall have their reward with their Lord; on them shall be no fear, nor shall they grieve.

63. And remember, We took your Covenant and We raised above you (the towering height) of Mount (Sinai): (saying): "Hold firmly to what We have given you and bring (ever) to remembrance what is therein: perchance you may fear Allah."

64. But you turned back thereafter: had it not been for the Grace and Mercy of Allah to you, you had surely been among the lost.

65. And you knew well those amongst you who transgressed in the matter of the Sabbath: We said to them: "Be you apes, despised and rejected."

66. So We made it an example to their own time and to their posterity, and a lesson to those who fear Allah.

67. And remember, Moses said to his people: "Allah commands that you sacrifice a heifer". They said: Do you wish to make a laughing-stock of us?" He said: "May Allah save me from being an ignorant (fool)!"

68. They said: "Beseech on our behalf your Lord to make plain to us what (heifer) it is!" He said; "He says: the heifer should be neither too old nor too young, but of middling age: now do what you are commanded!"

69. They said: "Beseech on our behalf your Lord to make plain to us her colour." He said: "He says: A fawn-coloured heifer, pure and rich in tone, the admiration of beholders!"

وَالنَّصٰرٰى وَالصّٰبِئِيْنَ مَنْ اٰمَنَ بِاللّٰهِ وَالْيَوْمِ الْاٰخِرِ وَعَمِلَ صَالِحًا فَلَهُمْ اَجْرُهُمْ عِنْدَ رَبِّهِمْ ۚ وَلَا خَوْفٌ عَلَيْهِمْ وَلَا هُمْ يَحْزَنُوْنَ ۞

وَاِذْ اَخَذْنَا مِيْثَاقَكُمْ وَرَفَعْنَا فَوْقَكُمُ الطُّوْرَ ؕ خُذُوْا مَا اٰتَيْنٰكُمْ بِقُوَّةٍ وَّ اذْكُرُوْا مَا فِيْهِ لَعَلَّكُمْ تَتَّقُوْنَ ۞

ثُمَّ تَوَلَّيْتُمْ مِّنْ بَعْدِ ذٰلِكَ ۚ فَلَوْلَا فَضْلُ اللّٰهِ عَلَيْكُمْ وَرَحْمَتُهٗ لَكُنْتُمْ مِّنَ الْخٰسِرِيْنَ ۞

وَلَقَدْ عَلِمْتُمُ الَّذِيْنَ اعْتَدَوْا مِنْكُمْ فِى السَّبْتِ فَقُلْنَا لَهُمْ كُوْنُوْا قِرَدَةً خٰسِئِيْنَ ۞

فَجَعَلْنٰهَا نَكَالًا لِّمَا بَيْنَ يَدَيْهَا وَمَا خَلْفَهَا وَمَوْعِظَةً لِّلْمُتَّقِيْنَ ۞

وَاِذْ قَالَ مُوْسٰى لِقَوْمِهٖ اِنَّ اللّٰهَ يَأْمُرُكُمْ اَنْ تَذْبَحُوْا بَقَرَةً ؕ قَالُوْا اَتَتَّخِذُنَا هُزُوًا ؕ قَالَ اَعُوْذُ بِاللّٰهِ اَنْ اَكُوْنَ مِنَ الْجٰهِلِيْنَ ۞

قَالُوا ادْعُ لَنَا رَبَّكَ يُبَيِّنْ لَّنَا مَا هِيَ ؕ قَالَ اِنَّهٗ يَقُوْلُ اِنَّهَا بَقَرَةٌ لَّا فَارِضٌ وَّلَا بِكْرٌ ؕ عَوَانٌ بَيْنَ ذٰلِكَ ؕ فَافْعَلُوْا مَا تُؤْمَرُوْنَ ۞

قَالُوا ادْعُ لَنَا رَبَّكَ يُبَيِّنْ لَّنَا مَا لَوْنُهَا ؕ قَالَ اِنَّهٗ يَقُوْلُ اِنَّهَا بَقَرَةٌ صَفْرَآءُ ۙ فَاقِعٌ لَّوْنُهَا تَسُرُّ النّٰظِرِيْنَ ۞

70. They said: "Beseech on our behalf your Lord to make plain to us what she is: to us all heifers are alike: we wish indeed for guidance, if Allah wills."

قَالُوا ادْعُ لَنَا رَبَّكَ يُبَيِّنْ لَّنَا مَا هِىَ ۙ اِنَّ الْبَقَرَ تَشَابَهَ عَلَيْنَا ۙ وَاِنَّا اِنْ شَآءَ اللّٰهُ لَمُهْتَدُوْنَ ۞

71. He said: "He says: a heifer not trained to till the soil or water the fields; sound and without blemish". They said: "Now you has brought the truth." Then they offered her in sacrifice, but not with good-will.

قَالَ اِنَّهٗ يَقُوْلُ اِنَّهَا بَقَرَةٌ لَّا ذَلُوْلٌ تُثِيرُ الْاَرْضَ وَلَا تَسْقِى الْحَرْثَ ۚ مُسَلَّمَةٌ لَّا شِيَةَ فِيْهَا ۙ قَالُوا الْـٰٔنَ جِئْتَ بِالْحَقِّ ۚ فَذَبَحُوْهَا وَمَا كَادُوْا يَفْعَلُوْنَ ۞

72. Remember, you slew a man and fell into a dispute among yourselves as to the crime: but Allah was to bring forth what you did hide.

وَاِذْ قَتَلْتُمْ نَفْسًا فَادّٰرَءْتُمْ فِيْهَا ۖ وَاللّٰهُ مُخْرِجٌ مَّا كُنْتُمْ تَكْتُمُوْنَ ۞

73. So We said: "Strike the (body) with a piece of the (heifer)." Thus Allah brings the dead to life and shows you His Signs: perchance you may understand.

فَقُلْنَا اضْرِبُوْهُ بِبَعْضِهَا ۚ كَذٰلِكَ يُحْيِ اللّٰهُ الْمَوْتٰى ۙ وَيُرِيْكُمْ اٰيٰتِهٖ لَعَلَّكُمْ تَعْقِلُوْنَ ۞

74. Thenceforth your hearts were hardened: they became like a rock and even worse in hardness. For among rocks there are some from which rivers gush forth; others there are which when split asunder send forth water; and others which sink for fear of Allah. And Allah is not unmindful of what you do.

ثُمَّ قَسَتْ قُلُوْبُكُمْ مِّنْ بَعْدِ ذٰلِكَ فَهِىَ كَالْحِجَارَةِ اَوْ اَشَدُّ قَسْوَةً ۚ وَاِنَّ مِنَ الْحِجَارَةِ لَمَا يَتَفَجَّرُ مِنْهُ الْاَنْهٰرُ ۚ وَاِنَّ مِنْهَا لَمَا يَشَّقَّقُ فَيَخْرُجُ مِنْهُ الْمَآءُ ۚ وَاِنَّ مِنْهَا لَمَا يَهْبِطُ مِنْ خَشْيَةِ اللّٰهِ ۗ وَمَا اللّٰهُ بِغَافِلٍ عَمَّا تَعْمَلُوْنَ ۞

75. Can you (O you men of Faith) entertain the hope that they will believe in you?- seeing that a party of them heard the Word of Allah, and perverted it knowingly after they understood it.

اَفَتَطْمَعُوْنَ اَنْ يُّؤْمِنُوْا لَكُمْ وَقَدْ كَانَ فَرِيْقٌ مِّنْهُمْ يَسْمَعُوْنَ كَلَامَ اللّٰهِ ثُمَّ يُحَرِّفُوْنَهٗ مِنْ بَعْدِ مَا عَقَلُوْهُ وَهُمْ يَعْلَمُوْنَ ۞

76. Behold! when they meet the men of Faith, they say: "We believe": but when they meet each other in private,

وَاِذَا لَقُوا الَّذِيْنَ اٰمَنُوا قَالُوْا اٰمَنَّا ۚ وَاِذَا خَلَا بَعْضُهُمْ اِلٰى بَعْضٍ

they say: "Shall you tell them what Allah has revealed to you, that they may engage you in argument about it before your Lord?"- do you not understand (their aim)?

77. Do they not know that Allah knows what they conceal and what they reveal?

78. And there are among them illiterates, who do not know the Book, but (see therein their own) desires, and they do nothing but conjecture.

79. Then woe to those who write the Book with their own hands, and then say:"This is from Allah," to traffic with it for a miserable price!- Woe to them for what their hands do write, and for the gain they make thereby.

80. And they say: "The Fire shall not touch us but for a few numbered days:" say: "Have you taken a promise from Allah, for He never breaks His promise? or is it that you say of Allah what you do not know?"

81. Nay, those who seek gain in evil, and are girt round by their sins,- they are Companions of the Fire: therein shall they abide (for ever).

82. But those who have faith and work righteousness, they are Companions of the Garden: therein shall they abide (for ever).

83. And remember, We took a Covenant from the Children of Israel (to this effect): worship none but Allah; treat with kindness your parents and kindred, and orphans and those in need; speak fair to the people;

قَالُوْٓا اَتُحَدِّثُوْنَهُمْ بِمَا فَتَحَ اللّٰهُ
عَلَيْكُمْ لِيُحَآجُّوْكُمْ بِهٖ عِنْدَ
رَبِّكُمْ ؕ اَفَلَا تَعْقِلُوْنَ ۝

اَوَلَا يَعْلَمُوْنَ اَنَّ اللّٰهَ يَعْلَمُ
مَا يُسِرُّوْنَ وَمَا يُعْلِنُوْنَ ۝

وَمِنْهُمْ اُمِّيُّوْنَ لَا يَعْلَمُوْنَ الْكِتٰبَ
اِلَّآ اَمَانِيَّ وَاِنْ هُمْ اِلَّا يَظُنُّوْنَ ۝

فَوَيْلٌ لِّلَّذِيْنَ يَكْتُبُوْنَ الْكِتٰبَ
بِاَيْدِيْهِمْ ٞ ثُمَّ يَقُوْلُوْنَ هٰذَا مِنْ
عِنْدِ اللّٰهِ لِيَشْتَرُوْا بِهٖ ثَمَنًا قَلِيْلًا ؕ
فَوَيْلٌ لَّهُمْ مِّمَّا كَتَبَتْ اَيْدِيْهِمْ
وَوَيْلٌ لَّهُمْ مِّمَّا يَكْسِبُوْنَ ۝

وَقَالُوا لَنْ تَمَسَّنَا النَّارُ اِلَّآ اَيَّامًا
مَّعْدُوْدَةً ؕ قُلْ اَتَّخَذْتُمْ عِنْدَ اللّٰهِ
عَهْدًا فَلَنْ يُّخْلِفَ اللّٰهُ عَهْدَهٗٓ اَمْ
تَقُوْلُوْنَ عَلَى اللّٰهِ مَا لَا تَعْلَمُوْنَ ۝

بَلٰى مَنْ كَسَبَ سَيِّئَةً وَّاَحَاطَتْ
بِهٖ خَطِيْٓئَتُهٗ فَاُولٰٓئِكَ اَصْحٰبُ النَّارِ ۚ
هُمْ فِيْهَا خٰلِدُوْنَ ۝

وَالَّذِيْنَ اٰمَنُوْا وَعَمِلُوا الصّٰلِحٰتِ
اُولٰٓئِكَ اَصْحٰبُ الْجَنَّةِ ۚ هُمْ فِيْهَا
خٰلِدُوْنَ ۝

وَاِذْ اَخَذْنَا مِيْثَاقَ بَنِيْٓ اِسْرَآئِيْلَ
لَا تَعْبُدُوْنَ اِلَّا اللّٰهَ ۫ وَبِالْوَالِدَيْنِ
اِحْسَانًا وَّذِي الْقُرْبٰى وَالْيَتٰمٰى
وَالْمَسٰكِيْنِ وَقُوْلُوْا لِلنَّاسِ حُسْنًا

be steadfast in prayer; and practise regular charity. Then you turned back, except a few among you, and you backslide (even now).

وَاَقِيْمُوا الصَّلٰوةَ وَاٰتُوا الزَّكٰوةَ ۚ ثُمَّ تَوَلَّيْتُمْ اِلَّا قَلِيْلًا مِّنْكُمْ وَاَنْتُمْ مُّعْرِضُوْنَ ۞

84. And remember We took your Covenant (to this effect): shed no blood amongst you, nor turn out your own people from your homes: and this you solemnly ratified, and to this you can bear witness.

وَاِذْ اَخَذْنَا مِيْثَاقَكُمْ لَا تَسْفِكُوْنَ دِمَآءَكُمْ وَلَا تُخْرِجُوْنَ اَنْفُسَكُمْ مِّنْ دِيَارِكُمْ ثُمَّ اَقْرَرْتُمْ وَاَنْتُمْ تَشْهَدُوْنَ ۞

85. After this it is you, the same people, who slay among yourselves, and banish a party of you from their homes; assist (their enemies) against them, in guilt and rancour; and if they come to you as captives, you ransom them, though it was not lawful for you to banish them. Then is it only a part of the Book that you believe in, and do you reject the rest? But what is the reward for those among you who behave like this but disgrace in this life?- and on the Day of Judgment they shall be consigned to the most grievous Chastisement. For Allah is not unmindful of what you do.

ثُمَّ اَنْتُمْ هٰٓؤُلَآءِ تَقْتُلُوْنَ اَنْفُسَكُمْ وَتُخْرِجُوْنَ فَرِيْقًا مِّنْكُمْ مِّنْ دِيَارِهِمْ تَظٰهَرُوْنَ عَلَيْهِمْ بِالْاِثْمِ وَالْعُدْوَانِ ۚ وَاِنْ يَّاْتُوْكُمْ اُسٰرٰى تُفٰدُوْهُمْ وَهُوَ مُحَرَّمٌ عَلَيْكُمْ اِخْرَاجُهُمْ ۚ اَفَتُؤْمِنُوْنَ بِبَعْضِ الْكِتٰبِ وَتَكْفُرُوْنَ بِبَعْضٍ ۚ فَمَا جَزَآءُ مَنْ يَّفْعَلُ ذٰلِكَ مِنْكُمْ اِلَّا خِزْيٌ فِى الْحَيٰوةِ الدُّنْيَا ۚ وَيَوْمَ الْقِيٰمَةِ يُرَدُّوْنَ اِلٰٓى اَشَدِّ الْعَذَابِ ۗ وَمَا اللّٰهُ بِغَافِلٍ عَمَّا تَعْمَلُوْنَ ۞

86. These are the people who buy the life of this world at the price of the Hereafter: their Chastisement shall not be lightened nor shall they be helped.

اُولٰٓئِكَ الَّذِيْنَ اشْتَرَوُا الْحَيٰوةَ الدُّنْيَا بِالْاٰخِرَةِ ۫ فَلَا يُخَفَّفُ عَنْهُمُ الْعَذَابُ وَلَا هُمْ يُنْصَرُوْنَ ۞

87. We gave Moses the Book and followed him up with a succession of Apostles; We gave Jesus the son of Mary, clear (Signs) and strengthened him with the holy spirit. Is it that whenever there comes to you an Apostle with what you your-selves do not desire, you are puffed up with pride?-

وَلَقَدْ اٰتَيْنَا مُوْسَى الْكِتٰبَ وَقَفَّيْنَا مِنْ بَعْدِهٖ بِالرُّسُلِ ۫ وَاٰتَيْنَا عِيْسَى ابْنَ مَرْيَمَ الْبَيِّنٰتِ وَاَيَّدْنٰهُ بِرُوْحِ الْقُدُسِ ۗ اَفَكُلَّمَا جَآءَكُمْ رَسُوْلٌ بِمَا لَا تَهْوٰى اَنْفُسُكُمُ اسْتَكْبَرْتُمْ

some you called impostors, and others you slay!

88. They say, "Our hearts are the wrappings (which preserve Allah's Word: we need no more)." Nay, Allah's curse is on them for their blasphemy: little is it they believe.

89. And when there comes to them a Book from Allah, confirming what is with them,- although from of old they had prayed for victory against those without Faith,- when there comes to them that which they (should) have recognized, they refuse to believe in it but the curse of Allah is on those without Faith.

90. Miserable is the price for which they have sold their souls, in that they deny (the revelation) which Allah has sent down, in insolent envy that Allah of His Grace should send it to any of His servants He pleases: thus they have drawn on themselves Wrath upon Wrath. And humiliating is the punishment of those who reject Faith.

91. When it is said to them, "Believe in what Allah has sent down," they say, "We believe in what was sent down to us:" yet they reject all besides, even if it be Truth confirming what is with them. Say: "Why then have you slain the prophets of Allah in times gone by, if you did indeed believe?"

92. There came to you Moses with clear (Signs); yet you worshipped the Calf (even) after that, and you did behave wrongfully.

93. And remember, We took your Covenant and We raised above you (the towering height) of Mount (Sinai): (saying): "Hold firmly to what We have given you and hearken (to the Law)": they said: "We hear, and we disobey:" and they had to drink into their hearts (of the taint) of the Calf

فَفَرِيقًا كَذَّبْتُمْ وَفَرِيقًا تَقْتُلُونَ ۝

وَقَالُوا قُلُوبُنَا غُلْفٌ ۚ بَل لَّعَنَهُمُ اللّٰهُ بِكُفْرِهِمْ فَقَلِيلًا مَّا يُؤْمِنُونَ ۝

وَلَمَّا جَاءَهُمْ كِتَبٌ مِّنْ عِنْدِ اللّٰهِ مُصَدِّقٌ لِّمَا مَعَهُمْ ۙ وَكَانُوا مِن قَبْلُ يَسْتَفْتِحُونَ عَلَى الَّذِينَ كَفَرُوا ۖ فَلَمَّا جَاءَهُم مَّا عَرَفُوا كَفَرُوا بِهِ ۚ فَلَعْنَةُ اللّٰهِ عَلَى الْكَٰفِرِينَ ۝

بِئْسَمَا اشْتَرَوْا بِهِ أَنفُسَهُمْ أَن يَكْفُرُوا بِمَا أَنزَلَ اللّٰهُ بَغْيًا أَن يُنَزِّلَ اللّٰهُ مِن فَضْلِهِ عَلَىٰ مَن يَشَآءُ مِنْ عِبَادِهِ ۖ فَبَاءُو بِغَضَبٍ عَلَىٰ غَضَبٍ ۚ وَلِلْكَٰفِرِينَ عَذَابٌ مُّهِينٌ ۝

وَإِذَا قِيلَ لَهُمْ آمِنُوا بِمَا أَنزَلَ اللّٰهُ قَالُوا نُؤْمِنُ بِمَا أُنزِلَ عَلَيْنَا وَيَكْفُرُونَ بِمَا وَرَآءَهُ وَهُوَ الْحَقُّ مُصَدِّقًا لِّمَا مَعَهُمْ ۗ قُلْ فَلِمَ تَقْتُلُونَ أَنبِيَآءَ اللّٰهِ مِن قَبْلُ إِن كُنتُم مُّؤْمِنِينَ ۝

وَلَقَدْ جَاءَكُم مُّوسَىٰ بِالْبَيِّنَٰتِ ثُمَّ اتَّخَذْتُمُ الْعِجْلَ مِنۢ بَعْدِهِ وَأَنتُمْ ظَٰلِمُونَ ۝

وَإِذْ أَخَذْنَا مِيثَٰقَكُمْ وَرَفَعْنَا فَوْقَكُمُ الطُّورَ خُذُوا مَا آتَيْنَٰكُم بِقُوَّةٍ وَاسْمَعُوا ۖ قَالُوا سَمِعْنَا وَعَصَيْنَا وَأُشْرِبُوا فِي قُلُوبِهِمُ الْعِجْلَ

because of their Faithlessness. Say: "Vile indeed are the behests of your Faith if you have any faith!"

94. Say: "If the last Home, with Allah, be for you specially, and not for anyone else, then you seek for death, if you are sincere."

95. But they will never seek for death, on account of the (sins) which their hands have sent on before them. And Allah is well-acquainted with the wrong-doers.

96. You will indeed find them, of all people, most greedy of life,- even more than the idolators: each one of them wishes he could be given a life of a thousand years: but the grant of such life will not save him from (due) punishment. For Allah sees well all that they do.

97. Say: Whoever is an enemy to Gabriel - for he brings down the (revelation) to your heart by Allah's will, a confirmation of what went before, and guidance and glad tidings for those who believe,

98. Whoever is an enemy to Allah and His Angels and Apostles, to Gabriel and Michael,- certainly Allah is an enemy to those who reject Faith.

99. We have sent down to you Manifest Signs (ayaat); and none reject them but those who are perverse.

100. Is it not (the case) that every time they make a Covenant, some party among them throw it aside?- Nay, most of them are faithless.

101. And when there came to them an Apostle from Allah, confirming what was with them, a party of the People of the Book threw away the Book of Allah

behind their backs, as if (it had been something) they did not know!

102. They followed what the evil ones gave out (falsely) against the power of Solomon: the blasphemers were, not Solomon, but the evil ones, teaching men magic, and such things as came down at Babylon to the angels Harut and Marut. But neither of these taught anyone (such things) without saying: "We are only for trial; so do not blaspheme." They learned from them the means to sow discord between man and wife. But they could not thus harm anyone except by Allah's permission. And they learned what harmed them, not what profited them. And they knew that the buyers of (magic) would have no share in the happiness of the Hereafter. And vile was the price for which they did sell their souls, if they but knew!

103. If they had kept their Faith and guarded themselves from evil, far better had been the reward from their Lord, if they but knew!

104. O you who believe! say not (to the Apostle) words of ambiguous import, but words of respect; and hearken (to him): to those without Faith is a grievous punishment.

105. It is never the wish of those without Faith among the People of the Book, nor of the Pagans, that anything good should come down to you from your Lord. But Allah will choose for His special Mercy whom He will - for Allah is Lord of grace abounding.

وَرَآءَ ظُهُوْرِهِمْ كَأَنَّهُمْ لَا يَعْلَمُوْنَ ۝

وَاتَّبَعُوْا مَا تَتْلُوا الشَّيٰطِيْنُ عَلٰى

مُلْكِ سُلَيْمٰنَ ۚ وَمَا كَفَرَ سُلَيْمٰنُ

وَلٰكِنَّ الشَّيٰطِيْنَ كَفَرُوْا يُعَلِّمُوْنَ

النَّاسَ السِّحْرَ ۚ وَمَا أُنْزِلَ عَلَى

الْمَلَكَيْنِ بِبَابِلَ هَارُوْتَ وَمَارُوْتَ ۚ

وَمَا يُعَلِّمٰنِ مِنْ أَحَدٍ حَتّٰى يَقُوْلَآ

اِنَّمَا نَحْنُ فِتْنَةٌ فَلَا تَكْفُرْ ۚ فَيَتَعَلَّمُوْنَ

مِنْهُمَا مَا يُفَرِّقُوْنَ بِهٖ بَيْنَ الْمَرْءِ

وَزَوْجِهٖ ۚ وَمَا هُمْ بِضَآرِّيْنَ بِهٖ

مِنْ أَحَدٍ اِلَّا بِاِذْنِ اللّٰهِ ۚ وَيَتَعَلَّمُوْنَ

مَا يَضُرُّهُمْ وَلَا يَنْفَعُهُمْ ۚ وَلَقَدْ

عَلِمُوْا لَمَنِ اشْتَرٰىهُ مَا لَهٗ فِى الْاٰخِرَةِ

مِنْ خَلَاقٍ ۚ وَلَبِئْسَ مَا شَرَوْا بِهٖٓ

أَنْفُسَهُمْ ۚ لَوْ كَانُوْا يَعْلَمُوْنَ ۝

وَلَوْ أَنَّهُمْ اٰمَنُوْا وَاتَّقَوْا لَمَثُوْبَةٌ

مِنْ عِنْدِ اللّٰهِ خَيْرٌ ۚ لَوْ كَانُوْا

يَعْلَمُوْنَ ۝

يٰٓأَيُّهَا الَّذِيْنَ اٰمَنُوْا لَا تَقُوْلُوْا

رَاعِنَا وَقُوْلُوا انْظُرْنَا وَاسْمَعُوْا ۚ

وَلِلْكٰفِرِيْنَ عَذَابٌ اَلِيْمٌ ۝

مَا يَوَدُّ الَّذِيْنَ كَفَرُوْا مِنْ أَهْلِ

الْكِتٰبِ وَلَا الْمُشْرِكِيْنَ أَنْ يُنَزَّلَ

عَلَيْكُمْ مِنْ خَيْرٍ مِّنْ رَّبِّكُمْ ۚ وَاللّٰهُ

يَخْتَصُّ بِرَحْمَتِهٖ مَنْ يَّشَآءُ ۚ وَاللّٰهُ

ذُو الْفَضْلِ الْعَظِيْمِ ۝

106. None of Our revelations do We abrogate or cause to be forgotten, but We substitute something better or similar: don't you know that Allah has power over all things?

مَا نَنْسَخْ مِنْ اٰيَةٍ أَوْ نُنْسِهَا نَأْتِ بِخَيْرٍ مِّنْهَا أَوْ مِثْلِهَا ۚ أَلَمْ تَعْلَمْ أَنَّ اللّٰهَ عَلٰى كُلِّ شَيْءٍ قَدِيْرٌ ۝

107. Don't you know that to Allah belongs the dominion of the heavens and the earth? And besides Him you have neither patron nor helper.

أَلَمْ تَعْلَمْ أَنَّ اللّٰهَ لَهُ مُلْكُ السَّمٰوٰتِ وَالْأَرْضِ ۚ وَمَا لَكُمْ مِّنْ دُوْنِ اللّٰهِ مِنْ وَّلِيٍّ وَّلَا نَصِيْرٍ ۝

108. Would you question your Apostle as Moses was questioned of old? But whoever changes from Faith to Unbelief, has strayed without doubt from the even way.

أَمْ تُرِيْدُوْنَ أَنْ تَسْئَلُوْا رَسُوْلَكُمْ كَمَا سُئِلَ مُوْسٰى مِنْ قَبْلُ ۗ وَمَنْ يَّتَبَدَّلِ الْكُفْرَ بِالْإِيْمَانِ فَقَدْ ضَلَّ سَوَاءَ السَّبِيْلِ ۝

109. Quite a number of the People of the Book wish they could turn you (people) back to infidelity after you have believed, from selfish envy, after the Truth has become manifest unto them: but forgive and overlook, till Allah accomplish His purpose; for Allah has power over all things.

وَدَّ كَثِيْرٌ مِّنْ أَهْلِ الْكِتٰبِ لَوْ يَرُدُّوْنَكُمْ مِّنْ بَعْدِ إِيْمَانِكُمْ كُفَّارًا ۚ حَسَدًا مِّنْ عِنْدِ أَنْفُسِهِمْ مِّنْ بَعْدِ مَا تَبَيَّنَ لَهُمُ الْحَقُّ ۚ فَاعْفُوْا وَاصْفَحُوْا حَتّٰى يَأْتِيَ اللّٰهُ بِأَمْرِهِ ۗ إِنَّ اللّٰهَ عَلٰى كُلِّ شَيْءٍ قَدِيْرٌ ۝

110. And be steadfast in prayer and regular in charity: and whatever good you send forth for your souls before you, you shall find it with Allah: for Allah sees well all that you do.

وَأَقِيْمُوا الصَّلٰوةَ وَاٰتُوا الزَّكٰوةَ ۚ وَمَا تُقَدِّمُوْا لِأَنْفُسِكُمْ مِّنْ خَيْرٍ تَجِدُوْهُ عِنْدَ اللّٰهِ ۗ إِنَّ اللّٰهَ بِمَا تَعْمَلُوْنَ بَصِيْرٌ ۝

111. And they say: "None shall enter Paradise unless he be a Jew or a Christian." Those are their (vain) desires. Say: "Produce your proof if you are truthful."

وَقَالُوْا لَنْ يَّدْخُلَ الْجَنَّةَ إِلَّا مَنْ كَانَ هُوْدًا أَوْ نَصَارٰى ۗ تِلْكَ أَمَانِيُّهُمْ ۗ قُلْ هَاتُوْا بُرْهَانَكُمْ إِنْ كُنْتُمْ صٰدِقِيْنَ ۝

112. Nay,- whoever submits his whole self to Allah and is a doer of good,- he will get his reward with his Lord; on such

بَلٰى ۚ مَنْ أَسْلَمَ وَجْهَهُ لِلّٰهِ وَهُوَ مُحْسِنٌ فَلَهُ أَجْرُهُ عِنْدَ رَبِّهِ ۚ وَلَا

shall be no fear, nor shall they grieve.

113. The Jews say: "The Christians have nothing (to stand) upon"; and the Christians say: "The Jews have nothing (to stand) upon." Yet they (profess to) study the (same) Book. Like unto their word is what those say who do not know; but Allah will judge between them in their dispute on the Day of Judgment.

114. And who is more unjust than he who forbids that in places for the worship of Allah, Allah's name should be celebrated?-whose zeal is (in fact) to ruin them? It was not fitting that such should themselves enter them except in fear. For them there is nothing but disgrace in this world, and in the world to come, an exceeding torment.

115. To Allah belong the East and the West: whithersoever you turn, there is the presence of Allah. For Allah is All-Pervading, All-Knowing.

116. They say: "Allah has begotten a son": glory be to Him.-Nay, to Him belongs all that is in the heavens and on earth: everything renders worship to Him.

117. To Him is due the primal origin of the heavens and the earth: when He decrees a matter, He says to it: "Be," and it is.

118. Those without knowledge say: "Why does not Allah speak to us? Or why does not a Sign come to us?" So said the people before them words of similar import. Their hearts are alike. We have indeed made clear the Signs for any people who hold firmly to Faith (in their hearts).

119. Surely We have sent you in truth as a bearer of glad tidings and a warner: but of you no question shall be asked of the Companions of the Blazing Fire.

120. Never will the Jews or the Christians be satisfied with you unless you follow their form of religion. Say: "The Guidance of Allah,- that is the (only) Guidance." If you were to follow their desires after the knowledge which has reached you, then you would find neither Protector nor Helper against Allah.

121. Those to whom We have sent the Book study it as it should be studied: they are the ones that believe therein: those who reject faith therein, - the loss is their own.

122. O Children of Israel! call to mind the special favour which I bestowed upon you, and that I preferred you to all others (for My Message).

123. Then guard yourselves against a Day when one soul shall not avail another, nor shall compensation be accepted from her nor shall intercession profit her nor shall anyone be helped (from outside).

124. And remember that Abraham was tried by his Lord with certain commands, which he fulfilled: He said: "I will make you an Imam to the Nations." He pleaded: "And also (Imams) from my offspring!" He answered: "But My Promise is not within the reach of evil-doers."

125. And remember, We made the House a place of assembly for men and a place of safety; and you take the Station of Abraham as a place of prayer; and We covenanted with Abraham and Isma'il, that they should sanctify My House for those who compass it round,

or use it as a retreat, or bow, or prostrate themselves (therein in prayer).

126. And remember, Abraham said: "My Lord, make this a City of Peace, and feed its people with fruits,- such of them as believe in Allah and the Last Day." He said: "(Yes), and such as reject Faith,- for a while will I grant them their pleasure, but will soon drive them to the torment of Fire, - an evil destination (indeed)!"

127. And remember, Abraham and Isma'il raised the foundations of the House (with this prayer): "Our Lord! accept (this service) from us: for You are the All-Hearing, the All-Knowing.

128. "Our Lord! make of us Muslims, bowing to Your (Will), and of our progeny a people Muslim, bowing to Your (Will); and show us our places for the celebration of (due) rites; and turn unto us (in Mercy); for You are the Oft-Returning, Most Merciful.

129. "Our Lord! send amongst them an Apostle of their own, who shall rehearse Your Signs to them and instruct them in Scripture and Wisdom, and sanctify them: for You are the Exalted in Might, the Wise."

130. And who turns away from the religion of Abraham but such as debase their souls with folly? Him We chose and rendered pure in this world: and he will be in the Hereafter in the ranks of the Righteous.

131. Behold! his Lord said to him: "Bow (your will to Me):" he said: "I bow (my will) to the Lord and Cherisher of the Universe."

132. And this was the legacy that Abraham left to his sons, and so did Jacob; "Oh my sons! Allah has chosen the Faith for you;

then do not die except in the Faith of Islam."

133. Were you witnesses when Death appeared before Jacob? Behold, he said to his sons: "What will you worship after me?" They said: "We shall worship your God (Allah) and the God (Allah) of your fathers, of Abraham, Isma'il and Isaac, - the One (True) God (Allah): to Him we bow (in Islam)."

134. That was a people who have passed away. They shall reap the fruit of what they did, and you of what you do! Of their merits there is no question in your case!

135. They say: "Become Jews or Christians if you would be guided (to salvation)." You say: "Nay! (I would rather) the Religion of Abraham the True, and he joined not gods with Allah."

136. You say: "We believe in Allah, and the revelation given to us, and to Abraham, Isma'il, Isaac, Jacob, and the Tribes, and that given to Moses and Jesus, and that given to (all) prophets from their Lord: we make no difference between one and another of them: and we bow to Allah (in Islam)."

137. So if they believe as you believe, they are indeed on the right path; but if they turn back, it is they who are in schism; but Allah will suffice you as against them, and He is the All-Hearing, the All-Knowing.

138. (Our religion is) the Baptism of Allah: and who can baptize better than Allah? And it is He Whom we worship.

139. Say: Will you dispute with us about Allah, seeing that He is our Lord and your Lord; that we are responsible for our doings and you for

yours; and that we are sincere (in our faith) in Him?

140. Or do you say that Abraham, Isma'il, Isaac, Jacob and the Tribes were Jews or Christians? Say: Do you know better than Allah? Ah! who is more unjust than those who conceal the testimony they have from Allah? But Allah is not unmindful of what you do!

اَعْمَالُكُمْ وَنَحْنُ لَهُ مُخْلِصُوْنَ ۞

اَمْ تَقُوْلُوْنَ اِنَّ اِبْرٰهٖمَ وَاِسْمٰعِيْلَ وَاِسْحٰقَ وَيَعْقُوْبَ وَالْاَسْبَاطَ كَانُوْا هُوْدًا اَوْ نَصٰرٰى ۗ قُلْ ءَاَنْتُمْ اَعْلَمُ اَمِ اللّٰهُ ۗ وَمَنْ اَظْلَمُ مِمَّنْ كَتَمَ شَهَادَةً عِنْدَهٗ مِنَ اللّٰهِ ۗ وَمَا اللّٰهُ بِغَافِلٍ عَمَّا تَعْمَلُوْنَ ۞

141. That was a people who have passed away. They shall reap the fruit of what they did, and you of what you do! Of their merits there is no question in your case.

تِلْكَ اُمَّةٌ قَدْ خَلَتْ ۚ لَهَا مَا كَسَبَتْ وَلَكُمْ مَّا كَسَبْتُمْ ۚ وَلَا تُسْـَٔلُوْنَ عَمَّا كَانُوْا يَعْمَلُوْنَ ۞

142. The fools among the people will say: "What has turned them from the Qibla to which they were used?" Say: To Allah belong both East and West: He guides whom He will to a Way that is straight.

سَيَقُوْلُ السُّفَهَاءُ مِنَ النَّاسِ مَا وَلّٰىهُمْ عَنْ قِبْلَتِهِمُ الَّتِيْ كَانُوْا عَلَيْهَا ۗ قُلْ لِّلّٰهِ الْمَشْرِقُ وَ الْمَغْرِبُ ۚ يَهْدِيْ مَنْ يَّشَاءُ اِلٰى صِرَاطٍ مُّسْتَقِيْمٍ ۞

143. Thus, have We made of you an Ummat justly balanced, that you might be witnesses over the nations, and the Apostle a witness over yourselves; and We appointed the Qibla to which you were used, only to test those who followed the Apostle from those who would turn on their heels (from the Faith). Indeed it was (a change) momentous, except to those guided by Allah. And never would Allah make your faith of no effect. For Allah is to all people most surely full of kindness, Most Merciful.

وَكَذٰلِكَ جَعَلْنٰكُمْ اُمَّةً وَّسَطًا لِّتَكُوْنُوْا شُهَدَاءَ عَلَى النَّاسِ وَيَكُوْنَ الرَّسُوْلُ عَلَيْكُمْ شَهِيْدًا ۗ وَمَا جَعَلْنَا الْقِبْلَةَ الَّتِيْ كُنْتَ عَلَيْهَا اِلَّا لِنَعْلَمَ مَنْ يَّتَّبِعُ الرَّسُوْلَ مِمَّنْ يَّنْقَلِبُ عَلٰى عَقِبَيْهِ ۗ وَاِنْ كَانَتْ لَكَبِيْرَةً اِلَّا عَلَى الَّذِيْنَ هَدَى اللّٰهُ ۗ وَمَا كَانَ اللّٰهُ لِيُضِيْعَ اِيْمَانَكُمْ ۗ اِنَّ اللّٰهَ بِالنَّاسِ لَرَءُوْفٌ رَّحِيْمٌ ۞

144. We see the turning of your face (for guidance) to the heavens: now shall We turn you to a Qibla that shall please you. Turn then

قَدْ نَرٰى تَقَلُّبَ وَجْهِكَ فِى السَّمَاءِ ۚ فَلَنُوَلِّيَنَّكَ قِبْلَةً تَرْضٰىهَا ۚ فَوَلِّ

your face in the direction of the sacred Mosque: wherever you are, turn your faces in that direction. The people of the Book know well that that is the truth from their Lord. Nor is Allah unmindful of what they do.

وَجْهَكَ شَطْرَ الْمَسْجِدِ الْحَرَامِ ۚ وَحَيْثُ مَا كُنْتُمْ فَوَلُّوا وُجُوهَكُمْ شَطْرَهُ ۚ وَإِنَّ الَّذِينَ أُوتُوا الْكِتَابَ لَيَعْلَمُونَ أَنَّهُ الْحَقُّ مِنْ رَبِّهِمْ ۗ وَمَا اللّٰهُ بِغَافِلٍ عَمَّا يَعْمَلُونَ ۞

145. Even if you were to bring to the people of the Book all the Signs (together), they would not follow your Qibla; nor are you going to follow their Qibla; nor indeed will they follow each other's Qibla. If you after the knowledge has reached you were to follow their (vain) desires,- then you were indeed (clearly) in the wrong.

وَلَئِنْ أَتَيْتَ الَّذِينَ أُوتُوا الْكِتَابَ بِكُلِّ آيَةٍ مَا تَبِعُوا قِبْلَتَكَ ۚ وَمَا أَنْتَ بِتَابِعٍ قِبْلَتَهُمْ ۚ وَمَا بَعْضُهُمْ بِتَابِعٍ قِبْلَةَ بَعْضٍ ۚ وَلَئِنِ اتَّبَعْتَ أَهْوَاءَهُمْ مِنْ بَعْدِ مَا جَاءَكَ مِنَ الْعِلْمِ ۙ إِنَّكَ إِذًا لَمِنَ الظَّالِمِينَ ۞

146. The people of the Book know this as they know their own sons; but some of them conceal the truth which they themselves know.

الَّذِينَ آتَيْنَاهُمُ الْكِتَابَ يَعْرِفُونَهُ كَمَا يَعْرِفُونَ أَبْنَاءَهُمْ ۖ وَإِنَّ فَرِيقًا مِنْهُمْ لَيَكْتُمُونَ الْحَقَّ وَهُمْ يَعْلَمُونَ ۞

147. The Truth is from your Lord; so be not at all in doubt.

الْحَقُّ مِنْ رَبِّكَ فَلَا تَكُونَنَّ مِنَ الْمُمْتَرِينَ ۞

148. To each is a goal to which Allah turns him; then strive together (as in a race) toward all that is good. Wheresoever you are, Allah will bring you together. For Allah has power over all things.

وَلِكُلٍّ وِجْهَةٌ هُوَ مُوَلِّيهَا ۖ فَاسْتَبِقُوا الْخَيْرَاتِ ۚ أَيْنَ مَا تَكُونُوا يَأْتِ بِكُمُ اللّٰهُ جَمِيعًا ۚ إِنَّ اللّٰهَ عَلَىٰ كُلِّ شَيْءٍ قَدِيرٌ ۞

149. From wheresoever you start forth, turn your face in the direction of the Sacred Mosque; that is indeed the truth from your Lord. And Allah is not unmindful of what you do.

وَمِنْ حَيْثُ خَرَجْتَ فَوَلِّ وَجْهَكَ شَطْرَ الْمَسْجِدِ الْحَرَامِ ۖ وَإِنَّهُ لَلْحَقُّ مِنْ رَبِّكَ ۗ وَمَا اللّٰهُ بِغَافِلٍ عَمَّا تَعْمَلُونَ ۞

150. So from wheresoever you start forth, turn your face in the direction of the Sacred Mosque; and wheresoever

وَمِنْ حَيْثُ خَرَجْتَ فَوَلِّ وَجْهَكَ شَطْرَ الْمَسْجِدِ الْحَرَامِ ۚ وَحَيْثُ مَا

you are, turn your face to it: that there be no ground of dispute against you among the people, except those of them that are bent on wickedness; so do not fear them, but fear Me; and that I may complete My favours on you, and you may (consent to) be guided;

كُنْتُمْ فَوَلُّوْا وُجُوْهَكُمْ شَطْرَهُ ۚ لِئَلَّا

يَكُوْنَ لِلنَّاسِ عَلَيْكُمْ حُجَّةٌ ۚ

اِلَّا الَّذِيْنَ ظَلَمُوْا مِنْهُمْ ۚ فَلَا

تَخْشَوْهُمْ وَاخْشَوْنِيْ ۚ وَلِاُتِمَّ نِعْمَتِيْ

عَلَيْكُمْ وَلَعَلَّكُمْ تَهْتَدُوْنَ ۙ

151. A similar (favour you have already received) in that We have sent among you an Apostle of your own, rehearsing to you Our Signs, and sanctifying you, and instructing you in Scripture and Wisdom, and in new Knowledge.

كَمَا اَرْسَلْنَا فِيْكُمْ رَسُوْلًا مِّنْكُمْ

يَتْلُوْا عَلَيْكُمْ اٰيٰتِنَا وَيُزَكِّيْكُمْ

وَيُعَلِّمُكُمُ الْكِتٰبَ وَالْحِكْمَةَ

وَيُعَلِّمُكُمْ مَّا لَمْ تَكُوْنُوْا تَعْلَمُوْنَ ۗ

152. Then you remember Me; I will remember you. Be grateful to Me, and do not reject Faith.

فَاذْكُرُوْنِيْٓ اَذْكُرْكُمْ وَاشْكُرُوْا لِيْ

وَلَا تَكْفُرُوْنِ ۙ

153. O you who believe! seek help with patient perseverance and prayer; for Allah is with those who patiently persevere.

يٰٓاَيُّهَا الَّذِيْنَ اٰمَنُوا اسْتَعِيْنُوْا بِالصَّبْرِ

وَالصَّلٰوةِ ۚ اِنَّ اللّٰهَ مَعَ الصّٰبِرِيْنَ ۟

154. And do not say of those who are slain in the way of Allah: "They are dead." Nay, they are living, though you do not perceive (it) not.

وَلَا تَقُوْلُوْا لِمَنْ يُّقْتَلُ فِيْ سَبِيْلِ اللّٰهِ

اَمْوَاتٌ ۚ بَلْ اَحْيَاءٌ وَّلٰكِنْ لَّا تَشْعُرُوْنَ ۟

155. Be sure We shall test you with something of fear and hunger, some loss in goods or lives or the fruits (of your toil), but give glad tidings to those who patiently persevere,

وَلَنَبْلُوَنَّكُمْ بِشَيْءٍ مِّنَ الْخَوْفِ وَالْجُوْعِ

وَنَقْصٍ مِّنَ الْاَمْوَالِ وَالْاَنْفُسِ

وَالثَّمَرٰتِ ۗ وَبَشِّرِ الصّٰبِرِيْنَ ۙ

156. Who say, when afflicted with calamity: "To Allah we belong, and to Him is our return":-

الَّذِيْنَ اِذَآ اَصَابَتْهُمْ مُّصِيْبَةٌ ۚ

قَالُوْٓا اِنَّا لِلّٰهِ وَاِنَّآ اِلَيْهِ رٰجِعُوْنَ ۟

157. They are those on whom (descend) blessings from Allah, and Mercy, and they are the ones that receive guidance.

اُولٰٓئِكَ عَلَيْهِمْ صَلَوٰتٌ مِّنْ رَّبِّهِمْ وَ

رَحْمَةٌ ۚ وَاُولٰٓئِكَ هُمُ الْمُهْتَدُوْنَ ۟

158. Behold! Safa and Marwa are among the Symbols of Allah. So if those who visit the House in the Season or at other times, should compass them round, it is no sin in them. And if any one obeys his own impulse to Good,- be sure that Allah is He Who recognises and knows.

اِنَّ الصَّفَا وَالْمَرْوَةَ مِنْ شَعَآئِرِ

اللّٰهِ ۚ فَمَنْ حَجَّ الْبَيْتَ اَوِ اعْتَمَرَ فَلَا

جُنَاحَ عَلَيْهِ اَنْ يَّطَّوَّفَ بِهِمَا ۚ وَمَنْ

تَطَوَّعَ خَيْرًا ۙ فَاِنَّ اللّٰهَ شَاكِرٌ عَلِيْمٌ ۟

159. Those who conceal the clear (Signs) We have sent down, and the Guidance, after We have made it clear for the People in the Book,- on them shall be Allah's curse, and the curse of those entitled to curse,-

160. Except those who repent and make amends and openly declare (the Truth): to them I turn; for I am Oft-Returning, Most Merciful.

161. Those who reject Faith, and die rejecting,- on them is Allah's curse, and the curse of angels, and of all mankind.

162. They will abide therein: their Chastisement will not be lightened, nor will respite be their (lot).

163. And your God (Allah) is One God (Allah): There is no god but He, Most Gracious, Most Merciful.

164. Behold! in the creation of the heavens and the earth; in the alternation of the night and the day; in the sailing of the ships through the ocean for the profit of mankind; in the rain which Allah sends down from the skies, and the life which He gives therewith to an earth that is dead; in the beasts of all kinds that He scatters through the earth; in the change of the winds, and the clouds which they trail like their slaves between the sky and the earth;- (here) indeed are Signs for a people that are wise.

165. Yet there are men who take (for worship) others besides Allah, as equal (with Allah): they love them as they should love Allah. But those of Faith are overflowing in their love for Allah. If

إِنَّ الَّذِينَ يَكْتُمُونَ مَا أَنْزَلْنَا مِنَ الْبَيِّنَاتِ وَالْهُدَى مِنْ بَعْدِ مَا بَيَّنَّاهُ لِلنَّاسِ فِي الْكِتَابِ أُولَٰئِكَ يَلْعَنُهُمُ اللهُ وَيَلْعَنُهُمُ اللَّاعِنُونَ ۞

إِلَّا الَّذِينَ تَابُوا وَأَصْلَحُوا وَبَيَّنُوا فَأُولَٰئِكَ أَتُوبُ عَلَيْهِمْ ۚ وَأَنَا التَّوَّابُ الرَّحِيمُ ۞

إِنَّ الَّذِينَ كَفَرُوا وَمَاتُوا وَهُمْ كُفَّارٌ أُولَٰئِكَ عَلَيْهِمْ لَعْنَةُ اللهِ وَالْمَلَائِكَةِ وَالنَّاسِ أَجْمَعِينَ ۞

خَالِدِينَ فِيهَا ۖ لَا يُخَفَّفُ عَنْهُمُ الْعَذَابُ وَلَا هُمْ يُنْظَرُونَ ۞

وَإِلَٰهُكُمْ إِلَٰهٌ وَاحِدٌ ۖ لَا إِلَٰهَ إِلَّا هُوَ الرَّحْمَٰنُ الرَّحِيمُ ۞

إِنَّ فِي خَلْقِ السَّمَاوَاتِ وَالْأَرْضِ وَ اخْتِلَافِ اللَّيْلِ وَالنَّهَارِ وَالْفُلْكِ الَّتِي تَجْرِي فِي الْبَحْرِ بِمَا يَنْفَعُ النَّاسَ وَمَا أَنْزَلَ اللهُ مِنَ السَّمَاءِ مِنْ مَاءٍ فَأَحْيَا بِهِ الْأَرْضَ بَعْدَ مَوْتِهَا وَبَثَّ فِيهَا مِنْ كُلِّ دَابَّةٍ وَتَصْرِيفِ الرِّيَاحِ وَالسَّحَابِ الْمُسَخَّرِ بَيْنَ السَّمَاءِ وَالْأَرْضِ لَآيَاتٍ لِقَوْمٍ يَعْقِلُونَ ۞

وَمِنَ النَّاسِ مَنْ يَتَّخِذُ مِنْ دُونِ اللهِ أَنْدَادًا يُحِبُّونَهُمْ كَحُبِّ اللهِ ۖ وَالَّذِينَ آمَنُوا أَشَدُّ حُبًّا لِلهِ ۗ وَلَوْ يَرَى

only the unrighteous could see,
behold, they would see the
Chastisement: that to Allah
belongs all power, and Allah will
strongly enforce the Chastisement.

166. Then would those who are
followed clear themselves of
those who follow (them): they
would see the Chastisement, and
all relations between them
would be cut off.

167. And those who followed
would say: "If only we had one
more chance, we would clear
ourselves of them, as they have
cleared themselves of us." Thus
will Allah show them (the fruits
of) their deeds as (nothing but)
regrets. Nor will there be a way
for them out of the Fire.

168. O you people! Eat of what
is on earth, lawful and good; and
do not follow the footsteps of the
Satan, for he is to you an avowed
enemy.

169. For he commands you
what is evil and shameful, and
that you should say of Allah that
of which you have no knowledge.

170. When it is said to them:
"Follow what Allah has revealed:" they say: "Nay! we shall
follow the ways of our fathers."
What! even though their fathers
were void of wisdom and
guidance?

171. The parable of those who
reject Faith is as if one were to
shout like a goat- herd, to things
that listen to nothing but calls
and cries: deaf, dumb, and blind,
they are void of wisdom.

172. O you who believe! Eat of
the good things that We have
provided for you and be grateful

to Allah, if it is Him you worship.

173. He has only forbidden you dead meat, and blood, and the flesh of swine, and that on which any other name has been invoked besides that of Allah. But if one is forced by necessity, without wilful disobedience, nor transgressing due limits,- then is he guiltless, for Allah is Oft-Forgiving, Most Merciful.

174. Those who conceal Allah's revelations in the Book, and purchase for them a miserable profit,- they swallow into themselves nothing but Fire; Allah will not address them on the Day of Resurrection, nor purify them: grievous will be their Chastisement.

175. They are the ones who buy Error in place of Guidance and Torment in place of Forgiveness. Ah! what boldness (they show) for the Fire!

176. (Their doom is) because Allah sent down the Book in truth but those who seek causes of dispute in the Book are in a schism far (from the purpose).

177. It is not righteousness that you turn your faces toward East or West; but it is righteousness - to believe in Allah and the Last Day, and the Angels, and the Book, and the Messengers; to spend of your substance, out of love for Him, for your kin, for orphans, for the needy, for the wayfarer, for those who ask, and for the ransom of slaves; to be steadfast in prayer, and practice regular charity; to fulfil the

بِاللّٰهِ اِنْ كُنْتُمْ اِيَّاهُ تَعْبُدُوْنَ ۝

اِنَّمَا حَرَّمَ عَلَيْكُمُ الْمَيْتَةَ وَالدَّمَ وَلَحْمَ الْخِنْزِيْرِ وَمَا اُهِلَّ بِهٖ لِغَيْرِ اللّٰهِ ۚ فَمَنِ اضْطُرَّ غَيْرَ بَاغٍ وَّلَا عَادٍ فَلَا اِثْمَ عَلَيْهِ ۚ اِنَّ اللّٰهَ غَفُوْرٌ رَّحِيْمٌ ۝

اِنَّ الَّذِيْنَ يَكْتُمُوْنَ مَا اَنْزَلَ اللّٰهُ مِنَ الْكِتٰبِ وَيَشْتَرُوْنَ بِهٖ ثَمَنًا قَلِيْلًا ۙ اُولٰٓئِكَ مَا يَأْكُلُوْنَ فِيْ بُطُوْنِهِمْ اِلَّا النَّارَ وَلَا يُكَلِّمُهُمُ اللّٰهُ يَوْمَ الْقِيٰمَةِ وَلَا يُزَكِّيْهِمْ ۖ وَلَهُمْ عَذَابٌ اَلِيْمٌ ۝

اُولٰٓئِكَ الَّذِيْنَ اشْتَرَوُا الضَّلٰلَةَ بِالْهُدٰى وَالْعَذَابَ بِالْمَغْفِرَةِ ۚ فَمَا اَصْبَرَهُمْ عَلَى النَّارِ ۝

ذٰلِكَ بِاَنَّ اللّٰهَ نَزَّلَ الْكِتٰبَ بِالْحَقِّ ۗ وَاِنَّ الَّذِيْنَ اخْتَلَفُوْا فِي الْكِتٰبِ لَفِيْ شِقَاقٍ بَعِيْدٍ ۝

لَيْسَ الْبِرَّ اَنْ تُوَلُّوْا وُجُوْهَكُمْ قِبَلَ الْمَشْرِقِ وَالْمَغْرِبِ وَلٰكِنَّ الْبِرَّ مَنْ اٰمَنَ بِاللّٰهِ وَالْيَوْمِ الْاٰخِرِ وَالْمَلٰٓئِكَةِ وَالْكِتٰبِ وَالنَّبِيّٖنَ ۚ وَاٰتَى الْمَالَ عَلٰى حُبِّهٖ ذَوِي الْقُرْبٰى وَالْيَتٰمٰى وَالْمَسٰكِيْنَ وَابْنَ السَّبِيْلِ ۙ وَالسَّآئِلِيْنَ وَفِي الرِّقَابِ ۚ وَاَقَامَ الصَّلٰوةَ وَاٰتَى الزَّكٰوةَ ۚ وَالْمُوْفُوْنَ

contracts which you have made; and to be firm and patient, in pain (or suffering) and adversity, and throughout all periods of panic. Such are the people of truth, those who fear Allah.

178. O you who believe! The law of equality is prescribed to you in cases of murder: the free for the free, the slave for the slave, the woman for the woman. But if any remission is made by the brother of the slain, then grant any reasonable demand, and compensate him with handsome gratitude. This is a concession and a Mercy from your Lord. After this whoever exceeds the limits shall be in grave Chastisement.

179. In the Law of Equality there is (saving of) Life to you, O you men of understanding; that you may restrain yourselves.

180. It is prescribed, when death approaches any of you, if he leave any goods that he make a bequest to parents and next of kin, according to reasonable usage; this is due from those who fear Allah.

181. If anyone changes the bequest after hearing it, the guilt shall be on those who make the change. For Allah hears and knows (all things).

182. But if anyone fears partiality or wrong-doing on the part of the testator, and makes peace between (the parties concerned), there is no wrong in him: for Allah is Oft-Forgiving, Most Merciful.

183. O you who believe! Fasting is prescribed to you as it was prescribed to those

before you, that you may (learn) self-restraint,-

184. (Fasting) for a fixed number of days; but if any of you is ill, or on a journey, the prescribed number (should be made up) from days later. For those who can do it (with hardship), is a ransom, the feeding of one that is indigent. But he that will give more, of his own free will,- it is better for him. And it is better for you that you fast, if you only knew.

185. Ramadhan is the (month) in which was sent down the Qur'an, as a guide to mankind, also clear (Signs) for guidance and judgment (between right and wrong). So every one of you who is present (at his home) during that month should spend it in fasting, but if any one is ill, or on a journey, the prescribed period (should be made up) by days later. Allah intends every facility for you; He does not want to put you to difficulties. (He wants you) to complete the prescribed period, and to glorify Him in that He has guided you; and perchance you shall be grateful.

186. When My servants ask you concerning Me, I am indeed close (to them): I listen to the prayer of every suppliant when he calls on Me: let them also, with a will, listen to My call, and believe in Me: that they may walk in the right way.

187. Permitted to you, on the night of the fasts, is the approach to your wives. They are your garments and you are their garments. Allah knows what you used to do secretly among yourselves; but He turned to you and forgave you; so now associate with them, and seek what Allah has ordained

for you, and eat and drink, until the white thread of dawn appear to you distinct from its black thread; then complete your fast till the night appears; but do not associate with your wives while you are in retreat in the mosques. Those are limits (set by) Allah: do not go near to those. Thus Allah makes clear His Signs to men: that they may learn self-restraint.

لَكُمْ ۫ وَكُلُوْا وَاشْرَبُوْا حَتّٰى يَتَبَيَّنَ لَكُمُ الْخَيْطُ الْاَبْيَضُ مِنَ الْخَيْطِ الْاَسْوَدِ مِنَ الْفَجْرِ ۫ ثُمَّ اَتِمُّوا الصِّيَامَ اِلَى الَّيْلِ ۚ وَلَا تُبَاشِرُوْهُنَّ وَاَنْتُمْ عٰكِفُوْنَ ۙ فِى الْمَسٰجِدِ ۗ تِلْكَ حُدُوْدُ اللّٰهِ فَلَا تَقْرَبُوْهَا ۗ كَذٰلِكَ يُبَيِّنُ اللّٰهُ اٰيٰتِهٖ لِلنَّاسِ لَعَلَّهُمْ يَتَّقُوْنَ ۝

188. And do not eat up your property among yourselves for vanities, nor use it as bait for the judges, with intent that you may eat up wrongfully and knowingly a little of (other) people's property.

وَلَا تَأْكُلُوْۤا اَمْوَالَكُمْ بَيْنَكُمْ بِالْبَاطِلِ وَتُدْلُوْا بِهَاۤ اِلَى الْحُكَّامِ لِتَأْكُلُوْا فَرِيْقًا مِّنْ اَمْوَالِ النَّاسِ بِالْاِثْمِ وَاَنْتُمْ تَعْلَمُوْنَ ۝

189. They ask you concerning the New Moons. Say: They are but signs to mark fixed periods of time in (the affairs of) men, and for Pilgrimage. It is no virtue if you enter your houses from the back: it is virtue if you fear Allah. Enter houses through the proper doors: and fear Allah: that you may achieve success.

يَسْـَٔلُوْنَكَ عَنِ الْاَهِلَّةِ ۗ قُلْ هِىَ مَوَاقِيْتُ لِلنَّاسِ وَالْحَجِّ ۗ وَلَيْسَ الْبِرُّ بِاَنْ تَأْتُوا الْبُيُوْتَ مِنْ ظُهُوْرِهَا وَلٰكِنَّ الْبِرَّ مَنِ اتَّقٰى ۚ وَأْتُوا الْبُيُوْتَ مِنْ اَبْوَابِهَا ۚ وَاتَّقُوا اللّٰهَ لَعَلَّكُمْ تُفْلِحُوْنَ ۝

190. Fight in the cause of Allah those who fight you, but do not transgress limits; for Allah does not love transgressors.

وَقَاتِلُوْا فِىْ سَبِيْلِ اللّٰهِ الَّذِيْنَ يُقَاتِلُوْنَكُمْ وَلَا تَعْتَدُوْا ۚ اِنَّ اللّٰهَ لَا يُحِبُّ الْمُعْتَدِيْنَ ۝

191. And slay them wherever you catch them, and turn them out from where they have turned you out; for tumult and oppression are worse than slaughter; but do not fight them at the Sacred Mosque, unless they (first) fight you there; but if they fight you,

وَاقْتُلُوْهُمْ حَيْثُ ثَقِفْتُمُوْهُمْ وَاَخْرِجُوْهُمْ مِّنْ حَيْثُ اَخْرَجُوْكُمْ وَالْفِتْنَةُ اَشَدُّ مِنَ الْقَتْلِ ۚ وَلَا تُقٰتِلُوْهُمْ عِنْدَ الْمَسْجِدِ الْحَرَامِ حَتّٰى يُقٰتِلُوْكُمْ فِيْهِ ۚ فَاِنْ قٰتَلُوْكُمْ

slay them. Such is the reward of those who suppress faith.

192. But if they cease, Allah is Oft-Forgiving, Most Merciful.

193. And fight them on until there is no more tumult or oppression, and there prevail justice and faith in Allah; but if they cease, let there be no hostility except to those who practise oppression.

194. The prohibited month for the prohibited month,- and so for all things prohibited,- there is the law of equality. If then any one transgresses the prohibition against you, transgress you likewise against him. But fear Allah, and know that Allah is with those who restrain themselves.

195. And spend of your substance in the cause of Allah, and do not make your own hands contribute to (your) destruction; but do good; for Allah loves those who do good.

196. And complete the Hajj or 'Umra in the service of Allah. But if you are prevented (from completing it), send an offering for sacrifice, such as you may find, and do not shave your heads until the offering reaches the place of sacrifice. And if any of you is ill, or has an ailment in his scalp, (necessitating shaving), (he should) in compensation either fast, or feed the poor, or offer sacrifice; and when you are in peaceful conditions (again), if any one wishes to continue the 'Umra or the Hajj, he must make an offering, such as he can afford, but if he cannot afford it, he should fast three days during the Hajj and seven days on his return, making ten days in all. This is for those whose household is not in (the precincts of) the Sacred Mosque. And fear Allah,

فَٱقْتُلُوهُمْ كَذَٰلِكَ جَزَآءُ ٱلْكَٰفِرِينَ ۝

فَإِنِ ٱنتَهَوْا۟ فَإِنَّ ٱللَّهَ غَفُورٌ رَّحِيمٌ ۝

وَقَٰتِلُوهُمْ حَتَّىٰ لَا تَكُونَ فِتْنَةٌ

وَيَكُونَ ٱلدِّينُ لِلَّهِ ۖ فَإِنِ ٱنتَهَوْا۟

فَلَا عُدْوَٰنَ إِلَّا عَلَى ٱلظَّٰلِمِينَ ۝

ٱلشَّهْرُ ٱلْحَرَامُ بِٱلشَّهْرِ ٱلْحَرَامِ

وَٱلْحُرُمَٰتُ قِصَاصٌ ۚ فَمَنِ ٱعْتَدَىٰ

عَلَيْكُمْ فَٱعْتَدُوا۟ عَلَيْهِ بِمِثْلِ

مَا ٱعْتَدَىٰ عَلَيْكُمْ ۚ وَٱتَّقُوا۟ ٱللَّهَ

وَٱعْلَمُوٓا۟ أَنَّ ٱللَّهَ مَعَ ٱلْمُتَّقِينَ ۝

وَأَنفِقُوا۟ فِى سَبِيلِ ٱللَّهِ وَلَا تُلْقُوا۟

بِأَيْدِيكُمْ إِلَى ٱلتَّهْلُكَةِ ۛ وَأَحْسِنُوٓا۟ ۛ

إِنَّ ٱللَّهَ يُحِبُّ ٱلْمُحْسِنِينَ ۝

وَأَتِمُّوا۟ ٱلْحَجَّ وَٱلْعُمْرَةَ لِلَّهِ ۚ فَإِنْ

أُحْصِرْتُمْ فَمَا ٱسْتَيْسَرَ مِنَ ٱلْهَدْىِ

وَلَا تَحْلِقُوا۟ رُءُوسَكُمْ حَتَّىٰ يَبْلُغَ

ٱلْهَدْىُ مَحِلَّهُۥ ۚ فَمَن كَانَ مِنكُم

مَّرِيضًا أَوْ بِهِۦٓ أَذًى مِّن رَّأْسِهِ

فَفِدْيَةٌ مِّن صِيَامٍ أَوْ صَدَقَةٍ

أَوْ نُسُكٍ ۚ فَإِذَآ أَمِنتُمْ فَمَن تَمَتَّعَ

بِٱلْعُمْرَةِ إِلَى ٱلْحَجِّ فَمَا ٱسْتَيْسَرَ

مِنَ ٱلْهَدْىِ ۚ فَمَن لَّمْ يَجِدْ فَصِيَامُ

ثَلَٰثَةِ أَيَّامٍ فِى ٱلْحَجِّ وَسَبْعَةٍ إِذَا

رَجَعْتُمْ ۗ تِلْكَ عَشَرَةٌ كَامِلَةٌ ۗ ذَٰلِكَ

لِمَن لَّمْ يَكُنْ أَهْلُهُۥ حَاضِرِى

ٱلْمَسْجِدِ ٱلْحَرَامِ ۚ وَٱتَّقُوا۟ ٱللَّهَ

and know that Allah is strict in punishment.

197. For Hajj are the months well known. If any one undertakes that duty therein, let there be no obscenity, nor wickedness, nor wrangling in the Hajj. And whatever good you do, (be sure) Allah knows it. And take a provision (with you) for the journey, but the best of provisions is right conduct. So fear Me, O you that are wise.

198. It is no crime in you if you seek of the bounty of your Lord (during pilgrimage). Then when you pour down from (Mount) 'Arafat, celebrate the praises of Allah at the Sacred Monument, and celebrate His praises as He has directed you, even though, before this, you went astray.

199. Then pass on at a quick pace from the place whence it is usual for the multitude to do so, and ask for Allah's forgiveness. For Allah is Oft-Forgiving, Most Merciful.

200. So when you have accomplished your holy rites, celebrate the praises of Allah, as you used to celebrate the praises of your fathers,- yes, with far more heart and soul. There are men who say: "Our Lord! Give us (Your bounties) in this world!" but they will have no portion in the Hereafter.

201. And there are men who say: "Our Lord! Give us good in this world and good in the Hereafter, and save us from the torment of the Fire!"

202. To these will be allotted what they have earned; and Allah is quick in account.

203. Celebrate the praises of Allah during the Appointed Days.

But if any one hastens to leave in two days, there is no blame on him, and if any one stays on, there is no blame on him, if his aim is to do right. Then fear Allah, and know that you will surely be gathered to Him.

204. There is the type of man whose speech about this world's life may dazzle you, and he calls Allah to witness about what is in his heart; yet he is the most contentious of enemies.

205. When he turns his back, his aim everywhere is to spread mischief through the earth and destroy crops and cattle. But Allah does not love mischief.

206. When it is said to him, "Fear Allah", he is led by arrogance to (more) crime. Enough for him is Hell; - an evil bed indeed (to lie on)!

207. And there is the type of man who gives his life to earn the pleasure of Allah: and Allah is full of kindness to (His) devotees.

208. O you who believe! Enter into Islam whole-heartedly; and do not follow the footsteps of the Satan; for he is to you an avowed enemy.

209. If you backslide after the clear (Signs) have come to you, then know that Allah is Exalted in Power, Wise.

210. Will they wait until Allah comes to them in canopies of clouds, with Angels (in His train) and the question is (thus) settled? but to Allah do all questions go back (for decision).

211. Ask the Children of Israel how many Clear (Signs) We have sent them. But if any one,

after Allah's favour has come to him, substitutes (something else), Allah is strict in punishment.

212. The life of this world is alluring to those who reject faith, and they scoff at those who believe. But the righteous will be above them on the Day of Resurrection; for Allah bestows His abundance without measure on whom He will.

213. Mankind was one single nation, and Allah sent Messengers with glad tidings and warnings; and with them He sent the Book in truth, to judge between people in matters wherein they differed; but the People of the Book, after the Clear Signs came to them, did not differ among themselves, except through selfish contumacy. Allah by His Grace guided the Believers to the Truth, concerning that wherein they differed. For Allah guides whom He will to a path that is straight.

214. Or do you think that you shall enter the Garden (of Bliss) without such (trials) as came to those who passed away before you? They encountered suffering and adversity, and were so shaken in spirit that even the Apostle and those of faith who were with him cried: "When (will come) the help of Allah?" Ah! Verily, the help of Allah is (always) near!

215. They ask you what they should spend (in charity). Say: Whatever you spend that is good, is for parents and kindred and orphans and those in want and for wayfarers. And whatever you do that is

good, - Allah knows it well.

216. Fighting is prescribed for you, and you dislike it. But it is possible that you dislike a thing which is good for you, and that you love a thing which is bad for you. But Allah knows, and you know not.

217. They ask you concerning fighting in the Prohibited Month. Say: "Fighting therein is a grave (offence); but graver is still in the sight of Allah to prevent access to the path of Allah, to deny Him, to prevent access to the Sacred Mosque, and drive out its members." Tumult and oppression are worse than slaughter. Nor will they cease fighting you until they turn you back from your faith if they can. And if any of you turn back from their faith and die in unbelief, their works will bear no fruit in this life and in the Hereafter; they will be companions of the Fire and will abide therein.

218. Those who believed and those who suffered exile and fought (and strove and struggled) in the path of Allah,- they have the hope of the Mercy of Allah: and Allah is Oft-Forgiving, Most Merciful.

219. They ask you concerning wine and gambling. Say: "In them is great sin, and some profit, for men; but the sin is greater than the profit." They ask you how much they are to spend; Say: "What is beyond your needs." Thus Allah makes clear to you

His Signs: in order that you may consider-

220. (Their bearings) on this life and the Hereafter. They ask you concerning orphans. Say: "The best thing to do is what is for their good; if you mix their affairs with yours, they are your brethren; but Allah knows the man who means mischief from the man who means good. And if Allah had wished, He could have put you into difficulties: He is indeed Exalted in Power, Wise."

221. Do not marry unbelieving women (idolators), until they believe: a slave woman who believes is better than an unbelieving woman, even though she allure you. Nor marry (your girls) to unbelievers until they believe: a man slave who believes is better than an unbeliever, even though he allure you. Unbelievers do (but) beckon you to the Fire. But Allah beckons by His Grace to the Garden (of Bliss) and forgiveness, and makes His Signs clear to mankind, so that they may celebrate His praise.

222. They ask you concerning women's courses. Say: They are a hurt and a pollution: so keep away from women in their courses, and do not approach them until they are clean. But when they have purified themselves, you may approach them in any manner, time, or place ordained for you by Allah. For Allah loves those who turn to Him constantly and He loves those who keep themselves pure and clean.

223. Your wives are a tilth unto you; so approach your tilth when or how you will; but do some good act for your souls beforehand; and fear Allah. And know that you are to meet Him (in the Hereafter), and give (these) good tidings to those who believe.

224. And make not Allah's (name) an excuse in your oaths

against doing good, or acting rightly, or making peace between persons; for Allah is One Who hears and knows all things.

225. Allah will not call you to account for thoughtlessness in your oaths, but for the intention in your hearts; and He is Oft-Forgiving, Most Forbearing.

226. For those who take an oath for abstention from their wives, a waiting for four months is ordained; if then they return, Allah is Oft-Forgiving, Most Merciful.

227. But if their intention is firm for divorce, Allah hears and knows all things.

228. Divorced women shall wait concerning themselves for three monthly periods. Nor is it lawful for them to hide what Allah has created in their wombs, if they have faith in Allah and the Last Day. And their husbands have the better right to take them back in that period, if they wish for reconciliation. And women shall have rights similar to the rights against them, according to what is equitable; but men have a degree (of advantage) over them. And Allah is Exalted in Power, Wise.

229. A divorce is only permissible twice: after that, the parties should either hold together on equitable terms, or separate with kindness. It is not lawful for you, (men), to take back any of your gifts (from your wives), except when both parties fear that they would be unable to keep the limits ordained by Allah. If you (judges) do indeed fear that they would be unable to keep the limits ordained by Allah, there is no blame on either of them if she give something for her freedom. These are the limits ordained by Allah; so do not

اَنْ تَبَرُّوْا وَ تَتَّقُوْا وَ تُصْلِحُوْا بَيْنَ النَّاسِ ۗ وَ اللّٰهُ سَمِيْعٌ عَلِيْمٌ ۝

لَا يُؤَاخِذُكُمُ اللّٰهُ بِاللَّغْوِ فِيْۤ اَيْمَانِكُمْ وَ لٰكِنْ يُّؤَاخِذُكُمْ بِمَا كَسَبَتْ قُلُوْبُكُمْ ۗ وَ اللّٰهُ غَفُوْرٌ حَلِيْمٌ ۝

لِلَّذِيْنَ يُؤْلُوْنَ مِنْ نِّسَآئِهِمْ تَرَبُّصُ اَرْبَعَةِ اَشْهُرٍ ۚ فَاِنْ فَآءُوْ فَاِنَّ اللّٰهَ غَفُوْرٌ رَّحِيْمٌ ۝

وَ اِنْ عَزَمُوا الطَّلَاقَ فَاِنَّ اللّٰهَ سَمِيْعٌ عَلِيْمٌ ۝

وَ الْمُطَلَّقٰتُ يَتَرَبَّصْنَ بِاَنْفُسِهِنَّ ثَلٰثَةَ قُرُوْٓءٍ ۗ وَ لَا يَحِلُّ لَهُنَّ اَنْ يَّكْتُمْنَ مَا خَلَقَ اللّٰهُ فِيْۤ اَرْحَامِهِنَّ اِنْ كُنَّ يُؤْمِنَّ بِاللّٰهِ وَ الْيَوْمِ الْاٰخِرِ ۗ وَ بُعُوْلَتُهُنَّ اَحَقُّ بِرَدِّهِنَّ فِيْ ذٰلِكَ اِنْ اَرَادُوْۤا اِصْلَاحًا ۗ وَ لَهُنَّ مِثْلُ الَّذِيْ عَلَيْهِنَّ بِالْمَعْرُوْفِ ۫ وَ لِلرِّجَالِ عَلَيْهِنَّ دَرَجَةٌ ۗ وَ اللّٰهُ عَزِيْزٌ حَكِيْمٌ ۝

اَلطَّلَاقُ مَرَّتٰنِ ۫ فَاِمْسَاكٌ بِمَعْرُوْفٍ اَوْ تَسْرِيْحٌۢ بِاِحْسَانٍ ۗ وَ لَا يَحِلُّ لَكُمْ اَنْ تَأْخُذُوْا مِمَّاۤ اٰتَيْتُمُوْهُنَّ شَيْئًا اِلَّاۤ اَنْ يَّخَافَاۤ اَلَّا يُقِيْمَا حُدُوْدَ اللّٰهِ ۚ فَاِنْ خِفْتُمْ اَلَّا يُقِيْمَا حُدُوْدَ اللّٰهِ ۙ فَلَا جُنَاحَ عَلَيْهِمَا فِيْمَا افْتَدَتْ بِهٖ ۗ تِلْكَ حُدُوْدُ اللّٰهِ فَلَا

transgress them, if any do transgress the limits ordained by Allah, such persons wrong (themselves as well as others).

تَعْتَدُوْهَا ۚ وَمَنْ يَّتَعَدَّ حُدُوْدَ اللّٰهِ فَأُولٰٓئِكَ هُمُ الظّٰلِمُوْنَ ۝

230. So if a husband divorces his wife (irrevocably), he cannot, after that, re- marry her until after she has married another husband and he has divorced her. In that case there is no blame on either of them if they re-unite, provided they feel that they can keep the limits ordained by Allah. Such are the limits ordained by Allah, which He makes plain to those who understand.

فَإِنْ طَلَّقَهَا فَلَا تَحِلُّ لَهٗ مِنْۢ بَعْدُ حَتّٰى تَنْكِحَ زَوْجًا غَيْرَهٗ ۗ فَإِنْ طَلَّقَهَا فَلَا جُنَاحَ عَلَيْهِمَآ اَنْ يَّتَرَاجَعَآ اِنْ ظَنَّآ اَنْ يُّقِيْمَا حُدُوْدَ اللّٰهِ ۗ وَتِلْكَ حُدُوْدُ اللّٰهِ يُبَيِّنُهَا لِقَوْمٍ يَّعْلَمُوْنَ ۝

231. When you divorce women, and they fulfil the term of their ('Iddat), either take them back on equitable terms or set them free on equitable terms; but do not take them back to injure them, (or) to take undue advantage; if any one does that; he wrongs his own soul. Do not treat Allah's Signs as a jest, but solemnly rehearse Allah's favours on you, and the fact that He sent down to you the Book and Wisdom, for your instruction. And fear Allah, and know that Allah is well acquainted with all things.

وَإِذَا طَلَّقْتُمُ النِّسَآءَ فَبَلَغْنَ اَجَلَهُنَّ فَأَمْسِكُوْهُنَّ بِمَعْرُوْفٍ اَوْ سَرِّحُوْهُنَّ بِمَعْرُوْفٍ ۖ وَلَا تُمْسِكُوْهُنَّ ضِرَارًا لِّتَعْتَدُوْا ۚ وَمَنْ يَّفْعَلْ ذٰلِكَ فَقَدْ ظَلَمَ نَفْسَهٗ ۚ وَلَا تَتَّخِذُوْٓا اٰيٰتِ اللّٰهِ هُزُوًا ۚ وَّاذْكُرُوْا نِعْمَتَ اللّٰهِ عَلَيْكُمْ وَمَآ اَنْزَلَ عَلَيْكُمْ مِّنَ الْكِتٰبِ وَالْحِكْمَةِ يَعِظُكُمْ بِهٖ ۚ وَاتَّقُوا اللّٰهَ وَاعْلَمُوْٓا اَنَّ اللّٰهَ بِكُلِّ شَيْءٍ عَلِيْمٌ ۝

232. When you divorce women, and they fulfil the term of their ('Iddat), do not prevent them from marrying their (former) husbands, if they mutually agree on equitable terms. This instruction is for all amongst you, who believe in Allah and the Last Day. That is (the course making for) most virtue and purity amongst you. And Allah knows, and you do not know.

وَإِذَا طَلَّقْتُمُ النِّسَآءَ فَبَلَغْنَ اَجَلَهُنَّ فَلَا تَعْضُلُوْهُنَّ اَنْ يَّنْكِحْنَ اَزْوَاجَهُنَّ اِذَا تَرَاضَوْا بَيْنَهُمْ بِالْمَعْرُوْفِ ۗ ذٰلِكَ يُوْعَظُ بِهٖ مَنْ كَانَ مِنْكُمْ يُؤْمِنُ بِاللّٰهِ وَالْيَوْمِ الْاٰخِرِ ۚ ذٰلِكُمْ اَزْكٰى لَكُمْ وَاَطْهَرُ ۚ وَاللّٰهُ يَعْلَمُ وَاَنْتُمْ لَا تَعْلَمُوْنَ ۝

233. The mothers shall give suck to their offspring

وَالْوَالِدٰتُ يُرْضِعْنَ اَوْلَادَهُنَّ

for two whole years, if the father desires to complete the term. But he shall bear the cost of their food and clothing on equitable terms. No soul shall have a burden laid on it greater than it can bear. No mother shall be treated unfairly on account of her child. Nor father on account of his child, an heir shall be chargeable in the same way. If they both decide on weaning, by mutual consent, and after due consultation, there is no blame on them. If you decide on a foster-mother for your offspring, there is no blame on you, provided you pay (the mother) what you offered, on equitable terms. But fear Allah and know that Allah sees well what you do.

234.   If any of you die and leave widows behind, they shall wait concerning themselves four months and ten days: when they have fulfilled their term, there is no blame on you if they dispose of themselves in a just and reasonable manner. And Allah is well acquainted with what you do.

235.   There is no blame on you if you make an offer of betrothal or hold it in your hearts. Allah knows that you cherish them in your hearts: but do not make a secret contract with them except in terms honourable, nor resolve on the tie of marriage till the term prescribed is fulfilled. And know that Allah knows what is

in your hearts, and take heed of Him; and know that Allah is Oft-Forgiving, Most Forbearing.

236. There is no blame on you if you divorce women before consummation or the fixation of their dower; but bestow on them (a suitable gift), the wealthy according to his means, and the poor according to his means;- a gift of a reasonable amount is due from those who wish to do the right thing.

237. And if you divorce them before consummation, but after the fixation of a dower for them, then the half of the dower (is due to them), unless they remit it or (the man's half) is remitted by him in whose hands is the marriage tie; and the remission (of the man's half) is the nearest to righteousness. And do not forget liberality between yourselves. For Allah sees well all that you do.

238. Guard strictly your (habit of) prayers, especially the Middle Prayer; and stand before Allah in a devout (frame of mind).

239. If you fear (an enemy), pray on foot, or riding, (as may be most convenient), but when you are in security, celebrate Allah's praises in the manner He has taught you, which you knew not (before).

240. Those of you who die and leave widows should bequeath for their widows a year's maintenance and residence; but if they leave (the residence), there is no blame on you for what they do with themselves, provided it is

reasonable. And Allah is Exalted in Power, Wise.

241. For divorced women maintenance (should be provided) on a reasonable (scale). This is a duty on the righteous.

242. Thus Allah Makes clear His Signs to you: in order that you may understand.

243. Did you not turn your vision to those who abandoned their homes, though they were thousands (in number), for fear of death? Allah said to them: "Die"! Then He restored them to life. For Allah is full of bounty to mankind, but most of them are ungrateful.

244. Then fight in the cause of Allah, and know that Allah hears and knows all things.

245. Who is he that will loan to Allah a beautiful loan, which Allah will double unto his credit and multiply many times? It is Allah that gives (you) Want or Plenty, and to Him shall be your return.

246. Have you not turned your vision to the Chiefs of the Children of Israel after (the time of) Moses? They said to a Prophet (that was) among them: "Appoint for us a King, that we may fight in the cause of Allah." He said: "Is it not possible, if you were commanded to fight, that you will not fight?" They said: "How could we refuse to fight in the cause of Allah, seeing that we were turned out of our homes and our families?" But when they were commanded to fight, they turned back, except a small band among them. But Allah has full knowledge of those who do wrong.

247. Their Prophet said to them: "Allah has appointed Talut as king over you." They said: "How can he exercise authority over us when we are better fitted than he to exercise authority, and he is not even gifted, with wealth in abundance?" He said: "Allah has chosen him above you, and has gifted him abundantly with knowledge and bodily prowess: Allah grants His authority to whom He pleases. Allah cares for all, and He knows all things."

وَقَالَ لَهُمْ نَبِيُّهُمْ اِنَّ اللّٰهَ قَدْ بَعَثَ لَكُمْ طَالُوْتَ مَلِكًا ۚ قَالُوْٓا اَنّٰى يَكُوْنُ لَهُ الْمُلْكُ عَلَيْنَا وَنَحْنُ اَحَقُّ بِالْمُلْكِ مِنْهُ وَلَمْ يُؤْتَ سَعَةً مِّنَ الْمَالِ ۚ قَالَ اِنَّ اللّٰهَ اصْطَفٰهُ عَلَيْكُمْ وَزَادَهُ بَسْطَةً فِى الْعِلْمِ وَالْجِسْمِ ۚ وَاللّٰهُ يُؤْتِىْ مُلْكَهٗ مَنْ يَّشَآءُ ۚ وَاللّٰهُ وَاسِعٌ عَلِيْمٌ ۞

248. And (further) their Prophet said to them: "A Sign of his authority is that there shall come to you the Ark of the Covenant, with (an assurance) therein of security from your Lord, and the relics left by the family of Moses and the family of Aaron, carried by Angels. In this is a symbol for you if you indeed have faith."

وَقَالَ لَهُمْ نَبِيُّهُمْ اِنَّ اٰيَةَ مُلْكِهٖٓ اَنْ يَّاْتِيَكُمُ التَّابُوْتُ فِيْهِ سَكِيْنَةٌ مِّنْ رَّبِّكُمْ وَبَقِيَّةٌ مِّمَّا تَرَكَ اٰلُ مُوْسٰى وَاٰلُ هٰرُوْنَ تَحْمِلُهُ الْمَلٰٓئِكَةُ ۚ اِنَّ فِىْ ذٰلِكَ لَاٰيَةً لَّكُمْ اِنْ كُنْتُمْ مُّؤْمِنِيْنَ ۞

249. When Talut set forth with the armies, he said: "Allah will test you at the stream: if any drinks of its water, he does not go with my army: only those who do not taste of it go with me: a mere sip out of the hand is excused." But they all drank of it, except a few. When they crossed the river,- he and the faithful ones with him,- they said: "This day We cannot cope with Goliath and his forces." But those who were convinced that they must meet Allah, said: "How oft, by Allah's will, has a small force vanquished a big one? Allah is with those who steadfastly persevere."

فَلَمَّا فَصَلَ طَالُوْتُ بِالْجُنُوْدِ ۙ قَالَ اِنَّ اللّٰهَ مُبْتَلِيْكُمْ بِنَهَرٍ ۚ فَمَنْ شَرِبَ مِنْهُ فَلَيْسَ مِنِّىْ ۚ وَمَنْ لَّمْ يَطْعَمْهُ فَاِنَّهٗ مِنِّىْٓ اِلَّا مَنِ اغْتَرَفَ غُرْفَةً بِيَدِهٖ ۚ فَشَرِبُوْا مِنْهُ اِلَّا قَلِيْلًا مِّنْهُمْ ۚ فَلَمَّا جَاوَزَهٗ هُوَ وَالَّذِيْنَ اٰمَنُوْا مَعَهٗ ۙ قَالُوْا لَا طَاقَةَ لَنَا الْيَوْمَ بِجَالُوْتَ وَجُنُوْدِهٖ ۚ قَالَ الَّذِيْنَ يَظُنُّوْنَ اَنَّهُمْ مُّلٰقُوا اللّٰهِ ۙ كَمْ مِّنْ فِئَةٍ قَلِيْلَةٍ غَلَبَتْ فِئَةً كَثِيْرَةً بِاِذْنِ اللّٰهِ ۚ وَاللّٰهُ مَعَ الصّٰبِرِيْنَ ۞

250. When they advanced to meet Goliath and his forces, they prayed: "Our Lord! Pour out constancy on us and make our steps firm: help us against those that reject faith."

وَلَمَّا بَرَزُوا لِجَالُوتَ وَجُنُودِهِ

قَالُوا رَبَّنَا أَفْرِغْ عَلَيْنَا صَبْرًا وَّثَبِّتْ

أَقْدَامَنَا وَانْصُرْنَا عَلَى الْقَوْمِ

الْكَافِرِينَ ۞

251. By Allah's will, they routed them; and David slew Goliath; and Allah gave him power and wisdom and taught him whatever (else) He willed. And did not Allah check one set of people by means of another, the earth would indeed be full of mischief: But Allah is full of bounty to all the worlds.

فَهَزَمُوهُمْ بِإِذْنِ اللَّهِ ۙ وَقَتَلَ

دَاوُدُ جَالُوتَ وَآتَاهُ اللَّهُ الْمُلْكَ

وَالْحِكْمَةَ وَعَلَّمَهُ مِمَّا يَشَاءُ ۗ

وَلَوْلَا دَفْعُ اللَّهِ النَّاسَ بَعْضَهُمْ

بِبَعْضٍ لَّفَسَدَتِ الْأَرْضُ وَلَكِنَّ

اللَّهَ ذُو فَضْلٍ عَلَى الْعَالَمِينَ ۞

252. These are the Signs of Allah: we rehearse them to you in truth: verily you are one of the Apostles.

تِلْكَ آيَاتُ اللَّهِ نَتْلُوهَا عَلَيْكَ

بِالْحَقِّ ۚ وَإِنَّكَ لَمِنَ الْمُرْسَلِينَ

253. Those Messengers We endowed with gifts, some above others: to one of them Allah spoke; others He raised to degrees (of honour); to Jesus the son of Mary We gave Clear (Signs), and strengthened him with the holy spirit. If Allah had so willed, succeeding generations would not have fought among each other, after Clear (Signs) had come to them, but they (chose) to wrangle, some believing and others rejecting. If Allah had so willed, they would not have fought each other; but Allah fulfills His plan.

تِلْكَ الرُّسُلُ فَضَّلْنَا بَعْضَهُمْ

عَلَى بَعْضٍ ۘ مِّنْهُمْ مَّنْ كَلَّمَ اللَّهُ

وَرَفَعَ بَعْضَهُمْ دَرَجَاتٍ ۚ وَآتَيْنَا

عِيسَى ابْنَ مَرْيَمَ الْبَيِّنَاتِ وَأَيَّدْنَاهُ

بِرُوحِ الْقُدُسِ ۗ وَلَوْ شَاءَ اللَّهُ مَا

اقْتَتَلَ الَّذِينَ مِنْ بَعْدِهِمْ مِّنْ

بَعْدِ مَا جَاءَتْهُمُ الْبَيِّنَاتُ وَلَكِنِ

اخْتَلَفُوا فَمِنْهُمْ مَّنْ آمَنَ وَمِنْهُمْ

مَّنْ كَفَرَ ۚ وَلَوْ شَاءَ اللَّهُ مَا اقْتَتَلُوا

وَلَكِنَّ اللَّهَ يَفْعَلُ مَا يُرِيدُ ۞

254. O you who believe! spend out of (the bounties) We have provided for you, before the Day comes when no bargaining (will avail), nor friendship nor intercession. Those who reject Faith- they are the wrong-doers.

يَا أَيُّهَا الَّذِينَ آمَنُوا أَنْفِقُوا مِمَّا

رَزَقْنَاكُمْ مِّنْ قَبْلِ أَنْ يَأْتِيَ يَوْمٌ

لَّا بَيْعٌ فِيهِ وَلَا خُلَّةٌ وَّلَا شَفَاعَةٌ ۗ

وَالْكَافِرُونَ هُمُ الظَّالِمُونَ ۞

255. Allah! There is no god but He,—the Living, the Self-subsisting, Eternal. No slumber can seize Him nor sleep. His are all things in the heavens and on earth. Who is there can intercede in His presence except as He permits? He knows what (appears to His creatures as) Before or After or Behind them. Nor shall they compass of His knowledge except as He wills. His Throne extends over the heavens and the earth, and He feels no fatigue in guarding and preserving them for He is the Most High, the Supreme (in glory).

256. Let there be no compulsion in religion: Truth stands out clear from Error: whoever rejects Evil and believes in Allah has grasped the most trust-worthy hand-hold, that never breaks. And Allah hears and knows all things.

257. Allah is the Protector of those who have faith: from the depths of darkness He will lead them forth into light. Of those who reject faith the patrons are the Evil Ones: from light they will lead them forth into the depths of darkness. They will be companions of the fire, to dwell therein (for ever).

258. Have you not turned your vision to one who disputed with Abraham about his Lord, because Allah had granted him power? Abraham said: "My Lord is He Who gives life and death."He said: "I give life and death". Said Abraham: "But it is Allah that causes the sun to rise from the East: do you then cause it to rise from the West."

Thus was he confounded who (in arrogance) rejected Faith. Nor does Allah give guidance to a people unjust.

259. Or (take) the similitude of one who passed by a hamlet, all in ruins to its roofs. He said: "Oh! how shall Allah bring it (ever) to life, after (this) its death?" but Allah caused him to die for a hundred years, then raised him up (again). He said: "How long did you tarry (thus)?" He said: (Perhaps) a day or part of a day." He said: "Nay, you have tarried thus a hundred years; but look at your food and your drink; they show no signs of age; and look at your donkey: And that We may make of you a Sign for the people, Look further at the bones, how We bring them together and clothe them with flesh." When this was shown clearly to him, he said: "I know that Allah has power over all things."

260. Behold! Abraham said: "My Lord! Show me how You give life to the dead." He said: "Do you not then believe?" He said: "Yes! but to satisfy my own understanding." He said: "Take four birds; tame them to turn to you; put a portion of them on every hill and call to them: they will come to you (flying) with speed. Then know that Allah is Exalted in Power, Wise."

261. The parable of those who spend their substance in the way of Allah is that of a grain of corn: it grows seven ears, and each ear has a hundred grains. Allah gives manifold increase to whom He pleases:

and Allah cares for all and He knows all things.

262. Those who spend their substance in the cause of Allah, and do not follow up their gifts with reminders of their generosity or with injury,-for them their reward is with their Lord: on them shall be no fear, nor shall they grieve.

263. Kind words and the covering of faults are better than charity followed by injury. Allah is Free of all wants, and He is Most Forbearing.

264. O you who believe! waste not your charity by reminders of your generosity or by injury,-like those who spend their substance to be seen of men, but believe neither in Allah nor in the Last Day. They are in parable like a hard, barren rock, on which is a little soil: on it falls heavy rain, which leaves it (Just) a bare stone. They will be able to do nothing with anything they have earned. And Allah does not guide those who reject faith.

265. And the likeness of those who spend their substance, seeking to please Allah and to strengthen their souls, is as a garden, high and fertile: heavy rain falls on it but makes it yield a double increase of harvest, and if it does not receive heavy rain, light moisture suffices it. Allah sees well whatever you do.

266. Does any of you wish that he should have a garden with date-palms and vines and streams flowing underneath, and

وَٱللّٰهُ وَاسِعٌ عَلِيمٌ ۝

ٱلَّذِينَ يُنفِقُونَ أَمْوَالَهُمْ فِى سَبِيلِ ٱللّٰهِ ثُمَّ لَا يُتْبِعُونَ مَآ أَنفَقُوا مَنًّا وَّلَآ أَذًى ۙ لَّهُمْ أَجْرُهُمْ عِندَ رَبِّهِمْ ۖ وَلَا خَوْفٌ عَلَيْهِمْ وَلَا هُمْ يَحْزَنُونَ ۝

قَوْلٌ مَّعْرُوفٌ وَّمَغْفِرَةٌ خَيْرٌ مِّن صَدَقَةٍ يَّتْبَعُهَآ أَذًى ۗ وَٱللّٰهُ غَنِيٌّ حَلِيمٌ ۝

يَٰٓأَيُّهَا ٱلَّذِينَ ءَامَنُوا لَا تُبْطِلُوا صَدَقَٰتِكُم بِٱلْمَنِّ وَٱلْأَذَىٰ ۙ كَٱلَّذِى يُنفِقُ مَالَهُ رِئَآءَ ٱلنَّاسِ وَلَا يُؤْمِنُ بِٱللّٰهِ وَٱلْيَوْمِ ٱلْءَاخِرِ ۖ فَمَثَلُهُۥ كَمَثَلِ صَفْوَانٍ عَلَيْهِ تُرَابٌ فَأَصَابَهُۥ وَابِلٌ فَتَرَكَهُۥ صَلْدًا ۖ لَّا يَقْدِرُونَ عَلَىٰ شَىْءٍ مِّمَّا كَسَبُوا ۗ وَٱللّٰهُ لَا يَهْدِى ٱلْقَوْمَ ٱلْكَٰفِرِينَ ۝

وَمَثَلُ ٱلَّذِينَ يُنفِقُونَ أَمْوَالَهُمُ ٱبْتِغَآءَ مَرْضَاتِ ٱللّٰهِ وَتَثْبِيتًا مِّنْ أَنفُسِهِمْ كَمَثَلِ جَنَّةٍ بِرَبْوَةٍ أَصَابَهَا وَابِلٌ فَآتَتْ أُكُلَهَا ضِعْفَيْنِ ۚ فَإِن لَّمْ يُصِبْهَا وَابِلٌ فَطَلٌّ ۗ وَٱللّٰهُ بِمَا تَعْمَلُونَ بَصِيرٌ ۝

أَيَوَدُّ أَحَدُكُمْ أَن تَكُونَ لَهُۥ جَنَّةٌ مِّن نَّخِيلٍ وَّأَعْنَابٍ تَجْرِى مِن تَحْتِهَا ٱلْأَنْهَٰرُ لَهُۥ فِيهَا مِن

all kinds of fruit, while he is stricken with old age, and his children are not strong (enough to look after themselves)- that it should be caught in a whirlwind, with fire therein, and be burnt up? Thus does Allah make clear to you (His) Signs; that you may consider.

267. O you who believe! Give of the good things which you have (honourably) earned, and of the fruits of the earth which We have produced for you, and do not even aim at getting anything which is bad, in order that out of it you may give away something, when you yourselves would not receive it except with closed eyes. And know that Allah is Free of all wants, and Worthy of all praise.

268. Satan threatens you with poverty and bids you to conduct unseemly. Allah promises you His forgiveness and bounties. And Allah cares for all and He knows all things.

269. He grants wisdom to whom He pleases; and he to whom wisdom is granted receives indeed a benefit overflowing; but none will grasp the Message but men of understanding.

270. And whatever you spend in charity or devotion, be sure Allah knows it all. But the wrong-doers have no helpers.

271. If you disclose (acts of) charity, even so it is well, but if you conceal them, and make them reach those (really) in need, that is best for you: It will remove from you some of your (stains of) evil. And Allah is well acquainted with what you do.

272. It is not required of you (O Apostle), to set them on the right path, but Allah sets on the right path whom He pleases. Whatever of

كُلِّ الثَّمَرٰتِ وَاَصَابَهُ الْكِبَرُ وَلَهٗ

ذُرِّيَّةٌ ضُعَفَآءُ ۖ فَاَصَابَهَآ اِعْصَارٌ

فِيْهِ نَارٌ فَاحْتَرَقَتْ ۖ كَذٰلِكَ يُبَيِّنُ

اللّٰهُ لَكُمُ الْاٰيٰتِ لَعَلَّكُمْ تَتَفَكَّرُوْنَ ۝

يٰٓاَيُّهَا الَّذِيْنَ اٰمَنُوْۤا اَنْفِقُوْا مِنْ

طَيِّبٰتِ مَا كَسَبْتُمْ وَمِمَّاۤ اَخْرَجْنَا

لَكُمْ مِّنَ الْاَرْضِ ۖ وَلَا تَيَمَّمُوا

الْخَبِيْثَ مِنْهُ تُنْفِقُوْنَ وَلَسْتُمْ

بِاٰخِذِيْهِ اِلَّاۤ اَنْ تُغْمِضُوْا فِيْهِ ۚ

وَاعْلَمُوْۤا اَنَّ اللّٰهَ غَنِيٌّ حَمِيْدٌ ۝

اَلشَّيْطٰنُ يَعِدُكُمُ الْفَقْرَ وَيَاْمُرُكُمْ

بِالْفَحْشَآءِ ۚ وَاللّٰهُ يَعِدُكُمْ مَّغْفِرَةً

مِّنْهُ وَفَضْلًا ۗ وَاللّٰهُ وَاسِعٌ عَلِيْمٌ ۝

يُّؤْتِي الْحِكْمَةَ مَنْ يَّشَآءُ ۚ وَمَنْ يُّؤْتَ

الْحِكْمَةَ فَقَدْ اُوْتِيَ خَيْرًا كَثِيْرًا ۗ

وَمَا يَذَّكَّرُ اِلَّاۤ اُولُوا الْاَلْبَابِ ۝

وَمَاۤ اَنْفَقْتُمْ مِّنْ نَّفَقَةٍ اَوْ

نَذَرْتُمْ مِّنْ نَّذْرٍ فَاِنَّ اللّٰهَ

يَعْلَمُهٗ ۗ وَمَا لِلظّٰلِمِيْنَ مِنْ اَنْصَارٍ ۝

اِنْ تُبْدُوا الصَّدَقٰتِ فَنِعِمَّا هِيَ ۚ

وَاِنْ تُخْفُوْهَا وَتُؤْتُوْهَا الْفُقَرَآءَ

فَهُوَ خَيْرٌ لَّكُمْ ۗ وَيُكَفِّرُ عَنْكُمْ

مِّنْ سَيِّاٰتِكُمْ ۗ وَاللّٰهُ بِمَا تَعْمَلُوْنَ

خَبِيْرٌ ۝

لَيْسَ عَلَيْكَ هُدٰىهُمْ وَلٰكِنَّ اللّٰهَ

يَهْدِيْ مَنْ يَّشَآءُ ۗ وَمَا تُنْفِقُوْا

good you give benefits your own souls, and you shall only do so seeking the "Face" of Allah. Whatever good you give, shall be rendered back to you, and you shall not be dealt with unjustly.

273. (Charity is) for those in need, who, in Allah's cause are restricted (from travel), and cannot move about in the land, seeking (for trade or work): the ignorant man thinks, because of their modesty, that they are free from want. You shall know them by their (unfailing) mark: they do not beg importunately from all and sundry. And whatever of good you give, be assured Allah knows it well.

274. Those who (in charity) spend of their goods by night and by day, in secret and in public, have their reward with their Lord: on them shall be no fear, nor shall they grieve.

275. Those who devour interest will not stand except as stands one whom the Satan One by his touch has driven to madness. That is because they say: "Trade is like interest," but Allah has permitted trade and forbidden interest. Those who after receiving direction from their Lord, desist, shall be pardoned for the past; their case is for Allah (to judge); but those who repeat (the offence) are companions of the Fire: they will abide therein (for ever).

276. Allah will deprive interest of all blessing, but will give increase for deeds of charity: for He does not love ungrateful and wicked creatures.

277. Those who believe, and do deeds of righteousness,

and establish regular prayers and regular charity, will have their reward with their Lord: on them shall be no fear, nor shall they grieve.

وَاَقَامُوا الصَّلٰوةَ وَاٰتَوُا الزَّكٰوةَ لَهُمْ اَجْرُهُمْ عِنْدَ رَبِّهِمْ ۚ وَلَا خَوْفٌ عَلَيْهِمْ وَلَا هُمْ يَحْزَنُوْنَ ۞

278. O you who believe! Fear Allah, and give up what remains of your demand for interest, if you are indeed believers.

يٰٓاَيُّهَا الَّذِيْنَ اٰمَنُوا اتَّقُوا اللّٰهَ وَذَرُوْا مَا بَقِيَ مِنَ الرِّبٰوٓا اِنْ كُنْتُمْ مُّؤْمِنِيْنَ ۞

279. If you do it not, take notice of war from Allah and His Apostle: but if you turn back, you shall have your capital sums, deal not unjustly, and you shall not be dealt with unjustly.

فَاِنْ لَّمْ تَفْعَلُوْا فَاْذَنُوْا بِحَرْبٍ مِّنَ اللّٰهِ وَرَسُوْلِهٖ ۚ وَاِنْ تُبْتُمْ فَلَكُمْ رُءُوْسُ اَمْوَالِكُمْ ۚ لَا تَظْلِمُوْنَ وَلَا تُظْلَمُوْنَ ۞

280. If the debtor is in a difficulty, grant him time till it is easy for him to repay. But if you remit it by way of charity, that is best for you if you only knew.

وَاِنْ كَانَ ذُوْ عُسْرَةٍ فَنَظِرَةٌ اِلٰى مَيْسَرَةٍ ۚ وَاَنْ تَصَدَّقُوْا خَيْرٌ لَّكُمْ اِنْ كُنْتُمْ تَعْلَمُوْنَ ۞

281. And fear the Day when you shall be brought back to Allah. Then shall every soul be paid what it earned, and none shall be dealt with unjustly.

وَاتَّقُوْا يَوْمًا تُرْجَعُوْنَ فِيْهِ اِلَى اللّٰهِ ۚ ثُمَّ تُوَفّٰى كُلُّ نَفْسٍ مَّا كَسَبَتْ وَهُمْ لَا يُظْلَمُوْنَ ۞

282. O you who believe! When you deal with each other, in transactions involving future obligations in a fixed period of time, reduce them to writing. Let a scribe write down faithfully as between the parties: let not the scribe refuse to write: as Allah has taught him, so let him write. Let him who incurs the liability dictate, but let him fear His Lord Allah, and not diminish anything of what he owes. If the party liable is mentally deficient, or weak, or unable himself to dictate, Let his guardian dictate faithfully. And get

يٰٓاَيُّهَا الَّذِيْنَ اٰمَنُوْٓا اِذَا تَدَايَنْتُمْ بِدَيْنٍ اِلٰٓى اَجَلٍ مُّسَمًّى فَاكْتُبُوْهُ ۚ وَلْيَكْتُبْ بَيْنَكُمْ كَاتِبٌ بِالْعَدْلِ ۚ وَلَا يَاْبَ كَاتِبٌ اَنْ يَّكْتُبَ كَمَا عَلَّمَهُ اللّٰهُ فَلْيَكْتُبْ ۚ وَلْيُمْلِلِ الَّذِيْ عَلَيْهِ الْحَقُّ وَلْيَتَّقِ اللّٰهَ رَبَّهٗ وَلَا يَبْخَسْ مِنْهُ شَيْئًا ۚ فَاِنْ كَانَ الَّذِيْ عَلَيْهِ الْحَقُّ سَفِيْهًا اَوْ ضَعِيْفًا اَوْ لَا يَسْتَطِيْعُ اَنْ يُّمِلَّ هُوَ فَلْيُمْلِلْ وَلِيُّهٗ بِالْعَدْلِ ۚ وَاسْتَشْهِدُوْا

two witnesses, out of your own men, and if there are not two men, then a man and two women, such as you choose, for witnesses, so that if one of them errs, the other can remind her. The witnesses should not refuse when they are called on (for evidence). Disdain not to reduce to writing (your contract) for a future period, whether it be small or big: it is juster in the sight of Allah, more suitable as evidence, and more convenient to prevent doubts among yourselves but if it be a transaction which you carry out on the spot among yourselves, there is no blame on you if you reduce it not to writing. But take witnesses whenever you make a commercial contract; and let neither scribe nor witness suffer harm. If you do (such harm), it would be wickedness in you. So fear Allah; for it is Allah that teaches you. And Allah is well acquainted with all things.

283. If you are on a journey, and cannot find a scribe, a pledge with possession (may serve the purpose). And if one of you deposits a thing on trust with another, Let the trustee (faithfully) discharge his trust, and let him fear his Lord. Conceal not evidence; for whoever conceals it,- his heart is tainted with sin. And Allah knows all that you do.

284. To Allah belongs all that is in the heavens and on earth. Whether you show what is in your minds or conceal it, Allah calls you to account for it.

شَهِيدَيْنِ مِنْ رِّجَالِكُمْ ۚ فَإِنْ لَّمْ يَكُوْنَا رَجُلَيْنِ فَرَجُلٌ وَّامْرَاَتٰنِ مِمَّنْ تَرْضَوْنَ مِنَ الشُّهَدَآءِ اَنْ تَضِلَّ اِحْدٰىهُمَا فَتُذَكِّرَ اِحْدٰىهُمَا الْاُخْرٰى ۚ وَلَا يَاْبَ الشُّهَدَآءُ اِذَا مَا دُعُوْا ۚ وَلَا تَسْـَٔمُوْۤا اَنْ تَكْتُبُوْهُ صَغِيْرًا اَوْ كَبِيْرًا اِلٰۤى اَجَلِهٖ ۚ ذٰلِكُمْ اَقْسَطُ عِنْدَ اللّٰهِ وَاَقْوَمُ لِلشَّهَادَةِ وَاَدْنٰۤى اَلَّا تَرْتَابُوْۤا اِلَّاۤ اَنْ تَكُوْنَ تِجَارَةً حَاضِرَةً تُدِيْرُوْنَهَا بَيْنَكُمْ فَلَيْسَ عَلَيْكُمْ جُنَاحٌ اَلَّا تَكْتُبُوْهَا ۚ وَاَشْهِدُوْۤا اِذَا تَبَايَعْتُمْ ۚ وَلَا يُضَآرَّ كَاتِبٌ وَّلَا شَهِيْدٌ ۚ وَاِنْ تَفْعَلُوْا فَاِنَّهٗ فُسُوْقٌ بِكُمْ ۗ وَاتَّقُوا اللّٰهَ ۚ وَيُعَلِّمُكُمُ اللّٰهُ ۚ وَاللّٰهُ بِكُلِّ شَيْءٍ عَلِيْمٌ ۝

وَاِنْ كُنْتُمْ عَلٰى سَفَرٍ وَّلَمْ تَجِدُوْا كَاتِبًا فَرِهٰنٌ مَّقْبُوْضَةٌ ۚ فَاِنْ اَمِنَ بَعْضُكُمْ بَعْضًا فَلْيُؤَدِّ الَّذِى اؤْتُمِنَ اَمَانَتَهٗ وَلْيَتَّقِ اللّٰهَ رَبَّهٗ ۚ وَلَا تَكْتُمُوا الشَّهَادَةَ ۚ وَمَنْ يَّكْتُمْهَا فَاِنَّهٗۤ اٰثِمٌ قَلْبُهٗ ۗ وَاللّٰهُ بِمَا تَعْمَلُوْنَ عَلِيْمٌ ۝

لِلّٰهِ مَا فِى السَّمٰوٰتِ وَمَا فِى الْاَرْضِ ۗ وَاِنْ تُبْدُوْا مَا فِىْۤ اَنْفُسِكُمْ اَوْ تُخْفُوْهُ يُحَاسِبْكُمْ بِهِ اللّٰهُ ۖ

SÛRAH-3
ÂL-I-'IMRÃN
(INTRODUCTION)

This Sûrah is cognate to Sûrah 2, but the matter is here treated from a different point of view. The references to Badr (Ramadhân, H. 2.) and Uḥud (Shawwâl, H. 3) give a clue to the dates of those passages.

Like Sûrah 2, it takes a general view of the religious history of mankind, with special reference to the People of the Book, proceeds to explain the birth of the new People of Islam and their ordinances, insists on the need of struggle and fighting in the cause of Truth, and exhorts those who have been blessed with Islam to remain constant in Faith, pray for guidance, and maintain their spiritual hope for the Future.

Then new points of view developed are: (1) The emphasis is here laid on the duty of the Christians to accept the new light; the Christians are here specially appealed to as the jews were specially appealed to in the last Sûrah; (2) the lessons of the battles of Badr and Uḥud are set out for the Muslim community; and (3) the responsibilities of that community are insisted on both internally and in their relations to those outside.

He forgives whom He pleases,
and punishes whom He pleases.
For Allah has power over all
things.

285. The Apostle believes in
what has been revealed to him
from his Lord, as do the men of
faith. Each one (of them)
believes in Allah, His Angels,
His Books, and His Apostles.
"We make no distinction (they
say) between one and another of
His Apostles." And they say:
"We hear, and we obey: (we
seek) Your forgiveness, Our
Lord, and to You is the end of all
journeys."

286. On no soul Allah places a
burden greater than it can bear.
It gets every good that it earns,
and it suffers every ill that it
earns. (Pray:) "Our Lord! do not
condemn us if we forget or fall
into error; our Lord! do not lay
on us a burden like that which
You did lay on those before us;
our Lord! do not lay on us a
burden greater than we have
strength to bear. Blot out our
sins, and grant us forgiveness.
Have mercy on us. You are our
Protector; help us against those
who stand against Faith.

---

3. The Family of 'Imran

In the name of Allah, Most
Gracious, Most Merciful.

1. Alif-Lam-Mim
2. Allah! There is no god but
He,-the Living, the Self-
Subsisting, Eternal.
3. It is He Who sent down to
you (step by step), in truth, the
Book, confirming what went
before it; and He sent down the
Law (of Moses) and the Gospel
(of Jesus).
4. Before this, as a guide to
mankind, and He sent down the
Criterion (of judgment between
right and wrong). Then those who
reject Faith in the Signs of

فَيَغْفِرُ لِمَنْ يَّشَآءُ وَيُعَذِّبُ مَنْ
يَّشَآءُ ؕ وَاللّٰهُ عَلٰى كُلِّ شَىْءٍ قَدِيْرٌ ۟

اٰمَنَ الرَّسُوْلُ بِمَاۤ اُنْزِلَ اِلَيْهِ
مِنْ رَّبِّهٖ وَالْمُؤْمِنُوْنَ ؕ كُلٌّ اٰمَنَ
بِاللّٰهِ وَمَلٰٓئِكَتِهٖ وَكُتُبِهٖ وَرُسُلِهٖ ۟
لَا نُفَرِّقُ بَيْنَ اَحَدٍ مِّنْ رُّسُلِهٖ ۟
وَقَالُوْا سَمِعْنَا وَاَطَعْنَا ۤ غُفْرَانَكَ
رَبَّنَا وَاِلَيْكَ الْمَصِيْرُ ۟

لَا يُكَلِّفُ اللّٰهُ نَفْسًا اِلَّا وُسْعَهَا ؕ لَهَا
مَا كَسَبَتْ وَعَلَيْهَا مَا اكْتَسَبَتْ ؕ
رَبَّنَا لَا تُؤَاخِذْنَاۤ اِنْ نَّسِيْنَاۤ اَوْ
اَخْطَاْنَا ۚ رَبَّنَا وَلَا تَحْمِلْ عَلَيْنَاۤ
اِصْرًا كَمَا حَمَلْتَهٗ عَلَى الَّذِيْنَ
مِنْ قَبْلِنَا ۚ رَبَّنَا وَلَا تُحَمِّلْنَا مَا
لَا طَاقَةَ لَنَا بِهٖ ۚ وَاعْفُ عَنَّا ۟
وَاغْفِرْ لَنَا ۟ وَارْحَمْنَا ۟ اَنْتَ مَوْلٰىنَا
فَانْصُرْنَا عَلَى الْقَوْمِ الْكٰفِرِيْنَ ۟

(٣) سُوْرَةُ اٰلِ عِمْرٰن مَدَنِيَّةٌ (٨٩)

بِسْمِ اللّٰهِ الرَّحْمٰنِ الرَّحِيْمِ

الٓمّٓ ۟
اللّٰهُ لَاۤ اِلٰهَ اِلَّا هُوَ الْحَىُّ الْقَيُّوْمُ ؕ
نَزَّلَ عَلَيْكَ الْكِتٰبَ بِالْحَقِّ
مُصَدِّقًا لِّمَا بَيْنَ يَدَيْهِ وَاَنْزَلَ
التَّوْرٰىةَ وَالْاِنْجِيْلَ ۟
مِنْ قَبْلُ هُدًى لِّلنَّاسِ وَاَنْزَلَ
الْفُرْقَانَ ؕ اِنَّ الَّذِيْنَ كَفَرُوْا بِاٰيٰتِ

Allah will suffer the severest chastisement, and Allah is Exalted in Might, Lord of Retribution.

5.   From Allah, verily nothing is hidden on earth or in the heavens.

6.   He it is Who shapes you in the wombs as He pleases. There is no god but He, the Exalted in Might, the Wise.

7.   He it is Who has sent down to you the Book: In it are verses basic or fundamental (of established meaning); they are the foundation of the Book: others are allegorical. But those in whose hearts is perversity follow the part thereof that is allegorical, seeking discord, and searching for its hidden meanings, but no one knows its hidden meanings except Allah. And those who are firmly grounded in knowledge say: "We believe in the Book; the whole of it is from our Lord:" and none will grasp the Message except men of understanding.

8.   "Our Lord!" (they say), "Let not our hearts deviate now after You have guided us, but grant us mercy from Your Own Presence; for You are the Grantor of bounties without measure.

9.   "Our Lord! You are He that will gather mankind together against a Day about which there is no doubt; for Allah never fails in His promise."

10.   Those who reject Faith,- neither their possessions nor their (numerous) progeny will avail them nothing against Allah: they are themselves but fuel for the Fire.

11. (Their plight will be) no better than that of the people of Pharaoh, and their predecessors: they denied our Signs, and Allah called them to account for their sins. For Allah is strict in punishment.

كَدَأْبِ اٰلِ فِرْعَوْنَ ۙ وَالَّذِيْنَ مِنْ قَبْلِهِمْ ۚ كَذَّبُوْا بِاٰيٰتِنَا ۚ فَاَخَذَهُمُ اللّٰهُ بِذُنُوْبِهِمْ ۙ وَاللّٰهُ شَدِيْدُ الْعِقَابِ ۝

12. Say to those who reject Faith: "Soon will you be vanquished and gathered together to Hell,-an evil bed indeed (to lie on)!

قُلْ لِّلَّذِيْنَ كَفَرُوْا سَتُغْلَبُوْنَ وَتُحْشَرُوْنَ اِلٰى جَهَنَّمَ ۚ وَبِئْسَ الْمِهَادُ ۝

13. "There has already been for you a Sign in the two armies that met (in combat): one was fighting in the cause of Allah, the other resisting Allah; these saw with their own eyes twice their number. But Allah supports with His aid whom He pleases. In this is a warning for such as have eyes to see."

قَدْ كَانَ لَكُمْ اٰيَةٌ فِيْ فِئَتَيْنِ الْتَقَتَا ۚ فِئَةٌ تُقَاتِلُ فِيْ سَبِيْلِ اللّٰهِ وَاُخْرٰى كَافِرَةٌ يَّرَوْنَهُمْ مِّثْلَيْهِمْ رَأْيَ الْعَيْنِ ۚ وَاللّٰهُ يُؤَيِّدُ بِنَصْرِهٖ مَنْ يَّشَاءُ ۚ اِنَّ فِيْ ذٰلِكَ لَعِبْرَةً لِّاُولِى الْاَبْصَارِ ۝

14. Fair in the eyes of men is the love of things they covet: Women and sons; heaped-up hoards of gold and silver; horses branded (for breed and excellence); and (wealth of) cattle and well-tilled land. Such are the possessions of this world's life; but in nearness to Allah is the best of the goals (to return to).

زُيِّنَ لِلنَّاسِ حُبُّ الشَّهَوٰتِ مِنَ النِّسَاءِ وَالْبَنِيْنَ وَالْقَنَاطِيْرِ الْمُقَنْطَرَةِ مِنَ الذَّهَبِ وَالْفِضَّةِ وَالْخَيْلِ الْمُسَوَّمَةِ وَالْاَنْعَامِ وَالْحَرْثِ ۚ ذٰلِكَ مَتَاعُ الْحَيٰوةِ الدُّنْيَا ۚ وَاللّٰهُ عِنْدَهٗ حُسْنُ الْمَاٰبِ ۝

15. Say: Shall I give you glad tidings of things for better than those? For the righteous are Gardens in nearness to their Lord, with rivers flowing beneath; therein is their eternal home; with Companions pure (and holy); and the good pleasure of Allah. For in Allah's sight are (all) His servants.

قُلْ اَؤُنَبِّئُكُمْ بِخَيْرٍ مِّنْ ذٰلِكُمْ ۚ لِلَّذِيْنَ اتَّقَوْا عِنْدَ رَبِّهِمْ جَنّٰتٌ تَجْرِيْ مِنْ تَحْتِهَا الْاَنْهٰرُ خٰلِدِيْنَ فِيْهَا وَاَزْوَاجٌ مُّطَهَّرَةٌ وَّرِضْوَانٌ مِّنَ اللّٰهِ ۗ وَاللّٰهُ بَصِيْرٌ بِالْعِبَادِ ۝

16. (Namely), those who say: "Our Lord! we have indeed believed: forgive us, then, our sins, and save us from the agony of the Fire;"-

اَلَّذِيْنَ يَقُوْلُوْنَ رَبَّنَآ اِنَّنَآ اٰمَنَّا فَاغْفِرْ لَنَا ذُنُوْبَنَا وَقِنَا عَذَابَ النَّارِ ۚ

17. Those who show patience, firmness and self-control; who are true (in word and deed); who worship devoutly; who spend (in the way of Allah); and who pray for forgiveness in the early hours of the morning.

18. There is no god but He: that is the witness of Allah, His angels, and those endued with knowledge, standing firm on justice. There is no god but He, the Exalted in Power, the Wise.

19. The Religion before Allah is Islam (submission to His Will): nor did the People of the Book dissent therefrom except through envy of each other, after knowledge had come to them. But if any deny the Signs of Allah, Allah is swift in calling to account.

20. So if they dispute with you, say: "I have submitted my whole self to Allah and so have those who follow me." And say to the People of the Book and to those who are unlearned: "Do you (also) submit yourselves?" If they do, they are in right guidance, but if they turn back, your duty is to convey the Message; and in Allah's sight are (all) His servants.

21. As to those who deny the Signs of Allah, and in defiance of right, slay the prophets, and slay those who teach just dealing with mankind, announce to them a grievous chastisement.

22. They are those whose works will bear no fruit in this world and in the Hereafter, nor will they have anyone to help.

23. Have you not turned your vision to those who have been given a portion of the Book? They are invited to the Book of Allah, to settle their dispute, but a party of them turn back and decline (the arbitration).

24. This because they say: "The Fire shall not touch us but for a few numbered days": for their forgeries deceive them as to their own religion.

ذٰلِكَ بِأَنَّهُمْ قَالُوا لَنْ تَمَسَّنَا النَّارُ اِلَّا اَيَّامًا مَّعْدُوْدٰتٍ ۖ وَّغَرَّهُمْ فِيْ دِيْنِهِمْ مَّا كَانُوْا يَفْتَرُوْنَ ۞

25. But how (will they fare) when We gather them together against a Day about which there is no doubt, and each soul will be paid out just what it has earned, without (favour or) injustice?

فَكَيْفَ اِذَا جَمَعْنٰهُمْ لِيَوْمٍ لَّا رَيْبَ فِيْهِ ۙ وَوُفِّيَتْ كُلُّ نَفْسٍ مَّا كَسَبَتْ وَهُمْ لَا يُظْلَمُوْنَ ۞

26. Say: "O Allah! Lord of Power (and Rule), You give power to whom You please, and You strip off power from whom You please: You endue with honour whom You please, and You bring low whom You please: In Your hand is all good. Verily, over all things You have power.

قُلِ اللّٰهُمَّ مٰلِكَ الْمُلْكِ تُؤْتِى الْمُلْكَ مَنْ تَشَآءُ وَتَنْزِعُ الْمُلْكَ مِمَّنْ تَشَآءُ وَتُعِزُّ مَنْ تَشَآءُ وَتُذِلُّ مَنْ تَشَآءُ ۖ بِيَدِكَ الْخَيْرُ ۖ اِنَّكَ عَلٰى كُلِّ شَيْءٍ قَدِيْرٌ ۞

27. "You cause the Night to gain on the Day, and You cause the Day to gain on the Night; You bring the Living out of the Dead, and You bring the Dead out of the Living; and You give sustenance to whom You please, without measure ."

تُوْلِجُ الَّيْلَ فِى النَّهَارِ وَتُوْلِجُ النَّهَارَ فِى الَّيْلِ ۖ وَتُخْرِجُ الْحَىَّ مِنَ الْمَيِّتِ وَتُخْرِجُ الْمَيِّتَ مِنَ الْحَىِّ ۖ وَتَرْزُقُ مَنْ تَشَآءُ بِغَيْرِ حِسَابٍ ۞

28. Let not the Believers take for friends or helpers Unbelievers rather than Believers: if any do that, in nothing will there be help from Allah: except by way of precaution, that you may guard yourselves from them. But Allah cautions you (to remember) Himself; for the final goal is to Allah.

لَا يَتَّخِذِ الْمُؤْمِنُوْنَ الْكٰفِرِيْنَ اَوْلِيَآءَ مِنْ دُوْنِ الْمُؤْمِنِيْنَ ۖ وَمَنْ يَّفْعَلْ ذٰلِكَ فَلَيْسَ مِنَ اللّٰهِ فِيْ شَيْءٍ اِلَّا اَنْ تَتَّقُوْا مِنْهُمْ تُقٰىةً ۖ وَيُحَذِّرُكُمُ اللّٰهُ نَفْسَهُ ۖ وَاِلَى اللّٰهِ الْمَصِيْرُ ۞

29. Say: "Whether you hide what is in your hearts or reveal it, Allah knows it all: He knows what is in the heavens, and what is on earth. And Allah has power over all things.

قُلْ اِنْ تُخْفُوْا مَا فِيْ صُدُوْرِكُمْ اَوْ تُبْدُوْهُ يَعْلَمْهُ اللّٰهُ ۖ وَيَعْلَمُ مَا فِى السَّمٰوٰتِ وَمَا فِى الْاَرْضِ ۖ وَاللّٰهُ عَلٰى كُلِّ شَيْءٍ قَدِيْرٌ ۞

30. "On the Day when every soul will be confronted with all

يَوْمَ تَجِدُ كُلُّ نَفْسٍ مَّا عَمِلَتْ مِنْ

the good it has done, and all the evil it has done, it will wish there were a great distance between it and its evil. But Allah cautions you (to remember) Himself. And Allah is full of kindness to those that serve Him."

31. Say: "If you do love Allah, follow me: Allah will love you and forgive you your sins: for Allah is Oft-Forgiving, Most Merciful."

32. Say: "Obey Allah and His Apostle": but if they turn back, Allah does not love those who reject Faith.

33. Allah chose Adam and Noah, the family of Abraham, and the family of 'Imran above all people,-

34. Offspring, one of the other: and Allah hears and knows all things.

35. Behold! a woman of 'Imran said: "O my Lord! I do dedicate unto You what is in my womb for Your special service: So accept this of me: for You hear and know all things."

36. When she delivered (the baby girl) she said: "O my Lord! Behold! I have delivered a female child!"- and Allah knew best what she brought forth- "And no wise is the male like the female. I have named her Mary, and I commend her and her offspring to Your protection from Satan, the Rejected."

37. Right graciously did her Lord accept her: He made her grow in purity and beauty: she was assigned to the care of Zakariya. Every time that he entered (Her) chamber to see her, He found her supplied with sustenance. He said:

"O Mary! Wherefrom (comes) this to you?" She said: "From Allah: for Allah provides sustenance to whom He pleases without measure."

38. Zakariya prayed there to his Lord, saying: "O my Lord! Grant unto me from Your presence a progeny that is pure: for You are He Who hears prayer!

39. While he was standing in prayer in the chamber, the angels called unto him: "Allah gives you the glad tidings of Yahya, confirming the truth of a Word from Allah, and be (besides) noble, chaste, and a prophet,- of the (goodly) company of the righteous."

40. He said: "O my Lord! how shall I have a son, seeing I am very old, and my wife is barren?" "Thus," was the answer, "Allah accomplishes what He wills."

41. He said: "O my Lord! give me a Sign!" "Your Sign," was the answer, "shall be that you shall speak to no man for three days but with signals. Then celebrate the praises of your Lord again and again, and glorify Him in the evening and in the morning."

42. Behold! the angels said: "O Mary! Allah has chosen you and purified you- chosen you above the women of all nations.

43 "O Mary! worship your Lord devoutly: Prostrate yourself and bow down (in prayer) with those who bow down."

44. This is part of the tidings of the things unseen, which We reveal unto you (O Apostle!) by inspiration: you were not with them when they cast lots with arrows, as to which of them should be charged with the care of Mary:

nor were you with them when they disputed (the point).

45. Behold! the angels said: "O Mary! Allah gives you glad tidings of a Word from Him: his name will be Christ Jesus, the son of Mary, held in honour in this world and the Hereafter and of (the company of) those nearest to Allah;

46. "He shall speak to the people in infancy and in maturity. And he shall be (of the company) of the righteous."

47. She said: "O my Lord! how shall I have a son when no man has touched me?" He said: "Even so: Allah creates what He wills: When He has decreed a Plan, He but says to it, 'Be,' and it is!

48. "And Allah will teach him the Book and Wisdom, the Torah and the Gospel,?

49. "And (appoint him) an Apostle to the Children of Israel, (with this message): "'I have come to you, with a Sign from your Lord, in that I make for you out of clay, as it were, the figure of a bird, and breathe into it, and it becomes a bird by Allah's leave: and I heal those born blind, and the lepers, and I quicken the dead, by Allah's leave; and I declare to you what you eat, and what you store in your houses. Surely therein is a Sign for you if you did believe;

50. "'(I have come to you), to attest the Torah which was before me. And to make lawful to you part of what was (before) forbidden to you; I have come to you with a Sign from

your Lord. So fear Allah, and obey me.

51. "'It is Allah Who is my Lord and your Lord; then worship Him. This is a Way that is straight.'"

52. When Jesus found unbelief on their part, he said: "Who will be my helpers to (the work of) Allah?" Said the disciples: "We are Allah's helpers: We believe in Allah, and you bear witness that we are Muslims.

53. "Our Lord! we believe in what You have revealed, and we follow the Apostle; then write us down among those who bear witness."

54. And (the unbelievers) plotted and planned, and Allah too planned, and the best of planners is Allah.

55. Behold! Allah said: "O Jesus! I will take you and raise you to Myself and clear you (of the falsehoods) of those who blaspheme; I will make those who follow you superior to those who reject faith, to the Day of Resurrection: then you shall all return to me, and I will judge between you of the matters wherein you dispute.

56. "As to those who reject faith, I will punish them with terrible agony in this world and in the Hereafter, nor will they have anyone to help."

57. "As to those who believe and work righteousness, Allah will pay them (in full) their reward; but Allah does not love those who do wrong."

58. "This is what We rehearse to you of the Signs and the Message of Wisdom."

59. The similitude of Jesus before Allah is as that of Adam; He created him from dust, then said to him: "Be". And he was.

اِنَّ مَثَلَ عِيْسٰى عِنْدَ اللّٰهِ كَمَثَلِ اٰدَمَ ۚ خَلَقَهٗ مِنْ تُرَابٍ ثُمَّ قَالَ لَهٗ كُنْ فَيَكُوْنُ ۞

60. The Truth (comes) from Allah alone; so be not of those who doubt.

اَلْحَقُّ مِنْ رَّبِّكَ فَلَا تَكُنْ مِّنَ الْمُمْتَرِيْنَ ۞

61. If any one disputes in this matter with you, now after (full) knowledge has come to you, say: "Come! let us gather together,- our sons and your sons, our women and your women, ourselves and yourselves: then let us earnestly pray, and invoke the curse of Allah on those who lie!"

فَمَنْ حَآجَّكَ فِيْهِ مِنْ بَعْدِ مَا جَآءَكَ مِنَ الْعِلْمِ فَقُلْ تَعَالَوْا نَدْعُ اَبْنَآءَنَا وَاَبْنَآءَكُمْ وَنِسَآءَنَا وَنِسَآءَكُمْ وَاَنْفُسَنَا وَاَنْفُسَكُمْ ۗ ثُمَّ نَبْتَهِلْ فَنَجْعَلْ لَّعْنَتَ اللّٰهِ عَلَى الْكٰذِبِيْنَ ۞

62. This is the true account: there is no god except Allah; and Allah-He is indeed the Exalted in Power, the Wise.

اِنَّ هٰذَا لَهُوَ الْقَصَصُ الْحَقُّ ۚ وَمَا مِنْ اِلٰهٍ اِلَّا اللّٰهُ ۗ وَاِنَّ اللّٰهَ لَهُوَ الْعَزِيْزُ الْحَكِيْمُ ۞

63. But if they turn back, Allah has full knowledge of those who do mischief.

فَاِنْ تَوَلَّوْا فَاِنَّ اللّٰهَ عَلِيْمٌ ۢ بِالْمُفْسِدِيْنَ ۞

64. Say: "O People of the Book! come to common terms as between us and you: that we worship none but Allah; that we associate no partners with Him; that we do not erect, from among ourselves, Lords and patrons other than Allah." If then they turn back, you say: "Bear witness that we (at least) are Muslims (bowing to Allah's Will).
65. You People of the Book! Why do you dispute about Abraham, when the Torah and the Gospel were not revealed till after him? Have you no understanding?

قُلْ يٰٓاَهْلَ الْكِتٰبِ تَعَالَوْا اِلٰى كَلِمَةٍ سَوَآءٍۢ بَيْنَنَا وَبَيْنَكُمْ اَلَّا نَعْبُدَ اِلَّا اللّٰهَ وَلَا نُشْرِكَ بِهٖ شَيْئًا وَّلَا يَتَّخِذَ بَعْضُنَا بَعْضًا اَرْبَابًا مِّنْ دُوْنِ اللّٰهِ ۚ فَاِنْ تَوَلَّوْا فَقُوْلُوا اشْهَدُوْا بِاَنَّا مُسْلِمُوْنَ ۞ يٰٓاَهْلَ الْكِتٰبِ لِمَ تُحَآجُّوْنَ فِيْٓ اِبْرٰهِيْمَ وَمَآ اُنْزِلَتِ التَّوْرٰىةُ وَالْاِنْجِيْلُ اِلَّا مِنْ بَعْدِهٖ ۗ اَفَلَا تَعْقِلُوْنَ ۞

66. Ah! You are those who fell to disputing (even) in matters of which you had some knowledge! but why do you dispute in matters of which you have no knowledge? It is Allah Who knows, and you who do not know!

هَآنْتُمْ هٰؤُلَآءِ حَاجَجْتُمْ فِيْمَا لَكُمْ بِهٖ عِلْمٌ فَلِمَ تُحَآجُّوْنَ فِيْمَا لَيْسَ لَكُمْ بِهٖ عِلْمٌ ۚ وَاللّٰهُ يَعْلَمُ وَاَنْتُمْ لَا تَعْلَمُوْنَ ۞

67. Abraham was not a Jew nor yet a Christian; but he was true in Faith, and bowed his will to Allah's (Which is Islam), and he did not join gods with Allah.

مَا كَانَ اِبْرٰهِيْمُ يَهُوْدِيًّا وَّلَا نَصْرَانِيًّا وَّلٰكِنْ كَانَ حَنِيْفًا مُّسْلِمًا ۚ وَمَا كَانَ مِنَ الْمُشْرِكِيْنَ ۞

68. Without doubt, among men, the nearest of kin to Abraham, are those who follow him, as are also this Apostle and those who believe: And Allah is the Protector of those who have Faith.

اِنَّ اَوْلَى النَّاسِ بِاِبْرٰهِيْمَ لَلَّذِيْنَ اتَّبَعُوْهُ وَهٰذَا النَّبِيُّ وَالَّذِيْنَ اٰمَنُوْا ۗ وَاللّٰهُ وَلِيُّ الْمُؤْمِنِيْنَ ۞

69. It is the wish of a section of the People of the Book to lead you astray. But they shall lead astray (not you), but themselves, and they do not perceive!

وَدَّتْ طَّآئِفَةٌ مِّنْ اَهْلِ الْكِتٰبِ لَوْ يُضِلُّوْنَكُمْ ۚ وَمَا يُضِلُّوْنَ اِلَّا اَنْفُسَهُمْ وَمَا يَشْعُرُوْنَ ۞

70. You People of the Book! Why do you reject the Signs of Allah, of which you are (yourselves) witnesses?

يٰٓاَهْلَ الْكِتٰبِ لِمَ تَكْفُرُوْنَ بِاٰيٰتِ اللّٰهِ وَاَنْتُمْ تَشْهَدُوْنَ ۞

71. You People of the Book! Why do you clothe Truth with falsehood, and conceal the Truth, while you have knowledge?

يٰٓاَهْلَ الْكِتٰبِ لِمَ تَلْبِسُوْنَ الْحَقَّ بِالْبَاطِلِ وَتَكْتُمُوْنَ الْحَقَّ وَاَنْتُمْ تَعْلَمُوْنَ ۞

72. A section of the People of the Book say: "Believe in the morning what is revealed to the Believers, but reject it at the end of the day; perchance they may (themselves) turn back;

وَقَالَتْ طَّآئِفَةٌ مِّنْ اَهْلِ الْكِتٰبِ اٰمِنُوْا بِالَّذِيْٓ اُنْزِلَ عَلَى الَّذِيْنَ اٰمَنُوْا وَجْهَ النَّهَارِ وَاكْفُرُوْٓا اٰخِرَهٗ لَعَلَّهُمْ يَرْجِعُوْنَ ۞

73. "And believe no one unless he follows your religion." Say: "True guidance is the guidance of Allah: (fear you) lest a revelation be sent to someone (else) like that which was sent to you? Or that those (receiving such revelation) should engage you in argument before your Lord?" Say:

وَلَا تُؤْمِنُوْٓا اِلَّا لِمَنْ تَبِعَ دِيْنَكُمْ ۗ قُلْ اِنَّ الْهُدٰى هُدَى اللّٰهِ ۙ اَنْ يُّؤْتٰٓى اَحَدٌ مِّثْلَ مَآ اُوْتِيْتُمْ اَوْ يُحَآجُّوْكُمْ عِنْدَ رَبِّكُمْ ۗ قُلْ اِنَّ

"All bounties are in the hand of Allah: He grants them to whom He pleases: and Allah cares for all, and He knows all things."

74. For His Mercy He specially chooses whom He pleases; for Allah is the Lord of bounties unbounded.

75. Among the People of the Book are some who, if entrusted with a hoard of gold, will (readily) pay it back; others, who, if entrusted with a single silver coin, will not repay it unless you constantly stood demanding, because, they say, "there is no call on us (to keep faith) with these ignorant (Pagans)." But they tell a lie against Allah, and (well) they know it.

76. Nay, those that keep their plighted faith and act aright, verily Allah loves those who act aright.

77. As for those who sell the faith they owe to Allah and their own plighted word for a small price, they shall have no portion in the Hereafter: nor will Allah speak to them or look at them on the Day of Judgment, nor will He cleanse them (of sin): they shall have a grievous Chastisement.

78. There is among them a section who distort the Book with their tongues: (as they read) you would think it is a part of the Book, but it is no part of the Book; and they say, "That is from Allah," but it is not from Allah: it is they who tell a lie against Allah, and (well) they know it!

79. It is not (possible) that a man, to whom is given

the Book, and Wisdom, and the Prophetic Office, should say to people: "You be my worshippers rather than Allah's": on the contrary (he would say) "You be worshippers of Him Who is truly the Cherisher of all: for you had taught the Book, and you have studied it earnestly."

80. Nor would he instruct you to take angels and prophets for Lords and Patrons. What! would he bid you to unbelief after you have bowed your will (to Allah in Islam)?

81. Behold! Allah took the Covenant of the Prophets, saying: "I give you a Book and Wisdom; then comes to you an Apostle, confirming what is with you; you believe in him and render him help." Allah said: "Do you agree, and take this My Covenant as binding on you?" They said: "We agree." He said: "Then bear witness, and I am with you among the witnesses."

82. If any turn back after this, they are perverted transgressors.

83. Do they seek for other than the Religion of Allah?- while all creatures in the heavens and on the earth have, willingly or unwillingly, bowed to His Will (accepted Islam), and to Him shall they all be brought back.

84. Say: "We believe in Allah, and in what has been revealed to us and what was revealed to Abraham, Isma'il, Isaac, Jacob, and the Tribes, and in (the Books) given to Moses, Jesus, and the Prophets, from their Lord: we make no distinction between one and another among them, and to Allah do we bow our will (in Islam)."

85. If anyone desires a religion other than Islam (submission to Allah), never will it be accepted of him; and in the Hereafter he will be in the ranks of those who have lost (all spiritual good).

86. How shall Allah guide those who reject Faith after they accepted it and bore witness that the Apostle was true and that Clear Signs had come to them? But Allah does not guide a people unjust.

87. Of such the reward is that on them (rests) the curse of Allah, of His angels, and of all mankind;-

88. In that will they dwell; nor will their Chastisement be lightened, nor respite be their (lot);-

89. Except for those that repent (even) after that, and make amends; for verily Allah is Oft-Forgiving, Most Merciful.

90. But those who reject Faith after they accepted it, and then go on adding to their defiance of Faith, - never will their repentance be accepted; for they are those who have (of set purpose) gone astray.

91. As to those who reject Faith, and die rejecting, - never would be accepted from any such as much gold as the earth contains, though they should offer it for ransom. For such is (in store) a Chastisement grievous, and they will find no helpers.

92. By no means shall you attain righteousness unless you give (freely) of that which you love; and whatever you give, of a truth Allah knows it well.

93. All food was lawful to the Children of Israel, except what Israel made unlawful for itself,

before the Law (of Moses) was revealed. Say: " you bring the Law and study it, if you be men of truth.

94. If any, after this, invent a lie and attribute it to Allah, they are indeed unjust wrong-doers.

95. Say: "Allah speaks the Truth: follow the religion of Abraham, the sane in faith; he was not of the Pagans."

96. The first House (of worship) appointed for men was that at Bakka (Makkah); full of blessing and of guidance for all kinds of beings:

97. In it are Signs manifest; (for example), the Station of Abraham; whoever enters it attains security; pilgrimage thereto is a duty men owe to Allah,- those who can afford the journey; but if any deny faith, Allah does not stand in need of any of His creatures.

98. Say: "O People of the Book! Why do you reject the Signs of Allah, when Allah is Himself witness to all you do?"

99. Say: "O you People of the Book! Why do you obstruct those who believe, from the path of Allah, seeking to make it crooked, while you were yourselves witnesses (to Allah's Covenant)? But Allah is not unmindful of all that you do."

100. O you who believe! If you listen to a faction among the People of the Book, they would (indeed) render you apostates after you have believed!

101. And how would you deny Faith while unto you are rehearsed the Signs of Allah, and among you lives the Apostle? Whoever holds firmly to Allah will be shown

a Way that is straight.

102. O you who believe! Fear
Allah as He should be feared,
and do not die except in a state
of Islam.

103. And hold fast, all together,
by the Rope which Allah
(stretches out for you), and be
not divided among yourselves;
and remember with gratitude
Allah's favour on you; for you
were enemies and He joined
your hearts in love, so that by His
Grace, you became brethren; and
you were on the brink of the Pit
of Fire, and He saved you from it.
Thus Allah makes His Signs
clear to you: that you may be
guided.

104. Let there arise out of you a
band of people inviting to all
that is good, enjoining what is
right, and forbidding what is
wrong: they are the ones to
attain felicity.

105. Be not like those who are
divided amongst themselves
and fall into disputations after
receiving Clear Signs: for them
is a dreadful Chastisement,-

106. On the Day when some
faces will be (lit up with) white,
and some faces will be (in the
gloom of) black: to those whose
faces will be black, (will be said):
"Did you reject Faith after
accepting it? Taste then the Chastisement for rejecting Faith."

107. But those whose faces will
be (lit with) white,- they will be
in (the light of) Allah's mercy:
therein to dwell (for ever).

108. These are the Signs of
Allah: We rehearse them to you
in Truth: and Allah means no
injustice to any of His creatures.

109. To Allah belongs all that is
in the heavens and on earth: to
Him do all questions go back
(for decision).

إِلٰى صِرَاطٍ مُّسْتَقِيْمٍ ۞

يٰۤاَيُّهَا الَّذِيْنَ اٰمَنُوا اتَّقُوا اللّٰهَ حَقَّ تُقٰتِهٖ وَلَا تَمُوْتُنَّ اِلَّا وَاَنْتُمْ مُّسْلِمُوْنَ ۞

وَاعْتَصِمُوْا بِحَبْلِ اللّٰهِ جَمِيْعًا وَّلَا تَفَرَّقُوْا ۪ وَاذْكُرُوْا نِعْمَتَ اللّٰهِ عَلَيْكُمْ اِذْ كُنْتُمْ اَعْدَآءً فَاَلَّفَ بَيْنَ قُلُوْبِكُمْ فَاَصْبَحْتُمْ بِنِعْمَتِهٖۤ اِخْوَانًا ۚ وَكُنْتُمْ عَلٰى شَفَا حُفْرَةٍ مِّنَ النَّارِ فَاَنْقَذَكُمْ مِّنْهَا ۗ كَذٰلِكَ يُبَيِّنُ اللّٰهُ لَكُمْ اٰيٰتِهٖ لَعَلَّكُمْ تَهْتَدُوْنَ ۞

وَلْتَكُنْ مِّنْكُمْ اُمَّةٌ يَّدْعُوْنَ اِلَى الْخَيْرِ وَيَاْمُرُوْنَ بِالْمَعْرُوْفِ وَيَنْهَوْنَ عَنِ الْمُنْكَرِ ۗ وَاُولٰٓئِكَ هُمُ الْمُفْلِحُوْنَ ۞

وَلَا تَكُوْنُوْا كَالَّذِيْنَ تَفَرَّقُوْا وَاخْتَلَفُوْا مِنْۢ بَعْدِ مَا جَآءَهُمُ الْبَيِّنٰتُ ۗ وَاُولٰٓئِكَ لَهُمْ عَذَابٌ عَظِيْمٌ ۞

يَّوْمَ تَبْيَضُّ وُجُوْهٌ وَّتَسْوَدُّ وُجُوْهٌ ۚ فَاَمَّا الَّذِيْنَ اسْوَدَّتْ وُجُوْهُهُمْ ۗ اَكَفَرْتُمْ بَعْدَ اِيْمَانِكُمْ فَذُوْقُوا الْعَذَابَ بِمَا كُنْتُمْ تَكْفُرُوْنَ ۞

وَاَمَّا الَّذِيْنَ ابْيَضَّتْ وُجُوْهُهُمْ فَفِيْ رَحْمَةِ اللّٰهِ ۗ هُمْ فِيْهَا خٰلِدُوْنَ ۞

تِلْكَ اٰيٰتُ اللّٰهِ نَتْلُوْهَا عَلَيْكَ بِالْحَقِّ ۗ وَمَا اللّٰهُ يُرِيْدُ ظُلْمًا لِّلْعٰلَمِيْنَ ۞

وَلِلّٰهِ مَا فِي السَّمٰوٰتِ وَمَا فِي الْاَرْضِ ۗ وَاِلَى اللّٰهِ تُرْجَعُ الْاُمُوْرُ ۞

110. You are the best of peoples, evolved for mankind, enjoining what is right, forbidding what is wrong, and believing in Allah. If only the People of the Book had faith, it were best for them: among them are some who have faith, but most of them are perverted transgressors.

كُنْتُمْ خَيْرَ اُمَّةٍ اُخْرِجَتْ لِلنَّاسِ
تَأْمُرُوْنَ بِالْمَعْرُوْفِ وَتَنْهَوْنَ عَنِ
الْمُنْكَرِ وَتُؤْمِنُوْنَ بِاللّٰهِ ؕ وَلَوْ اٰمَنَ
اَهْلُ الْكِتٰبِ لَكَانَ خَيْرًا لَّهُمْ ؕ مِنْهُمُ
الْمُؤْمِنُوْنَ وَاَكْثَرُهُمُ الْفٰسِقُوْنَ ۝

111. They will do you no harm, barring a trifling annoyance; if they come out to fight you, they will show you their backs, and no help shall they get.

لَنْ يَّضُرُّوْكُمْ اِلَّا اَذًى ؕ وَاِنْ
يُّقَاتِلُوْكُمْ يُوَلُّوْكُمُ الْاَدْبَارَ ۟
ثُمَّ لَا يُنْصَرُوْنَ ۝

112. Shame is pitched over them (like a tent) wherever they are found, except when under a covenant (of protection) from Allah and from men; they draw on themselves wrath from Allah, and pitched over them is (the tent of) destitution. This because they rejected the Signs of Allah, and slew the Prophets in defiance of right; this because they rebelled and transgressed beyond bounds.

ضُرِبَتْ عَلَيْهِمُ الذِّلَّةُ اَيْنَ مَا
ثُقِفُوْٓا اِلَّا بِحَبْلٍ مِّنَ اللّٰهِ وَحَبْلٍ
مِّنَ النَّاسِ وَبَآءُوْ بِغَضَبٍ مِّنَ اللّٰهِ
وَضُرِبَتْ عَلَيْهِمُ الْمَسْكَنَةُ ؕ ذٰلِكَ
بِاَنَّهُمْ كَانُوْا يَكْفُرُوْنَ بِاٰيٰتِ اللّٰهِ
وَيَقْتُلُوْنَ الْاَنْبِيَآءَ بِغَيْرِ حَقٍّ ؕ ذٰلِكَ
بِمَا عَصَوْا وَّكَانُوْا يَعْتَدُوْنَ ۝

113. Not all of them are alike: of the People of the Book are a portion that stand (for the right): they rehearse the Signs of Allah all night long, and they prostrate themselves in adoration.

لَيْسُوْا سَوَآءً ؕ مِنْ اَهْلِ الْكِتٰبِ اُمَّةٌ
قَآئِمَةٌ يَّتْلُوْنَ اٰيٰتِ اللّٰهِ اٰنَآءَ الَّيْلِ
وَهُمْ يَسْجُدُوْنَ ۝

114. They believe in Allah and the Last Day; they enjoin what is right, and they forbid what is wrong; and they hasten (in emulation) in (all) good works: they are in the ranks of the righteous.

يُؤْمِنُوْنَ بِاللّٰهِ وَالْيَوْمِ الْاٰخِرِ وَ
يَأْمُرُوْنَ بِالْمَعْرُوْفِ وَيَنْهَوْنَ
عَنِ الْمُنْكَرِ وَيُسَارِعُوْنَ فِى الْخَيْرٰتِ ؕ
وَاُولٰٓئِكَ مِنَ الصّٰلِحِيْنَ ۝

115. Of the good that they do, nothing will be rejected of them; for Allah knows well those that do right.

وَمَا يَفْعَلُوْا مِنْ خَيْرٍ فَلَنْ يُّكْفَرُوْهُ ؕ
وَاللّٰهُ عَلِيْمٌۢ بِالْمُتَّقِيْنَ ۝

116. Those who reject Faith,-neither their possessions nor their (numerous) progeny will avail them anything against Allah:

اِنَّ الَّذِيْنَ كَفَرُوْا لَنْ تُغْنِىَ عَنْهُمْ
اَمْوَالُهُمْ وَلَاۤ اَوْلَادُهُمْ مِّنَ اللّٰهِ

they will be Companions of the Fire,- dwelling therein (for ever).

117. What they spend in the life of this (material) world may be likened to a wind which brings a nipping frost: it strikes and destroys the harvest of men who have wronged their own souls:it is not Allah that has wronged them, but they wrong them-selves.

118. O you who believe! take not into your intimacy those outside your ranks: they will not fail to corrupt you. They only desire your ruin: rank hatred has already appeared from their mouths: what their hearts conceal is far worse. We have made plain to you the Signs, if you have wisdom.

119. Ah! you are those who love them, but they do not love you, though you believe in the whole of the Book. When they meet you, they say, "We believe": but when they are alone, they bite off the very tips of their fingers at you in their rage. Say: "Perish in your rage; Allah knows well all the secrets of the heart."

120. If anything that is good befalls you, it grieves them; but if some misfortune overtakes you, they rejoice at it. But if you are constant and do right, not the least harm will their cunning do to you; for Allah compasses round about all that they do.

121. Remember that morning you left your household (early) to post the Faithful at their stations for battle: and Allah hears and knows all things:

122. Remember two of your parties meditated cowardice; but Allah was their Protector, and in Allah the Faithful should (ever) put their trust.

اِذْ هَمَّتْ طَّآئِفَتٰنِ مِنْكُمْ اَنْ تَفْشَلَاۙ وَاللّٰهُ وَلِيُّهُمَا ؕ وَعَلَى اللّٰهِ فَلْيَتَوَكَّلِ الْمُؤْمِنُوْنَ ۟

123. Allah had helped you at Badr, when you were an insignificant little force; then fear Allah; thus you may show your gratitude.

وَلَقَدْ نَصَرَكُمُ اللّٰهُ بِبَدْرٍ وَّاَنْتُمْ اَذِلَّةٌ ۚ فَاتَّقُوا اللّٰهَ لَعَلَّكُمْ تَشْكُرُوْنَ ۟

124. Remember you said to the Faithful: "Is it not enough for you that Allah should help you with three thousand angels (specially) sent down?

اِذْ تَقُوْلُ لِلْمُؤْمِنِيْنَ اَلَنْ يَّكْفِيَكُمْ اَنْ يُّمِدَّكُمْ رَبُّكُمْ بِثَلٰثَةِ اٰلٰفٍ مِّنَ الْمَلٰٓئِكَةِ مُنْزَلِيْنَ ؕ

125. "Yes, - if you remain firm, and act aright, even if the enemy should rush here on you in hot haste, your Lord would help you with five thousand angels making a terrific onslaught.

بَلٰٓى ۙ اِنْ تَصْبِرُوْا وَتَتَّقُوْا وَيَأْتُوْكُمْ مِّنْ فَوْرِهِمْ هٰذَا يُمْدِدْكُمْ رَبُّكُمْ بِخَمْسَةِ اٰلٰفٍ مِّنَ الْمَلٰٓئِكَةِ مُسَوِّمِيْنَ ۟

126. Allah made it but a message of hope for you, and an assurance to your hearts: (in any case) there is no help except from Allah, the Exalted, the Wise:

وَمَا جَعَلَهُ اللّٰهُ اِلَّا بُشْرٰى لَكُمْ وَلِتَطْمَئِنَّ قُلُوْبُكُمْ بِهٖ ؕ وَمَا النَّصْرُ اِلَّا مِنْ عِنْدِ اللّٰهِ الْعَزِيْزِ الْحَكِيْمِ ۙ

127. That He might cut off a fringe of the Unbelievers or expose them to infamy, and they should then be turned back, frustrated of their purpose.

لِيَقْطَعَ طَرَفًا مِّنَ الَّذِيْنَ كَفَرُوْٓا اَوْ يَكْبِتَهُمْ فَيَنْقَلِبُوْا خَآئِبِيْنَ ۟

128. Not for you, (but for Allah), is the decision: whether He turn in mercy to them, or punish them; for they are indeed wrong-doers.

لَيْسَ لَكَ مِنَ الْاَمْرِ شَيْءٌ اَوْ يَتُوْبَ عَلَيْهِمْ اَوْ يُعَذِّبَهُمْ فَاِنَّهُمْ ظٰلِمُوْنَ ۟

129. To Allah belongs all that is in the heavens and on earth. He forgives whom He pleases and punishes whom He pleases; but Allah is Oft-Forgiving, Most Merciful.

وَلِلّٰهِ مَا فِى السَّمٰوٰتِ وَمَا فِى الْاَرْضِ ؕ يَغْفِرُ لِمَنْ يَّشَآءُ وَيُعَذِّبُ مَنْ يَّشَآءُ ؕ وَاللّٰهُ غَفُوْرٌ رَّحِيْمٌ ۟

130. O you who believe! Devour not interest, doubled and multiplied; but fear Allah; that you may (really) prosper.

يٰٓاَيُّهَا الَّذِيْنَ اٰمَنُوْا لَا تَأْكُلُوا الرِّبٰٓوا اَضْعَافًا مُّضٰعَفَةً ۪ وَاتَّقُوا اللّٰهَ لَعَلَّكُمْ تُفْلِحُوْنَ ۟

131. Fear the Fire, which is prepared for those who reject Faith:

132. And obey Allah and the Apostle; that you may obtain mercy.

133. Be quick in the race for seeking forgiveness from your Lord, and for a Garden whose width is that (of the whole) of the heavens and of the earth, prepared for the righteous,-

134. Those who spend (freely), whether in prosperity, or in adversity; who restrain anger, and pardon (all) men; - for Allah loves those who do good,-

135. And those who, having done something to be ashamed of, or wronged their own souls, earnestly bring Allah to mind, and ask for forgiveness for their sins, - and who can forgive sins except Allah? - and are never obstinate in persisting knowingly in (the wrong) they have done.

136. For such the reward is forgiveness from their Lord, and Gardens with rivers flowing underneath,- an eternal dwelling: how excellent a recompense for those who work (and strive)!

137. Many were the Ways of Life that have passed away before you: travel through the earth, and see what was the end of those who rejected Truth.

138. Here is a plain statement to men, a guidance and instruction to those who fear Allah.

139. So lose not heart, nor fall into despair: for you must gain mastery if you are true in Faith.

وَاتَّقُوا النَّارَ الَّتِيٓ أُعِدَّتْ لِلْكَافِرِينَ ۝

وَأَطِيعُوا اللَّهَ وَالرَّسُولَ لَعَلَّكُمْ تُرْحَمُونَ ۝

وَسَارِعُوٓا إِلَىٰ مَغْفِرَةٍ مِّن رَّبِّكُمْ وَجَنَّةٍ عَرْضُهَا السَّمَٰوَٰتُ وَالْأَرْضُ أُعِدَّتْ لِلْمُتَّقِينَ ۝

الَّذِينَ يُنفِقُونَ فِي السَّرَّآءِ وَالضَّرَّآءِ وَالْكَٰظِمِينَ الْغَيْظَ وَالْعَافِينَ عَنِ النَّاسِ ۗ وَاللَّهُ يُحِبُّ الْمُحْسِنِينَ ۝

وَالَّذِينَ إِذَا فَعَلُوا فَاحِشَةً أَوْ ظَلَمُوٓا أَنفُسَهُمْ ذَكَرُوا اللَّهَ فَاسْتَغْفَرُوا لِذُنُوبِهِمْ وَمَن يَغْفِرُ الذُّنُوبَ إِلَّا اللَّهُ وَلَمْ يُصِرُّوا عَلَىٰ مَا فَعَلُوا وَهُمْ يَعْلَمُونَ ۝

أُولَٰئِكَ جَزَآؤُهُم مَّغْفِرَةٌ مِّن رَّبِّهِمْ وَجَنَّٰتٌ تَجْرِي مِن تَحْتِهَا الْأَنْهَٰرُ خَٰلِدِينَ فِيهَا ۚ وَنِعْمَ أَجْرُ الْعَٰمِلِينَ ۝

قَدْ خَلَتْ مِن قَبْلِكُمْ سُنَنٌ فَسِيرُوا فِي الْأَرْضِ فَانظُرُوا كَيْفَ كَانَ عَٰقِبَةُ الْمُكَذِّبِينَ ۝

هَٰذَا بَيَانٌ لِّلنَّاسِ وَهُدًى وَمَوْعِظَةٌ لِّلْمُتَّقِينَ ۝

وَلَا تَهِنُوا وَلَا تَحْزَنُوا وَأَنتُمُ الْأَعْلَوْنَ إِن كُنتُم مُّؤْمِنِينَ ۝

140. If a wound has touched you, be sure a similar wound has touched the others. Such days (of varying fortunes) We give to men and men by turns: that Allah may know those that believe, and that He may take to Himself from your ranks Martyr-witnesses (to Truth). And Allah does not love those that do wrong.

141. Allah's object also is to purge those that are true in Faith and to deprive of blessing those that resist Faith.

142. Did you think that you would enter Heaven without Allah testing those of you who fought hard (in His Cause) and remained steadfast?

143. You did indeed wish for death before you met him: now you have seen him with your own eyes, (and you flinch!)

144. Muhammad is no more than an Apostle: many were the Apostles that passed away before him. If he died or were slain, will you then turn back on your heels? If any did turn back on his heels, not the least harm will he do to Allah; but Allah (on the other hand) will swiftly reward those who (serve Him) with gratitude.

145. Nor can a soul die except by Allah's leave, the term being fixed as by writing. If any do desire a reward in this life, We shall give it to him; and if any do desire a reward in the Hereafter, We shall give it to him. And swiftly shall We reward those that (serve Us with) gratitude.

146. How many of the prophets fought (in Allah's way), and with them (fought) large bands of godly men? But they never lost heart if they

إِنْ يَّمْسَسْكُمْ قَرْحٌ فَقَدْ مَسَّ الْقَوْمَ قَرْحٌ مِّثْلُهُ ۚ وَتِلْكَ الْاَيَّامُ نُدَاوِلُهَا بَيْنَ النَّاسِ ۚ وَلِيَعْلَمَ اللّٰهُ الَّذِيْنَ اٰمَنُوْا وَيَتَّخِذَ مِنْكُمْ شُهَدَآءَ ۚ وَاللّٰهُ لَا يُحِبُّ الظّٰلِمِيْنَ ۙ

وَلِيُمَحِّصَ اللّٰهُ الَّذِيْنَ اٰمَنُوْا وَيَمْحَقَ الْكٰفِرِيْنَ ۝

اَمْ حَسِبْتُمْ اَنْ تَدْخُلُوا الْجَنَّةَ وَلَمَّا يَعْلَمِ اللّٰهُ الَّذِيْنَ جٰهَدُوْا مِنْكُمْ وَيَعْلَمَ الصّٰبِرِيْنَ ۝

وَلَقَدْ كُنْتُمْ تَمَنَّوْنَ الْمَوْتَ مِنْ قَبْلِ اَنْ تَلْقَوْهُ ۠ فَقَدْ رَاَيْتُمُوْهُ وَاَنْتُمْ تَنْظُرُوْنَ ۝

وَمَا مُحَمَّدٌ اِلَّا رَسُوْلٌ ۚ قَدْ خَلَتْ مِنْ قَبْلِهِ الرُّسُلُ ۚ اَفَاۡئِنْ مَّاتَ اَوْ قُتِلَ انْقَلَبْتُمْ عَلٰۤى اَعْقَابِكُمْ ۚ وَمَنْ يَّنْقَلِبْ عَلٰى عَقِبَيْهِ فَلَنْ يَّضُرَّ اللّٰهَ شَيْئًا ۗ وَسَيَجْزِى اللّٰهُ الشّٰكِرِيْنَ ۝

وَمَا كَانَ لِنَفْسٍ اَنْ تَمُوْتَ اِلَّا بِاِذْنِ اللّٰهِ كِتٰبًا مُّؤَجَّلًا ۗ وَمَنْ يُّرِدْ ثَوَابَ الدُّنْيَا نُؤْتِهٖ مِنْهَا ۚ وَمَنْ يُّرِدْ ثَوَابَ الْاٰخِرَةِ نُؤْتِهٖ مِنْهَا ۗ وَسَنَجْزِى الشّٰكِرِيْنَ ۝

وَكَاَيِّنْ مِّنْ نَّبِيٍّ قٰتَلَ ۙ مَعَهٗ رِبِّيُّوْنَ كَثِيْرٌ ۚ فَمَا وَهَنُوْا لِمَا

met with disaster in Allah's way, nor did they weaken (in will) nor give in. And Allah loves those who are firm and steadfast.

147. All that they said was: "Our Lord! forgive us our sins and anything we may have done that transgressed our duty: establish our feet firmly, and help us against those that resist Faith."

148. And Allah gave them a reward in this world, and the excellent reward of the Hereafter. For Allah loves those who do good.

149. O you who believe! If you obey the Unbelievers, they will drive you back on your heels, and you will turn back (from Faith) to your own loss.

150. Nay, Allah is your protector, and He is the best of helpers.

151. Soon shall We cast terror into the hearts of the Unbelievers, for that they joined companions with Allah, for which He had sent no authority: their abode will be the Fire: and evil is the home of the wrong-doers!

152. Allah did indeed fulfil His promise to you when you with His permission were about to annihilate your enemy, - until you flinched and fell to disputing about the order, and disobeyed it after He brought you in sight (of the booty) which you covet. Among you are some that hanker after this world and some that desire the Hereafter. Then He diverted you from your foes in order to test you. But

أَصَابَهُمْ فِىْ سَبِيْلِ اللهِ وَمَا ضَعُفُوْا وَمَا اسْتَكَانُوْا ۚ وَاللهُ يُحِبُّ الصّٰبِرِيْنَ ۞

وَمَا كَانَ قَوْلَهُمْ اِلَّا اَنْ قَالُوْا رَبَّنَا اغْفِرْ لَنَا ذُنُوْبَنَا وَاِسْرَافَنَا فِىْ اَمْرِنَا وَثَبِّتْ اَقْدَامَنَا وَانْصُرْنَا عَلَى الْقَوْمِ الْكٰفِرِيْنَ ۞

فَاٰتٰهُمُ اللهُ ثَوَابَ الدُّنْيَا وَ حُسْنَ ثَوَابِ الْاٰخِرَةِ ۚ وَاللهُ يُحِبُّ الْمُحْسِنِيْنَ ۞

يٰٓاَيُّهَا الَّذِيْنَ اٰمَنُوْا اِنْ تُطِيْعُوا الَّذِيْنَ كَفَرُوْا يَرُدُّوْكُمْ عَلٰى اَعْقَابِكُمْ فَتَنْقَلِبُوْا خٰسِرِيْنَ ۞

بَلِ اللهُ مَوْلٰىكُمْ ۚ وَهُوَ خَيْرُ النّٰصِرِيْنَ ۞

سَنُلْقِىْ فِىْ قُلُوْبِ الَّذِيْنَ كَفَرُوا الرُّعْبَ بِمَا اَشْرَكُوْا بِاللهِ مَا لَمْ يُنَزِّلْ بِهٖ سُلْطٰنًا ۚ وَمَأْوٰىهُمُ النَّارُ ۚ وَبِئْسَ مَثْوَى الظّٰلِمِيْنَ ۞

وَلَقَدْ صَدَقَكُمُ اللهُ وَعْدَهٗ اِذْ تَحُسُّوْنَهُمْ بِاِذْنِهٖ ۚ حَتّٰى اِذَا فَشِلْتُمْ وَتَنَازَعْتُمْ فِى الْاَمْرِ وَعَصَيْتُمْ مِّنْ بَعْدِ مَا اَرٰىكُمْ مَّا تُحِبُّوْنَ ؕ مِنْكُمْ مَّنْ يُّرِيْدُ الدُّنْيَا وَ مِنْكُمْ مَّنْ يُّرِيْدُ الْاٰخِرَةَ ۚ ثُمَّ صَرَفَكُمْ عَنْهُمْ لِيَبْتَلِيَكُمْ ۚ وَلَقَدْ

He forgave you: for Allah is full of grace to those who believe.

153. Behold! you were climbing up the high ground, without even casting a side glance at any one, and the Apostle in your rear was calling you back. There did Allah give you one distress after another by way of requital, to teach you not to grieve for (the booty) that had escaped you and for (the ill) that had befallen you. For Allah is well aware of all that you do.

154. After (the excitement) of the distress, He sent down calm on a band of you overcome with slumber, while another band was stirred to anxiety by their own feelings, moved by wrong suspicions of Allah-suspicions due to ignorance. They said: "What affair is this of ours?" You say: "Indeed, this affair is wholly Allah's." They hide in their minds what they dare not reveal to you. They say (to themselves): "If we had had anything to do with this affair, We should not have been in the slaughter here ." Say: "Even if you had remained in your homes, those for whom death was decreed would certainly have gone forth to the place of their death"; but (all this was) that Allah might test what is in your breasts and purge what is in your hearts. For Allah knows well the secrets of your hearts.

155. Those of you who turned back on the day the two hosts met - it was Satan who caused them to fail, because of some (evil) they had done. But Allah has blotted out (their fault): for Allah is

Oft-Forgiving, Most Forbearing.

156. O you who believe! Be not
like the Unbelievers, who say of
their brethren, when they are
travelling through the earth or
engaged in fighting: "If they had
stayed with us, they would not
have died, or been slain." This
that Allah may make it a cause
of sighs and regrets in their
hearts. It is Allah that gives Life
and Death, and Allah sees well
all that you do.

157. And if you are slain, or die,
in the way of Allah, forgiveness
and mercy from Allah are far
better than all they could amass.

158. And if you die, or are slain,
lo! it is unto Allah that you are
brought together.

159. It is part of the Mercy of
Allah that you deal gently with
them. If you were severe or
harsh-hearted, they would have
broken away from about you: so
pass over (their faults), and ask
for (Allah's) forgiveness for
them; and consult them in
affairs (of moment). Then,
when you have taken a decision
put your trust in Allah. For Allah
loves those who put their trust
(in Him).

160. If Allah helps you, none
can overcome you: If He
forsakes you, who is there, after
that, that can help you? In Allah,
then, let Believers put their trust.

161. No prophet could (ever) be
false to his trust. If any person is
so false, he shall, on the Day of
Judgment, restore what he
misappropriated; then shall
every soul receive its due,
whatever it earned,-

and none shall be dealt with unjustly.

162. Is the man who follows the good pleasure of Allah like the man who draws on himself the wrath of Allah, and whose abode is in Hell?- a woeful refuge!

163. They are in varying grades in the sight of Allah, and Allah sees well all that they do.

164. Allah conferred a great favour on the Believers when He sent among them an Apostle from among themselves, rehearsing unto them the Signs of Allah, sanctifying them, and instructing them in Scripture and Wisdom, while, before that, they had been in manifest error.

165. What! When a single disaster smites you, although you smote (your enemies) with one twice as great, do you say?-"Wherefrom is this?" Say (to them): "It is from yourselves: for Allah has power over all things."

166. What you suffered on the day the two armies met, was with the leave of Allah, in order that He might test the Believers,

167. And the Hypocrites also. These were told: "Come, fight in the way of Allah, or (at least) drive (the foe from your city)." They said: "Had we known how to fight, we should certainly have followed you." They were that day nearer to Unbelief than to Faith, saying with their lips what was not in their hearts. But Allah has full knowledge of all they conceal.

168. (They are) the ones that say, (of their slain brethren), while they themselves sit (at ease): "If only they had listened to us they would not have been slain." Say: "Avert

death from your own selves, if you speak the truth."

169. Do not think of those who are slain in Allah's way as dead. Nay, they live, finding their sustenance in the presence of their Lord;

170. They rejoice in the Bounty provided by Allah: and with regard to those left behind, who have not yet joined them (in their bliss), the (Martyrs) glory in the fact that on them is no fear, nor have they (cause to) grieve.

171. They glory in the Grace and the Bounty from Allah, and in the fact that Allah lets not the reward of the Faithful to be lost (in the least).

172. Of those who answered the call of Allah and the Apostle, even after being wounded, those who do right and refrain from wrong, have a great reward;-

173. Men said to them: "A great army is gathering against you": and frightened them: but it (only) increased their Faith: they said: "For us Allah is sufficient, and He is the best Disposer of affairs."

174. And they returned with Grace and Bounty from Allah: no harm ever touched them: for they followed the good pleasure of Allah: and Allah is the Lord of bounties unbounded.

175. It is only the Satan that suggests to you the fear of his votaries: do not be afraid of them, but fear Me, if you have Faith.

176. Let not those grieve you who rush headlong into

أَنْفُسِكُمُ الْمَوْتَ اِنْ كُنْتُمْ صٰدِقِيْنَ ۞

وَلَا تَحْسَبَنَّ الَّذِيْنَ قُتِلُوْا فِيْ سَبِيْلِ اللّٰهِ اَمْوَاتًا ۚ بَلْ اَحْيَآءٌ عِنْدَ رَبِّهِمْ يُرْزَقُوْنَ ۞

فَرِحِيْنَ بِمَآ اٰتٰىهُمُ اللّٰهُ مِنْ فَضْلِهٖ ۙ وَيَسْتَبْشِرُوْنَ بِالَّذِيْنَ لَمْ يَلْحَقُوْا بِهِمْ مِّنْ خَلْفِهِمْ ۙ اَلَّا خَوْفٌ عَلَيْهِمْ وَلَا هُمْ يَحْزَنُوْنَ ۞

يَسْتَبْشِرُوْنَ بِنِعْمَةٍ مِّنَ اللّٰهِ وَفَضْلٍ ۙ وَّاَنَّ اللّٰهَ لَا يُضِيْعُ اَجْرَ الْمُؤْمِنِيْنَ ۞

اَلَّذِيْنَ اسْتَجَابُوْا لِلّٰهِ وَالرَّسُوْلِ مِنْۢ بَعْدِ مَآ اَصَابَهُمُ الْقَرْحُ ۛ لِلَّذِيْنَ اَحْسَنُوْا مِنْهُمْ وَاتَّقَوْا اَجْرٌ عَظِيْمٌ ۞

اَلَّذِيْنَ قَالَ لَهُمُ النَّاسُ اِنَّ النَّاسَ قَدْ جَمَعُوْا لَكُمْ فَاخْشَوْهُمْ فَزَادَهُمْ اِيْمَانًا ۙ وَّقَالُوْا حَسْبُنَا اللّٰهُ وَنِعْمَ الْوَكِيْلُ ۞

فَانْقَلَبُوْا بِنِعْمَةٍ مِّنَ اللّٰهِ وَفَضْلٍ لَّمْ يَمْسَسْهُمْ سُوْٓءٌ ۙ وَّاتَّبَعُوْا رِضْوَانَ اللّٰهِ ۗ وَاللّٰهُ ذُوْ فَضْلٍ عَظِيْمٍ ۞

اِنَّمَا ذٰلِكُمُ الشَّيْطٰنُ يُخَوِّفُ اَوْلِيَآءَهٗ ۖ فَلَا تَخَافُوْهُمْ وَخَافُوْنِ اِنْ كُنْتُمْ مُّؤْمِنِيْنَ ۞

وَلَا يَحْزُنْكَ الَّذِيْنَ يُسَارِعُوْنَ فِيْ

Unbelief: not the least harm will they do to Allah: Allah's plan is that He will give them no portion in the Hereafter, but a severe punishment.

177. Those who purchase Unbelief at the price of faith,- not the least harm will they do to Allah, but they will have a grievous punishment.

178. Let not the Unbelievers think that Our respite to them is good for themselves: We grant them respite that they may grow in their iniquity: but they will have a shameful punishment.

179. Allah will not leave the Believers in the state in which you are now, until He separates what is evil from what is good. Nor will He disclose to you the secrets of the Unseen, but He chooses of His Apostles (for the purpose) whom He pleases. So believe in Allah and His Apostles: and if you believe and do right, you have a reward without measure.

180. And let not those who covetously withhold of the gifts which Allah has given them of His Grace, think that it is good for them: nay, it will be the worse for them: soon shall the things which they covetously withheld be tied to their necks like a twisted collar, on the Day of Judgment. To Allah belongs the heritage of the heavens and the earth; and Allah is well-acquainted with all that you do.

181. Allah has heard the taunt of those who say: "Truly, Allah is indigent and we are rich!"-We shall certainly record their word and (their act) of slaying the Prophets

الْكُفْرَ اِنَّهُمْ لَنْ يَّضُرُّوا اللّٰهَ شَيْئًا

يُرِيْدُ اللّٰهُ اَلَّا يَجْعَلَ لَهُمْ حَظًّا فِي

الْاٰخِرَةِ ۚ وَلَهُمْ عَذَابٌ عَظِيْمٌ ۞

اِنَّ الَّذِيْنَ اشْتَرَوُا الْكُفْرَ بِالْاِيْمَانِ

لَنْ يَّضُرُّوا اللّٰهَ شَيْئًا ۚ وَ لَهُمْ

عَذَابٌ اَلِيْمٌ ۞

وَلَا يَحْسَبَنَّ الَّذِيْنَ كَفَرُوْا اَنَّمَا

نُمْلِيْ لَهُمْ خَيْرٌ لِّاَنْفُسِهِمْ ۚ اِنَّمَا

نُمْلِيْ لَهُمْ لِيَزْدَادُوْا اِثْمًا ۚ وَلَهُمْ

عَذَابٌ مُّهِيْنٌ ۞

مَا كَانَ اللّٰهُ لِيَذَرَ الْمُؤْمِنِيْنَ عَلٰى

مَا اَنْتُمْ عَلَيْهِ حَتّٰى يَمِيْزَ الْخَبِيْثَ

مِنَ الطَّيِّبِ ۗ وَمَا كَانَ اللّٰهُ لِيُطْلِعَكُمْ

عَلَى الْغَيْبِ وَلٰكِنَّ اللّٰهَ يَجْتَبِيْ مِنْ

رُّسُلِهٖ مَنْ يَّشَاءُ ۖ فَاٰمِنُوْا بِاللّٰهِ

وَرُسُلِهٖ ۚ وَاِنْ تُؤْمِنُوْا وَتَتَّقُوْا

فَلَكُمْ اَجْرٌ عَظِيْمٌ ۞

وَلَا يَحْسَبَنَّ الَّذِيْنَ يَبْخَلُوْنَ بِمَا

اٰتٰىهُمُ اللّٰهُ مِنْ فَضْلِهٖ هُوَ خَيْرًا

لَّهُمْ ۖ بَلْ هُوَ شَرٌّ لَّهُمْ ۚ سَيُطَوَّقُوْنَ

مَا بَخِلُوْا بِهٖ يَوْمَ الْقِيٰمَةِ ۗ وَلِلّٰهِ

مِيْرَاثُ السَّمٰوٰتِ وَالْاَرْضِ ۗ وَ

اللّٰهُ بِمَا تَعْمَلُوْنَ خَبِيْرٌ ۞

لَقَدْ سَمِعَ اللّٰهُ قَوْلَ الَّذِيْنَ قَالُوْۤا

اِنَّ اللّٰهَ فَقِيْرٌ وَّنَحْنُ اَغْنِيَاءُ ۘ

سَنَكْتُبُ مَا قَالُوْا وَقَتْلَهُمُ الْاَنْبِيَاءَ

in defiance of right, and We shall say: "You taste the Chastisement of the Scorching Fire!

182. "This is because of the (unrighteous deeds) which your hands sent on before you: for Allah never harms those who serve Him."

183. They (also) said: "Allah took our promise not to believe in an Apostle unless he showed us a sacrifice consumed by fire (from heaven)." Say: "There came to you Apostles before me, with Clear Signs and even with what you ask for: why then did you slay them, if you speak the truth?"

184. Then if they reject you, so were rejected Apostles before you, who came with Clear Signs, Books of dark prophe-cies, and the Book of Enlighten-ment.

185. Every soul shall have a taste of death: and only on the Day of Judgment shall you be paid your full recompense. Only he who is saved far from the Fire and admitted to the Garden will have attained the object (of Life): for the life of this world is but goods and chattels of deception.

186. You shall certainly be tried and tested in your possessions and in your personal selves; and you shall certainly hear much that will grieve you, from those who received the Book before you and from those who worship many gods. But if you persevere patiently, and guard against evil,- then that will be a determining factor in all affairs.

187. And remember Allah took a Covenant from the People of the Book, to make it known and clear to mankind, and not to hide it; but they threw it away behind their backs,

and purchased with it some
miserable gain! and vile was the
bargain they made!

188. Think not that those who
exult in what they have brought
about, and love to be praised for
what they have not done,- think
not that they can escape the
Chastisement. For them is a
Chastisement grievous indeed.

189. To Allah belongs the
dominion of the heavens and the
earth; and Allah has power over
all things.

190. Behold! In the creation of
the heavens and the earth, and
the alternation of Night and
Day,- there are indeed Signs for
men of understanding,-

191. Men who celebrate the
praises of Allah, standing, sitting,
and lying down on their sides,
and contemplate the (wonders of)
creation in the heavens and the
earth, (with the thought): "Our
Lord! You have created (all) this
not for nothing! Glory to You!
Give us salvation from the
Chastisement of the Fire.

192. "Our Lord! any whom You
admit to the Fire, truly You have
covered with shame, and never
will wrong-doers find any
helpers!

193. "Our Lord! we have heard
the call of one calling (us) to
Faith, 'you believe in the Lord,'
and we have believed. Our Lord!
forgive us our sins, blot out from
us our iniquities, and take to
Yourself our souls in the
company of the righteous.

194. "Our Lord! Grant us what
you promised to us through
Your Apostles, and save us from
shame on the Day of Judgment:
for You never break Your
promise."

195. And their Lord has accepted of them, and answered them:
"Never will I

suffer to be lost the work of any
of you, be he male or female:
you are members, one of
another: those who have left
their homes, or been driven out
therefrom, or suffered harm in
My Cause, or fought or been
slain,- verily, I will blot out from
them their iniquities, and admit
them into Gardens with rivers
flowing beneath; - a reward
from the Presence of Allah, and
from His Presence is the best of
rewards."

196. Let not the strutting about
of the Unbelievers through the
land deceive you:

197. Little is it for enjoyment:
their ultimate abode is Hell:
what an evil bed (to lie on)!

198. On the other hand, for
those who fear their Lord, are
Gardens, with rivers flowing
beneath; therein are they to
dwell (for ever),- a gift from the
presence of Allah; and that
which is in the Presence of Allah
is the best (bliss) for the
righteous.

199. And there are, certainly,
among the People of the Book,
those who believe in Allah, in
the revelation to you, and in the
revelation to them, bowing in
humility to Allah: they will not
sell the Signs of Allah for a
miserable gain! for them is a
reward with their Lord, and
Allah is swift in account.

200. O you who believe!
Persevere in patience and
constancy; vie in such
perseverance; strengthen each
other; and fear Allah; that you
may prosper.

SÛRAH-4
AN-NISÂ
(INTRODUCTION)

This Sûrah is closely connected chronologically with Sûrah 3. Its subject-matter deals with the social problems which the Muslim community had to face immediately after Uḥud. While the particular occasion made the necessity urgent, the principles laid down have permanently governed Muslim Law and social practice.

Broadly speaking, the Surah consists of two parts: (1) that dealing with women, orphans, inheritance, marriage and family rights generally, and (2) that dealing with the recalcitrants in the larger family, the community at Madinah, viz. the Hypocrites and their accomplices.

4. The Women
In the name of Allah. Most
Gracious, Most Merciful.

1.   O mankind! reverence your
Guardian-Lord, Who created
you from a single Person,
created, of like nature, his mate,
and from them twain scattered
(like seeds) countless men and
women;- reverence Allah,
through Whom you demand
your mutual (rights), and
(reverence) the wombs (that
bore you): for Allah ever
watches over you.

2.   To orphans restore their
property (when they reach their
age), nor substitute (your)
worthless things for (their) good
ones; and do not devour their
substance (by mixing it up) with
your own. For this is indeed a
great sin.

3.   If you fear that you shall not
be able to deal justly with the
orphans, marry women of your
choice, two or three or four; but
if you fear that you shall not be
able to deal justly (with them),
then only one, or (a captive) that
your right hands possess, that
will be more suitable, to prevent
you from doing injustice.

4.   And give the women (on
marriage) their dower as a free
gift; but if they, of their own
good pleasure, remit any part of
it to you, take it and enjoy it with
right good cheer.

5.   To those weak of understanding do not make over your
property, which Allah has made
a means of support for you, but
feed and clothe them therewith,
and speak to them words of
kindness and justice.

6.   Make trial of orphans until
they reach the age of marriage;
if then you find sound judgment
in them, release

their property to but consume it not wastefully, nor in haste against their growing up. If the guardian is well-off, let him claim no remuneration, but if he is poor, let him have for himself what is just and reasonable. When you release their property to them, take witnesses in their presence: but all-sufficient is Allah in taking account.

7. From what is left by parents and those nearest related there is a share for men and a share for women, whether the property be small or large,- a determinate share.

8. But if at the time of division other relatives, or orphans, or poor, are present, feed them out of the (property), and speak to them words of kindness and justice.

9. Let those (disposing of an estate) have the same fear in their minds as they would have for their own if they had left a helpless family behind: let them fear Allah, and speak words of appropriate (comfort).

10. Those who unjustly eat up the property of orphans, eat up a Fire into their own bodies: they will soon be enduring a blazing Fire!

11. Allah (thus) directs you as regards your children's (inheritance): to the male, a portion equal to that of two females: if only daughters, two or more, their share is two-thirds of the inheritance; if only one, her share is a half. For parents, a sixth share of the inheritance to each, if the deceased left children; if no children, and the parents are the (only) heirs, the mother has a third;

إِلَيْهِمْ أَمْوَالَهُمْ ۖ وَلَا تَأْكُلُوهَآ إِسْرَافًا

وَبِدَارًا أَن يَكْبَرُوا ۚ وَمَن كَانَ غَنِيًّا

فَلْيَسْتَعْفِفْ ۖ وَمَن كَانَ فَقِيرًا فَلْيَأْكُلْ

بِالْمَعْرُوفِ ۚ فَإِذَا دَفَعْتُمْ إِلَيْهِمْ

أَمْوَالَهُمْ فَأَشْهِدُوا عَلَيْهِمْ ۚ

وَكَفَىٰ بِاللَّهِ حَسِيبًا ۝

لِلرِّجَالِ نَصِيبٌ مِّمَّا تَرَكَ الْوَالِدَانِ

وَالْأَقْرَبُونَ ۚ وَلِلنِّسَاءِ نَصِيبٌ مِّمَّا

تَرَكَ الْوَالِدَانِ وَالْأَقْرَبُونَ مِمَّا قَلَّ

مِنْهُ أَوْ كَثُرَ ۚ نَصِيبًا مَّفْرُوضًا ۝

وَإِذَا حَضَرَ الْقِسْمَةَ أُولُو الْقُرْبَىٰ

وَالْيَتَامَىٰ وَالْمَسَاكِينُ فَارْزُقُوهُم مِّنْهُ

وَقُولُوا لَهُمْ قَوْلًا مَّعْرُوفًا ۝

وَلْيَخْشَ الَّذِينَ لَوْ تَرَكُوا مِنْ خَلْفِهِمْ

ذُرِّيَّةً ضِعَافًا خَافُوا عَلَيْهِمْ فَلْيَتَّقُوا

اللَّهَ وَلْيَقُولُوا قَوْلًا سَدِيدًا ۝

إِنَّ الَّذِينَ يَأْكُلُونَ أَمْوَالَ الْيَتَامَىٰ

ظُلْمًا إِنَّمَا يَأْكُلُونَ فِي بُطُونِهِمْ

نَارًا ۖ وَسَيَصْلَوْنَ سَعِيرًا ۝

يُوصِيكُمُ اللَّهُ فِي أَوْلَادِكُمْ ۖ لِلذَّكَرِ

مِثْلُ حَظِّ الْأُنثَيَيْنِ ۚ فَإِن كُنَّ نِسَاءً

فَوْقَ اثْنَتَيْنِ فَلَهُنَّ ثُلُثَا مَا تَرَكَ ۖ

وَإِن كَانَتْ وَاحِدَةً فَلَهَا النِّصْفُ ۚ

وَلِأَبَوَيْهِ لِكُلِّ وَاحِدٍ مِّنْهُمَا السُّدُسُ

مِمَّا تَرَكَ إِن كَانَ لَهُ وَلَدٌ ۚ فَإِن لَّمْ يَكُن

لَّهُ وَلَدٌ وَوَرِثَهُ أَبَوَاهُ فَلِأُمِّهِ الثُّلُثُ ۚ

فَإِنْ كَانَ لَهُ إِخْوَةٌ فَلِأُمِّهِ السُّدُسُ مِنْ بَعْدِ وَصِيَّةٍ يُوصِي بِهَا أَوْ دَيْنٍ ۗ آبَاؤُكُمْ وَأَبْنَاؤُكُمْ لَا تَدْرُونَ أَيُّهُمْ أَقْرَبُ لَكُمْ نَفْعًا ۚ فَرِيضَةً مِّنَ اللَّهِ ۗ إِنَّ اللَّهَ كَانَ عَلِيمًا حَكِيمًا ۝

وَلَكُمْ نِصْفُ مَا تَرَكَ أَزْوَاجُكُمْ إِنْ لَّمْ يَكُنْ لَّهُنَّ وَلَدٌ ۚ فَإِنْ كَانَ لَهُنَّ وَلَدٌ فَلَكُمُ الرُّبُعُ مِمَّا تَرَكْنَ ۚ مِنْ بَعْدِ وَصِيَّةٍ يُوصِينَ بِهَا أَوْ دَيْنٍ ۚ وَلَهُنَّ الرُّبُعُ مِمَّا تَرَكْتُمْ إِنْ لَّمْ يَكُنْ لَّكُمْ وَلَدٌ ۚ فَإِنْ كَانَ لَكُمْ وَلَدٌ فَلَهُنَّ الثُّمُنُ مِمَّا تَرَكْتُمْ ۚ مِّنْ بَعْدِ وَصِيَّةٍ تُوصُونَ بِهَا أَوْ دَيْنٍ ۗ وَإِنْ كَانَ رَجُلٌ يُورَثُ كَلَالَةً أَوِ امْرَأَةٌ وَلَهُ أَخٌ أَوْ أُخْتٌ فَلِكُلِّ وَاحِدٍ مِّنْهُمَا السُّدُسُ ۚ فَإِنْ كَانُوا أَكْثَرَ مِنْ ذَٰلِكَ فَهُمْ شُرَكَاءُ فِي الثُّلُثِ ۚ مِنْ بَعْدِ وَصِيَّةٍ يُوصَىٰ بِهَا أَوْ دَيْنٍ غَيْرَ مُضَارٍّ ۚ وَصِيَّةً مِّنَ اللَّهِ ۗ وَاللَّهُ عَلِيمٌ حَلِيمٌ ۝

تِلْكَ حُدُودُ اللَّهِ ۚ وَمَن يُطِعِ اللَّهَ وَرَسُولَهُ يُدْخِلْهُ جَنَّاتٍ تَجْرِي مِن تَحْتِهَا الْأَنْهَارُ خَالِدِينَ فِيهَا ۚ وَذَٰلِكَ الْفَوْزُ الْعَظِيمُ ۝

وَمَن يَعْصِ اللَّهَ وَرَسُولَهُ وَيَتَعَدَّ حُدُودَهُ يُدْخِلْهُ نَارًا خَالِدًا فِيهَا

and they shall have a humiliating punishment.

15. If any of your women are
guilty of lewdness, take the
evidence of four (reliable)
witnesses from amongst you
against them; and if they testify,
confine them to houses until
death do claim them, or Allah
ordain for them some (other)
way.

16. If two men among you are
guilty of lewdness, punish them
both. If they repent and amend,
leave them alone; for Allah is
Oft-returning, Most Merciful.

17. Allah accepts the repentance of those who do evil in
ignorance and repent soon
afterwards; to them will Allah
turn in mercy: for Allah is full of
knowledge and wisdom.

18. Of no effect is the
repentance of those who
continue to do evil, until death
faces one of them, and he says,
"Now have I repented indeed;"
nor of those who die rejecting
Faith: for them We have
prepared a punishment most
grievous.

19. O you who believe! you are
forbidden to inherit women
against their will. Nor should
you treat them with harshness,
that you may take away part of
the dower you have given
them,- except where they have
been guilty of open lewdness;
on the contrary live with them
on a footing of kindness and
equity. If you take a dislike to
them it may be that you dislike a
thing, and

وَلَهُمْ عَذَابٌ مُّهِيْنٌ ۞

وَالّٰتِيْ يَاْتِيْنَ الْفَاحِشَةَ مِنْ نِّسَآئِكُمْ

فَاسْتَشْهِدُوْا عَلَيْهِنَّ اَرْبَعَةً مِّنْكُمْ ۚ

فَاِنْ شَهِدُوْا فَاَمْسِكُوْهُنَّ فِي الْبُيُوْتِ

حَتّٰى يَتَوَفّٰهُنَّ الْمَوْتُ اَوْ يَجْعَلَ اللّٰهُ

لَهُنَّ سَبِيْلًا ۞

وَالَّذٰنِ يَاْتِيٰنِهَا مِنْكُمْ فَاٰذُوْهُمَا ۚ

فَاِنْ تَابَا وَاَصْلَحَا فَاَعْرِضُوْا عَنْهُمَا ۗ

اِنَّ اللّٰهَ كَانَ تَوَّابًا رَّحِيْمًا ۞

اِنَّمَا التَّوْبَةُ عَلَى اللّٰهِ لِلَّذِيْنَ

يَعْمَلُوْنَ السُّوْٓءَ بِجَهَالَةٍ ثُمَّ

يَتُوْبُوْنَ مِنْ قَرِيْبٍ فَاُولٰٓئِكَ يَتُوْبُ

اللّٰهُ عَلَيْهِمْ ۗ وَكَانَ اللّٰهُ

عَلِيْمًا حَكِيْمًا ۞

وَلَيْسَتِ التَّوْبَةُ لِلَّذِيْنَ يَعْمَلُوْنَ

السَّيِّاٰتِ ۚ حَتّٰى اِذَا حَضَرَ اَحَدَهُمُ

الْمَوْتُ قَالَ اِنِّيْ تُبْتُ الْـٰٔنَ وَلَا

الَّذِيْنَ يَمُوْتُوْنَ وَهُمْ كُفَّارٌ ۗ

اُولٰٓئِكَ اَعْتَدْنَا لَهُمْ عَذَابًا اَلِيْمًا ۞

يٰٓاَيُّهَا الَّذِيْنَ اٰمَنُوْا لَا يَحِلُّ

لَكُمْ اَنْ تَرِثُوا النِّسَآءَ كَرْهًا ۗ

وَلَا تَعْضُلُوْهُنَّ لِتَذْهَبُوْا بِبَعْضِ

مَآ اٰتَيْتُمُوْهُنَّ اِلَّا اَنْ يَّاْتِيْنَ

بِفَاحِشَةٍ مُّبَيِّنَةٍ ۚ وَعَاشِرُوْهُنَّ

بِالْمَعْرُوْفِ ۚ فَاِنْ كَرِهْتُمُوْهُنَّ

فَعَسٰٓى اَنْ تَكْرَهُوْا شَيْئًا وَّيَجْعَلَ

Allah brings about through it a great deal of good.

20. But if you decide to take one wife in place of another, even if you had given the latter a whole treasure for dower, take not the least bit of it back: would you take it by slander and a manifest wrong?

21. And how could you take it when you have gone in to each other, and they have taken from you a solemn covenant?

22. And marry not women whom your fathers married,- except what is past: it was shameful and odious,- an abominable custom indeed.

23. Prohibited to you (for marriage) are:- your mothers, daughters, sisters; father's sisters, mother's sisters; brother's daughters, sister's daughters; foster-mothers (who gave you suck), foster-sisters; your wives' mothers; your step-daughters under your guardian-ship, born of your wives to whom you have gone in, - no prohibition if you have not gone in; - (those who have been) wives of your sons proceeding from your loins; and two sisters in wedlock at one and the same time, except for what is past; for Allah is Oft-Forgiving, Most Merciful;-

24. Also (prohibited are) women already married, except those whom your right hands possess: thus has Allah ordained (prohibitions) against you: except for these, all others are lawful,

provided you seek (them in marriage) with gifts from your property,- desiring chastity, not lust. Seeing that you derive benefit from them, give them their dowers (at least) as prescribed; but if, after a dower is prescribed, you agree mutually (to vary it), there is no blame on you, and Allah is All-knowing, All-wise.

25. If any of you does not have the means wherewith to wed free believing women, they may wed believing girls from among those whom your right hands possess: and Allah has full knowledge about your Faith. You are one from another: wed them with the leave of their owners, and give them their dowers, according to what is reasonable: they should be chaste, not lustful, nor taking paramours: when they are taken in wedlock, if they fall into shame, their punishment is half that for free women. This (permission) is for those among you who fear sin; but it is better for you that you practise self-restraint. And Allah is Oft-forgiving, Most Merciful.

26. Allah wishes to make clear to you and to show you the ordinances of those before you; and (He wishes to) turn to you (in Mercy): and Allah is All-knowing, All-wise.

27. Allah wishes to turn to you, but the wish of those who follow their lusts is that you should turn away (from Him),- far, far away.

28. Allah wishes to lighten your (difficulties):

for man was created weak (in flesh).

وَخُلِقَ الْإِنْسَانُ ضَعِيفًا ۞

29. O you who believe! do not eat up your property among yourselves in vanities: but let there be amongst you traffic and trade by mutual good-will: nor kill (or destroy) yourselves: for verily Allah has been to you Most Merciful!

يَاأَيُّهَا الَّذِينَ آمَنُوا لَا تَأْكُلُوا أَمْوَالَكُمْ بَيْنَكُمْ بِالْبَاطِلِ إِلَّا أَنْ تَكُونَ تِجَارَةً عَنْ تَرَاضٍ مِنْكُمْ وَلَا تَقْتُلُوا أَنْفُسَكُمْ إِنَّ اللَّهَ كَانَ بِكُمْ رَحِيمًا ۞

30. If any do that in rancour and injustice,- soon shall We cast them into the Fire: and easy it is for Allah.

وَمَنْ يَفْعَلْ ذَلِكَ عُدْوَانًا وَظُلْمًا فَسَوْفَ نُصْلِيهِ نَارًا وَكَانَ ذَلِكَ عَلَى اللَّهِ يَسِيرًا ۞

31. If you (but) eschew the most heinous of the things which you are forbidden to do, We shall expel out of you all the evil in you, and admit you to a gate of great honour.

إِنْ تَجْتَنِبُوا كَبَائِرَ مَا تُنْهَوْنَ عَنْهُ نُكَفِّرْ عَنْكُمْ سَيِّئَاتِكُمْ وَنُدْخِلْكُمْ مُدْخَلًا كَرِيمًا ۞

32. And in no wise covet those things in which Allah has bestowed His gifts more freely on some of you than on others: to men is allotted what they earn, and to women what they earn: but ask Allah of His bounty. For Allah has full knowledge of all things.

وَلَا تَتَمَنَّوْا مَا فَضَّلَ اللَّهُ بِهِ بَعْضَكُمْ عَلَى بَعْضٍ لِلرِّجَالِ نَصِيبٌ مِمَّا اكْتَسَبُوا وَلِلنِّسَاءِ نَصِيبٌ مِمَّا اكْتَسَبْنَ وَسْئَلُوا اللَّهَ مِنْ فَضْلِهِ إِنَّ اللَّهَ كَانَ بِكُلِّ شَيْءٍ عَلِيمًا ۞

33. To (benefit) every one, We have appointed shares and heirs to property left by parents and relatives. To those, also, to whom your right hand was pledged, give their due portion. For truly Allah is Witness to all things.

وَلِكُلٍّ جَعَلْنَا مَوَالِيَ مِمَّا تَرَكَ الْوَالِدَانِ وَالْأَقْرَبُونَ وَالَّذِينَ عَقَدَتْ أَيْمَانُكُمْ فَآتُوهُمْ نَصِيبَهُمْ إِنَّ اللَّهَ كَانَ عَلَى كُلِّ شَيْءٍ شَهِيدًا ۞

34. Men are the protectors and maintainers of women, because Allah has given the one more (strength) than the other, and because they support them from their means. Therefore, the righteous women are devoutly obedient, and guard in (the husband's) absence what Allah would have them guard. As to those women on whose part you fear disloyalty and ill-conduct,

الرِّجَالُ قَوَّامُونَ عَلَى النِّسَاءِ بِمَا فَضَّلَ اللَّهُ بَعْضَهُمْ عَلَى بَعْضٍ وَبِمَا أَنْفَقُوا مِنْ أَمْوَالِهِمْ فَالصَّالِحَاتُ قَانِتَاتٌ حَافِظَاتٌ لِلْغَيْبِ بِمَا حَفِظَ اللَّهُ وَاللَّاتِي تَخَافُونَ نُشُوزَهُنَّ

admonish them (first), (next), refuse to share their beds, (and last) beat them (lightly); but if they return to obedience, do not seek against them means (of annoyance): for Allah is Most High, Great (above you all).

فَعِظُوْهُنَّ وَاهْجُرُوْهُنَّ فِي الْمَضَاجِعِ وَاضْرِبُوْهُنَّ ۚ فَاِنْ اَطَعْنَكُمْ فَلَا تَبْغُوْا عَلَيْهِنَّ سَبِيْلًا ۗ اِنَّ اللّٰهَ كَانَ عَلِيًّا كَبِيْرًا ۝

35. If you fear a breach between them twain, appoint (two) arbiters, one from his family, and the other from hers; if they wish for peace, Allah will cause their reconciliation: for Allah has full knowledge, and is acquainted with all things.

وَاِنْ خِفْتُمْ شِقَاقَ بَيْنِهِمَا فَابْعَثُوْا حَكَمًا مِّنْ اَهْلِهٖ وَحَكَمًا مِّنْ اَهْلِهَا ۚ اِنْ يُّرِيْدَا اِصْلَاحًا يُّوَفِّقِ اللّٰهُ بَيْنَهُمَا ۗ اِنَّ اللّٰهَ كَانَ عَلِيْمًا خَبِيْرًا ۝

36. Serve Allah, and join not any partners with Him; and do good - to parents, kinsfolk, orphans, those in need, neighbours who are near, neighbours who are strangers, the companion by your side, the way-farer (you meet), and what your right hands possess: for Allah does not love the arrogant, the vainglorious.

وَاعْبُدُوا اللّٰهَ وَلَا تُشْرِكُوْا بِهٖ شَيْئًا وَّبِالْوَالِدَيْنِ اِحْسَانًا وَّبِذِي الْقُرْبٰى وَالْيَتٰمٰى وَالْمَسٰكِيْنِ وَ الْجَارِ ذِي الْقُرْبٰى وَالْجَارِ الْجُنُبِ وَالصَّاحِبِ بِالْجَنْبِ وَابْنِ السَّبِيْلِ وَمَا مَلَكَتْ اَيْمَانُكُمْ ۗ اِنَّ اللّٰهَ لَا يُحِبُّ مَنْ كَانَ مُخْتَالًا فَخُوْرَا ۝

37. (Nor) those who are niggardly or enjoin niggardliness on others, or hide the bounties which Allah has bestowed on them; for We have prepared, for those who resist Faith, a Punishment that steeps them in contempt;-

اَلَّذِيْنَ يَبْخَلُوْنَ وَيَأْمُرُوْنَ النَّاسَ بِالْبُخْلِ وَ يَكْتُمُوْنَ مَا اٰتٰهُمُ اللّٰهُ مِنْ فَضْلِهٖ ۗ وَاَعْتَدْنَا لِلْكٰفِرِيْنَ عَذَابًا مُّهِيْنًا ۙ ۝

38. Nor those who spend of their substance, to be seen of men, but have no faith in Allah and the Last Day: If any take the Satan for their intimate, what a dreadful intimate he is!

وَالَّذِيْنَ يُنْفِقُوْنَ اَمْوَالَهُمْ رِئَاءَ النَّاسِ وَلَا يُؤْمِنُوْنَ بِاللّٰهِ وَلَا بِالْيَوْمِ الْاٰخِرِ ۗ وَمَنْ يَّكُنِ الشَّيْطٰنُ لَهٗ قَرِيْنًا فَسَاءَ قَرِيْنًا ۝

39. And what burden were it on them if they had faith in Allah and in the Last Day, and they spent out of what Allah has given them for sustenance?

وَمَاذَا عَلَيْهِمْ لَوْ اٰمَنُوْا بِاللّٰهِ وَ الْيَوْمِ الْاٰخِرِ وَاَنْفَقُوْا مِمَّا رَزَقَهُمُ

For Allah has full knowledge of them.

40. Allah is never unjust in the least degree: if there is any good (done), He doubles it, and gives from His Own Presence a great reward.

41. How then if We brought from each People a witness, and We brought you as a witness against these People!

اللهَ ۚ وَكَانَ اللهُ بِهِمْ عَلِيْمًا ۞

إِنَّ اللهَ لَا يَظْلِمُ مِثْقَالَ ذَرَّةٍ ۚ وَإِنْ

تَكُ حَسَنَةً يُّضٰعِفْهَا وَيُؤْتِ مِنْ

لَّدُنْهُ أَجْرًا عَظِيْمًا ۞

فَكَيْفَ إِذَا جِئْنَا مِنْ كُلِّ أُمَّةٍ

بِشَهِيْدٍ وَّجِئْنَا بِكَ عَلٰى هٰؤُلَاءِ

شَهِيْدًا ۞

42. On that day those who reject Faith and disobey the Apostle will wish that the earth were made one with them: but never will they hide a single fact from Allah!

43. O you who believe! do not approach prayers with a mind befogged, until you can understand all that you say,- nor in a state of ceremonial impurity (except when travelling on the road), until after washing your whole body. If you are ill, or on a journey, or one of you comes from offices of nature, or you have been in contact with women, and you find no water, then take for yourselves clean sand or earth, and rub there with your faces and hands. For Allah blots out sins and forgives again and again.

يَوْمَئِذٍ يَّوَدُّ الَّذِيْنَ كَفَرُوْا وَعَصَوُا

الرَّسُوْلَ لَوْ تُسَوّٰى بِهِمُ الْأَرْضُ ۚ

وَلَا يَكْتُمُوْنَ اللهَ حَدِيْثًا ۞

يٰٓأَيُّهَا الَّذِيْنَ اٰمَنُوْا لَا تَقْرَبُوا

الصَّلٰوةَ وَأَنْتُمْ سُكٰرٰى حَتّٰى تَعْلَمُوْا

مَا تَقُوْلُوْنَ وَلَا جُنُبًا إِلَّا عَابِرِيْ

سَبِيْلٍ حَتّٰى تَغْتَسِلُوْا ۚ وَإِنْ كُنْتُمْ

مَّرْضٰى أَوْ عَلٰى سَفَرٍ أَوْ جَاءَ أَحَدٌ

مِّنْكُمْ مِنَ الْغَائِطِ أَوْ لٰمَسْتُمُ

النِّسَاءَ فَلَمْ تَجِدُوْا مَاءً فَتَيَمَّمُوْا

صَعِيْدًا طَيِّبًا فَامْسَحُوْا بِوُجُوْهِكُمْ

وَأَيْدِيْكُمْ ۗ إِنَّ اللهَ كَانَ عَفُوًّا

غَفُوْرًا ۞

44. Have you not turned your vision to those who were given a portion of the Book? They traffic in error, and wish that you should lose the right path.

45. But Allah has full knowledge of your enemies: Allah is enough for a Protector, and Allah is enough for a Helper.

46. Of the Jews there are those who displace

أَلَمْ تَرَ إِلَى الَّذِيْنَ أُوْتُوْا نَصِيْبًا

مِّنَ الْكِتٰبِ يَشْتَرُوْنَ الضَّلٰلَةَ

وَيُرِيْدُوْنَ أَنْ تَضِلُّوا السَّبِيْلَ ۞

وَاللهُ أَعْلَمُ بِأَعْدَائِكُمْ ۚ وَكَفٰى بِاللهِ

وَلِيًّا ۚ وَكَفٰى بِاللهِ نَصِيْرًا ۞

مِنَ الَّذِيْنَ هَادُوْا يُحَرِّفُوْنَ

words from their (right) places,
and say: "We hear and we
disobey"; and "Hear what is not
heard"; and "Ra'ina"; with a
twist of their tongues and a
slander to Faith. If only they had
said: "We hear and we obey"; and
"Do hear"; and "Do look at us"; it
would have been better for them,
and more proper; but Allah has
cursed them for their Unbelief;
and but few of them will believe.

47. O you People of the Book!
believe in what We have (now)
revealed, confirming what was
(already) with you, before We
change the face and fame of
some (of you) beyond all
recognition, and turn them
hindwards, or curse them as We
cursed the Sabbath-breakers,
for the decision of Allah must be
carried out.

48. Allah does not forgive that
partners should be set up with
Him; but He forgives anything
else, to whom He pleases; to set
up partners with Allah is to
devise a sin most heinous
indeed.

49. Have you not turned your
vision to those who claim sanctity for themselves? Nay- but
Allah sanctifies whom He
pleases. But never will they fail
to receive justice in the least
little thing.

50. See! how they invent a lie
against Allah! but that by itself
is a manifest sin!

51. Have you not turned your
vision to those who were given a
portion of the Book? They
believe in sorcery and evil, and
say to the Unbelievers that they
are better guided in the (right)
way than the Believers!

الْكَلِمَ عَنْ مَّوَاضِعِهٖ وَيَقُوْلُوْنَ
سَمِعْنَا وَعَصَيْنَا وَاسْمَعْ غَيْرَ مُسْمَعٍ
وَّرَاعِنَا لَيًّا بِأَلْسِنَتِهِمْ وَطَعْنًا فِى
الدِّيْنِ ۚ وَلَوْ اَنَّهُمْ قَالُوْا سَمِعْنَا
وَاَطَعْنَا وَاسْمَعْ وَانْظُرْنَا لَكَانَ
خَيْرًا لَّهُمْ وَاَقْوَمَ ۙ وَلٰكِنْ لَّعَنَهُمُ اللّٰهُ
بِكُفْرِهِمْ فَلَا يُؤْمِنُوْنَ اِلَّا قَلِيْلًا ۟
يٰٓاَيُّهَا الَّذِيْنَ اُوْتُوا الْكِتٰبَ اٰمِنُوْا
بِمَا نَزَّلْنَا مُصَدِّقًا لِّمَا مَعَكُمْ
مِّنْ قَبْلِ اَنْ نَّطْمِسَ وُجُوْهًا
فَنَرُدَّهَا عَلٰٓى اَدْبَارِهَا اَوْ نَلْعَنَهُمْ
كَمَا لَعَنَّا اَصْحٰبَ السَّبْتِ ۚ وَكَانَ
اَمْرُ اللّٰهِ مَفْعُوْلًا ۟
اِنَّ اللّٰهَ لَا يَغْفِرُ اَنْ يُّشْرَكَ بِهٖ
وَيَغْفِرُ مَا دُوْنَ ذٰلِكَ لِمَنْ يَّشَآءُ ۚ
وَمَنْ يُّشْرِكْ بِاللّٰهِ فَقَدِ افْتَرٰٓى
اِثْمًا عَظِيْمًا ۟
اَلَمْ تَرَ اِلَى الَّذِيْنَ يُزَكُّوْنَ اَنْفُسَهُمْ ۚ
بَلِ اللّٰهُ يُزَكِّيْ مَنْ يَّشَآءُ وَلَا
يُظْلَمُوْنَ فَتِيْلًا ۟
اُنْظُرْ كَيْفَ يَفْتَرُوْنَ عَلَى اللّٰهِ
الْكَذِبَ ۚ وَكَفٰى بِهٖٓ اِثْمًا مُّبِيْنًا ۟
اَلَمْ تَرَ اِلَى الَّذِيْنَ اُوْتُوْا نَصِيْبًا مِّنَ
الْكِتٰبِ يُؤْمِنُوْنَ بِالْجِبْتِ وَالطَّاغُوْتِ
وَيَقُوْلُوْنَ لِلَّذِيْنَ كَفَرُوْا هٰٓؤُلَآءِ اَهْدٰى
مِنَ الَّذِيْنَ اٰمَنُوْا سَبِيْلًا ۟

52. They are (men) whom Allah has cursed: and those whom Allah has cursed, you will find, have no one to help.

53. Have they a share in dominion or power? Behold, they do not give a farthing to their fellow-men.

54. Or do they envy mankind for what Allah has given them of His bounty? But We had already given the people of Abraham the Book and wisdom, and conferred upon them a great kingdom.

55. Some of them believed, and some of them averted their faces from him: and enough is Hell for a burning fire.

56. Those who reject Our Signs, We shall soon cast (them) into the Fire: as often as their skins are roasted through, We shall change them for fresh skins, that they may taste the Chastisement: for Allah is Exalted in Power, Wise.

57. But those who believe and do deeds of righteousness, We shall soon admit (them) to Gardens, with rivers flowing beneath, - their eternal home: therein shall they have Companions pure and holy: We shall admit them to shades, cool and ever deepening.

58. Allah commands you to render back your trusts to those to whom they are due; and when you judge between man and man, that you judge with justice: verily how excellent is the teaching which He gives you! for Allah is He Who hears and sees all things.

59. O you who believe! obey Allah,

أُولَٰٓئِكَ الَّذِينَ لَعَنَهُمُ اللهُ ۖ وَمَن يَلْعَنِ اللهُ فَلَن تَجِدَ لَهُۥ نَصِيرًا ۞

أَمْ لَهُمْ نَصِيبٌ مِّنَ الْمُلْكِ فَإِذًا لَّا يُؤْتُونَ النَّاسَ نَقِيرًا ۞

أَمْ يَحْسُدُونَ النَّاسَ عَلَىٰ مَآ ءَاتَىٰهُمُ اللهُ مِن فَضْلِهِۦ ۖ فَقَدْ ءَاتَيْنَآ ءَالَ إِبْرَٰهِيمَ الْكِتَٰبَ وَالْحِكْمَةَ وَءَاتَيْنَٰهُم مُّلْكًا عَظِيمًا ۞

فَمِنْهُم مَّنْ ءَامَنَ بِهِۦ وَمِنْهُم مَّن صَدَّ عَنْهُ ۚ وَكَفَىٰ بِجَهَنَّمَ سَعِيرًا ۞

إِنَّ الَّذِينَ كَفَرُوا بِـَٔايَٰتِنَا سَوْفَ نُصْلِيهِمْ نَارًا كُلَّمَا نَضِجَتْ جُلُودُهُم بَدَّلْنَٰهُمْ جُلُودًا غَيْرَهَا لِيَذُوقُوا الْعَذَابَ ۗ إِنَّ اللهَ كَانَ عَزِيزًا حَكِيمًا ۞

وَالَّذِينَ ءَامَنُوا وَعَمِلُوا الصَّٰلِحَٰتِ سَنُدْخِلُهُمْ جَنَّٰتٍ تَجْرِى مِن تَحْتِهَا الْأَنْهَٰرُ خَٰلِدِينَ فِيهَآ أَبَدًا ۖ لَّهُمْ فِيهَآ أَزْوَٰجٌ مُّطَهَّرَةٌ ۖ وَنُدْخِلُهُمْ ظِلًّا ظَلِيلًا ۞

إِنَّ اللهَ يَأْمُرُكُمْ أَن تُؤَدُّوا الْأَمَٰنَٰتِ إِلَىٰٓ أَهْلِهَا ۙ وَإِذَا حَكَمْتُم بَيْنَ النَّاسِ أَن تَحْكُمُوا بِالْعَدْلِ ۚ إِنَّ اللهَ نِعِمَّا يَعِظُكُم بِهِۦ ۗ إِنَّ اللهَ كَانَ سَمِيعًا بَصِيرًا ۞

يَٰٓأَيُّهَا الَّذِينَ ءَامَنُوٓا أَطِيعُوا اللهَ

and obey the Apostle, and those charged with authority among you. If you differ in anything among yourselves, refer it to Allah and His Apostle, if you do believe in Allah and the Last Day: that is best, and most suitable for final determination.

وَأَطِيعُوا الرَّسُوۡلَ وَأُولِى الۡأَمۡرِ مِنۡكُمۡ ۚ فَإِنۡ تَنَازَعۡتُمۡ فِىۡ شَىۡءٍ فَرُدُّوۡهُ إِلَى اللّٰهِ وَالرَّسُوۡلِ إِنۡ كُنۡتُمۡ تُؤۡمِنُوۡنَ بِاللّٰهِ وَالۡيَوۡمِ الۡاٰخِرِ ۚ ذٰلِكَ خَيۡرٌ وَّأَحۡسَنُ تَأۡوِيۡلًا ۞

60. Have you not turned your vision to those who declare that they believe in the revelations that have come to you and to those before you? Their (real) wish is to resort together for judgment (in their disputes) to the Satan, though they were ordered to reject him. But Satan's wish is to lead them astray far away (from the right).

أَلَمۡ تَرَ إِلَى الَّذِيۡنَ يَزۡعُمُوۡنَ أَنَّهُمۡ اٰمَنُوۡا بِمَاۤ أُنۡزِلَ إِلَيۡكَ وَمَاۤ أُنۡزِلَ مِنۡ قَبۡلِكَ يُرِيۡدُوۡنَ أَنۡ يَّتَحَاكَمُوۤا إِلَى الطَّاغُوۡتِ وَقَدۡ أُمِرُوۤا أَنۡ يَّكۡفُرُوۡا بِهٖ ۖ وَيُرِيۡدُ الشَّيۡطٰنُ أَنۡ يُّضِلَّهُمۡ ضَلٰلًا بَعِيۡدًا ۞

61. When it is said to them: "Come to what Allah has revealed, and to the Apostle": you see the Hypocrites avert their faces from you in disgust.

وَإِذَا قِيۡلَ لَهُمۡ تَعَالَوۡا إِلَى مَاۤ أَنۡزَلَ اللّٰهُ وَإِلَى الرَّسُوۡلِ رَأَيۡتَ الۡمُنٰفِقِيۡنَ يَصُدُّوۡنَ عَنۡكَ صُدُوۡدًا ۞

62. How then, when they are seized by misfortune, because of the deeds which their hands have sent forth? Then they come to you, swearing by Allah: "We meant no more than good-will and conciliation!"

فَكَيۡفَ إِذَاۤ أَصَابَتۡهُمۡ مُّصِيۡبَةٌ بِمَا قَدَّمَتۡ أَيۡدِيۡهِمۡ ثُمَّ جَآءُوۡكَ يَحۡلِفُوۡنَ ۖ بِاللّٰهِ إِنۡ أَرَدۡنَاۤ إِلَّاۤ إِحۡسَانًا وَّتَوۡفِيۡقًا ۞

63. Those men, Allah knows what is in their hearts; so keep clear of them, but admonish them, and speak to them a word to reach their very souls.

أُولٰٓئِكَ الَّذِيۡنَ يَعۡلَمُ اللّٰهُ مَا فِىۡ قُلُوۡبِهِمۡ ۖ فَأَعۡرِضۡ عَنۡهُمۡ وَعِظۡهُمۡ وَقُلۡ لَّهُمۡ فِىۡۤ أَنۡفُسِهِمۡ قَوۡلًا بَلِيۡغًا ۞

64. We did not send an Apostle, but to be obeyed, in accordance with the Will of Allah. If they had only, when they were unjust to themselves, come to you and asked Allah's forgiveness, and the Apostle had asked forgiveness for them, they would have found Allah indeed Oft-returning, Most Merciful.

وَمَاۤ أَرۡسَلۡنَا مِنۡ رَّسُوۡلٍ إِلَّا لِيُطَاعَ بِإِذۡنِ اللّٰهِ ۚ وَلَوۡ أَنَّهُمۡ إِذۡ ظَّلَمُوۤا أَنۡفُسَهُمۡ جَآءُوۡكَ فَاسۡتَغۡفَرُوا اللّٰهَ وَاسۡتَغۡفَرَ لَهُمُ الرَّسُوۡلُ لَوَجَدُوا اللّٰهَ تَوَّابًا رَّحِيۡمًا ۞

65. But no, by your Lord, they can have no (real) Faith, until they make you judge in all disputes between them, and find in their souls no resistance against your decision, but accept them with the fullest conviction.

66. If We had ordered them to sacrifice their lives or to leave their homes, very few of them would have done it: but if they had done what they were (actually) told, it would have been best for them, and would have gone farthest to strengthen their (faith);

67. And We should then have given them from Our Presence a great reward;

68. And We should have shown them the Straight Way.

69. All who obey Allah and the Apostle are in the company of those on whom is the Grace of Allah, - of the Prophets (who teach), the Sincere (lovers of Truth), the Witnesses (who testify), and the Righteous (who do good): ah! what a beautiful Fellowship!

70. Such is the Bounty from Allah: and sufficient is it that Allah knows all.

71. O you who believe! take your precautions, and either go forth in parties or go forth all together.

72. There are certainly among you men who would tarry behind: if a misfortune befalls you, they say: "Allah favoured us in that we were not present among them."

73. But if good fortune comes to you from Allah, they would be sure to say - as if there had never been ties of affection between you and them - "Oh! I wish I had been with them; a fine thing should I then have made of it!"

فَلَا وَ رَبِّكَ لَا يُؤْمِنُوْنَ حَتّٰى يُحَكِّمُوْكَ فِيْمَا شَجَرَ بَيْنَهُمْ ثُمَّ لَا يَجِدُوْا فِىْٓ اَنْفُسِهِمْ حَرَجًا مِّمَّا قَضَيْتَ وَيُسَلِّمُوْا تَسْلِيْمًا ۞

وَلَوْ اَنَّا كَتَبْنَا عَلَيْهِمْ اَنِ اقْتُلُوْٓا اَنْفُسَكُمْ اَوِ اخْرُجُوْا مِنْ دِيَارِكُمْ مَّا فَعَلُوْهُ اِلَّا قَلِيْلٌ مِّنْهُمْ ۚ وَلَوْ اَنَّهُمْ فَعَلُوْا مَا يُوْعَظُوْنَ بِهٖ لَكَانَ خَيْرًا لَّهُمْ وَاَشَدَّ تَثْبِيْتًا ۞

وَّاِذًا لَّاٰتَيْنٰهُمْ مِّنْ لَّدُنَّآ اَجْرًا عَظِيْمًا ۞

وَّلَهَدَيْنٰهُمْ صِرَاطًا مُّسْتَقِيْمًا ۞

وَمَنْ يُّطِعِ اللّٰهَ وَالرَّسُوْلَ فَاُولٰٓئِكَ مَعَ الَّذِيْنَ اَنْعَمَ اللّٰهُ عَلَيْهِمْ مِّنَ النَّبِيّٖنَ وَالصِّدِّيْقِيْنَ وَالشُّهَدَآءِ وَالصّٰلِحِيْنَ ۚ وَحَسُنَ اُولٰٓئِكَ رَفِيْقًا ۞

ذٰلِكَ الْفَضْلُ مِنَ اللّٰهِ ۚ وَكَفٰى بِاللّٰهِ عَلِيْمًا ۞

يٰٓاَيُّهَا الَّذِيْنَ اٰمَنُوْا خُذُوْا حِذْرَكُمْ فَانْفِرُوْا ثُبَاتٍ اَوِ انْفِرُوْا جَمِيْعًا ۞

وَاِنَّ مِنْكُمْ لَمَنْ لَّيُبَطِّئَنَّ ۚ فَاِنْ اَصَابَتْكُمْ مُّصِيْبَةٌ قَالَ قَدْ اَنْعَمَ اللّٰهُ عَلَيَّ اِذْ لَمْ اَكُنْ مَّعَهُمْ شَهِيْدًا ۞

وَلَئِنْ اَصَابَكُمْ فَضْلٌ مِّنَ اللّٰهِ لَيَقُوْلَنَّ كَاَنْ لَّمْ تَكُنْ بَيْنَكُمْ وَبَيْنَهٗ مَوَدَّةٌ يّٰلَيْتَنِيْ كُنْتُ مَعَهُمْ فَاَفُوْزَ فَوْزًا عَظِيْمًا ۞

74. Let those fight in the cause of Allah who sell the life of this world for the Hereafter. To him who fights in the cause of Allah,- whether he is slain or gets victory - soon shall We give him a reward of great (value).

75. And why should you not fight in the cause of Allah and of those who, being weak, are ill-treated (and oppressed)?- men, women, and children, whose cry is: "Our Lord! Rescue us from this town, whose people are oppressors; and raise for us from You one who will protect; and raise for us from You one who will help!"

76. Those who believe fight in the cause of Allah, and those who reject Faith fight in the cause of Evil: so you fight against the friends of Satan: feeble indeed is the cunning of Satan.

77. Have you not turned your vision to those who were told to hold back their hands (from fight) but establish regular prayers and spend in regular charity? When (at length) the order for fighting was issued to them, behold! a section of them feared men as - or even more than - they should have feared Allah: they said: "Our Lord! Why have You ordered us to fight? Would You not grant us respite to our (natural) term, near (enough)?" Say: "Short is the enjoyment of this world: the Hereafter is the best for those who do right: never will you be dealt with unjustly in the very least!

78. "Wherever you are, death will find you out, even if you are in towers built up strong and high!" If some good befalls them, they say, "This is from

Allah"; but if evil, they say, "This is from you" (O Prophet). Say: "All things are from Allah." But what have come to these people, that they fail to understand a single fact?

79. Whatever good, (O man!) happens to you, is from Allah; but whatever evil happens to you, is from your (own) soul. And We have sent you as an Apostle to (instruct) mankind. And enough is Allah for a Witness.

80. He who obeys the Apostle, obeys Allah: but if any turn away, We have not sent you to watch over their (evil deeds).

81. They have "Obedience" on their lips; but when they leave you, a section of them meditate all night on things very different from what you tell them. But Allah records their nightly (plots): so keep clear of them, and put your trust in Allah, and enough is Allah as a disposer of affairs.

82. Do they not consider the Qur'an (with care)? Had it been from other than Allah, they would surely have found therein much discrepancy.

83. When there comes to them some matter touching (public) safety or fear, they divulge it. If they had only referred it to the Apostle, or to those charged with authority among them, the proper investigators would have tested it from them (direct). Were it not for the Grace and Mercy of Allah to you, all but a few of you would have fallen into the clutches of Satan.

84. Then fight in Allah's cause - you are held responsible only

for yourself - and motivate the Believers. It may be that Allah will restrain the fury of the Unbelievers; for Allah is the strongest in might and in punishment.

85. Whoever recommends and helps a good cause becomes a partner therein: and whoever recommends and helps an evil cause, shares in its burden: and Allah has power over all things.

86. When a (courteous) greeting is offered you, meet it with a greeting still more courteous, or (at least) of equal courtesy. Allah takes careful account of all things.

87. Allah! There is no god but He: of a surety He will gather you together against the Day of Judgment, about which there is no doubt. And whose word can be truer than Allah's?

88. Why should you be divided into two parties about the Hypocrites? Allah has upset them for their (evil) deeds. Would you guide those whom Allah has thrown out of the Way? For those whom Allah has thrown out of the Way, you will never find the Way.

89. They but wish that you should reject Faith, as they do, and thus be on the same footing (as they): but do not take friends from their ranks until they flee in the way of Allah (from what is forbidden). But if they turn renegades, seize them and slay them wherever you find them; and (in any case) take no friends or helpers from their ranks;-

90. Except those who join a group between whom and you there is a treaty (of peace), or those who approach you with hearts restraining them from fighting you

as well as fighting their own
people. If Allah had pleased, He
could have given them power
over you, and they would have
fought you: therefore if they
withdraw from you but do not
fight you, and (instead) send
you (guarantees) of peace, then
Allah has opened no way for
you (to war against them).

91. Others you will find that
wish to gain your confidence as
well as that of their people:
every time they are sent back to
temptation, they succumb
thereto: if they do not withdraw
from you nor give you
(guarantees) of peace besides
restraining their hands, seize
them and slay them wherever
you get them: in their case We
have provided you with a clear
argument against them.

92. Never should a Believer
kill a Believer; but (if it so
happens) by mistake, (compensation is due): if one (so) kills a
Believer, it is ordained that he
should free a believing slave,
and pay compensation to the
deceased's family, unless they
remit it freely. If the deceased
belonged to a people at war with
you, and he was a Believer, the
freeing of a believing slave (is
enough). If he belonged to a
people with whom you have
treaty of mutual alliance,
compensation should be paid to
his family, and a believing slave
be freed. For those who find this
beyond their means, (is
prescribed) a fast for two months
running: by way of repentance to
Allah: for Allah has all
knowledge and all wisdom.

93. If a man kills a Believer
intentionally, his recompense is

Hell, to abide therein (for ever): and the wrath and the curse of Allah are upon him, and a dreadful Chastisement is prepared for him.

94. O you who believe! When you go abroad in the cause of Allah, investigate carefully, and do not say to any one who offers you a salutation: "you are not a Believer!" coveting the perishable goods of this life: with Allah are profits and spoils abundant. Even thus were you yourselves before, till Allah conferred on you His favours: therefore carefully investigate. For Allah is well aware of all that you do.

95. Not equal are those Believers who sit (at home) and receive no hurt, and those who strive and fight in the cause of Allah with their goods and their persons. Allah has granted a grade higher to those who strive and fight with their goods and persons than to those who sit (at home). To all (in Faith) Allah has promised good: but those who strive and fight He has distinguished above those who sit (at home) by a special reward,-

96. Ranks specially bestowed by Him, and Forgiveness and Mercy. For Allah is Oft-forgiving, Most Merciful.

97. When angels take the souls of those who die in sin against their souls, they say: "In what (plight) were you?" They reply: "Weak and oppressed were we in the earth." They say: "Was not the earth of Allah spacious enough for you to move yourselves away (from evil)?" Such men will find their abode in Hell, - What an evil refuge! -

98. Except those who are (really) weak and oppressed - men, women, and children - who have no means in their power, nor (a guide-post) to direct their way.

99. For these, there is hope that Allah will forgive: for Allah blots out (sins) and forgives again and again.

100. He who forsakes his home in the cause of Allah, finds in the earth many a refuge, wide and spacious: should he die as a refugee from home for Allah and His Apostle, His reward becomes due and sure with Allah: And Allah is Oft-forgiving, Most Merciful.

101. When you travel through the earth, there is no blame on you if you shorten your prayers, for fear the Unbelievers may attack you: for the Unbelievers are open enemies to you.

102. When you (O Apostle) are with them, and stand to lead them in prayer, let one party of them stand up (in prayer) with you, taking their arms with them: when they finish their prostrations, let them take their position in the rear. And let the other party come up which has not yet prayed - and let them pray with you, taking all precautions, and bearing arms: the Unbelievers wish, if you were negligent of your arms and your baggage, to assault you in a single rush. But there is no blame

إِلَّا الْمُسْتَضْعَفِينَ مِنَ الرِّجَالِ وَالنِّسَاءِ وَالْوِلْدَانِ لَا يَسْتَطِيعُونَ حِيلَةً وَّلَا يَهْتَدُونَ سَبِيلًا ۞

فَأُولَٰئِكَ عَسَى اللَّهُ أَنْ يَّعْفُوَ عَنْهُمْ ۚ وَكَانَ اللَّهُ عَفُوًّا غَفُورًا ۞

وَمَنْ يُّهَاجِرْ فِي سَبِيلِ اللَّهِ يَجِدْ فِي الْأَرْضِ مُرَاغَمًا كَثِيرًا وَّسَعَةً ۚ وَمَنْ يَّخْرُجْ مِنْ بَيْتِهِ مُهَاجِرًا إِلَى اللَّهِ وَرَسُولِهِ ثُمَّ يُدْرِكْهُ الْمَوْتُ فَقَدْ وَقَعَ أَجْرُهُ عَلَى اللَّهِ ۗ وَكَانَ اللَّهُ غَفُورًا رَّحِيمًا ۞

وَإِذَا ضَرَبْتُمْ فِي الْأَرْضِ فَلَيْسَ عَلَيْكُمْ جُنَاحٌ أَنْ تَقْصُرُوا مِنَ الصَّلَاةِ ۖ إِنْ خِفْتُمْ أَنْ يَّفْتِنَكُمُ الَّذِينَ كَفَرُوا ۚ إِنَّ الْكَافِرِينَ كَانُوا لَكُمْ عَدُوًّا مُبِينًا ۞

وَإِذَا كُنْتَ فِيهِمْ فَأَقَمْتَ لَهُمُ الصَّلَاةَ فَلْتَقُمْ طَائِفَةٌ مِنْهُمْ مَعَكَ وَلْيَأْخُذُوا أَسْلِحَتَهُمْ ۖ فَإِذَا سَجَدُوا فَلْيَكُونُوا مِنْ وَرَائِكُمْ ۚ وَلْتَأْتِ طَائِفَةٌ أُخْرَى لَمْ يُصَلُّوا فَلْيُصَلُّوا مَعَكَ وَلْيَأْخُذُوا حِذْرَهُمْ وَأَسْلِحَتَهُمْ ۗ وَدَّ الَّذِينَ كَفَرُوا لَوْ تَغْفُلُونَ عَنْ أَسْلِحَتِكُمْ وَأَمْتِعَتِكُمْ فَيَمِيلُونَ عَلَيْكُمْ مَيْلَةً وَاحِدَةً ۚ وَلَا جُنَاحَ

on you if you put away your arms because of the inconvenience of rain or because you are ill; but take (every) precaution for yourselves. For the Unbelievers Allah has prepared a humiliating punishment.

103. When you pass (congregational) prayers, celebrate Allah's praises, standing, sitting down, or lying down on your sides; but when you are free from danger, set up regular Prayers: for such prayers are enjoined on Believers at stated times.

104. And slacken not in following up the enemy: if you are suffering hardships, they are suffering similar hardships; but you have hope from Allah, while they have none. And Allah is full of knowledge and wisdom.

105. We have sent down to you the Book in truth, that you might judge between men, as guided by Allah: so be not (used) as an advocate by those who betray their trust;

106. But seek the forgiveness of Allah; for Allah is Oft-forgiving, Most Merciful.

107. Do not contend on behalf of such as betray their own souls; for Allah does not love one given to perfidy and crime:

108. They may hide (their crimes) from men, but they cannot hide (them) from Allah, seeing that He is in their midst when they plot by night, in words that He cannot approve: and Allah compassess round all that they do.

عَلَيْكُمْ إِنْ كَانَ بِكُمْ أَذًى مِّنْ

مَّطَرٍ أَوْ كُنْتُمْ مَّرْضَى أَنْ تَضَعُوا

أَسْلِحَتَكُمْ وَخُذُوا حِذْرَكُمْ إِنَّ اللهَ

أَعَدَّ لِلْكَافِرِينَ عَذَابًا مُّهِينًا ۞

فَإِذَا قَضَيْتُمُ الصَّلَوةَ فَاذْكُرُوا

اللهَ قِيَامًا وَّقُعُودًا وَّعَلَى جُنُوبِكُمْ

فَإِذَا اطْمَأْنَنْتُمْ فَأَقِيمُوا الصَّلَوةَ

إِنَّ الصَّلَوةَ كَانَتْ عَلَى الْمُؤْمِنِينَ

كِتَابًا مَّوْقُوتًا

وَلَا تَهِنُوا فِي ابْتِغَاءِ الْقَوْمِ إِنْ

تَكُونُوا تَأْلَمُونَ فَإِنَّهُمْ يَأْلَمُونَ

كَمَا تَأْلَمُونَ وَتَرْجُونَ مِنَ اللهِ

مَا لَا يَرْجُونَ وَكَانَ اللهُ

عَلِيمًا حَكِيمًا ۞

إِنَّا أَنْزَلْنَا إِلَيْكَ الْكِتَابَ بِالْحَقِّ

لِتَحْكُمَ بَيْنَ النَّاسِ بِمَا أَرَاكَ اللهُ

وَلَا تَكُنْ لِّلْخَائِنِينَ خَصِيمًا ۞

وَّاسْتَغْفِرِ اللهَ إِنَّ اللهَ كَانَ

غَفُورًا رَّحِيمًا ۞

وَلَا تُجَادِلْ عَنِ الَّذِينَ يَخْتَانُونَ

أَنْفُسَهُمْ إِنَّ اللهَ لَا يُحِبُّ مَنْ

كَانَ خَوَّانًا أَثِيمًا ۞

يَسْتَخْفُونَ مِنَ النَّاسِ وَلَا يَسْتَخْفُونَ

مِنَ اللهِ وَهُوَ مَعَهُمْ إِذْ يُبَيِّتُونَ

مَا لَا يَرْضَى مِنَ الْقَوْلِ وَكَانَ

اللهُ بِمَا يَعْمَلُونَ مُحِيطًا

109. Ah! these are the sort of men on whose behalf you may contend in this world; but who will contend with Allah on their behalf on the Day of Judgment, or who will carry their affairs through?

هَآنْتُمْ هَٰؤُلَآءِ جَادَلْتُمْ عَنْهُمْ فِى الْحَيَوٰةِ الدُّنْيَا ۖ فَمَنْ يُّجَادِلُ اللّٰهَ عَنْهُمْ يَوْمَ الْقِيٰمَةِ اَمْ مَّنْ يَّكُوْنُ عَلَيْهِمْ وَكِيْلًا ۝

110. If any one does evil or wrongs his own soul but afterwards seeks Allah's forgiveness, he will find Allah Oft-forgiving, Most Merciful.

وَمَنْ يَّعْمَلْ سُوْٓءًا اَوْ يَظْلِمْ نَفْسَهٗ ثُمَّ يَسْتَغْفِرِ اللّٰهَ يَجِدِ اللّٰهَ غَفُوْرًا رَّحِيْمًا ۝

111. And if any one earns sin, he earns it against his own soul: for Allah is full of knowledge and wisdom.

وَمَنْ يَّكْسِبْ اِثْمًا فَاِنَّمَا يَكْسِبُهٗ عَلٰى نَفْسِهٖ ۖ وَكَانَ اللّٰهُ عَلِيْمًا حَكِيْمًا ۝

112. But if any one earns a fault or a sin and throws it on to one that is innocent, he carries (on himself) (both) a falsehood and a flagrant sin.

وَمَنْ يَّكْسِبْ خَطِيْٓئَةً اَوْ اِثْمًا ثُمَّ يَرْمِ بِهٖ بَرِيْٓئًا فَقَدِ احْتَمَلَ بُهْتَانًا وَّاِثْمًا مُّبِيْنًا ۝

113. But for the Grace of Allah to you and His Mercy, a party of them would certainly have plotted to lead you astray. But (in fact) they will only lead their own souls astray, and to you they can do no harm in the least. For Allah has sent down to you the Book and Wisdom and taught you what you did not know (before): and great is the Grace of Allah unto you.

وَلَوْلَا فَضْلُ اللّٰهِ عَلَيْكَ وَرَحْمَتُهٗ لَهَمَّتْ طَّآئِفَةٌ مِّنْهُمْ اَنْ يُّضِلُّوْكَ ۖ وَمَا يُضِلُّوْنَ اِلَّآ اَنْفُسَهُمْ وَمَا يَضُرُّوْنَكَ مِنْ شَيْءٍ ۖ وَاَنْزَلَ اللّٰهُ عَلَيْكَ الْكِتٰبَ وَالْحِكْمَةَ وَعَلَّمَكَ مَا لَمْ تَكُنْ تَعْلَمُ ۖ وَكَانَ فَضْلُ اللّٰهِ عَلَيْكَ عَظِيْمًا ۝

114. In most of their secret talks there is no good: but if one exhorts to a deed of charity or justice or conciliation between men, (secrecy is permissible): to him who does this, seeking the good pleasure of Allah, We shall soon give a reward of the highest (value).

لَاخَيْرَ فِىْ كَثِيْرٍ مِّنْ نَّجْوٰىهُمْ اِلَّا مَنْ اَمَرَ بِصَدَقَةٍ اَوْ مَعْرُوْفٍ اَوْ اِصْلَاحٍ بَيْنَ النَّاسِ ۖ وَمَنْ يَّفْعَلْ ذٰلِكَ ابْتِغَآءَ مَرْضَاتِ اللّٰهِ فَسَوْفَ نُؤْتِيْهِ اَجْرًا عَظِيْمًا ۝

115. If anyone contends with the Apostle even after

وَمَنْ يُّشَاقِقِ الرَّسُوْلَ مِنْ بَعْدِ

guidance has been plainly conveyed to him, and follows a path other than that becoming to men of Faith, We shall leave him in the path he has chosen, and land him in Hell, - what an evil refuge!

116. Allah does not forgive (the sin of) joining other gods with Him; but He forgives whom He pleases other sins than this: one who joins other gods with Allah has strayed far, far away (from the Right).

117. (The Pagans), leaving Him, call but upon female deities: they call but upon Satan the persistent rebel!

118. Allah did cursed him, but he said: "I will take of Your servants a portion marked off;

119. "I will mislead them, and I will create in them false desires; I will order them to slit the ears of cattle, and to deface the (fair) nature created by Allah." Whoever, forsaking Allah, takes Satan for a friend, of a surety has suffered a loss that is manifest.

120. Satan makes them promises, and creates in them false desires; but Satan's promises are nothing but deception.

121. They (his dupes) will have their dwelling in Hell, and from it they will find no way of escape.

122. But those who believe and do deeds of righteousness, - We shall soon admit them to Gardens, with rivers flowing beneath, - to dwell therein for ever. Allah's promise is the truth, and whose word can be truer than Allah's?

123. Not your desires, nor those of the People of

مَا تَبَيَّنَ لَهُ الْهُدَىٰ وَيَتَّبِعْ
غَيْرَ سَبِيلِ الْمُؤْمِنِينَ نُوَلِّهِ مَا تَوَلَّىٰ
وَنُصْلِهِ جَهَنَّمَ ۖ وَسَاءَتْ مَصِيرًا ۝
إِنَّ اللَّهَ لَا يَغْفِرُ أَن يُشْرَكَ بِهِ
وَيَغْفِرُ مَا دُونَ ذَٰلِكَ لِمَن يَشَاءُ ۚ
وَمَن يُشْرِكْ بِاللَّهِ فَقَدْ ضَلَّ
ضَلَالًا بَعِيدًا ۝
إِن يَدْعُونَ مِن دُونِهِ إِلَّا إِنَاثًا
وَإِن يَدْعُونَ إِلَّا شَيْطَانًا مَّرِيدًا ۝
لَّعَنَهُ اللَّهُ ۘ وَقَالَ لَأَتَّخِذَنَّ مِنْ
عِبَادِكَ نَصِيبًا مَّفْرُوضًا ۝
وَلَأُضِلَّنَّهُمْ وَلَأُمَنِّيَنَّهُمْ وَلَآمُرَنَّهُمْ
فَلَيُبَتِّكُنَّ آذَانَ الْأَنْعَامِ وَلَآمُرَنَّهُمْ
فَلَيُغَيِّرُنَّ خَلْقَ اللَّهِ ۚ وَمَن يَتَّخِذِ
الشَّيْطَانَ وَلِيًّا مِّن دُونِ اللَّهِ فَقَدْ
خَسِرَ خُسْرَانًا مُّبِينًا ۝
يَعِدُهُمْ وَيُمَنِّيهِمْ ۖ وَمَا يَعِدُهُمُ
الشَّيْطَانُ إِلَّا غُرُورًا ۝
أُولَٰئِكَ مَأْوَاهُمْ جَهَنَّمُ ۖ وَلَا
يَجِدُونَ عَنْهَا مَحِيصًا ۝
وَالَّذِينَ آمَنُوا وَعَمِلُوا الصَّالِحَاتِ
سَنُدْخِلُهُمْ جَنَّاتٍ تَجْرِي مِن
تَحْتِهَا الْأَنْهَارُ خَالِدِينَ فِيهَا أَبَدًا ۖ
وَعْدَ اللَّهِ حَقًّا ۚ وَمَنْ أَصْدَقُ
مِنَ اللَّهِ قِيلًا ۝
لَّيْسَ بِأَمَانِيِّكُمْ وَلَا أَمَانِيِّ أَهْلِ

the Book (can prevail): whoever works evil, will be requited accordingly. Nor will he find, besides Allah any protector or helper.

124. If any do deeds of righteousness,- be they male or female - and have faith, they will enter Heaven, and not the least injustice will be done to them.

125. Who can be better in religion than one who submits his whole self to Allah, does good, and follows the way of Abraham the true in faith? For Allah took Abraham for a friend.

126. But to Allah belong all things in the heavens and on earth: and He it is that encompasses all things.

127. They ask your instruction concerning the Women. Say: Allah instructed you about them: and (remember) what has been rehearsed unto you in the Book, concerning the orphans of women to whom you do not give the portions prescribed, and yet whom you desire to marry, as also concerning the children who are weak and oppressed: that you stand firm for justice to orphans. There is not a good deed which you do, but Allah is well-acquainted therewith.

128. If a wife fears cruelty or desertion on her husband's part, there is no blame on them if they arrange an amicable settlement between themselves; and such settlement is best; even though men's souls are

swayed by greed. But if you do good and practise self-restraint, Allah is well-acquainted with all that you do.

129. You are never able to be fair and just as between women, even if it is your ardent desire: but do not turn away (from a woman) altogether, so as to leave her (as it were) hanging (in the air). If you come to a friendly understanding, and practise self-restraint, Allah is Oft-forgiving, Most Merciful.

130. But if they disagree (and must part), Allah will provide abundance for all from His all-reaching bounty: for Allah is He that cares for all and is Wise.

131. To Allah belong all things in the heavens and on earth. Verily We have directed the People of the Book before you, and you (O Muslims) to fear Allah. But if you deny Him, lo! to Allah belong all things in the heavens and on earth, and Allah is free of all wants, worthy of all praise.

132. Yes, to Allah belong all things in the heavens and on earth, and enough is Allah to carry through all affairs.

133. If it were His Will, He could destroy you, O mankind, and create another race; for Allah has power to do this.

134. If any one desires a reward in this life, in Allah's (gift) is the reward (both) of this life and of the hereafter: for Allah is He that hears and sees (all things).

135. O you who believe! stand out firmly for justice, as witnesses to Allah, even as against yourselves, or your parents, or your kin,

and whether it be (against) rich or poor: for Allah can best protect both. Follow not the lusts (of your hearts), lest you swerve, and if you distort (justice) or decline to do justice, verily Allah is well- acquainted with all that you do.

اِنۡ یَّکُنۡ غَنِیًّا اَوۡ فَقِیۡرًا فَاللّٰهُ اَوۡلٰی بِهِمَا ۚ فَلَا تَتَّبِعُوا الۡهَوٰۤی اَنۡ تَعۡدِلُوۡا ۚ وَاِنۡ تَلۡوٗۤا اَوۡ تُعۡرِضُوۡا فَاِنَّ اللّٰهَ کَانَ بِمَا تَعۡمَلُوۡنَ خَبِیۡرًا ۟

136. O you who believe! Believe in Allah and His Apostle, and the scripture which He has sent to His Apostle and the scripture which He sent to those before (him). Any who denies Allah, His Angels, His Books, His Apostles, and the Day of Judgment, has gone far, far astray.

یٰۤاَیُّهَا الَّذِیۡنَ اٰمَنُوۡۤا اٰمِنُوۡا بِاللّٰهِ وَرَسُوۡلِهٖ وَالۡکِتٰبِ الَّذِیۡ نَزَّلَ عَلٰی رَسُوۡلِهٖ وَالۡکِتٰبِ الَّذِیۡۤ اَنۡزَلَ مِنۡ قَبۡلُ ۚ وَمَنۡ یَّکۡفُرۡ بِاللّٰهِ وَمَلٰٓئِکَتِهٖ وَکُتُبِهٖ وَرُسُلِهٖ وَالۡیَوۡمِ الۡاٰخِرِ فَقَدۡ ضَلَّ ضَلٰلًۢا بَعِیۡدًا ۟

137. Those who believe, then reject Faith, then believe (again) and (again) reject Faith, and go on increasing in Unbelief, - Allah will not forgive them nor guide them on the Way.

اِنَّ الَّذِیۡنَ اٰمَنُوۡا ثُمَّ کَفَرُوۡا ثُمَّ اٰمَنُوۡا ثُمَّ کَفَرُوۡا ثُمَّ ازۡدَادُوۡا کُفۡرًا لَّمۡ یَکُنِ اللّٰهُ لِیَغۡفِرَ لَهُمۡ وَلَا لِیَهۡدِیَهُمۡ سَبِیۡلًا ۟

138. To the Hypocrites give the glad tidings that there is for them (but) a grievous Chastisement.

بَشِّرِ الۡمُنٰفِقِیۡنَ بِاَنَّ لَهُمۡ عَذَابًا اَلِیۡمَا ۟ۙ

139. Yes, to those who take for friends Unbelievers rather than Believers: is it honour they seek among them? Nay,- all honour is with Allah.

الَّذِیۡنَ یَتَّخِذُوۡنَ الۡکٰفِرِیۡنَ اَوۡلِیَآءَ مِنۡ دُوۡنِ الۡمُؤۡمِنِیۡنَ ؕ اَیَبۡتَغُوۡنَ عِنۡدَهُمُ الۡعِزَّةَ فَاِنَّ الۡعِزَّةَ لِلّٰهِ جَمِیۡعًا ۟ؕ

140. Already He has sent you Word in the Book, that when you hear the Signs of Allah held in defiance and ridicule, you are not to sit with them unless they turn to a different theme: if you did, you would be like them. For Allah will collect the Hypocrites and those who defy Faith - all in Hell:-

وَقَدۡ نَزَّلَ عَلَیۡکُمۡ فِی الۡکِتٰبِ اَنۡ اِذَا سَمِعۡتُمۡ اٰیٰتِ اللّٰهِ یُکۡفَرُ بِهَا وَیُسۡتَهۡزَاُ بِهَا فَلَا تَقۡعُدُوۡا مَعَهُمۡ حَتّٰی یَخُوۡضُوۡا فِیۡ حَدِیۡثٍ غَیۡرِهٖۤ ۖ اِنَّکُمۡ اِذًا مِّثۡلُهُمۡ ؕ اِنَّ اللّٰهَ جَامِعُ الۡمُنٰفِقِیۡنَ وَالۡکٰفِرِیۡنَ فِیۡ جَهَنَّمَ جَمِیۡعَا ۟ۙ

141. (These are) the ones who wait and watch about you: if

الَّذِیۡنَ یَتَرَبَّصُوۡنَ بِکُمۡ ۚ فَاِنۡ کَانَ

you do gain a victory from Allah, they say: "Were we not with you?"- but if the Unbelievers gain a success, they say (to them): "Did we not gain an advantage over you, and did we not guard you from the Believers?" But Allah will judge between you on the Day of Judgment. And never will Allah grant to the Unbelievers a way (to triumph) over the Believers.

142. The Hypocrites - they think they are over-reaching Allah, but He will over- reach them: when they stand up to prayer, they stand without earnestness, to be seen of men, but little do they hold Allah in remembrance;

143. (They are) distracted in mind even in the midst of it,- being (sincerely) for neither one group nor for another. Whom Allah leaves straying,- never will you find for him the Way.

144. O you who believe! take not for friends Unbelievers rather than Believers: do you wish to offer Allah an open proof against yourselves?

145. The Hypocrites will be in the lowest depths of the Fire: no helper will you find for them;-

146. Except for those who repent, mend (their lives) hold fast to Allah, and purify their religion as in Allah's sight: if so they will be (numbered) with the Believers. And soon will Allah grant to the Believers a reward of immense value.

147. What can Allah gain by your punishment, if you are grateful and you believe? Nay, it is Allah that recognises (all good), and knows all things.

148. Allah does not love that

evil should be noised abroad in public speech, except where injustice has been done; for Allah is He who hears and knows all things.

149. Whether you publish a good deed or conceal it or cover evil with pardon, verily Allah blots out (sins) and has power (in the judgment of values).

150. Those who deny Allah and His Apostles, and (those who) wish to separate Allah from His Apostles, saying: "We believe in some but reject others": and (those who) wish to take a course midway,-

151. They are in truth (equally) Unbelievers; and We have prepared for Unbelievers a humiliating punishment.

152. To those who believe in Allah and His Apostles and make no distinction between any of the Apostles, We shall soon give their (due) rewards: for Allah is Oft-forgiving, Most Merciful.

153. The people of the Book ask you to cause a book to descend to them from heaven: Indeed they asked Moses for an even greater (miracle), for they said: "Show us Allah in public," but they were dazed for their presumption, with thunder and lightning. Yet they worshipped the calf even after Clear Signs had come to them; even so We forgave them; and gave Moses manifest proofs of authority.

154. And for their Covenant We raised over them (the towering height) of Mount (Sinai); and (on another occasion) We said:"Enter the gate with humility"; and (once again) We commanded them: "do not transgress in the matter of the Sabbath."

مِنَ الْقَوْلِ إِلَّا مَنْ ظُلِمَ ۚ وَكَانَ
اللهُ سَمِيعًا عَلِيمًا ۝

اِنْ تُبْدُوا خَيْرًا اَوْ تُخْفُوهُ اَوْ تَعْفُوا
عَنْ سُوءٍ فَاِنَّ اللهَ كَانَ عَفُوًّا قَدِيرًا۝

اِنَّ الَّذِيْنَ يَكْفُرُوْنَ بِاللهِ وَرُسُلِهِ
وَيُرِيْدُوْنَ اَنْ يُّفَرِّقُوْا بَيْنَ اللهِ
وَرُسُلِهِ وَيَقُوْلُوْنَ نُؤْمِنُ بِبَعْضٍ
وَّنَكْفُرُ بِبَعْضٍ ۙ وَّيُرِيْدُوْنَ اَنْ
يَّتَّخِذُوْا بَيْنَ ذٰلِكَ سَبِيْلًا ۙ۝

اُولٰٓئِكَ هُمُ الْكٰفِرُوْنَ حَقًّا ۚ وَاَعْتَدْنَا
لِلْكٰفِرِيْنَ عَذَابًا مُّهِيْنًا۝

وَالَّذِيْنَ اٰمَنُوْا بِاللهِ وَرُسُلِهِ وَلَمْ
يُفَرِّقُوْا بَيْنَ اَحَدٍ مِّنْهُمْ اُولٰٓئِكَ
سَوْفَ يُؤْتِيْهِمْ اُجُوْرَهُمْ ۗ وَكَانَ
اللهُ غَفُوْرًا رَّحِيْمًا ۝

يَسْئَلُكَ اَهْلُ الْكِتٰبِ اَنْ تُنَزِّلَ
عَلَيْهِمْ كِتٰبًا مِّنَ السَّمَاءِ فَقَدْ سَاَلُوْا
مُوْسٰى اَكْبَرَ مِنْ ذٰلِكَ فَقَالُوْٓا اَرِنَا
اللهَ جَهْرَةً فَاَخَذَتْهُمُ الصّٰعِقَةُ
بِظُلْمِهِمْ ۚ ثُمَّ اتَّخَذُوا الْعِجْلَ
مِنْ بَعْدِ مَا جَآءَتْهُمُ الْبَيِّنٰتُ
فَعَفَوْنَا عَنْ ذٰلِكَ ۚ وَاٰتَيْنَا مُوْسٰى
سُلْطٰنًا مُّبِيْنًا ۝

وَرَفَعْنَا فَوْقَهُمُ الطُّوْرَ بِمِيْثَاقِهِمْ
وَقُلْنَا لَهُمُ ادْخُلُوا الْبَابَ سُجَّدًا
وَّقُلْنَا لَهُمْ لَا تَعْدُوْا فِى السَّبْتِ

And We took from them a solemn Covenant.

155. (They have incurred divine displeasure): In that they broke their Covenant; that they rejected the Signs of Allah; that they slew the Messengers in defiance of right; that they said, "Our hearts are the wrappings (which preserve Allah's Word; We need no more)";- No, Allah has set the seal on their hearts for their blasphemy, and little is it they believe;-

156. That they rejected Faith; that they uttered against Mary a grave false charge;

157. That they said (in boast), "We killed Christ Jesus the son of Mary, the Apostle of Allah";- but they did not kill him, nor crucified him, but so it was made to appear to them, and those who differ therein are full of doubts, with no (certain) knowledge, but only conjecture to follow, for of a surety they did not kill him :-

158. Nay, Allah raised him up unto Himself; and Allah is Exalted in Power, Wise;-

159. And there is none of the People of the Book but must believe in him before his death; and on the Day of Judgment he will be a witness against them;-

160. For the iniquity of the Jews We made unlawful for them certain (foods) good and wholesome which had been lawful for them;- in that they hindered many from Allah's Way;-

161. That they took interest, though they were forbidden; and that they devoured men's substance wrongfully;- We have prepared for those among them who reject Faith a grievous punishment.

وَاَخَذْنَا مِنْهُمْ مِّيْثَاقًا غَلِيْظًا ۞

فَبِمَا نَقْضِهِمْ مِّيْثَاقَهُمْ وَكُفْرِهِمْ
بِاٰيٰتِ اللّٰهِ وَقَتْلِهِمُ الْاَنْبِيَآءَ بِغَيْرِ
حَقٍّ وَّقَوْلِهِمْ قُلُوْبُنَا غُلْفٌ ۚ بَلْ طَبَعَ
اللّٰهُ عَلَيْهَا بِكُفْرِهِمْ فَلَا يُؤْمِنُوْنَ
اِلَّا قَلِيْلًا ۙ۞

وَّبِكُفْرِهِمْ وَقَوْلِهِمْ عَلٰى مَرْيَمَ
بُهْتَانًا عَظِيْمًا ۙ۞

وَّقَوْلِهِمْ اِنَّا قَتَلْنَا الْمَسِيْحَ عِيْسَى
ابْنَ مَرْيَمَ رَسُوْلَ اللّٰهِ ۚ وَمَا قَتَلُوْهُ
وَمَا صَلَبُوْهُ وَلٰكِنْ شُبِّهَ لَهُمْ ۚ
وَاِنَّ الَّذِيْنَ اخْتَلَفُوْا فِيْهِ لَفِيْ شَكٍّ
مِّنْهُ ۚ مَا لَهُمْ بِهٖ مِنْ عِلْمٍ اِلَّا
اتِّبَاعَ الظَّنِّ ۚ وَمَا قَتَلُوْهُ يَقِيْنًا ۞

بَلْ رَّفَعَهُ اللّٰهُ اِلَيْهِ ۚ وَكَانَ اللّٰهُ
عَزِيْزًا حَكِيْمًا ۞

وَاِنْ مِّنْ اَهْلِ الْكِتٰبِ اِلَّا لَيُؤْمِنَنَّ
بِهٖ قَبْلَ مَوْتِهٖ ۚ وَيَوْمَ الْقِيٰمَةِ
يَكُوْنُ عَلَيْهِمْ شَهِيْدًا ۚ۞

فَبِظُلْمٍ مِّنَ الَّذِيْنَ هَادُوْا حَرَّمْنَا
عَلَيْهِمْ طَيِّبٰتٍ اُحِلَّتْ لَهُمْ وَبِصَدِّهِمْ
عَنْ سَبِيْلِ اللّٰهِ كَثِيْرًا ۙ۞

وَّاَخْذِهِمُ الرِّبٰوا وَقَدْ نُهُوْا عَنْهُ
وَاَكْلِهِمْ اَمْوَالَ النَّاسِ بِالْبَاطِلِ ۚ
وَاَعْتَدْنَا لِلْكٰفِرِيْنَ مِنْهُمْ عَذَابًا
اَلِيْمًا ۞

162. But those among them who are well-grounded in knowledge, and the Believers, believe in what has been revealed to you and what was revealed before you: and (especially) those who establish regular prayer and practise regular charity and believe in Allah and in the Last Day: to them shall We soon give a great reward.

لٰكِنِ الرّٰسِخُوْنَ فِى الْعِلْمِ مِنْهُمْ وَالْمُؤْمِنُوْنَ يُؤْمِنُوْنَ بِمَا أُنْزِلَ إِلَيْكَ وَمَا أُنْزِلَ مِنْ قَبْلِكَ وَ الْمُقِيْمِيْنَ الصَّلٰوةَ وَالْمُؤْتُوْنَ الزَّكٰوةَ وَالْمُؤْمِنُوْنَ بِاللّٰهِ وَالْيَوْمِ الْاٰخِرِ اُولٰٓئِكَ سَنُؤْتِيْهِمْ اَجْرًا عَظِيْمًا ۞

163. We have sent you inspiration, as We sent it to Noah and the Messengers after him: We sent inspiration to Abraham, Isma'il, Isaac, Jacob and the Tribes, to Jesus, Job, Jonah, Aaron, and Solomon, and to David We gave the Psalms.

إِنَّا أَوْحَيْنَا إِلَيْكَ كَمَا أَوْحَيْنَا إِلٰى نُوْحٍ وَّالنَّبِيّٖنَ مِنْ بَعْدِهٖ وَأَوْحَيْنَا إِلٰى إِبْرٰهِيْمَ وَإِسْمٰعِيْلَ وَإِسْحٰقَ وَيَعْقُوْبَ وَالْأَسْبَاطِ وَعِيْسٰى وَأَيُّوْبَ وَيُوْنُسَ وَهٰرُوْنَ وَسُلَيْمٰنَ وَاٰتَيْنَا دَاوٗدَ زَبُوْرًا ۞

164. Of some Apostles We have already told you the story; of others We have not;- and to Moses Allah spoke direct;-

وَرُسُلًا قَدْ قَصَصْنٰهُمْ عَلَيْكَ مِنْ قَبْلُ وَرُسُلًا لَّمْ نَقْصُصْهُمْ عَلَيْكَ وَكَلَّمَ اللّٰهُ مُوْسٰى تَكْلِيْمًا ۞

165. Apostles who gave good news as well as warning, that mankind, after (the coming) of the Apostles, should have no plea against Allah: for Allah is Exalted in Power, Wise.

رُسُلًا مُّبَشِّرِيْنَ وَمُنْذِرِيْنَ لِئَلَّا يَكُوْنَ لِلنَّاسِ عَلَى اللّٰهِ حُجَّةٌ بَعْدَ الرُّسُلِ وَكَانَ اللّٰهُ عَزِيْزًا حَكِيْمًا ۞

166. But Allah bears witness that what He has sent unto you He has sent from His (own) knowledge, and the Angels bear Witness: but enough is Allah for a Witness.

لٰكِنِ اللّٰهُ يَشْهَدُ بِمَا أَنْزَلَ إِلَيْكَ أَنْزَلَهٗ بِعِلْمِهٖ وَالْمَلٰٓئِكَةُ يَشْهَدُوْنَ وَكَفٰى بِاللّٰهِ شَهِيْدًا ۞

167. Those who reject Faith and keep off (men) from the way of Allah, have verily strayed far, far away from the Path.

إِنَّ الَّذِيْنَ كَفَرُوْا وَصَدُّوْا عَنْ سَبِيْلِ اللّٰهِ قَدْ ضَلُّوْا ضَلٰلًا بَعِيْدًا ۞

168. Those who reject Faith and do wrong,- Allah will not forgive them nor guide them to any way-

إِنَّ الَّذِيْنَ كَفَرُوْا وَظَلَمُوْا لَمْ يَكُنِ اللّٰهُ لِيَغْفِرَ لَهُمْ وَلَا لِيَهْدِيَهُمْ طَرِيْقًا ۞

169. Except the way of Hell, to dwell therein for ever. And this to Allah is easy.

170. O mankind! the Apostle has come to you in truth from Allah: believe in him: It is best for you. But if you reject Faith, to Allah belong all things in the heavens and on earth: And Allah is All-knowing, All-wise.

171. O People of the Book! commit no excesses in your religion: nor say of Allah anything but the truth. Christ Jesus the son of Mary was (no more than) an Apostle of Allah, and His Word, which He bestowed on Mary, and a spirit proceeding from Him: so believe in Allah and His Apostles. Do not say "Trinity" desist: it will be better for you: for Allah is One God: glory be to Him: (far Exalted is He) above having a son. To Him belong all things in the heavens and on earth. And enough is Allah as a Disposer of affairs.

172. Christ does not disdain to serve and worship Allah, nor do the angels, those nearest (to Allah): those who disdain His worship and are arrogant,-He will gather them all together unto Himself to (answer).

173. But to those who believe and do deeds of righteousness, He will give their (due) rewards,- and more, out of His bounty: but those who are disdainful and arrogant, He will punish with a grievous Chastisement; nor will they find, besides Allah, any to protect or help them.

إِلَّا طَرِيقَ جَهَنَّمَ خَلِدِينَ فِيهَآ
أَبَدًا ۚ وَكَانَ ذَٰلِكَ عَلَى اللَّهِ يَسِيرًا ۝
يَٰٓأَيُّهَا النَّاسُ قَدْ جَآءَكُمُ الرَّسُولُ
بِالْحَقِّ مِن رَّبِّكُمْ فَـَٔامِنُوا خَيْرًا
لَّكُمْ ۚ وَإِن تَكْفُرُوا فَإِنَّ لِلَّهِ مَا فِى
السَّمَٰوَٰتِ وَالْأَرْضِ ۚ وَكَانَ اللَّهُ
عَلِيمًا حَكِيمًا ۝
يَٰٓأَهْلَ الْكِتَٰبِ لَا تَغْلُوا فِى دِينِكُمْ
وَلَا تَقُولُوا عَلَى اللَّهِ إِلَّا الْحَقَّ ۚ إِنَّمَا
الْمَسِيحُ عِيسَى ابْنُ مَرْيَمَ رَسُولُ اللَّهِ
وَكَلِمَتُهُۥٓ أَلْقَىٰهَآ إِلَىٰ مَرْيَمَ وَرُوحٌ
مِّنْهُ ۖ فَـَٔامِنُوا بِاللَّهِ وَرُسُلِهِۦ ۖ وَلَا
تَقُولُوا ثَلَٰثَةٌ ۚ انتَهُوا خَيْرًا لَّكُمْ ۚ
إِنَّمَا اللَّهُ إِلَٰهٌ وَٰحِدٌ ۖ سُبْحَٰنَهُۥٓ أَن
يَكُونَ لَهُۥ وَلَدٌ ۘ لَّهُۥ مَا فِى السَّمَٰوَٰتِ
وَمَا فِى الْأَرْضِ ۗ وَكَفَىٰ بِاللَّهِ وَكِيلًا ۝
لَّن يَسْتَنكِفَ الْمَسِيحُ أَن يَكُونَ
عَبْدًا لِّلَّهِ وَلَا الْمَلَٰٓئِكَةُ الْمُقَرَّبُونَ ۚ
وَمَن يَسْتَنكِفْ عَنْ عِبَادَتِهِۦ
وَيَسْتَكْبِرْ فَسَيَحْشُرُهُمْ إِلَيْهِ جَمِيعًا ۝
فَأَمَّا الَّذِينَ ءَامَنُوا وَعَمِلُوا الصَّٰلِحَٰتِ
فَيُوَفِّيهِمْ أُجُورَهُمْ وَيَزِيدُهُم مِّن
فَضْلِهِۦ ۖ وَأَمَّا الَّذِينَ اسْتَنكَفُوا وَ
اسْتَكْبَرُوا فَيُعَذِّبُهُمْ عَذَابًا أَلِيمًا ۙ
وَلَا يَجِدُونَ لَهُم مِّن دُونِ اللَّهِ
وَلِيًّا وَلَا نَصِيرًا ۝

SÛRAH-5
AL-MÂ'ÎDAH
(INTRODUCTION)

This Sûrah deals, by way of recapitulation, with the backsliding of the Jews and Christians from their pure religions, to which the coping stone was placed by Islam. It refers particularly to the Christians, and to their solemn Sacrament of the Last Supper, to whose mystic meaning they are declared to have been false.

As a logical corollary to the corruption of the earlier religions of Allah, the practical precepts of Islam, about food cleanliness, justice, and fidelity are recapitulated.

The third verse contains the memorable declaration: "This day have I perfected your religion for you"; which was promulgated in 10 H., during the Apostle's last Pilgrimage to Makkah. Chronologically it was the last verse to be revealed.

174. O mankind! verily there has come to you a convincing proof from your Lord: for We have sent unto you a light (that is) manifest.

175. Then those who believe in Allah, and hold fast to Him,- soon will He admit them to Mercy and Grace from Himself, and guide them to Himself by a straight way.

176. They ask you for a legal decision. Say: Allah directs (thus) about those who leave no descendants or ascendants as heirs. If it is a man that dies, leaving a sister but no child, she shall have half the inheritance: If (such a deceased was) a woman, who left no child, her brother takes her inheritance: If there are two sisters, they shall have two-thirds of the inheritance (between them): if there are brothers and sisters, (they share), the male having twice the share of the female. Thus does Allah make clear to you (His law), lest you err. And Allah has knowledge of all things.

5. The Table Spread
In the name of Allah. Most Gracious, Most Merciful.

1. O you who believe! Fulfil (all) obligations. Lawful to you (for food) are all four-footed animals, with the exceptions named: But animals of the chase are forbidden while you are in the Sacred Precincts or in pilgrim garb: for Allah commands according to His Will and Plan.

2. O you who believe! violate not the sanctity of the Symbols of Allah, nor of the Sacred Month, nor of the animals brought for sacrifice, nor the Garlands that mark out such animals, nor the people resorting to the Sacred House, seeking of the bounty and good pleasure of their Lord.

But when you are clear of the Sacred Precincts and of pilgrim garb, you may hunt and let not the hatred of some people in (once) shutting you out of the Sacred Mosque lead you to transgression (and hostility on your part). You help one another in righteousness and piety, but do not help one another in sin and rancour: fear Allah: for Allah is strict in punishment.

3. Forbidden to you (for food) are: dead meat, blood, the flesh of swine, and that on which has been invoked the name of other than Allah; that which has been killed by strangling, or by a violent blow, or by a headlong fall, or by being gored to death; that which has been (partly) eaten by a wild animal; unless you are able to slaughter it (in due form); that which is sacrificed on stone (altars); (forbidden) also is the division (of meat) by raffling with arrows: that is impiety. This day those who reject faith have given up all hopes of your religion: yet fear them not but fear Me. This day have I perfected your religion for you, completed My favour upon you, and have chosen for you Islam as your religion. But if any is forced by hunger, with no inclination to transgression, Allah is indeed Oft-forgiving, Most Merciful.

4. They ask you what is lawful to them (as food). Say: lawful to you are (all) good and pure things: and what you have taught your trained hunting animals (to catch) in the manner directed to you by Allah: eat what they catch for you, but pronounce the name of Allah over it: and fear Allah; for Allah is swift in taking account.

5. This day (all) good and pure things are made lawful to you. The food of the People of the Book is lawful to you and

yours is lawful to them. (Lawful to you in marriage) are (not only) chaste women who are Believers, but chaste women among the People of the Book, revealed before your time,- when you give them their due dowers, and desire chastity, not lewdness, nor secret intrigues. If any one rejects faith, fruitless is his work, and in the Hereafter he will be in the ranks of those who have lost (all spiritual good).

6. O you who believe! when you prepare for prayer, wash your faces, and your hands (and arms) to the elbows; rub your heads (with water); and (wash) your feet to the ankles. If you are in a state of ceremonial impurity, bathe your whole body. But if you are ill, or on a journey, or one of you comes from offices of nature, or you have been in contact with women, and you find no water, then take for yourselves clean sand or earth, and rub therewith your faces and hands. Allah does not wish to place you in a difficulty, but to make you clean, and to complete His favour to you, that you may be grateful.

7. And call in remembrance the favour of Allah to you, and His Covenant, which He ratified with you, when you said: "We hear and we obey": and fear Allah, for Allah knows well the secrets of your hearts.

8. O you who believe! stand out firmly for Allah, as witnesses to fair dealing, and let not the hatred of others to you make you swerve to wrong and depart from justice. Be just:

that is next to piety: and fear Allah. For Allah is well-acquainted with all that you do.

9. To those who believe and do deeds of righteousness, Allah has promised forgiveness and a great reward.

10. Those who reject faith and deny Our Signs will be companions of Hell-fire.

11. O you who believe! call in remembrance the favour of Allah unto you when certain men formed the design to stretch out their hands against you, but (Allah) held back their hands from you: so fear Allah. And on Allah let Believers put (all) their trust.

12. Allah took (aforetime) a Covenant from the Children of Israel, and We appointed twelve captains among them. And Allah said: "I am with you: if you (but) establish regular prayers, practise regular charity, believe in My Apostles, honour and assist them, and loan to Allah a beautiful loan, verily I will wipe out from you your evils, and admit you to Gardens with rivers flowing beneath; but if any of you, after this, resists faith, he has truly wandered from the path of rectitude."

13. But because of their breach of their Covenant, We cursed them, and made their hearts grow hard; they change the words from their (right) places and forget a good part of the Message that was sent them, nor will you cease to find them - barring a few - ever bent on (new) deceits:

وَهُوَ أَقْرَبُ لِلتَّقْوَىٰ ۚ وَاتَّقُوا اللَّهَ ۚ إِنَّ اللَّهَ خَبِيرٌ بِمَا تَعْمَلُونَ ۝

وَعَدَ اللَّهُ الَّذِينَ آمَنُوا وَعَمِلُوا الصَّالِحَاتِ ۙ لَهُم مَّغْفِرَةٌ وَأَجْرٌ عَظِيمٌ ۝

وَالَّذِينَ كَفَرُوا وَكَذَّبُوا بِآيَاتِنَا أُولَٰئِكَ أَصْحَابُ الْجَحِيمِ ۝

يَا أَيُّهَا الَّذِينَ آمَنُوا اذْكُرُوا نِعْمَتَ اللَّهِ عَلَيْكُمْ إِذْ هَمَّ قَوْمٌ أَن يَبْسُطُوا إِلَيْكُمْ أَيْدِيَهُمْ فَكَفَّ أَيْدِيَهُمْ عَنكُمْ ۖ وَاتَّقُوا اللَّهَ ۚ وَعَلَى اللَّهِ فَلْيَتَوَكَّلِ الْمُؤْمِنُونَ ۝

وَلَقَدْ أَخَذَ اللَّهُ مِيثَاقَ بَنِي إِسْرَائِيلَ وَبَعَثْنَا مِنْهُمُ اثْنَيْ عَشَرَ نَقِيبًا ۖ وَقَالَ اللَّهُ إِنِّي مَعَكُمْ ۖ لَئِنْ أَقَمْتُمُ الصَّلَاةَ وَآتَيْتُمُ الزَّكَاةَ وَآمَنتُم بِرُسُلِي وَعَزَّرْتُمُوهُمْ وَأَقْرَضْتُمُ اللَّهَ قَرْضًا حَسَنًا لَّأُكَفِّرَنَّ عَنكُمْ سَيِّئَاتِكُمْ وَلَأُدْخِلَنَّكُمْ جَنَّاتٍ تَجْرِي مِن تَحْتِهَا الْأَنْهَارُ ۚ فَمَن كَفَرَ بَعْدَ ذَٰلِكَ مِنكُمْ فَقَدْ ضَلَّ سَوَاءَ السَّبِيلِ ۝

فَبِمَا نَقْضِهِم مِّيثَاقَهُمْ لَعَنَّاهُمْ وَجَعَلْنَا قُلُوبَهُمْ قَاسِيَةً ۖ يُحَرِّفُونَ الْكَلِمَ عَن مَّوَاضِعِهِ ۙ وَنَسُوا حَظًّا مِّمَّا ذُكِّرُوا بِهِ ۚ وَلَا تَزَالُ تَطَّلِعُ عَلَىٰ خَائِنَةٍ مِّنْهُمْ إِلَّا قَلِيلًا مِّنْهُمْ

but forgive them, and overlook (their misdeeds): for Allah loves those who are kind.

14. From those, too, who call themselves Christians, We did take a Covenant, but they forgot a good part of the message that was sent them: so We estranged them, with enmity and hatred between the one and the other, to the Day of judgment. And soon will Allah show them what it is they have done.

15. O people of the Book! there has come to you Our Apostle, revealing to you much that you used to hide in the Book, and passing over much (that is now unnecessary). There has come to you from Allah a (new) light and a perspicuous Book,

16. Wherewith Allah guides all who seek His good pleasure to ways of peace and safety, and leads them out of darkness, by His Will, unto the light,- guides them to a Path that is Straight.

17. In blasphemy indeed are those that say that Allah is Christ the son of Mary. Say: "Who then has the least power against Allah, if His Will were to destroy Christ the son of Mary, his mother, and all - every one that is on the earth? For to Allah belongs the dominion of the heavens and the earth, and all that is between. He creates what He pleases. For Allah has power over all things."

18. (Both) the Jews and the Christians say: "We are sons of Allah, and His beloved." Say: "Why then does He punish you for your sins? Nay, you are but men,- of the men He has created: He forgives whom He pleases, and He punishes

whom He pleases: and to Allah belongs the dominion of the heavens and the earth, and all that is between: and unto Him is the final goal (of all)".

19. O People of the Book! now has come to you, making (things) clear to you, Our Apostle, after the break in (the series of) Our Apostles, lest you should say: "There came unto us no bringer of glad tidings and no warner (from evil)": But now has come to you a bringer of glad tidings and a warner (from evil). And Allah has power over all things.

20. Remember Moses said to his people: "O my people! call in remembrance the favour of Allah to you, when He produced prophets among you, made you kings, and gave you what He had not given to any other among the people.

21. "O my people! enter the holy land which Allah has assigned unto you, and do not turn back ignominiously, for then will you be overthrown, to your own ruin.

22. They said: "O Moses! In this land are a people of exceeding strength: never shall we enter it until they leave it: if (once) they leave, then we shall enter."

23. (But) among (their) Allah-fearing men were two on whom Allah had bestowed His grace: they said: "Assault them at the (proper) Gate: when once you are in, victory will be yours; But on Allah put your trust if you have faith."

24. They said: "O Moses! while they remain there, never shall we be able to enter, to the end of time. You go,

and your Lord, and fight you two, while we sit here (and watch)."

25. He said: "O my Lord! I have power only over myself and my brother: so separate us from this rebellious people!"

26. Allah said: "Therefore the land will be out of their reach for forty years: In distraction they will wander through the land: but you do not grieve over these rebellious people.

27. Recite to them the truth of the story of the two sons of Adam. Behold! they each presented a sacrifice (to Allah): It was accepted from one, but not from the other. Said the latter: "Be sure I will slay you." "Surely," said the former, "Allah accepts of the sacrifice of those who are righteous.

28. "If you stretch your hand against me, to slay me, it is not for me to stretch my hand against you to slay you: for I do fear Allah, the Cherisher of the worlds.

29. "For me, I intend to let you draw on yourself my sin as well as yours, for you will be among the companions of the Fire, and that is the reward of those who do wrong."

30. The (selfish) soul of the other led him to the murder of his brother: he murdered him, and became (himself) one of the lost ones.

31. Then Allah sent a raven, who scratched the ground, to show him how to hide the shame of his brother. "Woe is me!" said he; "Was I not even able to be as this raven, and to hide the shame of my brother?" then he became full of regrets-

32. On that account: We ordained for the Children of

Israel that if any one slew a person - unless it be for murder or for spreading mischief in the land - it would be as if he slew the whole people: and if any one saved a life, it would be as if he saved the life of the whole people. Then although there came to them Our Apostles with Clear Signs, yet, even after that, many of them continued to commit excesses in the land.

33. The punishment of those who wage war against Allah and His Apostle, and strive with might and main for mischief through the land is: execution, or crucifixion, or the cutting off of hands and feet from opposite sides, or exile from the land: that is their disgrace in this world, and a heavy punishment is theirs in the Hereafter;

34. Except for those who repent before they fall into your power: in that case, know that Allah is Oft-forgiving, Most Merciful.

35. O you who believe! do your duty to Allah, seek the means of approach unto Him, and strive with might and main in His cause: that you may prosper.

36. As to those who reject Faith,- if they had everything on earth, and twice repeated, to give as ransom for the Chastisement of the Day of Judgment, it would never be accepted of them, theirs would be a grievous Chastisement.

37. Their wish will be to get out of the Fire, but never will they get out therefrom: their

Chastisement will be one that endures.

38. As to the thief, male or female, cut off his or her hands: a punishment by way of example, from Allah, for their crime: and Allah is Exalted in power.

39. But if the thief repents after his crime, and amends his conduct, Allah turns to him in forgiveness; for Allah is Oft-forgiving, Most Merciful.

40. Do you not know that to Allah (alone) belongs the dominion of the heavens and the earth? He punishes whom He pleases, and He forgives whom He pleases: and Allah has power over all things.

41. O Apostle! let not those grieve you, who race each other into Unbelief: (whether it be) among those who say "We believe" with their lips but whose hearts have no faith; or it be among the Jews,- men who will listen to any lie,- will listen even to others who have never so much as come to you. They change the words from their (right) times and places: they say, "If you are given this, take it, but if not, beware!" If any one's trial is intended by Allah you have no authority in the least for him against Allah. For such - it is not Allah's will to purify their hearts. For them there is disgrace in this world, and in the Hereafter a heavy punishment.

42. (They are fond of) listening to falsehood, of devouring anything forbidden.

If they do come to you, either judge between them, or decline to interfere. If you decline, they cannot hurt you in the least. If you judge, judge in equity between them. For Allah loves those who judge in equity.

فَإِنْ جَآءُوكَ فَاحْكُمْ بَيْنَهُمْ أَوْ اَعْرِضْ عَنْهُمْ وَاِنْ تُعْرِضْ عَنْهُمْ فَلَنْ يَّضُرُّوكَ شَيْئًا وَاِنْ حَكَمْتَ فَاحْكُمْ بَيْنَهُمْ بِالْقِسْطِ إِنَّ اللّٰهَ يُحِبُّ الْمُقْسِطِينَ ۝

43. But why do they come to you for decision, when they have (their own) law before them?- therein is the (plain) Command of Allah; yet even after that, they would turn away. For they are not (really) People of Faith.

وَكَيْفَ يُحَكِّمُوْنَكَ وَعِنْدَهُمُ التَّوْرٰىةُ فِيْهَا حُكْمُ اللّٰهِ ثُمَّ يَتَوَلَّوْنَ مِنْ بَعْدِ ذٰلِكَ وَمَا أُولٰٓئِكَ بِالْمُؤْمِنِيْنَ ۝

44. It was We Who revealed the Law (to Moses): therein was guidance and light. By its standard have been judged the Jews, by the prophets who bowed (as in Islam) to Allah's Will, by the Rabbis and the Doctors of Law: for to them was entrusted the protection of Allah's Book, and they were witnesses there to: therefore fear not men, but fear Me, and sell not My Signs for a miserable price. If any do fail to judge by (the light of) what Allah has revealed, they are (no better than) Unbelievers.

إِنَّا أَنْزَلْنَا التَّوْرٰىةَ فِيْهَا هُدًى وَّنُوْرٌ يَحْكُمُ بِهَا النَّبِيُّوْنَ الَّذِيْنَ أَسْلَمُوْا لِلَّذِيْنَ هَادُوْا وَالرَّبَّانِيُّوْنَ وَالْأَحْبَارُ بِمَا اسْتُحْفِظُوْا مِنْ كِتٰبِ اللّٰهِ وَكَانُوْا عَلَيْهِ شُهَدَآءَ فَلَا تَخْشَوُا النَّاسَ وَاخْشَوْنِ وَلَا تَشْتَرُوْا بِاٰيٰتِيْ ثَمَنًا قَلِيْلًا وَمَنْ لَّمْ يَحْكُمْ بِمَا أَنْزَلَ اللّٰهُ فَأُولٰٓئِكَ هُمُ الْكٰفِرُوْنَ ۝

45. We ordained therein for them: "Life for life, eye for eye, nose for nose, ear for ear, tooth for tooth, and wounds equal for equal." But if any one remits the retaliation by way of charity, it is an act of atonement for himself. And if any fail to judge by (the light of) what Allah has revealed, they are (no better than) wrong-doers.

وَكَتَبْنَا عَلَيْهِمْ فِيْهَا أَنَّ النَّفْسَ بِالنَّفْسِ وَالْعَيْنَ بِالْعَيْنِ وَالْأَنْفَ بِالْأَنْفِ وَالْأُذُنَ بِالْأُذُنِ وَالسِّنَّ بِالسِّنِّ وَالْجُرُوْحَ قِصَاصٌ فَمَنْ تَصَدَّقَ بِهِ فَهُوَ كَفَّارَةٌ لَّهُ وَمَنْ لَّمْ يَحْكُمْ بِمَا أَنْزَلَ اللّٰهُ فَأُولٰٓئِكَ هُمُ الظّٰلِمُوْنَ ۝

46. And in their footsteps We sent Jesus the son of

وَقَفَّيْنَا عَلٰٓى اٰثَارِهِمْ بِعِيْسَى ابْنِ

Mary, confirming the Law that had come before him: We sent him the Gospel: therein was guidance and light, and confirmation of the Law that had come before him: a guidance and an admonition to those who fear Allah.

مَرْيَمَ مُصَدِّقًا لِّمَا بَيْنَ يَدَيْهِ مِنَ التَّوْرَاةِ ۖ وَاٰتَيْنٰهُ الْاِنْجِيْلَ فِيْهِ هُدًى وَّنُوْرٌ ۙ وَّمُصَدِّقًا لِّمَا بَيْنَ يَدَيْهِ مِنَ التَّوْرَاةِ وَهُدًى وَّ مَوْعِظَةً لِّلْمُتَّقِيْنَ ۞

47. Let the people of the Gospel judge by what Allah has revealed therein. If any do fail to judge by (the light of) what Allah has revealed, they are (no better than) those who rebel.

وَلْيَحْكُمْ اَهْلُ الْاِنْجِيْلِ بِمَآ اَنْزَلَ اللّٰهُ فِيْهِ ۖ وَمَنْ لَّمْ يَحْكُمْ بِمَآ اَنْزَلَ اللّٰهُ فَاُولٰٓئِكَ هُمُ الْفٰسِقُوْنَ ۞

48. To you We sent the Scripture in truth, confirming the scripture that came before it, and guarding it in safety: so judge between them by what Allah has revealed, and do not follow their vain desires, diverging from the Truth that has come to you. To each among you We have prescribed a Law and an Open Way. If Allah had so willed, He would have made you a single people, but (His plan is) to test you in what He have given you: so strive as in a race in all virtues. The goal of you all is to Allah; it is He that will show you the truth of the matters in which you dispute;

وَ اَنْزَلْنَآ اِلَيْكَ الْكِتٰبَ بِالْحَقِّ مُصَدِّقًا لِّمَا بَيْنَ يَدَيْهِ مِنَ الْكِتٰبِ وَمُهَيْمِنًا عَلَيْهِ فَاحْكُمْ بَيْنَهُمْ بِمَآ اَنْزَلَ اللّٰهُ وَلَا تَتَّبِعْ اَهْوَآءَهُمْ عَمَّا جَآءَكَ مِنَ الْحَقِّ ۙ لِكُلٍّ جَعَلْنَا مِنْكُمْ شِرْعَةً وَّمِنْهَاجًا ۖ وَلَوْ شَآءَ اللّٰهُ لَجَعَلَكُمْ اُمَّةً وَّاحِدَةً وَّلٰكِنْ لِّيَبْلُوَكُمْ فِيْ مَآ اٰتٰكُمْ فَاسْتَبِقُوا الْخَيْرٰتِ ۖ اِلَى اللّٰهِ مَرْجِعُكُمْ جَمِيْعًا فَيُنَبِّئُكُمْ بِمَا كُنْتُمْ فِيْهِ تَخْتَلِفُوْنَ ۞

49. And this (He commands): you Judge between them by what Allah has revealed, and follow not their vain desires, but beware of them lest they beguile you from any of that (teaching) which Allah has sent down to you. And if they turn away, be assured that for some of their crimes it is Allah's purpose to punish them. And truly most men are rebellious.

وَاَنِ احْكُمْ بَيْنَهُمْ بِمَآ اَنْزَلَ اللّٰهُ وَلَا تَتَّبِعْ اَهْوَآءَهُمْ وَاحْذَرْهُمْ اَنْ يَّفْتِنُوْكَ عَنْ بَعْضِ مَآ اَنْزَلَ اللّٰهُ اِلَيْكَ ۖ فَاِنْ تَوَلَّوْا فَاعْلَمْ اَنَّمَا يُرِيْدُ اللّٰهُ اَنْ يُّصِيْبَهُمْ بِبَعْضِ ذُنُوْبِهِمْ ۖ وَاِنَّ كَثِيْرًا مِّنَ النَّاسِ لَفٰسِقُوْنَ ۞

50.   Do they then seek after a judgment of (the days of) ignorance? But who, for a people whose faith is assured, can give better judgment than Allah?

51.   O you who believe! take not the Jews and the Christians for your friends and protectors: they are but friends and protectors to each other. And he amongst you that turns to them (for friendship) is of them. Verily Allah guides not a people unjust.

52.   Those in whose hearts is a disease - you see how eagerly they run about amongst them, saying: "We do fear lest a change of fortune bring us disaster." Ah! perhaps Allah will give (you) victory, or a decision according to His Will. Then will they repent of the thoughts which they secretly harboured in their hearts.

53.   And those who believe will say: "Are these the men who swore their strongest oaths by Allah, that they were with you?" All that they do will be in vain, and they will fall into (nothing but) ruin.

54.   O you who believe! if any from among you turn back from his Faith, soon will Allah produce a people whom He will love as they will love Him,- lowly with the Believers, mighty against the Rejecters, fighting in the way of Allah, and never afraid of the reproaches of such as find fault. That is the Grace of Allah, which He will bestow on whom He pleases. And Allah encompasses all, and He knows all things.

55. Your (real) friends are (no less than) Allah, His Apostle, and the (fellowship of) Believers,- those who establish regular prayers and regular charity, and they bow down humbly (in worship).

56. As to those who turn (for friendship) to Allah, His Apostle, and the (Fellowship of) Believers,- it is the Fellowship of Allah that must certainly triumph.

57. O you who believe! take not for friends and protectors those who take your religion for a mockery or sport,- whether among those who received the Scripture before you, or among those who reject Faith; but you should fear Allah, if you have Faith (indeed).

58. When you proclaim your call to prayer, they take it (but) as mockery and sport; that is because they are a people without understanding.

59. Say: "O people of the Book! Do you disapprove of us for no other reason than that we believe in Allah, and the revelation that has come to us and that which came before (us), and (perhaps) that most of you are rebellious and disobedient?"

60. Say: "Shall I point out to you something much worse than this, (as judged) by the treatment it received from Allah? those who incurred the curse of Allah and His wrath, those of whom some He transformed into apes and swine, those who worshipped evil;- these are (many times) worse in rank, and far more astray from the even path!"

61. When they come to you, they say: "We believe": but in fact they enter with a mind against Faith, and they go out with the same. But Allah knows fully all that they hide.

إِنَّمَا وَلِيُّكُمُ اللهُ وَرَسُوْلُهٗ وَالَّذِيْنَ اٰمَنُوا الَّذِيْنَ يُقِيْمُوْنَ الصَّلٰوةَ وَيُؤْتُوْنَ الزَّكٰوةَ وَهُمْ رَاكِعُوْنَ ۝

وَمَنْ يَّتَوَلَّ اللهَ وَرَسُوْلَهٗ وَالَّذِيْنَ اٰمَنُوْا فَاِنَّ حِزْبَ اللهِ هُمُ الْغٰلِبُوْنَ ۝

يٰۤاَيُّهَا الَّذِيْنَ اٰمَنُوا لَا تَتَّخِذُوا الَّذِيْنَ اتَّخَذُوْا دِيْنَكُمْ هُزُوًا وَّلَعِبًا مِّنَ الَّذِيْنَ اُوْتُوا الْكِتٰبَ مِنْ قَبْلِكُمْ وَالْكُفَّارَ اَوْلِيَاءَ وَاتَّقُوا اللهَ اِنْ كُنْتُمْ مُّؤْمِنِيْنَ ۝

وَاِذَا نَادَيْتُمْ اِلَى الصَّلٰوةِ اتَّخَذُوْهَا هُزُوًا وَّلَعِبًا ذٰلِكَ بِاَنَّهُمْ قَوْمٌ لَّا يَعْقِلُوْنَ ۝

قُلْ يٰۤاَهْلَ الْكِتٰبِ هَلْ تَنْقِمُوْنَ مِنَّاۤ اِلَّاۤ اَنْ اٰمَنَّا بِاللهِ وَمَاۤ اُنْزِلَ اِلَيْنَا وَمَاۤ اُنْزِلَ مِنْ قَبْلُ ۙ وَاَنَّ اَكْثَرَكُمْ فٰسِقُوْنَ ۝

قُلْ هَلْ اُنَبِّئُكُمْ بِشَرٍّ مِّنْ ذٰلِكَ مَثُوْبَةً عِنْدَ اللهِ مَنْ لَّعَنَهُ اللهُ وَغَضِبَ عَلَيْهِ وَجَعَلَ مِنْهُمُ الْقِرَدَةَ وَالْخَنَازِيْرَ وَعَبَدَ الطَّاغُوْتَ اُولٰٓئِكَ شَرٌّ مَّكَانًا وَّاَضَلُّ عَنْ سَوَآءِ السَّبِيْلِ ۝

وَاِذَا جَآءُوْكُمْ قَالُوْۤا اٰمَنَّا وَقَدْ دَّخَلُوْا بِالْكُفْرِ وَهُمْ قَدْ خَرَجُوْا بِهٖ وَاللهُ اَعْلَمُ بِمَا كَانُوْا يَكْتُمُوْنَ ۝

62. You see many of them racing each other in sin and rancour, and their eating of things forbidden. Evil indeed are the things that they do.

63. Why do not the Rabbis and the Doctors of Law forbid them from their (habit of) uttering sinful words and eating things forbidden? Evil indeed are their works.

64. The Jews say: "Allah's hand is tied up." Be their hands tied up and be they accursed for the (blasphemy) they utter. Nay, both His hands are widely outstretched: He gives and spends (of His bounty) as He pleases. But the revelation that comes to you from Allah increases in most of them their obstinate rebellion and blasphemy. Amongst them we have placed enmity and hatred till the Day of Judgment. Every time they kindle the fire of war, Allah extinguishes it; but they (ever) strive to do mischief on earth. And Allah does not love those who do mischief.

65. If only the People of the Book had believed and been righteous, We should indeed have blotted out their iniquities and admitted them to Gardens of Bliss.

66. If only they had stood fast by the Law, the Gospel, and all the revelation that was sent to them from their Lord, they would have enjoyed happiness from every side. There is from among them a party on the right course: but many of them follow a course that is evil.

67. O Apostle! proclaim the (Message) which has been sent to you from your Lord. If you did not, you would not have fulfilled and proclaimed

His Mission. And Allah will defend you from men (who mean mischief). For Allah guides not those who reject Faith.

68. Say: "O People of the Book! you have no ground to stand upon unless you stand fast by the Law, the Gospel, and all the revelation that has come to you from your Lord." It is the revelation that comes to you from your Lord, that increases in most of them their obstinate rebellion and blasphemy. But you do not grieve over (these) people without Faith.

69. Those who believe (in the Qur'an), those who follow the Jewish (scriptures), and the Sabians and the Christians,- any who believe in Allah and the Last Day, and work righteous-ness,- on them shall be no fear, nor shall they grieve.

70. We took the Covenant of the Children of Israel and sent them Apostles. Every time there came to them an Apostle with what they themselves did not desire, some (of these) they called impostors, and some they (go so far as to) slay.

71. They thought there would be no trial (or punishment); so they became blind and deaf; yet Allah (in mercy) turned to them; yet again many of them became blind and deaf. But Allah sees well all that they do.

72. They do blaspheme who say: "Allah is Christ the son of Mary." But Christ said: "O Children of Israel! worship Allah, my Lord and your Lord." Whoever joins other gods with Allah,- Allah will forbid

him the Garden, and the Fire will be his abode. There will for the wrong-doers be no one to help.

73. They do blaspheme who say: Allah is one of three in a Trinity; for there is no god except One God. If they do not desist from their word (of blasphemy), verily a grievous Chastisement will befall the blasphemers among them.

74. Why do they not turn to Allah, and seek His forgiveness? For Allah is Oftforgiving, Most Merciful.

75. Christ the son of Mary was no more than an Apostle; many were the Apostles that passed away before him. His mother was a woman of truth. They had both to eat their (daily) food. See how Allah makes His Signs clear to them; yet see in what ways they are deluded away from the truth!

76. Say: "Will you worship, besides Allah, something which has no power either to harm or benefit you? But Allah,- He it is that hears and knows all things."

77. Say: "O people of the Book! exceed not in your religion the bounds (of what is proper), trespassing beyond the truth, nor follow the vain desires of people who went wrong in times gone by,- who misled many, and strayed (themselves) from the even way.

78. Curses were pronounced on those among the Children of Israel who rejected Faith, by the tongue of David and of Jesus the son of Mary: because they disobeyed and persisted in excesses.

79. Nor did they (usually) forbid one another the iniquities

عَلَيْهِ الْجَنَّةَ وَمَأْوَاهُ النَّارُ وَمَا لِلظَّالِمِينَ مِنْ أَنْصَارٍ ۝

لَقَدْ كَفَرَ الَّذِينَ قَالُوٓا إِنَّ اللَّهَ ثَالِثُ ثَلَٰثَةٍ وَمَا مِنْ إِلَٰهٍ إِلَّآ إِلَٰهٌ وَٰحِدٌ وَإِنْ لَمْ يَنْتَهُوا عَمَّا يَقُولُونَ لَيَمَسَّنَّ الَّذِينَ كَفَرُوا مِنْهُمْ عَذَابٌ أَلِيمٌ ۝

أَفَلَا يَتُوبُونَ إِلَى اللَّهِ وَيَسْتَغْفِرُونَهُ وَاللَّهُ غَفُورٌ رَّحِيمٌ ۝

مَّا الْمَسِيحُ ابْنُ مَرْيَمَ إِلَّا رَسُولٌ قَدْ خَلَتْ مِنْ قَبْلِهِ الرُّسُلُ وَأُمُّهُ صِدِّيقَةٌ كَانَا يَأْكُلَانِ الطَّعَامَ أُنْظُرْ كَيْفَ نُبَيِّنُ لَهُمُ الْآيَاتِ ثُمَّ انْظُرْ أَنَّىٰ يُؤْفَكُونَ ۝

قُلْ أَتَعْبُدُونَ مِنْ دُونِ اللَّهِ مَا لَا يَمْلِكُ لَكُمْ ضَرًّا وَلَا نَفْعًا وَاللَّهُ هُوَ السَّمِيعُ الْعَلِيمُ ۝

قُلْ يَا أَهْلَ الْكِتَابِ لَا تَغْلُوا فِي دِينِكُمْ غَيْرَ الْحَقِّ وَلَا تَتَّبِعُوٓا أَهْوَاءَ قَوْمٍ قَدْ ضَلُّوا مِنْ قَبْلُ وَأَضَلُّوا كَثِيرًا وَضَلُّوا عَنْ سَوَاءِ السَّبِيلِ ۝

لُعِنَ الَّذِينَ كَفَرُوا مِنْ بَنِي إِسْرَآئِيلَ عَلَىٰ لِسَانِ دَاوُدَ وَعِيسَى ابْنِ مَرْيَمَ ذَٰلِكَ بِمَا عَصَوْا وَكَانُوا يَعْتَدُونَ ۝

كَانُوا لَا يَتَنَاهَوْنَ عَنْ مُنْكَرٍ

which they committed: evil indeed were the deeds which they did.

80. You see many of them turning in friendship to the Unbelievers. Evil indeed are (the works) which their souls have sent forward before them (with the result), that Allah's wrath is on them, and in torment will they abide.

81. If only they had believed in Allah, in the Apostle, and in what has been revealed to him, never would they have taken them for friends and protectors, but most of them are rebellious wrong-doers.

82. Strongest among men in enmity to the Believers will you find the Jews and Pagans; and nearest among them in love to the Believers will you find those who say, "We are Christians": because amongst these are men devoted to learning and men who have renounced the world, and they are not arrogant.

83. And when they listen to the revelation received by the Apostle, you will see their eyes overflowing with tears, for they recognise the truth: they pray: "Our Lord! we believe; write us down among the witnesses.

84. "What cause can we have not to believe in Allah and the truth which has come to us, seeing that we long for our Lord to admit us to the company of the righteous?"

85. And for this their prayer Allah has rewarded them with Gardens, with rivers flowing underneath,- their eternal home. Such is the recompense of those who do good.

86. But those who reject Faith and belie our Signs,-

they shall be Companions of Hell-fire.

87. O you who believe! Do not make unlawful the good things which Allah has made lawful for you, but commit no excess: for Allah does not love those given to excess.

88. Eat of the things which Allah has provided for you, lawful and good; but fear Allah, in Whom you believe.

89. Allah will not call you to account for what is futile in your oaths, but He will call you to account for your deliberate oaths: for expiation, feed ten indigent persons, on a scale of the average for the food of your families; or clothe them; or give a slave his freedom. If that is beyond your means, fast for three days. That is the expiation for the oaths you have sworn. But keep to your oaths. Thus Allah makes clear to you His Signs, that you may be grateful.

90. O you who believe! Intoxicants and gambling, (dedication of) stones, and (divination by) arrows, are an abomination,- of Satan's handiwork: eschew such (abomination), that you may prosper.

91. Satan's plan is (but) to excite enmity and hatred between you, with intoxicants and gambling, and hinder you from the remembrance of Allah, and from prayer: will you not then abstain?

92. Obey Allah, and obey the Apostle, and beware (of evil): if you do turn back, you should know that it is Our Apostle's duty to proclaim (the Message) in the clearest manner.

93. On those who believe and do deeds of righteousness there is no blame for what they ate (in the past), when they guard themselves from evil, and believe, and do deeds of righteousness,- (or) again, guard themselves from evil and believe,- (or) again, guard themselves from evil and do good. For Allah loves those who do good.

94. O you who believe! Allah makes a trial of you in a little matter of game well within reach of your hands and your lances, that He may test who fears Him unseen: and who transgress thereafter, will have a grievous Chastisement.

95. O you who believe! do not kill game while in the Sacred Precincts or in pilgrim garb. If any of you does so intentionally, the compensation is an offering, brought to the Ka'ba, of a domestic animal equivalent to the one he killed, as adjudged by two just men among you; or by way of atonement, the feeding of the indigent; or its equivalent in fasts: that he may taste of the Chastisement of his deed. Allah forgives what is past: for repetition Allah will exact from him the Chastisement. For Allah is Exalted, and Lord of Retribution.

96. Lawful to you is the pursuit of water-game and its use for food,- for the benefit of your-selves and those who travel; but forbidden is the pursuit of land-game;- as long as you are in the Sacred Precincts or in pilgrim garb. And fear Allah, to Whom you shall be gathered back.

97. Allah made the Ka'ba, the Sacred House, an asylum of security for men, as also the Sacred Months, the animals for offerings, and the garlands that mark them: that you may know that Allah

لَيْسَ عَلَى الَّذِيْنَ اٰمَنُوْا وَعَمِلُوا الصّٰلِحٰتِ
جُنَاحٌ فِيْمَا طَعِمُوْا اِذَا مَا اتَّقَوْا
وَّاٰمَنُوْا وَعَمِلُوا الصّٰلِحٰتِ ثُمَّ اتَّقَوْا
وَّاٰمَنُوْا ثُمَّ اتَّقَوْا وَّاَحْسَنُوْا ۚ وَاللّٰهُ
يُحِبُّ الْمُحْسِنِيْنَ ۞

يٰۤاَيُّهَا الَّذِيْنَ اٰمَنُوْا لَيَبْلُوَنَّكُمُ اللّٰهُ
بِشَيْءٍ مِّنَ الصَّيْدِ تَنَالُهٗۤ اَيْدِيْكُمْ
وَرِمَاحُكُمْ لِيَعْلَمَ اللّٰهُ مَنْ يَّخَافُهٗ
بِالْغَيْبِ ۚ فَمَنِ اعْتَدٰى بَعْدَ ذٰلِكَ
فَلَهٗ عَذَابٌ اَلِيْمٌ ۞

يٰۤاَيُّهَا الَّذِيْنَ اٰمَنُوْا لَا تَقْتُلُوا الصَّيْدَ
وَاَنْتُمْ حُرُمٌ ۚ وَمَنْ قَتَلَهٗ مِنْكُمْ
مُّتَعَمِّدًا فَجَزَآءٌ مِّثْلُ مَا قَتَلَ مِنَ
النَّعَمِ يَحْكُمُ بِهٖ ذَوَا عَدْلٍ مِّنْكُمْ هَدْيًۢا
بٰلِغَ الْكَعْبَةِ اَوْ كَفَّارَةٌ طَعَامُ مَسٰكِيْنَ
اَوْ عَدْلُ ذٰلِكَ صِيَامًا لِّيَذُوْقَ وَبَالَ
اَمْرِهٖ ؕ عَفَا اللّٰهُ عَمَّا سَلَفَ ؕ وَمَنْ
عَادَ فَيَنْتَقِمُ اللّٰهُ مِنْهُ ؕ وَاللّٰهُ
عَزِيْزٌ ذُو انْتِقَامٍ ۞

اُحِلَّ لَكُمْ صَيْدُ الْبَحْرِ وَطَعَامُهٗ
مَتَاعًا لَّكُمْ وَلِلسَّيَّارَةِ ۚ وَحُرِّمَ عَلَيْكُمْ
صَيْدُ الْبَرِّ مَا دُمْتُمْ حُرُمًا ؕ وَاتَّقُوا
اللّٰهَ الَّذِيْۤ اِلَيْهِ تُحْشَرُوْنَ ۞

جَعَلَ اللّٰهُ الْكَعْبَةَ الْبَيْتَ الْحَرَامَ
قِيٰمًا لِّلنَّاسِ وَالشَّهْرَ الْحَرَامَ وَالْهَدْيَ
وَالْقَلَآئِدَ ؕ ذٰلِكَ لِتَعْلَمُوْۤا اَنَّ اللّٰهَ

ع ١٢

has knowledge of what is in the heavens and on earth and that Allah is well acquainted with all things.

98. You should know that Allah is strict in punishment and that Allah is Oft-forgiving, Most Merciful.

99. The Apostle's duty is but to proclaim (the Message). But Allah knows all that you reveal and all that you conceal.

100. Say: "Not equal are things that are bad and things that are good, even though the abundance of the bad may dazzle you; so fear Allah, O you that understand; that (so) you may prosper."

101. O you who believe! do not ask questions about things which, if made plain to you, may cause you trouble. But if you ask about things when the Qur'an is being revealed, they will be made plain to you, Allah will forgive those: for Allah is Oft-forgiving, Most Forbearing.

102. Some people before you did ask such questions, and on that account lost their faith.

103. It was not Allah Who instituted (superstitions like those of) a slit-ear she-camel, or a she-camel let loose for free pasture, or idol sacrifices for twin-births in animals, or stallion-camels freed from work: It is blasphemers who invent a lie against Allah; but most of them lack wisdom.

104. When it is said to them: "Come to what Allah has revealed; come to the Apostle": they say: "Enough for us are the ways we found our fathers following." what! even though their fathers were void of knowledge and guidance?

105. O you who believe! guard your own souls:

If you follow (right) guidance,
no hurt can come to you from
those who stray. The goal of you
all is to Allah: it is He that will
show you the truth of all that
you do.

106. O you who believe! When
death approaches any of you,
(take) witnesses among yourselves when making bequests,-
two just men of your own
(brotherhood) or others from
outside if you are journeying
through the earth, and the chance
of death befalls you (thus). If you
doubt (their truth), detain them
both after prayer, and let them
both swear by Allah: "We do not
wish in this for any worldly gain,
even though the (beneficiary) be
our near relation: we shall not
hide the evidence before Allah: if
we do, then behold! the sin be
upon us!"

107. But if it gets known that
these two were guilty of the sin
(of perjury), let two others stand
forth in their places,- nearest in
kin from among those who claim
a lawful right: let them swear by
Allah: "We affirm that our
witness is truer than that of those
two, and that we have not
trespassed (beyond the truth): if
we did, behold! the wrong be
upon us!"

108. That is most suitable: that
they may give the evidence in its
true nature and shape, or else
they would fear that other oaths
would be taken after their oaths.
But fear Allah, and listen (to His
counsel): for Allah does not
guide a rebellious people:

109. One day Allah will gather
the Apostles together, and ask:
"What was the response you
received (from men to your
teaching)?" They will say: "We
have no knowledge: it is You
Who knows in full all that is
hidden."

110. Then will Allah say: "O
Jesus the son of Mary! recount
My favour to you and to your
mother.

Behold! I strengthened you with the holy spirit, so that you did speak to the people in childhood and in maturity. Behold! I taught you the Book and Wisdom, the Law and the Gospel. And behold! you made out of clay, as it were, the figure of a bird, by My leave, and you breathed into it and it became a bird by My leave, and you healed those born blind, and the lepers, by My leave. And behold ! you brought forth the dead by My leave. And behold! I did restrain the Children of Israel from (violence to) you when you showed them the Clear Signs, and the Unbelievers among them said: 'This is nothing but evident magic.'

111. "And behold! I inspired the Disciples to have faith in Me and Mine Apostle: they said, 'We have faith, and you bear witness that we bow to Allah as Muslims'".

112. Behold! the Disciples said: "O Jesus the son of Mary! can your Lord send down to us a table set (with viands) from heaven?" Jesus said: "Fear Allah, if you have faith."

113. They said: "We only wish to eat thereof and satisfy our hearts, and to know that you have indeed told us the truth; and that we ourselves may be witnesses to the miracle."

114. Jesus the son of Mary said: "O Allah our Lord! send us from heaven a table set (with viands), that there may be for us - for the first and the last of us - a solemn festival and a Sign from You; and provide for our sustenance, for You are the best Sustainer (of our needs)."

115. Allah said: "I will send it down to you: But if any

SÛRAH-6
AL-AN'ÂM
(INTRODUCTION)

This is a Sûrah of the late Makkan period. The greater part of it was revealed entire. Its place in the traditional order of arrangement is justified by logical considerations. We have already had the spiritual history of mankind, a discussion to the earlier revelations and how they were lost or corrupted, the regulations for the outer life of the new Community and the points in which the Jews and Christians failed to maintain the central doctrine of Islam-the unity of Allah. The next step now taken is to expound this doctrine in relation to Pagan Arabia.

ٱلْأَنْعَام ٦

of you after that resists faith, I will punish him with a Chastisement such as I have not inflicted on any one among all the peoples."

116. And behold! Allah will say: "O Jesus the son of Mary! Did you say to men, worship me and my mother as gods in derogation of Allah'?" He will say: "Glory to You! never could I say what I had no right (to say). Had I said such a thing, You would indeed have known it. You know what is in my heart, though I do not know what is in Yours. For You know in full all that is hidden.

117. "Never said I to them anything except what You commanded me to say, to wit, 'Worship Allah, my Lord and your Lord'; and I was a witness over them while I dwelt amongst them; when You took me up, You were the Watcher over them, and You are a Witness to all things.

118. "If You punish them, they are Your servant: If You forgive them, You are the Exalted in power, the Wise."

119. Allah will say: "This is a day on which the truthful will profit from their truth: theirs are Gardens, with rivers flowing beneath,- their eternal home: Allah well-pleased with them, and they with Allah: that is the great salvation, (the fulfilment of all desires).

120. To Allah belongs the dominion of the heavens and the earth, and all that is therein, and it is He Who has power over all things.

6. The Cattle
In the name of Allah. Most Gracious, Most Merciful.

1. Praise be to Allah, Who created the heavens and

the earth, and made the darkness and the light. Yet those who reject Faith hold (others) as equal, with their Guardian-Lord.

2. He it is Who created you from clay, and then decreed a stated term (for you). And there is in His presence another determined term; yet you doubt within yourselves!

3. And He is Allah in the heavens and on earth. He knows what you hide, and what you reveal, and He knows the (recompense) which you earn (by your deeds).

4. But never did a single one of the Signs of their Lord reach them, but they turned away therefrom.

5. And now they reject the truth when it reaches them: but soon shall they learn the reality of what they used to mock at.

6. Don't they see how many of those before them We destroyed?- generations We had established on the earth, in strength such as We have not given to you - for whom We poured out rain from the skies in abundance, and gave (fertile) streams flowing beneath their (feet): yet for their sins We destroyed them, and raised in their wake fresh generations (to succeed them).

7. If We had sent to you a written (message) on parchment, so that they could touch it with their hands, the Unbelievers would have been sure to say: "This is nothing but obvious magic!"

8. They say: "Why is not an angel sent down to him?" If We sent down an angel, the matter would be settled at once, and no respite would be granted them.

9. If We had made it an angel, We should have sent him as a man, and We should certainly have caused them confusion in a matter which they have already covered with confusion.

10. Mocked were (many) Apostles before you; but their scoffers were hemmed in by the thing that they mocked.

11. Say: "Travel through the earth and see what was the end of those who rejected Truth."

12. Say: "To whom belongs all that is in the heavens and on earth?" Say: "To Allah. He has inscribed for Himself (the rule of) Mercy. That He will gather you together for the Day of Judgment, there is no doubt whatever. It is they who have lost their own souls, that will not believe.

13. To him belongs all that dwells (or lurks) in the Night and the Day. For He is the One Who hears and knows all things."

14. Say: "Shall I take for my protector any other than Allah, the Maker of the heavens and the earth? And He it is that feeds but is not fed." Say: "Nay! but I am commanded to be the first of those who bow to Allah (in Islam), and you be not of the company of those who join gods with Allah."

15. Say: "I would, if I disobeyed my Lord, indeed have fear of the Chastisement of a Mighty Day.

16. "On that day, if the Chastisement is averted from any, it is due to Allah's mercy; and that would be (Salvation), the obvious fulfilment of all desire.

17. "If Allah touch you with affliction, none can remove it but He; if He touch you with happiness, He has power over all things.

وَلَوْ جَعَلْنَاهُ مَلَكًا لَّجَعَلْنَاهُ رَجُلًا وَّ
لَلَبَسْنَا عَلَيْهِمْ مَّا يَلْبِسُوْنَ ۝

وَلَقَدِ اسْتُهْزِئَ بِرُسُلٍ مِّنْ قَبْلِكَ
فَحَاقَ بِالَّذِيْنَ سَخِرُوْا مِنْهُمْ
مَّا كَانُوْا بِهٖ يَسْتَهْزِءُوْنَ ۝

قُلْ سِيْرُوْا فِى الْأَرْضِ ثُمَّ انْظُرُوْا
كَيْفَ كَانَ عَاقِبَةُ الْمُكَذِّبِيْنَ ۝

قُلْ لِّمَنْ مَّا فِى السَّمٰوٰتِ وَالْأَرْضِ ۗ
قُلْ لِّلّٰهِ ۚ كَتَبَ عَلٰى نَفْسِهِ الرَّحْمَةَ ۚ
لَيَجْمَعَنَّكُمْ إِلٰى يَوْمِ الْقِيٰمَةِ لَا رَيْبَ
فِيْهِ ۚ اَلَّذِيْنَ خَسِرُوْا اَنْفُسَهُمْ فَهُمْ
لَا يُؤْمِنُوْنَ ۝

وَلَهُ مَا سَكَنَ فِى الَّيْلِ وَ النَّهَارِ ۚ
وَهُوَ السَّمِيْعُ الْعَلِيْمُ ۝

قُلْ اَغَيْرَ اللّٰهِ اَتَّخِذُ وَلِيًّا فَاطِرِ
السَّمٰوٰتِ وَالْأَرْضِ وَهُوَ يُطْعِمُ وَلَا
يُطْعَمُ ۗ قُلْ اِنِّيْ اُمِرْتُ اَنْ اَكُوْنَ
اَوَّلَ مَنْ اَسْلَمَ وَ لَا تَكُوْنَنَّ مِنَ
الْمُشْرِكِيْنَ ۝

قُلْ اِنِّيْ اَخَافُ اِنْ عَصَيْتُ رَبِّيْ
عَذَابَ يَوْمٍ عَظِيْمٍ ۝

مَنْ يُّصْرَفْ عَنْهُ يَوْمَئِذٍ فَقَدْ
رَحِمَهُ ۗ وَذٰلِكَ الْفَوْزُ الْمُبِيْنُ ۝

وَاِنْ يَّمْسَسْكَ اللّٰهُ بِضُرٍّ فَلَا كَاشِفَ
لَهُ اِلَّا هُوَ ۚ وَاِنْ يَّمْسَسْكَ بِخَيْرٍ فَهُوَ
عَلٰى كُلِّ شَيْءٍ قَدِيْرٌ ۝

18. "He is the Irresistible, (watching) from above over His worshippers; and He is the Wise, acquainted with all things."

19. Say: "What thing is most weighty in evidence?" Say: "Allah is Witness between me and you; this Qur'an has been revealed to me by inspiration, that I may warn you and all whom it reaches. Can you possibly bear witness that besides Allah there is another god?" Say: "Nay! I cannot bear witness!" Say: "But in truth He is the One God, and I truly am innocent of (your blasphemy of) joining others with Him."

20. Those to whom We have given the Book know this as they know their own sons. Those who have lost their own souls refuse therefore to believe.

21. Who does more wrong than he who invents a lie against Allah or rejects His Signs? But verily the wrong-doers shall never prosper.

22. One day We shall gather them all together: We shall say to those who ascribed partners (to Us): "Where are the partners whom you (invented and) talked about?"

23. There will then be (left) no subterfuge for them but to say: "By Allah, our Lord, we were not those who joined gods with Allah."

24. Behold! how they lie against their own souls! But the (lie) which they invented will leave them in the lurch.

25. Of them there are some who (pretend to) listen to you; but We have thrown veils on their hearts, So they do not understand it, and deafness in their ears; if they saw every one of the Signs, they will not believe in them; in so much that when they come to you,

they (but) dispute with you; the Unbelievers say: "These are nothing but tales of the ancients."

26. Others they keep away from it, and themselves they keep away; but they only destroy their own souls, and they do not perceive it.

27. If you could but see when they are confronted with the Fire! they will say: "Would that we were but sent back! then we would not reject the Signs of our Lord, but would be amongst those who believe!"

28. Yes, in their own (eyes) will become manifest what they concealed before. But if they were returned, they would certainly relapse to the things they were forbidden, for they are indeed liars.

29. And they (sometimes) say: "There is nothing except our life on this earth, and never shall we be raised up again."

30. If you could but see when they are confronted with their Lord! He will say: "Is not this the truth?" They will say: "Yes, by our Lord!" He will say: "You then test the Chastisement, because you rejected Faith."

31. Lost indeed are they who treat it as a falsehood that they must meet Allah,- until on a sudden the hour is on them, and they say: "Ah! woe unto us that we took no thought of it"; for they bear their burdens on their backs, and evil indeed are the burdens that they bear?

32. What is the life of this world but play and amusement? But best is the Home in the Hereafter, for those who are righteous. Will you not then understand?

33. We know indeed the grief which

their words do cause you: It is not you they reject: it is the Signs of Allah, which the wicked disdain.

34. Rejected were the Apostles before you: with patience and constancy they bore their rejection and their wrongs, until Our aid reached them: there is none that can alter the Words (and Decrees) of Allah. Already you have received some account of those Apostles.

35. If their spurning is hard on your mind, yet if you were able to seek a tunnel in the ground or a ladder to the skies and bring them a Sign,- (what good?). If it were Allah's Will, He could gather them together to true guidance: so you be not amongst those who are swayed by ignorance (and impatience)!

36. Those who listen (in truth), be sure, will accept: as to the dead, Allah will raise them up; then will they be turned unto Him.

37. They say: "Why is not a Sign sent down to him from his Lord?" Say: "Allah has certainly power to send down a Sign: but most of them do not understand.

38. There is not an animal (that lives) on the earth, nor a being that flies on its wings, but (forms part of) communities like you. Nothing have we omitted from the Book, and they (all) shall be gathered to their Lord in the end.

39. Those who reject Our Signs are deaf and dumb,- in the midst of profound darkness: whom Allah wills, He leaves to wander: whom He wills, He places on the Way that is Straight.

40. Say: "You think to yourselves, if there come upon you the Wrath of Allah, or the Hour (that you dread), would you then call upon other than Allah?-

(reply) if you are truthful!

إِنْ كُنْتُمْ صٰدِقِينَ ۞

41. "Nay,- On Him would you call, and if it be His Will, He would remove (the distress) which occasioned your call upon Him, and you would forget (the false gods) which you join with Him!"

بَلْ إِيَّاهُ تَدْعُوْنَ فَيَكْشِفُ مَا تَدْعُوْنَ إِلَيْهِ إِنْ شَاءَ وَتَنْسَوْنَ مَا تُشْرِكُوْنَ ۞

42. Before you We sent (Apostles) to many nations, and We afflicted the nations with suffering and adversity, that they might learn humility.

وَلَقَدْ أَرْسَلْنَا إِلَى أُمَمٍ مِّنْ قَبْلِكَ فَأَخَذْنَاهُمْ بِالْبَأْسَاءِ وَالضَّرَّاءِ لَعَلَّهُمْ يَتَضَرَّعُوْنَ ۞

43. When the suffering reached them from Us, why then did they not learn humility? On the contrary their hearts became hardened, and Satan made their (sinful) acts seem alluring to them.

فَلَوْلَا إِذْ جَاءَهُمْ بَأْسُنَا تَضَرَّعُوْا وَلٰكِنْ قَسَتْ قُلُوْبُهُمْ وَزَيَّنَ لَهُمُ الشَّيْطٰنُ مَا كَانُوْا يَعْمَلُوْنَ ۞

44. But when they forgot the warning they had received, We opened to them the gates of all (good) things, until, in the midst of their enjoyment of Our gifts, on a sudden, We called them to account, when lo! they were plunged in despair!

فَلَمَّا نَسُوْا مَا ذُكِّرُوْا بِهِ فَتَحْنَا عَلَيْهِمْ أَبْوَابَ كُلِّ شَيْءٍ ۚ حَتّٰى إِذَا فَرِحُوْا بِمَا أُوْتُوْا أَخَذْنَاهُمْ بَغْتَةً فَإِذَاهُمْ مُّبْلِسُوْنَ ۞

45. Of the wrong-doers the last remnant was cut off. Praise be to Allah, the Cherisher of the worlds.

فَقُطِعَ دَابِرُ الْقَوْمِ الَّذِيْنَ ظَلَمُوْا وَالْحَمْدُ لِلّٰهِ رَبِّ الْعٰلَمِيْنَ ۞

46. Say: "Do you think, if Allah took away your hearing and your sight, and sealed up your hearts, who - a god other than Allah - could restore them to you?" See how We explain the Signs by various (symbols); yet they turn aside.

قُلْ أَرَأَيْتُمْ إِنْ أَخَذَ اللّٰهُ سَمْعَكُمْ وَأَبْصَارَكُمْ وَخَتَمَ عَلٰى قُلُوْبِكُمْ مَّنْ إِلٰهٌ غَيْرُ اللّٰهِ يَأْتِيْكُمْ بِهِ ۚ أُنْظُرْ كَيْفَ نُصَرِّفُ الْأٰيٰتِ ثُمَّ هُمْ يَصْدِفُوْنَ ۞

47. Say: "Do you think, if the punishment of Allah comes to you, whether suddenly or openly, will any be destroyed except those who do wrong?

قُلْ أَرَأَيْتَكُمْ إِنْ أَتَاكُمْ عَذَابُ اللّٰهِ بَغْتَةً أَوْ جَهْرَةً هَلْ يُهْلَكُ إِلَّا الْقَوْمُ الظّٰلِمُوْنَ ۞

48. We send the Apostles only to give good news and to warn: so those who believe and mend (their lives),- upon them shall be no fear, nor shall they grieve.

وَمَا نُرْسِلُ الْمُرْسَلِيْنَ إِلَّا مُبَشِّرِيْنَ وَمُنْذِرِيْنَ ۚ فَمَنْ آمَنَ وَأَصْلَحَ فَلَا خَوْفٌ عَلَيْهِمْ وَلَا هُمْ يَحْزَنُوْنَ ۞

49. But those who reject Our Signs,- punishment shall touch them, for that they did not cease from transgressing.

50. Say: "I tell you not that with me are the treasures of Allah, nor do I know what is hidden, nor do I tell you I am an angel. I but follow what is revealed to me." Say: "can the blind be held equal to the seeing?" Will you then not consider?

51. Give this warning to those in whose (hearts) is the fear that they will be brought (to judgment) before their Lord except for Him they will have no protector nor intercessor: that they may guard (against evil).

52. Do not send away those who call on their Lord morning and evening, seeking His Face. In nothing are you accountable for them, and in nothing are they accountable for you, that you should turn them away, and thus be (one) of the unjust.

53. Thus did We try some of them by comparison with others that they should say: "Is it these then that Allah has favoured from amongst us?" Does not Allah know best those who are grateful?

54. When those come to you who believe in Our Signs, say: "Peace be on you: Your Lord has inscribed for Himself (the rule of) Mercy: verily, if any of you did evil in ignorance, and thereafter repented, and amended (his conduct), lo! He is Oftforgiving, Most Merciful.

55. Thus do We explain the Signs in detail: so that

وَالَّذِيْنَ كَذَّبُوْا بِاٰيٰتِنَا يَمَسُّهُمُ الْعَذَابُ بِمَا كَانُوْا يَفْسُقُوْنَ ۝

قُلْ لَّآ اَقُوْلُ لَكُمْ عِنْدِيْ خَزَآئِنُ اللهِ وَلَآ اَعْلَمُ الْغَيْبَ وَلَآ اَقُوْلُ لَكُمْ اِنِّيْ مَلَكٌ ۚ اِنْ اَتَّبِعُ اِلَّا مَا يُوْحٰى اِلَيَّ ؕ قُلْ هَلْ يَسْتَوِى الْاَعْمٰى وَالْبَصِيْرُ ؕ اَفَلَا تَتَفَكَّرُوْنَ ۝

وَاَنْذِرْ بِهِ الَّذِيْنَ يَخَافُوْنَ اَنْ يُّحْشَرُوْٓا اِلٰى رَبِّهِمْ لَيْسَ لَهُمْ مِّنْ دُوْنِهٖ وَلِيٌّ وَّلَا شَفِيْعٌ لَّعَلَّهُمْ يَتَّقُوْنَ ۝

وَلَا تَطْرُدِ الَّذِيْنَ يَدْعُوْنَ رَبَّهُمْ بِالْغَدٰوةِ وَالْعَشِيِّ يُرِيْدُوْنَ وَجْهَهٗ ؕ مَا عَلَيْكَ مِنْ حِسَابِهِمْ مِّنْ شَيْءٍ وَّمَا مِنْ حِسَابِكَ عَلَيْهِمْ مِّنْ شَيْءٍ فَتَطْرُدَهُمْ فَتَكُوْنَ مِنَ الظّٰلِمِيْنَ ۝

وَكَذٰلِكَ فَتَنَّا بَعْضَهُمْ بِبَعْضٍ لِّيَقُوْلُوْٓا اَهٰٓؤُلَآءِ مَنَّ اللهُ عَلَيْهِمْ مِّنْ بَيْنِنَا ؕ اَلَيْسَ اللهُ بِاَعْلَمَ بِالشّٰكِرِيْنَ ۝

وَاِذَا جَآءَكَ الَّذِيْنَ يُؤْمِنُوْنَ بِاٰيٰتِنَا فَقُلْ سَلٰمٌ عَلَيْكُمْ كَتَبَ رَبُّكُمْ عَلٰى نَفْسِهِ الرَّحْمَةَ ۙ اَنَّهٗ مَنْ عَمِلَ مِنْكُمْ سُوْٓءًا بِجَهَالَةٍ ثُمَّ تَابَ مِنْ بَعْدِهٖ وَاَصْلَحَ فَاَنَّهٗ غَفُوْرٌ رَّحِيْمٌ ۝

وَكَذٰلِكَ نُفَصِّلُ الْاٰيٰتِ وَلِتَسْتَبِيْنَ

the way of the sinners may be shown up.

56. Say: "I am forbidden to worship those - other than Allah - whom you call upon." Say: "I will not follow your vain desires: If I did, I would stray from the path, and be not of the company of those who receive guidance."

57. Say: "For me, I (work) on a clear Sign from my Lord, but you reject Him. What you would see hastened, is not in my power. The Command rests with none but Allah: He declares the Truth, and He is the best of judges."

58. Say: "If what you would see hastened were in my power, the matter would be settled at once between you and me. But Allah knows best those who do wrong."

59. With Him are the keys of the Unseen, the treasures that none knows but He. He knows whatever there is on the earth and in the sea. Not a leaf falls but with His knowledge: there is not a grain in the darkness (or depths) of the earth, nor anything fresh or dry (green or withered), but is (inscribed) in a Record clear (to those who can read).

60. It is He Who takes your souls by night, and has knowledge of all that you have done by day: by day He raises you up again that a term appointed be fulfilled; In the end unto Him will be your return; then will He show you the truth of all that you did.

61. He is the Irresistible, (watching) from above over His worshippers, and He sets guardians over you. At length, when death approaches one of you, Our angels take his soul,

سَبِيلُ الْمُجْرِمِينَ ۝

قُل إِنِّى نُهِيتُ أَنْ أَعْبُدَ الَّذِينَ تَدْعُونَ مِن دُونِ اللَّهِ ۔ قُل لَّا أَتَّبِعُ أَهْوَآءَكُمْ ۔ قَدْ ضَلَلْتُ إِذًا وَمَآ أَنَا مِنَ الْمُهْتَدِينَ ۝

قُلْ إِنِّى عَلَى بَيِّنَةٍ مِّن رَّبِّى وَكَذَّبْتُم بِهِ ۔ مَا عِندِى مَا تَسْتَعْجِلُونَ بِهِ ۔ إِنِ الْحُكْمُ إِلَّا لِلَّهِ ۔ يَقُصُّ الْحَقَّ وَهُوَ خَيْرُ الْفَصِلِينَ ۝

قُل لَّوْ أَنَّ عِندِى مَا تَسْتَعْجِلُونَ بِهِ لَقُضِىَ الْأَمْرُ بَيْنِى وَبَيْنَكُمْ ۔ وَاللَّهُ أَعْلَمُ بِالظَّالِمِينَ ۝

وَعِندَهُ مَفَاتِحُ الْغَيْبِ لَا يَعْلَمُهَا إِلَّا هُوَ ۔ وَيَعْلَمُ مَا فِى الْبَرِّ وَالْبَحْرِ ۔ وَمَا تَسْقُطُ مِن وَرَقَةٍ إِلَّا يَعْلَمُهَا وَلَا حَبَّةٍ فِى ظُلُمَاتِ الْأَرْضِ وَلَا رَطْبٍ وَلَا يَابِسٍ إِلَّا فِى كِتَٰبٍ مُّبِينٍ ۝

وَهُوَ الَّذِى يَتَوَفَّاكُم بِالَّيْلِ وَ يَعْلَمُ مَا جَرَحْتُم بِالنَّهَارِ ثُمَّ يَبْعَثُكُمْ فِيهِ لِيُقْضَى أَجَلٌ مُّسَمًّى ۚ ثُمَّ إِلَيْهِ مَرْجِعُكُمْ ثُمَّ يُنَبِّئُكُم بِمَا كُنتُمْ تَعْمَلُونَ ۝

وَهُوَ الْقَاهِرُ فَوْقَ عِبَادِهِ وَيُرْسِلُ عَلَيْكُمْ حَفَظَةً ۔ حَتَّى إِذَا جَآءَ أَحَدَكُمُ الْمَوْتُ تَوَفَّتْهُ رُسُلُنَا

and they never fail in their duty.

62. Then men are returned unto Allah, their Protector, the (only) Reality: Is not His the Command? and He is the Swiftest in taking account.

63. Say: "Who is it that deliveres you from the dark recesses of land and sea, when you call upon Him in humility and silent terror: 'If He only delivers us from these (dangers), (we vow) we shall truly show our gratitude'.?"

64. Say "It is Allah that delivers you from these and all (other) distresses: and yet you worship false gods!"

65. Say: "He has power to send calamities on you, from above and below, or to cover you with confusion in party strife, giving you a taste of mutual vengeance - each from the other." See how We explain the Signs by various (symbols); that they may understand.

66. But your people reject this, though it is the Truth. Say: "Not mine is the responsibility for arranging your affairs;

67. For every Message is a limit of time, and soon you shall know it."

68. When you see men engaged in vain discourse about Our Signs, turn away from them unless they turn to a different theme. If Satan ever makes you forget, then after recollection, do not sit in the company of those who do wrong.

69. On their account no responsibility falls on the righteous, but (their duty) is to remind them, that they may (learn to) fear Allah.

70. Leave alone those who take their religion to be mere play

and amusement, and are deceived by the life of this world. But proclaim (to them) this (truth): that every soul delivers itself to ruin by its own acts: it will find for itself no protector or intercessor except Allah: if it offered every ransom, (or reparation), none will be accepted: such is (the end of) those who deliver themselves to ruin by their own acts: they will have for drink (only) boiling water, and for punishment, one most grievous for they persisted in rejecting Allah.

71. Say: "Shall we indeed call on others besides Allah,- things that can do us neither good nor harm,- and turn on our heels after receiving guidance from Allah? - like one whom the evil ones have made into a fool, wandering bewildered through the earth, his friends calling, 'Come to us', (vainly) guiding him to the path." Say: "Allah's guidance is the (only) guidance, and we have been directed to submit ourselves to the Lord of the worlds;-

72. "To establish regular prayers and to fear Allah for it is to Him that we shall be gathered together."

73. It is He Who created the heavens and the earth in true (proportions): the day He says, "Be," Behold! it is. His Word is the Truth. His will be the dominion the day the trumpet will be blown. He knows the Unseen as well as that which is open. For He is the Wise, well acquainted (with all things).

74. Lo! Abraham said to his father Azar: "Do you take idols for gods? For I see you and your people in manifest error."

75. So also did We show Abraham the power and the laws of

the heavens and the earth, that he might (with understanding) have certitude.

76. When the night covered him over, he saw a star: He said: "This is my Lord." But when it set, he said: "I do not love those that set."

77. When he saw the moon rising in splendour, he said: "This is my Lord." But when the moon set, he said: "unless my Lord guide me, I shall surely be among those who go astray."

78. When he saw the sun rising in splendour, he said: "This is my Lord; this is the greatest (of all)." But when the sun set, he said: "O my people! I am indeed free from your (guilt) of giving partners to Allah.

79. "For me, I have set my face, firmly and truly, towards Him Who created the heavens and the earth, and never shall I give partners to Allah."

80. His people disputed with him. He said: "Do you (come) to dispute with me, about Allah, when He (Himself) has guided me? I do not fear (the beings) you associate with Allah: unless my Lord wills, (nothing can happen). My Lord comprehends in His knowledge all things. Will you not (yourselves) be admonished?

81. "How should I fear (the beings) you associate with Allah, when you do not fear to give partners to Allah without any warrant having been given to you? Which of (us) two parties has more right to security? (Tell me) if you know.

82. "It is those who believe and do not confuse their beliefs with wrong - that are (truly) in security, for they are on (right)

السَّمٰوٰتِ وَالْأَرْضِ وَ لِيَكُوْنَ مِنَ الْمُوْقِنِيْنَ ۞

فَلَمَّا جَنَّ عَلَيْهِ الَّيْلُ رَاٰ كَوْكَبًا قَالَ هٰذَا رَبِّيْ فَلَمَّآ أَفَلَ قَالَ لَاۤ أُحِبُّ الْاٰفِلِيْنَ ۞

فَلَمَّا رَاٰ الْقَمَرَ بَازِغًا قَالَ هٰذَا رَبِّيْ فَلَمَّآ أَفَلَ قَالَ لَئِنْ لَّمْ يَهْدِنِيْ رَبِّيْ لَأَكُوْنَنَّ مِنَ الْقَوْمِ الضَّآلِّيْنَ ۞

فَلَمَّا رَاٰ الشَّمْسَ بَازِغَةً قَالَ هٰذَا رَبِّيْ هٰذَاۤ أَكْبَرُ فَلَمَّآ أَفَلَتْ قَالَ يٰقَوْمِ اِنِّيْ بَرِيْٓءٌ مِّمَّا تُشْرِكُوْنَ ۞

اِنِّيْ وَجَّهْتُ وَجْهِيَ لِلَّذِيْ فَطَرَ السَّمٰوٰتِ وَالْأَرْضَ حَنِيْفًا وَّمَاۤ أَنَا مِنَ الْمُشْرِكِيْنَ ۞

وَحَآجَّهٗ قَوْمُهٗ قَالَ أَتُحَآجُّوْٓنِّيْ فِي اللّٰهِ وَقَدْ هَدٰىنِ وَلَاۤ أَخَافُ مَا تُشْرِكُوْنَ بِهٖۤ اِلَّاۤ أَنْ يَّشَآءَ رَبِّيْ شَيْئًا وَسِعَ رَبِّيْ كُلَّ شَيْءٍ عِلْمًا أَفَلَا تَتَذَكَّرُوْنَ ۞

وَكَيْفَ أَخَافُ مَاۤ أَشْرَكْتُمْ وَلَا تَخَافُوْنَ أَنَّكُمْ أَشْرَكْتُمْ بِاللّٰهِ مَا لَمْ يُنَزِّلْ بِهٖ عَلَيْكُمْ سُلْطٰنًا فَأَيُّ الْفَرِيْقَيْنِ أَحَقُّ بِالْأَمْنِ اِنْ كُنْتُمْ تَعْلَمُوْنَ ۞

الَّذِيْنَ اٰمَنُوْا وَلَمْ يَلْبِسُوْۤا اِيْمَانَهُمْ بِظُلْمٍ أُولٰٓئِكَ لَهُمُ الْأَمْنُ وَهُمْ

وقف لازم

guidance."

83. That was the reasoning about Us, which We gave to Abraham (to use) against his people: We raise whom We will, degree after degree: for your Lord is full of wisdom and knowledge.

84. We gave him Isaac and Jacob: all (three) We guided: and before him, We guided Noah, and among his progeny, David, Solomon, Job, Joseph, Moses, and Aaron: thus We reward those who do good:

85. And Zakariya and John, and Jesus and Elias all in the ranks of the Righteous:

86. And Isma'il and Elisha, and Jonas, and Lot: and to all We gave favour above the nations:

87. (To them) and to their fathers, and progeny and brethren: We chose them, and We guided them to a straight way.

88. This is the guidance of Allah: He gives that guidance to whom He pleases, of His worshippers. If they were to join other gods with Him, all that they did would be vain for them.

89. These were the men to whom We gave the Book, and Authority, and Prophethood: if these (their descendants) reject them, behold! We shall entrust their charge to a new people who do not reject them.

90. Those were the (prophets) who received Allah's guidance: follow the guidance they received; Say: "No reward for this do I ask of you: this is no less than a Message for the nations."

91. No just estimate of Allah do they make when they say: "Nothing does Allah send down to man (by way of revelation)" say: "Who then sent down the Book which Moses brought?- a light and guidance to man: but you make it into (separate) sheets for show, while you conceal much (of its contents): therein you were taught that which you did not know, neither you nor your fathers." Say: "Allah (sent it down)": then leave them to plunge in vain discourse and trifling.

92. And this is a Book which We have sent down, bringing blessings, and confirming (the revelations) which came before it: that you may warn the Mother of Cities and all around her. Those who believe in the Hereafter believe in this (Book), and they are constant in guarding their prayers.

93. Who can be more wicked than one who invents a lie against Allah, or says, "I have received inspiration," when he has received none, or (again) who says, "I can reveal the like of what Allah has revealed"? If you could but see how the wicked (do fare) in the flood of confusion at death! - the angels stretch forth their hands, (saying),"Yield up your souls: this day you shall receive your reward,- a Chastisement of shame, for that you used to tell lies against Allah, and scornfully to reject of His Signs!"

94. "And behold! you come to Us bare and alone as We created you for the first time: you have left behind you all (the favours) which We bestowed on you: We do not see with you your intercessors whom you thought to be partners in your affairs: so now all relations between you have been cut off, and your (pet) fancies have left you in the lurch!"

وَمَا قَدَرُوا اللّٰهَ حَقَّ قَدْرِهٖ إِذْ قَالُوا

مَآ أَنْزَلَ اللّٰهُ عَلٰى بَشَرٍ مِّنْ شَيْءٍ ۗ

قُلْ مَنْ أَنْزَلَ الْكِتٰبَ الَّذِيْ جَآءَ بِهٖ

مُوْسٰى نُوْرًا وَّهُدًى لِّلنَّاسِ تَجْعَلُوْنَهٗ

قَرَاطِيْسَ تُبْدُوْنَهَا وَتُخْفُوْنَ كَثِيْرًا ۚ

وَعُلِّمْتُمْ مَّا لَمْ تَعْلَمُوْٓا أَنْتُمْ وَلَآ اٰبَآؤُكُمْ ۗ

قُلِ اللّٰهُ ۙ ثُمَّ ذَرْهُمْ فِيْ خَوْضِهِمْ يَلْعَبُوْنَ ۝

وَهٰذَا كِتٰبٌ أَنْزَلْنٰهُ مُبٰرَكٌ مُّصَدِّقُ

الَّذِيْ بَيْنَ يَدَيْهِ وَلِتُنْذِرَ أُمَّ الْقُرٰى

وَمَنْ حَوْلَهَا ۚ وَالَّذِيْنَ يُؤْمِنُوْنَ

بِالْاٰخِرَةِ يُؤْمِنُوْنَ بِهٖ وَهُمْ عَلٰى

صَلَاتِهِمْ يُحَافِظُوْنَ ۝

وَمَنْ أَظْلَمُ مِمَّنِ افْتَرٰى عَلَى اللّٰهِ كَذِبًا

أَوْ قَالَ أُوْحِيَ إِلَيَّ وَلَمْ يُوْحَ إِلَيْهِ شَيْءٌ

وَمَنْ قَالَ سَأُنْزِلُ مِثْلَ مَآ أَنْزَلَ اللّٰهُ ۗ

وَلَوْ تَرٰٓى إِذِ الظّٰلِمُوْنَ فِيْ غَمَرٰتِ الْمَوْتِ

وَالْمَلٰٓئِكَةُ بَاسِطُوْٓا أَيْدِيْهِمْ ۚ أَخْرِجُوْٓا

أَنْفُسَكُمُ ۖ الْيَوْمَ تُجْزَوْنَ عَذَابَ الْهُوْنِ

بِمَا كُنْتُمْ تَقُوْلُوْنَ عَلَى اللّٰهِ غَيْرَ الْحَقِّ

وَكُنْتُمْ عَنْ اٰيٰتِهٖ تَسْتَكْبِرُوْنَ ۝

وَلَقَدْ جِئْتُمُوْنَا فُرَادٰى كَمَا خَلَقْنٰكُمْ

أَوَّلَ مَرَّةٍ وَّتَرَكْتُمْ مَّا خَوَّلْنٰكُمْ وَرَآءَ

ظُهُوْرِكُمْ ۚ وَمَا نَرٰى مَعَكُمْ شُفَعَآءَكُمُ

الَّذِيْنَ زَعَمْتُمْ أَنَّهُمْ فِيْكُمْ شُرَكٰٓؤُا ۗ

لَقَدْ تَّقَطَّعَ بَيْنَكُمْ وَضَلَّ عَنْكُمْ مَّا

كُنْتُمْ تَزْعُمُوْنَ ۝

95. It is Allah Who causes the seed-grain and the date-stone to split and sprout. He causes the living to issue from the dead, and He is the One to cause the dead to issue from the living. That is Allah: then how are you deluded away from the truth?

إِنَّ اللّهَ فَالِقُ الْحَبِّ وَالنَّوٰى ۖ يُخْرِجُ الْحَيَّ مِنَ الْمَيِّتِ وَمُخْرِجُ الْمَيِّتِ مِنَ الْحَيِّ ۚ ذٰلِكُمُ اللّهُ فَأَنّٰى تُؤْفَكُونَ ۝

96. He it is that cleaves the day-break (from the dark): He makes the night for rest and tranquillity, and the sun and moon for the reckoning (of time): Such is the judgment and ordering of (Him), the Exalted in Power, the Omniscient.

فَالِقُ الْإِصْبَاحِ ۖ وَجَعَلَ الَّيْلَ سَكَنًا وَّالشَّمْسَ وَالْقَمَرَ حُسْبَانًا ۚ ذٰلِكَ تَقْدِيرُ الْعَزِيزِ الْعَلِيمِ ۝

97. It is He Who makes the stars (as beacons) for you, that you may guide yourselves, with their help, through the dark spaces of land and sea: We detail Our Signs for people who know.

وَهُوَ الَّذِيْ جَعَلَ لَكُمُ النُّجُومَ لِتَهْتَدُوْا بِهَا فِيْ ظُلُمَاتِ الْبَرِّ وَالْبَحْرِ ۚ قَدْ فَصَّلْنَا الْأَيٰتِ لِقَوْمٍ يَّعْلَمُونَ ۝

98. It is He Who has produced you from a single person: here is a place of sojourn and a place of departure: We detail Our Signs for people who understand.

وَهُوَ الَّذِيْ أَنْشَأَكُمْ مِّنْ نَّفْسٍ وَّاحِدَةٍ فَمُسْتَقَرٌّ وَّمُسْتَوْدَعٌ ۗ قَدْ فَصَّلْنَا الْأَيٰتِ لِقَوْمٍ يَّفْقَهُونَ ۝

99. It is He Who sends down rain from the skies: with it We produce vegetation of all kinds: from some We produce green (crops), out of which We produce grain, heaped up (at harvest); out of the date-palm and its sheaths (or spathes) (come) clusters of dates hanging low and near: and (then there are) gardens of grapes, and olives, and pomegranates, each similar (in kind) yet different (in variety): when they begin to bear fruit, feast your eyes with the fruit and the ripeness thereof. Behold! in these things there are Signs for people who believe.

وَهُوَ الَّذِيْ أَنْزَلَ مِنَ السَّمَاءِ مَاءً ۚ فَأَخْرَجْنَا بِهٖ نَبَاتَ كُلِّ شَيْءٍ فَأَخْرَجْنَا مِنْهُ خَضِرًا نُّخْرِجُ مِنْهُ حَبًّا مُّتَرَاكِبًا ۚ وَمِنَ النَّخْلِ مِنْ طَلْعِهَا قِنْوَانٌ دَانِيَةٌ وَّجَنّٰتٍ مِّنْ أَعْنَابٍ وَّالزَّيْتُونَ وَالرُّمَّانَ مُشْتَبِهًا وَّغَيْرَ مُتَشَابِهٍ ۗ أُنْظُرُوْا إِلٰى ثَمَرِهٖ إِذَا أَثْمَرَ وَيَنْعِهٖ ۚ إِنَّ فِيْ ذٰلِكُمْ لَأَيٰتٍ لِّقَوْمٍ يُّؤْمِنُونَ ۝

100. Yet they make the Jinns equals with Allah, though Allah did create the Jinns; and they falsely, having no knowledge, attribute to Him sons and daughters. Praise and glory be to Him! (for He is) above what they attribute to Him!

وَجَعَلُوْا لِلّهِ شُرَكَاءَ الْجِنَّ وَخَلَقَهُمْ وَخَرَقُوْا لَهٗ بَنِيْنَ وَبَنَاتٍ بِغَيْرِ عِلْمٍ ۚ سُبْحٰنَهٗ وَتَعٰلٰى عَمَّا يَصِفُونَ ۝

101. To Him is due the primal origin of the heavens and the earth: how can He have a son when He has no consort? He created all things, and He has full knowledge of all things.

بَدِيْعُ السَّمٰوٰتِ وَالْأَرْضِ ۖ أَنّٰى يَكُونُ لَهٗ وَلَدٌ وَّلَمْ تَكُنْ لَّهٗ صَاحِبَةٌ ۖ وَخَلَقَ كُلَّ شَيْءٍ ۚ وَهُوَ بِكُلِّ شَيْءٍ عَلِيمٌ ۝

١٨

102. That is Allah, your Lord! there is no god but He, the Creator of all things: then worship Him and He has power to dispose of all affairs.

ذٰلِكُمُ اللهُ رَبُّكُمْ ۚ لَآ اِلٰهَ اِلَّا هُوَ ۚ خَالِقُ كُلِّ شَىْءٍ فَاعْبُدُوْهُ ۚ وَهُوَ عَلٰى كُلِّ شَىْءٍ وَّكِيْلٌ ۞

103. No vision can grasp Him, but His grasp is over all vision: He is above all comprehension, yet is acquainted with all things.

لَا تُدْرِكُهُ الْاَبْصَارُ ۖ وَهُوَ يُدْرِكُ الْاَبْصَارَ ۚ وَهُوَ اللَّطِيْفُ الْخَبِيْرُ ۞

104. "Now have come to you, from your Lord, proofs (to open your eyes): if any will see, it will be for (the good of) his own soul; if any will be blind, it will be to his own (harm): I am not (here) to watch over your doings."

قَدْ جَآءَكُمْ بَصَآئِرُ مِنْ رَّبِّكُمْ ۚ فَمَنْ اَبْصَرَ فَلِنَفْسِهٖ ۚ وَمَنْ عَمِيَ فَعَلَيْهَا ۚ وَمَاۤ اَنَا عَلَيْكُمْ بِحَفِيْظٍ ۞

105. Thus do We explain the Signs by various (symbols): that they may say, "You have taught (us) diligently," and that We may make the matter clear to those who know.

وَكَذٰلِكَ نُصَرِّفُ الْاٰيٰتِ وَلِيَقُوْلُوْا دَرَسْتَ وَلِنُبَيِّنَهٗ لِقَوْمٍ يَّعْلَمُوْنَ ۞

106. Follow what you are taught by inspiration from your Lord: there is no god but He: and turn aside from those who join gods with Allah.

اِتَّبِعْ مَاۤ اُوْحِيَ اِلَيْكَ مِنْ رَّبِّكَ ۚ لَاۤ اِلٰهَ اِلَّا هُوَ ۚ وَاَعْرِضْ عَنِ الْمُشْرِكِيْنَ ۞

107. If it had been Allah's plan, they would not have taken false gods: but We made you not one to watch over their doings, nor are you set over them to dispose of their affairs.

وَلَوْ شَآءَ اللهُ مَاۤ اَشْرَكُوْا ۗ وَمَا جَعَلْنٰكَ عَلَيْهِمْ حَفِيْظًا ۚ وَمَاۤ اَنْتَ عَلَيْهِمْ بِوَكِيْلٍ ۞

108. You do not revile those whom they call upon besides Allah, lest they out of spite revile Allah in their ignorance. Thus have We made alluring to each people its own doings. In the end will they return to their Lord, and We shall then tell them the truth of all that they did.

وَلَا تَسُبُّوا الَّذِيْنَ يَدْعُوْنَ مِنْ دُوْنِ اللهِ فَيَسُبُّوا اللهَ عَدْوًا بِغَيْرِ عِلْمٍ ۚ كَذٰلِكَ زَيَّنَّا لِكُلِّ اُمَّةٍ عَمَلَهُمْ ثُمَّ اِلٰى رَبِّهِمْ مَّرْجِعُهُمْ فَيُنَبِّئُهُمْ بِمَا كَانُوْا يَعْمَلُوْنَ ۞

109. They swear their strongest oaths by Allah, that if a (special) Sign came to them, by it they would believe. Say: "Certainly (all) Signs are in the power of Allah: but what will make you (Muslims) realize that (even) if (special) Signs came, they will not believe."?

وَاَقْسَمُوْا بِاللهِ جَهْدَ اَيْمَانِهِمْ لَئِنْ جَآءَتْهُمْ اٰيَةٌ لَّيُؤْمِنُنَّ بِهَا ۚ قُلْ اِنَّمَا الْاٰيٰتُ عِنْدَ اللهِ ۖ وَمَا يُشْعِرُكُمْ ۙ اَنَّهَاۤ اِذَا جَآءَتْ لَا يُؤْمِنُوْنَ ۞

110. We (too) shall turn to (confusion) their hearts and their eyes, even as they refused to believe in this in the first instance: We shall leave them in

وَنُقَلِّبُ اَفْئِدَتَهُمْ وَاَبْصَارَهُمْ كَمَا لَمْ يُؤْمِنُوْا بِهٖۤ اَوَّلَ مَرَّةٍ وَّنَذَرُهُمْ فِيْ

their trespasses, to wander in distraction.

111. Even if We sent angels to them, and the dead spoke to them, and We gathered together all things before their very eyes, they are not the ones to believe, unless it is in Allah's plan. But most of them ignore (the truth).

112. Likewise, We made for every Messenger an enemy, Satan among men and jinns, inspiring each other with flowery discourses by way of deception. If your Lord had so planned, they would not have done it: so leave them and their inventions alone.

113. To such (deceit) let the hearts of those incline, who have no faith in the Hereafter: let them delight in it, and let them earn from it what they may.

114. Say: "Shall I seek for judge other than Allah? - when He it is Who has sent to you the Book, explained in detail." They know full well, to whom We have given the Book, that it has been sent down from your Lord in truth. Never be then of those who doubt.

115. The Word of your Lord finds its fulfilment in truth and in justice: none can change His Words: for He is the One Who hears and knows all.

116. Were you to follow the common run of those on earth, they will lead you away from the Way of Allah. They follow nothing but conjecture: they do nothing but lie.

117. Your Lord knows best who strays

طُغْيَانِهِمْ يَعْمَهُونَ ۩

وَلَوْ أَنَّنَا نَزَّلْنَا إِلَيْهِمُ الْمَلَائِكَةَ

وَكَلَّمَهُمُ الْمَوْتَىٰ وَحَشَرْنَا عَلَيْهِمْ

كُلَّ شَيْءٍ قُبُلًا مَّا كَانُوا لِيُؤْمِنُوا

إِلَّا أَن يَشَاءَ اللَّهُ وَلَٰكِنَّ أَكْثَرَهُمْ

يَجْهَلُونَ ۞

وَكَذَٰلِكَ جَعَلْنَا لِكُلِّ نَبِيٍّ عَدُوًّا

شَيَاطِينَ الْإِنسِ وَالْجِنِّ يُوحِي

بَعْضُهُمْ إِلَىٰ بَعْضٍ زُخْرُفَ الْقَوْلِ

غُرُورًا ۚ وَلَوْ شَاءَ رَبُّكَ مَا فَعَلُوهُ

فَذَرْهُمْ وَمَا يَفْتَرُونَ ۞

وَلِتَصْغَىٰ إِلَيْهِ أَفْئِدَةُ الَّذِينَ

لَا يُؤْمِنُونَ بِالْآخِرَةِ وَلِيَرْضَوْهُ

وَلِيَقْتَرِفُوا مَا هُم مُّقْتَرِفُونَ ۞

أَفَغَيْرَ اللَّهِ أَبْتَغِي حَكَمًا وَهُوَ

الَّذِي أَنزَلَ إِلَيْكُمُ الْكِتَابَ

مُفَصَّلًا ۚ وَالَّذِينَ آتَيْنَاهُمُ الْكِتَابَ

يَعْلَمُونَ أَنَّهُ مُنَزَّلٌ مِّن رَّبِّكَ بِالْحَقِّ

فَلَا تَكُونَنَّ مِنَ الْمُمْتَرِينَ ۞

وَتَمَّتْ كَلِمَتُ رَبِّكَ صِدْقًا وَ

عَدْلًا ۚ لَّا مُبَدِّلَ لِكَلِمَاتِهِ ۚ

وَهُوَ السَّمِيعُ الْعَلِيمُ ۞

وَإِن تُطِعْ أَكْثَرَ مَن فِي الْأَرْضِ

يُضِلُّوكَ عَن سَبِيلِ اللَّهِ ۚ إِن يَتَّبِعُونَ

إِلَّا الظَّنَّ وَإِنْ هُمْ إِلَّا يَخْرُصُونَ ۞

إِنَّ رَبَّكَ هُوَ أَعْلَمُ مَن يَضِلُّ

from His Way: He knows best who they are that receive His guidance.

118. So eat of (meats) on which Allah's name has been pronounced, if you have faith in His Signs.

119. Why should you not eat of (meats) on which Allah's name has been pronounced, when He has explained to you in detail what is forbidden to you - except under compulsion of necessity? But many do mislead (men) by their appetites unchecked by knowledge. Your Lord knows best those who transgress.

120. Eschew all sin, open or secret: those who earn sin will get due recompense for their "earnings."

121. Do not eat of (meats) on which Allah's name has not been pronounced: that would be impiety. But the evil ones ever inspire their friends to contend with you if you were to obey them, you would indeed be Pagans.

122. Can he who was dead, to whom We gave life, and a light whereby he can walk amongst men, be like him who is in the depths of darkness, from which he can never come out? Thus to those without Faith their own deeds seem pleasing.

123. Thus have We placed leaders in every town, its wicked men, to plot (and burrow) therein: but they only plot against their own souls, and they do not perceive it.

124. When there comes to them a Sign (from Allah), they say: "We shall not believe until we receive one (exactly) like those received by Allah's Apostles."

Allah knows best where (and how) to carry out His mission. Soon will the wicked be overtaken by humiliation before Allah, and a severe punishment, for all their plots.

125. Those whom Allah (in His Plan) wills to guide,- He opens their breast to Islam; those whom He wills to leave straying,- He makes their breast close and constricted, as if they had to climb up to the skies: thus Allah (heaps) the Chastisement on those who refuse to believe.

126. This is the Way of your Lord, leading straight: We have detailed the Signs for those who receive admonition.

127. For them will be a Home of peace in the presence of their Lord: He will be their friend, because they practised (righteousness).

128. One day He will gather them all together, (and say): "O you assembly of Jinns! much (toll) did you take of men." Their friends amongst men will say: "Our Lord! we made profit from each other: but (alas!) we reached our term - which You appointed for us." He will say: "The Fire be your dwelling-place: you will dwell therein for ever, except as Allah wills." for your Lord is full of wisdom and knowledge.

129. Thus We make the wrong-doers turn to each other, because of what they earn.

130. "O you assembly of Jinns and men! did not the Messengers come to you from amongst you, setting forth unto you My Signs, and warning you of the meeting of this Day of yours?"

They will say: "We bear witness against ourselves." It was the life of this world that deceived them. So they will bear witness against themselves that they rejected Faith.

131. (The Apostles were sent) thus, for your Lord would not destroy men's habitations for their wrong-doing whilst their occupants were unwarned.

132. To all are degrees (or ranks) according to their deeds: for your Lord is not unmindful of anything that they do.

133. Your Lord is Self-sufficient, full of Mercy: if it were His Will, He could destroy you, and in your place appoint whom He will as your successors, even as He raised you up from the posterity of other people.

134. All that has been promised to you will come to pass: nor can you frustrate it (in the least bit).

135. Say: "O my people! do whatever you can: I will do (my part): soon will you know who it is whose end will be (best) in the Hereafter: certain it is that the wrong-doers will not prosper."

136. Out of what Allah has produced in abundance in tilth and in cattle, they assigned Him a share: they say, according to their fancies: "This is for Allah, and this" - for our "partners"! but the share of their "partners" does not reach Allah, whilst the share of Allah reaches their "partners" ! evil (and unjust) is their assignment!

137. Even so, in the eyes of most of the pagans, their "partners" made alluring the slaughter of their children, in order to lead them to their own destruction, and cause confusion in their religion. If Allah has willed,

هٰذَاۚ قَالُوْا شَهِدْنَا عَلٰٓى اَنْفُسِنَا وَغَرَّتْهُمُ الْحَيٰوةُ الدُّنْيَا وَشَهِدُوْا عَلٰٓى اَنْفُسِهِمْ اَنَّهُمْ كَانُوْا كٰفِرِيْنَ ۝

ذٰلِكَ اَنْ لَّمْ يَكُنْ رَّبُّكَ مُهْلِكَ الْقُرٰى بِظُلْمٍ وَّاَهْلُهَا غٰفِلُوْنَ ۝

وَلِكُلٍّ دَرَجٰتٌ مِّمَّا عَمِلُوْا ۚ وَمَا رَبُّكَ بِغَافِلٍ عَمَّا يَعْمَلُوْنَ ۝

وَرَبُّكَ الْغَنِيُّ ذُو الرَّحْمَةِ ۚ اِنْ يَّشَأْ يُذْهِبْكُمْ وَيَسْتَخْلِفْ مِنْ بَعْدِكُمْ مَّا يَشَآءُ كَمَآ اَنْشَاَكُمْ مِّنْ ذُرِّيَّةِ قَوْمٍ اٰخَرِيْنَ ۝

اِنَّ مَا تُوْعَدُوْنَ لَاٰتٍ ۙ وَّمَآ اَنْتُمْ بِمُعْجِزِيْنَ ۝

قُلْ يٰقَوْمِ اعْمَلُوْا عَلٰى مَكَانَتِكُمْ اِنِّيْ عَامِلٌ ۚ فَسَوْفَ تَعْلَمُوْنَ ۙ مَنْ تَكُوْنُ لَهٗ عَاقِبَةُ الدَّارِ ۚ اِنَّهٗ لَا يُفْلِحُ الظّٰلِمُوْنَ ۝

وَجَعَلُوْا لِلّٰهِ مِمَّا ذَرَاَ مِنَ الْحَرْثِ وَالْاَنْعَامِ نَصِيْبًا فَقَالُوْا هٰذَا لِلّٰهِ بِزَعْمِهِمْ وَهٰذَا لِشُرَكَآئِنَا ۚ فَمَا كَانَ لِشُرَكَآئِهِمْ فَلَا يَصِلُ اِلَى اللّٰهِ ۚ وَمَا كَانَ لِلّٰهِ فَهُوَ يَصِلُ اِلٰى شُرَكَآئِهِمْ ۗ سَآءَ مَا يَحْكُمُوْنَ ۝

وَكَذٰلِكَ زَيَّنَ لِكَثِيْرٍ مِّنَ الْمُشْرِكِيْنَ قَتْلَ اَوْلَادِهِمْ شُرَكَآؤُهُمْ لِيُرْدُوْهُمْ وَلِيَلْبِسُوْا عَلَيْهِمْ دِيْنَهُمْ ۚ وَلَوْ شَآءَ

they would not have done so: but leave them and their inventions alone.

138. And they say that such and such cattle and crops are taboo, and none should eat of them except those whom - so they say - We wish; further, there are cattle forbidden to yoke or burden, and cattle on which, (at slaughter), the name of Allah is not pronounced; - inventions against Allah's name: soon will He requite them for their inventions.

139. They say: "What is in the wombs of such and such cattle is specially reserved (for food) for our men, and forbidden to our women; but if it is still-born, then all have shares therein. For their (false) attribution (of superstitions to Allah), He will soon punish them: for He is full of wisdom and knowledge.

140. Lost are those who slay their children, from folly, without knowledge, and forbid food which Allah has provided for them, inventing (lies) against Allah. They have indeed gone astray and heeded no guidance.

141. It is He Who produces gardens, with trellises and without, and dates, and tilth with produce of all kinds, and olives and pomegranates, similar (in kind) and different (in variety): eat of their fruit in their season, but render the dues that are proper on the day that the harvest is gathered. But waste not by excess: for Allah does not love the wasters.

142. Of the cattle are some for burden and some for meat: eat what Allah has provided for you, and follow not the footsteps of Satan: for he is to you an avowed enemy.

143. (Take) eight (head of cattle) in (four) pairs: of sheep a pair, and of goats a pair; say, has He forbidden the two males,

اللّٰهُ مَا فَعَلُوْهُ فَذَرْهُمْ وَمَا يَفْتَرُوْنَ ۞

وَقَالُوْا هٰذِهٖۤ اَنْعَامٌ وَّحَرْثٌ حِجْرٌ ۖ

لَّا يَطْعَمُهَاۤ اِلَّا مَنْ نَّشَآءُ بِزَعْمِهِمْ

وَاَنْعَامٌ حُرِّمَتْ ظُهُوْرُهَا وَاَنْعَامٌ

لَّا يَذْكُرُوْنَ اسْمَ اللّٰهِ عَلَيْهَا افْتِرَآءً

عَلَيْهِ ؕ سَيَجْزِيْهِمْ بِمَا كَانُوْا يَفْتَرُوْنَ ۞

وَقَالُوْا مَا فِيْ بُطُوْنِ هٰذِهِ الْاَنْعَامِ

خَالِصَةٌ لِّذُكُوْرِنَا وَمُحَرَّمٌ عَلٰۤى

اَزْوَاجِنَا ۚ وَاِنْ يَّكُنْ مَّيْتَةً فَهُمْ

فِيْهِ شُرَكَآءُ ؕ سَيَجْزِيْهِمْ وَصْفَهُمْ ؕ

اِنَّهٗ حَكِيْمٌ عَلِيْمٌ ۞

قَدْ خَسِرَ الَّذِيْنَ قَتَلُوْۤا اَوْلَادَهُمْ

سَفَهًا بِغَيْرِ عِلْمٍ وَّحَرَّمُوْا مَا

رَزَقَهُمُ اللّٰهُ افْتِرَآءً عَلَى اللّٰهِ ؕ قَدْ

ضَلُّوْا وَمَا كَانُوْا مُهْتَدِيْنَ ۞

وَهُوَ الَّذِيْۤ اَنْشَاَ جَنّٰتٍ مَّعْرُوْشٰتٍ وَّغَيْرَ

مَعْرُوْشٰتٍ وَّالنَّخْلَ وَالزَّرْعَ مُخْتَلِفًا

اُكُلُهٗ وَالزَّيْتُوْنَ وَالرُّمَّانَ مُتَشَابِهًا

وَّغَيْرَ مُتَشَابِهٍ ؕ كُلُوْا مِنْ ثَمَرِهٖۤ اِذَاۤ

اَثْمَرَ وَاٰتُوْا حَقَّهٗ يَوْمَ حَصَادِهٖ ۖ وَلَا

تُسْرِفُوْا ؕ اِنَّهٗ لَا يُحِبُّ الْمُسْرِفِيْنَ ۞

وَمِنَ الْاَنْعَامِ حَمُوْلَةً وَّفَرْشًا ؕ كُلُوْا

مِمَّا رَزَقَكُمُ اللّٰهُ وَلَا تَتَّبِعُوْا خُطُوٰتِ

الشَّيْطٰنِ ؕ اِنَّهٗ لَكُمْ عَدُوٌّ مُّبِيْنٌ ۞

ثَمٰنِيَةَ اَزْوَاجٍ ۚ مِنَ الضَّأْنِ اثْنَيْنِ

وَمِنَ الْمَعْزِ اثْنَيْنِ ؕ قُلْ ءٰالذَّكَرَيْنِ

or the two females, or (the young) which the wombs of the two females enclose? Tell me with knowledge if you are truthful:

144. Of camels a pair, and of oxen a pair; say, has He forbidden the two males, or the two females, or (the young) which the wombs of the two females enclose? - Were you present when Allah ordered you such a thing? But who does more wrong than one who invents a lie against Allah, to lead astray men without knowledge? For Allah does not guide people who do wrong.

145. Say: "I do not find in the Message received by me by inspiration any (meat) forbidden to be eaten by one who wishes to eat it, unless it be dead meat, or blood poured forth, or the flesh of swine,- for it is an abomination - or, what is impious, (meat) on which a name has been invoked, other than Allah's". But (even so), if a person is forced by necessity, without wilful disobedience, nor transgressing due limits,- your Lord is Oft-forgiving, Most Merciful.

146. For those who followed the Jewish Law, We forbade every (animal) with undivided hoof, and We forbade them that fat of the ox and the sheep, except what adheres to their backs or their entrails, or is mixed up with a bone: this in recompense for their wilful disobedience: for We are true (in Our ordinances).

147. If they accuse you of falsehood, say: "Your Lord is full of mercy all- embracing; but from people in guilt never will His wrath be turned back.

حَرَّمَ اَمِ الْاُنْثَيَيْنِ اَمَّا اشْتَمَلَتْ
عَلَيْهِ اَرْحَامُ الْاُنْثَيَيْنِ ؕ نَبِّـُٔوْنِيْ
بِعِلْمٍ اِنْ كُنْتُمْ صٰدِقِيْنَ ۟
وَمِنَ الْاِبِلِ اثْنَيْنِ وَمِنَ الْبَقَرِ
اثْنَيْنِ ؕ قُلْ ءٰٓالذَّكَرَيْنِ حَرَّمَ اَمِ
الْاُنْثَيَيْنِ اَمَّا اشْتَمَلَتْ عَلَيْهِ
اَرْحَامُ الْاُنْثَيَيْنِ ؕ اَمْ كُنْتُمْ شُهَدَآءَ
اِذْ وَصّٰكُمُ اللّٰهُ بِهٰذَا ۚ فَمَنْ اَظْلَمُ
مِمَّنِ افْتَرٰى عَلَى اللّٰهِ كَذِبًا لِّيُضِلَّ
النَّاسَ بِغَيْرِ عِلْمٍ ؕ اِنَّ اللّٰهَ لَا
يَهْدِى الْقَوْمَ الظّٰلِمِيْنَ ۟
قُلْ لَّاۤ اَجِدُ فِيْ مَاۤ اُوْحِيَ اِلَيَّ مُحَرَّمًا
عَلٰى طَاعِمٍ يَّطْعَمُهٗٓ اِلَّاۤ اَنْ يَّكُوْنَ
مَيْتَةً اَوْ دَمًا مَّسْفُوْحًا اَوْ لَحْمَ
خِنْزِيْرٍ فَاِنَّهٗ رِجْسٌ اَوْ فِسْقًا اُهِلَّ
لِغَيْرِ اللّٰهِ بِهٖ ؕ فَمَنِ اضْطُرَّ غَيْرَ بَاغٍ
وَّلَا عَادٍ فَاِنَّ رَبَّكَ غَفُوْرٌ رَّحِيْمٌ ۟
وَعَلَى الَّذِيْنَ هَادُوْا حَرَّمْنَا كُلَّ
ذِيْ ظُفُرٍ ۚ وَمِنَ الْبَقَرِ وَالْغَنَمِ حَرَّمْنَا
عَلَيْهِمْ شُحُوْمَهُمَاۤ اِلَّا مَا حَمَلَتْ
ظُهُوْرُهُمَاۤ اَوِ الْحَوَايَاۤ اَوْ مَا اخْتَلَطَ
بِعَظْمٍ ؕ ذٰلِكَ جَزَيْنٰهُمْ بِبَغْيِهِمْ ۖ وَاِنَّا
لَصٰدِقُوْنَ ۟
فَاِنْ كَذَّبُوْكَ فَقُلْ رَّبُّكُمْ ذُوْ رَحْمَةٍ
وَّاسِعَةٍ ۚ وَلَا يُرَدُّ بَأْسُهٗ عَنِ
الْقَوْمِ الْمُجْرِمِيْنَ ۟

٤ ع

148. Those who give partners (to Allah) will say: "If Allah had wished, we should not have given partners to Him nor would our fathers; nor should we have had any taboos." So did their ancestors argue falsely, until they tasted of Our wrath. Say: "Have you any (certain) knowledge? If so, produce it before us. You follow nothing but conjecture: you do nothing but lie."

149. Say: "With Allah is the argument that reaches home: if it had been His Will, He could indeed have guided you all."

150. Say: "Bring forward your witnesses to prove that Allah forbade you so and so." If they bring such witnesses, you should not be amongst them: nor you should follow the vain desires of such as treat Our Signs as falsehoods, and such as do not believe in the Hereafter: for they hold others as equal with their Guardian-Lord.

151. Say: "Come, I will rehearse what Allah has (really) prohibited you from": Join not anything as equal with Him; be good to your parents; kill not your children on a plea of want;- We provide sustenance for you and for them;- do not come near to shameful deeds, whether open or secret; take not life, which Allah has made sacred, except by way of justice and law: thus does He command you, that you may learn wisdom.

152. And come not near to the orphan's property, except to improve it, until he attain the age of full strength; give measure and weight with (full) justice;-

سَيَقُولُ الَّذِينَ أَشْرَكُوا لَوْ شَاءَ اللهُ مَا أَشْرَكْنَا وَلَا آبَاؤُنَا وَلَا حَرَّمْنَا مِنْ شَيْءٍ ۚ كَذَٰلِكَ كَذَّبَ الَّذِينَ مِنْ قَبْلِهِمْ حَتَّىٰ ذَاقُوا بَأْسَنَا ۗ قُلْ هَلْ عِنْدَكُمْ مِنْ عِلْمٍ فَتُخْرِجُوهُ لَنَا ۖ إِنْ تَتَّبِعُونَ إِلَّا الظَّنَّ وَإِنْ أَنْتُمْ إِلَّا تَخْرُصُونَ ۝

قُلْ فَلِلَّهِ الْحُجَّةُ الْبَالِغَةُ ۖ فَلَوْ شَاءَ لَهَدَاكُمْ أَجْمَعِينَ ۝

قُلْ هَلُمَّ شُهَدَاءَكُمُ الَّذِينَ يَشْهَدُونَ أَنَّ اللهَ حَرَّمَ هَٰذَا ۖ فَإِنْ شَهِدُوا فَلَا تَشْهَدْ مَعَهُمْ ۚ وَلَا تَتَّبِعْ أَهْوَاءَ الَّذِينَ كَذَّبُوا بِآيَاتِنَا وَالَّذِينَ لَا يُؤْمِنُونَ بِالْآخِرَةِ وَهُمْ بِرَبِّهِمْ يَعْدِلُونَ ۝

قُلْ تَعَالَوْا أَتْلُ مَا حَرَّمَ رَبُّكُمْ عَلَيْكُمْ ۖ أَلَّا تُشْرِكُوا بِهِ شَيْئًا ۖ وَبِالْوَالِدَيْنِ إِحْسَانًا ۖ وَلَا تَقْتُلُوا أَوْلَادَكُمْ مِنْ إِمْلَاقٍ ۖ نَحْنُ نَرْزُقُكُمْ وَإِيَّاهُمْ ۖ وَلَا تَقْرَبُوا الْفَوَاحِشَ مَا ظَهَرَ مِنْهَا وَمَا بَطَنَ ۖ وَلَا تَقْتُلُوا النَّفْسَ الَّتِي حَرَّمَ اللهُ إِلَّا بِالْحَقِّ ۚ ذَٰلِكُمْ وَصَّاكُمْ بِهِ لَعَلَّكُمْ تَعْقِلُونَ ۝

وَلَا تَقْرَبُوا مَالَ الْيَتِيمِ إِلَّا بِالَّتِي هِيَ أَحْسَنُ حَتَّىٰ يَبْلُغَ أَشُدَّهُ ۖ وَ أَوْفُوا الْكَيْلَ وَالْمِيزَانَ بِالْقِسْطِ ۖ

no burden do We place on any soul, but that which it can bear;- whenever you speak, speak justly, even if a near relative is concerned; and fulfil the Covenant of Allah: thus He commands you, that you may remember.

153. Verily, this is My Way, leading straight: follow it: do not follow (other) paths: they will scatter you about from His (great) path: thus He commands you that you may be righteous.

154. Moreover, We gave Moses the Book, completing (Our favour) to those who would do right, and explained all things in detail,- and a guide and a mercy, that they might believe in the meeting with their Lord.

155. And this is a Book which We have revealed as a blessing: so follow it and be righteous, that you may receive mercy:

156. Lest you should say: "The Book was sent down to two Peoples before us, and for our part, we remained unacquainted with all that they learned by assiduous study:"

157. Or lest you should say: "If the Book had only been sent down to us, we should have followed its guidance better than they." Now then has come unto you a Clear (Sign) from your Lord,- and a guide and a mercy: then who could do more wrong than one who rejects Allah's Signs, and turns away therefrom? In good time shall We requite those who turn away from Our Signs, with a dreadful Chastisement, for their turning away.

158. Are they waiting to see if the angels come to them, or your Lord (Himself), or

لَا نُكَلِّفُ نَفْسًا إِلَّا وُسْعَهَا ۖ وَإِذَا قُلْتُمْ فَاعْدِلُوا وَلَوْ كَانَ ذَا قُرْبَىٰ ۖ وَبِعَهْدِ اللَّهِ أَوْفُوا ۚ ذَٰلِكُمْ وَصَّاكُم بِهِ لَعَلَّكُمْ تَذَكَّرُونَ ۞

وَأَنَّ هَٰذَا صِرَاطِي مُسْتَقِيمًا فَاتَّبِعُوهُ ۖ وَلَا تَتَّبِعُوا السُّبُلَ فَتَفَرَّقَ بِكُمْ عَن سَبِيلِهِ ۚ ذَٰلِكُمْ وَصَّاكُم بِهِ لَعَلَّكُمْ تَتَّقُونَ ۞

ثُمَّ آتَيْنَا مُوسَى الْكِتَابَ تَمَامًا عَلَى الَّذِي أَحْسَنَ وَتَفْصِيلًا لِّكُلِّ شَيْءٍ وَهُدًى وَرَحْمَةً لَّعَلَّهُم بِلِقَاءِ رَبِّهِمْ يُؤْمِنُونَ ۞

وَهَٰذَا كِتَابٌ أَنزَلْنَاهُ مُبَارَكٌ فَاتَّبِعُوهُ وَاتَّقُوا لَعَلَّكُمْ تُرْحَمُونَ ۞

أَن تَقُولُوا إِنَّمَا أُنزِلَ الْكِتَابُ عَلَىٰ طَائِفَتَيْنِ مِن قَبْلِنَا وَإِن كُنَّا عَن دِرَاسَتِهِمْ لَغَافِلِينَ ۞

أَوْ تَقُولُوا لَوْ أَنَّا أُنزِلَ عَلَيْنَا الْكِتَابُ لَكُنَّا أَهْدَىٰ مِنْهُمْ ۚ فَقَدْ جَاءَكُم بَيِّنَةٌ مِّن رَّبِّكُمْ وَهُدًى وَرَحْمَةٌ ۚ فَمَنْ أَظْلَمُ مِمَّن كَذَّبَ بِآيَاتِ اللَّهِ وَصَدَفَ عَنْهَا ۚ سَنَجْزِي الَّذِينَ يَصْدِفُونَ عَنْ آيَاتِنَا سُوءَ الْعَذَابِ بِمَا كَانُوا يَصْدِفُونَ ۞

هَلْ يَنظُرُونَ إِلَّا أَن تَأْتِيَهُمُ الْمَلَائِكَةُ أَوْ يَأْتِيَ رَبُّكَ أَوْ يَأْتِيَ

١٩
ع
٦

certain of the Signs of your Lord! the day that certain of the Signs of your Lord do come, no good will it do to a soul to believe in them then, if it believed not before nor earned righteousness through its Faith. Say: "You wait: we too are waiting."

159. As for those who divide their religion and break up into sects, you have no part in them in the least: their affair is with Allah: He will in the end tell them the truth of all that they did.

160. He that does good shall have ten times as much to his credit: he that does evil shall only be recompensed according to his evil: no wrong shall be done to (any of) them.

161. Say: "Verily, my Lord has guided me to a way that is straight,- a religion of right,- the path (trod) by Abraham, the true in faith, and he (certainly) did not join gods with Allah."

162. Say: "Truly, my prayer and my service of sacrifice, my life and my death, are (all) for Allah, the Cherisher of the Worlds:

163. No partner has He: this I am commanded, and I am the first of those who bow to His Will.

164. Say: "Shall I seek for (my) Cherisher other than Allah, when He is the Cherisher of all things (that exist)? Every soul draws the meed of its acts on none but itself: no bearer of burdens can bear the burden of another. Your goal in the end is towards Allah: He will tell you the truth of the things wherein you disputed."

165. It is He Who has made you (His) agents, inheritors of the earth: He has raised you in ranks, some above others:

SÛRAH-7
AL-A'RÂF
(INTRODUCTION)

This Sûrah is closely connected, both chronologically and in respect of the argument, with the previous Sûrah. But it expounds the doctrine of revelation and man's spiritual history by illustrations from Adam onwards, through various Prophets and the details of Moses's struggles, to the time of the Apostle Muhammad, in whom Allah's revelation is completed.

that He may try you in the gifts He has given you: for your Lord is quick in punishment: yet He is indeed Oft-forgiving, Most Merciful.

لِيَبْلُوَكُمْ فِيْ مَاۤ اٰتٰىكُمْ ۚ اِنَّ رَبَّكَ سَرِيْعُ الْعِقَابِ ۚ وَاِنَّهٗ لَغَفُوْرٌ رَّحِيْمٌ ۞

---

7. The Heights
In the name of Allah. Most Gracious, Most Merciful.

(٧) سُوْرَةُ الْاَعْرَافِ مَكِّيَّةٌ (٣٩)

بِسْمِ اللّٰهِ الرَّحْمٰنِ الرَّحِيْمِ

1. Alif, Lam, Mim, Sad.

الٓمّٓصٓ ۞

2. A Book revealed unto you,- So let your heart be oppressed no more by any difficulty on that account,- that with it you might warn (the erring) and teach the Believers.

كِتٰبٌ اُنْزِلَ اِلَيْكَ فَلَا يَكُنْ فِيْ صَدْرِكَ حَرَجٌ مِّنْهُ لِتُنْذِرَ بِهٖ وَذِكْرٰى لِلْمُؤْمِنِيْنَ ۞

3. Follow (O men!) the revelation given to you from your Lord, and follow not, as friends or protectors, other than Him. Little it is you remember of admonition.

اِتَّبِعُوْا مَاۤ اُنْزِلَ اِلَيْكُمْ مِّنْ رَّبِّكُمْ وَلَا تَتَّبِعُوْا مِنْ دُوْنِهٖۤ اَوْلِيَآءَ ۗ قَلِيْلًا مَّا تَذَكَّرُوْنَ ۞

4. How many towns have We destroyed (for their sins)? Our punishment took them on a sudden by night or while they slept for their afternoon rest.

وَكَمْ مِّنْ قَرْيَةٍ اَهْلَكْنٰهَا فَجَآءَهَا بَاْسُنَا بَيَاتًا اَوْ هُمْ قَآئِلُوْنَ ۞

5. When (thus) Our punishment took them, no cry did they utter but this: "Indeed we did wrong."

فَمَا كَانَ دَعْوٰىهُمْ اِذْ جَآءَهُمْ بَاْسُنَاۤ اِلَّاۤ اَنْ قَالُوْاۤ اِنَّا كُنَّا ظٰلِمِيْنَ ۞

6. Then shall We question those to whom Our Message was sent and those by whom We sent it.

فَلَنَسْئَلَنَّ الَّذِيْنَ اُرْسِلَ اِلَيْهِمْ وَلَنَسْئَلَنَّ الْمُرْسَلِيْنَ ۞

7. And verily, We shall recount their whole story with knowledge, for We were never absent (at any time or place).

فَلَنَقُصَّنَّ عَلَيْهِمْ بِعِلْمٍ وَّمَا كُنَّا غَآئِبِيْنَ ۞

8. The balance that day will be true (to a nicety): those whose scale (of good) will be heavy, will prosper:

وَالْوَزْنُ يَوْمَئِذِ ۨالْحَقُّ ۚ فَمَنْ ثَقُلَتْ مَوَازِيْنُهٗ فَاُولٰٓئِكَ هُمُ الْمُفْلِحُوْنَ ۞

9. Those whose scale will be light, will find their souls in perdition, for that they wrongfully treated Our Signs.

وَمَنْ خَفَّتْ مَوَازِيْنُهٗ فَاُولٰٓئِكَ الَّذِيْنَ خَسِرُوْۤا اَنْفُسَهُمْ بِمَا كَانُوْا بِاٰيٰتِنَا يَظْلِمُوْنَ ۞

10. It is We Who have placed you with authority on earth, and

وَلَقَدْ مَكَّنّٰكُمْ فِى الْاَرْضِ وَ

provided you therein with means for the fulfilment of your life: small are the thanks that you give!

11. It is We Who created you and gave you shape; then We said the angels bow down to Adam, and they bowed down; not so Iblis; He refused to be of those who bow down.

12. (Allah) said: "What prevented you from bowing down when I commanded you?" He said: "I am better than he: you created me from fire, and him from clay."

13. (Allah) said: "Get you down from here: it is not for you to be arrogant here: get out, for you are of the meanest(of creatures)."

14. He said: "Give me respite till the day they are raised up."

15. (Allah) said: "Be you among those who have respite."

16. He said: "Because You have thrown me out of the way, I will lie in wait for them on Your Straight Way:

17. "Then I will assault them from before them and behind them, from their right and their left: nor will You find gratitude in most of them, (for Your mercies)."

18. (Allah) said: "Get out from this, disgraced and expelled. If any of them follow you,- I will fill Hell with you all.

19. "O Adam! You and your wife dwell in the Garden, and enjoy (its good things) as you wish: but do not approach this tree, or you run into harm and transgression."

20. Then began Satan to whisper suggestions to them, in order to reveal to them

their shame that was hidden from them (before): he said: "Your Lord only forbade you this tree, lest you should become angels or such beings as live for ever."

21. And he swore to them both, that he was their sincere adviser.

22. So by deceit he brought about their fall: when they tasted of the tree, their shame became manifest to them, and they began to sew together the leaves of the Garden over their bodies. And their Lord called to them: "Did I not forbid you that tree, and tell you that Satan was an avowed enemy to you?"

23. They said: "Our Lord! We have wronged our own souls: If You do not forgive us and do not bestow upon us Your Mercy, we shall certainly be lost."

24. (Allah) said: "Get you down, with enmity between yourselves. On earth will be your dwelling-place and your means of livelihood,- for a time."

25. He said: "Therein you shall live, and therein you shall die; but from it you shall be taken out (at last)."

26. O you Children of Adam! We have bestowed raiment upon you to cover your shame, as well as to be an adornment to you. But the raiment of righteousness,- that is the best. Such are among the Signs of Allah, that they may receive admonition!

27. O you Children of Adam! let not Satan seduce you, in the same manner as He got your parents out of the Garden, stripping them of their raiment, to expose their shame:

مَا وُرِيَ عَنْهُمَا مِنْ سَوْءَاتِهِمَا وَ

قَالَ مَا نَهٰكُمَا رَبُّكُمَا عَنْ هٰذِهِ

الشَّجَرَةِ اِلَّا اَنْ تَكُوْنَا مَلَكَيْنِ

اَوْ تَكُوْنَا مِنَ الْخٰلِدِيْنَ ۞

وَقَاسَمَهُمَا اِنِّيْ لَكُمَا لَمِنَ النّٰصِحِيْنَ ۞

فَدَلّٰهُمَا بِغُرُوْرٍ ۚ فَلَمَّا ذَاقَا الشَّجَرَةَ

بَدَتْ لَهُمَا سَوْءَاتُهُمَا وَطَفِقَا يَخْصِفٰنِ

عَلَيْهِمَا مِنْ وَّرَقِ الْجَنَّةِ ۚ وَنَادٰهُمَا

رَبُّهُمَا اَلَمْ اَنْهَكُمَا عَنْ تِلْكُمَا

الشَّجَرَةِ وَاَقُلْ لَّكُمَا اِنَّ الشَّيْطٰنَ

لَكُمَا عَدُوٌّ مُّبِيْنٌ ۞

قَالَا رَبَّنَا ظَلَمْنَا اَنْفُسَنَا ۫ وَ

اِنْ لَّمْ تَغْفِرْ لَنَا وَتَرْحَمْنَا لَنَكُوْنَنَّ

مِنَ الْخٰسِرِيْنَ ۞

قَالَ اهْبِطُوْا بَعْضُكُمْ لِبَعْضٍ عَدُوٌّ ۚ

وَلَكُمْ فِى الْاَرْضِ مُسْتَقَرٌّ وَّمَتَاعٌ

اِلٰى حِيْنٍ ۞

قَالَ فِيْهَا تَحْيَوْنَ وَفِيْهَا تَمُوْتُوْنَ

وَمِنْهَا تُخْرَجُوْنَ ۞

يٰبَنِيْ اٰدَمَ قَدْ اَنْزَلْنَا عَلَيْكُمْ لِبَاسًا

يُّوَارِيْ سَوْءَاتِكُمْ وَرِيْشًا ۖ وَلِبَاسُ

التَّقْوٰى ۙ ذٰلِكَ خَيْرٌ ۚ ذٰلِكَ مِنْ

اٰيٰتِ اللّٰهِ لَعَلَّهُمْ يَذَّكَّرُوْنَ ۞

يٰبَنِيْ اٰدَمَ لَا يَفْتِنَنَّكُمُ الشَّيْطٰنُ كَمَا

اَخْرَجَ اَبَوَيْكُمْ مِّنَ الْجَنَّةِ يَنْزِعُ

عَنْهُمَا لِبَاسَهُمَا لِيُرِيَهُمَا سَوْءَاتِهِمَا ۗ

ع
٩

for he and his tribe watch you from a position where you cannot see them: We made the Satan friends (only) to those without Faith.

28. When they do anything that is shameful, they say: "We found our fathers doing so"; and "Allah commanded us thus": Say: "Nay, Allah never commands what is shameful: do you say of Allah what you do not know?"

29. Say: "My Lord has commanded justice; and that you set your whole selves (to Him) at every time and place of prayer, and call upon Him, making your devotion sincere as in His sight: such as He created you in the beginning, so shall you return."

30. Some He has guided: others have (by their choice) deserved the loss of their way; in that they took the Satan, in preference to Allah, for their friends and protectors, and think that they receive guidance.

31. O Children of Adam! wear your beautiful apparel at every time and place of prayer: eat and drink: but do not waste by excess, for Allah does not love the wasters.

32. Say: Who has forbidden the beautiful (gifts) of Allah, which He has produced for His servants, and the things, clean and pure, which (He has provided) for sustenance? Say: They are, in the life of this world, for those who believe, (and) purely for them on the Day of Judgment. Thus do We explain the Signs in detail for those who understand.

33. Say: The things that my Lord has indeed forbidden are: shameful deeds, whether open or secret; sins and trespasses against truth or reason; assigning of partners to Allah,

for which He has given no authority; and saying things about Allah of which you have no knowledge.

34. To every people is a term appointed: when their term is reached, not an hour can they cause delay, nor (an hour) can they advance (it in anticipation).

35. O you Children of Adam! whenever there come to you Apostles from amongst you, rehearsing My Signs to you,- those who are righteous and mend (their lives),- on them shall be no fear nor shall they grieve.

36. But those who reject Our Signs and treat them with arrogance,- they are Companions of the Fire, to dwell therein (for ever).

37. Who is more unjust than one who invents a lie against Allah or rejects His Signs? For such, their portion appointed must reach them from the Book (of Decrees): until, when our messengers (of death) arrive and take their souls, they say: "Where are the things that you used to invoke besides Allah?" They will reply, "They have left us in the lurch," and they will bear witness against themselves, that they had rejected Allah.

38. He will say: "You enter in the company of the peoples who passed away before you - men and jinns, - into the Fire." Every time a new people enters, it curses its sister-people (that went before), until they follow each other, all into the Fire. Says the last about the first: "Our Lord! it is these that misled us: so give them a double Chastisement in the Fire." He will say: "Doubled for all" : but this you do not

understand.

39. Then the first will say to the last: "See then! You do not have any advantage over us; so you taste of the Chastisement for all that you did."

40. To those who reject Our Signs and treat them with arrogance, no opening will there be of the gates of heaven, nor will they enter the Garden, until the camel can pass through the eye of the needle: such is Our reward for those in sin.

41. For them there is Hell, as a couch (below) and folds of covering above: such is Our requital of those who do wrong.

42. But those who believe and work righteousness,- no burden do We place on any soul, but that which it can bear,-they will be Companions of the Garden, therein to dwell (for ever).

43. And We shall remove from their hearts any lurking sense of injury;- beneath them will be rivers flowing;- and they shall say: "Praise be to Allah, Who has guided us to this (felicity): never could we have found guidance, had it not been for the guidance of Allah: indeed it was the truth, that the Apostles of our Lord brought to us." And they shall hear the cry: "Behold! the Garden before you! you have been made its inheritors, for your deeds (of righteousness)."

44. The Companions of the Garden will call out to the Companions of the Fire: "We have indeed found the promises of our Lord to us true: have you also found Your Lord's promises true?" They shall say, "Yes"; But

لَا تَعْلَمُونَ ۝

وَقَالَتْ أُولَاهُمْ لِأُخْرَاهُمْ فَمَا كَانَ لَكُمْ عَلَيْنَا مِنْ فَضْلٍ فَذُوقُوا الْعَذَابَ بِمَا كُنْتُمْ تَكْسِبُونَ ۝

إِنَّ الَّذِينَ كَذَّبُوا بِآيَاتِنَا وَاسْتَكْبَرُوا عَنْهَا لَا تُفَتَّحُ لَهُمْ أَبْوَابُ السَّمَاءِ وَلَا يَدْخُلُونَ الْجَنَّةَ حَتَّى يَلِجَ الْجَمَلُ فِي سَمِّ الْخِيَاطِ ۗ وَكَذَلِكَ نَجْزِي الْمُجْرِمِينَ ۝

لَهُمْ مِنْ جَهَنَّمَ مِهَادٌ وَمِنْ فَوْقِهِمْ غَوَاشٍ ۚ وَكَذَلِكَ نَجْزِي الظَّالِمِينَ ۝

وَالَّذِينَ آمَنُوا وَعَمِلُوا الصَّالِحَاتِ لَا نُكَلِّفُ نَفْسًا إِلَّا وُسْعَهَا ۚ أُولَئِكَ أَصْحَابُ الْجَنَّةِ ۖ هُمْ فِيهَا خَالِدُونَ ۝

وَنَزَعْنَا مَا فِي صُدُورِهِمْ مِنْ غِلٍّ تَجْرِي مِنْ تَحْتِهِمُ الْأَنْهَارُ ۖ وَقَالُوا الْحَمْدُ لِلَّهِ الَّذِي هَدَانَا لِهَذَا وَمَا كُنَّا لِنَهْتَدِيَ لَوْلَا أَنْ هَدَانَا اللَّهُ ۖ لَقَدْ جَاءَتْ رُسُلُ رَبِّنَا بِالْحَقِّ ۖ وَنُودُوا أَنْ تِلْكُمُ الْجَنَّةُ أُورِثْتُمُوهَا بِمَا كُنْتُمْ تَعْمَلُونَ ۝

وَنَادَى أَصْحَابُ الْجَنَّةِ أَصْحَابَ النَّارِ أَنْ قَدْ وَجَدْنَا مَا وَعَدَنَا رَبُّنَا حَقًّا فَهَلْ وَجَدْتُمْ مَا وَعَدَ رَبُّكُمْ حَقًّا ۖ قَالُوا نَعَمْ ۚ فَأَذَّنَ

a Crier shall proclaim between them: "The curse of Allah is on the wrong-doers;-

45. "Those who would hinder (men) from the path of Allah and would seek in it something crooked: they were those who denied the Hereafter."

46. Between them shall be a veil, and on the Heights will be men who would know every one by his marks: they will call out to the Companions of the Garden, "peace on you": they will not have entered, but they will have an assurance (thereof).

47. When their eyes shall be turned towards the Companions of the Fire, they will say: "Our Lord! do not send us to the company of the wrong-doers."

48. The men on the Heights will call to certain men whom they will know from their marks, saying: "Of what profit to you were your hoards and your arrogant ways?

49. "Behold! are these not the men whom you swore that Allah would never bless with His Mercy? you enter the Garden: no fear shall be on you, nor shall you grieve."

50. The Companions of the Fire will call to the Companions of the Garden: "Pour down to us water or anything that Allah provides for your sustenance." They will say: "Allah has forbidden both these things to those who rejected Him."

51. "Such as took their religion to be mere amusement and play, and were deceived by the life of the world." That day

We shall forget them as they forgot the meeting of this day of theirs, and as they were wont to reject Our Signs.

52. For We had certainly sent to them a Book, based on knowledge, which We explained in detail,- a guide and a mercy to all who believe.

53. Do they just wait for the final fulfilment of the event? On the day the event is finally fulfilled, those who disregarded it before will say: "The Apostles of our Lord did indeed bring true (tidings). Have we no intercessors now to intercede on our behalf? Or could we be sent back? Then should we behave differently from our behaviour in the past." In fact they will have lost their souls, and the things they invented will leave them in the lurch.

54. Your Guardian-Lord is Allah, Who created the heavens and the earth in six Days, and is firmly established on the Throne (of authority): He draws the night as a veil over the day, each seeking the other in rapid succession: He created the sun, the moon, and the stars, (all) governed by laws under His Command. Is it not His to create and to govern? Blessed be Allah, the Cherisher and Sustainer of the Worlds.

55. Call on your Lord with humility and in private: for Allah does not love those who trespass beyond bounds.

56. Do no mischief on the earth, after it has been set in order, but call on Him with fear and longing (in your hearts): for the Mercy of Allah is (always) near to those who do good.

57. It is He Who sends the winds like heralds of glad tidings, going before His mercy: when

نَنْسَاهُمْ كَمَا نَسُوا لِقَاءَ يَوْمِهِمْ هٰذَا ٢١

وَمَا كَانُوا بِاٰيٰتِنَا يَجْحَدُونَ ۝

وَلَقَدْ جِئْنٰهُمْ بِكِتٰبٍ فَصَّلْنٰهُ عَلٰى عِلْمٍ

هُدًى وَّرَحْمَةً لِّقَوْمٍ يُّؤْمِنُونَ ۝

هَلْ يَنْظُرُونَ إِلَّا تَأْوِيلَهُ يَوْمَ

يَأْتِي تَأْوِيلُهُ يَقُولُ الَّذِينَ نَسُوهُ

مِنْ قَبْلُ قَدْ جَاءَتْ رُسُلُ رَبِّنَا

بِالْحَقِّ فَهَلْ لَّنَا مِنْ شُفَعَاءَ

فَيَشْفَعُوا لَنَا أَوْ نُرَدُّ فَنَعْمَلَ غَيْرَ

الَّذِي كُنَّا نَعْمَلُ قَدْ خَسِرُوا

أَنْفُسَهُمْ وَضَلَّ عَنْهُمْ مَّا كَانُوا

يَفْتَرُونَ ۝

إِنَّ رَبَّكُمُ اللَّهُ الَّذِي خَلَقَ السَّمٰوٰتِ

وَالْأَرْضَ فِي سِتَّةِ أَيَّامٍ ثُمَّ اسْتَوٰى

عَلَى الْعَرْشِ يُغْشِي اللَّيْلَ النَّهَارَ

يَطْلُبُهُ حَثِيثًا وَّالشَّمْسَ وَالْقَمَرَ

وَالنُّجُومَ مُسَخَّرٰتٍ بِأَمْرِهِ أَلَا لَهُ

الْخَلْقُ وَالْأَمْرُ تَبَارَكَ اللَّهُ رَبُّ

الْعٰلَمِينَ ۝

اُدْعُوا رَبَّكُمْ تَضَرُّعًا وَّخُفْيَةً

إِنَّهُ لَا يُحِبُّ الْمُعْتَدِينَ ۝

وَلَا تُفْسِدُوا فِي الْأَرْضِ بَعْدَ إِصْلَاحِهَا

وَادْعُوهُ خَوْفًا وَّطَمَعًا إِنَّ رَحْمَتَ

اللَّهِ قَرِيبٌ مِّنَ الْمُحْسِنِينَ ۝

وَهُوَ الَّذِي يُرْسِلُ الرِّيٰحَ بُشْرًا

بَيْنَ يَدَيْ رَحْمَتِهِ حَتّٰى إِذَا

they have carried the heavy-laden clouds, We drive them to a land that is dead, make rain to descend thereon, and produce every kind of harvest therewith: thus shall We raise up the dead: perchance you may remember.

58. From the land that is clean and good, by the Will of its Cherisher, springs up produce, (rich) after its kind: but from the land that is bad, springs up nothing but that which is niggardly: thus do We explain the Signs by various (symbols) to those who are grateful.

59. We sent Noah to his people. He said: "O my people! worship Allah! you have no other god but Him. I fear for you the punishment of a dreadful Day!

60. The leaders of his people said: "Ah! we see you evidently wandering (in mind)."

61. He said: "O my people! no wandering is there in my (mind): on the contrary I am an Apostle from the Lord and Cherisher of the Worlds!

62. "I but fulfil towards you the duties of my Lord's mission: sincere is my advice to you, and I know from Allah something that you do not know.

63. "Do you wonder that there has come to you a message from your Lord, through a man of your own people, to warn you,-so that you may fear Allah and haply receive His Mercy?"

64. But they rejected him, and We delivered him, and those with him, in the Ark: but We overwhelmed in the Flood those who rejected Our Signs. They were indeed a blind people!

65. To the 'Ad people, (We sent) Hud, one of their (own) brethren: he said:

O my people! worship Allah! you have no other god but Him, will you not fear (Allah)?"

يٰقَوْمِ اعْبُدُوا اللّٰهَ مَا لَكُمْ مِّنْ اِلٰهٍ غَيْرُهٗ ۚ اَفَلَا تَتَّقُوْنَ ۞

66.   The leaders of the Unbelievers among his people said: "Ah! we see you are an imbecile!" and "We think you are a liar!"

قَالَ الْمَلَاُ الَّذِيْنَ كَفَرُوْا مِنْ قَوْمِهٖ اِنَّا لَنَرٰىكَ فِيْ سَفَاهَةٍ وَّ اِنَّا لَنَظُنُّكَ مِنَ الْكٰذِبِيْنَ ۞

67.   He said: "O my people! I am no imbecile, but (I am) an Apostle from the Lord and Cherisher of the worlds!

قَالَ يٰقَوْمِ لَيْسَ بِيْ سَفَاهَةٌ وَّ لٰكِنِّيْ رَسُوْلٌ مِّنْ رَّبِّ الْعٰلَمِيْنَ

68.   "I but fulfil towards you the duties of my Lord's mission: I am to you a sincere and trustworthy adviser.

اُبَلِّغُكُمْ رِسٰلٰتِ رَبِّيْ وَاَنَا لَكُمْ نَاصِحٌ اَمِيْنٌ ۞

69.   "Do you wonder that there has come to you a message from your Lord through a man of your own people, to warn you? Call in remembrance that He made you inheritors after the people of Noah, and gave you a stature tall among the nations. Call in remembrance the benefits (you have received) from Allah: that so you may prosper."

اَوَعَجِبْتُمْ اَنْ جَآءَكُمْ ذِكْرٌ مِّنْ رَّبِّكُمْ عَلٰى رَجُلٍ مِّنْكُمْ لِيُنْذِرَكُمْ ۚ وَاذْكُرُوْا اِذْ جَعَلَكُمْ خُلَفَآءَ مِنْ بَعْدِ قَوْمِ نُوْحٍ وَّزَادَكُمْ فِي الْخَلْقِ بَصْۜطَةً ۚ فَاذْكُرُوْا اٰلَآءَ اللّٰهِ لَعَلَّكُمْ تُفْلِحُوْنَ ۞

70.   They said: "Do you come to us that we may worship Allah alone, and give up the cult of our fathers? Bring us what you threaten us with, if so be that you tell the truth!"

قَالُوْا اَجِئْتَنَا لِنَعْبُدَ اللّٰهَ وَحْدَهٗ وَنَذَرَ مَا كَانَ يَعْبُدُ اٰبَآؤُنَا ۚ فَأْتِنَا بِمَا تَعِدُنَآ اِنْ كُنْتَ مِنَ الصّٰدِقِيْنَ ۞

71.   He said: "Punishment and wrath have already come upon you from your Lord: do you dispute with me over names which you have devised - you and your fathers,- without authority from Allah? Then wait: I am amongst you, also waiting."

قَالَ قَدْ وَقَعَ عَلَيْكُمْ مِّنْ رَّبِّكُمْ رِجْسٌ وَّغَضَبٌ ۚ اَتُجَادِلُوْنَنِيْ فِيْ اَسْمَآءٍ سَمَّيْتُمُوْهَآ اَنْتُمْ وَ اٰبَآؤُكُمْ مَّا نَزَّلَ اللّٰهُ بِهَا مِنْ سُلْطٰنٍ ۚ فَانْتَظِرُوْا اِنِّيْ مَعَكُمْ مِّنَ الْمُنْتَظِرِيْنَ ۞

72.   We saved him and those who adhered to him,

فَاَنْجَيْنٰهُ وَالَّذِيْنَ مَعَهٗ بِرَحْمَةٍ

by Our Mercy, and We cut off the roots of those who rejected Our Signs and did not believe.

مِنَّا وَقَطَعْنَا دَابِرَ الَّذِينَ كَذَّبُوا بِـَٔايَٰتِنَا وَمَا كَانُوا مُؤْمِنِينَ ۝

73. To the Thamud people (We sent) Salih, one of their own brethren: He said: "O my people! worship Allah: you have no other god but Him. Now has come to you a clear (Sign) from your Lord! This she-camel of Allah is a Sign to you: so leave her to graze in Allah's earth, and let her come to no harm, or you shall be seized with a grievous punishment.

وَإِلَىٰ ثَمُودَ أَخَاهُمْ صَٰلِحًا قَالَ يَٰقَوْمِ اعْبُدُوا اللَّهَ مَا لَكُم مِّنْ إِلَٰهٍ غَيْرُهُ قَدْ جَآءَتْكُم بَيِّنَةٌ مِّن رَّبِّكُمْ هَٰذِهِ نَاقَةُ اللَّهِ لَكُمْ ءَايَةً فَذَرُوهَا تَأْكُلْ فِىٓ أَرْضِ اللَّهِ وَلَا تَمَسُّوهَا بِسُوٓءٍ فَيَأْخُذَكُمْ عَذَابٌ أَلِيمٌ ۝

74. "And remember how He made you inheritors after the 'Ad people and gave you habitations in the land: you build for yourselves palaces and castles in (open) plains, and carve out homes in the mountains; so bring to remembrance the benefits (you have received) from Allah, and refrain from evil and mischief on the earth."

وَاذْكُرُوٓا إِذْ جَعَلَكُمْ خُلَفَآءَ مِنۢ بَعْدِ عَادٍ وَبَوَّأَكُمْ فِى الْأَرْضِ تَتَّخِذُونَ مِن سُهُولِهَا قُصُورًا وَتَنْحِتُونَ الْجِبَالَ بُيُوتًا فَاذْكُرُوٓا ءَالَآءَ اللَّهِ وَلَا تَعْثَوْا فِى الْأَرْضِ مُفْسِدِينَ ۝

75. The leaders of the arrogant party among his people said to those who were reckoned powerless - those among them who believed: "Do you know indeed that Salih is an Apostle from his Lord?" They said: "We do indeed believe in the revelation which has been sent through him."

قَالَ الْمَلَأُ الَّذِينَ اسْتَكْبَرُوا مِن قَوْمِهِ لِلَّذِينَ اسْتُضْعِفُوا لِمَنْ ءَامَنَ مِنْهُمْ أَتَعْلَمُونَ أَنَّ صَٰلِحًا مُّرْسَلٌ مِّن رَّبِّهِ قَالُوٓا إِنَّا بِمَآ أُرْسِلَ بِهِ مُؤْمِنُونَ ۝

76. The arrogant party said: "For our part, we reject what you believe in."

قَالَ الَّذِينَ اسْتَكْبَرُوٓا إِنَّا بِالَّذِىٓ ءَامَنتُم بِهِ كَٰفِرُونَ ۝

77. Then they ham-strung the she-camel, and insolently defied the order of their Lord, saying: "O Salih! bring about your threats, if you are an Apostle (of Allah)!"

فَعَقَرُوا النَّاقَةَ وَعَتَوْا عَنْ أَمْرِ رَبِّهِمْ وَقَالُوا يَٰصَٰلِحُ ائْتِنَا بِمَا تَعِدُنَآ إِن كُنتَ مِنَ الْمُرْسَلِينَ ۝

78. So the earthquake took them unawares, and they lay

فَأَخَذَتْهُمُ الرَّجْفَةُ فَأَصْبَحُوا فِى

prostrate in their homes in the morning!

79. So Salih left them, saying: "O my people! I did indeed convey to you the message for which I was sent by my Lord: I gave you good counsel, but you do not love good counsellors!"

80. We also (sent) Lut: he said to his people: "Do you commit lewdness such as no people in creation (ever) committed before you?

81. "For you practise your lusts on men in preference to women : you are indeed a people transgressing beyond bounds."

82. And his people gave no answer but this: they said, "Drive them out of your city: these are indeed men who want to be clean and pure!"

83. But We saved him and his family, except his wife: she was of those who lagged behind.

84. And We rained down on them a shower (of brimstone): then see what was the end of those who indulged in sin and crime!

85. To the Madyan people We sent Shu'aib, one of their own brethren: he said: "O my people! worship Allah; you have no other god but Him. Now has come unto you a clear (Sign) from your Lord! so give just measure and weight, nor withhold from the people the things that are their due; and do no mischief on the earth after it has been set in order: that will be best for you, if you have Faith.

86. "And do not squat on every road, breathing threats, hindering from the path of Allah those who believe in Him, and seeking in it something crooked;

but remember how you were small in numbers, and He gave you increase. And hold in your mind's eye what was the end of those who did mischief.

87. "And if there is a party among you who believes in the Message with which I have been sent, and a party which does not believe, hold yourselves in patience until Allah decides between us: for He is the best to decide.

88. The leaders, the arrogant party among his people, said: "O Shu'aib! we shall certainly drive you out of our city - (you) and those who believe with you; or else you (and they) shall have to return to our ways and religion." He said: "What! even though we do detest (them)?

89. "We should indeed invent a lie against Allah, if we returned to your ways after Allah has rescued us therefrom; nor could we by any manner of means return thereto unless it be as in the will and plan of Allah, our Lord. Our Lord can reach out to the utmost recesses of things by His knowledge. In Allah is our trust. Our Lord! You decide between us and our people in truth, for You are the best to decide."

90. The leaders, the Unbelievers among his people, said: "If you follow Shu'aib, be sure then you are ruined!"

91. But the earthquake took them unawares, and they lay prostrate in their homes before the morning!

92. The men who rejected Shu'aib became as if they had never been in the homes where they had flourished: the men who rejected Shu'aib - it was they who were ruined!

93. So Shu'aib left them, saying: "O my people! I did indeed

اذْكُرُوا اِذْ كُنْتُمْ قَلِيْلًا فَكَثَّرَكُمْ ۖ وَانْظُرُوْا كَيْفَ كَانَ عَاقِبَةُ الْمُفْسِدِيْنَ ۝

وَاِنْ كَانَ طَآئِفَةٌ مِّنْكُمْ اٰمَنُوْا بِالَّذِيْ اُرْسِلْتُ بِهٖ وَطَآئِفَةٌ لَّمْ يُؤْمِنُوْا فَاصْبِرُوْا حَتّٰى يَحْكُمَ اللّٰهُ بَيْنَنَا ۚ وَهُوَ خَيْرُ الْحٰكِمِيْنَ ۝

قَالَ الْمَلَاُ الَّذِيْنَ اسْتَكْبَرُوْا مِنْ قَوْمِهٖ لَنُخْرِجَنَّكَ يٰشُعَيْبُ وَالَّذِيْنَ اٰمَنُوْا مَعَكَ مِنْ قَرْيَتِنَآ اَوْ لَتَعُوْدُنَّ فِيْ مِلَّتِنَا ۗ قَالَ اَوَلَوْ كُنَّا كٰرِهِيْنَ ۝

قَدِ افْتَرَيْنَا عَلَى اللّٰهِ كَذِبًا اِنْ عُدْنَا فِيْ مِلَّتِكُمْ بَعْدَ اِذْ نَجّٰىنَا اللّٰهُ مِنْهَا ۗ وَمَا يَكُوْنُ لَنَآ اَنْ نَّعُوْدَ فِيْهَآ اِلَّآ اَنْ يَّشَآءَ اللّٰهُ رَبُّنَا ۗ وَسِعَ رَبُّنَا كُلَّ شَيْءٍ عِلْمًا ۗ عَلَى اللّٰهِ تَوَكَّلْنَا ۗ رَبَّنَا افْتَحْ بَيْنَنَا وَبَيْنَ قَوْمِنَا بِالْحَقِّ وَاَنْتَ خَيْرُ الْفٰتِحِيْنَ ۝

وَقَالَ الْمَلَاُ الَّذِيْنَ كَفَرُوْا مِنْ قَوْمِهٖ لَئِنِ اتَّبَعْتُمْ شُعَيْبًا اِنَّكُمْ اِذًا لَّخٰسِرُوْنَ ۝

فَاَخَذَتْهُمُ الرَّجْفَةُ فَاَصْبَحُوْا فِيْ دَارِهِمْ جٰثِمِيْنَ ۝

الَّذِيْنَ كَذَّبُوْا شُعَيْبًا كَاَنْ لَّمْ يَغْنَوْا فِيْهَا ۖ الَّذِيْنَ كَذَّبُوْا شُعَيْبًا كَانُوْا هُمُ الْخٰسِرِيْنَ ۝

فَتَوَلّٰى عَنْهُمْ وَقَالَ يٰقَوْمِ لَقَدْ

convey to you the Messages for which I was sent by my Lord: I gave you good counsel, but how shall I lament over a people who refuse to believe!"

94. Whenever We sent a prophet to a town, We took up its people in suffering and adversity, in order that they might learn humility.

95. Then We changed their suffering into prosperity, until they grew and multiplied, and began to say: "Our fathers (too) were touched by suffering and affluence" ... Behold! We called them to account of a sudden, while they did not realise (their peril).

96. If the people of the towns had but believed and feared Allah, We should indeed have opened out to them (all kinds of) blessings from heaven and earth; but they rejected (the truth), and We brought them to book for their misdeeds.

97. Did the people of the towns feel secure against the coming of Our wrath by night while they were asleep?

98. Or else did they feel secure against its coming in broad daylight while they played about (care-free)?

99. Did they then feel secure against the Plan of Allah?- but no one can feel secure from the Plan of Allah, except those (doomed) to ruin!

100. To those who inherit the earth in succession to its (previous) possessors, is it not a guiding, (lesson) that, if We so willed, We could punish them (too) for their sins, and seal up their hearts so that they could not hear?

101. Such were the towns whose story We (thus) relate unto you: there came indeed to them their Apostles with clear (Signs): But they would not believe what

أَبْلِغُكُمْ رِسَالَاتِ رَبِّى وَنَصَحْتُ لَكُمْ وَلٰكِنْ لَّا تُحِبُّونَ النَّاصِحِينَ ۝

فَكَيْفَ اٰسٰى عَلٰى قَوْمٍ كٰفِرِينَ ۝

وَمَاۤ اَرْسَلْنَا فِىۡ قَرْيَةٍ مِّنۡ نَّبِىٍّ اِلَّاۤ اَخَذْنَاۤ اَهْلَهَا بِالْبَاْسَاۤءِ وَالضَّرَّاۤءِ لَعَلَّهُمْ يَضَّرَّعُوۡنَ ۝

ثُمَّ بَدَّلْنَا مَكَانَ السَّيِّئَةِ الْحَسَنَةَ حَتّٰى عَفَوْا وَّقَالُوۡا قَدْ مَسَّ اٰبَاۤءَنَا الضَّرَّاۤءُ وَالسَّرَّاۤءُ فَاَخَذْنٰهُمۡ بَغْتَةً وَّهُمْ لَا يَشْعُرُوۡنَ ۝

وَلَوْ اَنَّ اَهْلَ الْقُرٰۤى اٰمَنُوۡا وَاتَّقَوْا لَفَتَحْنَا عَلَيْهِمۡ بَرَكٰتٍ مِّنَ السَّمَاۤءِ وَالْاَرْضِ وَلٰكِنۡ كَذَّبُوۡا فَاَخَذْنٰهُمۡ بِمَا كَانُوۡا يَكْسِبُوۡنَ ۝

اَفَاَمِنَ اَهْلُ الْقُرٰۤى اَنۡ يَّاْتِيَهُمۡ بَاْسُنَا بَيَاتًا وَّهُمْ نَاۤئِمُوۡنَ ۝

اَوَاَمِنَ اَهْلُ الْقُرٰۤى اَنۡ يَّاْتِيَهُمۡ بَاْسُنَا ضُحًى وَّهُمْ يَلْعَبُوۡنَ ۝

اَفَاَمِنُوۡا مَكْرَ اللّٰهِ ۚ فَلَا يَاْمَنُ مَكْرَ اللّٰهِ اِلَّا الْقَوْمُ الْخٰسِرُوۡنَ ۝

اَوَلَمْ يَهْدِ لِلَّذِيۡنَ يَرِثُوۡنَ الْاَرْضَ مِنۡ بَعْدِ اَهْلِهَاۤ اَنۡ لَّوْ نَشَاۤءُ اَصَبْنٰهُمۡ بِذُنُوۡبِهِمۡ ۚ وَنَطْبَعُ عَلٰى قُلُوۡبِهِمۡ فَهُمْ لَا يَسْمَعُوۡنَ ۝

تِلْكَ الْقُرٰى نَقُصُّ عَلَيْكَ مِنۡ اَنۡبَاۤئِهَا ۚ وَلَقَدۡ جَاۤءَتْهُمۡ رُسُلُهُمۡ بِالْبَيِّنٰتِ ۚ فَمَا كَانُوۡا لِيُؤْمِنُوۡا بِمَا

they had rejected before. Thus does Allah seal up the hearts of those who reject Faith.

102. Most of the men We did not find (true) to their covenant: but most of them We found rebellious and disobedient.

103. Then after them We sent Moses with Our Signs to Pharaoh and his chiefs, but they wrongfully rejected them: So see what was the end of those who made mischief.

104. Moses said: "O Pharaoh! I am an Apostle from the Lord of the worlds,-

105. One for whom it is right to say nothing but truth about Allah. Now I have come to you (people), from your Lord, with a clear (Sign): So let the Children of Israel depart along with me."

106. (Pharaoh) said: "If indeed you have come with a Sign, show it forth,- if you are telling the truth."

107. Then (Moses) threw his rod, and behold! it was a serpent, plain (for all to see)!

108. And he drew out his hand, and behold! it was white to all beholders!

109. Said the Chiefs of the people of Pharaoh: "This is indeed a sorcerer well-versed.

110. "His plan is to get you out of your land: then what is it you counsel?"

111. They said: "Keep him and his brother in suspense (for a while); and send to the cities men to collect-

112. And bring up to you all (our) sorcerers well-versed."

113. So there came the sorcerers to Pharaoh: they said, "of course we shall have a (suitable) reward if we win!"

114. He said: "Yes, (and more),- for you shall in that case be (raised to posts) nearest (to my person)."

115. They said: "O Moses! will you throw (first), or shall we have the (first) throw?"

116. Said Moses: "You throw (first)." So when they threw, they bewitched the eyes of the people, and struck terror into them: for they showed a great (feat of) magic.

117. We put it into Moses's mind by inspiration: "Throw (now) your rod": and behold! it swallows up straightway all the falsehoods which they fake!

118. Thus truth was confirmed, and all that they did was made of no effect.

119. So the (great ones) were vanquished there and then, and were made to look small.

120. But the sorcerers fell down prostrate in adoration.

121. Saying: "We believe in the Lord of the Worlds,-

122. "The Lord of Moses and Aaron."

123. Said Pharaoh: "Do you believe in Him before I give you permission? Surely this is a trick which you have planned in the city to drive out its people: but soon you shall know (the consequences).

124. "Be sure I will cut off your hands and your feet on opposite sides, and I will cause you all to die on the cross."

125. They said: "For us, we are but sent back to our Lord:

126. "But you wreak your vengeance on us simply because we believed in the Signs of our Lord when they reached us! Our Lord! pour out on us patience and constancy, and take our souls unto You as Muslims (who bow to Your Will)!

127. Said the chiefs of Pharaoh's people:" Will you leave Moses and his people, to spread mischief in the land, and to abandon you and your gods?" He said:

قَالُوا يَمُوسَى إِمَّا أَن تُلْقِىَ وَإِمَّا أَن نَّكُونَ نَحْنُ الْمُلْقِينَ ۝

قَالَ أَلْقُوا فَلَمَّا أَلْقَوْا سَحَرُوا أَعْيُنَ النَّاسِ وَاسْتَرْهَبُوهُمْ وَجَاءُو بِسِحْرٍ عَظِيمٍ ۝

وَأَوْحَيْنَا إِلَى مُوسَى أَنْ أَلْقِ عَصَاكَ فَإِذَا هِىَ تَلْقَفُ مَا يَأْفِكُونَ ۝

فَوَقَعَ الْحَقُّ وَبَطَلَ مَا كَانُوا يَعْمَلُونَ ۝

فَغُلِبُوا هُنَالِكَ وَانقَلَبُوا صَاغِرِينَ ۝

وَأُلْقِيَ السَّحَرَةُ سَاجِدِينَ ۝

قَالُوا آمَنَّا بِرَبِّ الْعَالَمِينَ ۝

رَبِّ مُوسَى وَهَارُونَ ۝

قَالَ فِرْعَوْنُ آمَنتُم بِهِ قَبْلَ أَنْ آذَنَ لَكُمْ إِنَّ هَذَا لَمَكْرٌ مَّكَرْتُمُوهُ فِى الْمَدِينَةِ لِتُخْرِجُوا مِنْهَا أَهْلَهَا فَسَوْفَ تَعْلَمُونَ ۝

لَأُقَطِّعَنَّ أَيْدِيَكُمْ وَأَرْجُلَكُم مِّنْ خِلَافٍ ثُمَّ لَأُصَلِّبَنَّكُمْ أَجْمَعِينَ ۝

قَالُوا إِنَّا إِلَى رَبِّنَا مُنقَلِبُونَ ۝

وَمَا تَنقِمُ مِنَّا إِلَّا أَنْ آمَنَّا بِآيَاتِ رَبِّنَا لَمَّا جَاءَتْنَا رَبَّنَا أَفْرِغْ عَلَيْنَا صَبْرًا وَتَوَفَّنَا مُسْلِمِينَ ۝

وَقَالَ الْمَلَأُ مِن قَوْمِ فِرْعَوْنَ أَتَذَرُ مُوسَى وَقَوْمَهُ لِيُفْسِدُوا فِى الْأَرْضِ وَيَذَرَكَ وَآلِهَتَكَ قَالَ

"We will slay their male children; we will save alive (only)
their females; and we have
irresistible (power) over them."

128. Moses said to his people:
"Pray for help from Allah, and
(wait) in patience and
constancy: for the earth is
Allah's, to give as a heritage to
such of His servants as He
pleases; and the end is (best) for
the righteous.

129. They said: "We have had
(nothing but) trouble, both
before and after you came to
us." He said: "It may be that
your Lord will destroy your
enemy and make you inheritors
in the earth; that so He may try
you by your deeds."

130. We punished the people of
Pharaoh with years (of drought)
and shortness of crops; that they
might receive admonition.

131. But when good (times)
came, they said, "This is due to
us;" when gripped by calamity,
they ascribed it to evil omens
connected with Moses and those
with him! Behold! in truth the
omens of evil are theirs in
Allah's sight, but most of them
do not understand!

132. They said (to Moses):
"Whatever be the Signs you
bring, to work therewith your
sorcery on us, we shall never
believe in you.

133. So We sent (plagues) on
them: wholesale Death,
Locusts, Lice, Frogs, and
Blood: Signs openly self-
explained: but they were
steeped in arrogance,- a people
given to sin.

134. Every time the Chastisement fell on them, they said: "O
Moses!

on our behalf call on your Lord in virtue of His promise to you: If you will remove the Chastisement from us, we shall truly believe in you, and we shall send away the Children of Israel with you."

135. But every time We removed the plague from them according to a fixed term which they had to fulfil,- Behold! they broke their word!

136. So We exacted retribution from them: We drowned them in the sea, because they rejected Our Signs and failed to take warning from them.

137. And We made a people, considered weak (and of no account), inheritors of lands in both East and West, - lands whereon We sent down Our blessings. The fair promise of your Lord was fulfilled for the Children of Israel, because they had patience and constancy, and We levelled to the ground the great works and fine buildings which Pharaoh and his people erected (with such pride).

138. We took the Children of Israel (with safety) across the sea. They came upon a people devoted entirely to some idols they had. They said: "O Moses! fashion for us a god like the gods they have." He said: "Surely you are a people without knowledge.

139. "As to these folks,- the cult they are in is (but) a fragment of a ruin, and vain is the (worship) which they practise."

140. He said: "Shall I seek for you a god other than the (true) God, when it is Allah Who has endowed you with gifts above the nations?"

141. And remember We rescued you from Pharaoh's people, who afflicted you with the worst of penalties, Who slew

your male children and saved alive your females: in that was a momentous trial from your Lord.

142. We appointed for Moses thirty nights, and completed (the period) with ten (more): thus was completed the term (of communion) with his Lord, forty nights. And Moses had charged his brother Aaron (before he went up): "Act for me amongst my people: do right, and do not follow the way of those who do mischief."

143. When Moses came to the place appointed by Us, and his Lord addressed him, he said: "O my Lord! show (Yourself) to me, that I may look upon You." Allah said: "By no means can you see Me (direct); But look upon the Mount; if it abide in its place, then shall you see Me." When his Lord manifested His glory on the Mount, He made it as dust, and Moses fell down in a swoon. When he recovered his senses he said: "Glory be to You! To You I turn in repentance, and I am the first to believe."

144. (Allah) said: "O Moses! I have chosen you above (other) men, by the mission I (have given you) and the words I (have spoken to you): take then the (revelation) which I give you, and be of those who give thanks."

145. And We ordained laws for him in the Tablets in all matters, both commanding and explaining all things, (and said): "Take and hold these with firmness, and enjoin your people to hold fast by the best in the precepts: soon shall I show you the homes of the wicked,- (how they lie desolate)."

146. Those who behave arrogantly on the earth in defiance of right - I will turn them away from My Signs: Even if they see all the Signs, they will not believe in them;

and if they see the way of right
conduct, they will not adopt it as
the way; but if they see the way
of error, that is the way they will
adopt. For they have rejected
Our Signs, and failed to take
warning from them.

147. Those who reject Our
Signs and the Meeting in the
Hereafter,- vain are their deeds:
can they expect to be rewarded
except as they have wrought?

148. The people of Moses
made, in his absence, out of their
ornaments, the image of a calf,
(for worship) having lowing
sound. Did they not see that it
could neither speak to them, nor
show them the way? They took it
for worship and they did wrong.

149. When they repented, and
saw that they had erred, they
said: "If our Lord have not
mercy upon us and forgive us,
we shall indeed be of those who
perish."

150. When Moses came back to
his people, angry and grieved,
he said: "Evil it is that you have
done in my place in my absence:
did you make haste to bring on
the judgment of your Lord?" He
put down the Tablets, seized his
brother by (the hair of) his head,
and dragged him to him. Aaron
said: "Son of my mother! The
people did indeed reckon me as
nothing, and went near to
slaying me! Make not the
enemies rejoice over my
misfortune, nor count you me
amongst the people of sin."

151. Moses prayed: "O my
Lord! forgive me and my
brother! Admit us to Your mercy!
for You are the Most Merciful of
those who show mercy!"

152. Those who took the calf
(for worship) will indeed be

overwhelmed with wrath from their Lord, and with shame in this life: thus do We recompense those who invent (falsehoods).

153. But those who do wrong but repent thereafter and (truly) believe,- verily your Lord is thereafter Oft-forgiving, Most Merciful.

154. When the anger of Moses was appeased, he took up the Tablets: in the writing thereon was Guidance and Mercy for such as fear their Lord.

155. And Moses chose seventy of his people for Our place of meeting: when they were seized with violent quaking, he prayed: "O my Lord! if it had been Your Will You could have destroyed, long before, both them and me: would You destroy us for the deeds of the foolish ones among us? this is no more than Your trial: by it You cause whom You will to stray, and You lead whom You will into the right path. You are our Protector: so forgive us and give us Your Mercy; for You are the best of those who forgive.

156. "And ordain for us that which is good, in this life and in the Hereafter: for we have turned unto You." He said: "With My punishment I visit whom I will; but My Mercy extends to all things. That (Mercy) I shall ordain for those who do right, and pay Zakat, and those who believe in Our Signs;-

157. "Those who follow the Apostle, the unlettered Prophet,

غَضَبٌ مِّنۡ رَّبِّهِمۡ وَذِلَّةٌ فِى الۡحَيٰوةِ الدُّنۡيَا ۚ وَكَذٰلِكَ نَجۡزِى الۡمُفۡتَرِيۡنَ ۞

وَالَّذِيۡنَ عَمِلُوا السَّيِّاٰتِ ثُمَّ تَابُوۡا مِنۡ بَعۡدِهَا وَاٰمَنُوۡۤا ۙ اِنَّ رَبَّكَ مِنۡۢ بَعۡدِهَا لَغَفُوۡرٌ رَّحِيۡمٌ ۞

وَلَمَّا سَكَتَ عَنۡ مُّوۡسَى الۡغَضَبُ اَخَذَ الۡاَلۡوَاحَ ۚ وَفِىۡ نُسۡخَتِهَا هُدًى وَّرَحۡمَةٌ لِّلَّذِيۡنَ هُمۡ لِرَبِّهِمۡ يَرۡهَبُوۡنَ ۞

وَاخۡتَارَ مُوۡسٰى قَوۡمَهٗ سَبۡعِيۡنَ رَجُلًا لِّمِيۡقَاتِنَا ۚ فَلَمَّاۤ اَخَذَتۡهُمُ الرَّجۡفَةُ قَالَ رَبِّ لَوۡ شِئۡتَ اَهۡلَكۡتَهُمۡ مِّنۡ قَبۡلُ وَاِيَّاىَ ۚ اَتُهۡلِكُنَا بِمَا فَعَلَ السُّفَهَاۤءُ مِنَّا ۚ اِنۡ هِىَ اِلَّا فِتۡنَتُكَ ۚ تُضِلُّ بِهَا مَنۡ تَشَاۤءُ وَتَهۡدِىۡ مَنۡ تَشَاۤءُ ۚ اَنۡتَ وَلِيُّنَا فَاغۡفِرۡ لَنَا وَارۡحَمۡنَا وَاَنۡتَ خَيۡرُ الۡغٰفِرِيۡنَ ۞

وَاكۡتُبۡ لَنَا فِىۡ هٰذِهِ الدُّنۡيَا حَسَنَةً وَّفِى الۡاٰخِرَةِ اِنَّا هُدۡنَاۤ اِلَيۡكَ ۚ قَالَ عَذَابِىۡۤ اُصِيۡبُ بِهٖ مَنۡ اَشَاۤءُ ۚ وَرَحۡمَتِىۡ وَسِعَتۡ كُلَّ شَىۡءٍ ۚ فَسَاَكۡتُبُهَا لِلَّذِيۡنَ يَتَّقُوۡنَ وَيُؤۡتُوۡنَ الزَّكٰوةَ وَالَّذِيۡنَ هُمۡ بِاٰيٰتِنَا يُؤۡمِنُوۡنَ ۞

اَلَّذِيۡنَ يَتَّبِعُوۡنَ الرَّسُوۡلَ النَّبِىَّ

whom they find mentioned in their own (Scriptures),- in theTourat and the Gospel;- for he commands them what is just and forbids them what is evil; he allows them as lawful what is good (and pure) and prohibits them from what is bad (and impure); He releases them from their heavy burdens and from the yokes that are upon them. So it is those who believe in him, honour him, help him, and follow the Light which is sent down with him,- it is they who will prosper."

158. Say: "O men! I am sent to you all, as the Apostle of Allah, to Whom belongs the dominion of the heavens and the earth: there is no god but He: it is He that gives both life and death. So believe in Allah and His Apostle, the unlettered Prophet, who believes in Allah and His Words: follow him that (so) you may be guided."

159. Of the people of Moses there is a section who guide and do justice in the light of truth.

160. We divided them into twelve tribes or nations. We directed Moses by inspiration, when his (thirsty) people asked him for water: "Strike the rock with your staff": out of it there gushed forth twelve springs: each group knew its own place for water. We gave them the shade of clouds, and sent down to them manna and quails, (saying): "Eat of the good things We have provided for you": (but they rebelled); to Us they did no harm,

but they harmed their own souls.

161. And remember it was said to them: "Dwell in this town and eat therein as you wish, but say the word of humility and enter the gate in a posture of humility: We shall forgive you your faults; We shall increase (the portion of) those who do good."

162. But the transgressors among them changed the word from that which had been given them so We sent on them a plague from heaven. For that they repeatedly transgressed.

163. Ask them concerning the town standing close by the sea. Behold! they transgressed in the matter of the Sabbath. For on the day of their Sabbath their fish did come to them, openly holding up their heads, but on the day they had no Sabbath, they did not come: thus did We make a trial of them, for they were given to transgression.

164. When some of them said: "Why do you preach to a people whom Allah will destroy or visit with a terrible punishment?"- said the preachers:" To discharge our duty to your Lord, and perchance they may fear Him."

165. When they disregarded the warnings that had been given them, We rescued those who forbade evil; but We visited the wrong-doers with a grievous punishment because they were given to transgre-ssion.

166. When in their insolence they transgressed (all) prohibi-tions, We said to them: "Be you apes, despised and rejected."

167. Behold! Your Lord did declare that He would send against them, to the Day of Judgment, those who would afflict them with

وَلَـٰكِن كَانُوٓا أَنفُسَهُمۡ يَظۡلِمُونَ ۝

وَإِذۡ قِيلَ لَهُمُ ٱسۡكُنُوا۟ هَـٰذِهِ ٱلۡقَرۡيَةَ وَكُلُوا۟ مِنۡهَا حَيۡثُ شِئۡتُمۡ وَقُولُوا۟ حِطَّةٌ وَٱدۡخُلُوا۟ ٱلۡبَابَ سُجَّدٗا نَّغۡفِرۡ لَكُمۡ خَطِيٓـَٰٔتِكُمۡ ۚ سَنَزِيدُ ٱلۡمُحۡسِنِينَ ۝

فَبَدَّلَ ٱلَّذِينَ ظَلَمُوا۟ مِنۡهُمۡ قَوۡلًا غَيۡرَ ٱلَّذِي قِيلَ لَهُمۡ فَأَرۡسَلۡنَا عَلَيۡهِمۡ رِجۡزٗا مِّنَ ٱلسَّمَآءِ بِمَا كَانُوا۟ يَظۡلِمُونَ ۝

وَسۡـَٔلۡهُمۡ عَنِ ٱلۡقَرۡيَةِ ٱلَّتِي كَانَتۡ حَاضِرَةَ ٱلۡبَحۡرِ إِذۡ يَعۡدُونَ فِي ٱلسَّبۡتِ إِذۡ تَأۡتِيهِمۡ حِيتَانُهُمۡ يَوۡمَ سَبۡتِهِمۡ شُرَّعٗا وَيَوۡمَ لَا يَسۡبِتُونَ لَا تَأۡتِيهِمۡ ۚ كَذَٰلِكَ نَبۡلُوهُم بِمَا كَانُوا۟ يَفۡسُقُونَ ۝

وَإِذۡ قَالَتۡ أُمَّةٌ مِّنۡهُمۡ لِمَ تَعِظُونَ قَوۡمًا ٱللَّهُ مُهۡلِكُهُمۡ أَوۡ مُعَذِّبُهُمۡ عَذَابٗا شَدِيدٗا ۖ قَالُوا۟ مَعۡذِرَةً إِلَىٰ رَبِّكُمۡ وَلَعَلَّهُمۡ يَتَّقُونَ ۝

فَلَمَّا نَسُوا۟ مَا ذُكِّرُوا۟ بِهِۦٓ أَنجَيۡنَا ٱلَّذِينَ يَنۡهَوۡنَ عَنِ ٱلسُّوٓءِ وَأَخَذۡنَا ٱلَّذِينَ ظَلَمُوا۟ بِعَذَابِۭ بَـِٔيسِۭ بِمَا كَانُوا۟ يَفۡسُقُونَ ۝

فَلَمَّا عَتَوۡا۟ عَن مَّا نُهُوا۟ عَنۡهُ قُلۡنَا لَهُمۡ كُونُوا۟ قِرَدَةً خَـٰسِـِٔينَ ۝

وَإِذۡ تَأَذَّنَ رَبُّكَ لَيَبۡعَثَنَّ عَلَيۡهِمۡ إِلَىٰ يَوۡمِ ٱلۡقِيَـٰمَةِ مَن يَسُومُهُمۡ

grievous chastisement. Your Lord is quick in retribution, but He is also Oft-forgiving, Most Merciful.

168. We broke them up into sections on this earth. There are among them some that are the righteous, and some that are the opposite. We have tried them with both prosperity and adversity: in order that they might turn (to Us).

169. After them succeeded an (evil) generation: they inherited the Book, but they chose (for themselves) the vanities of this world, saying (for excuse): "(Everything) will be forgiven us." (Even so), if similar vanities came their way, they would (again) seize them. Was not the Covenant of the Book taken from them, that they would not ascribe to Allah anything but the truth? And they study what is in the Book. But best for the righteous is the Home in the Hereafter. Will you not understand?

170. As to those who hold fast by the Book and establish regular prayer,- never shall We suffer the reward of the righteous to perish.

171. When We shook the Mount over them, as if it had been a canopy, and they thought it was going to fall on them (We said): "Hold firmly to what We have given you, and bring (ever) to remembrance what is therein; perchance you may fear Allah."

172. When your Lord drew forth from the Children of Adam- from their loins - their descendants, and made them testify concerning themselves, (saying): "Am I not your Lord (Who cherishes and sustains you)?"- they said: "Yes! We do testify!" (This), lest you should say on the Day of Judgment: "Of this we were never mindful":

173. Or lest you should say: "Our fathers before us may have taken false gods, but we are (their) descendants after them: will You then destroy us because of the deeds of men who followed falsehood?"

174. Thus do We explain the Signs in detail; and perchance they may turn (to Us).

175. Relate to them the story of the man to whom We sent Our Signs, but he passed them by: so Satan followed him up, and he went astray.

176. If it had been Our Will, We should have elevated him with Our Signs; but he inclined to the earth, and followed his own vain desires. His similitude is that of a dog: if you attack him, he lolls out his tongue, or if you leave him alone, he (still) lolls out his tongue. That is the similitude of those who reject Our Signs; so relate the story; perchance they may reflect.

177. Evil as an example are people who reject Our Signs and wrong their own souls.

178. Whom Allah does guide,- he is on the right path: whom He rejects from His guidance,- such are the persons who perish.

179. Many are the Jinns and men We have made for Hell: they have hearts wherewith they do not understand, eyes wherewith they do not see, and ears wherewith they do not hear. They are like cattle,- nay more misguided: for they are heedless (of warning).

180. The most beautiful names belong to Allah: so call on Him by them; but shun such men as use profanity in His names: for what they do, they will soon be requited.

181. Of those We have created are people who direct (others) with truth. And dispense justice therewith.

182. Those who reject Our Signs, We shall gradually visit with punishment, in ways they perceive not;

183. Respite I will grant to them: for My scheme is strong (and unfailing).

184. Do they not reflect? Their companion is not seized with madness: he is but a perspicuous warner.

185. Do they see nothing in the kingdom of the heavens and the earth and all that Allah has created? (Do they not see) that it may well be that their terms is near drawing to an end? In what Message after this will they then believe?

186. To such as Allah rejects from His guidance, there can be no guide: He will leave them in their trespasses, wandering in distraction.

187. They ask you about the (final) Hour - when will be its appointed time? Say: "The knowledge thereof is with my Lord (alone): none but He can reveal as to when it will occur. Heavy were its burden through the heavens and the earth. Only, all of a sudden will it come to you." They ask you as if you were eager in search thereof: say: "The knowledge thereof is with Allah (alone), but most men do not know."

188. Say: "I have no power over any good or harm to myself

except as Allah wills. If I had knowledge of the unseen, I should have multiplied all good, and no evil should have touched me: I am but a warner, and a bringer of glad tidings to those who have faith."

189. It is He Who created you from a single person, and made his mate of like nature, in order that he might dwell with her (in love). When they are united, she bears a light burden and carries it about (unnoticed). When she grows heavy, they both pray to Allah their Lord, (saying): "If you give us a goodly child, we vow we shall (ever) be grateful."

190. But when He gives them a goodly child, they ascribe to others a share in the gift they have received: but Allah is Exalted high above the partners they ascribe to Him.

191. Do they indeed ascribe to Him as partners things that can create nothing, but are themselves created?

192. No aid can they give them, nor can they aid themselves!

193. If you call them to guidance, they will not obey: for you it is the same whether you call them or you hold your peace!

194. Verily those whom you call upon besides Allah are servants like you: call upon them, and let them listen to your prayer, if you are (indeed) truthful!

195. Have they feet to walk with? Or

hands to lay hold with? Or eyes to see with? Or ears to hear with? Say: "Call your 'god-partners', scheme (your worst) against me, and give me no respite!

أَيْدٍ يَبْطِشُونَ بِهَا أَمْ لَهُمْ أَعْيُنٌ يُبْصِرُونَ بِهَا أَمْ لَهُمْ آذَانٌ يَسْمَعُونَ بِهَا قُلِ ادْعُوا شُرَكَاءَكُمْ ثُمَّ كِيدُونِ فَلَا تُنْظِرُونِ ۞

196. "For my Protector is Allah, Who revealed the Book (from time to time), and He will choose and befriend the righteous.

إِنَّ وَلِيِّيَ اللَّهُ الَّذِي نَزَّلَ الْكِتَابَ وَهُوَ يَتَوَلَّى الصَّالِحِينَ ۞

197. "But those you call upon besides Him, are unable to help you, and indeed to help themselves."

وَالَّذِينَ تَدْعُونَ مِنْ دُونِهِ لَا يَسْتَطِيعُونَ نَصْرَكُمْ وَلَا أَنْفُسَهُمْ يَنْصُرُونَ ۞

198. If you call them to guidance, they do not hear. You will see them looking at you, but they do not see.

وَإِنْ تَدْعُوهُمْ إِلَى الْهُدَى لَا يَسْمَعُوا وَتَرَاهُمْ يَنْظُرُونَ إِلَيْكَ وَهُمْ لَا يُبْصِرُونَ ۞

199. Hold to forgiveness; command what is right; but turn away from the ignorant.

خُذِ الْعَفْوَ وَأْمُرْ بِالْعُرْفِ وَأَعْرِضْ عَنِ الْجَاهِلِينَ ۞

200. If a suggestion from Satan assails your (mind), seek refuge with Allah; for He hears and knows (all things).

وَإِمَّا يَنْزَغَنَّكَ مِنَ الشَّيْطَانِ نَزْغٌ فَاسْتَعِذْ بِاللَّهِ إِنَّهُ سَمِيعٌ عَلِيمٌ

201. Those who fear Allah, when a thought of evil from Satan assaults them, bring Allah to remembrance, when lo! they see (aright)!

إِنَّ الَّذِينَ اتَّقَوْا إِذَا مَسَّهُمْ طَائِفٌ مِنَ الشَّيْطَانِ تَذَكَّرُوا فَإِذَا هُمْ مُبْصِرُونَ ۞

202. But their brethren (the evil ones) plunge them deeper into error, and never relax (their efforts).

وَإِخْوَانُهُمْ يَمُدُّونَهُمْ فِي الْغَيِّ ثُمَّ لَا يُقْصِرُونَ ۞

203. If you do not bring them a revelation, they say: "Why have you not got it together?" Say: "I but follow what is revealed to me from my Lord: this is (nothing but) Lights from your Lord, and Guidance, and Mercy, for any who have Faith."

وَإِذَا لَمْ تَأْتِهِمْ بِآيَةٍ قَالُوا لَوْلَا اجْتَبَيْتَهَا قُلْ إِنَّمَا أَتَّبِعُ مَا يُوحَى إِلَيَّ مِنْ رَبِّي هَذَا بَصَائِرُ مِنْ رَبِّكُمْ وَهُدًى وَرَحْمَةٌ لِقَوْمٍ يُؤْمِنُونَ ۞

SÛRAH-8
AL-ANFÃL
(INTRODUCTION)

In the previous Introductions to the Sûras we have shown how each Sûrah is a step or gradation in the teaching of the Qur'ân. The first seven Sûras, comprising a little less than onethird of the Qur'ân, form a gradation, sketching the early spiritual history of man and leading up to the formation of the new Ummat or Community of the Holy Apostle. Now we begin another gradation, consolidating that Ummat and directing us as to various phases in our new collective life.

In this chapter we have the lessons of the Battle of Badr enforced in their larger aspects: (1) the question of war booty; (2) the true virtues necessary for fighting the good fight; (3) victory against odds; (4) clemency and consideration for one's own and for others in the hour of victory.

As regards booty taken in battle, the first point to note is that should never be our aim in war. It is only an advertitious circumstance, a sort of windfall. Secondly, no soldier or troop has any inherent right to it. A righteous war is a community affair, and any accessions resulting from it belong to Allah, or the community or Cause. Thirdly, certain equitable principles of division should be laid down to check human greed and selfishness. A fifth share goes to the Commander, and he can use it at his discretion; for his own expenses, and for the relief of the poor and suffering, and the orphans and widows (8:41). The remainder was divided, according to the Prophet's practice, not only among those who were actually in the fight physically, but all who were in the enterprise, young and old, provided they loyally did some duty assigned to them. Fourthly, there should be no disputes, as they interfere with internal discipline and harmony.

These principles are followed in the best modem practice of civilised nations. All acquisition of war belong absolutely to the Sovereign as representing the commonwealth. In the distribution of booty not only the actual captors but also the "joint captors" and the "constructive captors" share. See   Sir R. Phillimore's *International Law* (1885), vol. 3,pp. 209-10,221 -4.

As regards the military virtues, which are the types of virtues throughout life, we are shown by an analysis of the incidents of Badr how, against the greatest odds, Allah's help will give the victory if men are fighting not for themselves but for the sacred Cause of Allah. And directions are given for the treatment of prisoners and for maintaining the solidarity of the Muslim community.

The date of this Sûrah is shortly after the battle of Badr, which was fought on Friday, the 17th of Ramadhân in the second year of the Hijra.

204. When the Qur'an is read, listen to it with attention, and hold your peace: that you may receive Mercy.

205. And you (O reader!) bring your Lord to remembrance in your (very) soul, with humility and in reverence, without loudness in words, in the mornings and evenings; and you be not of those who are unheedful.

206. Those who are near to your Lord, do not disdain to do Him worship: they celebrate His praises, and bow down before Him.

8. The Spoil of War
In the name of Allah. Most Gracious, Most Merciful.

1. They ask you concerning (things taken as) spoils of war. Say: "(Such) spoils are at the disposal of Allah and the Apostle: so fear Allah, and keep straight the relations between yourselves: obey Allah and His Apostle, if you do believe."

2. For, Believers are those who, when Allah is mentioned, feel a tremor in their hearts, and when they hear His Signs rehearsed, find their faith strengthened, and put (all) their trust in their Lord;

3. Who establish regular prayers and spend (freely) out of the gifts We have given them for sustenance:

4. Such in truth are the Believers: they have grades of dignity with their Lord, and forgiveness, and generous sustenance:

5. Just as your Lord ordered you out of your house in truth, even though a party among the Believers

وَإِذَا قُرِئَ الْقُرْاٰنُ فَاسْتَمِعُوْا لَهٗ وَاَنْصِتُوْا لَعَلَّكُمْ تُرْحَمُوْنَ ۝

وَاذْكُرْ رَّبَّكَ فِيْ نَفْسِكَ تَضَرُّعًا وَّخِيْفَةً وَّدُوْنَ الْجَهْرِ مِنَ الْقَوْلِ بِالْغُدُوِّ وَالْاٰصَالِ وَلَا تَكُنْ مِّنَ الْغٰفِلِيْنَ ۝

اِنَّ الَّذِيْنَ عِنْدَ رَبِّكَ لَا يَسْتَكْبِرُوْنَ عَنْ عِبَادَتِهٖ وَيُسَبِّحُوْنَهٗ وَلَهٗ يَسْجُدُوْنَ ۩

(٨) سُوْرَةُ الْاَنْفَالِ مَدَنِيَّةٌ (٨٨)

بِسْمِ اللّٰهِ الرَّحْمٰنِ الرَّحِيْمِ

يَسْئَلُوْنَكَ عَنِ الْاَنْفَالِ ۚ قُلِ الْاَنْفَالُ لِلّٰهِ وَالرَّسُوْلِ ۚ فَاتَّقُوا اللّٰهَ وَ اَصْلِحُوْا ذَاتَ بَيْنِكُمْ ۖ وَاَطِيْعُوا اللّٰهَ وَرَسُوْلَهٗ اِنْ كُنْتُمْ مُّؤْمِنِيْنَ ۝

اِنَّمَا الْمُؤْمِنُوْنَ الَّذِيْنَ اِذَا ذُكِرَ اللّٰهُ وَجِلَتْ قُلُوْبُهُمْ وَاِذَا تُلِيَتْ عَلَيْهِمْ اٰيٰتُهٗ زَادَتْهُمْ اِيْمَانًا وَّعَلٰى رَبِّهِمْ يَتَوَكَّلُوْنَ ۝

الَّذِيْنَ يُقِيْمُوْنَ الصَّلٰوةَ وَمِمَّا رَزَقْنٰهُمْ يُنْفِقُوْنَ ۝

اُولٰٓئِكَ هُمُ الْمُؤْمِنُوْنَ حَقًّا ۚ لَهُمْ دَرَجٰتٌ عِنْدَ رَبِّهِمْ وَمَغْفِرَةٌ وَّ رِزْقٌ كَرِيْمٌ ۝

كَمَا اَخْرَجَكَ رَبُّكَ مِنْ بَيْتِكَ بِالْحَقِّ ۖ وَاِنَّ فَرِيْقًا مِّنَ الْمُؤْمِنِيْنَ

disliked it.

6. Disputing with you concerning the truth after it was made manifest, as if they were being driven to death and they (actually) saw it.

7. Behold! Allah promised you one of the two (enemy) parties, that it should be yours: you wished that the one unarmed should be yours, but Allah willed to justify the Truth according to His words and to cut off the roots of the Unbelievers;-

8. That He might justify Truth and prove Falsehood false, distasteful though it be to those in guilt.

9. Remember you implored the assistance of your Lord, and He answered you: "I will assist you with a thousand of the angels, ranks on ranks."

10. Allah made it but a message of hope, and an assurance to your hearts: (in any case) there is no help except from Allah: and Allah is Exalted in Power, Wise.

11. Remember He covered you with a sort of drowsiness, to give you calm as from Himself, and He caused rain to descend on you from heaven, to clean you therewith, to remove from you the stain of Satan, to strengthen your hearts, and to plant your feet firmly therewith.

12. Remember your Lord inspired the angels (with the message): "I am with you: give firmness to the Believers: I will instil terror into the hearts of the Unbelievers: you smite above their necks

كَارِهُوْنَ ۟

يُجَادِلُوْنَكَ فِى الْحَقِّ بَعْدَ مَا

تَبَيَّنَ كَاَنَّمَا يُسَاقُوْنَ اِلَى الْمَوْتِ

وَهُمْ يَنْظُرُوْنَ ۟

وَاِذْ يَعِدُكُمُ اللّٰهُ اِحْدَى

الطَّآئِفَتَيْنِ اَنَّهَا لَكُمْ وَتَوَدُّوْنَ اَنَّ

غَيْرَ ذَاتِ الشَّوْكَةِ تَكُوْنُ لَكُمْ

وَيُرِيْدُ اللّٰهُ اَنْ يُّحِقَّ الْحَقَّ بِكَلِمٰتِهٖ

وَيَقْطَعَ دَابِرَ الْكٰفِرِيْنَ ۟

لِيُحِقَّ الْحَقَّ وَيُبْطِلَ الْبَاطِلَ وَ

لَوْ كَرِهَ الْمُجْرِمُوْنَ ۟

اِذْ تَسْتَغِيْثُوْنَ رَبَّكُمْ فَاسْتَجَابَ

لَكُمْ اَنِّيْ مُمِدُّكُمْ بِاَلْفٍ مِّنَ

الْمَلٰٓئِكَةِ مُرْدِفِيْنَ ۟

وَمَا جَعَلَهُ اللّٰهُ اِلَّا بُشْرٰى وَلِتَطْمَئِنَّ

بِهٖ قُلُوْبُكُمْ ۖ وَمَا النَّصْرُ اِلَّا مِنْ

عِنْدِ اللّٰهِ ۗ اِنَّ اللّٰهَ عَزِيْزٌ حَكِيْمٌ ۟

اِذْ يُغَشِّيْكُمُ النُّعَاسَ اَمَنَةً مِّنْهُ

وَيُنَزِّلُ عَلَيْكُمْ مِّنَ السَّمَآءِ مَآءً

لِّيُطَهِّرَكُمْ بِهٖ وَيُذْهِبَ عَنْكُمْ

رِجْزَ الشَّيْطٰنِ وَلِيَرْبِطَ عَلٰى

قُلُوْبِكُمْ وَيُثَبِّتَ بِهِ الْاَقْدَامَ ۟

اِذْ يُوْحِيْ رَبُّكَ اِلَى الْمَلٰٓئِكَةِ

اَنِّيْ مَعَكُمْ فَثَبِّتُوا الَّذِيْنَ اٰمَنُوْا ۗ

سَاُلْقِيْ فِيْ قُلُوْبِ الَّذِيْنَ كَفَرُوا

الرُّعْبَ فَاضْرِبُوْا فَوْقَ الْاَعْنَاقِ

ع
١٥

and smite all their finger-tips off them."

13. This because they contended against Allah and His Apostle: if any contend against Allah and His Apostle, Allah is strict in punishment.

14. Thus (will it be said): "You taste then of the (punishment): for those who resist Allah, is the Chastisement of the Fire."

15. O you who believe! when you meet the Unbelievers in hostile array, never turn your backs to them.

16. If any do turn his back to them on such a day - unless it be in a stratagem of war, or to retreat to a troop (of his own) - he draws on himself the wrath of Allah, and his abode is Hell,- an evil refuge (indeed)!

17. It is not you who slew them; it was Allah: when you threw (a handful of dust), it was not your act, but Allah's: in order that He might test the Believers by a gracious trial from Himself: for Allah is He Who hears and knows (all things).

18. That, and also because Allah is He Who makes feeble the plans and stratagems of the Unbelievers.

19. (O Unbelievers!) if you prayed for victory and judgment, now has the judgment come to you: if you desist (from wrong), it will be best for you: if you return (to the attack), so shall We. Not the least good will your forces be to you even if they were multiplied: for verily Allah is with those who believe!

20. O you who believe! Obey Allah and His Apostle, and do not turn away from him when you

hear (him speak).

21. Nor be like those who say, "We hear," but do not listen.

22. For the worst of beasts in the sight of Allah are the deaf and the dumb,- those who do not understand.

23. If Allah had found in them any good, He would indeed have made them listen: (as it is), if He had made them listen, they would but have turned back and declined (Faith).

24. O you who believe! give your response to Allah and His Apostle, when He calls you to that which will give you life; and know that Allah comes in between a man and his heart, and that it is He to Whom you shall (all) be gathered.

25. And fear tumult or oppression, which affects not in particular (only) those of you who do wrong: and know that Allah is strict in punishment.

26. Call to mind when you were a small (band), deemed weak through the land, and afraid that men might despoil and kidnap you; but He provided a safe asylum for you, strengthened you with His aid, and gave you good things for sustenance: that you might be grateful.

27. O you that believe! do not betray the trust of Allah and the Apostle, nor misappropriate knowingly things entrusted to you.

28. And you should know that your possessions and your progeny are but a trial; and that it is Allah with Whom lies your highest reward.

29. O you who believe! if you fear Allah, He will grant you a Criterion (to judge between right and wrong), remove from you (all) evil (that may afflict) you, and forgive you: for Allah

تَسْمَعُوْنَ ۞

وَلَا تَكُوْنُوْا كَالَّذِيْنَ قَالُوْا سَمِعْنَا وَهُمْ لَا يَسْمَعُوْنَ ۞

اِنَّ شَرَّ الدَّوَآبِّ عِنْدَ اللّٰهِ الصُّمُّ الْبُكْمُ الَّذِيْنَ لَا يَعْقِلُوْنَ ۞

وَلَوْ عَلِمَ اللّٰهُ فِيْهِمْ خَيْرًا لَّأَسْمَعَهُمْ وَلَوْ اَسْمَعَهُمْ لَتَوَلَّوْا وَّهُمْ مُّعْرِضُوْنَ ۞

يٰٓاَيُّهَا الَّذِيْنَ اٰمَنُوا اسْتَجِيْبُوْا لِلّٰهِ وَلِلرَّسُوْلِ اِذَا دَعَاكُمْ لِمَا يُحْيِيْكُمْ وَاعْلَمُوْٓا اَنَّ اللّٰهَ يَحُوْلُ بَيْنَ الْمَرْءِ وَقَلْبِهٖ وَاَنَّهٗٓ اِلَيْهِ تُحْشَرُوْنَ ۞

وَاتَّقُوْا فِتْنَةً لَّا تُصِيْبَنَّ الَّذِيْنَ ظَلَمُوْا مِنْكُمْ خَآصَّةً ۚ وَاعْلَمُوْٓا اَنَّ اللّٰهَ شَدِيْدُ الْعِقَابِ ۞

وَاذْكُرُوْٓا اِذْ اَنْتُمْ قَلِيْلٌ مُّسْتَضْعَفُوْنَ فِى الْاَرْضِ تَخَافُوْنَ اَنْ يَّتَخَطَّفَكُمُ النَّاسُ فَاٰوٰىكُمْ وَاَيَّدَكُمْ بِنَصْرِهٖ وَ رَزَقَكُمْ مِّنَ الطَّيِّبٰتِ لَعَلَّكُمْ تَشْكُرُوْنَ ۞

يٰٓاَيُّهَا الَّذِيْنَ اٰمَنُوْا لَا تَخُوْنُوا اللّٰهَ وَالرَّسُوْلَ وَتَخُوْنُوْٓا اَمٰنٰتِكُمْ وَاَنْتُمْ تَعْلَمُوْنَ ۞

وَاعْلَمُوْٓا اَنَّمَآ اَمْوَالُكُمْ وَاَوْلَادُكُمْ فِتْنَةٌ ۙ وَّاَنَّ اللّٰهَ عِنْدَهٗٓ اَجْرٌ عَظِيْمٌ ۞

يٰٓاَيُّهَا الَّذِيْنَ اٰمَنُوْٓا اِنْ تَتَّقُوا اللّٰهَ يَجْعَلْ لَّكُمْ فُرْقَانًا وَّيُكَفِّرْ عَنْكُمْ سَيِّاٰتِكُمْ وَيَغْفِرْ لَكُمْ ۖ وَاللّٰهُ

is the Lord of grace unbounded.

30. Remember how the Unbelievers plotted against you, to keep you in bonds, or slay you, or get you out (of your home). They plot and plan, and Allah too plans, but the best of planners is Allah.

31. When Our Signs are rehearsed to them, they say: "We have heard this (before): if we wished, we could say (words) like these: these are nothing but tales of the ancients."

32. Remember how they said: "O Allah! if this is indeed the Truth from You, rain down on us a shower of stones from the sky, or send us a grievous Chastisement."

33. But Allah was not going to send them a Chastisement whilst you were amongst them; nor was He going to send it whilst they could ask for pardon.

34. But what plea have they that Allah should not punish them, when they keep out (men) from the Sacred Mosque - and they are not its guardians? No men can be its guardians except the righteous; but most of them do not understand.

35. Their prayer at the House (of Allah) is nothing but whistling and clapping of hands: (its only answer can be), "You taste the Chastisement because you blasphemed."

36. The Unbelievers spend their wealth to hinder (men) from the path of Allah, and so will they continue to spend; but in the end they will have (only) regrets and sighs; at length they will be overcome: and the

Unbelievers will be gathered together to Hell;

37. In order that Allah may separate the impure from the pure, put the impure, one on another, heap them together, and cast them into Hell. They will be the ones to have lost.

38. Say to the Unbelievers, if (now) they desist (from Unbelief), their past would be forgiven them; but if they persist, the punishment of those before them is already (a matter of warning for them).

39. And fight them on until there is no more tumult or oppression, and religion becomes Allah's in its entirety, but if they cease, surely Allah sees all that they do.

40. If they refuse, be sure that Allah is your Protector - the Best to protect and the Best to help.

41. And know that out of all the booty that you may acquire (in war), a fifth share is assigned to Allah,- and to the Apostle, and to near relatives, orphans, the needy, and the wayfarer,- if you do believe in Allah and in the revelation We sent down to Our Servant on the Day of discrimination,- the Day of the meeting of the two forces. For Allah has power over all things.

42. Remember you were on the hither side of the valley, and they on the farther side, and the caravan on lower ground than you. Even if you had made a mutual appointment to meet, you would certainly have failed in the appointment: but (thus you met), that Allah might accomplish a matter already decided; that those who died might die after a Clear Sign (had been given), and those who lived might live after

a Clear Sign (had been given). And verily Allah is He Who hears and knows (all things).

43. Remember in your dream Allah showed them to you as few: if He had shown them to you as many, you would surely have been discouraged, and you would surely have disputed in (your) decision; but Allah saved (you): for He knows well the (secrets) of (all) hearts.

44. And remember when you met, He showed them to you as few in your eyes, and He made you appear as contemptible in their eyes: that Allah might accomplish a matter already decided. For to Allah do all questions go back (for decision).

45. O you who believe! When you meet a force, be firm, and call Allah in remembrance much (and often); that you may prosper:

46. And obey Allah and His Apostle; and fall into no disputes, lest you lose heart and your power depart; and be patient and persevering: for Allah is with those who patiently persevere:

47. And be not like those who started from their homes insolently and to be seen of men, and to hinder (men) from the path of Allah: for Allah compasses round about all that they do.

48. Remember Satan made their (sinful) acts seem alluring to them, and said: "No one among men can overcome you this day, while I am near to you": But when the two forces came in sight of each other, he turned on his heels, and said: "Lo! I am clear of you; Lo! I see what you do not see; Lo! I fear Allah: for Allah is strict in punishment."

49. Lo! the Hypocrites say, and those in whose hearts is a disease: "These people,- their religion has misled them." But if any trust in Allah, behold! Allah is Exalted in might, Wise.

إِذْ يَقُوْلُ الْمُنٰفِقُوْنَ وَ الَّذِيْنَ فِيْ قُلُوْبِهِمْ مَّرَضٌ غَرَّ هٰؤُلَاءِ دِيْنُهُمْ ۖ وَمَنْ يَّتَوَكَّلْ عَلَى اللّٰهِ فَاِنَّ اللّٰهَ عَزِيْزٌ حَكِيْمٌ ۞

50. If you could see, when the angels take the souls of the Unbelievers (at death), (how) they smite their faces and their backs, (saying): "Taste the Chastisement of the blazing Fire-

وَلَوْ تَرٰى إِذْ يَتَوَفَّى الَّذِيْنَ كَفَرُوا الْمَلٰٓئِكَةُ يَضْرِبُوْنَ وُجُوْهَهُمْ وَاَدْبَارَهُمْ ۚ وَذُوْقُوْا عَذَابَ الْحَرِيْقِ ۞

51. "Because of (the deeds) which your (own) hands sent forth; for Allah is never unjust to His servants:

ذٰلِكَ بِمَا قَدَّمَتْ اَيْدِيْكُمْ وَ اَنَّ اللّٰهَ لَيْسَ بِظَلَّامٍ لِّلْعَبِيْدِ ۞

52. "(Deeds) after the manner of the people of Pharaoh and of those before them: they rejected the Signs of Allah, and Allah punished them for their crimes: for Allah is Strong, and Strict in punishment:

كَدَأْبِ اٰلِ فِرْعَوْنَ ۙ وَالَّذِيْنَ مِنْ قَبْلِهِمْ ۚ كَفَرُوْا بِاٰيٰتِ اللّٰهِ فَاَخَذَهُمُ اللّٰهُ بِذُنُوْبِهِمْ ۚ اِنَّ اللّٰهَ قَوِيٌّ شَدِيْدُ الْعِقَابِ ۞

53. "Because Allah will never change the Grace which He has bestowed on a people until they change what is in their (own) souls, and surely Allah is He Who hears and knows (all things)."

ذٰلِكَ بِاَنَّ اللّٰهَ لَمْ يَكُ مُغَيِّرًا نِّعْمَةً اَنْعَمَهَا عَلٰى قَوْمٍ حَتّٰى يُغَيِّرُوْا مَا بِاَنْفُسِهِمْ ۙ وَ اَنَّ اللّٰهَ سَمِيْعٌ عَلِيْمٌ ۞

54. "(Deeds) after the manner of the people of Pharaoh and those before them": they treated as false the Signs of their Lord, so We destroyed them for their crimes, and We drowned the people of Pharaoh: for they were all oppressors and wrong-doers.

كَدَأْبِ اٰلِ فِرْعَوْنَ ۙ وَالَّذِيْنَ مِنْ قَبْلِهِمْ ۚ كَذَّبُوْا بِاٰيٰتِ رَبِّهِمْ ۚ فَاَهْلَكْنٰهُمْ بِذُنُوْبِهِمْ وَاَغْرَقْنَا اٰلَ فِرْعَوْنَ ۚ وَكُلٌّ كَانُوْا ظٰلِمِيْنَ ۞

55. For the worst of beasts in the sight of Allah are those who reject Him: they will not believe.

اِنَّ شَرَّ الدَّوَآبِّ عِنْدَ اللّٰهِ الَّذِيْنَ كَفَرُوْا فَهُمْ لَا يُؤْمِنُوْنَ ۙ

56. They are those with whom you made a covenant, but

الَّذِيْنَ عٰهَدْتَّ مِنْهُمْ ثُمَّ

they break their covenant every time, and they do not have the fear (of Allah).

57. If you encounter them in a battle deal severely with them so as to put terror in those who follow them, that they may remember.

58. If you fear treachery from any group, throw back (their covenant) to them, (so as to be) on equal terms: for Allah does not love the treacherous.

59. Let not the Unbelievers think that they can get the better (of the godly): they will never frustrate (them).

60. Against them make ready your strength to the utmost of your power, including steeds of war, to strike terror into (the hearts of) the enemies, of Allah and your enemies, and others besides, whom you may not know, but whom Allah knows. Whatever you shall spend in the Cause of Allah, shall be repaid to you, and you shall not be treated unjustly.

61. But if the enemy incline towards peace, you (also) incline towards peace, and trust in Allah: for He is the One that hears and knows (all things).

62. Should they intend to deceive you,- verily Allah suffices you: He it is that has strengthened you with His aid and with (the company of) the Believers;

63. And (moreover) He has put affection between their hearts: not if you had spent all that is in the earth, could you have produced that affection, but Allah has done it: for He is Exalted in might, Wise.

64. O Apostle! sufficient to you is Allah,- (to you) and to those who follow you among the Believers.

65. O Apostle! rouse the Believers to the fight. If there are twenty amongst you, patient and persevering, they will vanquish two hundred: if a hundred, they will vanquish a thousand of the Unbelievers: for these are a people without understanding.

66. For the present, Allah has lightened your (task), for He knows that there is a weak spot in you: but (even so), if there are a hundred of you, patient and persevering, they will vanquish two hundred, and if a thousand, they will vanquish two thousand, with the leave of Allah: for Allah is with those who patiently persevere.

67. It is not fitting for an Apostle that he should have prisoners of war until he has thoroughly subdued the land. You look for the temporal goods of this world; but Allah looks to the Hereafter: and Allah is Exalted in might, Wise.

68. Had it not been for a previous ordainment from Allah, a severe penalty would have reached you for the (ransom) that you took.

69. But (now) enjoy what you took in war, lawful and good: but fear Allah: for Allah is Oft-forgiving, Most Merciful.

70. O Apostle! say to those who are captives in your hands: "If Allah finds any good in your hearts, He will give you something better than what has been taken from you, and He will forgive you: for Allah is Oft-forgiving, Most Merciful."

71. But if they have treacherous designs against you,(O Apostle!), they have already been in treason against Allah, and so has He given (you) power over them. And Allah is He Who has (full) knowledge and wisdom.

وَاِنْ يُّرِيْدُوْا خِيَانَتَكَ فَقَدْ خَانُوا اللهَ مِنْ قَبْلُ فَاَمْكَنَ مِنْهُمْ ۖ وَاللهُ عَلِيْمٌ حَكِيْمٌ ۝

72. Those who believed, and adopted exile, and fought for the Faith, with their property and their persons, in the cause of Allah, as well as those who gave (them) asylum and aid,- these are (all) friends and protectors, one of another. As to those who believed but came not into exile, you owe no duty of protection to them until they come into exile; but if they seek your aid in religion, it is your duty to help them, except against a people with whom you have a treaty of mutual alliance. And (remember) Allah sees all that you do.

اِنَّ الَّذِيْنَ اٰمَنُوْا وَهَاجَرُوْا وَجَاهَدُوْا بِاَمْوَالِهِمْ وَاَنْفُسِهِمْ فِيْ سَبِيْلِ اللهِ وَالَّذِيْنَ اٰوَوْا وَّنَصَرُوْا اُولٰٓئِكَ بَعْضُهُمْ اَوْلِيَآءُ بَعْضٍ ۗ وَالَّذِيْنَ اٰمَنُوْا وَلَمْ يُهَاجِرُوْا مَا لَكُمْ مِّنْ وَّلَايَتِهِمْ مِّنْ شَيْءٍ حَتّٰى يُهَاجِرُوْا ۚ وَاِنِ اسْتَنْصَرُوْكُمْ فِي الدِّيْنِ فَعَلَيْكُمُ النَّصْرُ اِلَّا عَلٰى قَوْمٍۭ بَيْنَكُمْ وَبَيْنَهُمْ مِّيْثَاقٌ ۗ وَاللهُ بِمَا تَعْمَلُوْنَ بَصِيْرٌ ۝

73. The Unbelievers are protectors, one of another: unless you do this, (protect each other), there would be tumult and oppression on earth, and great mischief.

وَالَّذِيْنَ كَفَرُوْا بَعْضُهُمْ اَوْلِيَآءُ بَعْضٍ ۗ اِلَّا تَفْعَلُوْهُ تَكُنْ فِتْنَةٌ فِي الْاَرْضِ وَفَسَادٌ كَبِيْرٌ ۝

74. Those who believe, and adopt exile, and fight for the Faith, in the cause of Allah as well as those who give (them) asylum and aid,- these are (all) in very truth the Believers: for them is the forgiveness of sins and a provision most generous.

وَالَّذِيْنَ اٰمَنُوْا وَهَاجَرُوْا وَجَاهَدُوْا فِيْ سَبِيْلِ اللهِ وَالَّذِيْنَ اٰوَوْا وَّنَصَرُوْا اُولٰٓئِكَ هُمُ الْمُؤْمِنُوْنَ حَقًّا ۚ لَهُمْ مَّغْفِرَةٌ وَّرِزْقٌ كَرِيْمٌ ۝

75. And those who accept Faith subsequently, and adopt exile, and fight for the Faith in your company,- they are of you. But kindred by blood have prior rights against each other in the Book of Allah. Verily Allah is well-acquainted with all things.

وَالَّذِيْنَ اٰمَنُوْا مِنْ بَعْدُ وَهَاجَرُوْا وَجَاهَدُوْا مَعَكُمْ فَاُولٰٓئِكَ مِنْكُمْ ۗ وَاُولُوا الْاَرْحَامِ بَعْضُهُمْ اَوْلٰى بِبَعْضٍ فِيْ كِتٰبِ اللهِ ۗ اِنَّ اللهَ بِكُلِّ شَيْءٍ عَلِيْمٌ ۝

SÛRAH-9
AT-TAUBAH
(INTRODUCTION)

Logically this Sûrah follows up the argument of the last Sûrah (8), and indeed may be considered a part of it, although chronologically the two are separated by an interval of seven years.

We saw that Sûrah 8 dealt with the large questions arising at the outset of the life of a new Ummat or organised nation; questions of defence under attack, distribution of war acquisitions after victory, the virtues needed for concerted action, and clemency and consideration for one's own and for enemies in the hour of victory. We pass on in this Sûrah to deal with the question: What is to be done if the enemy breaks faith and is guilty of treachery? No nation can go on with a treaty if the other party violates it at will; but it is laid down that a period of four months should be allowed by way of notice after denunciation of the treaty; that due protection should be accorded in the intervening period; that there should always be open the door to repentance and reunion with the people of Allah; and that if all these fail, and war must be undertaken, it must be pushed with utmost vigour.

These are the general principles deducible from the Sûrah. The immediate occasion for their promulgation may be considered in connection with the chronological place of the Surah.

Chronologically, verses 1-29 were a notable declaration of State policy promulgated about the month of Shawwal, A.H. 9, and read out by Ḥadhrat ' Ali at the Pilgrimage two months later in order to give the policy the widest publicity possible. The remainder of the Sûrah, verses 30-129, was revealed a little earlier, say, about the month of Ramadhân, A.H. 9, and sums up the lessons of the Apostle's Tabûk expedition in the summer of A.H. 9 (say October 630).

Tabûk is a place near the frontier of Arabia, quite close to

what was then Byzantine territory in the Province of Syria
(which includes Palestine). It is about 350 miles northwest of
Madinah, and 150 miles south of Ma'an. It had a fort and a spring
of sweet water. In consequence of strong and persistent rumours
that the Byzantines (Romans) were preparing to invade Arabia
and that the Byzantine Emperor himself had arrived near the
frontier for the purpose, the Apostle collected as large a force as
he could, and marched to Tabûk. The Byzantine invasion did not
come off. But the Apostle took the opportunity of consolidating
the Muslim position in that direction and making treaties of
alliance with certain Christain and Jewish tribes near the Gulf of
'Aqaba. On his return to Madinah he considered the situation.
During his absence the Hypocrites had played, as always, a
double game, and the policy hitherto followed, of free access to
the sacred centre of Islam, to Muslims and Pagans alike, was now
altered, as it had been abused by the enemies of Islam.

This is the only Sûrah to which the usual formula of
Bismillâh is not prefixed. It was among the last of the Sûras
revealed, and though the Apostle had directed that it should
follow Sûrah 8, it was not clear whether it was to form a separate
Sûrah or only a part of Sûrah 8. It is now treated as a separate
Sûrah, but the *Bismillâh* is not prefixed to it, as there is no
warrant for supposing that the Apostle used the *Bismillâh* before
it in his recitation of the Qur'an. The Sûrah is known under many
names, the two most commonly used are (1) *Taubah*
(Repentance) with reference to 9: 104 and (2) *Barâat*
(Immunity), the opening word of the Surah.

9. Repentance or Immunity

بِسْمِ اللهِ الرَّحْمٰنِ الرَّحِيْمِ

١. سُوْرَةُ التَّوْبَةِ مَدَنِيَّةٌ (١١٣)

1. A (declaration) of immunity from Allah and His Apostle, to those of the Pagans with whom you have contracted mutual alliances:-

بَرَآءَةٌ مِّنَ اللهِ وَرَسُوْلِهٖۤ اِلَى الَّذِيْنَ عٰهَدْتُّمْ مِّنَ الْمُشْرِكِيْنَ ۗ

2. You go, then, for four months, backwards and forwards, (as you will), throughout the land, but know that you cannot frustrate Allah (by your falsehood) but that Allah will cover with shame those who reject Him.

فَسِيْحُوْا فِي الْاَرْضِ اَرْبَعَةَ اَشْهُرٍ وَّاعْلَمُوْۤا اَنَّكُمْ غَيْرُ مُعْجِزِى اللهِ ۙ وَاَنَّ اللهَ مُخْزِى الْكٰفِرِيْنَ ۞

3. And an announcement from Allah and His Apostle, to the people (assembled) on the day of the Great Pilgrimage,- that Allah and His Apostle dissolve (treaty) obligations with the Pagans. If then, you repent, it were best for you; but if you turn away, you (should) know that you cannot frustrate Allah. And proclaim a grievous Chastisement to those who reject Faith.

وَاَذَانٌ مِّنَ اللهِ وَرَسُوْلِهٖۤ اِلَى النَّاسِ يَوْمَ الْحَجِّ الْاَكْبَرِ اَنَّ اللهَ بَرِىْٓءٌ مِّنَ الْمُشْرِكِيْنَ ۙ۬ وَرَسُوْلُهٗ ۚ فَاِنْ تُبْتُمْ فَهُوَ خَيْرٌ لَّكُمْ ۚ وَاِنْ تَوَلَّيْتُمْ فَاعْلَمُوْۤا اَنَّكُمْ غَيْرُ مُعْجِزِى اللهِ ۗ وَبَشِّرِ الَّذِيْنَ كَفَرُوْا بِعَذَابٍ اَلِيْمٍ ۞

4. (But the treaties are) not dissolved with those Pagans with whom you have entered into alliance and who have not subsequently failed you in any thing, nor aided any one against you. So fulfil your agreements with them to the end of their term: for Allah loves the righteous.

اِلَّا الَّذِيْنَ عٰهَدْتُّمْ مِّنَ الْمُشْرِكِيْنَ ثُمَّ لَمْ يَنْقُصُوْكُمْ شَيْئًا وَّلَمْ يُظَاهِرُوْا عَلَيْكُمْ اَحَدًا فَاَتِمُّوْۤا اِلَيْهِمْ عَهْدَهُمْ اِلٰى مُدَّتِهِمْ ۗ اِنَّ اللهَ يُحِبُّ الْمُتَّقِيْنَ ۞

5. But when the forbidden months are past, then fight and slay the Pagans wherever you find them, and seize them, beleaguer them, and lie in wait for them in every strategem (of war); but if they repent, and establish regular prayers and practise regular charity, then open the way for them: for Allah is Oft-forgiving, Most Merciful.

فَاِذَا انْسَلَخَ الْاَشْهُرُ الْحُرُمُ فَاقْتُلُوا الْمُشْرِكِيْنَ حَيْثُ وَجَدْتُّمُوْهُمْ وَخُذُوْهُمْ وَاحْصُرُوْهُمْ وَاقْعُدُوْا لَهُمْ كُلَّ مَرْصَدٍ ۚ فَاِنْ تَابُوْا وَاَقَامُوا الصَّلٰوةَ وَاٰتَوُا الزَّكٰوةَ فَخَلُّوْا سَبِيْلَهُمْ ۗ اِنَّ اللهَ غَفُوْرٌ رَّحِيْمٌ ۞

6. If one amongst the Pagans ask you for asylum, grant it to him, so that he may hear the Word of Allah; and then escort him to where he can be secure. This is because they

وَاِنْ اَحَدٌ مِّنَ الْمُشْرِكِيْنَ اسْتَجَارَكَ فَاَجِرْهُ حَتّٰى يَسْمَعَ كَلٰمَ اللهِ ثُمَّ اَبْلِغْهُ مَاْمَنَهٗ ۗ ذٰلِكَ بِاَنَّهُمْ

men without knowledge.

7. How can there be a league, before Allah and His Apostle, with the Pagans, except those with whom you made a treaty near the Sacred Mosque? As long as these stand true to you, you stand true to them: for Allah loves the righteous.

8. How (can there be such a league), seeing that if they get an advantage over you, they do not respect in you the ties either of kinship or of covenant? With (fair words from) their mouths they please you, but their hearts are averse from you; and most of them are rebellious and wicked.

9. They have sold the Signs of Allah for a miserable price, and (many) have they hindered from His Way: evil indeed are the deeds they have done.

10. In a Believer they do not respect the ties either of kinship or of covenant! It is they who have transgressed all bounds.

11. But if (even so), if they repent, establish regular prayers, and practise regular charity,- then they are your brethren in Faith: (thus) do We explain the Signs in detail, for those who understand.

12. But if they violate their oaths after their covenant, and taunt you for your Faith,- you fight the chiefs of Unfaith: for their oaths are nothing to them: that thus they may be restrained.

13. Will you not fight people who violated their oaths, plotted to expel the Apostle, and took the aggressive by being the first (to assault) you? Do you fear them? Nay, it is Allah Whom you should more justly fear, if

قَوْمٌ لَّا يَعْلَمُوْنَ ۞

كَيْفَ يَكُوْنُ لِلْمُشْرِكِيْنَ عَهْدٌ عِنْدَ اللّٰهِ وَعِنْدَ رَسُوْلِهٖۤ اِلَّا الَّذِيْنَ عَاهَدْتُّمْ عِنْدَ الْمَسْجِدِ الْحَرَامِ ۚ فَمَا اسْتَقَامُوْا لَكُمْ فَاسْتَقِيْمُوْا لَهُمْ ؕ اِنَّ اللّٰهَ يُحِبُّ الْمُتَّقِيْنَ ۞

كَيْفَ وَاِنْ يَّظْهَرُوْا عَلَيْكُمْ لَا يَرْقُبُوْا فِيْكُمْ اِلًّا وَّلَا ذِمَّةً ؕ يُرْضُوْنَكُمْ بِاَفْوَاهِهِمْ وَتَأْبٰى قُلُوْبُهُمْ ۚ وَاَكْثَرُهُمْ فٰسِقُوْنَ ۞

اِشْتَرَوْا بِاٰيٰتِ اللّٰهِ ثَمَنًا قَلِيْلًا فَصَدُّوْا عَنْ سَبِيْلِهٖ ؕ اِنَّهُمْ سَآءَ مَا كَانُوْا يَعْمَلُوْنَ ۞

لَا يَرْقُبُوْنَ فِيْ مُؤْمِنٍ اِلًّا وَّلَا ذِمَّةً ؕ وَاُولٰٓئِكَ هُمُ الْمُعْتَدُوْنَ ۞

فَاِنْ تَابُوْا وَاَقَامُوا الصَّلٰوةَ وَاٰتَوُا الزَّكٰوةَ فَاِخْوَانُكُمْ فِى الدِّيْنِ ؕ وَنُفَصِّلُ الْاٰيٰتِ لِقَوْمٍ يَّعْلَمُوْنَ ۞

وَاِنْ نَّكَثُوْۤا اَيْمَانَهُمْ مِّنْ بَعْدِ عَهْدِهِمْ وَطَعَنُوْا فِيْ دِيْنِكُمْ فَقَاتِلُوْۤا اَئِمَّةَ الْكُفْرِ ۙ اِنَّهُمْ لَاۤ اَيْمَانَ لَهُمْ لَعَلَّهُمْ يَنْتَهُوْنَ ۞

اَلَا تُقَاتِلُوْنَ قَوْمًا نَّكَثُوْۤا اَيْمَانَهُمْ وَهَمُّوْا بِاِخْرَاجِ الرَّسُوْلِ وَهُمْ بَدَءُوْكُمْ اَوَّلَ مَرَّةٍ ؕ اَتَخْشَوْنَهُمْ ۚ فَاللّٰهُ اَحَقُّ اَنْ تَخْشَوْهُ اِنْ كُنْتُمْ

you believe!

مُّؤْمِنِيْنَ ۝

14. Fight them, and Allah will punish them by your hands, cover them with shame, help you (to victory) over them, heal the breasts of Believers,

قَاتِلُوْهُمْ يُعَذِّبْهُمُ اللهُ بِأَيْدِيْكُمْ وَيُخْزِهِمْ وَيَنْصُرْكُمْ عَلَيْهِمْ وَيَشْفِ صُدُوْرَ قَوْمٍ مُّؤْمِنِيْنَ ۝

15. And still the indignation of their hearts. For Allah will turn (in mercy) to whom He will; and Allah is All-Knowing, All-Wise.

وَيُذْهِبْ غَيْظَ قُلُوْبِهِمْ وَيَتُوْبُ اللهُ عَلٰى مَنْ يَّشَاءُ وَاللهُ عَلِيْمٌ حَكِيْمٌ ۝

16. Or do you think that you shall be abandoned, as though Allah did not know those among you who strive with might and main, and take none for friends and protectors except Allah, His Apostle, and the (community of) Believers? But Allah is well-acquainted with (all) that you do.

أَمْ حَسِبْتُمْ أَنْ تُتْرَكُوْا وَلَمَّا يَعْلَمِ اللهُ الَّذِيْنَ جَاهَدُوْا مِنْكُمْ وَلَمْ يَتَّخِذُوْا مِنْ دُوْنِ اللهِ وَلَا رَسُوْلِهِ وَلَا الْمُؤْمِنِيْنَ وَلِيْجَةً وَاللهُ خَبِيْرٌ بِمَا تَعْمَلُوْنَ ۝

17. It is not for such as join gods with Allah, to visit or maintain the mosques of Allah while they witness against their own souls to infidelity. The works of such bear no fruit: In Fire shall they dwell.

مَا كَانَ لِلْمُشْرِكِيْنَ أَنْ يَّعْمُرُوْا مَسٰجِدَ اللهِ شٰهِدِيْنَ عَلٰى أَنْفُسِهِمْ بِالْكُفْرِ أُولٰٓئِكَ حَبِطَتْ أَعْمَالُهُمْ وَفِي النَّارِ هُمْ خٰلِدُوْنَ ۝

18. The mosques of Allah shall be visited and maintained by such as believe in Allah and the Last Day, establish regular prayers, and practise regular charity, and fear none (at all) except Allah. It is they who are expected to be on true guidance.

إِنَّمَا يَعْمُرُ مَسٰجِدَ اللهِ مَنْ اٰمَنَ بِاللهِ وَالْيَوْمِ الْاٰخِرِ وَأَقَامَ الصَّلٰوةَ وَاٰتَى الزَّكٰوةَ وَلَمْ يَخْشَ إِلَّا اللهَ فَعَسٰى أُولٰٓئِكَ أَنْ يَّكُوْنُوْا مِنَ الْمُهْتَدِيْنَ ۝

19. Do you make the giving of drink to pilgrims, or the maintenance of the Sacred Mosque, equal to (the pious service of) those who believe in Allah and the Last Day, and strive with might and main in the cause of Allah? They are not comparable in the sight of Allah: and Allah does not guide those who do wrong.

أَجَعَلْتُمْ سِقَايَةَ الْحَاجِّ وَعِمَارَةَ الْمَسْجِدِ الْحَرَامِ كَمَنْ اٰمَنَ بِاللهِ وَالْيَوْمِ الْاٰخِرِ وَجٰهَدَ فِيْ سَبِيْلِ اللهِ لَا يَسْتَوْنَ عِنْدَ اللهِ وَاللهُ لَا يَهْدِي الْقَوْمَ الظّٰلِمِيْنَ ۝

20. Those who believe, and suffer exile and strive with might and main, in Allah's cause, with their goods and their persons, have the highest rank in the sight of Allah: they are the people who will achieve (salvation).

21. Their Lord gives them glad tidings of a Mercy from Himself, of His good pleasure, and of Gardens for them, wherein are delights that endure:

22. They will dwell therein for ever. Verily in Allah's presence is a reward, the greatest (of all).

23. O you who believe! Do not take for protectors your fathers and your brothers if they love infidelity above Faith: if any of you do so, they do wrong.

24. Say: If it be that your fathers, your sons, your brothers, your mates, or your kindred; the wealth that you have gained; the commerce in which you fear a decline: or the dwellings in which you delight - are dearer to you than Allah, or His Apostle, or the striving in His cause;- then wait until Allah brings about His Decision: and Allah does not guide the rebellious.

25. Assuredly Allah did help you in many battle-fields and on the day of Hunain: behold! your great numbers elated you, but they availed you nothing: the land, for all that it is wide,

did constrain you, and you turned back in retreat.

26.   But Allah poured His calm on the Apostle and on the Believers, and sent down forces which you did not see: He punished the Unbelievers; thus does He reward those without Faith.

27.   Again will Allah, after this, turn (in mercy) to whom He will: for Allah is Oft- forgiving, Most Merciful.

28.   O you who believe! Truly the Pagans are unclean; so let them not, after this year of theirs, approach the Sacred Mosque. And if you fear poverty, soon will Allah enrich you, if He wills, out of His bounty, for Allah is All-Knowing, All-Wise.

29.   Fight those who do not believe in Allah nor the Last Day, nor hold that forbidden which has been forbidden by Allah and His Apostle, nor acknowledge the Religion of Truth, (even if they are) of the People of the Book, until they pay the Jizya with willing submission, and feel themselves subdued.

30.   The Jews call 'Uzair a son of Allah, and the Christians call Christ the son of Allah. That is a saying from their mouth;(in this) they but imitate what the Unbelievers of old used to say. Allah's curse be on them: how they are deluded away from the Truth!

31.   They take their priests and their anchorites to be their lords in derogation of Allah, and (they take as their Lord) Christ the son of

Mary; yet they were commanded to worship but One God (Allah): there is no god but He. Praise and glory to Him: (far is He) from having the partners they associate (with Him).

32. Fain would they extinguish Allah's light with their mouths, but Allah will not allow but that His Light should be perfected, even though the Unbelievers may detest (it).

33. It is He Who has sent His Apostle with Guidance and the Religion of Truth, to proclaim it over all religion, even though the Pagans may detest (it).

34. O you who believe! there are indeed many among the priests and anchorites, who in falsehood devour the substance of men and hinder (them) from the Way of Allah. And there are those who bury gold and silver and do not spend it in the Way of Allah: announce to them a most grievous Chastisement-

35. On the Day when heat will be produced out of that (wealth) in the fire of Hell, and with it will be branded their foreheads, their flanks, and their backs-"This is the (treasure) which you buried for yourselves: you then taste the (treasures) you buried!"

36. The number of months in the sight of Allah is twelve (in a year)- so ordained by Him the day He created the heavens and the earth; of them four are sacred: that is the straight usage. So do not wrong yourselves therein,

and fight the Pagans all together
as they fight you all together.
But know that Allah is with
those who restrain themselves.

37. Verily the transposing (of
a prohibited month) is an
addition to Unbelief: the
Unbelievers are led to wrong
thereby: for they make it lawful
one year, and forbidden another
year, in order to adjust the
number of months forbidden by
Allah and make such forbidden
ones lawful. The evil of their
course seems pleasing to them.
But Allah does not guide those
who reject Faith.

38. O you who believe! what
is the matter with you, that,
when you are asked to go forth
in the Cause of Allah, you cling
heavily to the earth? Do you
prefer the life of this world to
the Hereafter? But little is the
comfort of this life, as compared
with the Hereafter.

39. Unless you go forth, He
will punish you with a grievous
Chastisement, and put others in
your place; but Him you would
not harm in the least. For Allah
has power over all things.

40. If you help not (your
leader), (it is no matter): for
Allah did indeed help him,
when the Unbelievers drove
him out: he had no more than
one companion; they two were
in the Cave, and he said to his
companion, "Have no fear, for
Allah is with us": then Allah
sent down His peace upon him,
and strengthened him with
forces which you did not see,
and humbled to the depths the
word of the Unbelievers. But
the word of Allah is exalted to
the heights: for Allah is Exalted
in might, Wise.

وَقَاتِلُوا الْمُشْرِكِيْنَ كَآفَّةً كَمَا
يُقَاتِلُوْنَكُمْ كَآفَّةً ۚ وَاعْلَمُوْٓا اَنَّ
اللّٰهَ مَعَ الْمُتَّقِيْنَ ۞

اِنَّمَا النَّسِيْٓءُ زِيَادَةٌ فِي الْكُفْرِ
يُضَلُّ بِهِ الَّذِيْنَ كَفَرُوْا يُحِلُّوْنَهٗ
عَامًا وَّيُحَرِّمُوْنَهٗ عَامًا لِّيُوَاطِئُوْا
عِدَّةَ مَا حَرَّمَ اللّٰهُ فَيُحِلُّوْا مَا حَرَّمَ
اللّٰهُ ۚ زُيِّنَ لَهُمْ سُوْٓءُ اَعْمَالِهِمْ ؕ
وَاللّٰهُ لَا يَهْدِي الْقَوْمَ الْكٰفِرِيْنَ ۞
يٰٓاَيُّهَا الَّذِيْنَ اٰمَنُوْا مَا لَكُمْ اِذَا
قِيْلَ لَكُمُ انْفِرُوْا فِيْ سَبِيْلِ اللّٰهِ
اثَّاقَلْتُمْ اِلَى الْاَرْضِ ؕ اَرَضِيْتُمْ
بِالْحَيٰوةِ الدُّنْيَا مِنَ الْاٰخِرَةِ ۚ فَمَا
مَتَاعُ الْحَيٰوةِ الدُّنْيَا فِي الْاٰخِرَةِ
اِلَّا قَلِيْلٌ ۞

اِلَّا تَنْفِرُوْا يُعَذِّبْكُمْ عَذَابًا اَلِيْمًا ۙ
وَّيَسْتَبْدِلْ قَوْمًا غَيْرَكُمْ وَلَا تَضُرُّوْهُ
شَيْئًا ؕ وَاللّٰهُ عَلٰى كُلِّ شَيْءٍ قَدِيْرٌ ۞

اِلَّا تَنْصُرُوْهُ فَقَدْ نَصَرَهُ اللّٰهُ اِذْ
اَخْرَجَهُ الَّذِيْنَ كَفَرُوْا ثَانِيَ اثْنَيْنِ
اِذْ هُمَا فِي الْغَارِ اِذْ يَقُوْلُ
لِصَاحِبِهٖ لَا تَحْزَنْ اِنَّ اللّٰهَ مَعَنَا ۚ
فَاَنْزَلَ اللّٰهُ سَكِيْنَتَهٗ عَلَيْهِ وَاَيَّدَهٗ
بِجُنُوْدٍ لَّمْ تَرَوْهَا وَجَعَلَ كَلِمَةَ
الَّذِيْنَ كَفَرُوا السُّفْلٰى ؕ وَكَلِمَةُ اللّٰهِ
هِيَ الْعُلْيَا ؕ وَاللّٰهُ عَزِيْزٌ حَكِيْمٌ ۞

41. You go forth, (whether equipped) lightly or heavily, and strive and struggle, with your goods and your persons, in the Cause of Allah. That is best for you, if you (but) knew.

42. If there had been imme-diate gain (in sight), and the journey easy, they would (all) without doubt have followed you, but the distance was long, (and weighed) on them. They would indeed swear by Allah, "If we only could, we should certainly have come out with you": they would destroy their own souls; for Allah knows that they are certainly lying.

43. Allah gave you grace! Why did you grant them exemption until those who told the truth were seen by you in a clear light, and you had proved the liars?

44. Those who believe in Allah and the Last Day ask you for no exemption from fighting with their goods and persons. And Allah knows well those who do their duty.

45. Only those ask you for exemption who do not believe in Allah and the Last Day, and whose hearts are in doubt, so that they are tossed in their doubts to and fro.

46. If they had intended to come out, they would certainly have made some preparation therefor; but Allah was averse to their being sent forth; so He made them lag behind, and they were told, "You sit among those who sit (inactive)."

47. If they had come out with you, they would not have added to your (strength) but

إِنْفِرُوْا خِفَافًا وَّثِقَالًا وَّجَاهِدُوْا بِأَمْوَالِكُمْ وَأَنْفُسِكُمْ فِيْ سَبِيْلِ اللّٰهِ ۦ ذٰلِكُمْ خَيْرٌ لَّكُمْ اِنْ كُنْتُمْ تَعْلَمُوْنَ ۞

لَوْكَانَ عَرَضًا قَرِيْبًا وَّسَفَرًا قَاصِدًا لَّاتَّبَعُوْكَ وَلٰكِنْ بَعُدَتْ عَلَيْهِمُ الشُّقَّةُ ۚ وَسَيَحْلِفُوْنَ بِاللّٰهِ لَوِ اسْتَطَعْنَا لَخَرَجْنَا مَعَكُمْ ۚ يُهْلِكُوْنَ أَنْفُسَهُمْ ۚ وَاللّٰهُ يَعْلَمُ اِنَّهُمْ لَكٰذِبُوْنَ ۞

عَفَا اللّٰهُ عَنْكَ ۚ لِمَ أَذِنْتَ لَهُمْ حَتّٰى يَتَبَيَّنَ لَكَ الَّذِيْنَ صَدَقُوْا وَتَعْلَمَ الْكٰذِبِيْنَ ۞

لَا يَسْتَأْذِنُكَ الَّذِيْنَ يُؤْمِنُوْنَ بِاللّٰهِ وَالْيَوْمِ الْاٰخِرِ أَنْ يُّجَاهِدُوْا بِأَمْوَالِهِمْ وَأَنْفُسِهِمْ ۚ وَاللّٰهُ عَلِيْمٌ بِالْمُتَّقِيْنَ ۞

اِنَّمَا يَسْتَأْذِنُكَ الَّذِيْنَ لَا يُؤْمِنُوْنَ بِاللّٰهِ وَالْيَوْمِ الْاٰخِرِ وَارْتَابَتْ قُلُوْبُهُمْ فَهُمْ فِيْ رَيْبِهِمْ يَتَرَدَّدُوْنَ ۞

وَلَوْ أَرَادُوا الْخُرُوْجَ لَأَعَدُّوْا لَهٗ عُدَّةً وَّلٰكِنْ كَرِهَ اللّٰهُ انْبِعَاثَهُمْ فَثَبَّطَهُمْ وَقِيْلَ اقْعُدُوْا مَعَ الْقٰعِدِيْنَ ۞

لَوْ خَرَجُوْا فِيْكُمْ مَّا زَادُوْكُمْ اِلَّا

only (made for) disorder,
hurrying here and there in your
midst and sowing sedition
among you, and there would
have been some among you who
would have listened to them .
But Allah knows well those who
do wrong.

48. Indeed they had plotted
sedition before, and upset
matters for you, until, the Truth
arrived, and the Decree of Allah
became manifest, much to their
disgust.

49. Among them is (many) a
man who says: "Grant me exemption and do not draw me
into trial." Have they not fallen
into trial already? and indeed
Hell surrounds the Unbelievers
(on all sides).

50. If good befalls you, it
grieves them; but if a misfortune
befalls you, they say, "We took
indeed our precautions
beforehand," and they turn
away rejoicing.

51. Say: "Nothing will happen
to us except what Allah has
decreed for us: He is our
Protector": and on Allah let the
Believers put their trust.

52. Say: "Can you expect for
us (any fate) other than one of
two glorious things- (martyr-
dom or victory)? But we can
expect for you either that Allah
will send His punishment from
Himself, or by our hands. So
wait (expectant); we too will
wait with you."

53. Say: "Spend (for the
Cause) willingly or unwillingly:
from you it will not be accepted:
for you are indeed a people
rebellious and wicked."

54. The only reasons why
their contributions are not

خَبَالًا وَّلَا أَوْضَعُوا خِلَلَكُمْ
يَبْغُونَكُمُ الْفِتْنَةَ ۚ وَفِيكُمْ
سَمّٰعُونَ لَهُمْ ؕ وَاللّٰهُ عَلِيْمٌۢ
بِالظّٰلِمِيْنَ ۝

لَقَدِ ابْتَغَوُا الْفِتْنَةَ مِنْ قَبْلُ
وَقَلَّبُوا لَكَ الْأُمُوْرَ حَتّٰى جَآءَ الْحَقُّ
وَظَهَرَ أَمْرُ اللّٰهِ وَهُمْ كٰرِهُوْنَ ۝

وَمِنْهُمْ مَّنْ يَّقُوْلُ ائْذَنْ لِّيْ وَلَا
تَفْتِنِّيْ ؕ اَلَا فِي الْفِتْنَةِ سَقَطُوْا ؕ
وَاِنَّ جَهَنَّمَ لَمُحِيْطَةٌۢ بِالْكٰفِرِيْنَ ۝

اِنْ تُصِبْكَ حَسَنَةٌ تَسُؤْهُمْ ۚ وَاِنْ
تُصِبْكَ مُصِيْبَةٌ يَّقُوْلُوْا قَدْ
اَخَذْنَا أَمْرَنَا مِنْ قَبْلُ وَيَتَوَلَّوْا
وَّهُمْ فَرِحُوْنَ ۝

قُلْ لَّنْ يُّصِيْبَنَا إِلَّا مَا كَتَبَ
اللّٰهُ لَنَا ۚ هُوَ مَوْلٰنَا ۚ وَعَلَى اللّٰهِ
فَلْيَتَوَكَّلِ الْمُؤْمِنُوْنَ ۝

قُلْ هَلْ تَرَبَّصُوْنَ بِنَا إِلَّا اِحْدَى
الْحُسْنَيَيْنِ ؕ وَنَحْنُ نَتَرَبَّصُ بِكُمْ
اَنْ يُّصِيْبَكُمُ اللّٰهُ بِعَذَابٍ مِّنْ
عِنْدِهٖ أَوْ بِأَيْدِيْنَا ۙ فَتَرَبَّصُوْا
اِنَّا مَعَكُمْ مُّتَرَبِّصُوْنَ ۝

قُلْ أَنْفِقُوْا طَوْعًا أَوْ كَرْهًا لَّنْ
يُّتَقَبَّلَ مِنْكُمْ ؕ اِنَّكُمْ كُنْتُمْ
قَوْمًا فٰسِقِيْنَ ۝

وَمَا مَنَعَهُمْ أَنْ تُقْبَلَ مِنْهُمْ

accepted are: that they reject Allah and His Apostle; that they come to prayer without earnestness; and that they offer contributions unwillingly.

55. Let not their wealth nor their (following in) sons dazzle you: in reality Allah's plan is to punish them with these things in this life, and that their souls may perish in their (very) denial of Allah.

56. They swear by Allah that they are indeed of you; but they are not of you: yet they are afraid (to appear in their true colours).

57. If they could find a place to flee to, or caves, or a place of concealment, they would turn straightway thereto, with an obstinate rush.

58. And among them are men who slander you in the matter of (the distribution of) the alms: if they are given part thereof, they are pleased, but if not, behold! they are indignant!

59. If only they had been content with what Allah and His Apostle gave them, and had said, "Sufficient unto us is Allah! Allah and His Apostle will soon give us of His bounty: to Allah do we turn our hopes!" (that would have been the right course).

60. Alms are for the poor and the needy, and those employed to administer the (funds); for those whose hearts have been (recently) reconciled (to Truth); for those in bondage and in debt; in the cause of Allah; and for the wayfarer: (thus is it) ordained by Allah, and Allah is full of knowledge and wisdom.

61. Among them are men who slander the Prophet and say, "He is (all) ear." Say, "He listens to what is best for you: he believes in Allah, has faith in the Believers, and is a Mercy to those of you who believe." But those who slander the Apostle will have a grievous Chastisement.

وَمِنْهُمُ الَّذِيْنَ يُؤْذُوْنَ النَّبِيَّ وَيَقُوْلُوْنَ هُوَ اُذُنٌ ۗ قُلْ اُذُنُ خَيْرٍ لَّكُمْ يُؤْمِنُ بِاللّٰهِ وَيُؤْمِنُ لِلْمُؤْمِنِيْنَ وَرَحْمَةٌ لِّلَّذِيْنَ اٰمَنُوْا مِنْكُمْ ۗ وَالَّذِيْنَ يُؤْذُوْنَ رَسُوْلَ اللّٰهِ لَهُمْ عَذَابٌ اَلِيْمٌ ۞

62. To you they swear by Allah, In order to please you: But it is more fitting that they should please Allah and His Apostle, if they are Believers.

يَحْلِفُوْنَ بِاللّٰهِ لَكُمْ لِيُرْضُوْكُمْ ۚ وَاللّٰهُ وَرَسُوْلُهٗ اَحَقُّ اَنْ يُّرْضُوْهُ اِنْ كَانُوْا مُؤْمِنِيْنَ ۞

63. Do they not know that for those who oppose Allah and His Apostle, is the Fire of Hell?- wherein they shall dwell. That is the supreme disgrace.

اَلَمْ يَعْلَمُوْا اَنَّهٗ مَنْ يُّحَادِدِ اللّٰهَ وَرَسُوْلَهٗ فَاَنَّ لَهٗ نَارَ جَهَنَّمَ خَالِدًا فِيْهَا ۗ ذٰلِكَ الْخِزْيُ الْعَظِيْمُ ۞

64. The Hypocrites are afraid lest a Sura should be sent down about them, showing them what is (really passing) in their hearts. Say: "Mock you! But verily Allah will bring to light all that you fear (should be revealed).

يَحْذَرُ الْمُنٰفِقُوْنَ اَنْ تُنَزَّلَ عَلَيْهِمْ سُوْرَةٌ تُنَبِّئُهُمْ بِمَا فِيْ قُلُوْبِهِمْ ۗ قُلِ اسْتَهْزِءُوْا ۚ اِنَّ اللّٰهَ مُخْرِجٌ مَّا تَحْذَرُوْنَ ۞

65. If you question them, they declare (with emphasis): "We were only talking idly and in play." Say: "Was it at Allah, and His Signs, and His Apostle, that you were mocking?"

وَلَئِنْ سَاَلْتَهُمْ لَيَقُوْلُنَّ اِنَّمَا كُنَّا نَخُوْضُ وَنَلْعَبُ ۗ قُلْ اَبِاللّٰهِ وَاٰيٰتِهٖ وَرَسُوْلِهٖ كُنْتُمْ تَسْتَهْزِءُوْنَ ۞

66. You do not make any excuses: you have rejected Faith after you had accepted it. If We pardon some of you, We will punish others amongst you, for that they are in sin.

لَا تَعْتَذِرُوْا قَدْ كَفَرْتُمْ بَعْدَ اِيْمَانِكُمْ ۗ اِنْ نَّعْفُ عَنْ طَآئِفَةٍ مِّنْكُمْ نُعَذِّبْ طَآئِفَةً بِاَنَّهُمْ كَانُوْا مُجْرِمِيْنَ ۞

67. The Hypocrites, men and women, (have an understanding) with each other: They enjoin evil, and forbid what is just, and are close

اَلْمُنٰفِقُوْنَ وَالْمُنٰفِقٰتُ بَعْضُهُمْ مِّنْ بَعْضٍ ۚ يَاْمُرُوْنَ بِالْمُنْكَرِ وَيَنْهَوْنَ عَنِ الْمَعْرُوْفِ وَيَقْبِضُوْنَ

with their hands. They have forgotten Allah; so He has forgotten them. Verily the Hypocrites
are rebellious and perverse.

68.   Allah has promised the
Hypocrites men and women,
and the rejecters, of Faith, the
fire of Hell: therein shall they
dwell: sufficient is it for them:
for them is the curse of Allah,
and an enduring punishment,-

69.   As in the case of those
before you: they were mightier
than you in power, and more
flourishing in wealth and
children. They had their
enjoyment of their portion: and
you have of yours, as did those
before you; and you indulge in
idle talk as they did. They!- their
works are fruitless in this world
and in the Hereafter, and they
will lose (all spiritual good).

70.   Has not the story reached
them of those before them?- the
People of Noah, and 'Ad, and
Thamud; the People of
Abraham, the men of Midian,
and the cities overthrown. To
them came their Apostles with
Clear Signs. It is not Allah Who
wrongs them, but they wrong
their own souls.

71.   The Believers, men and
women, are protectors, one of
another: they enjoin what is just,
and forbid what is evil: they
observe regular prayers,
practise regular charity, and
obey Allah and His Apostle. On
them will Allah pour His mercy:
for Allah is Exalted in power,

Wise.

72. Allah has promised to Believers, men and women, Gardens under which rivers flow, to dwell therein, and beautiful mansions in Gardens of everlasting bliss. But the greatest bliss is the Good pleasure of Allah: that is the supreme felicity.

73. O Prophet! strive hard against the Unbelievers and the Hypocrites, and be firm against them, their abode is Hell,- an evil refuge indeed.

74. They swear by Allah that they said nothing (evil), but indeed they uttered blasphemy, and they did it after accepting Islam; and they meditated a plot which they were unable to carry out: this revenge of theirs was (their) only return for the bounty with which Allah and His Apostle had enriched them! If they repent, it will be best for them; but if they turn back (to their evil ways), Allah will punish them with a grievous Chastisement in this life and in the Hereafter: they shall have none on earth to protect or help them.

75. Amongst them are men who made a Covenant with Allah, that if He bestowed on them of His bounty, they would give (largely) in charity, and be truly amongst those who are righteous.

76. But when He did bestow of His bounty, they became covetous, and turned back (from their Covenant), averse (from its fulfilment).

77. So He has put as a consequence Hypocrisy into their hearts, (to last) till the Day, whereon they shall meet Him: because they broke their

حَكِيمٌ ۞
وَعَدَ اللّٰهُ الْمُؤْمِنِيْنَ وَالْمُؤْمِنٰتِ
جَنّٰتٍ تَجْرِيْ مِنْ تَحْتِهَا الْأَنْهٰرُ
خٰلِدِيْنَ فِيْهَا وَمَسٰكِنَ طَيِّبَةً
فِيْ جَنّٰتِ عَدْنٍ ؕ وَرِضْوَانٌ مِّنَ
اللّٰهِ اَكْبَرُ ؕ ذٰلِكَ هُوَ الْفَوْزُ الْعَظِيْمُ ۞
يٰٓاَيُّهَا النَّبِيُّ جَاهِدِ الْكُفَّارَ
وَالْمُنٰفِقِيْنَ وَاغْلُظْ عَلَيْهِمْ ؕ وَ
مَأْوٰىهُمْ جَهَنَّمُ ؕ وَبِئْسَ الْمَصِيْرُ ۞
يَحْلِفُوْنَ بِاللّٰهِ مَا قَالُوْا ؕ وَ
لَقَدْ قَالُوْا كَلِمَةَ الْكُفْرِ وَ
كَفَرُوْا بَعْدَ اِسْلَامِهِمْ وَهَمُّوْا
بِمَا لَمْ يَنَالُوْا ؕ وَمَا نَقَمُوْٓا اِلَّآ
اَنْ اَغْنٰىهُمُ اللّٰهُ وَرَسُوْلُهٗ مِنْ
فَضْلِهٖ ؕ فَاِنْ يَّتُوْبُوْا يَكُ خَيْرًا
لَّهُمْ ؕ وَاِنْ يَّتَوَلَّوْا يُعَذِّبْهُمُ
اللّٰهُ عَذَابًا اَلِيْمًا ۙ فِي الدُّنْيَا وَ
الْاٰخِرَةِ ؕ وَمَا لَهُمْ فِي الْاَرْضِ
مِنْ وَّلِيٍّ وَّلَا نَصِيْرٍ ۞
وَمِنْهُمْ مَّنْ عٰهَدَ اللّٰهَ لَئِنْ
اٰتٰىنَا مِنْ فَضْلِهٖ لَنَصَّدَّقَنَّ
وَلَنَكُوْنَنَّ مِنَ الصّٰلِحِيْنَ ۞
فَلَمَّآ اٰتٰىهُمْ مِّنْ فَضْلِهٖ بَخِلُوْا
بِهٖ وَتَوَلَّوْا وَّهُمْ مُّعْرِضُوْنَ ۞
فَاَعْقَبَهُمْ نِفَاقًا فِيْ قُلُوْبِهِمْ اِلٰى
يَوْمِ يَلْقَوْنَهٗ بِمَآ اَخْلَفُوا اللّٰهَ مَا

Covenant with Allah, and because they lied (again and again).

78. Do they not know that Allah knows their secret (thoughts) and their secret counsels, and that Allah knows well all things unseen?

79. Those who slander such of the Believers as give themselves freely to (deeds of) charity, as well as such as can find nothing to give except the fruits of their labour,- and throw ridicule on them,- Allah will throw back their ridicule on them: and they shall have a grievous Chastisement.

80. Whether you ask for their forgiveness, or not, (their sin is unforgivable): if you ask seventy times for their forgiveness, Allah will not forgive them: because they have rejected Allah and His Apostle: and Allah does not guide those who are perversely rebellious.

81. Those who were left behind (in the Tabuk expedition) rejoiced in their inaction behind the back of the Apostle of Allah: they hated to strive and fight, with their goods and their persons, in the Cause of Allah: they said, "Do not go forth in the heat." Say, "The fire of Hell is fiercer in heat." If only they could understand!

82. Let them laugh a little: much will they weep: a recompense for the (evil) that they do.

83. If, then, Allah bring you back to any of them, and they ask your permission to come out (with you), say: "Never shall you come out with me, nor fight an enemy with me: for you preferred to sit inactive on the first occasion: then you sit (now) with those who lag behind."

84. Nor do you ever pray for any of them that dies,

وَعَدُّوهُ وَبِمَا كَانُوْا يَكْذِبُوْنَ ۝

اَلَمْ يَعْلَمُوْۤا اَنَّ اللّٰهَ يَعْلَمُ سِرَّهُمْ وَ نَجْوٰىهُمْ وَاَنَّ اللّٰهَ عَلَّامُ الْغُيُوْبِ ۝

اَلَّذِيْنَ يَلْمِزُوْنَ الْمُطَّوِّعِيْنَ مِنَ الْمُؤْمِنِيْنَ فِى الصَّدَقٰتِ وَالَّذِيْنَ لَا يَجِدُوْنَ اِلَّا جُهْدَهُمْ فَيَسْخَرُوْنَ مِنْهُمْ ۙ سَخِرَ اللّٰهُ مِنْهُمْ ۫ وَلَهُمْ عَذَابٌ اَلِيْمٌ ۝

اِسْتَغْفِرْ لَهُمْ اَوْ لَا تَسْتَغْفِرْ لَهُمْ ۗ اِنْ تَسْتَغْفِرْ لَهُمْ سَبْعِيْنَ مَرَّةً فَلَنْ يَّغْفِرَ اللّٰهُ لَهُمْ ۗ ذٰلِكَ بِاَنَّهُمْ كَفَرُوْا بِاللّٰهِ وَرَسُوْلِهٖ ۗ وَاللّٰهُ لَا يَهْدِى الْقَوْمَ الْفٰسِقِيْنَ ۝

فَرِحَ الْمُخَلَّفُوْنَ بِمَقْعَدِهِمْ خِلٰفَ رَسُوْلِ اللّٰهِ وَكَرِهُوْۤا اَنْ يُّجَاهِدُوْا بِاَمْوَالِهِمْ وَاَنْفُسِهِمْ فِىْ سَبِيْلِ اللّٰهِ وَقَالُوْا لَا تَنْفِرُوْا فِى الْحَرِّ ۗ قُلْ نَارُ جَهَنَّمَ اَشَدُّ حَرًّا ۗ لَوْ كَانُوْا يَفْقَهُوْنَ ۝

فَلْيَضْحَكُوْا قَلِيْلًا وَّلْيَبْكُوْا كَثِيْرًا ۚ جَزَآءً بِمَا كَانُوْا يَكْسِبُوْنَ ۝

فَاِنْ رَّجَعَكَ اللّٰهُ اِلٰى طَآئِفَةٍ مِّنْهُمْ فَاسْتَأْذَنُوْكَ لِلْخُرُوْجِ فَقُلْ لَّنْ تَخْرُجُوْا مَعِىَ اَبَدًا وَّلَنْ تُقَاتِلُوْا مَعِىَ عَدُوًّا ۗ اِنَّكُمْ رَضِيْتُمْ بِالْقُعُوْدِ اَوَّلَ مَرَّةٍ فَاقْعُدُوْا مَعَ الْخٰلِفِيْنَ ۝

وَلَا تُصَلِّ عَلٰۤى اَحَدٍ مِّنْهُمْ مَّاتَ

nor stand at his grave; for they rejected Allah and His Apostle, and died in a state of perverse rebellion.

85. Nor let their wealth nor their children dazzle you: Allah's plan is to punish them with these things in this world, and that their souls may perish in their (very) denial of Allah.

86. When a Sura comes down, enjoining them to believe in Allah and to strive and fight along with His Apostle, those with wealth and influence among them ask you for exemption, and say: "Leave us (behind): we would be with those who sit (at home)."

87. They prefer to be with (the women), who remain behind (at home): their hearts are sealed and so they do not understand.

88. But the Apostle, and those who believe with him, strive and fight with their wealth and their persons: for them are (all) good things: and it is they who will prosper.

89. Allah has prepared for them Gardens under which rivers flow, to dwell therein: that is the supreme felicity.

90. And there were, among the desert Arabs (also), men who made excuses and came to claim exemption; and those who were false to Allah and His Apostle (merely) sat inactive. Soon will a grievous Chastisement seize the Unbelievers among them.

91. There is no blame on those who are infirm, or ill, or who find no resources to spend (on the Cause), if they are sincere (in duty) to Allah and

His Apostle: no ground (of complaint) can there be against such as do right: and Allah is Oft-forgiving, Most Merciful.

92. Nor (is there blame) on those who came to you to be provided with mounts, and when you said, "I can not find any mounts for you," they turned back, their eyes streaming with tears of grief that they had no resources wherewith to provide the expenses.

93. The ground (of complaint) is against such as claim exemption while they are rich. They prefer to stay with the (women) who remain behind: Allah has sealed their hearts; so they do not know (what they miss).

94. They will present their excuses to you when you return to them. You say: "Present no excuses: we shall not believe you: Allah has already informed us of the true state of matters concerning you: It is your actions that Allah and His Apostle will observe: in the end you will be brought back to Him Who knows what is hidden and what is open: then He will show you the truth of all that you did."

95. They will swear to you by Allah, when you return to them, that you may leave them alone. So leave them alone: for they are an abomination, and Hell is their dwelling-place,—a fitting recompense for the (evil) that they did.

96. They will swear unto you, that you may be pleased with them, but if you are pleased with them, Allah is not pleased with those who disobey.

97 The Arabs of the desert are the worst in unbelief and hypocrisy, and most fitted

to be in ignorance of the
command which Allah has sent
down to His Apostle: But Allah
is All-knowing, All-Wise.

98. Some of the desert Arabs
look upon their payments as a
fine, and watch for disasters for
you: on them be the disaster of
evil: for Allah is He that hears
and knows (all things).

99. But some of the desert
Arabs believe in Allah and the
Last Day, and look on their
payments as pious gifts bringing
them nearer to Allah and
obtaining the prayers of the
Apostle. Yes, indeed they bring
them nearer (to Him): soon will
Allah admit them to His Mercy:
for Allah is Oft-forgiving, Most
Merciful.

100. The vanguard (of Islam)-
the first of those who forsook
(their homes) and of those who
gave them aid, and (also) those
who follow them in (all) good
deeds,- well- pleased is Allah
with them, as are they with Him:
for them He has prepared
Gardens under which rivers
flow, to dwell therein for ever:
that is the supreme felicity.

101. Certain of the desert Arabs
round about you are Hypocrites,
as well as (desert Arabs) among
the Medina folk: they are
obstinate in hypocrisy: you do
not know them: We know them:
twice shall We punish them: and
in addition they shall be sent to a
grievous Chastisement.

102. Others (there are who)
have acknowledged their
wrong-doings: they have mixed
an act that was good with
another that was evil. Perhaps
Allah will turn to them (in
Mercy): for Allah is Oft-
forgiving, Most Merciful.

103. Of their goods, take alms, that so you might purify and sanctify them; and pray on their behalf. Verily, your prayers are a source of security for them: and Allah is One Who hears and knows.

خُذْ مِنْ اَمْوَالِهِمْ صَدَقَةً تُطَهِّرُهُمْ وَتُزَكِّيْهِمْ بِهَا وَصَلِّ عَلَيْهِمْ ۭ اِنَّ صَلٰوتَكَ سَكَنٌ لَّهُمْ ۭ وَاللّٰهُ سَمِيْعٌ عَلِيْمٌ ۝

104. Do they not know that Allah accepts repentance from His votaries and receives their gifts of charity, and that Allah is verily He, the Oft-Returning, Most Merciful.

اَلَمْ يَعْلَمُوْٓا اَنَّ اللّٰهَ هُوَ يَقْبَلُ التَّوْبَةَ عَنْ عِبَادِهٖ وَيَأْخُذُ الصَّدَقٰتِ وَاَنَّ اللّٰهَ هُوَ التَّوَّابُ الرَّحِيْمُ ۝

105. And say: "Work (righteousness): soon will Allah observe your work, and His Apostle, and the Believers: soon will you be brought back to the Knower of what is hidden and what is open: then will He show you the truth of all that you did."

وَقُلِ اعْمَلُوْا فَسَيَرَى اللّٰهُ عَمَلَكُمْ وَرَسُوْلُهٗ وَالْمُؤْمِنُوْنَ ۭ وَسَتُرَدُّوْنَ اِلٰى عٰلِمِ الْغَيْبِ وَالشَّهَادَةِ فَيُنَبِّئُكُمْ بِمَا كُنْتُمْ تَعْمَلُوْنَ ۝

106. There are (yet) others, held in suspense for the command of Allah, whether He will punish them, or turn in mercy to them: and Allah is All-Knowing, Wise.

وَاٰخَرُوْنَ مُرْجَوْنَ لِاَمْرِ اللّٰهِ اِمَّا يُعَذِّبُهُمْ وَاِمَّا يَتُوْبُ عَلَيْهِمْ ۭ وَاللّٰهُ عَلِيْمٌ حَكِيْمٌ ۝

107. And there are those who put up a mosque by way of mischief and infidelity - to disunite the Believers - and in preparation for one who warred against Allah and His Apostle aforetime. They will indeed swear that their intention is nothing but good ; but Allah declares that they are certainly liars.

وَالَّذِيْنَ اتَّخَذُوْا مَسْجِدًا ضِرَارًا وَّكُفْرًا وَّتَفْرِيْقًاۢ بَيْنَ الْمُؤْمِنِيْنَ وَاِرْصَادًا لِّمَنْ حَارَبَ اللّٰهَ وَرَسُوْلَهٗ مِنْ قَبْلُ ۭ وَلَيَحْلِفُنَّ اِنْ اَرَدْنَآ اِلَّا الْحُسْنٰى ۭ وَاللّٰهُ يَشْهَدُ اِنَّهُمْ لَكٰذِبُوْنَ ۝

108. You never stand forth therein. There is a mosque whose foundation was laid from the first day on piety; it is more worthy of your standing forth (for prayer) therein. In it are men who love to be purified; and Allah loves those who make themselves pure.

لَا تَقُمْ فِيْهِ اَبَدًا ۭ لَمَسْجِدٌ اُسِّسَ عَلَى التَّقْوٰى مِنْ اَوَّلِ يَوْمٍ اَحَقُّ اَنْ تَقُوْمَ فِيْهِ ۭ فِيْهِ رِجَالٌ يُّحِبُّوْنَ اَنْ يَّتَطَهَّرُوْا ۭ وَاللّٰهُ يُحِبُّ الْمُطَّهِّرِيْنَ ۝

109. Which then is best? - he that lays his foundation on piety to Allah and His Good Pleasure? - or he

اَفَمَنْ اَسَّسَ بُنْيَانَهٗ عَلٰى تَقْوٰى مِنَ اللّٰهِ وَرِضْوَانٍ خَيْرٌ اَمْ مَّنْ

that lays his foundation on an undermined sand-cliff ready to crumble to pieces? And it crumbles to pieces with him, into the fire of Hell. And Allah does not guide people that do wrong.

110. The foundation of those who so build is never free from suspicion and shakiness in their hearts, until their hearts are cut to pieces. And Allah is All-Knowing, Wise.

111. Allah has purchased of the Believers their persons and their goods; for theirs (in return) is the Garden (of Paradise): they fight in His Cause, and slay and are slain: a promise binding on Him in Truth, through the Torah, the Gospel, and the Qur'an: and who is more faithful to his Covenant than Allah? Then rejoice in the bargain which you have concluded: that is the supreme achievement.

112. Those that turn (to Allah) in repentance; that serve Him, and praise Him; that wander in devotion to the Cause of Allah,: that bow down and prostrate themselves in prayer; that enjoin good and forbid evil; and observe the limits set by Allah;- (these do rejoice). So proclaim the glad tidings to the Believers.

113. It is not fitting, for the Prophet and those who believe, that they should pray for forgiveness for Pagans, even though they be of kin, after it is clear to them that they are companions of the Fire.

114. And Abraham prayed for his father's forgiveness only because of a promise he had made to him. But when it became clear to him that he was an enemy to Allah, he dissociated himself from him:

for Abraham was most tender-hearted, forbearing.

115. And Allah will not mislead a people after He has guided them, in order that He may make clear to them what to fear (and avoid)- for Allah has knowledge of all things.

116. To Allah belongs the dominion of the heavens and the earth. He gives life and He takes it. Except for Him you have no protector nor helper.

117. Allah turned with favour to the Prophet, the Muhajirs, and the Ansar,- who followed him in a time of distress, after that the hearts of a part of them had nearly swerved (from duty); but He turned to them (also): for He is to them Most Kind, Most Merciful.

118. (He turned in mercy also) to the three who were left behind; (they felt guilty) to such a degree that the earth seemed constrained to them, for all its spaciousness, and their (very) souls seemed straitened to them,- and they perceived that there is no fleeing from Allah (and no refuge) but to Himself. Then He turned to them, that they might repent: for Allah is Oft-Returning, Most Merciful.

119. O you who believe! Fear Allah and be with those who are true (in word and deed).

120. It was not fitting for the people of Medina and the Bedouin Arabs of the neighbour-hood, to refuse to follow Allah's Apostle, nor to prefer their own lives to his: because nothing could they suffer or do, but was reckoned to their credit as a deed of righteousness, whether they suffered thirst, or fatigue, or hunger, in the Cause of Allah, or trod paths to raise the ire of

the Unbelievers, or received any injury whatever from an enemy: for Allah does not suffer the reward to be lost of those who do good;-

الْكُفَّارَ وَلَا يَنَالُوْنَ مِنْ عَدُوٍّ نَّيْلًا اِلَّا كُتِبَ لَهُمْ بِهٖ عَمَلٌ صَالِحٌ ۭ اِنَّ اللّٰهَ لَا يُضِيْعُ اَجْرَ الْمُحْسِنِيْنَ ۙ

121. Nor could they spend anything (for the Cause) - small or great- nor cut across a valley, but the deed is inscribed to their credit: that Allah may requite their deed with the best (possible reward).

وَلَا يُنْفِقُوْنَ نَفَقَةً صَغِيْرَةً وَّلَا كَبِيْرَةً وَّلَا يَقْطَعُوْنَ وَادِيًا اِلَّا كُتِبَ لَهُمْ لِيَجْزِيَهُمُ اللّٰهُ اَحْسَنَ مَا كَانُوْا يَعْمَلُوْنَ ۞

122. Nor should the Believers all go forth together: if a contingent from every expedition remained behind, they could devote themselves to studies in religion, and admonish the people when they return to them,- that thus they (may learn) to guard themselves (against evil).

وَمَا كَانَ الْمُؤْمِنُوْنَ لِيَنْفِرُوْا كَآفَّةً ؕ فَلَوْلَا نَفَرَ مِنْ كُلِّ فِرْقَةٍ مِّنْهُمْ طَآئِفَةٌ لِّيَتَفَقَّهُوْا فِى الدِّيْنِ وَلِيُنْذِرُوْا قَوْمَهُمْ اِذَا رَجَعُوْٓا اِلَيْهِمْ لَعَلَّهُمْ يَحْذَرُوْنَ ۞

123. O you who believe! Fight the Unbelievers who gird you about, and let them find firmness in you: and know that Allah is with those who fear Him.

يٰٓاَيُّهَا الَّذِيْنَ اٰمَنُوْا قَاتِلُوا الَّذِيْنَ يَلُوْنَكُمْ مِّنَ الْكُفَّارِ وَلْيَجِدُوْا فِيْكُمْ غِلْظَةً ؕ وَاعْلَمُوْٓا اَنَّ اللّٰهَ مَعَ الْمُتَّقِيْنَ ۞

124. Whenever there comes down a Sura, some of them say: "Which of you has had his faith increased by it?" Yes, those who believe,- their faith is increased and they do rejoice.

وَاِذَا مَآ اُنْزِلَتْ سُوْرَةٌ فَمِنْهُمْ مَّنْ يَّقُوْلُ اَيُّكُمْ زَادَتْهُ هٰذِهٖٓ اِيْمَانًا ۚ فَاَمَّا الَّذِيْنَ اٰمَنُوْا فَزَادَتْهُمْ اِيْمَانًا وَّهُمْ يَسْتَبْشِرُوْنَ ۞

125. But those in whose hearts is a disease,- it will add doubt to their doubt, and they will die in a state of Unbelief.

وَاَمَّا الَّذِيْنَ فِيْ قُلُوْبِهِمْ مَّرَضٌ فَزَادَتْهُمْ رِجْسًا اِلٰى رِجْسِهِمْ وَمَاتُوْا وَهُمْ كٰفِرُوْنَ ۞

126. Don't they see that they are tried every year once or twice? Yet they do not turn in repentance, and they take no heed.

اَوَلَا يَرَوْنَ اَنَّهُمْ يُفْتَنُوْنَ فِيْ كُلِّ عَامٍ مَّرَّةً اَوْ مَرَّتَيْنِ ثُمَّ لَا يَتُوْبُوْنَ وَلَا هُمْ يَذَّكَّرُوْنَ ۞

SŪRAH-10
YŪNUS
(INTRODUCTION)

Chronologically this Sûrah and the five that follow (Suras 9, 12, 13, 14, and 15) are closely connected, and were revealed in the late Makkah period, as the great event of the Hijrat was gradually approaching down the stream of Time. But their chronology has no particular significance.

On the other hand their arrangement in the gradation of Qur'ânic teaching fits in with the subject-matter. S.8 and S. 9 were mainly concerned with the first questions that arose on the formation of the new and organised Community of Islam in its conflict with those who wished to suppress or destroy it or use force to prevent its growth and the consolidation of its ideals. See Introductions to those Sûras. The present group leads us to the questions that face us when external hostility has been met, and our relations to Allah have to be considered from a higher standpoint than that of sale-preservation. How does revelation work? What is the meaning of divine grace and its wihtdrawals How do the Messengers of Allah deliver their Message? How should we receive it?

All these question revolve round the revelation of the Qur'ân and each Sûrah of this group except the 13 has the Abbreviated Letters A.L.R. attached to it. S. 13 has the letters A.L.M.R., and we shall discuss this variation when we come to S. 13.

The Abbreviated Letters are mystic symbols, about whose meaning there is no authoritative explanation. If the present group A.L.R is cognate to the group A.L.M., we have to consider and form some idea in our minds as to the probable meaning of the variation. We think A.L.M. to be a symbol of those Suras that deal with the beginning, the middle, and the end of man's spiritual history,—the origin, the present position, and the things to come in the Last Days (eschatology, to use a theological term).

A.L. stand as symbols of the first two, and M. of the last. In the present group of Suras we find hardly any eschatological matter, and therefore we can understand the absence of M., the symbol standing for such matter. In its place comes R., which is phonetically allied to L.L. is produced by the impact of the tongue to the front of the palate, and R. to the middle of the palate. In many languages the letters L. and R. are interchangeable; e.g. in Arabic, al-Rahmân becomes ar-Rahmân, and R. in imperfect enunciation becomes L., as in Chinese lallations. If L. is a symbol of present-day things looking to the future, we may take R. as a symbol of present-day things looking within, i.e. into the interior of the organisation of the Ummat. And this symbolism fits in with the subject-matter of the Sûras in question. But no one should be dogmatic in speculation about mystic Symbols.

Let us now consider Sûrah 10 alone. The central theme is that Allah's wonderful Creation must not be viewed by us as a creation of material things only, once made and finished with. Most wonderful of all is how He reveals Himself to men through Apostles and Scriptures; how apostles are rejected by men, and the Message disbelieved until it is too late for repentance; and how, as in the case of Yûnus (Jonah) and his people, even the rejection (when repentance supervenes) does not prevent Allah's grace and mercy from working, and how far that working is beyond man's comprehension.

127. Whenever there comes down a Sura, they look at each other, (saying), "Does anyone see you?" Then they turn aside: Allah has turned their hearts (from the light); for they are a people that do not understand.

128. Now has come to you an Apostle from amongst yourselves: it grieves him that you should perish: he is ardently anxious over you: to the Believers he is most kind and merciful.

129. But if they turn away, say: "Allah is sufficient for me: there is no god but He: on Him is my trust,- He the Lord of the Throne (of Glory) Supreme!"

10. Yunus or Jonah
In the name of Allah. Most Gracious, Most Merciful.

1. Alif-Lam-Raa. These are the Ayats of the Book of Wisdom.

2. Is it a matter of wonderment to men that We have sent Our inspiration to a man from among themselves?- that he should warn mankind (of their danger), and give the good news to the Believers that they have before their Lord, the lofty rank of Truth. (But) the Unbelievers say: "This is indeed an evident sorcerer!"

3. Verily your Lord is Allah, Who created the heavens and the earth in six days, and is firmly established on the throne (of authority), regulating and governing all things. No intercessor (can plead with Him) except after His leave (has been obtai-ned). This is Allah your Lord; you therefore serve Him: will you not receive admonition?

4. To Him will be your return- of all of you. The promise of Allah is true and sure. It is He Who begins the process of creation, and repeats it, that He may reward with justice those who believe and work righteousness;

but those who reject Him will have draughts of boiling fluids, and a Chastisement grievous, because they did reject Him.

5. It is He Who made the sun to be a shining glory and the moon to be a light (of beauty), and measured out stages for it, that you might know the number of years and the count (of time). Nowise did Allah create this but in truth and righteousness. (Thus) He explains His Signs in detail, for those who understand.

6. Verily, in the alternation of the night and the day, and in all that Allah has created, in the heavens and the earth, are Signs for those who fear Him.

7. Those who do not rest their hope on their meeting with Us, but are pleased and satisfied with the life of the present, and those who do not heed Our Signs,-

8. Their abode is the Fire, because of the (evil) they earned.

9. Those who believe, and work righteousness,- their Lord will guide them because of their faith: beneath them will flow rivers in Gardens of Bliss.

10. (This will be) their cry therein: "Glory to You, O Allah!" And "Peace" will be their greeting therein! and the close of their cry will be: "Praise be to Allah, the Cherisher and Sustainer of the Worlds!"

11. If Allah were to hasten for men the ill (they have earned) as they would fain hasten on the good,- then would their respite be settled at once. But We leave those who do not rest their hope on their meeting with Us, in their trespasses, wandering in distraction to and fro.

12. When trouble touches a man, He cries unto Us (in all postures)- lying down on his side, or sitting, or standing. But when We have solved his trouble, he passes on his way as if he had never cried to us for a trouble that touched him! Thus do the deeds of transgressors seem fair in their eyes!

وَإِذَا مَسَّ الْإِنْسَانَ الضُّرُّ دَعَانَا لِجَنْبِهِ أَوْ قَاعِدًا أَوْ قَآئِمًا ۖ فَلَمَّا كَشَفْنَا عَنْهُ ضُرَّهُ مَرَّ كَأَنْ لَّمْ يَدْعُنَآ إِلَىٰ ضُرٍّ مَّسَّهُ ۚ كَذَٰلِكَ زُيِّنَ لِلْمُسْرِفِينَ مَا كَانُوْا يَعْمَلُوْنَ ۝

13. We destroyed generations before you when they did wrong: their Apostles came to them with Clear Signs, but they would not believe! Thus do We requite those who sin!

وَلَقَدْ أَهْلَكْنَا الْقُرُوْنَ مِنْ قَبْلِكُمْ لَمَّا ظَلَمُوْا ۙ وَجَآءَتْهُمْ رُسُلُهُمْ بِالْبَيِّنَاتِ وَمَا كَانُوْا لِيُؤْمِنُوْا ۚ كَذَٰلِكَ نَجْزِي الْقَوْمَ الْمُجْرِمِيْنَ ۝

14. Then We made you heirs in the land after them, to see how you would behave!

ثُمَّ جَعَلْنَاكُمْ خَلَآئِفَ فِي الْأَرْضِ مِنْ بَعْدِهِمْ لِنَنْظُرَ كَيْفَ تَعْمَلُوْنَ ۝

15. But when Our Clear Signs are rehearsed to them, those who do not rest their hope on their meeting with Us, say: "Bring us a Qur'an other than this, or change this," say: "It is not for me, of my own accord, to change it: I follow nothing but what is revealed to me: if I were to disobey my Lord, I should myself fear the Chastisement of a Great Day (to come)."

وَإِذَا تُتْلَىٰ عَلَيْهِمْ اٰيَاتُنَا بَيِّنَاتٍ ۙ قَالَ الَّذِيْنَ لَا يَرْجُوْنَ لِقَآءَنَا ائْتِ بِقُرْاٰنٍ غَيْرِ هٰذَآ أَوْ بَدِّلْهُ ۚ قُلْ مَا يَكُوْنُ لِيْٓ أَنْ أُبَدِّلَهُ مِنْ تِلْقَآيِٕ نَفْسِيْ ۖ إِنْ أَتَّبِعُ إِلَّا مَا يُوْحَىٰ إِلَيَّ ۖ إِنِّيْٓ أَخَافُ إِنْ عَصَيْتُ رَبِّيْ عَذَابَ يَوْمٍ عَظِيْمٍ ۝

16. Say: "If Allah had so willed, I should not have rehearsed it to you, nor would He have made it known to you. A whole life-time before this I have tarried amongst you: will you not then understand?"

قُلْ لَّوْ شَآءَ اللّٰهُ مَا تَلَوْتُهُ عَلَيْكُمْ وَلَآ أَدْرَاكُمْ بِهِ ۖ فَقَدْ لَبِثْتُ فِيْكُمْ عُمُرًا مِّنْ قَبْلِهِ ۚ أَفَلَا تَعْقِلُوْنَ ۝

17. Who does more wrong than such as forge a lie against Allah, or deny His Signs? But never will prosper those who sin.

فَمَنْ أَظْلَمُ مِمَّنِ افْتَرَىٰ عَلَى اللّٰهِ كَذِبًا أَوْ كَذَّبَ بِاٰيٰتِهِ ۚ إِنَّهُ لَا يُفْلِحُ الْمُجْرِمُوْنَ ۝

18. They serve, besides Allah, things that do not hurt them nor profit them, and they say:

وَيَعْبُدُوْنَ مِنْ دُوْنِ اللّٰهِ مَا لَا يَضُرُّهُمْ وَلَا يَنْفَعُهُمْ وَيَقُوْلُوْنَ

"These are our intercessors with Allah." Say: "Do you indeed inform Allah of something He knows not, in the heavens or on earth?- Glory to Him! and far is He above the partners they ascribe (to Him)!"

19. Mankind was but one nation, but differed (later). Had it not been for a Word that went forth before from your Lord, their differences would have been settled between them.

20. They say: "Why is not a Sign sent down to him from his Lord?" Say: "The Unseen is only for Allah (to know). Then you wait: I too will wait with you."

21. When We make mankind taste of some mercy after adversity has touched them, behold! they take to plotting against Our Signs! Say: "Swifter to plan is Allah!" Verily, Our angels record all the plots that you make.

22. He it is Who enables you to traverse through land and sea; so that you even board ships;- they sail with them with a favourable wind, and they rejoice thereat; then comes a stormy wind and the waves come to them from all sides, and they think they are being overwhelmed: they cry to Allah, sincerely offering (their) duty to Him saying, "If You deliver us from this, we shall truly show our gratitude!"

23. But when He delivers them, behold! they transgress insolently through the earth in defiance of right! O mankind! your insolence is against your own souls,- an enjoyment of the life of the present:

هٰؤُلَاءِ شُفَعَاؤُنَا عِنْدَ اللّٰهِ ۚ قُلْ اَتُنَبِّئُوْنَ اللّٰهَ بِمَا لَا يَعْلَمُ فِي السَّمٰوٰتِ وَلَا فِي الْاَرْضِ ۚ سُبْحٰنَهٗ وَتَعٰلٰى عَمَّا يُشْرِكُوْنَ ۞

وَمَا كَانَ النَّاسُ اِلَّا اُمَّةً وَّاحِدَةً فَاخْتَلَفُوْا ۚ وَلَوْلَا كَلِمَةٌ سَبَقَتْ مِنْ رَّبِّكَ لَقُضِيَ بَيْنَهُمْ فِيْمَا فِيْهِ يَخْتَلِفُوْنَ ۞

وَيَقُوْلُوْنَ لَوْلَا اُنْزِلَ عَلَيْهِ اٰيَةٌ مِّنْ رَّبِّهٖ ۚ فَقُلْ اِنَّمَا الْغَيْبُ لِلّٰهِ فَانْتَظِرُوْا ۚ اِنِّيْ مَعَكُمْ مِّنَ الْمُنْتَظِرِيْنَ ۞

وَاِذَا اَذَقْنَا النَّاسَ رَحْمَةً مِّنْ بَعْدِ ضَرَّاءَ مَسَّتْهُمْ اِذَا لَهُمْ مَّكْرٌ فِيْ اٰيَاتِنَا ۚ قُلِ اللّٰهُ اَسْرَعُ مَكْرًا ۚ اِنَّ رُسُلَنَا يَكْتُبُوْنَ مَا تَمْكُرُوْنَ ۞

هُوَ الَّذِيْ يُسَيِّرُكُمْ فِي الْبَرِّ وَالْبَحْرِ ۚ حَتّٰى اِذَا كُنْتُمْ فِي الْفُلْكِ ۚ وَجَرَيْنَ بِهِمْ بِرِيْحٍ طَيِّبَةٍ وَّفَرِحُوْا بِهَا جَاءَتْهَا رِيْحٌ عَاصِفٌ وَّجَاءَهُمُ الْمَوْجُ مِنْ كُلِّ مَكَانٍ وَّظَنُّوْا اَنَّهُمْ اُحِيْطَ بِهِمْ ۙ دَعَوُا اللّٰهَ مُخْلِصِيْنَ لَهُ الدِّيْنَ ۚ لَئِنْ اَنْجَيْتَنَا مِنْ هٰذِهٖ لَنَكُوْنَنَّ مِنَ الشّٰكِرِيْنَ ۞

فَلَمَّا اَنْجٰىهُمْ اِذَا هُمْ يَبْغُوْنَ فِي الْاَرْضِ بِغَيْرِ الْحَقِّ ۚ يٰاَيُّهَا النَّاسُ اِنَّمَا بَغْيُكُمْ عَلٰى اَنْفُسِكُمْ ۙ مَّتَاعَ الْحَيٰوةِ الدُّنْيَا

in the end, to Us is your return, and We shall show you the truth of all that you did.

24. The likeness of the life of the Present is as the rain which We send down from the skies: by its mingling arises the produce of the earth- which provides food for men and animals: (It grows) till the earth is clad with its golden ornaments and is decked out (in beauty): the people to whom it belongs think they have all powers of disposal over it: there reaches it Our command by night or by day, and We make it like a harvest clean-mown, as if it had not flourished only the day before! Thus do We explain the Signs in detail for those who reflect.

25. But Allah calls to the Home of Peace: He guides whom He pleases to a Way that is straight.

26. To those who do right is a goodly (reward)- Yes, more (than in measure)! No darkness nor shame shall cover their faces! They are companions of the Garden; they will abide therein (for ever).

27. But those who have earned evil will have a reward of like evil: ignominy will cover their (faces): no defender will they have from (the wrath of) Allah: their faces will be covered, as it were, with pieces from the depths of the darkness of Night : they are Companions of the Fire: they will abide therein (for ever)!

28. One Day We shall gather them all together. Then We shall say to those who joined gods (with Us): "To your place! you and those you joined as 'partners' We shall separate them, and their "Partners" shall say: "It was not us that you worshipped!

ثُمَّ اِلَيْنَا مَرْجِعُكُمْ فَنُنَبِّئُكُمْ بِمَا كُنْتُمْ تَعْمَلُوْنَ ۞

اِنَّمَا مَثَلُ الْحَيٰوةِ الدُّنْيَا كَمَآءٍ اَنْزَلْنٰهُ مِنَ السَّمَآءِ فَاخْتَلَطَ بِهٖ نَبَاتُ الْاَرْضِ مِمَّا يَأْكُلُ النَّاسُ وَ الْاَنْعَامُ ۫ حَتّٰى اِذَآ اَخَذَتِ الْاَرْضُ زُخْرُفَهَا وَازَّيَّنَتْ وَظَنَّ اَهْلُهَآ اَنَّهُمْ قٰدِرُوْنَ عَلَيْهَآ ۙ اَتٰىهَآ اَمْرُنَا لَيْلًا اَوْ نَهَارًا فَجَعَلْنٰهَا حَصِيْدًا كَاَنْ لَّمْ تَغْنَ بِالْاَمْسِ ۫ كَذٰلِكَ نُفَصِّلُ الْاٰيٰتِ لِقَوْمٍ يَّتَفَكَّرُوْنَ ۞

وَاللّٰهُ يَدْعُوْٓا اِلٰى دَارِ السَّلٰمِ ۫ وَيَهْدِيْ مَنْ يَّشَآءُ اِلٰى صِرَاطٍ مُّسْتَقِيْمٍ ۞

لِلَّذِيْنَ اَحْسَنُوا الْحُسْنٰى وَزِيَادَةٌ ۫ وَلَا يَرْهَقُ وُجُوْهَهُمْ قَتَرٌ وَّلَا ذِلَّةٌ ۫ اُولٰٓئِكَ اَصْحٰبُ الْجَنَّةِ ۫ هُمْ فِيْهَا خٰلِدُوْنَ ۞

وَالَّذِيْنَ كَسَبُوا السَّيِّاٰتِ جَزَآءُ سَيِّئَةٍ ۭ بِمِثْلِهَا ۙ وَتَرْهَقُهُمْ ذِلَّةٌ ۫ مَالَهُمْ مِّنَ اللّٰهِ مِنْ عَاصِمٍ ۫ كَاَنَّمَآ اُغْشِيَتْ وُجُوْهُهُمْ قِطَعًا مِّنَ الَّيْلِ مُظْلِمًا ۫ اُولٰٓئِكَ اَصْحٰبُ النَّارِ ۫ هُمْ فِيْهَا خٰلِدُوْنَ ۞

وَيَوْمَ نَحْشُرُهُمْ جَمِيْعًا ثُمَّ نَقُوْلُ لِلَّذِيْنَ اَشْرَكُوْا مَكَانَكُمْ اَنْتُمْ وَ شُرَكَآؤُكُمْ ۫ فَزَيَّلْنَا بَيْنَهُمْ وَقَالَ شُرَكَآؤُهُمْ مَّا كُنْتُمْ اِيَّانَا تَعْبُدُوْنَ ۞

29. "Enough is Allah for a witness between us and you: we certainly knew nothing of your worship of us!"

30. There will every soul prove (the fruits of) the deeds it sent before: they will be brought back to Allah, their rightful Lord, and their invented falsehoods will leave them in the lurch.

31. Say: "Who is it that sustains you (in life) from the sky and from the earth? Or who is it that has power over hearing and sight? And who is it that brings out the living from the dead and the dead from the living? And who is it that rules and regulates all affairs?" They will soon say, "Allah". Say, "Will you not then show piety (to Him)?"

32. Such is Allah, your real Cherisher and Sustainer; apart from Truth, what (remains) but error? How then are you turned away?

33. Thus is the Word of your Lord proved true against those who rebel: verily they will not believe.

34. Say: "Of your 'partners', can any originate creation and repeat it?" Say: "It is Allah Who originates creation and repeats it: then how are you deluded away (from the truth)?"

35. Say: "Of your 'partners' is there any that can give any guidance towards Truth?" Say: "It is Allah Who gives guidance towards Truth. Is then He Who gives guidance to truth more worthy to be followed, or he who finds not guidance (himself) unless he is guided? what then is the matter with you? How do you judge.

36. But most of them follow nothing but conjecture: truly conjecture can be of no avail against Truth.

فَكَفَى بِاللّٰهِ شَهِيْدًۢا بَيْنَنَا وَبَيْنَكُمْ اِنْ كُنَّا عَنْ عِبَادَتِكُمْ لَغٰفِلِيْنَ ۝

هُنَالِكَ تَبْلُوْا كُلُّ نَفْسٍ مَّاۤ اَسْلَفَتْ وَرُدُّوْۤا اِلَى اللّٰهِ مَوْلٰىهُمُ الْحَقِّ وَضَلَّ عَنْهُمْ مَّا كَانُوْا يَفْتَرُوْنَ ۝

قُلْ مَنْ يَّرْزُقُكُمْ مِّنَ السَّمَآءِ وَ الْاَرْضِ اَمَّنْ يَّمْلِكُ السَّمْعَ وَالْاَبْصَارَ وَمَنْ يُّخْرِجُ الْحَيَّ مِنَ الْمَيِّتِ وَيُخْرِجُ الْمَيِّتَ مِنَ الْحَيِّ وَمَنْ يُّدَبِّرُ الْاَمْرَ ۚ فَسَيَقُوْلُوْنَ اللّٰهُ ۚ فَقُلْ اَفَلَا تَتَّقُوْنَ ۝

فَذٰلِكُمُ اللّٰهُ رَبُّكُمُ الْحَقُّ ۚ فَمَاذَا بَعْدَ الْحَقِّ اِلَّا الضَّلٰلُ ۚ فَاَنّٰى تُصْرَفُوْنَ ۝

كَذٰلِكَ حَقَّتْ كَلِمَتُ رَبِّكَ عَلَى الَّذِيْنَ فَسَقُوْۤا اَنَّهُمْ لَا يُؤْمِنُوْنَ ۝

قُلْ هَلْ مِنْ شُرَكَآئِكُمْ مَّنْ يَّبْدَؤُا الْخَلْقَ ثُمَّ يُعِيْدُهٗ ۚ قُلِ اللّٰهُ يَبْدَؤُا الْخَلْقَ ثُمَّ يُعِيْدُهٗ ۚ فَاَنّٰى تُؤْفَكُوْنَ ۝

قُلْ هَلْ مِنْ شُرَكَآئِكُمْ مَّنْ يَّهْدِيْۤ اِلَى الْحَقِّ ۚ قُلِ اللّٰهُ يَهْدِيْ لِلْحَقِّ ۗ اَفَمَنْ يَّهْدِيْۤ اِلَى الْحَقِّ اَحَقُّ اَنْ يُّتَّبَعَ اَمَّنْ لَّا يَهِدِّيْۤ اِلَّاۤ اَنْ يُّهْدٰى ۚ فَمَا لَكُمْ ۚ كَيْفَ تَحْكُمُوْنَ ۝

وَمَا يَتَّبِعُ اَكْثَرُهُمْ اِلَّا ظَنًّا ۚ اِنَّ الظَّنَّ لَا يُغْنِيْ مِنَ الْحَقِّ شَيْئًا ۗ

Verily Allah is well aware of all that they do.

37. This Qur'an is not such as can be produced by other than Allah; on the contrary it is a confirmation of (revelations) that went before it, and a fuller explanation of the Book - wherein there is no doubt - from the Lord of the Worlds.

إِنَّ اللّٰهَ عَلِيمٌ بِمَا يَفْعَلُوْنَ ۝

وَمَا كَانَ هٰذَا الْقُرْاٰنُ اَنْ يُّفْتَرٰى مِنْ دُوْنِ اللّٰهِ وَلٰكِنْ تَصْدِيْقَ الَّذِيْ بَيْنَ يَدَيْهِ وَتَفْصِيْلَ الْكِتٰبِ لَا رَيْبَ فِيْهِ مِنْ رَّبِّ الْعٰلَمِيْنَ ۝

38. Or do they say, "He forged it"? Say: "Bring then a Sura like it, and call (to your aid) anyone you can, besides Allah, if it be you speak the truth!"

اَمْ يَقُوْلُوْنَ افْتَرٰىهُ ۭ قُلْ فَاْتُوْا بِسُوْرَةٍ مِّثْلِهٖ وَادْعُوْا مَنِ اسْتَطَعْتُمْ مِّنْ دُوْنِ اللّٰهِ اِنْ كُنْتُمْ صٰدِقِيْنَ ۝

39. Nay, they charge with falsehood that whose knowledge they cannot compass, even before the elucidation thereof has reached them: thus did those before them make charges of falsehood: but see what was the end of those who did wrong!

بَلْ كَذَّبُوْا بِمَا لَمْ يُحِيْطُوْا بِعِلْمِهٖ وَلَمَّا يَاْتِهِمْ تَاْوِيْلُهٗ ۭ كَذٰلِكَ كَذَّبَ الَّذِيْنَ مِنْ قَبْلِهِمْ فَانْظُرْ كَيْفَ كَانَ عَاقِبَةُ الظّٰلِمِيْنَ ۝

40. Of them there are some who believe therein, and some who do not: and your Lord knows best those who are out for mischief.

وَمِنْهُمْ مَّنْ يُّؤْمِنُ بِهٖ وَمِنْهُمْ مَّنْ لَّا يُؤْمِنُ بِهٖ ۭ وَرَبُّكَ اَعْلَمُ بِالْمُفْسِدِيْنَ ۝

41. If they charge you with falsehood, say: "My work to me, and yours to you! you are free from responsibility for what I do, and I for what you do!"

وَاِنْ كَذَّبُوْكَ فَقُلْ لِّيْ عَمَلِيْ وَلَكُمْ عَمَلُكُمْ ۚ اَنْتُمْ بَرِيْٓـُٔوْنَ مِمَّآ اَعْمَلُ وَاَنَا بَرِيْٓءٌ مِّمَّا تَعْمَلُوْنَ ۝

42. Among them are some who (pretend to) listen to you: but can you make the deaf to hear,- even though they are without understanding?

وَمِنْهُمْ مَّنْ يَّسْتَمِعُوْنَ اِلَيْكَ ۭ اَفَاَنْتَ تُسْمِعُ الصُّمَّ وَلَوْ كَانُوْا لَا يَعْقِلُوْنَ ۝

43. And among them are some who look at you: but can you guide the blind,- even though they will not see?

وَمِنْهُمْ مَّنْ يَّنْظُرُ اِلَيْكَ ۭ اَفَاَنْتَ تَهْدِي الْعُمْيَ وَلَوْ كَانُوْا لَا يُبْصِرُوْنَ ۝

44. Verily Allah will not deal unjustly with man in anything:

اِنَّ اللّٰهَ لَا يَظْلِمُ النَّاسَ شَيْـًٔا

It is man that wrongs his own soul.

45. One day He will gather them together: (It will be) as if they had tarried but an hour of a day: they will recognise each other: assuredly those will be lost who denied the meeting with Allah and refused to receive true guidance.

46. Whether We show you (realized in your life-time) some part of what We promise them,- or We take your soul (to Our Mercy) (before that),- in any case, to Us is their return: ultimately Allah is Witness to all that they do.

47. To every people (was sent) an Apostle: when their Apostle comes (before them), the matter will be judged between them with justice, and they will not be wronged.

48. They say: "When will this promise come to pass,- if you speak the truth?"

49. Say: "I have no power over any harm or profit to myself except as Allah wills. To every people is a term appointed: when their term is reached, not an hour can they cause delay, nor (an hour) can they advance (it in anticipation)."

50. Say: "Do you see,- if His punishment should come to you by night or by day,- what portion of it would the Sinners wish to hasten?

51. "Would you then believe in it at last, when it actually comes to pass? (It will then be said): 'Ah! now? and you wanted (aforetime) to hasten it on!'

52. "At length will be said to the wrong-doers: 'you taste the enduring punishment! You get the recompense of what you earned!'"

وَلٰكِنَّ النَّاسَ اَنْفُسَهُمْ يَظْلِمُوْنَ ۝

وَيَوْمَ يَحْشُرُهُمْ كَاَنْ لَّمْ يَلْبَثُوْٓا اِلَّا سَاعَةً مِّنَ النَّهَارِ يَتَعَارَفُوْنَ بَيْنَهُمْ ؕ قَدْ خَسِرَ الَّذِيْنَ كَذَّبُوْا بِلِقَآءِ اللّٰهِ وَمَا كَانُوْا مُهْتَدِيْنَ ۝

وَاِمَّا نُرِيَنَّكَ بَعْضَ الَّذِيْ نَعِدُهُمْ اَوْ نَتَوَفَّيَنَّكَ فَاِلَيْنَا مَرْجِعُهُمْ ثُمَّ اللّٰهُ شَهِيْدٌ عَلٰى مَا يَفْعَلُوْنَ ۝

وَلِكُلِّ اُمَّةٍ رَّسُوْلٌ ۚ فَاِذَا جَآءَ رَسُوْلُهُمْ قُضِيَ بَيْنَهُمْ بِالْقِسْطِ وَهُمْ لَا يُظْلَمُوْنَ ۝

وَيَقُوْلُوْنَ مَتٰى هٰذَا الْوَعْدُ اِنْ كُنْتُمْ صٰدِقِيْنَ ۝

قُلْ لَّاۤ اَمْلِكُ لِنَفْسِيْ ضَرًّا وَّلَا نَفْعًا اِلَّا مَا شَآءَ اللّٰهُ ؕ لِكُلِّ اُمَّةٍ اَجَلٌ ؕ اِذَا جَآءَ اَجَلُهُمْ فَلَا يَسْتَأْخِرُوْنَ سَاعَةً وَّلَا يَسْتَقْدِمُوْنَ ۝

قُلْ اَرَءَيْتُمْ اِنْ اَتٰىكُمْ عَذَابُهٗ بَيَاتًا اَوْ نَهَارًا مَّاذَا يَسْتَعْجِلُ مِنْهُ الْمُجْرِمُوْنَ ۝

اَثُمَّ اِذَا مَا وَقَعَ اٰمَنْتُمْ بِهٖ ؕ آلْـٰٔنَ وَقَدْ كُنْتُمْ بِهٖ تَسْتَعْجِلُوْنَ ۝

ثُمَّ قِيْلَ لِلَّذِيْنَ ظَلَمُوْا ذُوْقُوْا عَذَابَ الْخُلْدِ ۚ هَلْ تُجْزَوْنَ اِلَّا بِمَا كُنْتُمْ تَكْسِبُوْنَ ۝

53. They seek to be informed by you: "Is that true?" Say: "Yes, by my Lord! it is the very truth and you cannot frustrate it!"

54. Every soul that has sinned, if it possessed all that is on earth, would fain give it in ransom: they would declare (their) repentance when they see the Chastisement: but the judgment between them will be with justice, and no wrong will be done to them.

55. Is it not (the case) that to Allah belongs whatever is in the heavens and on earth? Is it not (the case) that Allah's promise is assuredly true? Yet most of them do not understand.

56. It is He Who gives life and who takes it, and to Him shall you all be brought back.

57. O mankind! there has come to you a direction from your Lord and a healing for the (diseases) in your hearts,- and for those who believe, a Guidance and a Mercy.

58. Say: "In the Bounty of Allah, and in His Mercy,- in that let them rejoice": that is better than the (wealth) they hoard.

59. Say: "Do you see what things Allah has sent down to you for sustenance? Yet you hold forbidden some things thereof and (some things) lawful." Say: "Has Allah indeed permitted you, or do you invent (things) to attribute to Allah?"

60. And what do those think who invent lies against Allah, of the Day of Judgment? Verily Allah is full of Bounty to mankind, but most of them are ungrateful.

61. In whatever business you may be, and whatever portion you may be reciting

from the Qur'an,- and whatever deed you (mankind) may be doing,- We are Witnesses thereof when you are deeply engrossed therein. Nor is hidden from your Lord (so much as) the weight of an atom on the earth or in heaven. And not the least and not the greatest of these things but are recorded in a clear Record.

مِنْهُ مِنْ قُرْآنٍ وَّلَا تَعْمَلُوْنَ مِنْ عَمَلٍ اِلَّا كُنَّا عَلَيْكُمْ شُهُوْدًا اِذْ تُفِيْضُوْنَ فِيْهِ ۖ وَمَا يَعْزُبُ عَنْ رَّبِّكَ مِنْ مِّثْقَالِ ذَرَّةٍ فِى الْاَرْضِ وَلَا فِى السَّمَآءِ وَلَا اَصْغَرَ مِنْ ذٰلِكَ وَلَا اَكْبَرَ اِلَّا فِىْ كِتٰبٍ مُّبِيْنٍ ۞

62. Behold! verily on the friends of Allah there is no fear, nor shall they grieve;

اَلَا اِنَّ اَوْلِيَآءَ اللّٰهِ لَا خَوْفٌ عَلَيْهِمْ وَلَا هُمْ يَحْزَنُوْنَ ۞

63. Those who believe and (constantly) guard against evil;-

الَّذِيْنَ اٰمَنُوْا وَكَانُوْا يَتَّقُوْنَ ۞

64. For them are Glad Tidings, in the life of the Present and in the Hereafter; no change can there be in the Words of Allah. This is indeed the supreme felicity.

لَهُمُ الْبُشْرٰى فِى الْحَيٰوةِ الدُّنْيَا وَفِى الْاٰخِرَةِ ۖ لَا تَبْدِيْلَ لِكَلِمٰتِ اللّٰهِ ۚ ذٰلِكَ هُوَ الْفَوْزُ الْعَظِيْمُ ۞

65. Let not their speech grieve you: for all power and honour belong to Allah: It is He Who hears and knows (all things).

وَلَا يَحْزُنْكَ قَوْلُهُمْ ۘ اِنَّ الْعِزَّةَ لِلّٰهِ جَمِيْعًا ۗ هُوَ السَّمِيْعُ الْعَلِيْمُ ۞

66. Behold! verily to Allah belong all creatures, in the heavens and on earth. What do they follow who worship as His "partners" other than Allah? They follow nothing but fancy, and they do nothing but lie.

اَلَا اِنَّ لِلّٰهِ مَنْ فِى السَّمٰوٰتِ وَمَنْ فِى الْاَرْضِ ۗ وَمَا يَتَّبِعُ الَّذِيْنَ يَدْعُوْنَ مِنْ دُوْنِ اللّٰهِ شُرَكَآءَ ۚ اِنْ يَّتَّبِعُوْنَ اِلَّا الظَّنَّ وَاِنْ هُمْ اِلَّا يَخْرُصُوْنَ ۞

67. He it is that has made for you the Night that you may rest therein, and the Day to make things visible (to you). Verily in this are Signs for those who listen (to His Message).

هُوَ الَّذِيْ جَعَلَ لَكُمُ الَّيْلَ لِتَسْكُنُوْا فِيْهِ وَالنَّهَارَ مُبْصِرًا ۚ اِنَّ فِىْ ذٰلِكَ لَاٰيٰتٍ لِّقَوْمٍ يَّسْمَعُوْنَ ۞

68. They say: "God (Alalh) has begotten a son!" - Glory be to Him! He is Self-Sufficient! His are all things in the heavens and on earth! No warrant have you

قَالُوا اتَّخَذَ اللّٰهُ وَلَدًا سُبْحٰنَهُ ۗ هُوَ الْغَنِيُّ ۗ لَهُ مَا فِى السَّمٰوٰتِ وَمَا فِى الْاَرْضِ ۗ اِنْ عِنْدَكُمْ مِّنْ

for this! Do you say about Allah what you do not know?

69. Say: "Those who invent a lie against Allah will never prosper."

70. A little enjoyment in this world!- and then, to Us will be their return, then shall We make them taste the severest Chastisement for their blasphemies.

71. Relate to them the story of Noah. Behold! he said to his people: "O my people, if it be hard on your (mind) that I should stay (with you) and commemorate the Signs of Allah,- yet I put my trust in Allah. You then get an agreement about your plan and among your partners, so your plan be not to you dark and dubious. Then pass your sentence on me, and give me no respite.

72. "But if you turn back, (consider): no reward have I asked of you: my reward is only due from Allah, and I have been commanded to be of those who submit to Allah's Will (in Islam)."

73. They rejected him, but We delivered him, and those with him, in the Ark, and We made them inherit (the earth), while We overwhelmed in the flood those who rejected Our Signs. Then see what was the end of those who were warned (but heeded not)!

74. Then after him We sent (many) Apostles to their peoples: they brought them Clear Signs, but they would not believe what they had already rejected beforehand. Thus do We seal the hearts of the transgressors.

75. Then after them We sent Moses and Aaron to Pharaoh and his chiefs with Our Signs. But they were arrogant: they were a people in sin.

76. When the Truth did come to them from Us, they said: "This is indeed evident sorcery!"

77. Moses said: "Do you say (this) about the Truth when it has (actually) reached you? Is sorcery (like) this? But sorcerers will not prosper."

78. They said: "Have you come to us to turn us away from the ways we found our fathers following,- in order that you and your brother may have greatness in the land? But we shall not believe in you!"

79. Pharaoh said: "Bring me every sorcerer well versed."

80. When the sorcerers came, Moses said to them: "You throw what you (wish) to throw!"

81. When they had had their throw, Moses said: "What you have brought is sorcery: Allah will surely make it of no effect: for Allah does not prosper the work of those who make mischief.

82. "And Allah by His Words proves and establishes His Truth, however much the Sinners may hate it!"

83. But none believed in Moses except some children of his people, because of the fear of Pharaoh and his chiefs, lest they should persecute them; and certainly Pharaoh was mighty on the earth and one who transgressed all bounds.

ثُمَّ بَعَثْنَا مِنْ بَعْدِهِمْ مُّوْسَى وَهَارُوْنَ

اِلَى فِرْعَوْنَ وَمَلَائِهِ بِاٰيٰتِنَا

فَاسْتَكْبَرُوْا وَكَانُوْا قَوْمًا مُّجْرِمِيْنَ ۝

فَلَمَّا جَآءَهُمُ الْحَقُّ مِنْ عِنْدِنَا قَالُوْٓا

اِنَّ هٰذَا لَسِحْرٌ مُّبِيْنٌ ۝

قَالَ مُوْسٰى اَتَقُوْلُوْنَ لِلْحَقِّ لَمَّا

جَآءَكُمْ ۖ اَسِحْرٌ هٰذَا ۖ وَلَا يُفْلِحُ

السّٰحِرُوْنَ ۝

قَالُوْٓا اَجِئْتَنَا لِتَلْفِتَنَا عَمَّا

وَجَدْنَا عَلَيْهِ اٰبَآءَنَا وَتَكُوْنَ

لَكُمَا الْكِبْرِيَآءُ فِي الْاَرْضِ ۖ وَمَا

نَحْنُ لَكُمَا بِمُؤْمِنِيْنَ ۝

وَقَالَ فِرْعَوْنُ ائْتُوْنِيْ بِكُلِّ

سٰحِرٍ عَلِيْمٍ ۝

فَلَمَّا جَآءَ السَّحَرَةُ قَالَ لَهُمْ

مُّوْسٰٓى اَلْقُوْا مَآ اَنْتُمْ مُّلْقُوْنَ ۝

فَلَمَّآ اَلْقَوْا قَالَ مُوْسٰى مَا جِئْتُمْ بِهِ

السِّحْرُ ۖ اِنَّ اللّٰهَ سَيُبْطِلُهُ ۖ اِنَّ

اللّٰهَ لَا يُصْلِحُ عَمَلَ الْمُفْسِدِيْنَ ۝

وَيُحِقُّ اللّٰهُ الْحَقَّ بِكَلِمٰتِهِ وَلَوْ كَرِهَ

الْمُجْرِمُوْنَ ۝

فَمَآ اٰمَنَ لِمُوْسٰٓى اِلَّا ذُرِّيَّةٌ مِّنْ

قَوْمِهٖ عَلٰى خَوْفٍ مِّنْ فِرْعَوْنَ

وَمَلَائِهِمْ اَنْ يَّفْتِنَهُمْ ۖ وَاِنَّ

فِرْعَوْنَ لَعَالٍ فِي الْاَرْضِ ۚ وَاِنَّهٗ

لَمِنَ الْمُسْرِفِيْنَ ۝

84. Moses said: "O my people! If you do (really) believe in Allah, then in Him put your trust if you submit (your will to His)."

وَقَالَ مُوْسَى يٰقَوْمِ اِنْ كُنْتُمْ اٰمَنْتُمْ بِاللّٰهِ فَعَلَيْهِ تَوَكَّلُوْۤا اِنْ كُنْتُمْ مُّسْلِمِيْنَ ۞

85. They said: "In Allah do we put our trust. Our Lord! do not make us a trial for those who practise oppression;

فَقَالُوْا عَلَى اللّٰهِ تَوَكَّلْنَا ۚ رَبَّنَا لَا تَجْعَلْنَا فِتْنَةً لِّلْقَوْمِ الظّٰلِمِيْنَ ۞

86. "And deliver us by Your Mercy from those who reject (You)."

وَنَجِّنَا بِرَحْمَتِكَ مِنَ الْقَوْمِ الْكٰفِرِيْنَ ۞

87. We inspired Moses and his brother with this Message: "Provide dwellings for your people in Egypt, make your dwellings into places of worship, and establish regular prayers: and give Glad Tidings to those who believe!"

وَاَوْحَيْنَاۤ اِلٰى مُوْسٰى وَاَخِيْهِ اَنْ تَبَوَّاٰ لِقَوْمِكُمَا بِمِصْرَ بُيُوْتًا وَّاجْعَلُوْا بُيُوْتَكُمْ قِبْلَةً وَّاَقِيْمُوا الصَّلٰوةَ ۚ وَبَشِّرِ الْمُؤْمِنِيْنَ ۞

88. Moses prayed: "Our Lord! You have indeed bestowed on Pharaoh and his Chiefs splendour and wealth in the life of the Present, and so, our Lord, they mislead (men) from Your Path. Our Lord, deface the features of their wealth, and send hardness to their hearts, so they will not believe until they see the grievous Chastisement."

وَقَالَ مُوْسٰى رَبَّنَاۤ اِنَّكَ اٰتَيْتَ فِرْعَوْنَ وَمَلَاَهٗ زِيْنَةً وَّاَمْوَالًا فِى الْحَيٰوةِ الدُّنْيَا ۙ رَبَّنَا لِيُضِلُّوْا عَنْ سَبِيْلِكَ ۚ رَبَّنَا اطْمِسْ عَلٰۤى اَمْوَالِهِمْ وَاشْدُدْ عَلٰى قُلُوْبِهِمْ فَلَا يُؤْمِنُوْا حَتّٰى يَرَوُا الْعَذَابَ الْاَلِيْمَ ۞

89. Allah said: "Accepted is your prayer (O Moses and Aaron)! So you stand straight, and do not follow the path of those who do not know."

قَالَ قَدْ اُجِيْبَتْ دَّعْوَتُكُمَا فَاسْتَقِيْمَا وَلَا تَتَّبِعٰٓنِّ سَبِيْلَ الَّذِيْنَ لَا يَعْلَمُوْنَ ۞

90. We took the Children of Israel across the sea: Pharaoh and his hosts followed them in insolence and spite. At length, when overwhelmed with the flood, he said: "I believe that there is no god except Him Whom the Children of Israel believe in: I am of those who submit (to Allah in Islam)."

وَجٰوَزْنَا بِبَنِيْۤ اِسْرَآءِيْلَ الْبَحْرَ فَاَتْبَعَهُمْ فِرْعَوْنُ وَجُنُوْدُهٗ بَغْيًا وَّعَدْوًا ۗ حَتّٰىۤ اِذَاۤ اَدْرَكَهُ الْغَرَقُ ۙ قَالَ اٰمَنْتُ اَنَّهٗ لَاۤ اِلٰهَ اِلَّا الَّذِيْۤ اٰمَنَتْ بِهٖ بَنُوْۤا اِسْرَآءِيْلَ وَاَنَا مِنَ الْمُسْلِمِيْنَ ۞

91. (It was said to him): "Ah now!- But a little while before, you were in rebellion!- and you did mischief (and violence)!

92. "This day shall We save you in your body, that you may be a Sign to those who come after you! but verily, many among mankind are heedless of Our Signs!"

93. We settled the Children of Israel in a beautiful dwelling-place, and provided for them sustenance of the best: it was after knowledge had been granted to them, that they fell into schisms. Verily Allah will judge between them as to the schisms amongst them, on the Day of Judgment.

94. If you were in doubt as to what We have revealed to you, then ask those who have been reading the Book before you: the Truth has indeed come to you from your Lord: so be in no wise of those in doubt.

95. Nor be of those who reject the Signs of Allah, or you shall be of those who perish.

96. Those against whom the Word of your Lord has been verified would not believe-

97. Even if every Sign was brought to them,- until they see (for themselves) the Chastisement grievous.

98. Why was there not a single township (among those We warned), which believed,- so its faith should have profited it,- except the people of Jonah? When they believed, We removed from them the Chastisement of ignominy in the life of the present, and permitted them to enjoy (their life) for a while.

ٱلْـٰٔنَ وَقَدْ عَصَيْتَ قَبْلُ وَكُنْتَ مِنَ الْمُفْسِدِيْنَ ۞

فَالْيَوْمَ نُنَجِّيْكَ بِبَدَنِكَ لِتَكُوْنَ لِمَنْ خَلْفَكَ اٰيَةً ۚ وَاِنَّ كَثِيْرًا مِّنَ النَّاسِ عَنْ اٰيٰتِنَا لَغٰفِلُوْنَ ۞

وَلَقَدْ بَوَّأْنَا بَنِيْ اِسْرَآءِيْلَ مُبَوَّأَ صِدْقٍ وَّرَزَقْنٰهُمْ مِّنَ الطَّيِّبٰتِ ۚ فَمَا اخْتَلَفُوْا حَتّٰى جَآءَهُمُ الْعِلْمُ ۚ اِنَّ رَبَّكَ يَقْضِيْ بَيْنَهُمْ يَوْمَ الْقِيٰمَةِ فِيْمَا كَانُوْا فِيْهِ يَخْتَلِفُوْنَ ۞

فَاِنْ كُنْتَ فِيْ شَكٍّ مِّمَّا اَنْزَلْنَا اِلَيْكَ فَسْـَٔلِ الَّذِيْنَ يَقْرَءُوْنَ الْكِتٰبَ مِنْ قَبْلِكَ ۚ لَقَدْ جَآءَكَ الْحَقُّ مِنْ رَّبِّكَ فَلَا تَكُوْنَنَّ مِنَ الْمُمْتَرِيْنَ ۞

وَلَا تَكُوْنَنَّ مِنَ الَّذِيْنَ كَذَّبُوْا بِاٰيٰتِ اللّٰهِ فَتَكُوْنَ مِنَ الْخٰسِرِيْنَ ۞

اِنَّ الَّذِيْنَ حَقَّتْ عَلَيْهِمْ كَلِمَتُ رَبِّكَ لَا يُؤْمِنُوْنَ ۞

وَلَوْ جَآءَتْهُمْ كُلُّ اٰيَةٍ حَتّٰى يَرَوُا الْعَذَابَ الْاَلِيْمَ ۞

فَلَوْلَا كَانَتْ قَرْيَةٌ اٰمَنَتْ فَنَفَعَهَا اِيْمَانُهَا اِلَّا قَوْمَ يُوْنُسَ ۚ لَمَّا اٰمَنُوْا كَشَفْنَا عَنْهُمْ عَذَابَ الْخِزْيِ فِي الْحَيٰوةِ الدُّنْيَا وَمَتَّعْنٰهُمْ اِلٰى حِيْنٍ ۞

99. If it had been your Lord's Will, they would all have believed,- all who are on earth! Will you then compel mankind, against their will, to believe!

وَلَوْ شَاءَ رَبُّكَ لَاٰمَنَ مَنْ فِى الْاَرْضِ كُلُّهُمْ جَمِيْعًا ۚ اَفَاَنْتَ تُكْرِهُ النَّاسَ حَتّٰى يَكُوْنُوْا مُؤْمِنِيْنَ ۝

100. No soul can believe, except by the Will of Allah, and He will place Doubt (or obscurity) on those who will not understand.

وَمَا كَانَ لِنَفْسٍ اَنْ تُؤْمِنَ اِلَّا بِاِذْنِ اللّٰهِ ۚ وَيَجْعَلُ الرِّجْسَ عَلَى الَّذِيْنَ لَا يَعْقِلُوْنَ ۝

101. Say: "Behold all that is in the heavens and on earth"; but neither Signs nor Warners profit those who do not believe.

قُلِ انْظُرُوْا مَا ذَا فِى السَّمٰوٰتِ وَالْاَرْضِ ۚ وَمَا تُغْنِى الْاٰيٰتُ وَالنُّذُرُ عَنْ قَوْمٍ لَّا يُؤْمِنُوْنَ ۝

102. Do they then expect (anything) but (what happened in) the days of the men who passed away before them? Say: "You wait then: for I, too, will wait with you."

فَهَلْ يَنْتَظِرُوْنَ اِلَّا مِثْلَ اَيَّامِ الَّذِيْنَ خَلَوْا مِنْ قَبْلِهِمْ ۚ قُلْ فَانْتَظِرُوْا اِنِّيْ مَعَكُمْ مِّنَ الْمُنْتَظِرِيْنَ ۝

103. In the end We deliver Our Apostles and those who believe: thus is it fitting on Our part that We should deliver those who believe!

ثُمَّ نُنَجِّيْ رُسُلَنَا وَالَّذِيْنَ اٰمَنُوْا كَذٰلِكَ ۚ حَقًّا عَلَيْنَا نُنْجِ الْمُؤْمِنِيْنَ ۝

104. Say: "O you men! If you are in doubt as to my religion, (behold!) I do not worship what you worship, other than Allah! But I worship Allah - Who will take your souls (at death): I am commanded to be (in the ranks) of the Believers,

قُلْ يٰٓاَيُّهَا النَّاسُ اِنْ كُنْتُمْ فِيْ شَكٍّ مِّنْ دِيْنِيْ فَلَا اَعْبُدُ الَّذِيْنَ تَعْبُدُوْنَ مِنْ دُوْنِ اللّٰهِ وَلٰكِنْ اَعْبُدُ اللّٰهَ الَّذِيْ يَتَوَفّٰىكُمْ ۚ وَاُمِرْتُ اَنْ اَكُوْنَ مِنَ الْمُؤْمِنِيْنَ ۙ

105. "And further (thus): 'set your face towards Religion with true piety, and never in any wise be of the Unbelievers;

وَاَنْ اَقِمْ وَجْهَكَ لِلدِّيْنِ حَنِيْفًا ۚ وَلَا تَكُوْنَنَّ مِنَ الْمُشْرِكِيْنَ ۝

106. "'Nor call on any, other than Allah;- Such will neither profit you nor hurt you: if you do so, behold! you shall certainly be of those who do wrong.'"

وَلَا تَدْعُ مِنْ دُوْنِ اللّٰهِ مَا لَا يَنْفَعُكَ وَلَا يَضُرُّكَ ۚ فَاِنْ فَعَلْتَ فَاِنَّكَ اِذًا مِّنَ الظّٰلِمِيْنَ ۝

107. If Allah touches you with hurt, there is none

وَاِنْ يَّمْسَسْكَ اللّٰهُ بِضُرٍّ فَلَا

SÛRAH-11
HÛD
(INTRODUCTION)

For the chronological place of this Sûrah and the general arguments of Sûras 10 to 15, see Introduction to S. 10.

In subject-matter this Sûrah supplements the preceding one. In the last Sûrah stress was laid on that side of Allah's dealings with man which leads to Mercy: here stress is laid on the side which deals with justice and the punishment of Sin when all Grace is resisted.

can remove it but He: if He
designs some benefit for you,
there is none can keep back His
favour: He causes it to reach
whomsoever of His servants He
pleases. And He is the Oft-
Forgiving, Most Merciful.

108. Say: "O you men! Now
Truth has reached you from
your Lord! those who receive
guidance, do so for the good of
their own souls; those who stray,
do so to their own loss: and I am
not (set) over you to arrange
your affairs."

109. You follow the inspiration
sent to you, and be patient and
constant, till Allah do decide:
for He is the Best to decide.

11. Hud (The Prophet Hud)
In the name of Allah. Most
Gracious, Most Merciful.

1. Alif - Lam - Raa (This is) a
Book, with verses basic or funda-
mental (of established meaning),
further explained in detail,- from
One Who is Wise and Well-
Acquainted (with all things):

2. (It teaches) that you should
worship none but Allah. (Say):
"Verily I am (sent) to you from
Him to warn and to bring glad
tidings:

3. "(And to preach thus),
'You seek the forgiveness of your
Lord, and turn to Him in
repentance; that He may grant
you enjoyment, good (and true),
for a term appointed, and bestow
His abounding grace on all who
abound in merit! But if you turn
away , then I fear for you the
Chastisement of a Great Day:

4. 'To Allah is your return,
and He has power over all
things."

5. Behold! they fold up their
hearts, that they may lie hid from
Him! Ah! even when

they cover themselves with their garments, He knows what they conceal, and what they reveal: for He knows well the (inmost secrets) of the hearts.

6. There is no moving creature on earth but its sustenance depends on Allah: He knows the time and place of its definite abode and its temporary deposit: all is in a clear Record.

7. He it is Who created the heavens and the earth in six Days - and His Throne was over the waters - that He might try you, which of you is best in conduct. But if you were to say to them, "You shall indeed be raised up after death", the Unbelievers would be sure to say, "This is nothing but obvious sorcery!"

8. If We delay the Chastisement for them for a definite term, they are sure to say, "What keeps it back?" Ah! On the day it (actually) reaches them, nothing will turn it away from them, and they will be completely encircled by that which they used to mock at!

9. If We give man a taste of Mercy from Ourselves, and then withdraw it from him, behold! he is in despair and (falls into) blasphemy.

10. But if We give him a taste of (Our) favours after adversity has touched him, he is sure to say, "All evil has departed from me:" behold! he falls into exultation and pride.

11. Not so do those who show patience and constancy, and work righteousness; for them is forgiveness (of sins) and a great reward.

12. Perchance you may (feel the inclination) to give up a part of what is revealed to you, and your heart feels straitened lest

they say, "Why is not a treasure sent down to him, or why does not an angel come down with him?" But you are there only to warn! It is Allah that arranges all affairs!

13. Or they may say, "He forged it," Say, "You then bring ten Suras forged, like unto it, and call (to your aid) whomsoever you can, other than Allah!- If you speak the truth!

14. "If then they (your false gods) do not answer your (call), you (should) know that this Revelation is sent down (replete) with the knowledge of Allah, and that there is no god but He! Will you even then submit (to Islam)?"

15. Those who desire the life of the present and its glitter,- to them We shall pay (the price of) their deeds therein,- without diminution.

16. They are those for whom there is nothing in the Hereafter but the Fire: vain are the designs they frame therein, and of no effect are the deeds that they do!

17. Can they be (like) those who accept a Clear (Sign) from their Lord, and whom a witness from Himself teaches, as did the Book of Moses before it,- a guide and a mercy? They believe therein; but those of the Sects that reject it,- the Fire will be their promised meeting-place. Be not then in doubt thereon: for it is the Truth from your Lord: yet many among men do not believe!

18. Who does more wrong than those who invent a lie against Allah? They will be turned back to the presence of their Lord, and the witnesses will say, "These are the ones

who lied against their Lord!
Behold! the Curse of Allah is on
those who do wrong!-

19. "Those who would hinder
(men) from the path of Allah
and would seek in it something
crooked: these were they who
denied the Hereafter!"

20. They will in no wise
frustrate (His design) on earth,
nor have they protectors besides
Allah! Their Chastisement will
be doubled! They lost the power
to hear and they did not see!

21. They are the ones who
have lost their own souls: and
the (fancies) they invented have
left them in the lurch!
22. Without a doubt, these are
the very ones who will lose most
in the Hereafter!

23. But those who believe and
work righteousness, and
humble themselves before their
Lord,- they will be Companions
of the Garden, to dwell therein
for ever!
24. These two kinds (of men)
may be compared to the blind
and deaf, and those who can see
and hear well. Are they equal
when compared? Will you not
then take heed?
25. We sent Noah to his people
(with a mission): "I have come
to you with a Clear Warning:

26. "That you serve none but
Allah: Verily I do fear for you
the Chastisement of a Grievous
Day."

27. But the chiefs of the
Unbelievers among his people
said: "We see (in) you nothing
but a man like ourselves:

nor do we see that any follow you but the meanest among us, in judgment immature: nor do we see in you (all) any merit above us: in fact we think you are liars!"

28. He said: "O my people! do you see if (it be that) I have a Clear Sign from my Lord, and that He has sent Mercy to me from His Own Presence, but that the Mercy has been obscured from your sight? Shall we compel you to accept it when you are averse to it?

29. "And O my people! I ask you for no wealth in return: my reward is from none but Allah: but I will not drive away (in contempt) those who believe: for verily they are to meet their Lord, and you, I see are the ignorant ones!

30. "And O my people! who would help me against Allah if I drove them away? Will you not then take heed?

31. "I do not tell you that with me are the Treasures of Allah, nor do I know what is hidden, nor I claim to be an angel. Nor yet do I say, of those whom your eyes do despise that Allah will not grant them (all) that is good: Allah knows best what is in their souls: I should, if I did, indeed be a wrong-doer."

32. They said: "O Noah! You have disputed with us, and much have you prolonged the dispute with us: now bring upon us what you threaten us with, if you speak the truth!?"

33. He said: "Truly, Allah will bring it on you if He wills,- and then, you will not be able to frustrate it!

34. "Of no profit will be my counsel to you, much as I desire

to give you (good) counsel, if it be that Allah wills to leave you astray: He is your Lord! and to Him will you return!"

اَنْ اَنْصَحَ لَكُمْ اِنْ كَانَ اللّٰهُ يُرِيْدُ اَنْ يُغْوِيَكُمْ هُوَ رَبُّكُمْ وَاِلَيْهِ تُرْجَعُوْنَ ۞

35. Or do they say, "He has forged it"? Say: "If I had forged it, on me were my sin! and I am free of the sins of which you are guilty!

اَمْ يَقُوْلُوْنَ افْتَرٰىهُ قُلْ اِنِ افْتَرَيْتُهُ فَعَلَيَّ اِجْرَامِيْ وَاَنَا بَرِيْٓءٌ مِّمَّا تُجْرِمُوْنَ ۞

36. It was revealed to Noah: "None of your people will believe except those who have believed already! So grieve no longer over their (evil) deeds.

وَاُوْحِيَ اِلٰى نُوْحٍ اَنَّهُ لَنْ يُّؤْمِنَ مِنْ قَوْمِكَ اِلَّا مَنْ قَدْ اٰمَنَ فَلَا تَبْتَئِسْ بِمَا كَانُوْا يَفْعَلُوْنَ ۞

37. "But construct an Ark under Our eyes and Our inspiration, and address Me no (further) on behalf of those who are in sin: for they are about to be overwhelmed (in the Flood)."

وَاصْنَعِ الْفُلْكَ بِاَعْيُنِنَا وَوَحْيِنَا وَلَا تُخَاطِبْنِيْ فِى الَّذِيْنَ ظَلَمُوْا اِنَّهُمْ مُّغْرَقُوْنَ ۞

38. Forthwith he (starts) constructing the Ark: every time that the Chiefs of his people passed by him, they threw ridicule on him. He said: "If you ridicule us now, we (in our turn) can look down on you with ridicule likewise!

وَيَصْنَعُ الْفُلْكَ وَكُلَّمَا مَرَّ عَلَيْهِ مَلَاٌ مِّنْ قَوْمِهِ سَخِرُوْا مِنْهُ قَالَ اِنْ تَسْخَرُوْا مِنَّا فَاِنَّا نَسْخَرُ مِنْكُمْ كَمَا تَسْخَرُوْنَ ۞

39. "But soon you will know who it is on whom will descend a Chastisement that will cover them with shame,- on whom will be unloosed a lasting Chastisement:"

فَسَوْفَ تَعْلَمُوْنَ مَنْ يَّأْتِيْهِ عَذَابٌ يُّخْزِيْهِ وَيَحِلُّ عَلَيْهِ عَذَابٌ مُّقِيْمٌ ۞

40. At length, behold! there came Our Command, and the fountains of the earth gushed forth! We said: "Embark therein, of each kind two, male and female, and your family - except those against whom the Word has already gone forth,- and the Believers." But only a few believed with him.

حَتّٰى اِذَا جَاءَ اَمْرُنَا وَفَارَ التَّنُّوْرُ قُلْنَا احْمِلْ فِيْهَا مِنْ كُلٍّ زَوْجَيْنِ اثْنَيْنِ وَاَهْلَكَ اِلَّا مَنْ سَبَقَ عَلَيْهِ الْقَوْلُ وَمَنْ اٰمَنَ وَمَاۤ اٰمَنَ مَعَهُ اِلَّا قَلِيْلٌ ۞

41. So he said: "You embark on the Ark, In the name of Allah, whether it move or be at rest! For my Lord is, be sure, Oft-Forgiving, Most Merciful!"

وَقَالَ ارْكَبُوْا فِيْهَا بِسْمِ اللّٰهِ مَجْرٖىٰهَا وَمُرْسٰىهَا اِنَّ رَبِّيْ لَغَفُوْرٌ رَّحِيْمٌ ۞

42. So the Ark floated with them on the waves (towering) like mountains,

وَهِيَ تَجْرِيْ بِهِمْ فِيْ مَوْجٍ كَالْجِبَالِ

and Noah called out to his son, who had separated himself (from the rest): "O my son! embark with us, and be not with the Unbelievers!"

وَنَادَىٰ نُوحُُۨ ابْنَهُ وَكَانَ فِي مَعْزِلٍ يَبُنَيَّ ارْكَبْ مَّعَنَا وَلَا تَكُنْ مَّعَ الْكَافِرِينَ ۞

43. The son replied: "I will betake myself to some mountain: it will save me from the water." Noah said: "This day nothing can save, from the Command of Allah, any but those on whom He has mercy! "And the waves came between them, and the son was among those overwhelmed in the Flood.

قَالَ سَاوِى إِلَىٰ جَبَلٍ يَعْصِمُنِي مِنَ الْمَاءِ قَالَ لَا عَاصِمَ الْيَوْمَ مِنْ أَمْرِ اللّهِ إِلَّا مَن رَّحِمَ وَحَالَ بَيْنَهُمَا الْمَوْجُ فَكَانَ مِنَ الْمُغْرَقِينَ ۞

44. Then the word went forth: "O earth! swallow up your water, and O sky! withhold (your rain)!" And the water abated, and the matter was ended. The Ark rested on Mount Judi, and the word went forth: "Away with those who do wrong!"

وَقِيلَ يَٰأَرْضُ ابْلَعِي مَاءَكِ وَيَٰسَمَاءُ أَقْلِعِي وَغِيضَ الْمَاءُ وَقُضِيَ الْأَمْرُ وَاسْتَوَتْ عَلَى الْجُودِيِّ وَقِيلَ بُعْدًا لِّلْقَوْمِ الظَّالِمِينَ ۞

45. And Noah called upon his Lord, and said: "O my Lord! surely my son is of my family! And Your promise is true, and You are the Justest of Judges!"

وَنَادَىٰ نُوحٌ رَّبَّهُ فَقَالَ رَبِّ إِنَّ ابْنِي مِنْ أَهْلِي وَإِنَّ وَعْدَكَ الْحَقُّ وَأَنتَ أَحْكَمُ الْحَاكِمِينَ ۞

46. He said: "O Noah! He is not of your family: for his conduct is unrighteous. So do not ask of Me that of which you have no knowledge! I give you counsel, lest you act like the ignorant!"

قَالَ يَٰنُوحُ إِنَّهُ لَيْسَ مِنْ أَهْلِكَ إِنَّهُ عَمَلٌ غَيْرُ صَالِحٍ فَلَا تَسْأَلْنِ مَا لَيْسَ لَكَ بِهِ عِلْمٌ إِنِّي أَعِظُكَ أَن تَكُونَ مِنَ الْجَاهِلِينَ ۞

47. Noah said: "O my Lord! I do seek refuge with You, lest I ask You for that of which I have no knowledge. And unless You forgive me and have Mercy on me, I should indeed be lost!"

قَالَ رَبِّ إِنِّي أَعُوذُ بِكَ أَنْ أَسْأَلَكَ مَا لَيْسَ لِي بِهِ عِلْمٌ وَإِلَّا تَغْفِرْ لِي وَتَرْحَمْنِي أَكُن مِّنَ الْخَاسِرِينَ ۞

48. The word came: "O Noah! come down (from the Ark) with peace from Us, and Blessing on you and on some of the peoples (who will spring) from those with you: but (there will be other) peoples to whom We shall grant their pleasures (for a time), but in the end a grievous Chastisement will reach them from Us."

قِيلَ يَٰنُوحُ اهْبِطْ بِسَلَامٍ مِّنَّا وَبَرَكَاتٍ عَلَيْكَ وَعَلَىٰ أُمَمٍ مِّمَّن مَّعَكَ وَأُمَمٌ سَنُمَتِّعُهُمْ ثُمَّ يَمَسُّهُم مِّنَّا عَذَابٌ أَلِيمٌ ۞

49. Such are some of the stories of the Unseen, which We have revealed

تِلْكَ مِنْ أَنبَاءِ الْغَيْبِ نُوحِيهَا

to you: before this, neither you
nor your people knew them. So
persevere patiently: for the End
is for those who are righteous.

إِلَيْكَ مَا كُنْتَ تَعْلَمُهَا أَنْتَ وَلَا
قَوْمُكَ مِنْ قَبْلِ هٰذَا ۖ فَاصْبِرْ ۚ
إِنَّ الْعَاقِبَةَ لِلْمُتَّقِينَ ۞

50. To the 'Ad People (We
sent) Hud, one of their own
brethren. He said: "O my people!
worship Allah! you have no
other god but Him. (Your other
gods) you do nothing but invent!

وَإِلَىٰ عَادٍ أَخَاهُمْ هُودًا ۚ قَالَ
يٰقَوْمِ اعْبُدُوا اللّٰهَ مَا لَكُمْ مِنْ
إِلٰهٍ غَيْرُهُ ۖ إِنْ أَنْتُمْ إِلَّا مُفْتَرُونَ

51. "O my people! I ask of you
no reward for this (Message).
My reward is from none but
Him Who created me: will you
not then understand?

يٰقَوْمِ لَا أَسْأَلُكُمْ عَلَيْهِ أَجْرًا ۖ إِنْ
أَجْرِيَ إِلَّا عَلَى الَّذِي فَطَرَنِي ۚ
أَفَلَا تَعْقِلُونَ ۞

52. "And O my people! Ask
forgiveness of your Lord, and
turn to Him (in repentance): He
will send you the skies pouring
abundant rain, and add strength
to your strength: so you do not
turn back in sin!"

وَيٰقَوْمِ اسْتَغْفِرُوا رَبَّكُمْ ثُمَّ تُوبُوا
إِلَيْهِ يُرْسِلِ السَّمَاءَ عَلَيْكُمْ مِدْرَارًا
وَيَزِدْكُمْ قُوَّةً إِلَىٰ قُوَّتِكُمْ وَلَا
تَتَوَلَّوْا مُجْرِمِينَ ۞

53. They said: "O Hud! You
have brought us no Clear (Sign),
and we are not the ones to desert
our gods on your word! Nor
shall we believe in you!

قَالُوا يٰهُودُ مَا جِئْتَنَا بِبَيِّنَةٍ وَمَا
نَحْنُ بِتَارِكِي آلِهَتِنَا عَنْ قَوْلِكَ وَمَا
نَحْنُ لَكَ بِمُؤْمِنِينَ ۞

54. "We say nothing but that
(perhaps) some of our gods may
have seized you with imbeci-
lity." He said: "I call Allah to
witness, and you do bear
witness, that I am free from the
sin of ascribing, to Him,

إِنْ نَقُولُ إِلَّا اعْتَرَاكَ بَعْضُ آلِهَتِنَا
بِسُوءٍ ۗ قَالَ إِنِّي أُشْهِدُ اللّٰهَ وَاشْهَدُوا
أَنِّي بَرِيءٌ مِمَّا تُشْرِكُونَ ۞

55. "Other gods as partners!
So scheme (your worst) against
me, all of you, and give me no
respite.

مِنْ دُونِهِ ۖ فَكِيدُونِي جَمِيعًا ثُمَّ
لَا تُنْظِرُونِ ۞

56. "I put my trust in Allah,
my Lord and your Lord! There
is not a moving creature, but He
has grasp of its fore-lock. Verily,
it is my Lord that is on a straight
Path.

إِنِّي تَوَكَّلْتُ عَلَى اللّٰهِ رَبِّي وَرَبِّكُمْ ۚ
مَا مِنْ دَابَّةٍ إِلَّا هُوَ آخِذٌ بِنَاصِيَتِهَا ۚ
إِنَّ رَبِّي عَلَىٰ صِرَاطٍ مُسْتَقِيمٍ ۞

57. "If you turn away,- I (at least)
have conveyed the Message with
which I was sent to you. My
Lord will make another

فَإِنْ تَوَلَّوْا فَقَدْ أَبْلَغْتُكُمْ مَا أُرْسِلْتُ
بِهِ إِلَيْكُمْ ۚ وَيَسْتَخْلِفُ رَبِّي قَوْمًا

people to succeed you, and you will not harm Him in the least. For my Lord has care and watch over all things."

58. So when Our decree issued, We saved Hud and those who believed with him, by (special) Grace from Ourselves: We saved them from a severe Chastisement.

59. Such were the 'Ad People: they rejected the Signs of their Lord and Cherisher; disobeyed His Apostles; and followed the command of every powerful, obstinate transgressor.

60. And they were pursued by a Curse in this life,- and on the Day of Judgment. Ah! Behold! For the 'Ad rejected their Lord and Cherisher! Ah! Behold! Removed (from sight) were 'Ad, the people of Hud!

61. To the Thamud People (We sent) Salih, one of their own brethren. He said: "O my people! Worship Allah: you have no other god but Him. It is He Who has produced you from the earth and settled you therein: then ask forgiveness of Him, and turn to Him (in repentance): for my Lord is (always) near, ready to answer."

62. They said: "O Salih! you have been of us!- a centre of our hopes hitherto! Do you (now) forbid us the worship of what our fathers worshipped? But we are really in suspicious (disquieting) doubt as to that to which you invite us."

63. He said: "O my people! Do you see? if I have a Clear (Sign) from my Lord and He has sent Mercy to me from Himself,- who then can help me against Allah if I were to disobey Him? What then would you add to my (portion) but perdition?

64. "And O my people! this she-camel of Allah is a symbol to

you: leave her to feed on Allah's (free) earth, and inflict no harm on her, or a swift Chastisement will seize you!"

65.   But they hamstrung her. So he said: "Enjoy yourselves in your homes for three days: (then will be your ruin): (behold) there is a promise not to be belied!"

66.   When Our Decree issued, We saved Salih and those who believed with him, by (special) Grace from Ourselves - and from the Ignominy of that Day. For your Lord - He is the Strong One, and Able to enforce His Will.

67.   The (mighty) Blast over- took the wrong-doers, and they lay prostrate in their homes before the morning,-

68.   As if they had never dwelt and flourished there. Ah! Behold! For the Thamud rejec- ted their Lord and Cherisher! Ah! Behold! Removed (from sight) were the Thamud!

69.   There came Our Messen- gers to Abraham with glad tidings. They said, "Peace!" He answered, "Peace!" and haste- ned to entertain them with a roasted calf.

70.   But when he saw their hands did not go towards the (meal), he felt some mistrust of them, and conceived a fear of them. They said: "Fear not: we have been sent against the people of Lut."

71.   And his wife was standing (there), and she laughed: but We gave her glad tidings of Isaac, and after him, of Jacob.

72.   She said: "Alas for me! shall I bear a child, seeing I am an old woman, and my husband here is an old man? That would indeed be a wonderful thing!"

73.   They said: "Do you won- der at Allah's decree? The Grace

of Allah and His blessings on you, O you people of the house! for He is indeed worthy of all praise, full of all glory!"

74. When fear had passed from (the mind of) Abraham and the glad tidings had reached him, he began to plead with Us for Lut's people.

75. For Abraham was, without doubt, forbearing (of faults), compassionate, and given to look to Allah.

76. O Abraham! Do not seek this. The decree of your Lord has gone forth: for them there comes a Chastisement that cannot be turned back!

77. When Our Messengers came to Lut, he was grieved on their account and felt himself powerless (to protect) them. He said: "This is a distressful day."

78. And his people came rushing towards him, and they had been long in the habit of practising abominations. He said: "O my people! Here are my daughters: they are purer for you (if you marry)! Now fear Allah, and do not cover me with shame about my guests! Isn't there among you a single right-minded man?"

79. They said: "You know well we have no need of your daughters: indeed you know quite well what we want!"

80. He said: "Would that I had power to suppress you or that I could betake myself to some powerful support."

81. (The Messengers) said: "O Lut! We are Messengers from your Lord! By no means they shall reach you! Now travel with your family while yet a part of the night remains, and let not any of you look back: but your wife (will remain behind): to her will happen what happens to the people. Morning is their appointed time:

is not the morning near?"

82. When Our decree issued, We turned (the cities) upside down, and rained down on them brimstones hard as baked clay, spread, layer on layer,-

83. Marked as from your Lord: nor are they ever far from those who do wrong!

84. To the Madyan People (We sent) Shu'aib, one of their own brethren: he said: "O my people! worship Allah: you have no other god but Him. And do not give short measure or weight: I see you in prosperity, but I fear for you the Chastisement of a Day that will compass (you) all round.

85. "And O my people! give just measure and weight, nor withhold from the people the things that are their due: do not commit evil in the land with intent to do mischief.

86. "That which is left you by Allah is best for you, if you (but) believed! but I am not set over you to keep watch!"

87. They said: "O Shu'aib! Does your (religion of) prayer command you that we leave off the worship which our fathers practised, or that we leave off doing what we like with our property? truly, you are the one that forbears with faults and is right-minded!"

88. He said: "O my people! Do you see whether I have a Clear (Sign) from my Lord, and He has given me sustenance (pure and) good as from Himself? I do not wish, in opposition to you, to do that which I forbid you to do. I only desire (your) betterment to the best of my power; and my success (in my task) can only come from Allah. In Him I trust,

اَلَيْسَ الصُّبْحُ بِقَرِيْبٍ ۝

فَلَمَّا جَآءَ اَمْرُنَا جَعَلْنَا عَالِيَهَا

سَافِلَهَا وَاَمْطَرْنَا عَلَيْهَا حِجَارَةً

مِّنْ سِجِّيْلٍ ۙ مَّنْضُوْدٍ ۝

مُّسَوَّمَةً عِنْدَ رَبِّكَ ۗ وَمَا هِيَ

مِنَ الظّٰلِمِيْنَ بِبَعِيْدٍ ۝

وَاِلٰى مَدْيَنَ اَخَاهُمْ شُعَيْبًا ۘ قَالَ

يٰقَوْمِ اعْبُدُوا اللّٰهَ مَا لَكُمْ مِّنْ

اِلٰهٍ غَيْرُهٗ ۗ وَلَا تَنْقُصُوا الْمِكْيَالَ

وَالْمِيْزَانَ اِنِّيْۤ اَرٰىكُمْ بِخَيْرٍ وَّاِنِّيْۤ اَخَافُ

عَلَيْكُمْ عَذَابَ يَوْمٍ مُّحِيْطٍ ۝

وَيٰقَوْمِ اَوْفُوا الْمِكْيَالَ وَالْمِيْزَانَ

بِالْقِسْطِ وَلَا تَبْخَسُوا النَّاسَ اَشْيَآءَهُمْ

وَلَا تَعْثَوْا فِى الْاَرْضِ مُفْسِدِيْنَ ۝

بَقِيَّتُ اللّٰهِ خَيْرٌ لَّكُمْ اِنْ كُنْتُمْ

مُّؤْمِنِيْنَ ۚ وَمَاۤ اَنَا عَلَيْكُمْ بِحَفِيْظٍ ۝

قَالُوْا يٰشُعَيْبُ اَصَلٰوتُكَ تَأْمُرُكَ اَنْ

نَّتْرُكَ مَا يَعْبُدُ اٰبَآؤُنَاۤ اَوْ اَنْ

نَّفْعَلَ فِيْۤ اَمْوَالِنَا مَا نَشٰٓؤُا ۗ اِنَّكَ

لَاَنْتَ الْحَلِيْمُ الرَّشِيْدُ ۝

قَالَ يٰقَوْمِ اَرَءَيْتُمْ اِنْ كُنْتُ عَلٰى

بَيِّنَةٍ مِّنْ رَّبِّيْ وَرَزَقَنِيْ مِنْهُ

رِزْقًا حَسَنًا ۗ وَمَاۤ اُرِيْدُ اَنْ اُخَالِفَكُمْ

اِلٰى مَاۤ اَنْهٰىكُمْ عَنْهُ ۗ اِنْ اُرِيْدُ اِلَّا

الْاِصْلَاحَ مَا اسْتَطَعْتُ ۗ وَمَا

تَوْفِيْقِيْۤ اِلَّا بِاللّٰهِ ۗ عَلَيْهِ تَوَكَّلْتُ

and to Him I turn.

89. "And O my people! let not my dissent (from you) cause you to sin, lest you suffer a fate similar to that of the people of Noah or of Hud or of Salih, nor are the people of Lut far off from you!

90. "But ask forgiveness of your Lord, and turn to Him (in repentance): for my Lord is indeed full of mercy and loving-kindness."

91. They said: "O Shu'aib! much of what you say we do not understand! In fact among us we see that you have no strength! Were it not for your family, we should certainly have stoned you! For you have among us no great position!"

92. He said: "O my people! is then my family of more consideration with you than Allah? For you cast Him away behind your backs (with contempt). But verily my Lord encompasses on all sides all that you do!

93. "And O my people! do whatever you can: I will do (my part): soon will you know who it is on whom descends the Chastisement of ignominy; and who is a liar! and you watch! for I too am watching with you!"

94. When Our decree issued, We saved Shu'aib and those who believed with him, by (special) Mercy from Our selves: but the (mighty) Blast seized the wrong-doers, and they lay prostrate in their homes by the morning,-

95. As if they had never dwelt and flourished there! Ah! Behold! How the Madyan were removed (from sight) as were removed the Thamud.

96. And We sent Moses, With Our Clear (Signs) and an authority manifest,

97. Unto Pharaoh and his Chiefs: but they followed the command of Pharaoh and the command of Pharaoh was no right (guide).

إِلَى فِرْعَوْنَ وَمَلَائِهِ فَاتَّبَعُوْٓا أَمْرَ

فِرْعَوْنَ ۚ وَمَآ أَمْرُ فِرْعَوْنَ بِرَشِيْدٍ ۞

98. He will go before his people on the Day of Judgment, and lead them into the Fire (as cattle are led to water): but woeful indeed will be the place to which they are led!

يَقْدُمُ قَوْمَهٗ يَوْمَ الْقِيٰمَةِ فَأَوْرَدَهُمُ

النَّارَ ۚ وَبِئْسَ الْوِرْدُ الْمَوْرُوْدُ ۞

99. And they are followed by a curse in this (life) and on the Day of Judgment: and woeful is the gift which shall be given (to them)!

وَأُتْبِعُوْا فِيْ هٰذِهٖ لَعْنَةً وَّيَوْمَ

الْقِيٰمَةِ ۚ بِئْسَ الرِّفْدُ الْمَرْفُوْدُ ۞

100. These are some of the stories of communities which We relate to you: of them some are standing, and some have been mown down (by the sickle of time).

ذٰلِكَ مِنْ أَنْبَآءِ الْقُرٰى نَقُصُّهٗ

عَلَيْكَ مِنْهَا قَآئِمٌ وَّحَصِيْدٌ ۞

101. It was not We that wronged them: they wronged their own souls: the deities, other than Allah, whom they invoked, profited them no whit when there issued the decree of your Lord: nor did they add anything (to their lot) but perdition!

وَمَا ظَلَمْنٰهُمْ وَلٰكِنْ ظَلَمُوْٓا أَنْفُسَهُمْ

فَمَآ أَغْنَتْ عَنْهُمْ آلِهَتُهُمُ الَّتِيْ

يَدْعُوْنَ مِنْ دُوْنِ اللّٰهِ مِنْ شَيْءٍ

لَّمَّا جَآءَ أَمْرُ رَبِّكَ ۚ وَمَا زَادُوْهُمْ

غَيْرَ تَتْبِيْبٍ ۞

102. Such is the chastisement of your Lord when He chastises communities in the midst of their wrong: grievous, indeed, and severe is His chastisement.

وَكَذٰلِكَ أَخْذُ رَبِّكَ إِذَآ أَخَذَ

الْقُرٰى وَهِيَ ظَالِمَةٌ ۚ إِنَّ أَخْذَهٗٓ

أَلِيْمٌ شَدِيْدٌ ۞

103. In that is a Sign for those who fear the Chastisement of the Hereafter: that is a Day for which mankind will be gathered together: that will be a Day of Testimony.

إِنَّ فِيْ ذٰلِكَ لَآيَةً لِّمَنْ خَافَ

عَذَابَ الْآخِرَةِ ۚ ذٰلِكَ يَوْمٌ مَّجْمُوْعٌ

لَّهُ النَّاسُ وَذٰلِكَ يَوْمٌ مَّشْهُوْدٌ ۞

104. Nor shall We delay it but for a term appointed.

وَمَا نُؤَخِّرُهٗٓ إِلَّا لِأَجَلٍ مَّعْدُوْدٍ ۞

105. The day it arrives, no soul shall speak except by His leave: of those (gathered) some will be wretched and some will be blessed.

يَوْمَ يَأْتِ لَا تَكَلَّمُ نَفْسٌ إِلَّا بِإِذْنِهٖ ۚ

فَمِنْهُمْ شَقِيٌّ وَّسَعِيْدٌ ۞

106. Those who are wretched shall be in the Fire: there will be for them therein (nothing but) the heaving of sighs and sobs:

فَأَمَّا الَّذِيْنَ شَقُوْا فَفِي النَّارِ

لَهُمْ فِيْهَا زَفِيْرٌ وَّشَهِيْقٌ ۞

107. They will dwell therein for all the time that the heavens and the earth endure, except as your Lord wills: for

خٰلِدِيْنَ فِيْهَا مَا دَامَتِ السَّمٰوٰتُ

وَالْأَرْضُ إِلَّا مَا شَآءَ رَبُّكَ ۚ إِنَّ

your Lord is the (sure) Accomplisher of what He plans.

108. And those who are blessed shall be in the Garden: they will dwell therein for all the time that the heavens and the earth endure, except as your Lord wills: a gift without break.

109. Be not then in doubt as to what these men worship. They worship nothing but what their fathers worshipped before (them): but verily We shall pay them back (in full) their portion without (the least) abatement.

110. We certainly gave the Book to Moses, but differences arose therein: had it not been that a Word had gone forth before from your Lord, the matter would have been decided between them, but they are in suspicious doubt concerning it.

111. And, of a surety, to all will your Lord pay back (in full the recompense) of their deeds: for He knows well all that they do.

112. Therefore stand firm (in the straight Path) as you are commanded,- you and those who with you turn (unto Allah); and do not transgress (from the Path): for He sees well all that you do.

113. And incline not to those who do wrong, or the Fire will seize you; and you have no protectors other than Allah, nor shall you be helped.

114. And establish regular prayers at the two ends of the day and at the approaches of the night: for those things, that are good remove those that are evil: be that the word of remembrance to those who remember (their Lord):

115. And be steadfast in patience; for verily Allah will not suffer the reward of the righteous to perish.

For the chronological place of this Sûrah and the general arguments of Sûras 10 to 15, see Introduction to 10.

In subject-matter this Sûrah is entirely taken up with the story (recapitulated rather than told) of Joseph, the youngest (but one) of the twelve sons of the patriarch Jacob. The story is called the most beautiful of stories (12:3) for many reasons: (1) it is the most detailed of any in the Qur'ân; (2) it is full of human vicissitudes, and has therefore deservedly appealed to men and women of all classes; (3) it paints in vivid colours, with their spiritual implications, the most varied aspects of life-the patriarch's old age and the confidence between him and his little best-beloved son, the elder brother's jealousy of this little son, their plot and their father's grief, the sale of the father's darling into slavery for a miserable little price, carnal love contrasted with purity and chastity, false charges, prison, the interpretation of dreams, low life and high life, Innocence raised to honour; the sweet "revenge" of Forgiveness and Benevolence, high matters of State and administration, humility in exaltation, filial love, and the beauty of Piety and Truth.

The story is similar to but not identical with the Biblical story; but the atmosphere is wholly different. The Biblical story is like a folk-tale in which morality has no place. Its tendency is to exalt the clever and financially-minded Jew against the Egyptian, and to explain certain ethnic and tribal peculiarities in later Jewish history. Joseph is shown as buying up all the cattle and the land of the poor Egyptians for the State under the stress of famine conditions, and making the Israelites "rulers" over Pharaoh's cattle. The Qur'anic story, one the other hand, is less a narrative than a highly spiritual sermon of allegory explaining the seeming contradictions in life, the enduring nature of virtue in a world full of flux and change, and the marvellous working of Allah's eternal purpose in His Plan as unfolded to us on the wide canvas of history. This aspect of the matter has been a favourite with Muslim poets and Sufi exegetists.

116. Why were there not, among the generations before you, persons possessed of balanced good sense, prohibiting (men) from mischief in the earth - except a few among them whom We saved (from harm)? But the wrong-doers pursued the enjoyment of the good things of life which were given them, and persisted in sin.

117. Nor would your Lord be the One to destroy communities for a single wrong- doing, if its members were likely to mend.

118. If your Lord had so willed, He could have made mankind one people: but they will not cease to dispute.

119. Except those on whom your Lord has bestowed His Mercy: and for this He created them: and the Word of your Lord shall be fulfilled: "I will fill Hell with (disobedient) jinns and men all together."

120. All that We relate to you of the stories of the Apostles,- with it We make firm your heart: in them there comes to you the Truth, as well as an exhortation and a message of remembrance to those who believe.

121. Say to those who do not believe: "Do whatever you can: we shall do our part;

122. "And you wait! we too shall wait."

123. To Allah do belong the unseen (secrets) of the heavens and the earth, and to Him goes back every affair (for decision): then worship Him, and put your trust in Him: and your Lord is not unmindful of anything that you do.

12. Yusuf or Joseph
In the name of Allah. Most Gracious, Most Merciful.

1. *Alif - Lam - Raa.* These are the Symbols (or Verses) of the Perspicuous Book.

فَلَوْلَا كَانَ مِنَ الْقُرُونِ مِنْ قَبْلِكُمْ أُولُوا بَقِيَّةٍ يَنْهَوْنَ عَنِ الْفَسَادِ فِي الْأَرْضِ إِلَّا قَلِيلًا مِّمَّنْ أَنْجَيْنَا مِنْهُمْ ۗ وَاتَّبَعَ الَّذِينَ ظَلَمُوا مَا أُتْرِفُوا فِيهِ وَكَانُوا مُجْرِمِينَ ۝

وَمَا كَانَ رَبُّكَ لِيُهْلِكَ الْقُرَىٰ بِظُلْمٍ وَأَهْلُهَا مُصْلِحُونَ ۝

وَلَوْ شَاءَ رَبُّكَ لَجَعَلَ النَّاسَ أُمَّةً وَاحِدَةً ۖ وَلَا يَزَالُونَ مُخْتَلِفِينَ ۝

إِلَّا مَنْ رَّحِمَ رَبُّكَ ۚ وَلِذَٰلِكَ خَلَقَهُمْ ۗ وَتَمَّتْ كَلِمَةُ رَبِّكَ لَأَمْلَأَنَّ جَهَنَّمَ مِنَ الْجِنَّةِ وَالنَّاسِ أَجْمَعِينَ ۝

وَكُلًّا نَّقُصُّ عَلَيْكَ مِنْ أَنْبَاءِ الرُّسُلِ مَا نُثَبِّتُ بِهِ فُؤَادَكَ ۚ وَجَاءَكَ فِي هَٰذِهِ الْحَقُّ وَمَوْعِظَةٌ وَذِكْرَىٰ لِلْمُؤْمِنِينَ ۝

وَقُلْ لِّلَّذِينَ لَا يُؤْمِنُونَ اعْمَلُوا عَلَىٰ مَكَانَتِكُمْ ۖ إِنَّا عَامِلُونَ ۝

وَانْتَظِرُوا إِنَّا مُنْتَظِرُونَ ۝

وَلِلَّهِ غَيْبُ السَّمَاوَاتِ وَالْأَرْضِ وَإِلَيْهِ يُرْجَعُ الْأَمْرُ كُلُّهُ فَاعْبُدْهُ وَتَوَكَّلْ عَلَيْهِ ۚ وَمَا رَبُّكَ بِغَافِلٍ عَمَّا تَعْمَلُونَ ۝

(١٢) سُورَةُ يُوسُفَ مَكِّيَّةٌ (٥٣)

بِسْمِ اللَّهِ الرَّحْمَٰنِ الرَّحِيمِ

الٓر ۚ تِلْكَ آيَاتُ الْكِتَابِ الْمُبِينِ ۝

2. We have sent it down as an Arabic Qur'an, in order that you may learn wisdom.

3. We do relate to you the most beautiful of stories, in that We reveal to you this (portion of the) Qur'an: before this, you too were among those who did not know it.

4. Behold! Joseph said to his father: "O my father! I saw eleven stars and the sun and the moon: I saw them prostrate themselves to me!"

5. Said (the father): "My (dear) little son! do not relate your vision to your brothers, lest they concoct a plot against you: for Satan is to man an avowed enemy!

6. "Thus will your Lord choose you and teach you the interpretation of stories (and events) and perfect His favour to you and to the posterity of Jacob - even as He perfected it to your fathers Abraham and Isaac aforetime! for Allah is full of knowledge and wisdom."

7. Verily in Joseph and his brethren are Signs (or Symbols) for Seekers (after Truth).

8. They said: "Truly Joseph and his brother are loved more by our father than we: but we are a goodly body! really our father is obviously wandering (in his mind)!

9. "You slay Joseph or cast him out to some (unknown) land, that so the favour of your father may be given to you alone: (there will be time enough) for you to be righteous after that!"

10. Said one of them: "do not slay Joseph, but if you must do

something, throw him down to the bottom of the well: he will be picked up by some caravan of travellers."

11. They said: "O our father! why do you not trust us with Joseph,- seeing we are indeed his sincere well-wishers?

12. "Send him with us tomorrow to enjoy himself and play, and we shall take every care of him."

13. (Jacob) said: "Really it saddens me that you should take him away: I fear lest the wolf should devour him while you do not attend to him."

14. They said: "If the wolf were to devour him while we are (so large) a party, then should we indeed (first) have perished ourselves!"

15. So they took him away, and they all agreed to throw him down to the bottom of the well: and We put into his heart (this Message): 'Of a surety you shall (one day) tell them the truth of this their affair while they do not know (you)'

16. Then they came to their father in the early part of the night, weeping.

17. They said: "O our father! We went racing with one another, and left Joseph with our things; and the wolf devoured him. But you will never believe us even though we tell the truth."

18. They stained his shirt with false blood. He said: "Nay, but your minds have made up a tale (that may pass) with you. (For me) patience is most fitting: against that which you assert, it is Allah (alone) Whose help can be sought"..

19. Then there came a caravan of travellers: they sent their water-carrier (for water), and he let down his bucket (into the well)...He said: "Ah there! Good news! Here is

وَأَلْقُوهُ فِي غَيَابَتِ الْجُبِّ يَلْتَقِطْهُ بَعْضُ السَّيَّارَةِ إِنْ كُنْتُمْ فَاعِلِينَ ۞

قَالُوا يَا أَبَانَا مَا لَكَ لَا تَأْمَنَّا عَلَى يُوسُفَ وَإِنَّا لَهُ لَنَاصِحُونَ ۞

أَرْسِلْهُ مَعَنَا غَدًا يَرْتَعْ وَيَلْعَبْ وَإِنَّا لَهُ لَحَافِظُونَ ۞

قَالَ إِنِّي لَيَحْزُنُنِي أَنْ تَذْهَبُوا بِهِ وَأَخَافُ أَنْ يَأْكُلَهُ الذِّئْبُ وَأَنْتُمْ عَنْهُ غَافِلُونَ ۞

قَالُوا لَئِنْ أَكَلَهُ الذِّئْبُ وَنَحْنُ عُصْبَةٌ إِنَّا إِذًا لَخَاسِرُونَ ۞

فَلَمَّا ذَهَبُوا بِهِ وَأَجْمَعُوا أَنْ يَجْعَلُوهُ فِي غَيَابَتِ الْجُبِّ ۚ وَأَوْحَيْنَا إِلَيْهِ لَتُنَبِّئَنَّهُمْ بِأَمْرِهِمْ هَذَا وَهُمْ لَا يَشْعُرُونَ ۞

وَجَاءُوا أَبَاهُمْ عِشَاءً يَبْكُونَ ۞

قَالُوا يَا أَبَانَا إِنَّا ذَهَبْنَا نَسْتَبِقُ وَتَرَكْنَا يُوسُفَ عِنْدَ مَتَاعِنَا فَأَكَلَهُ الذِّئْبُ ۚ وَمَا أَنْتَ بِمُؤْمِنٍ لَنَا وَلَوْ كُنَّا صَادِقِينَ ۞

وَجَاءُوا عَلَى قَمِيصِهِ بِدَمٍ كَذِبٍ قَالَ بَلْ سَوَّلَتْ لَكُمْ أَنْفُسُكُمْ أَمْرًا فَصَبْرٌ جَمِيلٌ ۖ وَاللَّهُ الْمُسْتَعَانُ عَلَى مَا تَصِفُونَ ۞

وَجَاءَتْ سَيَّارَةٌ فَأَرْسَلُوا وَارِدَهُمْ فَأَدْلَى دَلْوَهُ ۖ قَالَ يَا بُشْرَى هَذَا

a (fine) young man!" So they
concealed him as a treasure! But
Allah knows well all that they
do!

20. The (Brethren) sold him
for a miserable price, for a few
dirhams counted out: in such low
estimation did they hold him!

21. The man in Egypt who
bought him, said to his wife:
"Make his stay (among us)
honourable: may be he will
bring us much good, or we shall
adopt him as a son." Thus We
established Joseph in the land,
that We might teach him the
interpretation of stories (and
events). And Allah has full
power and control over His
affairs; but most among mankind do not know it.

22. When Joseph attained his
full manhood, We gave him
power and knowledge: thus do
We reward those who do right.

23. But she in whose house he
was, sought to seduce him from
his (true) self: she fastened the
doors, and said: "Now come,
you (dear one)!" He said: "Allah
forbid! truly (your husband) is
my lord! he made my sojourn
agreeable! truly to no good
come those who do wrong!"

24. And (with passion) she
desired him, and he would have
desired her, but that he saw the
evidence of his Lord: thus (did
We order) that We might turn
away from him (all) evil and
shameful deeds: for he was one
of Our servants, sincere and
purified.

25. So they both raced each
other to the door, and she tore
his shirt from the back: they
both found her lord near the
door. She said: "What is the
(fitting) punishment for one
who formed an evil design
against your wife, but prison or

غُلَامٌ ۗ وَأَسَرُّوهُ بِضَاعَةً ۚ وَاللّٰهُ
عَلِيمٌ بِمَا يَعْمَلُونَ ۞

وَشَرَوْهُ بِثَمَنٍ بَخْسٍ دَرَاهِمَ مَعْدُودَةٍ ۚ
وَكَانُوْا فِيْهِ مِنَ الزَّاهِدِيْنَ ۞

وَقَالَ الَّذِي اشْتَرَاهُ مِنْ مِّصْرَ
لِامْرَأَتِهٖ أَكْرِمِيْ مَثْوَاهُ عَسٰى أَنْ
يَّنْفَعَنَا أَوْ نَتَّخِذَهُ وَلَدًا ۚ وَكَذٰلِكَ
مَكَّنَّا لِيُوسُفَ فِى الْأَرْضِ وَلِنُعَلِّمَهٗ
مِنْ تَأْوِيْلِ الْأَحَادِيْثِ ۚ وَاللّٰهُ
غَالِبٌ عَلٰى أَمْرِهٖ وَلٰكِنَّ أَكْثَرَ النَّاسِ
لَا يَعْلَمُوْنَ ۞

وَلَمَّا بَلَغَ أَشُدَّهٗ اٰتَيْنٰهُ حُكْمًا
وَّعِلْمًا ۚ وَكَذٰلِكَ نَجْزِى الْمُحْسِنِيْنَ ۞

وَرَاوَدَتْهُ الَّتِيْ هُوَ فِيْ بَيْتِهَا عَنْ
نَّفْسِهٖ وَغَلَّقَتِ الْأَبْوَابَ وَقَالَتْ
هَيْتَ لَكَ ۚ قَالَ مَعَاذَ اللّٰهِ اِنَّهٗ
رَبِّيْ أَحْسَنَ مَثْوَايَ ۚ اِنَّهٗ لَا يُفْلِحُ
الظّٰلِمُوْنَ ۞

وَلَقَدْ هَمَّتْ بِهٖ ۚ وَهَمَّ بِهَا لَوْلَا
أَنْ رَّاٰ بُرْهَانَ رَبِّهٖ ۚ كَذٰلِكَ لِنَصْرِفَ
عَنْهُ السُّوْٓءَ وَالْفَحْشَآءَ ۚ اِنَّهٗ مِنْ
عِبَادِنَا الْمُخْلَصِيْنَ ۞

وَاسْتَبَقَا الْبَابَ وَقَدَّتْ قَمِيْصَهٗ
مِنْ دُبُرٍ وَّأَلْفَيَا سَيِّدَهَا لَدَا
الْبَابِ ۚ قَالَتْ مَا جَزَآءُ مَنْ أَرَادَ
بِأَهْلِكَ سُوْٓءًا اِلَّا أَنْ يُّسْجَنَ أَوْ

a grievous chastisement?"

عَذَابٌ أَلِيْمٌ ۞

26. He said: "It was she that sought to seduce me - from my (true) self." And one of her household saw (this) and bore witness, (thus):- "If it be that his shirt is torn from the front, then her tale is true, and he is a liar!

قَالَ هِيَ رَاوَدَتْنِيْ عَنْ نَّفْسِيْ وَشَهِدَ شَاهِدٌ مِّنْ أَهْلِهَا ۚ إِنْ كَانَ قَمِيْصُهُ قُدَّ مِنْ قُبُلٍ فَصَدَقَتْ وَهُوَ مِنَ الْكٰذِبِيْنَ

27. "But if it be that his shirt is torn from the back, then is she the liar, and he is telling the truth!"

وَإِنْ كَانَ قَمِيْصُهُ قُدَّ مِنْ دُبُرٍ فَكَذَبَتْ وَهُوَ مِنَ الصّٰدِقِيْنَ ۞

28. So when he saw his shirt,- that it was torn at the back,- (her husband) said: "Behold! It is a snare of you women! truly, mighty is your snare!

فَلَمَّا رَاٰ قَمِيْصَهُ قُدَّ مِنْ دُبُرٍ قَالَ إِنَّهُ مِنْ كَيْدِكُنَّ ۚ إِنَّ كَيْدَكُنَّ عَظِيْمٌ ۞

29. "O Joseph, pass this over! (O wife), ask forgiveness for your sin, for truly you have been at fault!"

يُوسُفُ أَعْرِضْ عَنْ هٰذَا ۚ وَاسْتَغْفِرِيْ لِذَنْبِكِ ۚ إِنَّكِ كُنْتِ مِنَ الْخَاطِئِيْنَ ۞

30. Ladies said in the City: "The wife of the (great) 'Aziz is seeking to seduce her slave from his (true) self: Truly he has inspired her with violent love: we see she is evidently going astray."

وَقَالَ نِسْوَةٌ فِي الْمَدِيْنَةِ امْرَأَتُ الْعَزِيْزِ تُرَاوِدُ فَتٰهَا عَنْ نَّفْسِهِ ۚ قَدْ شَغَفَهَا حُبًّا ۚ إِنَّا لَنَرٰهَا فِيْ ضَلٰلٍ مُّبِيْنٍ ۞

31. When she heard of their malicious talk, she sent for them and prepared a banquet for them: she gave each of them a knife: and she said (to Joseph), "Come out before them." When they saw him, they extolled him, and (in their amazement) cut their hands: they said, "Allah preserve us! no mortal is this! this is none other than a noble angel!"

فَلَمَّا سَمِعَتْ بِمَكْرِهِنَّ أَرْسَلَتْ إِلَيْهِنَّ وَأَعْتَدَتْ لَهُنَّ مُتَّكَأً وَّ آتَتْ كُلَّ وَاحِدَةٍ مِّنْهُنَّ سِكِّيْنًا وَّقَالَتِ اخْرُجْ عَلَيْهِنَّ ۚ فَلَمَّا رَأَيْنَهُ أَكْبَرْنَهُ وَقَطَّعْنَ أَيْدِيَهُنَّ وَقُلْنَ حَاشَ لِلّٰهِ مَا هٰذَا بَشَرًا ۚ إِنْ هٰذَا إِلَّا مَلَكٌ كَرِيْمٌ ۞

32. She said: "There before you is the man about whom you blamed me! I sought to seduce him from his (true) self but he firmly saved himself guiltless!....

قَالَتْ فَذٰلِكُنَّ الَّذِيْ لُمْتُنَّنِيْ فِيْهِ ۖ وَلَقَدْ رَاوَدْتُّهُ عَنْ نَّفْسِهِ فَاسْتَعْصَمَ

And now, if he does not my bidding, he shall certainly be cast into prison, and (what is more) be of the company of the vilest!"

33. He said: "O my Lord! the prison is more to my liking than that to which they invite me: unless You turn away their snare from me, I should (in my youthful folly) feel inclined toward them and join the ranks of the ignorant."

34. So his Lord hearkened to him (in his prayer), and turned away from him their snare: verily He hears and knows (all things).

35. Then it occurred to the men, after they had seen the Signs, (that it was best) to imprison him for a time.

36. Now with him there came into the prison two young men, said one of them: "I see myself (in a dream) pressing wine." Said the other: "I see myself (in a dream) carrying bread on my head, and birds are eating thereof." "Tell us" (they said) "the truth and meaning thereof: for we see you are one that does good (to all)."

37. He said: "Before any food comes (in due course) to feed either of you, I will surely reveal to you the truth and meaning of this ere it befall you: that is part of the (duty) which my Lord has taught me. I have (I assure you) abandoned the ways of a people that do not believe in Allah and that (even) deny the Hereafter.

38. "And I follow the ways of my fathers,- Abraham, Isaac, and Jacob; and never could we attribute any partners whatever to Allah: that (comes) of the grace of Allah to us and to mankind: yet most men are not grateful.

39. "O my two companions of the prison! (I ask you): are many lords differing among themselves

better, or the One God (Allah), Supreme and Irresistible?

40. "If not Him, you worship nothing but names which you have named,- you and your fathers,- for which Allah has sent down no authority: the Command is for none but Allah: He has commanded that you worship none but Him: that is the right religion, but most men do not understand.

41. "O my two companions of the prison! As to one of you, he will pour out the wine for his lord to drink: as for the other, he will hang from the cross, and the birds will eat from off his head. (So) has been decreed that matter whereof you twain do enquire"...

42. And of the two, to that one whom he considered about to be saved, he said: "Mention me to your lord." But Satan made him forget to mention him to his lord: and (Joseph) lingered in prison a few (more) years.

43. The king (of Egypt) said: "I do see (in a vision) seven fat kine, whom seven lean ones devour,- and seven green ears of corn, and seven (others) withered. O you chiefs! Expound to me my vision if it be that you can interpret visions."

44. They said: "A confused medley of dreams: and we are not skilled in the interpretation of dreams."

45. But the man who had been released, one of the two (who had been in prison) and who now remembered him after (so long) a space of time, said: "I will tell you the truth of its interpretation: you send me (therefore)."

46. "O Joseph!" (he said) "O man of truth! Expound to us

خَيْرٌ اَمِ اللهُ الْوَاحِدُ الْقَهَّارُ ۟

مَا تَعْبُدُوْنَ مِنْ دُوْنِهٖٓ اِلَّآ اَسْمَآءً سَمَّيْتُمُوْهَآ اَنْتُمْ وَاٰبَآؤُكُمْ مَّآ اَنْزَلَ اللهُ بِهَا مِنْ سُلْطٰنٍ ۭ اِنِ الْحُكْمُ اِلَّا لِلهِ ۭ اَمَرَ اَلَّا تَعْبُدُوْٓا اِلَّآ اِيَّاهُ ۭ ذٰلِكَ الدِّيْنُ الْقَيِّمُ وَلٰكِنَّ اَكْثَرَ النَّاسِ لَا يَعْلَمُوْنَ ۟

يٰصَاحِبَيِ السِّجْنِ اَمَّآ اَحَدُكُمَا فَيَسْقِىْ رَبَّهٗ خَمْرًا ۚ وَاَمَّا الْاٰخَرُ فَيُصْلَبُ فَتَأْكُلُ الطَّيْرُ مِنْ رَّأْسِهٖ ۭ قُضِيَ الْاَمْرُ الَّذِىْ فِيْهِ تَسْتَفْتِيٰنِ ۟

وَقَالَ لِلَّذِىْ ظَنَّ اَنَّهٗ نَاجٍ مِّنْهُمَا اذْكُرْنِىْ عِنْدَ رَبِّكَ ۡ فَاَنْسٰهُ الشَّيْطٰنُ ذِكْرَ رَبِّهٖ فَلَبِثَ فِى السِّجْنِ بِضْعَ سِنِيْنَ ۟

وَقَالَ الْمَلِكُ اِنِّىْٓ اَرٰى سَبْعَ بَقَرٰتٍ سِمَانٍ يَّأْكُلُهُنَّ سَبْعٌ عِجَافٌ وَّسَبْعَ سُنْبُلٰتٍ خُضْرٍ وَّاُخَرَ يٰبِسٰتٍ ۭ يٰٓاَيُّهَا الْمَلَاُ اَفْتُوْنِىْ فِىْ رُءْيَاىَ اِنْ كُنْتُمْ لِلرُّءْيَا تَعْبُرُوْنَ ۟

قَالُوْٓا اَضْغَاثُ اَحْلَامٍ ۚ وَمَا نَحْنُ بِتَأْوِيْلِ الْاَحْلَامِ بِعٰلِمِيْنَ ۟

وَقَالَ الَّذِىْ نَجَا مِنْهُمَا وَادَّكَرَ بَعْدَ اُمَّةٍ اَنَا اُنَبِّئُكُمْ بِتَأْوِيْلِهٖ فَاَرْسِلُوْنِ ۟

يُوْسُفُ اَيُّهَا الصِّدِّيْقُ اَفْتِنَا فِىْ

(the dream) of seven fat kine whom seven lean ones devour, and of seven green ears of corn and (seven) others withered: that I may return to the people, and that they may understand."

سَبْعِ بَقَرَٰتٍ سِمَانٍ يَّأْكُلُهُنَّ سَبْعٌ عِجَافٌ وَّسَبْعِ سُنْبُلَٰتٍ خُضْرٍ وَّ اُخَرَ يٰبِسٰتٍ ۚ لَّعَلِّيْٓ اَرْجِعُ اِلَى النَّاسِ لَعَلَّهُمْ يَعْلَمُوْنَ ۝

47. (Joseph) said: "For seven years you shall diligently sow as is your wont: and the harvests that you reap, you shall leave them in the ear,- except a little, of which you shall eat.

قَالَ تَزْرَعُوْنَ سَبْعَ سِنِيْنَ دَاَبًا ۚ فَمَا حَصَدْتُّمْ فَذَرُوْهُ فِيْ سُنْۢبُلِهٖٓ اِلَّا قَلِيْلًا مِّمَّا تَأْكُلُوْنَ ۝

48. "Then will come after that (period) seven dreadful (years), which will devour what you shall have laid by in advance for them,- (all) except a little which you shall have (specially) guarded.

ثُمَّ يَأْتِيْ مِنْۢ بَعْدِ ذٰلِكَ سَبْعٌ شِدَادٌ يَّأْكُلْنَ مَا قَدَّمْتُمْ لَهُنَّ اِلَّا قَلِيْلًا مِّمَّا تُحْصِنُوْنَ ۝

49. "Then will come after that (period) a year in which the people will have abundant water, and in which they will press (wine and oil)."

ثُمَّ يَأْتِيْ مِنْۢ بَعْدِ ذٰلِكَ عَامٌ فِيْهِ يُغَاثُ النَّاسُ وَفِيْهِ يَعْصِرُوْنَ ۝

50. So the king said: "You bring him to me." But when the messenger came to him, (Joseph) said: "You go back to your lord, and ask him, 'What is the state of mind of the ladies who cut their hands'? For my Lord is certainly well aware of their snare."

وَقَالَ الْمَلِكُ ائْتُوْنِيْ بِهٖ ۚ فَلَمَّا جَآءَهُ الرَّسُوْلُ قَالَ ارْجِعْ اِلٰى رَبِّكَ فَسْـَٔلْهُ مَا بَالُ النِّسْوَةِ الّٰتِيْ قَطَّعْنَ اَيْدِيَهُنَّ ۚ اِنَّ رَبِّيْ بِكَيْدِهِنَّ عَلِيْمٌ ۝

51. (The king) said (to the ladies): "What was your affair when you sought to seduce Joseph from his (true) self?" The ladies said: "Allah preserve us! We do not know any evil against him!" Said the 'Aziz's wife: "Now is the truth manifest (to all): it was I who sought to seduce him from his (true) self: he is indeed of those who are (ever) true (and virtuous).

قَالَ مَا خَطْبُكُنَّ اِذْ رَاوَدْتُّنَّ يُوْسُفَ عَنْ نَّفْسِهٖ ۚ قُلْنَ حَاشَ لِلّٰهِ مَا عَلِمْنَا عَلَيْهِ مِنْ سُوْٓءٍ ۚ قَالَتِ امْرَاَتُ الْعَزِيْزِ الْـٰٔنَ حَصْحَصَ الْحَقُّ ۖ اَنَا رَاوَدْتُّهٗ عَنْ نَّفْسِهٖ وَاِنَّهٗ لَمِنَ الصّٰدِقِيْنَ ۝

52. "This (I say), in order that he may know that I have never been false to him in his absence, and that Allah will never guide the snare of the false ones.

ذٰلِكَ لِيَعْلَمَ اَنِّيْ لَمْ اَخُنْهُ بِالْغَيْبِ وَاَنَّ اللّٰهَ لَا يَهْدِيْ كَيْدَ الْخَآئِنِيْنَ ۝

53. "Nor do I absolve my own self (of blame): the (human) soul is certainly prone to evil, unless my Lord bestows His Mercy: but surely my Lord is Oft- Forgiving, Most Merciful."

وَمَآ اُبَرِّئُ نَفْسِيْ ۚ اِنَّ النَّفْسَ لَاَمَّارَةٌۢ بِالسُّوْٓءِ اِلَّا مَا رَحِمَ رَبِّيْ ۚ اِنَّ رَبِّيْ غَفُوْرٌ رَّحِيْمٌ ۝

54. So the king said: "Bring him to me; I will take him specially to serve about my own person." Therefore when he had spoken to him, he said: "Be assured this day, you are, before our own presence, with rank firmly established, and fidelity fully proved!"

55. (Joseph) said: "Set me over the store-houses of the land: I will indeed guard them, as one that knows (their importance)."

56. Thus We gave established power to Joseph in the land, to take possession therein as, when, or where he pleased. We bestow of Our Mercy on whom We please, and We suffer not, to be lost, the reward of those who do good.

57. But verily the reward of the Hereafter is the best, for those who believe, and are constant in righteousness.

58. Then came Joseph's brethren: they entered his presence, and he knew them, but they did not know him.

59. And when he had furnished them forth with provisions (suitable) for them, he said: "Bring to me a brother you have, of the same father as yourselves, (but a different mother): do you not see that I pay out full measure, and that I do provide the best hospitality?

60. "Now if you do not bring him to me, you shall have no measure (of corn) from me, nor you shall (even) come near me."

61. They said: "We shall certainly seek to get our wish about him from his father: indeed we shall do it."

62. And (Joseph) told his servants to put their stock-in-trade (with which they had bartered) into their saddle-bags, so they should know it only when they returned to their people, in order that they might come back.

63. Now when they returned to their father, they said: "O our father! No more measure of grain shall we get (unless we take our brother): so send

وَقَالَ الْمَلِكُ ائْتُوْنِىْ بِهٖ اَسْتَخْلِصْهُ لِنَفْسِىْ ۚ فَلَمَّا كَلَّمَهٗ قَالَ اِنَّكَ الْيَوْمَ لَدَيْنَا مَكِيْنٌ اَمِيْنٌ ۝

قَالَ اجْعَلْنِىْ عَلٰى خَزَآئِنِ الْاَرْضِ ۚ اِنِّىْ حَفِيْظٌ عَلِيْمٌ ۝

وَكَذٰلِكَ مَكَّنَّا لِيُوْسُفَ فِى الْاَرْضِ ۚ يَتَبَوَّاُ مِنْهَا حَيْثُ يَشَآءُ ۚ نُصِيْبُ بِرَحْمَتِنَا مَنْ نَّشَآءُ وَلَا نُضِيْعُ اَجْرَ الْمُحْسِنِيْنَ ۝

وَلَاَجْرُ الْاٰخِرَةِ خَيْرٌ لِّلَّذِيْنَ اٰمَنُوْا وَكَانُوْا يَتَّقُوْنَ ۝

وَجَآءَ اِخْوَةُ يُوْسُفَ فَدَخَلُوْا عَلَيْهِ فَعَرَفَهُمْ وَهُمْ لَهٗ مُنْكِرُوْنَ ۝

وَلَمَّا جَهَّزَهُمْ بِجَهَازِهِمْ قَالَ ائْتُوْنِىْ بِاَخٍ لَّكُمْ مِّنْ اَبِيْكُمْ ۚ اَلَا تَرَوْنَ اَنِّىْ اُوْفِى الْكَيْلَ وَاَنَا خَيْرُ الْمُنْزِلِيْنَ ۝

فَاِنْ لَّمْ تَأْتُوْنِىْ بِهٖ فَلَا كَيْلَ لَكُمْ عِنْدِىْ وَلَا تَقْرَبُوْنِ ۝

قَالُوْا سَنُرَاوِدُ عَنْهُ اَبَاهُ وَاِنَّا لَفٰعِلُوْنَ ۝

وَقَالَ لِفِتْيٰنِهِ اجْعَلُوْا بِضَاعَتَهُمْ فِىْ رِحَالِهِمْ لَعَلَّهُمْ يَعْرِفُوْنَهَآ اِذَا انْقَلَبُوْا اِلٰٓى اَهْلِهِمْ لَعَلَّهُمْ يَرْجِعُوْنَ ۝

فَلَمَّا رَجَعُوْا اِلٰٓى اَبِيْهِمْ قَالُوْا يٰٓاَبَانَا مُنِعَ مِنَّا الْكَيْلُ فَاَرْسِلْ

ع

our brother with us, that we may get our measure; and we will indeed take every care of him."

64. He said: "Shall I trust you with him with any result other than when I trusted you with his brother aforetime? But Allah is the best to take care (of him), and He is the Most Merciful of those who show mercy!"

65. Then when they opened their baggage, they found their stock-in-trade had been returned to them. They said: "O our father! What (more) can we desire? this our stock-in-trade has been returned to us: we shall get (more) food for our family; we shall take care of our brother; and add (at the same time) a full camel's load (of grain to our provisions). This is but a small quantity.

66. (Jacob) said: "Never will I send him with you until you swear a solemn oath to me, in Allah's name, that you will be sure to bring him back to me unless you are yourselves hemmed in (and made powerless). And when they had sworn their solemn oath, he said: "Over all that we say, be Allah the Witness and Guardian!"

67. Further he said: "O my sons! enter not all by one gate: you enter by different gates. Not that I can profit you anything against Allah (with my advice): none can command except Allah: on Him do I put my trust: and let all that trust put their trust on Him."

68. And when they entered in the manner their father had enjoined, it did not profit them in the least against (the plan of) Allah: it was but a necessity of Jacob's soul, which he discharged. For he was, by Our instruction, full of knowledge (and experience): but most men do not know.

مَعَنَآ اَخَانَا نَكْتَلْ وَاِنَّا لَهٗ لَحٰفِظُوْنَ ۝

قَالَ هَلْ اٰمَنُكُمْ عَلَيْهِ اِلَّا كَمَآ اَمِنْتُكُمْ عَلٰۤى اَخِيْهِ مِنْ قَبْلُ ۚ فَاللّٰهُ خَيْرٌ حٰفِظًا ۫ وَّهُوَ اَرْحَمُ الرّٰحِمِيْنَ ۝

وَلَمَّا فَتَحُوْا مَتَاعَهُمْ وَجَدُوْا بِضَاعَتَهُمْ رُدَّتْ اِلَيْهِمْ ۭ قَالُوْا يَاۤاَبَانَا مَا نَبْغِيْ ۭ هٰذِهٖ بِضَاعَتُنَا رُدَّتْ اِلَيْنَا ۚ وَنَمِيْرُ اَهْلَنَا وَنَحْفَظُ اَخَانَا وَنَزْدَادُ كَيْلَ بَعِيْرٍ ۭ ذٰلِكَ كَيْلٌ يَّسِيْرٌ ۝

قَالَ لَنْ اُرْسِلَهٗ مَعَكُمْ حَتّٰى تُؤْتُوْنِ مَوْثِقًا مِّنَ اللّٰهِ لَتَأْتُنَّنِيْ بِهٖۤ اِلَّاۤ اَنْ يُّحَاطَ بِكُمْ ۚ فَلَمَّاۤ اٰتَوْهُ مَوْثِقَهُمْ قَالَ اللّٰهُ عَلٰى مَا نَقُوْلُ وَكِيْلٌ ۝

وَقَالَ يٰبَنِيَّ لَا تَدْخُلُوْا مِنْۢ بَابٍ وَّاحِدٍ وَّادْخُلُوْا مِنْ اَبْوَابٍ مُّتَفَرِّقَةٍ ۭ وَمَاۤ اُغْنِيْ عَنْكُمْ مِّنَ اللّٰهِ مِنْ شَيْءٍ ۭ اِنِ الْحُكْمُ اِلَّا لِلّٰهِ ۭ عَلَيْهِ تَوَكَّلْتُ ۚ وَعَلَيْهِ فَلْيَتَوَكَّلِ الْمُتَوَكِّلُوْنَ ۝

وَلَمَّا دَخَلُوْا مِنْ حَيْثُ اَمَرَهُمْ اَبُوْهُمْ ۭ مَا كَانَ يُغْنِيْ عَنْهُمْ مِّنَ اللّٰهِ مِنْ شَيْءٍ اِلَّا حَاجَةً فِيْ نَفْسِ يَعْقُوْبَ قَضٰىهَا ۭ وَاِنَّهٗ لَذُوْ عِلْمٍ لِّمَا عَلَّمْنٰهُ وَلٰكِنَّ اَكْثَرَ النَّاسِ لَا يَعْلَمُوْنَ ۝

69. Now when they came into Joseph's presence, he received his (full) brother to stay with him. He said (to him): "Behold! I am your (own) brother; so do not grieve at anything of their doings."

70. At length when he had furnished them forth with provisions (suitable) for them, he put the drinking cup into his brother's saddle-bag. Then shouted out a Crier:"O you (in) the caravan! behold! you are thieves, without doubt!"

71. They said, turning toward them: "What is it that you miss?"

72. They said: "We miss the great beaker of the King; for him who produces it, is (the reward of) a camel load; I will be bound by it."

73. (The brothers) said: "By Allah! you know well that we did not come to make mischief in the land, and we are no thieves!"

74. (The Egyptians) said: "What then shall be the penalty of this, if you are (proved) to have lied?"

75. They said: "The penalty should be that he in whose saddle-bag it is found, should be held (as bondman) to atone for the (crime). Thus it is we punish the wrong-doers!"

76. So he began (the search) with their baggage, before (he came to) the baggage of his brother: at length he brought it out of his brother's baggage. Thus did We plan for Joseph. He could not take his brother by the law of the king except that Allah willed it (so). We raise to degrees (of wisdom) whom We please: but over all endued with knowledge is One, the All-Knowing.

77. They said: "If he steals, there was a brother of his who stole before (him)." But these things Joseph kept locked in his heart, revealing not the secrets to them. He (simply) said (to himself): "You are the worse situated; and Allah knows best the truth of what you assert!"

وَلَمَّا دَخَلُوْا عَلٰى يُوْسُفَ اٰوٰٓى
اِلَيْهِ اَخَاهُ قَالَ اِنِّیْٓ اَنَا اَخُوْكَ
فَلَا تَبْتَئِسْ بِمَا كَانُوْا يَعْمَلُوْنَ ۞

فَلَمَّا جَهَّزَهُمْ بِجَهَازِهِمْ جَعَلَ
السِّقَايَةَ فِیْ رَحْلِ اَخِیْهِ ثُمَّ اَذَّنَ
مُؤَذِّنٌ اَيَّتُهَا الْعِيْرُ اِنَّكُمْ لَسٰرِقُوْنَ ۞

قَالُوْا وَاَقْبَلُوْا عَلَيْهِمْ مَّاذَا تَفْقِدُوْنَ ۞

قَالُوْا نَفْقِدُ صُوَاعَ الْمَلِكِ وَلِمَنْ
جَآءَ بِهٖ حِمْلُ بَعِيْرٍ وَّاَنَا بِهٖ زَعِيْمٌ ۞

قَالُوْا تَاللّٰهِ لَقَدْ عَلِمْتُمْ مَّا جِئْنَا لِنُفْسِدَ
فِی الْاَرْضِ وَمَا كُنَّا سٰرِقِیْنَ ۞

قَالُوْا فَمَا جَزَآؤُهٗٓ اِنْ كُنْتُمْ كٰذِبِیْنَ ۞

قَالُوْا جَزَآؤُهٗ مَنْ وُّجِدَ فِیْ رَحْلِهٖ
فَهُوَ جَزَآؤُهٗ ۚ كَذٰلِكَ نَجْزِی
الظّٰلِمِیْنَ ۞

فَبَدَاَ بِاَوْعِيَتِهِمْ قَبْلَ وِعَآءِ اَخِیْهِ
ثُمَّ اسْتَخْرَجَهَا مِنْ وِّعَآءِ اَخِیْهِ ۚ
كَذٰلِكَ كِدْنَا لِيُوْسُفَ ۚ مَا كَانَ
لِيَاْخُذَ اَخَاهُ فِیْ دِيْنِ الْمَلِكِ اِلَّآ
اَنْ يَّشَآءَ اللّٰهُ ۚ نَرْفَعُ دَرَجٰتٍ مَّنْ
نَّشَآءُ ۚ وَفَوْقَ كُلِّ ذِیْ عِلْمٍ عَلِيْمٌ ۞

قَالُوْٓا اِنْ يَّسْرِقْ فَقَدْ سَرَقَ اَخٌ لَّهٗ
مِنْ قَبْلُ ۚ فَاَسَرَّهَا يُوْسُفُ فِیْ
نَفْسِهٖ وَلَمْ يُبْدِهَا لَهُمْ ۚ قَالَ
اَنْتُمْ شَرٌّ مَّكَانًا ۚ وَاللّٰهُ اَعْلَمُ
بِمَا تَصِفُوْنَ ۞

78. They said: "O exalted one! Behold! he has a father, aged and venerable, (who will grieve for him); so take one of us in his place; for we see that you are (gracious) in doing good."

قَالُوا يَا أَيُّهَا الْعَزِيزُ إِنَّ لَهُ أَبًا شَيْخًا كَبِيرًا فَخُذْ أَحَدَنَا مَكَانَهُ إِنَّا نَرَاكَ مِنَ الْمُحْسِنِينَ ۝

79. He said: "Allah forbid that we take other than him with whom we found our property: indeed (if we did so), we should be acting wrongfully.

قَالَ مَعَاذَ اللّٰهِ أَنْ نَّأْخُذَ إِلَّا مَنْ وَّجَدْنَا مَتَاعَنَا عِنْدَهُ ۙ إِنَّا إِذًا لَّظَالِمُونَ ۝

80. Now when they saw no hope of his (yielding), they held a conference in private. The leader among them said: "Don't you know that your father took an oath from you in Allah's name, and how, before this, you failed in your duty with Joseph? Therefore I will not leave this land until my father permits me, or Allah commands me; and He is the best to command.

فَلَمَّا اسْتَيْأَسُوا مِنْهُ خَلَصُوا نَجِيًّا ۭ قَالَ كَبِيرُهُمْ أَلَمْ تَعْلَمُوا أَنَّ أَبَاكُمْ قَدْ أَخَذَ عَلَيْكُمْ مَّوْثِقًا مِّنَ اللّٰهِ وَمِنْ قَبْلُ مَا فَرَّطْتُمْ فِي يُوسُفَ ۚ فَلَنْ أَبْرَحَ الْأَرْضَ حَتّٰى يَأْذَنَ لِي أَبِي أَوْ يَحْكُمَ اللّٰهُ لِي ۚ وَهُوَ خَيْرُ الْحَاكِمِينَ ۝

81. "You turn back to your father, and say, 'O our father! Behold! your son committed theft! we bear witness only to what we know, and we could not well guard against the unseen!

اِرْجِعُوا إِلٰى أَبِيكُمْ فَقُولُوا يَا أَبَانَا إِنَّ ابْنَكَ سَرَقَ ۚ وَمَا شَهِدْنَا إِلَّا بِمَا عَلِمْنَا وَمَا كُنَّا لِلْغَيْبِ حَافِظِينَ ۝

82. "'Ask at the town where we have been and the caravan in which we returned, and (you will find) we are indeed telling the truth.'"

وَسْئَلِ الْقَرْيَةَ الَّتِي كُنَّا فِيهَا وَالْعِيرَ الَّتِي أَقْبَلْنَا فِيهَا ۚ وَإِنَّا لَصَادِقُونَ ۝

83. Jacob said: "Nay, but you have yourselves contrived a story (good enough) for you. So patience is most fitting (for me). May be Allah will bring them (back) all to me (in the end). For He is indeed full of knowledge and wisdom."

قَالَ بَلْ سَوَّلَتْ لَكُمْ أَنْفُسُكُمْ أَمْرًا ۚ فَصَبْرٌ جَمِيلٌ ۖ عَسَى اللّٰهُ أَنْ يَّأْتِيَنِي بِهِمْ جَمِيعًا ۚ إِنَّهُ هُوَ الْعَلِيمُ الْحَكِيمُ ۝

84. And he turned away from them, and said: "How great is my grief for Joseph!" And his eyes became white with

وَتَوَلّٰى عَنْهُمْ وَقَالَ يَا أَسَفَى عَلٰى يُوسُفَ وَابْيَضَّتْ عَيْنَاهُ مِنَ

sorrow, and he fell into silent melancholy.

85. They said: "By Allah! (Never) will you cease to remember Joseph until you reach the last extremity of illness, or until you die!"

86. He said: "I only complain of my distraction and anguish to Allah, and I know from Allah that which you do not know.

87. "O my sons! you go and enquire about Joseph and his brother, and never give up hope of Allah's soothing Mercy: truly no one despairs of Allah's soothing Mercy, except those who have no faith."

88. Then, when they came (back) into (Joseph's) presence they said: "O exalted one! distress has seized us and our family: we have (now) brought but scanty capital: so pay us full measure, (we pray you), and treat it as charity to us: for Allah rewards the charitable."

89. He said: "Do you know how you dealt with Joseph and his brother, not knowing (what you were doing)?"

90. They said: "Are you indeed Joseph?" He said, "I am Joseph, and this is my brother: Allah has indeed been gracious to us (all): behold, he that is righteous and patient,- never will Allah suffer the reward to be lost, of those who do right."

91. They said: "By Allah! indeed Allah has preferred you above us, and we certainly have been guilty of sin!"

92. He said: "This day let no reproach be (cast) on you: Allah will forgive you, and He is the Most Merciful of those who show mercy!

93. "Go with this my shirt, and cast it

الْحُزْنِ فَهُوَ كَظِيْمٌ ۝

قَالُوْا تَاللّٰهِ تَفْتَؤُا تَذْكُرُ يُوْسُفَ

حَتّٰى تَكُوْنَ حَرَضًا اَوْ تَكُوْنَ

مِنَ الْهٰلِكِيْنَ ۝

قَالَ اِنَّمَاۤ اَشْكُوْا بَثِّيْ وَحُزْنِيْۤ اِلَى

اللّٰهِ وَاَعْلَمُ مِنَ اللّٰهِ مَا لَا تَعْلَمُوْنَ ۝

يٰبَنِيَّ اذْهَبُوْا فَتَحَسَّسُوْا مِنْ يُّوْسُفَ

وَاَخِيْهِ وَلَا تَايْئَسُوْا مِنْ رَّوْحِ اللّٰهِ ؕ

اِنَّهٗ لَا يَايْئَسُ مِنْ رَّوْحِ اللّٰهِ اِلَّا

الْقَوْمُ الْكٰفِرُوْنَ ۝

فَلَمَّا دَخَلُوْا عَلَيْهِ قَالُوْا يٰۤاَيُّهَا

الْعَزِيْزُ مَسَّنَا وَاَهْلَنَا الضُّرُّ وَجِئْنَا

بِبِضَاعَةٍ مُّزْجٰةٍ فَاَوْفِ لَنَا الْكَيْلَ

وَتَصَدَّقْ عَلَيْنَا ؕ اِنَّ اللّٰهَ يَجْزِى

الْمُتَصَدِّقِيْنَ ۝

قَالَ هَلْ عَلِمْتُمْ مَّا فَعَلْتُمْ بِيُوْسُفَ

وَاَخِيْهِ اِذْ اَنْتُمْ جٰهِلُوْنَ ۝

قَالُوْا ءَاِنَّكَ لَاَنْتَ يُوْسُفُ ؕ قَالَ

اَنَا يُوْسُفُ وَهٰذَاۤ اَخِيْ ؗ قَدْ مَنَّ

اللّٰهُ عَلَيْنَا ؕ اِنَّهٗ مَنْ يَّتَّقِ وَيَصْبِرْ

فَاِنَّ اللّٰهَ لَا يُضِيْعُ اَجْرَ الْمُحْسِنِيْنَ ۝

قَالُوْا تَاللّٰهِ لَقَدْ اٰثَرَكَ اللّٰهُ عَلَيْنَا

وَاِنْ كُنَّا لَخٰطِئِيْنَ ۝

قَالَ لَا تَثْرِيْبَ عَلَيْكُمُ الْيَوْمَ ؕ يَغْفِرُ

اللّٰهُ لَكُمْ ؗ وَهُوَ اَرْحَمُ الرّٰحِمِيْنَ ۝

اِذْهَبُوْا بِقَمِيْصِيْ هٰذَا فَاَلْقُوْهُ

over the face of my father: he will come to see (clearly). Then you come (here) to me together with all your family."

94. When the Caravan left (Egypt), their father said: "I do indeed scent the presence of Joseph: nay, think me not a dotard."

95. They said: "By Allah! truly you are in your old wandering mind."

96. Then when the bearer of the good news came, he cast (the shirt) over his face, and he forthwith regained clear sight. He said: "Did I not say to you, 'I know from Allah that which you do not know?'"

97. They said: "O our father! ask for us forgiveness for our sins, for we were truly at fault."

98. He said: "Soon will I ask my Lord for forgiveness for you: for He is indeed Oft-Forgiving, Most Merciful."

99. Then when they entered the presence of Joseph, he provided a home for his parents with himself, and said: "you enter Egypt (all) in safety if it please Allah."

100. And he raised his parents high on the throne (of dignity), and they fell down in prostration, (all) before him. He said: "O my father! this is the fulfilment of my vision of old! Allah has made it come true! He was indeed good to me when He took me out of prison and brought you (all here) out of the desert, (even) after Satan had sown enmity between me and my brothers. Verily my Lord understands best the mysteries of all that He plans to do. For verily He is full of knowledge and wisdom.

101. "O my Lord! You have indeed bestowed on me some power, and taught me something of the interpretation of dreams and events,- O You Creator of the heavens and the earth! You are my Protector in this world and in the Hereafter. You take my soul (at death) as one submitting to Your Will (as a Muslim), and unite me with the righteous."

رَبِّ قَدْ اٰتَيْتَنِيْ مِنَ الْمُلْكِ وَعَلَّمْتَنِيْ مِنْ تَأْوِيْلِ الْاَحَادِيْثِ ۚ فَاطِرَ السَّمٰوٰتِ وَالْاَرْضِ ۛ اَنْتَ وَلِيٖ فِى الدُّنْيَا وَالْاٰخِرَةِ ۚ تَوَفَّنِيْ مُسْلِمًا وَّاَلْحِقْنِيْ بِالصّٰلِحِيْنَ ۝

102. Such is one of the stories of what happened unseen, which We reveal by inspiration unto you; nor were you (present) with them when they concerted their plans together in the process of weaving their plots.

ذٰلِكَ مِنْ اَنْۢبَاءِ الْغَيْبِ نُوْحِيْهِ اِلَيْكَ ۚ وَمَا كُنْتَ لَدَيْهِمْ اِذْ اَجْمَعُوْۤا اَمْرَهُمْ وَهُمْ يَمْكُرُوْنَ ۝

103. Yet no faith will the greater part of mankind have, however ardently you do desire it.

وَمَاۤ اَكْثَرُ النَّاسِ وَلَوْ حَرَصْتَ بِمُؤْمِنِيْنَ ۝

104. And no reward do you ask of them for this: it is no less than a message for all creatures.

وَمَا تَسْـَٔلُهُمْ عَلَيْهِ مِنْ اَجْرٍ ۭ اِنْ هُوَ اِلَّا ذِكْرٌ لِّلْعٰلَمِيْنَ ۝

105. And how many Signs in the heavens and the earth do they pass by? Yet they turn (their faces) away from them!

وَكَاَيِّنْ مِّنْ اٰيَةٍ فِى السَّمٰوٰتِ وَالْاَرْضِ يَمُرُّوْنَ عَلَيْهَا وَهُمْ عَنْهَا مُعْرِضُوْنَ ۝

106. And most of them do not believe in Allah without associating (others as partners) with Him!

وَمَا يُؤْمِنُ اَكْثَرُهُمْ بِاللّٰهِ اِلَّا وَهُمْ مُّشْرِكُوْنَ ۝

107. Do they then feel secure from the coming against them of the covering veil of the wrath of Allah,- or of the coming against them of the (final) Hour all of a sudden while they perceive not?

اَفَاَمِنُوْۤا اَنْ تَأْتِيَهُمْ غَاشِيَةٌ مِّنْ عَذَابِ اللّٰهِ اَوْ تَأْتِيَهُمُ السَّاعَةُ بَغْتَةً وَّهُمْ لَا يَشْعُرُوْنَ ۝

108. You say: "This is my way: I do invite to Allah,- on evidence clear as the seeing with one's eyes,- I and whoever follows me. Glory to Allah! and never will I join gods with Allah!"

قُلْ هٰذِهٖ سَبِيْلِيْۤ اَدْعُوْۤا اِلَى اللّٰهِ ۚ عَلٰى بَصِيْرَةٍ اَنَا وَمَنِ اتَّبَعَنِيْ ۭ وَسُبْحٰنَ اللّٰهِ وَمَاۤ اَنَا مِنَ الْمُشْرِكِيْنَ ۝

109. Nor did We send before you (as Messengers) any but men, whom We inspired,- (men) living in human habitations. Do they not travel through the earth, and see what

وَمَاۤ اَرْسَلْنَا مِنْ قَبْلِكَ اِلَّا رِجَالًا نُّوْحِيْۤ اِلَيْهِمْ مِّنْ اَهْلِ الْقُرٰى ۭ اَفَلَمْ يَسِيْرُوْا فِى الْاَرْضِ فَيَنْظُرُوْا كَيْفَ

SÛRAH-13
AR-RA'D
(INTRODUCTION)

The chronological place of this Sûra and the general argument of Sûras 10 to 15 has been described in the Introduction to S. 10.

The special argument of this Sûrah deals with that aspect of Allah's revelation of Himself to man and His dealings with him, which is concerned with certain contrasts which are here pointed out. There is the revelation to the Prophets, which comes in spoken words adapted to the language of the various men and groups of men to whom it comes; and there is the parallel revelation or signs in the constant laws of external nature, on this earth and in the visible heavens. There is the contrast between recurring life and death already in the external world: why should men disbelieve in the life after death? They mock at the idea of punishment because it is deferred: but can they not see Allah's power and glory in thunder and the forces of nature? All creation praises Him: it is the good that endures and the evil that is swept away like froth or scum. Not only in miracles but in the normal working of the world, are shown Allah's power and mercy. What is Punishment in this world, compared to that in the life to come? Even here there are Signs of the working of His law: plot or plan as men will, it is Allah's Will that must prevail. This is illustrated in Joseph's story in the preceding Sûrah.

was the end of those before them? But the home of the Hereafter is best, for those who do right. Will you not then understand?

110. (Respite will be granted) until, when the Messengers give up hope (of their people) and (come to) think that they were treated as liars, there reaches them Our help, and those whom We will are delivered into safety. But never will be warded off Our punishment from those who are in sin.

111. There is, in their stories, instruction for men endued with understanding. It is not a tale invented, but a confirmation of what went before it,- a detailed exposition of all things, and a Guide and a Mercy to any such as believe.

---

13. Thunder
In the name of Allah. Most Gracious, Most Merciful.

1. *Alif-Lam-Mim-Raa.* These are the Signs (or Verses) of the Book: that which has been revealed to you from your Lord is the Truth; but most men do not believe.

2. Allah is He Who raised the heavens without any pillars that you can see; is firmly established on the Throne (of Authority); He has subjected the sun and the moon (to His Law)! Each one runs (its course) for a term appointed. He regulates all affairs, explaining the Signs in detail, that you may believe with certainty in the meeting with your Lord.

3. And it is He Who spread out the earth, and set thereon mountains standing firm and (flowing) rivers: and fruit of every kind He made in pairs, two and two:

He draws the night as a veil over the day. Behold, verily in these things there are Signs for those who consider!

4. And in the earth are tracts (diverse though) neighboring, and gardens of vines and fields sown with corn, and palm-trees growing out of single roots or otherwise: watered with the same water, yet some of them We make more excellent than others to eat. Behold, verily in these things there are Signs for those who understand!

5. If you do marvel (at their want of faith), strange is their saying: "When we are (actually) dust, shall we indeed then be in a renewed creation?" They are those who deny their Lord! They are those round whose necks will be yokes (of servitude): they will be Companions of the Fire, to dwell therein (for ever)!

6. They ask you to hasten on the evil in preference to the good: yet before them, have come to pass, (many) exemplary punishments! But verily your Lord is full of forgiveness for mankind for their wrong-doing. And verily your Lord is (also) strict in punishment.

7. And the Unbelievers say: "Why is not a Sign sent down to him from his Lord?" But you are truly a warner, and to every people a guide.

8. Allah knows what every female (womb) bears, by how much the wombs fall short (of their time or number) or do exceed. Every single thing is before His sight, in (due) proportion.

9. He knows the unseen and that which is open:

يُغْشِى الَّيْلَ النَّهَارَ ۚ اِنَّ فِىْ ذٰلِكَ لَاٰيٰتٍ لِّقَوْمٍ يَّتَفَكَّرُوْنَ ۞

وَفِى الْاَرْضِ قِطَعٌ مُّتَجٰوِرٰتٌ وَّجَنّٰتٌ مِّنْ اَعْنَابٍ وَّزَرْعٌ وَّنَخِيْلٌ صِنْوَانٌ وَّغَيْرُ صِنْوَانٍ يُّسْقٰى بِمَآءٍ وَّاحِدٍ ۖ وَّنُفَضِّلُ بَعْضَهَا عَلٰى بَعْضٍ فِى الْاُكُلِ ۚ اِنَّ فِىْ ذٰلِكَ لَاٰيٰتٍ لِّقَوْمٍ يَّعْقِلُوْنَ ۞

وَاِنْ تَعْجَبْ فَعَجَبٌ قَوْلُهُمْ ءَاِذَا كُنَّا تُرٰبًا ءَاِنَّا لَفِىْ خَلْقٍ جَدِيْدٍ ۗ اُولٰۤئِكَ الَّذِيْنَ كَفَرُوْا بِرَبِّهِمْ ۚ وَاُولٰۤئِكَ الْاَغْلٰلُ فِىْۤ اَعْنَاقِهِمْ ۚ وَاُولٰۤئِكَ اَصْحٰبُ النَّارِ ۚ هُمْ فِيْهَا خٰلِدُوْنَ ۞

وَيَسْتَعْجِلُوْنَكَ بِالسَّيِّئَةِ قَبْلَ الْحَسَنَةِ وَقَدْ خَلَتْ مِنْ قَبْلِهِمُ الْمَثُلٰتُ ۗ وَاِنَّ رَبَّكَ لَذُوْ مَغْفِرَةٍ لِّلنَّاسِ عَلٰى ظُلْمِهِمْ ۚ وَاِنَّ رَبَّكَ لَشَدِيْدُ الْعِقَابِ ۞

وَيَقُوْلُ الَّذِيْنَ كَفَرُوْا لَوْلَاۤ اُنْزِلَ عَلَيْهِ اٰيَةٌ مِّنْ رَّبِّهٖ ۗ اِنَّمَآ اَنْتَ مُنْذِرٌ وَّلِكُلِّ قَوْمٍ هَادٍ ۞

اَللّٰهُ يَعْلَمُ مَا تَحْمِلُ كُلُّ اُنْثٰى وَمَا تَغِيْضُ الْاَرْحَامُ وَمَا تَزْدَادُ ۗ وَكُلُّ شَىْءٍ عِنْدَهٗ بِمِقْدَارٍ ۞

عٰلِمُ الْغَيْبِ وَالشَّهَادَةِ

ع

He is the Great, the Most High.

الْكَبِيرُ الْمُتَعَالِ ۞

10. It is the same (to Him) whether any of you conceal his speech or declare it openly; whether he lie hid by night or walk forth freely by day.

سَوَاءٌ مِّنْكُمْ مَّنْ أَسَرَّ الْقَوْلَ وَمَنْ جَهَرَ بِهِ وَمَنْ هُوَ مُسْتَخْفٍ بِالَّيْلِ وَسَارِبٌ بِالنَّهَارِ ۞

11. For each (such person) there are (angels) in succession, before and behind him: they guard him by command of Allah. Verily never will Allah change the condition of a people until they change it themselves (with their own souls). But when (once) Allah wills a people's punishment, there can be no turning it back, nor will they find, besides Him, any to protect.

لَهُ مُعَقِّبَاتٌ مِّنْ بَيْنِ يَدَيْهِ وَ مِنْ خَلْفِهِ يَحْفَظُونَهُ مِنْ أَمْرِ اللهِ طِرَانَ اللهَ لَا يُغَيِّرُ مَا بِقَوْمٍ حَتَّى يُغَيِّرُوا مَا بِأَنْفُسِهِمْ وَإِذَا أَرَادَ اللهُ بِقَوْمٍ سُوْءًا فَلَا مَرَدَّ لَهُ وَمَا لَهُمْ مِّنْ دُونِهِ مِنْ وَّالٍ ۞

12. It is He Who shows you the lightning, by way both of fear and of hope: it is He Who raises up the clouds, heavy with (fertilising) rain!

هُوَ الَّذِى يُرِيكُمُ الْبَرْقَ خَوْفًا وَّ طَمَعًا وَّيُنْشِئُ السَّحَابَ الثِّقَالَ ۚ

13. Nay, thunder repeats His praises, and so do the angels, with awe: He flings the loud-voiced thunder-bolts, and therewith He strikes whom-soever He will..Yet these (are the men) who (dare to) dispute about Allah, with the strength of His power (supreme)!

وَيُسَبِّحُ الرَّعْدُ بِحَمْدِهِ وَالْمَلٰئِكَةُ مِنْ خِيفَتِهِ وَيُرْسِلُ الصَّوَاعِقَ فَيُصِيبُ بِهَا مَنْ يَّشَاءُ وَهُمْ يُجَادِلُونَ فِى اللهِ ۚ وَهُوَ شَدِيدُ الْمِحَالِ ۚ

14. For Him (alone) is prayer in Truth: any others that they call upon besides Him hear them no more than if they were to stretch forth their hands for water to reach their mouths but it reaches them not: for the prayer of those without Faith is nothing but (futile) wandering (in the mind).

لَهُ دَعْوَةُ الْحَقِّ وَالَّذِينَ يَدْعُونَ مِنْ دُونِهِ لَا يَسْتَجِيبُونَ لَهُمْ بِشَيْءٍ إِلَّا كَبَاسِطِ كَفَّيْهِ إِلَى الْمَاءِ لِيَبْلُغَ فَاهُ وَمَا هُوَ بِبَالِغِهِ وَمَا دُعَاءُ الْكٰفِرِينَ إِلَّا فِى ضَلَالٍ ۞

15. Whatever beings there are in the heavens and the earth do prostrate themselves to Allah (acknowledging subjection),- with good-will or in spite of themselves: so do their shadows in the mornings and evenings.

وَلِلّٰهِ يَسْجُدُ مَنْ فِى السَّمٰوٰتِ وَالْأَرْضِ طَوْعًا وَّكَرْهًا وَّظِلَالُهُمْ بِالْغُدُوِّ وَالْأَصَالِ ۞

16. Say: "Who is the Lord and Sustainer of the heavens and the earth?"

قُلْ مَنْ رَّبُّ السَّمٰوٰتِ وَالْأَرْضِ ۚ

Say: "(It is) Allah." Say: "Do you then take (for worship) protectors other than Him, such as have no power either for good or for harm to themselves?" Say: "Are the blind equal with those who see? Or the depths of darkness equal with light?" Or do they assign to Allah partners who have created (anything) as He has created, so that the creation seemed to them similar? Say: "Allah is the Creator of all things: He is the One, the Supreme and Irresistible."

17. He sends down water from the skies, and the channels flow, each according to its measure: but the torrent bears away the foam that mounts up to the surface. Even so, from that (ore) which they heat in the fire, to make ornaments or utensils therewith, there is a scum likewise. Thus Allah (by parables) shows forth Truth and Vanity. For the scum disappears like forth cast out; while that which is for the good of mankind remains on the earth. Thus Allah sets forth parables.

18. For those who respond to their Lord, are (all) good things. But those who do not respond to Him,- even if they had all that is in the heavens and on earth, and as much more, (in vain) would they offer it for ransom. For them will the reckoning be terrible: their abode will be Hell,- what a bed of misery!

19. Is then one who knows that that which has been revealed to you from your Lord is the Truth, like one who is blind? It is those who are endued with understanding that receive admonition;-

20. Those who fulfil the Covenant of Allah and do not fail in their plighted word;

21. Those who join together those things which Allah has commanded to be joined, hold their Lord in awe, and fear the terrible reckoning;

22. Those who patiently persevere, seeking the countenance of their Lord; establish regular prayers; spend out of (the gifts) We have bestowed for their sustenance, secretly and openly; and turn off Evil with good: for such there is the final attainment of the (Eternal) Home,-

23. Gardens of perpetual bliss: they shall enter there, as well as the righteous among their fathers, their spouses, and their offspring: and angels shall enter unto them from every gate (with the salutation):

24. "Peace unto you for that you persevered in patience! Now how excellent is the final Home!"

25. But those who break the Covenant of Allah, after having plighted their word thereto, and cut asunder those things which Allah has commanded to be joined, and work mischief in the land;- on them is the Curse; for them is the terrible Home!

26. Allah enlarges, or grants by (strict) measure, the sustenance (which He gives) to whomso He pleases. (The worldly) rejoice in the life of this world: but the life of this world is but little comfort in the Hereafter.

27. The Unbelievers say: "Why is not a Sign sent down to him from his Lord?" Say: "Truly Allah leaves to stray, whom He will; But He guides

to Himself those who turn to
Him in penitence;

28. "Those who believe, and
whose hearts find satisfaction in
the remembrance of Allah: for
without doubt in the remembrance of Allah do hearts find
satisfaction.

29. "For those who believe
and work righteousness, is
(every) blessedness, and a
beautiful place of (final) return."

30. Thus We have sent you
amongst a People before whom
(long since) have (other)
Peoples (gone and) passed
away; in order that you might
rehearse unto them what We
send down to you by
inspiration; yet they reject
(Him), the Most Gracious! Say:
"He is my Lord! There is no god
but He! On Him is my trust, and
to Him do I turn!"

31. If there were a Qur'an with
which mountains were moved,
or the earth were cloven
asunder, or the dead were made
to speak, (this would be the
one!) but, truly, the Command is
with Allah in all things! Do not
the Believers know, that, had
Allah (so) willed, He could have
guided all mankind (to the
right)? But the Unbelievers,-
never will disaster cease to seize
them for their (ill) deeds, or to
settle close to their homes, until
the promise of Allah come to
pass, for, verily, Allah will not
fail in His promise.

32. Mocked were (many)
Messengers before you: but I
granted respite to the Unbelievers, and finally I punished
them: then how (terrible) was
My requital!

33. Is then He Who stands
over every soul (and knows) all
that it does, (like any others)?
And yet they ascribe partners to
Allah. Say:

إِلَيْهِ مَنْ أَنَابَ ۞

الَّذِيْنَ اٰمَنُوْا وَتَطْمَئِنُّ قُلُوْبُهُمْ

بِذِكْرِ اللّٰهِ ۗ اَلَا بِذِكْرِ اللّٰهِ

تَطْمَئِنُّ الْقُلُوْبُ ۞

اَلَّذِيْنَ اٰمَنُوْا وَعَمِلُوا الصّٰلِحٰتِ

طُوْبٰى لَهُمْ وَحُسْنُ مَاٰبٍ ۞

كَذٰلِكَ اَرْسَلْنٰكَ فِيْٓ اُمَّةٍ قَدْ

خَلَتْ مِنْ قَبْلِهَآ اُمَمٌ لِّتَتْلُوَا۟

عَلَيْهِمُ الَّذِيْٓ اَوْحَيْنَآ اِلَيْكَ وَهُمْ

يَكْفُرُوْنَ بِالرَّحْمٰنِ ۗ قُلْ هُوَ رَبِّيْ

لَآ اِلٰهَ اِلَّا هُوَ ۚ عَلَيْهِ تَوَكَّلْتُ

وَاِلَيْهِ مَتَابِ ۞

وَلَوْ اَنَّ قُرْاٰنًا سُيِّرَتْ بِهِ الْجِبَالُ

اَوْ قُطِّعَتْ بِهِ الْاَرْضُ اَوْ كُلِّمَ بِهِ

الْمَوْتٰى ۗ بَلْ لِّلّٰهِ الْاَمْرُ جَمِيْعًا ۗ

اَفَلَمْ يَايْـَٔسِ الَّذِيْنَ اٰمَنُوْٓا اَنْ لَّوْ

يَشَآءُ اللّٰهُ لَهَدَى النَّاسَ جَمِيْعًا ۗ

وَلَا يَزَالُ الَّذِيْنَ كَفَرُوْا تُصِيْبُهُمْ

بِمَا صَنَعُوْا قَارِعَةٌ اَوْ تَحُلُّ قَرِيْبًا

مِّنْ دَارِهِمْ حَتّٰى يَأْتِيَ وَعْدُ اللّٰهِ ۗ

اِنَّ اللّٰهَ لَا يُخْلِفُ الْمِيْعَادَ ۞

وَلَقَدِ اسْتُهْزِئَ بِرُسُلٍ مِّنْ قَبْلِكَ

فَاَمْلَيْتُ لِلَّذِيْنَ كَفَرُوْا ثُمَّ اَخَذْتُهُمْ ۖ

فَكَيْفَ كَانَ عِقَابِ ۞

اَفَمَنْ هُوَ قَآئِمٌ عَلٰى كُلِّ نَفْسٍ بِمَا

كَسَبَتْ ۚ وَجَعَلُوْا لِلّٰهِ شُرَكَآءَ ۗ قُلْ

"But name them! Is it that you will inform Him of something He does not know on earth, or is it (just) a show of words?" Nay! to those who believe not, their pretence seems pleasing, but they are kept back (thereby) from the Path. And those whom Allah leaves to stray, no one can guide.

34. For them is a Panalty in the life of this world, but harder, truly, is the Penalty of the Hereafter: and they do not have any defender against Allah.

35. The parable of the Garden which the righteous are pro- mised!- beneath it flow rivers: perpetual is the enjoyment thereof and the shade therein: such is the End of the Righteous; and the End of Unbelievers is the Fire.

36. Those to whom We have given the Book rejoice at what has been revealed unto you: but there are among the clans those who reject a part thereof. Say: "I am commanded to worship Allah, and not to join partners with Him. To Him I call, and to Him is my return."

37. Thus We have revealed it to be a judgment of authority in Arabic. Were you to follow their (vain) desires after the knowledge which has reached you, then you would find neither protector nor defender against Allah.

38. We sent Messengers before you, and appointed for them wives and children: and it was never the part of a Messenger to bring a Sign except as Allah permitted (or commanded). For each period is a Book (revealed).

39. Allah blots out or confirms what He pleases:

SÛRAH-14
IBRÂHÎM
(INTRODUCTION)

For the chronology and the general argument of this Sûrah in the series Sûras 10 to 15, see Introduction to S. 10.

The special subject-matter of this Sûrah is a continuation of the concluding portion of the last Sûrah, which explained how Allah's revelation gains ground in spite of selfish men's opposition. Here illustrations are given from the story of Moses and Abraham, and Abraham's Prayer for Makkah forms the core of the Sûrah.

with Him is the Mother of the Book.

40. Whether We shall show you (within your life-time) part of what We promised them or take to Ourselves your soul (before it is all accomplished),- your duty is to make (the Message) reach them: it is Our part to call them to account.

41. Don't they see that We gradually reduce the land (in their control) from its outlying borders? (Where) Allah commands, there is none to put back His command: and He is Swift in calling to account.

42. Those before them (also) devised plots; but in all things the master- planning is Allah's. He knows the doings of every soul: and soon will the Unbelievers know who gets home in the End.

43. The Unbelievers say: "No Messenger are you." Say: "Enough for a witness between me and you is Allah, and such as have knowledge of the Book."

14. Abraham
In the name of Allah. Most Gracious, Most Merciful.

1. *Alif - Lam - Raa.* A Book which We have revealed to you, in order that you might lead mankind out of the depths of darkness into light - by the leave of their Lord - to the Way of (Him) the Exalted in Power, worthy of all Praise!-

2. Of Allah, to Whom do belong all things in the heavens and on earth! But alas for the Unbelievers for a terrible Penalty (their Unfaith will bring them)!-

3. Those who love the life of this world more than the Hereafter, who hinder (men) from the Path of

Allah and seek therein something crooked: they are astray by a long distance.

4. We did not send a Messenger except (to teach) in the language of his (own) people, in order to make (things) clear to them. Now Allah leaves straying those whom He pleases and guides whom He pleases: and He is Exalted in Power, full of Wisdom.

5. We sent Moses with Our Signs (and the command). "Bring out your people from the depths of darkness into light, and teach them to remember the Days of Allah." Verily in this there are Signs for such as are firmly patient and constant,- grateful and appreciative.

6. Remember! Moses said to his people: "Call to mind the favour of Allah to you when He delivered you from the people of Pharaoh: they set you hard tasks and punishments, slaughtered your sons, and let your women-folk live: therein was a tremendous trial from your Lord."

7. And remember! your Lord caused to be declared (publicly): "If you are grateful, I will add more (favours) to you; But if you show ingratitude, truly My punishment is terrible indeed."

8. And Moses said: "If you show ingratitude, you and all on earth together, yet is Allah free of all wants, worthy of all praise.

9. Has not the story reached you, (O people!), of those who (went) before you? - of the people of Noah, and 'Ad, and Thamud? - and of those who (came) after them? None knows them but Allah. To them came Messengers with Clear (Signs);

اللهِ وَيَبْغُوْنَهَا عِوَجًا ۚ أُولٰٓئِكَ فِيْ

ضَلٰلٍ بَعِيْدٍ ۟

وَمَآ اَرْسَلْنَا مِنْ رَّسُوْلٍ اِلَّا بِلِسَانِ

قَوْمِهٖ لِيُبَيِّنَ لَهُمْ ۚ فَيُضِلُّ اللهُ مَنْ

يَّشَاءُ وَيَهْدِيْ مَنْ يَّشَاءُ ۚ وَهُوَ

الْعَزِيْزُ الْحَكِيْمُ ۟

وَلَقَدْ اَرْسَلْنَا مُوْسٰى بِاٰيٰتِنَآ اَنْ

اَخْرِجْ قَوْمَكَ مِنَ الظُّلُمٰتِ اِلَى النُّوْرِ ۙ۬

وَذَكِّرْهُمْ بِاَيّٰمِ اللهِ ۚ اِنَّ فِيْ ذٰلِكَ

لَاٰيٰتٍ لِّكُلِّ صَبَّارٍ شَكُوْرٍ ۟

وَاِذْ قَالَ مُوْسٰى لِقَوْمِهِ اذْكُرُوْا

نِعْمَةَ اللهِ عَلَيْكُمْ اِذْ اَنْجٰىكُمْ

مِّنْ اٰلِ فِرْعَوْنَ يَسُوْمُوْنَكُمْ سُوْۤءَ

الْعَذَابِ وَيُذَبِّحُوْنَ اَبْنَآءَكُمْ

وَيَسْتَحْيُوْنَ نِسَآءَكُمْ ۚ وَفِيْ ذٰلِكُمْ

بَلَآءٌ مِّنْ رَّبِّكُمْ عَظِيْمٌ ۟

وَاِذْ تَاَذَّنَ رَبُّكُمْ لَئِنْ شَكَرْتُمْ

لَاَزِيْدَنَّكُمْ وَلَئِنْ كَفَرْتُمْ اِنَّ عَذَابِيْ

لَشَدِيْدٌ ۟

وَقَالَ مُوْسٰٓى اِنْ تَكْفُرُوْۤا اَنْتُمْ

وَمَنْ فِى الْاَرْضِ جَمِيْعًا ۙ فَاِنَّ

اللهَ لَغَنِيٌّ حَمِيْدٌ ۟

اَلَمْ يَاْتِكُمْ نَبَؤُا الَّذِيْنَ مِنْ قَبْلِكُمْ

قَوْمِ نُوْحٍ وَّعَادٍ وَّثَمُوْدَ ۛ۬ وَالَّذِيْنَ

مِنْۢ بَعْدِهِمْ ۛ۬ لَا يَعْلَمُهُمْ اِلَّا

اللهُ ۚ جَآءَتْهُمْ رُسُلُهُمْ بِالْبَيِّنٰتِ ۙ

but they put their hands up to their mouths, and said: "We do deny (the mission) on which you have been sent, and we are really in suspicious (disquieting) doubt as to that to which you invite us."

10. Their Messengers said: "Is there a doubt about Allah, the Creator of the heavens and the earth? It is He Who invites you, in order that He may forgive you your sins and give you respite for a term appointed!" They said: "Ah! you are no more than human, like ourselves! You wish to turn us away from the (gods) our fathers used to worship: then bring us some clear authority."

11. Their Messengers said to them: "True, we are human like yourselves, but Allah grants His grace to such of His servants as He pleases. It is not for us to bring you an authority except as Allah permits. And on Allah let all men of faith put their trust.

12. "We do not have any reason why we should not put our trust on Allah. Indeed He has guided us to the Ways we (follow). We shall certainly bear with patience all the hurt you may cause us. For those who put their trust should put their trust on Allah."

13. And the Unbelievers said to their Messengers: "Be sure we shall drive you out of our land, or you shall return to our religion." But their Lord inspired (this Message) to them: "Verily We shall cause the wrong-doers to perish!

14. "And verily We shall cause you to abide in the land, and succeed them. This for such as fear the Time when they shall stand before My tribunal,- such as fear

the punishment denounced."

15. But they sought victory and decision (there and then), and frustration was the lot of every powerful obstinate transgressor.

16. In front of such a one is Hell, and he is given, for drink, boiling fetid water.

17. In gulps will he sip it, but never will he be near swallowing it down his throat: death will come to him from every quarter, yet he will not die: and in front of him will be a chastisement unrelenting.

18. The parable of those who reject their Lord is that their works are as ashes, on which the wind blows furiously on a tempestuous day: no power have they over anything that they have earned: that is the straying far, far (from the goal).

19. Don't you see that Allah created the heavens and the earth in Truth? If He so will, He can remove you and put (in your place) a new Creation?

20. Nor is that for Allah any great matter.

21. They will all be marshalled before Allah together: then will the weak say to those who were arrogant, "For us, we but followed you; can you then avail us at all against the Wrath of Allah?" They will reply, "If we had received the Guidance of Allah, we should have given it to you: to us it makes no difference (now) whether we rage, or bear (these torments) with patience: for ourselves there is no way of escape."

22. And Satan will say when the matter is decided:

وَعِيْدِ ۟

وَاسْتَفْتَحُوْا وَخَابَ كُلُّ جَبَّارٍ عَنِيْدٍ ۟

مِّنْ وَّرَآئِهِ جَهَنَّمُ وَيُسْقٰى مِنْ مَّآءٍ صَدِيْدٍ ۟

يَّتَجَرَّعُهٗ وَلَا يَكَادُ يُسِيْغُهٗ وَيَأْتِيْهِ الْمَوْتُ مِنْ كُلِّ مَكَانٍ وَّمَا هُوَ بِمَيِّتٍ ۖ وَمِنْ وَّرَآئِهٖ عَذَابٌ غَلِيْظٌ ۟

مَثَلُ الَّذِيْنَ كَفَرُوْا بِرَبِّهِمْ اَعْمَالُهُمْ كَرَمَادٍ اشْتَدَّتْ بِهِ الرِّيْحُ فِيْ يَوْمٍ عَاصِفٍ ۖ لَا يَقْدِرُوْنَ مِمَّا كَسَبُوْا عَلٰى شَيْءٍ ۖ ذٰلِكَ هُوَ الضَّلٰلُ الْبَعِيْدُ ۟

اَلَمْ تَرَ اَنَّ اللّٰهَ خَلَقَ السَّمٰوٰتِ وَ الْاَرْضَ بِالْحَقِّ ۚ اِنْ يَّشَأْ يُذْهِبْكُمْ وَيَأْتِ بِخَلْقٍ جَدِيْدٍ ۟

وَّمَا ذٰلِكَ عَلَى اللّٰهِ بِعَزِيْزٍ ۟

وَبَرَزُوْا لِلّٰهِ جَمِيْعًا فَقَالَ الضُّعَفٰٓؤُا لِلَّذِيْنَ اسْتَكْبَرُوْٓا اِنَّا كُنَّا لَكُمْ تَبَعًا فَهَلْ اَنْتُمْ مُّغْنُوْنَ عَنَّا مِنْ عَذَابِ اللّٰهِ مِنْ شَيْءٍ ۚ قَالُوْا لَوْ هَدٰىنَا اللّٰهُ لَهَدَيْنٰكُمْ ۖ سَوَآءٌ عَلَيْنَآ اَجَزِعْنَآ اَمْ صَبَرْنَا مَا لَنَا مِنْ مَّحِيْصٍ ۟

وَقَالَ الشَّيْطٰنُ لَمَّا قُضِيَ الْاَمْرُ

ع ١٥

"It was Allah Who gave you a promise of Truth: I too promised, but I failed in my promise to you. I had no authority over you except to call you, but you listened to me: then reproach not me, but reproach your own souls. I cannot listen to your cries, nor can you listen to mine. I reject your former act in associating me with Allah. For wrong-doers there must be a grievous Penalty."

إِنَّ اللهَ وَعَدَكُمْ وَعْدَ الْحَقِّ وَ
وَعَدْتُكُمْ فَأَخْلَفْتُكُمْ ۚ وَمَا كَانَ
لِيَ عَلَيْكُمْ مِّنْ سُلْطٰنٍ إِلَّا أَنْ
دَعَوْتُكُمْ فَاسْتَجَبْتُمْ لِيْ ۚ فَلَا تَلُوْمُوْنِيْ
وَلُوْمُوْا أَنْفُسَكُمْ ۚ مَا أَنَا بِمُصْرِخِكُمْ
وَمَا أَنْتُمْ بِمُصْرِخِيَّ ۚ إِنِّيْ كَفَرْتُ بِمَا
أَشْرَكْتُمُوْنِ مِنْ قَبْلُ ۚ إِنَّ الظّٰلِمِيْنَ
لَهُمْ عَذَابٌ أَلِيْمٌ ۝

23.   But those who believe and work righteousness will be admitted to Gardens beneath which rivers flow,- to dwell therein for ever with the leave of their Lord. Their greeting therein will be: "Peace!"

وَأُدْخِلَ الَّذِيْنَ اٰمَنُوْا وَعَمِلُوا
الصّٰلِحٰتِ جَنّٰتٍ تَجْرِيْ مِنْ تَحْتِهَا
الْأَنْهٰرُ خٰلِدِيْنَ فِيْهَا بِإِذْنِ رَبِّهِمْ ۚ
تَحِيَّتُهُمْ فِيْهَا سَلٰمٌ ۝

24.   Do you not see how Allah sets forth a parable? - a goodly Word like a goodly tree, whose root is firmly fixed, and its branches (reach) to the heavens.

أَلَمْ تَرَ كَيْفَ ضَرَبَ اللهُ مَثَلًا
كَلِمَةً طَيِّبَةً كَشَجَرَةٍ طَيِّبَةٍ
أَصْلُهَا ثَابِتٌ وَّفَرْعُهَا فِي السَّمَاءِ ۝

25.   It brings forth its fruit at all times, by the leave of its Lord. So Allah sets forth parables for men, in order that they may receive admonition.

تُؤْتِيْ أُكُلَهَا كُلَّ حِيْنٍ بِإِذْنِ رَبِّهَا ۚ
وَيَضْرِبُ اللهُ الْأَمْثَالَ لِلنَّاسِ
لَعَلَّهُمْ يَتَذَكَّرُوْنَ ۝

26.   And the parable of an evil Word is that of an evil tree: It is torn up by the root from the surface of the earth: it has no stability.

وَمَثَلُ كَلِمَةٍ خَبِيْثَةٍ كَشَجَرَةٍ
خَبِيْثَةٍ ۨ اجْتُثَّتْ مِنْ فَوْقِ
الْأَرْضِ مَا لَهَا مِنْ قَرَارٍ ۝

27.   Allah will establish in strength those who believe, with the Word that stands firm, in this world and in the Hereafter; but Allah will leave, to stray, those who do wrong: Allah does what He wills.

يُثَبِّتُ اللهُ الَّذِيْنَ اٰمَنُوْا بِالْقَوْلِ
الثَّابِتِ فِي الْحَيٰوةِ الدُّنْيَا وَفِي
الْاٰخِرَةِ ۚ وَيُضِلُّ اللهُ الظّٰلِمِيْنَ ۚ
وَيَفْعَلُ اللهُ مَا يَشَاءُ ۝

28.   Have you not turned your vision to those who have exchanged the favour of Allah

أَلَمْ تَرَ إِلَى الَّذِيْنَ بَدَّلُوْا نِعْمَتَ اللهِ

into blasphemy and caused their People to descend to the House of Perdition?-

29. Into Hell? They will burn therein,- an evil place to stay in!

30. And they set up (idols) as equal to Allah, to mislead (men) from the Path! Say: "Enjoy (your brief power)! But verily you are making straightway for Hell!"

31. Speak to My servants who have believed, that they may establish regular prayers, and spend (in charity) out of the Sustenance We have given them, secretly and openly, before the coming of a Day in which there will be neither mutual bargaining nor befriending.

32. It is Allah Who has created the heavens and the earth and sends down rain from the skies, and with it brings out fruits wherewith to feed you; it is He Who have made the ships subject to you, that they may sail through the sea by His Command; and He has made the rivers (also) subject to you.

33. And He has made subject to you the sun and the moon, both diligently pursuing their courses; and He has (also) made the Night and the Day subject to you.

34. And He gives you of all that you ask for. But if you count the favours of Allah, never will you be able to number them. Verily, man is given up to injustice and ingratitude.

35. Remember Abraham said: "O my Lord! make this city one of peace and security: and preserve me and my sons from worshipping idols.

36. "O my Lord! they have indeed led astray many among mankind; he then who follows my (ways) is of me, and he that disobeys me,- but You are indeed Oft-Forgiving, Most Merciful.

37. "O our Lord! I have made some of my offspring to dwell

in a valley without cultivation, by Your Sacred House; in order, O our Lord, that they may establish regular Prayer: so fill the hearts of some among men with love toward them, and feed them with fruits: so that they may give thanks.

38. "O our Lord! truly You do know what we conceal and what we reveal: for nothing whatever is hidden from Allah, whether on earth or in heaven.

39. "Praise be to Allah, Who has granted to me in old age Isma'il and Isaac: for truly my Lord is He, the Hearer of Prayer!

40. O my Lord! make me one who establishes regular Prayer, and also (raise such) among my offspring O our Lord! and You accept my Prayer.

41. "O our Lord! cover (us) with Your Forgiveness - me, my parents, and (all) Believers, on the Day that the Reckoning will be established!

42. Think not that Allah does not heed the deeds of those who do wrong. He but gives them respite against a Day when the eyes will fixedly stare in horror,-

43. They running forward with necks outstretched, their heads uplifted, their gaze returning not toward them, and their hearts a (gaping) void!

44. So warn mankind of the Day when the Wrath will reach them: then will the wrong-doers say: "Our Lord! respite us (if only) for a short Term: we will answer Your Call, and follow the Messengers!" "What! were you not wont to swear aforetime that you should suffer no

بِوَادٍ غَيْرِ ذِى زَرْعٍ عِنْدَ بَيْتِكَ الْمُحَرَّمِ ۙ رَبَّنَا لِيُقِيْمُوا الصَّلٰوةَ فَاجْعَلْ اَفْئِدَةً مِّنَ النَّاسِ تَهْوِىْۤ اِلَيْهِمْ وَارْزُقْهُمْ مِّنَ الثَّمَرٰتِ لَعَلَّهُمْ يَشْكُرُوْنَ ۞

رَبَّنَاۤ اِنَّكَ تَعْلَمُ مَا نُخْفِيْ وَمَا نُعْلِنُ ؕ وَمَا يَخْفٰى عَلَى اللّٰهِ مِنْ شَىْءٍ فِى الْاَرْضِ وَلَا فِى السَّمَآءِ ۞

اَلْحَمْدُ لِلّٰهِ الَّذِىْ وَهَبَ لِىْ عَلَى الْكِبَرِ اِسْمٰعِيْلَ وَاِسْحٰقَ ؕ اِنَّ رَبِّىْ لَسَمِيْعُ الدُّعَآءِ ۞

رَبِّ اجْعَلْنِىْ مُقِيْمَ الصَّلٰوةِ وَمِنْ ذُرِّيَّتِىْ ؗ رَبَّنَا وَتَقَبَّلْ دُعَآءِ ۞

رَبَّنَا اغْفِرْ لِىْ وَلِوَالِدَىَّ وَ لِلْمُؤْمِنِيْنَ يَوْمَ يَقُوْمُ الْحِسَابُ ۞

وَلَا تَحْسَبَنَّ اللّٰهَ غَافِلًا عَمَّا يَعْمَلُ الظّٰلِمُوْنَ ؕ اِنَّمَا يُؤَخِّرُهُمْ لِيَوْمٍ تَشْخَصُ فِيْهِ الْاَبْصَارُ ۞

مُهْطِعِيْنَ مُقْنِعِىْ رُءُوْسِهِمْ لَا يَرْتَدُّ اِلَيْهِمْ طَرْفُهُمْ ۚ وَ اَفْئِدَتُهُمْ هَوَآءٌ ۞

وَاَنْذِرِ النَّاسَ يَوْمَ يَأْتِيْهِمُ الْعَذَابُ فَيَقُوْلُ الَّذِيْنَ ظَلَمُوْا رَبَّنَاۤ اَخِّرْنَاۤ اِلٰۤى اَجَلٍ قَرِيْبٍ ۙ نُّجِبْ دَعْوَتَكَ وَنَتَّبِعِ الرُّسُلَ ؕ اَوَلَمْ تَكُوْنُوْۤا اَقْسَمْتُمْ مِّنْ قَبْلُ مَا لَكُمْ

SÛRA-15
AL-HIJR
(INTRODUCTION)

This is the last of the six Sûras of the A.L.M. series (10 to 15). Its place in chronology is the late Makkah period, probably somewhere near the middle of that period. See Introduction to S. 10 where will be found also an indication of the general subject-matter of the whole series in the gradation of Qur'ânic teaching.

The special subject-matter of this, Sûrah is the protection of Allah's Revelation and Allah's Truth. Evil arose from Pride and the warping of man's will, but Allah's Mercy is the antidote, as was proved in the case of Abraham and Lot, and might have been proved by the people of the Aike and the Hijr if they had only attended to Allah's "Signs". The Qur'ân, beginning with the Seven Oft-repeated Verses, is the precious vehicle for the praises of Allah.

decline?

قِّن زَوَالٍ ۞

45. "And you dwelt in the dwellings of men who wronged their own souls; you were clearly shown how We dealt with them; and We put forth (many) Parables in your behoof!"

وَسَكَنتُمْ فِى مَسْكِنِ الَّذِينَ ظَلَمُوْا
اَنفُسَهُمْ وَتَبَيَّنَ لَكُمْ كَيْفَ فَعَلْنَا
بِهِمْ وَضَرَبْنَا لَكُمُ الْاَمْثَالَ ۞

46. Mighty indeed were the plots which they made, but their plots were (well) within the sight of Allah, even though they were such as to shake the hills!

وَقَدْ مَكَرُوْا مَكْرَهُمْ وَعِنْدَ اللهِ
مَكْرُهُمْ ۗ وَاِنْ كَانَ مَكْرُهُمْ
لِتَزُوْلَ مِنْهُ الْجِبَالُ ۞

47. Never think that Allah would fail His Messengers in His promise: for Allah is Exalted in Power, - the Lord of Retribution.

فَلَا تَحْسَبَنَّ اللهَ مُخْلِفَ وَعْدِهٖ
رُسُلَهٗ ۗ اِنَّ اللهَ عَزِيزٌ ذُو انْتِقَامٍ ۞

48. One day the Earth will be changed to a different Earth, and so will be the Heavens, and (men) will be marshalled forth, before Allah, the One, the Irresistible;

يَوْمَ تُبَدَّلُ الْاَرْضُ غَيْرَ الْاَرْضِ
وَالسَّمٰوٰتُ وَبَرَزُوْا لِلّٰهِ الْوَاحِدِ
الْقَهَّارِ ۞

49. And you will see the Sinners that day bound together in fetters;-

وَتَرَى الْمُجْرِمِيْنَ يَوْمَئِذٍ
مُّقَرَّنِيْنَ فِى الْاَصْفَادِ ۚ

50. Their garments of liquid pitch, and their faces covered with Fire.

سَرَابِيْلُهُمْ مِّنْ قَطِرَانٍ وَّتَغْشٰى
وُجُوْهَهُمُ النَّارُ ۞

51. That Allah may requite each soul according to its deserts; and verily Allah is Swift in calling to account.

لِيَجْزِىَ اللهُ كُلَّ نَفْسٍ مَّا كَسَبَتْ ۚ
اِنَّ اللهَ سَرِيْعُ الْحِسَابِ ۞

52. Here is a Message for mankind: let them take warning therefrom, and let them know that He is (no other than) One God (Allah): let men of understanding take heed.

هٰذَا بَلٰغٌ لِّلنَّاسِ وَلِيُنْذَرُوْا بِهٖ
وَلِيَعْلَمُوْا اَنَّمَا هُوَ اِلٰهٌ وَّاحِدٌ
وَّلِيَذَّكَّرَ اُولُوا الْاَلْبَابِ ۞

14. The Rocky Tract
In the name of Allah. Most Gracious, Most Merciful.

۞ سُوْرَةُ الْحِجْرِ مَكِّيَّةٌ ۞ (١٥)
بِسْمِ اللهِ الرَّحْمٰنِ الرَّحِيْمِ

1. *Alif - Lam- Ra.* These are the Ayats of Revelation,- of a Qur'an that makes things clear.

الٓرٰ ۚ تِلْكَ اٰيٰتُ الْكِتٰبِ وَقُرْاٰنٍ
مُّبِيْنٍ ۞

2. Again and again will those who disbelieve, wish that they

رُبَمَا يَوَدُّ الَّذِينَ كَفَرُوْا لَوْ

had bowed (to Allah's Will) in Islam.

3. Leave them alone, to enjoy (the good things of this life) and to please themselves: let (false) hope amuse them: soon will knowledge (undeceive them).

4. We never destroyed a population that had not a term decreed and assigned beforehand.

5. Neither can a people anticipate its Term, nor delay it.

6. They say: "O you to whom the Message is being revealed! truly you are mad (or possessed)!

7. "Why don't you bring the angels to us if it be that you have the Truth?"

8. We do not send the angels down except for just cause: if they came (to the ungodly), behold! no respite would they have!

9. We have, without doubt, sent down the Message; and We will assuredly guard it (from corruption).

10. We sent Messengers before you amongst the religious sects of old:

11. But never came a Messenger to them but they mocked him.

12. Even so do We let it creep into the hearts of the sinners.

13. That they should not believe in the (Message); but the ways of the ancients have passed away.

14. Even if We opened out to them a gate from heaven, and they were to continue (all day) ascending therein,

15. They would only say: "Our eyes have been intoxicated: nay, we have been bewitched by sorcery."

كَانُوا مُسْلِمِينَ ۝

ذَرْهُمْ يَأْكُلُوا وَيَتَمَتَّعُوا وَيُلْهِهِمُ الْأَمَلُ فَسَوْفَ يَعْلَمُونَ ۝

وَمَا أَهْلَكْنَا مِن قَرْيَةٍ إِلَّا وَلَهَا كِتَابٌ مَّعْلُومٌ ۝

مَا تَسْبِقُ مِنْ أُمَّةٍ أَجَلَهَا وَمَا يَسْتَأْخِرُونَ ۝

وَقَالُوا يَا أَيُّهَا الَّذِي نُزِّلَ عَلَيْهِ الذِّكْرُ إِنَّكَ لَمَجْنُونٌ ۝

لَوْ مَا تَأْتِينَا بِالْمَلَائِكَةِ إِن كُنتَ مِنَ الصَّادِقِينَ ۝

مَا نُنَزِّلُ الْمَلَائِكَةَ إِلَّا بِالْحَقِّ وَمَا كَانُوا إِذًا مُّنظَرِينَ ۝

إِنَّا نَحْنُ نَزَّلْنَا الذِّكْرَ وَإِنَّا لَهُ لَحَافِظُونَ ۝

وَلَقَدْ أَرْسَلْنَا مِن قَبْلِكَ فِي شِيَعِ الْأَوَّلِينَ ۝

وَمَا يَأْتِيهِم مِّن رَّسُولٍ إِلَّا كَانُوا بِهِ يَسْتَهْزِئُونَ ۝

كَذَلِكَ نَسْلُكُهُ فِي قُلُوبِ الْمُجْرِمِينَ ۝

لَا يُؤْمِنُونَ بِهِ وَقَدْ خَلَتْ سُنَّةُ الْأَوَّلِينَ ۝

وَلَوْ فَتَحْنَا عَلَيْهِم بَابًا مِّنَ السَّمَاءِ فَظَلُّوا فِيهِ يَعْرُجُونَ ۝

لَقَالُوا إِنَّمَا سُكِّرَتْ أَبْصَارُنَا بَلْ نَحْنُ قَوْمٌ مَّسْحُورُونَ ۝

16. It is We Who have set out the Zodiacal Signs in the heavens, and made them fair-seeming to (all) beholders;

17. And (moreover) We have guarded them from every evil spirit accursed.

18. But any that gains a hearing by stealth, is pursued by a flaming fire, bright (to see).

وَلَقَدْ جَعَلْنَا فِي السَّمَآءِ بُرُوجًا وَزَيَّنَّاهَا لِلنَّاظِرِينَ ۝

وَحَفِظْنَاهَا مِنْ كُلِّ شَيْطَانٍ رَّجِيمٍ ۝

إِلَّا مَنِ اسْتَرَقَ السَّمْعَ فَأَتْبَعَهُ شِهَابٌ مُّبِينٌ ۝

19. And the earth We have spread out (like a carpet); set thereon mountains firm and immovable; and produced therein all kinds of things in due balance.

20. And We have provided therein means of subsistence,- for you and for those for whose sustenance you are not responsible.

21. And there is not a thing but its (sources and) treasures (inexhaustible) are with Us; but We only send down thereof in due and ascertainable measures.

وَالْأَرْضَ مَدَدْنَاهَا وَأَلْقَيْنَا فِيهَا رَوَاسِيَ وَأَنْبَتْنَا فِيهَا مِنْ كُلِّ شَيْءٍ مَّوْزُونٍ ۝

وَجَعَلْنَا لَكُمْ فِيهَا مَعَايِشَ وَمَنْ لَّسْتُمْ لَهُ بِرَازِقِينَ ۝

وَإِنْ مِّنْ شَيْءٍ إِلَّا عِنْدَنَا خَزَائِنُهُ وَمَا نُنَزِّلُهُ إِلَّا بِقَدَرٍ مَّعْلُومٍ ۝

22. And We send the fecundating winds, then cause the rain to descend from the sky, therewith providing you with water (in abundance), though you are not the guardians of its stores.

23. And verily, it is We Who give life, and Who give death: it is We Who remain inheritors (after all else passes away).

24. To Us are known those of you who hasten forward, and those who lag behind.

وَأَرْسَلْنَا الرِّيَاحَ لَوَاقِحَ فَأَنْزَلْنَا مِنَ السَّمَآءِ مَآءً فَأَسْقَيْنَاكُمُوهُ وَمَا أَنْتُمْ لَهُ بِخَازِنِينَ ۝

وَإِنَّا لَنَحْنُ نُحْيِي وَنُمِيتُ وَنَحْنُ الْوَارِثُونَ ۝

وَلَقَدْ عَلِمْنَا الْمُسْتَقْدِمِينَ مِنكُمْ وَلَقَدْ عَلِمْنَا الْمُسْتَأْخِرِينَ ۝

25. Assuredly it is your Lord Who will gather them together: for He is perfect in Wisdom and Knowledge.

26. We created man from sounding clay, from mud moulded into shape;

27. And the Jinn race, We had created before, from the fire of a scorching wind.

وَإِنَّ رَبَّكَ هُوَ يَحْشُرُهُمْ ۚ إِنَّهُ حَكِيمٌ عَلِيمٌ ۝

وَلَقَدْ خَلَقْنَا الْإِنْسَانَ مِنْ صَلْصَالٍ مِّنْ حَمَإٍ مَّسْنُونٍ ۝

وَالْجَآنَّ خَلَقْنَاهُ مِنْ قَبْلُ مِنْ نَّارِ السَّمُومِ ۝

28. Behold! your Lord said to the angels: "I am about to create man, from sounding clay from mud moulded into shape;

وَإِذْ قَالَ رَبُّكَ لِلْمَلَٰٓئِكَةِ إِنِّى خَالِقٌۢ بَشَرًا مِّن صَلْصَٰلٍ مِّنْ حَمَإٍ مَّسْنُونٍ ۝

29. "When I have fashioned him (in due proportion) and breathed into him of My spirit, you fall down in obeisance to him."

فَإِذَا سَوَّيْتُهُۥ وَنَفَخْتُ فِيهِ مِن رُّوحِى فَقَعُوا۟ لَهُۥ سَٰجِدِينَ ۝

30. So the angels prostrated themselves, all of them together:

فَسَجَدَ الْمَلَٰٓئِكَةُ كُلُّهُمْ أَجْمَعُونَ ۝

31. Not so Iblis: he refused to be among those who prostrated themselves.

إِلَّآ إِبْلِيسَ أَبَىٰٓ أَن يَكُونَ مَعَ السَّٰجِدِينَ ۝

32. (Allah) said: "O Iblis! what is your reason for not being among those who prostrated themselves?"

قَالَ يَٰٓإِبْلِيسُ مَا لَكَ أَلَّا تَكُونَ مَعَ السَّٰجِدِينَ ۝

33. (Iblis) said: "I am not one to prostrate myself to man, whom You created from sounding clay, from mud moulded into shape."

قَالَ لَمْ أَكُن لِّأَسْجُدَ لِبَشَرٍ خَلَقْتَهُۥ مِن صَلْصَٰلٍ مِّنْ حَمَإٍ مَّسْنُونٍ ۝

34. (Allah) said: "Then get out from here; for you are rejected, accursed.

قَالَ فَاخْرُجْ مِنْهَا فَإِنَّكَ رَجِيمٌ ۝

35. "And the curse shall be on you till the day of Judgment."

وَإِنَّ عَلَيْكَ اللَّعْنَةَ إِلَىٰ يَوْمِ الدِّينِ ۝

36. (Iblis) said: "O my Lord! give me then respite till the Day the (dead) are raised."

قَالَ رَبِّ فَأَنظِرْنِىٓ إِلَىٰ يَوْمِ يُبْعَثُونَ ۝

37. (Allah) said: "Respite is granted to you,

قَالَ فَإِنَّكَ مِنَ الْمُنظَرِينَ ۝

38. "Till the Day of the Time Appointed."

إِلَىٰ يَوْمِ الْوَقْتِ الْمَعْلُومِ ۝

39. (Iblis) said: "O my Lord! because You have put me in the wrong, I will make (wrong) fair-seeming to them on the earth, and I will put them all in the wrong,-

قَالَ رَبِّ بِمَآ أَغْوَيْتَنِى لَأُزَيِّنَنَّ لَهُمْ فِى الْأَرْضِ وَلَأُغْوِيَنَّهُمْ أَجْمَعِينَ ۝

40. "Except Your servants among them, sincere and purified (by Your Grace)."

إِلَّا عِبَادَكَ مِنْهُمُ الْمُخْلَصِينَ ۝

41. (Allah) said: "This (Way of My sincere servants) is indeed a Way that leads straight to Me.

قَالَ هَٰذَا صِرَٰطٌ عَلَىَّ مُسْتَقِيمٌ ۝

42. "For over My servants no authority shall you have, except such as put themselves

إِنَّ عِبَادِى لَيْسَ لَكَ عَلَيْهِمْ سُلْطَٰنٌ إِلَّا مَنِ اتَّبَعَكَ مِنَ

in the wrong and follow you."

43. And verily, Hell is the promised abode for them all!

44. To it are seven Gates: for each of those Gates is a (special) class (of sinners) assigned.

45. The righteous (will be) amid Gardens and fountains (of clear-flowing water):

46. (Their greeting will be): "You enter here in peace and security."

47. And We shall remove from their hearts any lurking sense of injury: (they will be) brothers (joyfully) facing each other on thrones (of dignity).

48. There no sense of fatigue shall touch them, nor shall they (ever) be asked to leave.

49. Tell My servants that I am indeed the Oft-Forgiving, Most Merciful;

50. And that My Penalty will be indeed the most grievous Penalty.

51. Tell them about the guests of Abraham.

52. When they entered his presence and said, "Peace!" he said, "We feel afraid of you!"

53. They said: "Fear not! We give you glad tidings of a son endowed with wisdom."

54. He said: "Do you give me glad tidings that old age has seized me? Of what, then, is your good news?"

55. They said: "We give you glad tidings in truth: be not then in despair!"

56. He said: "And who despairs of the mercy of his Lord, but such as go astray?"

57. Abraham said: "What then is the business on which you (have come), O you messengers (of Allah)?"

58. They said: "We have been sent to a people (deep) in sin,

59. "Excepting the adherents of Lut: we are certainly (charged) to save them (from harm),- all -

إِلَّا اٰلَ لُوْطٍ ۗ اِنَّا لَمُنَجُّوْهُمْ اَجْمَعِيْنَ ۝

60. "Except his wife, who, We have ascertained, will be among those who will lag behind."

إِلَّا امْرَاَتَهٗ قَدَّرْنَا ۙ اِنَّهَا لَمِنَ الْغٰبِرِيْنَ ۝

61. At length when the messengers arrived among the adherents of Lut,

فَلَمَّا جَآءَ اٰلَ لُوْطِۨ الْمُرْسَلُوْنَ ۝

62. He said: "You appear to be uncommon folk."

قَالَ اِنَّكُمْ قَوْمٌ مُّنْكَرُوْنَ ۝

63. They said: "Yes, we have come to you to accomplish that of which they doubt.

قَالُوْا بَلْ جِئْنٰكَ بِمَا كَانُوْا فِيْهِ يَمْتَرُوْنَ ۝

64. "We have brought to you that which is inevitably due, and assuredly we tell the truth.

وَاَتَيْنٰكَ بِالْحَقِّ وَاِنَّا لَصٰدِقُوْنَ ۝

65. "Then travel by night with your household, when a portion of the night (yet remains), and you bring up the rear: let no one amongst you look back, but pass on whither you are ordered."

فَاَسْرِ بِاَهْلِكَ بِقِطْعٍ مِّنَ الَّيْلِ وَاتَّبِعْ اَدْبَارَهُمْ وَلَا يَلْتَفِتْ مِنْكُمْ اَحَدٌ وَّامْضُوْا حَيْثُ تُؤْمَرُوْنَ ۝

66. And We made known this decree to him, that the last remnants of those (sinners) should be cut off by the morning.

وَقَضَيْنَآ اِلَيْهِ ذٰلِكَ الْاَمْرَ اَنَّ دَابِرَ هٰٓؤُلَاۤءِ مَقْطُوْعٌ مُّصْبِحِيْنَ ۝

67. The inhabitants of the city came in (mad) joy (at news of the young men).

وَجَآءَ اَهْلُ الْمَدِيْنَةِ يَسْتَبْشِرُوْنَ ۝

68. Lut said: "These are my guests: do not disgrace me:

قَالَ اِنَّ هٰٓؤُلَاۤءِ ضَيْفِيْ فَلَا تَفْضَحُوْنِ ۝

69. "But fear Allah, and shame me not."

وَاتَّقُوا اللّٰهَ وَلَا تُخْزُوْنِ ۝

70. They said: "Did we not forbid you (to speak) for all and sundry?"

قَالُوْٓا اَوَلَمْ نَنْهَكَ عَنِ الْعٰلَمِيْنَ ۝

71. He said: "There are my daughters (to marry), if you must act (so)."

قَالَ هٰٓؤُلَاۤءِ بَنٰتِيْٓ اِنْ كُنْتُمْ فٰعِلِيْنَ ۝

72. Verily, by your life (O Prophet), in their wild intoxication, they wander in distraction, to and fro.

لَعَمْرُكَ اِنَّهُمْ لَفِيْ سَكْرَتِهِمْ يَعْمَهُوْنَ ۝

73. But the (mighty) Blast overtook them before morning,

فَاَخَذَتْهُمُ الصَّيْحَةُ مُشْرِقِيْنَ ۝

74. And We turned (the cities) upside down, and rained down on them brimstones hard as baked clay.

فَجَعَلْنَا عَالِيَهَا سَافِلَهَا وَاَمْطَرْنَا عَلَيْهِمْ حِجَارَةً مِّنْ سِجِّيْلٍ ۝

75. Behold! in this are Signs for those who by tokens do understand.

اِنَّ فِيْ ذٰلِكَ لَاٰيٰتٍ لِّلْمُتَوَسِّمِيْنَ ۝

76. And the (cities were) right on the high-road.

77. Behold! in this is a Sign for those who believe!

78. And the Companions of the Wood were also wrong-doers;

79. So We exacted retribution from them. They were both on an open highway, plain to see.

80. The Companions of the Rocky Tract also rejected the Messengers:

81. We sent them Our Sings, but they persisted in turning away from them.

82. Out of the mountains did they hew (their) edifices, (feeling themselves) secure.

83. But the (mighty) Blast seized them of a morning,

84. And of no avail to them was all that they did (with such art and care)!

85. We did not create the heavens, the earth, and all between them, but for just ends. And the Hour is surely coming (when this will be manifest). So overlook (any human faults) with gracious forgiveness.

86. For verily it is your Lord Who is the Master-Creator, knowing all things.

87. And We have bestowed upon you the Seven Oft-repeated (verses) and the Grand Qur'an.

88. Do not strain your eyes (wistfully) at what We have bestowed on certain classes of them, nor grieve over them: but lower your wing (in gentleness) to the Believers.

89. And say: "I am indeed he that warns openly and without ambiguity,"-

90. (Of just such wrath) as We sent down on those who divided (Scripture into arbitrary parts),-

91. (So also on such) as have made Qur'an into shreds (as they please).

92. Therefore, by the Lord, We will, of a surety, call them to account.

SÛRAH-16
AN-NAHL
(INTRODUCTION)

Chronologically this Sûrah, like the six which preceded it, belongs to the late Makkah period, except perhaps verse 110 and some of the verses that follow, but the chronology has no significance. In subject-matter it sums up, from a new point of view, the arguments on the great questions of Allah's dealings with man, His Self-revelation to man and how the Messengers and the Message are writ large in every phase of Allah's Creation and the life of Man. The new point of view is that Nature points to Nature's Allah.

93. For all their deeds.

94. Therefore expound openly what you are commanded, and turn away from those who join false gods with Allah.

95. For sufficient are We to you against those who scoff,

96. Those who adopt, with Allah, another god: but soon will they come to know.

97. We do indeed know how your heart is distressed at what they say.

98. But celebrate the praises of your Lord, and be of those who prostrate themselves in adoration.

99. And serve your Lord until there come to you the Hour that is Certain.

---

16. The Bee
In the name of Allah. Most Gracious, Most Merciful.

1. (Inevitable) comes (to pass) the Command of Allah: do not then seek to hasten it: glory to Him, and far is He above having the partners they ascribe to Him!

2. He sends down His angels with inspiration of His Command, to such of His servants as He pleases, (saying): "Warn (Man) that there is no god but I: so do your duty to Me."

3. He has created the heavens and the earth for just ends: far is He above having the partners they ascribe to Him!

4. He has created man from a sperm-drop; and behold this same (man) becomes an open disputer!

5. And He has created cattle for you (men): from them you derive warmth, and numerous benefits, and of their (meat) you eat.

عَمَّا كَانُوْا يَعْمَلُوْنَ ۞

فَاصْدَعْ بِمَا تُؤْمَرُ وَاَعْرِضْ

عَنِ الْمُشْرِكِيْنَ ۞

اِنَّا كَفَيْنٰكَ الْمُسْتَهْزِءِيْنَ ۞

الَّذِيْنَ يَجْعَلُوْنَ مَعَ اللّٰهِ اِلٰهًا اٰخَرَ ۚ

فَسَوْفَ يَعْلَمُوْنَ ۞

وَلَقَدْ نَعْلَمُ اَنَّكَ يَضِيْقُ صَدْرُكَ

بِمَا يَقُوْلُوْنَ ۞

فَسَبِّحْ بِحَمْدِ رَبِّكَ وَكُنْ مِّنَ

السّٰجِدِيْنَ ۞

وَاعْبُدْ رَبَّكَ حَتّٰى يَأْتِيَكَ

الْيَقِيْنُ ۞

(١٦) سُوْرَةُ النَّحْلِ مَكِّيَّةٌ (٧٠)

بِسْمِ اللّٰهِ الرَّحْمٰنِ الرَّحِيْمِ

اَتٰى اَمْرُ اللّٰهِ فَلَا تَسْتَعْجِلُوْهُ ۚ

سُبْحٰنَهٗ وَتَعٰلٰى عَمَّا يُشْرِكُوْنَ ۞

يُنَزِّلُ الْمَلٰٓئِكَةَ بِالرُّوْحِ مِنْ اَمْرِهٖ

عَلٰى مَنْ يَّشَآءُ مِنْ عِبَادِهٖٓ اَنْ

اَنْذِرُوْٓا اَنَّهٗ لَاۤ اِلٰهَ اِلَّاۤ

اَنَا فَاتَّقُوْنِ ۞

خَلَقَ السَّمٰوٰتِ وَالْاَرْضَ بِالْحَقِّ ۚ

تَعٰلٰى عَمَّا يُشْرِكُوْنَ ۞

خَلَقَ الْاِنْسَانَ مِنْ نُّطْفَةٍ فَاِذَا

هُوَ خَصِيْمٌ مُّبِيْنٌ ۞

وَالْاَنْعَامَ خَلَقَهَا ۚ لَكُمْ فِيْهَا دِفْءٌ

وَّمَنَافِعُ وَمِنْهَا تَأْكُلُوْنَ ۞

6. And you have a sense of pride and beauty in them as you drive them home in the evening, and as you lead them forth to pasture in the morning.

7. And they carry your heavy loads to lands that you could not (otherwise) reach except with souls distressed: for your Lord is indeed Most Kind, Most Merciful.

8. And (He has created) horses, mules, and donkeys, for you to ride and use for show; and He has created (other) things of which you have no knowledge.

9. And to Allah leads straight the Way, but there are ways that turn aside: if Allah had willed, He could have guided all of you.

10. It is He Who sends down rain from the sky: from it you drink, and out of it (grows) the vegetation on which you feed your cattle.

11. With it He produces for you corn, olives, date-palms, grapes and every kind of fruit: verily in this is a Sign for those who give thought.

12. He has made subject to you the Night and the Day; the Sun and the Moon; and the Stars are in subjection by His Command: verily in this are Signs for men who are wise.

13. And the things on this earth which He has multiplied in varying colours (and qualities): verily in this is a Sign for men who celebrate the praises of Allah (in gratitude).

14. It is He Who has made the sea subject,

وَلَكُمْ فِيهَا جَمَالٌ حِيْنَ تُرِيْحُوْنَ وَحِيْنَ تَسْرَحُوْنَ ۞

وَتَحْمِلُ أَثْقَالَكُمْ إِلٰى بَلَدٍ لَّمْ تَكُوْنُوْا بٰلِغِيْهِ إِلَّا بِشِقِّ الْأَنْفُسِ ۚ اِنَّ رَبَّكُمْ لَرَءُوْفٌ رَّحِيْمٌ ۞

وَّالْخَيْلَ وَالْبِغَالَ وَالْحَمِيْرَ لِتَرْكَبُوْهَا وَزِيْنَةً ۚ وَ يَخْلُقُ مَا لَا تَعْلَمُوْنَ ۞

وَعَلَى اللّٰهِ قَصْدُ السَّبِيْلِ وَمِنْهَا جَآئِرٌ ۚ وَلَوْ شَآءَ لَهَدٰىكُمْ اَجْمَعِيْنَ ۞

هُوَ الَّذِيْ اَنْزَلَ مِنَ السَّمَآءِ مَآءً لَّكُمْ مِّنْهُ شَرَابٌ وَّمِنْهُ شَجَرٌ فِيْهِ تُسِيْمُوْنَ ۞

يُنْبِتُ لَكُمْ بِهِ الزَّرْعَ وَالزَّيْتُوْنَ وَالنَّخِيْلَ وَالْأَعْنَابَ وَمِنْ كُلِّ الثَّمَرٰتِ ۚ اِنَّ فِيْ ذٰلِكَ لَأٰيَةً لِّقَوْمٍ يَّتَفَكَّرُوْنَ ۞

وَسَخَّرَ لَكُمُ الَّيْلَ وَالنَّهَارَ وَ الشَّمْسَ وَالْقَمَرَ ۚ وَالنُّجُوْمُ مُسَخَّرٰتٌ بِاَمْرِهٖ ۚ اِنَّ فِيْ ذٰلِكَ لَأٰيٰتٍ لِّقَوْمٍ يَّعْقِلُوْنَ ۞

وَمَا ذَرَأَ لَكُمْ فِي الْأَرْضِ مُخْتَلِفًا اَلْوَانُهُ ۚ اِنَّ فِيْ ذٰلِكَ لَأٰيَةً لِّقَوْمٍ يَّذَّكَّرُوْنَ ۞

وَهُوَ الَّذِيْ سَخَّرَ الْبَحْرَ

that you may eat thereof flesh that is fresh and tender, and that you may extract therefrom ornaments to wear; and you see the ships therein that plough the waves, that you may seek (thus) of the bounty of Allah and that you may be grateful.

15. And He has set up on the earth mountains standing firm, lest it should shake with you; and rivers and roads; that you may guide yourselves;

16. And marks and sign-posts; and by the stars (men) guide themselves.

17. Is then He Who creates like one that creates not? Will you not receive admonition?

18. If you would count up the favours of Allah, never would you be able to number them: for Allah is Oft-Forgiving, Most Merciful.

19. And Allah knows what you conceal, and what you reveal.

20. Those whom they invoke besides Allah create nothing and are themselves created.

21. (They are things) dead, lifeless: nor do they know when they will be raised up.

22. Your God (Allah) is One God (Allah): as to those who do not believe in the Hereafter, their hearts refuse to know, and they are arrogant.

23. Undoubtedly Allah knows what they conceal, and what they reveal: verily He does not love the arrogant.

24. When it is said to them, "What is it that your Lord has

لِتَأْكُلُوْا مِنْهُ لَحْمًا طَرِيًّا

وَّتَسْتَخْرِجُوْا مِنْهُ حِلْيَةً

تَلْبَسُوْنَهَا ۖ وَتَرَى الْفُلْكَ مَوَاخِرَ

فِيْهِ وَلِتَبْتَغُوْا مِنْ فَضْلِهٖ

وَلَعَلَّكُمْ تَشْكُرُوْنَ ۝

وَاَلْقٰى فِى الْاَرْضِ رَوَاسِيَ اَنْ

تَمِيْدَ بِكُمْ وَاَنْهٰرًا وَّسُبُلًا لَّعَلَّكُمْ

تَهْتَدُوْنَ ۙ۝

وَعَلٰمٰتٍ ۚ وَبِالنَّجْمِ هُمْ يَهْتَدُوْنَ ۝

اَفَمَنْ يَّخْلُقُ كَمَنْ لَّا يَخْلُقُ ؕ

اَفَلَا تَذَكَّرُوْنَ ۝

وَاِنْ تَعُدُّوْا نِعْمَةَ اللّٰهِ لَا تُحْصُوْهَا ؕ

اِنَّ اللّٰهَ لَغَفُوْرٌ رَّحِيْمٌ ۝

وَاللّٰهُ يَعْلَمُ مَا تُسِرُّوْنَ وَمَا

تُعْلِنُوْنَ ۝

وَالَّذِيْنَ يَدْعُوْنَ مِنْ دُوْنِ اللّٰهِ

لَا يَخْلُقُوْنَ شَيْئًا وَّهُمْ يُخْلَقُوْنَ ۝

اَمْوَاتٌ غَيْرُ اَحْيَاءٍ ۚ وَمَا يَشْعُرُوْنَ ۙ

اَيَّانَ يُبْعَثُوْنَ ۝

اِلٰهُكُمْ اِلٰهٌ وَّاحِدٌ ۚ فَالَّذِيْنَ لَا

يُؤْمِنُوْنَ بِالْاٰخِرَةِ قُلُوْبُهُمْ

مُّنْكِرَةٌ وَّهُمْ مُّسْتَكْبِرُوْنَ ۝

لَا جَرَمَ اَنَّ اللّٰهَ يَعْلَمُ مَا يُسِرُّوْنَ

وَمَا يُعْلِنُوْنَ ؕ اِنَّهٗ لَا يُحِبُّ

الْمُسْتَكْبِرِيْنَ ۝

وَاِذَا قِيْلَ لَهُمْ مَّاذَآ اَنْزَلَ

revealed?" they say, "Tales of the ancients!"

25. Let them bear, on the Day of Judgment, their own burdens in full, and also (something) of the burdens of those without knowledge, whom they misled. Alas, how grievous the burdens they will bear!

26. Those before them also plotted (against Allah's Way): but Allah took their structures from their foundations, and the roof fell down on them from above; and the Wrath seized them from directions they did not perceive.

27. Then, on the Day of Judgment, He will cover them with shame, and say: "Where are My 'partners' concerning whom you used to dispute (with the godly)?" Those endued with knowledge will say: "This Day, indeed, are the Unbelievers covered with Shame and Misery,-

28. "(Namely) those whose lives the angels take in a state of wrong-doing to their own souls." Then would they offer submission (with the pretence), "We did no evil (knowingly)." (The angels will reply), "Nay, but verily Allah knows all that you did;

29. "So enter the gates of Hell, to dwell therein. Thus evil indeed is the abode of the arrogant."

30. To the righteous (when) it is said, "What is it that your Lord has revealed?" they say, "All that is good." To those who do good, there is good in this world, and the Home of the Hereafter is even better and excellent indeed is the Home of the righteous,-

31. Gardens of Eternity which they will enter: beneath them

رَبُّكُمْ ۙ قَالُوْۤا اَسَاطِيْرُ الْاَوَّلِيْنَ ۟

لِيَحْمِلُوْۤا اَوْزَارَهُمْ كَامِلَةً يَّوْمَ الْقِيٰمَةِ ۙ وَمِنْ اَوْزَارِ الَّذِيْنَ يُضِلُّوْنَهُمْ بِغَيْرِ عِلْمٍ ؕ اَلَا سَآءَ مَا يَزِرُوْنَ ۟

قَدْ مَكَرَ الَّذِيْنَ مِنْ قَبْلِهِمْ فَاَتَى اللّٰهُ بُنْيَانَهُمْ مِّنَ الْقَوَاعِدِ فَخَرَّ عَلَيْهِمُ السَّقْفُ مِنْ فَوْقِهِمْ وَاَتٰىهُمُ الْعَذَابُ مِنْ حَيْثُ لَا يَشْعُرُوْنَ ۟

ثُمَّ يَوْمَ الْقِيٰمَةِ يُخْزِيْهِمْ وَيَقُوْلُ اَيْنَ شُرَكَآءِيَ الَّذِيْنَ كُنْتُمْ تُشَآقُّوْنَ فِيْهِمْ ؕ قَالَ الَّذِيْنَ اُوْتُوا الْعِلْمَ اِنَّ الْخِزْيَ الْيَوْمَ وَالسُّوْٓءَ عَلَى الْكٰفِرِيْنَ ۟

الَّذِيْنَ تَتَوَفّٰىهُمُ الْمَلٰٓئِكَةُ ظَالِمِيْۤ اَنْفُسِهِمْ ۪ فَاَلْقَوُا السَّلَمَ مَا كُنَّا نَعْمَلُ مِنْ سُوْٓءٍ ؕ بَلٰٓى اِنَّ اللّٰهَ عَلِيْمٌ ۢ بِمَا كُنْتُمْ تَعْمَلُوْنَ ۟

فَادْخُلُوْۤا اَبْوَابَ جَهَنَّمَ خٰلِدِيْنَ فِيْهَا ؕ فَلَبِئْسَ مَثْوَى الْمُتَكَبِّرِيْنَ ۟

وَقِيْلَ لِلَّذِيْنَ اتَّقَوْا مَاذَاۤ اَنْزَلَ رَبُّكُمْ ؕ قَالُوْا خَيْرًا ؕ لِلَّذِيْنَ اَحْسَنُوْا فِيْ هٰذِهِ الدُّنْيَا حَسَنَةٌ ؕ وَلَدَارُ الْاٰخِرَةِ خَيْرٌ ؕ وَلَنِعْمَ دَارُ الْمُتَّقِيْنَ ۟

جَنّٰتُ عَدْنٍ يَّدْخُلُوْنَهَا تَجْرِيْ

flow (pleasant) rivers: they will have therein all that they wish: thus Allah rewards the righteous,-

مِنۡ تَحۡتِهَا الۡأَنۡهَٰرُ لَهُمۡ فِيهَا مَا يَشَآءُوۡنَ ۚ كَذَٰلِكَ يَجۡزِى اللّٰهُ الۡمُتَّقِيۡنَ ۟

32. (Namely) those whose lives the angels take in a state of purity, saying (to them), "Peace be on you; you enter the Garden, because of (the good) which you did (in the world)."

الَّذِيۡنَ تَتَوَفّٰهُمُ الۡمَلٰٓئِكَةُ طَيِّبِيۡنَ ۙ يَقُوۡلُوۡنَ سَلٰمٌ عَلَيۡكُمُ ۙ ادۡخُلُوا الۡجَنَّةَ بِمَا كُنۡتُمۡ تَعۡمَلُوۡنَ ۟

33. Do the (ungodly) wait until the angels come to them, or there comes the Command of your Lord (for their doom)? So did those who went before them. But Allah did not wrong them: nay, they wronged their own souls.

هَلۡ يَنۡظُرُوۡنَ اِلَّآ اَنۡ تَأۡتِيَهُمُ الۡمَلٰٓئِكَةُ اَوۡ يَأۡتِىَ اَمۡرُ رَبِّكَ ۚ كَذَٰلِكَ فَعَلَ الَّذِيۡنَ مِنۡ قَبۡلِهِمۡ ۚ وَمَا ظَلَمَهُمُ اللّٰهُ وَلٰكِنۡ كَانُوۡٓا اَنۡفُسَهُمۡ يَظۡلِمُوۡنَ ۟

34. But the evil results of their deeds overtook them, and that very (Wrath) at which they had scoffed hemmed them in.

فَاَصَابَهُمۡ سَيِّاٰتُ مَا عَمِلُوۡا وَحَاقَ بِهِمۡ مَّا كَانُوۡا بِهٖ يَسۡتَهۡزِءُوۡنَ ۟

35. The worshippers of false gods say: "If Allah had so willed, we should not have worshipped anything but Him - neither we nor our fathers,- nor should we have prescribed prohibitions other than His." So did those who went before them. But what is the mission of Messengers but to preach the Clear Message?

وَقَالَ الَّذِيۡنَ اَشۡرَكُوۡا لَوۡ شَآءَ اللّٰهُ مَا عَبَدۡنَا مِنۡ دُوۡنِهٖ مِنۡ شَىۡءٍ نَّحۡنُ وَلَآ اٰبَآؤُنَا وَلَا حَرَّمۡنَا مِنۡ دُوۡنِهٖ مِنۡ شَىۡءٍ ۚ كَذَٰلِكَ فَعَلَ الَّذِيۡنَ مِنۡ قَبۡلِهِمۡ ۚ فَهَلۡ عَلَى الرُّسُلِ اِلَّا الۡبَلٰغُ الۡمُبِيۡنُ ۟

36. For We assuredly sent amongst every People a Messenger, (with the Command), "Serve Allah, and eschew Evil": of the People were some whom Allah guided, and some on whom error became inevitably (established). So travel through the earth, and see what was the end of those who denied (the Truth).

وَلَقَدۡ بَعَثۡنَا فِىۡ كُلِّ اُمَّةٍ رَّسُوۡلًا اَنِ اعۡبُدُوا اللّٰهَ وَاجۡتَنِبُوا الطَّاغُوۡتَ ۚ فَمِنۡهُمۡ مَّنۡ هَدَى اللّٰهُ وَمِنۡهُمۡ مَّنۡ حَقَّتۡ عَلَيۡهِ الضَّلٰلَةُ ۚ فَسِيۡرُوۡا فِى الۡأَرۡضِ فَانۡظُرُوۡا كَيۡفَ كَانَ عَاقِبَةُ الۡمُكَذِّبِيۡنَ ۟

37. If you are anxious for their guidance, yet Allah

اِنۡ تَحۡرِصۡ عَلٰى هُدٰىهُمۡ فَاِنَّ اللّٰهَ

does not guide (any) such as He leaves to stray, and there is none to help them.

38. They swear their strongest oaths by Allah, that Allah will not raise up those who die: nay, but it is a promise (binding) on Him in truth: but most among mankind do not realize it.

39. (They must be raised up), in order that He may manifest to them the truth of that wherein they differ, and that the rejecters of Truth may realize that they had indeed (surrendered to) Falsehood.

40. For to anything which We have willed, We but say the Word, "Be", and it is.

41. To those who leave their homes in the cause of Allah, after suffering oppression,- We will assuredly give a goodly home in this world; but truly the reward of the Hereafter will be greater. If they only realized (this)!

42. (They are) those who persevere in patience, and put their trust on their Lord.

43. And before you also the Messengers We sent were but men, to whom We granted inspiration: if you do not realize this, ask of those who possess the Message.

44. (We sent them) with Clear Signs and Books of dark prophesies; and We have sent down to you (also) the Message; that you may explain clearly to men what is sent for them, and that they may give thought.

45. Do then those who devise evil (plots) feel secure that Allah will not cause the earth to swallow them up, or that the Wrath will not seize them from directions they little perceive?-

لَا يَهْدِىْ مَنْ يُّضِلُّ وَمَا لَهُمْ مِّنْ نّٰصِرِيْنَ ۞

وَاَقْسَمُوْا بِاللّٰهِ جَهْدَ اَيْمَانِهِمْ لَا يَبْعَثُ اللّٰهُ مَنْ يَّمُوْتُ ۗ بَلٰى وَعْدًا عَلَيْهِ حَقًّا وَّلٰكِنَّ اَكْثَرَ النَّاسِ لَا يَعْلَمُوْنَ ۞

لِيُبَيِّنَ لَهُمُ الَّذِىْ يَخْتَلِفُوْنَ فِيْهِ وَلِيَعْلَمَ الَّذِيْنَ كَفَرُوْٓا اَنَّهُمْ كَانُوْا كٰذِبِيْنَ ۞

اِنَّمَا قَوْلُنَا لِشَىْءٍ اِذَآ اَرَدْنٰهُ اَنْ نَّقُوْلَ لَهٗ كُنْ فَيَكُوْنُ ۞

وَالَّذِيْنَ هَاجَرُوْا فِى اللّٰهِ مِنْۢ بَعْدِ مَا ظُلِمُوْا لَنُبَوِّئَنَّهُمْ فِى الدُّنْيَا حَسَنَةً ۗ وَلَاَجْرُ الْاٰخِرَةِ اَكْبَرُ ۘ لَوْ كَانُوْا يَعْلَمُوْنَ ۞

الَّذِيْنَ صَبَرُوْا وَعَلٰى رَبِّهِمْ يَتَوَكَّلُوْنَ ۞

وَمَآ اَرْسَلْنَا مِنْ قَبْلِكَ اِلَّا رِجَالًا نُّوْحِىْٓ اِلَيْهِمْ فَسْـَٔلُوْٓا اَهْلَ الذِّكْرِ اِنْ كُنْتُمْ لَا تَعْلَمُوْنَ ۞

بِالْبَيِّنٰتِ وَالزُّبُرِ ۗ وَاَنْزَلْنَآ اِلَيْكَ الذِّكْرَ لِتُبَيِّنَ لِلنَّاسِ مَا نُزِّلَ اِلَيْهِمْ وَلَعَلَّهُمْ يَتَفَكَّرُوْنَ ۞

اَفَاَمِنَ الَّذِيْنَ مَكَرُوا السَّيِّاٰتِ اَنْ يَّخْسِفَ اللّٰهُ بِهِمُ الْاَرْضَ اَوْ يَأْتِيَهُمُ الْعَذَابُ مِنْ حَيْثُ لَا يَشْعُرُوْنَ ۞

46. Or that He may not call them to account in the midst of their goings to and fro, without a chance of their frustrating Him?

47. Or that He may not call them to account by a process of slow wastage - for your Lord is indeed full of kindness and mercy.

48. Do they not look at Allah's creation, (even) among (inanimate) things,- how their (very) shadows turn round, from the right and the left, prostrating themselves to Allah, and that in the humblest manner?

49. And to Allah does obeisance all that is in the heavens and on earth, whether moving (living) creatures or the angels: for none are arrogant (before their Lord).

50. They all revere their Lord, high above them, and they do all that they are commanded.

51. Allah has said: "Do not take (for worship) two gods: for He is just One God (Allah): then fear Me (and Me alone)."

52. To Him belongs whatever is in the heavens and on earth, and to Him is duty due always: then will you fear other than Allah?

53. And you have no good thing but is from Allah: and moreover, when you are touched by distress, to Him you cry with groans;

54. Yet, when He removes the distress from you, behold! some of you turn to other gods to join with their Lord-

55. (As if) to show their ingratitude for the favours We have bestowed on them! then enjoy (your brief day): but soon will you know (your folly)!

56. And they (even) assign, to things they do not know, a portion out of that which We have bestowed for your sustenance! By Allah, you shall certainly be called to account for your false inventions.

57.   And they assign daughters for Allah! - Glory be to Him! - and for themselves (sons,- the issue) they desire!

58.   When news is brought to one of them, of (the birth of) a female (child), his face darkens, and he is filled with inward grief!

59.   With shame he hides himself from his people, because of the bad news he has had! Shall he retain it on (sufferance and) contempt, or bury it in the dust? Ah! what an evil (choice) they decide on?

وَيَجْعَلُونَ لِلّٰهِ الْبَنٰتِ سُبْحٰنَهُۥ ۙ وَلَهُم مَّا يَشْتَهُونَ ۝

وَإِذَا بُشِّرَ أَحَدُهُم بِالْأُنثَىٰ ظَلَّ وَجْهُهُۥ مُسْوَدًّا وَّهُوَ كَظِيمٌ ۝

يَتَوَارَىٰ مِنَ الْقَوْمِ مِن سُوٓءِ مَا بُشِّرَ بِهِۦ ۚ أَيُمْسِكُهُۥ عَلَىٰ هُونٍ أَمْ يَدُسُّهُۥ فِى التُّرَابِ ۗ أَلَا سَآءَ مَا يَحْكُمُونَ ۝

60.   To those who believe not in the Hereafter, applies the similitude of evil: to Allah applies the highest similitude: for He is the Exalted in Power, full of Wisdom.

لِلَّذِينَ لَا يُؤْمِنُونَ بِالْأَخِرَةِ مَثَلُ السَّوْءِ ۖ وَلِلّٰهِ الْمَثَلُ الْأَعْلَىٰ ۚ وَهُوَ الْعَزِيزُ الْحَكِيمُ ۝

61.   If Allah were to punish men for their wrong-doing, He would not leave, on the (earth), a single living creature: but He gives them respite for a stated Term: when their Term expires, they would not be able to delay (the punishment) for a single hour, just as they would not be able to advance it (for a single hour).

وَلَوْ يُؤَاخِذُ اللّٰهُ النَّاسَ بِظُلْمِهِم مَّا تَرَكَ عَلَيْهَا مِن دَآبَّةٍ وَّلٰكِن يُؤَخِّرُهُمْ إِلَىٰٓ أَجَلٍ مُّسَمًّى ۖ فَإِذَا جَآءَ أَجَلُهُمْ لَا يَسْتَأْخِرُونَ سَاعَةً وَّلَا يَسْتَقْدِمُونَ ۝

62.   They attribute to Allah what they hate (for themselves), and their tongues assert the falsehood that all good things are for themselves: without doubt for them is the Fire, and they will be the first to be hastened on into it!

وَيَجْعَلُونَ لِلّٰهِ مَا يَكْرَهُونَ وَتَصِفُ أَلْسِنَتُهُمُ الْكَذِبَ أَنَّ لَهُمُ الْحُسْنَىٰ ۖ لَا جَرَمَ أَنَّ لَهُمُ النَّارَ وَأَنَّهُم مُّفْرَطُونَ ۝

63.   By Allah, We (also) sent (Our Messengers) to Peoples before you but Satan made, (to the wicked), their own acts seem alluring: he is also their patron today, but they shall have a most grievous Penalty.

تَاللّٰهِ لَقَدْ أَرْسَلْنَآ إِلَىٰٓ أُمَمٍ مِّن قَبْلِكَ فَزَيَّنَ لَهُمُ الشَّيْطٰنُ أَعْمَالَهُمْ فَهُوَ وَلِيُّهُمُ الْيَوْمَ وَلَهُمْ عَذَابٌ أَلِيمٌ ۝

64.   And We sent down the Book to you for the express purpose, that you should make clear to them those things in which they differ,

وَمَآ أَنزَلْنَا عَلَيْكَ الْكِتٰبَ إِلَّا لِتُبَيِّنَ لَهُمُ الَّذِى اخْتَلَفُوا فِيهِ

and that it should be a guide and a mercy to those who believe.

65. And Allah sends down rain from the skies, and gives therewith life to the earth after its death: verily in this is a Sign for those who listen.

66. And verily in cattle (too) will you find an instructive Sign. From what is within their bodies, between excretions and blood, We produce, for your drink, milk, pure and agreeable to those who drink it.

67. And from the fruit of the date-palm and the vine, you get out wholesome drink and food; behold, in this also is a Sign for those who are wise.

68. And your Lord taught the Bee to build its cells in hills, on trees, and in (men's) habitations;

69. Then to eat of all the produce (of the earth), and find with skill the spacious paths of its Lord: there issues from within their bodies a drink of varying colours, wherein is healing for men: verily in this is a Sign for those who give thought.

70. It is Allah Who creates you and takes your souls at death; and of you there are some who are sent back to a feeble age, so that they know nothing after having known (much): for Allah is All-Knowing, All-Powerful.

71. Allah has bestowed His gifts of sustenance more freely on some of you than on others:

وَهُدًى وَرَحْمَةً لِّقَوْمٍ يُّؤْمِنُوْنَ ۝

وَاللّٰهُ اَنْزَلَ مِنَ السَّمَاءِ مَاءً فَاَحْيَا بِهِ الْاَرْضَ بَعْدَ مَوْتِهَا ۚ اِنَّ فِيْ ذٰلِكَ لَاٰيَةً لِّقَوْمٍ يَّسْمَعُوْنَ ۝

وَاِنَّ لَكُمْ فِي الْاَنْعَامِ لَعِبْرَةً ۚ نُسْقِيْكُمْ مِّمَّا فِيْ بُطُوْنِهٖ مِنْۢ بَيْنِ فَرْثٍ وَّدَمٍ لَّبَنًا خَالِصًا سَآئِغًا لِّلشّٰرِبِيْنَ ۝

وَمِنْ ثَمَرٰتِ النَّخِيْلِ وَالْاَعْنَابِ تَتَّخِذُوْنَ مِنْهُ سَكَرًا وَّرِزْقًا حَسَنًا ۗ اِنَّ فِيْ ذٰلِكَ لَاٰيَةً لِّقَوْمٍ يَّعْقِلُوْنَ ۝

وَاَوْحٰى رَبُّكَ اِلَى النَّحْلِ اَنِ اتَّخِذِيْ مِنَ الْجِبَالِ بُيُوْتًا وَّمِنَ الشَّجَرِ وَمِمَّا يَعْرِشُوْنَ ۝

ثُمَّ كُلِيْ مِنْ كُلِّ الثَّمَرٰتِ فَاسْلُكِيْ سُبُلَ رَبِّكِ ذُلُلًا ۗ يَخْرُجُ مِنْۢ بُطُوْنِهَا شَرَابٌ مُّخْتَلِفٌ اَلْوَانُهٗ فِيْهِ شِفَآءٌ لِّلنَّاسِ ۗ اِنَّ فِيْ ذٰلِكَ لَاٰيَةً لِّقَوْمٍ يَّتَفَكَّرُوْنَ ۝

وَاللّٰهُ خَلَقَكُمْ ثُمَّ يَتَوَفّٰىكُمْ ۙ وَمِنْكُمْ مَّنْ يُّرَدُّ اِلٰۤى اَرْذَلِ الْعُمُرِ لِكَيْ لَا يَعْلَمَ بَعْدَ عِلْمٍ شَيْئًا ۚ اِنَّ اللّٰهَ عَلِيْمٌ قَدِيْرٌ ۝

وَاللّٰهُ فَضَّلَ بَعْضَكُمْ عَلٰى بَعْضٍ

those more favoured are not
going to throw back their gifts to
those whom their right hands
possess, so as to be equal in that
respect. Will they then deny the
favours of Allah?

72.   And Allah has made for
you mates (and companions) of
your own nature, and made for
you, out of them, sons and
daughters and grandchildren,
and provided for you sustenance
of the best: will they then
believe in vain things, and be
ungrateful for Allah's favours?-

73.   And worship others than
Allah,- such as have no power of
providing them, for sustenance,
with anything in heavens or
earth, and cannot possibly have
such power?

74.   Do not invent similitudes
for Allah: for Allah knows, and
you do not know.

75.   Allah sets forth the
Parable (of two men: one) a
slave under the dominion of
another; he has no power of any
sort; and (the other) a man on
whom We have bestowed
goodly favours from Ourselves,
and he spends thereof (freely),
privately and publicly: are the
two equal? (By no means;)
praise be to Allah. But most of
them do not understand.

76.   Allah sets forth (another)
Parable of two men: one of them
dumb, with no power of any
sort; a wearisome burden is he
to his master; whichever way he
directs him, he brings no good:
is such a man equal with one
who commands Justice, and is
on a Straight Way?

77.   To Allah belongs the
Mystery of the heavens and the
earth.

And the Decision of the Hour (of Judgment) is as the twinkling of an eye, or even quicker: for Allah has power over all things.

وَمَآ أَمْرُ السَّاعَةِ إِلَّا كَلَمْحِ الْبَصَرِ أَوْ هُوَ أَقْرَبُ ۚ إِنَّ اللّٰهَ عَلٰى كُلِّ شَيْءٍ قَدِيْرٌ ۝

78. It is He Who brought you forth from the wombs of your mothers when you knew nothing; and He gave you hearing and sight and intelligence and affections: that you may give thanks (to Allah).

وَاللّٰهُ أَخْرَجَكُمْ مِّنْ بُطُوْنِ أُمَّهٰتِكُمْ لَا تَعْلَمُوْنَ شَيْئًا ۙ وَّجَعَلَ لَكُمُ السَّمْعَ وَالْأَبْصَارَ وَالْأَفْئِدَةَ ۙ لَعَلَّكُمْ تَشْكُرُوْنَ ۝

79. Do they not look at the birds, held poised in the midst of (the air and) the sky? Nothing holds them up but (the power of) Allah. Verily in this are Signs for those who believe.

أَلَمْ يَرَوْا إِلَى الطَّيْرِ مُسَخَّرٰتٍ فِيْ جَوِّ السَّمَآءِ ۚ مَا يُمْسِكُهُنَّ إِلَّا اللّٰهُ ۗ إِنَّ فِيْ ذٰلِكَ لَأٰيٰتٍ لِّقَوْمٍ يُّؤْمِنُوْنَ ۝

80. It is Allah Who made your habitations homes of rest and quiet for you; and made for you, out of the skins of animals, (tents for) dwellings, which you find so light (and handy) when you travel and when you stop (in your travels); and out of their wool, and their soft fibres (between wool and hair),and their hair, rich stuff and articles of convenience (to serve you) for a time.

وَاللّٰهُ جَعَلَ لَكُمْ مِّنْ بُيُوْتِكُمْ سَكَنًا وَّجَعَلَ لَكُمْ مِّنْ جُلُوْدِ الْأَنْعَامِ بُيُوْتًا تَسْتَخِفُّوْنَهَا يَوْمَ ظَعْنِكُمْ وَيَوْمَ إِقَامَتِكُمْ ۙ وَمِنْ أَصْوَافِهَا وَأَوْبَارِهَا وَأَشْعَارِهَآ أَثَاثًا وَّمَتَاعًا إِلٰى حِيْنٍ ۝

81. It is Allah Who made. Out of the things He created, some things to give you shade; of the hills He made some for your shelter; He made you garments to protect you from heat, and coats of mail to protect you from your (mutual) violence. Thus He completes His favours on you, that you may bow to His Will (in Islam).

وَاللّٰهُ جَعَلَ لَكُمْ مِّمَّا خَلَقَ ظِلٰلًا وَّجَعَلَ لَكُمْ مِّنَ الْجِبَالِ أَكْنَانًا وَّجَعَلَ لَكُمْ سَرَابِيْلَ تَقِيْكُمُ الْحَرَّ وَسَرَابِيْلَ تَقِيْكُمْ بَأْسَكُمْ ۚ كَذٰلِكَ يُتِمُّ نِعْمَتَهٗ عَلَيْكُمْ لَعَلَّكُمْ تُسْلِمُوْنَ ۝

82. But if they turn away, your duty is only to preach the Clear Message.

فَإِنْ تَوَلَّوْا فَإِنَّمَا عَلَيْكَ الْبَلٰغُ الْمُبِيْنُ ۝

83. They recognise the favours of Allah; then they deny them;

يَعْرِفُوْنَ نِعْمَتَ اللّٰهِ ثُمَّ يُنْكِرُوْنَهَا

and most of them are (creatures) ungrateful.

84. One Day We shall raise from all Peoples a Witness: then will no excuse be accepted from Unbelievers, nor will they receive any favours.

85. When the wrong-doers (actually) see the Penalty, then it will in no way be mitigated, nor will they then receive respite.

86. When those who gave partners to Allah will see their "partners", they will say: "Our Lord! these are our 'partners,' those whom we used to invoke besides You." But they will throw back their word at them (and say): "Indeed you are liars!"

87. That day they shall (openly) show (their) submission to Allah; and all their inventions shall leave them in the lurch.

88. Those who reject Allah and hinder (men) from the Path of Allah - for them We will add Penalty to Penalty; for that they used to spread mischief.

89. One day We shall raise from all Peoples a witness against them, from amongst themselves: and We shall bring you as a witness against these (your people): and We have sent down to you the Book explaining all things, a Guide, a Mercy, and Glad Tidings to Muslims.

90. Allah commands justice, the doing of good, and liberality to kith and kin, and He forbids all shameful deeds, and injustice and rebellion: He instructs you, that you may receive admonition.

91. Fulfil the Covenant of Allah when you have entered into

it, and do not break your oaths
after you have confirmed them;
indeed you have made Allah
your surety; for Allah knows all
that you do.

92. And be not like a woman
who breaks into untwisted
strands the yarn which she has
spun, after it has become strong.
Nor take your oaths to practise
deception between yourselves,
lest one party should be more
numerous than another: for
Allah will test you by this; and
on the Day of Judgment He will
certainly make clear to you (the
truth of) that wherein you
disagree.

93. If Allah so willed, He
could make you all one People:
but He leaves straying whom He
pleases, and He guides whom
He pleases: but you shall certainly be called to account for all
your actions.

94. And do not take your oaths,
to practise deception between
yourselves, with the result that
someone's foot may slip after it
was firmly planted, and you may
have to taste the evil (consequences) of having hindered (men)
from the Path of Allah, and a
mighty Wrath descend on you.

95. Nor sell the Covenant of
Allah for a miserable price: for
with Allah is (a prize) far better
for you, if you only knew.

96. What is with you must
vanish: what is with Allah will
endure. And We will certainly
bestow, on those who patiently
persevere, their reward according to the best of their actions.

97. Whoever works righ-
teousness, man or woman, and
has Faith, verily, to him We will
give a new Life, a life that is
good and pure and We will
bestow on such

their reward according to the best of their actions.

98. When you read the Qur'an, seek Allah's protection from Satan the Rejected One.

99. He does not have any authority over those who believe and put their trust in their Lord.

100. His authority is over those only, who take him as a patron and who join partners with Allah.

101. When We substitute one revelation for another,- and Allah knows best what He reveals (in stages),- they say, "You are but a forger": but most of them do not understand.

102. Say, the Holy Spirit has brought the revelation from your Lord in Truth, in order to strengthen those who believe, and as a Guide and Glad Tidings to Muslims.

103. We know indeed that they say, "It is a man that teaches him." The tongue of him they wickedly point to is notably foreign, while this is Arabic, pure and clear.

104. Those who do not believe in the Signs of Allah,- Allah will not guide them, and theirs will be a grievous Penalty.

105. It is those who do not believe in the Signs of Allah, that forge falsehood: it is they who lie!

106. Any one who, after accepting faith in Allah, utters Unbelief,- except under compulsion, his heart remaining firm

أَجْرَهُمْ بِأَحْسَنِ مَا كَانُوا يَعْمَلُونَ ۝

فَإِذَا قَرَأْتَ الْقُرْآنَ فَاسْتَعِذْ بِاللهِ

مِنَ الشَّيْطَانِ الرَّجِيمِ ۝

إِنَّهُ لَيْسَ لَهُ سُلْطَانٌ عَلَى الَّذِينَ

آمَنُوا وَعَلَى رَبِّهِمْ يَتَوَكَّلُونَ ۝

إِنَّمَا سُلْطَانُهُ عَلَى الَّذِينَ يَتَوَلَّوْنَهُ

وَالَّذِينَ هُمْ بِهِ مُشْرِكُونَ ۝

وَإِذَا بَدَّلْنَا آيَةً مَكَانَ آيَةٍ ۙ

وَاللهُ أَعْلَمُ بِمَا يُنَزِّلُ قَالُوا إِنَّمَا

أَنْتَ مُفْتَرٍ ۚ بَلْ أَكْثَرُهُمْ

لَا يَعْلَمُونَ ۝

قُلْ نَزَّلَهُ رُوحُ الْقُدُسِ مِنْ

رَبِّكَ بِالْحَقِّ لِيُثَبِّتَ الَّذِينَ آمَنُوا

وَهُدًى وَبُشْرَى لِلْمُسْلِمِينَ ۝

وَلَقَدْ نَعْلَمُ أَنَّهُمْ يَقُولُونَ إِنَّمَا

يُعَلِّمُهُ بَشَرٌ ۗ لِسَانُ الَّذِي

يُلْحِدُونَ إِلَيْهِ أَعْجَمِيٌّ وَهٰذَا

لِسَانٌ عَرَبِيٌّ مُبِينٌ ۝

إِنَّ الَّذِينَ لَا يُؤْمِنُونَ بِآيَاتِ

اللهِ ۙ لَا يَهْدِيهِمُ اللهُ وَلَهُمْ

عَذَابٌ أَلِيمٌ ۝

إِنَّمَا يَفْتَرِي الْكَذِبَ الَّذِينَ

لَا يُؤْمِنُونَ بِآيَاتِ اللهِ ۚ وَأُولٰئِكَ

هُمُ الْكَاذِبُونَ ۝

مَنْ كَفَرَ بِاللهِ مِنْ بَعْدِ إِيمَانِهِ

إِلَّا مَنْ أُكْرِهَ وَقَلْبُهُ مُطْمَئِنٌّ

in Faith - but such as open their breast to Unbelief, on them is Wrath from Allah, and for them will be a dreadful Penalty.

بِالْإِيمَانِ وَلَكِنْ مَّنْ شَرَحَ بِالْكُفْرِ صَدْرًا فَعَلَيْهِمْ غَضَبٌ مِّنَ اللّٰهِ ۖ وَلَهُمْ عَذَابٌ عَظِيْمٌ ۝

107. This because they love the life of this world better than the Hereafter: and Allah will not guide those who reject Faith.

ذٰلِكَ بِأَنَّهُمُ اسْتَحَبُّوا الْحَيٰوةَ الدُّنْيَا عَلَى الْأٰخِرَةِ ۙ وَأَنَّ اللّٰهَ لَا يَهْدِى الْقَوْمَ الْكٰفِرِيْنَ ۝

108. Those are they whose hearts, ears, and eyes Allah has sealed up, and they take no heed.

أُولٰٓئِكَ الَّذِيْنَ طَبَعَ اللّٰهُ عَلٰى قُلُوْبِهِمْ وَسَمْعِهِمْ وَأَبْصَارِهِمْ ۖ وَأُولٰٓئِكَ هُمُ الْغٰفِلُوْنَ ۝

109. Without doubt, in the Hereafter they will perish.

لَا جَرَمَ أَنَّهُمْ فِى الْأٰخِرَةِ هُمُ الْخٰسِرُوْنَ ۝

110. But verily your Lord,- to those who leave their homes after trials and persecutions,- and who thereafter strive and fight for the faith and patiently persevere,- your Lord, after all this is Oft-Forgiving, Most Merciful.

ثُمَّ إِنَّ رَبَّكَ لِلَّذِيْنَ هَاجَرُوْا مِنْ بَعْدِ مَا فُتِنُوْا ثُمَّ جٰهَدُوْا وَصَبَرُوْا ۙ إِنَّ رَبَّكَ مِنْ بَعْدِهَا لَغَفُوْرٌ رَّحِيْمٌ ۝

111. One Day every soul will come up struggling for itself, and every soul will be recompensed (fully) for all its actions, and none will be unjustly dealt with.

يَوْمَ تَأْتِيْ كُلُّ نَفْسٍ تُجَادِلُ عَنْ نَفْسِهَا وَتُوَفّٰى كُلُّ نَفْسٍ مَّا عَمِلَتْ وَهُمْ لَا يُظْلَمُوْنَ ۝

112. Allah sets forth a Parable: a city enjoying security and quiet, abundantly supplied with sustenance from every place: yet was it ungrateful for the favours of Allah: so Allah made it taste of hunger and terror (in extremes) (closing in on it) like a garment (from every side), because of the (evil) which (its people) wrought.

وَضَرَبَ اللّٰهُ مَثَلًا قَرْيَةً كَانَتْ اٰمِنَةً مُّطْمَئِنَّةً يَّأْتِيْهَا رِزْقُهَا رَغَدًا مِّنْ كُلِّ مَكَانٍ فَكَفَرَتْ بِأَنْعُمِ اللّٰهِ فَأَذَاقَهَا اللّٰهُ لِبَاسَ الْجُوْعِ وَالْخَوْفِ بِمَا كَانُوْا يَصْنَعُوْنَ ۝

113. And there came to them a Messenger from among them-selves, but they falsely rejected him; so the Wrath seized them even in the midst of their iniquities.

وَلَقَدْ جَاءَهُمْ رَسُوْلٌ مِّنْهُمْ فَكَذَّبُوْهُ فَأَخَذَهُمُ الْعَذَابُ وَهُمْ ظٰلِمُوْنَ ۝

114. So eat of the sustenance which Allah has provided for you, lawful and good; and be grateful for the favours of Allah, if it is He Whom you serve.

115. He has only forbidden you dead meat, and blood, and the flesh of swine, and any (food) over which the name of other than Allah has been invoked. But if one is forced by necessity, without wilful disobedience, nor transgressing due limits,- then Allah is Oft-Forgiving, Most Merciful.

116. But say not - for any false thing that your tongues may put forth,- "This is lawful, and this is forbidden," so as to ascribe false things to Allah. For those who ascribe false things to Allah, will never prosper.

117. (In such falsehood) is but a paltry profit; but they will have a most grievous Penalty.

118. To the Jews We prohibited such things as We have mentioned to you before: We did them no wrong, but they were used to doing wrong to themselves.

119. But verily your Lord,- to those who do wrong in ignorance, but who thereafter repent and make amends,- your Lord, after all this, is Oft-Forgiving, Most Merciful.

120. Abraham was indeed a model, devoutly obedient to Allah, (and) true in Faith, and he did not join gods with Allah:

121. He showed his gratitude for the favours of Allah, Who chose him, and guided him to a

فَكُلُوْا مِمَّا رَزَقَكُمُ اللّٰهُ حَلٰلًا طَيِّبًا ۖ وَّاشْكُرُوْا نِعْمَتَ اللّٰهِ اِنْ كُنْتُمْ اِيَّاهُ تَعْبُدُوْنَ ۞

اِنَّمَا حَرَّمَ عَلَيْكُمُ الْمَيْتَةَ وَالدَّمَ وَلَحْمَ الْخِنْزِيْرِ وَمَاۤ اُهِلَّ لِغَيْرِ اللّٰهِ بِهٖ ۚ فَمَنِ اضْطُرَّ غَيْرَ بَاغٍ وَّلَا عَادٍ فَاِنَّ اللّٰهَ غَفُوْرٌ رَّحِيْمٌ ۞

وَلَا تَقُوْلُوْا لِمَا تَصِفُ اَلْسِنَتُكُمُ الْكَذِبَ هٰذَا حَلٰلٌ وَّهٰذَا حَرَامٌ لِّتَفْتَرُوْا عَلَى اللّٰهِ الْكَذِبَ ۚ اِنَّ الَّذِيْنَ يَفْتَرُوْنَ عَلَى اللّٰهِ الْكَذِبَ لَا يُفْلِحُوْنَ ۞

مَتَاعٌ قَلِيْلٌ ۖ وَّلَهُمْ عَذَابٌ اَلِيْمٌ ۞

وَعَلَى الَّذِيْنَ هَادُوْا حَرَّمْنَا مَا قَصَصْنَا عَلَيْكَ مِنْ قَبْلُ ۚ وَمَا ظَلَمْنٰهُمْ وَلٰكِنْ كَانُوْۤا اَنْفُسَهُمْ يَظْلِمُوْنَ ۞

ثُمَّ اِنَّ رَبَّكَ لِلَّذِيْنَ عَمِلُوا السُّوْٓءَ بِجَهَالَةٍ ثُمَّ تَابُوْا مِنْۢ بَعْدِ ذٰلِكَ وَاَصْلَحُوْۤا اِنَّ رَبَّكَ مِنْۢ بَعْدِهَا لَغَفُوْرٌ رَّحِيْمٌ ۞

اِنَّ اِبْرٰهِيْمَ كَانَ اُمَّةً قَانِتًا لِّلّٰهِ حَنِيْفًا ۚ وَلَمْ يَكُ مِنَ الْمُشْرِكِيْنَ ۙ ۞

شَاكِرًا لِّاَنْعُمِهِ ۚ اِجْتَبٰهُ وَهَدٰىهُ

SÛRA-17
BANÎ ISRA'IL
(INTRODUCTION)

In the gradation of spiritual teaching (see Introduction to Sûrah 7), we saw that the first seven Sûras sketched the early spiritual history of man, and led up to the formation of the new Ummat of Islam. Sûras 8 to 16 formed another series dealing with the formation of the new Umaat and its consolidation, and Allah's dealing with man taken as an Ummat and considered in his social relation in organised communities (see Introduction to Suras 8, 10, and 16). We now come to a fresh series, (Suras 17-21 begin with an allusion to the *Mi'râj* (of which more later), and proceed to spiritual histoiy as touching individuals rather than nations. The old prophets and stories of the past are now referred to from this point of view. Suras 22-25 refer to Hajj (pilgrimage), worship and prayer, chastity, privacy, etc., as related to a man's individual spiritual growth. Sûras 26-29 go back to the old prophets and stories of the past, as illustrating the growth of the individual soul in the reactions against the lives of the communities, and the reactions of the communities to the lives of its great individual souls.

Let us now consider S. 17 itself. It opens with the mystic Vision of the Ascension of the Holy Prophet: he was transported from the Sacred Mosque (of Makkah) to the Farthest Mosque (of Jerusalem) in a night and shown some of the Signs of Allah. The majority of Commentators take this Night Journey literally, but allow that there were other occasions on which a spiritual Journey or Vision occurred. Even on the supposition of a miraculous bodily Journey, it is conceded that the body was almost transformed into a spiritual fineness. The Hadith literature gives details of this Journey and its study helps to elucidate its mystic meaning. The Holy Prophet was first transported to the seat of the earlier revelations in Jerusalem, and then taken through the seven heavens, even to the Sublime Throne, and initiated into the spiritual mysteries of the human soul struggling in Space and Time. The Spaniard, Miguel Asin, Arabic Professor in the University of Madrid, has shown that this *Mi 'raj* literature had a great influence on the Mediaeval literature of Europe, and especially on the great Italian poem, the *Divine Comedy* (or Drama) of Dante, which towers like a landmark in mediaeval European literature.

The reference to this great mystic story of the *Mi'râj* is a fitting prelude to the journey of the human soul in its spiritual growth in life. The first steps in such growth must be through moral conduct-the reciprocal rights of parents and children, kindness to our fellow-men, courage and firmness in the hour of danger, a sense of personal responsibility, and a sense of Allah's Presence through prayer and praise.

The *Mi'râj* is usually dated to the 27th night of the month of Rajab (though other dates, e.g. 17thofRabi' 1, are also given) in the year before the Hijra. This fixes the date of the opening verse of the Sûrah, though portions of the Sûrah, may have been a little earlier.

Straight Way.

122. And We gave him Good in this world, and he will be, in the Hereafter, in the ranks of the Righteous.

123. So We have taught you the inspired (message), "Follow the ways of Abraham, the True in Faith, and he did not join gods with Allah."

124. The Sabbath was only made (strict) for those who disagreed (as to its observance); but Allah will judge between them on the Day of Judgment, as to their differences.

125. Invite (all) to the Way of your Lord with wisdom and beautiful preaching; and argue with them in ways that are best and most gracious: for your Lord knows best, who have strayed from His Path, and who receive guidance.

126. And if you do catch them out, catch them out no worse than they catch you out: but if you show patience, that is indeed the best (course) for those who are patient.

127. And you be patient, for your patience is but from Allah; nor grieve over them: and do not distress yourself because of their plots.

128. For Allah is with those who restrain themselves, and those who do good.

17. The Children of Israel
In the name of Allah. Most Gracious, Most Merciful.

1. Glory to (Allah) Who took His Servant for a Journey by night from the Sacred Mosque to the Farthest Mosque,

اِلٰى صِرَاطٍ مُّسْتَقِيْمٍ ۞

وَاٰتَيْنٰهُ فِى الدُّنْيَا حَسَنَةً ۖ وَاِنَّهٗ فِى الْاٰخِرَةِ لَمِنَ الصّٰلِحِيْنَ ۞

ثُمَّ اَوْحَيْنَآ اِلَيْكَ اَنِ اتَّبِعْ مِلَّةَ اِبْرٰهِيْمَ حَنِيْفًا ۖ وَمَا كَانَ مِنَ الْمُشْرِكِيْنَ ۞

اِنَّمَا جُعِلَ السَّبْتُ عَلَى الَّذِيْنَ اخْتَلَفُوْا فِيْهِ ۖ وَاِنَّ رَبَّكَ لَيَحْكُمُ بَيْنَهُمْ يَوْمَ الْقِيٰمَةِ فِيْمَا كَانُوْا فِيْهِ يَخْتَلِفُوْنَ ۞

اُدْعُ اِلٰى سَبِيْلِ رَبِّكَ بِالْحِكْمَةِ وَالْمَوْعِظَةِ الْحَسَنَةِ وَجَادِلْهُمْ بِالَّتِيْ هِيَ اَحْسَنُ ۚ اِنَّ رَبَّكَ هُوَ اَعْلَمُ بِمَنْ ضَلَّ عَنْ سَبِيْلِهٖ وَهُوَ اَعْلَمُ بِالْمُهْتَدِيْنَ ۞

وَاِنْ عَاقَبْتُمْ فَعَاقِبُوْا بِمِثْلِ مَا عُوْقِبْتُمْ بِهٖ ۖ وَلَئِنْ صَبَرْتُمْ لَهُوَ خَيْرٌ لِّلصّٰبِرِيْنَ ۞

وَاصْبِرْ وَمَا صَبْرُكَ اِلَّا بِاللّٰهِ وَلَا تَحْزَنْ عَلَيْهِمْ وَلَا تَكُ فِيْ ضَيْقٍ مِّمَّا يَمْكُرُوْنَ ۞

اِنَّ اللّٰهَ مَعَ الَّذِيْنَ اتَّقَوْا وَّالَّذِيْنَ هُمْ مُّحْسِنُوْنَ ۞

(١٧) سُوْرَةُ بَنِيْ اِسْرَآئِيْلَ مَكِّيَّةٌ (٥٠)

بِسْمِ اللّٰهِ الرَّحْمٰنِ الرَّحِيْمِ

سُبْحٰنَ الَّذِيْ اَسْرٰى بِعَبْدِهٖ لَيْلًا مِّنَ

whose precincts We did bless,- in order that We might show him some of Our Signs: for He is the One Who hears and sees (all things).

2. We gave Moses the Book, and made it a Guide to the Children of Israel, (commanding): "Do not take other than Me as Disposer of (your) affairs."

3. O you that are sprung from those whom We carried (in the Ark) with Noah! Verily he was a devotee most grateful.

4. And We gave (clear) warning to the Children of Israel in the Book, that twice would they do mischief on the earth and be elated with mighty arrogance (and twice would they be punished)!

5. When the first of the warnings came to pass, We sent against you Our servants given to terrible warfare: they entered the very inmost parts of your homes; and it was a warning (completely) fulfilled.

6. Then We granted you the Return as against them: We gave you increase in resources and sons, and made you the more numerous in man-power.

7. If you did well, you did well for yourselves; if you did evil, (you did it) against yourselves. So when the second of the warnings came to pass, (We permitted your enemies) to disfigure your faces, and to enter your Temple as they had entered it before, and to visit with destruction all that fell into their power.

8. It may be that your Lord may (yet) show Mercy to you; but if you revert (to your sins), We shall revert (to Our punishments): and We have made Hell a prison for those who reject (all Faith).

9. Verily this Qur'an guides to that which is

most right (or stable), and gives the glad tidings to the Believers who work deeds of righteousness, that they shall have a magnificent reward;

10. And to those who do not believe in the Hereafter, (it announces) that We have prepared for them a Penalty Grievous (indeed).

11. The prayer that man should make for good, he makes for evil; for man is given to hasty (deeds).

12. We have made the Night and the Day as two (of Our) Signs: the Sign of the Night We have obscured, while the Sign of the Day We have made to enlighten you; that you may seek bounty from your Lord, and that you may know the number and count of the years: We have explained all things in detail.

13. Every man's fate We have fastened on his own neck: on the Day of Judgment We shall bring out for him a scroll, which he will see spread open.

14. (It will be said to him:) "Read your (own) record: sufficient is your soul this day to make out an account against you."

15. Who receives guidance, receives it for his own benefit: who goes astray does so to his own loss: no bearer of burdens can bear the burden of another: nor would We visit with Our Wrath until We had sent a Messenger (to give warning).

16. When We decide to destroy a population, We (first) send a definite order to those among them who are given the good things of this life and yet transgress; so that the word is proved true against them: then (it is) We destroy them utterly.

17. How many generations have We destroyed after Noah? And enough is your Lord to note

and see the sins of His servants.

عِبَادِهٖ خَبِيۡرًۢا بَصِيۡرًا ۞

18. If any do wish for the transitory things (of this life), We readily grant them - such things as We will, to such persons as We will: in the end We have provided Hell for them: they will burn therein, disgraced and rejected.

مَنۡ كَانَ يُرِيۡدُ الۡعَاجِلَةَ عَجَّلۡنَا

لَهٗ فِيۡهَا مَا نَشَآءُ لِمَنۡ نُّرِيۡدُ

ثُمَّ جَعَلۡنَا لَهٗ جَهَنَّمَ ۚ يَصۡلٰىهَا

مَذۡمُوۡمًا مَّدۡحُوۡرًا ۞

19. Those who do wish for the (things of) the Hereafter, and strive therefor with all due striving, and have Faith,- they are the ones whose striving is acceptable (to Allah).

وَمَنۡ اَرَادَ الۡاٰخِرَةَ وَسَعٰى لَهَا

سَعۡيَهَا وَهُوَ مُؤۡمِنٌ فَاُولٰٓئِكَ كَانَ

سَعۡيُهُمۡ مَّشۡكُوۡرًا ۞

20. Of the bounties of your Lord We bestow freely on all- these as well as those: the bounties of your Lord are not closed (to anyone).

كُلًّا نُّمِدُّ هٰٓؤُلَآءِ وَهٰٓؤُلَآءِ مِنۡ عَطَآءِ رَبِّكَ ؕ

وَمَا كَانَ عَطَآءُ رَبِّكَ مَحۡظُوۡرًا ۞

21. See how We have besto- wed more on some than on others; but verily the Hereafter is more in rank and gradation and more in excellence.

اُنۡظُرۡ كَيۡفَ فَضَّلۡنَا بَعۡضَهُمۡ عَلٰى بَعۡضٍ ؕ

وَلَلۡاٰخِرَةُ اَكۡبَرُ دَرَجٰتٍ وَّاَكۡبَرُ تَفۡضِيۡلًا ۞

22. Take not with Allah another object of worship; or you (O man!) will sit in disgrace and destitution.

لَا تَجۡعَلۡ مَعَ اللّٰهِ اِلٰهًا اٰخَرَ فَتَقۡعُدَ

مَذۡمُوۡمًا مَّخۡذُوۡلًا ۞

23. Your Lord has decreed that you worship none but Him, and that you be kind to parents. Whether one or both of them attain old age in your life, say not to them a word of contempt, nor repel them, but address them in terms of honour.

وَقَضٰى رَبُّكَ اَلَّا تَعۡبُدُوۡۤا اِلَّاۤ اِيَّاهُ وَ

بِالۡوَالِدَيۡنِ اِحۡسَانًا ؕ اِمَّا يَبۡلُغَنَّ

عِنۡدَكَ الۡكِبَرَ اَحَدُهُمَاۤ اَوۡ كِلٰهُمَا فَلَا

تَقُلۡ لَّهُمَاۤ اُفٍّ وَّلَا تَنۡهَرۡهُمَا وَقُلۡ

لَّهُمَا قَوۡلًا كَرِيۡمًا ۞

24. And, out of kindness, lower to them the wing of humility, and say: "My Lord! bestow on them Your Mercy even as they cherished me in childhood."

وَاخۡفِضۡ لَهُمَا جَنَاحَ الذُّلِّ مِنَ

الرَّحۡمَةِ وَقُلۡ رَّبِّ ارۡحَمۡهُمَا كَمَا

رَبَّيٰنِىۡ صَغِيۡرًا ۞

25. Your Lord knows best what is in your hearts: If you do deeds of righteousness, verily He is Most Forgiving to those who turn to Him again and again (in true penitence).

رَبُّكُمۡ اَعۡلَمُ بِمَا فِىۡ نُفُوۡسِكُمۡ ؕ

اِنۡ تَكُوۡنُوۡا صٰلِحِيۡنَ فَاِنَّهٗ كَانَ

لِلۡاَوَّابِيۡنَ غَفُوۡرًا ۞

26. And render to the kindred their due rights, as (also) to those in want,

وَاٰتِ ذَا الۡقُرۡبٰى حَقَّهٗ وَالۡمِسۡكِيۡنَ

and to the wayfarer: but
squander not (your wealth) in
the manner of a spendthrift.

27. Verily spendthrifts are
brothers of the Evil Ones; and
the Evil One is to his Lord
(Himself) ungrateful.

28. And even if you have to
turn away from them in pursuit
of the Mercy from your Lord
which you do expect, yet speak
to them a word of easy kindness.

29. Make not your hand tied
(like a miser's) to your neck, nor
stretch it forth to its utmost
reach, so that you become
blameworthy and destitute.

30. Verily your Lord provides
sustenance in abundance for
whom He pleases, and He
provides in a just measure. For
He knows and regards all His
servants.

31. Do not kill your children
for fear of want: We shall
provide sustenance for them as
well as for you. Verily the
killing of them is a great sin.

32. Nor come near to adultery:
for it is a shameful (deed) and an
evil, opening the road (to other
evils).

33. Nor take life - which Allah
has made sacred - except for just
cause. And if anyone is slain
wrongfully, We have given his
heir authority (to demand Qisas
or to forgive): but let him not
exceed bounds in the matter of
taking life; for he is helped (by
the Law).

34. Come not near to the
orphan's property except to
improve it, until he attains the
age of full strength; and fulfil
(every) engagement, for (every)
engagement will be enquired
into (on the Day of Reckoning).

35. Give full measure when
you measure, and weigh

with a balance that is straight: that is the most fitting and the most advantageous in the final determination.

36. And do not pursue that of which you have no knowledge; for every act of hearing, or of seeing or of (feeling in) the heart will be enquired into (on the Day of Reckoning).

37. Nor walk on the earth with insolence: for you can not rend the earth asunder, nor reach the mountains in height.

38. Of all such things the evil is hateful in the sight of your Lord.

39. These are among the (precepts of) wisdom, which your Lord has revealed to you. Do not take, with Allah, another object of worship, lest you should be thrown into Hell, blameworthy and rejected.

40. Has then your Lord (O Pagans!) preferred for you sons, and taken for Himself daughters among the angels? Truly you utter a most dreadful saying!

41. We have explained (things) in various (ways) in this Qur'an, in order that they may receive admonition, but it only increases their flight (from the Truth)!

42. Say: If there had been (other) gods with Him, as they say,- behold, they would certainly have sought out a way to the Lord of the Throne!

43. Glory to Him! He is high above all that they say!- Exalted and Great (beyond measure)!

44. The seven heavens and the earth, and all beings therein, declare His glory: there is not a thing but celebrates

His praise; and yet you do not understand how they declare His glory! Verily He is Oft-Forbearing, Most Forgiving!

45. When you recite the Qur'an, We put between you and those who do not believe in the Hereafter, an invisible veil:

46. And We put coverings over their hearts (and minds) lest they should understand the Qur'an, and deafness into their ears: when you commemorate your Lord and Him alone in the Qur'an, they turn on their backs, fleeing (from the Truth).

47. We know best why it is they listen, when they listen to you: and when they meet in private conference, behold, the wicked say, "You follow none other than a man bewitched!"

48. See what similes they strike for you: but they have gone astray, and never can they find a way.

49. They say: "What! when we are reduced to bones and dust, should we really be raised up (to be) a new creation?"

50. Say: "(Nay!) be you stones or iron,

51. "Or any created matter which, in your minds, is hardest (to be raised up),- (yet you shall be raised up)!" Then they will say: "Who will cause us to return?" Say: "He Who created you first!" Then they will wag their heads toward you, and say, "When will that be?" Say, "May be it will be quite soon!

52. "It will be on a Day when He will call you, and you will answer (His call) with (words of) His praise, and you will think that you tarried but a little while!"

53. Say to My servants that they should (only) say those things that are

best: for Satan sows dissensions among them: for Satan is to man an avowed enemy.

54. It is your Lord that knows you best: If He please, He grants you mercy, or if He please, punishment: We have not sent you to be a disposer of their affairs for them.

55. And it is your Lord that knows best all beings that are in the heavens and on earth: We bestowed on some prophets more (and other) gifts than on others: and We gave to David (the gift of) the Psalms.

56. Say: "Call on those - besides Him - whom you fancy: they have neither the power to remove your troubles from you nor to change them."

57. Those whom they call upon do desire (for themselves) means of access to their Lord, - even those who are nearest: they hope for His Mercy and fear His Wrath: for the Wrath of your Lord is something to take heed of.

58. There is not a population but We shall destroy it before the Day of Judgment or punish it with a dreadful Penalty: that is written in the (eternal) Record.

59. And We refrain from sending the Signs, only because the men of former generations treated them as false: We sent the she-camel to the Thamud to open their eyes, but they treated her wrongfully: We only send the Signs by way of terror (and warning from evil).

60. Behold! We told you that your Lord encompasses mankind round about: We granted the vision which We showed you, but as a trial for men,- as also the Cursed Tree

(mentioned) in the Qur'an: We put terror (and warning) into them, but it only increases their inordinate transgression!

61. Behold! We said to the angels: "Bow down to Adam": They bowed down except Iblis: he said, "Shall I bow down to one whom You created from clay?"

62. He said: "Do You see? this is the one whom You have honoured above me! If You will but respite me to the Day of Judgment, I will surely bring his descendants under my sway - all but a few!"

63. (Allah) said: "Go you away; if any of them follow you, verily Hell will be the recompense of you (all)- an ample recompense.

64. "Lead to destruction those whom you can among them, with your (seductive) voice; make assaults on them with your cavalry and your infantry; mutually share with them wealth and children; and make promises to them." But Satan promises them nothing but deceit.

65. "As for My servants, no authority you shall have over them:" enough is your Lord for a Disposer of affairs.

66. Your Lord is He that makes the ship go smoothly for you through the sea, in order that you may seek of His Bounty. For He is to you most Merciful.

67. When distress seizes you at sea, those that you call upon - besides Himself - leave you in the lurch! but when He brings you back safe to land, you turn away (from Him). Most ungrateful is man!

68. Do you then feel secure that He will not cause you to be swallowed up beneath the earth when you are on land, or that He will not send against you a violent tornado (with showers of stones) so that you shall find no protector?

69. Or do you feel secure that He will not send you back a

second time to sea and send against you a heavy gale to drown you because of your ingratitude, so that you find no helper therein against Us?

70. We have honoured the sons of Adam; provided them with transport on land and sea; given them for sustenance things good and pure; and conferred on them special favours, above a great part of Our Creation.

71. One day We shall call together all human beings with their (respective) Imams: those who are given their record in their right hand will read it (with pleasure), and they will not be dealt with unjustly in the least.

72. But those who were blind in this world, will be blind in the Hereafter, and most astray from the Path.

73. And their purpose was to tempt you away from that which We had revealed to you, to substitute in Our name something quite different; (in that case), behold! they would certainly have made you (their) friend!

74. And had We not given you strength, you would nearly have inclined to them a little.

75. In that case, We should have made you taste a double portion (of punishment) in this life, and a double portion after death: and moreover you would have found none to help you against Us!

76. Their purpose was to scare you off the land, in order to expel you; but in that case they would not have stayed (therein) after you, except for a little while.

77. (This was Our) way with the Messengers We sent before you: you will find no change in Our ways.

78. Establish regular prayers at the sun's decline till the darkness of the night, and the recital of the Qur'an in morning prayer, for the recital in the morning

أُخْرَى فَيُرْسِلَ عَلَيْكُمْ قَاصِفًا مِّنَ الرِّيحِ فَيُغْرِقَكُمْ بِمَا كَفَرْتُمْ ثُمَّ لَا تَجِدُوا لَكُمْ عَلَيْنَا بِهِ تَبِيعًا ۝

وَلَقَدْ كَرَّمْنَا بَنِيٓ اٰدَمَ وَحَمَلْنَاهُمْ فِي الْبَرِّ وَالْبَحْرِ وَرَزَقْنَاهُمْ مِّنَ الطَّيِّبَاتِ وَفَضَّلْنَاهُمْ عَلَى كَثِيرٍ مِّمَّنْ خَلَقْنَا تَفْضِيلًا ۝

يَوْمَ نَدْعُوا كُلَّ اُنَاسٍ بِاِمَامِهِمْ فَمَنْ اُوتِيَ كِتَابَهُ بِيَمِينِهِ فَاُولٰئِكَ يَقْرَءُوْنَ كِتَابَهُمْ وَلَا يُظْلَمُوْنَ فَتِيلًا ۝

وَمَنْ كَانَ فِي هٰذِهٖٓ اَعْمٰى فَهُوَ فِي الْاٰخِرَةِ اَعْمٰى وَاَضَلُّ سَبِيلًا ۝

وَاِنْ كَادُوا لَيَفْتِنُوْنَكَ عَنِ الَّذِيٓ اَوْحَيْنَآ اِلَيْكَ لِتَفْتَرِيَ عَلَيْنَا غَيْرَهُ وَاِذًا لَّاتَّخَذُوْكَ خَلِيلًا ۝

وَلَوْلَا اَنْ ثَبَّتْنَاكَ لَقَدْ كِدتَّ تَرْكَنُ اِلَيْهِمْ شَيْئًا قَلِيلًا ۝

اِذًا لَّاَذَقْنَاكَ ضِعْفَ الْحَيَاةِ وَضِعْفَ الْمَمَاتِ ثُمَّ لَا تَجِدُ لَكَ عَلَيْنَا نَصِيرًا ۝

وَاِنْ كَادُوا لَيَسْتَفِزُّوْنَكَ مِنَ الْاَرْضِ لِيُخْرِجُوْكَ مِنْهَا وَاِذًا لَّا يَلْبَثُوْنَ خِلٰفَكَ اِلَّا قَلِيلًا ۝

سُنَّةَ مَنْ قَدْ اَرْسَلْنَا قَبْلَكَ مِنْ رُّسُلِنَا وَلَا تَجِدُ لِسُنَّتِنَا تَحْوِيْلًا ۝

اَقِمِ الصَّلٰوةَ لِدُلُوْكِ الشَّمْسِ اِلٰى غَسَقِ الَّيْلِ وَقُرْاٰنَ الْفَجْرِ اِنَّ قُرْاٰنَ الْفَجْرِ

carry (angels') testimony.

79. And as for the night keep awake a part of it as an additional prayer for you, soon will your Lord raise you to a Station of Praise and Glory!

80. Say: "O my Lord! Let my entry be by the Gate of Truth and Honour, and likewise my exit by the Gate of Truth and Honour; and grant me from Your Presence an authority to aid (me)."

81. And say: "Truth has (now) arrived, and Falsehood perished: for Falsehood is (by its nature) bound to perish."

82. We send down (stage by stage) in the Qur'an that which is a healing and a mercy to those who believe: to the unjust it causes nothing but loss after loss.

83. Yet when We bestow Our favours on man, he turns away and becomes remote on his side (instead of coming to Us), and when evil seizes him he gives himself up to despair.

84. Say: "Everyone acts according to his own disposition: but your Lord knows best who it is that is best guided on the Way."

85. They ask you concerning the Spirit (of inspiration). Say: "The Spirit (comes) by command of my Lord: of knowledge it is only a little that is communicated to you, (O men!)"

86. If it were Our Will, We could take away that which We have sent you by inspiration: then would you find none to plead your affair in that matter as against Us,-

87. Except for Mercy from your Lord: for His Bounty is to you (indeed) great.

88. Say: "If the whole of mankind and Jinns were to gather

together to produce the like of this Qur'an, they could not produce the like thereof, even if they backed up each other with help and support.

89. And We have explained to man, in this Qur'an, every kind of similitude: yet the greater part of men refuse (to receive it) except with ingratitude!

90. They say: "We shall not believe in you, until you cause a spring to gush forth for us from the earth,

91. "Or (until) you have a garden of date trees and vines, and cause rivers to gush forth in their midst, carrying abundant water;

92. "Or you cause the sky to fall in pieces, as you say (will happen), against us; or you bring Allah and the angels before (us) face to face:

93. "Or you have a house adorned with gold, or you mount a ladder right into the skies. No, we shall not even believe in your mounting until you send down to us a book that we could read." Say: "Glory to my Lord! Am I not but a man,- a Messenger?"

94. What kept men back from belief when Guidance came to them, was nothing but this: they said, "Has Allah sent a man (like us) to be (His) Messenger?"

95. Say, "If there were settled, on earth, angels walking about in peace and quiet, We should certainly have sent them down from the heavens an angel for a Messenger."

96. Say: "Enough is Allah for a Witness between me and you: for He is well acquainted with His servants, and He sees (all things).

97. It is he whom Allah guides, that is on true guidance; but he whom

عَلَىٰ أَن يَأْتُوا بِمِثْلِ هٰذَا الْقُرْآنِ لَا يَأْتُونَ بِمِثْلِهِ وَلَوْ كَانَ بَعْضُهُمْ لِبَعْضٍ ظَهِيرًا ۝

وَلَقَدْ صَرَّفْنَا لِلنَّاسِ فِى هٰذَا الْقُرْآنِ مِنْ كُلِّ مَثَلٍ فَأَبَىٰ أَكْثَرُ النَّاسِ إِلَّا كُفُورًا ۝

وَقَالُوا لَنْ نُؤْمِنَ لَكَ حَتَّىٰ تَفْجُرَ لَنَا مِنَ الْأَرْضِ يَنْبُوعًا ۝

أَوْ تَكُونَ لَكَ جَنَّةٌ مِّنْ نَّخِيلٍ وَّ عِنَبٍ فَتُفَجِّرَ الْأَنْهَارَ خِلَالَهَا تَفْجِيرًا ۝

أَوْ تُسْقِطَ السَّمَاءَ كَمَا زَعَمْتَ عَلَيْنَا كِسَفًا أَوْ تَأْتِيَ بِاللّٰهِ وَالْمَلَائِكَةِ قَبِيلًا ۝

أَوْ يَكُونَ لَكَ بَيْتٌ مِّنْ زُخْرُفٍ أَوْ تَرْقَىٰ فِى السَّمَاءِ وَلَنْ نُؤْمِنَ لِرُقِيِّكَ حَتَّىٰ تُنَزِّلَ عَلَيْنَا كِتَابًا نَّقْرَؤُهُ قُلْ سُبْحَانَ رَبِّى هَلْ كُنْتُ إِلَّا بَشَرًا رَّسُولًا ۝

وَمَا مَنَعَ النَّاسَ أَنْ يُؤْمِنُوا إِذْ جَاءَهُمُ الْهُدَىٰ إِلَّا أَنْ قَالُوا أَبَعَثَ اللّٰهُ بَشَرًا رَّسُولًا ۝

قُلْ لَّوْ كَانَ فِى الْأَرْضِ مَلَائِكَةٌ يَمْشُونَ مُطْمَئِنِّينَ لَنَزَّلْنَا عَلَيْهِمْ مِّنَ السَّمَاءِ مَلَكًا رَّسُولًا ۝

قُلْ كَفَىٰ بِاللّٰهِ شَهِيدًا بَيْنِى وَبَيْنَكُمْ إِنَّهُ كَانَ بِعِبَادِهِ خَبِيرًا بَصِيرًا ۝

وَمَنْ يَهْدِ اللّٰهُ فَهُوَ الْمُهْتَدِ وَمَنْ

He leaves astray - for such you will find no protector besides Him. On the Day of Judgment We shall gather them together, prone on their faces, blind, dumb, and deaf: their abode will be Hell: every time it shows abatement, We shall increase for them the fierceness of the Fire.

98. That is their recompense, because they rejected Our Signs, and said, "When we are reduced to bones and broken dust, should we really be raised up (to be) a new Creation?"

99. Don't they see that Allah, Who created the heavens and the earth, has power to create the like of them (anew)? Only He has decreed a term appointed, of which there is no doubt. But the unjust refuse (to receive it) except with ingratitude.

100. Say: "If you had control of the Treasures of the Mercy of my Lord, behold, you would keep them back, for fear of spending them: for man is (ever) miserly!"

101. To Moses We gave Nine Clear Signs: ask the Children of Israel: when he came to them, Pharaoh said to him: "O Moses! I consider you, indeed, to have been worked upon by sorcery!

102. Moses said, "You know well that these things have been sent down by none but the Lord of the heavens and the earth as eye-opening evidence: and I consider you indeed, O Pharaoh, to be one doomed to destruction!"

103. So he resolved to remove them from the face of the earth: but We drowned him and all who were with him.

104. And We said thereafter to the Children of Israel, "Dwell securely in the land (of promise)": but when the second of the warnings came to pass, We gathered you together in a mingled crowd.

SÛRAH-18
AL-KAHF
(INTRODUCTION)

It has been explained in the Introduction to S. 17 how the five Sûras 17 to 21 develop the theme of the individual soul's spiritual history, and how they fit into the general scheme of exposition.

This particular Makkah Sûrah may be called a lesson on the brevity and mystery of Life. First there is the story of the Companions of the Cave who slept therein for a long period, and yet thought they had been there only a day or less. Then there is the story of the mysterious Teacher who shows Moses how life itself is parable. And further there is the story of Zul-qarnain, the two horned one, the powerful ruler of west and east, who made an iron wall to protect the weak against the strong. The parables refer to the brevity, uncertainty, and vanity of this life; to the many paradoxes in it, which can only be understood by patience and the fulness of knowledge; and to the need of guarding our spiritual gains against the incursions of evil.

105. We sent down the (Qur'an) in Truth, and in Truth has it descended: and We sent you but to give Glad Tidings and to warn (sinners).

106. (It is) a Qur'an which We have divided (into parts from time to time), in order that you might recite it to men at intervals: We have revealed it by stages.

107. Say: "Whether you believe in it or not, it is true that those who were given knowledge beforehand, when it is recited to them, fall down on their faces in humble prostration,

108. "And they say: 'Glory to our Lord! Truly has the promise of our Lord been fulfilled!'"

109. They fall down on their faces in tears, and it increases their (earnest) humility.

110. Say: "Call upon Allah, or call upon Rahman: by whatever name you call upon Him, (it is well): for to Him belong the Most Beautiful Names. Neither speak your Prayer aloud, nor speak it in a low tone, but seek a middle course between."

111. Say: "Praise be to Allah, Who begets no son, and has no partner in (His) dominion: nor (needs) He any to protect Him from humiliation: yes, magnify Him for His greatness and glory!

18. The Cave
In the name of Allah. Most Gracious, Most Merciful.

1. Praise be to Allah, Who has sent to His Servant the Book, and has allowed therein no crookedness:

2. (He has made it) Straight (and Clear) in order that He may warn (the godless) of a terrible Punishment from Him, and that He may give Glad Tidings to the Believers who work righteous Deeds, that they shall have

وَبِالْحَقِّ اَنْزَلْنٰهُ وَبِالْحَقِّ نَزَلَ ۗ وَمَآ اَرْسَلْنٰكَ اِلَّا مُبَشِّرًا وَّ نَذِيْرًا ۞

وَقُرْاٰنًا فَرَقْنٰهُ لِتَقْرَاَهٗ عَلَى النَّاسِ عَلٰى مُكْثٍ وَّنَزَّلْنٰهُ تَنْزِيْلًا ۞

قُلْ اٰمِنُوْا بِهٖٓ اَوْ لَا تُؤْمِنُوْا ۗ اِنَّ الَّذِيْنَ اُوْتُوا الْعِلْمَ مِنْ قَبْلِهٖٓ اِذَا يُتْلٰى عَلَيْهِمْ يَخِرُّوْنَ لِلْاَذْقَانِ سُجَّدًا ۞

وَّيَقُوْلُوْنَ سُبْحٰنَ رَبِّنَآ اِنْ كَانَ وَعْدُ رَبِّنَا لَمَفْعُوْلًا ۞

وَيَخِرُّوْنَ لِلْاَذْقَانِ يَبْكُوْنَ وَ يَزِيْدُهُمْ خُشُوْعًا ۞

قُلِ ادْعُوا اللّٰهَ اَوِ ادْعُوا الرَّحْمٰنَ ۗ اَيًّا مَّا تَدْعُوْا فَلَهُ الْاَسْمَآءُ الْحُسْنٰى ۚ وَلَا تَجْهَرْ بِصَلَاتِكَ وَلَا تُخَافِتْ بِهَا وَابْتَغِ بَيْنَ ذٰلِكَ سَبِيْلًا ۞

وَقُلِ الْحَمْدُ لِلّٰهِ الَّذِيْ لَمْ يَتَّخِذْ وَلَدًا وَّلَمْ يَكُنْ لَّهٗ شَرِيْكٌ فِى الْمُلْكِ وَلَمْ يَكُنْ لَّهٗ وَلِيٌّ مِّنَ الذُّلِّ وَكَبِّرْهُ تَكْبِيْرًا ۞

(١٨) سُوْرَةُ الْكَهْفِ مَكِّيَّةٌ (٦٩)

بِسْمِ اللّٰهِ الرَّحْمٰنِ الرَّحِيْمِ

اَلْحَمْدُ لِلّٰهِ الَّذِيْٓ اَنْزَلَ عَلٰى عَبْدِهِ الْكِتٰبَ وَلَمْ يَجْعَلْ لَّهٗ عِوَجًا ۜ

قَيِّمًا لِّيُنْذِرَ بَأْسًا شَدِيْدًا مِّنْ لَّدُنْهُ وَيُبَشِّرَ الْمُؤْمِنِيْنَ الَّذِيْنَ يَعْمَلُوْنَ الصّٰلِحٰتِ اَنَّ لَهُمْ

a goodly Reward,

أَجْرًا حَسَنًا ۞

3. Wherein they shall remain for ever:

مَّاكِثِينَ فِيهِ أَبَدًا ۞

4. Further, that He may warn those (also) who say, "Allah has begotten a son":

وَّ يُنْذِرَ الَّذِينَ قَالُوا اتَّخَذَ

اللهُ وَلَدًا ۞

5. They do not have any knowledge of such a thing, nor had their fathers. It is a grievous thing that issues from their mouths as a saying. What they say is nothing but falsehood!

مَّا لَهُمْ بِهِ مِنْ عِلْمٍ وَّلَا لِآبَآئِهِمْ ۚ

كَبُرَتْ كَلِمَةً تَخْرُجُ مِنْ أَفْوَاهِهِمْ ۚ

إِنْ يَّقُولُونَ إِلَّا كَذِبًا ۞

6. You would only, per-chance, fret yourself to death, following after them, in grief, if they do not believe in this Message.

فَلَعَلَّكَ بَاخِعٌ نَّفْسَكَ عَلَى آثَارِهِمْ

إِنْ لَّمْ يُؤْمِنُوا بِهَذَا الْحَدِيْثِ

أَسَفًا ۞

7. That which is on earth We have made but as a glittering show for the earth, in order that We may test them - as to which of them are best in conduct.

إِنَّا جَعَلْنَا مَا عَلَى الْأَرْضِ زِينَةً

لَّهَا لِنَبْلُوَهُمْ أَيُّهُمْ أَحْسَنُ عَمَلًا ۞

8. Verily what is on earth We shall make but as dust and dry soil (without growth or herbage).

وَإِنَّا لَجَاعِلُونَ مَا عَلَيْهَا صَعِيدًا

جُرُزًا ۞

9. Or do you reflect that the Companions of the Cave and of the Inscription were wonders among Our Signs?

أَمْ حَسِبْتَ أَنَّ أَصْحَابَ الْكَهْفِ

وَالرَّقِيْمِ كَانُوا مِنْ آيَاتِنَا عَجَبًا ۞

10. Behold, the youths betook themselves to the Cave: they said, "Our Lord! bestow on us Mercy from Yourself, and dispose of our affair for us in the right way!"

إِذْ أَوَى الْفِتْيَةُ إِلَى الْكَهْفِ فَقَالُوا

رَبَّنَا آتِنَا مِنْ لَّدُنْكَ رَحْمَةً

وَّهَيِّئْ لَنَا مِنْ أَمْرِنَا رَشَدًا ۞

11. Then We drew (a veil) over their ears, for a number of years, in the Cave, (so that they did not hear):

فَضَرَبْنَا عَلَى آذَانِهِمْ فِي الْكَهْفِ

سِنِينَ عَدَدًا ۞

12. Then We roused them, in order to test which of the two parties was best at calculating the term of years they had tarried!

ثُمَّ بَعَثْنَاهُمْ لِنَعْلَمَ أَيُّ الْحِزْبَيْنِ

أَحْصَى لِمَا لَبِثُوا أَمَدًا ۞

13. We relate to you their story in truth: they were youths who believed in their Lord, and We advanced them in guidance:

نَحْنُ نَقُصُّ عَلَيْكَ نَبَأَهُمْ بِالْحَقِّ ۚ

إِنَّهُمْ فِتْيَةٌ آمَنُوا بِرَبِّهِمْ وَزِدْنَاهُمْ

هُدًى ۞

14.   We gave strength to their hearts: behold, they stood up and said: "Our Lord is the Lord of the heavens and of the earth: never shall we call upon any god other than Him: if we did, we should indeed have uttered an enormity!

15.   "These our people have taken for worship gods other than Him: why do they not bring forward an authority clear (and convincing) for what they do? Who does more wrong than such as invent a falsehood against Allah?

16.   "When you turn away from them and the things they worship other than Allah, betake yourselves to the Cave: your Lord will shower His mercies on you and dispose of your affair towards comfort and ease."

17.   You would have seen the sun, when it rose, declining to the right from their Cave, and when it set, turning away from them to the left, while they lay in the open space in the midst of the Cave. Such are among the Signs of Allah: He whom Allah guides is rightly guided; but he whom Allah leaves to stray,- for him you will find no protector to lead him to the Right Way.

18.   You would have deemed them awake, whilst they were asleep, and We turned them on their right and on their left sides: their dog stretching forth his two fore-legs on the threshold: if you had come up on to them, you would have certainly turned back from them in flight, and would certainly have been filled with terror of them.

19.   Such (being their state), We raised them up (from sleep), that they might question each other. Said one of them,

"How long have you stayed (here)?" They said, "We have stayed (perhaps) a day, or part of a day." (At length) they (all) said, "Allah (alone) knows best how long you have stayed here.... Now you send one of you with this money of yours to the town: let him find out which is the best food (to be had) and bring some to you, that (you may) satisfy your hunger therewith: and let him behave with care and courtesy, and let him not inform anyone about you.

20. "For if they should come upon you, they would stone you or force you to return to their cult, and in that case you would never attain prosperity."

21. Thus We made their case known to the people, that they might know that the promise of Allah is true, and that there can be no doubt about the Hour of Judgment. Behold, they dispute among themselves as to their affair. (Some) said, "Construct a building over them": Their Lord knows best about them: those who prevailed over their affair said, "Let us surely build a place of worship over them."

22. (Some) say they were three, the dog being the fourth among them; (others) say they were five, the dog being the sixth,- doubtfully guessing at the unknown; (yet others) say they were seven, the dog being the eighth. You say: "My Lord knows best their number; it is but few that know their (real case)." Do not enter, therefore, into controversies concerning them, except on a matter that is clear, nor consult any of them about (the affair of) the Sleepers.

23. Nor say of anything, "I shall be sure to do

so and so tomorrow"-

24. Without adding, "If Allah so wills" and call your Lord to mind when you forget, and say, "I hope that my Lord will guide me ever closer (even) than this to the right road."

25. So they stayed in their Cave three hundred years, and (some) add nine (more).

26. Say: "Allah knows best how long they stayed: with Him is (the knowledge of) the secrets of the heavens and the earth: how clearly He sees, how finely He hears (everything)! They have no protector other than Him; nor does He share His Command with any person whatsoever.

27. And recite (and teach) what has been revealed to you of the Book of your Lord: none can change His Words, and none will you find as a refuge other than Him.

28. And keep your soul content with those who call on their Lord morning and evening, seeking His Face; and let not your eyes pass beyond them, seeking the pomp and glitter of this Life; nor obey any whose heart We have permitted to neglect the remembrance of Us, one who follows his own desires, whose case has gone beyond all bounds.

29. Say, "The Truth is from your Lord": let him who will believe, and let him who will reject (it): for the wrong-doers We have prepared a Fire whose (smoke and flames), like the walls and roof of a tent, will hem them in: if they implore relief they will be granted water like melted brass, that will scald their faces.

ذٰلِكَ غَدًا ۞

اِلَّاۤ اَنْ يَّشَاۤءَ اللّٰهُ ۖ وَاذْكُرْ رَّبَّكَ اِذَا نَسِيْتَ وَقُلْ عَسٰۤى اَنْ يَّهْدِيَنِ رَبِّيْ لِاَقْرَبَ مِنْ هٰذَا رَشَدًا ۞

وَلَبِثُوْا فِيْ كَهْفِهِمْ ثَلٰثَ مِائَةٍ سِنِيْنَ وَازْدَادُوْا تِسْعًا ۞

قُلِ اللّٰهُ اَعْلَمُ بِمَا لَبِثُوْا ۖ لَهٗ غَيْبُ السَّمٰوٰتِ وَالْاَرْضِ ۖ اَبْصِرْ بِهٖ وَ اَسْمِعْ ۚ مَا لَهُمْ مِّنْ دُوْنِهٖ مِنْ وَّلِيٍّ ۖ وَّلَا يُشْرِكُ فِيْ حُكْمِهٖۤ اَحَدًا ۞

وَاتْلُ مَاۤ اُوْحِيَ اِلَيْكَ مِنْ كِتَابِ رَبِّكَ ۚ لَا مُبَدِّلَ لِكَلِمٰتِهٖ ۚ وَلَنْ تَجِدَ مِنْ دُوْنِهٖ مُلْتَحَدًا ۞

وَاصْبِرْ نَفْسَكَ مَعَ الَّذِيْنَ يَدْعُوْنَ رَبَّهُمْ بِالْغَدٰوةِ وَالْعَشِيِّ يُرِيْدُوْنَ وَجْهَهٗ وَلَا تَعْدُ عَيْنٰكَ عَنْهُمْ ۚ تُرِيْدُ زِيْنَةَ الْحَيٰوةِ الدُّنْيَا ۚ وَلَا تُطِعْ مَنْ اَغْفَلْنَا قَلْبَهٗ عَنْ ذِكْرِنَا وَاتَّبَعَ هَوٰىهُ وَكَانَ اَمْرُهٗ فُرُطًا ۞

وَقُلِ الْحَقُّ مِنْ رَّبِّكُمْ ۖ فَمَنْ شَاۤءَ فَلْيُؤْمِنْ وَّ مَنْ شَاۤءَ فَلْيَكْفُرْ ۙ اِنَّاۤ اَعْتَدْنَا لِلظّٰلِمِيْنَ نَارًا ۙ اَحَاطَ بِهِمْ سُرَادِقُهَا ۚ وَاِنْ يَّسْتَغِيْثُوْا يُغَاثُوْا بِمَاۤءٍ كَالْمُهْلِ يَشْوِي الْوُجُوْهَ ۚ

القبله

How dreadful the drink! How uncomfortable a couch to recline on!

30. As to those who believe and work righteousness, verily We shall not suffer to perish the reward of any who do a (single) righteous deed.

31. For them will be Gardens of Eternity; beneath them rivers will flow; they will be adorned therein with bracelets of gold, and they will wear green garments of fine silk and heavy brocade: they will recline therein on raised thrones. How good the recompense! How beautiful a couch to recline on!

32. Set forth to them the parable of two men: for one of them We provided two gardens of grape-vines and surrounded them with date palms; in between the two We placed corn-fields.

33. Each of those gardens brought forth its produce, and did not fail in the least therein: in the midst of them We caused a river to flow.

34. (Abundant) was the produce this man had : he said to his companion, in the course of a mutual argument: "I have more wealth than you, and more honour and power in (my following of) men."

35. He went into his garden in a state (of mind) unjust to his soul: he said, "I deem not that this will ever perish.

36. "Nor do I deem that the Hour (of Judgment) will (ever) come: even if I am brought back to my Lord, I shall surely find (there) something better in exchange."

37. His companion said to him, in the course of the argument with him: "Do you deny Him Who created you out of

dust, then out of a sperm-drop,
then fashioned you into a man?

تُرَابٍ ثُمَّ مِنْ نُّطْفَةٍ ثُمَّ

سَوّٰىكَ رَجُلًا ۚ

38. "But (I think) for my part
that He is Allah, my Lord, and
none shall I associate with my
Lord.

لٰكِنَّا۠ هُوَ اللّٰهُ رَبِّيْ وَلَاۤ اُشْرِكُ

بِرَبِّيْۤ اَحَدًا ۞

39. "Why did you not, as you
went into your garden, say:
'Allah's Will (be done)! There is
no power but with Allah!' If you
see me less than you in wealth
and sons,

وَلَوْلَاۤ اِذْ دَخَلْتَ جَنَّتَكَ قُلْتَ

مَا شَاۤءَ اللّٰهُ ۙ لَا قُوَّةَ اِلَّا بِاللّٰهِ ۚ

اِنْ تَرَنِ اَنَا اَقَلَّ مِنْكَ مَالًا

وَّوَلَدًا ۚ

40. "It may be that my Lord
will give me something better
than your garden, and that He
will send on your garden
thunderbolts (by way of
reckoning) from heaven,
making it (but) slippery sand!-

فَعَسٰى رَبِّيْۤ اَنْ يُّؤْتِيَنِ خَيْرًا

مِّنْ جَنَّتِكَ وَيُرْسِلَ عَلَيْهَا

حُسْبَانًا مِّنَ السَّمَاۤءِ فَتُصْبِحَ

صَعِيْدًا زَلَقًا ۚ

41. "Or the water of the garden
will run off underground so that
you will never be able to find it."

اَوْ يُصْبِحَ مَاۤؤُهَا غَوْرًا فَلَنْ

تَسْتَطِيْعَ لَهٗ طَلَبًا ۞

42. So his fruits (and enjoyment) were encompassed (with
ruin), and he remained twisting
and turning his hands over what
he had spent on his property,
which had (now) tumbled to
pieces to its very foundations,
and he could only say, "Woe is
me! Would I had never ascribed
partners to my Lord and
Cherisher!"

وَاُحِيْطَ بِثَمَرِهٖ فَاَصْبَحَ يُقَلِّبُ

كَفَّيْهِ عَلٰى مَاۤ اَنْفَقَ فِيْهَا

وَهِيَ خَاوِيَةٌ عَلٰى عُرُوْشِهَا

وَيَقُوْلُ يٰلَيْتَنِيْ لَمْ اُشْرِكْ

بِرَبِّيْۤ اَحَدًا ۞

43. Nor had he numbers to
help him against Allah, nor was
he able to deliver himself.

وَلَمْ تَكُنْ لَّهٗ فِئَةٌ

يَّنْصُرُوْنَهٗ مِنْ دُوْنِ اللّٰهِ

وَمَا كَانَ مُنْتَصِرًا ۞

44. There, the (only) protection comes from Allah, the True
One. He is the Best to reward,
and the Best to give success.

هُنَالِكَ الْوَلَايَةُ لِلّٰهِ الْحَقِّ ۚ هُوَ

خَيْرٌ ثَوَابًا وَّخَيْرٌ عُقْبًا ۞

45. Set forth to them the
similitude of the life of this
world: It is like the rain which
We send down from the skies:

وَاضْرِبْ لَهُمْ مَّثَلَ الْحَيٰوةِ الدُّنْيَا

كَمَاۤءٍ اَنْزَلْنٰهُ مِنَ السَّمَاۤءِ

the earth's vegetation absorbs it,
but soon it becomes dry stubble,
which the winds do scatter: it is
(only) Allah Who prevails over
all things.

46. Wealth and sons are
allurements of the life of this
world: but the things that
endure, Good Deeds, are best in
the sight of your Lord, as
rewards, and best as (the
foundation for) hopes.

47. One Day We shall remove
the mountains, and you will see
the earth as a level stretch, and
We shall gather them, all
together, nor shall We leave out
any one of them.

48. And they will be mar-
shalled before your Lord in
ranks, (with the announcement),
"Now you have come to Us
(bare) as We created you first:
yes, you thought We shall not
fulfil the appointment made to
you to meet (Us)!":

49. And the Book (of Deeds)
will be placed (before you); and
you will see the sinful in great
terror because of what is
(recorded) therein; they will
say, "Ah! woe to us! what a
Book is this! It leaves out
nothing small or great, but takes
account thereof!" They will find
all that they did, placed before
them: and not one will your
Lord treat with injustice.

50. Behold! We said to the
angels, "Bow down to Adam":
they bowed down except Iblis.
He was one of the Jinns, and he
broke the Command of his
Lord. Will you then take him
and his progeny as protectors
rather than Me? And they are
enemies to you! Evil would be
the exchange for the wrong-
doers!

51. I called them not to
witness the creation of the
heavens and the earth, nor
(even) their own creation: nor

is it for Me to take as helpers such as lead (men) astray!

52. One Day He will say, "Call on those whom you thought to be My partners," and they will call on them, but they will not listen to them; and We shall make for them a place of common perdition.

53. And the Sinful shall see the fire and apprehend that they have to fall therein: no means will they find to turn away therefrom.

54. We have explained in detail in this Qur'an, for the benefit of mankind, every kind of similitude: but man is, in most things, contentious.

55. And what is there to keep back men from believing, now that guidance has come to them, nor from praying for forgiveness from their Lord, but that (they ask that) the ways of the ancients be repeated with them, or the Wrath be brought to them face to face?

56. We only send the Messengers to give glad tidings and to give warning but the Unbelievers dispute with vain argument, in order therewith to weaken the Truth, and they treat My Signs as a jest as also the fact that they are warned.

57. And who does more wrong than one who is reminded of the Signs of his Lord, but turns away from them, forgetting the (deeds) which his hands have sent forth? Verily We have set veils over their hearts lest they should understand this, and over their ears, deafness. If you call them to guidance, even then they will never accept guidance.

كُنتُ مُتَّخِذَ الْمُضِلِّينَ عَضُدًا ۞

وَيَوْمَ يَقُولُ نَادُوا شُرَكَآءِیَ الَّذِينَ زَعَمْتُمْ فَدَعَوْهُمْ فَلَمْ يَسْتَجِيبُوا لَهُمْ وَجَعَلْنَا بَيْنَهُمْ مَّوْبِقًا ۞

وَرَاَ الْمُجْرِمُونَ النَّارَ فَظَنُّوْا اَنَّهُمْ مُّوَاقِعُوهَا وَلَمْ يَجِدُوا عَنْهَا مَصْرِفًا ۞

وَلَقَدْ صَرَّفْنَا فِي هٰذَا الْقُرْاٰنِ لِلنَّاسِ مِنْ كُلِّ مَثَلٍ ۚ وَكَانَ الْاِنْسَانُ اَكْثَرَ شَيْءٍ جَدَلًا ۞

وَمَا مَنَعَ النَّاسَ اَنْ يُّؤْمِنُوْا اِذْ جَآءَهُمُ الْهُدٰى وَيَسْتَغْفِرُوا رَبَّهُمْ اِلَّا اَنْ تَأْتِيَهُمْ سُنَّةُ الْاَوَّلِينَ اَوْ يَأْتِيَهُمُ الْعَذَابُ قُبُلًا ۞

وَمَا نُرْسِلُ الْمُرْسَلِينَ اِلَّا مُبَشِّرِينَ وَمُنْذِرِينَ ۚ وَيُجَادِلُ الَّذِينَ كَفَرُوا بِالْبَاطِلِ لِيُدْحِضُوا بِهِ الْحَقَّ وَاتَّخَذُوا اٰيٰتِي وَمَا اُنْذِرُوا هُزُوًا ۞

وَمَنْ اَظْلَمُ مِمَّنْ ذُكِّرَ بِاٰيٰتِ رَبِّهِ فَاَعْرَضَ عَنْهَا وَنَسِيَ مَا قَدَّمَتْ يَدَاهُ ۚ اِنَّا جَعَلْنَا عَلٰى قُلُوبِهِمْ اَكِنَّةً اَنْ يَّفْقَهُوهُ وَفِيْ اٰذَانِهِمْ وَقْرًا ۚ وَاِنْ تَدْعُهُمْ اِلَى الْهُدٰى فَلَنْ يَّهْتَدُوا اِذًا اَبَدًا ۞

ع
١٩

58. But your Lord is Most forgiving, full of Mercy. If He were to call them (at once) to account for what they have earned, then surely He would have hastened their punishment: but they have their appointed time, beyond which they will find no refuge.

59. Such were the populations We destroyed when they committed iniquities; but We fixed an appointed time for their destruction.

60. Behold, Moses said to his attendant, "I will not give up until I reach the junction of the two seas or (until) I spend years and years in travel."

61. But when they reached the Junction, they forgot (about) their Fish, which took its course through the sea (straight) as in a tunnel.

62. When they had passed on (some distance), Moses said to his attendant: "Bring us our early meal; truly we have suffered much fatigue at this (stage of) our journey."

63. He replied: "Did you see (what happened) when we betook ourselves to the rock? I indeed forgot (about) the Fish: none but Satan made me forget to tell (you) about it: it took its course through the sea in a marvellous way!"

64. Moses said: "That was what we were seeking after:" so they went back on their footsteps, following (the path they had come).

65. So they found one of Our servants, on whom We had bestowed Mercy from Ourselves and whom We had taught knowledge from Our Own Presence.

66. Moses said to him: "May I follow you, on the footing that you teach me something of the (Higher) Truth which you have been taught?"

67. (The other) said: "Verily you will not be able to have patience with me!"

68. "And how can you have patience about things about which your understanding is not complete?"

69. Moses said: "You will find me, if Allah so will, (truly) patient: nor shall I disobey you in any matter."

70. The other said: "If then you would follow me, ask me no questions about anything until I myself speak to you concerning it."

71. So they both proceeded: until, when they were in the boat, he scuttled it. Said Moses: "Have you scuttled it in order to drown those in it? Truly a strange thing you have done!"

72. He answered: "Did I not tell you that you can have no patience with me?"

73. Moses said: "Do not rebuke me for forgetting, nor grieve me by raising difficulties in my case."

74. Then they proceeded: until, when they met a young man, he slew him. Moses said: "Have you slain an innocent person who had slain none? Truly a foul (unheard-of) thing you have done!"

75. He answered: "Did I not tell you that you can have no patience with me?"

76. (Moses) said: "If ever I ask you about anything after this, do not keep me in your company: then you would have received (full) excuse from my side."

77. Then they proceeded: until, when they came to the inhabitants of a town, they asked them for food, but they refused them hospitality. They found there a wall on the point of falling down, but he set it up straight. (Moses) said:

قَالَ إِنَّكَ لَنْ تَسْتَطِيعَ مَعِيَ صَبْرًا

وَكَيْفَ تَصْبِرُ عَلَى مَا لَمْ تُحِطْ بِهِ خُبْرًا ۞

قَالَ سَتَجِدُنِي إِنْ شَاءَ اللَّهُ صَابِرًا وَلَا أَعْصِي لَكَ أَمْرًا ۞

قَالَ فَإِنِ اتَّبَعْتَنِي فَلَا تَسْأَلْنِي عَنْ شَيْءٍ حَتَّى أُحْدِثَ لَكَ مِنْهُ ذِكْرًا ۞

فَانْطَلَقَا ۞ حَتَّى إِذَا رَكِبَا فِي السَّفِينَةِ خَرَقَهَا ۚ قَالَ أَخَرَقْتَهَا لِتُغْرِقَ أَهْلَهَا ۚ لَقَدْ جِئْتَ شَيْئًا إِمْرًا ۞

قَالَ أَلَمْ أَقُلْ إِنَّكَ لَنْ تَسْتَطِيعَ مَعِيَ صَبْرًا ۞

قَالَ لَا تُؤَاخِذْنِي بِمَا نَسِيتُ وَلَا تُرْهِقْنِي مِنْ أَمْرِي عُسْرًا ۞

فَانْطَلَقَا ۞ حَتَّى إِذَا لَقِيَا غُلَامًا فَقَتَلَهُ ۙ قَالَ أَقَتَلْتَ نَفْسًا زَكِيَّةً بِغَيْرِ نَفْسٍ ۚ لَقَدْ جِئْتَ شَيْئًا نُكْرًا ۞

قَالَ أَلَمْ أَقُلْ لَكَ إِنَّكَ لَنْ تَسْتَطِيعَ مَعِيَ صَبْرًا ۞

قَالَ إِنْ سَأَلْتُكَ عَنْ شَيْءٍ بَعْدَهَا فَلَا تُصَاحِبْنِي ۖ قَدْ بَلَغْتَ مِنْ لَدُنِّي عُذْرًا ۞

فَانْطَلَقَا ۞ حَتَّى إِذَا أَتَيَا أَهْلَ قَرْيَةٍ اسْتَطْعَمَا أَهْلَهَا فَأَبَوْا أَنْ يُضَيِّفُوهُمَا فَوَجَدَا فِيهَا جِدَارًا يُرِيدُ أَنْ يَنْقَضَّ فَأَقَامَهُ ۖ قَالَ

"If you had wished, surely you could have exacted some recompense for it!"

78. He answered: "This is the parting between me and you: now will I tell you the interpretation of (those things) over which you were unable to hold patience.

79. "As for the boat, it belonged to certain men in dire want: they plied on the water: I but wished to render it unserviceable, for there was after them a certain king who seized on every boat by force.

80. "As for the youth, his parents were people of Faith, and we feared that he would grieve them by obstinate rebellion and ingratitude (to Allah).

81. "So we desired that their Lord would give them in exchange (a son) better in purity (of conduct) and closer in affection.

82. "As for the wall, it belonged to two youths, orphans, in the Town; there was, beneath it, a buried treasure, to which they were entitled: their father had been a righteous man: so your Lord desired that they should attain their age of full strength and get out their treasure - a mercy (and favour) from your Lord. I did it not of my own accord. Such is the interpretation of (those things) over which you were unable to hold patience."

83. They ask you concerning Zul-qarnain. Say, "I will rehearse to you something of his story."

84. Verily We established his power on earth, and We gave him the ways and the means to all ends.

85. One (such) way he followed,

86. Until, when he reached the setting of the sun, he found it set in a spring of murky water: near it he found

a People: We said: "O Zul-qarnain! (you have authority,) either to punish them, or to treat them with kindness."

87. He said: "Whoever does wrong, we shall punish him; then he shall be sent back to his Lord; and He will punish him with a punishment unheard-of (before).

88. "But whoever believes, and works righteousness,-he shall have a goodly reward, and his task will be easy as We order it by our command."

89. Then he followed (another) way,

90. Until, when he came to the rising of the sun, he found it rising on a people for whom We had provided no covering protection against the sun.

91. (He left them) as they were: We completely understood what was before him.

92. Then he followed (another) way,

93. Until, when he reached (a tract) between two mountains, he found, beneath them, a people who scarcely understood a word.

94. They said: "O Zul-qarnain! the Gog and Magog (People) do great mischief on earth: shall we then render you tribute in order that you might erect a barrier between us and them?

95. He said: "(The power) in which my Lord has established me is better (than tribute): help me therefore with strength (and labor): I will erect a strong barrier between you and them:

96. "Bring me blocks of iron." At length, when he had filled up the space between the two steep mountain-sides, he said, "Blow (with your bellows)"

then, when he had made it (red) as fire, he said: "Bring me, that I may pour over it, molten lead."

97. Thus they were made powerless to scale it or to dig through it.

98. He said: "This is a mercy from my Lord: but when the promise of my Lord comes to pass, He will make it into dust; and the promise of my Lord is true."

99. On that day We shall leave them to surge like waves on one another: the trumpet will be blown, and We shall collect them all together.

100. And We shall present Hell that day for Unbelievers to see, all spread out,-

101. (Unbelievers) whose eyes had been under a veil from remembrance of Me, and who had been unable even to hear.

102. Do the Unbelievers think that they can take My servants as protectors besides Me? Verily We have prepared Hell for the Unbelievers for (their) entertainment.

103. Say: "Shall we tell you of those who lose most in respect of their deeds?-

104. "Those whose efforts have been wasted in this life, while they thought that they were acquiring good by their works?"

105. They are those who deny the Signs of their Lord and the fact of their having to meet Him (in the Hereafter): vain will be their works, nor shall We, on the Day of Judgment, give them any weight.

106. That is their reward, Hell, because they rejected Faith, and took My Signs and My Messengers by way of jest.

SÛRAH-19
MARYAM
(INTRODUCTION)

The spiritual growth of man as an individual soul having been explained in S. 17 as beginning with the first principles of moral conduct and in S. 18 as being dependent upon our realisation of the brevity and mystery of this life and the true use of power as in the story of Zul-qarnain, we now pass on to the story of individual Messengers of Allah in their personal relations with their environment,-Yahya with his father Zakariya, Jesus with his mother Mary, Abraham with his unbelieving father, Moses with his brother Aaron, Isma'il with his family, and Idris in the high station to which he was called, seeing how these great ones fitted into the scheme of life, man is condemned for his want of faith, or for degrading his faith to superstition, and warned of the Hereafter.

In chronology, it was revealed before the first resort of the batch of Muslims to Abyssinia, say seven years before the Hijrat.

107. As to those who believe and work righteous deeds, they have, for their entertainment, the Gardens of Paradise,

108. Wherein they shall dwell (for ever), no change will they wish for from them.

109. Say: "If the ocean were ink (wherewith to write out) the words of my Lord, sooner would the ocean be exhausted than would the words of my Lord, even if we added another ocean like it, for its aid."

110. Say: "I am but a man like yourselves, (but) the inspiration has come to me, that your God is One God: whoever expects to meet his Lord, let him work righteousness, and, in the worship of his Lord, admit no one as partner.

19. Mary
In the name of Allah. Most Gracious, Most Merciful.

1. Kaf. Ha. Ya. 'Ain. Ṣad.

2. (This is) a recital of the Mercy of your Lord to His servant Zakariya.

3. Behold! he cried to his Lord in secret,

4. Praying: "O my Lord! infirm indeed are my bones, and the hair of my head glistens with grey: but never am I unblest, O my Lord, in my prayer to You!

5. "Now I fear (what) my relatives (and colleagues) (will do) after me: but my wife is barren: so give me an heir as from Yourself,-

6. "(One that) will (truly) represent me, and represent the posterity of Jacob; and make him, O my Lord! one with whom You are well-pleased!"

7. (His prayer was answered): "O Zakariya! We give you good news of a son: his name shall be Yahya: on none by that name have We conferred distinction before."

8. He said: "O my Lord! How shall I have a son, when

اِنَّ الَّذِيْنَ اٰمَنُوْا وَعَمِلُوا الصّٰلِحٰتِ

كَانَتْ لَهُمْ جَنّٰتُ الْفِرْدَوْسِ نُزُلًا ۞

خٰلِدِيْنَ فِيْهَا لَا يَبْغُوْنَ عَنْهَا حِوَلًا ۞

قُلْ لَّوْ كَانَ الْبَحْرُ مِدَادًا لِّكَلِمٰتِ رَبِّيْ

لَنَفِدَ الْبَحْرُ قَبْلَ اَنْ تَنْفَدَ كَلِمٰتُ

رَبِّيْ وَلَوْ جِئْنَا بِمِثْلِهٖ مَدَدًا ۞

قُلْ اِنَّمَآ اَنَا بَشَرٌ مِّثْلُكُمْ يُوْحٰى اِلَيَّ

اَنَّمَآ اِلٰهُكُمْ اِلٰهٌ وَّاحِدٌ ۚ فَمَنْ كَانَ يَرْجُوْا

لِقَآءَ رَبِّهٖ فَلْيَعْمَلْ عَمَلًا صَالِحًا وَّلَا

يُشْرِكْ بِعِبَادَةِ رَبِّهٖٓ اَحَدًا ۞

(١٩) سُوْرَةُ مَرْيَمَ مَكِّيَّةٌ (٩٨)

بِسْمِ اللّٰهِ الرَّحْمٰنِ الرَّحِيْمِ

كٓهٰيٰعٓصٓ ۞

ذِكْرُ رَحْمَتِ رَبِّكَ عَبْدَهٗ زَكَرِيَّا ۞

اِذْ نَادٰى رَبَّهٗ نِدَآءً خَفِيًّا ۞

قَالَ رَبِّ اِنِّيْ وَهَنَ الْعَظْمُ مِنِّيْ

وَاشْتَعَلَ الرَّأْسُ شَيْبًا وَّلَمْ اَكُنْ

بِدُعَآئِكَ رَبِّ شَقِيًّا ۞

وَاِنِّيْ خِفْتُ الْمَوَالِيَ مِنْ وَّرَآءِيْ

وَكَانَتِ امْرَاَتِيْ عَاقِرًا فَهَبْ لِيْ

مِنْ لَّدُنْكَ وَلِيًّا ۞

يَّرِثُنِيْ وَيَرِثُ مِنْ اٰلِ يَعْقُوْبَ ۖ

وَاجْعَلْهُ رَبِّ رَضِيًّا ۞

يٰزَكَرِيَّآ اِنَّا نُبَشِّرُكَ بِغُلٰمِ اسْمُهٗ يَحْيٰى ۙ

لَمْ نَجْعَلْ لَّهٗ مِنْ قَبْلُ سَمِيًّا ۞

قَالَ رَبِّ اَنّٰى يَكُوْنُ لِيْ غُلٰمٌ وَّ

my wife is barren and I have grown quite decrepit from old age?"

9.   He said: "So (it will be) your Lord says, 'That is easy for Me: I indeed created you before, when you had been nothing!'"

10.   (Zakariya) said: "O my Lord! give me a Sign." "your Sign," was the answer, "shall be that you shall speak to no man for three nights, although you are not dumb."

11.   So Zakariya came out to his people from his chamber: he told them by signs to celebrate Allah's praises in the morning and in the evening.

12.   (To his son came the command): "O Yahya! take hold of the Book with might," and We gave him Wisdom even as a youth,

13.   And piety (for all creatures) as from Us, and purity: he was devout,

14.   And kind to his parents, and he was not overbearing or rebellious.

15.   So Peace on him the day he was born, the day that he dies, and the day that he will be raised up to life (again)!

16.   Relate in the Book (the story of) Mary, when she withdrew from her family to a place in the East.

17.   She placed a screen (to screen herself) from them; then We sent to her Our angel, and he appeared before her as a man in all respects.

18.   She said: "I seek refuge from you to (Allah) Most Gracious: (come not near) if you fear Allah."

19.   He said: "Nay, I am only a messenger from your Lord, (to announce) to you the gift of a holy son."

20.   She said: "How shall I have a son, seeing that no man has touched me, and I am not unchaste?"

21. He said: "So (it will be):
your Lord says 'That is easy for
Me: and (We wish) to appoint
him as a Sign unto men and a
Mercy from Us':It is a matter
(so) decreed."

22. So she conceived him, and
she retired with him to a remote
place.

23. And the pains of childbirth
drove her to the trunk of a palm-
tree: She cried (in her anguish):
"Ah! would that I had died before
this! would that I had been a
thing forgotten and out of sight!"

24. But (a voice) cried to her
from beneath the (palm-tree):
"Do not grieve! for your Lord
has provided a rivulet beneath
you;

25. "And shake toward
yourself the trunk of the palm-
tree: it will let fall fresh ripe
dates upon you.

26. "So eat and drink and cool
(your) eye. And if you see any
man, say, 'I have vowed a fast to
(Allah) Most Gracious, and this
day I will not enter into talk with
any human being'"

27. At length she brought the
(babe) to her people, carrying
him (in her arms). They said: "O
Mary! truly an amazing thing
you have brought!

28. "O sister of Aaron! your
father was not a man of evil, nor
your mother an unchaste woman
!"

29. But she pointed to the
babe. They said: "How can we
talk to one who is a child in the
cradle?"

30. He said: "I am indeed a
servant of Allah: He has given
me Revelation and made me a
prophet;

31. "And He has made me
blessed wheresoever I be, and
has enjoined on me Prayer and
Charity as long as I live;

قَالَ كَذٰلِكِ ۚ قَالَ رَبُّكِ هُوَ عَلَيَّ
هَيِّنٌ ۚ وَلِنَجْعَلَهٗ اٰيَةً لِّلنَّاسِ وَرَحْمَةً
مِّنَّا ۚ وَكَانَ اَمْرًا مَّقْضِيًّا ۞

فَحَمَلَتْهُ فَانْتَبَذَتْ بِهٖ مَكَانًا قَصِيًّا ۞

فَاَجَآءَهَا الْمَخَاضُ اِلٰى جِذْعِ النَّخْلَةِ ۚ
قَالَتْ يٰلَيْتَنِيْ مِتُّ قَبْلَ هٰذَا وَ
كُنْتُ نَسْيًا مَّنْسِيًّا ۞

فَنَادٰىهَا مِنْ تَحْتِهَآ اَلَّا تَحْزَنِيْ قَدْ
جَعَلَ رَبُّكِ تَحْتَكِ سَرِيًّا ۞

وَهُزِّيْ اِلَيْكِ بِجِذْعِ النَّخْلَةِ تُسٰقِطْ
عَلَيْكِ رُطَبًا جَنِيًّا ۞

فَكُلِيْ وَاشْرَبِيْ وَقَرِّيْ عَيْنًا ۚ فَاِمَّا
تَرَيِنَّ مِنَ الْبَشَرِ اَحَدًا ۙ فَقُوْلِيْٓ اِنِّيْ
نَذَرْتُ لِلرَّحْمٰنِ صَوْمًا فَلَنْ اُكَلِّمَ
الْيَوْمَ اِنْسِيًّا ۞

فَاَتَتْ بِهٖ قَوْمَهَا تَحْمِلُهٗ ۚ قَالُوْا
يٰمَرْيَمُ لَقَدْ جِئْتِ شَيْئًا فَرِيًّا ۞

يٰٓاُخْتَ هٰرُوْنَ مَا كَانَ اَبُوْكِ امْرَاَ
سَوْءٍ وَّمَا كَانَتْ اُمُّكِ بَغِيًّا ۚ

فَاَشَارَتْ اِلَيْهِ ۚ قَالُوْا كَيْفَ نُكَلِّمُ
مَنْ كَانَ فِى الْمَهْدِ صَبِيًّا ۞

قَالَ اِنِّيْ عَبْدُ اللّٰهِ ۚ اٰتٰىنِيَ الْكِتٰبَ وَ
جَعَلَنِيْ نَبِيًّا ۞

وَّجَعَلَنِيْ مُبٰرَكًا اَيْنَ مَا كُنْتُ ۖ وَ
اَوْصٰنِيْ بِالصَّلٰوةِ وَالزَّكٰوةِ مَا
دُمْتُ حَيًّا ۞

32. "(He) has made me kind to my mother, and not overbearing or miserable;

وَبَرَّۢا بِوَالِدَتِیۡ وَلَمۡ یَجۡعَلۡنِیۡ جَبَّارًا شَقِیًّا ۟

33. "So peace is on me the day I was born, the day that I die, and the day that I shall be raised up to life (again)"!

وَالسَّلَامُ عَلَیَّ یَوۡمَ وُلِدۡتُّ وَیَوۡمَ اَمُوۡتُ وَیَوۡمَ اُبۡعَثُ حَیًّا ۟

34. Such (was) Jesus the son of Mary: (it is) a statement of truth, about which they (vainly) dispute.

ذٰلِكَ عِیۡسَی ابۡنُ مَرۡیَمَ ۚ قَوۡلَ الۡحَقِّ الَّذِیۡ فِیۡهِ یَمۡتَرُوۡنَ ۟

35. It is not befitting to (the majesty of) Allah that He should beget a son. Glory be to Him! when He determines a matter, He only says to it, "Be", and it is.

مَا كَانَ لِلّٰهِ اَنۡ یَّتَّخِذَ مِنۡ وَّلَدٍ ۙ سُبۡحٰنَهٗ ؕ اِذَا قَضٰۤی اَمۡرًا فَاِنَّمَا یَقُوۡلُ لَهٗ كُنۡ فَیَكُوۡنُ ؕ

36. Verily Allah is my Lord and your Lord: you, therefore serve Him: this is a Way that is straight.

وَاِنَّ اللّٰهَ رَبِّیۡ وَرَبُّكُمۡ فَاعۡبُدُوۡهُ ؕ هٰذَا صِرَاطٌ مُّسۡتَقِیۡمٌ ۟

37. But the sects differ among themselves: and woe to the Unbelievers because of the (coming) Judgment of a momentous Day!

فَاخۡتَلَفَ الۡاَحۡزَابُ مِنۢ بَیۡنِهِمۡ ۚ فَوَیۡلٌ لِّلَّذِیۡنَ كَفَرُوۡا مِنۡ مَّشۡهَدِ یَوۡمٍ عَظِیۡمٍ ۟

38. How plainly will they see and hear, the Day that they will appear before Us! but the unjust today are in manifest error!

اَسۡمِعۡ بِهِمۡ وَاَبۡصِرۡ ۙ یَوۡمَ یَاۡتُوۡنَنَا لٰكِنِ الظّٰلِمُوۡنَ الۡیَوۡمَ فِیۡ ضَلٰلٍ مُّبِیۡنٍ ۟

39. But warn them of the Day of Distress, when the matter will be determined: for (behold,) they are negligent and they do not believe!

وَاَنۡذِرۡهُمۡ یَوۡمَ الۡحَسۡرَةِ اِذۡ قُضِیَ الۡاَمۡرُ ۘ وَهُمۡ فِیۡ غَفۡلَةٍ وَّهُمۡ لَا یُؤۡمِنُوۡنَ ۟

40. It is We Who will inherit the earth, and all beings thereon: to Us will they all be returned.

اِنَّا نَحۡنُ نَرِثُ الۡاَرۡضَ وَمَنۡ عَلَیۡهَا وَاِلَیۡنَا یُرۡجَعُوۡنَ ۟

41. (Also) mention in the Book (the story of) Abraham: He was a man of Truth, a prophet.

وَاذۡكُرۡ فِی الۡكِتٰبِ اِبۡرٰهِیۡمَ ۚ اِنَّهٗ كَانَ صِدِّیۡقًا نَّبِیًّا ۟

42. Behold, he said to his father: "O my father! why worship that which does not hear and does not see, and can profit you nothing?

اِذۡ قَالَ لِاَبِیۡهِ یٰۤاَبَتِ لِمَ تَعۡبُدُ مَا لَا یَسۡمَعُ وَلَا یُبۡصِرُ وَلَا یُغۡنِیۡ عَنۡكَ شَیۡئًا ۟

43. "O my father! to me has come knowledge which has not reached you: so follow me: I will guide you to a Way that is even and straight.

یٰۤاَبَتِ اِنِّیۡ قَدۡ جَآءَنِیۡ مِنَ الۡعِلۡمِ مَا لَمۡ یَاۡتِكَ فَاتَّبِعۡنِیۤ اَهۡدِكَ صِرَاطًا سَوِیًّا ۟

44. "O my father! do not serve Satan: for Satan is a rebel against (Allah) Most Gracious.

يَا أَبَتِ لَا تَعْبُدِ الشَّيْطَنَ ۖ إِنَّ الشَّيْطَنَ كَانَ لِلرَّحْمَنِ عَصِيًّا ۝

45. "O my father! I fear lest a Penalty afflict you from (Allah) Most Gracious, so that you become a friend to Satan."

يَا أَبَتِ إِنِّي أَخَافُ أَنْ يَمَسَّكَ عَذَابٌ مِنَ الرَّحْمَنِ فَتَكُونَ لِلشَّيْطَنِ وَلِيًّا ۝

46. (The father) replied: "Do you hate my gods, O Abraham? If you do not forbear, I will indeed stone you: now get away from me for a good long while!"

قَالَ أَرَاغِبٌ أَنْتَ عَنْ آلِهَتِي يَا إِبْرَاهِيمُ ۖ لَئِنْ لَمْ تَنْتَهِ لَأَرْجُمَنَّكَ وَاهْجُرْنِي مَلِيًّا ۝

47. Abraham said: "Peace be on you: I will pray to my Lord for your forgiveness: for He is to me Most Gracious.

قَالَ سَلَامٌ عَلَيْكَ ۖ سَأَسْتَغْفِرُ لَكَ رَبِّي ۖ إِنَّهُ كَانَ بِي حَفِيًّا ۝

48. "And I will turn away from you (all) and from those whom you invoke besides Allah: I will call on my Lord: perhaps, by my prayer to my Lord, I shall be not unblest."

وَأَعْتَزِلُكُمْ وَمَا تَدْعُونَ مِنْ دُونِ اللَّهِ وَأَدْعُو رَبِّي عَسَى أَلَّا أَكُونَ بِدُعَاءِ رَبِّي شَقِيًّا ۝

49. When he had turned away from them and from those whom they worshipped besides Allah, We bestowed on him Isaac and Jacob, and each one of them We made a prophet.

فَلَمَّا اعْتَزَلَهُمْ وَمَا يَعْبُدُونَ مِنْ دُونِ اللَّهِ وَهَبْنَا لَهُ إِسْحَقَ وَيَعْقُوبَ ۖ وَكُلًّا جَعَلْنَا نَبِيًّا ۝

50. And We bestowed of Our Mercy on them, and We granted them lofty honour on the tongue of truth.

وَوَهَبْنَا لَهُمْ مِنْ رَحْمَتِنَا وَجَعَلْنَا لَهُمْ لِسَانَ صِدْقٍ عَلِيًّا ۝

51. Also mention in the Book (the story of) Moses: for he was specially chosen, and he was a Messenger (and) a prophet.

وَاذْكُرْ فِي الْكِتَابِ مُوسَى ۚ إِنَّهُ كَانَ مُخْلَصًا وَكَانَ رَسُولًا نَبِيًّا ۝

52. And We called him from the right side of Mount (Sinai), and made him draw near to Us, for mystic (converse).

وَنَادَيْنَاهُ مِنْ جَانِبِ الطُّورِ الْأَيْمَنِ وَقَرَّبْنَاهُ نَجِيًّا ۝

53. And, out of Our Mercy, We gave him his brother Aaron, (also) a prophet.

وَوَهَبْنَا لَهُ مِنْ رَحْمَتِنَا أَخَاهُ هَارُونَ نَبِيًّا ۝

54. Also mention in the Book (the story of) Isma'il: he was (strictly) true to what he promised, and he was a Messenger (and) a prophet.

وَاذْكُرْ فِي الْكِتَابِ إِسْمَاعِيلَ ۚ إِنَّهُ كَانَ صَادِقَ الْوَعْدِ وَكَانَ رَسُولًا نَبِيًّا ۝

55. He used to enjoin on his people Prayer and

وَكَانَ يَأْمُرُ أَهْلَهُ بِالصَّلَوةِ وَ

Charity, and he was most acceptable in the sight of his Lord.

56. Also mention in the Book
the case of Idris: he was a man of
truth (and sincerity), (and) a
prophet:

57. And We raised him to a
lofty station.

58. Those were some of the
prophets on whom Allah
bestowed His Grace,- of the
posterity of Adam, and of those
whom We carried (in the Ark)
with Noah, and of the posterity
of Abraham and Israel of those
whom We guided and chose.
Whenever the Signs of (Allah)
Most Gracious were rehearsed
to them, they would fall down in
prostrate adoration and in tears.

59. But after them there
followed a posterity who missed
prayers and followed after lusts
soon, then, they will face
Destruction,-

60. Except those who repent
and believe, and work righteousness: for these will enter
the Garden and will not be
wronged in the least,-

61. Gardens of Eternity, those
which (Allah) Most Gracious
has promised to His servants in
the Unseen: for His promise
must (necessarily) come to pass.

62. They will not hear any
vain discourse there, but only
salutations of Peace: and therein
they will have their sustenance,
morning and evening.

63. Such is the Garden which
We give as an inheritance to
those of Our servants who guard
against evil.

64. (The angels say:) "We do
not descend but by command of
your Lord: to Him belongs what
is before us and what is behind
us, and what is between: and
your Lord never forgets,-

65. "Lord of the heavens and
of the earth, and of all that is
between them;

الزَّكٰوةَ ۚ وَكَانَ عِنْدَ رَبِّهٖ مَرْضِيًّا ۞

وَاذْكُرْ فِى الْكِتٰبِ اِدْرِيْسَ ۫ اِنَّهٗ

كَانَ صِدِّيْقًا نَّبِيًّا ۙ۞

وَّرَفَعْنٰهُ مَكَانًا عَلِيًّا ۞

اُولٰٓئِكَ الَّذِيْنَ اَنْعَمَ اللّٰهُ عَلَيْهِمْ مِّنَ

النَّبِيّٖنَ مِنْ ذُرِّيَّةِ اٰدَمَ ۖ وَمِمَّنْ

حَمَلْنَا مَعَ نُوْحٍ ۖ وَّمِنْ ذُرِّيَّةِ

اِبْرٰهِيْمَ وَاِسْرَآءِيْلَ ۖ وَمِمَّنْ هَدَيْنَا

وَاجْتَبَيْنَا ۚ اِذَا تُتْلٰى عَلَيْهِمْ اٰيٰتُ

الرَّحْمٰنِ خَرُّوْا سُجَّدًا وَّبُكِيًّا ۩۞

فَخَلَفَ مِنْ بَعْدِهِمْ خَلْفٌ اَضَاعُوا

الصَّلٰوةَ وَاتَّبَعُوا الشَّهَوٰتِ ۖ فَسَوْفَ

يَلْقَوْنَ غَيًّا ۙ۞

اِلَّا مَنْ تَابَ وَاٰمَنَ وَعَمِلَ صَالِحًا

فَاُولٰٓئِكَ يَدْخُلُوْنَ الْجَنَّةَ وَلَا

يُظْلَمُوْنَ شَيْئًا ۙ۞

جَنّٰتِ عَدْنِۨ الَّتِيْ وَعَدَ الرَّحْمٰنُ عِبَادَهٗ

بِالْغَيْبِ ۚ اِنَّهٗ كَانَ وَعْدُهٗ مَأْتِيًّا ۞

لَا يَسْمَعُوْنَ فِيْهَا لَغْوًا اِلَّا سَلٰمًا ۚ

وَلَهُمْ رِزْقُهُمْ فِيْهَا بُكْرَةً وَّعَشِيًّا ۞

تِلْكَ الْجَنَّةُ الَّتِيْ نُوْرِثُ مِنْ عِبَادِنَا

مَنْ كَانَ تَقِيًّا ۞

وَمَا نَتَنَزَّلُ اِلَّا بِاَمْرِ رَبِّكَ ۚ لَهٗ مَا

بَيْنَ اَيْدِيْنَا وَمَا خَلْفَنَا وَمَا بَيْنَ

ذٰلِكَ ۚ وَمَا كَانَ رَبُّكَ نَسِيًّا ۞

رَبُّ السَّمٰوٰتِ وَالْاَرْضِ وَمَا بَيْنَهُمَا

so worship Him, and be constant and patient in His worship: do you know of any who is worthy of the same Name as He?"

66.   Man says: "What! When I am dead, shall I then be raised up alive?"

67.   But does not man call to mind that We created him before, out of nothing?

68.   So, by your Lord, without doubt, We shall gather them together, and (also) the Evil Ones (with them); then We shall bring them forth on their knees round about Hell:

69.   Then We shall certainly drag out from every sect all those who were worst in obstinate rebellion against (Allah) Most Gracious.

70.   And certainly We know best those who are most worthy of being burned therein.

71.   Not one of you but will pass over it: this is, with your Lord, a Decree which must be accomplished.

72.   But We shall save those who guarded against evil, and We shall leave the wrong-doers therein, (humbled) to their knees.

73.   When Our Clear Signs are rehearsed to them, the Unbelievers say to those who believe, "Which of the two sides is best in point of position? which makes the best show in Council?"

74.   But how many (countless) generations before them We have destroyed, who were even better in equipment and in glitter to the eye?

75.   Say: "If any men go astray, (Allah) Most Gracious extends (the rope) to them, until, when they see the warning of Allah (being fulfilled) - either in punishment or in (the approach of) the Hour,- they will at length realise who is worst

فَٱعْبُدْهُ وَٱصْطَبِرْ لِعِبَادَتِهِۦ ۚ هَلْ تَعْلَمُ لَهُۥ سَمِيًّا ۝

وَيَقُولُ ٱلْإِنسَٰنُ أَءِذَا مَا مِتُّ لَسَوْفَ أُخْرَجُ حَيًّا ۝

أَوَلَا يَذْكُرُ ٱلْإِنسَٰنُ أَنَّا خَلَقْنَٰهُ مِن قَبْلُ وَلَمْ يَكُ شَيْـًٔا ۝

فَوَرَبِّكَ لَنَحْشُرَنَّهُمْ وَٱلشَّيَٰطِينَ ثُمَّ لَنُحْضِرَنَّهُمْ حَوْلَ جَهَنَّمَ جِثِيًّا ۝

ثُمَّ لَنَنزِعَنَّ مِن كُلِّ شِيعَةٍ أَيُّهُمْ أَشَدُّ عَلَى ٱلرَّحْمَٰنِ عِتِيًّا ۝

ثُمَّ لَنَحْنُ أَعْلَمُ بِٱلَّذِينَ هُمْ أَوْلَىٰ بِهَا صِلِيًّا ۝

وَإِن مِّنكُمْ إِلَّا وَارِدُهَا ۚ كَانَ عَلَىٰ رَبِّكَ حَتْمًا مَّقْضِيًّا ۝

ثُمَّ نُنَجِّي ٱلَّذِينَ ٱتَّقَوا۟ وَّنَذَرُ ٱلظَّٰلِمِينَ فِيهَا جِثِيًّا ۝

وَإِذَا تُتْلَىٰ عَلَيْهِمْ ءَايَٰتُنَا بَيِّنَٰتٍ قَالَ ٱلَّذِينَ كَفَرُوا۟ لِلَّذِينَ ءَامَنُوٓا۟ أَيُّ ٱلْفَرِيقَيْنِ خَيْرٌ مَّقَامًا وَّأَحْسَنُ نَدِيًّا ۝

وَكَمْ أَهْلَكْنَا قَبْلَهُم مِّن قَرْنٍ هُمْ أَحْسَنُ أَثَٰثًا وَّرِءْيًا ۝

قُلْ مَن كَانَ فِي ٱلضَّلَٰلَةِ فَلْيَمْدُدْ لَهُ ٱلرَّحْمَٰنُ مَدًّا ۚ حَتَّىٰٓ إِذَا رَأَوْا۟ مَا يُوعَدُونَ إِمَّا ٱلْعَذَابَ وَإِمَّا ٱلسَّاعَةَ فَسَيَعْلَمُونَ مَنْ هُوَ شَرٌّ

in position, and (who) weakest in forces!

76. "And Allah advances those in guidance who seek guidance: and the things that endure, Good Deeds, are best in the sight of your Lord, as rewards, and best in respect of (their) eventual returns."

77. Have you then seen the (sort of) man who rejects Our Signs, yet says: "I shall certainly be given wealth and children?"

78. Has he penetrated to the Unseen, or has he taken a contract with (Allah) Most Gracious?

79. Nay! We shall record what he says, and We shall add and add to his punishment.

80. To Us shall return all that he talks of, and he shall appear before Us bare and alone.

81. And they have taken (for worship) gods other than Allah, to give them power and glory!

82. Instead, they shall reject their worship, and become adversaries against them.

83. Don't you see that We have set the Evil Ones on against the unbelievers, to incite them with fury?

84. So make no haste against them, for We but count out to them a (limited) number (of days).

85. The day We shall gather the righteous to (Allah) Most Gracious, like a band presented before a king for honours,

86. And We shall drive the sinners to Hell, like thirsty cattle driven down to water,-

87. None shall have the power of intercession, but such a one as has received permission (or promise) from (Allah) Most Gracious.

88. They say: "(Allah) Most Gracious has begotten a son!"

89. Indeed you have put forth a thing most monstrous!

مَّكَانًا وَّاَضْعَفُ جُنْدًا ۞

وَيَزِيدُ اللّٰهُ الَّذِيْنَ اهْتَدَوْا هُدًى ۚ وَالْبٰقِيٰتُ الصّٰلِحٰتُ خَيْرٌ عِنْدَ رَبِّكَ ثَوَابًا وَّخَيْرٌ مَّرَدًّا ۞

اَفَرَءَيْتَ الَّذِيْ كَفَرَ بِاٰيٰتِنَا وَقَالَ لَاُوْتَيَنَّ مَالًا وَّوَلَدًا ۞

اَطَّلَعَ الْغَيْبَ اَمِ اتَّخَذَ عِنْدَ الرَّحْمٰنِ عَهْدًا ۞

كَلَّا ۚ سَنَكْتُبُ مَا يَقُوْلُ وَنَمُدُّ لَهٗ مِنَ الْعَذَابِ مَدًّا ۞

وَّنَرِثُهٗ مَا يَقُوْلُ وَيَاْتِيْنَا فَرْدًا ۞

وَاتَّخَذُوْا مِنْ دُوْنِ اللّٰهِ اٰلِهَةً لِّيَكُوْنُوْا لَهُمْ عِزًّا ۞

كَلَّا ۚ سَيَكْفُرُوْنَ بِعِبَادَتِهِمْ وَيَكُوْنُوْنَ عَلَيْهِمْ ضِدًّا ۞

اَلَمْ تَرَ اَنَّا اَرْسَلْنَا الشَّيٰطِيْنَ عَلَى الْكٰفِرِيْنَ تَؤُزُّهُمْ اَزًّا ۞

فَلَا تَعْجَلْ عَلَيْهِمْ ۖ اِنَّمَا نَعُدُّ لَهُمْ عَدًّا ۞

يَوْمَ نَحْشُرُ الْمُتَّقِيْنَ اِلَى الرَّحْمٰنِ وَفْدًا ۞

وَّنَسُوْقُ الْمُجْرِمِيْنَ اِلٰى جَهَنَّمَ وِرْدًا ۞

لَا يَمْلِكُوْنَ الشَّفَاعَةَ اِلَّا مَنِ اتَّخَذَ عِنْدَ الرَّحْمٰنِ عَهْدًا ۞

وَقَالُوا اتَّخَذَ الرَّحْمٰنُ وَلَدًا ۞

لَقَدْ جِئْتُمْ شَيْئًا اِدًّا ۞

SÛRAH-20
TÂ-HA
(INTRODUCTION)

The chronology of this Sûrah has some significance: it has some relation to the spiritual lessons which it teaches.

It was used with great effect in that remarkable scene which resulted in Ḥaḍhrat 'Umar's conversion, and which took place about the seventh year before the Hijrat.

The scene is described with dramatic details by Ibn Hisham. 'Umar had previously been one of the greatest enemies and persecutors of Islam. Like his blood-thirsty kinsmen the Quraish, he meditated slaying the Prophet, when it was suggested to him that there were near relations of his that had embraced Islam. His sister Fatima and her husband Sa'id were Muslims, but in those days of persecution they had kept their faith secret. When 'Umar went to their house, he heard them reciting this Sûrah from a written copy they had. For a while they concealed the copy. 'Umar attacked his sister and her husband, but they bore the attack with exemplary patience, and declared their faith. 'Umar was so struck with their sincerity and fortitude that he asked to see the leaf from which they had been reading. It was given to him: his soul was touched, and he not only came into the Faith but became one of its strongest supporters and champions.

The leaf contained some portion of this Sûrah, perhaps the introductory portion. The mystic letters Ta-Ha are prefixed to this Sûrah. What do they mean? The earliest tradition is that they denote a dialectical interjection meaning "O man!" If so, the title is particularly appropriate in two ways: (1) It was a direct and personal address to a man in a high state of excitement tempted by his temper to do grievous wrong, but called by Allah's Grace, as by a personal appeal, to face the realities, for Allah knew his inmost secret thoughts (20: 7): the revelation was sent by Allah Most Gracious, out of His Grace and Mercy (20: 5). (2) It takes up the story from the last Sûrah, of man as a spiritual being and illustrates it in further details. It tells the story of Moses in the crisis of his life when he received Allah's Commission and in his personal relations with his mother, and how he came to be brought up in the Pharaoh's house, to learn all the wisdom of the Egyptians, for use in Allah's service, and in his personal relations with Pharaoh, whom we take to be his adoptive father (28: 9). If further tells the story of a fallen soul who misled the Israelites into idolatry, and recalls how man's Arch-enemy Satan caused his fall. Prayer and praise are necessary to man to cure his spiritual blindness and enable him to appreciate Allah's revelation.

90. At it the skies are ready to burst, the earth to split asunder, and the mountains to fall down in utter ruin,

91. That they should invoke a son for (Allah) Most Gracious.

92. For it is not consonant with the majesty of (Allah) Most Gracious that He should beget a son.

93. Not one of the beings in the heavens and the earth but must come to (Allah) Most Gracious as a servant.

94. He takes an account of them (all), and has numbered them (all) exactly.

95. And everyone of them will come to Him singly on the Day of Judgment.

96. On those who believe and work deeds of righteousness, (Allah) Most Gracious will bestow Love.

97. So We have made the (Qur'an) easy in your own tongue, that with it you may give glad tidings to the righteous, and warnings to people given to contention

98. But how many (countless) generations before them We have destroyed? Can you find a single one of them (now) or hear (so much as) a whisper of them?

---

20. Ta-Ha
(Mystic Letters, T. H.)

In the name of Allah. Most Gracious, Most Merciful.

1. Ta-Ha.

2. We have not sent down the Qur'an to you to be (an occasion) for your distress,

3. But only as an admonition to those who fear (Allah),-

4. A revelation from Him Who created the earth and the heavens on high.

5. (Allah) Most Gracious is firmly established on the throne (of authority).

6. To Him belongs what is in the heavens and on earth, and all between them, and all beneath the soil.

7. If you pronounce the word aloud, (it is no matter): for verily He knows what is secret

and what is yet more hidden.

وَأَخْفَى ۞

8.   Allah! there is no god but He! To Him belong the most Beautiful Names.

اللهُ لَا إِلَهَ إِلَّا هُوَ لَهُ الْأَسْمَاءُ الْحُسْنَى ۞

9.   Has the story of Moses reached you?

وَهَلْ أَتَاكَ حَدِيثُ مُوسَى ۞

10.   Behold, he saw a fire: so he said to his family, "You tarry; I perceive a fire; perhaps I can bring you some burning brand therefrom, or find some guidance at the fire."

إِذْ رَأَى نَارًا فَقَالَ لِأَهْلِهِ امْكُثُوا إِنِّي آنَسْتُ نَارًا لَّعَلِّي آتِيكُم مِّنْهَا بِقَبَسٍ أَوْ أَجِدُ عَلَى النَّارِ هُدًى ۞

11.   But when he came to the fire, a voice was heard: "O Moses!

فَلَمَّا أَتَاهَا نُودِيَ يَا مُوسَى ۞

12.   "Verily I am your Lord! Therefore (in My presence) put off your shoes: you are in the sacred valley Tuwa.

إِنِّي أَنَا رَبُّكَ فَاخْلَعْ نَعْلَيْكَ إِنَّكَ بِالْوَادِ الْمُقَدَّسِ طُوًى ۞

13.   "I have chosen you: listen, then, to the inspiration (sent to you).

وَأَنَا اخْتَرْتُكَ فَاسْتَمِعْ لِمَا يُوحَى ۞

14.   "Verily, I am Allah: There is no god but I: so you serve Me (only), and establish regular prayer for celebrating My praise.

إِنَّنِي أَنَا اللهُ لَا إِلَهَ إِلَّا أَنَا فَاعْبُدْنِي وَأَقِمِ الصَّلَوٰةَ لِذِكْرِي ۞

15.   "Verily the Hour is coming-My design is to keep it hidden- for every soul to receive its reward by the measure of its Endeavor.

إِنَّ السَّاعَةَ آتِيَةٌ أَكَادُ أُخْفِيهَا لِتُجْزَى كُلُّ نَفْسٍ بِمَا تَسْعَى ۞

16.   "Therefore let not such as do not believe therein but follow their own lusts, divert you therefrom, lest you perish!".

فَلَا يَصُدَّنَّكَ عَنْهَا مَن لَّا يُؤْمِنُ بِهَا وَاتَّبَعَ هَوَاهُ فَتَرْدَى ۞

17.   "And what is that in your right hand, O Moses?"

وَمَا تِلْكَ بِيَمِينِكَ يَا مُوسَى ۞

18.   He said, "It is my rod: on it I lean; with it I beat down fodder for my flocks; and in it I find other uses."

قَالَ هِيَ عَصَايَ أَتَوَكَّأُ عَلَيْهَا وَأَهُشُّ بِهَا عَلَى غَنَمِي وَلِيَ فِيهَا مَآرِبُ أُخْرَى ۞

19.   (Allah) said, "Throw it, O Moses!"

قَالَ أَلْقِهَا يَا مُوسَى ۞

20.   He threw it, and behold! it was a snake, active in motion.

فَأَلْقَاهَا فَإِذَا هِيَ حَيَّةٌ تَسْعَى ۞

21.   (Allah) said, "Seize it, and fear not: We shall return it at once to its former condition"..

قَالَ خُذْهَا وَلَا تَخَفْ سَنُعِيدُهَا سِيرَتَهَا الْأُولَى ۞

22.   "Now draw your hand close to your side: it shall come forth white (and shining), without harm (or stain),- as another Sign,-

وَاضْمُمْ يَدَكَ إِلَى جَنَاحِكَ تَخْرُجْ بَيْضَاءَ مِنْ غَيْرِ سُوءٍ آيَةً أُخْرَى ۞

23. "In order that We may show you (two) of our Greater Signs.

لِنُرِيَكَ مِنْ اٰيٰتِنَا الْكُبْرٰى ۟

24. "You go to Pharaoh, for he has indeed transgressed all bounds."

اِذْهَبْ اِلٰى فِرْعَوْنَ اِنَّهٗ طَغٰى ۟

25. (Moses) said: "O my Lord! expand me my breast;

قَالَ رَبِّ اشْرَحْ لِيْ صَدْرِيْ ۟

26. "Ease my task for me;

وَيَسِّرْ لِيْۤ اَمْرِيْ ۟

27. "And remove the impediment from my speech,

وَاحْلُلْ عُقْدَةً مِّنْ لِّسَانِيْ ۟

28. "So they may understand what I say:

يَفْقَهُوْا قَوْلِيْ ۟

29. "And give me a Minister from my family,

وَاجْعَلْ لِّيْ وَزِيْرًا مِّنْ اَهْلِيْ ۟

30. "Aaron, my brother;

هٰرُوْنَ اَخِيْ ۟

31. "Add to my strength through him,

اشْدُدْ بِهٖۤ اَزْرِيْ ۟

32. "And make him share my task:

وَاَشْرِكْهُ فِيْۤ اَمْرِيْ ۟

33. "That we may celebrate Your praise without stint,

كَيْ نُسَبِّحَكَ كَثِيْرًا ۟

34. "And remember You without stint:

وَّنَذْكُرَكَ كَثِيْرًا ۟

35. "For You are He that (ever) regards us."

اِنَّكَ كُنْتَ بِنَا بَصِيْرًا ۟

36. (Allah) said: "Granted is your prayer, O Moses!"

قَالَ قَدْ اُوْتِيْتَ سُؤْلَكَ يٰمُوْسٰى ۟

37. "And indeed We conferred a favour on you another time (before).

وَلَقَدْ مَنَنَّا عَلَيْكَ مَرَّةً اُخْرٰى ۟

38. "Behold! We sent to your mother, by inspiration, the message:

اِذْ اَوْحَيْنَاۤ اِلٰۤى اُمِّكَ مَا يُوْحٰى ۟

39. "'Throw (the child) into the chest, and throw (the chest) into the river: the river will cast him up on the bank, and he will be taken up by one who is an enemy to Me and an enemy to him': but I cast (the garment of) love over you from Me: and (this) in order that you may be reared under Mine eye.

اَنِ اقْذِفِيْهِ فِى التَّابُوْتِ فَاقْذِفِيْهِ فِى الْيَمِّ فَلْيُلْقِهِ الْيَمُّ بِالسَّاحِلِ يَأْخُذْهُ عَدُوٌّ لِّيْ وَعَدُوٌّ لَّهٗ ۟ وَاَلْقَيْتُ عَلَيْكَ مَحَبَّةً مِّنِّيْ ۟ وَلِتُصْنَعَ عَلٰى عَيْنِيْ ۟

40. "Behold! your sister goes forth and says, 'shall I show you one who will nurse and rear the (child)?' So We brought you back to your mother, that her eye might be cooled and she should not grieve. Then you slew a man, but We saved you from trouble, and We tried you in various ways. Then you tarried a number of years with the people of Midian. Then you came hither as ordained, O Moses!

اِذْ تَمْشِيْۤ اُخْتُكَ فَتَقُوْلُ هَلْ اَدُلُّكُمْ عَلٰى مَنْ يَّكْفُلُهٗ ۟ فَرَجَعْنٰكَ اِلٰۤى اُمِّكَ كَيْ تَقَرَّ عَيْنُهَا وَلَا تَحْزَنَ ۟ وَقَتَلْتَ نَفْسًا فَنَجَّيْنٰكَ مِنَ الْغَمِّ وَفَتَنّٰكَ فُتُوْنًا ۟ فَلَبِثْتَ سِنِيْنَ فِيْۤ اَهْلِ مَدْيَنَ ۟ ثُمَّ جِئْتَ عَلٰى قَدَرٍ يّٰمُوْسٰى ۟

41. "And I have prepared you for Myself (for service)"..

واصْطَنَعْتُكَ لِنَفْسِيٓ ۞

42. "Go, you and your brother, with My Signs, and slacken not, either of you, in keeping Me in remembrance.

اِذْهَبْ اَنْتَ وَاَخُوكَ بِاٰيٰتِيْ وَلَا تَنِيَا فِيْ ذِكْرِيْ ۞

43. "Go, both of you, to Pharaoh, for he has indeed transgressed all bounds;

اِذْهَبَآ اِلٰى فِرْعَوْنَ اِنَّهٗ طَغٰى ۞

44. "But speak to him mildly; perchance he may take warning or fear (Allah)."

فَقُوْلَا لَهٗ قَوْلًا لَّيِّنًا لَّعَلَّهٗ يَتَذَكَّرُ اَوْ يَخْشٰى ۞

45. They (Moses and Aaron) said: "Our Lord! We fear lest he hasten with insolence against us, or lest he transgress all bounds."

قَالَا رَبَّنَآ اِنَّنَا نَخَافُ اَنْ يَّفْرُطَ عَلَيْنَآ اَوْ اَنْ يَّطْغٰى ۞

46. He said: "Do not fear: for I am with you: I hear and see (everything).

قَالَ لَا تَخَافَآ اِنَّنِيْ مَعَكُمَآ اَسْمَعُ وَاَرٰى ۞

47. "So you both go to him, and say, 'Verily we are Messengers sent by your Lord: send forth, therefore, the Children of Israel with us, and afflict them not: with a Sign, indeed, we have come from your Lord! and peace to all who follow guidance!

فَأْتِيٰهُ فَقُوْلَآ اِنَّا رَسُوْلَا رَبِّكَ فَأَرْسِلْ مَعَنَا بَنِيْٓ اِسْرَآءِيْلَ وَلَا تُعَذِّبْهُمْ ۚ قَدْ جِئْنٰكَ بِاٰيَةٍ مِّنْ رَّبِّكَ وَالسَّلٰمُ عَلٰى مَنِ اتَّبَعَ الْهُدٰى ۞

48. "'Verily it has been revealed to us that the Chastisement (awaits) those who reject and turn away.'"

اِنَّا قَدْ اُوْحِيَ اِلَيْنَآ اَنَّ الْعَذَابَ عَلٰى مَنْ كَذَّبَ وَتَوَلّٰى ۞

49. (When this message was delivered), (Pharaoh) said: "Who, then, O Moses, is the Lord of you two?"

قَالَ فَمَنْ رَّبُّكُمَا يٰمُوْسٰى ۞

50. He said: "Our Lord is He Who gave to each (created) thing its form and nature, and further, gave (it) guidance."

قَالَ رَبُّنَا الَّذِيْٓ اَعْطٰى كُلَّ شَيْءٍ خَلْقَهٗ ثُمَّ هَدٰى ۞

51. (Pharaoh) said: "What then is the condition of previous generations?"

قَالَ فَمَا بَالُ الْقُرُوْنِ الْاُوْلٰى ۞

52. He replied: "The knowledge of that is with my Lord, duly recorded: my Lord never errs, nor forgets,-

قَالَ عِلْمُهَا عِنْدَ رَبِّيْ فِيْ كِتٰبٍ ۚ لَا يَضِلُّ رَبِّيْ وَلَا يَنْسَى ۞

53. "He Who has made for you the earth like a carpet spread out; has enabled you to go about therein by roads (and channels); and has sent down water from the sky." With it have We produced diverse pairs of plants each separate from the others.

الَّذِيْ جَعَلَ لَكُمُ الْاَرْضَ مَهْدًا وَّسَلَكَ لَكُمْ فِيْهَا سُبُلًا وَّاَنْزَلَ مِنَ السَّمَآءِ مَآءً ۚ فَأَخْرَجْنَا بِهٖٓ اَزْوَاجًا مِّنْ نَّبَاتٍ شَتّٰى ۞

54.   Eat (for yourselves) and pasture your cattle: verily, in this are Signs for men endued with understanding.

55.   From the (earth) We created you, and into it We shall return you, and from it We shall bring you out once again.

56.   And We showed Pharaoh all Our Signs, but he rejected and refused.

57.   He said: "Have you come to drive us out of our land with your magic, O Moses?

58.   "But we can surely produce magic to match yours! So make a tryst between us and you, which we shall not fail to keep - neither we nor you - in a place where both shall have even chances."

59.   Moses said: "Your tryst is the Day of the Festival, and let the people be assembled when the sun is well up."

60.   So Pharaoh withdrew: he concerted his plan, and then came (back).

61.   Moses said to him: Woe to you! You do not forge a lie against Allah, lest He destroy you (at once) utterly by chastisement: the forger must suffer frustration!"

62.   So they disputed, one with another, over their affair, but they kept their talk secret.

63.   They said: "These two are certainly (expert) magicians: their object is to drive you out from your land with their magic, and to do away with your most cherished institutions.

64.   "Therefore concert your plan, and then assemble in (serried) ranks: he wins (all along) today who gains the upper hand."

65.   They said: "O Moses! whether will you that you throw (first) or that we be the first to throw?"

66. He said, "Nay, you throw first!" Then behold their ropes and their rods-so it seemed to him on account of their magic - began to be in lively motion!

67. So Moses conceived in his mind a (sort of) fear.

68. We said: "Do not fear! for you have indeed the upper hand:

69. "Throw that which is in your right hand: quickly it will swallow up that which they have faked; what they have faked is but a magician's trick: and the magician does not thrive, (no matter) where he goes."

70. So the magicians were thrown down to prostration: they said, "We believe in the Lord of Aaron and Moses".

71. (Pharaoh) said: "Do you believe in Him before I give you permission? Surely this must be your leader, who has taught you magic! Be sure I will cut off your hands and feet on opposite sides, and I will have you crucified on trunks of palm-trees: so you shall know for certain, which of us can give the more severe and the more lasting punishment!"

72. They said: "Never shall we regard you as more than the Clear Sings that have come to us, or than Him Who created us! so decree whatever you desire to decree: for you can only decree (touching) the life of this world.

73. "For us, we have believed in our Lord: may He forgive us our faults, and the magic to which you compelled us: for Allah is Best and Most Abiding."

74. Verily he who comes to his Lord as a sinner (at Judgment),- for him is Hell: therein shall he neither die nor live.

75. But such as come to Him as Believers who have worked righteous deeds,-

for them are ranks exalted,-

فَأُولَٰئِكَ لَهُمُ الدَّرَجَاتُ الْعُلَىٰ ۞

76. Gardens of Eternity, beneath which flow rivers: they will dwell therein for ever: such is the reward of those who purify themselves (from evil).

جَنَّاتُ عَدْنٍ تَجْرِي مِنْ تَحْتِهَا الْأَنْهَارُ خَٰلِدِينَ فِيهَا ۚ وَذَٰلِكَ جَزَاءُ مَنْ تَزَكَّىٰ ۞

77. We sent an inspiration to Moses: "Travel by night with My servants, and strike a dry path for them through the sea, without fear of being overtaken (by Pharaoh) and without (any other) fear."

وَلَقَدْ أَوْحَيْنَا إِلَىٰ مُوسَىٰ أَنْ أَسْرِ بِعِبَادِي فَاضْرِبْ لَهُمْ طَرِيقًا فِي الْبَحْرِ يَبَسًا لَا تَخَافُ دَرَكًا وَلَا تَخْشَىٰ ۞

78. Then Pharaoh pursued them with his forces, but the waters completely overwhelmed them and covered them up.

فَأَتْبَعَهُمْ فِرْعَوْنُ بِجُنُودِهِ فَغَشِيَهُمْ مِنَ الْيَمِّ مَا غَشِيَهُمْ ۞

79. Pharaoh led his people astray instead of leading them aright.

وَأَضَلَّ فِرْعَوْنُ قَوْمَهُ وَمَا هَدَىٰ ۞

80. O you Children of Israel! We delivered you from your enemy, and We made a Covenant with you on the right side of Mount (Sinai), and We sent down to you Manna and quails:

يَٰبَنِي إِسْرَائِيلَ قَدْ أَنْجَيْنَاكُمْ مِنْ عَدُوِّكُمْ وَوَاعَدْنَاكُمْ جَانِبَ الطُّورِ الْأَيْمَنَ وَنَزَّلْنَا عَلَيْكُمُ الْمَنَّ وَالسَّلْوَىٰ ۞

81. (Saying): "Eat of the good things We have provided for your sustenance, but commit no excess therein, lest My Wrath should justly descend on you: and those on whom descends My Wrath, do perish indeed!

كُلُوا مِنْ طَيِّبَاتِ مَا رَزَقْنَاكُمْ وَلَا تَطْغَوْا فِيهِ فَيَحِلَّ عَلَيْكُمْ غَضَبِي ۖ وَمَنْ يَحْلِلْ عَلَيْهِ غَضَبِي فَقَدْ هَوَىٰ ۞

82. "But, without doubt, I am (also) He that forgives again and again, to those who repent, believe, and do right,- who, in fine, are ready to receive true guidance."

وَإِنِّي لَغَفَّارٌ لِمَنْ تَابَ وَآمَنَ وَعَمِلَ صَالِحًا ثُمَّ اهْتَدَىٰ ۞

83. (When Moses was up on the Mount, Allah said:) "What made you hasten in advance of your people, O Moses?"

وَمَا أَعْجَلَكَ عَنْ قَوْمِكَ يَٰمُوسَىٰ ۞

84. He replied: "Behold, they are close on my footsteps: I hastened to You, O my Lord, to please You."

قَالَ هُمْ أُولَاءِ عَلَىٰ أَثَرِي وَعَجِلْتُ إِلَيْكَ رَبِّ لِتَرْضَىٰ ۞

85. (Allah) said: "We have tested your people in your absence: the Samiri has led them astray."

قَالَ فَإِنَّا قَدْ فَتَنَّا قَوْمَكَ مِنْ بَعْدِكَ وَأَضَلَّهُمُ السَّامِرِيُّ ۞

86. So Moses returned to his people in a state of indignation

فَرَجَعَ مُوسَىٰ إِلَىٰ قَوْمِهِ غَضْبَانَ

and sorrow. He said: "O my people! did not your Lord make a handsome promise to you? Did then the promise seem to you long (in coming)? Or did you desire that Wrath should descend from your Lord on you, and so you broke your promise to me?"

87. They said: "We did not break the promise to you, as far as lay in our power: but we were made to carry the weight of the ornaments of the (whole) people, and we threw them (into the fire), and that was what the Samiri suggested.

88. "Then he brought out (of the fire) before the (people) the image of a calf: it seemed to low: so they said: This is your god, and the god of Moses, but (Moses) has forgotten!"

89. Could they not see that it could not return them a word (for answer), and that it had no power either to harm them or to do them good?

90. Aaron had already, before this said to them: "O my people! you are being tested in this: for verily your Lord is (Allah) Most Gracious; so follow me and obey my command."

91. They had said: "We will not cease to worship it, but we will devote ourselves to it until Moses returns to us."

92. (Moses) said: "O Aaron! what kept you back, when you saw them going wrong,

93. "From following me? Did you then disobey my order?"

94. (Aaron) replied: "O son of my mother! Do not seize (me) by my beard nor by (the hair of) my head! Truly I feared lest you should say, 'you have caused a division among the children of Israel, and you did not respect my word!'"

95. (Moses) said: "What then is your case, O Samiri?"

96. He replied: "I saw what they did not see: so I took a handful (of dust) from the footprint of the Messenger, and threw it (into the calf): thus did my soul suggest to me."

97. (Moses) said: "Get you gone! But your (punishment) in this life will be that you will say, 'Touch me not'; and moreover (for a future Penalty) you have a promise that will not fail: now look at your god, of whom you have become a devoted worshipper: we will certainly (melt) it in a blazing fire and scatter it broadcast in the sea!"

98. But the God of you all is the One God (Allah): there is no god but He: all things He comprehends in His knowledge.

99. Thus do We relate to you some stories of what happened before: for We have sent you a Message from Our Own Presence.

100. If any do turn away therefrom, verily they will bear a burden on the Day of judgment;

101. They will abide in this (state): and grievous will be the burden to them on that Day,-

102. The Day when the Trumpet will be sounded: that Day, We shall gather the sinful, blear-eyed (with terror).

103. In whispers will they consult each other: "You tarried not longer than ten (Days);"

104. We know best what they will say, when their leader most eminent in conduct will say: "You did not tarry longer than a day!"

105. They ask you concerning the Mountains: say, "My Lord will uproot them and scatter them as dust;

106. "He will leave them as plains smooth and level;

107. "Nothing crooked or curved will you see in their place."

108. On that Day they will follow the Caller (straight): no crookedness (can they show) him: all sounds shall humble themselves in the Presence of (Allah) Most Gracious: nothing shall you hear but the tramp of their feet (as they march).

109. On that Day no intercession shall avail except for those for whom permission has been granted by (Allah) Most Gracious and whose word is acceptable to Him.

110. He knows what (appears to His creatures as) before or after or behind them: but they shall not compass it with their knowledge.

111. (All) faces shall be humbled before (Him) - the Living, the Self-subsisting, Eternal: hopeless indeed will be the man that carries iniquity (on his back).

112. But he who works deeds of righteousness, and has faith, will have no fear of harm nor of any curtailment (of what is his due).

113. Thus have We sent this down - an Arabic Qur'an - and explained therein in detail some of the warnings, in order that they may fear Allah, or that it may cause their remembrance (of Him).

114. High above all is Allah, the King, the Truth! Be not in haste with the Qur'an before its revelation to you is completed, but say, "O my Lord! advance me in knowledge."

115. We had already, beforehand, taken the covenant of Adam, but he forgot: and We found on his part no firm resolve.

116. When We said to the angels, "Prostrate yourselves to Adam", they prostrated themselves, but not Iblis: he refused.

117. Then We said: "O Adam! verily, this is an enemy to you and your wife: so let him not get you both out of the Garden, so that you are landed in misery.

فَيَذَرُهَا قَاعًا صَفْصَفًا ۞

لَّا تَرَىٰ فِيهَا عِوَجًا وَّلَآ أَمْتًا ۞

يَوْمَئِذٍ يَّتَّبِعُونَ الدَّاعِيَ لَا عِوَجَ لَهُ ۖ

وَخَشَعَتِ الْأَصْوَاتُ لِلرَّحْمَٰنِ

فَلَا تَسْمَعُ إِلَّا هَمْسًا ۞

يَوْمَئِذٍ لَّا تَنفَعُ الشَّفَاعَةُ إِلَّا مَنْ

أَذِنَ لَهُ الرَّحْمَٰنُ وَرَضِيَ لَهُ قَوْلًا ۞

يَعْلَمُ مَا بَيْنَ أَيْدِيهِمْ وَمَا

خَلْفَهُمْ وَلَا يُحِيطُونَ بِهِ عِلْمًا ۞

وَعَنَتِ الْوُجُوهُ لِلْحَيِّ الْقَيُّومِ ۖ

وَقَدْ خَابَ مَنْ حَمَلَ ظُلْمًا ۞

وَمَن يَعْمَلْ مِنَ الصَّالِحَاتِ وَهُوَ

مُؤْمِنٌ فَلَا يَخَافُ ظُلْمًا وَّلَا هَضْمًا ۞

وَكَذَٰلِكَ أَنزَلْنَاهُ قُرْآنًا عَرَبِيًّا وَّ

صَرَّفْنَا فِيهِ مِنَ الْوَعِيدِ لَعَلَّهُمْ

يَتَّقُونَ أَوْ يُحْدِثُ لَهُمْ ذِكْرًا ۞

فَتَعَالَى اللَّهُ الْمَلِكُ الْحَقُّ ۗ وَلَا تَعْجَلْ

بِالْقُرْآنِ مِن قَبْلِ أَن يُقْضَىٰ إِلَيْكَ

وَحْيُهُ ۖ وَقُل رَّبِّ زِدْنِي عِلْمًا ۞

وَلَقَدْ عَهِدْنَا إِلَىٰ آدَمَ مِن قَبْلُ

فَنَسِيَ وَلَمْ نَجِدْ لَهُ عَزْمًا ۞

وَإِذْ قُلْنَا لِلْمَلَائِكَةِ اسْجُدُوا

لِآدَمَ فَسَجَدُوا إِلَّا إِبْلِيسَ أَبَىٰ ۞

فَقُلْنَا يَا آدَمُ إِنَّ هَٰذَا عَدُوٌّ لَّكَ

وَلِزَوْجِكَ فَلَا يُخْرِجَنَّكُمَا مِنَ

الْجَنَّةِ فَتَشْقَىٰ ۞

118. "There is therein (enough provision) for you not to go hungry nor to go naked,

إِنَّ لَكَ أَلَّا تَجُوعَ فِيهَا وَلَا تَعْرَىٰ ۞

119. "Nor to suffer from thirst, nor from the sun's heat."

وَأَنَّكَ لَا تَظْمَؤُا۟ فِيهَا وَلَا تَضْحَىٰ ۞

120. But Satan whispered evil to him: he said, "O Adam! shall I lead you to the Tree of Eternity and to a kingdom that never decays?"

فَوَسْوَسَ إِلَيْهِ الشَّيْطَٰنُ قَالَ يَٰٓأَادَمُ هَلْ أَدُلُّكَ عَلَىٰ شَجَرَةِ الْخُلْدِ وَمُلْكٍ لَّا يَبْلَىٰ ۞

121. In the result, they both ate of the tree, and so their nakedness appeared to them: they began to sew together, for their covering, leaves from the Garden: thus Adam disobeyed his Lord, and allowed himself to be seduced.

فَأَكَلَا مِنْهَا فَبَدَتْ لَهُمَا سَوْءَٰتُهُمَا وَطَفِقَا يَخْصِفَانِ عَلَيْهِمَا مِن وَرَقِ الْجَنَّةِ ۚ وَعَصَىٰٓ ءَادَمُ رَبَّهُ فَغَوَىٰ ۞

122. But his Lord chose him (for His Grace): He turned to him, and gave him guidance.

ثُمَّ اجْتَبَٰهُ رَبُّهُ فَتَابَ عَلَيْهِ وَهَدَىٰ ۞

123. He said: "Get you down, both of you,- all together, from the Garden, with enmity one to another: but if, as is sure, there comes to you guidance from Me, whosoever follows My guidance, will not lose his way, nor fall into misery.

قَالَ اهْبِطَا مِنْهَا جَمِيعًا ۖ بَعْضُكُمْ لِبَعْضٍ عَدُوٌّ ۖ فَإِمَّا يَأْتِيَنَّكُم مِّنِّى هُدًى فَمَنِ اتَّبَعَ هُدَاىَ فَلَا يَضِلُّ وَلَا يَشْقَىٰ ۞

124. "But whosoever turns away from My Message, verily for him is a life narrowed down, and We shall raise him up blind on the Day of Judgment."

وَمَنْ أَعْرَضَ عَن ذِكْرِى فَإِنَّ لَهُ مَعِيشَةً ضَنكًا وَنَحْشُرُهُ يَوْمَ الْقِيَٰمَةِ أَعْمَىٰ ۞

125. He will say: "O my Lord! why have you raised me up blind, while I had sight (before)?"

قَالَ رَبِّ لِمَ حَشَرْتَنِىٓ أَعْمَىٰ وَقَدْ كُنتُ بَصِيرًا ۞

126. (Allah) will say: "Thus did you, when Our Signs came unto you, disregard them: so will you, this day, be disregarded."

قَالَ كَذَٰلِكَ أَتَتْكَ ءَايَٰتُنَا فَنَسِيتَهَا ۖ وَكَذَٰلِكَ الْيَوْمَ تُنسَىٰ ۞

127. And thus do We recompense him who transgresses beyond bounds and does not believe in the Sings of his Lord: and the Chastisement of the Hereafter is far more grievous and more enduring.

وَكَذَٰلِكَ نَجْزِى مَنْ أَسْرَفَ وَلَمْ يُؤْمِن بِـَٔايَٰتِ رَبِّهِ ۚ وَلَعَذَابُ الْءَاخِرَةِ أَشَدُّ وَأَبْقَىٰ ۞

128. Is it not a warning to such men (to call to mind) how

أَفَلَمْ يَهْدِ لَهُمْ كَمْ أَهْلَكْنَا

many generations before them We destroyed, in whose haunts they (now) move? Verily, in this are Signs for men endued with understanding.

129. Had it not been for a Word that went forth before from your Lord, (their punishment) must necessarily have come; but there is a term appointed (for respite).

130. Therefore be patient with what they say, and celebrate (constantly) the praises of your Lord, before the rising of the sun, and before its setting; yes, celebrate them for part of the hours of the night, and at the sides of the day: that you may have (spiritual) joy.

131. Nor strain your eyes in longing for the things We have given for enjoyment to parties of them, the splendor of the life of this world, through which We test them: but the provision of your Lord is better and more enduring.

132. Enjoin prayer on your people, and be constant therein. We ask you not to provide sustenance: We provide it for you. But the (fruit of) the Hereafter is for righteousness.

133. They say: "Why does he not bring us a Sign from his Lord?" Has not a Clear Sign come to them of all that was in the former Books of revelation?

134. And if We had inflicted on them a penalty before this, they would have said: "Our Lord! If only You had sent us a Messenger, we should certainly have followed Your Signs before we were humbled and put to shame."

135. Say: "Each one (of us) is waiting: you wait, therefore, and soon you shall know who it is that is on the straight and even way, and who it is that has received guidance."

SURAH-21
AL-ANBIYA'
(INTRODUCTION)

The last Surah dealt with the individual story (spiritual of Moses and Aaron, and contrasted it with the growth of evil in individuals like Pharaoh and the Samirî, and ended with a warning against Evil, and an exhortation to the purification of the soul with prayer and praise. This Sûrah begins with the external obstacles placed by Evil against such purification, and gives the assurance of Allah's, power to defend men, illustrating this with reference to Abraham's fight against idolatry, Lot's fight against unnatural wickedness, Noah's fight against unbelief, that of David and Solomon against injustice and failure to proclaim Allah's glory by making full use of man's Allah-given faculties and powers, that of Job against impatience and want of self-confidence, that of Isma'îl Idris and Zul-kifl against want of steady perseverance, that of Zun-nun against hasty anger, that of Zakariya against spiritual isolation, and that of Mary against the lusts of this world. In each illusion there is a special point about the soul's purification. The common point is that the Prophets were not, as the vulgar suppose, just irresistible men. They had to win their ground inch by inch against all kinds of resistance from evil.

The chronology of this Sûrah has no significance. It probably dates from the middle of the Makkan period of inspiration.

21. The Prophets

In the name of Allah. Most Gracious, Most Merciful.

1. Closer and closer to mankind comes their Reckoning: yet they do not heed and they turn away.

2. Never comes (anything) to them of a renewed Message from their Lord, but they listen to it as in jest,-

3. Their hearts toying as with trifles. The wrong-doers conceal their private counsels, (saying), "Is this (one) more than a man like yourselves? Will you go to witchcraft with your eyes open?"

4. Say: "My Lord knows (every) word (spoken) in the heavens and on earth: He is the One that hears and knows (all things)."

5. "Nay," they say, "(these are) medleys of dreams! - Nay, he forged it! - Nay, he is (but) a poet! Let him then bring us a Sign like the ones that were sent to (Prophets) of old!"

6. (As to those) before them, not one of the populations which We destroyed believed: will these believe?

7. Before you, also, the Messengers We sent were but men, to whom We granted inspiration: if you do not realise this, ask of those who possess the Message.

8. Nor did We give them bodies that ate no food, nor were they exempt from death.

9. In the end We fulfilled to them Our Promise, and We saved them and those whom We pleased, but We destroyed those who transgressed beyond bounds.

10. We have revealed for you (O men!) a book in which is a Message for you: will you not then understand?

11. How many were the populations We utterly destroyed because of their iniquities, setting up in their places other peoples?

12. Yet, when they felt Our Punishment (coming), behold, they (tried to) flee from it.

13. Flee not, but return to the good things of this life which were given you, and to your homes, in order that you may be called to account.

14. They said: "Ah! woe to us! We were indeed wrong-doers!"

15. And that cry of theirs did not cease, till We made them as a field that is mown, as ashes silent and quenched.

16. Not for (idle) sport did We create the heavens and the earth and all that is between!

17. If it had been Our wish to take (just) a pastime, We should surely have taken it from the things nearest to Us, if We would do (such a thing)!

18. Nay, We hurl the Truth against falsehood, and it knocks out its brain, and behold, falsehood perishes! Ah! woe be to you for the (false) things you ascribe (to Us).

19. To Him belong all (creatures) in the heavens and on earth: even those who are in His (very) Presence are not too proud to serve Him, nor are they (ever) weary (of His service):

20. They celebrate His praises night and day, nor do they ever flag or intermit.

21. Or have they taken (for worship) gods from the earth who can raise (the dead)?

22. If there were, in the heavens and the earth, other gods besides Allah, there would have been confusion in both! But glory to Allah, the Lord of the Throne: (high is He) above what they attribute to Him!

23. He cannot be questioned for His acts, but they will be questioned (for theirs).

24. Or have they taken for worship (other) gods besides Him? Say, "Bring your convincing proof: this is the Message of those with me and the Message of those before me." But most of them do not know the Truth, and so turn away.

25. Not a Messenger did We send before you without this inspiration sent by Us to him: that there is no god but I; therefore worship and serve Me.

26. And they say: "(Allah) Most Gracious has begotten offspring." Glory to Him! They are (but) servants raised to honour.

27. They do not speak before He speaks, and they act (in all things) by His Command.

28. He knows what is before them, and what is behind them, and they offer no intercession except for those who are acceptable, and they stand in awe and reverence of His (glory).

29. If any of them should say, "I am a god besides Him", such a one We should reward with Hell: thus do We reward those who do wrong.

30. Do not the Unbelievers see that the heavens and the earth were joined together (as one unit of Creation), before We clove them asunder? We made from water every living thing. Will they not then believe?

31. And We have set on the earth mountains standing firm, lest it should shake with them, and We have made therein broad highways (between mountains) for them to pass through: that they may receive guidance.

32. And We have made the heavens as a canopy well guarded:

لَا يُسْـَٔلُ عَمَّا يَفْعَلُ وَهُمْ يُسْـَٔلُوْنَ ۞

اَمِ اتَّخَذُوْا مِنْ دُوْنِهٖۤ اٰلِهَةً ۚ قُلْ هَاتُوْا بُرْهَانَكُمْ ۚ هٰذَا ذِكْرُ مَنْ مَّعِيَ وَذِكْرُ مَنْ قَبْلِيْ ۚ بَلْ اَكْثَرُهُمْ لَا يَعْلَمُوْنَ الْحَقَّ فَهُمْ مُّعْرِضُوْنَ ۞

وَمَاۤ اَرْسَلْنَا مِنْ قَبْلِكَ مِنْ رَّسُوْلٍ اِلَّا نُوْحِيْۤ اِلَيْهِ اَنَّهٗ لَاۤ اِلٰهَ اِلَّاۤ اَنَا فَاعْبُدُوْنِ ۞

وَقَالُوا اتَّخَذَ الرَّحْمٰنُ وَلَدًا سُبْحٰنَهٗ ۚ بَلْ عِبَادٌ مُّكْرَمُوْنَ ۞

لَا يَسْبِقُوْنَهٗ بِالْقَوْلِ وَهُمْ بِاَمْرِهٖ يَعْمَلُوْنَ ۞

يَعْلَمُ مَا بَيْنَ اَيْدِيْهِمْ وَمَا خَلْفَهُمْ وَلَا يَشْفَعُوْنَ ۙ اِلَّا لِمَنِ ارْتَضٰى وَهُمْ مِّنْ خَشْيَتِهٖ مُشْفِقُوْنَ ۞

وَمَنْ يَّقُلْ مِنْهُمْ اِنِّيْۤ اِلٰهٌ مِّنْ دُوْنِهٖ فَذٰلِكَ نَجْزِيْهِ جَهَنَّمَ ۚ كَذٰلِكَ نَجْزِي الظّٰلِمِيْنَ ۞

اَوَلَمْ يَرَ الَّذِيْنَ كَفَرُوْۤا اَنَّ السَّمٰوٰتِ وَالْاَرْضَ كَانَتَا رَتْقًا فَفَتَقْنٰهُمَا ۚ وَجَعَلْنَا مِنَ الْمَآءِ كُلَّ شَيْءٍ حَيٍّ ۚ اَفَلَا يُؤْمِنُوْنَ ۞

وَجَعَلْنَا فِي الْاَرْضِ رَوَاسِيَ اَنْ تَمِيْدَ بِهِمْ ۖ وَجَعَلْنَا فِيْهَا فِجَاجًا سُبُلًا لَّعَلَّهُمْ يَهْتَدُوْنَ ۞

وَجَعَلْنَا السَّمَآءَ سَقْفًا مَّحْفُوْظًا ۖ

yet do they turn away from the Signs which these things (point to)!

33. It is He Who created the Night and the Day, and the sun and the moon: all (the celestial bodies) swim along, each in its rounded course.

34. We did not grant to any man before you permanent life (here): if then you should die, would they live permanently?

35. Every soul shall have a taste of death: and We test you by evil and by good by way of trial. To Us must you return.

36. When the Unbelievers see you, they do not treat you except with ridicule. "Is this," (they say), "the one who talks of your gods?" and they blaspheme at the mention of (Allah) Most Gracious!

37. Man is a creature of haste: soon (enough) will I show you My Signs; then you will not ask Me to hasten them!

38. They say: "When will this promise come to pass, if you are telling the truth?"

39. If only the Unbelievers knew (the time) when they will not be able to ward off the fire from their faces, nor yet from their backs, and (when) no help can reach them!

40. Nay, it may come to them all of a sudden and confound them: no power will they have then to avert it, nor will they (then) get respite.

41. Mocked were (many) Messengers before you; but their scoffers were hemmed in by the thing that they mocked.

وَهُمْ عَنْ اٰيٰتِهَا مُعْرِضُوْنَ ۝

وَهُوَ الَّذِىْ خَلَقَ الَّيْلَ وَالنَّهَارَ وَالشَّمْسَ وَالْقَمَرَ ۚ كُلٌّ فِىْ فَلَكٍ يَّسْبَحُوْنَ ۝

وَمَا جَعَلْنَا لِبَشَرٍ مِّنْ قَبْلِكَ الْخُلْدَ ۚ اَفَا۟ىِٕنْ مِّتَّ فَهُمُ الْخٰلِدُوْنَ ۝

كُلُّ نَفْسٍ ذَآئِقَةُ الْمَوْتِ ۚ وَنَبْلُوْكُمْ بِالشَّرِّ وَالْخَيْرِ فِتْنَةً ۚ وَاِلَيْنَا تُرْجَعُوْنَ ۝

وَاِذَا رَاٰكَ الَّذِيْنَ كَفَرُوْٓا اِنْ يَّتَّخِذُوْنَكَ اِلَّا هُزُوًا ۭ اَهٰذَا الَّذِىْ يَذْكُرُ اٰلِهَتَكُمْ ۚ وَهُمْ بِذِكْرِ الرَّحْمٰنِ هُمْ كٰفِرُوْنَ ۝

خُلِقَ الْاِنْسَانُ مِنْ عَجَلٍ ۭ سَاُورِيْكُمْ اٰيٰتِىْ فَلَا تَسْتَعْجِلُوْنِ ۝

وَيَقُوْلُوْنَ مَتٰى هٰذَا الْوَعْدُ اِنْ كُنْتُمْ صٰدِقِيْنَ ۝

لَوْ يَعْلَمُ الَّذِيْنَ كَفَرُوْا حِيْنَ لَا يَكُفُّوْنَ عَنْ وُّجُوْهِهِمُ النَّارَ وَلَا عَنْ ظُهُوْرِهِمْ وَلَا هُمْ يُنْصَرُوْنَ ۝

بَلْ تَأْتِيْهِمْ بَغْتَةً فَتَبْهَتُهُمْ فَلَا يَسْتَطِيْعُوْنَ رَدَّهَا وَلَا هُمْ يُنْظَرُوْنَ ۝

وَلَقَدِ اسْتُهْزِئَ بِرُسُلٍ مِّنْ قَبْلِكَ فَحَاقَ بِالَّذِيْنَ سَخِرُوْا مِنْهُمْ مَّا كَانُوْا بِهٖ يَسْتَهْزِءُوْنَ ۝

42. Say: "Who can keep you safe by night and by day from (the Wrath of) Allah Most Gracious?" Yet they turn away from the mention of their Lord.

قُلْ مَنْ يَّكْلَؤُكُمْ بِالَّيْلِ وَ النَّهَارِ مِنَ الرَّحْمٰنِ ۗ بَلْ هُمْ عَنْ ذِكْرِ رَبِّهِمْ مُّعْرِضُوْنَ ۝

43. Or have they gods that can guard them from Us? They have no power to aid themselves, nor can they be defended from Us.

أَمْ لَهُمْ اٰلِهَةٌ تَمْنَعُهُمْ مِّنْ دُوْنِنَا ۚ لَا يَسْتَطِيْعُوْنَ نَصْرَ أَنْفُسِهِمْ وَلَا هُمْ مِّنَّا يُصْحَبُوْنَ ۝

44. Nay, We gave the good things of this life to these men and their fathers until the period grew long for them; do not they see that We gradually reduce the land (in their control) from its outlying borders? Is it then they who will win?

بَلْ مَتَّعْنَا هٰؤُلَاءِ وَاٰبَاءَهُمْ حَتّٰى طَالَ عَلَيْهِمُ الْعُمُرُ ۗ أَفَلَا يَرَوْنَ أَنَّا نَأْتِي الْأَرْضَ نَنْقُصُهَا مِنْ أَطْرَافِهَا ۗ أَفَهُمُ الْغٰلِبُوْنَ ۝

45. Say, "I do but warn you according to revelation": but the deaf will not hear the call, (even) when they are warned!

قُلْ إِنَّمَا أُنْذِرُكُمْ بِالْوَحْيِ ۚ وَلَا يَسْمَعُ الصُّمُّ الدُّعَاءَ إِذَا مَا يُنْذَرُوْنَ ۝

46. If but a breath of the Wrath of your Lord do touch them, they will then say, "Woe to us! we did wrong indeed!"

وَلَئِنْ مَّسَّتْهُمْ نَفْحَةٌ مِّنْ عَذَابِ رَبِّكَ لَيَقُوْلُنَّ يٰوَيْلَنَا إِنَّا كُنَّا ظٰلِمِيْنَ ۝

47. We shall set up scales of justice for the Day of Judgment, so that not a soul will be dealt with unjustly in the least, and if there be (no more than) the weight of a mustard seed, We will bring it (to account): and enough are We to take account.

وَنَضَعُ الْمَوَازِيْنَ الْقِسْطَ لِيَوْمِ الْقِيٰمَةِ فَلَا تُظْلَمُ نَفْسٌ شَيْئًا ۗ وَإِنْ كَانَ مِثْقَالَ حَبَّةٍ مِّنْ خَرْدَلٍ أَتَيْنَا بِهَا ۗ وَكَفٰى بِنَا حٰسِبِيْنَ ۝

48. In the past We granted to Moses and Aaron the criterion (for judgment), and a Light and a Message for those who would do right,-

وَلَقَدْ اٰتَيْنَا مُوْسٰى وَهٰرُوْنَ الْفُرْقَانَ وَضِيَاءً وَّذِكْرًا لِّلْمُتَّقِيْنَ ۝

49. Those who fear their Lord in their most secret thoughts, and who hold the Hour (of Judgment) in awe.

الَّذِيْنَ يَخْشَوْنَ رَبَّهُمْ بِالْغَيْبِ وَهُمْ مِّنَ السَّاعَةِ مُشْفِقُوْنَ ۝

50. And this is a blessed Message which We have sent down: will you then

وَهٰذَا ذِكْرٌ مُّبٰرَكٌ أَنْزَلْنٰهُ ۚ أَفَأَنْتُمْ

reject it?

51. We bestowed aforetime on Abraham his rectitude of conduct, and We were well acquainted with him.

52. Behold! he said to his father and his people, "What are these images, to which you are (so assiduously) devoted?"

53. They said, "We found our fathers worshipping them."

54. He said, "Indeed you have been in manifest error - you and your fathers."

55. They said, "Have you brought us the Truth, or are you one of those who jest?"

56. He said, "Nay, your Lord is the Lord of the heavens and the earth, He Who created them (from nothing): and I am a witness to this (truth).

57. "And by Allah, I have a plan for your idols - after you go away and turn your backs".

58. So he broke them to pieces, (all) but the biggest of them, that they might turn (and address themselves) to it.

59. They said, "Who has done this to our gods? He must indeed be some man of impiety!"

60. They said, "We heard a youth talk of them: he is called Abraham."

61. They said, "Then bring him before the eyes of the people, that they may bear witness."

62. They said, "Are you the one that did this with our gods, O Abraham?"

63. He said: "Nay, this was done by - this is their biggest one!

ask them, if they can speak intelligently!"

64. So they turned to themselves and said, "Surely you are the ones in the wrong!"

65. Then they were confounded with shame: (they said), "you know full well that these (idols) do not speak!"

66. (Abraham) said, "Do you then worship, besides Allah, things that can neither be of any good to you nor do you harm?

67. "Fie upon you, and upon the things that you worship besides Allah! Have you no sense?".

68. They said, "Burn him and protect your gods, if you do (anything at all)!"

69. We said, "O Fire! you be cool, and (a means of) safety for Abraham!"

70. Then they sought a strategem against him: but We made them the ones that lost most!

71. But We delivered him and (his nephew) Lut (and directed them) to the land which We have blessed for the nations.

72. And We bestowed on him Isaac and, as an additional gift, (a grandson), Jacob, and We made righteous men of every one (of them).

73. And We made them leaders, guiding (men) by Our Command, and We sent them inspiration to do good deeds, to establish regular prayers, and to practise regular charity; and they constantly served Us (and Us only).

74. And to Lut, too, We gave Judgment and Knowledge, and We saved him from the town which practised abominations: truly they were

a people given to Evil, a rebellious people.

75. And We admitted him to Our Mercy: for he was one of the Righteous.

76. (Remember) Noah, when he cried (to Us) aforetime: We listened to his (prayer) and delivered him and his family from great distress.

77. We helped him against people who rejected Our Signs: truly they were a people given to Evil: so We drowned them (in the Flood) all together.

78. And remember David and Solomon, when they gave judgment in the matter of the field into which the sheep of certain people had strayed by night: We witnessed their judgment.

79. To Solomon We inspired the (right) understanding of the matter: to each (of them) We gave Judgment and Knowledge; it was Our power that made the hills and the birds celebrate Our praises, with David: it was We Who did (all these things).

80. It was We Who taught him the making of coats of mail for your benefit, to guard you from each other's violence: will you then be grateful?

81. (It was Our power that made) the violent (unruly) wind flow (tamely) for Solomon, to his order, to the land which We had blessed: for We do know all things.

82. And of the evil ones, were some who dived for him, and did other work besides; and it was We Who guarded them.

83. And (remember) Job, when He cried to his Lord, "Truly distress has seized me,

قَوْمَ سَوْءٍ فَٰسِقِينَ ۝

وَأَدْخَلْنَٰهُ فِى رَحْمَتِنَا إِنَّهُ مِنَ الصَّٰلِحِينَ ۝

وَنُوحًا إِذْ نَادَىٰ مِن قَبْلُ فَٱسْتَجَبْنَا لَهُ فَنَجَّيْنَٰهُ وَأَهْلَهُ مِنَ الْكَرْبِ الْعَظِيمِ ۝

وَنَصَرْنَٰهُ مِنَ الْقَوْمِ الَّذِينَ كَذَّبُوا بِـَٔايَٰتِنَا إِنَّهُمْ كَانُوا قَوْمَ سَوْءٍ فَأَغْرَقْنَٰهُمْ أَجْمَعِينَ ۝

وَدَاوُدَ وَسُلَيْمَٰنَ إِذْ يَحْكُمَٰنِ فِى الْحَرْثِ إِذْ نَفَشَتْ فِيهِ غَنَمُ الْقَوْمِ وَكُنَّا لِحُكْمِهِمْ شَٰهِدِينَ ۝

فَفَهَّمْنَٰهَا سُلَيْمَٰنَ وَكُلًّا آتَيْنَا حُكْمًا وَعِلْمًا وَسَخَّرْنَا مَعَ دَاوُدَ الْجِبَالَ يُسَبِّحْنَ وَالطَّيْرَ وَكُنَّا فَٰعِلِينَ ۝

وَعَلَّمْنَٰهُ صَنْعَةَ لَبُوسٍ لَّكُمْ لِتُحْصِنَكُم مِّنۢ بَأْسِكُمْ فَهَلْ أَنتُمْ شَٰكِرُونَ ۝

وَلِسُلَيْمَٰنَ الرِّيحَ عَاصِفَةً تَجْرِى بِأَمْرِهِ إِلَى الْأَرْضِ الَّتِى بَٰرَكْنَا فِيهَا وَكُنَّا بِكُلِّ شَىْءٍ عَٰلِمِينَ ۝

وَمِنَ الشَّيَٰطِينِ مَن يَغُوصُونَ لَهُ وَيَعْمَلُونَ عَمَلًا دُونَ ذَٰلِكَ وَكُنَّا لَهُمْ حَٰفِظِينَ ۝

وَأَيُّوبَ إِذْ نَادَىٰ رَبَّهُ أَنِّى مَسَّنِىَ

but you are the Most Merciful of those that are merciful."

84. So We listened to him: We removed the distress that was on him, and We restored his people to him, and doubled their number,- as a Grace from Ourselves, and a thing for commemoration, for all who serve Us.

الضُّرُّ وَأَنْتَ أَرْحَمُ الرَّاحِمِينَ ۞

فَاسْتَجَبْنَا لَهُ فَكَشَفْنَا مَا بِهِ مِنْ

ضُرٍّ وَآتَيْنَاهُ أَهْلَهُ وَمِثْلَهُمْ مَعَهُمْ

رَحْمَةً مِّنْ عِنْدِنَا وَ ذِكْرَى

لِلْعَابِدِينَ ۞

85. And (remember) Isma'il, Idris, and Zul-kifl, all (men) of constancy and patience;

وَ اِسْمَعِيلَ وَاِدْرِيسَ وَذَا الْكِفْلِ

كُلٌّ مِّنَ الصَّابِرِينَ ۞

86. We admitted them to Our Mercy: for they were of the righteous ones.

وَ اَدْخَلْنَاهُمْ فِي رَحْمَتِنَا إِنَّهُمْ

مِّنَ الصَّالِحِينَ ۞

87. And remember Zun-nun, when he departed in wrath: he imagined that We had no power over him! but he cried through the depths of darkness, "There is no god but You: glory to You: I was indeed wrong!"

وَذَا النُّونِ إِذْ ذَهَبَ مُغَاضِبًا

فَظَنَّ أَنْ لَّنْ نَّقْدِرَ عَلَيْهِ فَنَادَى

فِي الظُّلُمَاتِ أَنْ لَّا إِلٰهَ اِلَّا

أَنْتَ سُبْحَانَكَ ۖ اِنِّي كُنْتُ مِنَ

الظَّالِمِينَ ۞

88. So We listened to him: and delivered him from distress: and thus do We deliver those who have faith.

فَاسْتَجَبْنَا لَهُ ۙ وَنَجَّيْنَاهُ مِنَ

الْغَمِّ ۚ وَكَذَلِكَ نُنْجِى الْمُؤْمِنِينَ ۞

89. And (remember) Zakariya, when he cried to his Lord: "O my Lord! do not leave me without offspring, though You are the best of inheritors."

وَزَكَرِيَّا إِذْ نَادَى رَبَّهُ رَبِّ

لَا تَذَرْنِي فَرْدًا وَّأَنْتَ خَيْرُ

الْوَارِثِينَ ۞

90. So We listened to him: and We granted him Yahya: We cured his wife's (Barrenness) for him. These (three) were ever quick in emulation in good works; they used to call on Us with love and reverence, and humble themselves before Us.

فَاسْتَجَبْنَا لَهُ ۫ وَوَهَبْنَا لَهُ يَحْيَى

وَأَصْلَحْنَا لَهُ زَوْجَهُ ۚ إِنَّهُمْ

كَانُوا يُسَارِعُونَ فِي الْخَيْرَاتِ وَ

يَدْعُونَنَا رَغَبًا وَّرَهَبًا ۚ وَكَانُوا

لَنَا خَاشِعِينَ ۞

91. And (remember) her who guarded her chastity: We breathed into her of Our spirit, and We made her

وَالَّتِي أَحْصَنَتْ فَرْجَهَا فَنَفَخْنَا

فِيهَا مِنْ رُّوحِنَا وَجَعَلْنَاهَا

and her son a Sign for all peoples.

92. Verily, this brotherhood of yours is a single brotherhood, and I am your Lord and Cherisher: therefore serve Me (and no other).

93. But (later generations) cut off their affair (of unity), one from another: (yet) they will all return to Us.

94. Whoever works any act of righteousness and has faith,- his endeavour will not be rejected: We shall record it in his favour.

95. But there is a ban on any population which We have destroyed: that they shall not return,

96. Until the Gog and Magog (people) are let through (their barrier), and they swiftly swarm from every hill.

97. Then will the True Promise draw near (of fulfilment): then behold! the eyes of the Unbelievers will fixedly stare in horror: "Ah! woe to us! we were indeed heedless of this; nay, we truly did wrong!"

98. Verily you, (Unbelievers), and the (false) gods that you worship besides Allah, are (but) fuel for Hell! To it will you (surely) come!

99. If these had been gods, they would not have got there! but each one will abide therein.

100. There, sobbing will be their lot, nor will they there hear (anything else.)

101. Those for whom the Good (record) from Us has gone before, will be removed far therefrom.

102. Not the slightest sound will they hear of Hell:

وَابْنَهَا اٰيَةً لِّلْعٰلَمِيْنَ ۞

اِنَّ هٰذِهٖۤ اُمَّتُكُمْ اُمَّةً وَّاحِدَةً ۖ

وَّاَنَا رَبُّكُمْ فَاعْبُدُوْنِ ۞

وَتَقَطَّعُوْۤا اَمْرَهُمْ بَيْنَهُمْ ۖ كُلٌّ

اِلَيْنَا رٰجِعُوْنَ ۞

فَمَنْ يَّعْمَلْ مِنَ الصّٰلِحٰتِ وَهُوَ

مُؤْمِنٌ فَلَا كُفْرَانَ لِسَعْيِهٖ ۚ وَاِنَّا

لَهٗ كٰتِبُوْنَ ۞

وَحَرٰمٌ عَلٰى قَرْيَةٍ اَهْلَكْنٰهَاۤ

اَنَّهُمْ لَا يَرْجِعُوْنَ ۞

حَتّٰۤى اِذَا فُتِحَتْ يَاْجُوْجُ وَمَاْجُوْجُ

وَهُمْ مِّنْ كُلِّ حَدَبٍ يَّنْسِلُوْنَ ۞

وَاقْتَرَبَ الْوَعْدُ الْحَقُّ فَاِذَا هِيَ

شَاخِصَةٌ اَبْصَارُ الَّذِيْنَ كَفَرُوْا ۚ

يٰوَيْلَنَا قَدْ كُنَّا فِيْ غَفْلَةٍ مِّنْ

هٰذَا بَلْ كُنَّا ظٰلِمِيْنَ ۞

اِنَّكُمْ وَمَا تَعْبُدُوْنَ مِنْ دُوْنِ

اللّٰهِ حَصَبُ جَهَنَّمَ ۚ اَنْتُمْ لَهَا

وٰرِدُوْنَ ۞

لَوْ كَانَ هٰۤؤُلَآءِ اٰلِهَةً مَّا وَرَدُوْهَا ۚ

وَكُلٌّ فِيْهَا خٰلِدُوْنَ ۞

لَهُمْ فِيْهَا زَفِيْرٌ وَّهُمْ فِيْهَا

لَا يَسْمَعُوْنَ ۞

اِنَّ الَّذِيْنَ سَبَقَتْ لَهُمْ مِّنَّا الْحُسْنٰۤى ۙ

اُولٰٓئِكَ عَنْهَا مُبْعَدُوْنَ ۞

لَا يَسْمَعُوْنَ حَسِيْسَهَا ۚ وَهُمْ فِيْ

what their souls desired, in that they will dwell.

103. The Great Terror will bring them no grief: but the angels will meet them (with mutual greetings): "This is your Day,- (the Day) that you were promised."

104. The Day that We roll up the heavens like a scroll rolled up for books (completed),- even as We produced the first creation, so shall We produce a new one: a promise We have undertaken: truly shall We fulfil it.

105. Before this We wrote in the Psalms, after the Message (given to Moses): My servants, the righteous, shall inherit the earth."

106. Verily in this (Qur'an) is a Message for people who would (truly) worship Allah.

107. We sent you not, but as a Mercy for all creatures.

108. Say: "What has come to me by inspiration is that your God is One God: will you therefore bow to His Will (in Islam)?"

109. But if they turn back, say: "I have proclaimed the Message to you all alike and in truth; but I do not know whether that which you are promised is near or far.

110. "It is He Who knows what is open in speech and what you hide (in your hearts).

111. "I do not know but that it may be a trial for you, and a grant of (worldly) livelihood (to you) for a time."

112. Say: "O my Lord! You judge in truth!" "Our Lord Most Gracious is the One Whose assistance should be sought against the blasphemies you utter!

SÛRAH-22
AL-HAJJ
(INTRODUCTION)

We now come to a new series of four Sûras, dealing with the environments and methods contributing to our spiritual progress, as the last five Sûras dealt with the Messengers who came in various ways to proclaim the Truth and conquer evil. See Introduction to S: 17.

The subject-matter of this particular Sûrah is concerned mainly with the spiritual implications of the Sacred House, the Pilgrimage, the Sacrifices, Striving and Fighting in defence of Truth when attacked, and other acts that make for Unselfishness and uproot Falsehood.

On the chronology of this Sûrah, opinion is divided. Some parts were probably revealed in the later Makkan period, and some in Madinah. But the chronological question has no significance here.

22. The Pilgrimage
In the name of Allah. Most Gracious, Most Merciful.

(٢٢) سُوْرَةُ الْحَجّ مَدَنِيَّةٌ (١٠٣)

بِسْمِ اللهِ الرَّحْمٰنِ الرَّحِيْمِ

1. O mankind! fear your Lord! for the convulsion of the Hour (of Judgment) will be a thing terrible!

يَاَيُّهَا النَّاسُ اتَّقُوْا رَبَّكُمْ ۚ اِنَّ زَلْزَلَةَ السَّاعَةِ شَيْءٌ عَظِيْمٌ ۞

2. The Day you shall see it, every mother giving suck shall forget her suckling-babe, and every pregnant female shall drop her load (unformed): you shall see mankind as in a drunken riot, yet not drunk: but dreadful will be the Chastisement of Allah.

يَوْمَ تَرَوْنَهَا تَذْهَلُ كُلُّ مُرْضِعَةٍ عَمَّا اَرْضَعَتْ وَتَضَعُ كُلُّ ذَاتِ حَمْلٍ حَمْلَهَا وَتَرَى النَّاسَ سُكَارٰى وَمَا هُمْ بِسُكَارٰى وَلٰكِنَّ عَذَابَ اللهِ شَدِيْدٌ ۞

3. And yet among men there are such as dispute about Allah, without knowledge, and follow every evil one obstinate in rebellion!

وَمِنَ النَّاسِ مَنْ يُّجَادِلُ فِي اللهِ بِغَيْرِ عِلْمٍ وَّيَتَّبِعُ كُلَّ شَيْطٰنٍ مَّرِيْدٍ ۙ

4. About the (Evil One) it is decreed that whoever turns to him for friendship, he will lead him astray, and he will guide him to the Penalty of the Fire.

كُتِبَ عَلَيْهِ اَنَّهُ مَنْ تَوَلَّاهُ فَاَنَّهُ يُضِلُّهُ وَيَهْدِيْهِ اِلٰى عَذَابِ السَّعِيْرِ ۞

5. O mankind! if you have a doubt about the Resurrection, (consider) that We created you out of dust, then out of sperm, then out of a leech-like clot, then out of a morsel of flesh, partly formed and partly unformed, in order that We may manifest (Our power) to you; and We cause whom We will to rest in the wombs for an appointed term, then do We bring you out as babes, then (foster you) that you may reach your age of full strength; and some of you are called to die, and some are sent back to the feeblest old age, so that they know nothing after having known (much), and (further), you see the earth

يَاَيُّهَا النَّاسُ اِنْ كُنْتُمْ فِيْ رَيْبٍ مِّنَ الْبَعْثِ فَاِنَّا خَلَقْنٰكُمْ مِّنْ تُرَابٍ ثُمَّ مِنْ نُّطْفَةٍ ثُمَّ مِنْ عَلَقَةٍ ثُمَّ مِنْ مُّضْغَةٍ مُّخَلَّقَةٍ وَّغَيْرِ مُخَلَّقَةٍ لِّنُبَيِّنَ لَكُمْ ۚ وَنُقِرُّ فِي الْاَرْحَامِ مَا نَشَاءُ اِلٰى اَجَلٍ مُّسَمًّى ثُمَّ نُخْرِجُكُمْ طِفْلًا ثُمَّ لِتَبْلُغُوْا اَشُدَّكُمْ ۚ وَمِنْكُمْ مَّنْ يُّتَوَفّٰى وَمِنْكُمْ مَّنْ يُّرَدُّ اِلٰى اَرْذَلِ الْعُمُرِ لِكَيْلَا يَعْلَمَ مِنْ بَعْدِ عِلْمٍ شَيْئًا ۚ وَتَرَى الْاَرْضَ

barren and lifeless, but when We pour down rain on it, it is stirred (to life), it swells, and it puts forth every kind of beautiful growth (in pairs).

6.   This is so, because Allah is the Reality: it is He Who gives life to the dead, and it is He Who has power over all things.

7.   And verily the Hour will come: there can be no doubt about it, or about (the fact) that Allah will raise up all who are in the graves.

8.   Yet there is among men such a one as disputes about Allah, without knowledge, without guidance, and without a Book of Enlightenment,-

9.   (Disdainfully) bending his side, in order to lead (men) astray from the Path of Allah: for him there is disgrace in this life, and on the Day of Judgment We shall make him taste the Penalty of burning (Fire).

10.   (It will be said): "This is because of the deeds which your hands sent forth, for verily Allah is not unjust to His servants.

11.   There are among men some who serve Allah, as it were, on the verge: if good befalls them, they are, therewith, well content; but if a trial comes to them, they turn on their faces: they lose both this world and the Hereafter: that is loss for all to see!

12.   They call on such deities, besides Allah, as can neither hurt nor profit them: that is straying far indeed (from the Way)!

13.   (Perhaps) they call on one whose hurt is nearer than his profit: evil, indeed, is the patron, and evil the companion (for help)!

هَامِدَةً فَإِذَآ أَنزَلْنَا عَلَيْهَا الْمَآءَ اهْتَزَّتْ وَرَبَتْ وَأَنبَتَتْ مِن كُلِّ زَوْجٍ بَهِيجٍ ۞

ذَٰلِكَ بِأَنَّ اللَّهَ هُوَ الْحَقُّ وَأَنَّهُ يُحْيِ الْمَوْتَىٰ وَأَنَّهُ عَلَىٰ كُلِّ شَيْءٍ قَدِيرٌ ۞

وَأَنَّ السَّاعَةَ آتِيَةٌ لَّا رَيْبَ فِيهَا وَأَنَّ اللَّهَ يَبْعَثُ مَن فِي الْقُبُورِ ۞

وَمِنَ النَّاسِ مَن يُجَادِلُ فِي اللَّهِ بِغَيْرِ عِلْمٍ وَلَا هُدًى وَلَا كِتَابٍ مُّنِيرٍ ۞

ثَانِيَ عِطْفِهِ لِيُضِلَّ عَن سَبِيلِ اللَّهِ لَهُ فِي الدُّنْيَا خِزْيٌ وَنُذِيقُهُ يَوْمَ الْقِيَامَةِ عَذَابَ الْحَرِيقِ ۞

ذَٰلِكَ بِمَا قَدَّمَتْ يَدَاكَ وَأَنَّ اللَّهَ لَيْسَ بِظَلَّامٍ لِّلْعَبِيدِ ۞

وَمِنَ النَّاسِ مَن يَعْبُدُ اللَّهَ عَلَىٰ حَرْفٍ فَإِنْ أَصَابَهُ خَيْرٌ اطْمَأَنَّ بِهِ وَإِنْ أَصَابَتْهُ فِتْنَةٌ انقَلَبَ عَلَىٰ وَجْهِهِ خَسِرَ الدُّنْيَا وَالْآخِرَةَ ذَٰلِكَ هُوَ الْخُسْرَانُ الْمُبِينُ ۞

يَدْعُو مِن دُونِ اللَّهِ مَا لَا يَضُرُّهُ وَمَا لَا يَنفَعُهُ ذَٰلِكَ هُوَ الضَّلَالُ الْبَعِيدُ ۞

يَدْعُو لَمَن ضَرُّهُ أَقْرَبُ مِن نَّفْعِهِ لَبِئْسَ الْمَوْلَىٰ وَلَبِئْسَ الْعَشِيرُ ۞

٨ ع

14. Verily Allah will admit those who believe and work righteous deeds, to Gardens, beneath which rivers flow: for Allah carries out all that He plans.

15. If any think that Allah will not help him (His Messenger) in this world and the Hereafter, let him stretch out a rope to the ceiling and cut (himself) off: then let him see whether his plan will remove that which enrages (him)!

16. Thus We have sent down Clear Sings; and verily Allah guides whom He will!

17. Those who believe (in the Qur'an), those who follow the Jewish (scriptures), and the Sabians, Christians, Magians, and Polytheists,- Allah will judge between them on the Day of Judgment: for Allah is Witness of all things.

18. Do you not see that to Allah bow down in worship all things that are in the heavens and on earth,- the sun, the moon, the stars; the hills, the trees, the animals; and a great number among mankind? But a great number are (also) such as are fit for Punishment: and such as Allah shall disgrace,- none can raise to honour: for Allah carries out all that He wills.

19. These two antagonists dispute with each other about their Lord: but those who deny (their Lord),- for them will be cut out a garment of Fire: over their heads will be poured out boiling water.

20. With it will be scalded what is within their bodies, as well as (their) skins.

21. In addition there will be maces of iron (to punish) them.

22. Every time they wish to get away therefrom, from anguish, they will be forced back therein, and (it will be said), "You taste the Penalty of Burning!"

23. Allah will admit those who believe and work righteous deeds, to Gardens beneath which rivers flow: they shall be adorned therein with bracelets of gold and pearls; and their garments there will be of silk.

24. For they have been guided (in this life) to the purest of speeches; they have been guided to the Path of Him Who is Worthy of (all) Praise.

25. As to those who have rejected (Allah), and would keep back (men) from the Way of Allah, and from the Sacred Mosque, which We have made (open) to (all) men - equal is the dweller there and the visitor from the country - and any whose purpose therein is profanity or wrong-doing - them will We cause to taste of a most grievous Penalty.

26. Behold! We gave the site, to Abraham, of the (Sacred) House, (saying): "Do not associate anything (in worship) with Me; and sanctify My House for those who compass it round, or stand up, or bow, or prostrate themselves (therein in prayer).

27. "And proclaim the Pilgrimage among men: they will come to you on foot and (mounted) on every kind of camel, lean on account of journeys through deep and distant mountain highways;

28. "That they may witness the benefits (provided) for them, and celebrate

يُصْهَرُ بِهٖ مَا فِىْ بُطُوْنِهِمْ وَالْجُلُوْدُ ۞

وَلَهُمْ مَّقَامِعُ مِنْ حَدِيْدٍ ۞

كُلَّمَا اَرَادُوْا اَنْ يَّخْرُجُوْا مِنْهَا مِنْ غَمٍّ اُعِيْدُوْا فِيْهَا ۚ وَذُوْقُوْا عَذَابَ الْحَرِيْقِ ۞

اِنَّ اللّٰهَ يُدْخِلُ الَّذِيْنَ اٰمَنُوْا وَ عَمِلُوا الصّٰلِحٰتِ جَنّٰتٍ تَجْرِىْ مِنْ تَحْتِهَا الْاَنْهٰرُ يُحَلَّوْنَ فِيْهَا مِنْ اَسَاوِرَ مِنْ ذَهَبٍ وَّ لُؤْلُؤًا ۖ وَلِبَاسُهُمْ فِيْهَا حَرِيْرٌ ۞

وَهُدُوْا اِلَى الطَّيِّبِ مِنَ الْقَوْلِ ۚ وَهُدُوْا اِلٰى صِرَاطِ الْحَمِيْدِ ۞

اِنَّ الَّذِيْنَ كَفَرُوْا وَيَصُدُّوْنَ عَنْ سَبِيْلِ اللّٰهِ وَالْمَسْجِدِ الْحَرَامِ الَّذِىْ جَعَلْنٰهُ لِلنَّاسِ سَوَآءَ ۨ الْعَاكِفُ فِيْهِ وَالْبَادِ ۚ وَمَنْ يُّرِدْ فِيْهِ بِاِلْحَادٍ بِظُلْمٍ نُّذِقْهُ مِنْ عَذَابٍ اَلِيْمٍ ۞

وَاِذْ بَوَّاْنَا لِاِبْرٰهِيْمَ مَكَانَ الْبَيْتِ اَنْ لَّا تُشْرِكْ بِىْ شَيْئًا وَّطَهِّرْ بَيْتِىَ لِلطَّآئِفِيْنَ وَالْقَآئِمِيْنَ وَالرُّكَّعِ السُّجُوْدِ ۞

وَاَذِّنْ فِى النَّاسِ بِالْحَجِّ يَاْتُوْكَ رِجَالًا وَّعَلٰى كُلِّ ضَامِرٍ يَّاْتِيْنَ مِنْ كُلِّ فَجٍّ عَمِيْقٍ ۞

لِّيَشْهَدُوْا مَنَافِعَ لَهُمْ وَيَذْكُرُوا

the name of Allah, through the Days appointed, over the cattle which He has provided for them (for sacrifice): then you eat thereof and feed the distressed ones in want.

29. "Then let them complete the rites prescribed for them, perform their vows, and (again) circumambulate the Ancient House."

30. Such (is the Pilgrimage): whoever honours the sacred rites of Allah, for him it is good in the sight of his Lord. Lawful to you (for food in Pilgrimage) are cattle, except those mentioned to you (as exceptions): but shun the abomination of idols, and shun the word that is false,-

31. Being true in faith to Allah, and never assigning partners to Him: if anyone assigns partners to Allah, he is as if he had fallen from heaven and been snatched up by birds, or the wind had swooped (like a bird on its prey) and thrown him into a far-distant place.

32. Such (is his state): and whoever holds in honour the symbols of Allah, (in the sacrifice of animals), such (honour) should come truly from piety of heart.

33. In them you have benefits for a term appointed: in the end their place of sacrifice is near the Ancient House.

34. To every people We appointed rites (of sacrifice), that they might celebrate the name of Allah over the sustenance He gave them from animals (fit for food). But your God is One God (Allah): submit then your wills to Him (in Islam): and you give the good news to those who humble themselves,-

35. To those whose hearts, when Allah is mentioned, are filled with fear, who show patient perseverance over their afflictions, keep up regular prayer,

and spend (in charity) out of what We have bestowed upon them.

36. The sacrificial camels We have made for you as among the Symbols from Allah: in them is (much) good for you: then pronounce the name of Allah over them as they line up (for sacrifice): when they are down on their sides (after slaughter), you eat thereof, and feed such as (beg not but) live in contentment, and such as beg with due humility: thus have We made animals subject to you, that you may be grateful.

37. It is not their meat nor their blood, that reaches Allah: it is your piety that reaches Him: He has thus made them subject to you, that you may glorify Allah for His guidance to you and proclaim the good news to all who do right.

38. Verily Allah will defend (from ill) those who believe: verily, Allah does not love any that is a traitor to faith, or show ingratitude.

39. To those against whom war is made, permission is given (to fight), because they are wronged;- and verily, Allah is most powerful for their aid;-

40. (They are) those who have been expelled from their homes in defiance of right,- (for no cause) except that they say, "Our Lord is Allah". Did not Allah check one set of people by means of another, there would surely have been pulled down monasteries, churches, synagogues, and mosques, in which the name of Allah is commemorated in abundant measure. Allah will certainly aid those who aid His (cause);- for verily Allah is full of Strength, Exalted in Might, (able to enforce His Will).

41. (They are) those who, if We establish them in the land, establish regular prayer and give regular charity,

enjoin the right and forbid wrong: with Allah rests the end (and decision) of (all) affairs.

42.   If they treat your (mission) as false, so did the peoples before them (with their prophets),- the People of Noah, and 'Ad and Thamud;

43.   Those of Abraham and Lut;

44.   And the Companions of the Madyan People; and Moses was rejected (in the same way). But I granted respite to the Unbelievers, and (only) after that did I punish them: but how (terrible) was My rejection (of them)!

45.   How many populations have We destroyed, which were given to wrong-doing? They tumbled down on their roofs. And how many wells are lying idle and neglected, and castles lofty and well-built?

46.   Do they not travel through the land, so that their hearts (and minds) may thus learn wisdom and their ears may thus learn to hear? Truly it is not their eyes that are blind, but their hearts which are in their breasts.

47.   Yet they ask you to hasten on the Punishment! But Allah will not fail in His Promise. Verily a Day in the sight of your Lord is like a thousand years of your reckoning.

48.   And to how many populations did I give respite, which were given to wrong-doing? In the end I punished them. To Me is the destination (of all).

49.   Say: "O men! I am (sent) to you only to give a Clear Warning:

50. "Those who believe and work righteousness, for them is forgiveness and a sustenance most generous.

51. "But those who strive against Our Signs, to frustrate them,- they will be Companions of the Fire."

52. Never did We send a Messenger or a prophet before you, but, when he framed a desire, Satan threw some (vanity) into his desire: but Allah will cancel anything (vain) that Satan throws in, and Allah will confirm (and establish) His Signs: for Allah is full of Knowledge and Wisdom:

53. That He may make the suggestions thrown in by Satan, but a trial for those in whose hearts is a disease and who are hardened of heart: verily the wrong-doers are in a schism far (from the Truth):

54. And that those on whom knowledge has been bestowed may learn that the (Qur'an) is the Truth from your Lord, and that they may believe therein, and their hearts may be made humbly (open) to it: for verily Allah is the Guide of those who believe, to the Straight Way.

55. Those who reject Faith will not cease to be in doubt concerning (Revelation) until the Hour (of Judgment) comes suddenly upon them, or there comes to them the Penalty of a Day of Disaster.

56. On that Day the Dominion will be that of Allah: He will judge between them: so those who believe and work righteous deeds will be in Gardens of Delight.

57. And for those who reject Faith and deny Our Signs,

فَالَّذِينَ اٰمَنُوا وَعَمِلُوا الصّٰلِحٰتِ لَهُمۡ مَّغۡفِرَةٌ وَّرِزۡقٌ كَرِيۡمٌ ۝

وَالَّذِينَ سَعَوۡا فِىۡۤ اٰيٰتِنَا مُعٰجِزِيۡنَ اُولٰٓئِكَ اَصۡحٰبُ الۡجَحِيۡمِ ۝

وَمَاۤ اَرۡسَلۡنَا مِنۡ قَبۡلِكَ مِنۡ رَّسُوۡلٍ وَّلَا نَبِىٍّ اِلَّاۤ اِذَا تَمَنّٰۤى اَلۡقَى الشَّيۡطٰنُ فِىۡۤ اُمۡنِيَّتِهٖ ۚ فَيَنۡسَخُ اللّٰهُ مَا يُلۡقِى الشَّيۡطٰنُ ثُمَّ يُحۡكِمُ اللّٰهُ اٰيٰتِهٖ ؕ وَاللّٰهُ عَلِيۡمٌ حَكِيۡمٌ ۝

لِّيَجۡعَلَ مَا يُلۡقِى الشَّيۡطٰنُ فِتۡنَةً لِّلَّذِينَ فِىۡ قُلُوۡبِهِمۡ مَّرَضٌ وَّالۡقَاسِيَةِ قُلُوۡبُهُمۡ ؕ وَاِنَّ الظّٰلِمِيۡنَ لَفِىۡ شِقَاقٍ بَعِيۡدٍ ۝

وَّلِيَعۡلَمَ الَّذِينَ اُوۡتُوا الۡعِلۡمَ اَنَّهُ الۡحَقُّ مِنۡ رَّبِّكَ فَيُؤۡمِنُوۡا بِهٖ فَتُخۡبِتَ لَهٗ قُلُوۡبُهُمۡ ؕ وَاِنَّ اللّٰهَ لَهَادِ الَّذِينَ اٰمَنُوۡۤا اِلٰى صِرَاطٍ مُّسۡتَقِيۡمٍ ۝

وَلَا يَزَالُ الَّذِينَ كَفَرُوۡا فِىۡ مِرۡيَةٍ مِّنۡهُ حَتّٰى تَأۡتِيَهُمُ السَّاعَةُ بَغۡتَةً اَوۡ يَأۡتِيَهُمۡ عَذَابُ يَوۡمٍ عَقِيۡمٍ ۝

اَلۡمُلۡكُ يَوۡمَئِذٍ لِّلّٰهِ ؕ يَحۡكُمُ بَيۡنَهُمۡ ؕ فَالَّذِينَ اٰمَنُوۡا وَعَمِلُوا الصّٰلِحٰتِ فِىۡ جَنّٰتِ النَّعِيۡمِ ۝

وَالَّذِينَ كَفَرُوۡا وَكَذَّبُوۡا بِاٰيٰتِنَا

there will be a humiliating Punishment.

58. Those who leave their homes in the cause of Allah, and are then slain or die,- on them Allah will bestow verily a goodly Provision: truly Allah is He Who bestows the best Provision.

59. Verily He will admit them to a place with which they shall be well pleased: for Allah is All-Knowing, Most Forbearing.

60. That (is so). And if one has retaliated to no greater extent than the injury he received, and is again set upon inordinately, Allah will help him: for Allah is One that blots out (sins) and forgives (again and again).

61. That is because Allah merges night into day, and He merges day into night, and verily it is Allah Who hears and sees (all things).

62. That is because Allah - He is the Reality; and those besides Him whom they invoke,- they are but vain Falsehood: verily Allah is He, Most High, Most Great.

63. Don't you see that Allah sends down rain from the sky, and forthwith the earth becomes clothed with green? for Allah is He Who understands the finest mysteries, and is well-acquainted (with them).

64. To Him belongs all that is in the heavens and on earth: for verily Allah,- He is free of all wants, Worthy of all Praise.

65. Don't you see that Allah has made subject to you (men) all that is on the earth, and the ships that sail through the sea by His Command? He withholds the sky (rain) from failing on the earth except by His leave: for Allah is Most Kind and Most Merciful to man.

66. It is He Who gave you life, will cause you to die, and will again give you life: truly man is a most ungrateful creature!

وَهُوَ الَّذِىٓ اَحْيَاكُمْ ثُمَّ يُمِيْتُكُمْ ثُمَّ يُحْيِيْكُمْ ۗ اِنَّ الْاِنْسَانَ لَكَفُوْرٌ ۞

67. To every people We have appointed rites and ceremonies which they must follow: let them not then dispute with you on the matter, but you do invite (them) to your Lord: for you are assuredly on the Right Way.

لِكُلِّ اُمَّةٍ جَعَلْنَا مَنْسَكًا هُمْ نَاسِكُوْهُ فَلَا يُنَازِعُنَّكَ فِى الْاَمْرِ وَادْعُ اِلٰى رَبِّكَ ۗ اِنَّكَ لَعَلٰى هُدًى مُّسْتَقِيْمٍ ۞

68. If they do wrangle with you, say, "Allah knows best what it is you are doing."

وَاِنْ جَادَلُوْكَ فَقُلِ اللّٰهُ اَعْلَمُ بِمَا تَعْمَلُوْنَ ۞

69. "Allah will judge between you on the Day of Judgment concerning the matters in which you differ."

اَللّٰهُ يَحْكُمُ بَيْنَكُمْ يَوْمَ الْقِيٰمَةِ فِيْمَا كُنْتُمْ فِيْهِ تَخْتَلِفُوْنَ ۞

70. Don't you know that Allah knows all that is in heaven and on earth? Indeed it is all in a Record, and that is easy for Allah.

اَلَمْ تَعْلَمْ اَنَّ اللّٰهَ يَعْلَمُ مَا فِى السَّمَآءِ وَالْاَرْضِ ۗ اِنَّ ذٰلِكَ فِىْ كِتٰبٍ ۗ اِنَّ ذٰلِكَ عَلَى اللّٰهِ يَسِيْرٌ ۞

71. Yet they worship besides Allah, things for which no authority has been sent down to them, and of which they have (really) no knowledge: for those that do wrong there is no helper.

وَيَعْبُدُوْنَ مِنْ دُوْنِ اللّٰهِ مَا لَمْ يُنَزِّلْ بِهٖ سُلْطٰنًا وَّمَا لَيْسَ لَهُمْ بِهٖ عِلْمٌ ۗ وَمَا لِلظّٰلِمِيْنَ مِنْ نَّصِيْرٍ ۞

72. When Our Clear Signs are rehearsed to them, you will notice a denial on the faces of the Unbelievers! they nearly attack with violence those who rehearse Our Signs to them. Say, "Shall I tell you of something (far) worse than these Signs? It is the Fire (of Hell)! Allah has promised it to the Unbelievers! and evil is that destination!"

وَاِذَا تُتْلٰى عَلَيْهِمْ اٰيٰتُنَا بَيِّنٰتٍ تَعْرِفُ فِىْ وُجُوْهِ الَّذِيْنَ كَفَرُوا الْمُنْكَرَ ۗ يَكَادُوْنَ يَسْطُوْنَ بِالَّذِيْنَ يَتْلُوْنَ عَلَيْهِمْ اٰيٰتِنَا ۗ قُلْ اَفَاُنَبِّئُكُمْ بِشَرٍّ مِّنْ ذٰلِكُمْ ۗ اَلنَّارُ وَعَدَهَا اللّٰهُ الَّذِيْنَ كَفَرُوْا ۗ وَبِئْسَ الْمَصِيْرُ ۞

73. O men! Here is a parable set forth! listen to it! Those on whom, besides Allah, you call,

يٰٓاَيُّهَا النَّاسُ ضُرِبَ مَثَلٌ فَاسْتَمِعُوْا لَهٗ ۗ اِنَّ الَّذِيْنَ تَدْعُوْنَ

SÛRAH-23
AL-MU'MINÛN
(INTRODUCTION)

This Sûrah deals with the virtues which are the seed-bed of Faith, especially in an environment in which Truth is denied and its votaries insulted and persecuted. But Truth is One and must prevail. Those who do wrong will be filled with vain regrets when it is too late for repentance.

It belongs to the late Makkan period.

cannot create (even) a fly, if they all met together for the purpose! And if the fly should snatch away anything from them, they would have no power to release it from the fly. Feeble are those who petition and those whom they petition!

74. No just estimate have they made of Allah: for Allah is He Who is strong and able to carry out His Will.

75. Allah chooses Messengers from angels and from men, for Allah is He Who hears and sees (all things).

76. He knows what is before them and what is behind them: and to Allah go back all questions (for decision).

77. O you who believe! Bow down, prostrate yourselves, and adore your Lord; and do good; that you may prosper.

78. And strive in His cause as you ought to strive, (with sincerity and under discipline). He has chosen you, and has imposed no difficulties on you in religion; it is the cult of your father Abraham. It is He Who has named you Muslims, both before and in this (Revelation); that the Messenger may be a witness for you, and you be witnesses for mankind! So establish regular Prayer, give regular Charity, and hold fast to Allah! He is your Protector - the Best to protect and the Best to help!

23. The Believers
In the name of Allah. Most Gracious, Most Merciful.

1. The Believers must (eventually) win through,-

2.   Those who humble themselves in their prayers;

3.   Who avoid vain talk;

4.   Who are active in deeds of charity;

5.   Who abstain from sex,

6.   Except with those joined to them in the marriage bond, or (the captives) whom their right hands possess,- for (in their case) they are free from blame,

7.   But those whose desires exceed those limits are transgressors;-

8.   Those who faithfully observe their trusts and their covenants;

9.   And who (strictly) guard their prayers;-

10.   These will be the heirs,

11.   Who will inherit Paradise: they will dwell therein (for ever).

12.   We created man from a quintessence (of clay);

13.   Then We placed him as (a drop of) sperm in a place of rest, firmly fixed;

14.   Then We made the sperm into a clot of congealed blood; then of that clot We made a (foetus) lump; then We made out of that lump bones and clothed the bones with flesh; then We developed out of it another creature. So blessed be Allah, the Best to create!

15.   After that, at length you will die.

16.   Again, on the Day of Judgment, you will be raised up.

17. And We have made, above you, seven tracts; and We are never unmindful of (Our) Creation.

وَلَقَدْ خَلَقْنَا فَوْقَكُمْ سَبْعَ طَرَآئِقَ وَمَا كُنَّا عَنِ الْخَلْقِ غٰفِلِيْنَ ۝

18. And We send down water from the sky according to (due) measure, and We cause it to soak in the soil; and We certainly are able to drain it off (with ease).

وَاَنْزَلْنَا مِنَ السَّمَآءِ مَآءً بِقَدَرٍ فَاَسْكَنّٰهُ فِى الْاَرْضِ وَاِنَّا عَلٰى ذَهَابٍ بِهٖ لَقٰدِرُوْنَ ۝

19. With it We grow for you gardens of date-palms and vines: in them you have abundant fruits: and of them you eat (and have enjoyment),-

فَاَنْشَأْنَا لَكُمْ بِهٖ جَنّٰتٍ مِّنْ نَّخِيْلٍ وَّاَعْنَابٍ ۘ لَكُمْ فِيْهَا فَوَاكِهُ كَثِيْرَةٌ وَّمِنْهَا تَأْكُلُوْنَ ۝

20. Also a tree springing out of Mount Sinai, which produces oil, and relish for those who use it for food.

وَشَجَرَةً تَخْرُجُ مِنْ طُوْرِ سَيْنَآءَ تَنْبُتُ بِالدُّهْنِ وَصِبْغٍ لِّلْاٰكِلِيْنَ ۝

21. And in cattle (too) you have an instructive example: from within their bodies We produce (milk) for you to drink; there are, in them, (besides), numerous (other) benefits for you; and of their (meat) you eat;

وَاِنَّ لَكُمْ فِى الْاَنْعَامِ لَعِبْرَةً ۘ نُسْقِيْكُمْ مِّمَّا فِيْ بُطُوْنِهَا وَلَكُمْ فِيْهَا مَنَافِعُ كَثِيْرَةٌ وَّمِنْهَا تَأْكُلُوْنَ ۝

22. And on them, as well as in ships, you ride.

وَعَلَيْهَا وَعَلَى الْفُلْكِ تُحْمَلُوْنَ ۝

23. We sent Noah to his people: he said, "O my people; worship Allah, you have no other god but Him. Will you not fear (Him)?"

وَلَقَدْ اَرْسَلْنَا نُوْحًا اِلٰى قَوْمِهٖ فَقَالَ يٰقَوْمِ اعْبُدُوا اللّٰهَ مَا لَكُمْ مِّنْ اِلٰهٍ غَيْرُهٗ ۗ اَفَلَا تَتَّقُوْنَ ۝

24. The chiefs of the Unbelievers among his people said: "He is no more than a man like yourselves: his wish is to assert his superiority over you. If Allah had wished (to send Messengers), He could have sent down angels; never did we hear such a thing (as he says), among our ancestors of old."

فَقَالَ الْمَلَؤُا الَّذِيْنَ كَفَرُوْا مِنْ قَوْمِهٖ مَا هٰذَآ اِلَّا بَشَرٌ مِّثْلُكُمْ ۙ يُرِيْدُ اَنْ يَّتَفَضَّلَ عَلَيْكُمْ ۗ وَلَوْ شَآءَ اللّٰهُ لَاَنْزَلَ مَلٰٓئِكَةً ۖ مَّا سَمِعْنَا بِهٰذَا فِيْۤ اٰبَآئِنَا الْاَوَّلِيْنَ ۝

25. (And some said): "He is only a man possessed; wait (and have patience) with him for a time."

اِنْ هُوَ اِلَّا رَجُلٌۢ بِهٖ جِنَّةٌ فَتَرَبَّصُوْا بِهٖ حَتّٰى حِيْنٍ ۝

26. (Noah) said: "O my Lord! help me: for that they accuse me of falsehood!"

قَالَ رَبِّ انْصُرْنِيْ بِمَا كَذَّبُوْنِ ۝

27. So We inspired him (with this message): "Construct the Ark

فَاَوْحَيْنَآ اِلَيْهِ اَنِ اصْنَعِ الْفُلْكَ

within Our sight and under Our guidance: then when comes Our command, and the fountains of the earth gush forth, you take on board pairs of every species, male and female, and your family- except those of them against whom the Word has already gone forth: and do not address Me in favour of the wrong-doers; for they shall be drowned (in the Flood).

28. And when you have embarked on the Ark - you and those with you,- say: "Praise be to Allah, Who has saved us from the people who do wrong."

29. And say: "O my Lord! enable me to disembark with Your blessing: for You are the Best to enable (us) to disembark."

30. Verily in this there are Signs (for men to understand); (thus) do We try (men).

31. Then We raised after them another generation.

32. And We sent to them a Messenger from among themselves, (saying), "Worship Allah! you have no other god but Him. Will you not fear (Him)?"

33. And the chiefs of his people, who disbelieved and denied the Meeting in the Hereafter, and on whom We had bestowed the good things of this life, said: "He is no more than a man like yourselves: he eats of that of which you eat, and drinks of what you drink.

34. "If you obey a man like yourselves, behold, it is certain you will be lost.

35. "Does he promise that when you die and become dust and bones, you shall be brought forth (again)?

36. "Far, very far is that which you are promised!

بِأَعْيُنِنَا وَوَحْيِنَا فَإِذَا جَاءَ أَمْرُنَا

وَفَارَ التَّنُّورُ فَاسْلُكْ فِيهَا مِنْ كُلٍّ

زَوْجَيْنِ اثْنَيْنِ وَأَهْلَكَ إِلَّا مَنْ سَبَقَ

عَلَيْهِ الْقَوْلُ مِنْهُمْ وَلَا تُخَاطِبْنِي

فِي الَّذِينَ ظَلَمُوا إِنَّهُمْ مُغْرَقُونَ ۝

فَإِذَا اسْتَوَيْتَ أَنْتَ وَمَنْ مَعَكَ

عَلَى الْفُلْكِ فَقُلِ الْحَمْدُ لِلَّهِ الَّذِي

نَجَّانَا مِنَ الْقَوْمِ الظَّالِمِينَ ۝

وَقُلْ رَبِّ أَنْزِلْنِي مُنْزَلًا مُبَارَكًا وَّ

أَنْتَ خَيْرُ الْمُنْزِلِينَ ۝

إِنَّ فِي ذَلِكَ لَآيَاتٍ وَإِنْ كُنَّا

لَمُبْتَلِينَ ۝

ثُمَّ أَنْشَأْنَا مِنْ بَعْدِهِمْ قَرْنًا آخَرِينَ ۝

فَأَرْسَلْنَا فِيهِمْ رَسُولًا مِنْهُمْ أَنِ

اعْبُدُوا اللَّهَ مَا لَكُمْ مِنْ إِلَهٍ غَيْرُهُ

أَفَلَا تَتَّقُونَ ۝

وَقَالَ الْمَلَأُ مِنْ قَوْمِهِ الَّذِينَ كَفَرُوا

وَكَذَّبُوا بِلِقَاءِ الْآخِرَةِ وَأَتْرَفْنَاهُمْ

فِي الْحَيَاةِ الدُّنْيَا مَا هَذَا إِلَّا بَشَرٌ

مِثْلُكُمْ يَأْكُلُ مِمَّا تَأْكُلُونَ مِنْهُ

وَيَشْرَبُ مِمَّا تَشْرَبُونَ ۝

وَلَئِنْ أَطَعْتُمْ بَشَرًا مِثْلَكُمْ إِنَّكُمْ

إِذًا لَخَاسِرُونَ ۝

أَيَعِدُكُمْ أَنَّكُمْ إِذَا مِتُّمْ وَكُنْتُمْ تُرَابًا

وَعِظَامًا أَنَّكُمْ مُخْرَجُونَ ۝

هَيْهَاتَ هَيْهَاتَ لِمَا تُوعَدُونَ ۝

37. "There is nothing but our life in this world! We shall die and we live! But we shall never be raised up again!

38. "He is only a man who invents a lie against Allah, but we are not the ones to believe in him!"

39. (The prophet) said: "O my Lord! help me: for that they accuse me of falsehood."

40. (Alalh) said: "In but a little while, they are sure to be sorry!"

41. Then the Blast overtook them with justice, and We made them as rubbish of dead leaves (floating on the stream of Time)! So away with the people who do wrong!

42. Then We raised after them other generations.

43. No people can hasten their term, nor can they delay (it).

44. Then We sent Our Messengers in succession: every time there came to a people their Messenger, they accused him of falsehood: so We made them follow each other (in punishment): We made them as a tale (that is told): so away with a people that will not believe!

45. Then We sent Moses and his brother Aaron, with Our Signs and authority manifest,

46. To Pharaoh and his Chiefs: but these behaved insolently: they were an arrogant people.

47. They said: "Shall we believe in two men like ourselves? And their people are subject to us!"

48. So they (rejected) and accused them of falsehood, and they became of those who were destroyed.

49. And We gave Moses the Book, in order that they might receive guidance.

50. And We made the son of Mary and his mother as a Sign:

We gave them both shelter on high ground, affording rest and security and furnished with springs.

51. O you Messengers! enjoy (all) things good and pure, and work righteousness: for I am well-acquainted with (all) that you do.

52. And verily this Brotherhood of yours is a single Brotherhood, and I am your Lord and Cherisher: therefore fear Me (and no other).

53. But people have cut off their affair (of unity), between them, into sects: each party rejoices in that which is with itself

54. But leave them in their confused ignorance for a time.

55. Do they think that because We have granted them abundance of wealth and sons,

56. We would hasten them on in every good? Nay, they do not understand.

57. Verily those who live in awe for fear of their Lord;

58. Those who believe in the Signs of their Lord;

59. Those who do not join (in worship) partners with their Lord;

60. And those who dispense their charity with their hearts full of fear, because they will return to their Lord;-

61. It is these who hasten in every good work, and these who are foremost in them.

62. On no soul do We place a burden greater than it can bear: before Us is a record which clearly speaks the truth: they will never be wronged.

63. But their hearts are in confused ignorance of this;

and there are, besides that, deeds of theirs, which they will (continue) to do,-

64. Until, when We seize in Punishment those of them who received the good things of this world, behold, they will groan in supplication!

65. (It will be said): "Do not groan in supplication this day: for you shall certainly not be helped by Us.

66. "My Signs used to be rehearsed to you, but you used to turn back on your heels-

67. "In arrogance: talking nonsense about the (Qur'an), like one telling fables by night."

68. Do they not ponder over the Word (of Allah), or has anything (new) come to them that did not come to their fathers of old?

69. Or do they not recognise their Messenger, that they deny him?

70. Or do they say, "He is possessed"? Nay, he has brought them the Truth, but most of them hate the Truth.

71. If the Truth had been in accord with their desires, truly the heavens and the earth, and all beings therein would have been in confusion and corruption! Nay, We have sent them their admonition, but they turn away from their admonition.

72. Or is it that you ask them for some recompense? But the recompense of your Lord is best: He is the Best of those who give sustenance.

73. But verily you call them to the Straight Way;

74. And verily those who do not believe in the Hereafter are deviating from that Way.

75. If We had mercy on them and removed the distress which is on them,

they would obstinately persist in their transgression, wandering in distraction to and fro.

76. We inflicted Punishment on them, but they did not humble themselves to their Lord, nor do they submissively entreat (Him)!-

77. Until We open on them a gate leading to a severe Punishment: then lo! they will be plunged in despair therein!

78. It is He Who has created for you (the faculties of) hearing, sight, feeling and understanding: but little thanks it is you give!

79. And He has multiplied you through the earth, and to Him you shall be gathered back.

80. It is He Who gives life and death, and to Him (is due) the alternation of Night and Day: will you not then understand?

81. On the contrary they say things similar to what the ancients said.

82. They say: "What! when we die and become dust and bones, could we really be raised up again?

83. "Such things have been promised to us and to our fathers before! they are nothing but tales of the ancients!"

84. Say: "To whom belong the earth and all beings therein? (say) if you know!"

85. They will say, "To Allah!" say: "Yet will you not receive admonition?"

86. Say: "Who is the Lord of the seven heavens, and the Lord of the Throne (of Glory) Supreme?"

87. They will say, "(They belong) to Allah." Say: "Will you not then fear?"

88. Say: "Who is it in whose hands is the governance of all things,- who protects (all), but is not protected (of any)? (say) if you know."

لَّلَجُّوْا فِيْ طُغْيَانِهِمْ يَعْمَهُوْنَ ۝

وَلَقَدْ اَخَذْنٰهُمْ بِالْعَذَابِ فَمَا اسْتَكَانُوْا لِرَبِّهِمْ وَمَا يَتَضَرَّعُوْنَ ۝

حَتّٰى اِذَا فَتَحْنَا عَلَيْهِمْ بَابًا ذَا عَذَابٍ شَدِيْدٍ اِذَا هُمْ فِيْهِ مُبْلِسُوْنَ ۝

وَهُوَ الَّذِىْ اَنْشَاَ لَكُمُ السَّمْعَ وَالْاَبْصَارَ وَالْاَفْـئِدَةَ ۚ قَلِيْلًا مَّا تَشْكُرُوْنَ ۝

وَهُوَ الَّذِىْ ذَرَاَكُمْ فِى الْاَرْضِ وَاِلَيْهِ تُحْشَرُوْنَ ۝

وَهُوَ الَّذِىْ يُحْيٖ وَيُمِيْتُ وَلَهُ اخْتِلَافُ الَّيْلِ وَالنَّهَارِ ۚ اَفَلَا تَعْقِلُوْنَ ۝

بَلْ قَالُوْا مِثْلَ مَا قَالَ الْاَوَّلُوْنَ ۝

قَالُوْۤا ءَاِذَا مِتْنَا وَكُنَّا تُرَابًا وَّعِظَامًا ءَاِنَّا لَمَبْعُوْثُوْنَ ۝

لَقَدْ وُعِدْنَا نَحْنُ وَاٰبَاؤُنَا هٰذَا مِنْ قَبْلُ اِنْ هٰذَا اِلَّاۤ اَسَاطِيْرُ الْاَوَّلِيْنَ ۝

قُلْ لِّمَنِ الْاَرْضُ وَمَنْ فِيْهَاۤ اِنْ كُنْتُمْ تَعْلَمُوْنَ ۝

سَيَقُوْلُوْنَ لِلّٰهِ ۚ قُلْ اَفَلَا تَذَكَّرُوْنَ ۝

قُلْ مَنْ رَّبُّ السَّمٰوٰتِ السَّبْعِ وَرَبُّ الْعَرْشِ الْعَظِيْمِ ۝

سَيَقُوْلُوْنَ لِلّٰهِ ۚ قُلْ اَفَلَا تَتَّقُوْنَ ۝

قُلْ مَنْ بِيَدِهٖ مَلَكُوْتُ كُلِّ شَىْءٍ وَّهُوَ يُجِيْرُ وَلَا يُجَارُ عَلَيْهِ اِنْ كُنْتُمْ

89. They will say, "(It belongs) to Allah." Say: "Then how are you deluded?"

90. We have sent them the Truth: but they indeed practise Falsehood!

91. No son did Allah beget, nor is there any god along with Him: (if there were many gods), behold, each god would have taken away what he had created, and some would have lorded it over others! Glory to Allah! (He is free) from the (sort of) things they attribute to Him!

92. He knows what is hidden and what is open: too high is He for the partners they attribute to Him!

93. Say: "O my Lord! if You will show me (in my lifetime) that which they are warned against,-

94. "Then, O my Lord! put me not amongst the people who do wrong!"

95. And We are certainly able to show you (in fulfilment) that against which they are warned.

96. Repel evil with that which is best: We are well acquainted with the things they say.

97. And say "O my Lord! I seek refuge with You from the suggestions of the Evil Ones.

98. "And I seek refuge with You O my Lord! lest they should come near me."

99. (In Falsehood will they be) until, when death comes to one of them, he says: "O my Lord! send me back (to life),-

100. "In order that I may work righteousness in the things I neglected." - "By no means! It is but a word he says."- Before them is a Partition till the Day they are raised up.

101. Then when the Trumpet is blown, there will be no more relationships between them that Day, nor will one ask after another!

102. Then those whose balance (of good deeds) is heavy,- they will attain salvation:

فَمَنْ ثَقُلَتْ مَوَازِيْنُهُ فَاُولٰٓئِكَ هُمُ الْمُفْلِحُوْنَ ۝

103. But those whose balance is light, will be those who have lost their souls, in Hell will they abide.

وَمَنْ خَفَّتْ مَوَازِيْنُهُ فَاُولٰٓئِكَ الَّذِيْنَ خَسِرُوْٓا اَنْفُسَهُمْ فِيْ جَهَنَّمَ خٰلِدُوْنَ ۝

104. The Fire will burn their faces, and they will therein grin, with their lips displaced.

تَلْفَحُ وُجُوْهَهُمُ النَّارُ وَهُمْ فِيْهَا كٰلِحُوْنَ ۝

105. "Were not My Signs rehearsed to you, and you but treated them as falsehoods?"

اَلَمْ تَكُنْ اٰيٰتِيْ تُتْلٰى عَلَيْكُمْ فَكُنْتُمْ بِهَا تُكَذِّبُوْنَ ۝

106. They will say: "Our Lord! our misfortune overwhelmed us, and we became a people astray!

قَالُوْا رَبَّنَا غَلَبَتْ عَلَيْنَا شِقْوَتُنَا وَكُنَّا قَوْمًا ضَآلِّيْنَ ۝

107. "Our Lord! bring us out of this: if ever we return (to evil), then shall we be wrong-doers indeed!"

رَبَّنَآ اَخْرِجْنَا مِنْهَا فَاِنْ عُدْنَا فَاِنَّا ظٰلِمُوْنَ ۝

108. He will say: "Be you driven into it (with ignominy)! and do not speak to Me!

قَالَ اخْسَئُوْا فِيْهَا وَلَا تُكَلِّمُوْنِ ۝

109. "A part of My servants there was, who used to pray, Our Lord! we believe; then You forgive us, and have mercy upon us: for You are the Best of those who show mercy!"

اِنَّهُ كَانَ فَرِيْقٌ مِّنْ عِبَادِيْ يَقُوْلُوْنَ رَبَّنَآ اٰمَنَّا فَاغْفِرْ لَنَا وَارْحَمْنَا وَاَنْتَ خَيْرُ الرّٰحِمِيْنَ ۝

110. "But you treated them with ridicule, so much so that (ridicule of) them made you forget My Message while you were laughing at them!

فَاتَّخَذْتُمُوْهُمْ سِخْرِيًّا حَتّٰٓى اَنْسَوْكُمْ ذِكْرِيْ وَكُنْتُمْ مِّنْهُمْ تَضْحَكُوْنَ ۝

111. "I have rewarded them this day for their patience and constancy: they are indeed the ones that have achieved bliss..."

اِنِّيْ جَزَيْتُهُمُ الْيَوْمَ بِمَا صَبَرُوْٓا اَنَّهُمْ هُمُ الْفَآئِزُوْنَ ۝

112. He will say: "What number of years did you stay on earth?"

قٰلَ كَمْ لَبِثْتُمْ فِي الْاَرْضِ عَدَدَ سِنِيْنَ ۝

113. They will say: "We stayed a day or part of a day: but ask those who keep account."

قَالُوْا لَبِثْنَا يَوْمًا اَوْ بَعْضَ يَوْمٍ فَسْئَلِ الْعَآدِّيْنَ ۝

114. He will say: "You stayed not but a little,- if you had only known!

قٰلَ اِنْ لَّبِثْتُمْ اِلَّا قَلِيْلًا لَّوْ اَنَّكُمْ كُنْتُمْ تَعْلَمُوْنَ ۝

SÛRAH-24
AN-NÛR
(INTRODUCTION)

The environmental and social influences which most frequently wreck our spiritual ideals have to do with sex, and especially with its misuse, whether in the form of unregulated behaviour, of false charges or scandals, or breach of the refined conventions of personal or domestic privacy. Our complete conquest of all pitfalls in such matters enables us to rise to the higher regions of Light and of Allah-created Nature, about which a mystic doctrine is suggested. This subject is continued in the next Sûrah.

As the reprobation of false slanders about women (24: 11 - 20) is connected with an incident that happened to Ḥaḍhrat 'Âi-sha in A.H. 5-6, that fixes the chronological place of this Madinah Sûrah.

115. "Did you then think that We had created you in jest, and that you would not be brought back to Us (for account)?"

اَفَحَسِبْتُمْ اَنَّمَا خَلَقْنٰكُمْ عَبَثًا وَّاَنَّكُمْ اِلَيْنَا لَا تُرْجَعُوْنَ ۝

116. Therefore exalted be Allah, the King, the Reality: there is no god but He, the Lord of the Throne of Honour!

فَتَعٰلَى اللّٰهُ الْمَلِكُ الْحَقُّ ۚ لَاۤ اِلٰهَ اِلَّا هُوَ ۚ رَبُّ الْعَرْشِ الْكَرِيْمِ ۝

117. If anyone invokes, besides Allah, any other god, he has no authority therefor; and his reckoning will be only with his Lord! and verily the Unbelievers shall not prosper!

وَمَنْ يَّدْعُ مَعَ اللّٰهِ اِلٰهًا اٰخَرَ ۙ لَا بُرْهَانَ لَهٗ بِهٖ ۙ فَاِنَّمَا حِسَابُهٗ عِنْدَ رَبِّهٖ ۭ اِنَّهٗ لَا يُفْلِحُ الْكٰفِرُوْنَ ۝

118. So say: "O my Lord! Grant us forgiveness and mercy! for You are the Best of those who show mercy!"

وَقُلْ رَّبِّ اغْفِرْ وَارْحَمْ وَاَنْتَ خَيْرُ الرّٰحِمِيْنَ ۝

24. The Light
In the name of Allah. Most Gracious, Most Merciful.

(٢٤) سُوْرَةُ النُّوْرِ مَدَنِيَّةٌ (١٠٢)

بِسْمِ اللّٰهِ الرَّحْمٰنِ الرَّحِيْمِ

1. A Surah which We have sent down and which We have ordained: in it We have sent down Clear Signs, in order that you may receive admonition.

سُوْرَةٌ اَنْزَلْنٰهَا وَفَرَضْنٰهَا وَاَنْزَلْنَا فِيْهَاۤ اٰيٰتٍۢ بَيِّنٰتٍ لَّعَلَّكُمْ تَذَكَّرُوْنَ ۝

2. The woman and the man guilty of adultery or fornication,- flog each of them with a hundred stripes: let not compassion move you in their case, in a matter prescribed by Allah, if you believe in Allah and the Last Day: and let a party of the Believers witness their punishment.

اَلزَّانِيَةُ وَالزَّانِيْ فَاجْلِدُوْا كُلَّ وَاحِدٍ مِّنْهُمَا مِائَةَ جَلْدَةٍ ۪ وَّلَا تَأْخُذْكُمْ بِهِمَا رَأْفَةٌ فِيْ دِيْنِ اللّٰهِ اِنْ كُنْتُمْ تُؤْمِنُوْنَ بِاللّٰهِ وَالْيَوْمِ الْاٰخِرِ ۚ وَلْيَشْهَدْ عَذَابَهُمَا طَآئِفَةٌ مِّنَ الْمُؤْمِنِيْنَ ۝

3. Let no man guilty of adultery or fornication marry any but a woman similarly guilty, or an Unbeliever: nor let any but such a man or an Unbeliever marry such a woman: to the Believers such a thing is forbidden.

اَلزَّانِيْ لَا يَنْكِحُ اِلَّا زَانِيَةً اَوْ مُشْرِكَةً ۫ وَّالزَّانِيَةُ لَا يَنْكِحُهَاۤ اِلَّا زَانٍ اَوْ مُشْرِكٌ ۚ وَحُرِّمَ ذٰلِكَ عَلَى الْمُؤْمِنِيْنَ ۝

4. And those who launch a charge against chaste women, and produce not four witnesses (to support their allegations),- flog them with eighty stripes; and reject their evidence ever after: for such men are wicked transgressors;-

وَالَّذِيْنَ يَرْمُوْنَ الْمُحْصَنٰتِ ثُمَّ لَمْ يَأْتُوْا بِاَرْبَعَةِ شُهَدَآءَ فَاجْلِدُوْهُمْ ثَمٰنِيْنَ جَلْدَةً وَّلَا تَقْبَلُوْا لَهُمْ شَهَادَةً اَبَدًا ۚ وَاُولٰٓئِكَ هُمُ الْفٰسِقُوْنَ ۝

5. Unless they repent thereafter and mend (their conduct); for Allah is Oft-Forgiving, Most Merciful.

6. And for those who launch a charge against their spouses, and have (in support) no evidence but their own,- their solitary evidence (can be received) if they bear witness four times (with an oath) by Allah that they are solemnly telling the truth;

7. And the fifth (oath) (should be) that they solemnly invoke the curse of Allah on themselves if they tell a lie;

8. But it would avert the punishment from the wife, if she bears witness four times (with an oath) by Allah, that (her husband) is telling a lie;

9. And the fifth (oath) should be that she solemnly invokes the wrath of Allah on herself if (her accuser) is telling the truth.

10. If it were not for Allah's grace and mercy on you, and that Allah is Oft- Returning, full of Wisdom,- (you would be ruined indeed).

11. Those who brought forward the lie are a body among yourselves: think it not to be an evil to you; on the contrary it is good for you: to every man among them (will come the punishment) of the sin that he earned, and to him who took on himself the lead among them, will be a Penalty grievous.

12. Why did not the Believers - men and women - when you heard of the affair,- thought well of their people and say, "This (charge) is an obvious lie"?

13. Why did they not bring four witnesses to prove it? When they have not brought the witnesses, such men, in the sight of Allah, (stand forth) themselves as liars!

إِلَّا الَّذِينَ تَابُوا مِنْ بَعْدِ ذٰلِكَ وَأَصْلَحُوا فَإِنَّ اللهَ غَفُورٌ رَّحِيمٌ ۝

وَالَّذِينَ يَرْمُونَ أَزْوَاجَهُمْ وَلَمْ يَكُنْ لَّهُمْ شُهَدَاءُ إِلَّا أَنْفُسُهُمْ فَشَهَادَةُ أَحَدِهِمْ أَرْبَعُ شَهَادَاتٍ بِاللهِ ۙ إِنَّهُ لَمِنَ الصَّادِقِينَ ۝

وَالْخَامِسَةُ أَنَّ لَعْنَتَ اللهِ عَلَيْهِ إِنْ كَانَ مِنَ الْكَاذِبِينَ ۝

وَيَدْرَؤُا عَنْهَا الْعَذَابَ أَنْ تَشْهَدَ أَرْبَعَ شَهَادَاتٍ بِاللهِ ۙ إِنَّهُ لَمِنَ الْكَاذِبِينَ ۝

وَالْخَامِسَةَ أَنَّ غَضَبَ اللهِ عَلَيْهَا إِنْ كَانَ مِنَ الصَّادِقِينَ ۝

وَلَوْلَا فَضْلُ اللهِ عَلَيْكُمْ وَرَحْمَتُهُ وَأَنَّ اللهَ تَوَّابٌ حَكِيمٌ ۝

إِنَّ الَّذِينَ جَاءُوا بِالْإِفْكِ عُصْبَةٌ مِّنْكُمْ ۚ لَا تَحْسَبُوهُ شَرًّا لَّكُمْ ۖ بَلْ هُوَ خَيْرٌ لَّكُمْ ۚ لِكُلِّ امْرِئٍ مِّنْهُمْ مَّا اكْتَسَبَ مِنَ الْإِثْمِ ۚ وَالَّذِي تَوَلَّى كِبْرَهُ مِنْهُمْ لَهُ عَذَابٌ عَظِيمٌ ۝

لَوْلَا إِذْ سَمِعْتُمُوهُ ظَنَّ الْمُؤْمِنُونَ وَالْمُؤْمِنَاتُ بِأَنْفُسِهِمْ خَيْرًا ۙ وَقَالُوا هٰذَا إِفْكٌ مُّبِينٌ ۝

لَوْلَا جَاءُوا عَلَيْهِ بِأَرْبَعَةِ شُهَدَاءَ ۚ فَإِذْ لَمْ يَأْتُوا بِالشُّهَدَاءِ فَأُولٰئِكَ عِنْدَ اللهِ هُمُ الْكَاذِبُونَ ۝

14. Were it not for the grace and mercy of Allah on you, in this world and the Hereafter, a grievous Penalty would have seized you in that you rushed glibly into this affair.

15. Behold, you received it on your tongues, and said out of your mouths things of which you had no knowledge; and you thought it to be a light matter, while it was most serious in the sight of Allah.

16. And why did you not, when you heard it, say? - "It is not right of us to speak of this: Glory to Allah! this is a most serious slander!"

17. Allah admonishes you, that you may never repeat such (conduct), if you are (true) Believers.

18. And Allah makes the Signs plain to you: for Allah is full of knowledge and wisdom.

19. Those who love (to see) scandal published broadcast among the Believers, will have a grievous Penalty in this life and in the Hereafter: Allah knows, and you do not know.

20. Were it not for the grace and mercy of Allah on you, and that Allah is full of kindness and mercy, (you would be ruined indeed).

21. O you who believe! Do not follow Satan's footsteps: if any will follow the footsteps of Satan, he will (but) command what is shameful and wrong: and were it not for the grace and mercy of Allah on you, not one of you would ever have been pure: but Allah purifies whom He pleases:

And Allah is One Who hears and knows (all things).

22. Let not those among you who are endued with grace and amplitude of means resolve by oath against helping their kinsmen, those in want, and those who have left their homes in Allah's cause: let them forgive and overlook, do you not wish that Allah should forgive you? For Allah is Oft-Forgiving, Most Merciful.

23. Those who slander chaste women, indiscreet but believing, are cursed in this life and in the Hereafter: for them is a grievous Penalty,-

24. On the Day when their tongues, their hands, and their feet will bear witness against them as to their actions.

25. On that Day Allah will pay them back (all) their just dues, and they will realise that Allah is the (very) Truth, that makes all things manifest.

26. Women impure are for men impure, and men impure for women impure and women of purity are for men of purity, and men of purity are for women of purity: these are not affected by what people say: for them there is forgiveness, and a provision honourable.

27. O you who believe! Do not enter houses other than your own, until you have asked permission and saluted those in them: that is best for you, in order that you may heed (what is seemly).

28. If you find no one in the house, do not enter until permission is given to you: if

you are asked to go back, go back: that makes for greater purity for yourselves: and Allah knows well all that you do.

29.   It is no fault on your part to enter houses not used for living in, which serve some (other) use for you: And Allah has know-ledge of what you reveal and what you conceal.

30.   Say to the believing men that they should lower their gaze and guard their modesty: that will make for greater purity for them: and Allah is well acquainted with all that they do.

31.   And say to the believing women that they should lower their gaze and guard their modesty; that they should not display their beauty and ornaments except what (must ordinarily) appear thereof; that they should draw their veils over their bosoms and not display their beauty except to their husbands, their fathers, their husband's fathers, their sons, their husbands' sons, their brothers or their brothers' sons, or their sisters' sons, or their women, or the slaves whom their right hands possess, or male servants free of sexual urge, or small children who have no sense of the shame of sex; and that they should not strike their feet in order to draw attention to their hidden orna-ments. And O you Believers! You turn all together towards Allah, that you may attain Bliss.

قِيلَ لَكُمُ ارْجِعُوا فَارْجِعُوا هُوَ اَزْكٰى
لَكُمْ ۗ وَاللّٰهُ بِمَا تَعْمَلُوْنَ عَلِيْمٌ ۞

لَيْسَ عَلَيْكُمْ جُنَاحٌ اَنْ تَدْخُلُوْا
بُيُوْتًا غَيْرَ مَسْكُوْنَةٍ فِيْهَا مَتَاعٌ
لَكُمْ ۗ وَاللّٰهُ يَعْلَمُ مَا تُبْدُوْنَ وَمَا
تَكْتُمُوْنَ ۞

قُلْ لِّلْمُؤْمِنِيْنَ يَغُضُّوْا مِنْ اَبْصَارِهِمْ
وَيَحْفَظُوْا فُرُوْجَهُمْ ۗ ذٰلِكَ اَزْكٰى
لَهُمْ ۗ اِنَّ اللّٰهَ خَبِيْرٌ بِمَا يَصْنَعُوْنَ ۞

وَقُلْ لِّلْمُؤْمِنٰتِ يَغْضُضْنَ مِنْ
اَبْصَارِهِنَّ وَيَحْفَظْنَ فُرُوْجَهُنَّ
وَلَا يُبْدِيْنَ زِيْنَتَهُنَّ اِلَّا مَا ظَهَرَ
مِنْهَا وَلْيَضْرِبْنَ بِخُمُرِهِنَّ عَلٰى
جُيُوْبِهِنَّ ۖ وَلَا يُبْدِيْنَ زِيْنَتَهُنَّ
اِلَّا لِبُعُوْلَتِهِنَّ اَوْ اٰبَائِهِنَّ اَوْ
اٰبَاءِ بُعُوْلَتِهِنَّ اَوْ اَبْنَائِهِنَّ اَوْ اَبْنَاءِ
بُعُوْلَتِهِنَّ اَوْ اِخْوَانِهِنَّ اَوْ بَنِيْ
اِخْوَانِهِنَّ اَوْ بَنِيْ اَخَوٰتِهِنَّ اَوْ
نِسَائِهِنَّ اَوْ مَا مَلَكَتْ اَيْمَانُهُنَّ
اَوِ التَّابِعِيْنَ غَيْرِ اُولِي الْاِرْبَةِ
مِنَ الرِّجَالِ اَوِ الطِّفْلِ الَّذِيْنَ لَمْ
يَظْهَرُوْا عَلٰى عَوْرٰتِ النِّسَاءِ ۖ وَلَا
يَضْرِبْنَ بِاَرْجُلِهِنَّ لِيُعْلَمَ مَا يُخْفِيْنَ
مِنْ زِيْنَتِهِنَّ ۗ وَتُوْبُوْا اِلَى اللّٰهِ
جَمِيْعًا اَيُّهَ الْمُؤْمِنُوْنَ لَعَلَّكُمْ
تُفْلِحُوْنَ ۞

32. Marry those among you who are single, or the virtuous ones among your slaves, male or female: if they are in poverty, Allah will give them means out of His grace: for Allah encompasses all, and He knows all things.

33. Let those who find not the wherewithal for marriage keep themselves chaste, until Allah gives them means out of His grace. And if any of your slaves ask for a deed in writing (to enable them to earn their freedom for a certain sum), give them such a deed if you know any good in them: yes, give them something yourselves out of the means which Allah has given to you. But do not force your maids to prostitution when they desire chastity, in order that you may make a gain in the goods of this life. But if anyone compels them, yet, after such compulsion, is Allah, Oft-Forgiving, Most Merciful (to them),

34. We have already sent down to you verses making things clear, an illustration from (the story of) people who passed away before you, and an admonition for those who fear (Allah).

35. Allah is the Light of the heavens and the earth. The parable of His Light is as if there were a Niche and within it a Lamp: the Lamp enclosed in Glass: the glass as it were a brilliant star: lit from a blessed Tree, an Olive, neither of the East nor of the West, whose Oil is well-nigh Luminous, though fire scarce touched it: Light upon Light! Allah guides whom He will to His Light: Allah sets forth Parables for men: and Allah

وَأَنكِحُوا الْأَيَامَىٰ مِنكُمْ وَالصَّالِحِينَ
مِنْ عِبَادِكُمْ وَإِمَائِكُمْ إِن يَكُونُوا
فُقَرَاءَ يُغْنِهِمُ اللَّهُ مِن فَضْلِهِ ۗ
وَاللَّهُ وَاسِعٌ عَلِيمٌ ۝
وَلْيَسْتَعْفِفِ الَّذِينَ لَا يَجِدُونَ
نِكَاحًا حَتَّىٰ يُغْنِيَهُمُ اللَّهُ مِن
فَضْلِهِ ۗ وَالَّذِينَ يَبْتَغُونَ الْكِتَابَ
مِمَّا مَلَكَتْ أَيْمَانُكُمْ فَكَاتِبُوهُمْ إِنْ
عَلِمْتُمْ فِيهِمْ خَيْرًا ۖ وَآتُوهُم مِّن
مَّالِ اللَّهِ الَّذِي آتَاكُمْ ۚ وَلَا تُكْرِهُوا
فَتَيَاتِكُمْ عَلَى الْبِغَاءِ إِنْ أَرَدْنَ تَحَصُّنًا
لِّتَبْتَغُوا عَرَضَ الْحَيَاةِ الدُّنْيَا ۚ وَمَن
يُكْرِههُّنَّ فَإِنَّ اللَّهَ مِن بَعْدِ
إِكْرَاهِهِنَّ غَفُورٌ رَّحِيمٌ ۝
وَلَقَدْ أَنزَلْنَا إِلَيْكُمْ آيَاتٍ مُّبَيِّنَاتٍ
وَمَثَلًا مِّنَ الَّذِينَ خَلَوْا مِن
قَبْلِكُمْ وَمَوْعِظَةً لِّلْمُتَّقِينَ ۝
اللَّهُ نُورُ السَّمَاوَاتِ وَالْأَرْضِ ۚ مَثَلُ
نُورِهِ كَمِشْكَاةٍ فِيهَا مِصْبَاحٌ ۖ
الْمِصْبَاحُ فِي زُجَاجَةٍ ۖ الزُّجَاجَةُ
كَأَنَّهَا كَوْكَبٌ دُرِّيٌّ يُوقَدُ مِن شَجَرَةٍ
مُّبَارَكَةٍ زَيْتُونَةٍ لَّا شَرْقِيَّةٍ وَلَا
غَرْبِيَّةٍ يَكَادُ زَيْتُهَا يُضِيءُ وَلَوْ لَمْ
تَمْسَسْهُ نَارٌ ۚ نُّورٌ عَلَىٰ نُورٍ ۗ يَهْدِي
اللَّهُ لِنُورِهِ مَن يَشَاءُ ۚ وَيَضْرِبُ
اللَّهُ الْأَمْثَالَ لِلنَّاسِ ۗ وَاللَّهُ بِكُلِّ

ع

knows all things.

36. (Lit is such a Light) in
houses, which Allah has permitted to be raised to honour;
for the celebration, in them, of His
name: in them is He glorified in
the mornings and in the
evenings, (again and again),-

37. By men whom neither
traffic nor merchandise can
divert from the remembrance of
Allah, nor from regular Prayer,
nor from paying Zakat; their
(only) fear is for the Day when
hearts and eyes will be turned
about,-

38. That Allah may reward
them according to the best of
their deeds, and add even more
for them out of His Grace: for
Allah provides for those whom
He will, without measure.

39. But the Unbelievers,- their
deeds are like a mirage in sandy
deserts, which the man parched
with thirst mistakes for water;
until when he comes up to it, he
finds it to be nothing: but he
finds Allah (ever) with him, and
Allah will pay him his account:
and Allah is swift in taking
account.

40. Or (the Unbelievers' state)
is like the depths of darkness in a
vast deep ocean, overwhelmed
with billow topped by billow,
topped by (dark) clouds: depths
of darkness, one above another:
if a man stretches out his hand,
he can hardly see it! for any to
whom Allah does not give light,
there is no light!

41. Do not you see that it is
Allah Whose praises all beings
in the heavens and on earth do
celebrate, and the birds (of the
air) with wings outspread? Each
one knows its own (mode of)
prayer and praise. And Allah
knows well all that they do.

42. Yes, to Allah belongs the dominion of the heavens and the earth; and to Allah is the final goal (of all).

43. Don't you see that Allah makes the clouds move gently, then joins them together, then makes them into a heap? - then you will see rain issue forth from their midst. And He sends down from the sky mountain masses (of clouds) wherein is hail: He strikes therewith whom He pleases and He turns it away from whom He pleases. The vivid flash of His lightning well-nigh blinds the sight.

44. It is Allah Who alternates the Night and the Day: verily in these things is an instructive example for those who have vision!

45. And Allah has created every animal from water: of them there are some that creep on their bellies; some that walk on two legs; and some that walk on four. Allah creates what He wills; for verily Allah has power over all things.

46. We have indeed sent down signs that make things manifest: and Allah guides whom He wills to a way that is straight.

47. They say, "We believe in Allah and in the Messenger, and we obey": but even after that, some of them turn away: they are not (really) Believers.

48. When they are summoned to Allah and His Messenger, in order that He may judge between them, behold, some of them decline (to come).

وَلِلّٰهِ مُلْكُ السَّمٰوٰتِ وَالْاَرْضِ ۚ وَاِلَى اللّٰهِ الْمَصِيْرُ ۝

اَلَمْ تَرَ اَنَّ اللّٰهَ يُزْجِيْ سَحَابًا ثُمَّ يُؤَلِّفُ بَيْنَهٗ ثُمَّ يَجْعَلُهٗ رُكَامًا فَتَرَى الْوَدْقَ يَخْرُجُ مِنْ خِلٰلِهٖ ۚ وَيُنَزِّلُ مِنَ السَّمَآءِ مِنْ جِبَالٍ فِيْهَا مِنْۢ بَرَدٍ فَيُصِيْبُ بِهٖ مَنْ يَّشَآءُ وَيَصْرِفُهٗ عَنْ مَّنْ يَّشَآءُ ۚ يَكَادُ سَنَا بَرْقِهٖ يَذْهَبُ بِالْاَبْصَارِ ۝

يُقَلِّبُ اللّٰهُ الَّيْلَ وَالنَّهَارَ ۚ اِنَّ فِيْ ذٰلِكَ لَعِبْرَةً لِّاُولِى الْاَبْصَارِ ۝

وَاللّٰهُ خَلَقَ كُلَّ دَآبَّةٍ مِّنْ مَّآءٍ ۚ فَمِنْهُمْ مَّنْ يَّمْشِيْ عَلٰى بَطْنِهٖ ۚ وَمِنْهُمْ مَّنْ يَّمْشِيْ عَلٰى رِجْلَيْنِ ۚ وَمِنْهُمْ مَّنْ يَّمْشِيْ عَلٰٓى اَرْبَعٍ ۚ يَخْلُقُ اللّٰهُ مَا يَشَآءُ ۚ اِنَّ اللّٰهَ عَلٰى كُلِّ شَيْءٍ قَدِيْرٌ ۝

لَقَدْ اَنْزَلْنَآ اٰيٰتٍ مُّبَيِّنٰتٍ ۚ وَاللّٰهُ يَهْدِيْ مَنْ يَّشَآءُ اِلٰى صِرَاطٍ مُّسْتَقِيْمٍ ۝

وَيَقُوْلُوْنَ اٰمَنَّا بِاللّٰهِ وَبِالرَّسُوْلِ وَاَطَعْنَا ثُمَّ يَتَوَلّٰى فَرِيْقٌ مِّنْهُمْ مِّنْۢ بَعْدِ ذٰلِكَ ۚ وَمَآ اُولٰٓئِكَ بِالْمُؤْمِنِيْنَ ۝

وَاِذَا دُعُوْٓا اِلَى اللّٰهِ وَرَسُوْلِهٖ لِيَحْكُمَ بَيْنَهُمْ اِذَا فَرِيْقٌ مِّنْهُمْ مُّعْرِضُوْنَ ۝

49. But if the right is on their side, they come to him with all submission.

50. Is it that there is a disease in their hearts? or do they doubt, or are they in fear, that Allah and His Messenger will deal unjustly with them? Nay, it is they themselves who do wrong.

51. The answer of the Believers, when summoned to Allah and His Messenger, in order that he may judge between them, is no other than this: they say, "We hear and we obey": it is such as these that will attain felicity.

52. It is such as obey Allah and His Messenger, and fear Allah and do right, that will win (in the end).

53. They swear their strongest oaths by Allah that, if only you would command them, they would leave (their homes). Say: "Do not swear, obedience is (more) reasonable; verily, Allah is well acquainted with all that you do."

54. Say: "Obey Allah, and obey the Messenger: but if you turn away, he is only responsible for the duty placed on him and you for that placed on you. If you obey him, you shall be on right guidance. The Messenger's duty is only to preach the clear (Message).

55. Allah has promised, to those among you who believe and work righteous deeds, that He will, of a surety, grant them in the land, inheritance (of power), as He granted it to those before them; that He will establish in authority their religion - the one which He has chosen for them; and that He will change (their state), after the fear in which they (lived), to one of security and peace: 'They will worship Me (alone)

and not associate any one with Me. 'If any do reject Faith after this, they are rebellious and wicked.

56. So establish regular Prayer and give regular Charity; and obey the Messenger; that you may receive mercy.

57. You should never think that the Unbelievers are going to frustrate (Allah's Plan) on earth: their abode is the Fire,- and it is indeed an evil refuge!

58. O you who believe! Let those whom your right hands possess, and the (children) among you who have not come of age ask your permission (before they come to your presence), on three occasions: before morning prayer; the while you doff your clothes for the noonday heat; and after the late-night prayer: these are your three times of undress: outside those times it is not wrong for you or for them to move about attending to each other: Thus Allah makes clear the Signs to you: for Allah is full of knowledge and wisdom.

59. But when the children among you come of age, let them (also) ask for permission, as do those senior to them (in age): thus Allah makes clear His Signs to you: for Allah is full of knowledge and wisdom.

60. Such elderly women as are past the prospect of marriage,- there is no blame on them if they lay aside their (outer) garments, provided they make not a wanton display of their beauty: but it is best for them to be modest: and Allah is One Who sees and knows all things.

يُشْرِكُوْنَ بِىْ شَيْئًا ۚ وَمَنْ كَفَرَ بَعْدَ

ذٰلِكَ فَاُولٰئِكَ هُمُ الْفٰسِقُوْنَ ۞

وَاَقِيْمُوا الصَّلٰوةَ وَاٰتُوا الزَّكٰوةَ

وَاَطِيْعُوا الرَّسُوْلَ لَعَلَّكُمْ تُرْحَمُوْنَ ۞

لَا تَحْسَبَنَّ الَّذِيْنَ كَفَرُوْا مُعْجِزِيْنَ

فِى الْاَرْضِ ۚ وَمَاْوٰىهُمُ النَّارُ ۚ

وَلَبِئْسَ الْمَصِيْرُ ۞

يٰٓاَيُّهَا الَّذِيْنَ اٰمَنُوْا لِيَسْتَاْذِنْكُمُ

الَّذِيْنَ مَلَكَتْ اَيْمَانُكُمْ وَالَّذِيْنَ لَمْ

يَبْلُغُوا الْحُلُمَ مِنْكُمْ ثَلٰثَ مَرّٰتٍ ۚ مِنْ

قَبْلِ صَلٰوةِ الْفَجْرِ ۚ وَحِيْنَ تَضَعُوْنَ

ثِيَابَكُمْ مِّنَ الظَّهِيْرَةِ ۚ وَمِنْ بَعْدِ

صَلٰوةِ الْعِشَآءِ ۚ ثَلٰثُ عَوْرٰتٍ لَّكُمْ ۚ

لَيْسَ عَلَيْكُمْ وَلَا عَلَيْهِمْ جُنَاحٌ ۚ

بَعْدَهُنَّ ۚ طَوّٰفُوْنَ عَلَيْكُمْ بَعْضُكُمْ

عَلٰى بَعْضٍ ۚ كَذٰلِكَ يُبَيِّنُ اللّٰهُ

لَكُمُ الْاٰيٰتِ ۚ وَاللّٰهُ عَلِيْمٌ حَكِيْمٌ ۞

وَاِذَا بَلَغَ الْاَطْفَالُ مِنْكُمُ الْحُلُمَ

فَلْيَسْتَاْذِنُوْا كَمَا اسْتَاْذَنَ الَّذِيْنَ

مِنْ قَبْلِهِمْ ۚ كَذٰلِكَ يُبَيِّنُ اللّٰهُ

لَكُمْ اٰيٰتِهٖ ۚ وَاللّٰهُ عَلِيْمٌ حَكِيْمٌ ۞

وَالْقَوَاعِدُ مِنَ النِّسَآءِ الّٰتِىْ لَا

يَرْجُوْنَ نِكَاحًا فَلَيْسَ عَلَيْهِنَّ

جُنَاحٌ اَنْ يَّضَعْنَ ثِيَابَهُنَّ غَيْرَ

مُتَبَرِّجٰتٍ بِزِيْنَةٍ ۚ وَاَنْ يَّسْتَعْفِفْنَ

خَيْرٌ لَّهُنَّ ۚ وَاللّٰهُ سَمِيْعٌ عَلِيْمٌ ۞

61. It is no fault in the blind nor in one born lame, nor in one afflicted with illness, nor in yourselves, that you should eat in your own houses, or those of your fathers, or your mothers, or your brothers, or your sisters, or your father's brothers or your father's sisters, or your mohter's brothers, or your mother's sisters, or in houses of which the keys are in your possession, or in the house of a sincere friend of yours: there is no blame on you, whether you eat in company or separately. But if you enter houses, salute each other - a greeting of blessing and purity as from Allah. Thus Allah makes clear the Signs to you: that you may understand.

لَيْسَ عَلَى الْأَعْمٰى حَرَجٌ وَّلَا عَلَى الْأَعْرَجِ حَرَجٌ وَّلَا عَلَى الْمَرِيْضِ حَرَجٌ وَّلَا عَلٰى أَنْفُسِكُمْ أَنْ تَأْكُلُوْا مِنْ بُيُوْتِكُمْ أَوْ بُيُوْتِ اٰبَآئِكُمْ أَوْ بُيُوْتِ أُمَّهٰتِكُمْ أَوْ بُيُوْتِ اِخْوَانِكُمْ أَوْ بُيُوْتِ أَخَوٰتِكُمْ أَوْ بُيُوْتِ أَعْمَامِكُمْ أَوْ بُيُوْتِ عَمّٰتِكُمْ أَوْ بُيُوْتِ أَخْوَالِكُمْ أَوْ بُيُوْتِ خٰلٰتِكُمْ أَوْ مَا مَلَكْتُمْ مَّفَاتِحَهٗ أَوْ صَدِيْقِكُمْ ۚ لَيْسَ عَلَيْكُمْ جُنَاحٌ أَنْ تَأْكُلُوْا جَمِيْعًا أَوْ أَشْتَاتًا ۚ فَإِذَا دَخَلْتُمْ بُيُوْتًا فَسَلِّمُوْا عَلٰى أَنْفُسِكُمْ تَحِيَّةً مِّنْ عِنْدِ اللّٰهِ مُبٰرَكَةً طَيِّبَةً ۚ كَذٰلِكَ يُبَيِّنُ اللّٰهُ لَكُمُ الْاٰيٰتِ لَعَلَّكُمْ تَعْقِلُوْنَ ۟

62. Only those are Believers, who believe in Allah and His Messenger: when they are with him on a matter requiring collective action, they do not depart until they have asked for his leave; those who ask for your leave are those who believe in Allah and His Messenger; so when they ask for your leave, for some business of theirs, give leave to those of them whom you will, and ask Allah for their forgiveness: for Allah is Oft-Forgiving, Most Merciful.

اِنَّمَا الْمُؤْمِنُوْنَ الَّذِيْنَ اٰمَنُوْا بِاللّٰهِ وَرَسُوْلِهٖ وَإِذَا كَانُوْا مَعَهٗ عَلٰى أَمْرٍ جَامِعٍ لَّمْ يَذْهَبُوْا حَتّٰى يَسْتَأْذِنُوْهُ ۚ اِنَّ الَّذِيْنَ يَسْتَأْذِنُوْنَكَ أُولٰٓئِكَ الَّذِيْنَ يُؤْمِنُوْنَ بِاللّٰهِ وَ رَسُوْلِهٖ ۚ فَإِذَا اسْتَأْذَنُوْكَ لِبَعْضِ شَأْنِهِمْ فَأْذَنْ لِّمَنْ شِئْتَ مِنْهُمْ وَاسْتَغْفِرْ لَهُمُ اللّٰهَ ۚ اِنَّ اللّٰهَ غَفُوْرٌ رَّحِيْمٌ ۟

63. Deem not the summons of the Messenger among your-selves

لَا تَجْعَلُوْا دُعَآءَ الرَّسُوْلِ بَيْنَكُمْ

SÛRAH-25
AL-FURQÂN
(INTRODUCTION)

This Sûrah further develops the contrast between Light and Darkness, as symbolical of knowledge and ignorance, righteousness and sin, spiritual progress and degradation. It closes with a definition of the deeds by which the righteous are known in the environment of this world.

It is mainly an early Makkan Sûrah, but its date has no significance.

like the summons of one of you to another: Allah knows those of you who slip away under shelter of some excuse: then let those beware who withstand the Messenger's order, lest some trial befall them, or a grievous Penalty be inflicted on them.

كَدُعَاءِ بَعْضِكُمْ بَعْضًا ۚ قَدْ يَعْلَمُ اللّٰهُ الَّذِينَ يَتَسَلَّلُونَ مِنْكُمْ لِوَاذًا ۚ فَلْيَحْذَرِ الَّذِينَ يُخَالِفُونَ عَنْ أَمْرِهٖ أَنْ تُصِيبَهُمْ فِتْنَةٌ أَوْ يُصِيبَهُمْ عَذَابٌ أَلِيمٌ ۝

64. Be quite sure that to Allah belongs whatever is in the heavens and on earth. Well does He know what you are intent upon: and one day they will be brought back to Him, and He will tell them the truth of what they did: for Allah knows all things.

أَلَا إِنَّ لِلّٰهِ مَا فِي السَّمٰوٰتِ وَالْأَرْضِ ۚ قَدْ يَعْلَمُ مَا أَنْتُمْ عَلَيْهِ ۚ وَيَوْمَ يُرْجَعُونَ إِلَيْهِ فَيُنَبِّئُهُمْ بِمَا عَمِلُوا ۚ وَاللّٰهُ بِكُلِّ شَيْءٍ عَلِيمٌ ۝

25. The Criterion
In the name of Allah. Most Gracious, Most Merciful.

سُورَةُ الْفُرْقَانِ مَكِّيَّةٌ ﴿٢٥﴾
بِسْمِ اللّٰهِ الرَّحْمٰنِ الرَّحِيمِ

1. Blessed is He Who sent down the Criterion to His servant, that it may be an admonition to all creatures;-

تَبٰرَكَ الَّذِي نَزَّلَ الْفُرْقَانَ عَلٰى عَبْدِهٖ لِيَكُونَ لِلْعٰلَمِينَ نَذِيرًا ۝

2. He to Whom belongs the dominion of the heavens and the earth: no son has He begotten, nor has He a partner in His dominion: it is He who created all things, and ordered them in due proportions.

الَّذِي لَهُ مُلْكُ السَّمٰوٰتِ وَالْأَرْضِ وَلَمْ يَتَّخِذْ وَلَدًا وَّلَمْ يَكُنْ لَّهُ شَرِيكٌ فِي الْمُلْكِ وَخَلَقَ كُلَّ شَيْءٍ فَقَدَّرَهٗ تَقْدِيرًا ۝

3. Yet have they taken, besides Him, gods that can create nothing but are themselves created; that have no control of hurt or good to themselves; nor can they control death nor life nor resurrection.

وَاتَّخَذُوا مِنْ دُونِهٖ آلِهَةً لَّا يَخْلُقُونَ شَيْئًا وَّهُمْ يُخْلَقُونَ وَلَا يَمْلِكُونَ لِأَنْفُسِهِمْ ضَرًّا وَّلَا نَفْعًا وَّلَا يَمْلِكُونَ مَوْتًا وَّلَا حَيٰوةً وَّلَا نُشُورًا ۝

4. But the Misbelievers say: "Nothing is this but a lie which he has forged, and others have helped him at it." In truth it is they who have put forward an iniquity and a falsehood.

وَقَالَ الَّذِينَ كَفَرُوا إِنْ هٰذَا إِلَّا إِفْكٌ افْتَرَاهُ وَأَعَانَهُ عَلَيْهِ قَوْمٌ آخَرُونَ ۖ فَقَدْ جَاءُو ظُلْمًا وَّزُورًا ۝

5. And they say: "Tales of the ancients, which he has caused to be written: and they are dictated before him morning and evening."

وَقَالُوٓا أَسَاطِيرُ الْأَوَّلِينَ اكْتَتَبَهَا فَهِيَ تُمْلَىٰ عَلَيْهِ بُكْرَةً وَأَصِيلًا ۝

6. Say: "The (Qur'an) was sent down by Him Who knows the mystery (that is) in the heavens and the earth: verily He is Oft-Forgiving, Most Merciful."

قُلْ أَنزَلَهُ الَّذِي يَعْلَمُ السِّرَّ فِي السَّمَٰوَٰتِ وَالْأَرْضِ ۚ إِنَّهُۥ كَانَ غَفُورًا رَّحِيمًا ۝

7. And they say: "What sort of a Messenger is this, who eats food, and walks through the streets? Why has not an angel been sent down to him to give admonition with him?

وَقَالُوا مَالِ هَٰذَا الرَّسُولِ يَأْكُلُ الطَّعَامَ وَيَمْشِي فِي الْأَسْوَاقِ ۗ لَوْلَآ أُنزِلَ إِلَيْهِ مَلَكٌ فَيَكُونَ مَعَهُۥ نَذِيرًا ۝

8. "Or (Why) has not a treasure been bestowed on him, or why has he (not) a garden for enjoyment?" The wicked say: "You follow none other than a man bewitched."

أَوْ يُلْقَىٰٓ إِلَيْهِ كَنزٌ أَوْ تَكُونُ لَهُۥ جَنَّةٌ يَأْكُلُ مِنْهَا ۚ وَقَالَ الظَّٰلِمُونَ إِن تَتَّبِعُونَ إِلَّا رَجُلًا مَّسْحُورًا ۝

9. See what kinds of comparisons they make for you! But they have gone astray, and never a way will they be able to find!

انظُرْ كَيْفَ ضَرَبُوا لَكَ الْأَمْثَٰلَ فَضَلُّوا فَلَا يَسْتَطِيعُونَ سَبِيلًا ۝

10. Blessed is He Who, if that were His Will, could give you better (things) than those,- Gardens beneath which rivers flow; and He could give you palaces (secure to dwell in).

تَبَارَكَ الَّذِي إِن شَآءَ جَعَلَ لَكَ خَيْرًا مِّن ذَٰلِكَ جَنَّٰتٍ تَجْرِي مِن تَحْتِهَا الْأَنْهَٰرُ وَيَجْعَل لَّكَ قُصُورًا ۝

11. Nay, they deny the Hour (of the judgment to come): but We have prepared a blazing fire for such as deny the Hour:

بَلْ كَذَّبُوا بِالسَّاعَةِ ۖ وَأَعْتَدْنَا لِمَن كَذَّبَ بِالسَّاعَةِ سَعِيرًا ۝

12. When it sees them from a place far off, they will hear its fury and its raging sigh.

إِذَا رَأَتْهُم مِّن مَّكَانٍ بَعِيدٍ سَمِعُوا لَهَا تَغَيُّظًا وَزَفِيرًا ۝

13. And when they are cast, bound together into a constricted place therein, they will plead for destruction there and then!

وَإِذَآ أُلْقُوا مِنْهَا مَكَانًا ضَيِّقًا مُّقَرَّنِينَ دَعَوْا هُنَالِكَ ثُبُورًا ۝

14. "This day do not plead for a single destruction:

لَّا تَدْعُوا الْيَوْمَ ثُبُورًا وَاحِدًا

plead for destruction oft-repeated!"

15. Say: "Is that best, or the eternal Garden, promised to the righteous? for them, that is a reward as well as a goal (of attainment).

16. "For them there will be therein all that they wish for: they will dwell (there) for ever: a promise binding upon your Lord."

17. The day He will gather them together as well as those whom they worship besides Allah, He will ask: "Was it you who let these My servants astray, or did they stray from the Path themselves?"

18. They will say: "Glory to You! Not meet was it for us that we should take for protectors others besides You: but You bestowed on them and their fathers, good things (in life), until they forgot the Message: for they were a people (worthless and) lost."

19. (Allah will say): "Now have they proved you liars in what you say: so you cannot avert (your penalty) nor (get) help." And whoever among you does wrong, him shall We cause to taste of a grievous Penalty.

20. And the Messengers whom We sent before you were all (men) who ate food and walked through the streets: We have made some of you as a trial for others: will you have patience? for Allah is One Who sees (all things).

21. Such as do not fear the meeting with Us (for Judgment) say: "Why are not the angels sent down to us, or (why) do we not see

وَادْعُوا ثُبُورًا كَثِيرًا ۝

قُلْ أَذٰلِكَ خَيْرٌ أَمْ جَنَّةُ الْخُلْدِ الَّتِي وُعِدَ الْمُتَّقُوْنَ ۚ كَانَتْ لَهُمْ جَزَاءً وَّمَصِيْرًا ۝

لَهُمْ فِيْهَا مَا يَشَاءُوْنَ خٰلِدِيْنَ ۚ كَانَ عَلٰى رَبِّكَ وَعْدًا مَّسْئُوْلًا ۝

وَيَوْمَ يَحْشُرُهُمْ وَمَا يَعْبُدُوْنَ مِنْ دُوْنِ اللّٰهِ فَيَقُوْلُ ءَأَنْتُمْ أَضْلَلْتُمْ عِبَادِيْ هٰؤُلَاءِ أَمْ هُمْ ضَلُّوا السَّبِيْلَ ۝

قَالُوْا سُبْحٰنَكَ مَا كَانَ يَنْبَغِيْ لَنَا أَنْ نَّتَّخِذَ مِنْ دُوْنِكَ مِنْ أَوْلِيَاءَ وَلٰكِنْ مَّتَّعْتَهُمْ وَ اٰبَاءَهُمْ حَتّٰى نَسُوا الذِّكْرَ ۚ وَ كَانُوْا قَوْمًا بُوْرًا ۝

فَقَدْ كَذَّبُوْكُمْ بِمَا تَقُوْلُوْنَ ۙ فَمَا تَسْتَطِيْعُوْنَ صَرْفًا وَّلَا نَصْرًا ۚ وَمَنْ يَّظْلِمْ مِّنْكُمْ نُذِقْهُ عَذَابًا كَبِيْرًا ۝

وَمَا أَرْسَلْنَا قَبْلَكَ مِنَ الْمُرْسَلِيْنَ إِلَّا إِنَّهُمْ لَيَأْكُلُوْنَ الطَّعَامَ وَ يَمْشُوْنَ فِي الْأَسْوَاقِ ۚ وَجَعَلْنَا بَعْضَكُمْ لِبَعْضٍ فِتْنَةً ۚ أَتَصْبِرُوْنَ ۚ وَكَانَ رَبُّكَ بَصِيْرًا ۝

وَقَالَ الَّذِيْنَ لَا يَرْجُوْنَ لِقَاءَنَا لَوْلَا أُنْزِلَ عَلَيْنَا الْمَلٰئِكَةُ أَوْ نَرٰى

(angels), no joy will there be to

our Lord?" Indeed they have an arrogant conceit of themselves, and mighty is the insolence of their impiety!

22. The Day they see the angels,- no joy will there be to the sinners that Day: the (angels) will say: "There is a barrier forbidden (to you) altogether!"

23. And We shall turn to whatever deeds they did (in this life), and We shall make such deeds as floating dust scattered about.

24. The Companions of the Garden will be well, that Day, in their abode, and have the fairest of places for repose.

25. The Day the heaven shall be rent asunder with clouds, and angels shall be sent down, descending (in ranks),-

26. That Day, the dominion as of right and truth, shall be (wholly) for (Allah) Most Merciful: it will be a Day of dire difficulty for the Misbelievers.

27. The Day that the wrongdoer will bite at his hands, he will say, "Oh! would that I had taken a (straight) path with the Messenger!

28. "Ah! woe is me! Would that I had never taken such a one for a friend!

29. "He did lead me astray from the Message (of Allah) after it had come to me! Ah! the Evil One is but a traitor to man!"

30. Then the Messenger will say: "O my Lord! Truly my people took this Qur'an for just foolish nonsense."

31. Thus have We made for every prophet an enemy among the sinners: but enough is your Lord to guide and to help.

32. Those who reject Faith say: "Why is not the Qur'an revealed to him all at once? Thus (is it revealed), that We may strengthen your heart thereby, and We have rehearsed it to you in slow, well-arranged stages, gradually.

33. And no question do they bring to you but We reveal to you the truth and the best explanation (thereof).

34. Those who will be gathered to Hell (prone) on their faces,- they will be in an evil plight, and, as to Path, most astray.

35. (Before this,) We sent Moses the Book, and appointed his brother Aaron with him as Minister;

36. And We commanded: "You both go, to the people who have rejected Our Signs:" and those (people) We destroyed with utter destruction.

37. And the people of Noah,- when they rejected the Messengers, We drowned them, and We made them as a Sign for mankind; and We have prepared for (all) wrong-doers a grievous Penalty;-

38. As also 'Ad and Thamud, and the Companions of the Rass, and many a generation between them.

39. To each one We set forth parables and examples; and each one We broke to utter annihilation (for their sins).

40. And the (Unbelievers) must indeed have passed by the town on which was rained a shower of evil: did they not then see it (with their own eyes)? But they do not fear the Resurrection.

41. When they see you, they treat you no otherwise than in mockery: "Is this the one whom Allah has sent as a Messenger?"

42. "He indeed would wellnigh have misled us from our gods, had it not been that we were constant to them!" - Soon will they know,

when they see the Penalty, who it is that is most misled in Path!

43. Do you see such a one as takes for his god his own passion (or impulse)? Could you be a disposer of affairs for him?

44. Or do you think that most of them listen or understand? They are only like cattle;- nay, they are worse astray in Path.

45. Have you not turned your vision to your Lord?- How does He prolong the shadow! If He willed, He could make it stationary! then do We make the sun its guide;

46. Then We draw it in towards Ourselves,- a contraction by easy stages.

47. And He it is Who makes the Night as a Robe for you, and Sleep as Repose, and makes the Day (as it were) a Resurrection.

48. And He it is Who sends the winds as heralds of glad tidings, going before His mercy, and We send down pure water from the sky,-

49. That with it We may give life to a dead land, and slake the thirst of things We have created,- cattle and men in great numbers.

50. And We have distributed the (water) amongst them, in order that they may celebrate (Our) praises, but most men are averse (to anything) but (rank) ingratitude.

51. Had it been Our Will, We could have sent a warner to every centre of population.

52. Therefore do not listen to the Unbelievers, but strive against them with the utmost strenuousness, with the (Qur'an).

53. It is He Who has let free the two bodies of flowing water: One palatable and sweet, and the other salt and bitter; yet He has made

a barrier between them, a partition that is forbidden to be passed.

54. It is He Who has created man from water: then He has established relationships of lineage and marriage: for your Lord has power (over all things).

55. Yet do they worship, besides Allah, things that can neither profit them nor harm them: and the Misbeliever is a helper (of Evil), against his own Lord!

56. But We sent you only to give glad tidings and admonition.

57. Say: "No reward do I ask of you for it but this: that each one who will may take a (straight) Path to his Lord."

58. And put your trust in Him Who lives and dies not; and celebrate His praise; and enough is He to be acquainted with the faults of His servants;-

59. He Who created the heavens and the earth and all that is between, in six days, and is firmly established on the Throne (of Authority): Allah Most Gracious: you ask then, about Him of any acquainted (with such things).

60. When it is said to them, "You adore (Allah) Most Gracious!", they say, "And what is (Allah) Most Gracious? Shall we adore that which you command us?" And it increases their flight (from the Truth).

61. Blessed is He Who made constellations in the skies, and placed therein a Lamp and a Moon giving light;

62. And it is He Who made the Night and the Day to follow each other: for such as desire to be mindful or to show their gratitude.

63. And the servants of (Allah) Most Gracious are those who walk on the earth in humility, and when the

ignorant address them, they say, "Peace!";

64. Those who spend the night in adoration of their Lord prostrate and standing;

65. Those who say, "Our Lord! avert from us the Wrath of Hell, for its Wrath is indeed an affliction grievous,-

66. "Evil indeed is it as an abode, and as a place to rest in";

67. Those who, when they spend, are not extravagant and not niggardly, but hold a just (balance) between those (extremes).

68. Those who do not invoke, with Allah, any other god, nor slay such life as Allah has made sacred except for just cause, nor commit fornication; - and any that does this (not only) meets punishment.

69. (But) the Penalty on the Day of Judgment will be doubled to him, and he will dwell therein in ignominy,-

70. Unless he repents, believes, and works righteous deeds, for Allah will change the evil of such persons into good, and Allah is Oft-Forgiving, Most Merciful,

71. And whoever repents and does good has truly turned to Allah with an (acceptable) conversion;-

72. Those who witness no falsehood, and, if they pass by futility, they pass by it with honourable (avoidance);

73. Those who, when they are admonished with the Signs of their Lord, droop not down at them as if they were deaf or blind;

74. And those who pray, "Our Lord! Grant unto us wives and offspring who will be the comfort of our eyes, and

الْجٰهِلُوْنَ قَالُوْا سَلٰمًا ۟

وَالَّذِيْنَ يَبِيْتُوْنَ لِرَبِّهِمْ سُجَّدًا وَّقِيَامًا ۟

وَالَّذِيْنَ يَقُوْلُوْنَ رَبَّنَا اصْرِفْ عَنَّا عَذَابَ جَهَنَّمَ ۖ اِنَّ عَذَابَهَا كَانَ غَرَامًا ۟

اِنَّهَا سَآءَتْ مُسْتَقَرًّا وَّمُقَامًا ۟

وَالَّذِيْنَ اِذَآ اَنْفَقُوْا لَمْ يُسْرِفُوْا وَلَمْ يَقْتُرُوْا وَكَانَ بَيْنَ ذٰلِكَ قَوَامًا ۟

وَالَّذِيْنَ لَا يَدْعُوْنَ مَعَ اللّٰهِ اِلٰهًا اٰخَرَ وَلَا يَقْتُلُوْنَ النَّفْسَ الَّتِيْ حَرَّمَ اللّٰهُ اِلَّا بِالْحَقِّ وَلَا يَزْنُوْنَ ۚ وَمَنْ يَّفْعَلْ ذٰلِكَ يَلْقَ اَثَامًا ۟

يُّضٰعَفْ لَهُ الْعَذَابُ يَوْمَ الْقِيٰمَةِ وَيَخْلُدْ فِيْهِ مُهَانًا ۟

اِلَّا مَنْ تَابَ وَاٰمَنَ وَعَمِلَ عَمَلًا صَالِحًا فَاُولٰٓئِكَ يُبَدِّلُ اللّٰهُ سَيِّاٰتِهِمْ حَسَنٰتٍ ۚ وَكَانَ اللّٰهُ غَفُوْرًا رَّحِيْمًا ۟

وَمَنْ تَابَ وَعَمِلَ صَالِحًا فَاِنَّهٗ يَتُوْبُ اِلَى اللّٰهِ مَتَابًا ۟

وَالَّذِيْنَ لَا يَشْهَدُوْنَ الزُّوْرَ ۙ وَاِذَا مَرُّوْا بِاللَّغْوِ مَرُّوْا كِرَامًا ۟

وَالَّذِيْنَ اِذَا ذُكِّرُوْا بِاٰيٰتِ رَبِّهِمْ لَمْ يَخِرُّوْا عَلَيْهَا صُمًّا وَّعُمْيَانًا ۟

وَالَّذِيْنَ يَقُوْلُوْنَ رَبَّنَا هَبْ لَنَا مِنْ اَزْوَاجِنَا وَذُرِّيّٰتِنَا قُرَّةَ اَعْيُنٍ وَّ

SÛRAH-26
ASH-SHU'ARÂ
(INTRODUCTION)

This Sûrah begins a new series of four Sûras (26-29), which illustrate the contrast between the spirit of Prophecy and spiritual Light and the reaction to it in the communities among whom it appeared, by going back to old Prophets and the stories of the Past, as explained in the Introduction to S. 17.

In this particular Sûrah we have the story of Moses in his fight with Pharaoh and of Pharaoh's discomfiture. Other Prophets mentioned are Abraham, Noah, Hûd, Ṣâliḥ, Lût and Shu'aib. The lesson is drawn that the Qur'ân is a continuation and fulfilment of previous Revelations, and is pure Truth, unlike the poetry of vain poets.

Chronologically, the Sûrah belongs to the middle Makkan period, when the contact of the Light of Prophecy with the milieu of Pagan Makkah was testing the Makkans in their most arrogant mood.

give us (the grace) to lead the righteous."

75. Those are the ones who will be rewarded with the highest place in heaven, because of their patient constancy: therein shall they be met with salutations and peace,

76. Dwelling therein;- how beautiful an abode and place of rest!

77. Say (to the Rejecters): "My Lord is not uneasy because of you if you do not call on Him: but you have indeed rejected (Him), and soon will come the inevitable (punishment)!"

26. The Poets

In the name of Allah. Most Gracious, Most Merciful.

1. Ta. Sin. Mim.

2. These are Verses of the Book that makes (things) clear.

3. It may be you will kill yourself with grief, that they do not become Believers.

4. If (such) were Our Will, We could send down to them from the sky a Sign, to which they would bend their necks in humility.

5. But there doesn't come to them a newly-revealed Message from (Allah) Most Gracious, but they turn away therefrom.

6. They have indeed rejected (the Message): so they will know soon (enough) the truth of what they mocked at!

7. Do they not look at the earth,- how many noble things of all kinds We have produced therein?

8. Verily, in this is a Sign: but most of them do not believe.

9. And verily, your Lord is He, the Exalted in Might, Most Merciful.

10. Behold, your Lord called Moses: "Go to the people of iniquity,-

11. "The people of Pharaoh: will they not fear Allah?"

قَوْمَ فِرْعَوْنَ ۚ أَلَا يَتَّقُوْنَ ۙ ⑪

12. He said: "O my Lord! I do fear that they will charge me with falsehood:

قَالَ رَبِّ اِنِّى اَخَافُ اَنْ يُّكَذِّبُوْنِ ۙ

13. "My breast will be straitened. And my speech may not go (smoothly): so send unto Aaron.

وَيَضِيْقُ صَدْرِىْ وَ لَا يَنْطَلِقُ

14. "And (further), they have a charge of crime against me; and I fear they may slay me."

لِسَانِىْ فَاَرْسِلْ اِلٰى هٰرُوْنَ ⑬ وَلَهُمْ عَلَىَّ ذَنْۢبٌ فَاَخَافُ اَنْ يَّقْتُلُوْنِ ۚ

15. Allah said: "By no means! proceed then, both of you, with Our Signs; We are with you, and will listen (to your call).

قَالَ كَلَّا ۚ فَاذْهَبَا بِاٰيٰتِنَآ اِنَّا مَعَكُمْ مُّسْتَمِعُوْنَ ۙ ⑮

16. "So go forth, both of you, to Pharaoh, and say: 'We have been sent by the Lord and Cherisher of the worlds;

فَأْتِيَا فِرْعَوْنَ فَقُوْلَآ اِنَّا رَسُوْلُ رَبِّ الْعٰلَمِيْنَ ۙ

17. "'You send with us the Children of Israel.'"

اَنْ اَرْسِلْ مَعَنَا بَنِىْٓ اِسْرَآءِيْلَ ۙ ⑰

18. (Pharaoh) said: "Did we not cherish you as a child among us, and did you not stay in our midst many years of your life?

قَالَ اَلَمْ نُرَبِّكَ فِيْنَا وَلِيْدًا وَّلَبِثْتَ فِيْنَا مِنْ عُمُرِكَ سِنِيْنَ ۙ ⑱

19. "And you did a deed of yours which (you know) you did, and you are an ungrateful (wretch)!"

وَفَعَلْتَ فَعْلَتَكَ الَّتِىْ فَعَلْتَ وَاَنْتَ مِنَ الْكٰفِرِيْنَ ⑲

20. Moses said: "I did it then, when I was in error.

قَالَ فَعَلْتُهَآ اِذًا وَّاَنَا مِنَ الضَّآلِّيْنَ ۙ

21. "So I fled from you (all) when I feared you; but my Lord has (since) invested me with judgment (and wisdom) and appointed me as one of the Messengers.

فَفَرَرْتُ مِنْكُمْ لَمَّا خِفْتُكُمْ فَوَهَبَ لِىْ رَبِّىْ حُكْمًا وَّجَعَلَنِىْ مِنَ الْمُرْسَلِيْنَ

22. "And this is the favour with which you do reproach me,- that you have enslaved the Children of Israel!"

وَتِلْكَ نِعْمَةٌ تَمُنُّهَا عَلَىَّ اَنْ عَبَّدْتَّ بَنِىْٓ اِسْرَآءِيْلَ ۗ ㉒

23. Pharaoh said: "And what is the 'Lord and Cherisher of the worlds'?"

قَالَ فِرْعَوْنُ وَمَا رَبُّ الْعٰلَمِيْنَ ⑳

24. (Moses) said: "The Lord and Cherisher of the heavens and the earth, and all between,- if you want to be quite sure."

قَالَ رَبُّ السَّمٰوٰتِ وَالْاَرْضِ وَمَا بَيْنَهُمَا ۖ اِنْ كُنْتُمْ مُّوْقِنِيْنَ ⑳

25. (Pharaoh) said to those around: "Did you not listen (to what he says)?"

قَالَ لِمَنْ حَوْلَهٗٓ اَلَا تَسْتَمِعُوْنَ ⑳

26. (Moses) said: "Your Lord and the Lord of your fathers from the beginning!"

قَالَ رَبُّكُمْ وَرَبُّ اٰبَآئِكُمُ الْاَوَّلِيْنَ ⑳

27. (Pharaoh) said: "Truly your Messenger who has been sent

قَالَ اِنَّ رَسُوْلَكُمُ الَّذِىْٓ اُرْسِلَ

to you is a veritable madman!"

إِلَيْكُمْ لَمَجْنُونٌ ۝

28. (Moses) said: "Lord of the East and the West, and all between! if you only had sense!"

قَالَ رَبُّ الْمَشْرِقِ وَالْمَغْرِبِ وَمَا بَيْنَهُمَا ۖ إِن كُنتُمْ تَعْقِلُونَ ۝

29. (Pharaoh) said: "If you do put forward any god other than me, I will certainly put you in prison!"

قَالَ لَئِنِ اتَّخَذْتَ إِلَٰهًا غَيْرِي لَأَجْعَلَنَّكَ مِنَ الْمَسْجُونِينَ ۝

30. (Moses) said: "Even if I showed you something clear (and) convincing?"

قَالَ أَوَلَوْ جِئْتُكَ بِشَيْءٍ مُّبِينٍ ۝

31. (Pharaoh) said: "Show it then, if you tell the truth!"

قَالَ فَأْتِ بِهِ إِن كُنتَ مِنَ الصَّادِقِينَ ۝

32. So (Moses) threw his rod, and behold, it was a serpent, plain (for all to see)!

فَأَلْقَىٰ عَصَاهُ فَإِذَا هِيَ ثُعْبَانٌ مُّبِينٌ ۝

33. And he drew out his hand, and behold, it was white to all beholders!

وَنَزَعَ يَدَهُ فَإِذَا هِيَ بَيْضَاءُ لِلنَّاظِرِينَ ۝

34. (Pharaoh) said to the Chiefs around him: "This is indeed a sorcerer well-versed:

قَالَ لِلْمَلَإِ حَوْلَهُ إِنَّ هَٰذَا لَسَاحِرٌ عَلِيمٌ ۝

35. "His plan is to get you out of your land by his sorcery; then what is it you counsel?"

يُرِيدُ أَن يُخْرِجَكُم مِّنْ أَرْضِكُم بِسِحْرِهِ فَمَاذَا تَأْمُرُونَ ۝

36. They said: "Keep him and his brother in suspense (for a while), and dispatch to the Cities heralds to collect-

قَالُوا أَرْجِهْ وَأَخَاهُ وَابْعَثْ فِي الْمَدَائِنِ حَاشِرِينَ ۝

37. "And bring up to you all (our) sorcerers well-versed."

يَأْتُوكَ بِكُلِّ سَحَّارٍ عَلِيمٍ ۝

38. So the sorcerers were got together for the appointment of a day well-known,

فَجُمِعَ السَّحَرَةُ لِمِيقَاتِ يَوْمٍ مَّعْلُومٍ ۝

39. And the people were told: "Are you (now) assembled?-

وَقِيلَ لِلنَّاسِ هَلْ أَنتُم مُّجْتَمِعُونَ ۝

40. "That we may follow the sorcerers (in religion) if they win?"

لَعَلَّنَا نَتَّبِعُ السَّحَرَةَ إِن كَانُوا هُمُ الْغَالِبِينَ ۝

41. So when the sorcerers arrived, they said to Pharaoh:

فَلَمَّا جَاءَ السَّحَرَةُ قَالُوا لِفِرْعَوْنَ

"Of course - shall we have a (suitable) reward if we win?

42. He said: "Yes, (and more),- for you shall in that case be (raised to posts) nearest (to my person)."

43. Moses said to them: You "throw that which you are about to throw!"

44. So they threw their ropes and their rods, and said: "By the might of Pharaoh, it is we who will certainly win!"

45. Then Moses threw his rod, when, behold, it straightway swallows up all the falsehoods which they fake!

46. Then did the sorcerers fall down, prostrate in adoration,

47. Saying: "We believe in the Lord of the Worlds,

48. "The Lord of Moses and Aaron."

49. Said (Pharaoh): "You believe in Him before I give you permission? Surely he is your leader, who has taught you sorcery! but soon you shall know! "Be sure I will cut off your hands and your feet on opposite sides, and I will cause you all to die on the cross!"

50. They said: "No matter! for us, we shall but return to our Lord!

51. "Only, our desire is that our Lord will forgive us our faults, that we may become foremost among the Believers!"

52. By inspiration We told Moses: "Travel by night with My servants; for surely you shall be pursued."

53. Then Pharaoh sent heralds to (all) the Cities,

54. (Saying): "These (Israelites) are but a small band,

55. "And they are raging furiously against us;

56. "But we are a multitude amply fore-warned."

أَئِنَّ لَنَا لَأَجْرًا إِن كُنَّا نَحْنُ الْغَلِبِينَ ۝

قَالَ نَعَمْ وَإِنَّكُمْ إِذًا لَّمِنَ الْمُقَرَّبِينَ ۝

قَالَ لَهُم مُّوسَى أَلْقُوا مَآ أَنتُم مُّلْقُونَ ۝

فَأَلْقَوْا حِبَالَهُمْ وَعِصِيَّهُمْ وَقَالُوا بِعِزَّةِ فِرْعَوْنَ إِنَّا لَنَحْنُ الْغَلِبُونَ ۝

فَأَلْقَى مُوسَى عَصَاهُ فَإِذَا هِيَ تَلْقَفُ مَا يَأْفِكُونَ ۝

فَأُلْقِيَ السَّحَرَةُ سَاجِدِينَ ۝

قَالُوا آمَنَّا بِرَبِّ الْعَالَمِينَ ۝

رَبِّ مُوسَى وَهَارُونَ ۝

قَالَ آمَنتُمْ لَهُ قَبْلَ أَنْ آذَنَ لَكُمْ إِنَّهُ لَكَبِيرُكُمُ الَّذِي عَلَّمَكُمُ السِّحْرَ فَلَسَوْفَ تَعْلَمُونَ لَأُقَطِّعَنَّ أَيْدِيَكُمْ وَأَرْجُلَكُم مِّنْ خِلَافٍ وَلَأُصَلِّبَنَّكُمْ أَجْمَعِينَ ۝

قَالُوا لَا ضَيْرَ إِنَّا إِلَى رَبِّنَا مُنقَلِبُونَ ۝

إِنَّا نَطْمَعُ أَن يَغْفِرَ لَنَا رَبُّنَا خَطَايَانَا أَن كُنَّا أَوَّلَ الْمُؤْمِنِينَ ۝

وَأَوْحَيْنَا إِلَى مُوسَى أَنْ أَسْرِ بِعِبَادِي إِنَّكُم مُّتَّبَعُونَ ۝

فَأَرْسَلَ فِرْعَوْنُ فِي الْمَدَائِنِ حَاشِرِينَ ۝

إِنَّ هَٰؤُلَاءِ لَشِرْذِمَةٌ قَلِيلُونَ ۝

وَإِنَّهُمْ لَنَا لَغَائِظُونَ ۝

وَإِنَّا لَجَمِيعٌ حَاذِرُونَ ۝

57. So We expelled them from gardens, springs,

58. Treasures, and every kind of honourable position;

59. Thus it was, but We made the Children of Israel inheritors of such things.

60. So they pursued them at sunrise.

61. And when the two bodies saw each other, the people of Moses said: "We are sure to be overtaken."

62. (Moses) said: "By no means! My Lord is with me! soon will He guide me!"

63. Then We told Moses by inspiration: "Strike the sea with your rod." So it divided, and each separate part became like the huge, firm mass of a mountain.

64. And We made the other party approach there.

65. We delivered Moses and all who were with him;

66. But We drowned the others.

67. Verily in this is a Sign: but most of them do not believe.

68. And verily your Lord is He, the Exalted in Might, Most Merciful.

69. And rehearse to them (something of) Abraham's story.

70. Behold, he said to his father and his people: "What do you worship?"

71. They said: "We worship idols, and we remain constantly in attendance on them."

72. He said: "Do they listen to you when you call (on them),

73. Or they do you good or harm?"

74. They said: "Nay, but we found our fathers doing thus (what we do)."

75. He said: "Do you then see whom you have been worshipping,-

فَأَخْرَجْنَهُمْ مِّن جَنَّتٍ وَعُيُونٍ ۝

وَكُنُوزٍ وَمَقَامٍ كَرِيمٍ ۝

كَذَلِكَ وَأَوْرَثْنَهَا بَنِي إِسْرَائِيلَ ۝

فَأَتْبَعُوهُم مُّشْرِقِينَ ۝

فَلَمَّا تَرَاءَ الْجَمْعَانِ قَالَ أَصْحَابُ مُوسَى

إِنَّا لَمُدْرَكُونَ ۝

قَالَ كَلَّا إِنَّ مَعِيَ رَبِّي سَيَهْدِينِ ۝

فَأَوْحَيْنَا إِلَى مُوسَى أَنِ اضْرِب

بِّعَصَاكَ الْبَحْرَ فَانفَلَقَ فَكَانَ كُلُّ

فِرْقٍ كَالطَّوْدِ الْعَظِيمِ ۝

وَأَزْلَفْنَا ثَمَّ الْآخَرِينَ ۝

وَأَنجَيْنَا مُوسَى وَمَن مَّعَهُ

أَجْمَعِينَ ۝

ثُمَّ أَغْرَقْنَا الْآخَرِينَ ۝

إِنَّ فِي ذَلِكَ لَآيَةً وَمَا كَانَ

أَكْثَرُهُم مُّؤْمِنِينَ ۝

وَإِنَّ رَبَّكَ لَهُوَ الْعَزِيزُ الرَّحِيمُ ۝

وَاتْلُ عَلَيْهِمْ نَبَأَ إِبْرَاهِيمَ ۝

إِذْ قَالَ لِأَبِيهِ وَقَوْمِهِ مَا تَعْبُدُونَ ۝

قَالُوا نَعْبُدُ أَصْنَامًا فَنَظَلُّ لَهَا

عَاكِفِينَ ۝

قَالَ هَلْ يَسْمَعُونَكُمْ إِذْ تَدْعُونَ ۝

أَوْ يَنفَعُونَكُمْ أَوْ يَضُرُّونَ ۝

قَالُوا بَلْ وَجَدْنَا آبَاءَنَا كَذَلِكَ

يَفْعَلُونَ ۝

قَالَ أَفَرَأَيْتُم مَّا كُنتُمْ تَعْبُدُونَ ۝

76. "You and your fathers before you?-

77. "For they are enemies to me; not so the Lord and Cherisher of the Worlds;

78. "Who created me, and it is He Who guides me;

79. "Who gives me food and drink,

80. "And when I am ill, it is He Who cures me;

81. "Who will cause me to die, and then to life (again);

82. "And who, I hope, will forgive me my faults on the day of Judgment.

83. "O my Lord! bestow wisdom on me, and join me with the righteous;

84. "Grant me honourable mention on the tongue of truth among the latest (generations);

85. "Make me one of the inheritors of the Garden of Bliss;

86. "Forgive my father, for that he is among those astray;

87. "And let me not be in disgrace on the Day when (men) will be raised up;-

88. "The Day whereon neither wealth nor sons will avail,

89. "But only he (will prosper) that brings to Allah a sound heart;

90. "To the righteous, the Garden will be brought near,

91. "And to those straying in Evil, the Fire will be placed in full view;

92. "And it shall be said to them: 'Where are the (gods) you worshipped-

93. "'Besides Allah? Can they help you or help themselves?'

94. "Then they will be thrown headlong into the (Fire),- they and those straying in Evil,

95. "And the whole hosts of Iblis together.

96. "They will say there in their mutual bickerings:

97. "'By Allah, we were truly in an error manifest,-

98. "'When we held you as equals with the Lord of the Worlds;

إِذْ نُسَوِّيكُم بِرَبِّ الْعَٰلَمِينَ ۝

99. "'And our seducers were only those who were steeped in guilt.

وَمَآ أَضَلَّنَآ إِلَّا الْمُجْرِمُونَ ۝

100. "Now, then, we have none to intercede (for us),

فَمَا لَنَا مِن شَٰفِعِينَ ۝

101. "Nor a single friend to feel (for us).

وَلَا صَدِيقٍ حَمِيمٍ ۝

102. "Now if we only had a chance of return, we shall truly be of those who believe!"

فَلَوْ أَنَّ لَنَا كَرَّةً فَنَكُونَ مِنَ الْمُؤْمِنِينَ ۝

103. Verily in this is a Sign but most of them do not believe.

إِنَّ فِي ذَٰلِكَ لَآيَةً ۖ وَمَا كَانَ أَكْثَرُهُم مُّؤْمِنِينَ ۝

104. And verily your Lord is He, the Exalted in Might, Most Merciful.

وَإِنَّ رَبَّكَ لَهُوَ الْعَزِيزُ الرَّحِيمُ ۝

105. The people of Noah rejected the Messengers.

كَذَّبَتْ قَوْمُ نُوحٍ الْمُرْسَلِينَ ۝

106. Behold, their brother Noah said to them: "Will you not fear (Allah)?

إِذْ قَالَ لَهُمْ أَخُوهُمْ نُوحٌ أَلَا تَتَّقُونَ ۝

107. "I am to you a Messenger worthy of all trust:

إِنِّي لَكُمْ رَسُولٌ أَمِينٌ ۝

108. "So fear Allah, and obey me.

فَاتَّقُوا اللَّهَ وَأَطِيعُونِ ۝

109. "No reward do I ask of you for it: my reward is only from the Lord of the Worlds:

وَمَآ أَسْـَٔلُكُمْ عَلَيْهِ مِنْ أَجْرٍ ۖ إِنْ أَجْرِيَ إِلَّا عَلَىٰ رَبِّ الْعَٰلَمِينَ ۝

110. "So fear Allah, and obey me."

فَاتَّقُوا اللَّهَ وَأَطِيعُونِ ۝

111. They said: "Shall we believe in you when it is the meanest that follow you?"

قَالُوٓا أَنُؤْمِنُ لَكَ وَاتَّبَعَكَ الْأَرْذَلُونَ ۝

112. He said: "And what do I know as to what they do?

قَالَ وَمَا عِلْمِي بِمَا كَانُوا يَعْمَلُونَ ۝

113. "Their account is only with my Lord, if you could (but) understand.

إِنْ حِسَابُهُمْ إِلَّا عَلَىٰ رَبِّي ۖ لَوْ تَشْعُرُونَ ۝

114. "I am not one to drive away those who believe.

وَمَآ أَنَا بِطَارِدِ الْمُؤْمِنِينَ ۝

115. "I am sent only to warn plainly in public."

إِنْ أَنَا إِلَّا نَذِيرٌ مُّبِينٌ ۝

116. They said: "If you desist not, O Noah! you shall be stoned (to death)."

قَالُوا لَئِن لَّمْ تَنتَهِ يَٰنُوحُ لَتَكُونَنَّ مِنَ الْمَرْجُومِينَ ۝

117. He said: "O my Lord! truly my people have rejected me.

118. "You judge, then, between me and them openly, and deliver me and those of the Believers who are with me."

قَالَ رَبِّ إِنَّ قَوْمِي كَذَّبُونِ ۝

فَافْتَحْ بَيْنِي وَبَيْنَهُمْ فَتْحًا وَّنَجِّنِي وَمَنْ مَّعِي مِنَ الْمُؤْمِنِينَ ۝

119. So We delivered him and those with him, in the Ark filled (with all creatures).

فَأَنْجَيْنَاهُ وَمَنْ مَّعَهُ فِي الْفُلْكِ الْمَشْحُونِ ۝

120. Thereafter We drowned those who remained behind.

121. Verily in this is a Sign: but most of them do not believe.

ثُمَّ أَغْرَقْنَا بَعْدُ الْبَاقِينَ ۝

إِنَّ فِي ذَلِكَ لَآيَةً وَمَا كَانَ أَكْثَرُهُمْ مُّؤْمِنِينَ ۝

122. And verily your Lord is He, the Exalted in Might, Most Merciful.

123. The 'Ad (people) rejected the Messengers.

124. Behold, their brother Hud said to them: "Will you not fear (Allah)?

وَإِنَّ رَبَّكَ لَهُوَ الْعَزِيزُ الرَّحِيمُ ۝

كَذَّبَتْ عَادُ الْمُرْسَلِينَ ۝

إِذْ قَالَ لَهُمْ أَخُوهُمْ هُودٌ أَلَا تَتَّقُونَ ۝

125. "I am to you a Messenger worthy of all trust:

126. "So fear Allah and obey me.

127. "No reward do I ask of you for it: my reward is only from the Lord of the Worlds.

إِنِّي لَكُمْ رَسُولٌ أَمِينٌ ۝

فَاتَّقُوا اللَّهَ وَأَطِيعُونِ ۝

وَمَا أَسْأَلُكُمْ عَلَيْهِ مِنْ أَجْرٍ إِنْ أَجْرِيَ إِلَّا عَلَى رَبِّ الْعَالَمِينَ ۝

128. "Do you build a landmark on every high place to amuse yourselves?

129. "And do you get for yourselves fine buildings in the hope of living therein (for ever)?

أَتَبْنُونَ بِكُلِّ رِيعٍ آيَةً تَعْبَثُونَ ۝

وَتَتَّخِذُونَ مَصَانِعَ لَعَلَّكُمْ تَخْلُدُونَ ۝

130. "And when you strike, you strike like tyrants.

131. "Now fear Allah, and obey me.

وَإِذَا بَطَشْتُمْ بَطَشْتُمْ جَبَّارِينَ ۝

فَاتَّقُوا اللَّهَ وَأَطِيعُونِ ۝

132. "Yes, fear Him Who has bestowed on you freely all that you know.

133. "Freely has He bestowed on you cattle and sons,-

134. "And Gardens and Springs.

وَاتَّقُوا الَّذِي أَمَدَّكُمْ بِمَا تَعْلَمُونَ ۝

أَمَدَّكُمْ بِأَنْعَامٍ وَبَنِينَ ۝

وَجَنَّاتٍ وَعُيُونٍ ۝

135. "Truly I fear for you the Penalty of a Great Day."

إِنِّي أَخَافُ عَلَيْكُمْ عَذَابَ يَوْمٍ عَظِيمٍ ۝

136. They said: "It is the same
to us whether you admonish us
or be not among (our) admo-
nishers!

137. "This is no other than a
customary device of the ancients,

138. "And we are not the ones
to receive Pains and Penalties!"

139. So they rejected him, and
We destroyed them. Verily in
this is a Sign: but most of them
do not believe.

140. And verily your Lord is
He, the Exalted in Might, Most
Merciful.

141. The Thamud (people)
rejected the Messengers.

142. Behold, their brother Salih
said to them: "Will you not fear
(Allah)?

143. "I am to you a Messenger
worthy of all trust.

144. "So fear Allah, and obey
me.

145. "No reward do I ask of you
for it: my reward is only from
the Lord of the Worlds.

146. "Will you be left secure, in
(the enjoyment of) all that you
have here?-

147. "Gardens and Springs,

148. "And corn-fields and date-
palms with spathes near breaking
(with the weight of fruit)?

149. "And you carve houses out
of (rocky) mountains with great
skill.

150. "But fear Allah and obey
me;

151. "And do not follow the
bidding of those who are extravagant,-

152. "Who make mischief in
the land, and do not mend (their
ways)."

153. They said: "You are only
one of those bewitched!

154. "You are no more than a
mortal like us: then bring us a
Sign, if you tell the truth!"

قَالُوا سَوَآءٌ عَلَيْنَآ أَوَعَظْتَ أَمْ لَمْ
تَكُن مِّنَ ٱلْوَٰعِظِينَ ۝

إِنْ هَٰذَآ إِلَّا خُلُقُ ٱلْأَوَّلِينَ ۝

وَمَا نَحْنُ بِمُعَذَّبِينَ ۝

فَكَذَّبُوهُ فَأَهْلَكْنَٰهُمْ ۘ إِنَّ فِي
ذَٰلِكَ لَءَايَةً ۖ وَمَا كَانَ أَكْثَرُهُم
مُّؤْمِنِينَ ۝

وَإِنَّ رَبَّكَ لَهُوَ ٱلْعَزِيزُ ٱلرَّحِيمُ ۝

كَذَّبَتْ ثَمُودُ ٱلْمُرْسَلِينَ ۝

إِذْ قَالَ لَهُمْ أَخُوهُمْ صَٰلِحٌ أَلَا
تَتَّقُونَ ۝

إِنِّي لَكُمْ رَسُولٌ أَمِينٌ ۝

فَٱتَّقُوا ٱللَّهَ وَأَطِيعُونِ ۝

وَمَآ أَسْـَٔلُكُمْ عَلَيْهِ مِنْ أَجْرٍ ۖ إِنْ
أَجْرِيَ إِلَّا عَلَىٰ رَبِّ ٱلْعَٰلَمِينَ ۝

أَتُتْرَكُونَ فِي مَا هَٰهُنَآ ءَامِنِينَ ۝

فِي جَنَّٰتٍ وَعُيُونٍ ۝

وَزُرُوعٍ وَنَخْلٍ طَلْعُهَا هَضِيمٌ ۝

وَتَنْحِتُونَ مِنَ ٱلْجِبَالِ بُيُوتًا فَٰرِهِينَ ۝

فَٱتَّقُوا ٱللَّهَ وَأَطِيعُونِ ۝

وَلَا تُطِيعُوٓا أَمْرَ ٱلْمُسْرِفِينَ ۝

ٱلَّذِينَ يُفْسِدُونَ فِي ٱلْأَرْضِ
وَلَا يُصْلِحُونَ ۝

قَالُوٓا إِنَّمَآ أَنتَ مِنَ ٱلْمُسَحَّرِينَ ۝

مَآ أَنتَ إِلَّا بَشَرٌ مِّثْلُنَا فَأْتِ بِـَٔايَةٍ
إِن كُنتَ مِنَ ٱلصَّٰدِقِينَ ۝

155. He said: "Here is a she-camel: she has a right of watering, and you have a right of watering, (severally) on a day appointed.

قَالَ هٰذِهٖ نَاقَةٌ لَّهَا شِرْبٌ وَّلَكُمْ شِرْبُ يَوْمٍ مَّعْلُوْمٍ ۞

156. "Do not touch her with harm, lest the Penalty of a Great Day seize you."

وَلَا تَمَسُّوْهَا بِسُوْۤءٍ فَيَأْخُذَكُمْ عَذَابُ يَوْمٍ عَظِيْمٍ ۞

157. But they ham-strung her: then they became full of regrets.

فَعَقَرُوْهَا فَاَصْبَحُوْا نٰدِمِيْنَ ۞

158. But the Penalty seized them. Verily in this is a Sign: but most of them do not believe.

فَاَخَذَهُمُ الْعَذَابُ ۗ اِنَّ فِيْ ذٰلِكَ لَاٰيَةً ۗ وَمَا كَانَ اَكْثَرُهُمْ مُّؤْمِنِيْنَ ۞

159. And verily your Lord is He, the Exalted in Might, Most Merciful.

وَاِنَّ رَبَّكَ لَهُوَ الْعَزِيْزُ الرَّحِيْمُ ۞

160. The people of Lut rejected the Messengers.

كَذَّبَتْ قَوْمُ لُوْطِ الْمُرْسَلِيْنَ ۞

161. Behold, their brother Lut said to them: "Will you not fear (Allah)?

اِذْ قَالَ لَهُمْ اَخُوْهُمْ لُوْطٌ اَلَا تَتَّقُوْنَ ۞

162. "I am to you a Messenger worthy of all trust.

اِنِّيْ لَكُمْ رَسُوْلٌ اَمِيْنٌ ۞

163. "So fear Allah and obey me.

فَاتَّقُوا اللّٰهَ وَاَطِيْعُوْنِ ۞

164. "No reward do I ask of you for it: my reward is only from the Lord of the Worlds.

وَمَاۤ اَسْئَلُكُمْ عَلَيْهِ مِنْ اَجْرٍ ۚ اِنْ اَجْرِيَ اِلَّا عَلٰى رَبِّ الْعٰلَمِيْنَ ۞

165. "Of all the creatures in the world, will you approach males,

اَتَأْتُوْنَ الذُّكْرَانَ مِنَ الْعٰلَمِيْنَ ۞

166. "And leave those whom Allah has created for you to be your mates? Nay, you are a people transgressing (all limits)!"

وَتَذَرُوْنَ مَا خَلَقَ لَكُمْ رَبُّكُمْ مِّنْ اَزْوَاجِكُمْ ۗ بَلْ اَنْتُمْ قَوْمٌ عٰدُوْنَ ۞

167. They said: "If you do not desist, O Lut! you will assuredly be cast out!"

قَالُوْا لَئِنْ لَّمْ تَنْتَهِ يٰلُوْطُ لَتَكُوْنَنَّ مِنَ الْمُخْرَجِيْنَ ۞

168. He said: "I do detest your doings."

قَالَ اِنِّيْ لِعَمَلِكُمْ مِّنَ الْقَالِيْنَ ۞

169. "O my Lord! deliver me and my family from such things as they do!"

رَبِّ نَجِّنِيْ وَاَهْلِيْ مِمَّا يَعْمَلُوْنَ ۞

170. So We delivered him and his family,- all

فَنَجَّيْنٰهُ وَاَهْلَهٗۤ اَجْمَعِيْنَ ۞

171. Except an old woman who lingered behind.

اِلَّا عَجُوْزًا فِى الْغٰبِرِيْنَ ۞

172. But the rest We destroyed utterly.

ثُمَّ دَمَّرْنَا الْاٰخَرِيْنَ ۞

173. We rained down on them a shower (of brimstone): and evil was the shower on those who were admonished (but heeded not)!

وَاَمْطَرْنَا عَلَيْهِمْ مَّطَرًا ۚ فَسَآءَ مَطَرُ الْمُنْذَرِيْنَ ۞

١٩
١٢
ع

174. Verily in this is a Sign: but most of them do not believe.

اِنَّ فِي ذٰلِكَ لَاٰيَةً ۖ وَمَا كَانَ اَكْثَرُهُمْ مُّؤْمِنِيْنَ ۞

175. And verily your Lord is He, the Exalted in Might, Most Merciful.

وَاِنَّ رَبَّكَ لَهُوَ الْعَزِيْزُ الرَّحِيْمُ ۞

176. The Companions of the Wood rejected the Messengers.

كَذَّبَ اَصْحٰبُ لْئَيْكَةِ الْمُرْسَلِيْنَ ۞

177. Behold, Shu'aib said to them: "Will you not fear (Allah)?

اِذْ قَالَ لَهُمْ شُعَيْبٌ اَلَا تَتَّقُوْنَ ۞

178. "I am to you a Messenger worthy of all trust.

اِنِّيْ لَكُمْ رَسُوْلٌ اَمِيْنٌ ۞

179. "So fear Allah and obey me.

فَاتَّقُوا اللّٰهَ وَاَطِيْعُوْنِ ۞

180. "No reward do I ask of you for it: my reward is only from the Lord of the Worlds.

وَمَا اَسْئَلُكُمْ عَلَيْهِ مِنْ اَجْرٍ ۚ اِنْ اَجْرِيَ اِلَّا عَلٰى رَبِّ الْعٰلَمِيْنَ ۞

181. "Give just measure, and cause no loss (to others by fraud).

اَوْفُوا الْكَيْلَ وَلَا تَكُوْنُوْا مِنَ الْمُخْسِرِيْنَ ۞

182. "And weigh with scales true and upright.

وَزِنُوْا بِالْقِسْطَاسِ الْمُسْتَقِيْمِ ۞

183. "And do not withhold things justly due to men, nor do evil in the land, working mischief.

وَلَا تَبْخَسُوا النَّاسَ اَشْيَاءَهُمْ وَلَا تَعْثَوْا فِي الْاَرْضِ مُفْسِدِيْنَ ۞

184. "And fear Him Who created you and (Who created) the generations before (you)"

وَاتَّقُوا الَّذِيْ خَلَقَكُمْ وَالْجِبِلَّةَ الْاَوَّلِيْنَ ۞

185. They said: "You are only one of those bewitched!

قَالُوْٓا اِنَّمَآ اَنْتَ مِنَ الْمُسَحَّرِيْنَ ۞

186. "You are no more than a mortal like us, and indeed we think you are a liar!

وَمَآ اَنْتَ اِلَّا بَشَرٌ مِّثْلُنَا وَاِنْ نَّظُنُّكَ لَمِنَ الْكٰذِبِيْنَ ۞

187. "Now cause a piece of the sky to fall on us, if you are truthful!"

فَاَسْقِطْ عَلَيْنَا كِسَفًا مِّنَ السَّمَآءِ اِنْ كُنْتَ مِنَ الصّٰدِقِيْنَ ۞

188. He said: "My Lord knows best what you do."

قَالَ رَبِّيْٓ اَعْلَمُ بِمَا تَعْمَلُوْنَ ۞

189. But they rejected him. Then the punishment of a day of overshadowing gloom seized them, and that was the Penalty of a Great Day.

فَكَذَّبُوْهُ فَاَخَذَهُمْ عَذَابُ يَوْمِ الظُّلَّةِ ۖ اِنَّهُ كَانَ عَذَابَ يَوْمٍ عَظِيْمٍ ۞

190. Verily in that is a Sign: but

اِنَّ فِي ذٰلِكَ لَاٰيَةً ۖ وَمَا كَانَ

most of them do not believe.

191. And verily your Lord is He, the Exalted in Might, Most Merciful.

اَكْثَرُهُمْ مُّؤْمِنِيْنَ ۞

وَاِنَّ رَبَّكَ لَهُوَ الْعَزِيْزُ الرَّحِيْمُ ۞

192. Verily this is a Revelation from the Lord of the Worlds:

وَاِنَّهُ لَتَنْزِيْلُ رَبِّ الْعٰلَمِيْنَ ۞

193. With it came down the spirit of Faith and Truth-

نَزَلَ بِهِ الرُّوْحُ الْاَمِيْنُ ۞

194. To your heart and mind, that you may admonish.

عَلٰى قَلْبِكَ لِتَكُوْنَ مِنَ الْمُنْذِرِيْنَ ۞

195. In the perspicuous Arabic tongue.

بِلِسَانٍ عَرَبِيٍّ مُّبِيْنٍ ۞

196. Without doubt it is (announced) in the mystic Books of former peoples.

وَاِنَّهُ لَفِيْ زُبُرِ الْاَوَّلِيْنَ ۞

197. Is it not a Sign to them that the Learned of the Children of Israel knew it (as true)?

اَوَلَمْ يَكُنْ لَّهُمْ اٰيَةً اَنْ يَّعْلَمَهُ

عُلَمَاؤُا بَنِيْ اِسْرَآءِيْلَ ۞

198. Had We revealed it to any of the non-Arabs,

وَلَوْ نَزَّلْنٰهُ عَلٰى بَعْضِ الْاَعْجَمِيْنَ ۞

199. And had he recited it to them, they would not have believed in it.

فَقَرَاَهُ عَلَيْهِمْ مَّا كَانُوْا بِهٖ مُؤْمِنِيْنَ ۞

200. Thus have We caused it to enter the hearts of the sinners.

كَذٰلِكَ سَلَكْنٰهُ فِيْ قُلُوْبِ الْمُجْرِمِيْنَ ۞

201. They will not believe in it until they see the grievous Penalty;

لَا يُؤْمِنُوْنَ بِهٖ حَتّٰى يَرَوُا الْعَذَابَ

الْاَلِيْمَ ۞

202. But the (Penalty) will come to them of a sudden, while they perceive it not;

فَيَاْتِيَهُمْ بَغْتَةً وَّهُمْ لَا يَشْعُرُوْنَ ۞

203. Then they will say: "Shall we be respited?"

فَيَقُوْلُوْا هَلْ نَحْنُ مُنْظَرُوْنَ ۞

204. Do they then ask for Our Penalty to be hastened on?

اَفَبِعَذَابِنَا يَسْتَعْجِلُوْنَ ۞

205. Do you see? If We do let them enjoy (this life) for a few years,

اَفَرَءَيْتَ اِنْ مَّتَّعْنٰهُمْ سِنِيْنَ ۞

206. Yet there comes to them at length the (Punishment) which they were promised!

ثُمَّ جَآءَهُمْ مَّا كَانُوْا يُوْعَدُوْنَ ۞

207. It will not profit them that they enjoyed (this life)!

مَآ اَغْنٰى عَنْهُمْ مَّا كَانُوْا يُمَتَّعُوْنَ ۞

208. Never did We destroy a town, but had its warners—

وَمَآ اَهْلَكْنَا مِنْ قَرْيَةٍ اِلَّا لَهَا

مُنْذِرُوْنَ ۞

209. By way of reminder; and We are never unjust.

ذِكْرٰى ۚ وَمَا كُنَّا ظٰلِمِيْنَ ۞

210. No evil ones have brought down this (Revelation):

وَمَا تَنَزَّلَتْ بِهِ الشَّيٰطِيْنُ ۞

211. It would neither suit them nor would they be able (to produce it).

وَمَا يَنْبَغِيْ لَهُمْ وَمَا يَسْتَطِيْعُوْنَ ۞

212. Indeed they have been removed far from even (a chance of) hearing it.

اِنَّهُمْ عَنِ السَّمْعِ لَمَعْزُوْلُوْنَ ۞

SÛRAH-27
AN-NAML
(INTRODUCTION)

This Sûrah is cognate in subject to the one preceding it and the two following it. Its chronological place is also in the same group of four.

Here there is much mystic symbolism. Wonders in the physical world are types of greater wonders in the spiritual world. The Fire, the White Hand and the Rod, in the story of Moses; the speech of birds, the crowds of Jinns and men pitted against a humble ant, and the Hoopoe and the Queen of Sheba, in Solomon's story; the defeat of the plot of the nine wicked men in the story of Sâliḥ; and the crime of sin with open eyes in the story of Lot;-lead up to the lessons of true and false worship and the miracles of Allah's grace and revelation.

213. So do not call on any other god with Allah, or you will be among those under the Penalty.

فَلَا تَدْعُ مَعَ اللّٰهِ إِلٰهًا اٰخَرَ فَتَكُوْنَ مِنَ الْمُعَذَّبِيْنَ ۟

214. And admonish your nearest kinsmen,

وَاَنْذِرْ عَشِيْرَتَكَ الْاَقْرَبِيْنَ ۟

215. And lower your wing to the Believers who follow you.

وَاخْفِضْ جَنَاحَكَ لِمَنِ اتَّبَعَكَ مِنَ الْمُؤْمِنِيْنَ ۟

216. Then if they disobey you, say: "I am free (of responsibility) for what you do!"

فَاِنْ عَصَوْكَ فَقُلْ اِنِّيْ بَرِيْٓءٌ مِّمَّا تَعْمَلُوْنَ ۟

217. And put your trust on the Exalted in Might, the Merciful,

وَتَوَكَّلْ عَلَى الْعَزِيْزِ الرَّحِيْمِ ۟

218. Who sees you standing forth (in prayer),

الَّذِيْ يَرٰىكَ حِيْنَ تَقُوْمُ ۟

219. And your movements among those who prostrate themselves,

وَتَقَلُّبَكَ فِى السّٰجِدِيْنَ ۟

220. For it is He Who hears and knows all things.

اِنَّهٗ هُوَ السَّمِيْعُ الْعَلِيْمُ ۟

221. Shall I inform you, (O people!), on whom it is that the evil ones descend?

هَلْ اُنَبِّئُكُمْ عَلٰى مَنْ تَنَزَّلُ الشَّيٰطِيْنُ ۟

222. They descend on every lying, wicked person,

تَنَزَّلُ عَلٰى كُلِّ اَفَّاكٍ اَثِيْمٍ ۟

223. (Into whose ears) they pour hearsay vanities, and most of them are liars.

يُّلْقُوْنَ السَّمْعَ وَاَكْثَرُهُمْ كٰذِبُوْنَ ۟

224. And the Poets,- it is those straying in Evil, who follow them:

وَالشُّعَرَاۤءُ يَتَّبِعُهُمُ الْغَاوٗنَ ۟

225. Don't you see that they wander distracted in every valley?-

اَلَمْ تَرَ اَنَّهُمْ فِيْ كُلِّ وَادٍ يَّهِيْمُوْنَ ۟

226. And that they say what they do not practise?-

وَاَنَّهُمْ يَقُوْلُوْنَ مَا لَا يَفْعَلُوْنَ ۟

227. Except those who believe, work righteousness, engage much in the remembrance of Allah, and defend themselves only after they are unjustly attacked. And soon will the unjust assailants know what vicissitudes their affairs will take!

اِلَّا الَّذِيْنَ اٰمَنُوْا وَعَمِلُوا الصّٰلِحٰتِ وَذَكَرُوا اللّٰهَ كَثِيْرًا وَّانْتَصَرُوْا مِنْۢ بَعْدِ مَا ظُلِمُوْا ۚ وَسَيَعْلَمُ الَّذِيْنَ ظَلَمُوْۤا اَيَّ مُنْقَلَبٍ يَّنْقَلِبُوْنَ ۟

27. The Ants
In the name of Allah. Most Gracious, Most Merciful.

سُوْرَةُ النَّمْلِ مَكِّيَّةٌ (٢٨) (٢٧)

بِسْمِ اللّٰهِ الرَّحْمٰنِ الرَّحِيْمِ

1. *Ta-Sin.* These are verses of the Qur'an,-a Book that makes (things) clear;

طٰسٓ ۟ تِلْكَ اٰيٰتُ الْقُرْاٰنِ وَكِتَابٍ مُّبِيْنٍ ۟

2.   A Guide and Glad Tidings for the Believers,-

3.   Those who establish regular prayers and give in regular charity, and also have (full) assurance of the Hereafter.

4.   As to those who do not believe in the Hereafter, We have made their deeds pleasing in their eyes; and so they wander about in distraction.

5.   Such are they for whom a grievous Penalty is (waiting); and in the Hereafter theirs will be the greatest loss.

6.   As to you, the Qur'an is bestowed upon you from the presence of One Who is Wise and All-knowing.

7.   Behold! Moses said to his family: "I perceive a fire; soon will I bring you from there some information, or I will bring you a burning brand to light our fuel, that you may warm yourselves.

8.   But when he came to the (fire), a voice was heard: "Blessed are those in the fire and those around: and Glory to Allah, the Lord of the worlds.

9.   "O Moses! Verily, I am Allah, the Exalted in Might, the Wise!.

10.   "Now you throw your rod!" But when he saw it moving (of its own accord) as if it had been a snake, he turned back in retreat, and retraced not his steps: "O Moses!" (it was said), "Fear not: truly, in My presence, those called as Messengers have no fear,-

11.   "But if any have done wrong and have thereafter substituted good to take the place of evil, truly, I am Oft-Forgiving, Most Merciful.

12.   "Now put your hand into your bosom, and it will come forth white without stain (or harm): (these are) among the nine Signs (you will take) to Pharaoh and his people: for they are a people rebellious in transgression."

13. But when Our Signs came to them, that should have opened their eyes, they said: "This is sorcery manifest!"

14. And they rejected those Signs in iniquity and arrogance, though their souls were convinced thereof: so see what was the end of those who acted corruptly!

15. We gave (in the past) knowledge to David and Solomon: and they both said: "Praise be to Allah, Who has favoured us above many of His servants who believe!"

16. And Solomon was David's heir. He said: "O you people! we have been taught the speech of birds, and on us has been bestowed (a little) of all things: this is indeed Grace manifest (from Allah.)"

17. And before Solomon were marshalled his hosts,- of Jinns and men and birds, and they were all kept in order and ranks.

18. At length, when they came to a (lowly) valley of ants, one of the ants said: "O you ants, get into your habitations, lest Solomon and his hosts crush you (under foot) without knowing it."

19. So he smiled, amused at her speech; and he said: "O my Lord! so order me that I may be grateful for Your favours, which You have bestowed on me and on my parents, and that I may work the righteousness that will please You: and admit me, by Your Grace, to the ranks of Your Righteous Servants."

20. And he took a muster of the Birds; and he said: "Why is it I do not see

فَلَمَّا جَآءَتْهُمْ ءَايَتُنَا مُبْصِرَةً قَالُوا هَذَا سِحْرٌ مُّبِينٌ ۞

وَجَحَدُوا بِهَا وَاسْتَيْقَنَتْهَآ أَنْفُسُهُمْ ظُلْمًا وَعُلُوًّا ۚ فَانْظُرْ كَيْفَ كَانَ عَاقِبَةُ الْمُفْسِدِينَ ۞

وَلَقَدْ ءَاتَيْنَا دَاوُدَ وَسُلَيْمَنَ عِلْمًا ۖ وَقَالَا الْحَمْدُ لِلَّهِ الَّذِي فَضَّلَنَا عَلَىٰ كَثِيرٍ مِّنْ عِبَادِهِ الْمُؤْمِنِينَ ۞

وَوَرِثَ سُلَيْمَنُ دَاوُدَ ۖ وَقَالَ يَآأَيُّهَا النَّاسُ عُلِّمْنَا مَنْطِقَ الطَّيْرِ وَأُوتِينَا مِنْ كُلِّ شَيْءٍ ۖ إِنَّ هَذَا لَهُوَ الْفَضْلُ الْمُبِينُ ۞

وَحُشِرَ لِسُلَيْمَنَ جُنُودُهُ مِنَ الْجِنِّ وَالْإِنْسِ وَالطَّيْرِ فَهُمْ يُوزَعُونَ ۞

حَتَّىٰ إِذَآ أَتَوْا عَلَىٰ وَادِ النَّمْلِ قَالَتْ نَمْلَةٌ يَآأَيُّهَا النَّمْلُ ادْخُلُوا مَسَكِنَكُمْ ۚ لَا يَحْطِمَنَّكُمْ سُلَيْمَنُ وَجُنُودُهُ ۚ وَهُمْ لَا يَشْعُرُونَ ۞

فَتَبَسَّمَ ضَاحِكًا مِّنْ قَوْلِهَا وَقَالَ رَبِّ أَوْزِعْنِي أَنْ أَشْكُرَ نِعْمَتَكَ الَّتِي أَنْعَمْتَ عَلَيَّ وَعَلَىٰ وَالِدَيَّ وَأَنْ أَعْمَلَ صَالِحًا تَرْضَاهُ وَأَدْخِلْنِي بِرَحْمَتِكَ فِي عِبَادِكَ الصَّالِحِينَ ۞

وَتَفَقَّدَ الطَّيْرَ فَقَالَ مَالِيَ لَآ أَرَى

the Hoopoe? Or is he among the absentees?

21. "I will certainly punish him with a severe penalty, or execute him, unless he brings me a clear reason (for absence)."

22. But the Hoopoe did not tarry far: he (came up and) said: "I have compassed (territory) which you have not compassed, and I have come to you from Saba with true tidings.

23. "I found (there) a woman ruling over them and provided with every requisite; and she has a magnificent throne.

24. "I found her and her people worshipping the sun besides Allah: Satan has made their deeds seem pleasing in their eyes, and has kept them away from the Path,- so they receive no guidance,-

25. "(Kept them away from the Path), that they should not worship Allah, Who brings to light what is hidden in the heavens and the earth, and knows what you hide and what you reveal.

26. "Allah!- there is no god but He!- Lord of the Throne Supreme!"

27. (Solomon) said: "Soon shall we see whether you have told the truth or lied!

28. "You go, with this letter of mine, and deliver it to them: then draw back from them, and (wait to) see what answer they return".

29. (The queen) said: "You chiefs! here is delivered to me - a letter worthy of respect.

30. "It is from Solomon, and is (as follows): 'In the name of Allah, Most Gracious, Most Merciful:

31. "'You be not arrogant against me, but come to me in submission (to the true Religion).'

32. She said: "You chiefs! Advise me in (this) my affair: no affair have I decided except in your presence."

33. They said: "We are endued with strength, and given to vehement war: but the command is with you; so consider what you will command."

34. She said: "Kings, when they enter a country, despoil it, and make the noblest of its people its meanest, thus do they behave.

35. "But I am going to send him a present, and (wait) to see with what (answer) (my) ambassadors return."

36. Now when (the embassy) came to Solomon, he said: "Will you give me abundance in wealth? But that which Allah has given me is better than that which He has given you! Nay it is you who rejoice in your gift!

37. "Go back to them, and be sure we shall come to them with such hosts as they will never be able to meet: we shall expel them from there in disgrace, and they will feel humbled (indeed)."

38. He said (to his own men): "You Chiefs! which of you can bring me her throne before they come to me in submission?"

39. An 'Ifrit, of the Jinns said: "I will bring it to you before you rise from your Council: indeed I have full strength for the purpose, and may be trusted."

40. Said one who had knowledge of the Book: "I will bring it to you within the twinkling of

an eye!" Then when (Solomon) saw it placed firmly before him, he said: "This is by the Grace of my Lord!- to test me whether I am grateful or ungrateful! and if any is grateful, truly his gratitude is (a gain) for his own soul; but if any is ungrateful, truly my Lord is Free of all Needs, Supreme in Honour !"

41.   He said: "Transform her throne out of all recognition by her; let us see whether she is guided (to the truth) or is one of those who receive no guidance."

42.   So when she arrived, she was asked, "Is this your throne?" She said, "It was just like this; and knowledge was bestowed on us in advance of this, and we have submitted to Allah (in Islam)."

43.   And he diverted her from the worship of others besides Allah: for she was (sprung) of a people that had no faith.

44.   She was asked to enter the lofty Palace: but when she saw it, she thought it was a lake of water, and she (tucked up her skirts), uncovering her legs. He said: "This is but a palace paved smooth with slabs of glass." She said: "O my Lord! I have indeed wronged my soul: I do (now) submit (in Islam), with Solomon, to the Lord of the Worlds."

45.   We sent (aforetime), to the Thamud, their brother Salih, saying, "Serve Allah": But behold, they became two factions quarrelling with each other.

46.   He said: "O my people! why do you ask to hasten on the evil in preference to the good? If only you ask Allah for forgiveness, you may hope to receive mercy.

47.   They said: "We augur ill omen from you and those that are with you".

طَرْفُكَ فَلَمَّا رَآهُ مُسْتَقِرًّا عِنْدَهُ

قَالَ هٰذَا مِنْ فَضْلِ رَبِّي ۖ

لِيَبْلُوَنِي ءَأَشْكُرُ أَمْ أَكْفُرُ ۖ وَمَنْ

شَكَرَ فَإِنَّمَا يَشْكُرُ لِنَفْسِهِ ۖ وَمَنْ

كَفَرَ فَإِنَّ رَبِّي غَنِيٌّ كَرِيمٌ ۝

قَالَ نَكِّرُوا لَهَا عَرْشَهَا نَنْظُرْ

أَتَهْتَدِي أَمْ تَكُونُ مِنَ الَّذِينَ

لَا يَهْتَدُونَ ۝

فَلَمَّا جَآءَتْ قِيلَ أَهٰكَذَا عَرْشُكِ

قَالَتْ كَأَنَّهُ هُوَ ۚ وَأُوتِينَا الْعِلْمَ

مِنْ قَبْلِهَا وَكُنَّا مُسْلِمِينَ ۝

وَصَدَّهَا مَا كَانَتْ تَعْبُدُ مِنْ دُونِ

اللّٰهِ ۖ إِنَّهَا كَانَتْ مِنْ قَوْمٍ كٰفِرِينَ ۝

قِيلَ لَهَا ادْخُلِي الصَّرْحَ ۖ فَلَمَّا

رَأَتْهُ حَسِبَتْهُ لُجَّةً وَكَشَفَتْ عَنْ

سَاقَيْهَا ۚ قَالَ إِنَّهُ صَرْحٌ مُّمَرَّدٌ

مِّنْ قَوَارِيرَ ۗ قَالَتْ رَبِّ إِنِّي ظَلَمْتُ

نَفْسِي وَأَسْلَمْتُ مَعَ سُلَيْمٰنَ لِلّٰهِ

رَبِّ الْعٰلَمِينَ ۝

وَلَقَدْ أَرْسَلْنَا إِلَىٰ ثَمُودَ أَخَاهُمْ

صٰلِحًا أَنِ اعْبُدُوا اللّٰهَ فَإِذَا

هُمْ فَرِيقَانِ يَخْتَصِمُونَ ۝

قَالَ يٰقَوْمِ لِمَ تَسْتَعْجِلُونَ

بِالسَّيِّئَةِ قَبْلَ الْحَسَنَةِ ۖ لَوْلَا

تَسْتَغْفِرُونَ اللّٰهَ لَعَلَّكُمْ تُرْحَمُونَ ۝

قَالُوا اطَّيَّرْنَا بِكَ وَبِمَنْ مَّعَكَ ۚ

He said: "Your ill omen is with Allah; yes, you are a people under trial."

48. There were in the city nine men of a family, who made mischief in the land, and would not reform.

49. They said: "Swear a mutual oath by Allah that we shall make a secret night attack on him and his people, and that we shall then say to his heir (when he seeks vengeance): "We were not present at the slaughter of his people, and we are positively telling the truth.'"

50. They plotted and planned, but We too planned, even while they perceived it not.

51. Then see what was the end of their plot!- this, that We destroyed them and their people, all (of them).

52. Now such were their houses, - in utter ruin, - because they practised wrong-doing. Verily in this is a Sign for people of knowledge.

53. And We saved those who believed and practised righteousness.

54. (We also sent) Lut (as a Messenger): behold, he said to his people, "Do you do what is shameful though you see (its iniquity)?

55. Would you really approach men in your lusts rather than women? Nay, you are a people (grossly) ignorant!

56. But his people gave no other answer but this: they said, "Drive out the followers of Lut from your city: these are indeed men who want to be clean and pure!"

57. But We saved him and his family, except his wife;

her We destined to be of those who lagged behind.

58. And We rained down on them a shower (of brimstone): and evil was the shower on those who were admonished (but heeded not)!

59. Say: Praise be to Allah, and Peace on His servants whom He has chosen (for His Message). (Who) is better?- Allah or the false gods they associate (with Him)?

60. Or, who has created the heavens and the earth, and who sends you down rain from the sky? Yes, with it We cause to grow well-planted orchards full of beauty and delight: it is not in your power to cause the growth of the trees in them. (Can there be another) god besides Allah? Nay, they are a people who swerve from justice.

61. Or, who has made the earth firm to live in; made rivers in its midst; set thereon mountains immovable; and made a separating bar between the two bodies of flowing water? (can there be another) god besides Allah? Nay, most of them do not know.

62. Or, who listens to the (soul) distressed when it calls on Him, and Who relieves its suffering, and makes you (mankind) inheritors of the earth? (Can there be another) god besides Allah? Little it is that you heed.

63. Or, who guides you through the depths of darkness on land and sea, and who sends the winds as heralds of glad tidings, going before His Mercy? (Can there be another) god besides Allah?- High is Allah above what they associate with Him!

64. Or, who originates Creation, then repeats it, and who gives you sustenance from heaven and earth? (Can there be another) god besides Allah? Say, "Bring forth your argument, if you are telling the truth!"

قَدَّرْنَاهَا مِنَ الْغَٰبِرِينَ ۝

وَأَمْطَرْنَا عَلَيْهِمْ مَّطَرًا ۚ فَسَآءَ مَطَرُ الْمُنْذَرِينَ ۝

قُلِ الْحَمْدُ لِلّٰهِ وَسَلَٰمٌ عَلَىٰ عِبَادِهِ الَّذِينَ اصْطَفَىٰ ۗ ءَآللّٰهُ خَيْرٌ أَمَّا يُشْرِكُونَ ۝

أَمَّنْ خَلَقَ السَّمٰوٰتِ وَالْأَرْضَ وَأَنْزَلَ لَكُمْ مِّنَ السَّمَآءِ مَآءً ۚ فَأَنْبَتْنَا بِهِ حَدَآئِقَ ذَاتَ بَهْجَةٍ ۚ مَا كَانَ لَكُمْ أَنْ تُنْبِتُوا شَجَرَهَا ۗ ءَإِلٰهٌ مَّعَ اللّٰهِ ۚ بَلْ هُمْ قَوْمٌ يَعْدِلُونَ ۝

أَمَّنْ جَعَلَ الْأَرْضَ قَرَارًا وَّجَعَلَ خِلَٰلَهَا أَنْهٰرًا وَّجَعَلَ لَهَا رَوَاسِيَ وَجَعَلَ بَيْنَ الْبَحْرَيْنِ حَاجِزًا ۗ ءَإِلٰهٌ مَّعَ اللّٰهِ ۚ بَلْ أَكْثَرُهُمْ لَا يَعْلَمُونَ ۝

أَمَّنْ يُّجِيبُ الْمُضْطَرَّ إِذَا دَعَاهُ وَيَكْشِفُ السُّوٓءَ وَيَجْعَلُكُمْ خُلَفَآءَ الْأَرْضِ ۗ ءَإِلٰهٌ مَّعَ اللّٰهِ ۚ قَلِيلًا مَّا تَذَكَّرُونَ ۝

أَمَّنْ يَّهْدِيكُمْ فِي ظُلُمٰتِ الْبَرِّ وَالْبَحْرِ وَمَنْ يُّرْسِلُ الرِّيٰحَ بُشْرًا بَيْنَ يَدَيْ رَحْمَتِهِ ۗ ءَإِلٰهٌ مَّعَ اللّٰهِ ۚ تَعٰلَى اللّٰهُ عَمَّا يُشْرِكُونَ ۝

أَمَّنْ يَّبْدَؤُا الْخَلْقَ ثُمَّ يُعِيدُهُ وَمَنْ يَّرْزُقُكُمْ مِّنَ السَّمَآءِ وَالْأَرْضِ ۗ ءَإِلٰهٌ مَّعَ اللّٰهِ ۚ قُلْ هَاتُوا بُرْهَانَكُمْ إِنْ

65. Say: None in the heavens or on earth, except Allah, knows what is hidden: nor can they perceive when they shall be raised up (for Judgment).

66. Still less can their knowledge comprehend the Hereafter; nay, they are in doubt and uncertainty thereat; nay, they are blind thereunto.

67. The Unbelievers say: "What! when we become dust,- we and our fathers,- shall we really be raised (from the dead)?

68. "It is true we were promised this,- we and our fathers before (us): these are nothing but tales of the ancients."

69. Say: "You go through the earth and see what has been the end of those guilty (of sin)."

70. But grieve not over them, nor distress yourself because of their plots.

71. They also say: "When will this promise (come to pass)? (Say) if you are truthful."

72. Say: "It may be that some of the events which you wish to hasten on may be (close) in your pursuit!"

73. But verily your Lord is full of grace to mankind: yet most of them are ungrateful.

74. And verily your Lord knows all that their hearts hide, as well as all that they reveal.

75. Nor is there anything of the Unseen, in heaven or earth, but is (recorded) in a clear record.

76. Verily this Qur'an explains to the Children of Israel most of the matters in which they disagree.

كُنْتُمْ صَٰدِقِيْنَ ۞

قُلْ لَّا يَعْلَمُ مَنْ فِى السَّمٰوٰتِ وَالْاَرْضِ الْغَيْبَ اِلَّا اللّٰهُ ۚ وَمَا يَشْعُرُوْنَ اَيَّانَ يُبْعَثُوْنَ ۞

بَلِ ادّٰرَكَ عِلْمُهُمْ فِى الْاٰخِرَةِ ۛ بَلْ هُمْ فِىْ شَكٍّ مِّنْهَا ۛ بَلْ هُمْ مِّنْهَا عَمُوْنَ ۞

وَقَالَ الَّذِيْنَ كَفَرُوْۤا ءَاِذَا كُنَّا تُرٰبًا وَّاٰبَآؤُنَاۤ اَئِنَّا لَمُخْرَجُوْنَ ۞

لَقَدْ وُعِدْنَا هٰذَا نَحْنُ وَاٰبَآؤُنَا مِنْ قَبْلُ ۙ اِنْ هٰذَاۤ اِلَّاۤ اَسَاطِيْرُ الْاَوَّلِيْنَ ۞

قُلْ سِيْرُوْا فِى الْاَرْضِ فَانْظُرُوْا كَيْفَ كَانَ عَاقِبَةُ الْمُجْرِمِيْنَ ۞

وَلَا تَحْزَنْ عَلَيْهِمْ وَلَا تَكُنْ فِىْ ضَيْقٍ مِّمَّا يَمْكُرُوْنَ ۞

وَيَقُوْلُوْنَ مَتٰى هٰذَا الْوَعْدُ اِنْ كُنْتُمْ صٰدِقِيْنَ ۞

قُلْ عَسٰۤى اَنْ يَّكُوْنَ رَدِفَ لَكُمْ بَعْضُ الَّذِىْ تَسْتَعْجِلُوْنَ ۞

وَاِنَّ رَبَّكَ لَذُوْ فَضْلٍ عَلَى النَّاسِ وَلٰكِنَّ اَكْثَرَهُمْ لَا يَشْكُرُوْنَ ۞

وَاِنَّ رَبَّكَ لَيَعْلَمُ مَا تُكِنُّ صُدُوْرُهُمْ وَمَا يُعْلِنُوْنَ ۞

وَمَا مِنْ غَآئِبَةٍ فِى السَّمَآءِ وَالْاَرْضِ اِلَّا فِىْ كِتٰبٍ مُّبِيْنٍ ۞

اِنَّ هٰذَا الْقُرْاٰنَ يَقُصُّ عَلٰى بَنِىْۤ اِسْرَآءِيْلَ اَكْثَرَ الَّذِىْ هُمْ فِيْهِ

77. And it certainly is a Guide and a Mercy to those who believe.

78. Verily your Lord will decide between them by His Decree: and He is Exalted in Might, All-Knowing.

79. So put your trust in Allah: for you are on (the path of) manifest Truth.

يَخْتَلِفُونَ ۝

وَإِنَّهُ لَهُدًى وَرَحْمَةٌ لِّلْمُؤْمِنِينَ ۝

إِنَّ رَبَّكَ يَقْضِي بَيْنَهُم بِحُكْمِهِ ۚ

وَهُوَ الْعَزِيزُ الْعَلِيمُ ۝

فَتَوَكَّلْ عَلَى اللَّهِ ۖ إِنَّكَ عَلَى الْحَقِّ

الْمُبِينِ ۝

80. Truly you can not cause the dead to listen, nor can you cause the deaf to hear the call, (especially) when they turn back in retreat.

81. Nor can you be a guide to the Blind, (to prevent them) from straying: only those who will you get to listen who believe in Our Signs, and they will bow in Islam.

82. And when the Word is fulfilled against them (the unjust), We shall produce from the earth a Beast to (face) them: he will speak to them, for that mankind did not believe with assurance in Our Signs.

إِنَّكَ لَا تُسْمِعُ الْمَوْتَى وَلَا تُسْمِعُ

الصُّمَّ الدُّعَاءَ إِذَا وَلَّوْا مُدْبِرِينَ ۝

وَمَا أَنتَ بِهَادِي الْعُمْيِ عَن ضَلَالَتِهِمْ ۖ

إِن تُسْمِعُ إِلَّا مَن يُؤْمِنُ بِآيَاتِنَا

فَهُم مُّسْلِمُونَ ۝

وَإِذَا وَقَعَ الْقَوْلُ عَلَيْهِمْ أَخْرَجْنَا

لَهُمْ دَابَّةً مِّنَ الْأَرْضِ تُكَلِّمُهُمْ

أَنَّ النَّاسَ كَانُوا بِآيَاتِنَا لَا يُوقِنُونَ ۝

83. One Day We shall gather together from every people a troop of those who reject Our Signs, and they shall be kept in ranks,-

84. Until, when they come (before the Judgment-seat), (Allah) will say: "Did you reject My Signs, though you did not comprehend them in knowledge, or what was it you did?"

85. And the Word will be fulfilled against them, because of their wrong-doing, and they will be unable to speak (in plea).

وَيَوْمَ نَحْشُرُ مِن كُلِّ أُمَّةٍ فَوْجًا مِّمَّن

يُكَذِّبُ بِآيَاتِنَا فَهُمْ يُوزَعُونَ ۝

حَتَّى إِذَا جَاءُوا قَالَ أَكَذَّبْتُم بِآيَاتِي

وَلَمْ تُحِيطُوا بِهَا عِلْمًا أَمَّاذَا

كُنتُمْ تَعْمَلُونَ ۝

وَوَقَعَ الْقَوْلُ عَلَيْهِم بِمَا ظَلَمُوا

فَهُمْ لَا يَنطِقُونَ ۝

86. Do they not see that We have made the Night for them to rest in and the Day to give them light? Verily in this are Signs for any people that believe!

87. And the Day that the Trumpet will be sounded - then will be smitten with terror those who are in the heavens, and those who are on earth, except

أَلَمْ يَرَوْا أَنَّا جَعَلْنَا اللَّيْلَ لِيَسْكُنُوا

فِيهِ وَالنَّهَارَ مُبْصِرًا ۚ إِنَّ فِي ذَٰلِكَ

لَآيَاتٍ لِّقَوْمٍ يُؤْمِنُونَ ۝

وَيَوْمَ يُنفَخُ فِي الصُّورِ فَفَزِعَ مَن

فِي السَّمَاوَاتِ وَمَن فِي الْأَرْضِ إِلَّا

SÛRAH-28
AL-QAṢAṢ
(INTRODUCTION)

This Sûrah continues the subject of Revelation and its reception by those to whom it is sent. But it emphasis new points: how the recipient of inspiration is prepared for his high destiny, even in the growth of his ordinary life, and how the rejection of Allah's Message by groups of men or by individuals is caused by overweening arrogance or avarice. The plight of those who reject the Truth is contrasted with the reward of the righteous.

With the possible exception of a few verses, it belongs to the late Makkan period, just preceding the Hijrat.

such as Allah will please (to exempt): and all shall come to His (Presence) as beings conscious of their lowliness.

88. You see the mountains and think them firmly fixed: but they shall pass away as the clouds pass away: (such is) the artistry of Allah, Who disposes of all things in perfect order: for He is well acquainted with all that you do.

89. If any do good, good will (accrue) to them therefrom; and they will be secure from terror that Day.

90. And if any do evil, their faces will be thrown headlong into the Fire: "Do you receive a reward other than that which you have earned by your deeds?"

91. For me, I have been commanded to serve the Lord of this City, Him Who has sanctified it and to Whom (belong) all things: and I am commanded to be of those who bow in Islam to Allah's Will,-

92. And to rehearse the Qur'an: and if any accept guidance, they do it for the good of their own souls, and if any stray, say: "I am only a Warner".

93. And say: "Praise be to Allah, Who will soon show you His Signs, so that you shall know them"; and your Lord is not unmindful of all that you do.

28. The Narration
In the name of Allah. Most Gracious, Most Merciful.

1. Ta. Sin. Mim.

2. These are Verses of the Book that makes (things) clear.

3. We rehearse to you some of the story of Moses and Pharaoh in Truth, for people who believe.

4. Truly Pharaoh elated himself in the land and broke up its people into sections, depressing a small group among them: their sons he slew, but he kept alive their females: for he was indeed a maker of mischief.

‏اِنَّ فِرْعَوْنَ عَلَا فِي الْاَرْضِ وَجَعَلَ‎
‏اَهْلَهَا شِيَعًا يَّسْتَضْعِفُ طَآئِفَةً‎
‏مِّنْهُمْ يُذَبِّحُ اَبْنَآءَهُمْ وَيَسْتَحْيٖ نِسَآءَهُمْ‎
‏اِنَّهٗ كَانَ مِنَ الْمُفْسِدِيْنَ ۟‎

5. And We wished to be gracious to those who were being depressed in the land, to make them leaders (in Faith) and make them heirs,

‏وَنُرِيْدُ اَنْ نَّمُنَّ عَلَى الَّذِيْنَ‎
‏اسْتُضْعِفُوْا فِي الْاَرْضِ وَنَجْعَلَهُمْ‎
‏اَئِمَّةً وَّنَجْعَلَهُمُ الْوٰرِثِيْنَ ۟‎

6. To establish a firm place for them in the land, and to show Pharaoh, Haman, and their hosts, at their hands, the very things against which they were taking precautions.

‏وَنُمَكِّنَ لَهُمْ فِي الْاَرْضِ وَنُرِيَ‎
‏فِرْعَوْنَ وَهَامٰنَ وَجُنُوْدَهُمَا‎
‏مِنْهُمْ مَّا كَانُوْا يَحْذَرُوْنَ ۟‎

7. So We sent this inspiration to the mother of Moses: "Suckle (your child), but when you have fears about him, cast him into the river, but fear not nor grieve: for We shall restore him to you, and We shall make him one of Our Messengers."

‏وَاَوْحَيْنَآ اِلٰٓى اُمِّ مُوْسٰٓى اَنْ اَرْضِعِيْهِ‎
‏فَاِذَا خِفْتِ عَلَيْهِ فَاَلْقِيْهِ فِي الْيَمِّ‎
‏وَلَا تَخَافِيْ وَلَا تَحْزَنِيْ اِنَّا رَآدُّوْهُ‎
‏اِلَيْكِ وَجَاعِلُوْهُ مِنَ الْمُرْسَلِيْنَ ۟‎

8. Then the people of Pharaoh picked him up (from the river): (it was intended) that (Moses) should be to them an adversary and a cause of sorrow: for Pharaoh and Haman and (all) their hosts were men of sin.

‏فَالْتَقَطَهٗٓ اٰلُ فِرْعَوْنَ لِيَكُوْنَ لَهُمْ‎
‏عَدُوًّا وَّحَزَنًا اِنَّ فِرْعَوْنَ وَهَامٰنَ‎
‏وَجُنُوْدَهُمَا كَانُوْا خٰطِئِيْنَ ۟‎

9. The wife of Pharaoh said: "(Here is) a joy of the eye, for me and for you: do not slay him. It may be that he will be of use to us, or we may adopt him as a son." And they did not perceive (what they were doing)!

‏وَقَالَتِ امْرَاَتُ فِرْعَوْنَ قُرَّتُ عَيْنٍ‎
‏لِّيْ وَلَكَ ۚ لَا تَقْتُلُوْهُ ۖ عَسٰٓى اَنْ‎
‏يَّنْفَعَنَآ اَوْ نَتَّخِذَهٗ وَلَدًا وَّهُمْ‎
‏لَا يَشْعُرُوْنَ ۟‎

10. But there came to be a void in the heart of the mother of Moses: she was going almost to disclose his (case), had We not strengthened her heart (with faith), so that she might remain a (firm) believer.

‏وَاَصْبَحَ فُؤَادُ اُمِّ مُوْسٰى فٰرِغًا ۚ اِنْ‎
‏كَادَتْ لَتُبْدِيْ بِهٖ لَوْلَآ اَنْ رَّبَطْنَا‎
‏عَلٰى قَلْبِهَا لِتَكُوْنَ مِنَ الْمُؤْمِنِيْنَ ۟‎

11. And she said to the sister of (Moses), "Follow him". So she (the sister) watched him in the character of a stranger. And they did not know.

‏وَقَالَتْ لِاُخْتِهٖ قُصِّيْهِ ۖ فَبَصُرَتْ بِهٖ‎
‏عَنْ جُنُبٍ وَّهُمْ لَا يَشْعُرُوْنَ ۟‎

12. And We ordained that he refused suck at first, until (his sister came up and) said: "Shall I point out to you the people of a house that will nourish and bring him up for you and be sincerely attached to him?"...

13. Thus We restored him to his mother, that her eye might be comforted, that she might not grieve, and that she might know that the promise of Allah is true: but most of them do not understand.

14. When he reached full age, and was firmly established (in life), We bestowed on him wisdom and knowledge: for thus do We reward those who do good.

15. And he entered the City at a time when its people were not watching: and he found there two men fighting,- one of his own religion, and the other, of his foes. Now the man of his own religion appealed to him against his foe, and Moses struck him with his fist and made an end of him. He said: "This is a work of Evil (Satan): for he is an enemy that manifestly misleads!"

16. He prayed: "O my Lord! I have indeed wronged my soul! You then forgive me!" So (Allah) forgave him: for He is the Oft-Forgiving, Most Merciful.

17. He said: "O my Lord! For that You have bestowed Your Grace on me, never shall I be a help to those who sin!"

18. So he saw the morning in the City, looking about in a state of fear, when behold, the man who had, the day before, sought his help called aloud for his help (again). Moses said to him:" You are truly, it is clear, a quarrelsome fellow!"

19. Then, when he decided to lay his hands on

وَحَرَّمْنَا عَلَيْهِ الْمَرَاضِعَ مِنْ قَبْلُ فَقَالَتْ هَلْ أَدُلُّكُمْ عَلَى أَهْلِ بَيْتٍ يَكْفُلُونَهُ لَكُمْ وَهُمْ لَهُ نَاصِحُونَ ۝

فَرَدَدْنَاهُ إِلَى أُمِّهِ كَيْ تَقَرَّ عَيْنُهَا وَلَا تَحْزَنَ وَلِتَعْلَمَ أَنَّ وَعْدَ اللهِ حَقٌّ وَلَكِنَّ أَكْثَرَهُمْ لَا يَعْلَمُونَ ۝

وَلَمَّا بَلَغَ أَشُدَّهُ وَاسْتَوَى آتَيْنَاهُ حُكْمًا وَعِلْمًا وَكَذَلِكَ نَجْزِي الْمُحْسِنِينَ ۝

وَدَخَلَ الْمَدِينَةَ عَلَى حِينِ غَفْلَةٍ مِنْ أَهْلِهَا فَوَجَدَ فِيهَا رَجُلَيْنِ يَقْتَتِلَانِ هَذَا مِنْ شِيعَتِهِ وَهَذَا مِنْ عَدُوِّهِ فَاسْتَغَاثَهُ الَّذِي مِنْ شِيعَتِهِ عَلَى الَّذِي مِنْ عَدُوِّهِ فَوَكَزَهُ مُوسَى فَقَضَى عَلَيْهِ قَالَ هَذَا مِنْ عَمَلِ الشَّيْطَانِ إِنَّهُ عَدُوٌّ مُضِلٌّ مُبِينٌ ۝

قَالَ رَبِّ إِنِّي ظَلَمْتُ نَفْسِي فَاغْفِرْ لِي فَغَفَرَ لَهُ إِنَّهُ هُوَ الْغَفُورُ الرَّحِيمُ ۝

قَالَ رَبِّ بِمَا أَنْعَمْتَ عَلَيَّ فَلَنْ أَكُونَ ظَهِيرًا لِلْمُجْرِمِينَ ۝

فَأَصْبَحَ فِي الْمَدِينَةِ خَائِفًا يَتَرَقَّبُ فَإِذَا الَّذِي اسْتَنْصَرَهُ بِالْأَمْسِ يَسْتَصْرِخُهُ قَالَ لَهُ مُوسَى إِنَّكَ لَغَوِيٌّ مُبِينٌ ۝

فَلَمَّا أَنْ أَرَادَ أَنْ يَبْطِشَ بِالَّذِي

their enemy, that man said : "O Moses! is it your intention to slay me as you slew a man yesterday? Your intention is none other than to become a powerful violent man in the land, and not who sets things right!"

20. And there came a man, running, from the furthest end of the City. He said: "O Moses! the Chiefs are taking counsel together about you, to slay you: so you get away, for I do give you sincere advice."

21. He therefore got away therefrom, looking about, in a state of fear. He prayed "O my Lord! save me from people given to wrong-doing."

22. Then, when he turned his face towards (the land of) Madyan, he said: "I do hope that my Lord will show me the smooth and straight Path."

23. And when he arrived at the watering (place) in Madyan, he found there a group of men watering (their flocks), and besides them he found two women who were keeping back (their flocks). He said: "What is the matter with you?" They said: "We can not water (our flocks) until the shepherds take back (their flocks): and our father is a very old man."

24. So he watered (their flocks) for them; then he turned back to the shade, and said:"O my Lord! truly I am in (desperate) need of any good that You do send me!"

25. Afterwards one of the (damsels) came (back) to him, walking bashfully. She said: "My father invites you that he may reward you for having watered (our flocks) for us." So when he came to him and narrated the story,

he said: "you do not fear: (well) have you escaped from unjust people."

26. Said one of the (damsels): "O my (dear) father! engage him on wages: truly the best of men for you to employ is the (man) who is strong and trustworthy."

27. He said: "I intend to wed one of these my daughters to you, on condition that you serve me for eight years; but if you complete ten years, it will be (grace) from you. But I intend not to place you under a difficulty: you will find me, indeed, if Allah wills, one of the righteous."

28. He said: "Be that (the agreement) between me and you: whichever of the two terms I fulfil, let there be no ill-will to me. Be Allah a Witness to what we say."

29. Now when Moses had fulfilled the term, and was travelling with his family, he perceived a fire in the direction of Mount Tur. He said to his family: "You tarry; I perceive a fire; I hope to bring you from there some information, or a burning firebrand, that you may warm yourselves."

30. But when he came to the (Fire), a voice was heard from the right bank of the valley, from a tree in hallowed ground: "O Moses! Verily I am Allah, the Lord of the Worlds....

31. "Now you throw your rod!" but when he saw it moving (of its own accord) as if it had been a snake, he turned back in retreat, and did not retrace his steps: O Moses!" (It was said), "Draw near, and do not fear: for you are of those who are secure.

قَالَ لَا تَخَفْ نَجَوْتَ مِنَ الْقَوْمِ الظّٰلِمِيْنَ ۞

قَالَتْ اِحْدٰىهُمَا يٰٓاَبَتِ اسْتَأْجِرْهُ ۖ اِنَّ خَيْرَ مَنِ اسْتَأْجَرْتَ الْقَوِيُّ الْاَمِيْنُ ۞

قَالَ اِنِّيْٓ اُرِيْدُ اَنْ اُنْكِحَكَ اِحْدَى ابْنَتَيَّ هٰتَيْنِ عَلٰٓى اَنْ تَأْجُرَنِيْ ثَمٰنِيَ حِجَجٍ ۚ فَاِنْ اَتْمَمْتَ عَشْرًا فَمِنْ عِنْدِكَ ۚ وَمَآ اُرِيْدُ اَنْ اَشُقَّ عَلَيْكَ ۚ سَتَجِدُنِيْٓ اِنْ شَآءَ اللّٰهُ مِنَ الصّٰلِحِيْنَ ۞

قَالَ ذٰلِكَ بَيْنِيْ وَبَيْنَكَ ۖ اَيَّمَا الْاَجَلَيْنِ قَضَيْتُ فَلَا عُدْوَانَ عَلَيَّ ۚ وَاللّٰهُ عَلٰى مَا نَقُوْلُ وَكِيْلٌ ۞

فَلَمَّا قَضٰى مُوْسَى الْاَجَلَ وَسَارَ بِاَهْلِهٖٓ اٰنَسَ مِنْ جَانِبِ الطُّوْرِ نَارًا ۖ قَالَ لِاَهْلِهِ امْكُثُوْٓا اِنِّيْٓ اٰنَسْتُ نَارًا لَّعَلِّيْٓ اٰتِيْكُمْ مِّنْهَا بِخَبَرٍ اَوْ جَذْوَةٍ مِّنَ النَّارِ لَعَلَّكُمْ تَصْطَلُوْنَ ۞

فَلَمَّآ اَتٰىهَا نُوْدِيَ مِنْ شَاطِئِ الْوَادِ الْاَيْمَنِ فِي الْبُقْعَةِ الْمُبٰرَكَةِ مِنَ الشَّجَرَةِ اَنْ يّٰمُوْسَىٰٓ اِنِّيْٓ اَنَا اللّٰهُ رَبُّ الْعٰلَمِيْنَ ۞

وَاَنْ اَلْقِ عَصَاكَ ۖ فَلَمَّا رَاٰهَا تَهْتَزُّ كَاَنَّهَا جَآنٌّ وَّلّٰى مُدْبِرًا وَّلَمْ يُعَقِّبْ ۚ يٰمُوْسَىٰٓ اَقْبِلْ وَلَا تَخَفْ ۖ اِنَّكَ مِنَ الْاٰمِنِيْنَ ۞

32. "Move your hand into your bosom, and it will come forth white without stain (or harm), and draw your hand close to your side (to guard) against fear. Those are the two credentials from your Lord to Pharaoh and his Chiefs: for truly they are a people rebellious and wicked."

أَسْلُكْ يَدَكَ فِيْ جَيْبِكَ تَخْرُجْ بَيْضَآءَ مِنْ غَيْرِ سُوْٓءٍ ۫ وَّاضْمُمْ اِلَيْكَ جَنَاحَكَ مِنَ الرَّهْبِ فَذٰنِكَ بُرْهَانٰنِ مِنْ رَّبِّكَ اِلٰى فِرْعَوْنَ وَمَلَإِيْهِ ؕ اِنَّهُمْ كَانُوْا قَوْمًا فٰسِقِيْنَ ۝

33. He said: "O my Lord! I have slain a man among them, and I fear lest they slay me.

قَالَ رَبِّ اِنِّيْ قَتَلْتُ مِنْهُمْ نَفْسًا فَاَخَافُ اَنْ يَّقْتُلُوْنِ ۝

34. "And my brother Aaron - he is more eloquent in speech than I: so send him with me as a helper, to confirm (and strengthen) me: for I fear that they may accuse me of falsehood."

وَاَخِيْ هٰرُوْنُ هُوَ اَفْصَحُ مِنِّيْ لِسَانًا فَاَرْسِلْهُ مَعِيَ رِدْاً يُّصَدِّقُنِيْٓ ؕ اِنِّيْٓ اَخَافُ اَنْ يُّكَذِّبُوْنِ ۝

35. He said: "We will certainly strengthen your arm through your brother, and invest you both with authority, so they shall not be able to touch you: with Our Signs you shall triumph,- you two as well as those who follow you."

قَالَ سَنَشُدُّ عَضُدَكَ بِاَخِيْكَ وَنَجْعَلُ لَكُمَا سُلْطٰنًا فَلَا يَصِلُوْنَ اِلَيْكُمَا ۚ بِاٰيٰتِنَا ٓ ؕ اَنْتُمَا وَمَنِ اتَّبَعَكُمَا الْغٰلِبُوْنَ ۝

36. When Moses came to them with Our Clear Signs, they said: "This is nothing but sorcery faked up: never did we hear the like among our fathers of old!"

فَلَمَّا جَآءَهُمْ مُّوْسٰى بِاٰيٰتِنَا بَيِّنٰتٍ قَالُوْا مَا هٰذَآ اِلَّا سِحْرٌ مُّفْتَرًى وَّمَا سَمِعْنَا بِهٰذَا فِيْٓ اٰبَآئِنَا الْاَوَّلِيْنَ ۝

37. Moses said: "My Lord knows best who it is that comes with guidance from Him and whose End will be best in the Hereafter: certain it is that the wrong-doers will not prosper."

وَقَالَ مُوْسٰى رَبِّيْٓ اَعْلَمُ بِمَنْ جَآءَ بِالْهُدٰى مِنْ عِنْدِهٖ وَمَنْ تَكُوْنُ لَهٗ عَاقِبَةُ الدَّارِ ؕ اِنَّهٗ لَا يُفْلِحُ الظّٰلِمُوْنَ ۝

38. Pharaoh said: "O Chiefs! no god do I know for you but myself: therefore, O Haman! light me a (kiln to bake bricks) out of clay, and build me a lofty palace, that I may mount up to the god of Moses:

وَقَالَ فِرْعَوْنُ يٰٓاَيُّهَا الْمَلَاُ مَا عَلِمْتُ لَكُمْ مِّنْ اِلٰهٍ غَيْرِيْ ۚ فَاَوْقِدْ لِيْ يٰهَامٰنُ عَلَى الطِّيْنِ فَاجْعَلْ لِّيْ صَرْحًا لَّعَلِّيْٓ اَطَّلِعُ اِلٰٓى اِلٰهِ مُوْسٰى ۙ

but as far as I am concerned, I think he (Moses) is a liar!"

39. And he was arrogant and insolent in the land, beyond reason,- he and his hosts: they thought that they would not have to return to Us!

40. So We seized him and his hosts, and We flung them into the sea: now behold what was the End of those who did wrong!

41. And We made them (but) leaders inviting to the Fire; and on the Day of Judgment no help shall they find.

42. In this world We made a curse to follow them and on the Day of Judgment they will be among the loathed (and despised).

43. We revealed to Moses the Book after We had destroyed the earlier generations, (to give) Insight to men, and Guidance and Mercy, that they might receive admonition.

44. You were not on the Western side when We decreed the Commission to Moses, nor were you a witness (of those events).

45. But We raised up (new) generations, and long were the ages that passed over them; but you were not a dweller among the people of Madyan, rehearsing Our Signs to them; but it is We Who send Messengers (with inspiration).

46. Nor were you at the side of (the Mountain of) Tur when We called (to Moses). Yet (you are sent) as a Mercy from your Lord, to give warning to a people to whom no warner had come before you: in order that they may receive admonition.

وَاِنِّيْ لَاَظُنُّهُ مِنَ الْكٰذِبِيْنَ ۝

وَاسْتَكْبَرَ هُوَ وَجُنُوْدُهُ فِى الْاَرْضِ بِغَيْرِ الْحَقِّ وَظَنُّوْٓا اَنَّهُمْ اِلَيْنَا لَا يُرْجَعُوْنَ ۝

فَاَخَذْنٰهُ وَجُنُوْدَهُ فَنَبَذْنٰهُمْ فِى الْيَمِّ فَانْظُرْ كَيْفَ كَانَ عَاقِبَةُ الظّٰلِمِيْنَ

وَجَعَلْنٰهُمْ اَئِمَّةً يَّدْعُوْنَ اِلَى النَّارِ وَيَوْمَ الْقِيٰمَةِ لَا يُنْصَرُوْنَ ۝

وَاَتْبَعْنٰهُمْ فِىْ هٰذِهِ الدُّنْيَا لَعْنَةً وَيَوْمَ الْقِيٰمَةِ هُمْ مِّنَ الْمَقْبُوْحِيْنَ ۝

وَلَقَدْ اٰتَيْنَا مُوْسَى الْكِتٰبَ مِنْ بَعْدِ مَاۤ اَهْلَكْنَا الْقُرُوْنَ الْاُوْلٰى بَصَآئِرَ لِلنَّاسِ وَهُدًى وَّرَحْمَةً لَّعَلَّهُمْ يَتَذَكَّرُوْنَ ۝

وَمَا كُنْتَ بِجَانِبِ الْغَرْبِيِّ اِذْ قَضَيْنَاۤ اِلٰى مُوْسَى الْاَمْرَ وَمَا كُنْتَ مِنَ الشّٰهِدِيْنَ ۝

وَلٰكِنَّاۤ اَنْشَاْنَا قُرُوْنًا فَتَطَاوَلَ عَلَيْهِمُ الْعُمُرُ وَمَا كُنْتَ ثَاوِيًا فِىْۤ اَهْلِ مَدْيَنَ تَتْلُوْا عَلَيْهِمْ اٰيٰتِنَا وَلٰكِنَّا كُنَّا مُرْسِلِيْنَ ۝

وَمَا كُنْتَ بِجَانِبِ الطُّوْرِ اِذْ نَادَيْنَا وَلٰكِنْ رَّحْمَةً مِّنْ رَّبِّكَ لِتُنْذِرَ قَوْمًا مَّاۤ اَتٰهُمْ مِّنْ نَّذِيْرٍ مِّنْ قَبْلِكَ لَعَلَّهُمْ يَتَذَكَّرُوْنَ ۝

47. If (We had) not (sent you to the Quraish),- in case a calamity should seize them for (the deeds) that their hands have sent forth, they might say: "Our Lord! why did You not sent us a Messenger? We should then have followed Your Signs and been amongst those who believe!"

وَلَوْلَا أَنْ تُصِيبَهُمْ مُصِيبَةٌ بِمَا قَدَّمَتْ أَيْدِيهِمْ فَيَقُولُوا رَبَّنَا لَوْلَا أَرْسَلْتَ إِلَيْنَا رَسُولًا فَنَتَّبِعَ اٰيٰتِكَ وَنَكُونَ مِنَ الْمُؤْمِنِينَ ۝

48. But (now), when the Truth has come to them from Ourselves, they say, "Why are not (Signs) sent to him, like those which were sent to Moses?" Do they not then reject (the Signs) which were formerly sent to Moses? They say: "Two kinds of sorcery , each assisting the other!" And they say: "For us, we reject all (such things)!"

فَلَمَّا جَاءَهُمُ الْحَقُّ مِنْ عِنْدِنَا قَالُوا لَوْلَا أُوتِيَ مِثْلَ مَا أُوتِيَ مُوسٰى ۚ أَوَلَمْ يَكْفُرُوا بِمَا أُوتِيَ مُوسٰى مِنْ قَبْلُ ۚ قَالُوا سِحْرَانِ تَظَاهَرَا ۖ وَ قَالُوا إِنَّا بِكُلٍّ كٰفِرُونَ ۝

49. Say: "Then you bring a Book from Allah, which is a better guide than either of them, that I may follow it! (do), if you are truthful!"

قُلْ فَأْتُوا بِكِتٰبٍ مِنْ عِنْدِ اللّٰهِ هُوَ أَهْدٰى مِنْهُمَا أَتَّبِعْهُ إِنْ كُنْتُمْ صٰدِقِينَ ۝

50. But if they hearken not to you, know that they only follow their own lusts: and who is more astray than one who follow his own lusts, devoid of guidance from Allah? for Allah does not guide people given to wrong-doing.

فَإِنْ لَمْ يَسْتَجِيبُوا لَكَ فَاعْلَمْ أَنَّمَا يَتَّبِعُونَ أَهْوَاءَهُمْ ۚ وَمَنْ أَضَلُّ مِمَّنِ اتَّبَعَ هَوٰهُ بِغَيْرِ هُدًى مِنَ اللّٰهِ ۚ إِنَّ اللّٰهَ لَا يَهْدِي الْقَوْمَ الظّٰلِمِينَ ۝

51. Now We have caused the Word to reach them themselves, in order that they may receive admonition.

وَلَقَدْ وَصَّلْنَا لَهُمُ الْقَوْلَ لَعَلَّهُمْ يَتَذَكَّرُونَ ۝

52. Those to whom We sent the Book before this,- they do believe in this (Revelation):

اَلَّذِينَ اٰتَيْنٰهُمُ الْكِتٰبَ مِنْ قَبْلِهِ هُمْ بِهِ يُؤْمِنُونَ ۝

53. And when it is recited to them, they say: "We believe therein, for it is the Truth from our Lord: indeed we have been Muslims (bowing to Allah's Will) from before this.

وَإِذَا يُتْلٰى عَلَيْهِمْ قَالُوا اٰمَنَّا بِهِ إِنَّهُ الْحَقُّ مِنْ رَبِّنَا إِنَّا كُنَّا مِنْ قَبْلِهِ مُسْلِمِينَ ۝

54. Twice will they be given their reward, for that they have persevered, that they avert Evil with Good,

أُولٰئِكَ يُؤْتَوْنَ أَجْرَهُمْ مَرَّتَيْنِ بِمَا صَبَرُوا وَيَدْرَءُونَ بِالْحَسَنَةِ

and that they spend (in charity) out of what We have given them.

55. And when they hear vain talk, they turn away therefrom and say: "To us our deeds, and to you yours; Peace be on you: we do not seek the ignorant."

56. It is true you will not be able to guide everyone whom you love; but Allah guides those whom He will and He knows best those who receive guidance.

57. They say: "If we were to follow the guidance with you, we should be snatched away from our land." Have We not established for them a secure sanctuary, to which are brought as tribute fruits of all kinds,- a provision from Ourselves? but most of them do not understand.

58. And how many populations We destroyed, which exulted in their life (of ease and plenty)! now those habitations of theirs, after them, are deserted,- all but a (miserable) few! and We are their heirs!

59. Nor was your Lord the one to destroy a population until He had sent to its centre a Messenger, rehearsing to them Our Signs; nor are We going to destroy a population except when its members practise iniquity.

60. The (material) things which you are given are but the conveniences of this life and the glitter thereof; but that which is with Allah is better and more enduring: will you not then be wise?

61. Are (these two) alike?- one to whom We have made a goodly promise, and who is going to reach its (fulfilment), and one to whom We have given the good things of this life, but who, on the Day of Judgment,is to be among those brought up (for punishment)?

62. That Day (Allah) will call to them, and say "Where are My 'partners'?- whom you imagined (to be such)?"

مِنَ الْمُحْضَرِيْنَ ۞

وَيَوْمَ يُنَادِيْهِمْ فَيَقُوْلُ اَيْنَ شُرَكَآءِيَ

الَّذِيْنَ كُنْتُمْ تَزْعُمُوْنَ ۞

63. Those against whom the charge will be proved, will say: "Our Lord! These are the ones whom we led astray: we led them astray, as we were astray ourselves: we free ourselves (from them) in Your presence: it was not us they worshipped."

قَالَ الَّذِيْنَ حَقَّ عَلَيْهِمُ الْقَوْلُ رَبَّنَا

هٰٓؤُلَآءِ الَّذِيْنَ اَغْوَيْنَا ۚ اَغْوَيْنٰهُمْ

كَمَا غَوَيْنَا ۚ تَبَرَّأْنَا اِلَيْكَ مَا كَانُوْا

اِيَّانَا يَعْبُدُوْنَ ۞

64. It will be said (to them): "Call upon your 'partners' (for help)" :they will call upon them, but they will not listen to them; and they will see the Penalty (before them); (how they will wish) 'if only they had been open to guidance!'

وَقِيْلَ ادْعُوْا شُرَكَآءَكُمْ فَدَعَوْهُمْ

فَلَمْ يَسْتَجِيْبُوْا لَهُمْ وَرَاَوُا الْعَذَابَ ۚ

لَوْ اَنَّهُمْ كَانُوْا يَهْتَدُوْنَ ۞

65. That Day (Allah) will call to them, and say: "What was the answer you gave to the Messengers?"

وَيَوْمَ يُنَادِيْهِمْ فَيَقُوْلُ مَاذَآ

اَجَبْتُمُ الْمُرْسَلِيْنَ ۞

66. Then the (whole) story that Day will seem obscure to them (like light to the blind) and they will not be able (even) to question each other.

فَعَمِيَتْ عَلَيْهِمُ الْاَنْبَآءُ يَوْمَئِذٍ

فَهُمْ لَا يَتَسَآءَلُوْنَ ۞

67. But any that (in this life) had repented, believed, and worked righteousness, haply he shall be one of the successful.

فَاَمَّا مَنْ تَابَ وَاٰمَنَ وَعَمِلَ صَالِحًا

فَعَسٰٓى اَنْ يَّكُوْنَ مِنَ الْمُفْلِحِيْنَ ۞

68. Your Lord creates and chooses as He pleases: no choice have they (in the matter): Glory to Allah! and far is He above the partners they ascribe (to Him)!

وَرَبُّكَ يَخْلُقُ مَا يَشَآءُ وَيَخْتَارُ ۚ

مَا كَانَ لَهُمُ الْخِيَرَةُ ۚ سُبْحٰنَ

اللّٰهِ وَتَعٰلٰى عَمَّا يُشْرِكُوْنَ ۞

69. And your Lord knows all that their hearts conceal and all that they reveal.

وَرَبُّكَ يَعْلَمُ مَا تُكِنُّ صُدُوْرُهُمْ

وَمَا يُعْلِنُوْنَ ۞

70. And He is Allah: there is no god but He. To Him be praise, at the first and at the last: for Him is the Command, and to Him you shall (all) be brought back.

وَهُوَ اللّٰهُ لَآ اِلٰهَ اِلَّا هُوَ ۖ لَهُ

الْحَمْدُ فِى الْاُوْلٰى وَالْاٰخِرَةِ ۖ وَلَهُ

الْحُكْمُ وَاِلَيْهِ تُرْجَعُوْنَ ۞

71. Say, do you see? If Allah were to make the night perpetual over you to the Day of Judgment, what

قُلْ اَرَءَيْتُمْ اِنْ جَعَلَ اللّٰهُ عَلَيْكُمُ

الَّيْلَ سَرْمَدًا اِلٰى يَوْمِ الْقِيٰمَةِ مَنْ

god is there other than Allah, Who can give you enlightenment? Will you not then hearken?

72. Say, do you see? If Allah were to make the Day perpetual over you to the Day of Judgment, what god is there other than Allah, Who can give you a Night in which you can rest? Will you not then see?

73. It is out of His Mercy that He has made for you Night and Day,- that you may rest therein, and that you may seek of His Grace;- and in order that you may be grateful.

74. The Day that He will call on them, He will say: "Where are My 'partners'?- whom you imagined (to be such)?"

75. And from each people We shall draw a witness, and We shall say: "Produce your Proof": then they shall know that the Truth is in Allah (alone), and the (lies) which they invented will leave them in lurch.

76. Qarun was doubtless, of the people of Moses; but he acted insolently towards them: such were the treasures We had bestowed on him that their very keys would have been a burden to a body of strong men. Behold, his people said to him: "Do not exult, for Allah does not love those who exult (in riches).

77. "But seek, with the (wealth) which Allah has bestowed on you, the Home of the Hereafter, nor forget your portion in this world: but you do good, as Allah has been good to you, and do not seek (occasions for) mischief in the land: for Allah does not love those who do mischief."

78. He said: "This has been given to me because of a certain knowledge which I have." Did he not know that Allah had destroyed, before him, (whole) generations,- which were superior to him in strength and greater in the amount (of riches) they had collected? but the wicked are not called (immediately) to account for their sins.

79. So he went forth among his people in the (pride of his worldly) glitter. Said those whose aim is the Life of this World: "Oh! that we had the like of what Qarun has got! For he is truly a lord of mighty good fortune!"

80. But those who had been granted (true) knowledge said: "Alas for you! The reward of Allah (in the Hereafter) is best for those who believe and work righteousness: but this none shall attain, save those who steadfastly persevere (in good)."

81. Then We caused the earth to swallow up him and his house; and he had not (the least little) party to help him against Allah, nor could he defend himself.

82. And those who had envied his position the day before began to say on the morrow: "Ah! it is indeed Allah Who enlarges the provision or restricts it, to any of His servants He pleases! Had it not been that Allah was gracious to us, He could have caused the earth to swallow us up! Ah! those who reject Allah will assuredly never prosper."

83. That Home of the Hereafter We shall give to those who do not intend high-handedness or mischief on earth:

SÛRAH-29
AL-'ANKABÛT
(INTRODUCTION)

This Sûrah is the last of the series begun with S. 17 in which the growth of the spiritual man as an individual in considered, especially illustrated by the way in which the great apostles were prepared for their work and received their mission, and the nature of Revelation in relation to the environments in which it was promulgated. (See Introduction to S. 17). It also closes the subseries beginning with S. 26 which is concerned with the spiritual Light, and the reactions to it at certain periods of spiritual history. (See Introduction to S. 26).

The last Sûrah closed with a reference to the doctrine of the *Ma 'âd,* or final Return of man to Allah. This theme is further developed here, and as it is continued in the subsequent three Sûras all bearing the Abbreviated Letters A.L.M.. it forms a connecting link between the present series and those three Sûras.

In particular, emphasis is laid here on the necessity of linking actual conduct with the reception of Allah's revelation, and reference is again made to the stories of Noah, Abraham, and Lot among the apostles, and the stories of Midian, Âd, Thamûd, and Pharaoh among the rejecters of Allah's Message. This world's life is contrasted with the real Life of the Hereafter.

Chronologically, the main Sûrah belongs to the late Middle Makkan period, but the chronology has no significance except as showing how clearly the vision of the Future was revealed long before the Hijrat, to the struggling Brotherhood of Islam.

and the end is (best) for the righteous.

84. If any does good, the reward to him is better than his deed; but if any does evil, the doers of evil are only punished (to the extent) of their deeds.

85. Verily He Who ordained the Qur'an for you, will bring you back to the Place of Return. Say: "My Lord knows best who it is that brings true guidance, and who is in manifest error."

86. And you had not expected that the Book would be sent to you except as a Mercy from your Lord: therefore you do not lend support in any way to those who reject (Allah's Message).

87. And let nothing keep you back from the Signs of Allah after they have been revealed to you: and invite (men) to your Lord, and be not of the company of those who join gods with Allah.

88. And do not call, besides Allah, on another god. There is no god but He. Everything (that exists) will perish except His Own Face. To Him belongs the Command, and to Him will you (all) be brought back.

29. The Spider

In the name of Allah. Most Gracious, Most Merciful.

1. Alif- Lam- Mim.

2. Do men think that they will be left alone on saying, "We believe", and that they will not be tested?

3. We tested those before them, and Allah will certainly know those who are true

from those who are false.

وَلَيَعْلَمَنَّ الْكٰذِبِيْنَ ۞

4. Do those who practise evil think that they will get the better of Us? Evil is their judgment!

اَمْ حَسِبَ الَّذِيْنَ يَعْمَلُوْنَ السَّيِّاٰتِ اَنْ يَّسْبِقُوْنَا ۚ سَاءَ مَا يَحْكُمُوْنَ ۞

5. For those whose hopes are in the meeting with Allah (in the Hereafter, let them strive); for the term (appointed) by Allah is surely coming and He hears and knows (all things).

مَنْ كَانَ يَرْجُوْا لِقَآءَ اللّٰهِ فَاِنَّ اَجَلَ اللّٰهِ لَاٰتٍ ۚ وَهُوَ السَّمِيْعُ الْعَلِيْمُ ۞

6. And if any strive (with might and main), they do so for their own souls: for Allah is free of all needs from all creation.

وَمَنْ جَاهَدَ فَاِنَّمَا يُجَاهِدُ لِنَفْسِهٖ ۚ اِنَّ اللّٰهَ لَغَنِيٌّ عَنِ الْعٰلَمِيْنَ ۞

7. Those who believe and work righteous deeds,- from them We shall blot out all evil (that may be) in them, and We shall reward them according to the best of their deeds.

وَالَّذِيْنَ اٰمَنُوْا وَعَمِلُوا الصّٰلِحٰتِ لَنُكَفِّرَنَّ عَنْهُمْ سَيِّاٰتِهِمْ وَلَنَجْزِيَنَّهُمْ اَحْسَنَ الَّذِيْ كَانُوْا يَعْمَلُوْنَ ۞

8. We have enjoined on man kindness to parents: but if they (either of them) strive (to force) you to join with Me (in worship) anything of which you have no knowledge, do not obey them. You have (all) to return to Me, and I will tell you (the truth) of all that you did.

وَوَصَّيْنَا الْاِنْسَانَ بِوَالِدَيْهِ حُسْنًا ۚ وَاِنْ جَاهَدٰكَ لِتُشْرِكَ بِيْ مَا لَيْسَ لَكَ بِهٖ عِلْمٌ فَلَا تُطِعْهُمَا ۚ اِلَيَّ مَرْجِعُكُمْ فَاُنَبِّئُكُمْ بِمَا كُنْتُمْ تَعْمَلُوْنَ ۞

9. And those who believe and work righteous deeds,- them We shall admit to the company of the Righteous.

وَالَّذِيْنَ اٰمَنُوْا وَعَمِلُوا الصّٰلِحٰتِ لَنُدْخِلَنَّهُمْ فِي الصّٰلِحِيْنَ ۞

10. Then there are among men such as say, "We believe in Allah"; but when they suffer affliction in (the cause of) Allah, they treat men's oppression as if it were the Wrath of Allah! And if help comes (to you) from your Lord, they are sure to say, "We have (always) been with you!" Does not Allah know best all that is in the hearts of all creation?

وَمِنَ النَّاسِ مَنْ يَّقُوْلُ اٰمَنَّا بِاللّٰهِ فَاِذَآ اُوْذِيَ فِي اللّٰهِ جَعَلَ فِتْنَةَ النَّاسِ كَعَذَابِ اللّٰهِ ۚ وَلَئِنْ جَآءَ نَصْرٌ مِّنْ رَّبِّكَ لَيَقُوْلُنَّ اِنَّا كُنَّا مَعَكُمْ ۚ اَوَلَيْسَ اللّٰهُ بِاَعْلَمَ بِمَا فِيْ صُدُوْرِ الْعٰلَمِيْنَ ۞

11. And Allah most certainly knows those who believe, and as certainly those who are Hypocrites.

وَلَيَعْلَمَنَّ اللّٰهُ الَّذِيْنَ اٰمَنُوْا وَلَيَعْلَمَنَّ الْمُنٰفِقِيْنَ ۞

12. And the Unbelievers say to those who believe:

وَقَالَ الَّذِيْنَ كَفَرُوْا لِلَّذِيْنَ اٰمَنُوا

"Follow our path, and we will bear (the consequences) of your faults." Never in the least will they bear their faults: in fact they are liars!

اتَّبِعُوْا سَبِيْلَنَا وَلْنَحْمِلْ خَطٰيٰكُمْ ۚ وَمَا هُمْ بِحٰمِلِيْنَ مِنْ خَطٰيٰهُمْ مِّنْ شَيْءٍ ۭ اِنَّهُمْ لَكٰذِبُوْنَ ۝

13. They will bear their own burdens, and (other) burdens along with their own, and on the Day of Judgment they will be called to account for their falsehoods.

وَلَيَحْمِلُنَّ اَثْقَالَهُمْ وَاَثْقَالًا مَّعَ اَثْقَالِهِمْ ۫ وَلَيُسْـَٔلُنَّ يَوْمَ الْقِيٰمَةِ عَمَّا كَانُوْا يَفْتَرُوْنَ ۝

14. We (once) sent Noah to his people, and he tarried among them a thousand years less fifty: but the Deluge overwhelmed them while they (persisted in) sin.

وَلَقَدْ اَرْسَلْنَا نُوْحًا اِلٰى قَوْمِهٖ فَلَبِثَ فِيْهِمْ اَلْفَ سَنَةٍ اِلَّا خَمْسِيْنَ عَامًا ۭ فَاَخَذَهُمُ الطُّوْفَانُ وَهُمْ ظٰلِمُوْنَ ۝

15. But We saved him and the companions of the Ark, and We made the (Ark) a Sign for all peoples!

فَاَنْجَيْنٰهُ وَاَصْحٰبَ السَّفِيْنَةِ وَجَعَلْنٰهَآ اٰيَةً لِّلْعٰلَمِيْنَ ۝

16. And (We also saved) Abraham: behold, he said to his people, "Serve Allah and fear Him: that will be best for you- If you understand!

وَاِبْرٰهِيْمَ اِذْ قَالَ لِقَوْمِهِ اعْبُدُوا اللّٰهَ وَاتَّقُوْهُ ۭ ذٰلِكُمْ خَيْرٌ لَّكُمْ اِنْ كُنْتُمْ تَعْلَمُوْنَ ۝

17. "For you worship idols besides Allah, and you invent falsehood. The things that you worship besides Allah have no power to give you sustenance: then you seek sustenance from Allah, serve Him, and be grateful to Him: to Him will be your return.

اِنَّمَا تَعْبُدُوْنَ مِنْ دُوْنِ اللّٰهِ اَوْثَانًا وَّتَخْلُقُوْنَ اِفْكًا ۭ اِنَّ الَّذِيْنَ تَعْبُدُوْنَ مِنْ دُوْنِ اللّٰهِ لَا يَمْلِكُوْنَ لَكُمْ رِزْقًا فَابْتَغُوْا عِنْدَ اللّٰهِ الرِّزْقَ وَاعْبُدُوْهُ وَاشْكُرُوْا لَهٗ ۭ اِلَيْهِ تُرْجَعُوْنَ ۝

18. "And if you reject (the Message), so did generations before you: and the duty of the Messenger is only to preach publicly (and clearly)."

وَاِنْ تُكَذِّبُوْا فَقَدْ كَذَّبَ اُمَمٌ مِّنْ قَبْلِكُمْ ۭ وَمَا عَلَى الرَّسُوْلِ اِلَّا الْبَلٰغُ الْمُبِيْنُ ۝

19. Don't they see how Allah originates creation, then repeats it: truly that is easy for Allah.

اَوَلَمْ يَرَوْا كَيْفَ يُبْدِئُ اللّٰهُ الْخَلْقَ ثُمَّ يُعِيْدُهٗ ۭ اِنَّ ذٰلِكَ

20. Say: "Travel through the earth and see how Allah originated creation; so will Allah produce a later creation: for Allah has power over all things.

قُلْ سِيرُوا فِى ٱلْأَرْضِ فَٱنظُرُوا كَيْفَ بَدَأَ ٱلْخَلْقَ ثُمَّ ٱللَّهُ يُنشِئُ ٱلنَّشْأَةَ ٱلْءَاخِرَةَ ۚ إِنَّ ٱللَّهَ عَلَىٰ كُلِّ شَىْءٍ قَدِيرٌ ۝

21. "He punishes whom He pleases, and He grants Mercy to whom He pleases, and towards Him are you turned.

يُعَذِّبُ مَن يَشَآءُ وَيَرْحَمُ مَن يَشَآءُ ۖ وَإِلَيْهِ تُقْلَبُونَ ۝

22. "Not on earth nor in heaven will you be able (fleeing) to frustrate (His Plan), nor have you, besides Allah, any protector or helper."

وَمَآ أَنتُم بِمُعْجِزِينَ فِى ٱلْأَرْضِ وَلَا فِى ٱلسَّمَآءِ ۖ وَمَا لَكُم مِّن دُونِ ٱللَّهِ مِن وَلِىٍّ وَلَا نَصِيرٍ ۝

23. Those who reject the Signs of Allah and the Meeting with Him (in the Hereafter),- it is they who shall despair of My Mercy: it is they who will (suffer) a most grievous Penalty.

وَٱلَّذِينَ كَفَرُوا بِـَٔايَٰتِ ٱللَّهِ وَلِقَآئِهِۦٓ أُو۟لَٰٓئِكَ يَئِسُوا۟ مِن رَّحْمَتِى وَأُو۟لَٰٓئِكَ لَهُمْ عَذَابٌ أَلِيمٌ ۝

24. So nothing was the answer of (Abraham's) people except that they said: "Slay him or burn him." But Allah saved him from the Fire. Verily in this are Signs for people who believe.

فَمَا كَانَ جَوَابَ قَوْمِهِۦٓ إِلَّآ أَن قَالُوا۟ ٱقْتُلُوهُ أَوْ حَرِّقُوهُ فَأَنجَىٰهُ ٱللَّهُ مِنَ ٱلنَّارِ ۚ إِنَّ فِى ذَٰلِكَ لَءَايَٰتٍ لِّقَوْمٍ يُؤْمِنُونَ ۝

25. And he said: "For you, you have taken (for worship) idols besides Allah, out of mutual love and regard between yourselves in this life; but on the Day of Judgment you shall disown each other and curse each other: and your abode will be the Fire, and you shall have none to help."

وَقَالَ إِنَّمَا ٱتَّخَذْتُم مِّن دُونِ ٱللَّهِ أَوْثَٰنًا مَّوَدَّةَ بَيْنِكُمْ فِى ٱلْحَيَوٰةِ ٱلدُّنْيَا ۖ ثُمَّ يَوْمَ ٱلْقِيَٰمَةِ يَكْفُرُ بَعْضُكُم بِبَعْضٍ وَيَلْعَنُ بَعْضُكُم بَعْضًا وَمَأْوَىٰكُمُ ٱلنَّارُ وَمَا لَكُم مِّن نَّٰصِرِينَ ۝

26. But Lut had faith in Him: he said: "I will leave home for the sake of my Lord: for He is Exalted in Might, and Wise."

فَـَٔامَنَ لَهُۥ لُوطٌ ۘ وَقَالَ إِنِّى مُهَاجِرٌ إِلَىٰ رَبِّىٓ ۖ إِنَّهُۥ هُوَ ٱلْعَزِيزُ ٱلْحَكِيمُ ۝

27. And We gave (Abraham) Isaac and Jacob, and ordained among his progeny Prophethood and Revelation, and We granted him his reward in this life; and he will be in the Hereafter (of the company) of the Righteous.

28. And (remember) Lut: behold, he said to his people: "You commit lewdness, such as no people in Creation (ever) committed before you.

29. "Do you indeed approach men, and cut off the highway?- and practise wickedness (even) in your councils?" But his people gave no answer but this: they said: "Bring us the Wrath of Allah if you tell the truth."

30. He said: "O my Lord! You help me against people who do mischief!"

31. When Our Messengers came to Abraham with the good news, they said: "We are indeed going to destroy the people of this township: for truly they are (addicted to) crime."

32. He said: "But there is Lut there." They said: "Well do we know who is there : we will certainly save him and his following, except his wife: she is of those who lag behind!"

33. And when Our Messengers came to Lut, he was grieved on their account, and felt himself powerless (to protect) them: but they said: "Do not fear, nor grieve: we

are (here) to save you and your following, except your wife: she is of those who lag behind.

مُنَجُّوكَ وَأَهْلَكَ إِلَّا امْرَأَتَكَ كَانَتْ مِنَ الْغَبِرِينَ ۝

34. "For we are going to bring down on the people of this township a Punishment from heaven, because they have been wickedly rebellious."

إِنَّا مُنْزِلُونَ عَلَى أَهْلِ هَٰذِهِ الْقَرْيَةِ رِجْزًا مِنَ السَّمَاءِ بِمَا كَانُوا يَفْسُقُونَ ۝

35. And We have left thereof an evident Sign, for any people who (care to) understand.

وَلَقَدْ تَرَكْنَا مِنْهَا آيَةً بَيِّنَةً لِقَوْمٍ يَعْقِلُونَ ۝

36. To the Madyan (people) (We sent) their brother Shu'aib. Then he said: "O my people! serve Allah, and fear the Last Day: nor commit evil on the earth, with intent to do mischief."

وَإِلَى مَدْيَنَ أَخَاهُمْ شُعَيْبًا ۚ فَقَالَ يَقَوْمِ اعْبُدُوا اللَّهَ وَارْجُوا الْيَوْمَ الْآخِرَ وَلَا تَعْثَوْا فِي الْأَرْضِ مُفْسِدِينَ ۝

37. But they rejected him: then the mighty Blast seized them, and they lay prostrate in their homes by the morning.

فَكَذَّبُوهُ فَأَخَذَتْهُمُ الرَّجْفَةُ فَأَصْبَحُوا فِي دَارِهِمْ جَاثِمِينَ ۝

38. (Remember also) the 'Ad and the Thamud (people): clearly will appear to you from (the traces) of their buildings (their fate): the Evil One made their deeds alluring to them, and kept them back from the Path, though they were gifted with Intelligence and Skill.

وَعَادًا وَثَمُودَا وَقَدْ تَبَيَّنَ لَكُمْ مِنْ مَسَاكِنِهِمْ ۖ وَزَيَّنَ لَهُمُ الشَّيْطَانُ أَعْمَالَهُمْ فَصَدَّهُمْ عَنِ السَّبِيلِ وَكَانُوا مُسْتَبْصِرِينَ ۝

39. (Remember also) Qarun, Pharaoh, and Haman: there came to them Moses with Clear Signs, but they behaved with insolence on the earth; yet they could not overreach (Us).

وَقَارُونَ وَفِرْعَوْنَ وَهَامَانَ ۖ وَلَقَدْ جَاءَهُمْ مُوسَى بِالْبَيِّنَاتِ فَاسْتَكْبَرُوا فِي الْأَرْضِ وَمَا كَانُوا سَابِقِينَ ۝

40. Each one of them We seized for his crime: of them, against some We sent a violent tornado (with showers of stones); some were caught by a (mighty) Blast; some We caused the earth to swallow up; and some We drowned (in the waters): It was not Allah

فَكُلًّا أَخَذْنَا بِذَنْبِهِ ۖ فَمِنْهُمْ مَنْ أَرْسَلْنَا عَلَيْهِ حَاصِبًا ۖ وَمِنْهُمْ مَنْ أَخَذَتْهُ الصَّيْحَةُ ۖ وَمِنْهُمْ مَنْ خَسَفْنَا بِهِ الْأَرْضَ ۖ وَمِنْهُمْ مَنْ أَغْرَقْنَا ۚ وَمَا كَانَ اللَّهُ

Who injured (or oppressed) them: they injured (and oppressed) their own souls.

لِيَظْلِمَهُمْ وَلٰكِنْ كَانُوْا اَنْفُسَهُمْ يَظْلِمُوْنَ ۝

41. The parable of those who take protectors other than Allah is that of the Spider, who builds (to itself) a house; but truly the flimsiest of houses is the Spider's house;- if they but knew.

مَثَلُ الَّذِيْنَ اتَّخَذُوْا مِنْ دُوْنِ اللّٰهِ اَوْلِيَاءَ كَمَثَلِ الْعَنْكَبُوْتِ ۚ اتَّخَذَتْ بَيْتًا ۚ وَاِنَّ اَوْهَنَ الْبُيُوْتِ لَبَيْتُ الْعَنْكَبُوْتِ ۘ لَوْ كَانُوْا يَعْلَمُوْنَ ۝

42. Verily Allah knows of (every thing) whatever that they call upon besides Him: and He is Exalted (in power), Wise.

اِنَّ اللّٰهَ يَعْلَمُ مَا يَدْعُوْنَ مِنْ دُوْنِهٖ مِنْ شَيْءٍ ۚ وَهُوَ الْعَزِيْزُ الْحَكِيْمُ ۝

43. And such are the Parables We set forth for mankind, but only those understand them who have knowledge.

وَتِلْكَ الْاَمْثَالُ نَضْرِبُهَا لِلنَّاسِ ۚ وَمَا يَعْقِلُهَا اِلَّا الْعٰلِمُوْنَ ۝

44. Allah created the heavens and the earth in true (proportions): verily in that is a Sign for those who believe.

خَلَقَ اللّٰهُ السَّمٰوٰتِ وَالْاَرْضَ بِالْحَقِّ ۚ اِنَّ فِيْ ذٰلِكَ لَاٰيَةً لِّلْمُؤْمِنِيْنَ ۝

45. Recite what is sent of the Book by inspiration to you, and establish regular Prayer: for Prayer restrains from shameful and unjust deeds; and remembrance of Allah is the greatest (thing in life) without doubt. And Allah knows the (deeds) that you do.

اُتْلُ مَا اُوْحِيَ اِلَيْكَ مِنَ الْكِتٰبِ وَاَقِمِ الصَّلٰوةَ ۚ اِنَّ الصَّلٰوةَ تَنْهٰى عَنِ الْفَحْشَاءِ وَالْمُنْكَرِ ۗ وَلَذِكْرُ اللّٰهِ اَكْبَرُ ۗ وَاللّٰهُ يَعْلَمُ مَا تَصْنَعُوْنَ ۝

46. And you do not dispute with the People of the Book, except with means better (than mere disputation), unless it be with those of them who inflict wrong (and injury): but say, "We believe in the Revelation which has come down to us and in that which came down to you; our God and your God is One; and it is to Him we bow (in Islam)."

وَلَا تُجَادِلُوْا اَهْلَ الْكِتٰبِ اِلَّا بِالَّتِيْ هِيَ اَحْسَنُ ۗ اِلَّا الَّذِيْنَ ظَلَمُوْا مِنْهُمْ وَقُوْلُوْا اٰمَنَّا بِالَّذِيْ اُنْزِلَ اِلَيْنَا وَاُنْزِلَ اِلَيْكُمْ وَاِلٰهُنَا وَاِلٰهُكُمْ وَاحِدٌ وَّنَحْنُ لَهٗ مُسْلِمُوْنَ ۝

47. And thus (it is) that We have sent down the Book to you. So the People of the Book believe therein,

وَكَذٰلِكَ اَنْزَلْنَا اِلَيْكَ الْكِتٰبَ ۗ فَالَّذِيْنَ اٰتَيْنٰهُمُ الْكِتٰبَ يُؤْمِنُوْنَ بِهٖ

as also do some of these (pagan Arabs): and none but Unbelievers reject Our Signs.

48.   And you were not (able) to recite a Book before this (Book came), nor are you (able) to transcribe it with your right hand: in that case, indeed, would the talkers of vanities have doubted.

49.   Nay, here are Signs self-evident in the hearts of those endowed with knowledge: and none but the unjust reject Our Signs.

50.   Yet they say: "Why are not Signs sent down to him from his Lord?" Say: "The Signs are indeed with Allah: and I am indeed a clear Warner."

51.   And is it not enough for them that We have sent down to you the Book which is rehearsed to them? Verily, in it is Mercy and a Reminder to those who believe.

52.   Say: "Enough is Allah for a Witness between me and you: He knows what is in the heavens and on earth. And it is those who believe in vanities and reject Allah, that will perish (in the end).

53.   They ask you to hasten on the Punishment (for them): had it not been for a term (of respite) appointed, the Punishment would certainly have come to them: and it will certainly reach them,- of a sudden, while they perceive not!

54.   They ask you to hasten on the Punishment: but, of a surety, Hell will encompass the Rejecters of Faith!-

55.   On the Day that the Punishment shall cover them from above them and from below them, and (a Voice) shall say: "You taste (the fruits) of your deeds!"

وَمِنْ هَٰٓؤُلَآءِ مَن يُؤْمِنُ بِهِۦ ۚ وَمَا يَجْحَدُ بِـَٔايَٰتِنَآ إِلَّا ٱلْكَٰفِرُونَ ۝

وَمَا كُنتَ تَتْلُوا۟ مِن قَبْلِهِۦ مِن كِتَٰبٍ وَلَا تَخُطُّهُۥ بِيَمِينِكَ ۖ إِذًا لَّٱرْتَابَ ٱلْمُبْطِلُونَ ۝

بَلْ هُوَ ءَايَٰتٌۢ بَيِّنَٰتٌ فِى صُدُورِ ٱلَّذِينَ أُوتُوا۟ ٱلْعِلْمَ ۚ وَمَا يَجْحَدُ بِـَٔايَٰتِنَآ إِلَّا ٱلظَّٰلِمُونَ ۝

وَقَالُوا۟ لَوْلَآ أُنزِلَ عَلَيْهِ ءَايَٰتٌ مِّن رَّبِّهِۦ ۖ قُلْ إِنَّمَا ٱلْءَايَٰتُ عِندَ ٱللَّهِ وَإِنَّمَآ أَنَا۠ نَذِيرٌ مُّبِينٌ ۝

أَوَلَمْ يَكْفِهِمْ أَنَّآ أَنزَلْنَا عَلَيْكَ ٱلْكِتَٰبَ يُتْلَىٰ عَلَيْهِمْ ۚ إِنَّ فِى ذَٰلِكَ لَرَحْمَةً وَذِكْرَىٰ لِقَوْمٍ يُؤْمِنُونَ ۝

قُلْ كَفَىٰ بِٱللَّهِ بَيْنِى وَبَيْنَكُمْ شَهِيدًا ۖ يَعْلَمُ مَا فِى ٱلسَّمَٰوَٰتِ وَٱلْأَرْضِ ۗ وَٱلَّذِينَ ءَامَنُوا۟ بِٱلْبَٰطِلِ وَكَفَرُوا۟ بِٱللَّهِ أُو۟لَٰٓئِكَ هُمُ ٱلْخَٰسِرُونَ ۝

وَيَسْتَعْجِلُونَكَ بِٱلْعَذَابِ ۚ وَلَوْلَآ أَجَلٌ مُّسَمًّى لَّجَآءَهُمُ ٱلْعَذَابُ وَلَيَأْتِيَنَّهُم بَغْتَةً وَهُمْ لَا يَشْعُرُونَ ۝

يَسْتَعْجِلُونَكَ بِٱلْعَذَابِ ۚ وَإِنَّ جَهَنَّمَ لَمُحِيطَةٌۢ بِٱلْكَٰفِرِينَ ۝

يَوْمَ يَغْشَىٰهُمُ ٱلْعَذَابُ مِن فَوْقِهِمْ وَمِن تَحْتِ أَرْجُلِهِمْ وَيَقُولُ ذُوقُوا۟ مَا كُنتُمْ تَعْمَلُونَ ۝

ع

56. O My servants who believe! Truly, spacious is My Earth: therefore you serve Me - (and Me alone)!

يٰعِبَادِيَ الَّذِيْنَ اٰمَنُوْٓا اِنَّ اَرْضِىْ
وَاسِعَةٌ فَاِيَّايَ فَاعْبُدُوْنِ ۝

57. Every soul shall have a taste of death: in the end to Us you shall be brought back.

كُلُّ نَفْسٍ ذَآئِقَةُ الْمَوْتِ ثُمَّ
اِلَيْنَا تُرْجَعُوْنَ ۝

58. But those who believe and work deeds of righteousness - to them We shall give a Home in Heaven,- lofty mansions beneath which flow rivers,- to dwell therein for ever;- an excellent reward for those who do (good)!-

وَالَّذِيْنَ اٰمَنُوْا وَعَمِلُوا الصّٰلِحٰتِ
لَنُبَوِّئَنَّهُمْ مِّنَ الْجَنَّةِ غُرَفًا تَجْرِىْ
مِنْ تَحْتِهَا الْاَنْهٰرُ خٰلِدِيْنَ فِيْهَا ۖ
نِعْمَ اَجْرُ الْعٰمِلِيْنَ ۝

59. Those who persevere in patience, and put their trust in their Lord and Cherisher.

الَّذِيْنَ صَبَرُوْا وَعَلٰى رَبِّهِمْ
يَتَوَكَّلُوْنَ ۝

60. How many are the creatures that do not carry their own sustenance? It is Allah Who feeds (both) them and you: for He hears and knows (all things).

وَكَاَيِّنْ مِّنْ دَآبَّةٍ لَّا تَحْمِلُ رِزْقَهَا ۖ
اللّٰهُ يَرْزُقُهَا وَاِيَّاكُمْ ۚ وَهُوَ
السَّمِيْعُ الْعَلِيْمُ ۝

61. If indeed you ask them who has created the heavens and the earth and subjected the sun and the moon (to His Law), they will certainly reply, "Allah". How are they then deluded away (from the truth)?

وَلَئِنْ سَاَلْتَهُمْ مَّنْ خَلَقَ السَّمٰوٰتِ
وَالْاَرْضَ وَسَخَّرَ الشَّمْسَ وَالْقَمَرَ
لَيَقُوْلُنَّ اللّٰهُ ۖ فَاَنّٰى يُؤْفَكُوْنَ ۝

62. Allah enlarges the sustenance (which He gives) to whichever of His servants He pleases; and He (similarly) grants by (strict) measure, (as He pleases): for Allah has full knowledge of all things.

اللّٰهُ يَبْسُطُ الرِّزْقَ لِمَنْ يَّشَآءُ
مِنْ عِبَادِهٖ وَيَقْدِرُ لَهٗ ۚ اِنَّ اللّٰهَ
بِكُلِّ شَىْءٍ عَلِيْمٌ ۝

63. And if indeed you ask them Who it is that sends down rain from the sky, and gives life therewith to the earth after its death, they will certainly reply, "Allah!" Say, "Praise be to Allah!" But most of them do not understand.

وَلَئِنْ سَاَلْتَهُمْ مَّنْ نَّزَّلَ مِنَ
السَّمَآءِ مَآءً فَاَحْيَا بِهِ الْاَرْضَ مِنْ
بَعْدِ مَوْتِهَا لَيَقُوْلُنَّ اللّٰهُ ۚ قُلِ
الْحَمْدُ لِلّٰهِ ۚ بَلْ اَكْثَرُهُمْ
لَا يَعْقِلُوْنَ ۝

64. What is the life of this world but amusement and play? But verily the Home in the Hereafter,- that is

وَمَا هٰذِهِ الْحَيٰوةُ الدُّنْيَآ اِلَّا لَهْوٌ
وَّلَعِبٌ ۗ وَاِنَّ الدَّارَ الْاٰخِرَةَ لَهِىَ

SÛRAH-30
AR-RÛM
(INTRODUCTION)

This Sûrah, as remarked in the Introduction to the last Sûrah, deals with the question of Ma'âd or the Final End of Things, from various points of view. In the last Sûrah, we saw that Revelation was linked up with Life and Conduct, and Time (looking backwards and forwards) figured forth the frailty of this Life. In this Sûrah the Time theme and its mystery are brought into relation with human history in the foreground and the evolution of the world in all its aspects in the background. The corruption introduced by man is cleared away by Allah, Whose Universal Plan points to the Hereafter. We shall see that the next two Sûras (31 and 32) present the theme in other aspects. All four are introduced with the Abbreviated Letters A.L.M. which (without being dogmatic) I have suggested as symbolical of the Past, Present and Future.

The chronology of this Sûrah is significant. It was revealed about the 7th or the 6th year *before* the Hijrat, corresponding to 615-16 of the Christian era, when the tide of Persian conquest over the Roman Empire was running strong. The Christian Empire of Rome had lost Jerusalem to the Persians, and Christianity had been humbled in the dust. At that time it seemed outside the bounds of human possibility, even to one intimately acquainted with the inner resources and conditions of the Persian and Roman armies and empires, that the tables would be turned and the position reversed within the space of eight or nine years. The pro-Persian Pagan Quraish rejoiced exceedingly, and redoubled their taunts and persecution against the Holy Prophet, whose Message was a renewal of the Message of Christ preached in Jerusalem. Then was this passage 30: 1-6 revealed, clearly foreshadowing the final defeat of Persia as a prelude to the destruction of the Persian Empire. There is no doubt about the prophecy and its fulfilment. For the exulting Pagans of Makka laid a heavy wager against the fulfilment of the prophecy with

Hadhrat Abû Bakr, and they lost it on its fulfilment.

But the rise and fall even of such mighty empires as the Persian and Roman Empires were but small events on the chequer-board of Time, compared to a mightier movement that was taking birth in the promulgation of Islam. In the seventh or sixth year *before* the Hijrat, and for a year or two after the Hijrat, Islam was struggling in the world like the still small voice in the conscience of humanity. It was scarcely heeded, and when it sought to insist upon its divine claim, it was insulted, assaulted, persecuted, boycotted, and (as it seemed) suppressed. The agony of Ta-if (two years before the Hijrat) and the murder-plot on the eve of the Hijrat were yet to come. But the purpose of Allah is not to be thwarted. Badr (A.H. 2=A.D. 624), rightly called the critical Day of Decision, began to redress the balance of outward events in early Islam, in the same year in which Issus began to redress the balance of outward events in Perso-Roman relations. Mightier events were yet to come. A new inner World was being created through Islam. This spiritual Revolution was of infinitely greater moment in world-history. The toppling down of priestcraft and false worship, the restoration of simplicity in faith and life, the rehabilitation of this life as the first step to the understanding of the Hereafter, the displacement of superstition and hairsplitting theology by a spirit of rational inquiry and knowledge, and the recognition of the divine as covering not merely an isolated thing called "Religion" but the whole way of Life, Thought, and Feeling,-this was and is the true Message of Islam and its mission. Its struggle-its fight-continues, but it is not without effect, as may be seen in the march of centuries in world-history.

life indeed, if they but knew.

الْحَيَوَانُ ۚ لَوْ كَانُوْا يَعْلَمُوْنَ ۝

65.   Now, if they embark on a boat, they call on Allah, making their devotion sincerely (and exclusively) to Him; but when He has delivered them safely to (dry) land, behold, they give a share (of their worship to others)!-

فَاِذَا رَكِبُوْا فِي الْفُلْكِ دَعَوُا اللّٰهَ مُخْلِصِيْنَ لَهُ الدِّيْنَ ۚ فَلَمَّا نَجّٰهُمْ اِلَى الْبَرِّ اِذَا هُمْ يُشْرِكُوْنَ ۝

66.   Disdaining ungratefully Our gifts, and giving them-selves up to (worldly) enjoy-ment! But soon will they know.

لِيَكْفُرُوْا بِمَا اٰتَيْنٰهُمْ ۙ وَلِيَتَمَتَّعُوْا ۖ فَسَوْفَ يَعْلَمُوْنَ ۝

67.   Do they not then see that We have made a sanctuary secure, and that men are being snatched away from all around them? Then, do they believe in that which is vain, and reject the Grace of Allah?

اَوَلَمْ يَرَوْا اَنَّا جَعَلْنَا حَرَمًا اٰمِنًا وَّيُتَخَطَّفُ النَّاسُ مِنْ حَوْلِهِمْ ۚ اَفَبِالْبَاطِلِ يُؤْمِنُوْنَ وَبِنِعْمَةِ اللّٰهِ يَكْفُرُوْنَ ۝

68.   And who does more wrong than he who invents a lie against Allah or rejects the Truth when it reaches him? Is there not a home in Hell for those who reject Faith?

وَمَنْ اَظْلَمُ مِمَّنِ افْتَرٰى عَلَى اللّٰهِ كَذِبًا اَوْ كَذَّبَ بِالْحَقِّ لَمَّا جَآءَهٗ ۚ اَلَيْسَ فِيْ جَهَنَّمَ مَثْوًى لِّلْكٰفِرِيْنَ ۝

69.   And those who strive in Our (Cause),- We will certainly guide them to Our Paths: for verily Allah is with those who do right.

وَالَّذِيْنَ جَاهَدُوْا فِيْنَا لَنَهْدِيَنَّهُمْ سُبُلَنَا ۚ وَاِنَّ اللّٰهَ لَمَعَ الْمُحْسِنِيْنَ ۝

30. The Roman Empire
In the name of Allah. Most Gracious, Most Merciful.

(٣) سُوْرَةُ الرُّوْمِ مَكِّيَّةٌ (٨٣)

بِسْمِ اللّٰهِ الرَّحْمٰنِ الرَّحِيْمِ

1.   Alif - Lam - Mim.

الٓمّٓ ۝

2.   The Roman Empire has been defeated-

غُلِبَتِ الرُّوْمُ ۝

3.   In a land close by; but they, (even) after (this) defeat of theirs, will soon be victorious-

فِيْ اَدْنَى الْاَرْضِ وَهُمْ مِّنْ بَعْدِ غَلَبِهِمْ سَيَغْلِبُوْنَ ۝

4.   Within a few years. With Allah is the Command, in the Past and in the Future: on that Day shall the Believers rejoice-

فِيْ بِضْعِ سِنِيْنَ ۚ لِلّٰهِ الْاَمْرُ مِنْ قَبْلُ وَمِنْ بَعْدُ ۚ وَيَوْمَئِذٍ يَّفْرَحُ الْمُؤْمِنُوْنَ ۝

5.   With the help of Allah. He helps whom He will, and He is Exalted in Might, Most Merciful.

بِنَصْرِ اللّٰهِ ۚ يَنْصُرُ مَنْ يَّشَآءُ ۚ وَهُوَ الْعَزِيْزُ الرَّحِيْمُ ۝

6. (It is) the promise of Allah. Never does Allah depart from His promise: but most men do not understand.

7. They know but the outer (things) in the life of this world: but they are heedless of the Hereafter.

8. Do they not reflect in their own minds? Not but for just ends and for a term appointed, did Allah create the heavens and the earth, and all between them: yet there are truly many among men who deny the meeting with their Lord (at the Resurrection)!

وَعْدَ اللهِ ۖ لَا يُخْلِفُ اللهُ وَعْدَهُ
وَلٰكِنَّ أَكْثَرَ النَّاسِ لَا يَعْلَمُوْنَ ۝
يَعْلَمُوْنَ ظَاهِرًا مِّنَ الْحَيٰوةِ الدُّنْيَا ۚ
وَهُمْ عَنِ الْاٰخِرَةِ هُمْ غٰفِلُوْنَ ۝
اَوَلَمْ يَتَفَكَّرُوْا فِيْٓ اَنْفُسِهِمْ ۗ مَا
خَلَقَ اللهُ السَّمٰوٰتِ وَالْاَرْضَ وَمَا
بَيْنَهُمَآ اِلَّا بِالْحَقِّ وَاَجَلٍ مُّسَمًّى ۗ
وَاِنَّ كَثِيْرًا مِّنَ النَّاسِ بِلِقَآئِ
رَبِّهِمْ لَكٰفِرُوْنَ ۝

9. Do they not travel through the Earth, and see what was the End of those before them? They were superior to them in strength: they tilled the soil and populated it in greater numbers than these have done: there came to them their Messengers with Clear (Signs). (which they rejected, to their own destruction): it was not Allah Who wronged them, but they wronged their own souls.

اَوَلَمْ يَسِيْرُوْا فِي الْاَرْضِ فَيَنْظُرُوْا
كَيْفَ كَانَ عَاقِبَةُ الَّذِيْنَ مِنْ
قَبْلِهِمْ ۚ كَانُوْٓا اَشَدَّ مِنْهُمْ قُوَّةً
وَّاَثَارُوا الْاَرْضَ وَعَمَرُوْهَآ اَكْثَرَ
مِمَّا عَمَرُوْهَا وَجَآءَتْهُمْ رُسُلُهُمْ
بِالْبَيِّنٰتِ ۚ فَمَا كَانَ اللهُ لِيَظْلِمَهُمْ
وَلٰكِنْ كَانُوْٓا اَنْفُسَهُمْ يَظْلِمُوْنَ ۝

10. In the long run evil in the extreme will be the End of those who do evil; for that they rejected the Signs of Allah, and held them up to ridicule.

ثُمَّ كَانَ عَاقِبَةَ الَّذِيْنَ اَسَآءُوا
السُّوْٓاٰى اَنْ كَذَّبُوْا بِاٰيٰتِ اللهِ
وَكَانُوْا بِهَا يَسْتَهْزِئُوْنَ ۝

11. It is Allah Who begins (the process of) creation; then repeats it; then you shall be brought back to Him.

اللهُ يَبْدَؤُا الْخَلْقَ ثُمَّ يُعِيْدُهُ ثُمَّ
اِلَيْهِ تُرْجَعُوْنَ ۝

12. On the Day that the Hour will be established, the guilty will be struck dumb with despair.

وَيَوْمَ تَقُوْمُ السَّاعَةُ يُبْلِسُ
الْمُجْرِمُوْنَ ۝

13. No intercessor will they have among their "Partners" and they will (themselves) reject their "Partners".

وَلَمْ يَكُنْ لَّهُمْ مِّنْ شُرَكَآئِهِمْ شُفَعٰٓؤُا
وَكَانُوْا بِشُرَكَآئِهِمْ كٰفِرِيْنَ ۝

14. On the Day that the Hour will be established,- that Day shall (all men) be sorted out.

وَيَوْمَ تَقُوْمُ السَّاعَةُ يَوْمَئِذٍ

15. Then those who have believed and worked righteous deeds, shall be made happy in a Mead of Delight.

16. And those who have rejected Faith and falsely denied Our Signs and the meeting of the Hereafter,- such shall be brought forth to Punishment.

17. So (give) glory to Allah, when you reach eventide and when you rise in the morning;

18. Yes, to Him be praise, in the heavens and on earth; and in the late afternoon and when the day begins to decline.

19. It is He Who brings out the living from the dead, and brings out the dead from the living, and Who gives life to the earth after it is dead: and thus you shall be brought out (from the dead).

20. Among His Signs is this, that He created you from dust; and then,- behold, you are men scattered (far and wide)!

21. And among His Signs is this, that He created for you mates from among yourselves, that you may dwell in tranquillity with them, and He has put love and mercy between your (hearts): verily in that are Signs for those who reflect.

22. And among His Signs is the creation of the heavens and the earth, and the variations in your languages and your colours: verily in that are Signs for those who know.

23. And among His Signs is the sleep that you take by night and by day, and the quest that you (make for livelihood) out of His Bounty: verily in that are Signs for those who hearken.

24. And among His Signs, He shows you the lightning, by way both of fear

بَتَفَرَّقُوْنَ ۝

فَاَمَّا الَّذِيْنَ اٰمَنُوْا وَعَمِلُوا الصّٰلِحٰتِ
فَهُمْ فِيْ رَوْضَةٍ يُّحْبَرُوْنَ ۝

وَاَمَّا الَّذِيْنَ كَفَرُوْا وَكَذَّبُوْا بِاٰيٰتِنَا
وَلِقَآئِ الْاٰخِرَةِ فَاُولٰٓئِكَ فِي
الْعَذَابِ مُحْضَرُوْنَ ۝

فَسُبْحٰنَ اللهِ حِيْنَ تُمْسُوْنَ وَحِيْنَ
تُصْبِحُوْنَ ۝

وَلَهُ الْحَمْدُ فِي السَّمٰوٰتِ وَ
الْاَرْضِ وَعَشِيًّا وَّحِيْنَ تُظْهِرُوْنَ ۝

يُخْرِجُ الْحَيَّ مِنَ الْمَيِّتِ وَيُخْرِجُ
الْمَيِّتَ مِنَ الْحَيِّ وَيُحْيِ الْاَرْضَ
بَعْدَ مَوْتِهَا ۗ وَكَذٰلِكَ تُخْرَجُوْنَ ۝

وَمِنْ اٰيٰتِهٖٓ اَنْ خَلَقَكُمْ مِّنْ تُرَابٍ
ثُمَّ اِذَآ اَنْتُمْ بَشَرٌ تَنْتَشِرُوْنَ ۝

وَمِنْ اٰيٰتِهٖٓ اَنْ خَلَقَ لَكُمْ مِّنْ
اَنْفُسِكُمْ اَزْوَاجًا لِّتَسْكُنُوْٓا اِلَيْهَا
وَجَعَلَ بَيْنَكُمْ مَّوَدَّةً وَّرَحْمَةً ۗ
اِنَّ فِيْ ذٰلِكَ لَاٰيٰتٍ لِّقَوْمٍ يَّتَفَكَّرُوْنَ ۝

وَمِنْ اٰيٰتِهٖ خَلْقُ السَّمٰوٰتِ وَالْاَرْضِ
وَاخْتِلَافُ اَلْسِنَتِكُمْ وَاَلْوَانِكُمْ ۗ
اِنَّ فِيْ ذٰلِكَ لَاٰيٰتٍ لِّلْعٰلِمِيْنَ ۝

وَمِنْ اٰيٰتِهٖ مَنَامُكُمْ بِالَّيْلِ وَالنَّهَارِ
وَابْتِغَآؤُكُمْ مِّنْ فَضْلِهٖ ۗ اِنَّ فِيْ
ذٰلِكَ لَاٰيٰتٍ لِّقَوْمٍ يَّسْمَعُوْنَ ۝

وَمِنْ اٰيٰتِهٖ يُرِيْكُمُ الْبَرْقَ خَوْفًا

and of hope, and He sends down
rain from the sky and with it
gives life to the earth after it is
dead: verily in that are Signs for
those who are wise.

وَطَمَعًا وَّيُنَزِّلُ مِنَ السَّمَآءِ مَآءً
فَيُحْيٖ بِهِ الْأَرْضَ بَعْدَ مَوْتِهَا ؕ
اِنَّ فِىۡ ذٰلِكَ لَاٰيٰتٍ لِّقَوْمٍ
يَّعْقِلُوْنَ ۝

25. And among His Signs is
this, that heaven and earth stand
by His Command: then when
He calls you, by a single call,
from the earth, behold, you
(straightway) come forth.

وَمِنْ اٰيٰتِهٖٓ اَنْ تَقُوْمَ السَّمَآءُ وَ
الْاَرْضُ بِاَمْرِهٖ ؕ ثُمَّ اِذَا دَعَاكُمْ
دَعْوَةً ۖ مِّنَ الْاَرْضِ ۙ اِذَآ
اَنْتُمْ تَخْرُجُوْنَ ۝

26. To Him belongs every
being that is in the heavens and
on earth: all are devoutly obedient to Him.

وَلَهٗ مَنْ فِى السَّمٰوٰتِ وَالْاَرْضِ ؕ
كُلٌّ لَّهٗ قٰنِتُوْنَ ۝

27. It is He Who begins (the
process of) creation; then
repeats it; and for Him it is most
easy. To Him belongs the
loftiest similitude (we can think
of) in the heavens and the earth:
for He is Exalted in Might, full
of Wisdom.

وَهُوَ الَّذِىْ يَبْدَؤُا الْخَلْقَ ثُمَّ
يُعِيْدُهٗ وَهُوَ اَهْوَنُ عَلَيْهِ ؕ وَلَهُ
الْمَثَلُ الْاَعْلٰى فِى السَّمٰوٰتِ وَالْاَرْضِ ۚ
وَهُوَ الْعَزِيْزُ الْحَكِيْمُ ۝

28. He propounds to you a
similitude from your own
(experience): do you have
partners among those whom
your right hands possess, to
share as equals in the wealth We
have bestowed on you? Do you
fear them as you fear each
other? Thus do We explain the
Signs in detail to a people that
understand.

ضَرَبَ لَكُمْ مَّثَلًا مِّنْ اَنْفُسِكُمْ ؕ هَلْ
لَّكُمْ مِّنْ مَّا مَلَكَتْ اَيْمَانُكُمْ مِّنْ
شُرَكَآءَ فِىْ مَا رَزَقْنٰكُمْ فَاَنْتُمْ فِيْهِ
سَوَآءٌ تَخَافُوْنَهُمْ كَخِيْفَتِكُمْ اَنْفُسَكُمْ ؕ
كَذٰلِكَ نُفَصِّلُ الْاٰيٰتِ لِقَوْمٍ
يَّعْقِلُوْنَ ۝

29. Nay, the wrong-doers
(merely) follow their own lusts,
being devoid of knowledge. But
who will guide those whom
Allah leaves astray? To them
there will be no helpers.

بَلِ اتَّبَعَ الَّذِيْنَ ظَلَمُوْٓا اَهْوَآءَهُمْ
بِغَيْرِ عِلْمٍ ۚ فَمَنْ يَّهْدِىْ مَنْ اَضَلَّ
اللّٰهُ ؕ وَمَا لَهُمْ مِّنْ نّٰصِرِيْنَ ۝

30. So you set your face stea-
dily and truly to the Faith: (establish) Allah's handiwork according to the pattern on which He
has made mankind: no change
(let there be) in the work
(wrought) by Allah: that is the

فَاَقِمْ وَجْهَكَ لِلدِّيْنِ حَنِيْفًا ؕ فِطْرَتَ
اللّٰهِ الَّتِىْ فَطَرَ النَّاسَ عَلَيْهَا ؕ
لَا تَبْدِيْلَ لِخَلْقِ اللّٰهِ ؕ ذٰلِكَ الدِّيْنُ

standard Religion: but most among mankind do not understand.

31. You turn back in repentance to Him, and fear Him: establish regular prayers, and you be not among those who join gods with Allah,-

32. Those who split up their Religion, and become (mere) Sects,- each party rejoicing in that which is with itself!

33. When trouble touches men, they cry to their Lord, turning back to Him in repentance: but when He gives them a taste of Mercy as from Himself, behold, some of them pay part-worship to other gods besides their Lord,-

34. (As if) to show their ingratitude for the (favours) We have bestowed on them! Then enjoy (your brief day); but soon will you know (your folly)

35. Or have We sent down authority to them, which points out to them the things to which they pay part-worship?

36. When We give men a taste of Mercy, they exult thereat: and when some evil afflicts them because of what their (own) hands have sent forth, behold, they are in despair!

37. Do not they see that Allah enlarges the provision and restricts it, to whomsoever He pleases? Verily in that are Signs for those who believe.

38. So give what is due to kindred, the needy, and the wayfarer. That is best for those who seek the Countenance of Allah, and it is they who will prosper.

39. That which you lay out for increase through

the property of (other) people,
will have no increase with
Allah: but that which you lay out
for charity, seeking the Countenance of Allah, (will increase):
it is these who will get a
recompense multiplied.

40. It is Allah Who has created
you: further, He has provided for
your sustenance; then He will
cause you to die; and again He
will give you life. Are there any
of your (false) "Partners" who
can do any single one of these
things? Glory to Him! and High
is He above the partners they
attribute (to Him)!

41. Mischief has appeared on
land and sea because of (the
deed) that the hands of men
have earned, that (Allah) may
give them a taste of some of
their deeds: in order that they
may turn back (from Evil).

42. Say: "Travel through the
earth and see what was the end
of those before (you): most of
them worshipped others besides
Allah."

43. But you set your face to
the right Religion, before there
come from Allah the Day which
there is no chance of averting:
on that Day men shall be
divided (in two).

44. Those who reject Faith
will suffer from that rejection:
and those who work righteousness will make provision for
themselves (in heaven):

45. That He may reward those
who believe and work righteous
deeds, out of His Bounty. For
He does not love those who
reject Faith.

46. Among His Signs is this,
that He sends the Winds, as
heralds of Glad Tidings, giving
you a taste of His (Grace and)
Mercy,- that the ships may sail
(majestically) by His Command
and that you may seek of His
Bounty: in order that you may be
grateful.

أَمْوَالِ النَّاسِ فَلَا يَرْبُوا عِنْدَ اللّٰهِ ۚ

وَمَآ اٰتَيْتُمْ مِّنْ زَكٰوةٍ تُرِيْدُوْنَ وَجْهَ

اللّٰهِ فَأُولٰٓئِكَ هُمُ الْمُضْعِفُوْنَ ۞

اللّٰهُ الَّذِيْ خَلَقَكُمْ ثُمَّ رَزَقَكُمْ

ثُمَّ يُمِيْتُكُمْ ثُمَّ يُحْيِيْكُمْ ۚ هَلْ مِنْ

شُرَكَآئِكُمْ مَّنْ يَّفْعَلُ مِنْ ذٰلِكُمْ

مِّنْ شَيْءٍ ۚ سُبْحٰنَهٗ وَتَعٰلٰى عَمَّا

يُشْرِكُوْنَ ۞

ظَهَرَ الْفَسَادُ فِي الْبَرِّ وَالْبَحْرِ بِمَا

كَسَبَتْ أَيْدِي النَّاسِ لِيُذِيْقَهُمْ

بَعْضَ الَّذِيْ عَمِلُوْا لَعَلَّهُمْ يَرْجِعُوْنَ ۞

قُلْ سِيْرُوْا فِي الْأَرْضِ فَانْظُرُوْا

كَيْفَ كَانَ عَاقِبَةُ الَّذِيْنَ مِنْ

قَبْلُ ۚ كَانَ أَكْثَرُهُمْ مُّشْرِكِيْنَ ۞

فَأَقِمْ وَجْهَكَ لِلدِّيْنِ الْقَيِّمِ مِنْ

قَبْلِ أَنْ يَّأْتِيَ يَوْمٌ لَّا مَرَدَّ لَهٗ

مِنَ اللّٰهِ يَوْمَئِذٍ يَّصَّدَّعُوْنَ ۞

مَنْ كَفَرَ فَعَلَيْهِ كُفْرُهٗ ۚ وَمَنْ عَمِلَ

صَالِحًا فَلِأَنْفُسِهِمْ يَمْهَدُوْنَ ۞

لِيَجْزِيَ الَّذِيْنَ اٰمَنُوْا وَعَمِلُوا

الصّٰلِحٰتِ مِنْ فَضْلِهٖ ۚ إِنَّهٗ لَا

يُحِبُّ الْكٰفِرِيْنَ ۞

وَمِنْ اٰيٰتِهٖٓ أَنْ يُّرْسِلَ الرِّيَاحَ

مُبَشِّرٰتٍ وَّلِيُذِيْقَكُمْ مِّنْ رَّحْمَتِهٖ

وَلِتَجْرِيَ الْفُلْكُ بِأَمْرِهٖ وَلِتَبْتَغُوْا

مِنْ فَضْلِهٖ وَلَعَلَّكُمْ تَشْكُرُوْنَ ۞

47. We sent indeed, before you, Messengers to their (respective) peoples, and they came to them with Clear Signs: then, to those who transgressed, We meted out Retribution: and it was due from Us to aid those who believed.

48. It is Allah Who sends the Winds, and they raise the Clouds: then He spreads them in the sky as He wills, and breaks them into fragments, until you see rain-drops issue from the midst thereof: then when He has made them reach such of His servants as He wills, behold, they do rejoice!-

49. Even though, before they received (the rain) - just before this - they were dumb with despair!

50. Then contemplate (O man!) the memorials of Allah's Mercy!- how He gives life to the earth after its death: verily the same will give life to the men who are dead: for He has power over all things.

51. And if We (but) send a Wind from which they see (their tilth) turn yellow,- behold, they become, thereafter, Ungrateful (Unbelievers)!

52. So verily you can not make the dead to hear, nor can you make the deaf to hear the call, when they show their backs and turn away.

53. Nor can you lead back the blind from their straying: only those you will make to hear, who believe in Our Signs and submit (their wills in Islam).

54. It is Allah Who created you in a state of (helpless) weakness, then gave (you) strength after weakness, then, after strength, gave (you) weakness

وَلَقَدْ اَرْسَلْنَا مِنْ قَبْلِكَ رُسُلًا اِلٰى قَوْمِهِمْ فَجَآءُوْهُمْ بِالْبَيِّنٰتِ فَانْتَقَمْنَا مِنَ الَّذِيْنَ اَجْرَمُوْا ۚ وَكَانَ حَقًّا عَلَيْنَا نَصْرُ الْمُؤْمِنِيْنَ ۝

اَللّٰهُ الَّذِيْ يُرْسِلُ الرِّيٰحَ فَتُثِيْرُ سَحَابًا فَيَبْسُطُهٗ فِى السَّمَآءِ كَيْفَ يَشَآءُ وَيَجْعَلُهٗ كِسَفًا فَتَرَى الْوَدْقَ يَخْرُجُ مِنْ خِلٰلِهٖ ۚ فَاِذَآ اَصَابَ بِهٖ مَنْ يَّشَآءُ مِنْ عِبَادِهٖٓ اِذَا هُمْ يَسْتَبْشِرُوْنَ ۝

وَاِنْ كَانُوْا مِنْ قَبْلِ اَنْ يُّنَزَّلَ عَلَيْهِمْ مِّنْ قَبْلِهٖ لَمُبْلِسِيْنَ ۝ فَانْظُرْ اِلٰٓى اٰثٰرِ رَحْمَتِ اللّٰهِ كَيْفَ يُحْيِ الْاَرْضَ بَعْدَ مَوْتِهَا ۚ اِنَّ ذٰلِكَ لَمُحْيِ الْمَوْتٰى ۚ وَهُوَ عَلٰى كُلِّ شَيْءٍ قَدِيْرٌ ۝

وَلَئِنْ اَرْسَلْنَا رِيْحًا فَرَاَوْهُ مُصْفَرًّا لَّظَلُّوْا مِنْ بَعْدِهٖ يَكْفُرُوْنَ ۝ فَاِنَّكَ لَا تُسْمِعُ الْمَوْتٰى وَلَا تُسْمِعُ الصُّمَّ الدُّعَآءَ اِذَا وَلَّوْا مُدْبِرِيْنَ ۝ وَمَآ اَنْتَ بِهٰدِ الْعُمْيِ عَنْ ضَلٰلَتِهِمْ ۚ اِنْ تُسْمِعُ اِلَّا مَنْ يُّؤْمِنُ بِاٰيٰتِنَا فَهُمْ مُّسْلِمُوْنَ ۝

اَللّٰهُ الَّذِيْ خَلَقَكُمْ مِّنْ ضُعْفٍ ثُمَّ جَعَلَ مِنْ بَعْدِ ضُعْفٍ قُوَّةً ثُمَّ جَعَلَ مِنْ بَعْدِ قُوَّةٍ ضُعْفًا

SÛRAH-31
LUQMÂN
(INTRODUCTION)

The argument of the Final End of Things is here continued from another point of view. What is Wisdom? Where shall she be found? Will she solve the mysteries of Time and Nature, and that world higher than physical Nature, which brings us nearer to Allah? "Yes," is the answer: "if, as in the advice of Luqman the Wise, human wisdom looks to Allah in true worship, enables every act of life with true kindness, but avoids the false indulgence that infringes the divine law,-and in short follows the golden mean of virtue." And this is indicated by every Sign in Nature.

The Chronology of the Sûrah has no significance. In the main, it belongs to the late Makkan period.

and a hoary head: He creates as He wills, and it is He Who has all knowledge and power.

55. On the Day that the Hour (of Reckoning) will be established, the transgressors will swear that they did not tarry but an hour: thus were they used to being deluded!

56. But those endued with knowledge and faith will say: "Indeed you tarried within Allah's Decree, to the Day of Resurrection, and this is the Day of Resurrection: but you-you were not aware!"

57. So on that Day no excuse of theirs will avail the Transgressors, nor will they be invited (then) to seek grace (by repentance).

58. Verily We have propounded for men, in this Qur'an every kind of Parable: but if you bring to them any Sign, the Unbelievers are sure to say, "You do nothing but talk vanities."

59. Thus Allah seals up the hearts of those who do not understand.

60. So patiently persevere: for verily the promise of Allah is true: nor let those shake your firmness, who have (themselves) no certainty of faith.

31. The Wise
In the name of Allah. Most Gracious, Most Merciful.

1. Alif- Lam-Mim.

2. These are Verses of the Wise Book,-

3. A Guide and a Mercy to the Doers of Good,-

4. Those who establish regular Prayer, and give regular Charity, and have (in their hearts) the assurance of the Hereafter.

5. These are on (true) guidance from their Lord: and these are the ones who will prosper.

يُوْقِنُوْنَ ۗ

اُولٰٓئِكَ عَلٰى هُدًى مِّنْ رَّبِّهِمْ وَاُولٰٓئِكَ هُمُ الْمُفْلِحُوْنَ ۞

6. But there are, among men, those who purchase idle tales, without knowledge (or meaning), to mislead (men) from the Path of Allah and throw ridicule (on the Path): for such there will be a Humiliating Penalty.

وَمِنَ النَّاسِ مَنْ يَّشْتَرِيْ لَهْوَ الْحَدِيْثِ لِيُضِلَّ عَنْ سَبِيْلِ اللّٰهِ بِغَيْرِ عِلْمٍ ۗ وَّيَتَّخِذَهَا هُزُوًا ۗ اُولٰٓئِكَ لَهُمْ عَذَابٌ مُّهِيْنٌ ۞

7. When Our Signs are rehearsed to such a one, he turns away in arrogance, as if he did not hear them, as if there were deafness in both his ears: announce to him a grievous Penalty.

وَإِذَا تُتْلٰى عَلَيْهِ اٰيٰتُنَا وَلّٰى مُسْتَكْبِرًا كَأَنْ لَّمْ يَسْمَعْهَا كَأَنَّ فِيْ اُذُنَيْهِ وَقْرًا ۗ فَبَشِّرْهُ بِعَذَابٍ اَلِيْمٍ ۞

8. For those who believe and work righteous deeds, there will be Gardens of Bliss,-

إِنَّ الَّذِيْنَ اٰمَنُوْا وَعَمِلُوا الصّٰلِحٰتِ لَهُمْ جَنّٰتُ النَّعِيْمِ ۙ

9. To dwell therein. The promise of Allah is true: and He is Exalted in Power, Wise.

خٰلِدِيْنَ فِيْهَا ۗ وَعْدَ اللّٰهِ حَقًّا ۗ وَهُوَ الْعَزِيْزُ الْحَكِيْمُ ۞

10. He created the heavens without any pillars that you can see; He set on the earth mountains standing firm, lest it should shake with you; and He scattered through it beasts of all kinds. We send down rain from the sky, and produce on the earth every kind of noble creature, in pairs.

خَلَقَ السَّمٰوٰتِ بِغَيْرِ عَمَدٍ تَرَوْنَهَا وَاَلْقٰى فِى الْاَرْضِ رَوَاسِيَ اَنْ تَمِيْدَ بِكُمْ وَبَثَّ فِيْهَا مِنْ كُلِّ دَآبَّةٍ ۗ وَاَنْزَلْنَا مِنَ السَّمَآءِ مَآءً فَاَنْبَتْنَا فِيْهَا مِنْ كُلِّ زَوْجٍ كَرِيْمٍ ۞

11. Such is the Creation of Allah: now show Me what is there that others besides Him have created: nay, but the Transgressors are in manifest error.

هٰذَا خَلْقُ اللّٰهِ فَاَرُوْنِيْ مَاذَا خَلَقَ الَّذِيْنَ مِنْ دُوْنِهٖ ۗ بَلِ الظّٰلِمُوْنَ فِيْ ضَلٰلٍ مُّبِيْنٍ ۞

12. We bestowed (in the past) Wisdom on Luqmân: "Show (your) gratitude to Allah." and who is (so) grateful does so to the profit of his own soul: but if any is ungrateful, verily Allah is free of all wants, Worthy of all praise.

وَلَقَدْ اٰتَيْنَا لُقْمٰنَ الْحِكْمَةَ اَنِ اشْكُرْ لِلّٰهِ ۗ وَمَنْ يَّشْكُرْ فَإِنَّمَا يَشْكُرُ لِنَفْسِهٖ ۗ وَمَنْ كَفَرَ فَإِنَّ

١١ ع

13. Behold, Luqman said to his son by way of instruction: "O my son! do not join in worship (others) with Allah: for false worship is indeed the highest wrong-doing."

14. And We have enjoined on man (to be good) to his parents: in travail upon travail his mother bore him, and in two years was his weaning: (hear the command), "Show gratitude to Me and to your parents: to Me is (your final) Goal.

15. "But if they strive to make you join in worship with Me things of which you have no knowledge, do not obey them; yet bear them company in this life with justice (and consideration), and follow the way of those who turn to Me (in love): in the end the return of you all is to Me, and I will tell you the truth (and meaning) of all that you did."

16. "O my son!" (said Luqman), "If there be (but) the weight of a mustard-seed and it were (hidden) in a rock, or (anywhere) in the heavens or on earth, Allah will bring it forth: for Allah is Subtle and Aware.

17. "O my son! establish regular prayer, enjoin what is just, and forbid what is wrong: and bear with patient constancy whatever betide you; for this is firmness (of purpose) in (the conduct of) affairs.

18. "And do not swell your cheek (for pride) at men, nor walk in insolence through the earth; for Allah does not love any arrogant boaster.

19. "And be moderate in your pace, and lower

your voice; for the harshest of sounds without doubt is the braying of the ass."

20. Do you not see that Allah has subjected to your (use) all things in the heavens and on earth, and has made His bounties flow to you in exceeding measure, (both) seen and unseen? Yet there are among men those who dispute about Allah, without knowledge and without guidance, and without a Book to enlighten them!

21. When they are told to follow the (Revelation) that Allah has sent down, they say: "Nay, we shall follow the ways that we found our fathers (following)." What! even if it is Satan beckoning them to the Penalty of the (Blazing) Fire?

22. Whoever submits his whole self to Allah, and is a doer of good, has grasped indeed the most trustworthy hand-hold: and with Allah rests the End and Decision of (all) affairs.

23. But if any reject Faith, let not his rejection grieve you: to Us is their return, and We shall tell them the truth of their deeds: for Allah knows well all that is in (men's) hearts.

24. We grant them their pleasure for a little while: in the end We shall drive them to an unrelenting chastisement.

25. If you ask them, who is it that created the heavens and the earth. They will certainly say, "Allah". Say: "Praise be to Allah!" But most of them do not understand.

26. To Allah belong all things in heaven and earth: verily Allah is He (that is) free of all wants, worthy of all praise.

27. And if all the trees on earth
were pens and the ocean (were
ink), with seven oceans behind it
to add to its (supply), yet the
Words of Allah would not be
exhausted (in the writing): for
Allah is Exalted in Power, full of
Wisdom.

28. And your creation or your
resurrection is in no wise but as
an individual soul: for Allah is
He Who hears and sees (all
things).

29. Don't you see that Allah
merges Night into Day and he
merges Day into Night; that He
has subjected the sun, and the
moon (to His Law), each running its course for a term
appointed; and that Allah is
well-acquainted with all that
you do?

30. That is because Allah is the
(only) Reality, and because
whatever else they invoke
besides Him is Falsehood; and
because Allah,- He is the Most
High, Most Great.

31. Don't you see that the
ships sail through the ocean by
the Grace of Allah?- that He
may show you of His Signs?
Verily in this are Signs for all
who constantly persevere and
give thanks.

32. When a wave covers them
like the canopy (of clouds), they
call to Allah, offering Him
sincere devotion. But when He
has delivered them safely to
land, there are among them
those that halt between (right
and wrong). But none reject Our
Signs except only a perfidious
ungrateful (wretch)!

33. O mankind! do your duty
to your Lord, and fear (the
coming of) a Day when no
father can avail anything for his
son, nor a son

SÛRAH-32
AS-SAJDAH
(INTRODUCTION)

This short Sûrah closes the series of the four A.L.M. Sûras, which began with the 29th. Its theme is the mystery of Creation, the mystery of Time and the mystery of the *Ma 'ad(* the Final End) as viewed through the light of Allah's revelation. The contemplation of these mysteries should lead to Faith and the adoration of Allah. In Chronology it belongs to the middle Makkan period and is therefore a little earlier than the last, but its chronology has no significance.

avail anything for his father. Verily, the promise of Allah is true: let not then this present life deceive you, nor let the Chief Deceiver deceive you about Allah.

جَازٍ عَنْ وَّالِدِهٖ شَيْئًا ؕ اِنَّ وَعْدَ اللّٰهِ حَقٌّ فَلَا تَغُرَّنَّكُمُ الْحَيٰوةُ الدُّنْيَا ۽ وَلَا يَغُرَّنَّكُمْ بِاللّٰهِ الْغَرُوْرُ ۝

34. Verily the knowledge of the Hour is with Allah (alone). It is He Who sends down rain, and He Who knows what is in the wombs. Nor does any one know what it is that he will earn on the morrow: nor does any one know in what land he is to die. Verily with Allah is full knowledge and He is acquainted (with all things).

اِنَّ اللّٰهَ عِنْدَهٗ عِلْمُ السَّاعَةِ ۚ وَيُنَزِّلُ الْغَيْثَ ۚ وَيَعْلَمُ مَا فِي الْاَرْحَامِ ؕ وَمَا تَدْرِيْ نَفْسٌ مَّا ذَا تَكْسِبُ غَدًا ؕ وَمَا تَدْرِيْ نَفْسٌ بِاَيِّ اَرْضٍ تَمُوْتُ ؕ اِنَّ اللّٰهَ عَلِيْمٌ خَبِيْرٌ ۝

32. Adoration
In the name of Allah. Most Gracious, Most Merciful.

(٣٢) سُوْرَةُ السَّجْدَةِ مَكِّيَّةٌ (٣٠)

بِسْمِ اللّٰهِ الرَّحْمٰنِ الرَّحِيْمِ

1. Alif- Lam-Mim.

الٓمّٓ ۚ

2. (This is) the revelation of the Book in which there is no doubt,- from the Lord of the Worlds.

تَنْزِيْلُ الْكِتٰبِ لَا رَيْبَ فِيْهِ مِنْ رَّبِّ الْعٰلَمِيْنَ ۝

3. Or do they say, "He has forged it"? Nay, it is the Truth from your Lord, that you may admonish a people to whom no warner has come before you: in order that they may receive guidance.

اَمْ يَقُوْلُوْنَ افْتَرٰىهُ ۚ بَلْ هُوَ الْحَقُّ مِنْ رَّبِّكَ لِتُنْذِرَ قَوْمًا مَّآ اَتٰىهُمْ مِّنْ نَّذِيْرٍ مِّنْ قَبْلِكَ لَعَلَّهُمْ يَهْتَدُوْنَ ۝

4. It is Allah Who has created the heavens and the earth, and all between them, in six Days, and is firmly established on the Throne (of authority): you have none, besides Him, to protect or intercede (for you): will you not then receive admonition?

اَللّٰهُ الَّذِيْ خَلَقَ السَّمٰوٰتِ وَالْاَرْضَ وَمَا بَيْنَهُمَا فِيْ سِتَّةِ اَيَّامٍ ثُمَّ اسْتَوٰى عَلَى الْعَرْشِ ؕ مَا لَكُمْ مِّنْ دُوْنِهٖ مِنْ وَّلِيٍّ وَّلَا شَفِيْعٍ ؕ اَفَلَا تَتَذَكَّرُوْنَ ۝

5. He rules (all) affairs from the heavens to the earth: in the end (all affairs) will go up to Him, on

يُدَبِّرُ الْاَمْرَ مِنَ السَّمَآءِ اِلَى الْاَرْضِ ثُمَّ يَعْرُجُ اِلَيْهِ فِيْ

a Day, the space whereof will be (as) a thousand years of your reckoning.

6. Such is He, the Knower of all things, hidden and open, the Exalted (in power), the Merciful;-

7. He Who has made every-thing which He has created most good: He began the creation of man with (nothing more than) clay,

8. And made his progeny from a quintessence of the nature of a fluid despised:

9. But He fashioned him in due proportion, and breathed into him something of His spirit. And He gave you (the faculties of) hearing and sight and feeling (and understanding): little thanks do you give!

10. And they say: "What! when we lie, hidden and lost, in the earth, shall we indeed be in a Creation renewed? Nay, they deny the Meeting with their Lord.

11. Say: "The Angel of Death, put in charge of you, will (duly) take your souls: then you shall be brought back to your Lord."

12. If only you could see when the guilty ones will bend low their heads before their Lord, (saying:) "Our Lord! We have seen and we have heard: now then send us back (to the world): we will work righteousness: for we do indeed (now) believe."

13. If We had so willed, We could certainly have brought every soul its true guidance: but the Word from Me will come true, "I will fill Hell with Jinns and men all together."

14. "Then you taste - for you forgot the Meeting of this Day

of yours, and We too will forget you - you taste the Penalty of Eternity for your (evil) deeds!"

15. Only those believe in Our Signs, who, when these are recited to them, fall down in adoration, and celebrate the praises of their Lord, nor are they (ever) puffed up with pride.

16. Their limbs do forsake their beds of sleep, the while they call on their Lord, in Fear and Hope: and they spend (in charity) out of the sustenance which We have bestowed on them.

17. Now no person knows what delights of the eye are kept hidden (in reserve) for them - as a reward for their (good) deeds.

18. Is then the man who believes no better than the man who is rebellious and wicked? Not equal are they.

19. For those who believe and do righteous deeds are Gardens as hospitable homes, for their (good) deeds.

20. As to those who are rebellious and wicked, their abode will be the Fire: every time they wish to get away therefrom, they will be forced back thereinto, and it will be said to them: "You taste the Penalty of the Fire, the which you were wont to reject as false."

21. And indeed We will make them taste of the Penalty of this (life) prior to the supreme Penalty, in order that they may (repent and) return.

22. And who does more wrong than one to whom are recited the Signs of his Lord, and who then turns away therefrom? Verily from those

هٰذَا إِنَّا نَسِينٰكُمْ وَذُوقُوا عَذَابَ

الْخُلْدِ بِمَا كُنْتُمْ تَعْمَلُوْنَ ۞

إِنَّمَا يُؤْمِنُ بِاٰيٰتِنَا الَّذِيْنَ إِذَا

ذُكِّرُوْا بِهَا خَرُّوْا سُجَّدًا وَّسَبَّحُوْا

بِحَمْدِ رَبِّهِمْ وَهُمْ لَا يَسْتَكْبِرُوْنَ ۩

تَتَجَافٰى جُنُوْبُهُمْ عَنِ الْمَضَاجِعِ

يَدْعُوْنَ رَبَّهُمْ خَوْفًا وَّطَمَعًا ۫ وَّمِمَّا

رَزَقْنٰهُمْ يُنْفِقُوْنَ ۞

فَلَا تَعْلَمُ نَفْسٌ مَّا أُخْفِيَ لَهُمْ

مِّنْ قُرَّةِ أَعْيُنٍ ۚ جَزَآءًۢ بِمَا

كَانُوْا يَعْمَلُوْنَ ۞

أَفَمَنْ كَانَ مُؤْمِنًا كَمَنْ كَانَ

فَاسِقًا ۚ لَا يَسْتَوٗنَ ۞

أَمَّا الَّذِيْنَ اٰمَنُوْا وَعَمِلُوا الصّٰلِحٰتِ

فَلَهُمْ جَنّٰتُ الْمَاْوٰى ۫ نُزُلًۢا بِمَا

كَانُوْا يَعْمَلُوْنَ ۞

وَأَمَّا الَّذِيْنَ فَسَقُوْا فَمَاْوٰىهُمُ

النَّارُ ۚ كُلَّمَآ أَرَادُوْا أَنْ يَّخْرُجُوْا

مِنْهَا أُعِيْدُوْا فِيْهَا وَقِيْلَ لَهُمْ

ذُوْقُوْا عَذَابَ النَّارِ الَّذِيْ كُنْتُمْ

بِهٖ تُكَذِّبُوْنَ ۞

وَلَنُذِيْقَنَّهُمْ مِّنَ الْعَذَابِ

الْأَدْنٰى دُوْنَ الْعَذَابِ الْأَكْبَرِ

لَعَلَّهُمْ يَرْجِعُوْنَ ۞

وَمَنْ أَظْلَمُ مِمَّنْ ذُكِّرَ بِاٰيٰتِ

رَبِّهٖ ثُمَّ أَعْرَضَ عَنْهَا ۚ إِنَّا مِنَ

SÛRAH-33
AL-AḤZÂB
(INTRODUCTION)

The series of mystic Sûras beginning with S. 26 having been closed with the last Sûrah, we now come back to the hard facts of this life. Two questions are mainly considered there, viz. (1) the attempt by violence and brute force to crush the truth, and (2) the attempt, by slander or unseemly conduct, to poison the relations of women with men.

As regards the first, the story of the Aḥzâb or Confederates, who tried to surround and annihilate the Muslim community in Madinah, is full of underhand intrigues on the part of such diverse enemies as the Pagan Quraish, the Jews (Banû Nadhîr) who had been already expelled from Madinah for their treachery, the Gatafân tribe of Bedouin Arabs from the interior, and the Jewish tribe Band Quraiẓa in Madinah. This was the unholy Confederacy against Islam. But though they caused a great deal of anxiety and suffering to the beleaguered Muslims, Islam came triumphantly out of the trial and got more firmly established than ever.

The Quraish in Makkah had tried all sorts of persecution, boycott, insult, and bodily injuries to the Muslims, leading to their partial *hijrat* to Abyssinia and their Hijrat as a body to Madinah. The first armed conflict between them and the Muslims took place at Badr in Ramadhân A.H. 2, when the Quraish were signally defeated. Next year (Shawwal A.H. 3) they came to take revenge on Madinah. The battle was fought at Uhud, and though the Muslims suffered severely, Madinah was saved and the Makkans had to return to Makkah with their object frustrated. Then they began to make a network of intrigues and alliances, and besieged Madinah with a force of 10,000 men in Shawwal and Zul-qaʻd A.H. 5. This is the siege of the Confederates referred to in 33: 9-27, which lasted over two weeks: some accounts give 27 days. It caused much suffering, from hunger, cold, an unceasing shower of arrows, and constant general or concentrated assaults. But it ended in the discomfiture of the Confederates, and established Islam firmer than ever. It was a well organized and formidable attack, but the Muslims had made preparations to meet it. One of the preparations, which took the enemy by surprise, was the Trench *(Khandaq)* dug round Madinah by the Prophet's order and under the supervision of Salman the Persian. The siege and battle are therefore known as the Battle of the Trench or the Battle of the Confederates.

As regards the position and dignity of the ladies of the Prophet's Household and the Muslim women generally, salutary principles are laid down to safeguard their honour and protect them from slander and insult. The ladies of the Household interested themselves in social work and work of instruction for the Muslim women, and Muslim women were being trained more and more in community service. Two of them (the two Zainabs) devoted themselves to the poor. The nursing of the wounded on or by the battlefield was specially necessary in those days of warfare. The Prophet's daughter Fatima, then aged about 19 to 20, lovingly nursed her father's wounds at Uḥud (A.H. 3); Rufaida nursed Saʻd ibn Muâ'z's wounds at the Siege of Madinah by the Confederates (A.H. 5) and in the Khaibar expedition (A.H. 7) Muslim women went out from Madinah for nursing service.

A portion of this Sûrah sums up the lessons of the Battle of the Trench and must have been revealed sometime after that Battle (Shawwâl A.H. 5). The marriage with Zainab referred to in verse 37 also took place in the same year. Some portions (e.g. verse 27) were probably revealed in A.H. 7 after the Khaibar settlement.

who transgress We shall exact (due) Retribution.

23. We did indeed before this give the Book to Moses: be not then in doubt of its reaching (you): and We made it a guide to the Children of Israel.

24. And We appointed from among them, leaders, giving guidance under Our command, so long as they persevered with patience and continued to have faith in Our Signs.

25. Verily your Lord will judge between them on the Day of Judgment, in the matters wherein they differ (among themselves).

26. Does it not teach them a lesson, how many generations We destroyed before them, in whose dwellings they (now) go to and fro? Verily in that are Signs: do they not then listen?

27. And do they not see that We do drive rain to parched soil (bare of herbage), and produce therewith crops, providing food for their cattle and themselves? Have they not the vision?

28. They say: "When will this Decision be, if you are telling the truth?"

29. Say: "On the Day of Decision, no profit will it be to Unbelievers if they (then) believe! nor will they be granted a respite."

30. So turn away from them, and wait: they too are waiting.

33. The Confederates
In the name of Allah. Most Gracious, Most Merciful.

1. O Prophet! Fear Allah, and do not hearken to the

Unbelievers and the Hypocrites: verily Allah is full of Knowledge and Wisdom.

2. But follow that which comes to you by inspiration from your Lord: for Allah is well acquainted with (all) that you do.

3. And put your trust in Allah, and enough is Allah as a Disposer of affairs.

4. Allah has not made for any man two hearts in his (one) body: nor has He made your wives whom you divorce by Zihar your mothers: nor has He made your adopted sons your sons. Such is (only) your (manner of) speech by your mouths. But Allah tells (you) the Truth, and He shows the (right) Way.

5. Call them by (the names of) their fathers: that is juster in the sight of Allah. But if you do not know their father's (names, call them) your Brothers in faith, or your *Maulas*. But there is no blame on you if you make a mistake therein: (what counts is) the intention of your hearts: and Allah is Oft-Returning, Most Merciful.

6. The Prophet is closer to the Believers than their own selves, and his wives are their mothers. Blood-relations among each other have closer personal ties, in the Decree of Allah than (the Brotherhood of) Believers and *Muhajirs*: nevertheless you do what is just to your closest friends: such is the writing in the Decree (of Allah).

7. And remember We took from the prophets their Covenant:

as (We did) from you: from Noah, Abraham, Moses, and Jesus the son of Mary: We took from them a solemn Covenant:

وَمِنْكَ وَمِنْ نُّوحٍ وَّاِبْرٰهِيْمَ وَمُوْسٰى وَعِيْسَى ابْنِ مَرْيَمَ ۖ وَاَخَذْنَا مِنْهُمْ مِّيْثَاقًا غَلِيْظًا ۙ

8. So that (Allah) may question the (custodians) of Truth concerning the Truth they (were charged with): and He has prepared for the Unbelievers a grievous Penalty.

لِّيَسْئَلَ الصّٰدِقِيْنَ عَنْ صِدْقِهِمْ ۚ وَاَعَدَّ لِلْكٰفِرِيْنَ عَذَابًا اَلِيْمًا ۟

9. O you who believe! Remember the Grace of Allah, (bestowed) on you, when there came down on you hosts (to overwhelm you): but We sent against them a hurricane and forces that you did not see: but Allah sees (clearly) all that you do.

يٰٓاَيُّهَا الَّذِيْنَ اٰمَنُوا اذْكُرُوْا نِعْمَةَ اللّٰهِ عَلَيْكُمْ اِذْ جَآءَتْكُمْ جُنُوْدٌ فَاَرْسَلْنَا عَلَيْهِمْ رِيْحًا وَّجُنُوْدًا لَّمْ تَرَوْهَا ۚ وَكَانَ اللّٰهُ بِمَا تَعْمَلُوْنَ بَصِيْرًا ۟

10. Behold! They came on you from above you and from below you, and behold, the eyes became dim and the hearts gaped up to the throats, and you imagined various (vain) thoughts about Allah!

اِذْ جَآءُوْكُمْ مِّنْ فَوْقِكُمْ وَمِنْ اَسْفَلَ مِنْكُمْ وَاِذْ زَاغَتِ الْاَبْصَارُ وَبَلَغَتِ الْقُلُوْبُ الْحَنَاجِرَ وَتَظُنُّوْنَ بِاللّٰهِ الظُّنُوْنَا ۟

11. In that situation were the Believers tried: they were shaken as by a tremendous shaking.

هُنَالِكَ ابْتُلِيَ الْمُؤْمِنُوْنَ وَزُلْزِلُوْا زِلْزَالًا شَدِيْدًا ۟

12. And behold! The Hypocrites and those in whose hearts is a disease (even) say: "Allah and His Messenger promised us nothing but delusions."

وَاِذْ يَقُوْلُ الْمُنٰفِقُوْنَ وَالَّذِيْنَ فِيْ قُلُوْبِهِمْ مَّرَضٌ مَّا وَعَدَنَا اللّٰهُ وَرَسُوْلُهٗٓ اِلَّا غُرُوْرًا ۟

13. Behold! A party among them said: "You men of Yathrib! you cannot stand (the attack)! therefore go back!" And a band of them ask for leave of the Prophet, saying, "Truly our houses are bare and exposed," though they were not exposed: they intended nothing but to run away.

وَاِذْ قَالَتْ طَّآئِفَةٌ مِّنْهُمْ يٰٓاَهْلَ يَثْرِبَ لَا مُقَامَ لَكُمْ فَارْجِعُوْا ۚ وَيَسْتَأْذِنُ فَرِيْقٌ مِّنْهُمُ النَّبِيَّ يَقُوْلُوْنَ اِنَّ بُيُوْتَنَا عَوْرَةٌ ۛ وَمَا هِيَ بِعَوْرَةٍ ۛ اِنْ يُّرِيْدُوْنَ اِلَّا فِرَارًا ۟

14. And if an entry had been effected to them from the sides of the (City), and they had been incited to sedition, they would certainly have brought it

وَلَوْ دُخِلَتْ عَلَيْهِمْ مِّنْ اَقْطَارِهَا ثُمَّ سُئِلُوا الْفِتْنَةَ لَاٰتَوْهَا وَمَا

to pass, with none but a brief delay!

15. And yet they had already covenanted with Allah not to turn their backs, and a covenant with Allah must (surely) be answered for.

16. Say: "Running away will not profit you if you are running away from death or slaughter; and even if (you do escape), no more than a brief (respite) will you be allowed to enjoy!"

17. Say: "Who is it that can screen you from Allah if it be His wish to give you punishment or to give you Mercy?" Nor will they find for themselves, besides Allah, any protector or helper.

18. Verily Allah knows those among you who keep back (men) and those who say to their brethren, "Come along to us", but come not to the fight except for just a little while.

19. Covetous over you. Then when fear comes, you will see them looking to you, their eyes revolving, like (those of) one over whom death hovers: but when the fear is past, they will smite you with sharp tongues, covetous of goods. Such men have no faith, and so Allah has made their deeds of none effect: and that is easy for Allah.

20. They think that the Confederates have not withdrawn; and if the Confederates should come (again), they would wish they were in the deserts (wandering) among the Bedouins, and seeking news about you (from a safe distance); and if they were in your midst,

they would fight but little.

21.   You have indeed in the Messenger of Allah a beautiful pattern (of conduct) for any one whose hope is in Allah and the Final Day, and who engages much in the Praise of Allah.

22.   When the Believers saw the Confederate forces, they said: "This is what Allah and His Messenger had promised us, and Allah and His Messenger told us what was true." And it only added to their faith and their zeal in obedience.

23.   Among the Believers are men who have been true to their covenant with Allah: of them some have completed their vow (to the extreme), and some (still) wait: but they have never changed (their determination) in the least:

24.   That Allah may reward the men of Truth for their Truth, and punish the Hypocrites if that be His Will, or turn to them in Mercy: for Allah is Oft-Forgiving, Most Merciful.

25.   And Allah turned back the Unbelievers for (all) their fury, no advantage did they gain; and enough is Allah for the Believers in their fight. And Allah is full of Strength, Able to enforce His Will.

26.   And those of the People of the Book who aided them- Allah took them down from their strongholds and cast terror into their hearts, (so that) some you slew, and some you made prisoners.

27.   And He made you heirs of their lands, their houses, and their goods, and of a land which you had not frequented (before). And Allah has power over all things.

28. O Prophet! Say to your Consorts:"If it be that you desire the life of this World, and its glitter,- then come! I will provide for your enjoyment and set you free in a handsome manner.

29. But if you seek Allah and His Apostle, and the Home of the Hereafter, verily Allah has prepared for the well-doers amongst you a great reward.

30. O Consorts of the Prophet! If any of you were guilty of evident unseemly conduct, the Punishment would be doubled to her, and that is easy for Allah.

31. But any of you that is devout in the service of Allah and His Apostle, and works righteousness,- to her shall We grant her reward twice: and We have prepared for her a generous Sustenance.

32. O Consorts of the Prophet! You are not like any of the (other) women: if you do fear (Allah), be not too complaisant of speech, lest one in whose heart is a disease should be moved with desire: but you speak a speech (that is) just.

33. And stay quietly in your houses, and make not a dazzling display, like that of the former Times of Ignorance; and establish regular Prayer, and give regular Charity; and obey Allah and His Apostle. And Allah only wishes to remove all abomination from you, you members of the Family, and to make you pure and spotless.

34. And recite what is rehearsed to you in your homes, of the Signs of Allah and His Wisdom: for Allah

understands the finest mysteries and is well-acquainted (with them).

35. For Muslim men and women, - for believing men and women, for devout men and women, for true men and women, for men and women who are patient and constant, for men and women who humble themselves, for men and women who give in Charity, for men and women who fast (and deny themselves), for men and women who guard their chastity, and for men and women who engage much in Allah's praise, - for them Allah has prepared forgiveness and great reward.

36. It is not fitting for a Believer, man or woman, when a matter has been decided by Allah and His Apostle, to have any option about their decision: if any one disobeys Allah and His Apostle, he is indeed on a clearly wrong Path.

37. Behold! You said to one who had received the grace of Allah and your favour: "You retain (in wedlock) your wife, and fear Allah." But you hid in your heart that which Allah was about to make manifest: you feared the people, but it is more fitting that you should fear Allah. Then when Zaid had dissolved (his marriage) with her, with the necessary (formality), We joined her in marriage to you: in order that (in future) there may be no difficulty to the Believers in (the matter of) marriage with the wives of their adopted sons, when the latter have dissolved with the necessary (formality) (their marriage) with them. And Allah's command must be fulfilled.

38. There can be no difficulty to the Prophet in what Allah has indicated to him as a duty. It was the practice (approved) of Allah amongst

كَانَ لَطِيْفًا خَبِيْرًا ۟

اِنَّ الْمُسْلِمِيْنَ وَالْمُسْلِمٰتِ وَالْمُؤْمِنِيْنَ

وَالْمُؤْمِنٰتِ وَالْقٰنِتِيْنَ وَالْقٰنِتٰتِ

وَالصّٰدِقِيْنَ وَالصّٰدِقٰتِ وَالصّٰبِرِيْنَ

وَالصّٰبِرٰتِ وَالْخٰشِعِيْنَ وَالْخٰشِعٰتِ

وَالْمُتَصَدِّقِيْنَ وَ الْمُتَصَدِّقٰتِ

وَالصَّآئِمِيْنَ وَالصّٰٓئِمٰتِ وَالْحٰفِظِيْنَ

فُرُوْجَهُمْ وَالْحٰفِظٰتِ وَالذّٰكِرِيْنَ اللّٰهَ

كَثِيْرًا وَّالذّٰكِرٰتِ ۙ اَعَدَّ اللّٰهُ لَهُمْ

مَّغْفِرَةً وَّاَجْرًا عَظِيْمًا ۟

وَمَا كَانَ لِمُؤْمِنٍ وَّلَا مُؤْمِنَةٍ اِذَا

قَضَى اللّٰهُ وَرَسُوْلُهٗٓ اَمْرًا اَنْ يَّكُوْنَ

لَهُمُ الْخِيَرَةُ مِنْ اَمْرِهِمْ ۗ وَمَنْ

يَّعْصِ اللّٰهَ وَرَسُوْلَهٗ فَقَدْ ضَلَّ

ضَلٰلًا مُّبِيْنًا ۟

وَاِذْ تَقُوْلُ لِلَّذِيْٓ اَنْعَمَ اللّٰهُ عَلَيْهِ

وَاَنْعَمْتَ عَلَيْهِ اَمْسِكْ عَلَيْكَ

زَوْجَكَ وَاتَّقِ اللّٰهَ وَتُخْفِيْ فِيْ نَفْسِكَ

مَا اللّٰهُ مُبْدِيْهِ وَتَخْشَى النَّاسَ ۚ

وَاللّٰهُ اَحَقُّ اَنْ تَخْشٰهُ ۗ فَلَمَّا قَضٰى

زَيْدٌ مِّنْهَا وَطَرًا زَوَّجْنٰكَهَا لِكَيْ

لَا يَكُوْنَ عَلَى الْمُؤْمِنِيْنَ حَرَجٌ فِيْٓ

اَزْوَاجِ اَدْعِيَآئِهِمْ اِذَا قَضَوْا مِنْهُنَّ

وَطَرًا ۗ وَكَانَ اَمْرُ اللّٰهِ مَفْعُوْلًا ۟

مَا كَانَ عَلَى النَّبِيِّ مِنْ حَرَجٍ فِيْمَا

فَرَضَ اللّٰهُ لَهٗ ۗ سُنَّةَ اللّٰهِ فِى

those of old that have passed away. And the command of Allah is a decree determined.

الَّذِينَ خَلَوْا مِنْ قَبْلُ ۚ وَكَانَ أَمْرُ اللّٰهِ قَدَرًا مَّقْدُوْرًا ۞

39. (It is the practice of those) who preach the Messages of Allah, and fear Him, and fear none but Allah. And enough is Allah to call (men) to account.

الَّذِينَ يُبَلِّغُوْنَ رِسٰلٰتِ اللّٰهِ وَ يَخْشَوْنَهٗ وَلَا يَخْشَوْنَ أَحَدًا إِلَّا اللّٰهَ ۗ وَكَفٰى بِاللّٰهِ حَسِيْبًا ۞

40. Muhammad is not the father of any of your men, but (he is) the Apostle of Allah, and the Seal of the Prophets: and Allah has full knowledge of all things.

مَا كَانَ مُحَمَّدٌ أَبَا أَحَدٍ مِّنْ رِّجَالِكُمْ وَلٰكِنْ رَّسُوْلَ اللّٰهِ وَخَاتَمَ النَّبِيّٖنَ ۗ وَكَانَ اللّٰهُ بِكُلِّ شَيْءٍ عَلِيْمًا ۞

41. O you who believe! Celebrate the praises of Allah, and do this often;

يٰٓأَيُّهَا الَّذِينَ اٰمَنُوا اذْكُرُوا اللّٰهَ ذِكْرًا كَثِيْرًا ۞

42. And glorify Him morning and evening.

وَّسَبِّحُوْهُ بُكْرَةً وَّأَصِيْلًا ۞

43. He it is Who sends blessings on you, as do His angels, that He may bring you out from the depths of Darkness into Light: and He is Full of Mercy to the Believers.

هُوَ الَّذِي يُصَلِّي عَلَيْكُمْ وَمَلٰٓئِكَتُهٗ لِيُخْرِجَكُمْ مِّنَ الظُّلُمٰتِ إِلَى النُّوْرِ ۚ وَكَانَ بِالْمُؤْمِنِيْنَ رَحِيْمًا ۞

44. Their salutation on the Day they meet Him will be "Peace!"; and He has prepared for them a generous Reward.

تَحِيَّتُهُمْ يَوْمَ يَلْقَوْنَهٗ سَلٰمٌ ۚ وَأَعَدَّ لَهُمْ أَجْرًا كَرِيْمًا ۞

45. O Prophet! Truly We have sent you as a Witness, a Bearer of Glad Tidings, and a Warner,-

يٰٓأَيُّهَا النَّبِيُّ إِنَّا أَرْسَلْنٰكَ شَاهِدًا وَّمُبَشِّرًا وَّنَذِيْرًا ۞

46. And as one who invites to Allah's (Grace) by His leave, and as a Lamp spreading Light.

وَّدَاعِيًا إِلَى اللّٰهِ بِإِذْنِهٖ وَسِرَاجًا مُّنِيْرًا ۞

47. Then give the glad tidings to the Believers, that they shall have from Allah a very great Bounty.

وَبَشِّرِ الْمُؤْمِنِيْنَ بِأَنَّ لَهُمْ مِّنَ اللّٰهِ فَضْلًا كَبِيْرًا ۞

48. And do not obey (the behests) of the Unbelievers and the Hypocrites, and do not heed their annoyances, but put your trust in Allah. For enough is Allah as a Disposer of affairs.

وَلَا تُطِعِ الْكٰفِرِيْنَ وَالْمُنٰفِقِيْنَ وَدَعْ أَذٰىهُمْ وَتَوَكَّلْ عَلَى اللّٰهِ ۚ وَكَفٰى بِاللّٰهِ وَكِيْلًا ۞

49. O you who believe! When you marry

يٰٓأَيُّهَا الَّذِينَ اٰمَنُوا إِذَا نَكَحْتُمُ

believing women, and then divorce them before you have touched them, no period of 'Iddat have you to count in respect of them: so give them a present, and set them free in a handsome manner.

الْمُؤْمِنَٰتِ ثُمَّ طَلَّقْتُمُوهُنَّ مِنْ قَبْلِ أَن تَمَسُّوهُنَّ فَمَا لَكُمْ عَلَيْهِنَّ مِنْ عِدَّةٍ تَعْتَدُّونَهَا فَمَتِّعُوهُنَّ وَسَرِّحُوهُنَّ سَرَاحًا جَمِيلًا ۝

50. O Prophet! We have made lawful to you your wives to whom you have paid their dowers; and those whom your right hand possesses out of the prisoners of war whom Allah has assigned to you; and daughters of your paternal uncles and aunts, and daughters of your maternal uncles and aunts, who migrated (from Makkah) with you; and any believing woman who dedicates her soul to the Prophet if the Prophet wishes to wed her;- this only for you, and not for the Believers (at large); We know what We have appointed for them as to their wives and the captives whom their right hands possess;- in order that there should be no difficulty for you. And Allah is Oft-Forgiving, Most Merciful.

يَٰٓأَيُّهَا النَّبِيُّ إِنَّآ أَحْلَلْنَا لَكَ أَزْوَٰجَكَ الَّٰتِيٓ ءَاتَيْتَ أُجُورَهُنَّ وَمَا مَلَكَتْ يَمِينُكَ مِمَّآ أَفَآءَ اللَّهُ عَلَيْكَ وَبَنَاتِ عَمِّكَ وَبَنَاتِ عَمَّٰتِكَ وَبَنَاتِ خَالِكَ وَبَنَاتِ خَٰلَٰتِكَ الَّٰتِي هَاجَرْنَ مَعَكَ وَامْرَأَةً مُّؤْمِنَةً إِن وَهَبَتْ نَفْسَهَا لِلنَّبِيِّ إِنْ أَرَادَ النَّبِيُّ أَن يَسْتَنكِحَهَا خَالِصَةً لَّكَ مِن دُونِ الْمُؤْمِنِينَ ۗ قَدْ عَلِمْنَا مَا فَرَضْنَا عَلَيْهِمْ فِيٓ أَزْوَٰجِهِمْ وَمَا مَلَكَتْ أَيْمَٰنُهُمْ لِكَيْلَا يَكُونَ عَلَيْكَ حَرَجٌ ۗ وَكَانَ اللَّهُ غَفُورًا رَّحِيمًا ۝

51. You may defer (the turn of) any of them that you please, and you may receive any you please: and there is no blame on you if you invite one whose (turn) you had set aside. This were nearer to the cooling of their eyes, the prevention of their grief, and their satisfaction - that of all of them - with that which you have to give them: and Allah knows (all) that is in your hearts: and Allah is All-Knowing, Most Forbearing.

تُرْجِي مَن تَشَآءُ مِنْهُنَّ وَتُؤْوِيٓ إِلَيْكَ مَن تَشَآءُ ۖ وَمَنِ ابْتَغَيْتَ مِمَّنْ عَزَلْتَ فَلَا جُنَاحَ عَلَيْكَ ۚ ذَٰلِكَ أَدْنَىٰٓ أَن تَقَرَّ أَعْيُنُهُنَّ وَلَا يَحْزَنَّ وَيَرْضَيْنَ بِمَآ ءَاتَيْتَهُنَّ كُلُّهُنَّ ۚ وَاللَّهُ يَعْلَمُ مَا فِي قُلُوبِكُمْ ۚ وَكَانَ اللَّهُ عَلِيمًا حَلِيمًا ۝

52. It is not lawful for you (to marry more) women after this, nor to change them for (other) wives, even though

لَّا يَحِلُّ لَكَ النِّسَآءُ مِنۢ بَعْدُ وَلَآ أَن تَبَدَّلَ بِهِنَّ مِنْ أَزْوَٰجٍ وَلَوْ

their beauty attract you, except any your right hand should possess (as handmaidens): and Allah watches over all things.

53. O you who believe! Do not enter the Prophet's houses,- until leave is given you,- for a meal, (and then) not (so early as) to wait for its preparation: but when you are invited, enter; and when you have taken your meal, disperse, without seeking familiar talk. Such (behaviour) annoys the Prophet: he is ashamed to dismiss you, but Allah is not ashamed (to tell you) the truth. And when you ask (his ladies) for anything you want, ask them from before a screen: that makes for greater purity for your hearts and for theirs. Nor is it right for you that you should annoy Allah's Apostle, or that you should marry his widows after him at any time. Truly such a thing is in Allah's sight an enormity.

54. Whether you reveal anything or conceal it, verily Allah has full knowledge of all things.

55. There is no blame (on these ladies if they appear) before their fathers or their sons, their brothers, or their brother's sons, or their sisters' sons, or their women, or the (slaves) whom their right hands possess. And (ladies), fear Allah; for Allah is Witness to all things.

56. Allah and His angels send blessings on the Prophet: O you that believe! you send blessings on him, and salute him with all respect.

اَعْجَبَكَ حُسْنُهُنَّ اِلَّا مَا مَلَكَتْ يَمِيْنُكَ ۚ وَكَانَ اللّٰهُ عَلٰى كُلِّ شَيْءٍ رَّقِيْبًا ۞

يٰۤاَيُّهَا الَّذِيْنَ اٰمَنُوْا لَا تَدْخُلُوْا بُيُوْتَ النَّبِيِّ اِلَّاۤ اَنْ يُّؤْذَنَ لَكُمْ اِلٰى طَعَامٍ غَيْرَ نٰظِرِيْنَ اِنٰىهُ ۙ وَلٰكِنْ اِذَا دُعِيْتُمْ فَادْخُلُوْا فَاِذَا طَعِمْتُمْ فَانْتَشِرُوْا وَلَا مُسْتَاْنِسِيْنَ لِحَدِيْثٍ ۚ اِنَّ ذٰلِكُمْ كَانَ يُؤْذِى النَّبِيَّ فَيَسْتَحْيٖ مِنْكُمْ ۖ وَاللّٰهُ لَا يَسْتَحْيٖ مِنَ الْحَقِّ ۚ وَاِذَا سَاَلْتُمُوْهُنَّ مَتَاعًا فَسْـَٔلُوْهُنَّ مِنْ وَّرَآءِ حِجَابٍ ۚ ذٰلِكُمْ اَطْهَرُ لِقُلُوْبِكُمْ وَقُلُوْبِهِنَّ ۚ وَمَا كَانَ لَكُمْ اَنْ تُؤْذُوْا رَسُوْلَ اللّٰهِ وَلَاۤ اَنْ تَنْكِحُوْۤا اَزْوَاجَهٗ مِنْۢ بَعْدِهٖۤ اَبَدًا ۚ اِنَّ ذٰلِكُمْ كَانَ عِنْدَ اللّٰهِ عَظِيْمًا ۞

اِنْ تُبْدُوْا شَيْئًا اَوْ تُخْفُوْهُ فَاِنَّ اللّٰهَ كَانَ بِكُلِّ شَيْءٍ عَلِيْمًا ۞

لَا جُنَاحَ عَلَيْهِنَّ فِيْۤ اٰبَآئِهِنَّ وَلَاۤ اَبْنَآئِهِنَّ وَلَاۤ اِخْوَانِهِنَّ وَلَاۤ اَبْنَآءِ اِخْوَانِهِنَّ وَلَاۤ اَبْنَآءِ اَخَوٰتِهِنَّ وَلَا نِسَآئِهِنَّ وَلَا مَا مَلَكَتْ اَيْمَانُهُنَّ ۚ وَاتَّقِيْنَ اللّٰهَ ۚ اِنَّ اللّٰهَ كَانَ عَلٰى كُلِّ شَيْءٍ شَهِيْدًا ۞

اِنَّ اللّٰهَ وَمَلٰٓئِكَتَهٗ يُصَلُّوْنَ عَلَى النَّبِيِّ ۚ يٰۤاَيُّهَا الَّذِيْنَ اٰمَنُوْا صَلُّوْا

57. Those who annoy Allah and His Apostle - Allah has cursed them in this World and in the Hereafter, and has prepared for them a humiliating Punishment.

58. And those who annoy believing men and women undeservedly, bear (on themselves) a calumny and a glaring sin.

59. O Prophet! Tell your wives and daughters, and the believing women, that they should cast their outer garments over their persons (when abroad): that is most convenient, that they should be known (as such) and not molested. And Allah is Oft-Forgiving, Most Merciful.

60. Truly, if the Hypocrites, and those in whose hearts is a disease, and those who stir up sedition in the City, desist not, We shall certainly stir you up against them: then will they not be able to stay in it as your neighbours for any length of time:

61. They shall have a curse on them: wherever they are found, they shall be seized and slain (without mercy).

62. (Such was) the practice (approved) of Allah among those who lived aforetime: no change you will find in the practice (approved) of Allah.

63. Men ask you concerning the Hour: say, "The knowledge thereof is with Allah (alone)": and what will make you understand?- perchance the Hour is near!

64. Verily Allah has cursed the Unbelievers and prepared for them a Blazing Fire.

65. To dwell therein for ever: no protector will they find, nor helper.

عَلَيْهِ وَسَلِّمُوْا تَسْلِيْمًا ۝

اِنَّ الَّذِيْنَ يُؤْذُوْنَ اللّٰهَ وَرَسُوْلَهٗ

لَعَنَهُمُ اللّٰهُ فِى الدُّنْيَا وَالْاٰخِرَةِ

وَاَعَدَّ لَهُمْ عَذَابًا مُّهِيْنًا ۝

وَالَّذِيْنَ يُؤْذُوْنَ الْمُؤْمِنِيْنَ وَالْمُؤْمِنٰتِ

بِغَيْرِ مَا اكْتَسَبُوْا فَقَدِ احْتَمَلُوْا

بُهْتَانًا وَّاِثْمًا مُّبِيْنًا ۝

يٰٓاَيُّهَا النَّبِيُّ قُلْ لِّاَزْوَاجِكَ وَبَنٰتِكَ

وَنِسَآءِ الْمُؤْمِنِيْنَ يُدْنِيْنَ عَلَيْهِنَّ

مِنْ جَلَابِيْبِهِنَّ ۚ ذٰلِكَ اَدْنٰٓى اَنْ

يُّعْرَفْنَ فَلَا يُؤْذَيْنَ ۗ وَكَانَ اللّٰهُ

غَفُوْرًا رَّحِيْمًا ۝

لَئِنْ لَّمْ يَنْتَهِ الْمُنٰفِقُوْنَ وَالَّذِيْنَ

فِيْ قُلُوْبِهِمْ مَّرَضٌ وَّالْمُرْجِفُوْنَ فِى

الْمَدِيْنَةِ لَنُغْرِيَنَّكَ بِهِمْ ثُمَّ لَا

يُجَاوِرُوْنَكَ فِيْهَآ اِلَّا قَلِيْلًا ۝

مَلْعُوْنِيْنَ ۛ اَيْنَمَا ثُقِفُوْٓا اُخِذُوْا

وَقُتِّلُوْا تَقْتِيْلًا ۝

سُنَّةَ اللّٰهِ فِى الَّذِيْنَ خَلَوْا مِنْ قَبْلُ ۚ

وَلَنْ تَجِدَ لِسُنَّةِ اللّٰهِ تَبْدِيْلًا ۝

يَسْـَٔلُكَ النَّاسُ عَنِ السَّاعَةِ ۗ قُلْ اِنَّمَا

عِلْمُهَا عِنْدَ اللّٰهِ ۚ وَمَا يُدْرِيْكَ لَعَلَّ

السَّاعَةَ تَكُوْنُ قَرِيْبًا ۝

اِنَّ اللّٰهَ لَعَنَ الْكٰفِرِيْنَ وَاَعَدَّ لَهُمْ

سَعِيْرًا ۝

خٰلِدِيْنَ فِيْهَآ اَبَدًا ۚ لَا يَجِدُوْنَ وَلِيًّا

SÛRAH-34
SABÂ'
(INTRODUCTION)

Now we begin a series of the Sûras, S. 34 to S. 39, which recapitulate some of the features of the spiritual world. This sûrah leads off with emphasis on Allah's Mercy and Power and Truth. Then (in S. 35) we are told how angles manifest the Power of Allah, and how different is Good from Evil and Truth from Falsehood. S. 34 is devoted to the Holy Prophet and the Qur'ân that came through him. In S. 37 the emphasis is on the snares of the Evil One; in S. 38, on the conquest of evil by wisdom and power as in the case of David and Solomon, and by Patience and Constancy as in the case of Job: and in S. 39 on the Final Judgment, which will sort out Faith from Unfaith and give to each its due.

The chronology has here no significance. This sûrah belongs to the early Makkan period.

66. The Day that their faces will be turned upside down in the Fire, they will say: "Woe to us! would that we had obeyed Allah and obeyed the Apostle!"

67. And they would say: "Our Lord! We obeyed our chiefs and our great ones, and they misled us as to the (right) Path.

68. "Our Lord! Give them double Chastisement and curse them with a very great Curse!"

69. O you who believe! You do not be like those who vexed and insulted Moses, but Allah cleared him of the (calumnies) they had uttered: and he was honourable in Allah's sight.

70. O you who believe! Fear Allah, and (always) say a word directed to the Right:

71. That He may make your conduct whole and sound and forgive you your sins: he that obeys Allah and His Apostle, has already attained the highest Achievement.

72. We did indeed offer the Trust to the Heavens and the Earth and the Mountains; but they refused to undertake it, being afraid thereof: but man undertook it;- he was indeed unjust and foolish;

73. (With the result) that Allah has to punish the Hypocrites, men and women, and the Unbelievers, men and women, and Allah turns in Mercy to the Believers, men and women: for Allah is Oft-Forgiving, Most Merciful.

34. The City of Saba
In the name of Allah. Most Gracious, Most Merciful.

1. Praise be to Allah, to Whom belong all things in the heavens

and on earth: to Him be Praise in the Hereafter: and He is Full of Wisdom, acquainted with all things.

2. He knows all that goes into the earth, and all that comes out thereof; and all that comes down from the sky and all that ascends thereto and He is the Most Merciful, the Oft-Forgiving.

3. The Unbelievers say, "Never to us will come the Hour": Say, "Nay! but most surely, by my Lord, it will come upon you;- by Him Who knows the unseen,- from Whom is not hidden the least little atom in the heavens or on earth: nor is there anything less than that, or greater, but is in the Record Perspicuous.

4. That He may reward those who believe and work deeds of righteousness: for such is Forgiveness and a Sustenance Most Generous."

5. But those who strive against Our Signs, to frustrate them,- for such will be a Chastisement,- a Punishment most humiliating.

6. And those to whom knowledge has come see that the (Revelation) sent down to you from your Lord - that is the Truth, and that it guides to the Path of the Exalted (in Might), Worthy of all praise.

7. The Unbelievers say (in ridicule): "Shall we point out to you a man that will tell you, when you are all scattered to pieces in disintegration, that you shall (then be raised) in a New Creation?

8. "Has he invented a falsehood against Allah, or has a spirit (seized) him?"- nay, it is those who do not believe in the Hereafter, that are in (real) Chastisement, and in farthest error.

9. See they not what is before them and

behind them, of the sky and the earth? If We wished, We could cause the earth to swallow them up, or cause a piece of the sky to fall upon them. Verily in this is a Sign for every devotee that turns to Allah (in repentance).

10. We bestowed Grace afore-time on David from ourselves: "O you Mountains! You sing back the Praises of Allah with him! and you birds (also)! And We made the iron soft for him;-

11. (Commanding), "You make coats of mail, balancing well the rings of chain armour, and you work righteousness; for be sure I see (clearly) all that you do."

12. And to Solomon (We made) the Wind (obedient): its early morning (stride) was a month's (journey), and its evening (stride) was a month's (journey); and We made a Font of molten brass to flow for him; and there were Jinns that worked in front of him, by the leave of his Lord, and if any of them turned aside from Our command, We made him taste of the Chastisement of the Blazing Fire.

13. They worked for him as he desired, (making) Arches, Images, Basins as large as Reservoirs, and (cooking) Caul-drons fixed (in their places): "You work, sons of David, with thanks! but few of My servants are grateful!"

14. Then, when We decreed (Solomon's) death, nothing showed them his death except a little worm of the earth, which kept (slowly) gnawing away at his staff: so when he fell down, the Jinns saw plainly that if they had known the unseen, they would not have tarried in the humiliating Chastisement (of their task).

15. There was, for Saba, aforetime, a Sign in their home-land - two Gardens to the right and to the left. "Eat

خَلْفَهُمْ مِّنَ السَّمَآءِ وَالْاَرْضِ اِنْ نَّشَأْ نَخْسِفْ بِهِمُ الْاَرْضَ اَوْ نُسْقِطْ عَلَيْهِمْ كِسَفًا مِّنَ السَّمَآءِ ط اِنَّ فِيْ ذٰلِكَ لَاٰيَةً لِّكُلِّ عَبْدٍ مُّنِيْبٍ ۞

وَلَقَدْ اٰتَيْنَا دَاوٗدَ مِنَّا فَضْلًا ط يٰجِبَالُ اَوِّبِيْ مَعَهٗ وَالطَّيْرَ ۚ وَاَلَنَّا لَهُ الْحَدِيْدَ ۞

اَنِ اعْمَلْ سٰبِغٰتٍ وَّقَدِّرْ فِي السَّرْدِ وَاعْمَلُوْا صَالِحًا ط اِنِّيْ بِمَا تَعْمَلُوْنَ بَصِيْرٌ ۞

وَلِسُلَيْمٰنَ الرِّيْحَ غُدُوُّهَا شَهْرٌ وَّرَوَاحُهَا شَهْرٌ ۚ وَاَسَلْنَا لَهٗ عَيْنَ الْقِطْرِ ط وَمِنَ الْجِنِّ مَنْ يَّعْمَلُ بَيْنَ يَدَيْهِ بِاِذْنِ رَبِّهٖ ط وَمَنْ يَّزِغْ مِنْهُمْ عَنْ اَمْرِنَا نُذِقْهُ مِنْ عَذَابِ السَّعِيْرِ ۞

يَعْمَلُوْنَ لَهٗ مَا يَشَآءُ مِنْ مَّحَارِيْبَ وَتَمَاثِيْلَ وَجِفَانٍ كَالْجَوَابِ وَقُدُوْرٍ رّٰسِيٰتٍ ط اِعْمَلُوْا اٰلَ دَاوٗدَ شُكْرًا ط وَقَلِيْلٌ مِّنْ عِبَادِيَ الشَّكُوْرُ ۞

فَلَمَّا قَضَيْنَا عَلَيْهِ الْمَوْتَ مَا دَلَّهُمْ عَلٰى مَوْتِهٖ اِلَّا دَآبَّةُ الْاَرْضِ تَأْكُلُ مِنْسَاَتَهٗ ۚ فَلَمَّا خَرَّ تَبَيَّنَتِ الْجِنُّ اَنْ لَّوْ كَانُوْا يَعْلَمُوْنَ الْغَيْبَ مَا لَبِثُوْا فِي الْعَذَابِ الْمُهِيْنِ ۞

لَقَدْ كَانَ لِسَبَاٍ فِيْ مَسْكَنِهِمْ اٰيَةٌ ۚ جَنَّتٰنِ عَنْ يَّمِيْنٍ وَّشِمَالٍ ط كُلُوْا

of the Sustenance (provided) by your Lord, and be grateful to Him: a territory fair and happy, and a Lord Oft-Forgiving!

16. But they turned away (from Allah), and We sent against them the flood (released) from the Dams, and We converted their two garden (rows) into "gardens" producing bitter fruit, and tamarisks, and some few (stunted) Lote-trees.

17. That was the Requital We gave them because they ungratefully rejected Faith: and never do We give (such) requital except to such as are ungrateful rejecters.

18. Between them and the Cities on which We had poured Our blessings, We had placed Cities in prominent positions, and between them We had appointed stages of journey in due proportion: "Travel therein, secure, by night and by day."

19. But they said: "Our Lord! Place longer distances between our journey-stages": but they wronged themselves (therein). At length We made them as a tale (that is told), and We dispersed them all in scattered fragments. Verily in this are Signs for every (soul that is) patiently constant and grateful.

20. And on them Satan proved true his idea, and they followed him, all but a party that believed.

21. But he had no authority over them,- except that We might test the man who believes in the Hereafter from him who is in doubt concerning it: and your Lord watches over all things.

22. Say: "Call upon other (gods) whom you fancy, besides Allah: they have no power,- not the weight of an atom,- in the heavens or on earth: no (sort of) share have they therein, nor is any of them a helper to Allah.

مِنْ رِّزْقِ رَبِّكُمْ وَاشْكُرُوْا لَهُ ۚ بَلْدَةٌ طَيِّبَةٌ وَّرَبٌّ غَفُوْرٌ ۝

فَاَعْرَضُوْا فَاَرْسَلْنَا عَلَيْهِمْ سَيْلَ الْعَرِمِ وَبَدَّلْنٰهُمْ بِجَنَّتَيْهِمْ جَنَّتَيْنِ ذَوَاتَيْ اُكُلٍ خَمْطٍ وَّاَثْلٍ وَّشَيْءٍ مِّنْ سِدْرٍ قَلِيْلٍ ۝

ذٰلِكَ جَزَيْنٰهُمْ بِمَا كَفَرُوْا ۚ وَهَلْ نُجٰزِيْ اِلَّا الْكَفُوْرَ ۝

وَجَعَلْنَا بَيْنَهُمْ وَبَيْنَ الْقُرَى الَّتِيْ بٰرَكْنَا فِيْهَا قُرًى ظَاهِرَةً وَّ قَدَّرْنَا فِيْهَا السَّيْرَ ۚ سِيْرُوْا فِيْهَا لَيَالِيَ وَاَيَّامًا اٰمِنِيْنَ ۝

فَقَالُوْا رَبَّنَا بٰعِدْ بَيْنَ اَسْفَارِنَا وَظَلَمُوْا اَنْفُسَهُمْ فَجَعَلْنٰهُمْ اَحَادِيْثَ وَمَزَّقْنٰهُمْ كُلَّ مُمَزَّقٍ ۚ اِنَّ فِيْ ذٰلِكَ لَاٰيٰتٍ لِّكُلِّ صَبَّارٍ شَكُوْرٍ ۝

وَلَقَدْ صَدَّقَ عَلَيْهِمْ اِبْلِيْسُ ظَنَّهٗ فَاتَّبَعُوْهُ اِلَّا فَرِيْقًا مِّنَ الْمُؤْمِنِيْنَ ۝

وَمَا كَانَ لَهٗ عَلَيْهِمْ مِّنْ سُلْطٰنٍ اِلَّا لِنَعْلَمَ مَنْ يُّؤْمِنُ بِالْاٰخِرَةِ مِمَّنْ هُوَ مِنْهَا فِيْ شَكٍّ ۗ وَرَبُّكَ عَلٰى كُلِّ شَيْءٍ حَفِيْظٌ ۝

قُلِ ادْعُوا الَّذِيْنَ زَعَمْتُمْ مِّنْ دُوْنِ اللهِ ۚ لَا يَمْلِكُوْنَ مِثْقَالَ ذَرَّةٍ فِي السَّمٰوٰتِ وَلَا فِي الْاَرْضِ وَمَا لَهُمْ فِيْهِمَا مِنْ شِرْكٍ وَّمَا لَهٗ مِنْهُمْ

23. "No intercession can avail in His Presence, except for those for whom He has granted permission. So far (is this the case) that, when terror is removed from their hearts (at the Day of Judgment) they will say, 'What is it that your Lord commanded?' They will say, 'That which is true and just; and He is the Most High, Most Great'."

24. Say: "Who gives you sustenance, from the heavens and the earth?" Say: "It is Allah; and certain it is that either we or you are on right guidance or in manifest error!"

25. Say: "You shall not be questioned as to our sins, nor shall we be questioned as to what you do."

26. Say: "Our Lord will gather us together and will in the end decide the matter between us (and you) in truth and justice: and He is the One to decide, the One Who knows all."

27. Say: "Show me those whom you have joined with Him as partners: by no means (can you). Nay, He is Allah, the Exalted in Power, the Wise."

28. We have not sent you but as a universal (Messenger) to men, giving them glad tidings, and warning them (against sin), but most men do not understand.

29. They say: "When will this promise (come to pass) if you are telling the truth?"

30. Say: "The appointment to you is for a Day, which you cannot put back for an hour nor put forward."

31. The Unbelievers say: "We shall neither believe in this scripture nor in (any) that (came) before it." Could you but see when the wrong-doers will be made to stand before their Lord, throwing back the word (of blame) on one another! Those who had been despised will say

مِّن ظَهِيرٍ ۝

وَلَا تَنفَعُ الشَّفَاعَةُ عِندَهُ إِلَّا لِمَنْ اَذِنَ لَهُ ۚ حَتَّىٰ إِذَا فُزِّعَ عَن قُلُوبِهِمْ قَالُوا مَاذَا ۙ قَالَ رَبُّكُمْ ۖ قَالُوا الْحَقَّ ۖ وَهُوَ الْعَلِيُّ الْكَبِيرُ ۝

قُلْ مَن يَرْزُقُكُم مِّنَ السَّمَٰوَٰتِ وَالْأَرْضِ ۖ قُلِ اللَّهُ ۖ وَإِنَّآ أَوْ إِيَّاكُمْ لَعَلَىٰ هُدًى أَوْ فِى ضَلَٰلٍ مُّبِينٍ ۝

قُل لَّا تُسْـَٔلُونَ عَمَّآ أَجْرَمْنَا وَلَا نُسْـَٔلُ عَمَّا تَعْمَلُونَ ۝

قُلْ يَجْمَعُ بَيْنَنَا رَبُّنَا ثُمَّ يَفْتَحُ بَيْنَنَا بِالْحَقِّ ۖ وَهُوَ الْفَتَّاحُ الْعَلِيمُ ۝

قُلْ أَرُونِىَ الَّذِينَ أَلْحَقْتُم بِهِ شُرَكَآءَ ۖ كَلَّا ۚ بَلْ هُوَ اللَّهُ الْعَزِيزُ الْحَكِيمُ ۝

وَمَآ أَرْسَلْنَٰكَ إِلَّا كَآفَّةً لِّلنَّاسِ بَشِيرًا وَنَذِيرًا وَلَٰكِنَّ أَكْثَرَ النَّاسِ لَا يَعْلَمُونَ ۝

وَيَقُولُونَ مَتَىٰ هَٰذَا الْوَعْدُ إِن كُنتُمْ صَٰدِقِينَ ۝

قُل لَّكُم مِّيعَادُ يَوْمٍ لَّا تَسْتَـْٔخِرُونَ عَنْهُ سَاعَةً وَلَا تَسْتَقْدِمُونَ ۝

وَقَالَ الَّذِينَ كَفَرُوا لَن نُّؤْمِنَ بِهَٰذَا الْقُرْءَانِ وَلَا بِالَّذِى بَيْنَ يَدَيْهِ ۗ وَلَوْ تَرَىٰٓ إِذِ الظَّٰلِمُونَ مَوْقُوفُونَ عِندَ رَبِّهِمْ يَرْجِعُ بَعْضُهُمْ إِلَىٰ بَعْضٍ الْقَوْلَ ۚ يَقُولُ الَّذِينَ اسْتُضْعِفُوا

to the arrogant ones: "Had it not been for you, we should certainly have been believers!"

لِلَّذِيْنَ اسْتَكْبَرُوْا لَوْلَا اَنْتُمْ لَكُنَّا مُؤْمِنِيْنَ ۞

32.   The arrogant ones will say to those who had been despised: "Was it we who kept you back from Guidance after it reached you? Nay, rather, it was you who transgressed.

قَالَ الَّذِيْنَ اسْتَكْبَرُوْا لِلَّذِيْنَ اسْتُضْعِفُوْا اَنَحْنُ صَدَدْنٰكُمْ عَنِ الْهُدٰى بَعْدَ اِذْ جَآءَكُمْ بَلْ كُنْتُمْ مُّجْرِمِيْنَ ۞

33.   Those who had been despised will say to the arrogant ones: "Nay! it was a plot (of yours) by day and by night: behold! you (constantly) ordered us to be ungrateful to Allah and to attribute equals to Him!" They will declare (their) repentance when they see the Chastisement: We shall put yokes on the necks of the Unbelievers: it would only be a requital for their (ill) Deeds.

وَقَالَ الَّذِيْنَ اسْتُضْعِفُوْا لِلَّذِيْنَ اسْتَكْبَرُوْا بَلْ مَكْرُ الَّيْلِ وَالنَّهَارِ اِذْ تَاْمُرُوْنَنَا اَنْ نَّكْفُرَ بِاللهِ وَنَجْعَلَ لَهٗٓ اَنْدَادًا ۚ وَاَسَرُّوا النَّدَامَةَ لَمَّا رَاَوُا الْعَذَابَ ۚ وَجَعَلْنَا الْاَغْلٰلَ فِيْ اَعْنَاقِ الَّذِيْنَ كَفَرُوْا ۚ هَلْ يُجْزَوْنَ اِلَّا مَا كَانُوْا يَعْمَلُوْنَ ۞

34.   Never did We send a Warner to a population, but the wealthy ones among them said: "We do not believe in the (Message) with which you have been sent."

وَمَآ اَرْسَلْنَا فِيْ قَرْيَةٍ مِّنْ نَّذِيْرٍ اِلَّا قَالَ مُتْرَفُوْهَآ اِنَّا بِمَآ اُرْسِلْتُمْ بِهٖ كٰفِرُوْنَ ۞

35.   They said: "We have more in wealth and in sons, and we cannot be punished."

وَقَالُوْا نَحْنُ اَكْثَرُ اَمْوَالًا وَّاَوْلَادًا ۙ وَّمَا نَحْنُ بِمُعَذَّبِيْنَ ۞

36.   Say: "Verily my Lord enlarges and restricts the Provision to whom He pleases, but most men do not understand."

قُلْ اِنَّ رَبِّيْ يَبْسُطُ الرِّزْقَ لِمَنْ يَّشَآءُ وَيَقْدِرُ وَلٰكِنَّ اَكْثَرَ النَّاسِ لَا يَعْلَمُوْنَ ۞

37.   It is not your wealth nor your sons, that will bring you nearer to Us in degree: but only those who believe and work righteousness - these are the ones for whom there is a multiplied Reward for their deeds, while secure they (reside) in the dwellings on high!

وَمَآ اَمْوَالُكُمْ وَلَآ اَوْلَادُكُمْ بِالَّتِيْ تُقَرِّبُكُمْ عِنْدَنَا زُلْفٰى اِلَّا مَنْ اٰمَنَ وَعَمِلَ صَالِحًا فَاُولٰٓئِكَ لَهُمْ جَزَآءُ الضِّعْفِ بِمَا عَمِلُوْا وَهُمْ فِي الْغُرُفٰتِ اٰمِنُوْنَ ۞

38. Those who strive against Our Signs, to frustrate them, will be given over into Punishment.

وَالَّذِيْنَ يَسْعَوْنَ فِيْٓ اٰيٰتِنَا مُعٰجِزِيْنَ اُولٰٓئِكَ فِي الْعَذَابِ مُحْضَرُوْنَ ۝

39. Say: "Verily my Lord enlarges and restricts the Sustenance to such of His servants as He pleases: and nothing do you spend in the least (in His Cause) but He replaces it: for He is the Best of those who grant Sustenance.

قُلْ اِنَّ رَبِّيْ يَبْسُطُ الرِّزْقَ لِمَنْ يَّشَاءُ مِنْ عِبَادِهٖ وَيَقْدِرُ لَهٗ ۚ وَمَآ اَنْفَقْتُمْ مِّنْ شَيْءٍ فَهُوَ يُخْلِفُهٗ ۚ وَهُوَ خَيْرُ الرّٰزِقِيْنَ ۝

40. One Day He will gather them all together, and say to the angels, "Were it you that these men used to worship?"

وَيَوْمَ يَحْشُرُهُمْ جَمِيْعًا ثُمَّ يَقُوْلُ لِلْمَلٰٓئِكَةِ اَهٰٓؤُلَاءِ اِيَّاكُمْ كَانُوْا يَعْبُدُوْنَ ۝

41. They will say, "Glory to You! our (tie) is with You - as Protector - not with them. Nay, but they worshipped the Jinns: most of them believed in them."

قَالُوْا سُبْحٰنَكَ اَنْتَ وَلِيُّنَا مِنْ دُوْنِهِمْ ۚ بَلْ كَانُوْا يَعْبُدُوْنَ الْجِنَّ ۚ اَكْثَرُهُمْ بِهِمْ مُّؤْمِنُوْنَ ۝

42. So on that Day no power shall they have over each other, for profit or harm: and We shall say to the wrong-doers, "You taste the Chastisement of the Fire,- the which you were wont to deny!"

فَالْيَوْمَ لَا يَمْلِكُ بَعْضُكُمْ لِبَعْضٍ نَّفْعًا وَّلَا ضَرًّا ۚ وَنَقُوْلُ لِلَّذِيْنَ ظَلَمُوْا ذُوْقُوْا عَذَابَ النَّارِ الَّتِيْ كُنْتُمْ بِهَا تُكَذِّبُوْنَ ۝

43. When Our Clear Signs are rehearsed to them, they say, "This is only a man who wishes to hinder you from the (worship) which your fathers practised." And they say, "This is only a falsehood invented!" And the Unbelievers say of the Truth when it comes to them, "This is nothing but evident magic!"

وَاِذَا تُتْلٰى عَلَيْهِمْ اٰيٰتُنَا بَيِّنٰتٍ قَالُوْا مَا هٰذَآ اِلَّا رَجُلٌ يُّرِيْدُ اَنْ يَّصُدَّكُمْ عَمَّا كَانَ يَعْبُدُ اٰبَاؤُكُمْ ۚ وَقَالُوْا مَا هٰذَآ اِلَّآ اِفْكٌ مُّفْتَرًى ۚ وَقَالَ الَّذِيْنَ كَفَرُوْا لِلْحَقِّ لَمَّا جَاءَهُمْ ۙ اِنْ هٰذَآ اِلَّا سِحْرٌ مُّبِيْنٌ ۝

44. But We had not given them Books which they could study, nor sent Apostles to them before you as Warners.

وَمَآ اٰتَيْنٰهُمْ مِّنْ كُتُبٍ يَّدْرُسُوْنَهَا وَمَآ اَرْسَلْنَآ اِلَيْهِمْ قَبْلَكَ مِنْ نَّذِيْرٍ ۝

45. And their predecessors rejected (the Truth); these have not

وَكَذَّبَ الَّذِيْنَ مِنْ قَبْلِهِمْ ۙ وَمَا

received a tenth of what We had granted to those: yet when they rejected My Apostles, how (terrible) was My rejection (of them)!

بَلَغُوْا مِعْشَارَ مَاۤ اٰتَیْنٰهُمْ فَكَذَّبُوْا رُسُلِیْ ۚ فَكَیْفَ كَانَ نَكِیْرِ ۟

46. Say: "I do admonish you on one point: that you do stand up before Allah,- (It may be) in pairs, or (it may be) singly,- and reflect (within yourselves): your Companion is not possessed: he is no less than a Warner to you, in face of a terrible Chastisement."

قُلْ اِنَّمَاۤ اَعِظُكُمْ بِوَاحِدَةٍ ۚ اَنْ تَقُوْمُوْا لِلّٰهِ مَثْنٰی وَفُرَادٰی ثُمَّ تَتَفَكَّرُوْا ۫ مَا بِصَاحِبِكُمْ مِّنْ جِنَّةٍ ؕ اِنْ هُوَ اِلَّا نَذِیْرٌ لَّكُمْ بَیْنَ یَدَیْ عَذَابٍ شَدِیْدٍ ۟

47. Say: "No reward do I ask of you: it is (all) in your interest: my reward is only due from Allah: and He is Witness to all things."

قُلْ مَا سَاَلْتُكُمْ مِّنْ اَجْرٍ فَهُوَ لَكُمْ ؕ اِنْ اَجْرِیَ اِلَّا عَلَی اللّٰهِ ۚ وَهُوَ عَلٰی كُلِّ شَیْءٍ شَهِیْدٌ ۟

48. Say: "Verily my Lord casts the (mantle of) Truth (over His servants),- He that has full knowledge of (all) that is hidden."

قُلْ اِنَّ رَبِّیْ یَقْذِفُ بِالْحَقِّ ۚ عَلَّامُ الْغُیُوْبِ ۟

49. Say: "The Truth has arrived, and Falsehood neither creates anything new, nor restores anything."

قُلْ جَاۤءَ الْحَقُّ وَمَا یُبْدِئُ الْبَاطِلُ وَمَا یُعِیْدُ ۟

50. Say: "If I am astray, I only stray to the loss of my own soul: but if I receive guidance, it is because of the inspiration of my Lord to me: it is He Who hears all things, and is (ever) near."

قُلْ اِنْ ضَلَلْتُ فَاِنَّمَاۤ اَضِلُّ عَلٰی نَفْسِیْ ۚ وَاِنِ اهْتَدَیْتُ فَبِمَا یُوْحِیْۤ اِلَیَّ رَبِّیْ ؕ اِنَّهٗ سَمِیْعٌ قَرِیْبٌ ۟

51. If you could but see when they will quake with terror; but then there will be no escape (for them), and they will be seized from a position (quite) near.

وَلَوْ تَرٰۤی اِذْ فَزِعُوْا فَلَا فَوْتَ وَاُخِذُوْا مِنْ مَّكَانٍ قَرِیْبٍ ۟

52. And they will say, "We do believe (now) in the (Truth)"; but how could they receive (Faith) from a position (so) far off,-

وَّقَالُوْۤا اٰمَنَّا بِهٖ ۚ وَاَنّٰی لَهُمُ التَّنَاوُشُ مِنْ مَّكَانٍ بَعِیْدٍ ۟

53. Seeing that they did reject Faith (entirely) before, and that they (continually) cast (slanders) on the Unseen from a position far off?

وَّقَدْ كَفَرُوْا بِهٖ مِنْ قَبْلُ ۚ وَیَقْذِفُوْنَ بِالْغَیْبِ مِنْ مَّكَانٍ بَعِیْدٍ ۟

54. And between them and their desires, is placed a barrier, as was done in the past with their partisans: for they were indeed in suspicious (disquieting) doubt.

وَحِیْلَ بَیْنَهُمْ وَبَیْنَ مَا یَشْتَهُوْنَ كَمَا فُعِلَ بِاَشْیَاعِهِمْ مِّنْ قَبْلُ ؕ اِنَّهُمْ كَانُوْا فِیْ شَكٍّ مُّرِیْبٍ ۟

SÛRAH-35
FÂṬIR
(INTRODUCTION)

See Introduction to the last Sûrah.

This Sûrah deals with the mystery of Creation and its maintenance, with various forces typified by the wings of Angels. Whether we look to outer nature or to man, Allah's Grace proclaims His Glory, and protects His votaries from Evil.

It is an early Makkan Sûrah, but its chronology has no significance.

35. The Originator of Creation

In the name of Allah, Most Gracious, Most Merciful.

1. Praise be to Allah, Who created (out of nothing) the heavens and the earth, Who made the angels messengers with wings,- two, or three, or four (pairs): He adds to Creation as He pleases: for Allah has power over all things.

2. What Allah out of His Mercy bestows on mankind there is none can withhold: what He withholds, there is none can grant, apart from Him: and He is the Exalted in Power, full of Wisdom.

3. O men! Call to mind the grace of Allah unto you! Is there a creator, other than Allah, to give you sustenance from heaven or earth? There is no god but He: how then are you deluded away from the Truth?

4. And if they reject you, so were Apostles rejected before you: to Allah go back for decision all affairs.

5. O men! Certainly the promise of Allah is true. Let not then this present life deceive you, nor let the Chief Deceiver deceive you about Allah.

6. Verily Satan is an enemy to you: so treat him as an enemy. He only invites his adherents, that they may become companions of the Blazing Fire.

7. For those who reject Allah, is a terrible Chastisement: but for those who believe and work righteous deeds, is Forgiveness, and a magnificent Reward.

8. Is he, then, to whom the evil of his conduct is made alluring, so that he looks upon it as good, (equal to one who is rightly guided)? For Allah leaves to stray whom He wills, and guides whom He wills. So let not your soul go out in (vainly) sighing after them: for Allah knows well all that they do!

9. It is Allah Who sends forth the Winds, so that they raise up the Clouds, and We drive them to a land that is dead, and revive the earth therewith after its death: even so (will be) the Resurrection!

10. If any do seek for glory and power,- to Allah belong all glory and power. To Him mount up (all) Words of Purity: it is He Who exalts each Deed of Righteousness. Those that lay Plots of Evil,- for them is a terrible penalty; and the plotting of such will be void (of result).

11. And Allah created you from dust; then from a sperm-drop; then He made you in pairs. And no female conceives, or lays down (her load), but with His knowledge. Nor is a man long-lived granted length of days, nor is a part cut off from his life, but is in a Decree (ordained). All this is easy to Allah.

12. Nor are the two bodies of flowing water alike,- the one palatable, sweet, and pleasant to drink, and the other, salt and bitter. Yet from each (kind of water) you eat flesh fresh and tender, and you extract ornaments to wear; and you see the ships therein that plough the waves, that you may seek

اَفَمَنْ زُيِّنَ لَهٗ سُوْٓءُ عَمَلِهٖ فَرَاٰهُ حَسَنًا ۚ فَاِنَّ اللّٰهَ يُضِلُّ مَنْ يَّشَآءُ وَيَهْدِيْ مَنْ يَّشَآءُ ۖ فَلَا تَذْهَبْ نَفْسُكَ عَلَيْهِمْ حَسَرٰتٍ ؕ اِنَّ اللّٰهَ عَلِيْمٌۢ بِمَا يَصْنَعُوْنَ ۟

وَاللّٰهُ الَّذِيْٓ اَرْسَلَ الرِّيٰحَ فَتُثِيْرُ سَحَابًا فَسُقْنٰهُ اِلٰى بَلَدٍ مَّيِّتٍ فَاَحْيَيْنَا بِهِ الْاَرْضَ بَعْدَ مَوْتِهَا ؕ كَذٰلِكَ النُّشُوْرُ ۟

مَنْ كَانَ يُرِيْدُ الْعِزَّةَ فَلِلّٰهِ الْعِزَّةُ جَمِيْعًا ؕ اِلَيْهِ يَصْعَدُ الْكَلِمُ الطَّيِّبُ وَالْعَمَلُ الصَّالِحُ يَرْفَعُهٗ ؕ وَالَّذِيْنَ يَمْكُرُوْنَ السَّيِّاٰتِ لَهُمْ عَذَابٌ شَدِيْدٌ ؕ وَمَكْرُ اُولٰٓئِكَ هُوَ يَبُوْرُ ۟

وَاللّٰهُ خَلَقَكُمْ مِّنْ تُرَابٍ ثُمَّ مِنْ نُّطْفَةٍ ثُمَّ جَعَلَكُمْ اَزْوَاجًا ؕ وَمَا تَحْمِلُ مِنْ اُنْثٰى وَلَا تَضَعُ اِلَّا بِعِلْمِهٖ ؕ وَمَا يُعَمَّرُ مِنْ مُّعَمَّرٍ وَّلَا يُنْقَصُ مِنْ عُمُرِهٖٓ اِلَّا فِيْ كِتٰبٍ ؕ اِنَّ ذٰلِكَ عَلَى اللّٰهِ يَسِيْرٌ ۟

وَمَا يَسْتَوِى الْبَحْرٰنِ ۖ هٰذَا عَذْبٌ فُرَاتٌ سَآئِغٌ شَرَابُهٗ وَهٰذَا مِلْحٌ اُجَاجٌ ؕ وَمِنْ كُلٍّ تَأْكُلُوْنَ لَحْمًا طَرِيًّا وَّتَسْتَخْرِجُوْنَ حِلْيَةً تَلْبَسُوْنَهَا ۚ وَتَرَى الْفُلْكَ فِيْهِ مَوَاخِرَ لِتَبْتَغُوْا

(thus) of the Bounty of Allah that you may be grateful.

13. He merges Night into Day, and He merges Day into Night, and He has subjected the sun and the moon (to His Law): each one runs its course for a term appointed. Such is Allah your Lord: to Him belongs all Dominion. And those whom you invoke besides Him have not the least power.

14. If you invoke them, they will not listen to your call, and if they were to listen, they cannot answer your (prayer). On the Day of Judgment they will reject your "Partnership". And none, (O man!) can tell you (the Truth) like the One Who is acquainted with all things.

15. O you men! It is you that have need of Allah: but Allah is the One Free of all wants, Worthy of all praise.

16. If He so pleased, He could blot you out and bring in a New Creation.

17. Nor is that (at all) difficult for Allah.

18. Nor can a bearer of burdens bear another's burden. If one heavily laden should call another to (bear) his load, not the least portion of it can be carried (by the other), even though he be nearly related. You can but admonish such as fear their Lord unseen and establish regular Prayer. And whoever purifies himself does so for the benefit of his own soul; and the destination (of all) is to Allah.

19. The blind and the seeing are not alike;

20. Nor are the depths of Darkness and the Light;

21. Nor are the (chilly) shade and the (genial) heat of the sun:

22. Nor are alike those that are living and those that are dead. Allah can make any that He wills to hear; but you cannot make those to hear who are (buried) in graves.

23. You are no other than a warner.

24. Verily We have sent you in truth, as a bearer of glad tidings, and as a warner: and there never was a people, without a warner having lived among them (in the past).

25. And if they reject you, so did their predecessors, to whom came their Apostles with Clear Signs, Books of dark prophecies, and the Book of Enlightenment.

26. In the end I punished those who rejected Faith: and how (terrible) was My rejection (of them)!

27. Do you not see that Allah sends down rain from the sky? With it We then bring out produce of various colours. And in the mountains are tracts white and red, of various shades of colour, and black intense in hue.

28. And so amongst men and crawling creatures and cattle, they are of various colours. Those truly fear Allah, among His servants, who have knowledge: for Allah is Exalted in Might, Oft-Forgiving.

29. Those who rehearse the Book of Allah, establish regular Prayer, and spend (in charity) out of what We have provided for them, secretly and openly, hope for a commerce that will never fail:

30. For He will pay them their meed, nay, He will give them (even) more out of His Bounty: for He is Oft-Forgiving, Most Ready to appreciate (service).

31. That which We have revealed to you of the Book

وَمَا يَسْتَوِى الْأَحْيَاءُ وَلَا الْأَمْوَاتُ ۚ إِنَّ اللّٰهَ يُسْمِعُ مَنْ يَشَاءُ ۖ وَمَا أَنْتَ بِمُسْمِعٍ مَّنْ فِى الْقُبُورِ ۝

إِنْ أَنْتَ إِلَّا نَذِيرٌ ۝

إِنَّا أَرْسَلْنٰكَ بِالْحَقِّ بَشِيرًا وَّنَذِيرًا ۚ وَإِنْ مِّنْ أُمَّةٍ إِلَّا خَلَا فِيهَا نَذِيرٌ ۝

وَإِنْ يُّكَذِّبُوكَ فَقَدْ كَذَّبَ الَّذِينَ مِنْ قَبْلِهِمْ ۚ جَاءَتْهُمْ رُسُلُهُمْ بِالْبَيِّنٰتِ وَبِالزُّبُرِ وَبِالْكِتٰبِ الْمُنِيرِ ۝

ثُمَّ أَخَذْتُ الَّذِينَ كَفَرُوا فَكَيْفَ كَانَ نَكِيرِ ۝

أَلَمْ تَرَ أَنَّ اللّٰهَ أَنْزَلَ مِنَ السَّمَاءِ مَاءً ۚ فَأَخْرَجْنَا بِهِ ثَمَرٰتٍ مُّخْتَلِفًا أَلْوَانُهَا ۚ وَمِنَ الْجِبَالِ جُدَدٌ بِيضٌ وَّحُمْرٌ مُّخْتَلِفٌ أَلْوَانُهَا وَغَرَابِيبُ سُودٌ ۝

وَمِنَ النَّاسِ وَالدَّوَابِّ وَالْأَنْعَامِ مُخْتَلِفٌ أَلْوَانُهُ كَذٰلِكَ ۗ إِنَّمَا يَخْشَى اللّٰهَ مِنْ عِبَادِهِ الْعُلَمٰؤُا ۗ إِنَّ اللّٰهَ عَزِيزٌ غَفُورٌ ۝

إِنَّ الَّذِينَ يَتْلُونَ كِتٰبَ اللّٰهِ وَأَقَامُوا الصَّلٰوةَ وَأَنْفَقُوا مِمَّا رَزَقْنٰهُمْ سِرًّا وَّعَلَانِيَةً يَّرْجُونَ تِجَارَةً لَّنْ تَبُورَ ۝

لِيُوَفِّيَهُمْ أُجُورَهُمْ وَيَزِيدَهُمْ مِّنْ فَضْلِهِ ۚ إِنَّهُ غَفُورٌ شَكُورٌ ۝

وَالَّذِى أَوْحَيْنَا إِلَيْكَ مِنَ الْكِتٰبِ

is the Truth,- confirming what was (revealed) before it: for Allah is assuredly- with respect to His servants - well acquainted and fully Observant.

32. Then We have given the Book for inheritance to such of Our Servants as We have chosen: but there are among them some who wrong their own souls; some who follow a middle course; and some who are, by Allah's leave, foremost in good deeds; that is the highest Grace.

33. Gardens of Eternity will they enter: therein they will be adorned with bracelets of gold and pearls; and their garments there will be of silk.

34. And they will say: "Praise be to Allah, Who has removed from us (all) sorrow: for our Lord is indeed Oft-Forgiving ready to appreciate (service):

35. "Who has, out of His Bounty, settled us in a Home that will last: no toil nor sense of weariness shall touch us therein."

36. But those who reject (Allah) - for them will be the Fire of Hell: no term shall be determined for them, so they should die, nor shall its Chastisement be lightened for them. Thus do We reward every ungrateful one!

37. Therein they will cry aloud (for assistance): "Our Lord! Bring us out: we shall work righteousness, not the (deeds) we used to do!" "Did We not give you long enough life so that he that would should receive admonition? And (moreover) the warner came to you. So you taste (the fruits of your deeds): for the wrong-doers there is no helper."

38. Verily Allah knows (all) the hidden things of the heavens and the earth: verily He has full knowledge of all that is in (men's) hearts.

39. He it is that has made you inheritors in the earth: if, then, any do reject (Allah), their rejection (works) against themselves: their rejection but adds to the odium for the Unbelievers in the sight of their Lord: their rejection but adds to (their own) undoing.

40. Say: "Have you seen (these) 'Partners' of yours whom you call upon besides Allah? Show me what it is they have created in the (wide) earth. Or have they a share in the heavens? Or have We given them a Book from which they (can derive) clear (evidence)?- Nay, the wrong-doers promise each other nothing but delusions.

41. It is Allah Who sustains the heavens and the earth, lest they cease (to function): and if they should fail, there is none - not one - can sustain them thereafter: Verily He is Most Forbearing, Oft-Forgiving.

42. They swore their strongest oaths by Allah that if a warner came to them, they would follow his guidance better than any (other) of the Peoples: but when a warner came to them, it has only increased their flight (from righteousness),-

43. On account of their arrogance in the land and their plotting of Evil. But the plotting of Evil will hem in only the authors thereof. Now are they but looking for the way the ancients were dealt with? But no change will you find in Allah's way (of dealing): no turning off will you find in Allah's way (of dealing).

44. Do they not travel through the earth, and see what was the End of those

هُوَ الَّذِيْ جَعَلَكُمْ خَلٰٓئِفَ فِى
الْأَرْضِ ۚ فَمَنْ كَفَرَ فَعَلَيْهِ كُفْرُهٗ ۚ
وَلَا يَزِيْدُ الْكٰفِرِيْنَ كُفْرُهُمْ عِنْدَ
رَبِّهِمْ اِلَّا مَقْتًا ۚ وَلَا يَزِيْدُ الْكٰفِرِيْنَ
كُفْرُهُمْ اِلَّا خَسَارًا ۝

قُلْ اَرَءَيْتُمْ شُرَكَآءَكُمُ الَّذِيْنَ
تَدْعُوْنَ مِنْ دُوْنِ اللّٰهِ ۚ اَرُوْنِيْ مَاذَا
خَلَقُوْا مِنَ الْأَرْضِ اَمْ لَهُمْ شِرْكٌ
فِى السَّمٰوٰتِ ۚ اَمْ اٰتَيْنٰهُمْ كِتٰبًا فَهُمْ
عَلٰى بَيِّنَتٍ مِّنْهُ ۚ بَلْ اِنْ يَّعِدُ
الظّٰلِمُوْنَ بَعْضُهُمْ بَعْضًا اِلَّا غُرُوْرًا ۝

اِنَّ اللّٰهَ يُمْسِكُ السَّمٰوٰتِ وَالْاَرْضَ
اَنْ تَزُوْلَا ۚ وَلَئِنْ زَالَتَا اِنْ اَمْسَكَهُمَا
مِنْ اَحَدٍ مِّنْ بَعْدِهٖ ۚ اِنَّهٗ كَانَ
حَلِيْمًا غَفُوْرًا ۝

وَاَقْسَمُوْا بِاللّٰهِ جَهْدَ اَيْمَانِهِمْ لَئِنْ
جَآءَهُمْ نَذِيْرٌ لَّيَكُوْنُنَّ اَهْدٰى مِنْ
اِحْدَى الْاُمَمِ ۚ فَلَمَّا جَآءَهُمْ نَذِيْرٌ
مَّا زَادَهُمْ اِلَّا نُفُوْرًا ۙ۝

اسْتِكْبَارًا فِى الْاَرْضِ وَمَكْرَ السَّيِّئِ ۚ
وَلَا يَحِيْقُ الْمَكْرُ السَّيِّئُ اِلَّا بِاَهْلِهٖ ۚ
فَهَلْ يَنْظُرُوْنَ اِلَّا سُنَّتَ الْاَوَّلِيْنَ ۚ
فَلَنْ تَجِدَ لِسُنَّتِ اللّٰهِ تَبْدِيْلًا ۚ وَ
لَنْ تَجِدَ لِسُنَّتِ اللّٰهِ تَحْوِيْلًا ۝

اَوَلَمْ يَسِيْرُوْا فِى الْاَرْضِ فَيَنْظُرُوْا
كَيْفَ كَانَ عَاقِبَةُ الَّذِيْنَ مِنْ

SÛRAH-36
YÂ-SÎN
(INTRODUCTION)

See Introduction to S. 34. This particular Sûrah is devoted to the Holy Prophet and the Revelation which he brought. The Abbreviated Letters Yâ-Sîn are usually construed as a title of the Holy Prophet. But it is not permissible to be dogmatic about the meaning of Abbreviated Letters. This Sûrah is considered to be "the heart of the Qur'ân," as it concerns the central figure in the teaching of Islam and central doctrine of Revelation and the Hereafter. As referring to the Hereafter, it is appropriately read in solemn ceremonies after death.

In chronology it belongs to the middle or early Makkan period.

In S. 37:130 (a cognate Sûrah) occurs the word *Il-yâ-sîn*.

before them,- though they were superior to them in strength? Nor is Allah to be frustrated by anything whatever in the heavens or on earth: for He is All-Knowing, All-Powerful.

قَبْلِهِمْ وَكَانُوٓا أَشَدَّ مِنْهُمْ قُوَّةً ۚ

وَمَا كَانَ اللّٰهُ لِيُعْجِزَهُ مِنْ شَيْءٍ فِى

السَّمٰوٰتِ وَلَا فِى الْأَرْضِ ۚ إِنَّهُ كَانَ

عَلِيْمًا قَدِيْرًا ۞

45. If Allah were to punish men according to what they deserve, He would not leave on the back of the (earth) a single living creature: but He gives them respite for a stated Term: when their Term expires, verily Allah has in His sight all His servants.

وَلَوْ يُؤَاخِذُ اللّٰهُ النَّاسَ بِمَا

كَسَبُوْا مَا تَرَكَ عَلَىٰ ظَهْرِهَا مِنْ

دَآبَّةٍ وَّلٰكِنْ يُّؤَخِّرُهُمْ إِلَىٰٓ أَجَلٍ

مُّسَمًّى ۚ فَإِذَا جَآءَ أَجَلُهُمْ فَإِنَّ

اللّٰهَ كَانَ بِعِبَادِهِ بَصِيْرًا ۞

36. Ya-Sin
In the name of Allah. Most Gracious, Most Merciful.

(٣٦) سُوْرَةُ يٓس مَكِّيَّةٌ (٣١)

بِسْمِ اللّٰهِ الرَّحْمٰنِ الرَّحِيْمِ

1.   Ya-Sin.

يٓس ۞

2.   By the Qur'an, full of Wisdom,-

وَالْقُرْآنِ الْحَكِيْمِ ۞

3.   You are indeed one of the Apostles,

إِنَّكَ لَمِنَ الْمُرْسَلِيْنَ ۞

4.   On a Straight Way.

عَلَىٰ صِرَاطٍ مُّسْتَقِيْمٍ ۞

5.   It is a Revelation sent down by (Him), the Exalted in Might, Most Merciful.

تَنْزِيْلَ الْعَزِيْزِ الرَّحِيْمِ ۞

6.   In order that you may admonish a people, whose fathers had received no admonition, and who therefore remain heedless (of the Signs of Allah).

لِتُنْذِرَ قَوْمًا مَّآ أُنْذِرَ اٰبَآؤُهُمْ فَهُمْ

غٰفِلُوْنَ ۞

7.   The Word is proved true against the greater part of them: for they do not believe.

لَقَدْ حَقَّ الْقَوْلُ عَلَىٰٓ أَكْثَرِهِمْ فَهُمْ

لَا يُؤْمِنُوْنَ ۞

8.   We have put yokes round their necks right up to their chins, so that their heads are forced up (and they cannot see).

إِنَّا جَعَلْنَا فِىٓ أَعْنَاقِهِمْ أَغْلٰلًا فَهِىَ

إِلَى الْأَذْقَانِ فَهُمْ مُّقْمَحُوْنَ ۞

9.   And We have put a bar in front of them and a bar behind them, and further, We have covered them up; so that they cannot see.

وَجَعَلْنَا مِنْ بَيْنِ أَيْدِيْهِمْ سَدًّا

وَّمِنْ خَلْفِهِمْ سَدًّا فَأَغْشَيْنٰهُمْ

فَهُمْ لَا يُبْصِرُوْنَ ۞

10.   The same is it to them whether you admonish them or you do not

وَسَوَآءٌ عَلَيْهِمْ ءَأَنْذَرْتَهُمْ أَمْ لَمْ

admonish them: they will not believe.

11. You can but admonish such a one as follows the Message and fears the (Lord) Most Gracious, unseen: give such a one, therefore, good tidings of Forgiveness and a Reward most generous.

12. Verily We shall give life to the dead, and We record that which they send before and that which they leave behind, and of all things have We taken account in a clear Book (of evidence).

13. Set forth to them, by way of a parable, the (story of) the Companions of the City. Behold! there came Apostles to it.

14. When We (first) sent to them two Apostles, they rejected them: but We strengthened them with a third: they said, "Truly, we have been sent on a mission to you."

15. The (people) said: "You are only men like ourselves; and (Allah) Most Gracious sends no sort of revelation: you do nothing but lie."

16. They said: "Our Lord knows that we have been sent on a mission to you:

17. "And our duty is only to proclaim the clear Message."

18. The (people) said: "For us, we augur an evil omen from you: if you do not desist, we will certainly stone you. And a grievous punishment indeed will be inflicted on you by us."

19. They said: "Your evil omens are with yourselves: (you deem this an evil omen), if you are admonished: Nay, but you are a people transgressing all bounds!"

20. Then there came running from the farthest part of the City, a man, saying, "O my people! Obey the Apostles:

21. "Obey those who ask no reward of you (for themselves), and who have themselves received Guidance.

تُنْذِرْهُمْ لَا يُؤْمِنُوْنَ ۝

اِنَّمَا تُنْذِرُ مَنِ اتَّبَعَ الذِّكْرَ وَخَشِيَ الرَّحْمٰنَ بِالْغَيْبِ ۚ فَبَشِّرْهُ بِمَغْفِرَةٍ وَّاَجْرٍ كَرِيْمٍ ۝

اِنَّا نَحْنُ نُحْيِ الْمَوْتٰى وَنَكْتُبُ مَا قَدَّمُوْا وَاٰثَارَهُمْ ۚ وَكُلَّ شَيْءٍ اَحْصَيْنٰهُ فِيْٓ اِمَامٍ مُّبِيْنٍ ۝

وَاضْرِبْ لَهُمْ مَّثَلًا اَصْحٰبَ الْقَرْيَةِ ۘ اِذْ جَآءَهَا الْمُرْسَلُوْنَ ۝

اِذْ اَرْسَلْنَآ اِلَيْهِمُ اثْنَيْنِ فَكَذَّبُوْهُمَا فَعَزَّزْنَا بِثَالِثٍ فَقَالُوْٓا اِنَّآ اِلَيْكُمْ مُّرْسَلُوْنَ ۝

قَالُوْا مَآ اَنْتُمْ اِلَّا بَشَرٌ مِّثْلُنَا ۙ وَمَآ اَنْزَلَ الرَّحْمٰنُ مِنْ شَيْءٍ ۙ اِنْ اَنْتُمْ اِلَّا تَكْذِبُوْنَ ۝

قَالُوْا رَبُّنَا يَعْلَمُ اِنَّآ اِلَيْكُمْ لَمُرْسَلُوْنَ ۝ وَمَا عَلَيْنَآ اِلَّا الْبَلٰغُ الْمُبِيْنُ ۝

قَالُوْٓا اِنَّا تَطَيَّرْنَا بِكُمْ ۚ لَئِنْ لَّمْ تَنْتَهُوْا لَنَرْجُمَنَّكُمْ وَلَيَمَسَّنَّكُمْ مِّنَّا عَذَابٌ اَلِيْمٌ ۝

قَالُوْا طَآئِرُكُمْ مَّعَكُمْ ۚ اَئِنْ ذُكِّرْتُمْ ۚ بَلْ اَنْتُمْ قَوْمٌ مُّسْرِفُوْنَ ۝

وَجَآءَ مِنْ اَقْصَا الْمَدِيْنَةِ رَجُلٌ يَّسْعٰى قَالَ يٰقَوْمِ اتَّبِعُوا الْمُرْسَلِيْنَ ۝

اتَّبِعُوْا مَنْ لَّا يَسْـَٔلُكُمْ اَجْرًا وَّهُمْ مُّهْتَدُوْنَ ۝

22. "It would not be reasonable in me if I did not serve Him Who created me, and to Whom you shall (all) be brought back.

23. "Shall I take (other) gods besides Him? If (Allah) Most Gracious should intend some adversity for me, of no use whatever will be their intercession for me, nor can they deliver me.

24. "I would indeed, if I were to do so, be in manifest Error.

25. "For me, I have faith in the Lord of you (all): listen, then, to me!"

26. It was said: "You enter the Garden." He said: "Ah me! Would that my People knew (what I know)!-

27. "For that my Lord has granted me Forgiveness and has enrolled me among those held in honour!"

28. And We did not send down against his People, after him, any hosts from heaven, nor was it needful for Us so to do.

29. It was no more than a single mighty Blast, and behold! they were (like ashes) quenched and silent.

30. Ah! Alas for (My) servants! There comes not an Apostle to them but they mock him!

31. Don't they see how many generations before them We destroyed? Not to them will they return:

32. But each one of them all - will be brought before Us (for judgment):

33. A Sign for them is the earth that is dead: We do give it life, and produce grain therefrom, of which you do eat.

34. And We produce therein orchards with date-palms and vines, and We cause springs to gush forth therein:

35. That they may enjoy the fruits of this (artistry): it was not

their hands that made this: will they not then give thanks?

36. Glory to Allah, Who created in pairs all things that the earth produces, as well as their own (human) kind and (other) things of which they have no knowledge.

اَيْدِيهِمْ ۖ اَفَلَا يَشْكُرُوْنَ ۝

سُبْحٰنَ الَّذِيْ خَلَقَ الْاَزْوَاجَ كُلَّهَا مِمَّا تُنْۢبِتُ الْاَرْضُ وَمِنْ اَنْفُسِهِمْ وَمِمَّا لَا يَعْلَمُوْنَ ۝

37. And a Sign for them is the Night: We withdraw therefrom the Day, and behold they are plunged in darkness;

وَاٰيَةٌ لَّهُمُ الَّيْلُ ۖ نَسْلَخُ مِنْهُ النَّهَارَ فَاِذَا هُمْ مُّظْلِمُوْنَ ۝

38. And the Sun runs his course for a period determined for him: that is the decree of (Him), the Exalted in Might, the All-Knowing.

وَالشَّمْسُ تَجْرِيْ لِمُسْتَقَرٍّ لَّهَا ۖ ذٰلِكَ تَقْدِيْرُ الْعَزِيْزِ الْعَلِيْمِ ۝

39. And the Moon,- We have measured for her mansions (to traverse) till she returns like the old (and withered) lower part of a date-stalk.

وَالْقَمَرَ قَدَّرْنٰهُ مَنَازِلَ حَتّٰى عَادَ كَالْعُرْجُوْنِ الْقَدِيْمِ ۝

40. It is not permitted to the Sun to catch up the Moon, nor can the Night outstrip the Day: each (just) swims along in (its own) orbit (according to Law).

لَا الشَّمْسُ يَنْۢبَغِيْ لَهَا اَنْ تُدْرِكَ الْقَمَرَ وَلَا الَّيْلُ سَابِقُ النَّهَارِ ۖ وَ كُلٌّ فِيْ فَلَكٍ يَّسْبَحُوْنَ ۝

41. And a Sign for them is that We bore their race (through the Flood) in the loaded Ark;

وَاٰيَةٌ لَّهُمْ اَنَّا حَمَلْنَا ذُرِّيَّتَهُمْ فِي الْفُلْكِ الْمَشْحُوْنِ ۝

42. And We have created for them similar (vessels) on which they ride.

وَخَلَقْنَا لَهُمْ مِّنْ مِّثْلِهٖ مَا يَرْكَبُوْنَ ۝

43. If it were Our Will, We could drown them: then would there be no helper (to hear their cry), nor could they be delivered,

وَاِنْ نَّشَأْ نُغْرِقْهُمْ فَلَا صَرِيْخَ لَهُمْ وَلَا هُمْ يُنْقَذُوْنَ ۝

44. Except by way of Mercy from Us, and by way of (worldly) convenience (to serve them) for a time.

اِلَّا رَحْمَةً مِّنَّا وَمَتَاعًا اِلٰى حِيْنٍ ۝

45. When they are told, "You fear that which is before you and that which will be after you, in order that you may receive Mercy," (they turn back).

وَاِذَا قِيْلَ لَهُمُ اتَّقُوْا مَا بَيْنَ اَيْدِيْكُمْ وَمَا خَلْفَكُمْ لَعَلَّكُمْ تُرْحَمُوْنَ ۝

46. Not a Sign comes to them from among the Signs of their Lord, but they turn away therefrom.

وَمَا تَأْتِيْهِمْ مِّنْ اٰيَةٍ مِّنْ اٰيٰتِ رَبِّهِمْ اِلَّا كَانُوْا عَنْهَا مُعْرِضِيْنَ ۝

47. And when they are told, "You spend of (the bounties) with which Allah has provided you," the Unbelievers say to those who believe:

وَاِذَا قِيْلَ لَهُمْ اَنْفِقُوْا مِمَّا رَزَقَكُمُ اللّٰهُ ۙ قَالَ الَّذِيْنَ كَفَرُوْا لِلَّذِيْنَ اٰمَنُوْا

"Shall we then feed those whom, if Allah had so willed, He would have fed, (Himself)?- you are in nothing but manifest error."

48. Further, they say, "When will this promise (come to pass), if what you say is true?"

49. They will not (have to) wait for anything but a single Blast: it will seize them while they are yet disputing among themselves!

50. No (chance) will they then have, by will, to dispose (of their affairs), nor to return to their own people!

51. The trumpet shall be sounded, when behold! from the sepulchres (men) will rush forth to their Lord!

52. They will say: "Ah! woe unto us! Who has raised us up from our beds of repose?"... (A voice will say:) "This is what (Allah) Most Gracious had promised. And true was the word of the Apostles!"

53. It will be no more than a single Blast, when lo! they will all be brought up before Us!

54. Then, on that Day, not a soul will be wronged in the least, and you shall but be repaid the meeds of your past Deeds.

55. Verily the Companions of the Garden shall that Day have joy in all that they do;

56. They and their associates will be in groves of (cool) shade, reclining on Thrones (of dignity);

57. (Every) fruit (enjoyment) will be there for them; they shall have whatever they call for;

58. "Peace!"-a Word (of salutation) from a Lord, Most Merciful!

59. "And O you in sin! You get apart this Day!

60. "Did I not enjoin on you, O you children of Adam,

that you should not worship Satan; for that he was to you an enemy avowed?-

اَنْ لَّا تَعْبُدُوا الشَّيْطٰنَ ۚ اِنَّهٗ لَكُمْ عَدُوٌّ مُّبِيْنٌ ۚ

61. "And that you should worship Me, (for that) this was the Straight Way?

وَّاَنِ اعْبُدُوْنِيْ ۚ هٰذَا صِرَاطٌ مُّسْتَقِيْمٌ

62. "But he did lead astray a great multitude of you. Did you not, then, understand?

وَلَقَدْ اَضَلَّ مِنْكُمْ جِبِلًّا كَثِيْرًا ۚ اَفَلَمْ تَكُوْنُوْا تَعْقِلُوْنَ

63. "This is the Hell of which you were (repeatedly) warned!

هٰذِهٖ جَهَنَّمُ الَّتِيْ كُنْتُمْ تُوْعَدُوْنَ

64. "You embrace the (fire) this Day, for that you (persistently) rejected (Truth)."

اِصْلَوْهَا الْيَوْمَ بِمَا كُنْتُمْ تَكْفُرُوْنَ

65. That Day We shall set a seal on their mouths. But their hands will speak to Us, and their feet bear witness, to all that they did.

اَلْيَوْمَ نَخْتِمُ عَلٰى اَفْوَاهِهِمْ وَتُكَلِّمُنَا اَيْدِيْهِمْ وَتَشْهَدُ اَرْجُلُهُمْ بِمَا كَانُوْا يَكْسِبُوْنَ

66. If it had been Our Will, We could surely have blotted out their eyes; then should they have run about groping for the Path, but how could they have seen?

وَلَوْ نَشَاءُ لَطَمَسْنَا عَلٰى اَعْيُنِهِمْ فَاسْتَبَقُوا الصِّرَاطَ فَاَنّٰى يُبْصِرُوْنَ

67. And if it had been Our Will, We could have transformed them (to remain) in their places; then they should have been unable to move about, nor could they have returned (after error).

وَلَوْ نَشَاءُ لَمَسَخْنٰهُمْ عَلٰى مَكَانَتِهِمْ فَمَا اسْتَطَاعُوْا مُضِيًّا وَّلَا يَرْجِعُوْنَ

68. If We grant long life to any, We cause him to be reversed in nature: will they not then understand?

وَمَنْ نُّعَمِّرْهُ نُنَكِّسْهُ فِى الْخَلْقِ ۚ اَفَلَا يَعْقِلُوْنَ

69. We have not instructed the (Prophet) in Poetry, nor is it meet for him: this is no less than a Message and a Qur'an making things clear:

وَمَا عَلَّمْنٰهُ الشِّعْرَ وَمَا يَنْۢبَغِيْ لَهٗ ۚ اِنْ هُوَ اِلَّا ذِكْرٌ وَّقُرْاٰنٌ مُّبِيْنٌ

70. That it may give admonition to any (who are) alive, and that the charge may be proved against those who reject (Truth).

لِّيُنْذِرَ مَنْ كَانَ حَيًّا وَّيَحِقَّ الْقَوْلُ عَلَى الْكٰفِرِيْنَ

71. Don't they see that it is We Who have created for them - among the things which Our hands have fashioned - cattle, which are under their dominion?-

اَوَلَمْ يَرَوْا اَنَّا خَلَقْنَا لَهُمْ مِّمَّا عَمِلَتْ اَيْدِيْنَا اَنْعَامًا فَهُمْ لَهَا مٰلِكُوْنَ

72. And that We have subjected them to their (use)? of them some do carry them and some they eat:

وَذَلَّلْنٰهَا لَهُمْ فَمِنْهَا رَكُوْبُهُمْ وَمِنْهَا يَاْكُلُوْنَ

SÛRAH-37
AŞ-ŞÂFFÂT
(INTRODUCTION)

As explained in the Introduction to S. 34, this is the fourth of a series of Sûras in which the mystries of the spiritual world are manifested in different ways, tending to the defeat and final extirpation of Evil. The defeat of Evil is throughout connected with Revelation, and here the ranged fight is illustrated by a reference to the angels in heaven and to the earlier Prophets in our earthly history, from Noah to Jonah. In chronology this Sûrah belongs to the early middle Makkan period.

73. And they have (other) profits from them (besides), and they get (milk) to drink. Will they not then be grateful?

وَلَهُمْ فِيهَا مَنَافِعُ وَمَشَارِبُ ۖ اَفَلَا يَشْكُرُوْنَ ۝

74. Yet they take (for worship) gods other than Allah, (hoping) that they might be helped!

وَاتَّخَذُوْا مِنْ دُوْنِ اللّٰهِ اٰلِهَةً لَّعَلَّهُمْ يُنْصَرُوْنَ ۝

75. They have not the power to help them: but they will be brought up (before Our Judgment-seat) as a troop (to be condemned).

لَا يَسْتَطِيْعُوْنَ نَصْرَهُمْ ۙ وَهُمْ لَهُمْ جُنْدٌ مُّحْضَرُوْنَ ۝

76. Let not their speech, then, grieve you. Verily We know what they hide as well as what they disclose.

فَلَا يَحْزُنْكَ قَوْلُهُمْ ۘ اِنَّا نَعْلَمُ مَا يُسِرُّوْنَ وَمَا يُعْلِنُوْنَ ۝

77. Does not man see that it is We Who created him from sperm? Yet behold! he (stands forth) as an open adversary!

اَوَلَمْ يَرَ الْاِنْسَانُ اَنَّا خَلَقْنٰهُ مِنْ نُّطْفَةٍ فَاِذَا هُوَ خَصِيْمٌ مُّبِيْنٌ ۝

78. And he makes comparisons for Us, and forgets his own (origin and) Creation: he says, "Who can give life to (dry) bones and decomposed ones (at that)?"

وَضَرَبَ لَنَا مَثَلًا وَّنَسِيَ خَلْقَهٗ ۖ قَالَ مَنْ يُّحْيِ الْعِظَامَ وَهِيَ رَمِيْمٌ ۝

79. Say, "He will give them life Who created them for the first time! for He is Well-versed in every kind of creation!-

قُلْ يُحْيِيْهَا الَّذِيْۤ اَنْشَاَهَاۤ اَوَّلَ مَرَّةٍ ۖ وَهُوَ بِكُلِّ خَلْقٍ عَلِيْمُۨ ۝

80. "The same Who produces for you fire out of the green tree, when behold! you kindle therewith (your own fires)!

الَّذِيْ جَعَلَ لَكُمْ مِّنَ الشَّجَرِ الْاَخْضَرِ نَارًا فَاِذَاۤ اَنْتُمْ مِّنْهُ تُوْقِدُوْنَ ۝

81. "Is not He Who created the heavens and the earth able to create the like thereof?" - yes, indeed! for He is the Creator Supreme, of skill and knowledge (infinite)!

اَوَلَيْسَ الَّذِيْ خَلَقَ السَّمٰوٰتِ وَالْاَرْضَ بِقٰدِرٍ عَلٰۤى اَنْ يَّخْلُقَ مِثْلَهُمْ ۚ بَلٰى ۖ وَهُوَ الْخَلّٰقُ الْعَلِيْمُ ۝

82. Verily, when He intends a thing, His Command is, "Be", and it is!

اِنَّمَاۤ اَمْرُهٗۤ اِذَاۤ اَرَادَ شَيْئًا اَنْ يَّقُوْلَ لَهٗ كُنْ فَيَكُوْنُ ۝

83. So glory to Him in Whose hands is the dominion of all things: and to Him will you be all brought back.

فَسُبْحٰنَ الَّذِيْ بِيَدِهٖ مَلَكُوْتُ كُلِّ شَيْءٍ وَّاِلَيْهِ تُرْجَعُوْنَ ۝

37. Those ranged in Ranks
In the name of Allah. Most Gracious, Most Merciful.

(٣٧) سُوْرَةُ الصّٰفّٰتِ مَكِّيَّةٌ (٥٦)

بِسْمِ اللّٰهِ الرَّحْمٰنِ الرَّحِيْمِ

1. By those who range themselves in ranks,

وَالصّٰفّٰتِ صَفًّا ۝

2. And so are strong in repelling (evil),

فَالزّٰجِرٰتِ زَجۡرًا ۙ

3. And thus proclaim the Message (of Allah)!

فَالتّٰلِيٰتِ ذِكۡرًا ۙ

4. Verily, verily, your God (Allah) is One!-

اِنَّ اِلٰهَكُمۡ لَوَاحِدٌ ؕ

5. Lord of the heavens and of the earth and all between them, and Lord of every point at the rising of the sun!

رَبُّ السَّمٰوٰتِ وَالۡاَرۡضِ وَمَا بَيۡنَهُمَا وَرَبُّ الۡمَشَارِقِ ؕ

6. We have indeed decked the lower heaven with beauty (in) the stars,-

اِنَّا زَيَّنَّا السَّمَآءَ الدُّنۡيَا بِزِيۡنَةِ الۡكَوَاكِبِ ۙ

7. (For beauty) and for guard against all obstinate rebellious evil spirits,

وَحِفۡظًا مِّنۡ كُلِّ شَيۡطٰنٍ مَّارِدٍ ۚ

8. (So) they should not strain their ears in the direction of the Exalted Assembly but be cast away from every side,

لَا يَسَّمَّعُوۡنَ اِلَى الۡمَلَاِ الۡاَعۡلٰى وَ يُقۡذَفُوۡنَ مِنۡ كُلِّ جَانِبٍ ۙ

9. Repulsed, for they are under a perpetual Chastisement,

دُحُوۡرًا وَّلَهُمۡ عَذَابٌ وَّاصِبٌ ۙ

10. Except such as snatch away something by stealth, and they are pursued by a flaming Fire, of piercing brightness.

اِلَّا مَنۡ خَطِفَ الۡخَطۡفَةَ فَاَتۡبَعَهُ شِهَابٌ ثَاقِبٌ ۝

11. Just ask their opinion: are they the more difficult to create, or the (other) beings We have created? We have created them out of a sticky clay!

فَاسۡتَفۡتِهِمۡ اَهُمۡ اَشَدُّ خَلۡقًا اَمۡ مَّنۡ خَلَقۡنَا ؕ اِنَّا خَلَقۡنٰهُمۡ مِّنۡ طِيۡنٍ لَّازِبٍ ۝

12. Truly you marvel, while they ridicule,-

بَلۡ عَجِبۡتَ وَيَسۡخَرُوۡنَ ۪

13. And, when they are admonished, pay no heed,-

وَاِذَا ذُكِّرُوۡا لَا يَذۡكُرُوۡنَ ۪

14. And, when they see a Sign, turn it to mockery,-

وَاِذَا رَاَوۡا اٰيَةً يَّسۡتَسۡخِرُوۡنَ ۪

15. And say, "This is nothing but evident sorcery!

وَقَالُوۡا اِنۡ هٰذَآ اِلَّا سِحۡرٌ مُّبِيۡنٌ ۚ

16. "What! when we die, and become dust and bones, shall we (then) be raised up (again)

ءَاِذَا مِتۡنَا وَكُنَّا تُرَابًا وَّعِظَامًا ءَاِنَّا لَمَبۡعُوۡثُوۡنَ ۙ

17. "And also our fathers of old?"

اَوَاٰبَآؤُنَا الۡاَوَّلُوۡنَ ؕ

18. You say: "Yes, and you shall then be humiliated (on account of your evil)."

قُلۡ نَعَمۡ وَاَنۡتُمۡ دَاخِرُوۡنَ ۚ

19. Then it will be a single (compelling) cry; and behold, they will begin to see!

فَاِنَّمَا هِيَ زَجۡرَةٌ وَّاحِدَةٌ فَاِذَا هُمۡ يَنۡظُرُوۡنَ ۝

20. They will say, "Ah! woe to us! this is the Day of Judgment!"

21. (A voice will say,) "This is the Day of Sorting Out, whose Truth you (once) denied!"

22. "Bring you up", it shall be said, "The wrong-doers and their wives, and the things they worshipped-

23. "Besides Allah, and lead them to the Way to the (fierce) Fire.

24. "But stop them, for they must be asked:

25. ""What is the matter with you that you do not help each other?""

26. Nay, but that day they shall submit (to Judgment);

27. And they will turn to one another, and question one another.

28. They will say: "It was you who used to come to us from the right hand (of power and authority)!"

29. They will reply: "Nay, you yourselves had no Faith!

30. "Nor had we any authority over you. Nay, it was you who were a people in obstinate rebellion!

31. "So now has been proved true, against us, the Word of our Lord that we shall indeed (have to) taste (the punishment of our sins).

32. "We led you astray: for truly we were ourselves astray."

33. Truly, that Day, they will (all) share in the Chastisement.

34. Verily that is how We shall deal with sinners.

35. For they, when they were told that there is no god except Allah, would puff themselves up with pride,

36. And say: "What! shall we give up our gods for the sake of a Poet possessed?"

37. Nay! he has come with the (very) Truth, and he confirms (the Message of) the Apostles (before him).

وَقَالُوْا يٰوَيْلَنَا هٰذَا يَوْمُ الدِّيْنِ ۟

هٰذَا يَوْمُ الْفَصْلِ الَّذِيْ كُنْتُمْ بِهٖ تُكَذِّبُوْنَ ۟

اُحْشُرُوا الَّذِيْنَ ظَلَمُوْا وَاَزْوَاجَهُمْ وَمَا كَانُوْا يَعْبُدُوْنَ ۟

مِنْ دُوْنِ اللّٰهِ فَاهْدُوْهُمْ اِلٰى صِرَاطِ الْجَحِيْمِ ۟

وَقِفُوْهُمْ اِنَّهُمْ مَّسْئُوْلُوْنَ ۟

مَا لَكُمْ لَا تَنَاصَرُوْنَ ۟

بَلْ هُمُ الْيَوْمَ مُسْتَسْلِمُوْنَ ۟

وَاَقْبَلَ بَعْضُهُمْ عَلٰى بَعْضٍ يَّتَسَآءَلُوْنَ ۟

قَالُوْا اِنَّكُمْ كُنْتُمْ تَأْتُوْنَنَا عَنِ الْيَمِيْنِ ۟

قَالُوْا بَلْ لَّمْ تَكُوْنُوْا مُؤْمِنِيْنَ ۟

وَمَا كَانَ لَنَا عَلَيْكُمْ مِّنْ سُلْطٰنٍ ۚ بَلْ كُنْتُمْ قَوْمًا طٰغِيْنَ ۟

فَحَقَّ عَلَيْنَا قَوْلُ رَبِّنَا ۖ اِنَّا لَذَآئِقُوْنَ ۟

فَاَغْوَيْنٰكُمْ اِنَّا كُنَّا غٰوِيْنَ ۟

فَاِنَّهُمْ يَوْمَئِذٍ فِى الْعَذَابِ مُشْتَرِكُوْنَ ۟

اِنَّا كَذٰلِكَ نَفْعَلُ بِالْمُجْرِمِيْنَ ۟

اِنَّهُمْ كَانُوْا اِذَا قِيْلَ لَهُمْ لَا اِلٰهَ اِلَّا اللّٰهُ ۙ يَسْتَكْبِرُوْنَ ۟

وَيَقُوْلُوْنَ اَئِنَّا لَتَارِكُوْا اٰلِهَتِنَا لِشَاعِرٍ مَّجْنُوْنٍ ۟

بَلْ جَآءَ بِالْحَقِّ وَصَدَّقَ الْمُرْسَلِيْنَ ۟

38. You shall indeed taste of the grievous Chastisement;-

اِنَّكُمْ لَذَآئِقُوا الْعَذَابِ الْاَلِيْمِ ۚ

39. But it will be no more than the retribution of (the Evil) that you have wrought;-

وَمَا تُجْزَوْنَ اِلَّا مَا كُنْتُمْ تَعْمَلُوْنَ ۙ

40. But the sincere (and devoted) Servants of Allah,-

اِلَّا عِبَادَ اللهِ الْمُخْلَصِيْنَ ۙ

41. For them is a Sustenance determined,

اُولٰٓئِكَ لَهُمْ رِزْقٌ مَّعْلُوْمٌ ۙ

42. Fruits (Delights); and they (shall enjoy) honour and dignity,

فَوَاكِهُ ۚ وَهُمْ مُّكْرَمُوْنَ ۙ

43. In Gardens of Felicity,

فِيْ جَنّٰتِ النَّعِيْمِ ۙ

44. Facing each other on Thrones (of dignity):

عَلٰى سُرُرٍ مُّتَقٰبِلِيْنَ ۙ

45. Round will be passed to them a cup from a clear-flowing fountain,

يُطَافُ عَلَيْهِمْ بِكَأْسٍ مِّنْ مَّعِيْنٍ ۙ

46. Crystal-white, of a taste delicious to those who drink (thereof),

بَيْضَآءَ لَذَّةٍ لِّلشّٰرِبِيْنَ ۚ

47. Free from headiness; nor will they suffer intoxication therefrom.

لَا فِيْهَا غَوْلٌ وَّلَا هُمْ عَنْهَا يُنْزَفُوْنَ ۙ

48. And besides them will be chaste women, restraining their glances, with big eyes (of wonder and beauty)!

وَعِنْدَهُمْ قٰصِرٰتُ الطَّرْفِ عِيْنٌ ۙ

49. As if they were (delicate) eggs closely guarded.

كَاَنَّهُنَّ بَيْضٌ مَّكْنُوْنٌ ۙ

50. Then they will turn to one another and question one another.

فَاَقْبَلَ بَعْضُهُمْ عَلٰى بَعْضٍ يَّتَسَآءَلُوْنَ ۙ

51. One of them will start the talk and say: "I had an intimate companion (on the earth),

قَالَ قَائِلٌ مِّنْهُمْ اِنِّيْ كَانَ لِيْ قَرِيْنٌ ۙ

52. Who used to say, "What! are you among those who bear witness to the truth (of the Message)?"

يَّقُوْلُ اَئِنَّكَ لَمِنَ الْمُصَدِّقِيْنَ ۙ

53. "'When we die and become dust and bones, shall we indeed receive rewards and punishments?'

ءَاِذَا مِتْنَا وَكُنَّا تُرَابًا وَّعِظَامًا ءَاِنَّا لَمَدِيْنُوْنَ ۙ

54. (A voice) said: "Would you like to look down?"

قَالَ هَلْ اَنْتُمْ مُّطَّلِعُوْنَ ۙ

55. He looked down and saw him in the midst of the Fire.

فَاطَّلَعَ فَرَاٰهُ فِيْ سَوَآءِ الْجَحِيْمِ ۙ

56. He said: "By Allah! you were little short of bringing me to perdition!

قَالَ تَاللهِ اِنْ كِدْتَّ لَتُرْدِيْنِ ۙ

57. "Had it not been for the Grace of my Lord, I should certainly have been among those brought (there)!

وَلَوْلَا نِعْمَةُ رَبِّيْ لَكُنْتُ مِنَ الْمُحْضَرِيْنَ ۙ

58. "Is it (the case) that we shall not die,

اَفَمَا نَحْنُ بِمَيِّتِيْنَ ۙ

59. "Except our first death, and that we shall not be punished?"

اِلَّا مَوْتَتَنَا الْاُوْلٰى وَمَا نَحْنُ

60. Verily this is the supreme achievement!

61. For the like of this let all strive, who wish to strive.

62. Is that the better entertainment or the Tree of Zaqqum?

63. For We have truly made it (as) a trial for the wrong-doers.

64. For it is a tree that springs out of the bottom of Hell-fire:

65. The shoots of its fruit-stalks are like the heads of devils:

66. Truly they will eat thereof and fill their bellies therewith.

67. Then on top of that they will be given a mixture made of boiling water.

68. Then their return shall be to the (Blazing) Fire.

69. Truly they found their fathers on the wrong Path;

70. So they (too) were rushed down on their footsteps!

71. And truly before them, many of the ancients went astray;

72. But We sent aforetime, among them, (Apostles) to admonish them;-

73. Then see what was the end of those who were admonished (but heeded not),-

74. Except the sincere (and devoted) Servants of Allah.

75. (In the days of old), Noah cried to Us, and We are the best to hear prayer.

76. And We delivered him and his people from the Great Calamity,

77. And made his progeny to endure (on the earth)

78. And We left (this blessing) for him among generations to come in later times:

79. "Peace and salutation to Noah among the nations!"

80. Thus indeed do We reward those who do right.

اِنَّا كَذٰلِكَ نَجْزِى الْمُحْسِنِيْنَ ۞

81. For he was one of Our believing Servants.

اِنَّهٗ مِنْ عِبَادِنَا الْمُؤْمِنِيْنَ ۞

82. Then the rest We over-whelmed in the Flood.

ثُمَّ اَغْرَقْنَا الْاٰخَرِيْنَ ۞

83. Verily among those who followed his Way was Abraham.

وَاِنَّ مِنْ شِيْعَتِهٖ لَاِبْرٰهِيْمَ ۞

84. Behold! he approached his Lord with a sound heart.

اِذْ جَآءَ رَبَّهٗ بِقَلْبٍ سَلِيْمٍ ۞

85. Behold! he said to his father and to his people, "What is that which you worship?

اِذْ قَالَ لِاَبِيْهِ وَقَوْمِهٖ مَاذَا تَعْبُدُوْنَ ۞

86. "Is it a falsehood - gods other than Allah- that you desire?

اَئِفْكًا اٰلِهَةً دُوْنَ اللّٰهِ تُرِيْدُوْنَ ۞

87. "Then what is your idea about the Lord of the Worlds?"

فَمَا ظَنُّكُمْ بِرَبِّ الْعٰلَمِيْنَ ۞

88. Then did he cast a glance at the Stars.

فَنَظَرَ نَظْرَةً فِى النُّجُوْمِ ۞

89. And he said, "I am indeed sick (at heart)!"

فَقَالَ اِنِّىْ سَقِيْمٌ ۞

90. So they turned away from him, and departed.

فَتَوَلَّوْا عَنْهُ مُدْبِرِيْنَ ۞

91. Then he turned to their gods and said, "Will you not eat (of the offerings before you)?...

فَرَاغَ اِلٰٓى اٰلِهَتِهِمْ فَقَالَ اَلَا تَاْكُلُوْنَ ۞

92. "What is the matter with you that you speak not (intelligently)?"

مَا لَكُمْ لَا تَنْطِقُوْنَ ۞

93. Then he turned upon them, striking (them) with the right hand.

فَرَاغَ عَلَيْهِمْ ضَرْبًا بِالْيَمِيْنِ ۞

94. Then came (the worship-pers) with hurried steps, and faced (him).

فَاَقْبَلُوْا اِلَيْهِ يَزِفُّوْنَ ۞

95. He said: "Do you worship that which you have (yourselves) carved?

قَالَ اَتَعْبُدُوْنَ مَا تَنْحِتُوْنَ ۞

96. "But Allah has created you and your handiwork!"

وَاللّٰهُ خَلَقَكُمْ وَمَا تَعْمَلُوْنَ ۞

97. They said, "Build him a furnace, and throw him into the blazing fire!"

قَالُوا ابْنُوْا لَهٗ بُنْيَانًا فَاَلْقُوْهُ فِى الْجَحِيْمِ ۞

98. (This failing), they then sought a stratagem against him, but We made them the ones most humiliated!

فَاَرَادُوْا بِهٖ كَيْدًا فَجَعَلْنٰهُمُ الْاَسْفَلِيْنَ ۞

99. He said: "I will go to my Lord! He will surely guide me!

وَقَالَ اِنِّىْ ذَاهِبٌ اِلٰى رَبِّىْ سَيَهْدِيْنِ ۞

100. "O my Lord! Grant me a righteous (son)!"

رَبِّ هَبْ لِىْ مِنَ الصّٰلِحِيْنَ ۞

101. So We gave him the good news of a boy ready to suffer and forbear.

فَبَشَّرْنَٰهُ بِغُلَٰمٍ حَلِيمٍ ۞

102. Then, when (the son) reached (the age of) (serious) work with him, he said: "O my son! I see in vision that I offer you in sacrifice: now see what is your view!" (The son) said: "O my father! Do as you are commanded: you will find me, if Allah so wills, one practising patience and constancy!"

فَلَمَّا بَلَغَ مَعَهُ ٱلسَّعْىَ قَالَ يَٰبُنَىَّ إِنِّىٓ أَرَىٰ فِى ٱلْمَنَامِ أَنِّىٓ أَذْبَحُكَ فَٱنظُرْ مَاذَا تَرَىٰ ۚ قَالَ يَٰٓأَبَتِ ٱفْعَلْ مَا تُؤْمَرُ ۖ سَتَجِدُنِىٓ إِن شَآءَ ٱللَّهُ مِنَ ٱلصَّٰبِرِينَ ۞

103. So when they had both submitted their wills (to Allah), and he had laid him prostrate on his forehead (for sacrifice),

فَلَمَّآ أَسْلَمَا وَتَلَّهُۥ لِلْجَبِينِ ۞

104. We called out to him "O Abraham!

وَنَٰدَيْنَٰهُ أَن يَٰٓإِبْرَٰهِيمُ ۞

105. "You have already fulfilled the vision!" - thus indeed do We reward those who do right.

قَدْ صَدَّقْتَ ٱلرُّءْيَآ ۚ إِنَّا كَذَٰلِكَ نَجْزِى ٱلْمُحْسِنِينَ ۞

106. For this was obviously a trial,-

إِنَّ هَٰذَا لَهُوَ ٱلْبَلَٰٓؤُا۟ ٱلْمُبِينُ ۞

107. And We ransomed him with a momentous sacrifice:

وَفَدَيْنَٰهُ بِذِبْحٍ عَظِيمٍ ۞

108. And We left (this blessing) for him among generations (to come) in later times:

وَتَرَكْنَا عَلَيْهِ فِى ٱلْءَاخِرِينَ ۞

109. "Peace and salutation to Abraham!"

سَلَٰمٌ عَلَىٰٓ إِبْرَٰهِيمَ ۞

110. Thus indeed do We reward those who do right.

كَذَٰلِكَ نَجْزِى ٱلْمُحْسِنِينَ ۞

111. For he was one of Our believing Servants.

إِنَّهُۥ مِنْ عِبَادِنَا ٱلْمُؤْمِنِينَ ۞

112. And We gave him the good news of Isaac - a prophet,- one of the Righteous.

وَبَشَّرْنَٰهُ بِإِسْحَٰقَ نَبِيًّا مِّنَ ٱلصَّٰلِحِينَ ۞

113. We blessed him and Isaac: but of their progeny are (some) that do right, and (some) that obviously do wrong, to their own souls.

وَبَٰرَكْنَا عَلَيْهِ وَعَلَىٰٓ إِسْحَٰقَ ۚ وَمِن ذُرِّيَّتِهِمَا مُحْسِنٌ وَظَالِمٌ لِّنَفْسِهِۦ مُبِينٌ ۞

114. Again (of old) We bestowed Our favour on Moses and Aaron,

وَلَقَدْ مَنَنَّا عَلَىٰ مُوسَىٰ وَهَٰرُونَ ۞

115. And We delivered them and their people from (their) Great Calamity;

وَنَجَّيْنَٰهُمَا وَقَوْمَهُمَا مِنَ ٱلْكَرْبِ ٱلْعَظِيمِ ۞

116. And We helped them, so they overcame (their troubles);

وَنَصَرْنَٰهُمْ فَكَانُوا۟ هُمُ ٱلْغَٰلِبِينَ ۞

117. And We gave them the Book which helps to make things clear;

وَءَاتَيْنَٰهُمَا ٱلْكِتَٰبَ ٱلْمُسْتَبِينَ ۞

118. And We guided them to the Straight Way.

وَهَدَيْنَٰهُمَا الصِّرَاطَ الْمُسْتَقِيمَ ۝

119. And We left (this blessing) for them among generations (to come) in later times:

وَتَرَكْنَا عَلَيْهِمَا فِي الْءَاخِرِينَ ۝

120. "Peace and salutation to Moses and Aaron!"

سَلَٰمٌ عَلَىٰ مُوسَىٰ وَهَٰرُونَ ۝

121. Thus indeed do We reward those who do right.

إِنَّا كَذَٰلِكَ نَجْزِى الْمُحْسِنِينَ ۝

122. For they were two of Our believing Servants.

إِنَّهُمَا مِنْ عِبَادِنَا الْمُؤْمِنِينَ ۝

123. So also was Elias among those sent (by Us).

وَإِنَّ إِلْيَاسَ لَمِنَ الْمُرْسَلِينَ ۝

124. Behold, he said to his people, "Will you not fear (Allah)?

إِذْ قَالَ لِقَوْمِهِ أَلَا تَتَّقُونَ ۝

125. "Will you call upon Baal and forsake the Best of Creators,

أَتَدْعُونَ بَعْلًا وَتَذَرُونَ أَحْسَنَ الْخَٰلِقِينَ ۝

126. "Allah, your Lord and Cherisher and the Lord and Cherisher of your fathers of old?"

اللَّهَ رَبَّكُمْ وَرَبَّ ءَابَآئِكُمُ الْأَوَّلِينَ ۝

127. But they rejected him, and they will certainly be called up (for punishment),-

فَكَذَّبُوهُ فَإِنَّهُمْ لَمُحْضَرُونَ ۝

128. Except the sincere and devoted Servants of Allah (among them).

إِلَّا عِبَادَ اللَّهِ الْمُخْلَصِينَ ۝

129. And We left (this blessing) for him among generations (to come) in later times:

وَتَرَكْنَا عَلَيْهِ فِي الْءَاخِرِينَ ۝

130. "Peace and salutation to such as Elias!"

سَلَٰمٌ عَلَىٰ إِلْ يَاسِينَ ۝

131. Thus indeed do We reward those who do right.

إِنَّا كَذَٰلِكَ نَجْزِى الْمُحْسِنِينَ ۝

132. For he was one of Our believing Servants.

إِنَّهُ مِنْ عِبَادِنَا الْمُؤْمِنِينَ ۝

133. So also was Lut among those sent (by Us).

وَإِنَّ لُوطًا لَمِنَ الْمُرْسَلِينَ ۝

134. Behold, We delivered him and his adherents, all,

إِذْ نَجَّيْنَٰهُ وَأَهْلَهُ أَجْمَعِينَ ۝

135. Except an old woman who was among those who lagged behind:

إِلَّا عَجُوزًا فِي الْغَٰبِرِينَ ۝

136. Then We destroyed the rest.

ثُمَّ دَمَّرْنَا الْءَاخَرِينَ ۝

137. Verily, you pass by their (sites), by day-

وَإِنَّكُمْ لَتَمُرُّونَ عَلَيْهِمْ مُصْبِحِينَ ۝

138. And by night: will you not understand?

وَبِالَّيْلِ أَفَلَا تَعْقِلُونَ ۝

139. So also was Jonah among those sent (by Us).

وَإِنَّ يُونُسَ لَمِنَ الْمُرْسَلِينَ ۝

140. When he ran away (like a slave from captivity) to the ship (fully) laden,

إِذْ أَبَقَ إِلَى الْفُلْكِ الْمَشْحُونِ ۝

141. He (agreed to) cast lots, and he was condemned:

فَسَاهَمَ فَكَانَ مِنَ الْمُدْحَضِينَ ۝

142. Then the big fish swallowed him, and he had done acts worthy of blame.

فَالْتَقَمَهُ الْحُوتُ وَهُوَ مُلِيمٌ ۝

143. Had it not been that he (repented and) glorified Allah,

144. He would certainly have remained inside the fish till the Day of Resurrection.

145. But We cast him forth on the naked shore in a state of sickness,

146. And We caused to grow, over him, a spreading plant of the gourd kind.

147. And We sent him (on a mission) to a hundred thousand (men) or more.

148. And they believe; so We permitted them to enjoy (their life) for a while.

149. Now ask them their opinion: is it that your Lord has (only) daughters, and they have sons?-

150. Or that We created the angels female, and they are witnesses (thereto)?

151. Is it not, that they say, from their own invention,

152. "Allah has begotten children"? But they are liars!

153. Did He (then) choose daughters rather than sons?

154. What is the matter with you? How do you judge?

155. Will you not then receive admonition.

156. Or do you have an authority manifest?

157. Then you bring your Book (of authority) if you be truthful!

158. And they have invented a blood-relationship between Him and the Jinns: but the Jinns know (quite well) that they have indeed to appear (before His Judgment-seat)!

159. Glory to Allah! (He is free) from the things they ascribe (to Him)!

160. Not (so do) the Servants of Allah, sincere and devoted.

161. For, verily, neither you nor those you worship-

162. Can lead (any) into temptation concerning Allah,

163. Except such as are (themselves) going to the blazing Fire!

164. (Those ranged in ranks say): "Not one of us but has a place appointed;

SÛRAH-38
ṢÂD
(INTRODUCTION)

For the place of this Sûrah, in the series of six, dealing with some of the mysteries of the spiritual world, see Introduction to S. 34.

This Sûrah, both in chronology and subject-matter, is cognate to S. 37, and carries forward the same argument. But here the emphasis is laid on the working of earthly power when combined with spiritual power, and it is pointed out how much more significant (and real) spiritual power is. For this reason the illustrative stories are mainly those of David and Solomon who were kings as well as prophets, and a parallel is suggested with the unfolding public life of our Holy Prophet.

165. "And we are verily ranged in ranks (for service);

166. "And we are verily those who declare (Allah's) glory!"

167. And there were those who said,

168. "If only we had had before us a Message from those of old,

169. "We should certainly have been Servants of Allah, sincere (and devoted)!"

170. But (now that the Qur'an has come), they reject it: but soon will they know!

171. Already has Our Word been passed before (this) to Our Servants sent (by Us),

172. That they would certainly be assisted,

173. And that Our forces,- they surely must conquer.

174. So you turn away from them for a little while,

175. And watch them (how they fare), and they soon shall see (how you fare)!

176. Do they wish (indeed) to hurry on our Punishment?

177. But when it descends into the open space before them, evil will be the morning for those who were warned (and heeded not)!

178. So you turn away from them for a little while,

179. And watch (how they fare) and they soon shall see (how you fare)!

180. Glory to your Lord, the Lord of Honor and Power! (He is free) from what they ascribe (to Him)!

181. And Peace on the Apostles!

182. And praise to Allah, the Lord and Cherisher of the Worlds!

38. Saad

In the name of Allah, Most Gracious, Most Merciful.

1. Saad: By the Qur'an, full of Admonition: (this is the Truth).

2. But the Unbelievers (are steeped) in Self-glory and Separatism.

3. How many generations before them did We destroy?

وَإِنَّا لَنَحْنُ الصَّآفُّونَ ۙ

وَإِنَّا لَنَحْنُ الْمُسَبِّحُونَ ۞

وَإِنْ كَانُوا لَيَقُولُونَ ۙ

لَوْ أَنَّ عِنْدَنَا ذِكْرًا مِّنَ الْأَوَّلِينَ ۙ

لَكُنَّا عِبَادَ اللّٰهِ الْمُخْلَصِينَ ۞

فَكَفَرُوْا بِهٖ فَسَوْفَ يَعْلَمُوْنَ ۞

وَلَقَدْ سَبَقَتْ كَلِمَتُنَا لِعِبَادِنَا الْمُرْسَلِينَ ۚ

إِنَّهُمْ لَهُمُ الْمَنْصُوْرُوْنَ ۪

وَإِنَّ جُنْدَنَا لَهُمُ الْغَالِبُوْنَ ۞

فَتَوَلَّ عَنْهُمْ حَتّٰى حِيْنٍ ۙ

وَّأَبْصِرْهُمْ فَسَوْفَ يُبْصِرُوْنَ ۞

أَفَبِعَذَابِنَا يَسْتَعْجِلُوْنَ ۞

فَإِذَا نَزَلَ بِسَاحَتِهِمْ فَسَآءَ صَبَاحُ الْمُنْذَرِيْنَ ۞

وَتَوَلَّ عَنْهُمْ حَتّٰى حِيْنٍ ۙ

وَّأَبْصِرْ فَسَوْفَ يُبْصِرُوْنَ ۞

سُبْحٰنَ رَبِّكَ رَبِّ الْعِزَّةِ عَمَّا يَصِفُوْنَ ۚ

وَسَلٰمٌ عَلَى الْمُرْسَلِيْنَ ۞

وَالْحَمْدُ لِلّٰهِ رَبِّ الْعٰلَمِيْنَ ۞

(٣٨) سُوْرَةُ صٓ مَكِّيَّةٌ (٨٨)

بِسْمِ اللّٰهِ الرَّحْمٰنِ الرَّحِيْمِ

صٓ ۚ وَالْقُرْآنِ ذِي الذِّكْرِ ۚ

بَلِ الَّذِيْنَ كَفَرُوْا فِيْ عِزَّةٍ وَّشِقَاقٍ ۞

كَمْ أَهْلَكْنَا مِنْ قَبْلِهِمْ مِّنْ قَرْنٍ

In the end they cried (for mercy)-
when there was no longer time
for being saved!

فَنَادَوْا وَّلَاتَ حِيْنَ مَنَاصٍ ۝

4. So they wonder that a
Warner has come to them from
among themselves! and the
Unbelievers say, "This is a sorcerer telling lies!

وَعَجِبُوْٓا اَنْ جَآءَهُمْ مُّنْذِرٌ مِّنْهُمْ وَ
قَالَ الْكٰفِرُوْنَ هٰذَا سٰحِرٌ كَذَّابٌ ۝

5. "Has he made the gods
(all) into one God (Allah)?
Truly this is a wonderful thing!"

اَجَعَلَ الْاٰلِهَةَ اِلٰهًا وَّاحِدًا ۚ اِنَّ
هٰذَا لَشَيْءٌ عُجَابٌ ۝

6. And the leaders among
them go away (impatiently),
(saying), "You walk away, and
remain constant to your gods!
For this is truly a thing designed
(against you)!

وَانْطَلَقَ الْمَلَاُ مِنْهُمْ اَنِ امْشُوْا
وَاصْبِرُوْا عَلٰٓى اٰلِهَتِكُمْ ۚ اِنَّ هٰذَا
لَشَيْءٌ يُّرَادُ ۝

7. "We never heard (the like)
of this among the people of
these latter days: this is nothing
but a made-up tale!"

مَا سَمِعْنَا بِهٰذَا فِى الْمِلَّةِ الْاٰخِرَةِ ۚ
اِنْ هٰذَآ اِلَّا اخْتِلَاقٌ ۝

8. "What! Has the Message
been sent to him - (of all
persons) among us?"...But they
are in doubt concerning My
(Own) Message! Nay, they have
not yet tasted My Punishment!

ءَاُنْزِلَ عَلَيْهِ الذِّكْرُ مِنْ بَيْنِنَا ۚ
بَلْ هُمْ فِى شَكٍّ مِّنْ ذِكْرِىْ ۚ بَلْ
لَّمَّا يَذُوْقُوْا عَذَابِ ۝

9. Or have they the Treasures
of the Mercy of your Lord,- the
Exalted in Power, the Grantor of
Bounties without measure?

اَمْ عِنْدَهُمْ خَزَآئِنُ رَحْمَةِ رَبِّكَ
الْعَزِيْزِ الْوَهَّابِ ۝

10. Or have they the dominion
of the heavens and the earth and
all between? If so, let them
mount up with the ropes and
means (to reach that end)!

اَمْ لَهُمْ مُّلْكُ السَّمٰوٰتِ وَالْاَرْضِ وَمَا
بَيْنَهُمَا ۚ فَلْيَرْتَقُوْا فِى الْاَسْبَابِ ۝

11. But there - will be put to
flight even a host of
confederates.

جُنْدٌ مَّا هُنَالِكَ مَهْزُوْمٌ مِّنَ
الْاَحْزَابِ ۝

12. Before them (were many
who) rejected Apostles,- the
People of Noah, and 'Ad, and
Pharaoh, the Lord of Stakes,

كَذَّبَتْ قَبْلَهُمْ قَوْمُ نُوْحٍ وَّعَادٌ وَّ
فِرْعَوْنُ ذُو الْاَوْتَادِ ۝

13. And Thamud, and the
people of Lut, and the
Companions of the Wood; -
such were the Confederates.

وَثَمُوْدُ وَقَوْمُ لُوْطٍ وَّاَصْحٰبُ لْـَٔيْكَةِ ۚ
اُولٰٓئِكَ الْاَحْزَابُ ۝

14. Not one (of them) but
rejected the Apostles, but My
Punishment came justly and
inevitably (on them).

اِنْ كُلٌّ اِلَّا كَذَّبَ الرُّسُلَ فَحَقَّ
عِقَابِ ۝

15. These (today) only wait
for a single mighty Blast,

وَمَا يَنْظُرُ هٰٓؤُلَآءِ اِلَّا صَيْحَةً

which (when it comes) will brook no delay.

16. They say: "Our Lord! hasten to us our sentence (even) before the Day of Account!"

17. Have patience at what they say, and remember Our Servant David, the man of strength: for he ever turned (to Allah).

18. It was We that made the hills declare, in unison with him, Our praises, at eventide and at break of day,

19. And the birds gathered (in assemblies): all with him turned (to Allah).

20. We strengthened his kingdom, and gave him wisdom and sound judgment in speech and decision.

21. Has the story of the Disputants reached you? Behold, they climbed over the wall of the private chamber;

22. When they entered the presence of David, and he was terrified of them, they said: "Fear not: we are two disputants, one of whom has wronged the other: decide now between us with truth, and treat us not with injustice, but guide us to the even Path.

23. "This man is my brother: he has nine and ninety ewes, and I have (but) one: yet he says, 'Commit her to my care,' and is (moreover) harsh to me in speech."

24. (David) said: "He has undoubtedly wronged you in demanding your (single) ewe to be added to his (flock of) ewes: truly many are the partners (in business) who wrong each other: not so do those who believe and work deeds of righteousness, and how few are they?"...and David gathered that We had tried him: he asked forgiveness of his Lord, fell down, bowing (in prostration), and turned (to Allah in repentance).

25. So We forgave him this (lapse): he enjoyed, indeed, a Near Approach to Us,

وَّاحِدَةٌ مَّا لَهَا مِنْ فَوَاقٍ ۞

وَقَالُوْا رَبَّنَا عَجِّلْ لَّنَا قِطَّنَا قَبْلَ يَوْمِ الْحِسَابِ ۞

اِصْبِرْ عَلٰى مَا يَقُوْلُوْنَ وَاذْكُرْ عَبْدَنَا دَاوٗدَ ذَا الْاَيْدِ ۚ اِنَّهٗ اَوَّابٌ ۞

اِنَّا سَخَّرْنَا الْجِبَالَ مَعَهٗ يُسَبِّحْنَ بِالْعَشِيِّ وَالْاِشْرَاقِ ۙ

وَالطَّيْرَ مَحْشُوْرَةً ۚ كُلٌّ لَّهٗٓ اَوَّابٌ ۞

وَشَدَدْنَا مُلْكَهٗ وَاٰتَيْنٰهُ الْحِكْمَةَ وَفَصْلَ الْخِطَابِ ۞

وَهَلْ اَتٰىكَ نَبَؤُا الْخَصْمِ ۘ اِذْ تَسَوَّرُوا الْمِحْرَابَ ۚ

اِذْ دَخَلُوْا عَلٰى دَاوٗدَ فَفَزِعَ مِنْهُمْ قَالُوْا لَا تَخَفْ ۚ خَصْمٰنِ بَغٰى بَعْضُنَا عَلٰى بَعْضٍ فَاحْكُمْ بَيْنَنَا بِالْحَقِّ وَلَا تُشْطِطْ وَاهْدِنَآ اِلٰى سَوَآءِ الصِّرَاطِ ۞

اِنَّ هٰذَآ اَخِيْ ۗ لَهٗ تِسْعٌ وَّتِسْعُوْنَ نَعْجَةً وَّلِيَ نَعْجَةٌ وَّاحِدَةٌ ۚ فَقَالَ اَكْفِلْنِيْهَا وَعَزَّنِيْ فِي الْخِطَابِ ۞

قَالَ لَقَدْ ظَلَمَكَ بِسُؤَالِ نَعْجَتِكَ اِلٰى نِعَاجِهٖ ۗ وَاِنَّ كَثِيْرًا مِّنَ الْخُلَطَآءِ لَيَبْغِيْ بَعْضُهُمْ عَلٰى بَعْضٍ اِلَّا الَّذِيْنَ اٰمَنُوْا وَعَمِلُوا الصّٰلِحٰتِ وَقَلِيْلٌ مَّا هُمْ ۗ وَظَنَّ دَاوٗدُ اَنَّمَا فَتَنّٰهُ فَاسْتَغْفَرَ رَبَّهٗ وَخَرَّ رَاكِعًا وَّاَنَابَ ۩ ۞

فَغَفَرْنَا لَهٗ ذٰلِكَ ۖ وَاِنَّ لَهٗ عِنْدَنَا

and a beautiful Place of (Final) Return.

26. O David! We did indeed make you a vicegerent on earth: so you judge between men in truth (and justice): nor do you follow the lusts (of your heart), for they will mislead you from the Path of Allah: for those who wander astray from the Path of Allah, is a Chastisement Grievous, for that they forget the Day of Account.

27. Not without purpose did We create heaven and earth and all between! that were the thought of Unbelievers! but woe to the Unbelievers because of the Fire (of Hell)!

28. Shall We treat those who believe and work deeds of righteousness, the same as those who do mischief on earth? Shall We treat those who guard against evil, the same as those who turn aside from the right?

29. (Here is) a Book which We have sent down unto you, full of blessings, that they may meditate on its Signs, and that men of understanding may receive admonition.

30. To David We gave Solomon (for a son),- how excellent in Our service! ever did he turn (to Us).

31. Behold, there were brought before him, at eventide, coursers of the highest breeding, and swift of foot;

32. And he said, "Truly do I love the love of Good, with a view to the glory of my Lord," until (the sun) was hidden in the veil (of Night):

33. "Bring them back to me." Then he began to pass his hand over (their) legs and their necks.

34. And We did try Solomon: We placed on his throne a body (without life); but he turned (to Us in true devotion):

لَزُلْفَىٰ وَحُسْنَ مَـَٔابٍ ۝

يٰدَاوٗدُ إِنَّا جَعَلْنٰكَ خَلِيفَةً فِى الْأَرْضِ فَاحْكُمْ بَيْنَ النَّاسِ بِالْحَقِّ وَلَا تَتَّبِعِ الْهَوٰىٰ فَيُضِلَّكَ عَنْ سَبِيلِ اللّٰهِ ۚ إِنَّ الَّذِيْنَ يَضِلُّوْنَ عَنْ سَبِيلِ اللّٰهِ لَهُمْ عَذَابٌ شَدِيْدٌۢ بِمَا نَسُوْا يَوْمَ الْحِسَابِ ۝

وَمَا خَلَقْنَا السَّمَآءَ وَالْأَرْضَ وَمَا بَيْنَهُمَا بَاطِلًا ۚ ذٰلِكَ ظَنُّ الَّذِيْنَ كَفَرُوْا ۚ فَوَيْلٌ لِّلَّذِيْنَ كَفَرُوْا مِنَ النَّارِ ۝

أَمْ نَجْعَلُ الَّذِيْنَ اٰمَنُوْا وَعَمِلُوا الصّٰلِحٰتِ كَالْمُفْسِدِيْنَ فِى الْأَرْضِ أَمْ نَجْعَلُ الْمُتَّقِيْنَ كَالْفُجَّارِ ۝

كِتٰبٌ أَنْزَلْنٰهُ إِلَيْكَ مُبٰرَكٌ لِّيَدَّبَّرُوْا اٰيٰتِهٖ وَلِيَتَذَكَّرَ أُولُوا الْأَلْبَابِ ۝

وَوَهَبْنَا لِدَاوٗدَ سُلَيْمٰنَ ۘ نِعْمَ الْعَبْدُ ۚ إِنَّهٗۤ أَوَّابٌ ۝

إِذْ عُرِضَ عَلَيْهِ بِالْعَشِيِّ الصّٰفِنٰتُ الْجِيَادُ ۝

فَقَالَ إِنِّيۤ أَحْبَبْتُ حُبَّ الْخَيْرِ عَنْ ذِكْرِ رَبِّيْ ۖ حَتّٰى تَوَارَتْ بِالْحِجَابِ ۝

رُدُّوْهَا عَلَيَّ ۖ فَطَفِقَ مَسْحًۢا بِالسُّوْقِ وَالْأَعْنَاقِ ۝

وَلَقَدْ فَتَنَّا سُلَيْمٰنَ وَأَلْقَيْنَا عَلٰى كُرْسِيِّهٖ جَسَدًا ثُمَّ أَنَابَ ۝

35. He said, "O my Lord! Forgive me, and grant me a kingdom which, (it may be), does not suit another after me: for You are the Grantor of Bounties (without measure)."

قَالَ رَبِّ اغْفِرْ لِيْ وَهَبْ لِيْ مُلْكًا لَّا يَنْبَغِيْ لِاَحَدٍ مِّنْ بَعْدِيْ ۚ اِنَّكَ اَنْتَ الْوَهَّابُ ۝

36. Then We subjected the wind to his power, to flow gently to his order, whithersoever he willed,-

فَسَخَّرْنَا لَهُ الرِّيْحَ تَجْرِيْ بِاَمْرِهٖ رُخَآءً حَيْثُ اَصَابَ ۝

37. As also the evil ones, (including) every kind of builder and diver,-

وَالشَّيٰطِيْنَ كُلَّ بَنَّآءٍ وَّغَوَّاصٍ ۝

38. As also others bound together in fetters.

وَّاٰخَرِيْنَ مُقَرَّنِيْنَ فِي الْاَصْفَادِ ۝

39. "Such are Our Bounties: whether you bestow them (on others) or withhold them, no account will be asked."

هٰذَا عَطَآؤُنَا فَامْنُنْ اَوْ اَمْسِكْ بِغَيْرِ حِسَابٍ ۝

40. And he enjoyed, indeed, a Near Approach to Us, and a beautiful Place of (Final) Return.

وَاِنَّ لَهٗ عِنْدَنَا لَزُلْفٰى وَحُسْنَ مَاٰبٍ ۝

41. Commemorate Our Servant Job. Behold! he cried to his Lord: "The Evil One has afflicted me with distress and suffering!"

وَاذْكُرْ عَبْدَنَا اَيُّوْبَ ۘ اِذْ نَادٰى رَبَّهٗ اَنِّيْ مَسَّنِيَ الشَّيْطٰنُ بِنُصْبٍ وَّعَذَابٍ ۝

42. (The command was given:) "Strike with your foot: here is (water) wherein to wash, cool and refreshing, and (water) to drink."

اُرْكُضْ بِرِجْلِكَ ۚ هٰذَا مُغْتَسَلٌ بَارِدٌ وَّشَرَابٌ ۝

43. And We gave him (back) his people, and doubled their number,- as a Grace from Ourselves, and a thing for commemoration, for all who have Understanding.

وَوَهَبْنَا لَهٗ اَهْلَهٗ وَمِثْلَهُمْ مَّعَهُمْ رَحْمَةً مِّنَّا وَذِكْرٰى لِاُولِي الْاَلْبَابِ ۝

44. "And take in your hand a little grass, and strike therewith: and do not break (your oath)." Truly We found him full of patience and constancy. How excellent in Our service! ever did he turn (to Us)!

وَخُذْ بِيَدِكَ ضِغْثًا فَاضْرِبْ بِّهٖ وَلَا تَحْنَثْ ۚ اِنَّا وَجَدْنٰهُ صَابِرًا ۘ نِعْمَ الْعَبْدُ ۚ اِنَّهٗ اَوَّابٌ ۝

45. And commemorate Our Servants Abraham, Isaac, and Jacob, possessors of Power and Vision.

وَاذْكُرْ عِبٰدَنَا اِبْرٰهِيْمَ وَاِسْحٰقَ وَيَعْقُوْبَ اُولِي الْاَيْدِيْ وَالْاَبْصَارِ ۝

46. Verily We chose them for a special (purpose)- proclaiming the Message of the Hereafter.

اِنَّا اَخْلَصْنٰهُمْ بِخَالِصَةٍ ذِكْرَى الدَّارِ ۝

47. They were, in Our sight, truly, of the company of the Elect and the Good.

وَاِنَّهُمْ عِنْدَنَا لَمِنَ الْمُصْطَفَيْنَ

48. And commemorate Ismail, Elisha, and Zul-Kifl: each of them was of the company of the Good.

49. This is a Message (of admonition): and verily, for the Righteous, is a beautiful place of (final) Return,-

50. Gardens of Eternity, whose doors will (ever) be open to them;

51. Therein will they recline (at ease): therein can they call (at pleasure) for fruit in abundance, and (delicious) drink;

52. And beside them will be chaste women restraining their glances, (companions) of equal age.

53. Such is the Promise made to you for the Day of Account!

54. Truly such will be Our Bounty (to you); it will never fail;-

55. Yes, such! but - for the wrong-doers will be an evil place of (final) Return!-

56. Hell!- They will burn therein,- an evil bed (indeed, to lie on)!-

57. Yes, such!- Then shall they taste it, - a boiling fluid, and a fluid dark murky, intensely cold!-

58. And other penalties of a similar kind, to match them!

59. Here is a troop rushing headlong with you! No welcome for them! truly, they shall burn in the Fire!

60. (Then followers shall cry to the misleaders:) "Nay, you (too)! No welcome for you! It is you who have brought this upon us! Now evil is (this) place to stay in!"

61. They will say: "Our Lord! Whoever brought this upon us,- add to him a double Chastisement in the Fire!"

62. And they will say: "What has happened to us that we do not see men whom we used to number among the bad ones?

63. "Did we treat them (as such) in ridicule, or have (our) eyes failed to perceive them?"

64. Truly that is just and fitting,-the mutual recriminations of the People of the Fire!

65. Say: "Truly I am a Warner: no god is there but the One God (Allah), Supreme and Irresistible,-

قُلْ إِنَّمَا أَنَا مُنذِرٌ ۖ وَمَا مِنْ إِلَٰهٍ إِلَّا اللَّهُ الْوَاحِدُ الْقَهَّارُ ۝

66. The Lord of the heavens and the earth, and all between,- Exalted in Might, able to enforce His Will, forgiving again and again."

رَبُّ السَّمَاوَاتِ وَالْأَرْضِ وَمَا بَيْنَهُمَا الْعَزِيزُ الْغَفَّارُ ۝

67. Say: "That is a Message Supreme (above all)-

قُلْ هُوَ نَبَؤٌا عَظِيمٌ ۝

68. "From which you do turn away!

أَنتُمْ عَنْهُ مُعْرِضُونَ ۝

69. "No knowledge have I of the chiefs on high, when they discuss (matters) among themselves.

مَا كَانَ لِيَ مِنْ عِلْمٍ بِالْمَلَإِ الْأَعْلَىٰ إِذْ يَخْتَصِمُونَ ۝

70. 'Only this has been revealed to me: that I am to give warning plainly and publicly."

إِن يُوحَىٰ إِلَيَّ إِلَّا أَنَّمَا أَنَا نَذِيرٌ مُّبِينٌ ۝

71. Behold, your Lord said to the angels: "I am about to create man from clay:

إِذْ قَالَ رَبُّكَ لِلْمَلَائِكَةِ إِنِّي خَالِقٌ بَشَرًا مِّن طِينٍ ۝

72. "When I have fashioned him (in due proportion) and breathed into him of My spirit, you fall down in obeisance to him."

فَإِذَا سَوَّيْتُهُ وَنَفَخْتُ فِيهِ مِن رُّوحِي فَقَعُوا لَهُ سَاجِدِينَ ۝

73. So the angels prostrated themselves, all of them together.

فَسَجَدَ الْمَلَائِكَةُ كُلُّهُمْ أَجْمَعُونَ ۝

74. Not so Iblis: he was haughty, and became one of those who reject Faith.

إِلَّا إِبْلِيسَ اسْتَكْبَرَ وَكَانَ مِنَ الْكَافِرِينَ ۝

75. (Allah) said: "O Iblis! What prevents you from prostrating yourself to one whom I have created with My hands? Are you haughty? Or are you one of the high (and mighty) ones?"

قَالَ يَا إِبْلِيسُ مَا مَنَعَكَ أَن تَسْجُدَ لِمَا خَلَقْتُ بِيَدَيَّ أَسْتَكْبَرْتَ أَمْ كُنتَ مِنَ الْعَالِينَ ۝

76. (Iblis) said: "I am better than he: You created me from fire, and him You created from clay."

قَالَ أَنَا خَيْرٌ مِّنْهُ خَلَقْتَنِي مِن نَّارٍ وَخَلَقْتَهُ مِن طِينٍ ۝

77. (Allah) said: "Then you get out from here: for you are rejected, accursed.

قَالَ فَاخْرُجْ مِنْهَا فَإِنَّكَ رَجِيمٌ ۝

78. "And My Curse shall be on you till the Day of Judgment."

وَإِنَّ عَلَيْكَ لَعْنَتِي إِلَىٰ يَوْمِ الدِّينِ ۝

79. (Iblis) said: "O my Lord! Give me then respite till the Day the (dead) are raised."

قَالَ رَبِّ فَأَنظِرْنِي إِلَىٰ يَوْمِ يُبْعَثُونَ ۝

SÛRAH-39
AZ-ZUMAR
(INTRODUCTION)

This is the last of the series of six Sûras beginning with S. 34, which deal with the mysteries of the spiritual world, as leading up to the *Ma 'âd,* or the Hereafter. See Introduction to S. 34.

Its subject-matter is how Creation in its great variety is yet sorted out in Groups or Classes, all governed by one Plan, and created and sustained by One Allah, Who will separate Good from Evil at the last Day. The word *Zumar* occurs in verses 71 and 73.

Its chronology has no significance. It belongs to the late Makkan period.

80. (Allah) said: "Respite then is granted to you-

81. "Till the Day of the Time Appointed."

82. (Iblis) said: "Then, by Your Power, I will put them all in the wrong,-

83. "Except Your Servants amongst them, sincere and purified (by Your grace).

84. (Allah) said: "Then it is just and fitting - and I say what is just and fitting-

85. "That I will certainly fill Hell with you and those that follow you,- every one."

86. Say: "No reward do I ask of you for this (Qur'an), nor I am a pretender.

87. "This is no less than a Message to (all) the Worlds.

88. "And you shall certainly know the truth of it (all) after a while."

39. The Crowds

In the name of Allah. Most Gracious, Most Merciful.

1. The revelation of this Book is from Allah, the Exalted in Power, full of Wisdom.

2. Verily it is We Who have revealed the Book to you in Truth: so serve Allah, offering Him sincere devotion.

3. Is it not to Allah that sincere devotion is due? But those who take for protectors others than Allah (say): "We only serve them in order that they may bring us nearer to Allah." Truly Allah will judge between them in that wherein they differ. But Allah does not guide such as are false and ungrateful.

4. Had Allah wished to take to Himself a son, He could have chosen whom He pleased out of those whom He creates: but Glory be to Him! (He is above such things.) He is Allah, the One, the Irresistible.

قَالَ فَإِنَّكَ مِنَ الْمُنْظَرِينَ ۞

إِلَىٰ يَوْمِ الْوَقْتِ الْمَعْلُومِ ۞

قَالَ فَبِعِزَّتِكَ لَأُغْوِيَنَّهُمْ أَجْمَعِينَ ۞

إِلَّا عِبَادَكَ مِنْهُمُ الْمُخْلَصِينَ ۞

قَالَ فَالْحَقُّ وَالْحَقَّ أَقُولُ ۞

لَأَمْلَأَنَّ جَهَنَّمَ مِنْكَ وَمِمَّنْ تَبِعَكَ مِنْهُمْ أَجْمَعِينَ ۞

قُلْ مَا أَسْأَلُكُمْ عَلَيْهِ مِنْ أَجْرٍ وَمَا أَنَا مِنَ الْمُتَكَلِّفِينَ ۞

إِنْ هُوَ إِلَّا ذِكْرٌ لِلْعَالَمِينَ ۞

وَلَتَعْلَمُنَّ نَبَأَهُ بَعْدَ حِينٍ ۞

(٣٩) سُورَةُ الزُّمَرِ مَكِّيَّةٌ (٥٩)

بِسْمِ اللهِ الرَّحْمٰنِ الرَّحِيمِ

تَنْزِيلُ الْكِتَابِ مِنَ اللهِ الْعَزِيزِ الْحَكِيمِ ۞

إِنَّا أَنْزَلْنَا إِلَيْكَ الْكِتَابَ بِالْحَقِّ فَاعْبُدِ اللهَ مُخْلِصًا لَهُ الدِّينَ ۞

أَلَا لِلّٰهِ الدِّينُ الْخَالِصُ وَالَّذِينَ اتَّخَذُوا مِنْ دُونِهِ أَوْلِيَاءَ مَا نَعْبُدُهُمْ إِلَّا لِيُقَرِّبُونَا إِلَى اللهِ زُلْفَىٰ إِنَّ اللهَ يَحْكُمُ بَيْنَهُمْ فِي مَا هُمْ فِيهِ يَخْتَلِفُونَ ۞ إِنَّ اللهَ لَا يَهْدِي مَنْ هُوَ كَاذِبٌ كَفَّارٌ ۞

لَوْ أَرَادَ اللهُ أَنْ يَتَّخِذَ وَلَدًا لَاصْطَفَىٰ مِمَّا يَخْلُقُ مَا يَشَاءُ سُبْحَانَهُ هُوَ اللهُ الْوَاحِدُ الْقَهَّارُ ۞

5.   He created the heavens and the earth in true (proportions): He makes the Night overlap the Day, and the Day overlap the Night: He has subjected the sun and the moon (to His law): each one follows a course for a time appointed. Is not He the Exalted in Power - He Who forgives again and again?

خَلَقَ السَّمٰوٰتِ وَ الْأَرْضَ بِالْحَقِّ ۚ

يُكَوِّرُ الَّيْلَ عَلَى النَّهَارِ وَ يُكَوِّرُ

النَّهَارَ عَلَى الَّيْلِ وَ سَخَّرَ الشَّمْسَ

وَ الْقَمَرَ ۖ كُلٌّ يَّجْرِيْ لِأَجَلٍ

مُّسَمًّى ۚ اَلَا هُوَ الْعَزِيْزُ الْغَفَّارُ ۞

6.   He created you (all) from a single person: then created, of like nature, his mate; and He sent down for you eight head of cattle in pairs: He makes you, in the wombs of your mothers, in stages, one after another, in three veils of darkness. Such is Allah, your Lord and Cherisher: to Him belongs (all) dominion. There is no god but He: then how are you turned away (from your true Centre)?

خَلَقَكُمْ مِّنْ نَّفْسٍ وَّاحِدَةٍ ثُمَّ جَعَلَ

مِنْهَا زَوْجَهَا وَ اَنْزَلَ لَكُمْ مِّنَ

الْأَنْعَامِ ثَمٰنِيَةَ اَزْوَاجٍ ۚ يَخْلُقُكُمْ

فِيْ بُطُوْنِ اُمَّهٰتِكُمْ خَلْقًا مِّنْ بَعْدِ

خَلْقٍ فِيْ ظُلُمٰتٍ ثَلٰثٍ ۚ ذٰلِكُمُ اللّٰهُ

رَبُّكُمْ لَهُ الْمُلْكُ ۖ لَا اِلٰهَ اِلَّا هُوَ ۖ

فَاَنّٰى تُصْرَفُوْنَ ۞

7.   If you reject (Allah), truly Allah has no need of you; but He does not like ingratitude from His servants: if you are grateful, He is pleased with you. No bearer of burdens can bear the burden of another. In the end, to your Lord is your Return, when He will tell you the truth of all that you did (in this life). For He knows well all that is in (men's) hearts.

اِنْ تَكْفُرُوْا فَاِنَّ اللّٰهَ غَنِيٌّ عَنْكُمْ ۖ

وَ لَا يَرْضٰى لِعِبَادِهِ الْكُفْرَ ۚ وَ اِنْ تَشْكُرُوْا

يَرْضَهُ لَكُمْ ۗ وَ لَا تَزِرُ وَازِرَةٌ وِّزْرَ

اُخْرٰى ۗ ثُمَّ اِلٰى رَبِّكُمْ مَّرْجِعُكُمْ

فَيُنَبِّئُكُمْ بِمَا كُنْتُمْ تَعْمَلُوْنَ ۗ اِنَّهُ

عَلِيْمٌ بِذَاتِ الصُّدُوْرِ ۞

8.   When some trouble touches man, he cries to his Lord, turning to Him in repentance: but when He bestows a favour upon him as from Himself, (man) forgets what he cried and prayed for before, and he sets up rivals to Allah, thus misleading others from Allah's Path. Say, "Enjoy your blasphemy for a little while: verily you are (one) of the Companions of the Fire!"

وَ اِذَا مَسَّ الْاِنْسَانَ ضُرٌّ دَعَا رَبَّهٗ

مُنِيْبًا اِلَيْهِ ثُمَّ اِذَا خَوَّلَهٗ نِعْمَةً

مِّنْهُ نَسِيَ مَا كَانَ يَدْعُوْا اِلَيْهِ مِنْ

قَبْلُ وَ جَعَلَ لِلّٰهِ اَنْدَادًا لِّيُضِلَّ

عَنْ سَبِيْلِهٖ ۗ قُلْ تَمَتَّعْ بِكُفْرِكَ

قَلِيْلًا ۚ اِنَّكَ مِنْ اَصْحٰبِ النَّارِ ۞

9.   Is one who worships devoutly during the hours of the night prostrating himself or standing (in adoration), who takes heed of the Hereafter, and who places his hope in

اَمَّنْ هُوَ قَانِتٌ اٰنَاءَ الَّيْلِ سَاجِدًا

وَّ قَائِمًا يَّحْذَرُ الْاٰخِرَةَ وَ يَرْجُوْا

the Mercy of his Lord - (like one who does not)? Say: "Are those equal, those who know and those who do not know? It is those who are endued with understanding that receive admonition.

10. Say: "O you My servants who believe! Fear your Lord, good is (the reward) for those who do good in this world. Spacious is Allah's earth! those who patiently persevere will truly receive a reward without measure!"

11. Say: "Verily, I am commanded to serve Allah with sincere devotion;

12. "And I am commanded to be the first of those who bow to Allah in Islam."

13. Say: "I would, if I disobeyed my Lord, indeed have fear of the Penalty of a Mighty Day."

14. Say: "It is Allah I serve, with my sincere (and exclusive) devotion:

15. "You serve what you will besides Him." Say: "Truly, those in loss are those who lose their own souls and their People on the Day of Judgment: Ah! that is indeed the (real and) evident Loss!

16. They shall have Layers of Fire above them, and Layers (of Fire) below them: with this Allah warns off His servants: "O My servants! then you fear Me!"

17. Those who eschew Evil,- and do not fall into its worship,- and turn to Allah (in repentance),- for them is Good News: so announce the Good News to My servants,-

18. Those who listen to the Word, and follow the best (meaning) in it: those are the ones whom Allah has guided,

ع
١٥

رَحْمَةَ رَبِّهِ ۚ قُلْ هَلْ يَسْتَوِى الَّذِيْنَ يَعْلَمُوْنَ وَالَّذِيْنَ لَا يَعْلَمُوْنَ ۗ إِنَّمَا يَتَذَكَّرُ أُولُوا الْأَلْبَابِ ۞

قُلْ يٰعِبَادِ الَّذِيْنَ اٰمَنُوا اتَّقُوْا رَبَّكُمْ ۚ لِلَّذِيْنَ أَحْسَنُوْا فِيْ هٰذِهِ الدُّنْيَا حَسَنَةٌ ۗ وَأَرْضُ اللّٰهِ وَاسِعَةٌ ۗ إِنَّمَا يُوَفَّى الصّٰبِرُوْنَ أَجْرَهُمْ بِغَيْرِ حِسَابٍ ۞

قُلْ إِنِّيْ أُمِرْتُ أَنْ أَعْبُدَ اللّٰهَ مُخْلِصًا لَّهُ الدِّيْنَ ۞ وَأُمِرْتُ لِأَنْ أَكُوْنَ أَوَّلَ الْمُسْلِمِيْنَ ۞ قُلْ إِنِّيْ أَخَافُ إِنْ عَصَيْتُ رَبِّيْ عَذَابَ يَوْمٍ عَظِيْمٍ ۞

قُلِ اللّٰهَ أَعْبُدُ مُخْلِصًا لَّهُ دِيْنِيْ ۞ فَاعْبُدُوْا مَا شِئْتُمْ مِّنْ دُوْنِهٖ ۗ قُلْ إِنَّ الْخٰسِرِيْنَ الَّذِيْنَ خَسِرُوْا أَنْفُسَهُمْ وَأَهْلِيْهِمْ يَوْمَ الْقِيٰمَةِ ۗ أَلَا ذٰلِكَ هُوَ الْخُسْرَانُ الْمُبِيْنُ ۞

لَهُمْ مِّنْ فَوْقِهِمْ ظُلَلٌ مِّنَ النَّارِ وَمِنْ تَحْتِهِمْ ظُلَلٌ ۗ ذٰلِكَ يُخَوِّفُ اللّٰهُ بِهٖ عِبَادَهٗ ۗ يٰعِبَادِ فَاتَّقُوْنِ ۞

وَالَّذِيْنَ اجْتَنَبُوا الطَّاغُوْتَ أَنْ يَّعْبُدُوْهَا وَأَنَابُوْا إِلَى اللّٰهِ لَهُمُ الْبُشْرٰى ۚ فَبَشِّرْ عِبَادِ ۞ الَّذِيْنَ يَسْتَمِعُوْنَ الْقَوْلَ فَيَتَّبِعُوْنَ أَحْسَنَهٗ ۗ أُولٰئِكَ الَّذِيْنَ هَدٰىهُمُ

and those are the ones endued with understanding.

19. Is, then, one against whom the decree of Punishment is justly due (equal to one who eschews Evil)? Would you, then, deliver one (who is) in the Fire?

20. But it is for those who fear their Lord. That lofty mansions, one above another, have been built: beneath them flow rivers (of delight): (such is) the Promise of Allah: never does Allah fail in (His) promise.

21. Do not you see that Allah sends down rain from the sky, and leads it through springs in the earth? Then He causes to grow, therewith, produce of various colours: then it withers; you will see it grow yellow; then He makes it dry up and crumble away. Truly, in this, is a Message of remembrance to men of understanding.

22. Is one whose heart Allah has opened to Islam, so that he has received Enlightenment from Allah, (no better than one hard-hearted)? Woe then to those whose hearts are hardened against celebrating the praises of Allah! they are manifestly wandering (in error)

23. Allah has revealed (from time to time) the most beautiful Message in the form of a Book, consistent with itself, (yet) repeating (its teaching in various aspects): the skins of those who fear their Lord tremble thereat; then their skins and their hearts do soften to the celebration of Allah's praises. Such is the guidance of Allah: He guides herewith whom He pleases, but such as Allah leaves to stray, can have none to guide.

24. Is, then, one who has to fear the brunt of the Chastisement on the Day of Judgment (and receive it) on his face, (like one guarded therefrom)? It will be said to the wrong-doers: "You taste (the fruits of) what you earned!"

اللّٰهُ وَأُولٰٓئِكَ هُمْ أُولُوا الْأَلْبَابِ ۞

أَفَمَنْ حَقَّ عَلَيْهِ كَلِمَةُ الْعَذَابِ ۖ

أَفَأَنْتَ تُنْقِذُ مَنْ فِي النَّارِ ۞

لٰكِنِ الَّذِيْنَ اتَّقَوْا رَبَّهُمْ لَهُمْ غُرَفٌ

مِّنْ فَوْقِهَا غُرَفٌ مَّبْنِيَّةٌ ۙ تَجْرِيْ

مِنْ تَحْتِهَا الْأَنْهَارُ ۖ وَعْدَ اللّٰهِ ۖ لَا

يُخْلِفُ اللّٰهُ الْمِيْعَادَ ۞

أَلَمْ تَرَ أَنَّ اللّٰهَ أَنْزَلَ مِنَ السَّمَاءِ

مَاءً فَسَلَكَهُ يَنَابِيْعَ فِي الْأَرْضِ ثُمَّ

يُخْرِجُ بِهٖ زَرْعًا مُّخْتَلِفًا أَلْوَانُهٗ ثُمَّ

يَهِيْجُ فَتَرَاهُ مُصْفَرًّا ثُمَّ يَجْعَلُهُ

حُطَامًا ۚ إِنَّ فِيْ ذٰلِكَ لَذِكْرٰى

لِأُولِي الْأَلْبَابِ ۞

أَفَمَنْ شَرَحَ اللّٰهُ صَدْرَهٗ لِلْإِسْلَامِ

فَهُوَ عَلٰى نُوْرٍ مِّنْ رَّبِّهٖ ۚ فَوَيْلٌ

لِّلْقَاسِيَةِ قُلُوْبُهُمْ مِّنْ ذِكْرِ

اللّٰهِ ۚ أُولٰٓئِكَ فِيْ ضَلٰلٍ مُّبِيْنٍ ۞

اللّٰهُ نَزَّلَ أَحْسَنَ الْحَدِيْثِ كِتٰبًا

مُّتَشَابِهًا مَّثَانِيَ ۖ تَقْشَعِرُّ مِنْهُ

جُلُوْدُ الَّذِيْنَ يَخْشَوْنَ رَبَّهُمْ ۚ ثُمَّ

تَلِيْنُ جُلُوْدُهُمْ وَقُلُوْبُهُمْ إِلٰى ذِكْرِ

اللّٰهِ ۚ ذٰلِكَ هُدَى اللّٰهِ يَهْدِيْ بِهٖ

مَنْ يَّشَاءُ ۚ وَمَنْ يُّضْلِلِ اللّٰهُ فَمَا

لَهٗ مِنْ هَادٍ ۞

أَفَمَنْ يَّتَّقِيْ بِوَجْهِهٖ سُوْءَ الْعَذَابِ

يَوْمَ الْقِيٰمَةِ ۚ وَقِيْلَ لِلظّٰلِمِيْنَ ذُوْقُوْا

25. Those before them (also) rejected (revelation), and so the Punishment came to them from directions they did not perceive.

مَا كَانُوا يَكْسِبُونَ ۝

كَذَّبَ الَّذِينَ مِنْ قَبْلِهِمْ فَأَتَاهُمُ

26. So Allah gave them a taste of humiliation in the present life, but greater is the punishment of the Hereafter, if they only knew!

الْعَذَابُ مِنْ حَيْثُ لَا يَشْعُرُونَ ۝

فَأَذَاقَهُمُ اللّٰهُ الْخِزْيَ فِى الْحَيٰوةِ

الدُّنْيَا ۖ وَلَعَذَابُ الْاٰخِرَةِ أَكْبَرُ ۚ

27. We have put forth for men, in this Qur'an every kind of Parable, in order that they may receive admonition.

لَوْ كَانُوا يَعْلَمُونَ ۝

وَلَقَدْ ضَرَبْنَا لِلنَّاسِ فِى هٰذَا

الْقُرْاٰنِ مِنْ كُلِّ مَثَلٍ لَّعَلَّهُمْ

28. (It is) a Qur'an in Arabic, without any crookedness (therein): in order that they may guard against Evil.

يَتَذَكَّرُونَ ۝

قُرْاٰنًا عَرَبِيًّا غَيْرَ ذِى عِوَجٍ

29. Allah puts forth a Parable - a man belonging to many partners at variance with each other, and a man belonging entirely to one master: are those two equal in comparison? Praise be to Allah! but most of them have no knowledge.

لَّعَلَّهُمْ يَتَّقُونَ ۝

ضَرَبَ اللّٰهُ مَثَلًا رَّجُلًا فِيهِ شُرَكَاءُ

مُتَشَاكِسُونَ وَرَجُلًا سَلَمًا لِّرَجُلٍ ۚ

هَلْ يَسْتَوِيٰنِ مَثَلًا ۚ اَلْحَمْدُ لِلّٰهِ ۚ

30. Truly you will die (one day), and truly they (too) will die (one day).

بَلْ أَكْثَرُهُمْ لَا يَعْلَمُونَ ۝

اِنَّكَ مَيِّتٌ وَّاِنَّهُمْ مَّيِّتُونَ ۝

31. In the end you will (all), on the Day of Judgment, settle your disputes in the presence of your Lord.

ثُمَّ اِنَّكُمْ يَوْمَ الْقِيٰمَةِ عِنْدَ رَبِّكُمْ

تَخْتَصِمُونَ ۝

32. Who, then, does more wrong than one who utters a lie concerning Allah, and rejects the Truth when it comes to him; is there not in Hell an abode for blasphemers?

فَمَنْ أَظْلَمُ مِمَّنْ كَذَبَ عَلَى اللّٰهِ

وَكَذَّبَ بِالصِّدْقِ اِذْ جَاءَهُ ۚ أَلَيْسَ

33. And he who brings the Truth and he who confirms (and supports) it - such are the men who do right.

فِى جَهَنَّمَ مَثْوًى لِّلْكَافِرِينَ ۝

وَالَّذِى جَاءَ بِالصِّدْقِ وَصَدَّقَ بِهِ

34. They shall have all that they wish for, in the presence of their Lord: such is the reward of those who do good:

اُولٰئِكَ هُمُ الْمُتَّقُونَ ۝

لَهُمْ مَّا يَشَاءُونَ عِنْدَ رَبِّهِمْ ۚ ذٰلِكَ

35. So that Allah will turn off from them (even) the worst in their deeds

جَزَاءُ الْمُحْسِنِينَ ۝

لِيُكَفِّرَ اللّٰهُ عَنْهُمْ أَسْوَأَ الَّذِى عَمِلُوا

and give them their reward according to the best of what they have done.

وَيَجْزِيَهُمْ أَجْرَهُمْ بِأَحْسَنِ الَّذِىْ
كَانُوْا يَعْمَلُوْنَ ۞

36. Is not Allah enough for his servant? But they try to frighten you with other (gods) besides Him! for such as Allah leaves to stray, there can be no guide.

اَلَيْسَ اللّٰهُ بِكَافٍ عَبْدَهٗ وَيُخَوِّفُوْنَكَ
بِالَّذِيْنَ مِنْ دُوْنِهٖ وَمَنْ يُّضْلِلِ اللّٰهُ
فَمَا لَهٗ مِنْ هَادٍ ۞

37. And such as Allah guides there can be none to lead astray. Is not Allah Exalted in Power, (Able to enforce His Will), Lord of Retribution?

وَمَنْ يَّهْدِ اللّٰهُ فَمَا لَهٗ مِنْ مُّضِلٍّ ۚ
اَلَيْسَ اللّٰهُ بِعَزِيْزٍ ذِى انْتِقَامٍ ۞

38. If indeed you ask them who it is that created the heavens and the earth, they would be sure to say, "Allah". Say: "Do you see then? the things that you invoke besides Allah,- can they, if Allah wills some Penalty for me, remove His Penalty?- Or if He wills some Grace for me, can they keep back His Grace?" Say: "Sufficient is Allah for me! In Him trust those who put their trust."

وَلَئِنْ سَاَلْتَهُمْ مَّنْ خَلَقَ السَّمٰوٰتِ
وَالْاَرْضَ لَيَقُوْلُنَّ اللّٰهُ ۚ قُلْ اَفَرَءَيْتُمْ
مَّا تَدْعُوْنَ مِنْ دُوْنِ اللّٰهِ اِنْ اَرَادَنِىَ
اللّٰهُ بِضُرٍّ هَلْ هُنَّ كٰشِفٰتُ ضُرِّهٖ اَوْ
اَرَادَنِىْ بِرَحْمَةٍ هَلْ هُنَّ مُمْسِكٰتُ
رَحْمَتِهٖ ۚ قُلْ حَسْبِىَ اللّٰهُ ۚ عَلَيْهِ يَتَوَكَّلُ
الْمُتَوَكِّلُوْنَ ۞

39. Say: "O my People! Do whatever you can: I will do (my part): but soon you will know-

قُلْ يٰقَوْمِ اعْمَلُوْا عَلٰى مَكَانَتِكُمْ اِنِّىْ
عَامِلٌ ۚ فَسَوْفَ تَعْلَمُوْنَ ۙ

40. "Who it is to whom comes a Chastisement of ignomiy, and on whom descends a Penalty that abides."

مَنْ يَّأْتِيْهِ عَذَابٌ يُّخْزِيْهِ وَيَحِلُّ
عَلَيْهِ عَذَابٌ مُّقِيْمٌ ۞

41. Verily We have revealed the Book to you in Truth, for (instructing) mankind. He, then, that receives guidance benefits his own soul: but he that strays injures his own soul. Nor you are set over them to dispose of their affairs.

اِنَّا اَنْزَلْنَا عَلَيْكَ الْكِتٰبَ لِلنَّاسِ
بِالْحَقِّ ۚ فَمَنِ اهْتَدٰى فَلِنَفْسِهٖ ۚ وَمَنْ
ضَلَّ فَاِنَّمَا يَضِلُّ عَلَيْهَا ۚ وَمَا اَنْتَ
عَلَيْهِمْ بِوَكِيْلٍ ۞

42. It is Allah that takes the souls (of men) at death; and those that die not (He takes) during their sleep: those on whom He has passed the decree of death, He keeps back (from returning to life), but the rest He sends (to their bodies) for a term appointed. Verily in

اَللّٰهُ يَتَوَفَّى الْاَنْفُسَ حِيْنَ مَوْتِهَا وَ
الَّتِىْ لَمْ تَمُتْ فِىْ مَنَامِهَا ۚ فَيُمْسِكُ
الَّتِىْ قَضٰى عَلَيْهَا الْمَوْتَ وَيُرْسِلُ
الْاُخْرٰى اِلٰى اَجَلٍ مُّسَمًّى ۚ اِنَّ فِىْ

this are Signs for those who reflect.

43. What! Do they take for intercessors others besides Allah? Say: "Even if they have no power whatever and no intelligence?"

44. Say: "To Allah belongs exclusively (the right to grant) intercession: to Him belongs the dominion of the heavens and the earth: In the End, it is to Him that you shall be brought back."

45. When Allah, the One and Only, is mentioned, the hearts of those who do not believe in the Hereafter are filled with disgust and horror; but when (gods) other than He are mentioned, behold, they are filled with joy!

46. Say: "O Allah! Creator of the heavens and the earth! Knower of all that is hidden and open! it is You that will judge between Your servants in those matters about which they have differed."

47. Even if the wrong-doers had all that there is on earth, and as much more, (in vain) would they offer it for ransom from the pain of the Chastisement on the Day of Judgment: but something will confront them from Allah, which they could never have counted upon!

48. For the evils of their deeds will confront them, and they will be (completely) encircled by that which they used to mock at!

49. Now, when trouble touches man, he cries to Us: but when We bestow a favour upon him as from Ourselves, he says, "This has been given to me because of a certain knowledge (I have)!" Nay, but this is but a trial, but most of them do not understand!

50. Thus did the (generations) before them say! But all that they did was of no profit to them.

51. Nay, the evil results of their deeds overtook them.

And the wrong-doers of this (generation)-the evil results of their deeds will soon overtake them (too), and they shall never escape.

ظَلَمُوْا مِنْ هٰٓؤُلَآءِ سَيُصِيْبُهُمْ سَيِّاٰتُ مَا كَسَبُوْا ۖ وَمَا هُمْ بِمُعْجِزِيْنَ ۝

52. Do they not know that Allah enlarges the provision or restricts it, for any He pleases? Verily, in this are Signs for those who believe!

اَوَلَمْ يَعْلَمُوْٓا اَنَّ اللّٰهَ يَبْسُطُ الرِّزْقَ لِمَنْ يَّشَآءُ وَيَقْدِرُ ۚ اِنَّ فِيْ ذٰلِكَ لَاٰيٰتٍ لِّقَوْمٍ يُّؤْمِنُوْنَ ۝

53. Say: "O My servants who have transgressed against their souls! do not despair of the Mercy of Allah: for Allah forgives all sins: for He is Oft-Forgiving, Most Merciful.

قُلْ يٰعِبَادِيَ الَّذِيْنَ اَسْرَفُوْا عَلٰٓى اَنْفُسِهِمْ لَا تَقْنَطُوْا مِنْ رَّحْمَةِ اللّٰهِ ۚ اِنَّ اللّٰهَ يَغْفِرُ الذُّنُوْبَ جَمِيْعًا ۗ اِنَّهٗ هُوَ الْغَفُوْرُ الرَّحِيْمُ ۝

54. "You turn to your Lord (in repentance) and bow to His (Will), before the Chastisement comes on you: after that you shall not be helped.

وَاَنِيْبُوْٓا اِلٰى رَبِّكُمْ وَاَسْلِمُوْا لَهٗ مِنْ قَبْلِ اَنْ يَّأْتِيَكُمُ الْعَذَابُ ثُمَّ لَا تُنْصَرُوْنَ ۝

55. "And follow the best of (the courses) revealed to you from your Lord, before the Chastisement comes on you - of a sudden, while you do not perceive!-

وَاتَّبِعُوْٓا اَحْسَنَ مَآ اُنْزِلَ اِلَيْكُمْ مِّنْ رَّبِّكُمْ مِّنْ قَبْلِ اَنْ يَّأْتِيَكُمُ الْعَذَابُ بَغْتَةً وَّاَنْتُمْ لَا تَشْعُرُوْنَ ۝

56. "Lest the soul should (then) say: 'Ah! woe is me!- In that I neglected (my duty) towards Allah, and was but among those who mocked!'-

اَنْ تَقُوْلَ نَفْسٌ يّٰحَسْرَتٰى عَلٰى مَا فَرَّطْتُ فِيْ جَنْبِ اللّٰهِ وَاِنْ كُنْتُ لَمِنَ السّٰخِرِيْنَ ۝

57. "Or (lest) it should say: 'If only Allah had guided me, I should certainly have been among the righteous!'

اَوْ تَقُوْلَ لَوْ اَنَّ اللّٰهَ هَدٰىنِيْ لَكُنْتُ مِنَ الْمُتَّقِيْنَ ۝

58. "Or (lest) it should say when it (actually) sees the Chastisement: 'If only I had another chance, I should certainly be among those who do good!'

اَوْ تَقُوْلَ حِيْنَ تَرَى الْعَذَابَ لَوْ اَنَّ لِيْ كَرَّةً فَاَكُوْنَ مِنَ الْمُحْسِنِيْنَ ۝

59. "(The reply will be:) 'Nay, but there came to you My Signs, and you rejected them: you were haughty, and became one of those who reject faith!'

بَلٰى قَدْ جَآءَتْكَ اٰيٰتِيْ فَكَذَّبْتَ بِهَا وَاسْتَكْبَرْتَ وَكُنْتَ مِنَ الْكٰفِرِيْنَ ۝

60. On the Day of Judgment you will see those who told lies against Allah;- their faces will be turned black; Is there not in

وَيَوْمَ الْقِيٰمَةِ تَرَى الَّذِيْنَ كَذَبُوْا عَلَى اللّٰهِ وُجُوْهُهُمْ مُّسْوَدَّةٌ ۗ اَلَيْسَ فِيْ

Hell an abode for the haughty?

جَهَنَّمُ مَثْوًى لِّلْمُتَكَبِّرِينَ ۞

61. But Allah will deliver the righteous to their place of salvation: no evil shall touch them, nor shall they grieve.

وَيُنَجِّى اللّٰهُ الَّذِينَ اتَّقَوْا بِمَفَازَتِهِمْ لَا يَمَسُّهُمُ السُّوٓءُ وَلَا هُمْ يَحْزَنُونَ ۞

62. Allah is the Creator of all things, and He is the Guardian and Disposer of all affairs.

اللّٰهُ خَالِقُ كُلِّ شَىْءٍ ۖ وَهُوَ عَلَىٰ كُلِّ شَىْءٍ وَكِيلٌ ۞

63. To Him belong the keys of the heavens and the earth: and those who reject the Signs of Allah,- it is they who will be in loss.

لَهُ مَقَالِيدُ السَّمٰوٰتِ وَالْأَرْضِ ۗ وَالَّذِينَ كَفَرُوا بِآيٰتِ اللّٰهِ أُولٰٓئِكَ هُمُ الْخٰسِرُونَ ۞

64. Say: "Is it someone other than Allah that you order me to worship, O you ignorant ones?"

قُلْ أَفَغَيْرَ اللّٰهِ تَأْمُرُوٓنِّى أَعْبُدُ أَيُّهَا الْجٰهِلُونَ ۞

65. But it has already been revealed to you,- as it was to those before you,- "If you were to join (gods with Allah), truly fruitless will be your work (in life), and you will surely be in the ranks of those who lose (all spirtualy good)".

وَلَقَدْ أُوحِىَ إِلَيْكَ وَإِلَى الَّذِينَ مِنْ قَبْلِكَ ۖ لَئِنْ أَشْرَكْتَ لَيَحْبَطَنَّ عَمَلُكَ وَلَتَكُونَنَّ مِنَ الْخٰسِرِينَ ۞

66. Nay, but worship Allah, and be of those who give thanks.

بَلِ اللّٰهَ فَاعْبُدْ وَكُنْ مِّنَ الشّٰكِرِينَ ۞

67. Nay just estimate have they made of Allah, such as is due to Him: on the Day of Judgment the whole of the earth will be but His handful, and the heavens will be rolled up in His right hand: glory to Him! High is He above the Partners they attribute to Him!

وَمَا قَدَرُوا اللّٰهَ حَقَّ قَدْرِهِ ۗ وَالْأَرْضُ جَمِيعًا قَبْضَتُهُ يَوْمَ الْقِيٰمَةِ وَ السَّمٰوٰتُ مَطْوِيّٰتٌ بِيَمِينِهِ ۚ سُبْحٰنَهُ وَتَعٰلَىٰ عَمَّا يُشْرِكُونَ ۞

68. The Trumpet will (just) be sounded, when all that are in the heavens and on earth will swoon, except such as it will please Allah (to exempt). Then will a second one be sounded, when, behold, they will be standing and looking on!

وَنُفِخَ فِى الصُّورِ فَصَعِقَ مَنْ فِى السَّمٰوٰتِ وَمَنْ فِى الْأَرْضِ إِلَّا مَنْ شَاۤءَ اللّٰهُ ۖ ثُمَّ نُفِخَ فِيهِ أُخْرَىٰ فَإِذَا هُمْ قِيَامٌ يَنْظُرُونَ ۞

69. And the Earth will shine with the glory of its Lord: the Record (of deeds) will be placed (open); the prophets and the witnesses will be brought forward and a just decision pronounced between them; and they will not be wronged (in the least).

وَأَشْرَقَتِ الْأَرْضُ بِنُورِ رَبِّهَا وَوُضِعَ الْكِتٰبُ وَجِاۤئَ بِالنَّبِيِّينَ وَالشُّهَدَاۤءِ وَقُضِىَ بَيْنَهُمْ بِالْحَقِّ وَهُمْ لَا يُظْلَمُونَ ۞

70. And to every soul will be paid in full (the fruit) of its deeds; and (Allah) knows best all that they do.

وَوُفِّيَتْ كُلُّ نَفْسٍ مَّا عَمِلَتْ وَهُوَ أَعْلَمُ بِمَا يَفْعَلُونَ ۞

SÛRAH-40
AL-MU'MIN
(INTRODUCTION)

This Sûrah is called "The Believer" *(Mu'-min)* from the story of the individual Believer among the people of Pharaoh, who declares his faith and looks to the Future (verses 28-45). It is also called *Ghâfir* (He who forgives, see verse 3). In S. 23, called *The Believers (Mu'minûn),* the argument was about the collective force of Faith and Virtue. Here it is about the Individual's witness to Faith and Virtue, and his triumph in the End.

We now begin a series of seven Sûras (40-46) to which are affixed the abbreviated Letters *Hâ-Mim.* Chronologically they all belong to the same period, the later Makkan Period, and they immediately follow the last Sûrah in time. As to the precise meaning of *Hâ-Mim* no authoritative explanation is available. If *Mim* here has a signification similar to Mim in A.L.M. it means the End of things, the Last Day, and all these Suras direct our special attention to that. *Hâ,* the emphatic guttural, in contrast with the softer breathing of Alif, may be meant to suggest that the Beginning is only for the End, the Present for the future, and to emphasise the eschatological element in Faith. But this is mere conjecture, and should be taken, for no more than it is worth.

The general theme of the whole series is the relation of Faith to Unfaith, Revelation to Rejection, Goodness to Evil, Truth to Falsehood. It is shown that the first in each of these pairs is the real friend, helper, and protector of man, while the second is his enemy. The very word *Hâmim* in that sense is used in Sûras 40 and 41 (40: 18 and 41: 34), while in the other Sûras we have words of equivalent import, e.g. *wali* or *nâṣir* (42: 8 and 31); *qarîn* (43: 36, 38); maulâ (44: 41); *auliyâa* or *nâṣirîn* (45: 19,34); *and auliyâ (46: 32).* Is it permissible, to connect the Abbreviated Letters *Hâ-Mîm* with these ideas as expressed in the word *Ḥamiml*

Another suggestion worthy of consideration is that *Hâ* stands for *Hâiy,* and *Mîm* for *Qaiyûm.* These are two attributes of Allah,

meaning, (1) the Living, and (2) the Self-Subsisting, Eternal.
The one points to Life and Revelation, and the other to the
Hereafter and Eternity; and both these matters are specially dealt
with in the seven *Hâ-Mîm* Sûras. The first letter of *Hâiy (Hâ)* is
appropriate for life, and the last letter of *Qaiyûm* is appropriate
for the last Days, the *Ma'âd,* the Hereafter. Again, this is mere
conjecture; and should not be taken for more than it is worth.

71. The Unbelievers will be led to Hell in crowd: until, when they arrive there, its gates will be opened. And its keepers will say, "Did not Apostles come to you from among yourselves, rehearsing to you the Signs of your Lord, and warning you of the Meeting of This Day of yours?" The answer will be: "True: but the Decree of Punishment has been proved true against the Unbelievers!"

وَسِيقَ الَّذِينَ كَفَرُوا إِلَى جَهَنَّمَ
زُمَرًا ۖ حَتَّى إِذَا جَاءُوهَا فُتِحَتْ
أَبْوَابُهَا وَقَالَ لَهُمْ خَزَنَتُهَا أَلَمْ
يَأْتِكُمْ رُسُلٌ مِّنكُمْ يَتْلُونَ عَلَيْكُمْ
آيَاتِ رَبِّكُمْ وَيُنذِرُونَكُمْ لِقَاءَ يَوْمِكُمْ
هَـٰذَا ۚ قَالُوا بَلَىٰ وَلَـٰكِنْ حَقَّتْ كَلِمَةُ
الْعَذَابِ عَلَى الْكَافِرِينَ ۝

72. (To them) will be said: "You enter the gates of Hell, to dwell therein: and evil is (this) abode of the arrogant!"

قِيلَ ادْخُلُوا أَبْوَابَ جَهَنَّمَ خَالِدِينَ
فِيهَا ۖ فَبِئْسَ مَثْوَى الْمُتَكَبِّرِينَ ۝

73. And those who feared their Lord will be led to the Garden in crowds: until behold, they arrive there; its gates will be opened; and its Keepers will say: "Peace be upon you! you have done well you enter here, to dwell therein."

وَسِيقَ الَّذِينَ اتَّقَوْا رَبَّهُمْ إِلَى الْجَنَّةِ
زُمَرًا ۖ حَتَّى إِذَا جَاءُوهَا وَفُتِحَتْ
أَبْوَابُهَا وَقَالَ لَهُمْ خَزَنَتُهَا سَلَامٌ
عَلَيْكُمْ طِبْتُمْ فَادْخُلُوهَا خَالِدِينَ ۝

74. They will say: "Praise be to Allah, Who has truly fulfilled His Promise to us, and has given us (this) land in heritage: we can dwell in the Garden as we will: how excellent a reward for those who work (righteousness)!"

وَقَالُوا الْحَمْدُ لِلَّهِ الَّذِي صَدَقَنَا
وَعْدَهُ وَأَوْرَثَنَا الْأَرْضَ نَتَبَوَّأُ
مِنَ الْجَنَّةِ حَيْثُ نَشَاءُ ۖ فَنِعْمَ
أَجْرُ الْعَامِلِينَ ۝

75. And you will see the angels surrounding the Throne (Divine) on all sides, singing Glory and Praise to their Lord. The Decision between them (at Judgment) will be in (perfect) justice, and the cry (on all sides) will be, "Praise be to Allah, the Lord of the Worlds!"

وَتَرَى الْمَلَائِكَةَ حَافِّينَ مِنْ
حَوْلِ الْعَرْشِ يُسَبِّحُونَ بِحَمْدِ رَبِّهِمْ ۖ
وَقُضِيَ بَيْنَهُم بِالْحَقِّ وَقِيلَ الْحَمْدُ
لِلَّهِ رَبِّ الْعَالَمِينَ ۝

---

40. The Believer
In the name of Allah. Most Gracious, Most Merciful.

(٤٠) سُورَةُ الْمُؤْمِنِ مَكِّيَّةٌ (٨٠)
بِسْمِ اللَّهِ الرَّحْمَـٰنِ الرَّحِيمِ

1. Ha-Mim

حم ۝

2. The revelation of this Book is from Allah, Exalted in Power, full of Knowledge,-

تَنزِيلُ الْكِتَابِ مِنَ اللَّهِ الْعَزِيزِ
الْعَلِيمِ ۝

3. Who forgives sin, accepts repentance, is Strict in punishment, and has a long reach (in all things). There is no god but He: to Him is the final goal.

4. None can dispute about the Signs of Allah but the Unbelievers. Let not, then, their strutting about through the land deceive you!

5. But (there were people) before them, who denied (the Signs),- the People of Noah, and the Confederates (of Evil) after them; and every People plotted against their prophet, to seize him, and disputed by means of vanities, therewith to condemn the Truth; but it was I that seized them! and how (terrible) was My Requital!

6. Thus was the Decree of your Lord proved true against the Unbelievers; that truly they are Companions of the Fire!

7. Those who sustain the Throne (of Allah) and those around it sing Glory and Praise to their Lord; believe in Him; and implore Forgiveness for those who believe: "Our Lord! Your Reach is over all things, in Mercy and Knowledge. Forgive, then, those who turn in Repentance, and follow Your Path; and preserve them from the Chastisement of the Blazing Fire!

8. "And grant, our Lord! that they enter the Gardens of Eternity, which You have promised to them, and to the righteous among their fathers, their wives, and their posterity! For You are (He), the Exalted in Might, full of Wisdom.

9. "And preserve them from (all) ills; and any whom You preserve from ills that Day,- on them You will have bestowed Mercy indeed: and that will be truly (for them) the highest Achievement".

10. The Unbelievers will be addressed: "Greater was the aversion of Allah to you than (is) your aversion to yourselves, seeing that you were called to the Faith and you used to refuse."

إِنَّ الَّذِينَ كَفَرُوا يُنَادَوْنَ لَمَقْتُ اللهِ أَكْبَرُ مِنْ مَّقْتِكُمْ أَنْفُسَكُمْ إِذْ تُدْعَوْنَ إِلَى الْإِيْمَانِ فَتَكْفُرُوْنَ ۝

11. They will say: "Our Lord! Twice have You made us without life, and twice have You given us Life! Now we have recognised our sins: Is there any way out (of this)?"

قَالُوْا رَبَّنَا أَمَتَّنَا اثْنَتَيْنِ وَأَحْيَيْتَنَا اثْنَتَيْنِ فَاعْتَرَفْنَا بِذُنُوْبِنَا فَهَلْ إِلَى خُرُوْجٍ مِّنْ سَبِيْلٍ ۝

12. (The answer will be:) "This is because, when Allah was invoked as the Only (object of worship), you rejected Faith, but when partners were joined to Him, you believed! the Command is with Allah, Most High, Most Great!"

ذٰلِكُمْ بِأَنَّهُ إِذَا دُعِيَ اللهُ وَحْدَهُ كَفَرْتُمْ وَإِنْ يُّشْرَكْ بِهِ تُؤْمِنُوْا فَالْحُكْمُ لِلّٰهِ الْعَلِيِّ الْكَبِيْرِ ۝

13. He it is Who shows you His Signs, and sends down sustenance for you from the sky: but only those receive admonition who turn (to Allah).

هُوَ الَّذِيْ يُرِيْكُمْ اٰيٰتِهِ وَيُنَزِّلُ لَكُمْ مِّنَ السَّمَاءِ رِزْقًا ۗ وَمَا يَتَذَكَّرُ إِلَّا مَنْ يُّنِيْبُ ۝

14. You call, then, upon Allah with sincere devotion to Him, even though the Unbelievers may detest it.

فَادْعُوا اللهَ مُخْلِصِيْنَ لَهُ الدِّيْنَ وَلَوْ كَرِهَ الْكٰفِرُوْنَ ۝

15. Raised high above ranks (or degrees), (He is) the Lord of the Throne (of Authority): by His Command He sends the Spirit (of inspiration) to any of His servants He pleases, that it may warn (men) of the Day of Mutual Meeting,-

رَفِيْعُ الدَّرَجٰتِ ذُو الْعَرْشِ ۚ يُلْقِي الرُّوْحَ مِنْ أَمْرِهِ عَلٰى مَنْ يَّشَاءُ مِنْ عِبَادِهِ لِيُنْذِرَ يَوْمَ التَّلَاقِ ۝

16. The Day whereon they will (all) come forth: not a single thing concerning them is hidden from Allah. Whose will be the dominion that Day?" That of Allah, the One, the Irresistible!

يَوْمَ هُمْ بَارِزُوْنَ ۚ لَا يَخْفٰى عَلَى اللهِ مِنْهُمْ شَيْءٌ ۗ لِمَنِ الْمُلْكُ الْيَوْمَ ۗ لِلّٰهِ الْوَاحِدِ الْقَهَّارِ ۝

17. That Day will every soul be requited for what it earned; no injustice will there be that Day, for Allah is Swift in taking account.

الْيَوْمَ تُجْزٰى كُلُّ نَفْسٍ بِمَا كَسَبَتْ ۗ لَا ظُلْمَ الْيَوْمَ ۗ إِنَّ اللهَ سَرِيْعُ الْحِسَابِ ۝

18. Warn them of the Day that is (ever) drawing near, when the hearts will (come) right up to the throats to choke (them); no intimate friend nor intercessor will the wrong-doers have, who could be listened to.

وَأَنْذِرْهُمْ يَوْمَ الْاٰزِفَةِ إِذِ الْقُلُوْبُ لَدَى الْحَنَاجِرِ كٰظِمِيْنَ ۚ مَا لِلظّٰلِمِيْنَ مِنْ حَمِيْمٍ وَّلَا شَفِيْعٍ

19. (Allah) knows of (the tricks) that deceive with the eyes, and all that the hearts (of men) conceal.

20. And Allah will judge with (justice and) Truth: but those whom (men) invoke besides Him, will not (be in a position) to judge at all. Verily it is Allah (alone) Who hears and sees (all things).

21. Do they not travel through the earth and see what was the End of those before them? They were even superior to them in strength, and in the traces (they have left) in the land: but Allah called them to account for their sins, and none had they to defend them against Allah.

22. That was because there came to them their Apostles with Clear (Signs), but they rejected them: so Allah called them to account: for He is full of Strength, Strict in Punishment.

23. Of old We sent Moses, with Our Signs and an Authority manifest,

24. To Pharaoh, Haman, and Qarun; but they called (him)" a sorcerer telling lies!"...

25. Now, when he came to them in Truth, from Us, they said, "Slay the sons of those who believe with him, and keep alive their females," but the plots of Unbelievers (end) in nothing but errors (and delusions)!...

26. Said Pharaoh: "Leave me to slay Moses; and let him call on his Lord! What I fear is lest he should change your religion, or lest he should cause mischief to appear in the land!"

يُطَاعُ ۞

يَعْلَمُ خَآئِنَةَ الْأَعْيُنِ وَمَا تُخْفِي الصُّدُورُ ۞

وَاللهُ يَقْضِي بِالْحَقِّ ۖ وَالَّذِينَ يَدْعُونَ مِنْ دُونِهِ لَا يَقْضُونَ بِشَيْءٍ ۗ إِنَّ اللهَ هُوَ السَّمِيعُ الْبَصِيرُ ۞

أَوَلَمْ يَسِيرُوا فِي الْأَرْضِ فَيَنْظُرُوا كَيْفَ كَانَ عَاقِبَةُ الَّذِينَ كَانُوا مِنْ قَبْلِهِمْ ۚ كَانُوا هُمْ أَشَدَّ مِنْهُمْ قُوَّةً وَّآثَارًا فِي الْأَرْضِ فَأَخَذَهُمُ اللهُ بِذُنُوبِهِمْ ۖ وَمَا كَانَ لَهُمْ مِّنَ اللهِ مِنْ وَّاقٍ ۞

ذَلِكَ بِأَنَّهُمْ كَانَتْ تَأْتِيهِمْ رُسُلُهُمْ بِالْبَيِّنَاتِ فَكَفَرُوا فَأَخَذَهُمُ اللهُ ۚ إِنَّهُ قَوِيٌّ شَدِيدُ الْعِقَابِ ۞

وَلَقَدْ أَرْسَلْنَا مُوسَى بِآيَاتِنَا وَ سُلْطَانٍ مُّبِينٍ ۞

إِلَى فِرْعَوْنَ وَهَامَانَ وَقَارُونَ فَقَالُوا سَاحِرٌ كَذَّابٌ ۞

فَلَمَّا جَآءَهُمْ بِالْحَقِّ مِنْ عِنْدِنَا قَالُوا اقْتُلُوا أَبْنَاءَ الَّذِينَ آمَنُوا مَعَهُ وَاسْتَحْيُوا نِسَاءَهُمْ ۚ وَمَا كَيْدُ الْكَافِرِينَ إِلَّا فِي ضَلَالٍ ۞

وَقَالَ فِرْعَوْنُ ذَرُونِي أَقْتُلْ مُوسَى وَلْيَدْعُ رَبَّهُ ۖ إِنِّي أَخَافُ أَنْ يُبَدِّلَ دِينَكُمْ أَوْ أَنْ يُظْهِرَ فِي

27. Moses said: "I have indeed called upon my Lord and your Lord (for protection) from every arrogant one who does not believe in the Day of Account!"

28. A believer, a man from among the people of Pharaoh, who had concealed his faith, said: "Will you slay a man because he says, 'My Lord is Allah'?- when he has indeed come to you with Clear (Signs) from your Lord? and if he be a liar, on him is (the sin of) his lie: but, if he is telling the Truth, then will fall on you something of the (calamity) of which he warns you: truly Allah does not guide one who transgresses and lies!

29. "O my People! Yours is the dominion this day: you have the upper hand in the land: but who will help us from the Punishment of Allah, should it befall us?" Pharaoh said: "I but point out to you that which I see (myself); nor do I guide you but to the Path of Right!"

30. Then said the man who believed: "O my people! Truly I do fear for you something like the Day (of disaster) of the Confederates (in sin)!-

31. "Something like the fate of the People of Noah, the 'Ad, and the Thamud, and those who came after them: but Allah never wishes injustice to His servants.

32. "And O my people! I fear for you a Day when there will be mutual calling (and wailing),-

33. "A Day when you shall turn your backs and flee: no defender shall you have from Allah: any whom Allah leaves to stray, there is none to guide.

الْأَرْضِ الْفَسَادَ ۝

وَقَالَ مُوسَى إِنِّي عُذْتُ بِرَبِّي وَرَبِّكُمْ

مِنْ كُلِّ مُتَكَبِّرٍ لَّا يُؤْمِنُ بِيَوْمِ

الْحِسَابِ ۝

وَقَالَ رَجُلٌ مُؤْمِنٌ مِّنْ الِ

فِرْعَوْنَ يَكْتُمُ إِيمَانَهُ أَتَقْتُلُونَ

رَجُلًا أَنْ يَقُولَ رَبِّيَ اللَّهُ وَقَدْ

جَاءَكُمْ بِالْبَيِّنَاتِ مِنْ رَبِّكُمْ وَإِنْ

يَكُ كَاذِبًا فَعَلَيْهِ كَذِبُهُ وَإِنْ

يَكُ صَادِقًا يُصِبْكُمْ بَعْضُ الَّذِي

يَعِدُكُمْ إِنَّ اللَّهَ لَا يَهْدِي مَنْ

هُوَ مُسْرِفٌ كَذَّابٌ ۝

يَقَوْمِ لَكُمُ الْمُلْكُ الْيَوْمَ ظَاهِرِينَ

فِي الْأَرْضِ فَمَنْ يَنْصُرُنَا مِنْ بَأْسِ

اللَّهِ إِنْ جَاءَنَا قَالَ فِرْعَوْنُ مَا

أُرِيكُمْ إِلَّا مَا أَرَى وَمَا أَهْدِيكُمْ

إِلَّا سَبِيلَ الرَّشَادِ ۝

وَقَالَ الَّذِي آمَنَ يَقَوْمِ إِنِّي أَخَافُ

عَلَيْكُمْ مِثْلَ يَوْمِ الْأَحْزَابِ ۝

مِثْلَ دَأْبِ قَوْمِ نُوحٍ وَعَادٍ وَثَمُودَ

وَالَّذِينَ مِنْ بَعْدِهِمْ وَمَا اللَّهُ

يُرِيدُ ظُلْمًا لِلْعِبَادِ ۝

وَيَقَوْمِ إِنِّي أَخَافُ عَلَيْكُمْ يَوْمَ

التَّنَادِ ۝

يَوْمَ تُوَلُّونَ مُدْبِرِينَ مَا لَكُمْ مِنَ

اللَّهِ مِنْ عَاصِمٍ وَمَنْ يُضْلِلِ اللَّهُ

34. "And to you there came Joseph in times gone by, with Clear Signs, but you did not cease to doubt of the (mission) for which he had come: at length, when he died, you said: Allah will not send any Messenger after him. Thus Allah leaves to stray such as transgress and live in doubt,-

فَمَا لَهُ مِنْ هَادٍ ۝

وَلَقَدْ جَاءَكُمْ يُوْسُفُ مِنْ قَبْلُ

بِالْبَيِّنَاتِ فَمَا زِلْتُمْ فِيْ شَكٍّ مِّمَّا

جَاءَكُمْ بِهِ ۖ حَتّٰى اِذَا هَلَكَ قُلْتُمْ

لَنْ يَّبْعَثَ اللّٰهُ مِنْ بَعْدِهٖ رَسُوْلًا ۚ

كَذٰلِكَ يُضِلُّ اللّٰهُ مَنْ هُوَ مُسْرِفٌ

مُّرْتَابٌ ۝

35. "(Such) as dispute about the Signs of Allah, without any authority that has reached them, grievous and odious (is such conduct) in the sight of Allah and of the Believers. Thus Allah seals up every heart of arrogant and obstinate transgressors."

الَّذِيْنَ يُجَادِلُوْنَ فِيْ اٰيٰتِ اللّٰهِ

بِغَيْرِ سُلْطٰنٍ اَتٰىهُمْ ۖ كَبُرَ مَقْتًا عِنْدَ

اللّٰهِ وَعِنْدَ الَّذِيْنَ اٰمَنُوْا ۚ كَذٰلِكَ

يَطْبَعُ اللّٰهُ عَلٰى كُلِّ قَلْبِ مُتَكَبِّرٍ

جَبَّارٍ ۝

36. Pharaoh said: "O Haman! build me a lofty palace, that I may attain the ways and means,-

وَقَالَ فِرْعَوْنُ يٰهَامٰنُ ابْنِ لِيْ

صَرْحًا لَّعَلِّيْٓ اَبْلُغُ الْاَسْبَابَ ۝

37. "The ways and means of (reaching) the heavens, and that I may mount up to the God of Moses: But as far as I am concerned, I think (Moses) is a liar!" Thus was made alluring, in Pharaoh's eyes, the evil of his deeds, and he was hindered from the Path; and the plot of Pharaoh led to nothing but perdition (for him).

اَسْبَابَ السَّمٰوٰتِ فَاَطَّلِعَ اِلٰٓى اِلٰهِ

مُوْسٰى وَاِنِّيْ لَاَظُنُّهٗ كَاذِبًا ۚ وَكَذٰلِكَ

زُيِّنَ لِفِرْعَوْنَ سُوْٓءُ عَمَلِهٖ وَصُدَّ عَنِ

السَّبِيْلِ ۚ وَمَا كَيْدُ فِرْعَوْنَ اِلَّا

فِيْ تَبَابٍ ۝

38. The man who believed said further: "O my people! follow me: I will lead you to the Path of Right.

وَقَالَ الَّذِيْٓ اٰمَنَ يٰقَوْمِ اتَّبِعُوْنِ

اَهْدِكُمْ سَبِيْلَ الرَّشَادِ ۝

39. "O my people! This life of the present is nothing but (temporary) convenience: It is the Hereafter that is the Home that will last.

يٰقَوْمِ اِنَّمَا هٰذِهِ الْحَيٰوةُ الدُّنْيَا

مَتَاعٌ ۖ وَّاِنَّ الْاٰخِرَةَ هِيَ دَارُ الْقَرَارِ

40. "He that works evil will not be requited but by the like thereof: and he that works a righteous deed - whether man or woman - and is a Believer- such

مَنْ عَمِلَ سَيِّئَةً فَلَا يُجْزٰٓى اِلَّا

مِثْلَهَا ۚ وَمَنْ عَمِلَ صَالِحًا مِّنْ

ذَكَرٍ اَوْ اُنْثٰى وَهُوَ مُؤْمِنٌ فَاُولٰٓئِكَ

will enter the Garden (of Bliss):therein will they have abundance without measure.

41. "And O my people! How (strange) it is for me to call you to Salvation while you call me to the Fire!

42. "You do call upon me to blaspheme against Allah, and to join with Him partners of whom I have no knowledge; and I call you to the Exalted in Power, Who forgives again and again!"

43. "Without doubt you do call me to one who is not fit to be called to, whether in this world, or in the Hereafter; our return will be to Allah; and the transgressors will be Companions of the Fire!

44. "Soon will you remember what I say to you (now)-My (own) affair I commit to Allah: for Allah (ever) watches over His servants."

45. Then Allah saved him from (every) ill that they plotted (against him), but the burnt of the Penalty encompassed on all sides the People of Pharaoh.

46. In front of the Fire will they be brought, morning and evening: and (the sentence will be) on the Day that Judgment will be established: "You cast the People of Pharaoh into the severest Chastisement!"

47. Behold, they will dispute with each other in the Fire! The weak ones (who followed) will say to those who had been arrogant, "We but followed you: can you then take (on yourselves) from us some share of the Fire?

48. Those who had been arrogant will say: "We are all in this (Fire)! Truly, Allah has judged between (His) servants!"

49. Those in the Fire will say to the Keepers of

Hell: "Pray to your Lord to lighten us the Penalty for a day (at least)!"

50. They will say: "Did there not come to you your Apostles with Clear Signs?" They will say, "Yes". They will reply, "Then pray (as you like)! But the prayer of those without Faith is nothing but (futile wandering) in (mazes of) error!"

51. We will, without doubt, help Our Apostles and those who believe, (both) in this world's life and on the Day when the Witnesses will stand forth,-

52. The Day when no profit will it be to Wrong-doers to present their excuses, but they will (only) have the Curse and the Home of Misery.

53. We did aforetime give Moses the (Book of) Guidance, and We gave the Book in inheritance to the Children of Israel,-

54. A Guide and a Message to men of Understanding.

55. Patiently, then, persevere: for the Promise of Allah is true: and ask forgiveness for your fault, and celebrate the Praises of your Lord in the evening and in the morning.

56. Those who dispute about the Signs of Allah without any authority bestowed on them,- there is nothing in their breasts but (the quest of) greatness, which they shall never attain to: seek refuge, then, in Allah: It is He Who hears and sees (all things).

57. Assuredly the creation of the heavens and the earth is a greater (matter) than the creation of men: yet most men do not understand.

58. Not equal are the blind and those who (clearly) see: nor are (equal) those who believe and work deeds of righteousness, and those who do evil. Little do you learn by admonition!

59. The Hour will certainly come: therein is no doubt: yet most men do not believe.

إِنَّ السَّاعَةَ لَآتِيَةٌ لَّا رَيْبَ فِيهَا وَلَٰكِنَّ أَكْثَرَ النَّاسِ لَا يُؤْمِنُونَ ۝

60. And your Lord says: "Call on Me; I will answer your (Prayer): but those who are too arrogant to serve Me will surely find themselves in Hell - in humiliation!"

وَقَالَ رَبُّكُمُ ادْعُونِي أَسْتَجِبْ لَكُمْ إِنَّ الَّذِينَ يَسْتَكْبِرُونَ عَنْ عِبَادَتِي سَيَدْخُلُونَ جَهَنَّمَ دَاخِرِينَ ۝

61. It is Allah Who has made the Night for you, that you may rest therein, and the Day as that which helps (you) to see. Verily Allah is full of Grace and Bounty to men: yet most men give no thanks.

اللَّهُ الَّذِي جَعَلَ لَكُمُ اللَّيْلَ لِتَسْكُنُوا فِيهِ وَالنَّهَارَ مُبْصِرًا إِنَّ اللَّهَ لَذُو فَضْلٍ عَلَى النَّاسِ وَلَٰكِنَّ أَكْثَرَ النَّاسِ لَا يَشْكُرُونَ ۝

62. Such is Allah, your Lord, the Creator of all things, there is no god but He: then how you are deluded away from the Truth!

ذَٰلِكُمُ اللَّهُ رَبُّكُمْ خَالِقُ كُلِّ شَيْءٍ لَّا إِلَٰهَ إِلَّا هُوَ فَأَنَّىٰ تُؤْفَكُونَ ۝

63. Thus are deluded those who are wont to reject the Signs of Allah.

كَذَٰلِكَ يُؤْفَكُ الَّذِينَ كَانُوا بِآيَاتِ اللَّهِ يَجْحَدُونَ ۝

64. It is Allah Who has made for you the earth as a resting place, and the sky as a canopy, and has given you shape- and made your shapes beautiful,- and has provided for you Sustenance, of things pure and good;- such is Allah your Lord. So Glory to Allah, the Lord of the Worlds!

اللَّهُ الَّذِي جَعَلَ لَكُمُ الْأَرْضَ قَرَارًا وَالسَّمَاءَ بِنَاءً وَصَوَّرَكُمْ فَأَحْسَنَ صُوَرَكُمْ وَرَزَقَكُمْ مِّنَ الطَّيِّبَاتِ ذَٰلِكُمُ اللَّهُ رَبُّكُمْ فَتَبَارَكَ اللَّهُ رَبُّ الْعَالَمِينَ ۝

65. He is the Living (One): there is no god but He: call upon Him, giving Him sincere devotion. Praise be to Allah, Lord of the Worlds!

هُوَ الْحَيُّ لَا إِلَٰهَ إِلَّا هُوَ فَادْعُوهُ مُخْلِصِينَ لَهُ الدِّينَ الْحَمْدُ لِلَّهِ رَبِّ الْعَالَمِينَ ۝

66. Say: "I have been forbidden to invoke those whom you invoke besides Allah,- seeing that the Clear Sings have come to me from my Lord; and I have been commanded to submit (in Islam) to the Lord of the Worlds."

قُلْ إِنِّي نُهِيتُ أَنْ أَعْبُدَ الَّذِينَ تَدْعُونَ مِن دُونِ اللَّهِ لَمَّا جَاءَنِيَ الْبَيِّنَاتُ مِن رَّبِّي وَأُمِرْتُ أَنْ أُسْلِمَ لِرَبِّ الْعَالَمِينَ ۝

67. It is He Who has created you from dust, then

هُوَ الَّذِي خَلَقَكُمْ مِّن تُرَابٍ ثُمَّ

from a sperm-drop, then from a leech-like clot; then He gets you out (into the light) as a child: then lets you (grow and) reach your age of full strength; then lets you become old,- though of you there are some who die before;- and lets you reach a term appointed; in order that you may learn wisdom.

68. It is He Who gives Life and Death; and when He decides upon an affair, He says to it, "Be", and it is.

69. Don't you see those that dispute concerning the Sings of Allah? How are they turned away (from Reality)?-

70. Those who reject the Book and the (revelations) with which We sent Our Apostles: but soon shall they know,-

71. When the yokes (shall be) round their necks, and the chains; they shall be dragged along-

72. In the boiling fetid fluid: then in the Fire they shall be burned;

73. Then shall it be said to them: "Where are the (deities) to which you gave part- worship-

74. "Besides Allah?" They will reply: "They have left us in the lurch: nay, we did not invoke of old, anything (that had real existence)." Thus does Allah leave the Unbelievers to stray.

75. "That was because you were wont to rejoice on the earth in things other than the Truth, and that you were wont to be insolent.

76. "You enter the gates of Hell, to dwell therein: and evil is (this) abode of the arrogant!"

77. So persevere in patience; for the Promise of Allah is true: and whether

We show you (in this life) some part of what We promise them,- or We take your soul (to Our Mercy) (before that),-(in any case) it is to Us that they shall (all) return.

78. We did aforetime send Apostles before you: of them there are some whose story We have related to you, and some whose story We have not related to you. It was not (possible) for any Apostle to bring a Sign except by the leave of Allah: but when the Command of Allah issued, the matter was decided in truth and justice, and there perished, there and then those who stood on Falsehoods.

79. It is Allah Who made cattle for you, that you may use some for riding and some for food;

80. And there are (other) advantages in them for you (besides); that you may through them attain to any need (there may be) in your hearts; and on them and on ships you are carried.

81. And He shows you (always) His Signs: then which of the Signs of Allah will you deny?

82. Do they not travel through the earth and see what was the End of those before them? They were more numerous than these and superior in strength and in the traces (they have left) in the land: yet all that they accomplished was of no profit to them.

83. For when their Apostles came to them with Clear Signs, they exulted in such knowledge (and skill) as they had; but that very (wrath) at which they were wont to scoff hemmed them in.

84. But when they saw Our Punishment, they said: "We believe in Allah,- the One Allah - and we reject the partners we used to join with Him."

85. But their professing the Faith when they (actually) saw

SÛRAH-41
HÂ-MÎM AS-SAJDAH
(INTRODUCTION)

This is the second of the series of seven Sûras bearing the Abbreviated Letters *Hâ-Mim*, as explained in the Introduction to S. 40. To prevent confusion with other Sûras of the *Hâ-Mim* series, the word *Sajdah* is sometimes added to the title, making it *Hâ-Mim as-Sajdah*, the double title being necessary as there is another sûrah called *Sajdah* (S. 32). To avoid the double title it is sometimes called *Fuṣṣilat*, from the occurrence of the word in verse 3.

The meaning of *Hâ-Mim* has been explained in the Introduction to S. 40, where will also be found a note on the chronology and general theme of the seven *Hâ-Mim* Sûras.

For this particular Sûrah the theme is that the basis of Faith and Revelation is Allah's Power and Goodness, and the fruit of both is man's righteousness and healing.

Our Punishment, was not going to profit them. (Such has been) Allah's Way of dealing with His servants (from the most ancient times). And even thus did the Rejecters of Allah perish (utterly)!

بِأْسَنَا سُنَّتَ اللهِ الَّتِي قَدْ خَلَتْ

فِيْ عِبَادِهٖ ۚ وَخَسِرَ هُنَالِكَ

الْكٰفِرُوْنَ ۞

41. Ha Mim Sajda
In the name of Allah. Most Gracious, Most Merciful.

(٣١) سُوْرَةُ حٰمٓ السَّجْدَةِ مَكِّيَّةٌ (٦١)

بِسْمِ اللهِ الرَّحْمٰنِ الرَّحِيْمِ

1.   Ha -Mim:

حٰمٓ ۞

2.   A Revelation from (Allah), Most Gracious, Most Merciful;-

تَنْزِيْلٌ مِّنَ الرَّحْمٰنِ الرَّحِيْمِ ۞

3.   A Book, whereof the verses are explained in detail;- a Qur'an in Arabic, for people who understand;-

كِتٰبٌ فُصِّلَتْ اٰيٰتُهٗ قُرْاٰنًا

عَرَبِيًّا لِّقَوْمٍ يَّعْلَمُوْنَ ۞

4.   Giving good news and admonition: yet most of them turn away, and so they do not hear.

بَشِيْرًا وَّنَذِيْرًا ۚ فَاَعْرَضَ اَكْثَرُهُمْ

فَهُمْ لَا يَسْمَعُوْنَ ۞

5.   They say: "Our hearts are under veils, (concealed) from that to which you invite us, and in our ears is a deafness, and between us and you is a screen: so you do (what you will); for us, we shall do (what we will!)"

وَقَالُوْا قُلُوْبُنَا فِيْ اَكِنَّةٍ مِّمَّا

تَدْعُوْنَا اِلَيْهِ وَفِيْ اٰذَانِنَا وَقْرٌ

وَّمِنْ بَيْنِنَا وَبَيْنِكَ حِجَابٌ

فَاعْمَلْ اِنَّنَا عٰمِلُوْنَ ۞

6.   You say : "I am but a man like you: It is revealed to me by Inspiration, that your God is One God: so stand true to Him, and ask for His Forgiveness." And woe to those who join gods with Allah,-

قُلْ اِنَّمَا اَنَا بَشَرٌ مِّثْلُكُمْ يُوْحٰى

اِلَيَّ اَنَّمَا اِلٰهُكُمْ اِلٰهٌ وَّاحِدٌ

فَاسْتَقِيْمُوْا اِلَيْهِ وَاسْتَغْفِرُوْهُ ۗ

وَوَيْلٌ لِّلْمُشْرِكِيْنَ ۞

7.   Those who do not practise regular Charity, and who even deny the Hereafter.

الَّذِيْنَ لَا يُؤْتُوْنَ الزَّكٰوةَ وَهُمْ

بِالْاٰخِرَةِ هُمْ كٰفِرُوْنَ ۞

8.   For those who believe and work deeds of righteousness is a reward that will never fail.

اِنَّ الَّذِيْنَ اٰمَنُوْا وَعَمِلُوا الصّٰلِحٰتِ

لَهُمْ اَجْرٌ غَيْرُ مَمْنُوْنٍ ۞

9.   Say: Is it that you deny Him Who created the earth in two Days? And do you join equals with Him? He is the Lord of (all) the Worlds.

قُلْ اَئِنَّكُمْ لَتَكْفُرُوْنَ بِالَّذِيْ خَلَقَ

الْاَرْضَ فِيْ يَوْمَيْنِ وَتَجْعَلُوْنَ لَهٗ

اَنْدَادًا ذٰلِكَ رَبُّ الْعٰلَمِيْنَ ۞

10. He set on the (earth), mountains standing firm, high above it, and bestowed blessings on the earth, and measured therein its sustenance in four Days, alike for (all) who ask.

وَجَعَلَ فِيهَا رَوَاسِىَ مِن فَوْقِهَا
وَبَارَكَ فِيهَا وَقَدَّرَ فِيهَا أَقْوَاتَهَا
فِىۤ أَرْبَعَةِ أَيَّامٍ سَوَآءً لِّلسَّآئِلِينَ ۞

11. Moreover He comprehended in His design the sky, and it had been (as) smoke: He said to it and to the earth: "You come together, willingly or unwillingly." They said: "We do come (together), in willing obedience."

ثُمَّ اسْتَوَىۤ إِلَى السَّمَآءِ وَهِىَ
دُخَانٌ فَقَالَ لَهَا وَلِلْأَرْضِ
ائْتِيَا طَوْعًا أَوْ كَرْهًا ۖ قَالَتَآ
أَتَيْنَا طَآئِعِينَ ۞

12. So He completed them as seven firmaments in two Days, and He assigned to each heaven its duty and command. And We adorned the lower heaven with lights, and (provided it) with guard. Such is the Decree of (Him) the Exalted in Might, Full of Knowledge.

فَقَضَىٰهُنَّ سَبْعَ سَمٰوَاتٍ فِى
يَوْمَيْنِ وَأَوْحَىٰ فِى كُلِّ سَمَآءٍ
أَمْرَهَا ۚ وَزَيَّنَّا السَّمَآءَ الدُّنْيَا
بِمَصَابِيحَ ۖ وَحِفْظًا ۚ ذٰلِكَ
تَقْدِيرُ الْعَزِيزِ الْعَلِيمِ ۞

13. But if they turn away, you say: "I have warned you of a stunning Punishment (as of thunder and lightning) like that which (overtook) the ʿAd and the Thamud!"

فَإِنْ أَعْرَضُوا فَقُلْ أَنذَرْتُكُمْ
صٰعِقَةً مِّثْلَ صٰعِقَةِ عَادٍ وَثَمُودَ ۞

14. Behold, the Apostles came to them, from before them and behind them, (preaching): "Serve none but Allah." They said, "If our Lord had so pleased, He would certainly have sent down angels (to preach). Now we reject your mission (altogether)."

إِذْ جَآءَتْهُمُ الرُّسُلُ مِن بَيْنِ أَيْدِيهِمْ
وَمِنْ خَلْفِهِمْ أَلَّا تَعْبُدُوا إِلَّا اللهَ ۖ
قَالُوا لَوْ شَآءَ رَبُّنَا لَأَنزَلَ مَلٰئِكَةً
فَإِنَّا بِمَآ أُرْسِلْتُم بِهِ كٰفِرُونَ ۞

15. Now the ʿAd behaved arrogantly through the land, against (all) truth and reason, and said: "Who is superior to us in strength?" What! did they not see that Allah, Who created them, was superior to them in strength? But they continued to reject Our Signs!

فَأَمَّا عَادٌ فَاسْتَكْبَرُوا فِى الْأَرْضِ
بِغَيْرِ الْحَقِّ وَقَالُوا مَنْ أَشَدُّ مِنَّا
قُوَّةً ۖ أَوَلَمْ يَرَوْا أَنَّ اللهَ الَّذِى
خَلَقَهُمْ هُوَ أَشَدُّ مِنْهُمْ قُوَّةً ۖ وَ
كَانُوا بِآيٰتِنَا يَجْحَدُونَ ۞

16. So We sent against them a furious wind through days of disaster, that We might give them a taste of a Chastisement of humiliation in this life;

فَأَرْسَلْنَا عَلَيْهِمْ رِيحًا صَرْصَرًا فِىۤ
أَيَّامٍ نَّحِسَاتٍ لِّنُذِيقَهُمْ عَذَابَ
الْخِزْىِ فِى الْحَيٰوةِ الدُّنْيَا ۖ وَ

but the Chastisement of the Hereafter will be more humiliating still: and they will find no help.

17. As to the Thamud, We gave them Guidance, but they preferred blindness (of heart) to Guidance: so the stunning Punishment of humiliation seized them, because of what they had earned.

18. But We delivered those who believed and practised righteousness.

19. On the Day that the enemies of Allah will be gathered together to the Fire, they will be marched in ranks.

20. At length, when they reach the (Fire), their hearing, their sight, and their skins will bear witness against them, as to (all) their deeds.

21. They will say to their skins: "Why do you bear witness against us?" They will say: "Allah has given us speech,- (He) Who gives speech to everything: He created you for the first time, and unto Him were you to return.

22. "You did not seek to hide yourselves, lest your hearing, your sight, and your skins should bear witness against you! But you thought that Allah did not know many of the things that you used to do!

23. "But this thought of yours which you entertained concerning your Lord, has brought you to destruction, and (now) you have become of those utterly lost!"

24. If, then, they have patience, the Fire will be a home for them! and if they beg to be received into favour, into favour will they not (then) be received.

لَعَذَابُ الْاٰخِرَةِ اَخْزٰى وَهُمْ لَا يُنْصَرُوْنَ ۝

وَاَمَّا ثَمُوْدُ فَهَدَيْنٰهُمْ فَاسْتَحَبُّوا الْعَمٰى عَلَى الْهُدٰى فَاَخَذَتْهُمْ صٰعِقَةُ الْعَذَابِ الْهُوْنِ بِمَا كَانُوْا يَكْسِبُوْنَ ۝

وَنَجَّيْنَا الَّذِيْنَ اٰمَنُوْا وَكَانُوْا يَتَّقُوْنَ ۝

وَيَوْمَ يُحْشَرُ اَعْدَآءُ اللّٰهِ اِلَى النَّارِ فَهُمْ يُوْزَعُوْنَ ۝

حَتّٰى اِذَا مَا جَآءُوْهَا شَهِدَ عَلَيْهِمْ سَمْعُهُمْ وَاَبْصَارُهُمْ وَجُلُوْدُهُمْ بِمَا كَانُوْا يَعْمَلُوْنَ ۝

وَقَالُوْا لِجُلُوْدِهِمْ لِمَ شَهِدْتُمْ عَلَيْنَا ۚ قَالُوْا اَنْطَقَنَا اللّٰهُ الَّذِيْ اَنْطَقَ كُلَّ شَيْءٍ وَهُوَ خَلَقَكُمْ اَوَّلَ مَرَّةٍ وَّ اِلَيْهِ تُرْجَعُوْنَ ۝

وَمَا كُنْتُمْ تَسْتَتِرُوْنَ اَنْ يَّشْهَدَ عَلَيْكُمْ سَمْعُكُمْ وَلَا اَبْصَارُكُمْ وَلَا جُلُوْدُكُمْ وَلٰكِنْ ظَنَنْتُمْ اَنَّ اللّٰهَ لَا يَعْلَمُ كَثِيْرًا مِّمَّا تَعْمَلُوْنَ ۝

وَذٰلِكُمْ ظَنُّكُمُ الَّذِيْ ظَنَنْتُمْ بِرَبِّكُمْ اَرْدٰىكُمْ فَاَصْبَحْتُمْ مِّنَ الْخٰسِرِيْنَ ۝

فَاِنْ يَّصْبِرُوْا فَالنَّارُ مَثْوًى لَّهُمْ ۚ وَاِنْ يَّسْتَعْتِبُوْا فَمَا هُمْ مِّنَ الْمُعْتَبِيْنَ ۝

25. And We have destined for them intimate companions (of like nature), who made alluring to them what was before them and behind them; and the sentence among the previous generations of Jinns and men, who have passed away, is proved against them; for they are utterly lost.

وَقَيَّضۡنَا لَهُمۡ قُرَنَآءَ فَزَيَّنُوۡا لَهُمۡ

مَّا بَيۡنَ اَيۡدِيۡهِمۡ وَمَا خَلۡفَهُمۡ

وَحَقَّ عَلَيۡهِمُ الۡقَوۡلُ فِيۡٓ اُمَمٍ قَدۡ

خَلَتۡ مِنۡ قَبۡلِهِمۡ مِّنَ الۡجِنِّ وَ

الۡاِنۡسِ ۚ اِنَّهُمۡ كَانُوۡا خٰسِرِيۡنَ ۞

26. The Unbelievers say: "Do not listen to this Qur'an, but talk at random in the midst of its (reading), that you may gain the upper hand!"

وَقَالَ الَّذِيۡنَ كَفَرُوۡا لَا تَسۡمَعُوۡا

لِهٰذَا الۡقُرۡاٰنِ وَالۡغَوۡا فِيۡهِ لَعَلَّكُمۡ

تَغۡلِبُوۡنَ ۞

27. But We will certainly give the Unbelievers a taste of a severe Chastisement, and We will requite them for the worst of their deeds.

فَلَنُذِيۡقَنَّ الَّذِيۡنَ كَفَرُوۡا عَذَابًا

شَدِيۡدًا ۙ وَّلَنَجۡزِيَنَّهُمۡ اَسۡوَاَ الَّذِيۡ

كَانُوۡا يَعۡمَلُوۡنَ ۞

28. Such is the requital of the enemies of Allah,- the Fire: therein will be for them the Eternal Home: a (fit) requital, for that they were wont to reject Our Signs.

ذٰلِكَ جَزَآءُ اَعۡدَآءِ اللّٰهِ النَّارُ ۚ

لَهُمۡ فِيۡهَا دَارُ الۡخُلۡدِ ۚ جَزَآءًۢ بِمَا

كَانُوۡا بِاٰيٰتِنَا يَجۡحَدُوۡنَ ۞

29. And the Unbelievers will say: "Our Lord! Show us those, among Jinns and men, who misled us: We shall crush them beneath our feet, so that they become the vilest (before all)."

وَقَالَ الَّذِيۡنَ كَفَرُوۡا رَبَّنَآ اَرِنَا

الَّذَيۡنِ اَضَلّٰنَا مِنَ الۡجِنِّ وَالۡاِنۡسِ

نَجۡعَلۡهُمَا تَحۡتَ اَقۡدَامِنَا لِيَكُوۡنَا

مِنَ الۡاَسۡفَلِيۡنَ ۞

30. In the case of those who say, "Our Lord is Allah", and, further, stand straight and steadfast, the angels descend on them (from time to time): "Fear you not!" (they suggest), "Nor grieve! but receive the Glad Tidings of the Garden (of Bliss), the which you were promised!

اِنَّ الَّذِيۡنَ قَالُوۡا رَبُّنَا اللّٰهُ ثُمَّ

اسۡتَقَامُوۡا تَتَنَزَّلُ عَلَيۡهِمُ الۡمَلٰٓئِكَةُ

اَلَّا تَخَافُوۡا وَلَا تَحۡزَنُوۡا وَاَبۡشِرُوۡا

بِالۡجَنَّةِ الَّتِيۡ كُنۡتُمۡ تُوۡعَدُوۡنَ ۞

31. "We are your protectors in this life and in the Hereafter: therein you shall have all that your souls shall desire; therein you shall have all that you ask for!-

نَحۡنُ اَوۡلِيَآؤُكُمۡ فِى الۡحَيٰوةِ الدُّنۡيَا

وَفِى الۡاٰخِرَةِ ۚ وَلَكُمۡ فِيۡهَا مَا

تَشۡتَهِيۡٓ اَنۡفُسُكُمۡ وَلَكُمۡ فِيۡهَا مَا

تَدَّعُوۡنَ ۞

32. "A hospitable gift from One Oft-Forgiving, Most Merciful!"

33. Who is better in speech than one who calls (men) to Allah, works righteousness, and says, "I am of those who bow in Islam"?

34. Nor can Goodness and Evil be equal. Repel (Evil) with what is better: then will he between whom and you was hatred, become as it were your friend and intimate!

35. And no one will be granted such goodness except those who exercise patience and self-restraint,- none but persons of the greatest good fortune.

36. And if (at any time) an incitement to discord is made to you by the Evil One, seek refuge in Allah. He is the One Who hears and knows all things.

37. Among His Signs are the Night and the Day, and the Sun and the Moon. Do not adore the sun and the moon, but adore Allah, Who created them, if it is Him you wish to serve.

38. But if the (Unbelievers) are arrogant, (no matter): for in the presence of your Lord are those who celebrate His praises by night and by day. And they never flag (nor feel themselves above it).

39. And among His Signs is this: that you see the earth barren and desolate; but when We send down rain to it, it is stirred to life and yields increase. Truly, He Who gives life to the (dead) earth can surely give life to (men) who are dead. For He has power over all things.

40. Those who pervert the Truth in Our Signs are

not hidden from Us. Which is better?- he that is cast into the Fire, or he that comes safe through, on the Day of Judgment? Do what you will: verily He sees (clearly) all that you do.

لَا يَخْفَوْنَ عَلَيْنَا ۗ أَفَمَنْ يُلْقٰى فِى النَّارِ خَيْرٌ أَمْ مَّنْ يَّأْتِىۡ اٰمِنًا يَّوْمَ الْقِيٰمَةِ ۚ اِعْمَلُوْا مَا شِئْتُمْ ۙ اِنَّهٗ بِمَا تَعْمَلُوْنَ بَصِيْرٌ ۝

41. Those who reject the Message when it comes to them (are not hidden from Us). And indeed it is a Book of exalted power.

اِنَّ الَّذِيْنَ كَفَرُوْا بِالذِّكْرِ لَمَّا جَآءَهُمْ ۚ وَاِنَّهٗ لَكِتٰبٌ عَزِيْزٌ ۝

42. No falsehood can approach it from before or behind it: It is sent down by One full of Wisdom, Worthy of all Praise.

لَّا يَأْتِيْهِ الْبَاطِلُ مِنْۢ بَيْنِ يَدَيْهِ وَلَا مِنْ خَلْفِهٖ ۚ تَنْزِيْلٌ مِّنْ حَكِيْمٍ حَمِيْدٍ ۝

43. Nothing is said to you that was not said to the Apostles before you: that your Lord has at His Command (all) forgiveness as well as a most Grievous Chastisement.

مَا يُقَالُ لَكَ اِلَّا مَا قَدْ قِيْلَ لِلرُّسُلِ مِنْ قَبْلِكَ ۗ اِنَّ رَبَّكَ لَذُوْ مَغْفِرَةٍ وَّذُوْ عِقَابٍ اَلِيْمٍ ۝

44. Had We sent this as a Qur'an (in a language) other than Arabic, they would have said: "Why are not its verses explained in detail? What! (a Book) not in Arabic and (a Messenger) an Arab?" Say: "It is a Guide and a Healing to those who believe ; and for those who do not believe, there is a deafness in their ears, and it is blindness in their (eyes): they are (as it were) being called from a place far distant!"

وَلَوْ جَعَلْنٰهُ قُرْاٰنًا اَعْجَمِيًّا لَّقَالُوْا لَوْلَا فُصِّلَتْ اٰيٰتُهٗ ؕ ءَاَعْجَمِيٌّ وَّعَرَبِيٌّ ؕ قُلْ هُوَ لِلَّذِيْنَ اٰمَنُوْا هُدًى وَّشِفَآءٌ ؕ وَالَّذِيْنَ لَا يُؤْمِنُوْنَ فِىْۤ اٰذَانِهِمْ وَقْرٌ وَّهُوَ عَلَيْهِمْ عَمًى ؕ اُولٰٓئِكَ يُنَادَوْنَ مِنْ مَّكَانٍۭ بَعِيْدٍ ۝

45. We certainly gave Moses the Book aforetime: but disputes arose therein. Had it not been for a Word that went forth before from your Lord, (their differences) would have been settled between them: but they remained in suspicious disquieting doubt thereon.

وَلَقَدْ اٰتَيْنَا مُوْسَى الْكِتٰبَ فَاخْتُلِفَ فِيْهِ ؕ وَلَوْلَا كَلِمَةٌ سَبَقَتْ مِنْ رَّبِّكَ لَقُضِىَ بَيْنَهُمْ ؕ وَاِنَّهُمْ لَفِىْ شَكٍّ مِّنْهُ مُرِيْبٍ ۝

46. Whoever works righteousness benefits his own soul; whoever works evil, it is against his own soul: nor is your Lord ever unjust (in the least) to His servants.

مَنْ عَمِلَ صَالِحًا فَلِنَفْسِهٖ وَمَنْ اَسَآءَ فَعَلَيْهَا ؕ وَمَا رَبُّكَ بِظَلَّامٍ لِّلْعَبِيْدِ ۝

47. To Him is referred the Knowledge of the Hour (of Judgment: He knows all): No

اِلَيْهِ يُرَدُّ عِلْمُ السَّاعَةِ ؕ وَمَا

date-fruit comes out of its sheath,
nor does a female conceive
(within her womb) nor bring
forth (young), but by His
knowledge. The Day that (Allah)
will propound to them the
(question), "Where are the
partners (you attributed) to Me?"
They will say, "We do assure You
not one of us can bear witness!"

تَخْرُجُ مِنْ ثَمَرٰتٍ مِّنْ أَكْمَامِهَا

وَمَا تَحْمِلُ مِنْ أُنْثٰى وَلَا تَضَعُ

إِلَّا بِعِلْمِهٖ ۚ وَيَوْمَ يُنَادِيْهِمْ

أَيْنَ شُرَكَآءِيْ ۙ قَالُوٓا اٰذَنّٰكَ ۙ

مَا مِنَّا مِنْ شَهِيْدٍ ﴿٤٧﴾

48. The (deities) they used to
invoke aforetime will leave them
in the lurch, and they will
perceive that they have no way of
escape.

وَضَلَّ عَنْهُمْ مَّا كَانُوْا يَدْعُوْنَ

مِنْ قَبْلُ وَظَنُّوْا مَا لَهُمْ مِّنْ

مَّحِيْصٍ ﴿٤٨﴾

49. Man does not weary of
asking for good (things), but if ill
touches him, he gives up all hope
(and) is lost in despair.

لَا يَسْـَٔمُ الْإِنْسَانُ مِنْ دُعَآءِ الْخَيْرِ ۖ

وَإِنْ مَّسَّهُ الشَّرُّ فَيَـُٔوْسٌ قَنُوْطٌ ﴿٤٩﴾

50. When We give him a taste
of some Mercy from Ourselves,
after some adversity has touched
him, he is sure to say, "This is due
to my (merit): I do not think that
the Hour (of Judgment) will
(ever) be established; but if I am
brought back to my Lord, I have
(much) good (stored) in His
sight!" But We will show the
Unbelievers the truth of all that
they did, and We shall give them
the taste of a severe Chastisement.

وَلَئِنْ أَذَقْنٰهُ رَحْمَةً مِّنَّا مِنْ بَعْدِ

ضَرَّآءَ مَسَّتْهُ لَيَقُوْلَنَّ هٰذَا لِيْ ۙ

وَمَآ أَظُنُّ السَّاعَةَ قَآئِمَةً ۙ وَّلَئِنْ

رُّجِعْتُ إِلٰى رَبِّيْ إِنَّ لِيْ عِنْدَهٗ

لَلْحُسْنٰى ۚ فَلَنُنَبِّئَنَّ الَّذِيْنَ كَفَرُوْا

بِمَا عَمِلُوْا ۖ وَلَنُذِيْقَنَّهُمْ مِّنْ

عَذَابٍ غَلِيْظٍ ﴿٥٠﴾

51. When We bestow favours
on man, he turns away, and gets
himself remote on his side
(instead of coming to Us); and
when evil seizes him, (he comes)
full of prolonged prayer!

وَإِذَآ أَنْعَمْنَا عَلَى الْإِنْسَانِ أَعْرَضَ

وَنَـَٔا بِجَانِبِهٖ ۚ وَإِذَا مَسَّهُ الشَّرُّ فَذُوْ

دُعَآءٍ عَرِيْضٍ ﴿٥١﴾

52. Say: "Do you see if the
(Revelation) is (really) from
Allah, and yet do you reject it?
Who is more astray than one who
is in a schism far (from any
purpose)?"

قُلْ أَرَءَيْتُمْ إِنْ كَانَ مِنْ عِنْدِ

اللّٰهِ ثُمَّ كَفَرْتُمْ بِهٖ مَنْ أَضَلُّ

مِمَّنْ هُوَ فِيْ شِقَاقٍ بَعِيْدٍ ﴿٥٢﴾

53. Soon will We show them
Our Signs in the (furthest)
regions (of the earth), and in their
own souls, until it becomes
manifest to them that this is the
Truth. Is it not enough that your
Lord

سَنُرِيْهِمْ اٰيٰتِنَا فِي الْاٰفَاقِ وَفِيْٓ

أَنْفُسِهِمْ حَتّٰى يَتَبَيَّنَ لَهُمْ أَنَّهُ

الْحَقُّ ۗ أَوَلَمْ يَكْفِ بِرَبِّكَ أَنَّهُ

SÛRAH-42
ASH-SHÛRÂ
(INTRODUCTION)

This is the third Sûrah of the *Hâ-Mim* series of seven Sûras, for which see the Introduction to S. 40.

The theme is how evil and blasphemy can be cured by the Mercy and Guidance of Allah, which come through His Revelation. Men are asked to settle their differences in patience by mutual Consultation (42: 38), which explains the title of the Sûrah.

Witnessess all things?

54. Ah indeed! Are they in doubt concerning the Meeting with their Lord? Ah indeed! It is He that encompasses all things!

42. Consultation
In the name of Allah. Most Gracious, Most Merciful.

1. *Ha-Mim*

2. *Ain. Sin. Qaf.*

3. Thus (He) sends inspiration to you as (He did) to those before you,- Allah, Exalted in Power, full of Wisdom.

4. To Him belongs all that is in the heavens and on earth: and He is Most High, Most Great.

5. The heavens are almost rent asunder from above them (by His Glory): and the angels celebrate the Praises of their Lord, and pray for forgiveness for (all) beings on earth: behold! Verily Allah is He, the Oft-Forgiving, Most Merciful.

6. And those who take as protectors others besides Him,- Allah watches over them; and you are not the disposer of their affairs.

7. Thus We have sent by inspiration to you an Arabic Qur'an: that you may warn the Mother of Cities and all around her,- and warn (them) of the Day of Assembly, of which there is no doubt: (when) some will be in the Garden, and some in the Blazing Fire.

8. If Allah had so willed, He could have made them a single people; but He admits whom He will

to His Mercy; and the wrong-doers will have no protector nor helper.

فِىْ رَحْمَتِهِ ۖ وَالظّٰلِمُوْنَ مَا لَهُمْ مِّنْ وَّلِيٍّ وَّلَا نَصِيْرٍ ۞

9. What! Have they taken (for worship) protectors besides Him? But it is Allah,- He is the Protector, and it is He Who gives life to the dead: It is He Who has power over all things.

أَمِ اتَّخَذُوْا مِنْ دُوْنِهٖ أَوْلِيَآءَ ۖ فَاللّٰهُ هُوَ الْوَلِيُّ وَهُوَ يُحْيِ الْمَوْتٰى ۖ وَهُوَ عَلٰى كُلِّ شَىْءٍ قَدِيْرٌ ۞

10. Whatever it be wherein you differ, the decision thereof is with Allah: such is Allah my Lord: In Him I trust, and to Him I turn.

وَمَا اخْتَلَفْتُمْ فِيْهِ مِنْ شَىْءٍ فَحُكْمُهٗٓ إِلَى اللّٰهِ ۚ ذٰلِكُمُ اللّٰهُ رَبِّيْ عَلَيْهِ تَوَكَّلْتُ ۖ وَإِلَيْهِ أُنِيْبُ ۞

11. (He is) the Creator of the heavens and the earth: He has made for you pairs from among yourselves, and pairs among cattle: by this means does He multiply you: there is nothing whatever like unto Him, and He is the One that hears and sees (all things).

فَاطِرُ السَّمٰوٰتِ وَالْأَرْضِ ۚ جَعَلَ لَكُمْ مِّنْ أَنْفُسِكُمْ أَزْوَاجًا وَّمِنَ الْأَنْعَامِ أَزْوَاجًا ۖ يَذْرَؤُكُمْ فِيْهِ ۚ لَيْسَ كَمِثْلِهٖ شَىْءٌ ۖ وَهُوَ السَّمِيْعُ الْبَصِيْرُ ۞

12. To Him belong the keys of the heavens and the earth: He enlarges and restricts the sustenance to whom He will: for He knows full well all things.

لَهٗ مَقَالِيْدُ السَّمٰوٰتِ وَالْأَرْضِ ۖ يَبْسُطُ الرِّزْقَ لِمَنْ يَّشَآءُ وَيَقْدِرُ ۚ إِنَّهٗ بِكُلِّ شَىْءٍ عَلِيْمٌ ۞

13. The same Religion He has established for you as that which He enjoined on Noah - the which We have sent by inspiration to you - and that which We enjoined on Abraham, Moses, and Jesus: namely, that you should remain steadfast in Religion, and make no divisions therein: to those who worship other things than Allah, hard is the (way) to which you call them. Allah chooses to Himself those whom He pleases, and guides to Himself those who turn (to Him).

شَرَعَ لَكُمْ مِّنَ الدِّيْنِ مَا وَصّٰى بِهٖ نُوْحًا وَّالَّذِيْٓ أَوْحَيْنَآ إِلَيْكَ وَمَا وَصَّيْنَا بِهٖٓ إِبْرٰهِيْمَ وَمُوْسٰى وَعِيْسٰىٓ أَنْ أَقِيْمُوا الدِّيْنَ وَلَا تَتَفَرَّقُوْا فِيْهِ ۚ كَبُرَ عَلَى الْمُشْرِكِيْنَ مَا تَدْعُوْهُمْ إِلَيْهِ ۚ اللّٰهُ يَجْتَبِيْٓ إِلَيْهِ مَنْ يَّشَآءُ وَيَهْدِيْٓ إِلَيْهِ مَنْ يُّنِيْبُ ۞

14. And they became divided only after Knowledge reached them,- through selfish envy as between themselves. Had it not been for

وَمَا تَفَرَّقُوْٓا إِلَّا مِنْ بَعْدِ مَا جَآءَهُمُ الْعِلْمُ بَغْيًا بَيْنَهُمْ ۚ وَلَوْلَا

a Word that went forth before
from your Lord, (tending) to a
term appointed, the matter would
have been settled between them:
but truly those who have
inherited the Book after them are
in suspicious (disquieting) doubt
concerning it.

15. Now then, for that (reason),
call (them to the Faith), and stand
steadfast as you are commanded,
nor you follow their vain desires;
but say: "I believe in the Book
which Allah has sent down; and I
am commanded to judge justly
between you. Allah is our Lord
and your Lord: for us (is the
responsibility for) our deeds, and
for you for your deeds. There is
no contention between us and
you. Allah will bring us together,
and to Him is (our) Final Goal.

16. But those who dispute
concerning Allah after He has
been accepted,- futile is their
dispute in the Sight of their
Lord: on them is wrath, and for
them will be a Chastisement
terrible.

17. It is Allah Who has sent
down the Book in Truth, and the
Balance (by which to weigh
conduct). And what will make
you realise that perhaps the
Hour is close at hand?

18. Only those wish to hasten
it who do not believe in it: those
who believe hold it in awe, and
know that it is the Truth.
Behold, verily those that dispute
concerning the Hour are far
astray.

19. Gracious is Allah to His
servants: He gives sustenance to
whom He pleases: and He is
Strong, the Mighty.

20. To any that desires the tilth
of the Hereafter,

We give increase in his tilth, and to any that desires the tilth of this world, We grant somewhat thereof, but he has no share or lot in the Hereafter.

21. What! have they partners (in godhead), who have established for them some religion without the permission of Allah? Had it not been for the Decree of Judgment, the matter would have been decided between them (at once). But verily the Wrong-doers will have a grievous Chastisement.

22. You will see the Wrong-doers in fear on account of what they have earned, and (the burden of) that must (necessarily) fall on them. But those who believe and work righteous deeds will be in the luxuriant meads of the Gardens: they shall have, before their Lord, all that they wish for. That will indeed be the magnificent Bounty (of Allah).

23. That is (the Bounty) whereof Allah gives Glad Tidings to His Servants who believe and do righteous deeds. Say: "No reward do I ask of you for this except the love of those near of kin." And if any one earns any good, We shall give him an increase of good in respect thereof: for Allah is Oft-Forgiving, Most Ready to appreciate (service).

24. What! Do they say, "He has forged a falsehood against Allah"? But if Allah willed, He could seal up your heart. And Allah blots out Vanity, and proves the Truth by His Words. For He knows well the secrets of all hearts.

25. He is the One that accepts repentance from His servants and forgives sins: and He knows all that you do.

26. And He listens to those who believe and do deeds of righteousness, and gives them increase of His Bounty: but for the Unbelievers their is a terrible Chastisement.

وَيَسْتَجِيبُ الَّذِينَ اٰمَنُوا وَعَمِلُوا الصّٰلِحٰتِ وَيَزِيدُهُمْ مِّنْ فَضْلِهِ ۚ وَالْكٰفِرُوْنَ لَهُمْ عَذَابٌ شَدِيدٌ ۝

27. If Allah were to enlarge the provision for His servants, they would indeed transgress beyond all bounds through the earth; but He sends (it) down in due measure as He pleases. For He is with His servants Well-acquainted, Watchful.

وَلَوْ بَسَطَ اللّٰهُ الرِّزْقَ لِعِبَادِهِ لَبَغَوْا فِي الْاَرْضِ وَلٰكِنْ يُّنَزِّلُ بِقَدَرٍ مَّا يَشَآءُ ۚ إِنَّهُ بِعِبَادِهِ خَبِيرٌ بَصِيرٌ ۝

28. He is the One that sends down rain (even) after (men) have given up all hope, and scatters His Mercy (far and wide). And He is the Protector, Worthy of all Praise.

وَهُوَ الَّذِي يُنَزِّلُ الْغَيْثَ مِنْ بَعْدِ مَا قَنَطُوا وَيَنْشُرُ رَحْمَتَهُ ۚ وَهُوَ الْوَلِيُّ الْحَمِيدُ ۝

29. And among His Signs is the creation of the heavens and the earth, and the living creatures that He has scattered through them: and He has power to gather them together when He wills.

وَمِنْ اٰيٰتِهِ خَلْقُ السَّمٰوٰتِ وَالْاَرْضِ وَمَا بَثَّ فِيهِمَا مِنْ دَآبَّةٍ ۚ وَهُوَ عَلَىٰ جَمْعِهِمْ إِذَا يَشَآءُ قَدِيرٌ ۝

30. Whatever misfortune happens to you, is because of the things your hands have wrought, and for many (of them) He grants forgiveness.

وَمَا أَصَابَكُمْ مِّنْ مُّصِيبَةٍ فَبِمَا كَسَبَتْ أَيْدِيكُمْ وَيَعْفُوا عَنْ كَثِيرٍ ۝

31. Nor can you frustrate (anything), (fleeing) through the earth; nor have you, besides Allah, any one to protect or to help.

وَمَا أَنْتُمْ بِمُعْجِزِينَ فِي الْاَرْضِ ۚ وَمَا لَكُمْ مِّنْ دُوْنِ اللّٰهِ مِنْ وَّلِيٍّ وَّلَا نَصِيرٍ ۝

32. And among His Signs are the ships, smooth-running through the ocean, (tall) as mountains.

وَمِنْ اٰيٰتِهِ الْجَوَارِ فِي الْبَحْرِ كَالْاَعْلَامِ ۝

33. If it be His Will, He can still the Wind: then would they become motionless on the back of the (ocean). Verily in this are Signs for everyone who patiently perseveres and is grateful.

إِنْ يَّشَأْ يُسْكِنِ الرِّيحَ فَيَظْلَلْنَ رَوَاكِدَ عَلَىٰ ظَهْرِهِ ۚ إِنَّ فِي ذٰلِكَ لَاٰيٰتٍ لِّكُلِّ صَبَّارٍ شَكُورٍ ۝

34. Or He can cause them to perish because of the (evil) which (the men) have earned; but much does He forgive.

أَوْ يُوبِقْهُنَّ بِمَا كَسَبُوا وَيَعْفُ عَنْ كَثِيرٍ ۝

35. But let those know, who dispute about Our Signs, that there is for them no way of escape.

وَيَعْلَمَ الَّذِينَ يُجَادِلُونَ فِي اٰيٰتِنَا ۚ مَا لَهُمْ مِّنْ مَّحِيصٍ ۝

36. Whatever you are given (here) is (but) a convenience of this life: but that which is with Allah is better and more lasting: (it is) for those who believe and put their trust in their Lord.

فَمَا أُوتِيتُمۡ مِّنۡ شَیۡءٍ فَمَتَاعُ الۡحَیٰوةِ الدُّنۡیَا ۖ وَمَا عِنۡدَ اللّٰهِ خَیۡرٌ وَّاَبۡقٰی لِلَّذِیۡنَ اٰمَنُوۡا وَعَلٰی رَبِّهِمۡ یَتَوَکَّلُوۡنَ ۞

37. Those who avoid the greater crimes and shameful deeds, and, when they are angry even then forgive;

وَالَّذِیۡنَ یَجۡتَنِبُوۡنَ کَبٰٓئِرَ الۡاِثۡمِ وَالۡفَوَاحِشَ وَاِذَا مَا غَضِبُوۡا هُمۡ یَغۡفِرُوۡنَ ۞

38. Those who hearken to their Lord, and establish regular Prayer; who (conduct) their affairs by mutual consultation; who spend out of what We bestow on them for Sustenance;

وَالَّذِیۡنَ اسۡتَجَابُوۡا لِرَبِّهِمۡ وَاَقَامُوا الصَّلٰوةَ ۖ وَاَمۡرُهُمۡ شُوۡرٰی بَیۡنَهُمۡ ۖ وَمِمَّا رَزَقۡنٰهُمۡ یُنۡفِقُوۡنَ ۞

39. And those who, when an oppressive wrong is inflicted on them, (are not cowed but) help and defend themselves.

وَالَّذِیۡنَ اِذَاۤ اَصَابَهُمُ الۡبَغۡیُ هُمۡ یَنۡتَصِرُوۡنَ ۞

40. The recompense for an injury is an injury equal thereto (in degree): but if a person forgives and makes reconciliation, his reward is due from Allah: for (Allah) does not love those who do wrong.

وَجَزٰٓؤُا سَیِّئَةٍ سَیِّئَةٌ مِّثۡلُهَا ۖ فَمَنۡ عَفَا وَاَصۡلَحَ فَاَجۡرُهُ عَلَی اللّٰهِ ۖ اِنَّهُ لَا یُحِبُّ الظّٰلِمِیۡنَ ۞

41. But indeed if any do help and defend themselves after a wrong (done) to them, against such there is no cause of blame.

وَلَمَنِ انۡتَصَرَ بَعۡدَ ظُلۡمِهِ فَاُولٰٓئِکَ مَا عَلَیۡهِمۡ مِّنۡ سَبِیۡلٍ ۞

42. The blame is only against those who oppress men with wrong-doing and insolently transgress beyond bounds through the land, defying right and justice: for such there will be a Chastisement grievous.

اِنَّمَا السَّبِیۡلُ عَلَی الَّذِیۡنَ یَظۡلِمُوۡنَ النَّاسَ وَیَبۡغُوۡنَ فِی الۡاَرۡضِ بِغَیۡرِ الۡحَقِّ ؕ اُولٰٓئِکَ لَهُمۡ عَذَابٌ اَلِیۡمٌ ۞

43. But indeed if any show patience and forgive, that would truly be an affair of great resolution.

وَلَمَنۡ صَبَرَ وَغَفَرَ اِنَّ ذٰلِکَ لَمِنۡ عَزۡمِ الۡاُمُوۡرِ ۞

44. For any whom Allah leaves astray, there is no protector thereafter. And you will see the Wrong-doers, when in sight of the Penalty, say: "Is there any way (to effect) a return?"

وَمَنۡ یُّضۡلِلِ اللّٰهُ فَمَا لَهُ مِنۡ وَّلِیٍّ مِّنۡ بَعۡدِهِ ؕ وَتَرَی الظّٰلِمِیۡنَ لَمَّا رَاَوُا الۡعَذَابَ یَقُوۡلُوۡنَ هَلۡ اِلٰی مَرَدٍّ مِّنۡ سَبِیۡلٍ ۞

45. And you will see them brought forward to the (Chastisement), in a humble frame of mind because of (their) disgrace, (and) looking with a stealthy glance. And the Believers will say: "Those are indeed in loss, who have given to perdition their own selves and those belonging to them on the Day of Judgment. Behold! Truly the Wrong-doers are in a lasting Chastisement!"

وَتَرَاهُمْ يُعْرَضُوْنَ عَلَيْهَا خٰشِعِيْنَ مِنَ الذُّلِّ يَنْظُرُوْنَ مِنْ طَرْفٍ خَفِيٍّ ۚ وَقَالَ الَّذِيْنَ اٰمَنُوْۤا اِنَّ الْخٰسِرِيْنَ الَّذِيْنَ خَسِرُوْۤا اَنْفُسَهُمْ وَاَهْلِيْهِمْ يَوْمَ الْقِيٰمَةِ ؕ اَلَاۤ اِنَّ الظّٰلِمِيْنَ فِيْ عَذَابٍ مُّقِيْمٍ ۝

46. And no protectors have they to help them, other than Allah. And for any whom Allah leaves to stray, there is no way (to the Goal).

وَمَا كَانَ لَهُمْ مِّنْ اَوْلِيَآءَ يَنْصُرُوْنَهُمْ مِّنْ دُوْنِ اللّٰهِ ؕ وَمَنْ يُّضْلِلِ اللّٰهُ فَمَا لَهٗ مِنْ سَبِيْلٍ ؕ ۝

47. You hearken to your Lord, before there come a Day which there will be no putting back, because of (the ordainment of) Allah! that Day there will be for you no place of refuge nor will there be for you any room for denial (of your sins)!

اِسْتَجِيْبُوْا لِرَبِّكُمْ مِّنْ قَبْلِ اَنْ يَّاْتِيَ يَوْمٌ لَّا مَرَدَّ لَهٗ مِنَ اللّٰهِ ؕ مَا لَكُمْ مِّنْ مَّلْجَاٍ يَّوْمَىِٕذٍ وَّمَا لَكُمْ مِّنْ نَّكِيْرٍ ۝

48. If then they turn away, We have not sent you as a guard over them. Your duty is but to convey (the Message). And truly, when We give man a taste of a Mercy from Ourselves, he exults thereat, but when some ill happens to him, on account of the deeds which his hands have sent forth, truly then man is ungrateful!

فَاِنْ اَعْرَضُوْا فَمَاۤ اَرْسَلْنٰكَ عَلَيْهِمْ حَفِيْظًا ؕ اِنْ عَلَيْكَ اِلَّا الْبَلٰغُ ؕ وَاِنَّاۤ اِذَاۤ اَذَقْنَا الْاِنْسَانَ مِنَّا رَحْمَةً فَرِحَ بِهَا ۚ وَاِنْ تُصِبْهُمْ سَيِّئَةٌۢ بِمَا قَدَّمَتْ اَيْدِيْهِمْ فَاِنَّ الْاِنْسَانَ كَفُوْرٌ ۝

49. To Allah belongs the dominion of the heavens and the earth. He creates what He wills (and plans). He bestows (children) male or female according to His Will (and Plan),

لِلّٰهِ مُلْكُ السَّمٰوٰتِ وَالْاَرْضِ ؕ يَخْلُقُ مَا يَشَآءُ ؕ يَهَبُ لِمَنْ يَّشَآءُ اِنَاثًا وَّيَهَبُ لِمَنْ يَّشَآءُ الذُّكُوْرَ ۝

50. Or He bestows both males and females, and He leaves barren whom He will: for He is full of Knowledge and Power.

اَوْ يُزَوِّجُهُمْ ذُكْرَانًا وَّاِنَاثًا ۚ وَيَجْعَلُ مَنْ يَّشَآءُ عَقِيْمًا ؕ اِنَّهٗ عَلِيْمٌ قَدِيْرٌ ۝

51. It is not fitting for a man that Allah should speak to him except by inspiration, or from behind a veil, or

وَمَا كَانَ لِبَشَرٍ اَنْ يُّكَلِّمَهُ اللّٰهُ اِلَّا وَحْيًا اَوْ مِنْ وَّرَآئِ حِجَابٍ اَوْ

SÛRAH-43
AZ-ZUKHRUF
(INTRODUCTION)

This is the fourth Sûrah of the *Hâ-Mim* series of seven Sûras. For their chronology and general theme see the Introduction to S. 40.

This Sûrah deals with the contrasts between the real glory of Truth and Revelation and the false glitter of what people like to believe and worship. It cites the examples of Abraham, Moses, and Jesus, as exposing the False holding up the Truth. The keyword *Zukhruf* (Gold Adornments) occurs in verse 38; but the idea occurs all through the Sûrah.

by the sending of a Messenger to reveal, with Allah's permission, what Allah wills: for He is Most High, Most Wise.

52.   And thus We have, by Our Command, sent inspiration to you: you did not know (before) what was Revelation, and what was Faith; but We have made the (Qur'an) a Light, wherewith We guide such of Our servants as We will; and verily you do guide (men) to the Straight Way,-

53.   The Way of Allah, to Whom belongs whatever is in the heavens and whatever is on earth. Behold (how) all affairs tend towards Allah!

43. Gold Adornments
In the name of Allah. Most Gracious, Most Merciful.

1.   *Ha-Mim*

2.   By the Book that makes things clear,-

3.   We have made it a Qur'an in Arabic, that you may be able to understand (and learn wisdom).

4.   And verily, it is in the Mother of the Book, in Our Presence, high (in dignity), full of wisdom.

5.   Shall We then take away the Message from you and repel (you) for that you are a people transgressing beyond bounds?

6.   But how many were the prophets We sent amongst the peoples of old?

7.   And never came there a prophet to them but they mocked him.

8.   So We destroyed (them)- stronger in power than these;- and (thus) has passed on the Parable of the peoples of old.

9.   If you were to question them, 'Who created the heavens

and the earth?' They would be sure to reply, 'they were created by (Him), the Exalted in Power, full of Knowledge';-

10. (Yes, the same that) has made for you the earth (like a carpet) spread out, and has made for you roads (and channels) therein, in order that you may find guidance (on the way);

11. Who sends down (from time to time) rain from the sky in due measure;- and We raise to life therewith a land that is dead; even so will you be raised (from the dead);-

12. That has created pairs in all things, and has made for you ships and cattle on which you ride,

13. In order that you may sit firm and square on their backs, and when so seated, you may celebrate the (kind) favour of your Lord, and say, "Glory to Him Who has subjected these to our (use), for we could never have accomplished this (by ourselves),

14. "And to our Lord, surely, must we turn back!"

15. Yet they attribute to some of His servants a share with Him (in His godhead)! truly is man a blasphemous ingrate avowed!

16. What! Has He taken daughters out of what He Himself creates, and granted to you sons for choice?

17. When news is brought to one of them (the birth of) what he sets up as a likeness to (Allah) Most Gracious, his face darkens, and he is filled with inward grief!

18. Is then one brought up among trinkets, and unable to give a clear account in a dispute (to be associated with Allah)?

19. And they make into females angels who themselves

serve Allah. Did they witness their creation? Their evidence will be recorded, and they will be called to account!

20. ("Ah!") they say, "If it had been the Will of (Allah) Most Gracious, we should not have worshipped such (deities)!" Of that they have no knowledge! they do nothing but lie!

21. What! have We given them a Book before this, to which they are holding fast?

22. Nay! they say: "We found our fathers following a certain religion, and we do guide ourselves by their footsteps."

23. Just in the same way, whenever We sent a Warner before you to any people, the wealthy ones among them said: "We found our fathers following a certain religion, and we will certainly follow in their footsteps."

24. He said: "What! Even if I brought you better guidance than that which you found your fathers following?" They said: "For us, we deny that you (prophets) are sent (on a mission at all)."

25. So We exacted retribution from them: now see what was the end of those who rejected (Truth)!

26. Behold! Abraham said to his father and his people: "I do indeed clear myself of what you worship:

27. "(I worship) only Him Who made me, and He will certainly guide me."

28. And he left it as a Word to endure among those who came after him, that they may turn back (to Allah).

29. Yes, I have given the good things of this life to these (men) and their fathers, until the Truth has come to them, and an Apostle making things clear.

30. But when the Truth came to them, they said: "This is sorcery, and we do reject it."

31. Also, they say: "Why is not this Qur'an sent down to some leading man in either of the two (chief) cities?"

32. Is it they who would portion out the Mercy of your Lord? It is We Who portion out between them their livelihood in the life of this world: and We raise some of them above others in ranks, so that some may command work from others. But the Mercy of your Lord is better than the (wealth) which they amass.

33. And were it not that (all) men might become of one community, We would provide, for everyone that blasphemes against (Allah) Most Gracious, silver roofs for their houses and (silver) stair-ways on which to go up,

34. And (silver) doors to their houses, and thrones (of silver) on which they could recline,

35. And also adornments of gold. But all this were nothing but enjoyment of the present life: The Hereafter, in the sight of your Lord is for the Righteous.

36. If anyone withdraws himself from remembrance of (Allah) Most Gracious, We appoint for him an evil one, to be an intimate companion to him.

37. Such (evil ones) really hinder them from the Path, but they think that they are being guided aright!

38. At length, when (such a one) comes to Us, he says (to his evil companion): "Would that between me and you were the distance of East and West!" Ah! evil is the companion (indeed)!

39. When you have done wrong, it will avail you nothing, that Day, that you shall be partners in Punishment!

وَإِنَّا بِهِ كَفِرُونَ ۝

وَقَالُوا لَوْلَا نُزِّلَ هٰذَا الْقُرْآنُ عَلٰى رَجُلٍ مِّنَ الْقَرْيَتَيْنِ عَظِيمٍ ۝

أَهُمْ يَقْسِمُونَ رَحْمَتَ رَبِّكَ ۚ نَحْنُ قَسَمْنَا بَيْنَهُمْ مَّعِيشَتَهُمْ فِي الْحَيٰوةِ الدُّنْيَا وَرَفَعْنَا بَعْضَهُمْ فَوْقَ بَعْضٍ دَرَجٰتٍ لِّيَتَّخِذَ بَعْضُهُمْ بَعْضًا سُخْرِيًّا ۚ وَرَحْمَتُ رَبِّكَ خَيْرٌ مِّمَّا يَجْمَعُونَ ۝

وَلَوْلَا أَنْ يَكُونَ النَّاسُ أُمَّةً وَّاحِدَةً لَّجَعَلْنَا لِمَنْ يَكْفُرُ بِالرَّحْمٰنِ لِبُيُوتِهِمْ سُقُفًا مِّنْ فِضَّةٍ وَّمَعَارِجَ عَلَيْهَا يَظْهَرُونَ ۝

وَلِبُيُوتِهِمْ أَبْوَابًا وَّسُرُرًا عَلَيْهَا يَتَّكِئُونَ ۝

وَزُخْرُفًا ۚ وَإِنْ كُلُّ ذٰلِكَ لَمَّا مَتَاعُ الْحَيٰوةِ الدُّنْيَا ۚ وَالْآخِرَةُ عِنْدَ رَبِّكَ لِلْمُتَّقِينَ ۝

وَمَنْ يَعْشُ عَنْ ذِكْرِ الرَّحْمٰنِ نُقَيِّضْ لَهُ شَيْطٰنًا فَهُوَ لَهُ قَرِينٌ ۝

وَإِنَّهُمْ لَيَصُدُّونَهُمْ عَنِ السَّبِيلِ وَيَحْسَبُونَ أَنَّهُمْ مُّهْتَدُونَ ۝

حَتّٰى إِذَا جَاءَنَا قَالَ يٰلَيْتَ بَيْنِي وَبَيْنَكَ بُعْدَ الْمَشْرِقَيْنِ فَبِئْسَ الْقَرِينُ ۝

وَلَنْ يَنْفَعَكُمُ الْيَوْمَ إِذْ ظَلَمْتُمْ أَنَّكُمْ فِي الْعَذَابِ مُشْتَرِكُونَ ۝

40. Can you then make the deaf to hear, or give direction to the blind or to such as (wander) in manifest error?

أَفَأَنْتَ تُسْمِعُ الصُّمَّ أَوْ تَهْدِي الْعُمْيَ وَمَنْ كَانَ فِي ضَلَالٍ مُّبِينٍ ۝

41. Even if We take you away, We shall be sure to exact retribution from them,

فَإِمَّا نَذْهَبَنَّ بِكَ فَإِنَّا مِنْهُمْ مُّنْتَقِمُونَ ۝

42. Or We shall show you that (accomplished) which We have promised them: for verily We shall prevail over them.

أَوْ نُرِيَنَّكَ الَّذِي وَعَدْنَاهُمْ فَإِنَّا عَلَيْهِمْ مُّقْتَدِرُونَ ۝

43. So you hold fast to the Revelation sent down to you; verily you are on a Straight Way.

فَاسْتَمْسِكْ بِالَّذِي أُوحِيَ إِلَيْكَ إِنَّكَ عَلَى صِرَاطٍ مُّسْتَقِيمٍ ۝

44. The (Qur'an) is indeed the message, for you and for your people; and soon shall you (all) be brought to account.

وَإِنَّهُ لَذِكْرٌ لَّكَ وَلِقَوْمِكَ وَسَوْفَ تُسْئَلُونَ ۝

45. And you question our Apostles whom We sent before you; did We appoint any deities other than (Allah) Most Gracious, to be worshipped?

وَسْئَلْ مَنْ أَرْسَلْنَا مِنْ قَبْلِكَ مِنْ رُّسُلِنَا أَجَعَلْنَا مِنْ دُونِ الرَّحْمَنِ آلِهَةً يُّعْبَدُونَ ۝

46. We sent Moses afore time, with Our Signs, to Pharaoh and his Chiefs: he said, "I am an Apostle of the Lord of the Worlds."

وَلَقَدْ أَرْسَلْنَا مُوسَى بِآيَاتِنَا إِلَى فِرْعَوْنَ وَمَلَائِهِ فَقَالَ إِنِّي رَسُولُ رَبِّ الْعَالَمِينَ ۝

47. But when he came to them with Our Signs, behold they ridiculed them.

فَلَمَّا جَاءَهُمْ بِآيَاتِنَا إِذَا هُمْ مِّنْهَا يَضْحَكُونَ ۝

48. We showed them Sign after Sign, each greater than its fellow, and We seized them with Punishment, in order that they might turn (to Us).

وَمَا نُرِيهِمْ مِنْ آيَةٍ إِلَّا هِيَ أَكْبَرُ مِنْ أُخْتِهَا وَأَخَذْنَاهُمْ بِالْعَذَابِ لَعَلَّهُمْ يَرْجِعُونَ ۝

49. And they said, "O you sorcerer! Invoke your Lord for us according to His covenant with you; for we shall truly accept guidance."

وَقَالُوا يَا أَيُّهَ السَّاحِرُ ادْعُ لَنَا رَبَّكَ بِمَا عَهِدَ عِنْدَكَ إِنَّنَا لَمُهْتَدُونَ ۝

50. But when We removed the Penalty from them, behold, they broke their word.

فَلَمَّا كَشَفْنَا عَنْهُمُ الْعَذَابَ إِذَا هُمْ يَنْكُثُونَ ۝

51. And Pharaoh proclaimed among his people, saying:

وَنَادَى فِرْعَوْنُ فِي قَوْمِهِ قَالَ يَا قَوْمِ

Does not the dominion of Egypt belong to me, (witness) these streams flowing underneath my (palace)? Do you not see then?

52. "Am I not better than this (Moses), who is a contemptible wretch and can scarcely express himself clearly?

53. "Then why are not gold bracelets bestowed on him, or (why) come (not) with him angels accompanying him in procession?"

54. Thus he made fools of his people, and they obeyed him: truly they were a rebellious people (against Allah).

55. When at length they provoked Us, We exacted retribution from them, and We drowned them all.

56. And We made them (a people) of the Past and an Example to later ages.

57. When (Jesus) the son of Mary is held up as an example, behold, your people raise a clamour thereat (in ridicule)!

58. And they say, "Are our gods best, or he?" This they set forth to you, only by way of disputation: yes, they are a contentious people.

59. He was no more than a servant: We granted Our favour to him, and We made him an example to the Children of Israel.

60. And if it were Our Will, We could make angels from amongst you, succeeding each other on the earth.

61. And (Jesus) shall be a Sign (for the coming of) the Hour (of Judgment): therefore have no doubt about the (Hour), but you follow Me: this is a Straight Way.

62. Let not the Evil One hinder you: for he is to you an avowed enemy.

63. When Jesus came with Clear Signs, he said: "Now I have come to you with Wisdom, and in order to make clear to you

أَلَيْسَ لِى مُلْكُ مِصْرَ وَهٰذِهِ الْأَنْهٰرُ

تَجْرِى مِنْ تَحْتِىْ أَفَلَا تُبْصِرُوْنَ ۞

أَمْ أَنَا خَيْرٌ مِّنْ هٰذَا الَّذِى هُوَ

مَهِيْنٌ ۙ وَّلَا يَكَادُ يُبِيْنُ ۞

فَلَوْلَا أُلْقِىَ عَلَيْهِ أَسْوِرَةٌ مِّنْ ذَهَبٍ

أَوْ جَاءَ مَعَهُ الْمَلٰئِكَةُ مُقْتَرِنِيْنَ ۞

فَاسْتَخَفَّ قَوْمَهُ فَأَطَاعُوْهُ ۗ إِنَّهُمْ

كَانُوْا قَوْمًا فٰسِقِيْنَ ۞

فَلَمَّآ اٰسَفُوْنَا انْتَقَمْنَا مِنْهُمْ

فَأَغْرَقْنٰهُمْ أَجْمَعِيْنَ ۞

فَجَعَلْنٰهُمْ سَلَفًا وَّمَثَلًا لِّلْاٰخِرِيْنَ ۞

وَلَمَّا ضُرِبَ ابْنُ مَرْيَمَ مَثَلًا إِذَا قَوْمُكَ

مِنْهُ يَصِدُّوْنَ ۞

وَقَالُوْٓا ءَاٰلِهَتُنَا خَيْرٌ أَمْ هُوَ ۗ مَا

ضَرَبُوْهُ لَكَ إِلَّا جَدَلًا ۗ بَلْ هُمْ

قَوْمٌ خَصِمُوْنَ ۞

إِنْ هُوَ إِلَّا عَبْدٌ أَنْعَمْنَا عَلَيْهِ وَجَعَلْنٰهُ

مَثَلًا لِّبَنِىْٓ إِسْرَآءِيْلَ ۗ

وَلَوْ نَشَاءُ لَجَعَلْنَا مِنْكُمْ مَّلٰئِكَةً

فِى الْأَرْضِ يَخْلُفُوْنَ ۞

وَإِنَّهُ لَعِلْمٌ لِّلسَّاعَةِ فَلَا تَمْتَرُنَّ بِهَا

وَاتَّبِعُوْنِ ۗ هٰذَا صِرَاطٌ مُّسْتَقِيْمٌ ۞

وَلَا يَصُدَّنَّكُمُ الشَّيْطٰنُ ۗ إِنَّهُ لَكُمْ

عَدُوٌّ مُّبِيْنٌ ۞

وَلَمَّا جَاءَ عِيْسٰى بِالْبَيِّنٰتِ قَالَ قَدْ

جِئْتُكُمْ بِالْحِكْمَةِ وَلِأُبَيِّنَ لَكُمْ

some of the (points) on which
you dispute: therefore fear Allah
and obey me.

بَعْضَ الَّذِى تَخْتَلِفُونَ فِيهِ فَاتَّقُوا
اللهَ وَأَطِيعُونِ ۝

64. "For Allah, He is my Lord
and your Lord: so you worship
Him: this is a Straight Way."

اِنَّ اللهَ هُوَ رَبِّى وَرَبُّكُمْ فَاعْبُدُوهُ
هٰذَا صِرَاطٌ مُّسْتَقِيمٌ ۝

65. But sects from among
themselves fell into disagree-
ment: then woe to the wrong-
doers, from the Chastisement of
a Grievous Day!

فَاخْتَلَفَ الْأَحْزَابُ مِنْ بَيْنِهِمْ
فَوَيْلٌ لِّلَّذِينَ ظَلَمُوا مِنْ عَذَابِ
يَوْمٍ أَلِيمٍ ۝

66. Do they only wait for the
Hour - that it should come on
them all of a sudden, while they
do not perceive?

هَلْ يَنْظُرُونَ إِلَّا السَّاعَةَ أَن
تَأْتِيَهُمْ بَغْتَةً وَّهُمْ لَا يَشْعُرُونَ ۝

67. Friends on that day will be
foes, one to another,- except the
Righteous.

الْأَخِلَّاءُ يَوْمَئِذٍ بَعْضُهُمْ لِبَعْضٍ
عَدُوٌّ إِلَّا الْمُتَّقِينَ ۝

68. My devotees! no fear shall
be on you that Day, nor shall you
grieve,-

يٰعِبَادِ لَا خَوْفٌ عَلَيْكُمُ الْيَوْمَ وَلَا
أَنْتُمْ تَحْزَنُونَ ۝

69. (Being) those who have
believed in Our Signs and bowed
(their wills to Ours) in Islam.

الَّذِينَ آمَنُوا بِآيَاتِنَا وَكَانُوا
مُسْلِمِينَ ۝

70. You enter the Garden, you
and your wives, in (beauty and)
rejoicing.

ادْخُلُوا الْجَنَّةَ أَنْتُمْ وَأَزْوَاجُكُمْ
تُحْبَرُونَ ۝

71. To them will be passed
round, dishes and goblets of
gold: there will be there all that
the souls could desire, all that the
eyes could delight in: and you
shall abide therein (for ever).

يُطَافُ عَلَيْهِمْ بِصِحَافٍ مِّنْ ذَهَبٍ
وَّأَكْوَابٍ ۚ وَفِيهَا مَا تَشْتَهِيهِ
الْأَنْفُسُ وَتَلَذُّ الْأَعْيُنُ ۚ وَأَنْتُمْ فِيهَا
خَالِدُونَ ۝

72. Such will be the Garden of
which you are made heirs for
your (good) deeds (in life).

وَتِلْكَ الْجَنَّةُ الَّتِي أُورِثْتُمُوهَا بِمَا
كُنْتُمْ تَعْمَلُونَ ۝

73. You shall have therein
abundance of fruit, from which
you shall have satisfaction.

لَكُمْ فِيهَا فَاكِهَةٌ كَثِيرَةٌ مِّنْهَا
تَأْكُلُونَ ۝

74. The sinners will be in the
Punishment of Hell, to dwell
therein (for ever):

اِنَّ الْمُجْرِمِينَ فِي عَذَابِ جَهَنَّمَ

75. Nowise will the (punishment) be lightened for them, and in despair will they be there overwhelmed.

76. Nowise shall We be unjust to them: but it is they who have been unjust themselves.

77. They will cry: "O Malik! would that your Lord put an end to us!" He will say, "Nay, but you shall abide!"

78. Verily We have brought the Truth to you: but most of you have a hatred for Truth.

79. What! have they settled some plan (among themselves)? But it is We Who settle things.

80. Or do they think that We do not hear their secrets and their private counsels? Indeed (We do), and Our Messengers are by them, to record.

81. Say: "If (Allah) Most Gracious had a son, I would be the first to worship."

82. Glory to the Lord of the heavens and the earth, the Lord of the Throne (of Authority)! (He is free) from the things they attribute (to Him)!

83. So leave them to babble and play (with vanities) until they meet that Day of theirs, which they have been promised.

84. It is He Who is Allah in heaven and Allah on earth; and He is full of Wisdom and Knowledge.

85. And blessed is He to Whom belongs the dominion of the heavens and the earth, and all between them: with Him is the Knowledge of the Hour (of Judgment): and to Him shall you be brought back.

86. And those whom they invoke besides Allah have no power of intercession;- only he who bears witness to the Truth, and they know (him).

SÛRAH-44
AD-DUKHÂN
(INTRODUCTION)

For the chronology and the general theme of the Sûras of the *Hâ-Mim* series, of which this is the fifth, see the Introduction to S. 40.

The theme of this particular Sûrah is how worldly pride and power are humbled in the dust if they resist spiritual forces, and how Evil and Good find their true setting in the Hereafter.

The title-word *Dukhân* occurs in verse 10. It means smoke or mist, and may refer to a drought or famine.

87. If you ask them, Who created them, they will certainly say, Allah: how then are they deluded away (from the Truth)?

88. (Allah has knowledge) of the (Prophet's) cry, "O my Lord! Truly these are a people who will not believe!"

89. But turn away from them, and say "Peace!" But soon shall they know!

---

44. Smoke or Mist
In the name of Allah. Most Gracious, Most Merciful.

1. *Ha-Mim.*

2. By the Book that makes things clear;-

3. We sent it down during a Blessed Night: for We (ever) wish to warn (against Evil).

4. In that (Night) is made distinct every affair of wisdom,

5. By command, from Our Presence. For We (ever) send (revelations),

6. As a Mercy from your Lord: for He hears and knows (all things);

7. The Lord of the heavens and the earth and all between them, if you (but) have an assured faith.

8. There is no god but He: It is He Who gives life and gives death,- the Lord and Cherisher to you and your earliest ancestors.

9. Yet they play about in doubt.

10. Then you watch for the Day that the sky will bring forth a kind of smoke (or mist) plainly visible,

11. Enveloping the people: this will be a Grievous Chastisement.

12. (They will say:) "Our Lord! remove the Chastisement from us, for we do really believe!"

13. How shall the Message be (effectual) for them, seeing that an Apostle explaining things clearly has (already) come to them,-

14. Yet they turn away from him and say: "Tutored (by others), a man possessed!"

15. We shall indeed remove the Chastisement for a while, (but) truly you will revert (to your ways).

16. One day We shall seize you with a mighty onslaught: We will indeed (then) exact Retribution!

17. We tried, before them, the people of Pharaoh: there came to them an Apostle most honourable,

18. Saying: "Restore to me the servants of Allah: I am to you an Apostle worthy of all trust;

19. "And be not arrogant as against Allah: for I come to you with authority manifest.

20. "For me, I have sought safety with my Lord and your Lord, against your injuring me.

21. And if you do not believe me, at least keep yourselves away from me.".

22. (But they were aggressive:) then he cried to his Lord: "These are indeed a people given to sin."

23. (The reply came:) "March forth with My servants by night: for you are sure to be pursued.

24. "And leave the sea as a furrow (divided): for they are a host (destined) to be drowned."

25. How many were the gardens and springs they left behind,

26. And corn-fields and noble buildings,

27. And wealth (and conveniences of lief), wherein they had taken such delight!

28. Thus (was their end)! And We made other people inherit (those things)!

اَنّٰى لَهُمُ الذِّكْرٰى وَقَدْ جَآءَهُمْ رَسُوْلٌ مُّبِيْنٌ ۞

ثُمَّ تَوَلَّوْا عَنْهُ وَقَالُوْا مُعَلَّمٌ مَّجْنُوْنٌ ۞

اِنَّا كَاشِفُوا الْعَذَابِ قَلِيْلًا اِنَّكُمْ عَآئِدُوْنَ ۞

يَوْمَ نَبْطِشُ الْبَطْشَةَ الْكُبْرٰى اِنَّا مُنْتَقِمُوْنَ ۞

وَلَقَدْ فَتَنَّا قَبْلَهُمْ قَوْمَ فِرْعَوْنَ وَجَآءَهُمْ رَسُوْلٌ كَرِيْمٌ ۞

اَنْ اَدُّوْا اِلَيَّ عِبَادَ اللّٰهِ اِنِّيْ لَكُمْ رَسُوْلٌ اَمِيْنٌ ۞

وَّاَنْ لَّا تَعْلُوْا عَلَى اللّٰهِ اِنِّيْ اٰتِيْكُمْ بِسُلْطٰنٍ مُّبِيْنٍ ۞

وَاِنِّيْ عُذْتُ بِرَبِّيْ وَرَبِّكُمْ اَنْ تَرْجُمُوْنِ ۞

وَاِنْ لَّمْ تُؤْمِنُوْا لِيْ فَاعْتَزِلُوْنِ ۞

فَدَعَا رَبَّهٗٓ اَنَّ هٰٓؤُلَآءِ قَوْمٌ مُّجْرِمُوْنَ ۞

فَاَسْرِ بِعِبَادِيْ لَيْلًا اِنَّكُمْ مُّتَّبَعُوْنَ ۞

وَاتْرُكِ الْبَحْرَ رَهْوًا اِنَّهُمْ جُنْدٌ مُّغْرَقُوْنَ ۞

كَمْ تَرَكُوْا مِنْ جَنّٰتٍ وَّعُيُوْنٍ ۞

وَّزُرُوْعٍ وَّمَقَامٍ كَرِيْمٍ ۞

وَّنَعْمَةٍ كَانُوْا فِيْهَا فٰكِهِيْنَ ۞

كَذٰلِكَ وَاَوْرَثْنٰهَا قَوْمًا اٰخَرِيْنَ ۞

29. And neither heaven nor earth shed a tear over them: nor were they given a respite (again).

فَمَا بَكَتْ عَلَيْهِمُ السَّمَآءُ وَالْاَرْضُ وَمَا كَانُوْا مُنْظَرِيْنَ ۞

30. We delivered aforetime the Children of Israel from humiliating Punishment,

وَلَقَدْ نَجَّيْنَا بَنِيٓ اِسْرَآءِيْلَ مِنَ الْعَذَابِ الْمُهِيْنِ ۙ

31. Inflicted by Pharaoh, for he was arrogant (even) among inordinate transgressors.

مِنْ فِرْعَوْنَ ؕ اِنَّهٗ كَانَ عَالِيًا مِّنَ الْمُسْرِفِيْنَ ۞

32. And We chose them aforetime above the nations, knowingly,

وَلَقَدِ اخْتَرْنٰهُمْ عَلٰى عِلْمٍ عَلَى الْعٰلَمِيْنَ ۚ

33. And granted them Signs in which there was a manifest trial.

وَاٰتَيْنٰهُمْ مِّنَ الْاٰيٰتِ مَا فِيْهِ بَلٰٓؤُا مُّبِيْنٌ ۞

34. As to these (Quraish), they say forsooth:

اِنَّ هٰٓؤُلَآءِ لَيَقُوْلُوْنَ ۙ ۞

35. "There is nothing beyond our first death, and we shall not be raised again.

اِنْ هِيَ اِلَّا مَوْتَتُنَا الْاُوْلٰى وَمَا نَحْنُ بِمُنْشَرِيْنَ ۞

36. "Then bring (back) our forefathers, if what you say is true!"

فَاْتُوْا بِاٰبَآئِنَا اِنْ كُنْتُمْ صٰدِقِيْنَ ۞

37. What! Are they better than the people of Tubba and those who were before them? We destroyed them because they were guilty of sin.

اَهُمْ خَيْرٌ اَمْ قَوْمُ تُبَّعٍ ۙ وَّالَّذِيْنَ مِنْ قَبْلِهِمْ ؕ اَهْلَكْنٰهُمْ ۫ اِنَّهُمْ كَانُوْا مُجْرِمِيْنَ ۞

38. We did not create the heavens, the earth, and all between them, merely in (idle) sport:

وَمَا خَلَقْنَا السَّمٰوٰتِ وَالْاَرْضَ وَمَا بَيْنَهُمَا لٰعِبِيْنَ ۞

39. We did not create them except for just ends: but most of them do not understand.

مَا خَلَقْنٰهُمَآ اِلَّا بِالْحَقِّ وَلٰكِنَّ اَكْثَرَهُمْ لَا يَعْلَمُوْنَ ۞

40. Verily the Day of sorting out is the time appointed for all of them,-

اِنَّ يَوْمَ الْفَصْلِ مِيْقَاتُهُمْ اَجْمَعِيْنَ ۙ

41. The Day when no protector can avail his client in any thing, and no help can they receive,

يَوْمَ لَا يُغْنِيْ مَوْلًى عَنْ مَّوْلًى شَيْئًا وَّلَا هُمْ يُنْصَرُوْنَ ۙ

42. Except such as receive Allah's Mercy: for He is Exalted in Might,

اِلَّا مَنْ رَّحِمَ اللّٰهُ ؕ اِنَّهٗ هُوَ الْعَزِيْزُ

Most Merciful.

الرَّحِيْمُ ۞

43. Verily the tree of Zaqqum,-

اِنَّ شَجَرَتَ الزَّقُّوْمِ ۞

44. Will be the food of the Sinful,-

طَعَامُ الْاَثِيْمِ ۞

45. Like molten brass; it will boil in their insides.

كَالْمُهْلِ ۞ يَغْلِيْ فِي الْبُطُوْنِ ۞

46. Like the boiling of scalding water.

كَغَلْيِ الْحَمِيْمِ ۞

47. (A voice will cry): "You seize him and drag him into the midst of the Blazing Fire!

خُذُوْهُ فَاعْتِلُوْهُ اِلٰى سَوَآءِ الْجَحِيْمِ ۞

48. "Then pour over his head the Chastisement of Boiling Water,

ثُمَّ صُبُّوْا فَوْقَ رَأْسِهٖ مِنْ عَذَابِ الْحَمِيْمِ ۞

49. You "taste (this)! Truly you were mighty, full of honour!

ذُقْ ۞ اِنَّكَ اَنْتَ الْعَزِيْزُ الْكَرِيْمُ ۞

50. "Truly this is what you used to doubt!"

اِنَّ هٰذَا مَا كُنْتُمْ بِهٖ تَمْتَرُوْنَ ۞

51. As to the Righteous (they will be) in a position of security,

اِنَّ الْمُتَّقِيْنَ فِيْ مَقَامٍ اَمِيْنٍ ۞

52. Among Gardens and Springs;

فِيْ جَنّٰتٍ وَّعُيُوْنٍ ۞

53. Dressed in fine silk and in rich brocade, they will face each other;

يَلْبَسُوْنَ مِنْ سُنْدُسٍ وَّاِسْتَبْرَقٍ مُّتَقٰبِلِيْنَ ۞

54. So; and We shall join them to Companions with beautiful, big and lustrous eyes.

كَذٰلِكَ ۚ وَزَوَّجْنٰهُمْ بِحُوْرٍ عِيْنٍ ۞

55. There can they call for every kind of fruit in peace and security;

يَدْعُوْنَ فِيْهَا بِكُلِّ فَاكِهَةٍ اٰمِنِيْنَ ۞

56. Nor will they there taste Death, except the first death; and He will preserve them from the Chastisement of the Blazing Fire,

لَا يَذُوْقُوْنَ فِيْهَا الْمَوْتَ اِلَّا الْمَوْتَةَ الْاُوْلٰى ۚ وَوَقٰهُمْ عَذَابَ الْجَحِيْمِ ۞

57. As a Bounty from your Lord! that will be the supreme achievement!

فَضْلًا مِّنْ رَّبِّكَ ۚ ذٰلِكَ هُوَ الْفَوْزُ الْعَظِيْمُ ۞

58. Verily, We have made this (Qur'an) easy, in your tongue, in order that they may give heed.

فَاِنَّمَا يَسَّرْنٰهُ بِلِسَانِكَ لَعَلَّهُمْ يَتَذَكَّرُوْنَ ۞

59. So you wait and watch; for they (too) are waiting.

فَارْتَقِبْ اِنَّهُمْ مُّرْتَقِبُوْنَ ۞

SÛRAH-45
AL-JÂSIYAH
(INTRODUCTION)

This is the sixth Sûrah of *Hâ-Mim* series: for their general theme and chronology, see the Introduction to S. 40.

Al-Jathiya, or Bowing the Knee

In the name of Allah, Most Gracious, Most Merciful.

1. *Ha-Mim.*

2. The revelation of the Book is from Allah, the Exalted in Power, full of Wisdom.

3. Verily in the heavens and the earth, are Signs for those who believe.

4. And in the creation of yourselves and the fact that animals are scattered (through the earth), are Signs for those of assured Faith.

5. And in the alternation of Night and Day, and the fact that Allah sends down Sustenance from the sky, and revives therewith the earth after its death, and in the change of the winds,- are Signs for those that are wise.

6. These are the Signs of Allah, which We rehearse to you in Truth; then in what exposition will they believe after (rejecting) Allah and His Signs?

7. Woe to each sinful dealer in Falsehoods:

8. He hears the Signs of Allah rehearsed to him, yet is obstinate and lofty, as if he had not heard them: then announce to him a Chastisement Grievous!

9. And when he learns something of Our Signs, he takes them in jest: for such there will be a humiliating Penalty.

10. In front of them is Hell: and of no profit to them is anything they may have earned, nor any protectors they may have taken to themselves besides Allah:

for them is a tremendous Chastisement.

11. This is (true) Guidance and for those who reject the Signs of their Lord, is a grievous Chastisement of abomination.

لَهُمْ عَذَابٌ عَظِيْمٌ ۞

هٰذَا هُدًى ۖ وَالَّذِيْنَ كَفَرُوْا بِاٰيٰتِ رَبِّهِمْ لَهُمْ عَذَابٌ مِّنْ رِّجْزٍ اَلِيْمٌ ۞

12. It is Allah Who has subjected the sea to you, that ships may sail through it by His command, that you may seek of His Bounty, and that you may be grateful.

اَللّٰهُ الَّذِيْ سَخَّرَ لَكُمُ الْبَحْرَ لِتَجْرِيَ الْفُلْكُ فِيْهِ بِاَمْرِهِ وَلِتَبْتَغُوْا مِنْ فَضْلِهِ وَلَعَلَّكُمْ تَشْكُرُوْنَ ۞

13. And He has subjected to you, as from Him, all that is in the heavens and on earth: behold, in that are Signs indeed for those who reflect.

وَسَخَّرَ لَكُمْ مَّا فِي السَّمٰوٰتِ وَمَا فِي الْاَرْضِ جَمِيْعًا مِّنْهُ ۚ اِنَّ فِيْ ذٰلِكَ لَاٰيٰتٍ لِّقَوْمٍ يَّتَفَكَّرُوْنَ ۞

14. Tell those who believe, to forgive those who do not look forward to the Days of Allah: It is for Him to recompense (for good or ill) each People according to what they have earned.

قُلْ لِّلَّذِيْنَ اٰمَنُوْا يَغْفِرُوْا لِلَّذِيْنَ لَا يَرْجُوْنَ اَيَّامَ اللّٰهِ لِيَجْزِيَ قَوْمًا بِمَا كَانُوْا يَكْسِبُوْنَ ۞

15. If any one does a righteous deed, it ensures to the benefit of his own soul; if he does evil, it works against (his own soul). In the end will you (all) be brought back to your Lord.

مَنْ عَمِلَ صَالِحًا فَلِنَفْسِهِ ۚ وَمَنْ اَسَآءَ فَعَلَيْهَا ۖ ثُمَّ اِلٰى رَبِّكُمْ تُرْجَعُوْنَ ۞

16. We did aforetime grant to the Children of Israel the Book, the Power of Command, and Prophethood; We gave them, for Sustenance, things good and pure; and We favoured them above the nations.

وَلَقَدْ اٰتَيْنَا بَنِيْ اِسْرَآءِيْلَ الْكِتٰبَ وَالْحُكْمَ وَالنُّبُوَّةَ وَ رَزَقْنٰهُمْ مِّنَ الطَّيِّبٰتِ وَفَضَّلْنٰهُمْ عَلَى الْعٰلَمِيْنَ ۞

17. And We granted them Clear Signs in affairs (of Religion): it was only after knowledge had been granted to them that they fell into schisms, through insolent envy among themselves. Verily your Lord will judge between them on the Day of Judgment as to those matters in which they set up differences.

وَاٰتَيْنٰهُمْ بَيِّنٰتٍ مِّنَ الْاَمْرِ ۚ فَمَا اخْتَلَفُوْا اِلَّا مِنْ بَعْدِ مَا جَآءَهُمُ الْعِلْمُ ۙ بَغْيًا بَيْنَهُمْ ۚ اِنَّ رَبَّكَ يَقْضِيْ بَيْنَهُمْ يَوْمَ الْقِيٰمَةِ فِيْمَا كَانُوْا فِيْهِ يَخْتَلِفُوْنَ ۞

18. Then We put you on the (right) Way of Religion:

ثُمَّ جَعَلْنٰكَ عَلٰى شَرِيْعَةٍ مِّنَ الْاَمْرِ

so you follow that (Way), and do not follow the desires of those who do not know.

فَاتَّبِعْهَا وَلَا تَتَّبِعْ أَهْوَآءَ الَّذِينَ لَا يَعْلَمُونَ ۞

19. They will be of no use to you in the sight of Allah: it is only Wrong-doers (that stand as) protectors, one to another: but Allah is the Protector of the Righteous.

إِنَّهُمْ لَنْ يُغْنُوا عَنْكَ مِنَ اللّٰهِ شَيْئًا ۚ وَإِنَّ الظّٰلِمِينَ بَعْضُهُمْ أَوْلِيَآءُ بَعْضٍ ۚ وَاللّٰهُ وَلِيُّ الْمُتَّقِينَ ۞

20. These are clear evidences to men and a Guidance and Mercy to those of assured Faith.

هٰذَا بَصَآئِرُ لِلنَّاسِ وَهُدًى وَرَحْمَةٌ لِّقَوْمٍ يُّوقِنُونَ ۞

21. What! do those who seek after evil ways think that We shall hold them equal with those who believe and do righteous deeds,- that equal will be their life and their death? Ill is the judgment that they make.

أَمْ حَسِبَ الَّذِينَ اجْتَرَحُوا السَّيِّاٰتِ أَنْ نَّجْعَلَهُمْ كَالَّذِينَ اٰمَنُوا وَعَمِلُوا الصّٰلِحٰتِ سَوَآءً مَّحْيَاهُمْ وَمَمَاتُهُمْ ۚ سَآءَ مَا يَحْكُمُونَ ۞

22. Allah created the heavens and the earth for just ends, and in order that each soul may find the recompense of what it has earned, and none of them be wronged.

وَخَلَقَ اللّٰهُ السَّمٰوٰتِ وَالْأَرْضَ بِالْحَقِّ وَلِتُجْزٰى كُلُّ نَفْسٍ بِمَا كَسَبَتْ وَهُمْ لَا يُظْلَمُونَ ۞

23. Do you see such a one as takes as his god his own vain desire? Allah has, knowing (him as such), left him astray, and sealed his hearing and his heart (and understanding), and put a cover on his sight. Who, then, will guide him after Allah (has withdrawn Guidance)? Will you not then receive admonition?

أَفَرَءَيْتَ مَنِ اتَّخَذَ إِلٰهَهُ هَوٰهُ وَأَضَلَّهُ اللّٰهُ عَلٰى عِلْمٍ وَّخَتَمَ عَلٰى سَمْعِهِ وَقَلْبِهِ وَجَعَلَ عَلٰى بَصَرِهِ غِشٰوَةً ۚ فَمَنْ يَّهْدِيهِ مِنْ بَعْدِ اللّٰهِ ۚ أَفَلَا تَذَكَّرُونَ ۞

24. And they say: "What is there but our life in this world? We shall die and we live, and nothing but Time can destroy us." But of that they have no knowledge: they merely conjecture:

وَقَالُوا مَا هِيَ إِلَّا حَيَاتُنَا الدُّنْيَا نَمُوتُ وَنَحْيَا وَمَا يُهْلِكُنَا إِلَّا الدَّهْرُ ۚ وَمَا لَهُمْ بِذٰلِكَ مِنْ عِلْمٍ ۚ إِنْ هُمْ إِلَّا يَظُنُّونَ ۞

25. And when Our Clear Signs are rehearsed to them, their argument is nothing but this:

وَإِذَا تُتْلٰى عَلَيْهِمْ اٰيَاتُنَا بَيِّنٰتٍ مَّا كَانَ حُجَّتَهُمْ إِلَّا أَنْ

they say, "Bring (back) our forefathers, if what you say is true!"

26. Say: "It is Allah Who gives you life, then gives you death; then He will gather you together for the Day of Judgment about which there is no doubt": But most men do not understand.

27. To Allah belongs the dominion of the heavens and the earth, and the Day that the Hour of Judgment is established,- that Day will the dealers in Falsehood perish!

28. And you will see every nation bowing the knee: every nation will be called to its Record: "This Day you shall be recompensed for all that you did!

29. "This Our Record speaks about you with truth: for We were wont to put on Record all that you did."

30. Then, as to those who believed and did righteous deeds, their Lord will admit them to His Mercy, that will be the achievement for all to see.

31. But as to those who rejected Allah, (to them will be said): "Were not Our Signs rehearsed to you? But you were arrogant, and were a people given to sin!

32. "And when it was said that the promise of Allah was true, and that the Hour- there was no doubt about its (coming), you used to say, 'We do not know what is the Hour: we only think it is an idea, and we have no firm assurance.'"

33. Then will appear to them the evil (fruits) of what they did, and they will be completely encircled

قَالُوا ائْتُوا بِآبَائِنَا إِنْ كُنْتُمْ
صَٰدِقِينَ ۝

قُلِ اللّٰهُ يُحْيِيكُمْ ثُمَّ يُمِيتُكُمْ
ثُمَّ يَجْمَعُكُمْ إِلَىٰ يَوْمِ الْقِيٰمَةِ
لَا رَيْبَ فِيهِ وَلٰكِنَّ أَكْثَرَ
النَّاسِ لَا يَعْلَمُونَ ۝

وَلِلّٰهِ مُلْكُ السَّمٰوٰتِ وَالْأَرْضِ
وَيَوْمَ تَقُومُ السَّاعَةُ يَوْمَئِذٍ
يَخْسَرُ الْمُبْطِلُونَ ۝

وَتَرَىٰ كُلَّ أُمَّةٍ جَاثِيَةً كُلُّ
أُمَّةٍ تُدْعَىٰ إِلَىٰ كِتٰبِهَا الْيَوْمَ
تُجْزَوْنَ مَا كُنْتُمْ تَعْمَلُونَ ۝

هٰذَا كِتٰبُنَا يَنْطِقُ عَلَيْكُمْ
بِالْحَقِّ إِنَّا كُنَّا نَسْتَنْسِخُ
مَا كُنْتُمْ تَعْمَلُونَ ۝

فَأَمَّا الَّذِينَ آمَنُوا وَعَمِلُوا
الصّٰلِحٰتِ فَيُدْخِلُهُمْ رَبُّهُمْ فِي
رَحْمَتِهِ ذٰلِكَ هُوَ الْفَوْزُ الْمُبِينُ ۝

وَأَمَّا الَّذِينَ كَفَرُوا أَفَلَمْ تَكُنْ
آيٰتِي تُتْلَىٰ عَلَيْكُمْ فَاسْتَكْبَرْتُمْ
وَكُنْتُمْ قَوْمًا مُجْرِمِينَ ۝

وَإِذَا قِيلَ إِنَّ وَعْدَ اللّٰهِ حَقٌّ
وَالسَّاعَةُ لَا رَيْبَ فِيهَا قُلْتُمْ مَا
نَدْرِي مَا السَّاعَةُ إِنْ نَظُنُّ إِلَّا
ظَنًّا وَمَا نَحْنُ بِمُسْتَيْقِنِينَ ۝

وَبَدَا لَهُمْ سَيِّئَاتُ مَا عَمِلُوا وَحَاقَ

SÛRAH-46
AL-AHQÂF
(INTRODUCTION)

This is the seventh and last Sûrah of the *Hâ-Mim* series. For the general theme and chronological place of these Sûras see the Introduction to S. 40.

The *Ahqâf* (mentioned in verse 21) are the long and winding crooked tracts of sand-hills, characteristic of the country of the 'Ãd people, adjoining Hadhramaut and Yaman: See 7: 65. These people had, at that time, probably a fertile irrigated country, but their sins brought on the calamity, mentioned in 46: 24-25. The lesson of this Sûrah is that if the Truth is challenged, the challenge will be duly answered, and Truth vindicated.

by that which they used to mock at!

34. It will also be said: "This Day We will forget you as you forgot the meeting of this Day of yours! and your abode is the Fire, and you do not have any helpers!

35. "This, because you used to take the Signs of Allah in jest, and the life of the world deceived you:" (from) that Day, therefore, they shall not be taken out thence, nor shall they be received into Grace.

36. Then Praise be to Allah, Lord of the heavens and Lord of the earth,- Lord and Cherisher of all the Worlds!

37. To Him be glory throughout the heavens and the earth and He is Exalted in Power. Full of Wisdom.

46. Winding Sand-tracts
In the name of Allah. Most Gracious, Most Merciful.

1. *Ha-Mim.*

2. The Revelation of the Book is from Allah, the Exalted in Power, full of Wisdom.

3. We did not create the heavens and the earth and all between them but with truth, and for a term appointed. But those who reject Faith turn away from that whereof they are warned.

4. Say: "Do you see what it is you invoke besides Allah? Show me what it is they have created on earth, or have they a share in the heavens, bring me a book (revealed) before this, or any remnant of knowledge (you may have), if you are telling the truth!

5.   And who is more astray than one who invokes besides Allah, such as will not answer him to the Day of Judgment, and who (in fact) are unconscious of their call (to them)?

وَمَنْ أَضَلُّ مِمَّنْ يَّدْعُوا مِنْ دُوْنِ اللّٰهِ مَنْ لَّا يَسْتَجِيْبُ لَهٗٓ إِلٰى يَوْمِ الْقِيٰمَةِ وَهُمْ عَنْ دُعَآئِهِمْ غٰفِلُوْنَ ۝

6.   And when mankind are gathered together (at the Resurrection), they will be hostile to them and reject their worship (altogether)!

وَإِذَا حُشِرَ النَّاسُ كَانُوْا لَهُمْ أَعْدَآءً وَّكَانُوْا بِعِبَادَتِهِمْ كٰفِرِيْنَ ۝

7.   When Our Clear Signs are rehearsed to them, the Unbelievers say, of the Truth when it comes to them: "This is evident sorcery!"

وَإِذَا تُتْلٰى عَلَيْهِمْ اٰيٰتُنَا بَيِّنٰتٍ قَالَ الَّذِيْنَ كَفَرُوْا لِلْحَقِّ لَمَّا جَآءَهُمْ ۙ هٰذَا سِحْرٌ مُّبِيْنٌ ؕ

8.   Or do they say, "He has forged it"? Say: "Had I forged it, then you will not at all be able to save me from the wrath of Allah. He knows best of that whereof you talk (so glibly)! Enough is He for a witness between me and you! And He is Oft-Forgiving, Most Merciful."

أَمْ يَقُوْلُوْنَ افْتَرٰىهُ ؕ قُلْ إِنِ افْتَرَيْتُهٗ فَلَا تَمْلِكُوْنَ لِيْ مِنَ اللّٰهِ شَيْئًا ؕ هُوَ أَعْلَمُ بِمَا تُفِيْضُوْنَ فِيْهِ ؕ كَفٰى بِهٖ شَهِيْدًا بَيْنِيْ وَبَيْنَكُمْ ؕ وَهُوَ الْغَفُوْرُ الرَّحِيْمُ ۝

9.   Say: "I am no bringer of new-fangled doctrine among the Apostles, nor do I know what will be done with me or with you. I follow but that which is revealed to me by inspiration; I am but a Warner open and clear."

قُلْ مَا كُنْتُ بِدْعًا مِّنَ الرُّسُلِ وَمَآ أَدْرِيْ مَا يُفْعَلُ بِيْ وَلَا بِكُمْ ؕ إِنْ أَتَّبِعُ إِلَّا مَا يُوْحٰى إِلَيَّ وَمَآ أَنَا إِلَّا نَذِيْرٌ مُّبِيْنٌ ۝

10.   Say: "Do you see? If (this teaching) be from Allah, and you reject it, and a witness from among the Children of Israel testifies to its similarity (with earlier scripture), and has believed while you are arrogant, (how unjust you are!) truly, Allah does not guide a people unjust."

قُلْ أَرَأَيْتُمْ إِنْ كَانَ مِنْ عِنْدِ اللّٰهِ وَكَفَرْتُمْ بِهٖ وَشَهِدَ شَاهِدٌ مِّنْ بَنِيْ إِسْرَآءِيْلَ عَلٰى مِثْلِهٖ فَاٰمَنَ وَاسْتَكْبَرْتُمْ ؕ إِنَّ اللّٰهَ لَا يَهْدِى الْقَوْمَ الظّٰلِمِيْنَ ۝

11.   The Unbelievers say of those who believe: "If (this Message) were a good thing, (such men) would not have gone to it first, before us!" And seeing that they do not guide themselves thereby, they will say,

وَقَالَ الَّذِيْنَ كَفَرُوْا لِلَّذِيْنَ اٰمَنُوْا لَوْ كَانَ خَيْرًا مَّا سَبَقُوْنَآ إِلَيْهِ ؕ وَإِذْ لَمْ يَهْتَدُوْا بِهٖ فَسَيَقُوْلُوْنَ

ع

"this is an old falsehood!"

هٰذَآ إِفْكٌ قَدِيمٌ ۝

12.   And before this, was the Book of Moses as a guide and a mercy: and this Book confirms (it) in the Arabic tongue; to admonish the unjust, and as glad tidings to those who do right.

وَمِنْ قَبْلِهٖ كِتٰبُ مُوْسٰٓى اِمَامًا وَّرَحْمَةً ۖ وَهٰذَا كِتٰبٌ مُّصَدِّقٌ لِّسَانًا عَرَبِيًّا لِّيُنْذِرَ الَّذِيْنَ ظَلَمُوْا ۖ وَبُشْرٰى لِلْمُحْسِنِيْنَ ۝

13.   Verily those who say, "Our Lord is Allah," and remain firm (on that Path),- on them shall be no fear, nor shall they grieve.

اِنَّ الَّذِيْنَ قَالُوْا رَبُّنَا اللهُ ثُمَّ اسْتَقَامُوْا فَلَا خَوْفٌ عَلَيْهِمْ وَلَا هُمْ يَحْزَنُوْنَ ۝

14.   Such shall be Companions of the Garden, dwelling therein (for ever): a recompense for their (good) deeds.

اُولٰٓئِكَ اَصْحٰبُ الْجَنَّةِ خٰلِدِيْنَ فِيْهَا ۚ جَزَآءً بِمَا كَانُوْا يَعْمَلُوْنَ ۝

15.   We have enjoined on man kindness to his parents: In pain did his mother bear him, and in pain did she give him birth. The carrying of the (child) to his weaning is (a period of) thirty months. At length, when he reaches the age of full strength and attains forty years, he says, "O my Lord! Grant me that I may be grateful for Your favour which You have bestowed upon me, and upon both my parents, and that I may work righteous-ness such as You may approve; and be gracious to me in my issue. Truly have I turned to You and truly do I bow (to You) in Islam."

وَوَصَّيْنَا الْاِنْسَانَ بِوَالِدَيْهِ اِحْسٰنًا ۖ حَمَلَتْهُ اُمُّهٗ كُرْهًا وَّ وَضَعَتْهُ كُرْهًا ۖ وَحَمْلُهٗ وَفِصٰلُهٗ ثَلٰثُوْنَ شَهْرًا ۚ حَتّٰٓى اِذَا بَلَغَ اَشُدَّهٗ وَبَلَغَ اَرْبَعِيْنَ سَنَةً ۙ قَالَ رَبِّ اَوْزِعْنِيْٓ اَنْ اَشْكُرَ نِعْمَتَكَ الَّتِيْٓ اَنْعَمْتَ عَلَيَّ وَعَلٰى وَالِدَيَّ وَاَنْ اَعْمَلَ صَالِحًا تَرْضٰهُ وَاَصْلِحْ لِيْ فِيْ ذُرِّيَّتِيْ ۚ اِنِّيْ تُبْتُ اِلَيْكَ وَاِنِّيْ مِنَ الْمُسْلِمِيْنَ ۝

16.   Such are they from whom We shall accept the best of their deeds and pass by their ill deeds: (they shall be) among the Companions of the Garden: a promise of truth, which was made to them (in this life).

اُولٰٓئِكَ الَّذِيْنَ نَتَقَبَّلُ عَنْهُمْ اَحْسَنَ مَا عَمِلُوْا وَنَتَجَاوَزُ عَنْ سَيِّاٰتِهِمْ فِيْٓ اَصْحٰبِ الْجَنَّةِ ۖ وَعْدَ الصِّدْقِ الَّذِيْ كَانُوْا يُوْعَدُوْنَ ۝

17.   But (there is one) who says to his parents, "Fie on you! Do you hold out the promise to me that I shall be raised up,

وَالَّذِيْ قَالَ لِوَالِدَيْهِ اُفٍّ لَّكُمَآ اَتَعِدٰنِنِيْٓ اَنْ اُخْرَجَ وَقَدْ خَلَتِ

even though generations have passed before me (without rising again)?" And they two seek Allah's aid, (and rebuke the son): "Woe to you! Have Faith! for the promise of Allah is true." But he says, "This is nothing but tales of the ancients!"

18. Such are they against whom is proved the sentence among the previous generations of Jinns and men, that have passed away; for they will be (utterly) lost.

19. And to all are (assigned) degrees according to the deeds which they (have done), and in order that (Allah) may recompense their deeds, and no injustice be done to them.

20. And on the Day that the Unbelievers will be placed before the Fire, (It will be said to them): "You received your good things in the life of the world, and you took your pleasure out of them: but today you shall be recompensed with a Chastisement of humiliation: for that you were arrogant on earth without just cause, and that you (ever) transgressed."

21. Mention (Hud) one of 'Ad's (own) brethren: behold, he warned his people about the winding Sand-tracts: and there have been warners before him and after him: "Warship you none other than Allah: Truly I fear for you the Chastisement of a Mighty Day."

22. They said: "Have you come in order to turn us aside from our gods? Then bring upon us the (calamity) with which you threaten us, if you are telling the truth?"

23. He said: "The Knowledge (of when it will come) is only with Allah: I proclaim to you the mission on which I have been sent: but I see that you are a people in ignorance!"..

ٱلۡقُرُونُ مِن قَبۡلِي وَهُمَا يَسۡتَغِيثٰنِ

ٱللَّهَ وَيۡلَكَ ءَامِنۡ ۖ إِنَّ وَعۡدَ ٱللَّهِ

حَقٌّ فَيَقُولُ مَا هَٰذَآ إِلَّآ أَسَٰطِيرُ

ٱلۡأَوَّلِينَ ۝

أُوْلَٰٓئِكَ ٱلَّذِينَ حَقَّ عَلَيۡهِمُ ٱلۡقَوۡلُ

فِيٓ أُمَمٍ قَدۡ خَلَتۡ مِن قَبۡلِهِم مِّنَ

ٱلۡجِنِّ وَٱلۡإِنسِ ۖ إِنَّهُمۡ كَانُوا۟ خَٰسِرِينَ ۝

وَلِكُلٍّ دَرَجَٰتٌ مِّمَّا عَمِلُوا۟ ۖ وَلِيُوَفِّيَهُمۡ

أَعۡمَٰلَهُمۡ وَهُمۡ لَا يُظۡلَمُونَ ۝

وَيَوۡمَ يُعۡرَضُ ٱلَّذِينَ كَفَرُوا۟ عَلَى

ٱلنَّارِ أَذۡهَبۡتُمۡ طَيِّبَٰتِكُمۡ فِي

حَيَاتِكُمُ ٱلدُّنۡيَا وَٱسۡتَمۡتَعۡتُم بِهَا

فَٱلۡيَوۡمَ تُجۡزَوۡنَ عَذَابَ ٱلۡهُونِ

بِمَا كُنتُمۡ تَسۡتَكۡبِرُونَ فِي ٱلۡأَرۡضِ

بِغَيۡرِ ٱلۡحَقِّ وَبِمَا كُنتُمۡ تَفۡسُقُونَ ۝

وَٱذۡكُرۡ أَخَا عَادٍ إِذۡ أَنذَرَ قَوۡمَهُۥ

بِٱلۡأَحۡقَافِ وَقَدۡ خَلَتِ ٱلنُّذُرُ

مِنۢ بَيۡنِ يَدَيۡهِ وَمِنۡ خَلۡفِهِۦٓ أَلَّا

تَعۡبُدُوٓا۟ إِلَّا ٱللَّهَ ۖ إِنِّيٓ أَخَافُ عَلَيۡكُمۡ

عَذَابَ يَوۡمٍ عَظِيمٍ ۝

قَالُوٓا۟ أَجِئۡتَنَا لِتَأۡفِكَنَا عَنۡ ءَالِهَتِنَا

فَأۡتِنَا بِمَا تَعِدُنَآ إِن كُنتَ مِنَ

ٱلصَّٰدِقِينَ ۝

قَالَ إِنَّمَا ٱلۡعِلۡمُ عِندَ ٱللَّهِ

وَأُبَلِّغُكُم مَّآ أُرۡسِلۡتُ بِهِۦ وَلَٰكِنِّيٓ

أَرَىٰكُمۡ قَوۡمًا تَجۡهَلُونَ ۝

24. Then, when they saw a cloud advancing towards their valleys, they said, "This cloud will give us rain!" "Nay, it is the (calamity) you were asking to be hastened, a wind wherein is a grievous Chastisement

فَلَمَّا رَأَوْهُ عَارِضًا مُّسْتَقْبِلَ أَوْ
دِيَتِهِمْ قَالُوا هٰذَا عَارِضٌ مُّمْطِرُنَا ۚ
بَلْ هُوَ مَا اسْتَعْجَلْتُمْ بِهٖ رِيْحٌ فِيْهَا
عَذَابٌ أَلِيْمٌ ۙ

25. "Everything will it destroy by the command of its Lord!" Then by the morning they became such that nothing was to be seen but (the ruins of) their houses! Thus do We recompense those given to sin!

تُدَمِّرُ كُلَّ شَيْءٍ بِأَمْرِ رَبِّهَا
فَأَصْبَحُوا لَا يُرَىٰ إِلَّا مَسٰكِنُهُمْ ۗ
كَذٰلِكَ نَجْزِي الْقَوْمَ الْمُجْرِمِيْنَ ۟

26. And We had firmly established them in a (prosperity and) power which We have not given to you (you Quraish!) and We had endowed them with (faculties of) hearing, sight, heart and intellect: but of no profit to them were their (faculties of) hearing, sight, and heart and intellect, when they went on rejecting the Signs of Allah; and they were (completely) encircled by that which they used to mock at!

وَلَقَدْ مَكَّنّٰهُمْ فِيْمَا إِنْ مَّكَّنّٰكُمْ
فِيْهِ وَجَعَلْنَا لَهُمْ سَمْعًا وَّأَبْصَارًا
وَّأَفْئِدَةً ۖ فَمَا أَغْنَىٰ عَنْهُمْ سَمْعُهُمْ
وَلَا أَبْصَارُهُمْ وَلَا أَفْئِدَتُهُمْ
مِّنْ شَيْءٍ إِذْ كَانُوا يَجْحَدُوْنَ ۙ
بِأَيٰتِ اللّٰهِ وَحَاقَ بِهِمْ مَّا كَانُوا
بِهٖ يَسْتَهْزِءُوْنَ ۟

27. We destroyed (aforetime) populations round about you; and We have shown the Signs in various ways, that they may turn (to Us).

وَلَقَدْ أَهْلَكْنَا مَا حَوْلَكُمْ مِّنَ الْقُرٰى
وَصَرَّفْنَا الْاٰيٰتِ لَعَلَّهُمْ يَرْجِعُوْنَ ۟

28. Why then was there no help forthcoming to them from those whom they worshipped as gods, besides Allah, as a means of access (to Allah)? Nay, they left them in the lurch: but that was their falsehood and their invention.

فَلَوْلَا نَصَرَهُمُ الَّذِيْنَ اتَّخَذُوا مِنْ
دُوْنِ اللّٰهِ قُرْبَانًا اٰلِهَةً ۖ بَلْ
ضَلُّوا عَنْهُمْ ۚ وَذٰلِكَ إِفْكُهُمْ
وَمَا كَانُوا يَفْتَرُوْنَ ۟

29. Behold, We turned towards you a company of Jinns (quietly) listening to the Qur'an: when they stood in the presence thereof, they said, "Listen in silence!" When the (reading) was finished, they returned to their people, to warn (them of their sins).

وَإِذْ صَرَفْنَا إِلَيْكَ نَفَرًا مِّنَ الْجِنِّ
يَسْتَمِعُوْنَ الْقُرْاٰنَ ۖ فَلَمَّا حَضَرُوْهُ
قَالُوا أَنْصِتُوا ۖ فَلَمَّا قُضِيَ وَلَّوْا
إِلَىٰ قَوْمِهِمْ مُّنْذِرِيْنَ ۟

30. They said, "O our people! We have heard a Book revealed after Moses, confirming

قَالُوا يٰقَوْمَنَا إِنَّا سَمِعْنَا كِتٰبًا
أُنْزِلَ مِنْ بَعْدِ مُوْسَىٰ مُصَدِّقًا

SÛRAH-47
MUHAMMAD
(INTRODUCTION)

We have examined and followed the current arrangement of the Sûras according to subject-matter and independently of Chronology, and we have found that a logical thread runs through them. We have now finished more than five-sixths of the Qur'ân. The remaining sixth consists of short Sûras, but these are again grouped according to subject-matter.

We begin the first of such groups with a group of three Sûras (47 to 49), which deal with the organization of the Muslim Ummat or community both for external defence and in internal relations. The present Sûrah deals with the necessity of defence against external foes by courage and strenous fighting, and dates from about the first of the Hijra, when the Muslims were under threat of extinction by invasion from Makkah.

what came before it: it guides (men) to the Truth and to a Straight Path.

لِّمَا بَيْنَ يَدَيْهِ يَهْدِىٓ إِلَى الْحَقِّ
وَإِلَى طَرِيْقٍ مُّسْتَقِيْمٍ ۝

31. "O our people, hearken to the one who invites (you) to Allah, and believe in him: He will forgive you your faults, and deliver you from a Chastisement Grievous.

يٰقَوْمَنَا أَجِيْبُوْا دَاعِىَ اللّٰهِ وَاٰمِنُوْا
بِهٖ يَغْفِرْ لَكُمْ مِّنْ ذُنُوْبِكُمْ
وَيُجِرْكُمْ مِّنْ عَذَابٍ أَلِيْمٍ ۝

32. "If any does not hearken to the one who invites (us) to Allah, he cannot frustrate (Allah's Plan) on earth, and no protectors can he have besides Allah: such men (wander) in manifest error."

وَمَنْ لَّا يُجِبْ دَاعِىَ اللّٰهِ فَلَيْسَ
بِمُعْجِزٍ فِى الْأَرْضِ وَلَيْسَ لَهٗ
مِنْ دُوْنِهٖ أَوْلِيَآءُ أُولٰٓئِكَ فِىْ
ضَلٰلٍ مُّبِيْنٍ ۝

33. Don't they see that Allah, Who created the heavens and the earth, and never wearied with their creation, is able to give life to the dead? Yes, verily He has power over all things.

أَوَلَمْ يَرَوْا أَنَّ اللّٰهَ الَّذِىْ خَلَقَ
السَّمٰوٰتِ وَالْأَرْضَ وَلَمْ يَعْىَ
بِخَلْقِهِنَّ بِقٰدِرٍ عَلٰٓى أَنْ يُّحْيِىَ
الْمَوْتٰى ۚ بَلٰٓى إِنَّهٗ عَلٰى كُلِّ
شَىْءٍ قَدِيْرٌ ۝

34. And on the Day that the Unbelievers will be placed before the Fire, (they will be asked,) "Is this not the Truth?" they will say, "Yes, by our Lord!" (One will say:) "Then you taste the Chastisement, for that you were wont to deny (Truth)!"

وَيَوْمَ يُعْرَضُ الَّذِيْنَ كَفَرُوْا عَلَى
النَّارِ ۚ أَلَيْسَ هٰذَا بِالْحَقِّ ۚ
قَالُوْا بَلٰى وَرَبِّنَا ۚ قَالَ فَذُوْقُوا
الْعَذَابَ بِمَا كُنْتُمْ تَكْفُرُوْنَ ۝

35. Therefore patiently persevere, as did (all) Apostles of inflexible purpose; and be in no haste about the (Unbelievers). On the Day that they see the (Punishment) promised them, (it will be) as if they had not tarried more than an hour in a single day. (Yours but) to proclaim the Message: but shall any be destroyed except those who transgress?

فَاصْبِرْ كَمَا صَبَرَ أُولُوا الْعَزْمِ
مِنَ الرُّسُلِ وَلَا تَسْتَعْجِلْ لَّهُمْ ۚ
كَأَنَّهُمْ يَوْمَ يَرَوْنَ مَا يُوْعَدُوْنَ ۙ لَمْ
يَلْبَثُوْا إِلَّا سَاعَةً مِّنْ نَّهَارٍ ۚ بَلٰغٌ ۚ
فَهَلْ يُهْلَكُ إِلَّا الْقَوْمُ الْفٰسِقُوْنَ ۝

47. (The Prophet) Muhammad
In the name of Allah. Most Gracious, Most Merciful.

(٤٧) سُوْرَةُ مُحَمَّدٍ مَّدَنِيَّةٌ (٩٥)
بِسْمِ اللّٰهِ الرَّحْمٰنِ الرَّحِيْمِ

1. Those who reject Allah and hinder (men) from the Path

الَّذِيْنَ كَفَرُوْا وَصَدُّوْا عَنْ سَبِيْلِ

of Allah,- Allah will render their deeds astray (from their mark).

2. But those who believe and work deeds of righteousness, and believe in the (Revelation) sent down to Muhammad - for it is the Truth from their Lord,- He will remove from them their ills and improve their condition.

3. This is because those who reject Allah, follow falsehood, while those who believe follow the Truth from their Lord: thus Allah sets forth for men their lessons by similitudes.

4. Therefore, when you meet the Unbelievers (in fight), smite at their necks; at length, when you have thoroughly subdued them, bind a bond firmly (on them): thereafter (is the time for) either generosity or ransom: until the war lays down its burdens. Thus (are you commanded): but if it had been Allah's Will, He could certainly have exacted retribution from them (Himself); but (He lets you fight) in order to test you, some with others. But those who are slain in the Way of Allah,- He will never let their deeds be lost.

5. Soon He will guide them and improve their condition,

6. And admit them to the Garden which He has announced for them.

7. O you who believe! If you will aid (the cause of) Allah, He will aid you, and plant your feet firmly.

8. But those who reject (Allah),- for them is destruction, and (Allah) will render their deeds worthless.

9. That is because they hate the Revelation of Allah; so He has made their deeds fruitless.

10. Do they not travel through the earth, and see

اللهُ اَضَلَّ اَعْمَالَهُمْ ۝

وَالَّذِيْنَ اٰمَنُوْا وَعَمِلُوا الصّٰلِحٰتِ وَاٰمَنُوْا بِمَا نُزِّلَ عَلٰى مُحَمَّدٍ وَّهُوَ الْحَقُّ مِنْ رَّبِّهِمْ ۙ كَفَّرَ عَنْهُمْ سَيِّاٰتِهِمْ وَاَصْلَحَ بَالَهُمْ ۝

ذٰلِكَ بِاَنَّ الَّذِيْنَ كَفَرُوا اتَّبَعُوا الْبَاطِلَ وَاَنَّ الَّذِيْنَ اٰمَنُوا اتَّبَعُوا الْحَقَّ مِنْ رَّبِّهِمْ ۗ كَذٰلِكَ يَضْرِبُ اللهُ لِلنَّاسِ اَمْثَالَهُمْ ۝

فَاِذَا لَقِيْتُمُ الَّذِيْنَ كَفَرُوْا فَضَرْبَ الرِّقَابِ ۗ حَتّٰى اِذَآ اَثْخَنْتُمُوْهُمْ فَشُدُّوا الْوَثَاقَ ۙ فَاِمَّا مَنًّا بَعْدُ وَاِمَّا فِدَآءً حَتّٰى تَضَعَ الْحَرْبُ اَوْزَارَهَا ۛۚ ذٰلِكَ ۛ وَلَوْ يَشَآءُ اللهُ لَانْتَصَرَ مِنْهُمْ ۙ وَلٰكِنْ لِّيَبْلُوَا بَعْضَكُمْ بِبَعْضٍ ۗ وَالَّذِيْنَ قُتِلُوْا فِيْ سَبِيْلِ اللهِ فَلَنْ يُّضِلَّ اَعْمَالَهُمْ ۝

سَيَهْدِيْهِمْ وَيُصْلِحُ بَالَهُمْ ۝

وَيُدْخِلُهُمُ الْجَنَّةَ عَرَّفَهَا لَهُمْ ۝

يٰاَيُّهَا الَّذِيْنَ اٰمَنُوْا اِنْ تَنْصُرُوا اللهَ يَنْصُرْكُمْ وَيُثَبِّتْ اَقْدَامَكُمْ ۝

وَالَّذِيْنَ كَفَرُوْا فَتَعْسًا لَّهُمْ وَاَضَلَّ اَعْمَالَهُمْ ۝

ذٰلِكَ بِاَنَّهُمْ كَرِهُوْا مَآ اَنْزَلَ اللهُ فَاَحْبَطَ اَعْمَالَهُمْ ۝

اَفَلَمْ يَسِيْرُوْا فِي الْاَرْضِ فَيَنْظُرُوْا

what was the End of those before them (who did evil)? Allah brought utter destruction on them, and similar (fates await) those who reject Allah.

11. That is because Allah is the Protector of those who believe, but those who reject Allah have no protector.

12. Verily Allah will admit those who believe and do righteous deeds, to Gardens beneath which rivers flow; while those who reject Allah will enjoy (this world) and eat as cattle eat; and the Fire will be their abode.

13. And how many cities, with more power than your city which has driven you out, have We destroyed (for their sins)? and there was none to aid them.

14. Is then one who is on a clear (Path) from his Lord, no better than one to whom the evil of his conduct seems pleasing, and such as follow their own lusts?

15. (Here is) a parable of the Garden which the righteous are promised: in it are rivers of water unstaling; rivers of milk of which the taste never changes; rivers of wine, a joy to those who drink; and rivers of honey pure and clear. In it there are for them all kinds of fruits; and Grace from their Lord. (Can those in such Bliss) be compared to such as shall dwell for ever in the Fire, and be given, to drink, boiling water, so that it cuts up their bowels (to pieces)?

16. And among them are men who listen to you, but in the end, when they go out from you, they say to those who

have received Knowledge,
"What is it he said just then?"
Such are men whose hearts
Allah has sealed, and who
follow their own lusts.

17. But to those who receive
Guidance, He increases the
(light of) Guidance, and bestows
on them their Piety and Restraint
(from evil).

18. Do they then only wait for
the Hour,- that it should come
on them of a sudden? But
already have come some tokens
thereof, and when it (actually) is
on, them, how can, they benefit
then by their admonition?

19. Know, therefore, that there
is no god but Allah, and ask
forgiveness for your fault, and
for the men and women who
believe: for Allah knows how
you move about and how you
dwell in your homes.

20. Those who believe say,
"Why is not a Sura sent down
(for us)?" But when a Sura of
basic or categorical meaning is
revealed, and fighting is
mentioned therein, you will see
those in whose hearts is a
disease looking at you with a
look of one in swoon at the
approach of death. But more
fitting for them-

21. Were it to obey and say
what is just, and when a matter
is resolved on, it were best for
them if they were true to Allah.

22. Then, is it to be expected
of you, if you were put in
authority, that you will do
mischief in the land, and break
your ties of kith and kin?

23. Such are the men whom
Allah has cursed for He has
made them deaf and blinded
their sight.

24. Do they not then earnestly
seek to understand the Qur'an, or
are their

hearts locked up by them?

قُلُوبٌ اَقْفَالُهَا ۝

25. Those who turn back as apostates after Guidance was clearly shown to them,- the Evil One has instigated them and buoyed them up with false hopes.

اِنَّ الَّذِيْنَ ارْتَدُّوْا عَلٰۤى اَدْبَارِهِمْ

مِّنْ بَعْدِ مَا تَبَيَّنَ لَهُمُ الْهُدَى ۙ

الشَّيْطٰنُ سَوَّلَ لَهُمْ ۫ وَاَمْلٰى لَهُمْ ۝

26. This is, because they said to those who hate what Allah has revealed, "We will obey you in part of (this) matter"; but Allah knows their (inner) secrets.

ذٰلِكَ بِاَنَّهُمْ قَالُوْا لِلَّذِيْنَ كَرِهُوْا

مَا نَزَّلَ اللّٰهُ سَنُطِيْعُكُمْ فِيْ بَعْضِ

الْاَمْرِ ۚ وَاللّٰهُ يَعْلَمُ اِسْرَارَهُمْ ۝

27. But how (will it be) when the angels take their souls at death, and smite their faces and their backs?

فَكَيْفَ اِذَا تَوَفَّتْهُمُ الْمَلٰٓئِكَةُ

يَضْرِبُوْنَ وُجُوْهَهُمْ وَاَدْبَارَهُمْ ۝

28. This is because they followed that which called forth the Wrath of Allah, and they hated Allah's good pleasure; so He made their deeds of no effect.

ذٰلِكَ بِاَنَّهُمُ اتَّبَعُوْا مَاۤ اَسْخَطَ

اللّٰهَ وَكَرِهُوْا رِضْوَانَهٗ فَاَحْبَطَ

اَعْمَالَهُمْ ۝

29. Or do those in whose hearts is a disease, think that Allah will not bring to light all their rancour?

اَمْ حَسِبَ الَّذِيْنَ فِيْ قُلُوْبِهِمْ

مَّرَضٌ اَنْ لَّنْ يُّخْرِجَ اللّٰهُ اَضْغَانَهُمْ ۝

30. If We had so willed, We could have shown them up to you, and you should have known them by their marks: but surely you will know them by the tone of their speech! And Allah knows all that you do.

وَلَوْ نَشَآءُ لَاَرَيْنٰكَهُمْ فَلَعَرَفْتَهُمْ

بِسِيْمٰهُمْ ۚ وَلَتَعْرِفَنَّهُمْ فِيْ لَحْنِ الْقَوْلِ ۚ

وَاللّٰهُ يَعْلَمُ اَعْمَالَكُمْ ۝

31. And We shall try you until We test those among you who strive their utmost and persevere in patience; and We shall try your reported (mettle).

وَلَنَبْلُوَنَّكُمْ حَتّٰى نَعْلَمَ الْمُجٰهِدِيْنَ

مِنْكُمْ وَالصّٰبِرِيْنَ ۙ وَنَبْلُوَا۟

اَخْبَارَكُمْ ۝

32. Those who reject Allah, hinder (men) from the Path of Allah, and resist the Apostle, after Guidance has been clearly shown to them, will not injure Allah in the least, but He will make their deeds of no effect.

اِنَّ الَّذِيْنَ كَفَرُوْا وَصَدُّوْا عَنْ

سَبِيْلِ اللّٰهِ وَشَآقُّوا الرَّسُوْلَ مِنْۢ

بَعْدِ مَا تَبَيَّنَ لَهُمُ الْهُدَى ۙ

لَنْ يَّضُرُّوا اللّٰهَ شَيْئًا ۚ وَسَيُحْبِطُ

اَعْمَالَهُمْ ۝

33. O you who believe! Obey Allah,

يٰۤاَيُّهَا الَّذِيْنَ اٰمَنُوْۤا اَطِيْعُوا اللّٰهَ

SÛRAH-48
AL-FATH
(INTRODUCTION)

1. This is the second of the group of three Madinah Sûras described in the Introduction to S. 47. Its date is fixed by the mention of the Treaty of Hudaibiya, Zul-qa'dA.H. 6=Feb. 628.

2. Hudaibiya is a plain, a short day's march to the north of Makkah, a little to the west of the Madinah-Makkah road, as used in the Prophet's time. Six years had passed since the Prophet had left his beloved City, and it had been in the hands of the Pagan autocracy. But Islam had grown during these six years. Its Qibla was towards the Ka'ba. The Pagans had tried to attack Islam at various times and had been foiled. By Arab custom every Arab was entitled to visit the Sacred Enclosure unarmed, and fighting of any kind was prohibited during the Sacred Months which included the month of Zul-qa'd. InZul-qa'dA.H. 6, therefore, the Prophet desired to perform the 'Umra or lesser Pilgrimage, unarmed but accompanied with his followers. A large following joined him, to the number of fourteen to fifteen hundred.

3. This was not to the liking of the Pagan autocracy at Makkah, which took alarm, and in breach of all Arab tradition and usage, prepared to prevent the peaceful party from performing the rites of Pilgrimage. They marched out to fight the unarmed party. The Prophet turned a little to the west of the road, and encamped at Hudaibiya, where negotiations took place. On the one hand the Prophet was unwilling to give the Quraish any pretended excuse for violence in the Sacred Territory; on the other, the Quraish had learnt, by six years' bitter experience, that their power was crumbling on all sides, and Islam was growing with its moral and spiritual forces, which were also reflected in its powers of organisation and resistance. The enthusiasm with which the Covenant of Fealty was entered into under a tree in Hudaibiya (48: 18) by that great multitude united in devotion to their great leader, was evidence of the great power which he

commanded even in a worldly sense if the Quraish had chosen to try conclusions with him.

4. A peaceful Treaty was therefore concluded, known as the Treaty of Ḥudaibiya. It stipulated: (1) that there was to be peace between the parties for ten years; (2) that any tribe or person was free to join either party or make an alliance with it; (3) that if a Quraish person from Makkah, under guardianship, should join the Prophet without the guardian's permission, he (or she) should be sent back to the guardian but in the contrary case, they should not be sent back; and (4) that the Prophet and his party were not to enter Makkah that year, but that they could enter unarmed the following year.

(5.) Item (3), not being reciprocal was objected to in the Muslim camp, but it really was of little importance. Muslims under guardianship, sent back to Makkah, were not likely to renounce the blessings of Islam: on the other hand, Muslims going to Makkah would be centers of influence for Islam, and it was more important that they should be allowed to remain there than that they should be sent back to Madinah. It was impossible to think that there would be apostates or renegades to Paganism! "Look on this picture, and on that!"

6. The Muslims faithfully observed the tenns of the Treaty. The following year (A.H. 7) they performed the lesser Pilgrimage in great state for three days. It is true that the Makkans later on broke the Peace in the attack which one of their allied tribes (the Banû Bakr) made on the Muslim Banu Khuzâ'a (who were in alliance with the Prophet), but this led to the conquest of Makkah and the sweeping away of the autocracy. Meanwhile Ḥudaibiya was a great victory, moral and social, as well as political, and its lessons are expounded in this Sûrah, as the lessons of Badr were expounded in 8:42-48, and of Uḥud in 3: 121-129,149-180.

and obey the Apostle, and do not make your deeds vain!

34. Those who reject Allah, and hinder (men) from the Path of Allah, then die rejecting Allah,- Allah will not forgive them.

35. Be not weary and faint-hearted, crying for peace, when you should be uppermost: for Allah is with you, and will never put you in loss for your (good) deeds.

36. The life of this world is but play and amusement: and if you believe and guard against Evil, He will grant you your recom-pense, and will not ask you (to give up) your possessions.

37. If He were to ask you for all of them, and press you, you would covetously withhold, and He would bring out all your ill-feeling.

38. Behold, you are those invited to spend (of your sub-stance) in the Way of Allah: but among you are some that are niggardly. But any who are niggardly are so at the expense of their own souls. But Allah is free of all wants, and it is you that are needy. If you turn back (from the Path), He will substitute in your stead another people; then they would not be like you!

---

48. Victory
In the name of Allah. Most Gracious, Most Merciful.

1. Verily We have granted you a manifest Victory:

2. That Allah may forgive you your faults of the past and those to follow; fulfil His favour to you; and guide you on the Straight Way;

3. And that Allah may help you with powerful help.

4. It is He Who sent down tranquillity into the hearts of the Believers, that they may add faith to their faith;- for to Allah belong the Forces of the heavens and the earth; and Allah is full of Knowledge and Wisdom;-

هُوَ الَّذِيَّ اَنْزَلَ السَّكِيْنَةَ فِيْ قُلُوْبِ الْمُؤْمِنِيْنَ لِيَزْدَادُوْا اِيْمَانًا مَّعَ اِيْمَانِهِمْ ٭ وَ لِلّٰهِ جُنُوْدُ السَّمٰوٰتِ وَالْاَرْضِ ٭ وَكَانَ اللّٰهُ عَلِيْمًا حَكِيْمًا ۞

5. That He may admit the men and women who believe, to Gardens beneath which rivers flow, to dwell therein for ever, and remove their ills from them;- and that is, in the sight of Allah, the highest achievement (for man),-

لِيُدْخِلَ الْمُؤْمِنِيْنَ وَالْمُؤْمِنٰتِ جَنّٰتٍ تَجْرِيْ مِنْ تَحْتِهَا الْاَنْهٰرُ خٰلِدِيْنَ فِيْهَا وَيُكَفِّرَ عَنْهُمْ سَيِّاٰتِهِمْ ٭ وَكَانَ ذٰلِكَ عِنْدَ اللّٰهِ فَوْزًا عَظِيْمًا ۙ

6. And that He may punish the Hypocrites, men and women, and the Polytheists, men and women, who imagine an evil opinion of Allah. On them is a round of Evil: the Wrath of Allah is on them: He has cursed them and got Hell ready for them: and evil is it for a destination.

وَّيُعَذِّبَ الْمُنٰفِقِيْنَ وَالْمُنٰفِقٰتِ وَالْمُشْرِكِيْنَ وَالْمُشْرِكٰتِ الظَّآنِّيْنَ بِاللّٰهِ ظَنَّ السَّوْءِ ٭ عَلَيْهِمْ دَآئِرَةُ السَّوْءِ ٭ وَغَضِبَ اللّٰهُ عَلَيْهِمْ وَلَعَنَهُمْ وَاَعَدَّ لَهُمْ جَهَنَّمَ ٭ وَسَآءَتْ مَصِيْرًا ۞

7. For to Allah belong the Forces of the heavens and the earth; and Allah is Exalted in Power, full of Wisdom.

وَلِلّٰهِ جُنُوْدُ السَّمٰوٰتِ وَالْاَرْضِ ٭ وَكَانَ اللّٰهُ عَزِيْزًا حَكِيْمًا ۞

8. We have truly sent you as a witness, as a bringer of Glad Tidings, and as a Warner:

اِنَّاۤ اَرْسَلْنٰكَ شَاهِدًا وَّمُبَشِّرًا وَّنَذِيْرًا ۙ

9. In order that you (O men) may believe in Allah and His Apostle, that you may assist and honour Him, and celebrate His praises morning and evening.

لِّتُؤْمِنُوْا بِاللّٰهِ وَرَسُوْلِهٖ وَتُعَزِّرُوْهُ وَتُوَقِّرُوْهُ ٭ وَتُسَبِّحُوْهُ بُكْرَةً وَّاَصِيْلًا ۞

10. Verily those who were swearing allegiance to you, were indeed swearing allegiance to Allah: the Hand of Allah is over their hands: then any one who violates His oath, does so to the harm of His own soul, and any one who fulfils what he has covenanted with Allah,-

اِنَّ الَّذِيْنَ يُبَايِعُوْنَكَ اِنَّمَا يُبَايِعُوْنَ اللّٰهَ ٭ يَدُ اللّٰهِ فَوْقَ اَيْدِيْهِمْ ٭ فَمَنْ نَّكَثَ فَاِنَّمَا يَنْكُثُ عَلٰى نَفْسِهٖ ٭ وَمَنْ اَوْفٰى بِمَا عٰهَدَ عَلَيْهُ

Allah will soon grant him a great Reward.

11. The desert Arabs who lagged behind will say to you: "We were engaged in (looking after) our flocks and herds, and our families: you then ask forgiveness for us." They say with their tongues what is not in their hearts. Say: "Who then has any power at all (to intervene) on your behalf with Allah, if His Will is to give you some loss or to give you some profit? But Allah is well acquainted with all that you do.

12. "Nay, you thought that the Apostle and the Believers would never return to their families; this seemed pleasing in your hearts, and you conceived an evil thought, for you are a people lost (in wickedness)."

13. And if any do not believe in Allah and His Apostle, We have prepared, for those who reject Allah, a Blazing Fire!

14. To Allah belongs the dominion of the heavens and the earth: He forgives whom He wills, and He punishes whom He wills: but Allah is Oft-Forgiving, Most Merciful.

15. Those who lagged behind (will say), when you (are free to) march and take booty (in war): "Permit us to follow you." They wish to change Allah's decree: say: "Not thus will you follow us: Allah has already declared (this) beforehand": then they will say, "But you are jealous of us." Nay, but little do they understand (such things).

16. Say to the desert Arabs who lagged behind:

"You shall be summoned (to fight) against a people given to vehement war: then you shall fight, or they shall submit. Then if you show obedience, Allah will grant you a goodly reward, but if you turn back as you did before, He will punish you with a grievous Chastisement."

17. No blame is there on the blind, nor is there blame on the lame, nor on one ill (if he does not join the war): but he that obeys Allah and His Apostle,- (Allah) will admit him to Gardens beneath which rivers flow; and he who turns back, (Allah) will punish him with a grievous Chastisement.

18. Allah's Good Pleasure was on the Believers when they swore allegiance to you under the Tree: He knew what was in their hearts, and He sent down Tranquillity to them; and He rewarded them with a speedy Victory;

19. And many gains will they acquire (besides): and Allah is Exalted in Power, full of Wisdom.

20. Allah has promised you many gains that you shall acquire, and He has given you these beforehand; and He has restrained the hands of men from you; that it may be a Sign for the Believers, and that He may guide you to a Straight Path;

21. And other (gains there are), which are not within your power, but which Allah has compassed and Allah has power over all things.

22. If the Unbelievers should fight you, they would certainly

سَتُدْعَوْنَ إِلَىٰ قَوْمٍ أُولِى بَأْسٍ شَدِيدٍ تُقَاتِلُوْنَهُمْ أَوْ يُسْلِمُوْنَ ۖ فَإِنْ تُطِيعُوا يُؤْتِكُمُ اللّٰهُ أَجْرًا حَسَنًا ۖ وَإِنْ تَتَوَلَّوْا كَمَا تَوَلَّيْتُمْ مِنْ قَبْلُ يُعَذِّبْكُمْ عَذَابًا أَلِيمًا ۝

لَيْسَ عَلَى الْأَعْمَىٰ حَرَجٌ وَّلَا عَلَى الْأَعْرَجِ حَرَجٌ وَّلَا عَلَى الْمَرِيضِ حَرَجٌ ۖ وَمَنْ يُّطِعِ اللّٰهَ وَرَسُوْلَهٗ يُدْخِلْهُ جَنّٰتٍ تَجْرِيْ مِنْ تَحْتِهَا الْأَنْهٰرُ ۖ وَمَنْ يَّتَوَلَّ يُعَذِّبْهُ عَذَابًا أَلِيمًا ۝

لَقَدْ رَضِيَ اللّٰهُ عَنِ الْمُؤْمِنِيْنَ إِذْ يُبَايِعُوْنَكَ تَحْتَ الشَّجَرَةِ فَعَلِمَ مَا فِيْ قُلُوْبِهِمْ فَأَنْزَلَ السَّكِيْنَةَ عَلَيْهِمْ وَأَثَابَهُمْ فَتْحًا قَرِيْبًا ۝

وَّمَغَانِمَ كَثِيْرَةً يَّأْخُذُوْنَهَا ۖ وَكَانَ اللّٰهُ عَزِيْزًا حَكِيْمًا ۝

وَعَدَكُمُ اللّٰهُ مَغَانِمَ كَثِيْرَةً تَأْخُذُوْنَهَا فَعَجَّلَ لَكُمْ هٰذِهٖ وَكَفَّ أَيْدِيَ النَّاسِ عَنْكُمْ ۖ وَلِتَكُوْنَ اٰيَةً لِّلْمُؤْمِنِيْنَ وَيَهْدِيَكُمْ صِرَاطًا مُّسْتَقِيْمًا ۝

وَأُخْرَىٰ لَمْ تَقْدِرُوْا عَلَيْهَا قَدْ أَحَاطَ اللّٰهُ بِهَا ۖ وَكَانَ اللّٰهُ عَلَىٰ كُلِّ شَيْءٍ قَدِيْرًا ۝

وَلَوْ قَاتَلَكُمُ الَّذِيْنَ كَفَرُوْا لَوَلَّوُا

turn their backs; then would they find neither protector nor helper.

الْأَدْبَارَ ثُمَّ لَا يَجِدُوْنَ وَلِيًّا وَّلَا نَصِيْرًا ۟

23. (Such has been) the practice (approved) of Allah already in the past: no change will you find in the practice (approved) of Allah.

سُنَّةَ اللّٰهِ الَّتِيْ قَدْ خَلَتْ مِنْ قَبْلُ ۚ وَلَنْ تَجِدَ لِسُنَّةِ اللّٰهِ تَبْدِيْلًا ۟

24. And it is He Who has restrained their hands from you and your hands from them in the midst of Makka, after that He gave you the victory over them. And Allah sees well all that you do.

وَهُوَ الَّذِيْ كَفَّ اَيْدِيَهُمْ عَنْكُمْ وَاَيْدِيَكُمْ عَنْهُمْ بِبَطْنِ مَكَّةَ مِنْ بَعْدِ اَنْ اَظْفَرَكُمْ عَلَيْهِمْ ۭ وَكَانَ اللّٰهُ بِمَا تَعْمَلُوْنَ بَصِيْرًا ۟

25. They are the ones who denied Revelation and hindered you from the Sacred Mosque and the sacrificial animals, detained from reaching their place of sacrifice. Had there not been believing men and believing women whom you did not know that you were trampling down and on whose account a crime would have accrued to you without (your) knowledge, (Allah would have allowed you to force your way, but He held back your hands) that Allah may admit to His Mercy whom He will. If they had been apart, We should certainly have punished the Unbelievers among them with a grievous Punishment.

هُمُ الَّذِيْنَ كَفَرُوْا وَصَدُّوْكُمْ عَنِ الْمَسْجِدِ الْحَرَامِ وَالْهَدْيَ مَعْكُوْفًا اَنْ يَّبْلُغَ مَحِلَّهٗ ۭ وَلَوْلَا رِجَالٌ مُّؤْمِنُوْنَ وَنِسَاءٌ مُّؤْمِنٰتٌ لَّمْ تَعْلَمُوْهُمْ اَنْ تَطَـُٔوْهُمْ فَتُصِيْبَكُمْ مِّنْهُمْ مَّعَرَّةٌ بِغَيْرِ عِلْمٍ ۚ لِيُدْخِلَ اللّٰهُ فِيْ رَحْمَتِهٖ مَنْ يَّشَاءُ ۚ لَوْ تَزَيَّلُوْا لَعَذَّبْنَا الَّذِيْنَ كَفَرُوْا مِنْهُمْ عَذَابًا اَلِيْمًا ۟

26. While the Unbelievers got up in their hearts heat and cant – the heat and cant of ignorance, – Allah sent down His Tranquillity to His Apostle and to the Believers, and made them stick close to the command of self-restraint; and well were they entitled to it and worthy of it. And Allah has full knowledge of all things.

اِذْ جَعَلَ الَّذِيْنَ كَفَرُوْا فِيْ قُلُوْبِهِمُ الْحَمِيَّةَ حَمِيَّةَ الْجَاهِلِيَّةِ فَاَنْزَلَ اللّٰهُ سَكِيْنَتَهٗ عَلٰى رَسُوْلِهٖ وَعَلَى الْمُؤْمِنِيْنَ وَاَلْزَمَهُمْ كَلِمَةَ التَّقْوٰى وَكَانُوْا اَحَقَّ بِهَا وَاَهْلَهَا ۭ وَكَانَ اللّٰهُ بِكُلِّ شَيْءٍ عَلِيْمًا ۟

27. Truly did Allah fulfil the vision for His Apostle: you shall enter the Sacred Mosque,

لَقَدْ صَدَقَ اللّٰهُ رَسُوْلَهُ الرُّءْيَا بِالْحَقِّ ۚ لَتَدْخُلُنَّ الْمَسْجِدَ الْحَرَامَ

SÛRAH-49
AL-ḤUJURÂH
(INTRODUCTION)

This is the third of the group of three Madinah Sûras, which began with S. 47. See the Introduction to that Sûrah.

Its subject-matter is the manners to be observed by the members of the rapidly-growing Muslim community, among themselves and towards its Leader. The key-word *"Hujurât"* (Inner Apartments) occurs in verse 4.

Its date is referred to the Year of Deputations, A.H. 9, when a large number of deputations of all kinds visited Madinah to offer their allegiance to Islam.

if Allah wills, with minds secure, heads shaved, hair cut short, and without fear. For He knew what you did not know, and He granted, besides this, a speedy victory.

28. It is He Who has sent His Apostle with Guidance and the Religion of Truth, to proclaim it over all religion: and enough is Allah for a Witness.

29. Muhammad is the Apostle of Allah; and those who are with him are strong against Unbelievers, (but) compassionate amongst each other. You will see them bow and prostrate themselves (in prayer), seeking Grace from Allah and (His) Good Pleasure. On their faces are their marks, (being) the traces of their prostration. This is their similitude in the Taurat; and their similitude in the Gospel is: like a seed which sends forth its blade, then makes it strong; it then becomes thick, and it stands on its own stem, (filling) the sowers with wonder and delight. As a result, it fills the Unbelievers with rage at them. Allah has promised those among them who believe and do righteous deeds forgiveness, and a great Reward.

49. The Inner Apartments

In the name of Allah, Most Gracious, Most Merciful.

1. O you who believe! Do not put yourselves forward before Allah and His Apostle; but fear Allah: for Allah is He Who hears and knows all things.

2. O you who believe! Do not raise your voices above the voice of the Prophet,

nor speak aloud to him in talk, as
you may speak aloud to one
another, lest your deeds become
vain and you do not perceive.

3.   Those that lower their
voices in the presence of Allah's
Apostle,- their hearts Allah has
tested for piety: for them is
Forgiveness and a great
Reward.

4.   Those who shout out to
you from without the inner
Apartments - most of them lack
understanding.

5.   If only they had patience
until you could come out to
them, it would be best for them:
but Allah is Oft-Forgiving,
Most Merciful.

6.   O you who believe! If a
wicked person comes to you
with any news, ascertain the
truth, lest you harm people
unwittingly, and afterwards
become full of repentance for
what you have done.

7.   And know that among you
is Allah's Apostle: were he, in
many matters, to follow your
(wishes), you would certainly
fall into misfortune: but Allah
has endeared the Faith to you,
and has made it beautiful in your
hearts, and He has made hateful
to you Unbelief, wickedness,
and rebellion: such indeed are
those who walk in righteousness;-

8.   A Grace and Favour from
Allah; and Allah is full of
Knowledge and Wisdom.

9.   If two parties among the
Believers fall into a quarrel, you
make peace between them: but
if

تَجْهَرُوا لَهُ بِالْقَوْلِ كَجَهْرِ بَعْضِكُمْ
لِبَعْضٍ اَنْ تَحْبَطَ اَعْمَالُكُمْ
وَاَنْتُمْ لَا تَشْعُرُوْنَ ۞
اِنَّ الَّذِيْنَ يَغُضُّوْنَ اَصْوَاتَهُمْ
عِنْدَ رَسُوْلِ اللّٰهِ اُولٰٓئِكَ الَّذِيْنَ
امْتَحَنَ اللّٰهُ قُلُوْبَهُمْ لِلتَّقْوٰى ۗ
لَهُمْ مَّغْفِرَةٌ وَّاَجْرٌ عَظِيْمٌ ۞
اِنَّ الَّذِيْنَ يُنَادُوْنَكَ مِنْ وَّرَآءِ
الْحُجُرٰتِ اَكْثَرُهُمْ لَا يَعْقِلُوْنَ۞
وَلَوْ اَنَّهُمْ صَبَرُوْا حَتّٰى تَخْرُجَ
اِلَيْهِمْ لَكَانَ خَيْرًا لَّهُمْ ۗ وَاللّٰهُ
غَفُوْرٌ رَّحِيْمٌ ۞
يٰٓاَيُّهَا الَّذِيْنَ اٰمَنُوْا اِنْ جَآءَكُمْ
فَاسِقٌ بِنَبَاٍ فَتَبَيَّنُوْا اَنْ تُصِيْبُوْا
قَوْمًا بِجَهَالَةٍ فَتُصْبِحُوْا عَلٰى مَا
فَعَلْتُمْ نٰدِمِيْنَ ۞
وَاعْلَمُوْا اَنَّ فِيْكُمْ رَسُوْلَ اللّٰهِ ۗ
لَوْ يُطِيْعُكُمْ فِيْ كَثِيْرٍ مِّنَ الْاَمْرِ
لَعَنِتُّمْ وَلٰكِنَّ اللّٰهَ حَبَّبَ اِلَيْكُمُ
الْاِيْمَانَ وَزَيَّنَهُ فِيْ قُلُوْبِكُمْ وَكَرَّهَ
اِلَيْكُمُ الْكُفْرَ وَالْفُسُوْقَ وَالْعِصْيَانَ ۚ
اُولٰٓئِكَ هُمُ الرّٰشِدُوْنَ ۞
فَضْلًا مِّنَ اللّٰهِ وَنِعْمَةً ۗ وَاللّٰهُ
عَلِيْمٌ حَكِيْمٌ ۞
وَاِنْ طَآئِفَتٰنِ مِنَ الْمُؤْمِنِيْنَ
اقْتَتَلُوْا فَاَصْلِحُوْا بَيْنَهُمَا ۚ فَاِنْ

one of them transgresses beyond bounds against the other, then you (all) fight against the one that transgresses until it complies with the command of Allah; but if it complies, then make peace between them with justice, and be fair: for Allah loves those who are fair (and just).

10. The Believers are but a single Brotherhood: so make peace and reconciliation between your two (contending) brothers; and fear Allah, that you may receive Mercy.

11. O you who believe! Let not some men among you laugh at others: It may be that the (latter) are better than the (former): nor let some women laugh at others: It may be that the (latter) are better than the (former): nor defame nor be sarcastic to each other, nor call each other by (offensive) nicknames: Ill-seeming is a name connoting wickedness, (to be used of one) after he has believed: and those who do not desist are (indeed) doing wrong.

12. O you who believe! Avoid suspicion as much (as possible): for suspicion in some cases is a sin: and spy not on each other, nor speak ill of each other behind their backs. Would any of you like to eat the flesh of his dead brother? Nay, you would abhor it...But fear Allah: For Allah is Oft-Returning, Most Merciful.

13. O mankind! We created you from a single (pair) of a male and a female, and made you into nations and tribes, that you may know each other (not that you may despise each other). Verily the most honoured of you

بَغَتْ إِحْدَىٰهُمَا عَلَى ٱلْأُخْرَىٰ

فَقَاتِلُوا ٱلَّتِي تَبْغِي حَتَّىٰ تَفِيٓءَ إِلَىٰٓ

أَمْرِ ٱللَّهِ ۚ فَإِن فَآءَتْ فَأَصْلِحُوا

بَيْنَهُمَا بِٱلْعَدْلِ وَأَقْسِطُوٓا ۖ

إِنَّ ٱللَّهَ يُحِبُّ ٱلْمُقْسِطِينَ ۝

إِنَّمَا ٱلْمُؤْمِنُونَ إِخْوَةٌ فَأَصْلِحُوا

بَيْنَ أَخَوَيْكُمْ ۚ وَٱتَّقُوا ٱللَّهَ لَعَلَّكُمْ

تُرْحَمُونَ ۝

يَٰٓأَيُّهَا ٱلَّذِينَ ءَامَنُوا لَا يَسْخَرْ

قَوْمٌ مِّن قَوْمٍ عَسَىٰٓ أَن يَكُونُوا

خَيْرًا مِّنْهُمْ وَلَا نِسَآءٌ مِّن نِّسَآءٍ

عَسَىٰٓ أَن يَكُنَّ خَيْرًا مِّنْهُنَّ ۖ

وَلَا تَلْمِزُوٓا أَنفُسَكُمْ وَلَا تَنَابَزُوا

بِٱلْأَلْقَٰبِ ۖ بِئْسَ ٱلِٱسْمُ ٱلْفُسُوقُ

بَعْدَ ٱلْإِيمَٰنِ ۚ وَمَن لَّمْ يَتُبْ

فَأُو۟لَٰٓئِكَ هُمُ ٱلظَّٰلِمُونَ ۝

يَٰٓأَيُّهَا ٱلَّذِينَ ءَامَنُوا ٱجْتَنِبُوا

كَثِيرًا مِّنَ ٱلظَّنِّ إِنَّ بَعْضَ

ٱلظَّنِّ إِثْمٌ ۖ وَلَا تَجَسَّسُوا وَلَا

يَغْتَب بَّعْضُكُم بَعْضًا ۚ أَيُحِبُّ

أَحَدُكُمْ أَن يَأْكُلَ لَحْمَ أَخِيهِ

مَيْتًا فَكَرِهْتُمُوهُ ۚ وَٱتَّقُوا ٱللَّهَ ۚ

إِنَّ ٱللَّهَ تَوَّابٌ رَّحِيمٌ ۝

يَٰٓأَيُّهَا ٱلنَّاسُ إِنَّا خَلَقْنَٰكُم مِّن

ذَكَرٍ وَأُنثَىٰ وَجَعَلْنَٰكُمْ شُعُوبًا

وَقَبَآئِلَ لِتَعَارَفُوٓا ۚ إِنَّ أَكْرَمَكُمْ

SÛRAH-50
QÂF
(INTRODUCTION)

We now conic to a group of seven Makkan Sûras (50-56) dealing with Allah's revelation through nature, through history, anil through the mouths of the prophets, and pointing to the Hereafter. We saw that the lust group of three (47-49) dealt with the external and internal relations of live Ummnt when formed. In the present group our attention is more particularly directed to aspects eschatological,—the Future before us when this life is done

This particular Sûrah belongs to the early Makkan period. After an appeal to nature and to the fate of wicked peoples in history, it removes as it were the evil (verse 22) from the Future after death.

in the sight of Allah is (he who is) the most righteous of you. And Allah has full knowledge and is well acquainted (with all things).

عِنْدَ اللّٰهِ أَتْقَىٰكُمْ ۚ إِنَّ اللّٰهَ عَلِيمٌ خَبِيرٌ ۝

14. The desert Arabs say, "We believe." Say, "You have no faith; but you (only) say, 'We have submitted our wills to Allah,' for Faith has not yet entered your hearts. But if you obey Allah and His Apostle, He will not belittle anything of your deeds: for Allah is Oft-Forgiving, Most Merciful."

قَالَتِ الْأَعْرَابُ اٰمَنَّا ۖ قُلْ لَمْ تُؤْمِنُوا وَلٰكِنْ قُولُوا أَسْلَمْنَا وَلَمَّا يَدْخُلِ الْإِيْمَانُ فِيْ قُلُوبِكُمْ ۖ وَإِنْ تُطِيْعُوا اللّٰهَ وَرَسُولَهُ لَا يَلِتْكُمْ مِّنْ أَعْمَالِكُمْ شَيْئًا ۚ إِنَّ اللّٰهَ غَفُورٌ رَّحِيمٌ ۝

15. Only those are Believers who have believed in Allah and His Apostle, and have never since doubted, but have striven with their belongings and their persons in the Cause of Allah: such are the sincere ones.

إِنَّمَا الْمُؤْمِنُونَ الَّذِينَ اٰمَنُوا بِاللّٰهِ وَرَسُولِهِ ثُمَّ لَمْ يَرْتَابُوا وَجَاهَدُوا بِأَمْوَالِهِمْ وَأَنْفُسِهِمْ فِيْ سَبِيلِ اللّٰهِ ۚ أُولٰئِكَ هُمُ الصّٰدِقُونَ ۝

16. Say: "What! Will you instruct Allah about your religion? But Allah knows all that is in the heavens and on earth: He has full knowledge of all things.

قُلْ أَتُعَلِّمُونَ اللّٰهَ بِدِيْنِكُمْ ۚ وَاللّٰهُ يَعْلَمُ مَا فِي السَّمٰوٰتِ وَمَا فِي الْأَرْضِ ۚ وَاللّٰهُ بِكُلِّ شَيْءٍ عَلِيمٌ ۝

17. They impress on you as a favour that they have embraced Islam. Say, "Do not count your Islam as a favour upon me: nay, Allah has conferred a favour upon you that He has guided you to the Faith, if you be true and sincere.

يَمُنُّونَ عَلَيْكَ أَنْ أَسْلَمُوا ۖ قُلْ لَا تَمُنُّوا عَلَيَّ إِسْلَامَكُمْ ۖ بَلِ اللّٰهُ يَمُنُّ عَلَيْكُمْ أَنْ هَدٰىكُمْ لِلْإِيْمَانِ إِنْ كُنْتُمْ صٰدِقِينَ ۝

18. "Verily Allah knows the secrets of the heavens and the earth: and Allah sees well all that you do."

إِنَّ اللّٰهَ يَعْلَمُ غَيْبَ السَّمٰوٰتِ وَالْأَرْضِ ۚ وَاللّٰهُ بَصِيرٌ بِمَا تَعْمَلُونَ ۝

---

50. Qaf
In the name of Allah, Most Gracious, Most Merciful.

(٥٠) سُورَةُ قٓ مَكِّيَّةٌ (٣٣)

بِسْمِ اللّٰهِ الرَّحْمٰنِ الرَّحِيمِ

1. Qaf: By the Glorious Qur'an (You are Allah's Apostle).

قٓ ۚ وَالْقُرْاٰنِ الْمَجِيدِ ۝

2. But they wonder that there has come to them a Warner

بَلْ عَجِبُوا أَنْ جَاءَهُمْ مُنْذِرٌ

from among themselves. So the Unbelievers say: "This is a wonderful thing

مِنْهُمْ فَقَالَ الْكٰفِرُوْنَ هٰذَا شَىْءٌ عَجِيْبٌ ۞

3. "What! When we die and become dust, (shall we live again?) That is a (sort of) return far (from our understanding)."

ءَاِذَا مِتْنَا وَكُنَّا تُرَابًا ۚ ذٰلِكَ رَجْعٌ بَعِيْدٌ ۞

4. We already know how much of them the earth takes away: with Us is a record guarding (the full account).

قَدْ عَلِمْنَا مَا تَنْقُصُ الْاَرْضُ مِنْهُمْ ۚ وَعِنْدَنَا كِتٰبٌ حَفِيْظٌ ۞

5. But they deny the Truth when it comes to them: so they are in a confused state.

بَلْ كَذَّبُوْا بِالْحَقِّ لَمَّا جَآءَهُمْ فَهُمْ فِيْٓ اَمْرٍ مَّرِيْجٍ ۞

6. Do they not look at the sky above them?- How We have made it and adorned it, and there are no flaws in it?

اَفَلَمْ يَنْظُرُوْٓا اِلَى السَّمَآءِ فَوْقَهُمْ كَيْفَ بَنَيْنٰهَا وَزَيَّنّٰهَا وَمَا لَهَا مِنْ فُرُوْجٍ ۞

7. And the earth- We have spread it out, and set thereon mountains standing firm, and produced therein every kind of beautiful growth (in pairs)-

وَالْاَرْضَ مَدَدْنٰهَا وَاَلْقَيْنَا فِيْهَا رَوَاسِيَ وَاَنْۢبَتْنَا فِيْهَا مِنْ كُلِّ زَوْجٍ بَهِيْجٍ ۞

8. To be observed and commemorated by every devotee turning (to Allah).

تَبْصِرَةً وَّذِكْرٰى لِكُلِّ عَبْدٍ مُّنِيْبٍ ۞

9. And We send down from the sky rain charted with blessing, and We produce therewith gardens and grain for harvests;

وَنَزَّلْنَا مِنَ السَّمَآءِ مَآءً مُّبٰرَكًا فَاَنْۢبَتْنَا بِهٖ جَنّٰتٍ وَّحَبَّ الْحَصِيْدِ ۞

10. And tall (and stately) palm-trees, with shoots of fruit-stalks, piled one over another;-

وَالنَّخْلَ بٰسِقٰتٍ لَّهَا طَلْعٌ نَّضِيْدٌ ۙ

11. As sustenance for (Allah's) servants;- and We give (new) life therewith to land that is dead: thus will be the Resurrection.

رِّزْقًا لِّلْعِبَادِ ۙ وَاَحْيَيْنَا بِهٖ بَلْدَةً مَّيْتًا ۚ كَذٰلِكَ الْخُرُوْجُ ۞

12. Before them was denied (the Hereafter) by the People of Noah, the Companions of the Rass, the Thamud,

كَذَّبَتْ قَبْلَهُمْ قَوْمُ نُوْحٍ وَّاَصْحٰبُ الرَّسِّ وَثَمُوْدُ ۞

13. The 'Ad, Pharaoh, the Brethren of Lut,

وَعَادٌ وَّفِرْعَوْنُ وَاِخْوَانُ لُوْطٍ ۙ

14. The Companions of the Wood, and the People of Tubba'; each one (of them) rejected the Apostles, and My warning was duly fulfilled (in them).

وَاَصْحٰبُ الْاَيْكَةِ وَقَوْمُ تُبَّعٍ ۚ كُلٌّ كَذَّبَ الرُّسُلَ فَحَقَّ وَعِيْدِ ۞

15. Were We then weary with the first Creation, that they should be in confused doubt about a new Creation?

اَفَعَيِيْنَا بِالْخَلْقِ الْاَوَّلِ ۚ بَلْ هُمْ فِيْ لَبْسٍ مِّنْ خَلْقٍ جَدِيْدٍ ۟

16. It was We Who created man, and We know what dark suggestions his soul makes to him: for We are nearer to him than (his) jugular vein.

وَلَقَدْ خَلَقْنَا الْاِنْسَانَ وَنَعْلَمُ مَا تُوَسْوِسُ بِهٖ نَفْسُهٗ ۚ وَنَحْنُ اَقْرَبُ اِلَيْهِ مِنْ حَبْلِ الْوَرِيْدِ ۟

17. Behold, two (watchful angels) appointed to record (his doings) one sitting on the right and one on the left.

اِذْ يَتَلَقَّى الْمُتَلَقِّيٰنِ عَنِ الْيَمِيْنِ وَعَنِ الشِّمَالِ قَعِيْدٌ ۟

18. Not a word does he utter but there is a watcher by him, ready (to note it).

مَا يَلْفِظُ مِنْ قَوْلٍ اِلَّا لَدَيْهِ رَقِيْبٌ عَتِيْدٌ ۟

19. And the stupor of death will bring Truth (before his eyes): "This was the thing which you were trying to escape!"

وَجَآءَتْ سَكْرَةُ الْمَوْتِ بِالْحَقِّ ۚ ذٰلِكَ مَا كُنْتَ مِنْهُ تَحِيْدُ ۟

20. And the Trumpet shall be blown: that will be the Day whereof Warning (had been given).

وَنُفِخَ فِى الصُّوْرِ ۚ ذٰلِكَ يَوْمُ الْوَعِيْدِ ۟

21. And there will come forth every soul: with each will be an (angel) to drive, and an (angel) to bear witness.

وَجَآءَتْ كُلُّ نَفْسٍ مَّعَهَا سَآئِقٌ وَّشَهِيْدٌ ۟

22. (It will be said:) "You were heedless of this; now have We removed your veil, and sharp is your sight this Day!"

لَقَدْ كُنْتَ فِيْ غَفْلَةٍ مِّنْ هٰذَا فَكَشَفْنَا عَنْكَ غِطَآءَكَ فَبَصَرُكَ الْيَوْمَ حَدِيْدٌ ۟

23. And his Companion will say: "Here is (his Record) ready with me!"

وَقَالَ قَرِيْنُهٗ هٰذَا مَا لَدَيَّ عَتِيْدٌ ۟

24. (The sentence will be:) "Throw, both of you into Hell every contumacious rejecter (of Allah)!-

اَلْقِيَا فِيْ جَهَنَّمَ كُلَّ كَفَّارٍ عَنِيْدٍ ۟

25. "Who forbade what was good, transgressed all bounds, cast doubts and suspicions;

مَّنَّاعٍ لِّلْخَيْرِ مُعْتَدٍ مُّرِيْبٍ ۟

26. "Who set up another god beside Allah: throw him into a severe Chastisement."

الَّذِيْ جَعَلَ مَعَ اللهِ اِلٰهًا اٰخَرَ فَاَلْقِيٰهُ فِى الْعَذَابِ الشَّدِيْدِ ۟

27. His Companion will say: "Our Lord! I did not make him transgress,

قَالَ قَرِيْنُهٗ رَبَّنَا مَاۤ اَطْغَيْتُهٗ

but he was (himself) far astray."

وَلَكِنْ كَانَ فِى ضَلَلٍ بَعِيْدٍ ۞

28. He will say: "Do not dispute with each other in My Presence: I had already in advance sent you Warning.

قَالَ لَا تَخْتَصِمُوْا لَدَىَّ وَقَدْ قَدَّمْتُ اِلَيْكُمْ بِالْوَعِيْدِ ۞

29. "The Word does not change before Me, and I do not do the least injustice to My servants."

مَا يُبَدَّلُ الْقَوْلُ لَدَىَّ وَمَا أَنَا بِظَلَّامٍ لِلْعَبِيْدِ ۞

30. That Day We will ask Hell, "Are you filled to the full?" It will say, "Are there any more (to come)?"

يَوْمَ نَقُوْلُ لِجَهَنَّمَ هَلِ امْتَلَأْتِ وَتَقُوْلُ هَلْ مِنْ مَزِيْدٍ ۞

31. And the Garden will be brought near to the Righteous,- no more a thing distant.

وَأُزْلِفَتِ الْجَنَّةُ لِلْمُتَّقِيْنَ غَيْرَ بَعِيْدٍ ۞

32. (A voice will say:) "This is what was promised for you,- for every one who turned (to Allah) in sincere repentance, Who kept (His Law),

هٰذَا مَا تُوْعَدُوْنَ لِكُلِّ أَوَّابٍ حَفِيْظٍ ۞

33. "Who feared (Allah) Most Gracious Unseen, and brought a heart turned in devotion (to Him):

مَنْ خَشِىَ الرَّحْمٰنَ بِالْغَيْبِ وَجَاءَ بِقَلْبٍ مُّنِيْبٍ ۞

34. "You enter therein in Peace and Security; this is a Day of Eternal Life!"

ادْخُلُوْهَا بِسَلٰمٍ ذٰلِكَ يَوْمُ الْخُلُوْدِ ۞

35. There will be for them therein all that they wish,- and more besides in Our Presence.

لَهُمْ مَّا يَشَاءُوْنَ فِيْهَا وَلَدَيْنَا مَزِيْدٌ ۞

36. But how many generations before them did We destroy (for their sins),- stronger in power than they? Then did they wander through the land: was there any place of escape (for them)?

وَكَمْ أَهْلَكْنَا قَبْلَهُمْ مِّنْ قَرْنٍ هُمْ أَشَدُّ مِنْهُمْ بَطْشًا فَنَقَّبُوْا فِى الْبِلَادِ ۦ هَلْ مِنْ مَّحِيْصٍ ۞

37. Verily in this is a Message for any that has a heart and understanding or who gives ear and earnestly witnesses (the truth).

اِنَّ فِى ذٰلِكَ لَذِكْرَى لِمَنْ كَانَ لَهُ قَلْبٌ أَوْ أَلْقَى السَّمْعَ وَهُوَ شَهِيْدٌ ۞

38. We created the heavens and the earth and all between them in Six Days, nor did any sense of weariness touch Us.

وَلَقَدْ خَلَقْنَا السَّمٰوٰتِ وَالْأَرْضَ وَمَا بَيْنَهُمَا فِى سِتَّةِ أَيَّامٍ وَّمَا مَسَّنَا مِنْ لُّغُوْبٍ ۞

39. Bear, then, with patience, all that they say, and celebrate the praises of your Lord, before the rising of the sun

فَاصْبِرْ عَلٰى مَا يَقُوْلُوْنَ وَسَبِّحْ بِحَمْدِ رَبِّكَ قَبْلَ طُلُوْعِ الشَّمْسِ

SÛRA-51
AZ-ZARIYÂT
(INTRODUCTION)

This is an early Makkan Sûrah, with a highly mystic meaning. It is the second of live seven Sûras forming a group dealing with Revelation anil the Hereafter. See Introduction to S. 50. This Sûrah deals with the varying ways in which Truth prevails irresistibly even against all human probabilities.

and before (its) setting.

وَقَبْلَ الْغُرُوبِ ۞

40. And during part of the night, (also,) celebrate His praises, and (so likewise) after the postures of adoration.

وَمِنَ الَّيْلِ فَسَبِّحْهُ وَاَدْبَارَ السُّجُوْدِ ۞

41. And listen for the Day when the Caller will call out from a place quiet near,-

وَاسْتَمِعْ يَوْمَ يُنَادِ الْمُنَادِ مِنْ مَّكَانٍ قَرِيْبِ ۞

42. The Day when they will hear a (mighty) Blast in (very) truth: that will be the Day of Resurrection.

يَّوْمَ يَسْمَعُوْنَ الصَّيْحَةَ بِالْحَقِّ ط ذٰلِكَ يَوْمُ الْخُرُوْجِ ۞

43. Verily it is We Who give Life and Death; and to Us is the Final Goal-

اِنَّا نَحْنُ نُحْيٖ وَنُمِيْتُ وَاِلَيْنَا الْمَصِيْرُ ۞

44. The Day when the Earth will be rent asunder, from (men) hurrying out: that will be a gathering together,- quite easy for Us.

يَوْمَ تَشَقَّقُ الْاَرْضُ عَنْهُمْ سِرَاعًا ذٰلِكَ حَشْرٌ عَلَيْنَا يَسِيْرٌ ۞

45. We know best what they say; and you are not one to overawe them by force. So admonish with the Qur'an such as fear My Warning!

نَحْنُ اَعْلَمُ بِمَا يَقُوْلُوْنَ وَمَا اَنْتَ عَلَيْهِمْ بِجَبَّارٍ فَذَكِّرْ بِالْقُرْاٰنِ مَنْ يَّخَافُ وَعِيْدِ ۞

51. The Winds that Scatter
In the name of Allah, Most Gracious, Most Merciful.

(٥١) سُوْرَةُ الذّٰرِيٰتِ مَكِّيَّةٌ (٦٧)

بِسْمِ اللهِ الرَّحْمٰنِ الرَّحِيْمِ

1. By the (winds) that scatter broadcast;

وَالذّٰرِيٰتِ ذَرْوًا ۞

2. And those that lift and bear away heavy weights;

فَالْحٰمِلٰتِ وِقْرًا ۞

3. And those that flow with ease and gentleness;

فَالْجٰرِيٰتِ يُسْرًا ۞

4. And those that distribute and apportion by Command;

فَالْمُقَسِّمٰتِ اَمْرًا ۞

5. Verily that which you are promised is true;

اِنَّمَا تُوْعَدُوْنَ لَصَادِقٌ ۞

6. And verily Judgment and Justice must indeed come to pass.

وَّاِنَّ الدِّيْنَ لَوَاقِعٌ ط

7. By the Sky with (its) numerous Paths,

وَالسَّمَاءِ ذَاتِ الْحُبُكِ ۞

8. Truly you are in a doctrine discordant,

اِنَّكُمْ لَفِيْ قَوْلٍ مُّخْتَلِفٍ ۞

9. Through which are deluded (away from the Truth) such as would be deluded.

يُّؤْفَكُ عَنْهُ مَنْ اُفِكَ ۞

10. Woe to the falsehoodmongers,-

قُتِلَ الْخَرّٰصُوْنَ ۞

11. Those who (flounder) heedless in a flood of confusion:

الَّذِينَ هُمْ فِي غَمْرَةٍ سَاهُونَ ۞

12. They ask, "When will be the Day of Judgment and Justice?"

يَسْـَٔلُونَ اَيَّانَ يَوْمُ الدِّينِ ۞

13. (It will be) a Day when they will be tried (and tested) over the Fire!

يَوْمَهُمْ عَلَى النَّارِ يُفْتَنُونَ ۞

14. "You taste your trial! This is what you used to ask to be hastened!"

ذُوقُوا فِتْنَتَكُمْ هٰذَا الَّذِي كُنْتُمْ بِهٖ تَسْتَعْجِلُونَ ۞

15. As to the Righteous, they will be in the midst of Gardens and Springs,

اِنَّ الْمُتَّقِينَ فِي جَنّٰتٍ وَّعُيُونٍ ۞

16. Taking joy in the things which their Lord gives them, because, before then, they lived a good life.

اٰخِذِينَ مَاۤ اٰتٰىهُمْ رَبُّهُمْ ۗ اِنَّهُمْ كَانُوا قَبْلَ ذٰلِكَ مُحْسِنِينَ ۞

17. They were in the habit of sleeping but little by night,

كَانُوا قَلِيلًا مِّنَ الَّيْلِ مَا يَهْجَعُونَ ۞

18. And in the hours of early dawn, they (were found) praying for Forgiveness;

وَبِالْاَسْحَارِهُمْ يَسْتَغْفِرُونَ ۞

19. And in their wealth the beggar and the outcast had due share.

وَفِيۤ اَمْوَالِهِمْ حَقٌّ لِّلسَّآئِلِ وَالْمَحْرُومِ ۞

20. On the earth are Signs for those of assured Faith,

وَفِي الْاَرْضِ اٰيٰتٌ لِّلْمُوقِنِينَ ۞

21. As also in your own selves: will you not then see?

وَفِيۤ اَنْفُسِكُمْ ۚ اَفَلَا تُبْصِرُونَ ۞

22. And in heaven is your Sustenance, as (also) that which you are promised.

وَفِي السَّمَآءِ رِزْقُكُمْ وَمَا تُوعَدُونَ ۞

23. Then, by the Lord of heaven and earth, this is the very Truth, as much as the fact that you can speak intelligently to each other.

فَوَرَبِّ السَّمَآءِ وَالْاَرْضِ اِنَّهٗ لَحَقٌّ مِّثْلَ مَاۤ اَنَّكُمْ تَنْطِقُونَ ۞

24. Has the story reached you, of the honoured guests of Abraham?

هَلْ اَتٰىكَ حَدِيثُ ضَيْفِ اِبْرٰهِيمَ الْمُكْرَمِينَ ۞

25. Behold, they entered his presence, and said: "Peace!" He said, "Peace!" (and thought, "These seem) unusual people.

اِذْ دَخَلُوا عَلَيْهِ فَقَالُوا سَلٰمًا ۖ قَالَ سَلٰمٌ ۚ قَوْمٌ مُّنْكَرُونَ ۞

26. Then he turned quickly to his household, brought out a fatted calf,

فَرَاغَ اِلٰۤى اَهْلِهٖ فَجَآءَ بِعِجْلٍ سَمِينٍ ۞

27. And placed it before them.. he said, "Will you not eat?"

فَقَرَّبَهٗۤ اِلَيْهِمْ قَالَ اَلَا تَأْكُلُونَ ۞

28. (When they did not eat), He conceived a fear of them. They said, "Fear not," and they gave him glad tidings of a son endowed with knowledge.

فَاَوْجَسَ مِنْهُمْ خِيفَةً ۖ قَالُوا لَا تَخَفْ ۖ وَبَشَّرُوهُ بِغُلٰمٍ عَلِيمٍ ۞

29. But his wife came forward (laughing) aloud: she smote

فَاَقْبَلَتِ امْرَاَتُهٗ فِي صَرَّةٍ فَصَكَّتْ

her face and said: "A barren old woman!"

30. They said, "Even so your Lord has spoken: and He is full of Wisdom and Knowledge."

وَجْهَهَا وَقَالَتْ عَجُوزٌ عَقِيمٌ ۝

قَالُوا كَذَلِكِ ۙ قَالَ رَبُّكِ ۚ إِنَّهُ هُوَ الْحَكِيمُ الْعَلِيمُ ۝

31. (Abraham) said: "And what, O you Messengers, is your errand (now)?"

قَالَ فَمَا خَطْبُكُمْ أَيُّهَا الْمُرْسَلُونَ ۝

32. They said, "We have been sent to a people (deep) in sin;-

قَالُوا إِنَّا أُرْسِلْنَا إِلَى قَوْمٍ مُّجْرِمِينَ ۝

33. "To bring on, on them, (a shower of) stones of clay (brimstone),

لِنُرْسِلَ عَلَيْهِمْ حِجَارَةً مِّن طِينٍ ۝

34. "Marked as from your Lord for those who trespass beyond bounds."

مُّسَوَّمَةً عِندَ رَبِّكَ لِلْمُسْرِفِينَ ۝

35. Then We evacuated those of the Believers who were there,

فَأَخْرَجْنَا مَن كَانَ فِيهَا مِنَ الْمُؤْمِنِينَ ۝

36. But We did not find there any just (Muslim) persons except in one house:

فَمَا وَجَدْنَا فِيهَا غَيْرَ بَيْتٍ مِّنَ الْمُسْلِمِينَ ۝

37. And We left there a Sign for such as fear the Grievous Chastisement.

وَتَرَكْنَا فِيهَا آيَةً لِّلَّذِينَ يَخَافُونَ الْعَذَابَ الْأَلِيمَ ۝

38. And in Moses (was another Sign): behold, We sent him to Pharaoh, with authority manifest.

وَفِي مُوسَى إِذْ أَرْسَلْنَاهُ إِلَى فِرْعَوْنَ بِسُلْطَانٍ مُّبِينٍ ۝

39. But (Pharaoh) turned back with his Chiefs, and said, "A sorcerer, or one possessed!"

فَتَوَلَّى بِرُكْنِهِ وَقَالَ سَاحِرٌ أَوْ مَجْنُونٌ ۝

40. So We took him and his forces, and threw them into the sea; and his was the blame.

فَأَخَذْنَاهُ وَجُنُودَهُ فَنَبَذْنَاهُمْ فِي الْيَمِّ وَهُوَ مُلِيمٌ ۝

41. And in the 'Ad (people) (was another Sign): behold, We sent against them the devastating Wind:

وَفِي عَادٍ إِذْ أَرْسَلْنَا عَلَيْهِمُ الرِّيحَ الْعَقِيمَ ۝

42. It left nothing whatever that it came up against, but reduced it to ruin and rottenness.

مَا تَذَرُ مِن شَيْءٍ أَتَتْ عَلَيْهِ إِلَّا جَعَلَتْهُ كَالرَّمِيمِ ۝

43. And in the Thamud (was another Sign): behold, they were told, "Enjoy (your brief day) for a little while!"

وَفِي ثَمُودَ إِذْ قِيلَ لَهُمْ تَمَتَّعُوا حَتَّى حِينٍ ۝

44. But they insolently defied the Command of their Lord: so the stunning noise (of an

فَعَتَوْا عَنْ أَمْرِ رَبِّهِمْ فَأَخَذَتْهُمُ

earthquake) seized them, even while they were looking on.

45. Then they could not even stand (on their feet), nor could they help themselves.

46. So were the People of Noah before them for they wickedly transgressed.

47. With power and skill We constructed the Firmament: for it is We Who create the vastness of space.

48. And We have spread out the (spacious) earth: how excellently We do spread out!

49. And of every thing We have created pairs: that you may receive instruction.

50. Then you hasten (at once) to Allah: I am from Him a Warner to you, clear and open!

51. And make not another an object of worship with Allah: I am from Him a Warner to you, clear and open!

52. Similarly, no Apostle came to the Peoples before them, but they said (of him) in like manner, "A sorcerer, or one possessed"!

53. Is this the legacy they have transmitted, one to another? Nay, they are themselves a people transgressing beyond bounds!

54. So turn away from them: not blame on you.

55. But teach (your Message) for teaching benefits the Believers.

56. And I have not created Jinns and men, except that they may serve (worship) Me.

57. No Sustenance do I require of them, nor do I require that they should feed Me.

58. For Allah is He Who gives (all) Sustenance,- Lord of Power,- Steadfast (for ever).

59. For the Wrong-doers, their portion is like unto the portion of their fellows (of earlier generations): then let them not ask Me to hasten (that portion)!

60. Woe, then, to the Unbelievers, on account of that Day of theirs

الصّٰعِقَةُ وَهُمْ يَنْظُرُوْنَ ۞

فَمَا اسْتَطَاعُوْا مِنْ قِيَامٍ وَّمَا كَانُوْا مُنْتَصِرِيْنَ ۞

وَقَوْمَ نُوْحٍ مِّنْ قَبْلُ ۖ إِنَّهُمْ كَانُوْا قَوْمًا فٰسِقِيْنَ ۞

وَالسَّمَآءَ بَنَيْنٰهَا بِأَيْيْدٍ وَّإِنَّا لَمُوْسِعُوْنَ ۞

وَالْأَرْضَ فَرَشْنٰهَا فَنِعْمَ الْمٰهِدُوْنَ ۞

وَمِنْ كُلِّ شَيْءٍ خَلَقْنَا زَوْجَيْنِ لَعَلَّكُمْ تَذَكَّرُوْنَ ۞

فَفِرُّوْا إِلَى اللّٰهِ ۖ إِنِّيْ لَكُمْ مِّنْهُ نَذِيْرٌ مُّبِيْنٌ ۞

وَلَا تَجْعَلُوْا مَعَ اللّٰهِ إِلٰهًا اخَرَ ۖ إِنِّيْ لَكُمْ مِّنْهُ نَذِيْرٌ مُّبِيْنٌ ۞

كَذٰلِكَ مَآ أَتَى الَّذِيْنَ مِنْ قَبْلِهِمْ مِّنْ رَّسُوْلٍ إِلَّا قَالُوْا سَاحِرٌ أَوْ مَجْنُوْنٌ ۞

أَتَوَاصَوْا بِهٖ ۚ بَلْ هُمْ قَوْمٌ طَاغُوْنَ ۞

فَتَوَلَّ عَنْهُمْ فَمَآ أَنْتَ بِمَلُوْمٍ ۞

وَذَكِّرْ فَإِنَّ الذِّكْرٰى تَنْفَعُ الْمُؤْمِنِيْنَ ۞

وَمَا خَلَقْتُ الْجِنَّ وَالْإِنْسَ إِلَّا لِيَعْبُدُوْنِ ۞

مَآ أُرِيْدُ مِنْهُمْ مِّنْ رِّزْقٍ وَّمَآ أُرِيْدُ أَنْ يُّطْعِمُوْنِ ۞

إِنَّ اللّٰهَ هُوَ الرَّزَّاقُ ذُو الْقُوَّةِ الْمَتِيْنُ ۞

فَإِنَّ لِلَّذِيْنَ ظَلَمُوْا ذَنُوْبًا مِّثْلَ ذَنُوْبِ أَصْحٰبِهِمْ فَلَا يَسْتَعْجِلُوْنِ ۞

فَوَيْلٌ لِّلَّذِيْنَ كَفَرُوْا مِنْ يَّوْمِهِمُ

SÛRAH-52
AT-TÛR
(INTRODUCTION)

This is the third of the group of seven Makkan Sûras described in the Introduction to S. 50.

It is, like its predecessor, an early Makkan Sûrah. The points here emphasised arc: that Revelation is in accord with all Allah's Signs, including previous Revelations, and that the Hereafter is inevitable, and we must prepare for it.

which they have been promised!

الَّذِى يُوعَدُونَ ۞

52. The Mount
In the name of Allah, Most Gracious, Most Merciful.

(٥٢) سُوْرَةُ الطُّوْرِ مَكِّيَّةٌ (٤٧)

بِسْمِ اللهِ الرَّحْمٰنِ الرَّحِيْمِ

1. By the Mount (of Revelation);

وَالطُّوْرِ ۞

2. By a Decree inscribed;

وَكِتٰبٍ مَّسْطُوْرٍ ۞

3. In a Scroll unfolded;

فِىْ رَقٍّ مَّنْشُوْرٍ ۞

4. And by the much-frequented Fane;

وَالْبَيْتِ الْمَعْمُوْرِ ۞

5. And by the Canopy raised High;

وَالسَّقْفِ الْمَرْفُوْعِ ۞

6. And by the Ocean filled with Swell;-

وَالْبَحْرِ الْمَسْجُوْرِ ۞

7. Verily, the Doom of your Lord will indeed come to pass;-

إِنَّ عَذَابَ رَبِّكَ لَوَاقِعٌ ۞

8. There is none can avert it;-

مَّا لَهٗ مِنْ دَافِعٍ ۞

9. On the Day when the firmament will be in dreadful commotion.

يَّوْمَ تَمُوْرُ السَّمَآءُ مَوْرًا ۞

10. And the mountains will fly hither and thither.

وَّتَسِيْرُ الْجِبَالُ سَيْرًا ۞

11. Then woe that Day to those that treat (Truth) as Falsehood;-

فَوَيْلٌ يَّوْمَئِذٍ لِّلْمُكَذِّبِيْنَ ۞

12. That play (and paddle) in shallow trifles.

الَّذِيْنَ هُمْ فِىْ خَوْضٍ يَّلْعَبُوْنَ ۞

13. That Day they shall be thrust down to the Fire of Hell, irresistibly.

يَوْمَ يُدَعُّوْنَ إِلٰى نَارِ جَهَنَّمَ دَعًّا ۞

14. "This:, it will be said, "Is the Fire,- which you were wont to deny!

هٰذِهِ النَّارُ الَّتِىْ كُنْتُمْ بِهَا

15. "Is this then a fake, or is it you that do not see?

تُكَذِّبُوْنَ ۞

16. "You burn therein: the same is it to you whether you bear it with patience, or not: you but receive the recompense of your (own) deeds."

أَفَسِحْرٌ هٰذَآ أَمْ أَنْتُمْ لَا تُبْصِرُوْنَ ۞ اِصْلَوْهَا فَاصْبِرُوْا أَوْ لَا تَصْبِرُوْا سَوَآءٌ عَلَيْكُمْ إِنَّمَا تُجْزَوْنَ مَا

17. As to the Righteous, they will be in Gardens, and in Happiness,-

كُنْتُمْ تَعْمَلُوْنَ ۞

18. Enjoying the (Bliss) which their Lord has bestowed on them, and their Lord shall deliver them from the Chastisement of the Fire.

إِنَّ الْمُتَّقِيْنَ فِىْ جَنّٰتٍ وَّنَعِيْمٍ ۞ فٰكِهِيْنَ بِمَآ اٰتٰهُمْ رَبُّهُمْ وَوَقٰهُمْ

19. (To them will be said:) "You eat and drink with good pleasure, because of your (good) deeds."

رَبُّهُمْ عَذَابَ الْجَحِيْمِ ۞ كُلُوْا وَاشْرَبُوْا هَنِيْٓئًا بِمَا كُنْتُمْ

20. They will recline (with ease) on Thrones (of dignity) arranged in ranks; and We shall join them to Companions, with beautiful, big and lustrous eyes.

21. And those who believe and whose families follow them in Faith,- to them We shall join their families: nor shall We deprive them (of the fruit) of anything of their works: (yet) each individual is in pledge for his deeds.

22. And We shall bestow on them, of fruit and meat, anything they shall desire.

23. They shall exchange there one with another, a (loving) cup free of frivolity, free of all taint of ill.

24. Round about them will serve, (devoted) to them, youths (handsome) as Pearls well-guarded.

25. They will advance to each other, engaging in mutual enquiry.

26. They will say: "Surely, aforetime, we were not without fear for the sake of our people.

27. "But Allah has been gracious to us, and has delivered us from the Penalty of the Scorching Wind.

28. "Truly, we called Him from of old: truly it is He, the Beneficent, the Merciful!"

29. Therefore you proclaim the praises (of your Lord): for by the Grace of your Lord, you are no (vulgar) soothsayer, nor you are one possessed.

30. Or do they say:- "A Poet! for him we await some calamity (hatched) by Time!"

31. You say: "You await!- I too will wait along with you!"

تَعْمَلُوْنَ ۞

مُتَّكِئِيْنَ عَلٰى سُرُرٍ مَّصْفُوْفَةٍ ۖ وَ زَوَّجْنٰهُمْ بِحُوْرٍ عِيْنٍ ۞

وَالَّذِيْنَ اٰمَنُوْا وَاتَّبَعَتْهُمْ ذُرِّيَّتُهُمْ بِاِيْمَانٍ اَلْحَقْنَا بِهِمْ ذُرِّيَّتَهُمْ وَمَاۤ اَلَتْنٰهُمْ مِّنْ عَمَلِهِمْ مِّنْ شَيْءٍ ۚ كُلُّ امْرِئٍ بِمَا كَسَبَ رَهِيْنٌ ۞

وَاَمْدَدْنٰهُمْ بِفَاكِهَةٍ وَّلَحْمٍ مِّمَّا يَشْتَهُوْنَ ۞

يَتَنَازَعُوْنَ فِيْهَا كَاْسًا لَّا لَغْوٌ فِيْهَا وَلَا تَاْثِيْمٌ ۞

وَيَطُوْفُ عَلَيْهِمْ غِلْمَانٌ لَّهُمْ كَاَنَّهُمْ لُؤْلُؤٌ مَّكْنُوْنٌ ۞

وَاَقْبَلَ بَعْضُهُمْ عَلٰى بَعْضٍ يَّتَسَآءَلُوْنَ ۞

قَالُوْۤا اِنَّا كُنَّا قَبْلُ فِيْۤ اَهْلِنَا مُشْفِقِيْنَ ۞

فَمَنَّ اللّٰهُ عَلَيْنَا وَوَقٰىنَا عَذَابَ السَّمُوْمِ ۞

اِنَّا كُنَّا مِنْ قَبْلُ نَدْعُوْهُ ۗ اِنَّهُ هُوَ الْبَرُّ الرَّحِيْمُ ۞

فَذَكِّرْ فَمَاۤ اَنْتَ بِنِعْمَتِ رَبِّكَ بِكَاهِنٍ وَّلَا مَجْنُوْنٍ ۞

اَمْ يَقُوْلُوْنَ شَاعِرٌ نَّتَرَبَّصُ بِهٖ رَيْبَ الْمَنُوْنِ ۞

قُلْ تَرَبَّصُوْا فَاِنِّيْ مَعَكُمْ مِّنَ

32. Is it that their faculties of understanding urge them to this, or are they but a people transgressing beyond bounds?

33. Or do they say, "He fabricated the (Message)"? Nay, they have no faith!

34. Let them then produce a recital like it,- If (it be) they speak the truth!

35. Were they created of nothing, or were they themselves the creators?

36. Or did they create the heavens and the earth? Nay, they have no firm belief.

37. Or are the Treasures of your Lord with them, or are they the managers (of affairs)?

38. Or have they a ladder, by which they can (climb up to heaven and) listen (to its secrets)? Then let (such a) listener of theirs produce a manifest proof.

39. Or has He only daughters and you have sons?

40. Or is it that you do ask for a reward, so that they are burdened with a load of debt?-

41. Or that the Unseen is in their hands, and they write it down?

42. Or do they intend a plot (against you)? But those who defy Allah are themselves involved in a Plot!

43. Or have they a god other than Allah? Exalted is Allah far above the things they associate with Him!

44. Were they to see a piece of the sky falling (on them), they would (only) say: "Clouds gathered in heaps!"

45. So leave them alone until they encounter that Day of theirs, wherein they shall (perforce) swoon (with terror),-

SÛRAH-53
AN-NAJM
(INTRODUCTION)

This is an early Makkan Sûrah, and is the fourth of the series seven which were described in the Introduction to S. 50.

The particular theme of this Sûrah is that Revelation is not N illusion: the illusion is in the minds of those who doubt and have false ideas of Allah: Allah is the source and goal of all things.

In some Sûras the consecutive arrangement is shown or suggested by a cue-word. Here the cue-word is "star," corresponding to "stars" in the last verse of the last Surah. So in 46-1. the words: "Exalted in Power. Full of Wisdom": are carried forward from the last verse of S. 45. and indeed the same words occur in the first verse of S. 45. So, again the words: "Most Merciful, Oft-Forgiving": in 34: 2. refer back to the words: "Oft- Forgiving, Most Mervi lul": in the last line of S. 33. In S. 54:1. the nearness of Judgment recalls the same idea at the end of the previous Sûrah (53:57). Other examples will also be found.

46. The Day when their plotting will avail them nothing and no help shall be given them.

يَوْمَ لَا يُغْنِيْ عَنْهُمْ كَيْدُهُمْ شَيْئًا وَّلَا هُمْ يُنْصَرُوْنَ ۚ

47. And verily, for those who do wrong, there is another punishment besides this: but most of them do not understand.

وَإِنَّ لِلَّذِيْنَ ظَلَمُوْا عَذَابًا دُوْنَ ذٰلِكَ وَلٰكِنَّ اَكْثَرَهُمْ لَا يَعْلَمُوْنَ

48. Now await in patience the command of your Lord: for verily you are in Our eyes: and celebrate the praises of your Lord the while you stand forth,

وَاصْبِرْ لِحُكْمِ رَبِّكَ فَإِنَّكَ بِاَعْيُنِنَا وَسَبِّحْ بِحَمْدِ رَبِّكَ حِيْنَ تَقُوْمُ ۙ

49. And for part of the night also you praise Him,- and at the retreat of the stars!

وَمِنَ الَّيْلِ فَسَبِّحْهُ وَإِدْبَارَ النُّجُوْمِ

53. The Star
In the name of Allah, Most Gracious, Most Merciful.

(٥٣) سُوْرَةُ النَّجْمِ مَكِّيَّةٌ (٢٣)

بِسْمِ اللهِ الرَّحْمٰنِ الرَّحِيْمِ

1. By the Star when it goes down,-

وَالنَّجْمِ اِذَا هَوٰى ۙ

2. Your Companion is neither astray nor being misled.

مَا ضَلَّ صَاحِبُكُمْ وَمَا غَوٰى ۙ

3. Nor does he say (anything) of (his own) Desire.

وَمَا يَنْطِقُ عَنِ الْهَوٰى ؕ

4. It is no less than inspiration sent down to him:

اِنْ هُوَ اِلَّا وَحْيٌ يُّوْحٰى ۙ

5. He was taught by one Mighty in Power,

عَلَّمَهُ شَدِيْدُ الْقُوٰى ۙ

6. Endued with Wisdom: for he appeared (in stately form);

ذُوْ مِرَّةٍ ؕ فَاسْتَوٰى ۙ

7. While he was in the highest part of the horizon:

وَهُوَ بِالْاُفُقِ الْاَعْلٰى ؕ

8. Then he approached and came closer,

ثُمَّ دَنَا فَتَدَلّٰى ۙ

9. And was at a distance of but two bow-lengths or (even) nearer;

فَكَانَ قَابَ قَوْسَيْنِ اَوْ اَدْنٰى ۚ

10. So did (Allah) convey the inspiration to His Servant (conveyed) what He (meant) to convey.

فَاَوْحٰى اِلٰى عَبْدِهٖ مَا اَوْحٰى ؕ

11. The (Prophet's) (mind and) heart in no way falsified that which he saw.

مَا كَذَبَ الْفُؤَادُ مَا رَاٰى

12. Will you then dispute with him concerning what he saw?

اَفَتُمٰرُوْنَهٗ عَلٰى مَا يَرٰى

13. For indeed he saw him at a second descent,

وَلَقَدْ رَاٰهُ نَزْلَةً اُخْرٰى ۙ

14. Near the Lote-tree beyond which none may pass:

عِنْدَ سِدْرَةِ الْمُنْتَهٰى ؕ

15. Near it is the Garden of Abode.

عِنْدَهَا جَنَّةُ الْمَاْوٰى ؕ

16. Behold, the Lote-tree was shrouded (in mystery unspeakable!)

اِذْ يَغْشَى السِّدْرَةَ مَا يَغْشٰى ۙ

17. (His) sight never swerved, nor did it go wrong!

مَا زَاغَ الْبَصَرُ وَمَا طَغٰى

18. For truly he saw of the Signs of his Lord, the Greatest!

19. Have you seen Lat and 'Uzza,

20. And another, the third (goddess), Manat?

21. What! for you the male sex, and for Him, the female?

22. Behold, such would be indeed a division most unfair!

23. These are nothing but names which you have devised,- you and your fathers,- for which Allah has sent down no authority (whatever). They follow nothing but conjecture and what their own souls desire!- Even though there has already come to them Guidance from their Lord!

24. Nay, shall man have (just) anything he hankers after?

25. But it is to Allah that the End and the Beginning (of all things) belong.

26. How many-so-ever be the angels in the heavens, their intercession will avail nothing except after Allah has given leave for whom He pleases and that he is acceptable to Him.

27. Those who do not believe in the Hereafter, name the angels with female names.

28. But they have no knowledge therein. They follow nothing but conjecture; and conjecture avails nothing against Truth.

29. Therefore shun those who turn away from Our Message and desire nothing but the life of this world.

30. That is as far as knowledge will reach them. Verily your Lord knows best those who stray from His Path, and He knows best those who receive guidance.

31. Yes, to Allah belongs all that is in the heavens and on earth:

so that He rewards those who do evil, according to their deeds, and He rewards those who do good, with what is best.

32. Those who avoid great sins and shameful deeds, only (falling into) small faults,- verily your Lord is ample in forgiveness. He knows you well when He brings you out of the earth, and when you are hidden in your mothers' wombs. Therefore, do not justify your-selves: He knows best who it is that guards against evil.

33. Do you see one who turns back,

34. Gives a little, then hardens (his heart)?

35. What! Has he knowledge of the Unseen so that he can see?

36. Or hath he not bad news of what is in book of Moses.

37. And of Abraham who fulfilled his engagements?-

38. That no laden one shall bear another's load.

39. That man can have nothing but what he strives for;

40. That (the fruit of) his striving will soon come in sight:

41. Then will he be rewarded with a reward complete;

42. That to your Lord is the final Goal;

43. That it is He Who grants Laughter and Tears;

44. That it is He Who grants Death and Life;

45. That He created in pairs,-male and female,

46. From a seed when lodged (in its place);

47. That He has promised a Second Creation (raising of the Dead);

48. That it is He Who gives wealth and satisfaction;

49. That He is the Lord of Sirius (the Mighty Star);

لِيَجْزِىَ الَّذِيْنَ اَسَاءُوْا بِمَا عَمِلُوْا

وَيَجْزِىَ الَّذِيْنَ اَحْسَنُوْا بِالْحُسْنَىٰ ۚ

اَلَّذِيْنَ يَجْتَنِبُوْنَ كَبَآئِرَ الْاِثْمِ

وَالْفَوَاحِشَ اِلَّا اللَّمَمَ ؕ اِنَّ رَبَّكَ

وَاسِعُ الْمَغْفِرَةِ ؕ هُوَ اَعْلَمُ بِكُمْ اِذْ

اَنْشَاَكُمْ مِّنَ الْاَرْضِ وَاِذْ اَنْتُمْ اَجِنَّةٌ

فِىْ بُطُوْنِ اُمَّهٰتِكُمْ ۚ فَلَا تُزَكُّوْا

اَنْفُسَكُمْ ؕ هُوَ اَعْلَمُ بِمَنِ اتَّقٰى ۚ ع

اَفَرَءَيْتَ الَّذِىْ تَوَلّٰى ۙ

وَاَعْطٰى قَلِيْلًا وَّاَكْدٰى ۞

اَعِنْدَهٗ عِلْمُ الْغَيْبِ فَهُوَ يَرٰى ۞

اَمْ لَمْ يُنَبَّأْ بِمَا فِىْ صُحُفِ مُوْسٰى ۙ

وَاِبْرٰهِيْمَ الَّذِىْ وَفّٰى ۙ

اَلَّا تَزِرُ وَازِرَةٌ وِّزْرَ اُخْرٰى ۙ

وَاَنْ لَّيْسَ لِلْاِنْسَانِ اِلَّا مَا سَعٰى ۙ

وَاَنَّ سَعْيَهٗ سَوْفَ يُرٰى ۙ

ثُمَّ يُجْزٰىهُ الْجَزَآءَ الْاَوْفٰى ۙ

وَاَنَّ اِلٰى رَبِّكَ الْمُنْتَهٰى ۙ

وَاَنَّهٗ هُوَ اَضْحَكَ وَاَبْكٰى ۙ

وَاَنَّهٗ هُوَ اَمَاتَ وَاَحْيَا ۙ

وَاَنَّهٗ خَلَقَ الزَّوْجَيْنِ الذَّكَرَ

وَالْاُنْثٰى ۙ

مِنْ نُّطْفَةٍ اِذَا تُمْنٰى ۙ

وَاَنَّ عَلَيْهِ النَّشْاَةَ الْاُخْرٰى ۙ

وَاَنَّهٗ هُوَ اَغْنٰى وَاَقْنٰى ۙ

وَاَنَّهٗ هُوَ رَبُّ الشِّعْرٰى ۙ

SÛRAH-54
AL-QAMAR
(INTRODUCTION)

This is an early Makkan Sûrah., the fifth in the series dealing with Judgment, and the truth of Revelation, as explained in the Introduction to S. 50.

The theme of thc Sûrah is explained by the refrain: "Is there any that will receive admonition?" which occurs six times, at the end of each reference to a past story of sin and rejection of warnings and in thc appeal to the simplicity of the Qur'ân (verses 15, 17, 22. 32, 40. and 51). There is an invitation to listen to Message and turn to Truth and Righteousness.

50. And that it is He Who destroyed the former (tribe of) 'Aad,

وَاَنَّهٗۤ اَهْلَكَ عَادَۨ الْاُوْلٰی ۙ

51. And the Thamud, nor gave them a lease of perpetual life.

وَثَمُوْدَا۟ فَمَاۤ اَبْقٰی ۙ

52. And before them, the people of Noah, for that they were (all) most unjust and most insolent transgressors,

وَقَوْمَ نُوْحٍ مِّنْ قَبْلُ ؕ اِنَّهُمْ كَانُوْا

هُمْ اَظْلَمَ وَاَطْغٰی ؕ

53. And He destroyed the Overthrown Cities (of Sodom and Gomorrah),

وَالْمُؤْتَفِكَةَ اَهْوٰی ۙ

54. So that (ruins unknown) have covered them up.

فَغَشّٰىهَا مَا غَشّٰی ۚ

55. Then which of the gifts of your Lord, (O man,) will you dispute about?

فَبِاَیِّ اٰلَآءِ رَبِّكَ تَتَمَارٰی

56. This is a Warner, of the (series of) Warners of old!

هٰذَا نَذِیْرٌ مِّنَ النُّذُرِ الْاُوْلٰی

57. The (Judgment) ever approaching draws near:

اَزِفَتِ الْاٰزِفَةُ ۚ

58. No (soul) but Allah can lay it bare.

لَیْسَ لَهَا مِنْ دُوْنِ اللّٰهِ كَاشِفَةٌ ؕ

59. Do you then wonder at this recital?

اَفَمِنْ هٰذَا الْحَدِیْثِ تَعْجَبُوْنَ ۙ

60. And will you laugh and not weep,-

وَتَضْحَكُوْنَ وَلَا تَبْكُوْنَ ۙ

61. Wasting your time in vanities?

وَاَنْتُمْ سٰمِدُوْنَ

62. But you fall down in prostration to Allah, and adore (Him)

فَاسْجُدُوْا لِلّٰهِ وَاعْبُدُوْا ۩

54. The Moon

In the name of Allah, Most Gracious, Most Merciful.

(٥٤) سُوْرَةُ الْقَمَرِ مَكِّیَّةٌ (٣٤)

بِسْمِ اللّٰهِ الرَّحْمٰنِ الرَّحِیْمِ

1. The Hour (of judgement) is near and the moon is cleft asunder.

اِقْتَرَبَتِ السَّاعَةُ وَانْشَقَّ الْقَمَرُ ۝

2. But if they see a Sign, they turn away, and say, "This is (but) transient magic."

وَاِنْ یَّرَوْا اٰیَةً یُّعْرِضُوْا وَیَقُوْلُوْا

سِحْرٌ مُّسْتَمِرٌّ ۝

3. They reject (the warning) and follow their (own) lusts but every matter has its appointed time.

وَكَذَّبُوْا وَاتَّبَعُوْۤا اَهْوَآءَهُمْ وَكُلُّ

اَمْرٍ مُّسْتَقِرٌّ ۝

4. There have already come to them such tidings as contain a deterrent-

وَلَقَدْ جَآءَهُمْ مِّنَ الْاَنْبَآءِ مَا

فِیْهِ مُزْدَجَرٌ ۙ

5. Mature wisdom; but (the preaching of) Warners does not profit them.

حِكْمَةٌ بَالِغَةٌ فَمَا تُغْنِ النُّذُرُ ۙ

6. Therefore, (O Prophet,) turn away from them. The Day that the Caller will call (them) to a terrible affair,

فَتَوَلَّ عَنْهُمْ ۘ یَوْمَ یَدْعُ الدَّاعِ اِلٰی

شَیْءٍ نُّكُرٍ ۙ

7. They will come forth,- their eyes humbled - from (their) graves, (torpid) like locusts scattered abroad,

8. Hastening, with eyes transfixed, towards the Caller!- "Hard is this Day!", the Unbelievers will say.

9. Before them the People of Noah rejected (their Apostle): they rejected Our servant, and said, "Here is one possessed!", and he was driven out.

10. Then he called on his Lord: "I am one overcome: do You then help (me)!"

11. So We opened the gates of heaven, with water pouring forth.

12. And We caused the earth to gush forth with springs, so the waters met (and rose) to the extent decreed.

13. But We bore him on an (Ark) made of broad planks and caulked with palm-fiber:,

14. She floats under our eyes (and care): a recompense to one who had been rejected (with scorn)!

15. And We have left this as a Sign (for all time): then is there any that will receive admonition?

16. But how (terrible) was My Chastisement and My Warning?

17. And We have indeed made the Qur'an easy to understand and remember: then is there any that will receive admonition?

18. The 'Ad (people) (too) rejected (Truth): then how terrible was My Chastisement and My Warning?

19. For We sent against them a furious wind, on a Day of violent Disaster,

20. Plucking out men as if they were roots of palm-trees torn up (from the ground).

21. Yes, how (terrible) was My Chastisement and My Warning!

22. But We have indeed made the Qur'an easy to understand and remember:

then is there any that will receive admonition?

23. The Thamud (also) rejected (their) Warners.

24. For they said: "What! a man! a solitary one from among ourselves! shall we follow such a one? Truly we should then be straying in mind, and mad!

25. "Is it that the Message is sent to him, of all people amongst us? Nay, he is a liar, an insolent one!"

26. Ah! they will know on the morrow, which is the liar, the insolent one!

27. For We will send the she-camel by way of trial for them. So watch them, (O Salih), and possess yourself in patience!

28. And inform them that the water is to be shared between them. each one's right to drink being brought forward (by suitable turns).

29. But they called to their companion, and he took a sword in hand, and hamstrung (her).

30. Ah! how (terrible) was My Chastisement and My Warning!

31. For We sent against them a single Mighty Blast, and they became like the dry stubble used by one who pens cattle.

32. And We have indeed made the Qur'an easy to understand and remember: then is there any that will receive admonition?

33. The people of Lut rejected (his) warning.

34. We sent against them a violent tornado with showers of stones, (which destroyed them), except Lut's household: We delivered them by early Dawn,-

35. As a Grace from Us: thus do We reward those who give thanks.

36. And (Lut) warned them of Our Punishment, but they disputed about the Warning.

37. And they even sought to snatch away his guests from him, but We blinded their eyes. (They heard:) "Now you taste My Wrath and My Warning."

فَهَلْ مِنْ مُّدَّكِرٍ ۞

كَذَّبَتْ ثَمُوْدُ بِالنُّذُرِ ۞

فَقَالُوْٓا اَبَشَرًا مِّنَّا وَاحِدًا نَّتَّبِعُهٗٓ

اِنَّآ اِذًا لَّفِيْ ضَلٰلٍ وَّسُعُرٍ ۞

ءَاُلْقِيَ الذِّكْرُ عَلَيْهِ مِنْۢ بَيْنِنَا

بَلْ هُوَ كَذَّابٌ اَشِرٌ ۞

سَيَعْلَمُوْنَ غَدًا مَّنِ الْكَذَّابُ الْاَشِرُ ۞

اِنَّا مُرْسِلُوا النَّاقَةِ فِتْنَةً لَّهُمْ

فَارْتَقِبْهُمْ وَاصْطَبِرْ ۞

وَنَبِّئْهُمْ اَنَّ الْمَآءَ قِسْمَةٌۢ بَيْنَهُمْ ۚ

كُلُّ شِرْبٍ مُّحْتَضَرٌ ۞

فَنَادَوْا صَاحِبَهُمْ فَتَعَاطٰى فَعَقَرَ ۞

فَكَيْفَ كَانَ عَذَابِيْ وَنُذُرِ ۞

اِنَّآ اَرْسَلْنَا عَلَيْهِمْ صَيْحَةً وَّاحِدَةً

فَكَانُوْا كَهَشِيْمِ الْمُحْتَظِرِ ۞

وَلَقَدْ يَسَّرْنَا الْقُرْاٰنَ لِلذِّكْرِ

فَهَلْ مِنْ مُّدَّكِرٍ ۞

كَذَّبَتْ قَوْمُ لُوْطٍۭ بِالنُّذُرِ ۞

اِنَّآ اَرْسَلْنَا عَلَيْهِمْ حَاصِبًا اِلَّآ اٰلَ

لُوْطٍ ۚ نَّجَّيْنٰهُمْ بِسَحَرٍ ۞

نِّعْمَةً مِّنْ عِنْدِنَا ۚ كَذٰلِكَ نَجْزِيْ

مَنْ شَكَرَ ۞

وَلَقَدْ اَنْذَرَهُمْ بَطْشَتَنَا فَتَمَارَوْا

بِالنُّذُرِ ۞

وَلَقَدْ رَاوَدُوْهُ عَنْ ضَيْفِهٖ فَطَمَسْنَآ

اَعْيُنَهُمْ فَذُوْقُوْا عَذَابِيْ وَنُذُرِ ۞

38. Early on the morrow an abiding Punishment seized them:

وَلَقَدْ صَبَّحَهُمْ بُكْرَةً عَذَابٌ مُّسْتَقِرٌّ ۝

39. "So you taste My Wrath and My Warning."

فَذُوقُوا عَذَابِي وَنُذُرِ ۝

40. And We have indeed made the Qur'an easy to understand and remember: then is there any that will receive admonition?

وَلَقَدْ يَسَّرْنَا الْقُرْآنَ لِلذِّكْرِ فَهَلْ مِنْ مُّدَّكِرٍ ۝

41. To the People of Pharaoh, too, aforetime, came Warners (from Allah).

وَلَقَدْ جَاءَ آلَ فِرْعَوْنَ النُّذُرُ ۝

42. The (people) rejected all Our Signs; but We seized them with such Chastisement (as comes) from One Exalted in Power, able to carry out His Will.

كَذَّبُوا بِآيَاتِنَا كُلِّهَا فَأَخَذْنَاهُمْ أَخْذَ عَزِيزٍ مُّقْتَدِرٍ ۝

43. Are you Unbelievers, (O Quraish), better than they? Or do you have an immunity in the Sacred Books?

أَكُفَّارُكُمْ خَيْرٌ مِّنْ أُولَئِكُمْ أَمْ لَكُمْ بَرَاءَةٌ فِي الزُّبُرِ ۝

44. Or do they say: "We acting together can defend ourselves"?

أَمْ يَقُولُونَ نَحْنُ جَمِيعٌ مُّنْتَصِرٌ ۝

45. Soon will their multitude be put to flight, and they will show their backs.

سَيُهْزَمُ الْجَمْعُ وَيُوَلُّونَ الدُّبُرَ ۝

46. Nay, the Hour (of Judgment) is the time promised them (for their full recompense): and that Hour will be most grievous and most bitter.

بَلِ السَّاعَةُ مَوْعِدُهُمْ وَالسَّاعَةُ أَدْهَى وَأَمَرُّ ۝

47. Truly those in sin are the ones straying in mind, and mad.

إِنَّ الْمُجْرِمِينَ فِي ضَلَالٍ وَسُعُرٍ ۝

48. The Day they will be dragged through the Fire on their faces, (they will hear:) "you taste the touch of Hell!"

يَوْمَ يُسْحَبُونَ فِي النَّارِ عَلَى وُجُوهِهِمْ ذُوقُوا مَسَّ سَقَرَ ۝

49. Verily! We have created every thing by measure.

إِنَّا كُلَّ شَيْءٍ خَلَقْنَاهُ بِقَدَرٍ ۝

50. And Our Command is but a single (Act),- like the twinkling of an eye.

وَمَا أَمْرُنَا إِلَّا وَاحِدَةٌ كَلَمْحٍ بِالْبَصَرِ ۝

51. And (oft) in the past, We have destroyed gangs like you: then is there any that will receive admonition?

وَلَقَدْ أَهْلَكْنَا أَشْيَاعَكُمْ فَهَلْ مِنْ مُّدَّكِرٍ ۝

52. All that they do is noted in (their) Books (of Deeds):

وَكُلُّ شَيْءٍ فَعَلُوهُ فِي الزُّبُرِ ۝

53. Every matter, small and great, is on record.

وَكُلُّ صَغِيرٍ وَكَبِيرٍ مُّسْتَطَرٌ ۝

54. As to the Righteous, they will be in the midst of Gardens and Rivers,

إِنَّ الْمُتَّقِينَ فِي جَنَّاتٍ وَنَهَرٍ ۝

55. In an Assembly of Truth, in the Presence of a Sovereign Omnipotent.

فِي مَقْعَدِ صِدْقٍ عِنْدَ مَلِيكٍ مُّقْتَدِرٍ ۝

SÛRAH-55
AR-RAHMÂN
(INTRODUCTION)

The majority of Commentators consider this an early Makkan Sûrah, though some consider at least a part of it as dating from Madinah. The greater part of it is undoubtedly early Makkan.

It is highly poetical and mystical, and lire refrain "Then which of the favours of your Lord will ye deny?" is interspersed 31 times among its 78 verses.

It is the sixth of the series of seven dealing with Revelation, the favours of Allah, and the Hereafter: see Introduction to S. 50.

Here the special theme is indicated by the refrain. The rhyme in most eases is in the Dual grammatical form and the Argument implies that though things are created m pairs, there is an underlying Unity, through the Creator, in the favours which He bestows, and in the goal to which they arc marching.

55. The Most Gracious
In the name of Allah, Most Gracious, Most Merciful.

سُوْرَةُ الرَّحْمٰنِ مَدَنِيَّةٌ (٩٧) (٥٥)

بِسْمِ اللهِ الرَّحْمٰنِ الرَّحِيْمِ

1. (Allah) Most Gracious!

اَلرَّحْمٰنُ ۙ

2. It is He Who has taught the Qur'an.

عَلَّمَ الْقُرْاٰنَ ۙ

3. He has created man:

خَلَقَ الْاِنْسَانَ ۙ

4. He has taught him speech (and given him intelligence).

عَلَّمَهُ الْبَيَانَ ۙ

5. The sun and the moon follow courses (exactly) computed;

اَلشَّمْسُ وَ الْقَمَرُ بِحُسْبَانٍ ۙ

6. The stars and the trees adore.

وَّالنَّجْمُ وَالشَّجَرُ يَسْجُدٰنِ ۙ

7. And He has uplifted the sky and He has set up the balance.

وَالسَّمَآءَ رَفَعَهَا وَوَضَعَ الْمِيْزَانَ ۙ

8. In order that you may not transgress (due) balance.

اَلَّا تَطْغَوْا فِي الْمِيْزَانِ ۙ

9. So establish weight with justice and do not fall short in the balance.

وَاَقِيْمُوا الْوَزْنَ بِالْقِسْطِ وَلَا تُخْسِرُوا الْمِيْزَانَ ۙ

10. It is He Who has spread out the earth for (His) creatures:

وَالْاَرْضَ وَضَعَهَا لِلْاَنَامِ ۙ

11. Therein is fruit and date-palms, producing spathes (enclosing dates);

فِيْهَا فَاكِهَةٌ ۙ وَّالنَّخْلُ ذَاتُ الْاَكْمَامِ ۙ

12. Also corn, with (its) leaves and stalk for fodder, and sweet-smelling plants.

وَالْحَبُّ ذُو الْعَصْفِ وَالرَّيْحَانُ ۙ

13. Then which of the favours of your Lord will you deny?

فَبِاَيِّ اٰلَآءِ رَبِّكُمَا تُكَذِّبٰنِ ۙ

14. He created man from sounding clay like unto pottery,

خَلَقَ الْاِنْسَانَ مِنْ صَلْصَالٍ كَالْفَخَّارِ ۙ

15. And He created Jinns from fire free of smoke:

وَخَلَقَ الْجَآنَّ مِنْ مَّارِجٍ مِّنْ نَّارٍ ۚ

16. Then which of the favours of your Lord will you deny?

فَبِاَيِّ اٰلَآءِ رَبِّكُمَا تُكَذِّبٰنِ ۙ

17. (He is) Lord of the two Easts and Lord of the two Wests:

رَبُّ الْمَشْرِقَيْنِ وَرَبُّ الْمَغْرِبَيْنِ ۙ

18. Then which of the favours of your Lord will you deny?

فَبِاَيِّ اٰلَآءِ رَبِّكُمَا تُكَذِّبٰنِ ۙ

19. He has let free the two seas meeting together.

مَرَجَ الْبَحْرَيْنِ يَلْتَقِيٰنِ ۙ

20. Between them is a Barrier which they do not transgress:

بَيْنَهُمَا بَرْزَخٌ لَّا يَبْغِيٰنِ ۙ

21. Then which of the favours of your Lord will you deny?

فَبِاَيِّ اٰلَآءِ رَبِّكُمَا تُكَذِّبٰنِ ۙ

22. Out of them come Pearls and Coral:

يَخْرُجُ مِنْهُمَا اللُّؤْلُؤُ وَالْمَرْجَانُ ۚ

23. Then which of the favours of your Lord will you deny?

فَبِاَيِّ اٰلَاءِ رَبِّكُمَا تُكَذِّبٰنِ ۞

24. And His are the Ships sailing smoothly through the seas, lofty as mountains:

وَلَهُ الْجَوَارِ الْمُنْشَئٰتُ فِى الْبَحْرِ كَالْاَعْلَامِ ۚ

25. Then which of the favours of your Lord will you deny?

فَبِاَيِّ اٰلَاءِ رَبِّكُمَا تُكَذِّبٰنِ ۞

26. All that is on earth will perish:

كُلُّ مَنْ عَلَيْهَا فَانٍ ۚ

27. But will abide (for ever) the Face of your Lord,- full of Majesty, Bounty and Honour.

وَّيَبْقٰى وَجْهُ رَبِّكَ ذُو الْجَلٰلِ وَالْاِكْرَامِ ۚ

28. Then which of the favours of your Lord will you deny?

فَبِاَيِّ اٰلَاءِ رَبِّكُمَا تُكَذِّبٰنِ ۞

29. Of Him seeks (its need) every creature in the heavens and on earth: every day He (shines) in (new) Splendour!

يَسْئَلُهُ مَنْ فِى السَّمٰوٰتِ وَالْاَرْضِ كُلَّ يَوْمٍ هُوَ فِى شَأْنٍ ۚ

30. Then which of the favours of your Lord will you deny?

فَبِاَيِّ اٰلَاءِ رَبِّكُمَا تُكَذِّبٰنِ ۞

31. Soon We shall settle your affairs, O both you worlds.

سَنَفْرُغُ لَكُمْ اَيُّهَ الثَّقَلٰنِ ۚ

32. Then which of the favours of your Lord will you deny?

فَبِاَيِّ اٰلَاءِ رَبِّكُمَا تُكَذِّبٰنِ ۞

33. O you assembly of Jinns and men! If it be you can pass beyond the zones of the heavens and the earth, you pass! not without authority shall you be able to pass!

يٰمَعْشَرَ الْجِنِّ وَالْاِنْسِ اِنِ اسْتَطَعْتُمْ اَنْ تَنْفُذُوْا مِنْ اَقْطَارِ السَّمٰوٰتِ وَالْاَرْضِ فَانْفُذُوْا ۚ لَا تَنْفُذُوْنَ اِلَّا بِسُلْطٰنٍ ۚ

34. Then which of the favours of your Lord will you deny?

فَبِاَيِّ اٰلَاءِ رَبِّكُمَا تُكَذِّبٰنِ ۞

35. On you will be sent (O you evil ones twain) a flame of fire (to burn) and a smoke (to choke): no defence will you have:

يُرْسَلُ عَلَيْكُمَا شُوَاظٌ مِّنْ نَّارٍ ۙ وَّنُحَاسٌ فَلَا تَنْتَصِرٰنِ ۚ

36. Then which of the favours of your Lord will you deny?

فَبِاَيِّ اٰلَاءِ رَبِّكُمَا تُكَذِّبٰنِ ۞

37. When the sky is rent asunder, and it becomes red like ointment:

فَاِذَا انْشَقَّتِ السَّمَاءُ فَكَانَتْ وَرْدَةً كَالدِّهَانِ ۚ

38. Then which of the favours of your Lord will you deny?

فَبِاَيِّ اٰلَاءِ رَبِّكُمَا تُكَذِّبٰنِ ۞

39. On that Day no question will be asked of man

فَيَوْمَئِذٍ لَّا يُسْئَلُ عَنْ ذَنْبِهٖ اِنْسٌ

or Jinn as to his sin.

وَلَا جَانٌّ ۖ

40. Then which of the favours of your Lord will you deny?

فَبِاَىِّ اٰلَاءِ رَبِّكُمَا تُكَذِّبٰنِ ۞

41. (For) the sinners will be known by their marks: and they will be seized by their forelocks and their feet.

يُعْرَفُ الْمُجْرِمُوْنَ بِسِيْمٰهُمْ فَيُؤْخَذُ بِالنَّوَاصِىْ وَالْاَقْدَامِ ۖ

42. Then which of the favours of your Lord will you deny?

فَبِاَىِّ اٰلَاءِ رَبِّكُمَا تُكَذِّبٰنِ ۞

43. This is the Hell which the Sinners deny:

هٰذِهٖ جَهَنَّمُ الَّتِىْ يُكَذِّبُ بِهَا الْمُجْرِمُوْنَ ۞

44. In its midst and in the midst of boiling hot water will they wander round!

يَطُوْفُوْنَ بَيْنَهَا وَبَيْنَ حَمِيْمٍ اٰنٍ ۖ

45. Then which of the favours of your Lord will you deny?

فَبِاَىِّ اٰلَاءِ رَبِّكُمَا تُكَذِّبٰنِ ۞

46. But for him who fear the standing before his Lord there will be two gardens.

وَلِمَنْ خَافَ مَقَامَ رَبِّهٖ جَنَّتٰنِ ۖ

47. Then which of the favours of your Lord will you deny?-

فَبِاَىِّ اٰلَاءِ رَبِّكُمَا تُكَذِّبٰنِ ۞

48. Containing all kinds (of trees and delights);-

ذَوَاتَآ اَفْنَانٍ ۖ

49. Then which of the favours of your Lord will you deny?-

فَبِاَىِّ اٰلَاءِ رَبِّكُمَا تُكَذِّبٰنِ ۞

50. In them (each) will be two springs flowing (free);

فِيْهِمَا عَيْنٰنِ تَجْرِيٰنِ ۖ

51. Then which of the favours of your Lord will you deny?-

فَبِاَىِّ اٰلَاءِ رَبِّكُمَا تُكَذِّبٰنِ ۞

52. In them will be Fruits of every kind, two and two.

فِيْهِمَا مِنْ كُلِّ فَاكِهَةٍ زَوْجٰنِ ۖ

53. Then which of the favours of your Lord will you deny?

فَبِاَىِّ اٰلَاءِ رَبِّكُمَا تُكَذِّبٰنِ ۞

54. They will recline on carpets, whose inner linings will be of rich brocade: the Fruit of the Gardens will be near (and easy of reach).

مُتَّكِئِيْنَ عَلٰى فُرُشٍ بَطَائِنُهَا مِنْ اِسْتَبْرَقٍ ۖ وَجَنَى الْجَنَّتَيْنِ دَانٍ ۖ

55. Then which of the favours of your Lord will you deny?

فَبِاَىِّ اٰلَاءِ رَبِّكُمَا تُكَذِّبٰنِ ۞

56. In them will be (Maidens), chaste, restraining their glances, whom no man or Jinn before them has touched;-

فِيْهِنَّ قٰصِرٰتُ الطَّرْفِ ۖ لَمْ يَطْمِثْهُنَّ اِنْسٌ قَبْلَهُمْ وَلَا جَانٌّ ۖ

57. Then which of the favours of your Lord will you deny?-

فَبِاَىِّ اٰلَاءِ رَبِّكُمَا تُكَذِّبٰنِ ۞

58. Like unto rubies and coral.

كَاَنَّهُنَّ الْيَاقُوْتُ وَالْمَرْجَانُ ۖ

59. Then which of the favours of your Lord will you deny?

فَبِاَىِّ اٰلَاءِ رَبِّكُمَا تُكَذِّبٰنِ ۞

60. Is there any Reward for Good - other than Good?

هَلْ جَزَآءُ الْاِحْسَانِ اِلَّا الْاِحْسَانُ ۖ

SÛRAH-56
AL-WÂQIÂ
(INTRODUCTION)

This is the seventh and last Sûrah of the series devoted to Revelation and the Hereafter, as explained in the Introduction to S. 50.

It belongs to the early Makkan period, with the possible exception of one or two verses.

The theme is the certainty of the Day of Judgment and its adjustment of true Values (56: 1-561; Allah's Power. Goodness and Glory (56: 57-74); and the truth or Revelation (56:75-96).

61. Then which of the favours of your Lord will you deny?

فَبِأَيِّ آلَاءِ رَبِّكُمَا تُكَذِّبَانِ ۞

62. And besides these two, there are two other Gardens,-

وَمِن دُونِهِمَا جَنَّتَانِ ۞

63. Then which of the favours of your Lord will you deny?-

فَبِأَيِّ آلَاءِ رَبِّكُمَا تُكَذِّبَانِ ۞

64. Dark-green in colour (from plentiful watering).

مُدْهَامَّتَانِ ۞

65. Then which of the favours of your Lord will you deny?

فَبِأَيِّ آلَاءِ رَبِّكُمَا تُكَذِّبَانِ ۞

66. In them (each) will be two springs pouring forth water in continuous abundance.

فِيهِمَا عَيْنَانِ نَضَّاخَتَانِ ۞

67. Then which of the favours of your Lord will you deny?

فَبِأَيِّ آلَاءِ رَبِّكُمَا تُكَذِّبَانِ ۞

68. In them will be Fruits, and dates and pomegranates:

فِيهِمَا فَاكِهَةٌ وَنَخْلٌ وَرُمَّانٌ ۞

69. Then which of the favours of your Lord will you deny?

فَبِأَيِّ آلَاءِ رَبِّكُمَا تُكَذِّبَانِ ۞

70. In them will be fair (Companions), good, beautiful;-

فِيهِنَّ خَيْرَاتٌ حِسَانٌ ۞

71. Then which of the favours of your Lord will you deny?-

فَبِأَيِّ آلَاءِ رَبِّكُمَا تُكَذِّبَانِ ۞

72. Maidens restrained (as to their glances), in (goodly) pavilions.

حُورٌ مَّقْصُورَاتٌ فِي الْخِيَامِ ۞

73. Then which of the favours of your Lord will you deny?-

فَبِأَيِّ آلَاءِ رَبِّكُمَا تُكَذِّبَانِ ۞

74. Whom no man or Jinn before them has touched;-

لَمْ يَطْمِثْهُنَّ إِنسٌ قَبْلَهُمْ وَلَا جَانٌّ ۞

75. Then which of the favours of your Lord will you deny?-

فَبِأَيِّ آلَاءِ رَبِّكُمَا تُكَذِّبَانِ ۞

76. Reclining on green cushions and rich carpets of beauty.

مُتَّكِئِينَ عَلَىٰ رَفْرَفٍ خُضْرٍ وَعَبْقَرِيٍّ حِسَانٍ ۞

77. Then which of the favours of your Lord will you deny?

فَبِأَيِّ آلَاءِ رَبِّكُمَا تُكَذِّبَانِ ۞

78. Blessed be the name of your Lord, full of Majesty, Bounty and Honour.

تَبَارَكَ اسْمُ رَبِّكَ ذِي الْجَلَالِ وَالْإِكْرَامِ ۞

56. The Inevitable Event
In the name of Allah, Most Gracious, Most Merciful.

(٥٦) سُورَةُ الْوَاقِعَةِ مَكِّيَّةٌ (٩٦)

بِسْمِ اللَّهِ الرَّحْمَٰنِ الرَّحِيمِ

1. When the inevitable event comes to pass,

إِذَا وَقَعَتِ الْوَاقِعَةُ ۞

2. Then will no (soul) deny its coming.

لَيْسَ لِوَقْعَتِهَا كَاذِبَةٌ ۞

3. (Many) will it bring low; (many) will it exalt;

خَافِضَةٌ رَّافِعَةٌ ۞

4. When the earth shall be shaken to its depths,

إِذَا رُجَّتِ الْأَرْضُ رَجًّا ۞

5. And the mountains shall be crumbled to atoms,

6. Becoming dust scattered abroad,

7. And you shall be sorted out into three classes.

8. Then (there will be) the Companions of the Right Hand;— What will be the Companions of the Right Hand?

9. And the Companions of the Left Hand,—what will be the Companions of the Left Hand?

10. And those Foremost (in Faith) will be Foremost (in the Hereafter)

11. These will be those Nearest to Allah:

12. In Gardens of Bliss:

13. A number of people from those of old,

14. And a few from those of later times.

15. (They will be) on couches encrusted (with gold and precious stones),

16. Reclining on them, facing each other.

17. Round about them will (serve) youths of perpetual (freshness),

18. With goblets, (shining) beakers, and cups (filled) out of clear-flowing fountains:

19. No after-ache will they receive therefrom, nor will they suffer intoxication:

20. And with fruits, any that they may select:

21. And the flesh of fowls, any that they may desire.

22. And (there will be) Companions with beautiful, big, and lustrous eyes,—

23. Like unto Pearls well-guarded.

24. A Reward for the deeds of their past (life).

25. No frivolity will they hear therein, nor any taint of ill,-

26. Only the saying, "Peace! Peace".

27. The Companions of the Right Hand,- what will be the Companions of the Right Hand?

وَبُسَّتِ الْجِبَالُ بَسًّا ۞

فَكَانَتْ هَبَآءً مُّنْبَثًّا ۞

وَكُنْتُمْ أَزْوَاجًا ثَلٰثَةً ۞

فَأَصْحٰبُ الْمَيْمَنَةِ ۬ۙ مَآ أَصْحٰبُ

الْمَيْمَنَةِ ۞ۙ

وَأَصْحٰبُ الْمَشْئَمَةِ ۬ۙ مَآ أَصْحٰبُ

الْمَشْئَمَةِ ۞ۙ

وَالسّٰبِقُوْنَ السّٰبِقُوْنَ ۞ۙ

أُولٰٓئِكَ الْمُقَرَّبُوْنَ ۞ۚ

فِيْ جَنّٰتِ النَّعِيْمِ ۞

ثُلَّةٌ مِّنَ الْأَوَّلِيْنَ ۞ۙ

وَقَلِيْلٌ مِّنَ الْأٰخِرِيْنَ ۞ؕ

عَلٰى سُرُرٍ مَّوْضُوْنَةٍ ۞ۙ

مُّتَّكِئِيْنَ عَلَيْهَا مُتَقٰبِلِيْنَ ۞

يَطُوْفُ عَلَيْهِمْ وِلْدَانٌ مُّخَلَّدُوْنَ ۞ۙ

بِأَكْوَابٍ وَّأَبَارِيْقَ ۬ۙ وَكَأْسٍ

مِّنْ مَّعِيْنٍ ۞ۙ

لَّا يُصَدَّعُوْنَ عَنْهَا وَلَا يُنْزِفُوْنَ ۞ۙ

وَفَاكِهَةٍ مِّمَّا يَتَخَيَّرُوْنَ ۞ۙ

وَلَحْمِ طَيْرٍ مِّمَّا يَشْتَهُوْنَ ۞ؕ

وَحُوْرٌ عِيْنٌ ۞ۙ

كَأَمْثَالِ اللُّؤْلُؤِ الْمَكْنُوْنِ ۞ۚ

جَزَآءً بِمَا كَانُوْا يَعْمَلُوْنَ ۞

لَا يَسْمَعُوْنَ فِيْهَا لَغْوًا وَّلَا تَأْثِيْمًا ۞ۙ

إِلَّا قِيْلًا سَلٰمًا سَلٰمًا ۞

وَأَصْحٰبُ الْيَمِيْنِ ۬ۙ مَآ أَصْحٰبُ

28. (They will be) among lote-trees without thorns,

فِيْ سِدْرٍ مَّخْضُوْدٍ ۙ

29. Among Talh trees with flowers (or fruits) piled one above another,—

وَّطَلْحٍ مَّنْضُوْدٍ ۙ

30. In shade long-extended,

وَّظِلٍّ مَّمْدُوْدٍ ۙ

31. By water flowing constantly.

وَّمَاۤءٍ مَّسْكُوْبٍ ۙ

32. And fruit in abundance.

وَّفَاكِهَةٍ كَثِيْرَةٍ ۙ

33. Whose season is not limited, nor (supply) forbidden,

لَّا مَقْطُوْعَةٍ وَّلَا مَمْنُوْعَةٍ ۙ

34. And on Thrones (of Dignity), raised high.

وَّفُرُشٍ مَّرْفُوْعَةٍ ؕ

35. We have created them a (new) creation.

إِنَّاۤ أَنْشَأْنٰهُنَّ إِنْشَاۤءً ۙ

36. And made them virgin–pure (and undefiled),—

فَجَعَلْنٰهُنَّ أَبْكَارًا ۙ

37. Beloved (by nature), equal in age-

عُرُبًا أَتْرَابًا ۙ

38. For the Companions of the Right Hand.

لِّأَصْحٰبِ الْيَمِيْنِ ؕ

39. A (goodly) number from those of old,

ثُلَّةٌ مِّنَ الْأَوَّلِيْنَ ۙ

40. And a (goodly) number from those of later times.

وَثُلَّةٌ مِّنَ الْأٰخِرِيْنَ ؕ

41. The Companions of the Left Hand,- what will be the Companions of the Left Hand?

وَأَصْحٰبُ الشِّمَالِ ۙ مَاۤ أَصْحٰبُ الشِّمَالِ ؕ

42. In scorching wind and scalding water.

فِيْ سَمُوْمٍ وَّحَمِيْمٍ ۙ

43. And in the shades of Black Smoke:

وَّظِلٍّ مِّنْ يَّحْمُوْمٍ ۙ

44. Nothing (will there be) to refresh, nor to please:

لَّا بَارِدٍ وَّلَا كَرِيْمٍ ۝

45. For that they were wont to be indulged, before that, in wealth and luxury,

إِنَّهُمْ كَانُوْا قَبْلَ ذٰلِكَ مُتْرَفِيْنَ ۚ

46. And persisted obstinately in supreme wickedness!

وَكَانُوْا يُصِرُّوْنَ عَلَى الْحِنْثِ الْعَظِيْمِ ۚ

47. And they used to say, "What! when we die and become dust and bones, shall we then indeed be raised up again?-

وَكَانُوْا يَقُوْلُوْنَ ەۙ أَئِذَا مِتْنَا وَكُنَّا تُرَابًا وَّعِظَامًا ءَإِنَّا لَمَبْعُوْثُوْنَ ۙ

48. "(We) and our fathers of old?"

أَوَ اٰبَاۤؤُنَا الْأَوَّلُوْنَ ۝

49. Say: "Yes, those of old and those of later times,

قُلْ إِنَّ الْأَوَّلِيْنَ وَالْأٰخِرِيْنَ ۙ

50. "All will certainly be gathered together for the meeting appointed for a Day well-known.

لَمَجْمُوعُوْنَ ۙ إِلَىٰ مِيْقَاتِ يَوْمٍ مَّعْلُوْمٍ ۞

51. "Then will you truly,– O you that go wrong, and deny (the Truth)

ثُمَّ إِنَّكُمْ أَيُّهَا الضَّآلُّوْنَ الْمُكَذِّبُوْنَ ۞

52. "You will surely taste of the Tree of Zaqqum.

لَأَكِلُوْنَ مِنْ شَجَرٍ مِّنْ زَقُّوْمٍ ۞

53. "Then will you fill your insides therewith,

فَمَالِئُوْنَ مِنْهَا الْبُطُوْنَ ۞

54. "And drink Boiling Water on top of it:

فَشَارِبُوْنَ عَلَيْهِ مِنَ الْحَمِيْمِ ۞

55. "Indeed you shall drink like diseased camels raging with thirst!".

فَشَارِبُوْنَ شُرْبَ الْهِيْمِ ۞

56. This will be their welcome on the Day of Judgment.

هٰذَا نُزُلُهُمْ يَوْمَ الدِّيْنِ ۞

57. It is We Who have created you: why will you not admit the Truth?

نَحْنُ خَلَقْنٰكُمْ فَلَوْلَا تُصَدِّقُوْنَ ۞

58. Do you then see? the (human seed) that you throw out,–

أَفَرَءَيْتُمْ مَّا تُمْنُوْنَ ۞

59. Is it you who create it, or are We the Creators?

ءَأَنْتُمْ تَخْلُقُوْنَهٗ أَمْ نَحْنُ الْخٰلِقُوْنَ ۞

60. We have decreed Death to be your common lot, and We are not to be frustrated-

نَحْنُ قَدَّرْنَا بَيْنَكُمُ الْمَوْتَ وَمَا نَحْنُ بِمَسْبُوْقِيْنَ ۞

61. from changing your Forms and creating you (again) in (forms) that you do not know.

عَلَىٰ أَنْ نُّبَدِّلَ أَمْثَالَكُمْ وَنُنْشِئَكُمْ فِيْ مَا لَا تَعْلَمُوْنَ ۞

62. And you certainly know already the first form of creation: why then do you not celebrate His praises?

وَلَقَدْ عَلِمْتُمُ النَّشْأَةَ الْأُوْلٰى فَلَوْلَا تَذَكَّرُوْنَ ۞

63. Do you see the seed that you sow in the ground?

أَفَرَءَيْتُمْ مَّا تَحْرُثُوْنَ ۞

64. Is it you that cause it to grow, or are We the Cause?

ءَأَنْتُمْ تَزْرَعُوْنَهٗ أَمْ نَحْنُ الزَّارِعُوْنَ ۞

65. Were it Our Will, We could make it broken orts. And you would be left in wonderment,

لَوْ نَشَآءُ لَجَعَلْنٰهُ حُطَامًا فَظَلْتُمْ تَفَكَّهُوْنَ ۞

66. (Saying), "We are indeed left with debts (for nothing):

إِنَّا لَمُغْرَمُوْنَ ۞

67. "Indeed are we shut out (of the fruits of our labour)"

بَلْ نَحْنُ مَحْرُوْمُوْنَ ۞

68. Do you see the water which you drink?

أَفَرَءَيْتُمُ الْمَآءَ الَّذِيْ تَشْرَبُوْنَ ۞

69. Do you bring it down (in rain) from the cloud or do We?

ءَأَنْتُمْ أَنْزَلْتُمُوْهُ مِنَ الْمُزْنِ أَمْ نَحْنُ الْمُنْزِلُوْنَ ۞

70. Were it Our Will, We could make it salt (and unpalatable): then why do you not give thanks?

71. Do you see the Fire which you kindle?

72. Is it you who grow the tree which feeds the fire, or do We grow it?

73. We have made it a memorial (of Our handiwork), and an article of comfort and convenience for the denizens of deserts.

74. Then celebrate with praises the name of your Lord, the Supreme!

75. Furthermore I call to witness the setting of the Stars,-

76. And! that is indeed a tremendous oath, if you but knew—

77. That this is indeed a Qur'an Most Honourable,

78. In a Book well-guarded,

79. Which none shall touch but those who are clean:

80. A Revelation from the Lord of the Worlds.

81. Is it such a Message that you would hold in light esteem?

82. And have you made it your livelihood that you should declare it false?

83. Then why do you not (intervene) when (the soul of the dying man) reaches the throat,—

84. And you the while (sit) looking on,-

85. But We are nearer to him than you, and yet do not see ,-

86. Then why do you not,—if you are exempt from (future) account,—

87. Call back the soul, if you are true (in your claim of Independence)?

88. Thus, then, if he be of those Nearest to Allah,

89. (There is for him) Rest and Satisfaction, and a Garden of Delights. .

90. And if he be of the Companions of the Right Hand,

91. (For him is the salutation), "Peace be unto you", from the Companions of the Right Hand.

لَوْ نَشَآءُ جَعَلْنَٰهُ أُجَاجًا فَلَوْلَا تَشْكُرُونَ ۝

أَفَرَءَيْتُمُ النَّارَ الَّتِى تُورُونَ ۝

ءَأَنتُمْ أَنشَأْتُمْ شَجَرَتَهَآ أَمْ نَحْنُ الْمُنشِـُٔونَ ۝

نَحْنُ جَعَلْنَٰهَا تَذْكِرَةً وَمَتَٰعًا لِّلْمُقْوِينَ ۝

فَسَبِّحْ بِاسْمِ رَبِّكَ الْعَظِيمِ ۝

فَلَآ أُقْسِمُ بِمَوَٰقِعِ النُّجُومِ ۝

وَإِنَّهُۥ لَقَسَمٌ لَّوْ تَعْلَمُونَ عَظِيمٌ ۝

إِنَّهُۥ لَقُرْءَانٌ كَرِيمٌ ۝

فِى كِتَٰبٍ مَّكْنُونٍ ۝

لَّا يَمَسُّهُۥٓ إِلَّا الْمُطَهَّرُونَ ۝

تَنزِيلٌ مِّن رَّبِّ الْعَٰلَمِينَ ۝

أَفَبِهَٰذَا الْحَدِيثِ أَنتُم مُّدْهِنُونَ ۝

وَتَجْعَلُونَ رِزْقَكُمْ أَنَّكُمْ تُكَذِّبُونَ ۝

فَلَوْلَآ إِذَا بَلَغَتِ الْحُلْقُومَ ۝

وَأَنتُمْ حِينَئِذٍ تَنظُرُونَ ۝

وَنَحْنُ أَقْرَبُ إِلَيْهِ مِنكُمْ وَلَٰكِن لَّا تُبْصِرُونَ ۝

فَلَوْلَآ إِن كُنتُمْ غَيْرَ مَدِينِينَ ۝

تَرْجِعُونَهَآ إِن كُنتُمْ صَٰدِقِينَ ۝

فَأَمَّآ إِن كَانَ مِنَ الْمُقَرَّبِينَ ۝

فَرَوْحٌ وَرَيْحَانٌ وَجَنَّتُ نَعِيمٍ ۝

وَأَمَّآ إِن كَانَ مِنْ أَصْحَٰبِ الْيَمِينِ ۝

فَسَلَٰمٌ لَّكَ مِنْ أَصْحَٰبِ الْيَمِينِ ۝

SÛRAH-57
AL-ḤADÎD
(INTRODUCTION)

We have now studied the contents of nearly nine-tenths of the Qur'ân. We have found that the arrangement of the Sûras in the present Text is not haphazard, but that they follow a distinct logical order more he'plul for study than the chronological order. The comprehensive scheme of building up the new *Ummat* or Brotherhood and its spiritual implications is now complete. The remaining tenth of the Qur'an may bo roughly considered in two parts The first contains ten Sûras (S. 57 to 66), all revealed in Madinah, and each dealing with some special point which needs emphasis in the social life Of the Ummat. The second (S. 67 to S. 114) contains shop Makkan lyrics, each dealing with some aspect of spiritual life, expressed in language of great mystic beauty.

The present Madinah Sûrah is chiefly concerned with spiritual humility and the avoidance of arrogance, and a warning that retirement from the world may not be the best way of seeking the good pleasure of Allah. Its probable date is after the Conquest of Makkah, A.H. 8.

92. And if he be of those who treat (Truth) as Falsehood, who go wrong,

93. For him is Entertainment with Boiling Water.

94. And burning in Hell-Fire.

95. Verily, this is the very Truth of assured certainty.

96. So celebrate with praises the name of your Lord, the Supreme.

57. Iron

In the name of Allah, Most Gracious, Most Merciful.

1. Whatever is in the heavens and on the earth glorifies Allah; and He is the Mighty, the Wise.

2. To Him belongs the dominion of the heavens and the earth: it is He Who gives Life and Death; and He has Power over all things.

3. He is the First and the Last, the Evident and theHidden: and He has full knowledge of all things.

4. He it is Who created the heavens and the earth in Six Days, and is moreover firmly established on the Throne (of Authority). He knows what enters within the earth and what comes forth out of it, what comes down from heaven and what mounts up to it. And He is with you wheresoever you may be. And Allah sees well all that you do.

5. To Him belongs the dominion of the heavens and the earth: and all affairs are referred back to Allah.

6. He merges Night into Day, and He merges Day into Night; and He has full knowledge of the secrets of (all) hearts.

7.   Believe in Allah and His Apostle, and spend (in charity) out of the (substance) whereof He has made you heirs. For, those of you who believe and spend (in charity),- for them is a great Reward.

8.   What cause do you have why you should not believe in Allah?- and the Apostle invites you to believe in your Lord, and has indeed taken your Covenant, if you are men of Faith.

9.   He is the One Who sends to His Servant Manifest Signs, that He may lead you from the depths of Darkness into the Light and verily Allah is to you most kind and Merciful.

10.   And what cause do you have why you should not spend in the cause of Allah? For to Allah belongs the heritage of the heavens and the earth. Not equal among you are those who spent (freely) and fought, before the Victory, (with those who did so later). Those are higher in rank than those who spent (freely) and fought afterwards. But to all has Allah promised a goodly (reward). And Allah is well acquainted with all that you do.

11.   Who is he that will loan to Allah a beautiful loan? for (Allah) will increase it manifold to his credit, and he will have (besides) a liberal reward.

12.   One Day you will see the believing men and the believing women- how their Light runs forward before them and by their right hands: (their greeting will be): "Good News for you this Day! Gardens beneath which flow rivers to dwell therein for ever! This is indeed the highest Achievement!"

آمِنُوْا بِاللّٰهِ وَرَسُوْلِهٖ وَاَنْفِقُوْا مِمَّا جَعَلَكُمْ مُّسْتَخْلَفِيْنَ فِيْهِ ۚ فَالَّذِيْنَ اٰمَنُوْا مِنْكُمْ وَاَنْفَقُوْا لَهُمْ اَجْرٌ كَبِيْرٌ ۝

وَمَا لَكُمْ لَا تُؤْمِنُوْنَ بِاللّٰهِ ۚ وَ الرَّسُوْلُ يَدْعُوْكُمْ لِتُؤْمِنُوْا بِرَبِّكُمْ وَقَدْ اَخَذَ مِيْثَاقَكُمْ اِنْ كُنْتُمْ مُّؤْمِنِيْنَ ۝

هُوَ الَّذِيْ يُنَزِّلُ عَلٰى عَبْدِهٖ اٰيٰتٍۢ بَيِّنٰتٍ لِّيُخْرِجَكُمْ مِّنَ الظُّلُمٰتِ اِلَى النُّوْرِ ۚ وَاِنَّ اللّٰهَ بِكُمْ لَرَءُوْفٌ رَّحِيْمٌ ۝

وَمَا لَكُمْ اَلَّا تُنْفِقُوْا فِيْ سَبِيْلِ اللّٰهِ وَلِلّٰهِ مِيْرَاثُ السَّمٰوٰتِ وَالْاَرْضِ ۚ لَا يَسْتَوِيْ مِنْكُمْ مَّنْ اَنْفَقَ مِنْ قَبْلِ الْفَتْحِ وَقَاتَلَ ۚ اُولٰٓئِكَ اَعْظَمُ دَرَجَةً مِّنَ الَّذِيْنَ اَنْفَقُوْا مِنْۢ بَعْدُ وَ قَاتَلُوْا ۚ وَكُلًّا وَّعَدَ اللّٰهُ الْحُسْنٰى ۚ وَاللّٰهُ بِمَا تَعْمَلُوْنَ خَبِيْرٌ ۝

مَنْ ذَا الَّذِيْ يُقْرِضُ اللّٰهَ قَرْضًا حَسَنًا فَيُضٰعِفَهٗ لَهٗ وَلَهٗٓ اَجْرٌ كَرِيْمٌ ۝

يَوْمَ تَرَى الْمُؤْمِنِيْنَ وَالْمُؤْمِنٰتِ يَسْعٰى نُوْرُهُمْ بَيْنَ اَيْدِيْهِمْ وَبِاَيْمَانِهِمْ بُشْرٰىكُمُ الْيَوْمَ جَنّٰتٌ تَجْرِيْ مِنْ تَحْتِهَا الْاَنْهٰرُ خٰلِدِيْنَ فِيْهَا ۚ ذٰلِكَ هُوَ الْفَوْزُ الْعَظِيْمُ ۝

13. One Day will the Hypocrites- men and women - say to the Believers: "Wait for us! Let us borrow (a light) from your Light!" It will be said: "You turn back to your rear! then seek a Light (where you can)!" So a wall will be put up between them, with a gate therein. Within it will be Mercy throughout, and without it, all alongside, will be (Wrath and) Punishment!

14. (Those without) will call out, "Were we not with you?" (The others) will reply, "True! but you led yourselves into temptation; you looked forward (to our ruin); you doubted (Allah's Promise); and (your false) desires deceived you; until there issued the Command of Allah. And the Deceiver deceived you in respect of Allah.

15. "This Day shall no ransom be accepted of you, nor of those who rejected Allah." Your abode is the Fire: that is the proper place to claim you: and an evil refuge it is!"

16. Has not the time arrived for the Believers that their hearts in all humility should engage in the remembrance of Allah and of the Truth which has been revealed (to them), and that they should not become like those to whom was given Revelation aforetime, but long ages passed over them and their hearts grew hard? For many among them are rebellious transgressors.

17. You (all) know that Allah gives life to the earth after its death! already have We shown the Signs plainly to you, that you may learn wisdom.

18. For those who give in charity, men and women, and loan to Allah a beautiful loan, it shall be increased manifold (to their credit), and they shall have (besides) a liberal reward.

19. And those who believe in Allah and His Apostles- they are the Sincere (lovers of Truth), and the witnesses (who testify), in the eyes of their Lord: they shall have their Reward and their Light. But those who reject Allah and deny Our Signs,- they are the Companions of Hell-Fire.

20. You (all) know that the life of this world is but play and amusement, pomp and mutual boasting and multiplying, (in rivalry) among yourselves, riches and children. Here is a similitude: how rain and the growth which it brings forth, delight (the hearts of) the tillers; soon it withers; you will see it grow yellow; then it becomes dry and crumbles away. But in the Hereafter is a Chastisement severe (for the devotees of wrong). And Forgiveness from Allah and (His) Good Pleasure (for the devotees of Allah). And what is the life of this world, but goods and chattels of deception?

21. You be foremost (in seeking) Forgiveness from your Lord, and a Garden (of Bliss), the width whereof is as the width of heaven and earth, prepared for those who believe in Allah and His Apostles: that is the Grace of Allah, which He bestows on whom He pleases: and Allah is the Lord of Grace abounding.

22. No misfortune can happen on earth or in your souls but is recorded in a decree before We bring it into existence: that is truly easy for Allah:

23. In order that you may not despair over matters that pass you by, nor exult over favours bestowed upon you. For Allah

وَالَّذِينَ اٰمَنُوا بِاللهِ وَرُسُلِهٖ أُولٰٓئِكَ

هُمُ الصِّدِّيقُوۡنَ ۖ وَالشُّهَدَآءُ عِنۡدَ

رَبِّهِمۡ ۖ لَهُمۡ أَجۡرُهُمۡ وَنُورُهُمۡ ۖ

وَالَّذِينَ كَفَرُوا وَكَذَّبُوا بِاٰيٰتِنَا

أُولٰٓئِكَ أَصۡحٰبُ الۡجَحِيۡمِ ۞

اِعۡلَمُوٓا أَنَّمَا الۡحَيٰوةُ الدُّنۡيَا

لَعِبٌ وَلَهۡوٌ وَزِينَةٌ وَتَفَاخُرٌ

بَيۡنَكُمۡ وَتَكَاثُرٌ فِي الۡأَمۡوَالِ

وَالۡأَوۡلَادِ ۖ كَمَثَلِ غَيۡثٍ أَعۡجَبَ

الۡكُفَّارَ نَبَاتُهٗ ثُمَّ يَهِيۡجُ فَتَرٰىهُ

مُصۡفَرًّا ثُمَّ يَكُوۡنُ حُطَامًا ۖ

وَفِي الۡأٰخِرَةِ عَذَابٌ شَدِيۡدٌ ۖ وَ

مَغۡفِرَةٌ مِّنَ اللهِ وَرِضۡوَانٌ ۖ وَمَا

الۡحَيٰوةُ الدُّنۡيَا إِلَّا مَتَاعُ الۡغُرُوۡرِ ۞

سَابِقُوٓا إِلٰى مَغۡفِرَةٍ مِّنۡ رَّبِّكُمۡ

وَجَنَّةٍ عَرۡضُهَا كَعَرۡضِ السَّمَآءِ

وَالۡأَرۡضِ ۖ أُعِدَّتۡ لِلَّذِينَ

اٰمَنُوا بِاللهِ وَرُسُلِهٖ ۖ ذٰلِكَ

فَضۡلُ اللهِ يُؤۡتِيۡهِ مَنۡ يَّشَآءُ ۖ

وَاللهُ ذُو الۡفَضۡلِ الۡعَظِيۡمِ ۞

مَآ أَصَابَ مِنۡ مُّصِيۡبَةٍ فِي

الۡأَرۡضِ وَلَا فِيۡ أَنۡفُسِكُمۡ إِلَّا

فِيۡ كِتٰبٍ مِّنۡ قَبۡلِ أَنۡ نَّبۡرَأَهَا ۚ

إِنَّ ذٰلِكَ عَلَى اللهِ يَسِيۡرٌ ۞

لِكَيۡلَا تَأۡسَوۡا عَلٰى مَا فَاتَكُمۡ

وَلَا تَفۡرَحُوا بِمَآ اٰتٰىكُمۡ ۖ وَاللهُ

does not love any vainglorious boaster,-

24. Such persons as are covetous and commend covetousness to men. And if any turn back (from Allah's Way), verily Allah is Free of all needs, Worthy of all Praise.

25. We sent aforetime Our Apostles with Clear Signs and sent down with them the Book and the Balance (of Right and Wrong), that men may stand forth in justice; and We sent down Iron, in which is (material for) mighty war, as well as many benefits for mankind, that Allah may test who it is that will help, unseen, Him and His Apostles: for Allah is Full of Strength, Exalted in Might (and able to enforce His Will).

26. And We sent Noah and Abraham, and established in their line Prophethood and Revelation: and some of them were on right guidance. But many of them became rebellious transgressors.

27. Then, in their wake, We followed them up with (others of) Our Apostles: We sent after them Jesus the son of Mary, and bestowed on him the Gospel; and We ordained in the hearts of those who followed him compassion and mercy. But the Monasticism which they invented for themselves, We did not prescribe for them: (We commanded) only the seeking for the Good Pleasure of Allah; but that they did not foster as they should have done. Yet We bestowed, on those among them who believed, their (due) reward, but many of them are rebellious transgressors.

28. O you that believe! Fear Allah, and believe in His Apostle, and He will bestow on you a double portion

لَا يُحِبُّ كُلَّ مُخْتَالٍ فَخُورٍ ۙ

الَّذِينَ يَبْخَلُوْنَ وَيَأْمُرُوْنَ النَّاسَ بِالْبُخْلِ ۚ وَمَنْ يَّتَوَلَّ فَاِنَّ اللّٰهَ هُوَ الْغَنِيُّ الْحَمِيْدُ ۟

لَقَدْ اَرْسَلْنَا رُسُلَنَا بِالْبَيِّنٰتِ وَ اَنْزَلْنَا مَعَهُمُ الْكِتٰبَ وَ الْمِيْزَانَ لِيَقُوْمَ النَّاسُ بِالْقِسْطِ ۚ وَ اَنْزَلْنَا الْحَدِيْدَ فِيْهِ بَأْسٌ شَدِيْدٌ وَّمَنَافِعُ لِلنَّاسِ وَلِيَعْلَمَ اللّٰهُ مَنْ يَّنْصُرُهُ وَرُسُلَهُ بِالْغَيْبِ ۚ اِنَّ اللّٰهَ قَوِيٌّ عَزِيْزٌ ۟

وَلَقَدْ اَرْسَلْنَا نُوْحًا وَّاِبْرٰهِيْمَ وَجَعَلْنَا فِيْ ذُرِّيَّتِهِمَا النُّبُوَّةَ وَالْكِتٰبَ فَمِنْهُمْ مُّهْتَدٍ ۚ وَكَثِيْرٌ مِّنْهُمْ فٰسِقُوْنَ ۟

ثُمَّ قَفَّيْنَا عَلٰۤى اٰثَارِهِمْ بِرُسُلِنَا وَقَفَّيْنَا بِعِيْسَى ابْنِ مَرْيَمَ وَاٰتَيْنٰهُ الْاِنْجِيْلَ ۙ وَجَعَلْنَا فِيْ قُلُوْبِ الَّذِيْنَ اتَّبَعُوْهُ رَأْفَةً وَّرَحْمَةً ۭ وَ رَهْبَانِيَّةَ ۨ ابْتَدَعُوْهَا مَا كَتَبْنٰهَا عَلَيْهِمْ اِلَّا ابْتِغَآءَ رِضْوَانِ اللّٰهِ فَمَا رَعَوْهَا حَقَّ رِعَايَتِهَا ۚ فَاٰتَيْنَا الَّذِيْنَ اٰمَنُوْا مِنْهُمْ اَجْرَهُمْ ۚ وَ كَثِيْرٌ مِّنْهُمْ فٰسِقُوْنَ ۟

يٰۤاَيُّهَا الَّذِيْنَ اٰمَنُوا اتَّقُوا اللّٰهَ وَاٰمِنُوْا بِرَسُوْلِهٖ يُؤْتِكُمْ كِفْلَيْنِ

SÛRAH-58
AL-MUJÂDILAH
(INTRODUCTION)

This is the second of the ten Madinah Sûras referred to in the Introduction to the last Sûrah. Its subject-matter is the acceptance of a women's Plea on behalf of herself and her children and a condemnation of all secret counsels and intrigues in the Muslim Brotherhood.

The date is somewhat close to that of S. 33, say between A H. 5. and A. H.7.

of His Mercy: He will provide for you a Light by which you shall walk (straight in your path), and He will forgive you (your past): for Allah is Oft-Forgiving, Most Merciful.

29. That the People of the Book may know that they have no power whatever over the Grace of Allah, that (His) Grace is (entirely) in His Hand, to bestow it on whomsoever He wills. For Allah is the Lord of Grace abounding.

58. The Women Who Pleads
In the name of Allah, Most Gracious, Most Merciful.

1. Allah has indeed heard (and accepted) the statement of the woman who pleads with you concerning her husband and carries her complaint (in prayer) to Allah: and Allah (always) hears the arguments between both sides among you: for Allah hears and sees (all things).

2. If any men among you divorce their wives by Zihar (calling them mothers), they cannot be their mothers: none can be their mothers except those who gave them birth. And in fact they use words (both) iniquitous and false: but truly Allah is One that blots out (sins), and forgives (again and again).

3. But those who divorce their wives by Zihar, then wish to go back on the words they uttered,- (It is ordained that such a one) should free a slave before they touch each other: this you are admonished to perform: and Allah is well-acquainted with (all) that you do.

4. And if any has not (the wherewithal), he should fast for two months consecutively before they touch each other. But if any is unable to do so, he should feed sixty indigent ones, this, that you may show your faith in Allah and His Apostle.

Those are limits (set by) Allah. For those who reject (Him), there is a grievous Chastisement.

5.   Those who resist Allah and His Apostle will be humbled to dust, as were those before them: for We have already sent down Clear Signs. And the Unbelievers (will have) a humiliating Chastisement,-

6.   On the Day that Allah will raise them all up (again) and show them the Truth (and meaning) of their conduct. Allah has reckoned its (value), though they may have forgotten it, for Allah is Witness to all things.

7.   Don't you see that Allah knows (all) that is in the heavens and on earth? There is not a secret consultation between three, but He makes the fourth among them, - Nor between five but He makes the sixth,- nor between fewer nor more, but He is in their midst, wheresoever they be: in the end He will tell them the truth of their conduct, on the Day of Judgment. For Allah has full knowledge of all things.

8.   Don't you turn your sight towards those who were forbidden secret counsels yet revert to that which they were forbidden (to do)? And they hold secret counsels among themselves for iniquity and hostility, and disobedience to the Apostle. And when they come to you, they salute you, not as Allah salutes you, (but in crooked ways): and they say to themselves, "Why does not Allah punish us for our words?" Enough for them is Hell: in it they will burn, and evil is that destination!

9.   O you who believe! When you hold secret counsel, do not do it for iniquity and hostility, and disobedience to the Prophet; but do it for righteousness

and self- restraint; and fear Allah, to Whom you shall be brought back.

10. Secret counsels are only (inspired) by the Evil One, in order that he may cause grief to the Believers; but he cannot harm them in the least, except as Allah permits; and on Allah let the Believers put their trust.

11. O you who believe! When you are told to make room in the assemblies, (spread out and) make room: (ample) room will Allah provide for you. And when you are told to rise up, rise up, Allah will raise up, to (suitable) ranks (and degrees) those of you who believe and who have been granted (mystic) Knowledge. And Allah is well- acquainted with all you do.

12. O you who believe! When you consult the Apostle in private, spend something in charity before your private consultation. That will be best for you, and most conducive to purity (of conduct). But if you do not find (the wherewithal), Allah is Oft- Forgiving, Most Merciful.

13. Is it that you are afraid of spending sums in charity before your private consultation (with him)? If, then, you do not so, and Allah forgives you, then (at least) establish regular prayer; practise regular charity; and obey Allah and His Apostle. And Allah is well-acquainted with all that you do.

14. Don't you turn your attention to those who turn (in friendship) to such as have the Wrath of Allah upon them? They are neither of you nor of them, and they swear to falsehood knowingly.

15. Allah has prepared for them a severe Chastisement: evil indeed are their deeds.

أَعَدَّ اللّٰهُ لَهُمْ عَذَابًا شَدِيْدًا ۖ إِنَّهُمْ سَآءَ مَا كَانُوْا يَعْمَلُوْنَ ۞

16. They have made their oaths a screen (for their misdeeds): thus they obstruct (men) from the Path of Allah: therefore they shall have a humiliating Chastisement.

اِتَّخَذُوْۤا اَيْمَانَهُمْ جُنَّةً فَصَدُّوْا عَنْ سَبِيْلِ اللّٰهِ فَلَهُمْ عَذَابٌ مُّهِيْنٌ ۞

17. Of no profit whatever to them, against Allah, will be their riches nor their sons: they will be Companions of the Fire, to dwell therein (for ever)!

لَنْ تُغْنِيَ عَنْهُمْ اَمْوَالُهُمْ وَلَاۤ اَوْلَادُهُمْ مِّنَ اللّٰهِ شَيْئًا ۖ اُولٰٓئِكَ اَصْحَابُ النَّارِ هُمْ فِيْهَا خَالِدُوْنَ ۞

18. One day Allah will raise them all up (for Judgment): then will they swear to Him as they swear to you: and they think that they have something (to stand upon). No, indeed! they are but liars!

يَوْمَ يَبْعَثُهُمُ اللّٰهُ جَمِيْعًا فَيَحْلِفُوْنَ لَهٗ كَمَا يَحْلِفُوْنَ لَكُمْ وَ يَحْسَبُوْنَ اَنَّهُمْ عَلٰى شَيْءٍ ۖ اَلَاۤ اِنَّهُمْ هُمُ الْكٰذِبُوْنَ ۞

19. The Evil One has got the better of them: so he has made them lose the remembrance of Allah. They are the Party of the Evil One. Truly, it is the Party of the Evil One that will perish!

اِسْتَحْوَذَ عَلَيْهِمُ الشَّيْطٰنُ فَاَنْسٰهُمْ ذِكْرَ اللّٰهِ ۖ اُولٰٓئِكَ حِزْبُ الشَّيْطٰنِ ۖ اَلَاۤ اِنَّ حِزْبَ الشَّيْطٰنِ هُمُ الْخٰسِرُوْنَ ۞

20. Those who resist Allah and His Apostle will be among those most humiliated.

اِنَّ الَّذِيْنَ يُحَآدُّوْنَ اللّٰهَ وَرَسُوْلَهٗۤ اُولٰٓئِكَ فِى الْاَذَلِّيْنَ ۞

21. Allah has decreed: "It is I and My Apostles who must prevail": for Allah is One full of strength, able to enforce His Will.

كَتَبَ اللّٰهُ لَاَغْلِبَنَّ اَنَا وَرُسُلِيْ ۚ اِنَّ اللّٰهَ قَوِيٌّ عَزِيْزٌ ۞

22. You will not find any people who believe in Allah and the Last Day, loving those who resist Allah and His Apostle, even though they were their fathers or their sons, or their brothers, or their kindred. For such He has written Faith in their hearts, and strengthened them with a spirit from Himself. And He will admit them to Gardens beneath which Rivers flow, to dwell therein (for ever). Allah will be well pleased with them, and they with Him. They are the Party of

لَا تَجِدُ قَوْمًا يُّؤْمِنُوْنَ بِاللّٰهِ وَالْيَوْمِ الْاٰخِرِ يُوَآدُّوْنَ مَنْ حَآدَّ اللّٰهَ وَ رَسُوْلَهٗ وَلَوْ كَانُوْۤا اٰبَآءَهُمْ اَوْ اَبْنَآءَهُمْ اَوْ اِخْوَانَهُمْ اَوْ عَشِيْرَتَهُمْ ۚ اُولٰٓئِكَ كَتَبَ فِيْ قُلُوْبِهِمُ الْاِيْمَانَ وَاَيَّدَهُمْ بِرُوْحٍ مِّنْهُ ۖ وَيُدْخِلُهُمْ جَنّٰتٍ تَجْرِيْ مِنْ تَحْتِهَا الْاَنْهٰرُ خٰلِدِيْنَ فِيْهَا ۚ رَضِيَ اللّٰهُ عَنْهُمْ وَرَضُوْا عَنْهُ ۚ اُولٰٓئِكَ حِزْبُ

SÛRAH-59
AL-ḤASHR
(INTRODUCTION)

This is the third of the series often short Madinah Sûras, dealing each with a special point in the life of the Ummat: see Introduction to S. 57. The special theme here is how treachery to the Ummat on the pan of it' enemies recoils on the enemies themselves, while it strengthens the bond between the different sections of the Ummat itself, and this is illustrated by the story of the expulsion of the Jewish tribe of the Band Nadhîr in Rabî || I. A. H .4.

This fixes the date of the sûrah.

Allah. Truly it is the Party of Allah that will achieve Felicity.

59. The Gathering

In the name of Allah, Most Gracious, Most Merciful.

1. Whatever is in the heavens and on earth, let it declare the Praises and Glory of Allah: for He is the Exalted in Might, the Wise.

2. It is He Who got out the Unbelievers among the People of the Book from their homes at the first gathering (of the forces). Little did you think that they would get out: and they thought that their fortresses would defend them from Allah! But the (Wrath of) Allah came to them from quarters from which they little expected (it), and cast terror into their hearts, so that they destroyed their dwellings by their own hands and the hands of the Believers. Take warning, then, O you with eyes (to see)!

3. And had it not been that Allah had decreed banishment for them, He would certainly have punished them in this world: and in the Hereafter they shall (certainly) have the Punishment of the Fire.

4. That is because they resisted Allah and His Apostle: and if any one resists Allah, verily Allah is severe in Punishment.

5. Whether you cut down (O you Muslims) the tender palm-trees, or you left them standing on their roots, it was by leave of Allah, and in order that He might cover with shame the rebellious transgressors.

6. What Allah has bestowed on His Apostle (and taken away) from them - for this you made no expedition with either cavalry or camelry: but Allah gives power to His Apostles over any He pleases: and Allah has power over all things.

7. What Allah has bestowed on His Apostle (and taken away) from the people of the townships,- belongs to Allah,- to His Apostle and to kindred and orphans, the needy and the wayfarer; In order that it may not (merely) make a circuit between the wealthy among you. So take what the Apostle assigns to you, and deny yourselves that which he withholds from you. And fear Allah; for Allah is strict in Punishment.

مَا أَفَاءَ اللَّهُ عَلَى رَسُولِهِ مِنْ أَهْلِ
الْقُرَى فَلِلَّهِ وَلِلرَّسُولِ وَلِذِي الْقُرْبَى
وَالْيَتَامَى وَالْمَسَاكِينِ وَابْنِ السَّبِيلِ
كَيْ لَا يَكُونَ دُولَةً بَيْنَ الْأَغْنِيَاءِ
مِنْكُمْ ۚ وَمَا آتَاكُمُ الرَّسُولُ فَخُذُوهُ
وَمَا نَهَاكُمْ عَنْهُ فَانْتَهُوا ۚ وَاتَّقُوا
اللَّهَ ۖ إِنَّ اللَّهَ شَدِيدُ الْعِقَابِ ۞

8. (Some part is due) to the indigent Muhajirs, those who were expelled from their homes and their property, while seeking Grace from Allah and (His) Good Pleasure, and aiding Allah and His Apostle: such are indeed the sincere ones:-

لِلْفُقَرَاءِ الْمُهَاجِرِينَ الَّذِينَ أُخْرِجُوا
مِنْ دِيَارِهِمْ وَأَمْوَالِهِمْ يَبْتَغُونَ
فَضْلًا مِنَ اللَّهِ وَرِضْوَانًا وَّ
يَنْصُرُونَ اللَّهَ وَرَسُولَهُ ۚ أُولَٰئِكَ
هُمُ الصَّادِقُونَ ۞

9. But those who before them, had homes (in Medina) and had adopted the Faith,- show their affection to such as came to them for refuge, and entertain no desire in their hearts for things given to the (latter), but give them preference over themselves, even though poverty was their (own lot). And those saved from the covetousness of their own souls,- they are the ones that achieve prosperity.

وَالَّذِينَ تَبَوَّءُو الدَّارَ وَالْإِيمَانَ
مِنْ قَبْلِهِمْ يُحِبُّونَ مَنْ هَاجَرَ
إِلَيْهِمْ وَلَا يَجِدُونَ فِي صُدُورِهِمْ
حَاجَةً مِمَّا أُوتُوا وَيُؤْثِرُونَ عَلَىٰ
أَنْفُسِهِمْ وَلَوْ كَانَ بِهِمْ خَصَاصَةٌ ۚ
وَمَنْ يُوقَ شُحَّ نَفْسِهِ فَأُولَٰئِكَ
هُمُ الْمُفْلِحُونَ ۞

10. And those who came after them say: "Our Lord! Forgive us, and our brethren who came before us into the Faith, and leave not, in our hearts, rancour (or sense of injury) against those who have believed. Our Lord! You are indeed Full of Kindness, Most Merciful."

وَالَّذِينَ جَاءُو مِنْ بَعْدِهِمْ يَقُولُونَ
رَبَّنَا اغْفِرْ لَنَا وَلِإِخْوَانِنَا الَّذِينَ
سَبَقُونَا بِالْإِيمَانِ وَلَا تَجْعَلْ فِي
قُلُوبِنَا غِلًّا لِلَّذِينَ آمَنُوا رَبَّنَا إِنَّكَ
رَءُوفٌ رَّحِيمٌ ۞

11. Have you not observed the Hypocrites say to their misbelieving brethren among the

أَلَمْ تَرَ إِلَى الَّذِينَ نَافَقُوا يَقُولُونَ
لِإِخْوَانِهِمُ الَّذِينَ كَفَرُوا مِنْ

People of the Book? - "If you are expelled, we too will go out with you, and we will never hearken to any one in your affair; and if you are attacked (in fight) we will help you". But Allah is Witness that they are indeed liars.

12. If they are expelled, never will they go out with them; and if they are attacked (in fight), they will never help them; and if they do help them, they will turn their backs; so they will receive no help.

13. Of a truth you are stronger (than they) because of the terror in their hearts, (sent) by Allah. This is because they are men devoid of understanding.

14. They will not fight you (even) together, except in fortified townships, or from behind walls. Strong is their fighting (spirit) amongst themselves: you would think they were united, but their hearts are divided: that is because they are a people devoid of wisdom.

15. Like those who lately preceded them, they have tasted the evil result of their conduct; and (in the Hereafter there is) for them a grievous Chastisement;-

16. (Their allies deceived them), like the Evil One, when he says to man, "Deny Allah": but when (man) denies Allah, (the Evil One) says, "I am free of you: I do fear Allah, the Lord of the Worlds!"

17. The end of both will be that they will go into the Fire, dwelling therein for ever. Such is the reward of the wrong-doers.

18. O you who believe! Fear Allah, and let every soul look to what (provision) he has sent forth for the morrow. Yes, fear Allah: for Allah is well-acquainted with (all) that you do.

SÛRAH-60
AL-MUMTAHANAH
(INTRODUCTION)

This is the fourth of the ten Madinah Sûras, each dealing with a special point in the life of the Ummat.

Here the point is: what social relations are possible with the Unbelievers? A distinction is made between those who persecute you for your Faith and want to destroy you and your Faith, and those who have shown no such rancour. For the latter there is hope of mercy and forgiveness. The question of women and cross-marriages is equitably dealt with.

The date is after the Pagans had broken the treaty of Hudaibiya, for which see Introduction to S. 47- say about A. H. 8, not long before the conquest of Makkah.

Part 28

19. And you be not like those who forgot Allah; and He made them forget their own souls! Such are the rebellious transgressors!

20. Not equal are the Companions of the Fire and the Companions of the Garden: it is the Companions of the Garden that will achieve Felicity.

21. Had We sent down this Qur'an on a mountain, verily, you would have seen it humble itself and cleave asunder for fear of Allah. Such are the similitudes which We propound to men, that they may reflect.

22. Allah is He, than Whom there is no other god;- Who knows (all things) both secret and open; He, Most Gracious, Most Merciful.

23. Allah is He, than Whom there is no other god;- the Sovereign, the Holy One, the Source of Peace (and Perfection), the Guardian of Faith, the Preserver of Safety, the Exalted in Might, the Irresistible, the Supreme: Glory to Allah! (High is He) above the partners they attribute to Him.

24. He is Allah, the Creator, the Evolver, the Bestower of Forms (or Colours). To Him belong the Most Beautiful Names: whatever is in the heavens and on earth, declares His Praises and Glory: and He is the Exalted in Might, the Wise.

60. The Women to be Examined
In the name of Allah, Most Gracious, Most Merciful.

1. O you who believe! Take not my enemies and yours as friends (or protectors),- offering them (your) love, even though they have rejected the Truth that has come to you, and have (on the contrary) driven out

تَعْمَلُوْنَ ۞

وَلَا تَكُوْنُوْا كَالَّذِيْنَ نَسُوا اللّٰهَ فَأَنْسٰهُمْ اَنْفُسَهُمْ ۚ اُولٰٓئِكَ هُمُ الْفٰسِقُوْنَ ۞

لَا يَسْتَوِيْٓ اَصْحٰبُ النَّارِ وَاَصْحٰبُ الْجَنَّةِ ۚ اَصْحٰبُ الْجَنَّةِ هُمُ الْفَآئِزُوْنَ ۞

لَوْ اَنْزَلْنَا هٰذَا الْقُرْاٰنَ عَلٰى جَبَلٍ لَّرَاَيْتَهٗ خَاشِعًا مُّتَصَدِّعًا مِّنْ خَشْيَةِ اللّٰهِ ۚ وَتِلْكَ الْاَمْثَالُ نَضْرِبُهَا لِلنَّاسِ لَعَلَّهُمْ يَتَفَكَّرُوْنَ ۞

هُوَ اللّٰهُ الَّذِيْ لَاۤ اِلٰهَ اِلَّا هُوَ ۚ عٰلِمُ الْغَيْبِ وَالشَّهَادَةِ ۚ هُوَ الرَّحْمٰنُ الرَّحِيْمُ ۞

هُوَ اللّٰهُ الَّذِيْ لَاۤ اِلٰهَ اِلَّا هُوَ ۚ اَلْمَلِكُ الْقُدُّوْسُ السَّلٰمُ الْمُؤْمِنُ الْمُهَيْمِنُ الْعَزِيْزُ الْجَبَّارُ الْمُتَكَبِّرُ ۚ سُبْحٰنَ اللّٰهِ عَمَّا يُشْرِكُوْنَ ۞

هُوَ اللّٰهُ الْخَالِقُ الْبَارِئُ الْمُصَوِّرُ لَهُ الْاَسْمَآءُ الْحُسْنٰى ۚ يُسَبِّحُ لَهٗ مَا فِى السَّمٰوٰتِ وَالْاَرْضِ ۚ وَهُوَ الْعَزِيْزُ الْحَكِيْمُ ۞

(٦٠) سُوْرَةُ الْمُمْتَحَنَةِ مَدَنِيَّةٌ (٩١)

بِسْمِ اللّٰهِ الرَّحْمٰنِ الرَّحِيْمِ

يٰٓاَيُّهَا الَّذِيْنَ اٰمَنُوْا لَا تَتَّخِذُوْا عَدُوِّيْ وَعَدُوَّكُمْ اَوْلِيَآءَ تُلْقُوْنَ اِلَيْهِمْ بِالْمَوَدَّةِ وَقَدْ كَفَرُوْا بِمَا جَآءَكُمْ مِّنَ الْحَقِّ ۚ يُخْرِجُوْنَ

Part 28

the Prophet and yourselves (from your homes), (simply) because you believe in Allah your Lord! If you have come out to strive in My Way and to seek My Good Pleasure, (take them not as friends), holding secret converse of love (and friendship) with them: for I know full well all that you conceal and all that you reveal. And any of you that does this has strayed from the Straight Path.

2. If they were to get the better of you, they would behave to you as enemies, and stretch forth their hands and their tongues against you for evil: and they desire that you should reject the Truth.

3. Of no profit to you will be your relatives and your children on the Day of Judgment: He will judge between you: for Allah sees well all that you do.

4. There is for you an excellent example (to follow) in Abraham and those with him, when they said to their people: "We are clear of you and of whatever you worship besides Allah: we have rejected you, and there has arisen, between us and you, enmity and hatred for ever,- unless you believe in Allah and Him alone": But not when Abraham said to his father: "I will pray for forgiveness for you, though I have no power (to get) anything on your behalf from Allah." (They prayed): "Our Lord! in You do we trust, and to You do we turn in repentance: to You is (our) Final Goal.

5. "Our Lord! Make us not a (test and) trial for the Unbelievers, but forgive us, our Lord! for You are the Exalted in Might, the Wise."

6. There was indeed in them an excellent example for you to follow,-

Part 28

for those whose hope is in Allah and in the Last Day. But if any turn away, truly Allah is Free of all Wants, Worthy of all Praise.

7. It may be that Allah will grant love (and friendship) between you and those whom you (now) hold as enemies. For Allah has power (over all things); and Allah is Oft-Forgiving, Most Merciful.

8. Allah does not forbid you, with regard to those who do not fight you for (your) Faith nor drive you out of your homes, from dealing kindly and justly with them: for Allah loves those who are just.

9. Allah only forbids you, with regard to those who fight you for (your) Faith, and drive you out of your homes, and support (others) in driving you out, from turning to them (for friendship and protection). It is such as turn to them (in these circumstances), that do wrong.

10. O you who believe! When there come to you believing women refugees, examine (and test) them: Allah knows best as to their Faith: if you ascertain that they are Believers, then do not send them back to the Unbelievers. They are not lawful (wives) for the Unbelievers, nor are the (Unbelievers) lawful (husbands) for them. But pay the Unbelievers what they have spent (on their dower), and there will be no blame on you if you marry them on payment of their dower to them. But do not hold to the guardianship of unbelieving women: ask for what you have spent on their dowers, and let the (Unbelievers) ask for what they have spent (on the dowers of women who come over to you). Such is the command of Allah: He judges (with justice) between you. And Allah is Full of Knowledge and Wisdom.

SÛRAH-61
AS-ṢAFF
(INTRODUCTION)

This is the fifth Sûrah of the series of short Madinah Sûras beginning with S. 57. Its subject-matter is the need for discipline, practical work, and self-sacrifice in the cause of the Ummat. Its date is uncertain, hut it was probably shortly after the battle of Uḥud, which was fought in Shawwal, A.H.3.

11. And if any of your wives deserts you to the Unbelievers, and you have an accession (by the coming over of a woman from the other side), then pay to those whose wives have deserted the equivalent of what they had spent (on their dower). And fear Allah, in Whom you believe.

12. O Prophet! When believing women come to you to take the oath of fealty to you, that they will not associate in worship any other thing whatever with Allah, that they will not steal, that they will not commit adultery (or fornication), that they will not kill their children, that they will not utter slander, intentionally forging falsehood, and that they will not disobey you in any just matter,- then you receive their fealty, and pray to Allah for the forgiveness (of their sins): for Allah is Oft-Forgiving, Most Merciful.

13. O you who believe! Do not turn (for friendship) to people on whom is the Wrath of Allah. Of the Hereafter they are already in despair, just as the Unbelievers are in despair about those (buried) in graves.

61. Battle Array
In the name of Allah, Most Gracious, Most Merciful.

1. Whatever is in the heavens and on earth, let it declare the Praises and Glory of Allah: for He is the Exalted in Might, the Wise.

2. O you who believe, why do you say that which you do not?

3. Grievously odious is it in the sight of Allah that you say that which you do not.

4. Truly Allah loves those who fight

وَإِنْ فَاتَكُمْ شَيْءٌ مِّنْ أَزْوَاجِكُمْ
إِلَى الْكُفَّارِ فَعَاقَبْتُمْ فَاٰتُوا
الَّذِينَ ذَهَبَتْ أَزْوَاجُهُمْ مِّثْلَ مَا
أَنْفَقُوا ۚ وَاتَّقُوا اللّٰهَ الَّذِيْ أَنْتُمْ
بِهٖ مُؤْمِنُوْنَ ۝

يَاأَيُّهَا النَّبِيُّ إِذَا جَاءَكَ الْمُؤْمِنٰتُ
يُبَايِعْنَكَ عَلٰى أَنْ لَّا يُشْرِكْنَ
بِاللّٰهِ شَيْئًا وَّلَا يَسْرِقْنَ وَلَا يَزْنِيْنَ
وَلَا يَقْتُلْنَ أَوْلَادَهُنَّ وَلَا يَأْتِيْنَ
بِبُهْتَانٍ يَّفْتَرِيْنَهٗ بَيْنَ أَيْدِيْهِنَّ وَ
أَرْجُلِهِنَّ وَلَا يَعْصِيْنَكَ فِيْ مَعْرُوْفٍ
فَبَايِعْهُنَّ وَاسْتَغْفِرْ لَهُنَّ اللّٰهَ ۚ إِنَّ
اللّٰهَ غَفُوْرٌ رَّحِيْمٌ ۝

يَاأَيُّهَا الَّذِيْنَ اٰمَنُوْا لَا تَتَوَلَّوْا قَوْمًا
غَضِبَ اللّٰهُ عَلَيْهِمْ قَدْ يَئِسُوْا مِنَ
الْاٰخِرَةِ كَمَا يَئِسَ الْكُفَّارُ مِنْ
أَصْحٰبِ الْقُبُوْرِ ۝

(٦١) سُوْرَةُ الصَّفِّ مَدَنِيَّةٌ (١٠٩)
بِسْمِ اللّٰهِ الرَّحْمٰنِ الرَّحِيْمِ
سَبَّحَ لِلّٰهِ مَا فِي السَّمٰوٰتِ وَمَا فِي الْأَرْضِ ۖ
وَهُوَ الْعَزِيْزُ الْحَكِيْمُ ۝
يَاأَيُّهَا الَّذِيْنَ اٰمَنُوْا لِمَ تَقُوْلُوْنَ
مَا لَا تَفْعَلُوْنَ ۝
كَبُرَ مَقْتًا عِنْدَ اللّٰهِ أَنْ تَقُوْلُوْا
مَا لَا تَفْعَلُوْنَ ۝
إِنَّ اللّٰهَ يُحِبُّ الَّذِيْنَ يُقَاتِلُوْنَ

in His Cause in battle array, as if they were a solid cemented structure.

5. And remember, Moses said to his people: "O my people! why do you vex and insult me, though you know that I am the Apostle of Allah (sent) to you?" Then when they went wrong, Allah let their hearts go wrong. For Allah does not guide those who are rebellious transgressors.

6. And remember, Jesus, the son of Mary, said: "O Children of Israel! I am the Apostle of Allah (sent) to you, confirming the Law (which came) before me, and giving Glad Tidings of an Apostle to come after me, whose name shall be Ahmad." But when he came to them with Clear Signs, they said, "this is evident sorcery!"

7. Who does greater wrong than one who invents falsehood against Allah, even as he is being invited to Islam? And Allah does not guide those who do wrong.

8. Their intention is to extinguish Allah's Light (by blowing) with their mouths: but Allah will complete (the revelation of) His Light, even though the Unbelievers may detest (it).

9. It is He Who has sent His Apostle with Guidance and the Religion of Truth, that he may proclaim it over all religion, even though the Pagans may detest (it).

10. O you who believe! Shall I lead you to a bargain that will save you from a grievous Chastisement?-

11. That you believe in Allah and His Apostle, and that you strive (your utmost) in the Cause of Allah, with your property and your persons:

SÛRAH-62
AL-JUMU'A
(INTRODUCTION)

This is the sixth Sûrah in the Madinah series of shod Sûras which began with S. 57.

The special theme here is the need for mutual contact in the Community for worship and understanding for the spirit of the Message is for all, ignorant and learned, in order that they may be purified and may learn wisdom.

The date has no special significance: it may he placed in the early Madinah period, say. between A .11.2 ami 5.

that will be best for you, if you but knew!

12. He will forgive you your sins, and admit you to Gardens beneath which Rivers flow, and to beautiful mansions in Gardens of Eternity: that is indeed the Supreme Achievement.

13. And another (favour will He bestow,) which you do love,- help from Allah and a speedy victory. So give the Glad Tidings to the Believers.

14. O you who believe! You be helpers of Allah: as said Jesus the son of Mary to the Disciples, "Who will be my helpers to (the work of) Allah?" Said the Disciples, "We are Allah's helpers!" then a portion of the Children of Israel believed, and a portion disbelieved: but We gave power to those who believed, against their enemies, and they became the ones that prevailed.

62. The Assembly - Friday Prayer
In the name of Allah, Most Gracious, Most Merciful.

1. Whatever is in the heavens and on earth, declares the Praises and Glory of Allah,- the Sovereign, the Holy One, the Exalted in Might, the Wise.

2. It is He Who has sent amongst the Unlettered an Apostle from among themselves, to rehearse to them His Signs, to purify them, and to instruct them in Scripture and Wisdom,- although they had been, before, in manifest error;-

3. As well as (to confer all these benefits upon) others of them, who have not already joined them: and He is Exalted in Might, Wise.

4. Such is the Bounty of Allah, which He bestows on whom He will:

ذٰلِكُمۡ خَيۡرٌ لَّكُمۡ اِنۡ كُنۡتُمۡ تَعۡلَمُوۡنَ ۝

يَغۡفِرۡ لَكُمۡ ذُنُوۡبَكُمۡ وَيُدۡخِلۡكُمۡ جَنّٰتٍ تَجۡرِىۡ مِنۡ تَحۡتِهَا الۡاَنۡهٰرُ وَمَسٰكِنَ طَيِّبَةً فِىۡ جَنّٰتِ عَدۡنٍ ؕ ذٰلِكَ الۡفَوۡزُ الۡعَظِيۡمُ ۝

وَاُخۡرٰى تُحِبُّوۡنَهَا ؕ نَصۡرٌ مِّنَ اللّٰهِ وَفَتۡحٌ قَرِيۡبٌ ؕ وَبَشِّرِ الۡمُؤۡمِنِيۡنَ ۝

يٰۤاَيُّهَا الَّذِيۡنَ اٰمَنُوۡا كُوۡنُوۡۤا اَنۡصَارَ اللّٰهِ كَمَا قَالَ عِيۡسَى ابۡنُ مَرۡيَمَ لِلۡحَوَارِيّٖنَ مَنۡ اَنۡصَارِىۡۤ اِلَى اللّٰهِ ؕ قَالَ الۡحَوَارِيُّوۡنَ نَحۡنُ اَنۡصَارُ اللّٰهِ فَاٰمَنَتۡ طَّآئِفَةٌ مِّنۡۢ بَنِىۡۤ اِسۡرَآءِيۡلَ وَكَفَرَتۡ طَّآئِفَةٌ ۚ فَاَيَّدۡنَا الَّذِيۡنَ اٰمَنُوۡا عَلٰى عَدُوِّهِمۡ فَاَصۡبَحُوۡا ظٰهِرِيۡنَ ۝

(۲۲) سُوۡرَةُ الۡجُمُعَةِ مَدَنِيَّةٌ (۱۱۰) بِسۡمِ اللّٰهِ الرَّحۡمٰنِ الرَّحِيۡمِ

يُسَبِّحُ لِلّٰهِ مَا فِى السَّمٰوٰتِ وَمَا فِى الۡاَرۡضِ الۡمَلِكِ الۡقُدُّوۡسِ الۡعَزِيۡزِ الۡحَكِيۡمِ ۝

هُوَ الَّذِىۡ بَعَثَ فِى الۡاُمِّيّٖنَ رَسُوۡلًا مِّنۡهُمۡ يَتۡلُوۡا عَلَيۡهِمۡ اٰيٰتِهٖ وَيُزَكِّيۡهِمۡ وَيُعَلِّمُهُمُ الۡكِتٰبَ وَالۡحِكۡمَةَ ۖ وَاِنۡ كَانُوۡا مِنۡ قَبۡلُ لَفِىۡ ضَلٰلٍ مُّبِيۡنٍ ۝

وَّاٰخَرِيۡنَ مِنۡهُمۡ لَمَّا يَلۡحَقُوۡا بِهِمۡ ؕ وَهُوَ الۡعَزِيۡزُ الۡحَكِيۡمُ ۝

ذٰلِكَ فَضۡلُ اللّٰهِ يُؤۡتِيۡهِ مَنۡ يَّشَآءُ ؕ

and Allah is the Lord of the highest bounty.

5. The similitude of those who were charged with the (obligations of the) Mosaic Law, but who subsequently failed in those (obligations), is that of a donkey which carries huge tomes (but does not understand them). Evil is the similitude of people who falsify the Signs of Allah: and Allah does not guide people who do wrong.

6. Say: "O you that stand on Judaism! If you think that you are friends to Allah, to the exclusion of (other) men, then express your desire for Death, if you are truthful!"

7. But never will they express their desire (for Death), because of the (deeds) their hands have sent on before them! and Allah knows well those that do wrong!

8. Say: "The Death from which you flee will truly overtake you: then you will be sent back to the Knower of things secret and open: and He will tell you (the truth of) the things that you did!"

9. O you who believe! When the call is proclaimed to prayer on Friday (the Day of Assembly), hasten earnestly to the Remembrance of Allah, and leave off business (and traffic): That is best for you if you but knew!

10. And when the Prayer is finished, then you may disperse through the land, and seek of the Bounty of Allah: and celebrate the Praises of Allah often (and without stint): that you may prosper.

11. But when they see some bargain or some amusement, they disperse headlong to it, and leave you standing. Say: "The (blessing) from the Presence of Allah is better than any amusement or

SÛRAH-63
AL-MUNÂFÎQÛN
(INTRODUCTION)

This is the seventh of the ten short Madinah Sûras dealing with a special feature in the social life of the Brotherhood.

The special feature here dealt with is the wiles and mischief of the Hypocrite element in any community, and the need of guarding against it and against the temptation it throws in the way of the Believers.

The battle of Uḥud (Shawwal A.H 3) unmasked the Hypocrites in Madinah: see 3: 167. This Sûrah may be referred to sometime after that event, say about 4 A.H. or possibly 5 A.H. if the words reported in verse 8 were uttered in the expedition against the Banu Muṣṭaliq A.H. 5.

bargain! and Allah is the Best to provide (for all needs)."

التِّجَارَةُ ۖ وَاللّٰهُ خَيْرُ الرّٰزِقِيْنَ ۞

63. The Hypocrites

In the name of Allah, Most Gracious, Most Merciful.

(١٣) سُوْرَةُ الْمُنٰفِقُوْنَ مَدَنِيَّةٌ (١٠٢)

بِسْمِ اللّٰهِ الرَّحْمٰنِ الرَّحِيْمِ

1. When the Hypocrites come to you, they say, "We bear witness that you are indeed the Apostle of Allah." Yes, Allah knows that you are indeed His Apostle, and Allah bears witness that the Hypocrites are indeed liars.

إِذَا جَآءَكَ الْمُنٰفِقُوْنَ قَالُوْا نَشْهَدُ

إِنَّكَ لَرَسُوْلُ اللّٰهِ ۘ وَاللّٰهُ يَعْلَمُ

إِنَّكَ لَرَسُوْلُهٗ ۗ وَاللّٰهُ يَشْهَدُ إِنَّ

الْمُنٰفِقِيْنَ لَكٰذِبُوْنَ ۞

2. They have made their oaths a screen (for their misdeeds): thus they obstruct (men) from the Path of Allah: truly evil are their deeds.

اِتَّخَذُوْا أَيْمَانَهُمْ جُنَّةً فَصَدُّوْا

عَنْ سَبِيْلِ اللّٰهِ ۗ إِنَّهُمْ سَآءَ مَا

كَانُوْا يَعْمَلُوْنَ ۞

3. That is because they believed, then they rejected Faith: so a seal was set on their hearts: therefore they do not understand.

ذٰلِكَ بِأَنَّهُمْ اٰمَنُوْا ثُمَّ كَفَرُوْا فَطُبِعَ

عَلٰى قُلُوْبِهِمْ فَهُمْ لَا يَفْقَهُوْنَ ۞

4. When you look at them, their exteriors please you; and when they speak, you listen to their words. They are as (worthless as hollow) pieces of timber propped up, (unable to stand on their own). They think that every cry is against them. They are the enemies; so beware of them. The curse of Allah be on them! How are they deluded (away from the Truth)!

وَإِذَا رَأَيْتَهُمْ تُعْجِبُكَ أَجْسَامُهُمْ ۗ

وَإِنْ يَّقُوْلُوْا تَسْمَعْ لِقَوْلِهِمْ ۗ كَأَنَّهُمْ

خُشُبٌ مُّسَنَّدَةٌ ۗ يَحْسَبُوْنَ كُلَّ صَيْحَةٍ

عَلَيْهِمْ ۗ هُمُ الْعَدُوُّ فَاحْذَرْهُمْ ۗ

قَاتَلَهُمُ اللّٰهُ ۗ أَنّٰى يُؤْفَكُوْنَ ۞

5. And when it is said to them, "Come, the Apostle of Allah will pray for your forgiveness", they turn aside their heads, and you would see them turning away their faces in arrogance.

وَإِذَا قِيْلَ لَهُمْ تَعَالَوْا يَسْتَغْفِرْ لَكُمْ

رَسُوْلُ اللّٰهِ لَوَّوْا رُءُوْسَهُمْ وَرَأَيْتَهُمْ

يَصُدُّوْنَ وَهُمْ مُّسْتَكْبِرُوْنَ ۞

6. It is equal to them whether you pray for their forgiveness or not. Allah will not forgive them. Truly Allah does not guide rebellious transgressors.

سَوَآءٌ عَلَيْهِمْ أَسْتَغْفَرْتَ لَهُمْ

أَمْ لَمْ تَسْتَغْفِرْ لَهُمْ ۗ لَنْ يَّغْفِرَ

اللّٰهُ لَهُمْ ۗ إِنَّ اللّٰهَ لَا يَهْدِي

الْقَوْمَ الْفٰسِقِيْنَ ۞

7. They are the ones who say, "Spend nothing on those who are with Allah's Apostle, to the end that they may disperse

هُمُ الَّذِيْنَ يَقُوْلُوْنَ لَا تُنْفِقُوْا عَلٰى

مَنْ عِنْدَ رَسُوْلِ اللّٰهِ حَتّٰى يَنْفَضُّوْا

SÛRAH-64
AT-TAGHÂBUN
(INTRODUCTION)

This is the eighth of the ten short Madinah Sûras, each dealing with a special aspect of the life of the Community

The special aspect spoke of here is the mutual gain and loss of Good and Evil, contrasted in this life and in the Hereafter

It is an early Madinah Surah, of the year I of (he Hijra or possibly even of (he Makkan period just before the Hijrat.

(and quit Medina)." But to Allah belong the treasures of the heavens and the earth; but the Hypocrites do not understand.

وَلِلّٰهِ خَزَآئِنُ السَّمٰوٰتِ وَالْأَرْضِ وَلٰكِنَّ الْمُنٰفِقِيْنَ لَا يَفْقَهُوْنَ ۞

8. They say, "If we return to Medina, surely the more honourable (element) will expel therefrom the meaner." But honour belongs to Allah and His Apostle, and to the Believers; but the Hypocrites do not know.

يَقُوْلُوْنَ لَئِنْ رَّجَعْنَآ اِلَى الْمَدِيْنَةِ لَيُخْرِجَنَّ الْأَعَزُّ مِنْهَا الْأَذَلَّ ۚ وَ لِلّٰهِ الْعِزَّةُ وَلِرَسُوْلِهٖ وَلِلْمُؤْمِنِيْنَ وَلٰكِنَّ الْمُنٰفِقِيْنَ لَا يَعْلَمُوْنَ ۞

9. O you who believe! Let not your riches or your children divert you from the remembrance of Allah. If any act thus, the loss is their own.

يٰٓاَيُّهَا الَّذِيْنَ اٰمَنُوْا لَا تُلْهِكُمْ اَمْوَالُكُمْ وَلَآ اَوْلَادُكُمْ عَنْ ذِكْرِ اللّٰهِ ۚ وَمَنْ يَّفْعَلْ ذٰلِكَ فَاُولٰٓئِكَ هُمُ الْخٰسِرُوْنَ ۞

10. And spend something (in charity) out of the substance which We have bestowed on you, before Death should come to any of you and he should say, "O my Lord! why did You not give me respite for a little while? I should then have given (largely) in charity, and I should have been one of the doers of good".

وَاَنْفِقُوْا مِنْ مَّا رَزَقْنٰكُمْ مِّنْ قَبْلِ اَنْ يَّاْتِيَ اَحَدَكُمُ الْمَوْتُ فَيَقُوْلَ رَبِّ لَوْلَآ اَخَّرْتَنِيْ اِلٰٓى اَجَلٍ قَرِيْبٍ ۙ فَاَصَّدَّقَ وَاَكُنْ مِّنَ الصّٰلِحِيْنَ ۞

11. But to no soul will Allah grant respite when the time appointed (for it) has come; and Allah is well acquainted with (all) that you do.

وَلَنْ يُّؤَخِّرَ اللّٰهُ نَفْسًا اِذَا جَآءَ اَجَلُهَا ۚ وَاللّٰهُ خَبِيْرٌۢ بِمَا تَعْمَلُوْنَ ۞

64. Mutual Loss and Gain
In the name of Allah. Most Gracious, Most Merciful.

(٦٤) سُوْرَةُ التَّغَابُنِ مَدَنِيَّةٌ (١٠٨) بِسْمِ اللّٰهِ الرَّحْمٰنِ الرَّحِيْمِ

1. Whatever is in the heavens and on earth, declares the Praises and Glory of Allah: to Him belongs dominion, and to Him belongs praise: and He has power over all things.

يُسَبِّحُ لِلّٰهِ مَا فِى السَّمٰوٰتِ وَمَا فِى الْأَرْضِ ۚ لَهُ الْمُلْكُ وَلَهُ الْحَمْدُ وَهُوَ عَلٰى كُلِّ شَيْءٍ قَدِيْرٌ ۞

2. It is He Who has created you; and of you are some that are Unbelievers, and some that are Believers: and Allah sees well all that you do.

هُوَ الَّذِيْ خَلَقَكُمْ فَمِنْكُمْ كَافِرٌ وَّمِنْكُمْ مُّؤْمِنٌ ۚ وَاللّٰهُ بِمَا تَعْمَلُوْنَ بَصِيْرٌ ۞

3. He has created the heavens and the earth in just proportions,

خَلَقَ السَّمٰوٰتِ وَالْأَرْضَ بِالْحَقِّ

and has given you shape, and
made your shapes beautiful: and
to Him is the final Goal.

4. He knows what is in the
heavens and on earth; and He
knows what you conceal and
what you reveal: yes, Allah
knows well the (secrets) of (all)
hearts.

5. Has not the story reached
you, of those who rejected Faith
aforetime? So they tasted the evil
result of their conduct; and they
had a grievous Chastisement.

6. That was because there
came to them Apostles with Clear
Signs, but they said: "Shall
(mere) human beings direct us?"
So they rejected (the Message)
and turned away. But Allah can
do without (them): and Allah is
free of all needs, worthy of all
praise.

7. The Unbelievers think that
they will not be raised up (for
Judgment). Say: "Yes, by my
Lord, you shall surely be raised
up: then you shall be told (the
truth) of all that you did. And that
is easy for Allah."

8. Believe, therefore, in Allah
and His Apostle, and in the Light
which We have sent down. And
Allah is well acquainted with all
that you do.

9. The Day that He assem-
bles you (all) for a Day of
Assembly,- that will be a Day of
mutual loss and gain (among
you), and those who believe in
Allah and work righteousness,-
He will remove from them their
ills, and He will admit them to
Gardens beneath which Rivers
flow, to dwell therein for ever:
that will be the Supreme
Achievement.

10. But those who reject Faith
and treat Our Signs as falsehoods, they will be Companions
of the Fire, to dwell therein for
ever: and evil is that Goal.

SÛRAH-65
AT-ṬALÂQ
(INTRODUCTION)

This is the ninth of the ten short Madinah Sûras dealing with the social life of the Community. The aspect dealt with here is Divorce and the necessity of precautions to guard against its abuse. The relations of the sexes are an important factor in the social life of the Community, and this and the following Sûrah deal with certain aspects of it. "Of all things permitted by law," said the Prophet, "divorce is the most hateful in the sight of Allah" (Abû Da-ûd, *Sunan,* 13:3). While the sanctity of marriage is the essential basis of family life, the incompatibility of individuals and the weaknesses of human nature require certain outlets' and safeguards if that sanctity is not to be made into a fetish at the expense of human life. That is why the question of Divorce is in the Sûrah linked with the question of insolent impiety and its punishment.

The date is somewhere about A.H. 6, but the chronology has no significance.

11. No kind of calamity can occur, except by the leave of Allah: and if any one believes in Allah, (Allah) guides his heart (aright): for Allah knows all things.

12. So obey Allah, and obey His Apostle: but if you turn back, the duty of Our Apostle is but to proclaim (the Message) clearly and openly.

13. Allah! There is no god but He: and on Allah, therefore, let the Believers put their trust.

14. O you who believe! Truly, among your wives and your children are (some that are) enemies to yourselves: so beware of them! But if you forgive and overlook, and cover up (their faults), verily Allah is Oft-Forgiving, Most Merciful.

15. Your riches and your children may be but a trial: but in the Presence of Allah, is the highest Reward.

16. So fear Allah as much as you can; listen and obey and spend in charity for the benefit of your own souls. And those saved from the covetousness of their own souls,- they are the ones that achieve prosperity.

17. If you loan to Allah a beautiful loan, He will double it to your (credit), and He will grant you Forgiveness: for Allah is most ready to appreciate (service), Most Forbearing,-

18. Knower of what is hidden and what is open, Exalted in Might, Full of Wisdom.

65. Divorce
In the name of Allah. Most Gracious, Most Merciful.

1. O Prophet! When you do divorce women,

مَآ أَصَابَ مِنْ مُّصِيبَةٍ إِلَّا بِإِذْنِ اللّٰهِ ۗ وَمَنْ يُّؤْمِنْ بِاللّٰهِ يَهْدِ قَلْبَهُ ۚ وَاللّٰهُ بِكُلِّ شَىْءٍ عَلِيمٌ ۝

وَأَطِيعُوا اللّٰهَ وَأَطِيعُوا الرَّسُولَ ۚ فَإِنْ تَوَلَّيْتُمْ فَإِنَّمَا عَلٰى رَسُولِنَا الْبَلَاغُ الْمُبِينُ ۝

اللّٰهُ لَآ إِلٰهَ إِلَّا هُوَ ۚ وَعَلَى اللّٰهِ فَلْيَتَوَكَّلِ الْمُؤْمِنُونَ ۝

يَٰٓأَيُّهَا الَّذِينَ اٰمَنُوٓا إِنَّ مِنْ أَزْوَاجِكُمْ وَأَوْلَادِكُمْ عَدُوًّا لَّكُمْ فَاحْذَرُوهُمْ ۚ وَإِنْ تَعْفُوا وَتَصْفَحُوا وَتَغْفِرُوا فَإِنَّ اللّٰهَ غَفُورٌ رَّحِيمٌ ۝

إِنَّمَآ أَمْوَالُكُمْ وَأَوْلَادُكُمْ فِتْنَةٌ ۚ وَاللّٰهُ عِنْدَهُ أَجْرٌ عَظِيمٌ ۝

فَاتَّقُوا اللّٰهَ مَا اسْتَطَعْتُمْ وَاسْمَعُوا وَأَطِيعُوا وَأَنْفِقُوا خَيْرًا لِّأَنْفُسِكُمْ ۗ وَمَنْ يُّوقَ شُحَّ نَفْسِهِ فَأُولٰٓئِكَ هُمُ الْمُفْلِحُونَ ۝

إِنْ تُقْرِضُوا اللّٰهَ قَرْضًا حَسَنًا يُّضَاعِفْهُ لَكُمْ وَيَغْفِرْ لَكُمْ ۗ وَاللّٰهُ شَكُورٌ حَلِيمٌ ۝

عٰلِمُ الْغَيْبِ وَالشَّهَادَةِ الْعَزِيزُ الْحَكِيمُ ۝

(٦٥) سُورَةُ الطَّلَاقِ مَدَنِيَّةٌ (٩٩)
بِسْمِ اللّٰهِ الرَّحْمٰنِ الرَّحِيمِ

يَٰٓأَيُّهَا النَّبِيُّ إِذَا طَلَّقْتُمُ النِّسَآءَ

divorce them at their prescribed periods, and count (accurately), their prescribed periods: and fear Allah your Lord: and do not turn them out of their houses, nor shall they (themselves) leave, except in case they are guilty of some open lewdness, those are limits set by Allah: and any who transgresses the limits of Allah, does verily wrong his (own) soul: you do not know if perchance Allah will bring about thereafter some new situation.

2. Thus when they fulfil their term appointed, either take them back on equitable terms or part with them on equitable terms; and take for witness two persons from among you, endued with justice, and establish the evidence (as) before Allah. Such is the admonition given to him who believes in Allah and the Last Day. And for those who fear Allah, He (ever) prepares a way out,

3. And He provides for him from (sources) he never could imagine. And if any one puts his trust in Allah, sufficient is (Allah) for him. For Allah will surely accomplish His purpose: verily, for all things has Allah appointed a due proportion.

4. Such of your women as have passed the age of monthly courses, for them the prescribed period, if you have any doubts, is three months, and for those who have no courses (it is the same): for those who carry (life within their wombs), their period is until they deliver their burdens: and for those who fear Allah, He will make their path easy.

5. That is the Command of Allah, which He has sent down to you: and if any one

فَطَلِّقُوْهُنَّ لِعِدَّتِهِنَّ وَ اَحْصُوا
الْعِدَّةَ ۚ وَاتَّقُوا اللّٰهَ رَبَّكُمْ ۚ لَا
تُخْرِجُوْهُنَّ مِنْ بُيُوْتِهِنَّ وَلَا
يَخْرُجْنَ اِلَّا اَنْ يَّاْتِيْنَ بِفَاحِشَةٍ
مُّبَيِّنَةٍ ۚ وَتِلْكَ حُدُوْدُ اللّٰهِ ۚ
وَمَنْ يَّتَعَدَّ حُدُوْدَ اللّٰهِ فَقَدْ
ظَلَمَ نَفْسَهٗ ۚ لَا تَدْرِيْ لَعَلَّ اللّٰهَ
يُحْدِثُ بَعْدَ ذٰلِكَ اَمْرًا ۞

فَاِذَا بَلَغْنَ اَجَلَهُنَّ فَاَمْسِكُوْهُنَّ
بِمَعْرُوْفٍ اَوْ فَارِقُوْهُنَّ بِمَعْرُوْفٍ
وَّاَشْهِدُوْا ذَوَيْ عَدْلٍ مِّنْكُمْ
وَاَقِيْمُوا الشَّهَادَةَ لِلّٰهِ ۚ ذٰلِكُمْ
يُوْعَظُ بِهٖ مَنْ كَانَ يُؤْمِنُ بِاللّٰهِ
وَالْيَوْمِ الْاٰخِرِ ۚ وَمَنْ يَّتَّقِ اللّٰهَ
يَجْعَلْ لَّهٗ مَخْرَجًا ۞

وَّيَرْزُقْهُ مِنْ حَيْثُ لَا يَحْتَسِبُ ۚ
وَمَنْ يَّتَوَكَّلْ عَلَى اللّٰهِ فَهُوَ حَسْبُهٗ ۚ
اِنَّ اللّٰهَ بَالِغُ اَمْرِهٖ ۚ قَدْ جَعَلَ
اللّٰهُ لِكُلِّ شَيْءٍ قَدْرًا ۞

وَالّٰٓئِيْ يَئِسْنَ مِنَ الْمَحِيْضِ مِنْ
نِّسَآئِكُمْ اِنِ ارْتَبْتُمْ فَعِدَّتُهُنَّ
ثَلٰثَةُ اَشْهُرٍ ۙ وَّالّٰٓئِيْ لَمْ يَحِضْنَ ۚ
وَاُولَاتُ الْاَحْمَالِ اَجَلُهُنَّ اَنْ
يَّضَعْنَ حَمْلَهُنَّ ۚ وَمَنْ يَّتَّقِ اللّٰهَ
يَجْعَلْ لَّهٗ مِنْ اَمْرِهٖ يُسْرًا ۞

ذٰلِكَ اَمْرُ اللّٰهِ اَنْزَلَهٗٓ اِلَيْكُمْ ۚ وَمَنْ

fears Allah, He will remove his ills from him, and will enlarge his reward.

يَتَّقِ اللهَ يُكَفِّرْ عَنْهُ سَيِّاٰتِهٖ وَ يُعْظِمْ لَهٗٓ اَجْرًا ۝

6. Let the women live (in 'iddat) in the same style as you live, according to your means: do not annoy them, so as to restrict them. And if they carry (life in their wombs), then spend (your substance) on them until they deliver their burden: and if they suckle your (offspring), give them their recompense: and take mutual counsel together, according to what is just and reasonable. And if you find yourselves in difficulties, let another woman suckle the child) on the (father's) behalf.

اَسْكِنُوْهُنَّ مِنْ حَيْثُ سَكَنْتُمْ مِّنْ وُّجْدِكُمْ وَلَا تُضَآرُّوْهُنَّ لِتُضَيِّقُوْا عَلَيْهِنَّ ۗ وَاِنْ كُنَّ اُولَاتِ حَمْلٍ فَاَنْفِقُوْا عَلَيْهِنَّ حَتّٰى يَضَعْنَ حَمْلَهُنَّ ۚ فَاِنْ اَرْضَعْنَ لَكُمْ فَاٰتُوْهُنَّ اُجُوْرَهُنَّ ۚ وَاْتَمِرُوْا بَيْنَكُمْ بِمَعْرُوْفٍ ۚ وَاِنْ تَعَاسَرْتُمْ فَسَتُرْضِعُ لَهٗٓ اُخْرٰى ۝

7. Let the man of means spend according to his means: and the man whose resources are restricted, let him spend according to what Allah has given him. Allah puts no burden on any person beyond what He has given him. After a difficulty, Allah will soon grant relief.

لِيُنْفِقْ ذُوْ سَعَةٍ مِّنْ سَعَتِهٖ ۗ وَمَنْ قُدِرَ عَلَيْهِ رِزْقُهٗ فَلْيُنْفِقْ مِمَّآ اٰتٰىهُ اللهُ ۗ لَا يُكَلِّفُ اللهُ نَفْسًا اِلَّا مَآ اٰتٰىهَا ۗ سَيَجْعَلُ اللهُ بَعْدَ عُسْرٍ يُّسْرًا ۝

8. How many populations that insolently opposed the Command of their Lord and of His Apostles, did We not then call to account,- to severe account?- and We imposed on them an exemplary Punishment.

وَكَاَيِّنْ مِّنْ قَرْيَةٍ عَتَتْ عَنْ اَمْرِ رَبِّهَا وَرُسُلِهٖ فَحَاسَبْنٰهَا حِسَابًا شَدِيْدًا ۙ وَّعَذَّبْنٰهَا عَذَابًا نُّكْرًا ۝

9. Then they tasted the evil result of their conduct, and the End of their conduct was Perdition.

فَذَاقَتْ وَبَالَ اَمْرِهَا وَكَانَ عَاقِبَةُ اَمْرِهَا خُسْرًا ۝

10. Allah has prepared for them a severe Punishment (in the Hereafter). Therefore fear Allah, O you men of under-standing - who have believed!- for Allah has indeed sent down to you a Message,-

اَعَدَّ اللهُ لَهُمْ عَذَابًا شَدِيْدًا ۖ فَاتَّقُوا اللهَ يٰٓاُولِي الْاَلْبَابِ ۛ الَّذِيْنَ اٰمَنُوْا ۛ قَدْ اَنْزَلَ اللهُ اِلَيْكُمْ ذِكْرًا ۝

11. An Apostle, who rehearses to you the Signs of Allah containing clear explanations, that he may lead forth those who believe

رَّسُوْلًا يَّتْلُوْا عَلَيْكُمْ اٰيٰتِ اللهِ مُبَيِّنٰتٍ لِّيُخْرِجَ الَّذِيْنَ اٰمَنُوْا

SÛRAH-66
AT-TAḤRÎM
(INTRODUCTION)

This is the tenth and last of the series of ten short Madinah Sûras which began with S. 57: see Introduction to that Sûrah. The point dealt with here is: how far the turning away from sex or the opposition of one sex against another or a want of harmony between the sexes may injure the higher interests of society.

The date may be taken to be somewhere about A.H. 7.

and do righteous deeds from the depths of Darkness into Light. And those who believe in Allah and work righteousness, He will admit to Gardens beneath which Rivers flow, to dwell therein for ever: Allah has indeed granted for them a most excellent Provision.

وَعَمِلُوا الصّٰلِحٰتِ مِنَ الظُّلُمٰتِ
اِلَى النُّوْرِ ۖ وَمَنْ يُّؤْمِنْۢ بِاللّٰهِ
وَيَعْمَلْ صَالِحًا يُّدْخِلْهُ
جَنّٰتٍ تَجْرِيْ مِنْ تَحْتِهَا الْاَنْهٰرُ
خٰلِدِيْنَ فِيْهَاۤ اَبَدًا ۖ قَدْ اَحْسَنَ
اللّٰهُ لَهٗ رِزْقًا ۞

12. Allah is He Who created seven Firmaments and of the earth a similar number. Through the midst of them (all) descends His Command: that you may know that Allah has power over all things, and that Allah comprehends all things in (His) Knowledge.

اَللّٰهُ الَّذِيْ خَلَقَ سَبْعَ سَمٰوٰتٍ
وَّمِنَ الْاَرْضِ مِثْلَهُنَّ ۖ يَتَنَزَّلُ
الْاَمْرُ بَيْنَهُنَّ لِتَعْلَمُوْۤا اَنَّ اللّٰهَ
عَلٰى كُلِّ شَيْءٍ قَدِيْرٌ ۙ وَّاَنَّ اللّٰهَ قَدْ
اَحَاطَ بِكُلِّ شَيْءٍ عِلْمًا ۞

66. Holding-something – to be Forbidden

In the name of Allah. Most Gracious, Most Merciful.

(٦٦) سُوْرَةُ التَّحْرِيْمِ مَدَنِيَّةٌ (١٠٧)
بِسْمِ اللّٰهِ الرَّحْمٰنِ الرَّحِيْمِ

1. O Prophet! Why do you hold to be forbidden that which Allah has made lawful to you? You seek to please your consorts. But Allah is Oft-Forgiving, Most Merciful.

يٰۤاَيُّهَا النَّبِيُّ لِمَ تُحَرِّمُ مَاۤ اَحَلَّ
اللّٰهُ لَكَ ۖ تَبْتَغِيْ مَرْضَاتَ اَزْوَاجِكَ ۚ
وَاللّٰهُ غَفُوْرٌ رَّحِيْمٌ ۞

2. Allah has already ordained for you, (O men), the dissolution of your oaths (in some cases): and Allah is your Protector, and He is Full of Knowledge and Wisdom.

قَدْ فَرَضَ اللّٰهُ لَكُمْ تَحِلَّةَ
اَيْمَانِكُمْ ۚ وَاللّٰهُ مَوْلٰىكُمْ ۚ وَهُوَ
الْعَلِيْمُ الْحَكِيْمُ ۞

3. When the Prophet disclosed a matter in confidence to one of his consorts, and she then divulged it (to another), and Allah made it known to him, he confirmed part thereof and repudiated a part. Then when he told her thereof, she said, "Who told you this? "He said, "He told me Who knows and is well-acquainted (with all things)."

وَاِذْ اَسَرَّ النَّبِيُّ اِلٰى بَعْضِ اَزْوَاجِهٖ
حَدِيْثًا ۚ فَلَمَّا نَبَّاَتْ بِهٖ وَاَظْهَرَهُ
اللّٰهُ عَلَيْهِ عَرَّفَ بَعْضَهٗ وَاَعْرَضَ
عَنْۢ بَعْضٍ ۚ فَلَمَّا نَبَّاَهَا بِهٖ قَالَتْ
مَنْ اَنْۢبَاَكَ هٰذَا ۖ قَالَ نَبَّاَنِۦَ
الْعَلِيْمُ الْخَبِيْرُ ۞

4. If you two turn in repentance to Him, your

اِنْ تَتُوْبَاۤ اِلَى اللّٰهِ فَقَدْ صَغَتْ

hearts are indeed so inclined; but if you back up each other against him, truly Allah is His Protector, and Gabriel, and (every) righteous one among those who believe,- and furthermore, the angels - will back (him) up.

قُلُوبُكُمَا ۚ وَ إِن تَظَاهَرَا عَلَيْهِ فَإِنَّ اللَّهَ هُوَ مَوْلَاهُ وَ جِبْرِيلُ وَصَالِحُ الْمُؤْمِنِينَ ۚ وَالْمَلَائِكَةُ بَعْدَ ذَٰلِكَ ظَهِيرٌ ۞

5. It may be, if he divorced you (all), that Allah will give him in exchange consorts better than you,- who submit (their wills), who believe, who are devout, who turn to Allah in repentance, who worship (in humility), who travel (for Faith) and fast, - previously married or virgins.

عَسَىٰ رَبُّهُ إِن طَلَّقَكُنَّ أَن يُبْدِلَهُ أَزْوَاجًا خَيْرًا مِّنكُنَّ مُسْلِمَاتٍ مُؤْمِنَاتٍ قَانِتَاتٍ تَائِبَاتٍ عَابِدَاتٍ سَائِحَاتٍ ثَيِّبَاتٍ وَ أَبْكَارًا ۞

6. O you who believe! save yourselves and your families from a Fire whose fuel is Men and Stones, over which are (appointed) angels stern (and) severe, who do not flinch (from executing) the Commands they receive from Allah, but do (precisely) what they are commanded.

يَا أَيُّهَا الَّذِينَ آمَنُوا قُوا أَنفُسَكُمْ وَ أَهْلِيكُمْ نَارًا وَّ قُودُهَا النَّاسُ وَالْحِجَارَةُ عَلَيْهَا مَلَائِكَةٌ غِلَاظٌ شِدَادٌ لَّا يَعْصُونَ اللَّهَ مَا أَمَرَهُمْ وَ يَفْعَلُونَ مَا يُؤْمَرُونَ ۞

7. (They will say), "O you Unbelievers! Make no excuses this Day! You are being but requited for all that you did!"

يَا أَيُّهَا الَّذِينَ كَفَرُوا لَا تَعْتَذِرُوا الْيَوْمَ ۖ إِنَّمَا تُجْزَوْنَ مَا كُنتُمْ تَعْمَلُونَ ۞

8. O you who believe! Turn to Allah with sincere repentance: in the hope that your Lord will remove from you your ills and admit you to Gardens beneath which Rivers flow,- the Day that Allah will not permit to be humiliated the Prophet and those who believe with him. Their Light will run forward before them and by their right hands, while they say, "Our Lord! Perfect our Light for us, and grant us Forgiveness: for You have power over all things."

يَا أَيُّهَا الَّذِينَ آمَنُوا تُوبُوا إِلَى اللَّهِ تَوْبَةً نَّصُوحًا عَسَىٰ رَبُّكُمْ أَن يُكَفِّرَ عَنكُمْ سَيِّئَاتِكُمْ وَ يُدْخِلَكُمْ جَنَّاتٍ تَجْرِي مِن تَحْتِهَا الْأَنْهَارُ يَوْمَ لَا يُخْزِي اللَّهُ النَّبِيَّ وَ الَّذِينَ آمَنُوا مَعَهُ ۖ نُورُهُمْ يَسْعَىٰ بَيْنَ أَيْدِيهِمْ وَ بِأَيْمَانِهِمْ يَقُولُونَ رَبَّنَا أَتْمِمْ لَنَا نُورَنَا وَ اغْفِرْ لَنَا ۖ إِنَّكَ عَلَىٰ كُلِّ شَيْءٍ قَدِيرٌ ۞

SÛRAH-67
AL-MULK
(INTRODUCTION)

We have now done fourteen-fifteenths of the Qur'ân, and have followed step by step the development of its argument establishing the *Ummat* or Brotherhood of Islam.

There is a logical break here. The remaining fifteenth consists of short spiritual Lyrics, mostly of the Makkan period, dealing mainly with the inner life of man, and in its individual aspects. They may be compared to Hymns or Psalms in other religious literature. But these short Qur'ânic Sûras have a grandeur, a beauty, a mystic meaning, and a force of earnestness under persecution, all their own. With their sources in the sublimest regions of the Empyrean, their light penetrates into the darkest recesses of Life, into the concrete facts which are often mistaken for the whole of Reality, though they are but an insignificant portion and on the surface and fleeting. There is much symbolism in language and thought, in describing the spiritual in terms of the things we see and understand.

It is the contrast between the shadows of Reality here and the eternal Reality, between the surface world and the profound inner World, that is urged on our attention here.

This Sûrah of 30 verses belongs to the middle Makkan period, just before S. 69 and S. 70. Allah is mentioned here by the name *Rahmân* (Most Gracious), as He is mentioned by the names -of *Rabb* (Lord and Cherisher) and *Rahmân* (Most Gracious) in S. 19.

9. O Prophet! Strive hard against the Unbelievers and the Hypocrites, and be firm against them. Their abode is Hell,- an evil refuge (indeed).

يَا أَيُّهَا النَّبِيُّ جَاهِدِ الْكُفَّارَ وَالْمُنَافِقِينَ وَاغْلُظْ عَلَيْهِمْ وَ مَأْوَاهُمْ جَهَنَّمُ وَبِئْسَ الْمَصِيرُ ۞

10. Allah sets forth, for an example to the Unbelievers, the wife of Noah and the wife of Lut: they were (respectively) under two of our righteous servants, but they were false to their (husbands), and they profited nothing before Allah on their account, but were told: "You enter the Fire along with (others) that enter!"

ضَرَبَ اللهُ مَثَلًا لِّلَّذِينَ كَفَرُوا امْرَأَتَ نُوحٍ وَّامْرَأَتَ لُوطٍ ۖ كَانَتَا تَحْتَ عَبْدَيْنِ مِنْ عِبَادِنَا صَالِحَيْنِ فَخَانَتَاهُمَا فَلَمْ يُغْنِيَا عَنْهُمَا مِنَ اللهِ شَيْئًا وَّقِيلَ ادْخُلَا النَّارَ مَعَ الدَّاخِلِينَ ۞

11. And Allah sets forth, as an example to those who believe, the wife of Pharaoh: behold she said: "O my Lord! build for me, in nearness to You, a mansion in the Garden, and save me from Pharaoh and his doings, and save me from those that do wrong"

وَضَرَبَ اللهُ مَثَلًا لِّلَّذِينَ امَنُوا امْرَأَتَ فِرْعَوْنَ ۘ اِذْ قَالَتْ رَبِّ ابْنِ لِي عِنْدَكَ بَيْتًا فِي الْجَنَّةِ وَنَجِّنِي مِنْ فِرْعَوْنَ وَعَمَلِهِ وَ نَجِّنِي مِنَ الْقَوْمِ الظّٰلِمِينَ ۞

12. And Mary the daughter of 'Imran, who guarded her chastity; and We breathed into (her body) of Our spirit; and she testified to the truth of the words of her Lord and of His Revelations, and was one of the devout (servants).

وَمَرْيَمَ ابْنَتَ عِمْرَانَ الَّتِي اَحْصَنَتْ فَرْجَهَا فَنَفَخْنَا فِيهِ مِنْ رُّوحِنَا وَصَدَّقَتْ بِكَلِمٰتِ رَبِّهَا وَكُتُبِهِ وَكَانَتْ مِنَ الْقٰنِتِينَ ۞

67. Dominion
In the name of Allah. Most Gracious, Most Merciful.

(٦٧) سُوْرَةُ الْمُلْكِ مَكِّيَّةٌ (٦٧)
بِسْمِ اللهِ الرَّحْمٰنِ الرَّحِيْمِ

1. Blessed be He in Whose hands is Dominion; and He over all things has Power;-

تَبٰرَكَ الَّذِي بِيَدِهِ الْمُلْكُ وَهُوَ عَلٰى كُلِّ شَيْءٍ قَدِيْرُ ۞

2. He Who created Death and Life, that He may try which of you is best in deed: and He is the Exalted in Might, Oft-Forgiving;-

الَّذِي خَلَقَ الْمَوْتَ وَالْحَيٰوةَ لِيَبْلُوَكُمْ اَيُّكُمْ اَحْسَنُ عَمَلًا ۚ وَهُوَ الْعَزِيْزُ الْغَفُوْرُ ۞

3. He Who created the seven heavens one above another: no

الَّذِي خَلَقَ سَبْعَ سَمٰوٰتٍ طِبَاقًا ۗ مَا

want of proportion will you see in the Creation of (Allah) Most Gracious. So turn your vision again: do you see any flaw?

4.　　Again turn your vision a second time: (your) vision will come back to you dull and discomfited, in a state worn out.

5.　　And We have, (from of old), adorned the lowest heaven with Lamps, and We have made such (Lamps) (as) missiles to drive away the Evil Ones, and have prepared for them the Chastisement of the Blazing Fire.

6.　　For those who reject their Lord (and Cherisher) is the Penalty of Hell: and evil is (such), destination.

7.　　When they are cast therein, they will hear the (terrible) drawing in of its breath even as it blazes forth,

8.　　Almost bursting with fury: every time a Group is cast therein, its Keepers will ask, "Did no Warner come to you?"

9.　　They will say: "Yes indeed; a Warner did come to us, but we rejected him and said, 'Allah never sent down any (Message): you are in nothing but an egregious delusion!'"

10.　　They will further say: "had we but listened or used our intelligence, we should not (now) be among the Companions of the Blazing Fire!"

11.　　They will then confess their sins: but far will be (Forgiveness) from the Companions of the Blazing Fire!

12.　　As for those who fear their Lord unseen, for them is Forgiveness and a great Reward.

13.　　And whether you hide your word or publish it, He certainly has (full) knowledge, of the secrets of (all) hearts.

14.　　Should He not know,- He that created? and He is the One that understands the finest mysteries (and) is well-acquainted (with them).

تَرَى فِى خَلْقِ الرَّحْمٰنِ مِنْ تَفٰوُتٍ ۖ

فَارْجِعِ الْبَصَرَ هَلْ تَرٰى مِنْ فُطُوْرٍ ۝

ثُمَّ ارْجِعِ الْبَصَرَ كَرَّتَيْنِ يَنْقَلِبْ

اِلَيْكَ الْبَصَرُ خَاسِئًا وَّهُوَ حَسِيْرٌ ۝

وَلَقَدْ زَيَّنَّا السَّمَآءَ الدُّنْيَا بِمَصَابِيْحَ

وَجَعَلْنٰهَا رُجُوْمًا لِّلشَّيٰطِيْنِ وَاَعْتَدْنَا

لَهُمْ عَذَابَ السَّعِيْرِ ۝

وَلِلَّذِيْنَ كَفَرُوْا بِرَبِّهِمْ عَذَابُ

جَهَنَّمَ ۖ وَبِئْسَ الْمَصِيْرُ ۝

اِذَآ اُلْقُوْا فِيْهَا سَمِعُوْا لَهَا شَهِيْقًا

وَّهِىَ تَفُوْرُ ۝

تَكَادُ تَمَيَّزُ مِنَ الْغَيْظِ ۖ كُلَّمَآ اُلْقِىَ

فِيْهَا فَوْجٌ سَاَلَهُمْ خَزَنَتُهَآ اَلَمْ

يَاْتِكُمْ نَذِيْرٌ ۝

قَالُوْا بَلٰى قَدْ جَآءَنَا نَذِيْرٌ ۖ ە

فَكَذَّبْنَا وَقُلْنَا مَا نَزَّلَ اللّٰهُ مِنْ

شَىْءٍ ۚ اِنْ اَنْتُمْ اِلَّا فِىْ ضَلٰلٍ كَبِيْرٍ ۝

وَقَالُوْا لَوْ كُنَّا نَسْمَعُ اَوْ نَعْقِلُ مَا

كُنَّا فِىْٓ اَصْحٰبِ السَّعِيْرِ ۝

فَاعْتَرَفُوْا بِذَنْبِهِمْ ۖ فَسُحْقًا

لِّاَصْحٰبِ السَّعِيْرِ ۝

اِنَّ الَّذِيْنَ يَخْشَوْنَ رَبَّهُمْ بِالْغَيْبِ

لَهُمْ مَّغْفِرَةٌ وَّاَجْرٌ كَبِيْرٌ ۝

وَاَسِرُّوْا قَوْلَكُمْ اَوِ اجْهَرُوْا بِهٖ ۖ اِنَّهٗ

عَلِيْمٌۢ بِذَاتِ الصُّدُوْرِ ۝

اَلَا يَعْلَمُ مَنْ خَلَقَ ۖ وَهُوَ اللَّطِيْفُ

15.　It is He Who has made the earth manageable for you, so you traverse through its tracts and enjoy of the Sustenance which He furnishes: but unto Him is the Resurrection.

16.　Do you feel secure that He Who is in Heaven will not cause you to be swallowed up by the earth even it shakes (as in an earthquake)?

17.　Or do you feel secure that He Who is in Heaven will not send against you a violent tornado (with showers of stones), so that you shall know how (terrible) was My warning?

18.　But indeed men before them rejected (My warning): then how (terrible) was My rejection (of them)?

19.　Do they not observe the birds above them, spreading their wings and folding them in? None can uphold them except (Allah) Most Gracious: truly it is He that watches over all things.

20.　Nay, who is there that can help you, (even as) an army, besides (Allah) Most Merciful? In nothing but delusion are the Unbelievers.

21.　Or who is there that can provide you with Sustenance if He were to withhold His provision? Nay, they obstinately persist in insolent impiety and flight (from the Truth).

22.　Is then one who walks headlong, with his face grovelling, better guided,- or one who walks evenly on a Straight Way?

23.　Say: "It is He Who has created you (and made you grow), and made for you the faculties of hearing, seeing, feeling and understanding: little thanks it is you give.

24.　Say: "It is He Who has multiplied you through the earth,

SÛRAH-68
AL-QALAM
(INTRODUCTION)

This is a very early Makkan revelation. The general Muslim opinion is that a great part of it was second in order of revelation, the first being S. 96. *(Iqraa)*, verses 1-5: see *Itqân*, Chapter 7.

The last Sûrah having defined the true Reality in contrast with the false standards set up by men, this illustrates the theme by an actual historical example. Our Holy Prophet was the sanest and wisest of man: those who could not understand him called him mad or possessed. So, in every age, it is the habit of the world to call Truth Falsehood and Wisdom Madness, and, on the other hand, to exalt Selfishness as Planning, and Arrogance as Power. The contrast is shown up between the two kinds of men and their inner worth.

and to Him shall you be gathered together."

25. They ask: When will this promise be (fulfilled)? - If you are telling the truth.

وَاِلَيْهِ تُحْشَرُوْنَ ۝

وَيَقُوْلُوْنَ مَتٰى هٰذَا الْوَعْدُ اِنْ كُنْتُمْ صٰدِقِيْنَ ۝

26. Say: "As to the knowledge of the time, it is with Allah alone: I am (sent) only to warn plainly in public."

قُلْ اِنَّمَا الْعِلْمُ عِنْدَ اللهِ ۫ وَاِنَّمَاۤ اَنَا نَذِيْرٌ مُّبِيْنٌ ۝

27. At length, when they see it close at hand, grieved will be the faces of the Unbelievers, and it will be said (to them): "This is (the promise fulfilled), which you were calling for!"

فَلَمَّا رَاَوْهُ زُلْفَةً سِيْٓئَتْ وُجُوْهُ الَّذِيْنَ كَفَرُوْا وَقِيْلَ هٰذَا الَّذِىْ كُنْتُمْ بِهٖ تَدَّعُوْنَ ۝

28. Say: "You see?- If Allah were to destroy me, and those with me, or if He bestows His Mercy on us,- yet who can deliver the Unbelievers from a grievous Chastisement?"

قُلْ اَرَءَيْتُمْ اِنْ اَهْلَكَنِىَ اللهُ وَمَنْ مَّعِىَ اَوْ رَحِمَنَا فَمَنْ يُّجِيْرُ الْكٰفِرِيْنَ مِنْ عَذَابٍ اَلِيْمٍ ۝

29. Say: "He is (Allah) Most Gracious: we have believed in Him, and on Him have we put our trust: so, soon will you know which (of us) it is that is in manifest error."

قُلْ هُوَ الرَّحْمٰنُ اٰمَنَّا بِهٖ وَعَلَيْهِ تَوَكَّلْنَا ۫ فَسَتَعْلَمُوْنَ مَنْ هُوَ فِىْ ضَلٰلٍ مُّبِيْنٍ ۝

30. Say: "You see?- If your stream be some morning lost (in the underground earth), who then can supply you with clear-flowing water?"

قُلْ اَرَءَيْتُمْ اِنْ اَصْبَحَ مَآؤُكُمْ غَوْرًا فَمَنْ يَّأْتِيْكُمْ بِمَآءٍ مَّعِيْنٍ ۝

68. The Pen
In the name of Allah. Most Gracious, Most Merciful.

(٢) سُوْرَةُ الْقَلَمِ مَكِّيَّةٌ (٦٨)

بِسْمِ اللهِ الرَّحْمٰنِ الرَّحِيْمِ

1. Nun. By the Pen and by the (Record) which (men) write,-

نٓ ۚ وَالْقَلَمِ وَمَا يَسْطُرُوْنَ ۝

2. You are not, by the Grace of your Lord, mad or possessed.

مَآ اَنْتَ بِنِعْمَةِ رَبِّكَ بِمَجْنُوْنٍ ۝

3. Nay, verily for you is a Reward unfailing.

وَاِنَّ لَكَ لَاَجْرًا غَيْرَ مَمْنُوْنٍ ۝

4. And you (stand) on an exalted standard of character.

وَاِنَّكَ لَعَلٰى خُلُقٍ عَظِيْمٍ ۝

5. Soon will you see, and they will see,

فَسَتُبْصِرُ وَيُبْصِرُوْنَ ۝

6. Which of you is afflicted with madness.

بِاَيِّكُمُ الْمَفْتُوْنُ ۝

7. Verily it is your Lord that knows best, which (among men) have strayed from His Path: and He knows best those who receive (true) Guidance.

اِنَّ رَبَّكَ هُوَ اَعْلَمُ بِمَنْ ضَلَّ عَنْ سَبِيْلِهٖ ۫ وَهُوَ اَعْلَمُ بِالْمُهْتَدِيْنَ ۝

8.   So hearken not to those who deny (the Truth).

9.   Their desire is that you should be pliant: so would they be pliant.

10.   Do not obey every mean swearer;

11.   A slanderer, going about with calumnies,

12.   (Habitually) hindering (all) good, transgressing beyond bounds, deep in sin,

13.   Violent (and cruel),- with all that, base-born,-

14.   Because he possesses wealth and (numerous) sons.

15.   When to him are rehearsed Our Signs, he cries "Tales of the ancients", !

16.   Soon shall We brand (the beast) on the snout!

17.   Verily We have tried them as We tried the People of the Garden, when they resolved to gather the fruits of the (garden) in the morning,

18.   But made no reservation, ("If it be Allah's Will").

19.   Then there came on the (garden) a visitation from your Lord, (which swept away) all around, while they were asleep.

20.   So the (garden) became, by the morning, like a dark and desolate spot, (whose fruit had been gathered).

21.   As the morning broke, they called out, one to another,-

22.   "You go to your tilth (betimes) in the morning, if you would gather the fruits."

23.   So they departed, conversing in secret low tones, (saying)-

24.   "Let not a single indigent person break in upon you into the (garden) this day."

25.   And they opened the morning, strong in an (unjust) resolve.

26.   But when they saw the (garden), they said: "We have surely lost our way.

27.   "Indeed we are shut out (of the fruits of our labour)!"

28.   Said one of them, more just (than the rest): "Did I not say to you,

فَلَا تُطِعِ الْمُكَذِّبِيْنَ ۞

وَدُّوْا لَوْ تُدْهِنُ فَيُدْهِنُوْنَ ۞

وَلَا تُطِعْ كُلَّ حَلَّافٍ مَّهِيْنٍ ۞

هَمَّازٍ مَّشَّآءٍ بِنَمِيْمٍ ۞

مَّنَّاعٍ لِّلْخَيْرِ مُعْتَدٍ اَثِيْمٍ ۞

عُتُلٍّ بَعْدَ ذٰلِكَ زَنِيْمٍ ۞

اَنْ كَانَ ذَا مَالٍ وَّبَنِيْنَ ۞

اِذَا تُتْلٰى عَلَيْهِ اٰيَاتُنَا قَالَ اَسَاطِيْرُ

الْاَوَّلِيْنَ ۞

سَنَسِمُهٗ عَلَى الْخُرْطُوْمِ ۞

اِنَّا بَلَوْنٰهُمْ كَمَا بَلَوْنَا اَصْحٰبَ الْجَنَّةِ ۚ

اِذْ اَقْسَمُوْا لَيَصْرِمُنَّهَا مُصْبِحِيْنَ ۞

وَلَا يَسْتَثْنُوْنَ ۞

فَطَافَ عَلَيْهَا طَآئِفٌ مِّنْ رَّبِّكَ

وَهُمْ نَآئِمُوْنَ ۞

فَاَصْبَحَتْ كَالصَّرِيْمِ ۞

فَتَنَادَوْا مُصْبِحِيْنَ ۞

اَنِ اغْدُوْا عَلٰى حَرْثِكُمْ اِنْ

كُنْتُمْ صٰرِمِيْنَ ۞

فَانْطَلَقُوْا وَهُمْ يَتَخَافَتُوْنَ ۞

اَنْ لَّا يَدْخُلَنَّهَا الْيَوْمَ عَلَيْكُمْ

مِّسْكِيْنٌ ۞

وَّغَدَوْا عَلٰى حَرْدٍ قٰدِرِيْنَ ۞

فَلَمَّا رَاَوْهَا قَالُوْۤا اِنَّا لَضَآلُّوْنَ ۞

بَلْ نَحْنُ مَحْرُوْمُوْنَ ۞

قَالَ اَوْسَطُهُمْ اَلَمْ اَقُلْ لَّكُمْ

"Why not glorify (Allah)?"

لَوْلَا تُسَبِّحُونَ ۝

29. They said: "Glory to our Lord! Verily we have been doing wrong!"

قَالُوا سُبْحَانَ رَبِّنَا إِنَّا كُنَّا ظَالِمِينَ ۝

30. Then they turned, one against another, in reproach.

فَأَقْبَلَ بَعْضُهُمْ عَلَى بَعْضٍ يَتَلَاوَمُونَ ۝

31. They said: "Alas for us! We have indeed transgressed!

قَالُوا يَا وَيْلَنَا إِنَّا كُنَّا طَاغِينَ ۝

32. "It may be that our Lord will give us in exchange a better (garden) than this: for we do turn to Him (in repentance)!"

عَسَى رَبُّنَا أَنْ يُبْدِلَنَا خَيْرًا مِنْهَا إِنَّا إِلَى رَبِّنَا رَاغِبُونَ ۝

33. Such is the Punishment (in this life); but greater is the Punishment in the Hereafter,- if only they knew!

كَذَلِكَ الْعَذَابُ وَلَعَذَابُ الْآخِرَةِ أَكْبَرُ لَوْ كَانُوا يَعْلَمُونَ ۝

34. Verily, for the Righteous, are Gardens of Delight, in the Presence of their Lord.

إِنَّ لِلْمُتَّقِينَ عِنْدَ رَبِّهِمْ جَنَّاتِ النَّعِيمِ ۝

35. Shall We then treat the People of Faith like the People of Sin?

أَفَنَجْعَلُ الْمُسْلِمِينَ كَالْمُجْرِمِينَ ۝

36. What is the matter with you? How judge you?

مَا لَكُمْ كَيْفَ تَحْكُمُونَ ۝

37. Or do you have a book through which you learn-

أَمْ لَكُمْ كِتَابٌ فِيهِ تَدْرُسُونَ ۝

38. That you shall have, through it whatever you choose?

إِنَّ لَكُمْ فِيهِ لَمَا تَخَيَّرُونَ ۝

39. Or do you have Covenants with Us on oath, reaching to the Day of Judgment, (providing) that you shall have whatever you shall demand?

أَمْ لَكُمْ أَيْمَانٌ عَلَيْنَا بَالِغَةٌ إِلَى يَوْمِ الْقِيَامَةِ إِنَّ لَكُمْ لَمَا تَحْكُمُونَ ۝

40. You ask them, which of them will stand surety for that!

سَلْهُمْ أَيُّهُمْ بِذَلِكَ زَعِيمٌ ۝

41. Or have they some "Partners" (in Godhead)? Then let them produce their "partners", if they are truthful!

أَمْ لَهُمْ شُرَكَاءُ فَلْيَأْتُوا بِشُرَكَائِهِمْ إِنْ كَانُوا صَادِقِينَ ۝

42. The Day that the shin shall be laid bare, and they shall be summoned to bow in adoration, but they shall not be able,-

يَوْمَ يُكْشَفُ عَنْ سَاقٍ وَيُدْعَوْنَ إِلَى السُّجُودِ فَلَا يَسْتَطِيعُونَ ۝

43. Their eyes will be cast down,- ignominy will cover them; seeing that they had been summoned aforetime to bow in adoration, while they were hale and healthy, (and had refused).

خَاشِعَةً أَبْصَارُهُمْ تَرْهَقُهُمْ ذِلَّةٌ وَقَدْ كَانُوا يُدْعَوْنَ إِلَى السُّجُودِ وَهُمْ سَالِمُونَ ۝

44. Then leave Me alone with such as reject this Message: by degrees shall We punish them from directions they do not perceive.

فَذَرْنِي وَمَنْ يُكَذِّبُ بِهَذَا الْحَدِيثِ سَنَسْتَدْرِجُهُمْ مِنْ حَيْثُ لَا يَعْلَمُونَ ۝

SÛRAH-69
AL-HÂQQA
(INTRODUCTION)

This Sûrah belongs to the early middle period of Makkan Revelation. The eschatological argument is pressed home: "the absolute Truth cannot fail; it must prevail; therefore, be not lured by false appearances in this life; it is Revelation that points to the sure and certain Reality."

45. A (long) respite will I grant them: truly powerful is My Plan.

وَأُمْلِى لَهُمْ ۚ إِنَّ كَيْدِى مَتِينٌ ۝

46. Or is it that you does ask them for a reward, so that they are burdened with a load of debt?-

أَمْ تَسْـَٔلُهُمْ أَجْرًا فَهُم مِّن مَّغْرَمٍ مُّثْقَلُونَ ۝

47. Or that the Unseen is in their hands, so that they can write it down?

أَمْ عِندَهُمُ الْغَيْبُ فَهُمْ يَكْتُبُونَ ۝

48. So wait with patience for the Command of your Lord, and be not like the Companion of the Fish,- when he cried out in agony.

فَاصْبِرْ لِحُكْمِ رَبِّكَ وَلَا تَكُن كَصَاحِبِ الْحُوتِ إِذْ نَادَىٰ وَهُوَ مَكْظُومٌ ۝

49. Had not Grace from his Lord reached him, he would indeed have been cast off on the naked shore, in disgrace.

لَّوْلَا أَن تَدَارَكَهُ نِعْمَةٌ مِّن رَّبِّهِ لَنُبِذَ بِالْعَرَاءِ وَهُوَ مَذْمُومٌ ۝

50. Thus did his Lord choose him and make him of the Company of the Righteous.

فَاجْتَبَاهُ رَبُّهُ فَجَعَلَهُ مِنَ الصَّالِحِينَ ۝

51. And the Unbelievers would almost trip you up with their eyes when they hear the Message; and they say: "Surely he is possessed!"

وَإِن يَكَادُ الَّذِينَ كَفَرُوا لَيُزْلِقُونَكَ بِأَبْصَارِهِمْ لَمَّا سَمِعُوا الذِّكْرَ وَيَقُولُونَ إِنَّهُ لَمَجْنُونٌ ۝

52. But it is nothing less than a Message to all the worlds.

وَمَا هُوَ إِلَّا ذِكْرٌ لِّلْعَالَمِينَ ۝

---

69. The Sure Reality
In the name of Allah. Most Gracious, Most Merciful.

سُورَةُ الْحَاقَّةِ مَكِّيَّةٌ (٥٢)
بِسْمِ اللَّهِ الرَّحْمَٰنِ الرَّحِيمِ

1. The Sure Reality!

الْحَاقَّةُ ۝

2. What is the Sure Reality?

مَا الْحَاقَّةُ ۝

3. And what will make you realize what the Sure Reality is?

وَمَا أَدْرَاكَ مَا الْحَاقَّةُ ۝

4. The Thamûd and the 'Ad People (branded) as false the Stunning Calamity!

كَذَّبَتْ ثَمُودُ وَعَادٌ بِالْقَارِعَةِ ۝

5. As for Thamûd, they were destroyed by a terrible Storm of thunder and lightning!

فَأَمَّا ثَمُودُ فَأُهْلِكُوا بِالطَّاغِيَةِ ۝

6. And the 'Ad, they were destroyed by a furious Wind, exceedingly violent;

وَأَمَّا عَادٌ فَأُهْلِكُوا بِرِيحٍ صَرْصَرٍ عَاتِيَةٍ ۝

7. He made it rage against them seven nights and eight days in succession: so that you could see the (whole) people lying

سَخَّرَهَا عَلَيْهِمْ سَبْعَ لَيَالٍ وَثَمَانِيَةَ أَيَّامٍ حُسُومًا فَتَرَى الْقَوْمَ فِيهَا

prostrate in its (path), as if they
had been roots of hollow palm-
trees tumbled down!

8. Then do you see any of
them left surviving?

9. And Pharaoh, and those
before him, and the Cities Overthrown, committed habitual Sin.

10. And disobeyed (each) the
Apostle of their Lord; so He
punished them with an abundant
Chastisement.

11. We, when the water (of
Noah's Flood) overflowed
beyond its limits, carried you
(mankind), in the floating (Ark),

12. That We might make it a
Message unto you, and that ears
(that should hear the tale and)
retain its memory should bear its
(lessons) in remembrance.

13. Then, when one blast is
sounded on the Trumpet,

14. And the earth is moved,
and its mountains, and they are
crushed to powder at one stroke,-

15. On that Day shall the
(Great) Event come to pass.

16. And the sky will be rent
asunder, for it will that Day be
flimsy,

17. And the angels will be on
its sides, and eight will, that
Day, bear the Throne of your
Lord above them.

18. On that day you shall be
exposed; not a secret of you will
be hidden.

19. Then he that will be given
his Record in his right hand will
say: "Ah here! You read my
Record!

20. "I did really understand
that my Account would (One
Day) reach me!"

21. And he will be in a life of
Bliss,

22. In a Garden on high,

23. The Fruits whereof (will
hang in bunches) low and near.

24. "You eat and you drink, with full satisfaction; because of the (good) that you sent before you, in the days that are gone!"

كُلُوا وَاشْرَبُوا هَنِيئًا بِمَا أَسْلَفْتُمْ فِي الْأَيَّامِ الْخَالِيَةِ ۝

25. And he that will be given his Record in his left hand, will say: "Ah! Would that my Record had not been given to me!

وَأَمَّا مَنْ أُوتِيَ كِتٰبَهُ بِشِمَالِهِ ۙ فَيَقُولُ يٰلَيْتَنِي لَمْ أُوتَ كِتٰبِيَهْ ۝

26. "And that I had never realised how my account (stood)!

وَلَمْ أَدْرِ مَا حِسَابِيَهْ ۝

27. "Ah! Would that (Death) had made an end of me!

يٰلَيْتَهَا كَانَتِ الْقَاضِيَةَ ۝

28. "Of no profit to me has been my wealth!

مَا أَغْنٰى عَنِّي مَالِيَهْ ۝

29. "My power has perished from me!"...

هَلَكَ عَنِّي سُلْطٰنِيَهْ ۝

30. (The stern command will say): "You seize him, and you bind him,

خُذُوهُ فَغُلُّوهُ ۝

31. "And you burn him in the Blazing Fire.

ثُمَّ الْجَحِيمَ صَلُّوهُ ۝

32. "Further, make him march in a chain, whereof the length is seventy cubits!

ثُمَّ فِي سِلْسِلَةٍ ذَرْعُهَا سَبْعُونَ ذِرَاعًا فَاسْلُكُوهُ ۝

33. "This was he that would not believe in Allah Most High.

إِنَّهُ كَانَ لَا يُؤْمِنُ بِاللّٰهِ الْعَظِيمِ ۝

34. "And would not encourage the feeding of the indigent!

وَلَا يَحُضُّ عَلٰى طَعَامِ الْمِسْكِينِ ۝

35. "So no friend he has here this Day.

فَلَيْسَ لَهُ الْيَوْمَ هٰهُنَا حَمِيمٌ ۝

36. "Nor he has any food except the corruption from the washing of wounds,

وَلَا طَعَامٌ إِلَّا مِنْ غِسْلِينٍ ۝

37. "Which none do eat but those in sin."

لَا يَأْكُلُهُ إِلَّا الْخَاطِئُونَ ۝

38. So I do call to witness what you see,

فَلَا أُقْسِمُ بِمَا تُبْصِرُونَ ۝

39. And what you do not see,

وَمَا لَا تُبْصِرُونَ ۝

40. That this is verily the word of an honoured Apostle;

إِنَّهُ لَقَوْلُ رَسُولٍ كَرِيمٍ ۝

41. It is not the word of a poet: little it is you believe!

وَمَا هُوَ بِقَوْلِ شَاعِرٍ قَلِيلًا مَا تُؤْمِنُونَ ۝

42. Nor is it the word of a soothsayer: little admonition it is you receive.

وَلَا بِقَوْلِ كَاهِنٍ ۙ قَلِيلًا مَا تَذَكَّرُونَ ۝

43. (This is) a Message sent down from the Lord of the Worlds.

تَنْزِيلٌ مِّنْ رَّبِّ الْعٰلَمِينَ ۝

44. And if the Apostle were to invent any sayings in Our name,

وَلَوْ تَقَوَّلَ عَلَيْنَا بَعْضَ الْأَقَاوِيلِ ۝

SÛRAH-70
AL-MA'ÂRIJ
(INTRODUCTION)

This is another eschatological Sûrah closely connected in subject-matter with the last one. Patience and the mystery of Time will show the ways that climb to Heaven. Sin and Goodness must each eventually come to its own.

Chronologically it belongs to the late early or early middle Makkan period, possibly soon after S. 69.

45. We should certainly seize him by his right hand,

46. An We should certainly then cut off the artery of his heart:

47. Nor could any of you withhold him (from Our wrath).

48. But verily this is a Message for the God-fearing.

49. And We certainly know that there are amongst you those that reject (it).

50. But truly (Revelation) is a cause of sorrow for the Unbelievers.

51. But verily it is Truth of assured certainty.

52. So glorify the name of your Lord Most High.

كَاخُذُ نَامِنْهُ بِالْيَمِيْنِ ۞

ثُمَّ لَقَطَعْنَا مِنْهُ الْوَتِيْنَ ۞

فَمَا مِنْكُمْ مِّنْ اَحَدٍ عَنْهُ حٰجِزِيْنَ ۞

وَاِنَّهُ لَتَذْكِرَةٌ لِّلْمُتَّقِيْنَ ۞

وَاِنَّا لَنَعْلَمُ اَنَّ مِنْكُمْ مُّكَذِّبِيْنَ ۞

وَاِنَّهُ لَحَسْرَةٌ عَلَى الْكٰفِرِيْنَ ۞

وَاِنَّهُ لَحَقُّ الْيَقِيْنِ ۞

فَسَبِّحْ بِاسْمِ رَبِّكَ الْعَظِيْمِ ۞

70. The Ways of Ascent
In the name of Allah. Most Gracious, Most Merciful.

سُوْرَةُ الْمَعَارِجِ مَكِّيَّةٌ (٧٠) (٢٩)

بِسْمِ اللّٰهِ الرَّحْمٰنِ الرَّحِيْمِ

1. A questioner asked about a Chastisement to befall-

2. The Unbelievers, the which there is none to ward off,-

3. (A Penalty) from Allah, Lord of the Ways of Ascent.

4. The angels and the spirit ascend unto Him in a Day the measure whereof is (as) fifty thousand years:

5. Therefore you hold patience,–a patience of beautiful (contentment).

6. They see the (Day) indeed as a far-off (event):

7. But We see it (quite) near.

8. The Day that the sky will be like molten brass,

9. And the mountains will be like wool,

10. And no friend will ask after a friend,

11. Though they will be put in sight of each other,–the sinner's desire will be: would that he could redeem himself from the Chastisement of that Day by (sacrificing) his children.

12. His wife and his brother,

13. His kindred who sheltered him,

سَاَلَ سَائِلٌ بِعَذَابٍ وَّاقِعٍ ۞

لِّلْكٰفِرِيْنَ لَيْسَ لَهُ دَافِعٌ ۞

مِّنَ اللّٰهِ ذِى الْمَعَارِجِ ۞

تَعْرُجُ الْمَلٰئِكَةُ وَالرُّوْحُ اِلَيْهِ فِيْ

يَوْمٍ كَانَ مِقْدَارُهُ خَمْسِيْنَ

اَلْفَ سَنَةٍ ۞

فَاصْبِرْ صَبْرًا جَمِيْلًا ۞

اِنَّهُمْ يَرَوْنَهُ بَعِيْدًا ۞

وَّنَرٰىهُ قَرِيْبًا ۞

يَوْمَ تَكُوْنُ السَّمَاءُ كَالْمُهْلِ ۞

وَتَكُوْنُ الْجِبَالُ كَالْعِهْنِ ۞

وَلَا يَسْئَلُ حَمِيْمٌ حَمِيْمًا ۞

يُبَصَّرُوْنَهُمْ يَوَدُّ الْمُجْرِمُ لَوْ يَفْتَدِيْ

مِنْ عَذَابِ يَوْمِئِذٍ بِبَنِيْهِ ۞

وَصَاحِبَتِهِ وَاَخِيْهِ ۞

وَفَصِيْلَتِهِ الَّتِيْ تُـٔوِيْهِ ۞

14. And all, all that is on earth,- so it could deliver him:

وَمَنْ فِي الْأَرْضِ جَمِيعًا ثُمَّ يُنْجِيهِ ۞

15. By no means! for it would be the Fire of Hell!-

كَلَّا إِنَّهَا لَظَىٰ ۞

16. Plucking out (his being) right to the skull!-

نَزَّاعَةً لِّلشَّوَىٰ ۞

17. Inviting (all) such as turn their backs and turn away their faces (from the Right),

تَدْعُوا مَنْ أَدْبَرَ وَتَوَلَّىٰ ۞

18. And collect (wealth) and hide it (from use)!

وَجَمَعَ فَأَوْعَىٰ ۞

19. Truly man was created very impatient;-

إِنَّ الْإِنْسَانَ خُلِقَ هَلُوعًا ۞

20. Fretful when evil touches him;

إِذَا مَسَّهُ الشَّرُّ جَزُوعًا ۞

21. And niggardly when good reaches him;-

وَإِذَا مَسَّهُ الْخَيْرُ مَنُوعًا ۞

22. Not so those devoted to Prayer;-

إِلَّا الْمُصَلِّينَ ۞

23. Those who remain steadfast to their prayer;

الَّذِينَ هُمْ عَلَىٰ صَلَاتِهِمْ دَائِمُونَ ۞

24. And those in whose wealth is a recognised right.

وَالَّذِينَ فِي أَمْوَالِهِمْ حَقٌّ مَّعْلُومٌ ۞

25. For the beggar and the destitute;

لِّلسَّائِلِ وَالْمَحْرُومِ ۞

26. And those who hold to the truth of the Day of Judgment;

وَالَّذِينَ يُصَدِّقُونَ بِيَوْمِ الدِّينِ ۞

27. And those who fear the displeasure of their Lord,-

وَالَّذِينَ هُم مِّنْ عَذَابِ رَبِّهِم مُّشْفِقُونَ ۞

28. For their Lord's displeasure is the opposite of Peace and Tranquillity;-

إِنَّ عَذَابَ رَبِّهِمْ غَيْرُ مَأْمُونٍ ۞

29. And those who guard their chastity,

وَالَّذِينَ هُمْ لِفُرُوجِهِمْ حَافِظُونَ ۞

30. Except with their wives and the (captives) whom their right hands possess,- for (then) they are not to be blamed,

إِلَّا عَلَىٰ أَزْوَاجِهِمْ أَوْ مَا مَلَكَتْ أَيْمَانُهُمْ فَإِنَّهُمْ غَيْرُ مَلُومِينَ ۞

31. But those who trespass beyond this are transgressors;

فَمَنِ ابْتَغَىٰ وَرَاءَ ذَٰلِكَ فَأُولَٰئِكَ هُمُ الْعَادُونَ ۞

32. And those who respect their trusts and covenants;

وَالَّذِينَ هُمْ لِأَمَانَاتِهِمْ وَعَهْدِهِمْ رَاعُونَ ۞

33. And those who stand firm in their testimonies;

وَالَّذِينَ هُم بِشَهَادَاتِهِمْ قَائِمُونَ ۞

34. And those who guard (the sacredness) of their worship;-

وَالَّذِينَ هُمْ عَلَىٰ صَلَاتِهِمْ يُحَافِظُونَ ۞

SÛRAH-71
NÛḤ
(INTRODUCTION)

This is another early Makkan Sûrah, of which the date has no significance. The theme is that while Good must uphold the standard of Truth and Righteousness, a stage is reached when it must definitely part company with Evil, lest Evil should spread its corruption abroad. This theme is embodied in the prayer of Noah just before the Flood. The story of Noah's agony is almost a Parable for the Holy Prophet's persecution in the Makkan period.

35. Such will be the honoured ones in the Gardens (of Bliss).

اُولٰٓئِكَ فِيْ جَنّٰتٍ مُّكْرَمُوْنَ ۟

36. Now what is the matter with the Unbelievers that they rush madly before you—

فَمَالِ الَّذِيْنَ كَفَرُوْا قِبَلَكَ

37. From the right and from the left, in crowds?

مُهْطِعِيْنَ ۟ عَنِ الْيَمِيْنِ وَعَنِ الشِّمَالِ عِزِيْنَ ۟

38. Does every man of them long to enter the Garden of Bliss?

اَيَطْمَعُ كُلُّ امْرِئٍ مِّنْهُمْ اَنْ يُّدْخَلَ جَنَّةَ نَعِيْمٍ ۟

39. By no means! For We have created them out of the (base matter) they know about.

كَلَّا ۚ اِنَّا خَلَقْنٰهُمْ مِّمَّا يَعْلَمُوْنَ ۟

40. Now I do call to witness the Lord of all points in the East and the West that We can certainly-

فَلَاۤ اُقْسِمُ بِرَبِّ الْمَشٰرِقِ وَالْمَغٰرِبِ اِنَّا لَقٰدِرُوْنَ ۟

41. Substitute for them better (men) than they; and We are not to be defeated (in Our Plan).

عَلٰۤى اَنْ نُّبَدِّلَ خَيْرًا مِّنْهُمْ ۙ وَمَا نَحْنُ بِمَسْبُوْقِيْنَ ۟

42. So leave them to plunge in vain talk and play about, until they encounter that Day of theirs which they have been promised!-

فَذَرْهُمْ يَخُوْضُوْا وَيَلْعَبُوْا حَتّٰى يُلٰقُوْا يَوْمَهُمُ الَّذِيْ يُوْعَدُوْنَ ۟

43. The day when they come forth from the graves in haste, as racing to a goal.

يَوْمَ يَخْرُجُوْنَ مِنَ الْاَجْدَاثِ سِرَاعًا كَاَنَّهُمْ اِلٰى نُصُبٍ يُّوْفِضُوْنَ ۟

44. Their eyes lowered in dejection,- ignominy covering them (all over)! such is the Day the which they are promised!

خَاشِعَةً اَبْصَارُهُمْ تَرْهَقُهُمْ ذِلَّةٌ ۚ ذٰلِكَ الْيَوْمُ الَّذِيْ كَانُوْا يُوْعَدُوْنَ ۟

71. Noah - The Prophet
In the name of Allah. Most Gracious, Most Merciful.

سُوْرَةُ نُوْحٍ مَكِّيَّةٌ (٢٨)

بِسْمِ اللّٰهِ الرَّحْمٰنِ الرَّحِيْمِ

1. We sent Noah to his People (with the Command): "Warn your People before there comes to them a grievous Chastisement."

اِنَّاۤ اَرْسَلْنَا نُوْحًا اِلٰى قَوْمِهٖۤ اَنْ اَنْذِرْ قَوْمَكَ مِنْ قَبْلِ اَنْ يَّاْتِيَهُمْ عَذَابٌ اَلِيْمٌ ۟

2. He said: O my People! I am a plain warner unto you.

قَالَ يٰقَوْمِ اِنِّيْ لَكُمْ نَذِيْرٌ مُّبِيْنٌ ۟

3. "That you should worship Allah, fear Him and obey me:

اَنِ اعْبُدُوا اللّٰهَ وَاتَّقُوْهُ وَاَطِيْعُوْنِ ۟

4. "So that He may forgive you your sins and give you respite for a stated Term: for when the Term given by Allah is

يَغْفِرْ لَكُمْ مِّنْ ذُنُوْبِكُمْ وَيُؤَخِّرْكُمْ اِلٰٓى اَجَلٍ مُّسَمًّى ۚ اِنَّ اَجَلَ اللّٰهِ اِذَا

accomplished, it cannot be put forward: if you only knew."

5.   He said: "O my Lord! I have called to my People night and day:

6.   ''But my call only increases (their) flight (from the Right).

7.   "And every time I have called to them, that You might forgive them, they have (only) thrust their fingers into their ears, covered themselves up with their garments, grown obstinate, and given themselves up to arrogance.

8.   "So I have called to them aloud;

9.   "Further I have spoken to them in public and secretly in private,

10.   "Saying, 'Ask forgiveness from your Lord; for He is Oft-Forgiving;

11.   "He will send rain to you in abundance;

12.   "'Give you increase in wealth and sons; and bestow on you gardens and bestow on you rivers (of flowing water).

13.   " 'What is the matter with you, that you are not conscious of Allah's Majesty,—

14.   " 'Seeing that it is He that has created you in diverse stages?

15.   'Don't you see how Allah has created the seven heavens one above another,

16.   "'And made the moon a light in their midst, and made the sun as a (Glorious) Lamp?

17.   "'And Allah has produced you from the earth growing (gradually),

18.   "'And in the End He will return you into the (earth), and raise you forth (again at the Resurrection)?

19.   And Allah has made the earth for you as a carpet (spread out),.

جَآءَ لَا يُؤَخَّرُ لَوْ كُنْتُمْ تَعْلَمُوْنَ ۝

قَالَ رَبِّ اِنِّيْ دَعَوْتُ قَوْمِيْ لَيْلًا

وَّنَهَارًا ۝

فَلَمْ يَزِدْهُمْ دُعَآءِيْ اِلَّا فِرَارًا ۝

وَاِنِّيْ كُلَّمَا دَعَوْتُهُمْ لِتَغْفِرَ لَهُمْ

جَعَلُوْۤا اَصَابِعَهُمْ فِيْۤ اٰذَانِهِمْ وَ

اسْتَغْشَوْا ثِيَابَهُمْ وَاَصَرُّوْا وَ

اسْتَكْبَرُوا اسْتِكْبَارًا ۝

ثُمَّ اِنِّيْ دَعَوْتُهُمْ جِهَارًا ۝

ثُمَّ اِنِّيْۤ اَعْلَنْتُ لَهُمْ وَاَسْرَرْتُ

لَهُمْ اِسْرَارًا ۝

فَقُلْتُ اسْتَغْفِرُوْا رَبَّكُمْ اِنَّهٗ

كَانَ غَفَّارًا ۝

يُّرْسِلِ السَّمَآءَ عَلَيْكُمْ مِّدْرَارًا ۝

وَّيُمْدِدْكُمْ بِاَمْوَالٍ وَّبَنِيْنَ وَيَجْعَلْ

لَّكُمْ جَنّٰتٍ وَّيَجْعَلْ لَّكُمْ اَنْهٰرًا ۝

مَا لَكُمْ لَا تَرْجُوْنَ لِلّٰهِ وَقَارًا ۝

وَقَدْ خَلَقَكُمْ اَطْوَارًا ۝

اَلَمْ تَرَوْا كَيْفَ خَلَقَ اللّٰهُ سَبْعَ

سَمٰوٰتٍ طِبَاقًا ۝

وَّجَعَلَ الْقَمَرَ فِيْهِنَّ نُوْرًا وَّجَعَلَ

الشَّمْسَ سِرَاجًا ۝

وَاللّٰهُ اَنْبَتَكُمْ مِّنَ الْاَرْضِ نَبَاتًا ۝

ثُمَّ يُعِيْدُكُمْ فِيْهَا وَيُخْرِجُكُمْ

اِخْرَاجًا ۝

وَاللّٰهُ جَعَلَ لَكُمُ الْاَرْضَ بِسَاطًا ۝

SÛRAH-72
AL-JINN
(INTRODUCTION)

This is a late Makkan Sûrah, of which we can be tolerably certain of the date. It was two years before the Hijrat, when the Prophet, despised and rejected in his native city of Makkah, went to evangelise the lordly men of Taif. They maltreated him and nearly killed him; what caused him even greater pain was the maltreatment of the humble and lowly men who went with him. Tabari has handed down that memorable Prayer of faith and humility which he offered in the midst of his suffering. On his return journey to Makkah, a glorious vision was revealed to him, -hidden spiritual forces working for him, -people not known to him accepting his mission while his own people were still rejecting him. Within two months some strangers from Madinah had privately met him and laid the foundations of that Hijrat which was to change the fate of Arabia and the course of world history.

20. 'That you may go about therein, in spacious roads.'

لِتَسْلُكُوا مِنْهَا سُبُلًا فِجَاجًا ۞

21. Noah said: "O my Lord! They have disobeyed me, but they follow (men) whose wealth and children give them no increase but only loss.

قَالَ نُوحٌ رَّبِّ إِنَّهُمْ عَصَوْنِي وَ اتَّبَعُوا مَنْ لَّمْ يَزِدْهُ مَالُهُ وَ وَلَدُهُ إِلَّا خَسَارًا ۞

22. "And they have devised a tremendous Plot.

وَمَكَرُوا مَكْرًا كُبَّارًا ۞

23. "And they have said (to each other), 'Do not abandon your gods: abandon neither Wadd nor Suwa', neither Yaguth nor Ya'uq, nor Nasr';-

وَقَالُوا لَا تَذَرُنَّ الِهَتَكُمْ وَلَا تَذَرُنَّ وَدًّا وَّلَا سُوَاعًا وَّلَا يَغُوثَ وَيَعُوقَ وَنَسْرًا ۞

24. "They have already misled many; and You grant no increase to the wrong- doers but in straying (from their mark)."

وَقَدْ أَضَلُّوا كَثِيرًا ۖ وَلَا تَزِدِ الظَّالِمِينَ إِلَّا ضَلَالًا ۞

25. Because of their sins they were drowned (in the flood), and were made to enter the Fire (of Punishment): and they found in lieu of Allah- none to help them.

مِمَّا خَطِيئَاتِهِمْ أُغْرِقُوا فَأُدْخِلُوا نَارًا ۖ فَلَمْ يَجِدُوا لَهُمْ مِّنْ دُونِ اللهِ أَنْصَارًا ۞

26. And Noah said: "O my Lord! Do not leave of the Unbelievers, a single one on earth!

وَقَالَ نُوحٌ رَّبِّ لَا تَذَرْ عَلَى الْأَرْضِ مِنَ الْكَافِرِينَ دَيَّارًا ۞

27. "For, if You leave (any of) them, they will but mislead Your devotees, and they willy breed none but wicked ungrateful ones.

إِنَّكَ إِنْ تَذَرْهُمْ يُضِلُّوا عِبَادَكَ وَلَا يَلِدُوا إِلَّا فَاجِرًا كَفَّارًا ۞

28. "O my Lord! Forgive me, my parents, all who enter my house in Faith, and (all) believing men and believing women: and to the wrong-doers You grant no increase but in perdition!"

رَبِّ اغْفِرْ لِي وَلِوَالِدَيَّ وَلِمَنْ دَخَلَ بَيْتِيَ مُؤْمِنًا وَّلِلْمُؤْمِنِينَ وَالْمُؤْمِنَاتِ ۖ وَلَا تَزِدِ الظَّالِمِينَ إِلَّا تَبَارًا ۞

72. The Spirits
In the name of Allah. Most Gracious, Most Merciful.

(۷۲) سُوْرَةُ الْجِنّ مَكِّيَّةٌ (۲۸)
بِسْمِ اللهِ الرَّحْمٰنِ الرَّحِيمِ

1. Say: It has been revealed to me that a company of Jinns listened (to the Qur'an). They said, 'We have really heard a wonderful Recital!

قُلْ أُوحِيَ إِلَيَّ أَنَّهُ اسْتَمَعَ نَفَرٌ مِّنَ الْجِنِّ فَقَالُوا إِنَّا سَمِعْنَا قُرْآنًا عَجَبًا ۞

2.   'It gives guidance to the Right, and we have believed therein: we shall not join (in worship) any (gods) with our Lord.

3.   'And Exalted is the Majesty of our Lord: He has taken neither a wife nor a son.

4.   'There were some foolish ones among us, who used to utter extravagant lies against Allah;

5.   'But we do think that no man or spirit should say anything that is untrue against Allah.

6.   'True, there were persons among mankind who took shelter with persons among the Jinns, but they increased them in folly.

7.   'And they (came to) think as you thought, that Allah would not raise up any one (to Judgment).

8.   'And we pried into the secrets of heaven; but we found it filled with stern guards and flaming fires.

9.   'We used, indeed, to sit there in (hidden) stations, to (steal) a hearing; but any who listens now will find a flaming fire watching him in ambush.

10.   And we understand not whether ill is intended to those on earth, or whether their Lord (really) intends to guide them to right conduct.

11.   'There are among us some that are righteous, and some the contrary: we follow divergent paths.

12.   'But we think that we can by no means frustrate Allah throughout the earth, nor can we frustrate Him by flight.

13.   'And as for us, since we have listened to the Guidance, we have accepted it: and any who believes in his Lord has no fear,

either of a short (account) or of any injustice.

14. 'Amongst us are some that submit their wills (to Allah), and some that swerve from justice. Now those who submit their wills - they have sought out (the path) of right conduct:

15. 'But those who swerve,- they are (but) fuel for Hell-fire'-

16. (And Allah's Message is): "if they (the Pagans) had (only) remained on the (right) Way, We should certainly have bestowed on them Rain in abundance.

17. "That We might try them by that (means). But if any turns away from the remembrance of his Lord, He will cause him to undergo a severe Chastisement.

18. "And the places of worship are for Allah (alone): so invoke not any one along with Allah;

19. "Yet when the Devotee of Allah stands forth to invoke Him, they just make round him a dense crowd."

20. Say: "I do no more than invoke my Lord, and I do not join with Him any (false god)."

21. Say: "It is not in my power to cause you harm, or to bring you to right conduct."

22. Say: "No one can deliver me from Allah (If I were to disobey Him), nor should I find refuge except in Him,

23. "Unless I proclaim what I receive from Allah and His Messages: for any that disobey Allah and His Apostle,- for them is Hell: they shall dwell therein for ever."

24. At length, when they see (with their own eyes) that which they are promised,- then will they know who it is that is weakest in (his) helper and least important in point of numbers.

25. Say: "I do not know whether the (Punishment) which you are promised is near,

SÛRAH-73
AL-MUZZAMMIL
(INTRODUCTION)

This is one of the earliest Sûras to have been revealed. The first was S. 96: 1-5 (*Iqraa*), in the fortieth year of the Prophet's life, say about 12 years before the Hijra. Then there was an interruption (*Fatra*), of which the duration cannot be exactly ascertained, as there was no external history connected with it. The usual estimate puts it at about six months, but it may have been a year or two years. The years were then counted by the lunisolar calendar: The second Sûrah in chronological order was probably a great portion of S. 68 (*Qalam*), which came after the *Fatra* was over. About the same time came this Sûrah (say third) and S. 74, which follows (say fourth), and the remainder of 96. We may roughly put the date of this Sûrah at about 11 to 10 years before the Hijra.

The subject-matter is the significance of Prayer and Humility in spiritual life and the terrible fate of those who reject Faith and Revelation.

Part 29

or whether my Lord will appoint for it a distant term.

أَمْ يَجْعَلُ لَهُ رَبِّيْ أَمَدًا ۟

26. "He (alone) knows the Unseen, nor does He make any one acquainted with His mysteries,-

عَٰلِمُ الْغَيْبِ فَلَا يُظْهِرُ عَلٰى غَيْبِهٖٓ اَحَدًا ۟

27. "Except an Apostle whom He has chosen: and then He makes a band of watchers march before him and behind him,

اِلَّا مَنِ ارْتَضٰى مِنْ رَّسُوْلٍ فَاِنَّهٗ يَسْلُكُ مِنْ بَيْنِ يَدَيْهِ وَمِنْ خَلْفِهٖ رَصَدًا ۟

28. "That he may know that they have (truly) brought and delivered the Messages of their Lord and He surrounds that are with them, and takes account of every single thing.

لِّيَعْلَمَ اَنْ قَدْ اَبْلَغُوْا رِسٰلٰتِ رَبِّهِمْ وَاَحَاطَ بِمَا لَدَيْهِمْ وَاَحْصٰى كُلَّ شَيْءٍ عَدَدًا ۟

73. Folded in Garments
In the name of Allah. Most Gracious, Most Merciful.

(٧٣) سُوْرَةُ الْمُزَّمِّلِ مَكِّيَّةٌ (٣)

بِسْمِ اللّٰهِ الرَّحْمٰنِ الرَّحِيْمِ

1. O you folded in garments!

يٰۤاَيُّهَا الْمُزَّمِّلُ ۟

2. Stand (to prayer) by night, but not all night,-

قُمِ الَّيْلَ اِلَّا قَلِيْلًا ۟

3. Half of it,- or a little less,

نِّصْفَهٗۤ اَوِ انْقُصْ مِنْهُ قَلِيْلًا ۟

4. Or a little more; and recite the Qur'an in slow, measured rhythmic tones.

اَوْ زِدْ عَلَيْهِ وَرَتِّلِ الْقُرْاٰنَ تَرْتِيْلًا ۟

5. Soon shall We send down to you a weighty Message.

اِنَّا سَنُلْقِيْ عَلَيْكَ قَوْلًا ثَقِيْلًا ۟

6. Truly the rising by night is a time when impression is more keen and speech more certain.

اِنَّ نَاشِئَةَ الَّيْلِ هِيَ اَشَدُّ وَطْاً وَّاَقْوَمُ قِيْلًا ۟

7. True, there is for you by day prolonged occupation with manifold duties.

اِنَّ لَكَ فِى النَّهَارِ سَبْحًا طَوِيْلًا ۟

8. But keep in remembrance the name of your Lord and devote yourself to Him wholeheartedly.

وَاذْكُرِ اسْمَ رَبِّكَ وَتَبَتَّلْ اِلَيْهِ تَبْتِيْلًا ۟

9. (He is) Lord of the East and the West: there is no god but He: take Him therefore for (your) Disposer of Affairs.

رَبُّ الْمَشْرِقِ وَالْمَغْرِبِ لَاۤ اِلٰهَ اِلَّا هُوَ فَاتَّخِذْهُ وَكِيْلًا ۟

10. And have patience with what they say, and leave them with noble (dignity).

وَاصْبِرْ عَلٰى مَا يَقُوْلُوْنَ وَاهْجُرْهُمْ هَجْرًا جَمِيْلًا ۟

11. And leave Me (alone to deal with) those in possession of the good things of life,

وَذَرْنِيْ وَالْمُكَذِّبِيْنَ اُولِى النَّعْمَةِ

Part 29

who (yet) deny the Truth; and bear with them for a little while.

12. With Us are Fetters (to bind them), and a Fire (to burn them).

13. And a Food that chokes, and a Chastisement Grievous.

14. On the Day when the earth and the mountains will be in violent commotion. And the mountains will be as a heap of sand poured out and flowing down.

15. We have sent to you, (O men!) an Apostle, to be a witness concerning you, even as We sent an Apostle to Pharaoh.

16. But Pharaoh disobeyed the Apostle; so We seized him with a heavy Punishment.

17. Then how shall you, if you deny (Allah), guard your-selves against a Day that will make children hoary-headed?-

18. Whereon the sky will be cleft asunder? His Promise needs must be accomplished.

19. Verily this is an Admonition: therefore, whoso will, let him take a (straight) path to his Lord!

20. Your Lord knows that you stand forth (to prayer) nearly two-thirds of the night, or half the night, or a third of the night, and so does a party of those with you. But Allah appoints night and day in due measure. He knows that you are unable to keep count thereof. So He has turned to you (in mercy): you read, therefore, of the Qur'an as much as may be easy (for you) He knows that there may be (some) among you in ill-health; others travelling through the land, seeking of Allah's bounty; yet others fighting in Allah's Cause, you read, therefore,

وَمَهِّلْهُمْ قَلِيلًا ۝

اِنَّ لَدَيْنَآ اَنْكَالًا وَّجَحِيمًا ۝

وَّطَعَامًا ذَا غُصَّةٍ وَّعَذَابًا اَلِيمًا ۝

يَوْمَ تَرْجُفُ الْاَرْضُ وَالْجِبَالُ وَ كَانَتِ الْجِبَالُ كَثِيبًا مَّهِيلًا ۝

اِنَّآ اَرْسَلْنَآ اِلَيْكُمْ رَسُوْلًا ۙ شَاهِدًا عَلَيْكُمْ كَمَآ اَرْسَلْنَآ اِلٰى فِرْعَوْنَ رَسُوْلًا ۝

فَعَصٰى فِرْعَوْنُ الرَّسُوْلَ فَاَخَذْنٰهُ اَخْذًا وَّبِيْلًا ۝

فَكَيْفَ تَتَّقُوْنَ اِنْ كَفَرْتُمْ يَوْمًا يَّجْعَلُ الْوِلْدَانَ شِيْبًا ۝ السَّمَآءُ مُنْفَطِرٌ ۢ بِهٖ ۚ كَانَ وَعْدُهٗ مَفْعُوْلًا ۝

اِنَّ هٰذِهٖ تَذْكِرَةٌ ۚ فَمَنْ شَآءَ اتَّخَذَ اِلٰى رَبِّهٖ سَبِيْلًا ۝

اِنَّ رَبَّكَ يَعْلَمُ اَنَّكَ تَقُوْمُ اَدْنٰى مِنْ ثُلُثَيِ الَّيْلِ وَنِصْفَهٗ وَثُلُثَهٗ وَطَآئِفَةٌ مِّنَ الَّذِيْنَ مَعَكَ ۚ وَاللّٰهُ يُقَدِّرُ الَّيْلَ وَالنَّهَارَ ۚ عَلِمَ اَنْ لَّنْ تُحْصُوْهُ فَتَابَ عَلَيْكُمْ فَاقْرَءُوْا مَا تَيَسَّرَ مِنَ الْقُرْاٰنِ ۙ عَلِمَ اَنْ سَيَكُوْنُ مِنْكُمْ مَّرْضٰى ۙ وَاٰخَرُوْنَ يَضْرِبُوْنَ فِى الْاَرْضِ يَبْتَغُوْنَ مِنْ فَضْلِ اللّٰهِ وَاٰخَرُوْنَ يُقَاتِلُوْنَ فِىْ سَبِيْلِ اللّٰهِ ۖ فَاقْرَءُوْا

SÛRAH-74
AL-MUDDSSIR
(INTRODUCTION)

This Sûrah dates from about the same time as the last one. Its subject-matter is also similar: Prayer, and Praise, and the need of patience in period of great spiritual stress; the unjust who cause sorrow and suffering now will themselves experience agony in the Hereafter.

as much of the Qur'an as may be easy (for you); and establish regular Prayer and give regular Charity; and loan to Allah a Beautiful Loan. And whatever good you send forth for your souls, you shall find it in Allah's Presence,- yes, better and greater, in Reward and seek you the Grace of Allah: for Allah is Oft-Forgiving, Most Merciful.

74. The One Wrapped Up
In the name of Allah. Most Gracious, Most Merciful.

1. O you wrapped up (in the mantle)!
2. Arise and deliver thy warning!
3. And your Lord do thou magnify!
4. And thy garments keep free from stain!
5. And shun all abomination!

6. Nor expect, in giving, any increase (for yourself)!
7. But, for your Lord's (Cause), be patient and constant!
8. Finally, when the trumpet is sounded,
9. That will be- that Day - a Day of Distress,-
10. Far from easy for those without Faith.
11. Leave Me alone (to deal) with the (creature) whom I created alone,
12. To whom I granted resources in abundance,
13. And sons to be by his side!-
14. To whom I made (life) smooth and comfortable!
15. Yet is he greedy-that I should add (yet more);-
16. By no means! For to Our Signs he has been refractory!
17. Soon will I visit him with a mount of calamities!
18. For he thought and he plotted;-

19. And woe to him! How he plotted!-

20. Yes, woe to him; How he plotted!-

21. Then he looked round;

22. Then he frowned and he scowled;

23. Then he turned back and was haughty;

24. Then he said; "This is nothing but magic, derived from of old;

25. "This is nothing but the word of a mortal!"

26. Soon will I cast him into Hell-Fire!

27. And what will explain to you what Hell-Fire is?

28. Nothing does it permit to endure, and nothing does it leave alone!—

29. Darkening and changing the colour of man!

30. Over it are Nineteen.

31. And We have set none but angels as Guardians of the Fire; and We have fixed their number only as a trial for Unbelievers,-in order that the People of the Book may arrive at certainty, and the Believers may increase in Faith,- and that no doubts may be left for the People of the Book and the Believers, and that those in whose hearts is a disease and the Unbelievers may say, "What symbol does Allah intend by this ?" Thus Allah leaves to stray whom He pleases, and guide whom He pleases: and none can know the forces of your Lord, except He and this is no other than a warning to mankind.

32. Nay, verily: by the Moon,

33. And by the Night as it retreats,

فَقُتِلَ كَيْفَ قَدَّرَ ۞

ثُمَّ قُتِلَ كَيْفَ قَدَّرَ ۞

ثُمَّ نَظَرَ ۞

ثُمَّ عَبَسَ وَبَسَرَ ۞

ثُمَّ أَدْبَرَ وَاسْتَكْبَرَ ۞

فَقَالَ إِنْ هٰذَا إِلَّا سِحْرٌ يُؤْثَرُ ۞

إِنْ هٰذَا إِلَّا قَوْلُ الْبَشَرِ ۞

سَأُصْلِيهِ سَقَرَ ۞

وَمَا أَدْرَاكَ مَا سَقَرُ ۞

لَا تُبْقِي وَلَا تَذَرُ ۞

لَوَّاحَةٌ لِلْبَشَرِ ۞

عَلَيْهَا تِسْعَةَ عَشَرَ ۞

وَمَا جَعَلْنَا أَصْحَابَ النَّارِ إِلَّا

مَلٰئِكَةً وَمَا جَعَلْنَا عِدَّتَهُمْ

إِلَّا فِتْنَةً لِّلَّذِينَ كَفَرُوا

لِيَسْتَيْقِنَ الَّذِينَ أُوتُوا الْكِتٰبَ

وَيَزْدَادَ الَّذِينَ اٰمَنُوا إِيمَانًا وَلَا

يَرْتَابَ الَّذِينَ أُوتُوا الْكِتٰبَ وَ

الْمُؤْمِنُونَ وَلِيَقُولَ الَّذِينَ فِي

قُلُوبِهِمْ مَرَضٌ وَالْكَافِرُونَ مَاذَا

أَرَادَ اللّٰهُ بِهٰذَا مَثَلًا ۞ كَذٰلِكَ

يُضِلُّ اللّٰهُ مَنْ يَشَاءُ وَيَهْدِي مَنْ

يَشَاءُ ۞ وَمَا يَعْلَمُ جُنُودَ رَبِّكَ إِلَّا

هُوَ ۞ وَمَا هِيَ إِلَّا ذِكْرَى لِلْبَشَرِ ۞

كَلَّا وَالْقَمَرِ ۞

وَالَّيْلِ إِذْ أَدْبَرَ ۞

34. And by the Dawn as it shines forth,-

وَالصُّبْحِ إِذَآ أَسْفَرَ ۝

35. This is but one of the mighty (portents),

إِنَّهَا لَإِحْدَى الْكُبَرِ ۝

36. A warning to mankind,-

نَذِيرًا لِّلْبَشَرِ ۝

37. To any of you that chooses to press forward, or to follow behind;-

لِمَن شَآءَ مِنكُمْ أَن يَتَقَدَّمَ أَوْ يَتَأَخَّرَ ۝

38. Every soul will be (held) in pledge for its deeds.

كُلُّ نَفْسٍ بِمَا كَسَبَتْ رَهِينَةٌ ۝

39. Except the Companions of the Right Hand.

إِلَّا أَصْحَابَ الْيَمِينِ ۝

40. In Gardens they will ask one another,

فِي جَنَّاتٍ يَتَسَآءَلُونَ ۝

41. And (ask) of the Sinners:

عَنِ الْمُجْرِمِينَ ۝

42. "What led you into Hell–Fire?"

مَا سَلَكَكُمْ فِي سَقَرَ ۝

43. They will say: "We were not of those who prayed;

قَالُوا لَمْ نَكُ مِنَ الْمُصَلِّينَ ۝

44. "Nor were we of those who fed the indigent;

وَلَمْ نَكُ نُطْعِمُ الْمِسْكِينَ ۝

45. "But we used to talk vanities with vain talkers;

وَكُنَّا نَخُوضُ مَعَ الْخَآئِضِينَ ۝

46. "And we used to deny the Day of Judgment,

وَكُنَّا نُكَذِّبُ بِيَوْمِ الدِّينِ ۝

47. "Until there came to us (the Hour) that is certain."

حَتَّى أَتَانَا الْيَقِينُ ۝

48. Then will no intercession of (any) intercessors profit them.

فَمَا تَنفَعُهُمْ شَفَاعَةُ الشَّافِعِينَ ۝

49. Then what is the matter with them that they turn away from admonition?—,

فَمَا لَهُمْ عَنِ التَّذْكِرَةِ مُعْرِضِينَ ۝

50. As if they were affrighted asses,

كَأَنَّهُمْ حُمُرٌ مُّسْتَنفِرَةٌ ۝

51. Fleeing from a lion!

فَرَّتْ مِن قَسْوَرَةٍ ۝

52. Forsooth, each one of them wants to be given scrolls (of revelation) spread out!

بَلْ يُرِيدُ كُلُّ امْرِئٍ مِّنْهُمْ أَن يُؤْتَى صُحُفًا مُّنَشَّرَةً ۝

53. By no means! But they do not fear the Hereafter,

كَلَّا بَل لَّا يَخَافُونَ الْآخِرَةَ ۝

54. Nay, this surely is an admonition:

كَلَّا إِنَّهُ تَذْكِرَةٌ ۝

55. Let any who will, keep it in remembrance!

فَمَن شَآءَ ذَكَرَهُ ۝

56. But none will keep it in remembrance except as Allah wills: He is the Lord of Righteousness, and the Lord of Forgiveness.

وَمَا يَذْكُرُونَ إِلَّا أَن يَشَآءَ اللَّهُ هُوَ أَهْلُ التَّقْوَى وَأَهْلُ الْمَغْفِرَةِ ۝

SÛRAH-75
AL-QIYÂMAH
(INTRODUCTION)

This Sûrah belongs to the early Makkan period, but comes chronologically a good deal later than the last two Sûras.

Its subject-matter is the Resurrection, viewed from the point of view of Man, especially unregenerate Man, as he is now, and as he will be then,-his inner and psychological history.

75. The Resurrection

In the name of Allah. Most
Gracious, Most Merciful.

سورة القِيٰمةِ مَكِّيَّةٌ (٣١) (٤٥)

بِسْمِ اللهِ الرَّحْمٰنِ الرَّحِيمِ

1. I do call to witness the Resurrection Day;

لَا أُقْسِمُ بِيَوْمِ الْقِيٰمَةِ ۚ

2. And I do call to witness the self-reproaching spirit: (eschew Evil).

وَلَا أُقْسِمُ بِالنَّفْسِ اللَّوَّامَةِ ۚ

3. Does man think that We cannot assemble his bones?

أَيَحْسَبُ الْإِنْسَانُ أَلَّنْ نَّجْمَعَ

4. Nay, We are able to put together in perfect order the very tips of his fingers.

عِظَامَهُ ۚ

5. But man wishes to do wrong (even) in the time in front of him.

بَلَىٰ قٰدِرِينَ عَلَىٰ أَنْ نُّسَوِّيَ بَنَانَهُ ۚ

بَلْ يُرِيدُ الْإِنْسَانُ لِيَفْجُرَ أَمَامَهُ ۚ

6. He questions: "When is the Day of Resurrection?"

يَسْأَلُ أَيَّانَ يَوْمُ الْقِيٰمَةِ ۚ

7. At length, when the sight is dazed,

فَإِذَا بَرِقَ الْبَصَرُ ۚ

8. And the moon is buried in darkness,

وَخَسَفَ الْقَمَرُ ۚ

9. And the sun and moon are joined together,-

وَجُمِعَ الشَّمْسُ وَالْقَمَرُ ۚ

10. That Day Man will say: "Where is the refuge?"

يَقُولُ الْإِنْسَانُ يَوْمَئِذٍ أَيْنَ الْمَفَرُّ ۚ

11. By no means! No place of safety!

كَلَّا لَا وَزَرَ ۚ

12. Before your Lord (alone), that Day will be the place of rest.

إِلَىٰ رَبِّكَ يَوْمَئِذٍ الْمُسْتَقَرُّ ۚ

13. That Day Man will be told (all) that he put forward, and all that he put back.

يُنَبَّؤُا الْإِنْسَانُ يَوْمَئِذٍ بِمَا قَدَّمَ

14. Nay, man will be evidence against himself,

وَأَخَّرَ ۚ

15. Even though he were to put up his excuses.

بَلِ الْإِنْسَانُ عَلَىٰ نَفْسِهِ بَصِيرَةٌ ۚ

16. Do not move your tongue concerning the (Qur'an) to make haste therewith.

وَلَوْ أَلْقَىٰ مَعَاذِيرَهُ ۚ

17. It is for Us to collect it and to promulgate it:

لَا تُحَرِّكْ بِهِ لِسَانَكَ لِتَعْجَلَ بِهِ ۚ

18. But when We have promulgated it, you follow its recital (as promulgated):

إِنَّ عَلَيْنَا جَمْعَهُ وَقُرْآنَهُ ۚ

19. Nay more, it is for Us to explain it (and make it clear):

فَإِذَا قَرَأْنَاهُ فَاتَّبِعْ قُرْآنَهُ ۚ

20. Nay, (you men!) but you love the fleeting life,

ثُمَّ إِنَّ عَلَيْنَا بَيَانَهُ ۚ

21. And leave alone the Hereafter.

كَلَّا بَلْ تُحِبُّونَ الْعَاجِلَةَ ۚ

22. Some faces, that Day, will beam (in brightness and beauty);-

وَتَذَرُونَ الْآخِرَةَ ۚ

وُجُوهٌ يَوْمَئِذٍ نَّاضِرَةٌ ۚ

SÛRAH-76
AL-INSÂN OR AD-DAHR
(INTRODUCTION)

The revelation of this Sûrah was probably in the early Makkan period, with the possible exception of some verse, but its date has no significance.

Its theme is the contrast between the two classes of men, those who choose good and those who choose evil, with special reference to the former.

The title of the Sûrah recalls a Pagan Arab idea, which personified Time as existing spontaneously form eternity to entemity and responsible for the misery or the happiness of mankind. In 45: 24 we read: "They say.... 'nothing but Time can destroy us.'" This attitude is of course wrong. Time is a created thing: it has its mysteries, but it is no more eternal than matter. It is also relative to our conceptions and not absolute, as Einstein has proved. It is only Allah Who is Self-Subsisting, Eternal from the beginning and Eternal to the end, the absolute Existence and Reality. We must not transfer His attributes to any figments of our imagination.

This deification of Time *(Dahr)* as against a living personal Allah has given rise to the term *dahrîya,* as applied to an atheist or a materialist.

The whole of the Sûrah is full of the highest symbolism, as is generally the case with Makkan Sûras, and this should always by remembered in their interpretation.

23. Looking towards their Lord;

24. And some faces, that Day, will be sad and dismal,

25. In the thought that some back-breaking calamity was about to be inflicted on them;

26. Yes, when (the soul) reaches to the collar-bone (in its exit),

27. And there will be a cry, "Who is a magician (to restore him)?

28. And he will conclude that it was (the Time) of Parting;

29. And one leg will be joined with another:

30. That Day the Drive will be (all) to your Lord!

31. So he gave nothing in charity, nor did he pray!-

32. But on the contrary, he rejected Truth and turned away!

33. Then he stalked to his family in full conceit!

34. Woe to you, (O man!), yes, woe!

35. Again, woe to you, (O man!), yes, woe!

36. Does man think that he will be left uncontrolled, (without purpose)?

37. Was he not a drop of sperm emitted (in lowly form)?

38. Then he became a leach-like clot; then (Allah) made and fashioned (him) in due proportion.

39. And of him He made two sexes, male and female.

40. Has He not, (the same), the power to give life to the dead?

إِلَىٰ رَبِّهَا نَاظِرَةٌ ۝

وَوُجُوهٌ يَوْمَئِذٍ بَاسِرَةٌ ۝

تَظُنُّ أَن يُفْعَلَ بِهَا فَاقِرَةٌ ۝

كَلَّا إِذَا بَلَغَتِ التَّرَاقِيَ ۝

وَقِيلَ مَنْ رَاقٍ ۝

وَظَنَّ أَنَّهُ الْفِرَاقُ ۝

وَالْتَفَّتِ السَّاقُ بِالسَّاقِ ۝

إِلَىٰ رَبِّكَ يَوْمَئِذٍ الْمَسَاقُ ۝

فَلَا صَدَّقَ وَلَا صَلَّىٰ ۝

وَلَٰكِن كَذَّبَ وَتَوَلَّىٰ ۝

ثُمَّ ذَهَبَ إِلَىٰ أَهْلِهِ يَتَمَطَّىٰ ۝

أَوْلَىٰ لَكَ فَأَوْلَىٰ ۝

ثُمَّ أَوْلَىٰ لَكَ فَأَوْلَىٰ ۝

أَيَحْسَبُ الْإِنسَانُ أَن يُتْرَكَ سُدًى ۝

أَلَمْ يَكُ نُطْفَةً مِّن مَّنِيٍّ يُمْنَىٰ ۝

ثُمَّ كَانَ عَلَقَةً فَخَلَقَ فَسَوَّىٰ ۝

فَجَعَلَ مِنْهُ الزَّوْجَيْنِ الذَّكَرَ وَالْأُنثَىٰ ۝

أَلَيْسَ ذَٰلِكَ بِقَادِرٍ عَلَىٰ أَن يُحْيِيَ الْمَوْتَىٰ ۝

76. Time; or Man

In the name of Allah. Most Gracious, Most Merciful.

1. Has there not been over Man a long period of Time, when he was nothing - (not even) mentioned?

2. Verily We created Man from a drop of mingled sperm, in order to try him: so We gave him (the gifts), of Hearing and Sight.

(٧٦) سُورَةُ الدَّهْرِ مَدَنِيَّةٌ (٩٨)

بِسْمِ اللَّهِ الرَّحْمَٰنِ الرَّحِيمِ

هَلْ أَتَىٰ عَلَى الْإِنسَانِ حِينٌ مِّنَ الدَّهْرِ لَمْ يَكُن شَيْئًا مَّذْكُورًا ۝

إِنَّا خَلَقْنَا الْإِنسَانَ مِن نُّطْفَةٍ أَمْشَاجٍ نَّبْتَلِيهِ فَجَعَلْنَاهُ سَمِيعًا

3.   We showed him the Way: whether he be grateful or ungrateful (rests on his will).

4.   For the Rejecters We have prepared chains, yokes, and a blazing Fire.

5.   As to the Righteous, they shall drink of a Cup mixed with Kafur,-

6.   A Fountain where the Devotees of Allah do drink, making it flow in unstinted abundance.

7.   They perform (their) vows, and they fear a Day whose evil flies far and wide.

8.   And they feed, for the love of Allah, the indigent, the orphan, and the captive,-

9.   (Saying),"We feed you for the sake of Allah alone: no reward do we desire from you, nor thanks.

10.   "We only fear a Day of distressful Wrath from the side of our Lord."

11.   But Allah will deliver them from the evil of that Day, and will shed over them a Light of Beauty and a (blissful) Joy.

12.   And because they were patient and constant, He will reward them with a Garden and (garments of) silk.

13.   Reclining in the (Garden) on raised thrones, they will see there neither the sun's (excessive heat) nor excessive cold.

14.   And the shades of the (Garden) will come low over them, and the bunches (of fruit), there, will hang low in humility.

15.   And amongst them will be passed round vessels of silver and goblets of crystal,-

16. Crystal-clear, made of silver: they will determine the measure thereof (according to their wishes).

17. And they will be given to drink there of a Cup (of Wine) mixed with Zanjabil,-

18. A fountain there, called Salsabil.

19. And round about them will (serve) youths of perpetual (freshness): If you see them, you would think them scattered Pearls.

20. And when you look, it is there you will see a Bliss and a Realm Magnificent.

21. Upon them will be green Garments of fine silk and heavy brocade, and they will be adorned with Bracelets of silver; and their Lord will give to them to drink a drink pure and holy.

22. "Verily this is a Reward for you, and your Endeavour is accepted and recognised."

23. It is We Who have sent down the Qur'an to you by stages.

24. Therefore, be patient with constancy to the Command of your Lord, and do not obey the sinner or the ingrate among them.

25. And celebrate the name of your Lord morning and evening,

26. And part of the night, prostrate yourself to Him; and glorify Him a long night through.

27. As to these, they love the fleeting life, and put away behind them a Day (that will be) hard.

28. It is We Who created them, and We have made their joints strong; but, when We will, We can substitute the like of them by a complete change.

قَوَارِيْرَا۟ مِنْ فِضَّةٍ قَدَّرُوْهَا تَقْدِيْرًا ۝

وَيُسْقَوْنَ فِيْهَا كَأْسًا كَانَ مِزَاجُهَا زَنْجَبِيْلًا ۝

عَيْنًا فِيْهَا تُسَمّٰى سَلْسَبِيْلًا ۝

وَيَطُوْفُ عَلَيْهِمْ وِلْدَانٌ مُّخَلَّدُوْنَ ۚ اِذَا رَاَيْتَهُمْ حَسِبْتَهُمْ لُؤْلُؤًا مَّنْثُوْرًا ۝

وَاِذَا رَاَيْتَ ثَمَّ رَاَيْتَ نَعِيْمًا وَّمُلْكًا كَبِيْرًا ۝

عٰلِيَهُمْ ثِيَابُ سُنْدُسٍ خُضْرٌ وَّاِسْتَبْرَقٌ ۫ وَّحُلُّوْٓا اَسَاوِرَ مِنْ فِضَّةٍ ۚ وَسَقٰىهُمْ رَبُّهُمْ شَرَابًا طَهُوْرًا ۝

اِنَّ هٰذَا كَانَ لَكُمْ جَزَآءً وَّكَانَ سَعْيُكُمْ مَّشْكُوْرًا ۝

اِنَّا نَحْنُ نَزَّلْنَا عَلَيْكَ الْقُرْاٰنَ تَنْزِيْلًا ۝

فَاصْبِرْ لِحُكْمِ رَبِّكَ وَلَا تُطِعْ مِنْهُمْ اٰثِمًا اَوْ كَفُوْرًا ۝

وَاذْكُرِ اسْمَ رَبِّكَ بُكْرَةً وَّاَصِيْلًا ۝

وَمِنَ الَّيْلِ فَاسْجُدْ لَهٗ وَسَبِّحْهُ لَيْلًا طَوِيْلًا ۝

اِنَّ هٰٓؤُلَآءِ يُحِبُّوْنَ الْعَاجِلَةَ وَيَذَرُوْنَ وَرَآءَهُمْ يَوْمًا ثَقِيْلًا ۝

نَحْنُ خَلَقْنٰهُمْ وَشَدَدْنَآ اَسْرَهُمْ ۚ وَاِذَا شِئْنَا بَدَّلْنَآ اَمْثَالَهُمْ تَبْدِيْلًا ۝

SÛRAH-77
AL-MURSALAT
(INTRODUCTION)

This Sûrah belongs to the early Makkan period, somewhere near to S. 75 *(Qiyâmah)*. The theme is some what similar. It denounces the horrors of the Hereafter, for those who rejected Truth. Then refrain, "Ah woe, that Day, to the Rejecters of Truth!" which occurs ten times in its fifty verses, or on an average, once in every five verses, indicates the *leitmotif*.

29. This is an admonition: whosoever will, let him take a (straight) Path to his Lord.

اِنَّ هٰذِهٖ تَذْكِرَةٌ ۚ فَمَنْ شَآءَ اتَّخَذَ اِلٰى رَبِّهٖ سَبِيْلًا ۞

30. But you will not, except as Allah wills; for Allah is full of Knowledge and Wisdom.

وَمَا تَشَآءُوْنَ اِلَّاۤ اَنْ يَّشَآءَ اللّٰهُ ۚ اِنَّ اللّٰهَ كَانَ عَلِيْمًا حَكِيْمًا ۞

31. He will admit to His Mercy whom He will; but the wrong-doers,- for them He has prepared a grievous Chastisement.

يُّدْخِلُ مَنْ يَّشَآءُ فِيْ رَحْمَتِهٖ ۚ وَ الظّٰلِمِيْنَ اَعَدَّ لَهُمْ عَذَابًا اَلِيْمًا ۞

---

77. Those Sent Forth
In the name of Allah. Most Gracious, Most Merciful.

(٤٤) سُوْرَةُ الْمُرْسَلٰتِ مَكِّيَّةٌ (٣٣)

بِسْمِ اللّٰهِ الرَّحْمٰنِ الرَّحِيْمِ

1. By the (Winds) sent forth one after another (to man's profit);

وَالْمُرْسَلٰتِ عُرْفًا ۞

2. Which then blow violently in tempestuous gusts,

فَالْعٰصِفٰتِ عَصْفًا ۞

3. And scatter (things) far and wide,

وَّ النّٰشِرٰتِ نَشْرًا ۞

4. Then separate them, one from another,

فَالْفٰرِقٰتِ فَرْقًا ۞

5. Then spread abroad a Message,

فَالْمُلْقِيٰتِ ذِكْرًا ۞

6. Whether of Justification or of Warning;-

عُذْرًا اَوْ نُذْرًا ۞

7. Assuredly, what you are promised must come to pass.

اِنَّمَا تُوْعَدُوْنَ لَوَاقِعٌ ۚ

8. Then when the stars become dim;

فَاِذَا النُّجُوْمُ طُمِسَتْ ۞

9. When the heaven is cleft asunder;

وَ اِذَا السَّمَآءُ فُرِجَتْ ۞

10. When the mountains are scattered (to the winds) as dust;

وَ اِذَا الْجِبَالُ نُسِفَتْ ۞

11. And when the time fixed for the gathering of all Apostles comes.

وَ اِذَا الرُّسُلُ اُقِّتَتْ ۞

12. For what Day are these (portents) deferred?

لِاَيِّ يَوْمٍ اُجِّلَتْ ۞

13. For the Day of Sorting out.

لِيَوْمِ الْفَصْلِ ۚ

14. And what will explain to you what is the Day of Sorting out?

وَمَاۤ اَدْرٰىكَ مَا يَوْمُ الْفَصْلِ ۞

15. Ah woe, that Day, to the Rejecters of Truth!

وَيْلٌ يَّوْمَئِذٍ لِّلْمُكَذِّبِيْنَ ۞

16. Did We not destroy the men of old (for their evil)?

اَلَمْ نُهْلِكِ الْاَوَّلِيْنَ ۚ

17. So shall We make later (generations) follow them.

ثُمَّ نُتْبِعُهُمُ الْاٰخِرِيْنَ ۞

18. Thus do We deal with men of sin.

كَذٰلِكَ نَفْعَلُ بِالْمُجْرِمِيْنَ ۞

19. Ah woe, that Day, to the Rejecters of Truth!

20. Have We not created you from a fluid (held) despicable?

21. Which We placed in a place of rest, firmly fixed,

22. For a period (of gestation), determined (according to need)?

23. For We do determine (according to need); for We are the Best to determine (things).

24. Ah woe, that Day! to the Rejecters of Truth!

25. Have We not made the earth (as a place) to draw together.

26. The living and the dead,

27. And made therein mountains standing firm, lofty (in stature); and provided for you sweet (and wholesome) water?

28. Ah woe, that Day, to the Rejecters of Truth!

29. (It will be said:) "You depart to that which you used to reject as false!

30. You depart to a Shadow (of smoke ascending) in three columns.

31. "(Which yields) no shade of coolness, and is of no use against the fierce Blaze.

32. "Indeed it throws about sparks (huge) as Forts,

33. "As if there were (a string of) yellow camels (marching swiftly)."

34. Ah woe, that Day, to the Rejecters of Truth!

35. That will be a Day when they shall not be able to speak.

36. Nor will it be open to them to put forth pleas.

37. Ah woe, that Day, to the Rejecters of Truth!

38. That will be a Day of Sorting out! We shall gather you together and those before (you)!

39. Now, if you have a trick (or plot), use it against Me!

40. Ah woe, that Day, to the Rejecters of Truth!

41. As to the Righteous, they shall be amidst (cool) shades and springs (of water).

42. And (they shall have) fruits,- all they desire.

وَيْلٌ يَوْمَئِذٍ لِّلْمُكَذِّبِيْنَ ۟

اَلَمْ نَخْلُقْكُّمْ مِّنْ مَّآءٍ مَّهِيْنٍ ۟

فَجَعَلْنٰهُ فِيْ قَرَارٍ مَّكِيْنٍ ۟

اِلٰى قَدَرٍ مَّعْلُوْمٍ ۟

فَقَدَرْنَا ۖ فَنِعْمَ الْقٰدِرُوْنَ ۟

وَيْلٌ يَوْمَئِذٍ لِّلْمُكَذِّبِيْنَ ۟

اَلَمْ نَجْعَلِ الْاَرْضَ كِفَاتًا ۟

اَحْيَآءً وَّاَمْوَاتًا ۟

وَّجَعَلْنَا فِيْهَا رَوَاسِيَ شٰمِخٰتٍ وَّاَسْقَيْنٰكُمْ مَّآءً فُرَاتًا ۟

وَيْلٌ يَوْمَئِذٍ لِّلْمُكَذِّبِيْنَ ۟

اِنْطَلِقُوْا اِلٰى مَا كُنْتُمْ بِهِ تُكَذِّبُوْنَ ۟

اِنْطَلِقُوْا اِلٰى ظِلٍّ ذِيْ ثَلٰثِ شُعَبٍ ۟

لَّا ظَلِيْلٍ وَّلَا يُغْنِيْ مِنَ اللَّهَبِ ۟

اِنَّهَا تَرْمِيْ بِشَرَرٍ كَالْقَصْرِ ۟

كَاَنَّهٗ جِمٰلَتٌ صُفْرٌ ۟

وَيْلٌ يَوْمَئِذٍ لِّلْمُكَذِّبِيْنَ ۟

هٰذَا يَوْمُ لَا يَنْطِقُوْنَ ۟

وَلَا يُؤْذَنُ لَهُمْ فَيَعْتَذِرُوْنَ ۟

وَيْلٌ يَوْمَئِذٍ لِّلْمُكَذِّبِيْنَ ۟

هٰذَا يَوْمُ الْفَصْلِ ۚ جَمَعْنٰكُمْ وَالْاَوَّلِيْنَ ۟

فَاِنْ كَانَ لَكُمْ كَيْدٌ فَكِيْدُوْنِ ۟

وَيْلٌ يَوْمَئِذٍ لِّلْمُكَذِّبِيْنَ ۟

اِنَّ الْمُتَّقِيْنَ فِيْ ظِلٰلٍ وَّعُيُوْنٍ ۟

وَّفَوَاكِهَ مِمَّا يَشْتَهُوْنَ ۟

SÛRAH-78
AN-NABA'
(INTRODUCTION)

This beautiful Makkan Sûrah is not quite so early as the last (S. 77), nor quite so late as S. 76, but nearer in time to the latter.

It sets forth Allah's loving care in a fine nature-passage, and deduces from it the Promise of the Future, when Evil will be destroyed and Good will come to its own; and invites all who have the will, to seek refuge with their Lord.

43. "You eat and you drink to your heart's content: for that you worked (Righteousness).

كُلُوا وَاشْرَبُوا هَنِيٓئًا بِمَا كُنتُمْ تَعْمَلُونَ ۝

44. Thus do We certainly reward the Doers of Good.

اِنَّا كَذَٰلِكَ نَجْزِے الْمُحْسِنِينَ ۝

45. Ah woe, that Day, to the Rejecters of Truth!

وَيْلٌ يَوْمَئِذٍ لِّلْمُكَذِّبِينَ ۝

46. (O you unjust!) You eat and enjoy yourselves (but) a little while, for that you are Sinners.

كُلُوا وَتَمَتَّعُوا قَلِيلًا اِنَّكُم مُّجْرِمُونَ ۝

47. Ah woe, that Day, to the Rejecters of Truth!

وَيْلٌ يَوْمَئِذٍ لِّلْمُكَذِّبِينَ ۝

48. And when it is said to them: bow down, they bow not down!

وَاِذَا قِيلَ لَهُمُ ارْكَعُوا لَا يَرْكَعُونَ ۝

49. Ah woe, that Day, to the Rejecters of Truth!

وَيْلٌ يَوْمَئِذٍ لِّلْمُكَذِّبِينَ ۝

50. Then what Message, after that, will they believe in?

فَبِأَيِّ حَدِيثٍۭ بَعْدَهُ يُؤْمِنُونَ ۝

78. The (Great) News
In the name of Allah. Most Gracious, Most Merciful.

(٤٨) سُورَةُ النَّبَا مَكِّيَّةٌ (٨٠)

بِسْمِ اللّٰهِ الرَّحْمٰنِ الرَّحِيمِ

1. Concerning what are they disputing?

عَمَّ يَتَسَآءَلُونَ ۝

2. Concerning the Great News,

عَنِ النَّبَاِ الْعَظِيمِ ۝

3. About which they cannot agree.

الَّذِے هُمْ فِيهِ مُخْتَلِفُونَ ۝

4. Verily, they shall soon (come to) know!

كَلَّا سَيَعْلَمُونَ ۝

5. Verily, verily they shall soon (come to) know!

ثُمَّ كَلَّا سَيَعْلَمُونَ ۝

6. Have We not made the earth as a wide expanse,

اَلَمْ نَجْعَلِ الْاَرْضَ مِهَادًا ۝

7. And the mountains as pegs?

وَالْجِبَالَ اَوْتَادًا ۝

8. And (have We not) created you in pairs,

وَخَلَقْنَاكُمْ اَزْوَاجًا ۝

9. And made your sleep for rest,

وَجَعَلْنَا نَوْمَكُمْ سُبَاتًا ۝

10. And made the night as a covering,

وَجَعَلْنَا الَّيْلَ لِبَاسًا ۝

11. And made the day as a means of subsistence?

وَجَعَلْنَا النَّهَارَ مَعَاشًا ۝

12. And (have We not) built over you the seven firmaments,

وَبَنَيْنَا فَوْقَكُمْ سَبْعًا شِدَادًا ۝

13. And placed (therein) a Light of Splendour?

وَجَعَلْنَا سِرَاجًا وَهَّاجًا ۝

14. And do We not send down from the clouds water in abundance,

وَاَنْزَلْنَا مِنَ الْمُعْصِرَاتِ مَآءً ثَجَّاجًا ۝

15. That We may produce therewith corn and vegetables,

لِنُخْرِجَ بِهٖ حَبًّا وَّنَبَاتًا ۙ

16. And gardens of luxurious growth?

وَّجَنّٰتٍ اَلْفَافًا ؕ

17. Verily the Day of Sorting out is a thing appointed,

اِنَّ يَوْمَ الْفَصْلِ كَانَ مِيْقَاتًا ۙ

18. The Day that the Trumpet shall be sounded, and you will come forth in crowds;

يَّوْمَ يُنْفَخُ فِى الصُّوْرِ فَتَاْتُوْنَ اَفْوَاجًا ۙ

19. And the heavens shall be opened as if there were doors,

وَّفُتِحَتِ السَّمَآءُ فَكَانَتْ اَبْوَابًا ۙ

20. And the mountains shall vanish, as if they were a mirage.

وَّسُيِّرَتِ الْجِبَالُ فَكَانَتْ سَرَابًا ؕ

21. Truly Hell is as a place of ambush,

اِنَّ جَهَنَّمَ كَانَتْ مِرْصَادًا ۙ

22. For the transgressors a place of destination:

لِّلطَّاغِيْنَ مَاٰبًا ۙ

23. They will dwell therein for ages.

لّٰبِثِيْنَ فِيْهَآ اَحْقَابًا ۚ

24. Nothing cool shall they taste therein, nor any drink,

لَا يَذُوْقُوْنَ فِيْهَا بَرْدًا وَّلَا شَرَابًا ۙ

25. Save a boiling fluid and a fluid, dark, murky, intensely cold,—:

اِلَّا حَمِيْمًا وَّغَسَّاقًا ۙ

26. A fitting recompense (for them).

جَزَآءً وِّفَاقًا ؕ

27. For that they used not to fear any account (for their deeds),

اِنَّهُمْ كَانُوْا لَا يَرْجُوْنَ حِسَابًا ۙ

28. But they (impudently) treated Our Signs as false.

وَّكَذَّبُوْا بِاٰيٰتِنَا كِذَّابًا ؕ

29. And all things have We preserved on record.

وَكُلَّ شَىْءٍ اَحْصَيْنٰهُ كِتٰبًا ۙ

30. "So you taste (the fruits of your deeds); for no increase shall We grant you, except in Chastisement.

فَذُوْقُوْا فَلَنْ نَّزِيْدَكُمْ اِلَّا عَذَابًا ۟

31. Verily for the Righteous there will be an Achievement.

اِنَّ لِلْمُتَّقِيْنَ مَفَازًا ۙ

32. Gardens enclosed, and grapevines;

حَدَآئِقَ وَاَعْنَابًا ۙ

33. Companions of equal age;

وَّكَوَاعِبَ اَتْرَابًا ۙ

34. And a cup full (to the brim).

وَّكَاْسًا دِهَاقًا ؕ

35. No vanity shall they hear therein, nor Untruth:-

لَا يَسْمَعُوْنَ فِيْهَا لَغْوًا وَّلَا كِذَّابًا ۚ

36. Recompense from your Lord, a gift, (amply) sufficient,

جَزَآءً مِّنْ رَّبِّكَ عَطَآءً حِسَابًا ۙ

37. (From) the Lord of the heavens and the earth, and all between,— the Most Gracious: none shall have power to argue with Him..

رَّبِّ السَّمٰوٰتِ وَالْاَرْضِ وَمَا بَيْنَهُمَا الرَّحْمٰنِ لَا يَمْلِكُوْنَ مِنْهُ خِطَابًا ۚ

38. The Day that the Spirit and the angels will stand forth in ranks,

يَوْمَ يَقُوْمُ الرُّوْحُ وَالْمَلٰٓئِكَةُ صَفًّا ۙ

SÛRAH-79
AN-NÂZI'ÂT
(INTRODUCTION)

This is also an early Makkan Sûrah, of about the same date as the last, and deals with the mystic theme of Judgment from the point of view of Pride and its Fall. The parable of Pharaoh occupies a central place in the argument: for he said, "I am your Lord Most High," and perished with his followers.

none shall speak except any who is permitted by (Allah) Most Gracious, and He will say what is right.

لَا يَتَكَلَّمُوْنَ إِلَّا مَنْ أَذِنَ لَهُ الرَّحْمٰنُ وَقَالَ صَوَابًا ۟

39. That Day will be the sure Reality: therefore, whoso will, let him take a (straight) return to his Lord!

ذٰلِكَ الْيَوْمُ الْحَقُّ ۚ فَمَنْ شَآءَ اتَّخَذَ إِلٰى رَبِّهٖ مَاٰبًا ۟

40. Verily, We have warned you of a Chastisement near, the Day when man will see (the deeds) which his hands have sent forth, and the Unbeliever will say, "Woe unto me! Would that I were (mere) dust!

إِنَّآ أَنْذَرْنٰكُمْ عَذَابًا قَرِيْبًا ۚ يَوْمَ يَنْظُرُ الْمَرْءُ مَا قَدَّمَتْ يَدٰهُ وَيَقُوْلُ الْكٰفِرُ يٰلَيْتَنِيْ كُنْتُ تُرٰبًا ۟

79. Those Who Tear Out
In the name of Allah. Most Gracious, Most Merciful.

(٧٩) سُوْرَةُ النَّزِعْتِ مَكِّيَّةٌ (٨١)

بِسْمِ اللّٰهِ الرَّحْمٰنِ الرَّحِيْمِ

1. By the (angels) who tear out (the souls of the wicked) with violence;

وَالنّٰزِعٰتِ غَرْقًا ۟

2. By those who gently draw out (the souls of the blessed);

وَّالنّٰشِطٰتِ نَشْطًا ۟

3. And by those who glide along (on errands of mercy),

وَّالسّٰبِحٰتِ سَبْحًا ۟

4. Then press forward as in a race,

فَالسّٰبِقٰتِ سَبْقًا ۟

5. Then arrange to do (the Commands of their Lord),

فَالْمُدَبِّرٰتِ أَمْرًا ۟

6. The Day everything that can be in commotion, will be in violent commotion,

يَوْمَ تَرْجُفُ الرَّاجِفَةُ ۟

7. Followed by oft-repeated (commotions):

تَتْبَعُهَا الرَّادِفَةُ ۟

8. Hearts that Day will be in agitation;

قُلُوْبٌ يَّوْمَئِذٍ وَّاجِفَةٌ ۟

9. Cast down will be (their owners') eyes.

أَبْصَارُهَا خَاشِعَةٌ ۟

10. They say (now): "What! shall we indeed be returned to (our) former state?

يَقُوْلُوْنَ أَءِنَّا لَمَرْدُوْدُوْنَ فِي الْحَافِرَةِ ۟

11. "What! - when we shall have become rotten bones?"

أَءِذَا كُنَّا عِظَامًا نَّخِرَةً ۟

12. They say: "It would, in that case, be a return with loss!"

قَالُوْا تِلْكَ إِذًا كَرَّةٌ خَاسِرَةٌ ۟

13. But verily, it will be but a single (compelling) Cry,

فَإِنَّمَا هِيَ زَجْرَةٌ وَّاحِدَةٌ ۟

14. When, behold, they will be brought out to the open.

فَإِذَا هُمْ بِالسَّاهِرَةِ ۟

15. Has the story of Moses reached you?

هَلْ أَتٰكَ حَدِيْثُ مُوْسٰى ۟

16. Behold, your Lord called him in the sacred valley of Tuwa:-

إِذْ نَادٰهُ رَبُّهٗ بِالْوَادِ الْمُقَدَّسِ طُوًى ۟

17. "You go to Pharaoh, for he has indeed transgressed all bounds:

اذْهَبْ اِلٰى فِرْعَوْنَ اِنَّهٗ طَغٰى ۚ۞

18. "And say to him, 'Would you (like) that you should be purified (from sin)?'—

فَقُلْ هَلْ لَّكَ اِلٰٓى اَنْ تَزَكّٰى ۙ۞

19. "'And that I guide you to your Lord, so you should fear Him?'"

وَاَهْدِيَكَ اِلٰى رَبِّكَ فَتَخْشٰى ۚ۞

20. Then (Moses) showed him the Great Sign.

فَاَرٰىهُ الْاٰيَةَ الْكُبْرٰى ۫۞

21. But (Pharaoh) rejected it and disobeyed (guidance);

فَكَذَّبَ وَعَصٰى ۙ۞

22. Further, he turned his back, striving hard (against Allah).

ثُمَّ اَدْبَرَ يَسْعٰى ۚ۞

23. Then he collected (his men) and made a proclamation,

فَحَشَرَ فَنَادٰى ۙ۞

24. Saying, "I am your Lord, Most High".

فَقَالَ اَنَا رَبُّكُمُ الْاَعْلٰى ۫۞

25. But Allah seized him, with punishment (and made an) example of him,—in the Hereafter, as in this life.

فَاَخَذَهُ اللّٰهُ نَكَالَ الْاٰخِرَةِ وَالْاُوْلٰى ۗ۞

26. Verily in this is a lesson for whosoever fears (Allah).

اِنَّ فِيْ ذٰلِكَ لَعِبْرَةً لِّمَنْ يَّخْشٰى ۚ۞

27. What! Are you the more difficult to create or the heaven (above)? (Allah) has constructed it:

ءَاَنْتُمْ اَشَدُّ خَلْقًا اَمِ السَّمَآءُ ۚ بَنٰىهَا ۫۞

28. On high has He raised its canopy, and He has given it order and perfection.

رَفَعَ سَمْكَهَا فَسَوّٰىهَا ۙ۞

29. Its night does He endow with darkness, and its splendour does He bring out (with light).

وَاَغْطَشَ لَيْلَهَا وَاَخْرَجَ ضُحٰىهَا ۪۞

30. And the earth, moreover, He has extended (to a wide expanse);

وَالْاَرْضَ بَعْدَ ذٰلِكَ دَحٰىهَا ؕ۞

31. He draws out therefrom its moisture and its pasture;

اَخْرَجَ مِنْهَا مَآءَهَا وَمَرْعٰىهَا ۪۞

32. And the mountains He has firmly fixed;-

وَالْجِبَالَ اَرْسٰىهَا ۙ۞

33. A provision for you and your cattle.

مَتَاعًا لَّكُمْ وَلِاَنْعَامِكُمْ ؕ۞

34. Therefore, when there comes the great, overwhelming (Event),—

فَاِذَا جَآءَتِ الطَّآمَّةُ الْكُبْرٰى ۫۞

35. The Day when Man shall remember (all) that he strove for,

يَوْمَ يَتَذَكَّرُ الْاِنْسَانُ مَا سَعٰى ۙ۞

36. And Hell-Fire shall be placed in full view for him who sees.—

وَبُرِّزَتِ الْجَحِيْمُ لِمَنْ يَّرٰى ۞

37. Then, for such as had transgressed all bounds,

فَاَمَّا مَنْ طَغٰى ۙ۞

38. And had preferred the life of this world,

وَاٰثَرَ الْحَيٰوةَ الدُّنْيَا ۙ۞

39. The Abode will be Hell-Fire;

فَاِنَّ الْجَحِيْمَ هِيَ الْمَاْوٰى ؕ۞

40. And for such as had entertained the fear of standing before their Lord's (tribunal) and had restrained (their) soul from lower desires,

وَاَمَّا مَنْ خَافَ مَقَامَ رَبِّهٖ وَنَهَى النَّفْسَ عَنِ الْهَوٰى ۙ۞

SÛRAH-80
'ABASA
(INTRODUCTION)

This is an early Makkan Sûrah, and is connected with an incident which reflects the highest honour on the Prophet's sincerity in the Revelations that were vouchsafed to him even if they seemed to reprove him for some natural and human zeal that led him to a false step in his mission according to his own high standards.

He was once deeply and earnestly engaged in trying to explain the Holy Qur'ân to Pagan Quraish leaders, when he was interrupted by blind man, 'Abdullah Umm Maktûm, one who was also poor, so that no one took any notice of him. He wanted to learn the Qur'ân. The Holy Prophet naturally disliked the interruption and showed impatience. Perhaps the poor man's feelings were hurt. But he whose gentle heart ever sympathised with the poor and the afflicted got new Light from above, and without the least hesitation published this revelation, which forms part of the sacred scripture of Islam, as described in verses 13-16. And the Prophet always afterwards held the man in high honour.

The incident was only a passing incident, but after explaining the eternal principles of revelation, the Sûrah recapitulates the Mercies of Allah to man, and the consequences of a good or a wicked life here, as seen in the spiritual world to come, in the Hereafter.

41. Their abode will be the Garden.

فَاَنَّ الْجَنَّةَ هِيَ الْمَاْوٰى ﴿

42. They ask you about the Hour,—'When will be its appointed time?'

يَسْـَٔلُوْنَكَ عَنِ السَّاعَةِ اَيَّانَ مُرْسٰىهَا ﴿

43. Wherein are you (concerned) with the declaration thereof?

فِيْمَ اَنْتَ مِنْ ذِكْرٰىهَا ﴿

44. With your Lord is the time fixed therefor.

اِلٰى رَبِّكَ مُنْتَهٰىهَا ﴿

45. You are but a Warner for such as fear it.

اِنَّمَاۤ اَنْتَ مُنْذِرُ مَنْ يَّخْشٰىهَا ﴿

46. The Day they see it, (it will be) as if they had tarried but a single evening, or (at most till) the following morn!

كَاَنَّهُمْ يَوْمَ يَرَوْنَهَا لَمْ يَلْبَثُوْۤا اِلَّا عَشِيَّةً اَوْ ضُحٰىهَا ﴿

80. He Frowned

In the name of Allah. Most Gracious, Most Merciful.

(٨٠) سُوْرَةُ عَبَسَ مَكِّيَّةٌ (٢٣)

بِسْمِ اللّٰهِ الرَّحْمٰنِ الرَّحِيْمِ

1. He (The Prophet) frowned and turned away,

عَبَسَ وَتَوَلّٰى ﴿

2. Because there came to him the blind man (interrupting).

اَنْ جَآءَهُ الْاَعْمٰى ﴿

3. But what could tell you but that perchance he might grow in purity?

وَمَا يُدْرِيْكَ لَعَلَّهُ يَزَّكّٰى ﴿

4. Or that he might receive admonition, and the teaching might profit him?

اَوْ يَذَّكَّرُ فَتَنْفَعَهُ الذِّكْرٰى ﴿

5. As to one who regards himself as self-sufficient,

اَمَّا مَنِ اسْتَغْنٰى ﴿

6. To him you do attend;

فَاَنْتَ لَهُ تَصَدّٰى ﴿

7. Though it is no blame to you if he grow not in purity.

وَمَا عَلَيْكَ اَلَّا يَزَّكّٰى ﴿

8. But as to him who came to you striving earnestly.

وَاَمَّا مَنْ جَآءَكَ يَسْعٰى ﴿

9. And with fear (in his heart),

وَهُوَ يَخْشٰى ﴿

10. Of him you were unmindful.

فَاَنْتَ عَنْهُ تَلَهّٰى ﴿

11. Nay, but verily it is an Admonishment,

كَلَّاۤ اِنَّهَا تَذْكِرَةٌ ﴿

12. Therefore let whoso will, keep it in remembrance.

فَمَنْ شَآءَ ذَكَرَهُ ﴿

13. (It is) in Books held (greatly) in honour,

فِيْ صُحُفٍ مُّكَرَّمَةٍ ﴿

14. Exalted (in dignity), kept pure and holy,

مَّرْفُوْعَةٍ مُّطَهَّرَةٍ ﴿

15. (Written) by the hands of scribes-

بِاَيْدِيْ سَفَرَةٍ ﴿

16. Honourable and Pious and Just.

كِرَامٍ بَرَرَةٍ ﴿

17. Woe to man! What has made him reject Allah;

قُتِلَ الْاِنْسَانُ مَاۤ اَكْفَرَهُ ﴿

18. From what stuff has He created him?

مِنْ أَيِّ شَيْءٍ خَلَقَهُ ۞

19. From a sperm-drop: He has created him, and then moulded him in due Proportion;

مِنْ نُّطْفَةٍ خَلَقَهُ فَقَدَّرَهُ ۞

20. Then He makes his path smooth for him;

ثُمَّ السَّبِيلَ يَسَّرَهُ ۞

21. Then He causes him to die, and puts him in his grave;

ثُمَّ أَمَاتَهُ فَأَقْبَرَهُ ۞

22. Then, when it is His Will, He will raise him up (again).

ثُمَّ إِذَا شَاءَ أَنْشَرَهُ ۞

23. By no means he has fulfilled what Allah has commanded him.

كَلَّا لَمَّا يَقْضِ مَا أَمَرَهُ ۞

24. Then let man look at his food, (and how We provide it):

فَلْيَنْظُرِ الْإِنْسَانُ إِلَى طَعَامِهِ ۞

25. For that We pour forth water in abundance,

أَنَّا صَبَبْنَا الْمَاءَ صَبًّا ۞

26. And We split the earth in fragments,

ثُمَّ شَقَقْنَا الْأَرْضَ شَقًّا ۞

27. And produce therein corn,

فَأَنْبَتْنَا فِيهَا حَبًّا ۞

28. And Grapes and nutritious plants,

وَعِنَبًا وَقَضْبًا ۞

29. And Olives and Dates,

وَزَيْتُونًا وَنَخْلًا ۞

30. And enclosed Gardens, dense with lofty trees,

وَحَدَائِقَ غُلْبًا ۞

31. And fruits and fodder,-

وَفَاكِهَةً وَأَبًّا ۞

32. For use and convenience to you and your cattle.

مَتَاعًا لَّكُمْ وَلِأَنْعَامِكُمْ ۞

33. At length, when there comes the Deafening Noise,-

فَإِذَا جَاءَتِ الصَّاخَّةُ ۞

34. That Day shall a man flee from his own brother,

يَوْمَ يَفِرُّ الْمَرْءُ مِنْ أَخِيهِ ۞

35. And from his mother and his father,

وَأُمِّهِ وَأَبِيهِ ۞

36. And from his wife and his children.

وَصَاحِبَتِهِ وَبَنِيهِ ۞

37. Each one of them, that Day, will have enough concern (of his own) to make him unmindful to the others.

لِكُلِّ امْرِئٍ مِّنْهُمْ يَوْمَئِذٍ شَأْنٌ يُغْنِيهِ ۞

38. Some faces that Day will be beaming,

وُجُوهٌ يَوْمَئِذٍ مُّسْفِرَةٌ ۞

39. Laughing, rejoicing.

ضَاحِكَةٌ مُّسْتَبْشِرَةٌ ۞

40. And other faces that Day will be dust-stained,

وَوُجُوهٌ يَوْمَئِذٍ عَلَيْهَا غَبَرَةٌ ۞

41. Blackness will cover them:

تَرْهَقُهَا قَتَرَةٌ ۞

42. Such will be the Rejecters of Allah, the Doers of iniquity.

أُولَئِكَ هُمُ الْكَفَرَةُ الْفَجَرَةُ ۞

SÛRAH-81
AT-TAKWÎR
(INTRODUCTION)

This is quite an early Makkan Sûrah, perhaps the sixth or seventh in chronological order. It opens with a series of highly mystical metaphors suggesting the break-up or the world as we know it (verses 1-13) and the enforcement of complete personal responsibility for each soul (verse 14). Then there is a mystical passage showing how the Qur'ânic Revelation was true, and revealed through the angel Gabriel, and not merely a rhepsody from one possessed. Revelation is given for man's spiritual guidance (verses 14-29).

Comparable with this Sûrah are the Sûras 82 and 84 which may be read with this.

81. The Folding Up

In the name of Allah. Most Gracious, Most Merciful.

١. سُوْرَةُ التَّكْوِيْرِ مَكِّيَّةٌ (٨١)

بِسْمِ اللّٰهِ الرَّحْمٰنِ الرَّحِيْمِ

1. When the sun (with its spacious light) is folded up;

إِذَا الشَّمْسُ كُوِّرَتْ ۞

2. When the stars fall, losing their lustre;

وَإِذَا النُّجُوْمُ انْكَدَرَتْ ۞

3. When the mountains vanish (like a mirage);

وَإِذَا الْجِبَالُ سُيِّرَتْ ۞

4. When the she-camels, ten months with young, are left untended;

وَإِذَا الْعِشَارُ عُطِّلَتْ ۞

5. When the wild beasts are herded together,

وَإِذَا الْوُحُوْشُ حُشِرَتْ ۞

6. When the oceans boil over with a swell;

وَإِذَا الْبِحَارُ سُجِّرَتْ ۞

7. When the souls are sorted out, (being joined, like with like);

وَإِذَا النُّفُوْسُ زُوِّجَتْ ۞

8. When the female (infant), buried alive, is questioned -

وَإِذَا الْمَوْءُوْدَةُ سُئِلَتْ ۞

9. For what crime she was killed;

بِأَيِّ ذَنْبٍ قُتِلَتْ ۞

10. When the scrolls are laid open;

وَإِذَا الصُّحُفُ نُشِرَتْ ۞

11. When the sky is unveiled;

وَإِذَا السَّمَاءُ كُشِطَتْ ۞

12. When the Blazing Fire is kindled to fierce heat;

وَإِذَا الْجَحِيْمُ سُعِّرَتْ ۞

13. And when the Garden is brought near;-

وَإِذَا الْجَنَّةُ أُزْلِفَتْ ۞

14. (Then) shall each soul know what it has put forward.

عَلِمَتْ نَفْسٌ مَّا أَحْضَرَتْ ۞

15. So verily I call to witness the planets - that recede,

فَلَا أُقْسِمُ بِالْخُنَّسِ ۞

16. Go straight, or hide;

17. And the Night as it dissipates;

الْجَوَارِ الْكُنَّسِ ۞

18. And the Dawn as it breathes away the darkness;-

وَالَّيْلِ إِذَا عَسْعَسَ ۞

وَالصُّبْحِ إِذَا تَنَفَّسَ ۞

19. Verily this is the word of a most honourable Messenger,

إِنَّهُ لَقَوْلُ رَسُوْلٍ كَرِيْمٍ ۞

20. Endued with Power, held in honour by the Lord of the Throne,

ذِيْ قُوَّةٍ عِنْدَ ذِي الْعَرْشِ مَكِيْنٍ ۞

21. With authority there, (and) faithful to his trust.

مُّطَاعٍ ثَمَّ أَمِيْنٍ ۞

22. And (O people!) your companion is not one possessed;

وَمَا صَاحِبُكُمْ بِمَجْنُوْنٍ ۞

23. And without doubt he saw him in the clear horizon.

وَلَقَدْ رَاٰهُ بِالْأُفُقِ الْمُبِيْنِ ۞

24. Neither does he withhold grudgingly a knowledge of the Unseen.

وَمَا هُوَ عَلَى الْغَيْبِ بِضَنِيْنٍ ۞

SÛRAH-82
AL-INFIṬÂR
(INTRODUCTION)

In subject-matter this Sûrah is cognate to the last, though the best authorities consider it a good deal later in chronology in the early Makkan period.

Its argument is subject to the threefold interpretation referring (1) to the final Day of Judgment, (2) to the Lesser Judgment, on an individual's death, and (3) to the awakening of the Inner Light in the soul at any time, that being considered as Death to the Falsities of this life and a Rebirth to the true spiritual Reality.

25. Nor is it the word of an evil spirit accursed.

وَمَاهُوَ بِقَوْلِ شَيْطَانٍ رَّجِيْمٍ ۞

26. When whither do you go?

فَاَيْنَ تَذْهَبُوْنَ ۞

27. Verily this is no less than a Message to (all) the Worlds:

اِنْ هُوَ اِلَّا ذِكْرٌ لِّلْعَالَمِيْنَ ۞

28. (With profit) to whoever among you wills to go straight:

لِمَنْ شَاءَ مِنْكُمْ اَنْ يَّسْتَقِيْمَ ۞

29. But you shall not will except as Allah wills,- the Cherisher of the Worlds.

وَمَا تَشَآءُوْنَ اِلَّا اَنْ يَّشَآءَ اللهُ رَبُّ الْعَالَمِيْنَ ۞

82. The Cleaving Asunder
In the name of Allah. Most Gracious, Most Merciful.

(٨٢) سُوْرَةُ الْاِنْفِطَارِ مَكِّيَّةٌ (٨٢)

بِسْمِ اللهِ الرَّحْمٰنِ الرَّحِيْمِ

1. When the Sky is cleft asunder;

اِذَا السَّمَآءُ انْفَطَرَتْ ۞

2. When the Stars are scattered;

وَاِذَا الْكَوَاكِبُ انْتَثَرَتْ ۞

3. When the Oceans are suffered to burst forth;

وَاِذَا الْبِحَارُ فُجِّرَتْ ۞

4. And when the Graves are turned upside down;-

وَاِذَا الْقُبُوْرُ بُعْثِرَتْ ۞

5. (Then) shall each soul know what it has sent forward and (what it has) kept back..

عَلِمَتْ نَفْسٌ مَّا قَدَّمَتْ وَاَخَّرَتْ ۞

6. O man! What has seduced you from your Lord Most Beneficent?-

يَاَيُّهَا الْاِنْسَانُ مَا غَرَّكَ بِرَبِّكَ الْكَرِيْمِ ۞

7. Him Who created you, fashioned you in due proportion, and gave you a just bias;

الَّذِيْ خَلَقَكَ فَسَوّٰىكَ فَعَدَلَكَ ۞

8. In whatever form He wills, He puts you together.

فِيْ اَيِّ صُوْرَةٍ مَّا شَآءَ رَكَّبَكَ ۞

9. Nay, but you do reject Right and Judgment!

كَلَّا بَلْ تُكَذِّبُوْنَ بِالدِّيْنِ ۞

10. But verily over you (are appointed angels) to protect you,—

وَاِنَّ عَلَيْكُمْ لَحٰفِظِيْنَ ۞

11. Kind and honourable,- writing down (your deeds):

كِرَامًا كَاتِبِيْنَ ۞

12. They know (and understand) all that you do.

يَعْلَمُوْنَ مَا تَفْعَلُوْنَ ۞

13. As for the Righteous, they will be in bliss;

اِنَّ الْاَبْرَارَ لَفِيْ نَعِيْمٍ ۞

14. And the Wicked - they will be in the Hell,

وَاِنَّ الْفُجَّارَ لَفِيْ جَحِيْمٍ ۞

15. Which they will enter on the Day of Judgment,

يَصْلَوْنَهَا يَوْمَ الدِّيْنِ ۞

16. And they will not be able to keep away therefrom.

وَمَا هُمْ عَنْهَا بِغَآئِبِيْنَ ۞

17. And what will explain to you what the Day of Judgment is?

وَمَا اَدْرٰىكَ مَا يَوْمُ الدِّيْنِ ۞

SÛRAH-83
AL-MUTAFFIFÎN
(INTRODUCTION)

This Sûrah is close in time to the last one and the next one.

It condemns all fraud-in daily dealings, as well as and especially in matters of Religion and the higher spiritual Life.

18. Again, what will explain to you what the Day of Judgment is?

ثُمَّ مَا أَدْرَاكَ مَا يَوْمُ الدِّيِنِ ۞

19. (It will be) the Day when no soul shall have power (to do) anything for another: for the command, that Day, will be (wholly) with Allah.

يَوْمَ لَا تَمْلِكُ نَفْسٌ لِّنَفْسٍ شَيْئًا ۖ وَالْأَمْرُ يَوْمَئِذٍ لِّلَّهِ ۞

(Al-Mutaffifin, or The Dealers in Fraud)

In the name of Allah, Most Gracious, Most Merciful.

(٨٣) سُورَةُ الْمُطَفِّفِينَ مَكِّيَّةٌ (٨٦)

بِسْمِ اللهِ الرَّحْمٰنِ الرَّحِيمِ

1. Woe to those that deal in fraud,-

وَيْلٌ لِّلْمُطَفِّفِينَ ۞

2. Those who, when they have to receive by measure from men, exact full measure,

الَّذِينَ إِذَا اكْتَالُوا عَلَى النَّاسِ يَسْتَوْفُونَ ۞

3. But when they have to give by measure or weight to men, give less than due.

وَإِذَا كَالُوهُمْ أَوْ وَزَنُوهُمْ يُخْسِرُونَ ۞

4. Do they not think that they will be called to account?-

أَلَا يَظُنُّ أُولَٰئِكَ أَنَّهُم مَّبْعُوثُونَ ۞

5. On a Mighty Day,

لِيَوْمٍ عَظِيمٍ ۞

6. The day when (all) mankind stand before the Lord of the Worlds?

يَوْمَ يَقُومُ النَّاسُ لِرَبِّ الْعَالَمِينَ ۞

7. Nay! Surely the record of the wicked is (preserved) in *Sijjin*.

كَلَّا إِنَّ كِتَابَ الْفُجَّارِ لَفِي سِجِّينٍ ۞

8. And what will explain to you what *Sijjin* is?

وَمَا أَدْرَاكَ مَا سِجِّينٌ ۞

9. (There is) a Register (fully) inscribed.

كِتَابٌ مَّرْقُومٌ ۞

10. Woe, that Day, to those that deny-

وَيْلٌ يَوْمَئِذٍ لِّلْمُكَذِّبِينَ ۞

11. Those that deny the Day of Judgment.

الَّذِينَ يُكَذِّبُونَ بِيَوْمِ الدِّينِ ۞

12. And none can deny it but the transgressor beyond bounds, the sinner!

وَمَا يُكَذِّبُ بِهِ إِلَّا كُلُّ مُعْتَدٍ أَثِيمٍ ۞

13. When Our Signs are rehearsed to him, he says, "Tales of the ancients!"

إِذَا تُتْلَىٰ عَلَيْهِ آيَاتُنَا قَالَ أَسَاطِيرُ الْأَوَّلِينَ ۞

14. By no means! but on their hearts is the stain of the (ill) which they do!

كَلَّا بَلْ رَانَ عَلَىٰ قُلُوبِهِم مَّا كَانُوا يَكْسِبُونَ ۞

15. Verily, from (the Light of) their Lord, that Day, will they be veiled.

كَلَّا إِنَّهُمْ عَن رَّبِّهِمْ يَوْمَئِذٍ لَّمَحْجُوبُونَ ۞

16. Further, they will enter the Fire of Hell.

ثُمَّ إِنَّهُمْ لَصَالُوا الْجَحِيمِ ۞

17. Further, it will be said to them: "This is the (reality)

ثُمَّ يُقَالُ هَٰذَا الَّذِي كُنتُم بِهِ

SÛRAH-84
AL-INSHIQÂQ
(INTRODUCTION)

Chronologically this Sûrah is closely connected with the last one. In subject-matter it resembles more S. 82, and 81 with which it may be compared.

By a number or mystic metaphors it is shown that the present phenomenal order will not last, and Allah's full Judgment will certainly be established: man should therefore strive for that World of Eternity and True Values.

which you rejected as false!

كَذِّبُوْنَ ۟

18. Nay, but the record of the righteous is in 'Illiyin!—

كَلَّا اِنَّ كِتٰبَ الْاَبْرَارِ لَفِيْ عِلِّيِّيْنَ ۟

19. And what will explain to you what 'Illiyin is?

وَمَا اَدْرٰىكَ مَا عِلِّيُّوْنَ ۟

20. (There is) a Register (fully) inscribed,

كِتٰبٌ مَّرْقُوْمٌ ۟

21. To which bear witness those Nearest (to Allah).

يَّشْهَدُهُ الْمُقَرَّبُوْنَ ۟

22. Truly the Righteous will be in Bliss:

اِنَّ الْاَبْرَارَ لَفِيْ نَعِيْمٍ ۟

23. On raised couches will they command a sight (of all things):

عَلَى الْاَرَآئِكِ يَنْظُرُوْنَ ۟

24. You will recognise in their faces the beaming brightness of Bliss.

تَعْرِفُ فِيْ وُجُوْهِهِمْ نَضْرَةَ النَّعِيْمِ ۟

25. Their thirst will be slaked with Pure Wine sealed:

يُسْقَوْنَ مِنْ رَّحِيْقٍ مَّخْتُوْمٍ ۟

26. The seal thereof will be musk: and for this let those aspire, who have aspirations:

خِتٰمُهُ مِسْكٌ ۭ وَفِيْ ذٰلِكَ فَلْيَتَنَافَسِ الْمُتَنَافِسُوْنَ ۟

27. With it will be (given) a mixture of Tasnim.

وَمِزَاجُهُ مِنْ تَسْنِيْمٍ ۟

28. A spring, from (the waters) whereof drink those Nearest to Allah.

عَيْنًا يَّشْرَبُ بِهَا الْمُقَرَّبُوْنَ ۟

29. Those in sin used to laugh at those who believed,

اِنَّ الَّذِيْنَ اَجْرَمُوْا كَانُوْا مِنَ الَّذِيْنَ

30. And whenever they passed by them, used to wink at each other (in mockery);

اٰمَنُوْا يَضْحَكُوْنَ ۟ وَاِذَا مَرُّوْا بِهِمْ يَتَغَامَزُوْنَ ۟

31. And when they returned to their own people, they returned jesting;

وَاِذَا انْقَلَبُوْا اِلٰٓى اَهْلِهِمُ انْقَلَبُوْا فَكِهِيْنَ ۟

32. And whenever they saw them, they would say, "Behold! These are the people truly astray!"

وَاِذَا رَاَوْهُمْ قَالُوْٓا اِنَّ هٰٓؤُلَاءِ لَضَآلُّوْنَ ۟

33. But they had not been sent as keepers over them!

وَمَآ اُرْسِلُوْا عَلَيْهِمْ حٰفِظِيْنَ ۟

34. But on this Day the Believers will laugh at the Unbelievers:

فَالْيَوْمَ الَّذِيْنَ اٰمَنُوْا مِنَ الْكُفَّارِ

35. On raised couches they will command (a sight) (of all things).

يَضْحَكُوْنَ ۟ عَلَى الْاَرَآئِكِ يَنْظُرُوْنَ ۟

36. Will not the Unbelievers have been paid back for what they did?

هَلْ ثُوِّبَ الْكُفَّارُ مَا كَانُوْا يَفْعَلُوْنَ ۟

84. The Rending Asunder
In the name of Allah. Most Gracious, Most Merciful.

سُوْرَةُ الْاِنْشِقَاقِ مَكِّيَّةٌ ۟

بِسْمِ اللّٰهِ الرَّحْمٰنِ الرَّحِيْمِ

1. When the Sky is rent asunder,

اِذَا السَّمَآءُ انْشَقَّتْ ۟

2.   And attentive to her Lord in fear,

وَأَذِنَتْ لِرَبِّهَا وَحُقَّتْ ۝

3.   And when the earth is flattened out,

وَإِذَا الْأَرْضُ مُدَّتْ ۝

4.   And hath casts out all that was in her, and is empty.

وَأَلْقَتْ مَا فِيهَا وَتَخَلَّتْ ۝

5.   And attentive to her Lord in fear!

وَأَذِنَتْ لِرَبِّهَا وَحُقَّتْ ۝

6.   O you man! Verily you are ever toiling on towards your Lord- painfully toiling,- but you shall meet Him.

يَا أَيُّهَا الْإِنْسَانُ إِنَّكَ كَادِحٌ إِلَى رَبِّكَ كَدْحًا فَمُلَاقِيهِ ۝

7.   Then he who is given his Record in his right hand,

فَأَمَّا مَنْ أُوتِيَ كِتَابَهُ بِيَمِينِهِ ۝

8.   Soon will his account be taken by an easy reckoning,

فَسَوْفَ يُحَاسَبُ حِسَابًا يَسِيرًا ۝

9.   And he will turn to his people, rejoicing!

وَيَنْقَلِبُ إِلَى أَهْلِهِ مَسْرُورًا ۝

10.   But he who is given his Record behind his back,-

وَأَمَّا مَنْ أُوتِيَ كِتَابَهُ وَرَاءَ ظَهْرِهِ ۝

11.   Soon will he cry for perdition,

فَسَوْفَ يَدْعُو ثُبُورًا ۝

12.   And he will enter a Blazing Fire.

وَيَصْلَى سَعِيرًا ۝

13.   Truly, did he go about among his people, rejoicing!

إِنَّهُ كَانَ فِي أَهْلِهِ مَسْرُورًا ۝

14.   Truly, did he think that he would not have to return (to Us)!

إِنَّهُ ظَنَّ أَنْ لَنْ يَحُورَ ۝

15.   Nay, nay! for his Lord was (ever) watchful of him!

بَلَى إِنَّ رَبَّهُ كَانَ بِهِ بَصِيرًا ۝

16.   So I do call to witness the ruddy glow of Sunset;

فَلَا أُقْسِمُ بِالشَّفَقِ ۝

17.   The Night and its Homing;

وَاللَّيْلِ وَمَا وَسَقَ ۝

18.   And the Moon in her fullness:

وَالْقَمَرِ إِذَا اتَّسَقَ ۝

19.   You shall surely travel from stage to stage.

لَتَرْكَبُنَّ طَبَقًا عَنْ طَبَقٍ ۝

20.   What then is the matter with them, that they do not believe?-

فَمَا لَهُمْ لَا يُؤْمِنُونَ ۝

21.   And when the Qur'an is read to them, they do not fall prostrate,

وَإِذَا قُرِئَ عَلَيْهِمُ الْقُرْآنُ لَا يَسْجُدُونَ ۩

22.   But on the contrary the Unbelievers reject (it).

بَلِ الَّذِينَ كَفَرُوا يُكَذِّبُونَ ۝

23.   And Allah knows best what they are hiding,

وَاللَّهُ أَعْلَمُ بِمَا يُوعُونَ ۝

24.   So announce to them a Chastisement Grievous,

فَبَشِّرْهُمْ بِعَذَابٍ أَلِيمٍ ۝

25.   Except to those who believe and work righteous deeds:

إِلَّا الَّذِينَ آمَنُوا وَعَمِلُوا الصَّالِحَاتِ

SÛRAH-85
AL-BURÛJ
(INTRODUCTION)

This is one of the earlier Makkan Sûras, chronologically cognate with S. 91. The subject-matter is the persecution of Allah's votaries. Allah watches over His own, and will deal with the enemies of Truth as He dealt with them in the past.

for them is a Reward that will never fail.

لَهُمْ اَجْرٌ غَيْرُ مَمْنُوْنٍ ۞

85. The Zodiacal Signs
In the name of Allah. Most Gracious, Most Merciful.

(٨٥) سُوْرَةُ الْبُرُوْجِ مَكِّيَّةٌ (٢٧)

بِسْمِ اللّٰهِ الرَّحْمٰنِ الرَّحِيْمِ

1.   By the Sky, with its constellations.

وَالسَّمَآءِ ذَاتِ الْبُرُوْجِ ۙ

2.   By the promised Day (of Judgment);

وَالْيَوْمِ الْمَوْعُوْدِ ۙ

3.   By one that witnesses, and the subject of the witness;-

وَشَاهِدٍ وَّمَشْهُوْدٍ ؕ

4.   Woe to the makers of the pit (of fire),

قُتِلَ اَصْحٰبُ الْاُخْدُوْدِ ۙ

5.   Fire supplied (abundantly) with fuel:

النَّارِ ذَاتِ الْوَقُوْدِ ۙ

6.   Behold! They sat over against the (fire),

اِذْ هُمْ عَلَيْهَا قُعُوْدٌ ۙ

7.   And they witnessed (all) that they were doing against the Believers.

وَّهُمْ عَلٰى مَا يَفْعَلُوْنَ بِالْمُؤْمِنِيْنَ شُهُوْدٌ ؕ

8.   And they ill-treated them for no other reason than that they believed in Allah, Exalted in Power, Worthy of all Praise!-

وَمَا نَقَمُوْا مِنْهُمْ اِلَّا اَنْ يُّؤْمِنُوْا بِاللّٰهِ الْعَزِيْزِ الْحَمِيْدِ ۙ

9.   Him to Whom belongs the dominion of the heavens and the earth! And Allah is Witness to all things.

الَّذِيْ لَهٗ مُلْكُ السَّمٰوٰتِ وَالْاَرْضِ ؕ وَ اللّٰهُ عَلٰى كُلِّ شَيْءٍ شَهِيْدٌ ؕ

10.   Those who persecute (or draw into temptation) the Believers, men and women, and do not turn in repentance, will have the Chastisement of Hell: they will have the Chastisement of the Burning Fire.

اِنَّ الَّذِيْنَ فَتَنُوا الْمُؤْمِنِيْنَ وَالْمُؤْمِنٰتِ ثُمَّ لَمْ يَتُوْبُوْا فَلَهُمْ عَذَابُ جَهَنَّمَ وَلَهُمْ عَذَابُ الْحَرِيْقِ ؕ

11.   For those who believe and do righteous deeds, will be in the Gardens; beneath which rivers flow: that is the great Salvation, (the fulfilment of all desires),

اِنَّ الَّذِيْنَ اٰمَنُوْا وَعَمِلُوا الصّٰلِحٰتِ لَهُمْ جَنّٰتٌ تَجْرِيْ مِنْ تَحْتِهَا الْاَنْهٰرُ ؕ ذٰلِكَ الْفَوْزُ الْكَبِيْرُ ؕ

12.   Truly strong is the Grip (and Power) of your Lord.

اِنَّ بَطْشَ رَبِّكَ لَشَدِيْدٌ ؕ

13.   It is He Who creates from the very beginning, and He can restore (life).

اِنَّهٗ هُوَ يُبْدِئُ وَيُعِيْدُ ۚ

14.   And He is the Oft-Forgiving, full of loving-kindness,

وَهُوَ الْغَفُوْرُ الْوَدُوْدُ ۙ

15.   Lord of the Throne of Glory,

ذُو الْعَرْشِ الْمَجِيْدُ ۙ

16.   Doer (without let) of all that He intends.

فَعَّالٌ لِّمَا يُرِيْدُ ؕ

SÛRAH-86
AT-TÂRIQ
(INTRODUCTION)

This Sûrah also belongs to the early Makkan period, perhaps not far removed from the last Sûrah.

Its subject-matter is the protection afforded to every soul in the darkest period of its spiritual history. The physical nature of man may be insignificant, but the soul given to him by Allah must win a glorious Future in the end.

17. Has the story reached you, of the forces-

هَلْ أَتٰىكَ حَدِيثُ الْجُنُوْدِ ۞

18. Of Pharaoh and the Thamud?

فِرْعَوْنَ وَثَمُوْدَ ۫

19. And yet the Unbelievers (persist) in rejecting (the Truth)!

بَلِ الَّذِيْنَ كَفَرُوْا فِيْ تَكْذِيْبٍ ۞

20. But Allah encompasses them from behind!

وَّاللّٰهُ مِنْ وَّرَآئِهِمْ مُّحِيْطٌ ۞

21. Nay, this is a Glorious Qur'an,

بَلْ هُوَ قُرْاٰنٌ مَّجِيْدٌ ۙ ۞

22. (Inscribed) in a Tablet Preserved.

فِيْ لَوْحٍ مَّحْفُوْظٍ ۞

86. The Night-Visitant
In the name of Allah. Most Gracious, Most Merciful.

(٨٢) سُوْرَةُ الطَّارِقِ مَكِّيَّةٌ (٣١)

بِسْمِ اللّٰهِ الرَّحْمٰنِ الرَّحِيْمِ

1. By the Sky and the Night-Visitant (therein);-

وَالسَّمَآءِ وَالطَّارِقِ ۙ ۞

2. And what will explain to you what the Night-Visitant is?

وَمَآ أَدْرٰىكَ مَا الطَّارِقُ ۙ ۞

3. (It is) the Star of piercing brightness;-

النَّجْمُ الثَّاقِبُ ۞

4. There is no soul but has a protector over it.

إِنْ كُلُّ نَفْسٍ لَّمَّا عَلَيْهَا حَافِظٌ ۞

5. Now let man but think from what he is created!

فَلْيَنْظُرِ الْإِنْسَانُ مِمَّ خُلِقَ ۞

6. He is created from a drop emitted-

خُلِقَ مِنْ مَّآءٍ دَافِقٍ ۙ ۞

7. Proceeding from between the backbone and the ribs:

يَخْرُجُ مِنْ بَيْنِ الصُّلْبِ وَالتَّرَآئِبِ ۙ ۞

8. Surely (Allah) is able to bring him back (to life)!

إِنَّهُ عَلٰى رَجْعِهِ لَقَادِرٌ ۞

9. The Day that (all) hidden things shall be made manifest.

يَوْمَ تُبْلَى السَّرَآئِرُ ۙ ۞

10. (Man) will have no power, and no helper.

فَمَا لَهُ مِنْ قُوَّةٍ وَّلَا نَاصِرٍ ۞

11. By the Firmament which gives the recurring rain,

وَالسَّمَآءِ ذَاتِ الرَّجْعِ ۙ ۞

12. And by the Earth which opens out (for the gushing of springs or the sprouting of vegetation),—

وَالْأَرْضِ ذَاتِ الصَّدْعِ ۙ ۞

13. Lo! This (Qur'an) is a conclusive word,

إِنَّهُ لَقَوْلٌ فَصْلٌ ۙ ۞

14. It is not a thing for amusement.

وَّمَا هُوَ بِالْهَزْلِ ۞

15. As for them, they are but plotting a scheme,

إِنَّهُمْ يَكِيْدُوْنَ كَيْدًا ۙ ۞

16. And I am planning a scheme.

وَّأَكِيْدُ كَيْدًا ۙ ۞

17. Therefore grant a delay to the Unbelievers: give respite to them gently (for awhile).

فَمَهِّلِ الْكٰفِرِيْنَ أَمْهِلْهُمْ رُوَيْدًا ۞

SÛRAH-87
AL-A'LÂ
(INTRODUCTION)

This is one of the earliest of the Makkan Sûras, being usually placed eighth in chronological order, and immediately after S. 81.

The argument is that Allah has made man capable of progress by ordered steps, and by His Revelation will lead him still higher to purification and perfection.

SÛRAH-88
AL-GHÂSHIYAH
(INTRODUCTION)

This is a late Sûrah of the early Makkan period, perhaps close in date to S. 52. Its subject-matter is the contrast between the destinies of the Good and the Evil in the Hereafter,—on the Day when the true balance will be restored: the Signs of Allah even in this life should remind us of the Day of Account, for Allah is good and just, and His creation is for a just Purpose.

87. The Most High
In the name of Allah. Most Gracious, Most Merciful.

(٨٤) سُوْرَةُ الْاَعْلٰى مَكِّيَّتُهَا (٨)

بِسْمِ اللّٰهِ الرَّحْمٰنِ الرَّحِيْمِ

1. Glorify the name of your Guardian-Lord, Most High,

سَبِّحِ اسْمَ رَبِّكَ الْاَعْلَى ۞

2. Who has created, and further, given order and proportion;

الَّذِيْ خَلَقَ فَسَوّٰى ۞

3. Who has ordained law, and granted guidance;

وَالَّذِيْ قَدَّرَ فَهَدٰى ۞

4. And Who brings out the (green and luscious) pasture,

وَالَّذِيْٓ اَخْرَجَ الْمَرْعٰى ۞

5. And then makes it (but) swarthy stubble.

فَجَعَلَهٗ غُثَآءً اَحْوٰى ۞

6. By degrees shall We teach you to declare (the Message), so you shall not forget,

سَنُقْرِئُكَ فَلَا تَنْسٰى ۞

7. Except as Allah wills: for He knows what is manifest and what is hidden.

اِلَّا مَا شَآءَ اللّٰهُ ۭ اِنَّهٗ يَعْلَمُ الْجَهْرَ وَمَا يَخْفٰى ۞

8. An We will make it easy for you (to follow) the simple (Path).

وَنُيَسِّرُكَ لِلْيُسْرٰى ۞

9. Therefore give admonition in case the admonition profits (the hearer).

فَذَكِّرْ اِنْ نَّفَعَتِ الذِّكْرٰى ۞

10. The admonition will be received by those who fear (Allah)

سَيَذَّكَّرُ مَنْ يَّخْشٰى ۞

11. But it will be avoided by those most unfortunate ones,

وَيَتَجَنَّبُهَا الْاَشْقَى ۞

12. Who will enter the Great Fire,

الَّذِيْ يَصْلَى النَّارَ الْكُبْرٰى ۞

13. In which they will then neither die nor live.

ثُمَّ لَا يَمُوْتُ فِيْهَا وَلَا يَحْيٰى ۞

14. But those will prosper who purify themselves,

قَدْ اَفْلَحَ مَنْ تَزَكّٰى ۞

15. And glorify the name of their Guardian - Lord, and pray.

وَذَكَرَ اسْمَ رَبِّهٖ فَصَلّٰى ۞

16. Nay, (behold) you prefer the life of this world;

بَلْ تُؤْثِرُوْنَ الْحَيٰوةَ الدُّنْيَا ۞

17. But the Hereafter is better and more enduring.

وَالْاٰخِرَةُ خَيْرٌ وَّاَبْقٰى ۞

18. And this is in the Books of the earliest (Revelations),-

اِنَّ هٰذَا لَفِي الصُّحُفِ الْاُوْلٰى ۞

19. The Books of Abraham and Moses.

صُحُفِ اِبْرٰهِيْمَ وَمُوْسٰى ۞

88. The Overwhelming Event
In the name of Allah. Most Gracious, Most Merciful.

(٨٨) سُوْرَةُ الْغَاشِيَةِ مَكِّيَّتُهَا (٢٨)

بِسْمِ اللّٰهِ الرَّحْمٰنِ الرَّحِيْمِ

1. Has the story reached you, of the Overwhelming (Event)?

هَلْ اَتٰىكَ حَدِيْثُ الْغَاشِيَةِ ۞

2. Some faces, that Day, will be humiliated,

وُجُوْهٌ يَّوْمَئِذٍ خَاشِعَةٌ ۞

3. Labouring (hard), weary,-

عَامِلَةٌ نَّاصِبَةٌ ۞

4. The while they enter the Blazing Fire,-

تَصْلَىٰ نَارًا حَامِيَةً ۞

5. The while they are given, to drink, of a boiling hot spring,

تُسْقَىٰ مِنْ عَيْنٍ اٰنِيَةٍ ۞

6. There will be no food for them but a bitter Dhari'

لَّيْسَ لَهُمْ طَعَامٌ إِلَّا مِنْ ضَرِيعٍ ۞

7. Which will neither nourish nor satisfy hunger.

لَّا يُسْمِنُ وَلَا يُغْنِى مِنْ جُوعٍ ۞

8. (Other) faces that Day will be joyful,

وُجُوهٌ يَّوْمَئِذٍ نَّاعِمَةٌ ۞

9. Pleased with their striving,-

لِّسَعْيِهَا رَاضِيَةٌ ۞

10. In a Garden on high,

فِى جَنَّةٍ عَالِيَةٍ ۞

11. Where they shall hear no (word) of vanity:

لَّا تَسْمَعُ فِيهَا لَاغِيَةً ۞

12. Therein will be a bubbling spring:

فِيهَا عَيْنٌ جَارِيَةٌ ۞

13. Therein will be Thrones (of dignity), raised on high,

فِيهَا سُرُرٌ مَّرْفُوعَةٌ ۞

14. Goblets placed (ready),

وَّأَكْوَابٌ مَّوْضُوعَةٌ ۞

15. And cushions set in rows,

وَّنَمَارِقُ مَصْفُوفَةٌ ۞

16. And rich carpets (all) spread out.

وَّزَرَابِيُّ مَبْثُوثَةٌ ۞

17. Do they not look at the Camels, how they are made?-

أَفَلَا يَنْظُرُونَ إِلَى الْإِبِلِ كَيْفَ خُلِقَتْ ۞

18. And at the Sky, how it is raised high?-

وَإِلَى السَّمَاءِ كَيْفَ رُفِعَتْ ۞

19. And at the Mountains, how they are fixed firm?-

وَإِلَى الْجِبَالِ كَيْفَ نُصِبَتْ ۞

20. And at the Earth, how it is spread out?

وَإِلَى الْأَرْضِ كَيْفَ سُطِحَتْ ۞

21. Therefore you give admonition, for you are one to admonish.

فَذَكِّرْ إِنَّمَا أَنْتَ مُذَكِّرٌ ۞

22. You are not one to manage (men's) affairs.

لَّسْتَ عَلَيْهِمْ بِمُصَيْطِرٍ ۞

23. But if any turn away and reject Allah,-

إِلَّا مَنْ تَوَلَّىٰ وَكَفَرَ ۞

24. Allah will punish him with a mighty Punishment,

فَيُعَذِّبُهُ اللّٰهُ الْعَذَابَ الْأَكْبَرَ ۞

25. For to Us will be their return;

إِنَّ إِلَيْنَا إِيَابَهُمْ ۞

26. Then it will be for Us to call them to account.

ثُمَّ إِنَّ عَلَيْنَا حِسَابَهُمْ ۞

SÛRAH-89
AL-FAJR
(INTRODUCTION)

This is one of the earliest of the Sûras to be revealed,- probably within the first ten in chronological order.

Its mystic meaning is suggested by contrasts,-contrasts in nature and in man's long history. Thus does it enforce the lesson of Faith in the Hereafter to "those who understand". Man's history and legendary lore show that greatness does not last and the proudest are brought low. For enforcing moral and spiritual truths, the strictest history is no better than legend. Indeed all artistic history is legend, for it is written from a special point of view.

Man is easily cowed by contrasts in his own fortunes, and yet he does not learn from them the lesson of forbearance and kindness to others, and the final elevation of goodness in the Hereafter. When all the things on which his mind and heart are set on this earth shall be crushed to nothingness, he will see the real glory and power, love and beauty, of Allah, for these are the light of the Garden of Paradise,

89. The Break of Day

In the name of Allah. Most Gracious, Most Merciful.

(٨٩) سُوْرَةُ الْفَجْرِ مَكِّيَّةٌ (١٠)

بِسْمِ اللّٰهِ الرَّحْمٰنِ الرَّحِيْمِ

1. By the break of Day;

وَالْفَجْرِ ۙ

2. By the ten Nights.

وَلَيَالٍ عَشْرٍ ۙ

3. By the even and odd (contrasted);

وَّالشَّفْعِ وَالْوَتْرِ ۙ

4. And by the Night when it passes away;-

وَالَّيْلِ اِذَا يَسْرِ ۚ

5. Is there (not) in these an adjuration (or evidence) for those who understand?.

هَلْ فِيْ ذٰلِكَ قَسَمٌ لِّذِيْ حِجْرٍ ؕ

6. Don't you see how your Lord dealt with the 'Ad (people),

اَلَمْ تَرَ كَيْفَ فَعَلَ رَبُّكَ بِعَادٍ ۙ

7. Of the (city of) Iram, with lofty pillars,

اِرَمَ ذَاتِ الْعِمَادِ ۙ

8. The like of which were not produced in (all) the land?

الَّتِيْ لَمْ يُخْلَقْ مِثْلُهَا فِى الْبِلَادِ ۙ

9. And with the Thamud (people), who cut out (huge) rocks in the valley?-

وَثَمُوْدَ الَّذِيْنَ جَابُوا الصَّخْرَ بِالْوَادِ ۙ

10. And with Pharaoh, lord of stakes?

وَفِرْعَوْنَ ذِى الْاَوْتَادِ ۙ

11. (All) these transgressed beyond bounds in the lands,

الَّذِيْنَ طَغَوْا فِى الْبِلَادِ ۙ

12. And heaped therein mischief (on mischief).

فَاَكْثَرُوْا فِيْهَا الْفَسَادَ ۙ

13. Therefore your Lord poured on them a scourge of diverse chastisements:

فَصَبَّ عَلَيْهِمْ رَبُّكَ سَوْطَ عَذَابٍ ۙ

14. For your Lord is (as a Guardian) on a watch-tower.

اِنَّ رَبَّكَ لَبِالْمِرْصَادِ ؕ

15. Now, as for man, when his Lord tries him, giving him honour and gifts, then he says, (puffed up), "My Lord has honoured me."

فَاَمَّا الْاِنْسَانُ اِذَا مَا ابْتَلٰهُ رَبُّهٗ فَاَكْرَمَهٗ وَنَعَّمَهٗ ۙ فَيَقُوْلُ رَبِّيْٓ اَكْرَمَنِ ؕ

16. But when He tries him, restricting his subsistence for him, then he says (in despair), "My Lord has humiliated me!"

وَاَمَّآ اِذَا مَا ابْتَلٰهُ فَقَدَرَ عَلَيْهِ رِزْقَهٗ ۙ فَيَقُوْلُ رَبِّيْٓ اَهَانَنِ ۚ

17. Nay, nay! but you do not honour the orphans!

كَلَّا بَلْ لَّا تُكْرِمُوْنَ الْيَتِيْمَ ۙ

18. Nor do you encourage one another to feed the poor!-

وَلَا تَحٰضُّوْنَ عَلٰى طَعَامِ الْمِسْكِيْنِ ۙ

19. And you devour inheritance - all with greed,

وَتَأْكُلُوْنَ التُّرَاثَ اَكْلًا لَّمًّا ۙ

20. And you love wealth with inordinate love!

وَّتُحِبُّوْنَ الْمَالَ حُبًّا جَمًّا ؕ

21. Nay! When the earth is pounded to powder,

كَلَّآ اِذَا دُكَّتِ الْاَرْضُ دَكًّا دَكًّا ۙ

22. And your Lord comes, and His angels rank upon rank,

وَّجَآءَ رَبُّكَ وَالْمَلَكُ صَفًّا صَفًّا ۙ

SÛRAH-90
AL-BALAD
(INTRODUCTION)

This is an early Makkan revelation, and refers to the mystic relation (by divine sanction) of the Holy Prophet with the city of Makkah. He was born in that City, which had already been sacred for ages before. He was nurtured in that City and had (to use a modem phrase) the freedom of that City, belonging, as he did, to the noble family which held the government of its sacred precincts in its hands. But he was an orphan, and orphans in his day had a poor time. But his mind was turned to things divine He protested against the prevailing idolatry and sin, and his parent City persecuted him and cast him out. He made another City Yathrib, his own: it became the *Madinat un-Nabî,* the City of the Prophet, and it has ever since been Madinah. We can speak of Madinah as the Prophet's child. But the Prophet ever cherished in his heart the love of his parent City of Makkah, and in the fulness of time was received in triumph there. He purified it from all idols and abominations, re-established the worship of the One True Allah, overthrew the purse-proud selfish autocracy, restored the sway of the righteous (people of the Right Hand), the liberty of the slave, and the rights of the poor and downtrodden. What a wonderful career centering round a City! It becomes a symbol of the world's spiritual history.

23. And Hell,—that Day, is brought (face to face), on that Day man will remember, but how will that remembrance profit him?

وَجِاْئَ يَوْمَئِذٍ بِجَهَنَّمَ ۞ يَوْمَئِذٍ

24. He will say: "Ah! Would that I had sent forth (good deeds) for (this) my (Future) Life!"

يَتَذَكَّرُ الْإِنْسَانُ وَأَنَّى لَهُ الذِّكْرَىٰ ۞

25. For, that Day, His Chastisement will be such as none (else) can inflict,

يَقُولُ يَٰلَيْتَنِي قَدَّمْتُ لِحَيَاتِي ۞

26. And His bonds will be such as none (other) can bind.

فَيَوْمَئِذٍ لَّا يُعَذِّبُ عَذَابَهُ أَحَدٌ ۞

27. (To the righteous soul will be said:) "O (you) soul, in (complete) rest and satisfaction!

وَلَا يُوثِقُ وَثَاقَهُ أَحَدٌ ۞

28. You come back to your Lord,- well pleased (yourself), and well-pleasing unto Him!

يَٰأَيَّتُهَا النَّفْسُ الْمُطْمَئِنَّةُ ۞

29. "You enter, then, among My Devotees!

ارْجِعِي إِلَىٰ رَبِّكِ رَاضِيَةً مَّرْضِيَّةً ۞

30. "Yes, you enter My Heaven!

فَادْخُلِي فِي عِبَادِي ۞

وَادْخُلِي جَنَّتِي ۞

90. The City
In the name of Allah. Most Gracious, Most Merciful.

(٩٠) سُورَةُ الْبَلَدِ مَكِّيَّةٌ (٣٥)

بِسْمِ اللّٰهِ الرَّحْمٰنِ الرَّحِيمِ

1. I do call to witness this City;-

لَا أُقْسِمُ بِهَٰذَا الْبَلَدِ ۞

2. And you are a freeman of this City;-

وَأَنْتَ حِلٌّ بِهَٰذَا الْبَلَدِ ۞

3. And (the mystic ties of) parent and child;-

وَوَالِدٍ وَمَا وَلَدَ ۞

4. Verily We have created Man into toil and struggle.

لَقَدْ خَلَقْنَا الْإِنْسَانَ فِي كَبَدٍ ۞

5. Does he think that none has power over him?

أَيَحْسَبُ أَنْ لَّنْ يَقْدِرَ عَلَيْهِ أَحَدٌ ۞

6. He may say (boastfully): " I have squandered Wealth in abundance!"

يَقُولُ أَهْلَكْتُ مَالًا لُّبَدًا ۞

7. Does he think that none beholds him?

أَيَحْسَبُ أَنْ لَّمْ يَرَهُ أَحَدٌ ۞

8. Have We not made for him a pair of eyes?-

أَلَمْ نَجْعَلْ لَّهُ عَيْنَيْنِ ۞

9. And a tongue, and a pair of lips?-

وَلِسَانًا وَشَفَتَيْنِ ۞

10. And shown him the two highways?

وَهَدَيْنَاهُ النَّجْدَيْنِ ۞

11. But he has made no haste on the path that is steep.

فَلَا اقْتَحَمَ الْعَقَبَةَ ۞

12. And what will explain to you the path that is steep?-

وَمَا أَدْرَاكَ مَا الْعَقَبَةُ ۞

13. (It is:) freeing the bondman;

فَكُّ رَقَبَةٍ ۞

14. Or the giving of food in a day of privation.

أَوْ إِطْعَامٌ فِي يَوْمٍ ذِي مَسْغَبَةٍ ۞

15. To the orphan with claims of relationship,

يَتِيمًا ذَا مَقْرَبَةٍ ۞

SÛRAH-91
ASH-SHAMS
(INTRODUCTION)

This is one of the early Makkan revelations. Beginning with a fine nature passage, and leading up to man's need of realising his spiritual responsibility, it ends with a warning of the terrible consequences for those who fear not the Hereafter.

16. Or to the indigent (down) in the dust.

اَوۡ مِسۡكِیۡنًا ذَا مَتۡرَبَةٍ ۞

17. Then he will be of those who believe, and enjoin patience,(constancy, and self-restraint), and enjoin deeds of kindness and compassion.

ثُمَّ كَانَ مِنَ الَّذِیۡنَ اٰمَنُوۡا وَتَوَاصَوۡا بِالصَّبۡرِ وَتَوَاصَوۡا بِالۡمَرۡحَمَةِ ۞

18. Such are the Companions of the Right Hand.

اُولٰٓئِكَ اَصۡحٰبُ الۡمَیۡمَنَةِ ۞

19. But those who reject Our Signs, they are the (unhappy) Companions of the Left Hand.

وَالَّذِیۡنَ كَفَرُوۡا بِاٰیٰتِنَا هُمۡ اَصۡحٰبُ الۡمَشۡـَٔمَةِ ۞

20. On them will be Fire vaulted over (all round).

عَلَیۡهِمۡ نَارٌ مُّؤۡصَدَةٌ ۞

91. The Sun
In the name of Allah. Most Gracious, Most Merciful.

(۹۱) سُوۡرَةُ الشَّمۡسِ مَكِّیَّةٌ (۲۱)

بِسۡمِ اللهِ الرَّحۡمٰنِ الرَّحِیۡمِ

1. By the Sun and his (glorious) splendour;

وَالشَّمۡسِ وَضُحٰىهَا ۞

2. By the Moon as she follows him;

وَالۡقَمَرِ اِذَا تَلٰىهَا ۞

3. By the Day as it shows up (the Sun's) glory;

وَالنَّهَارِ اِذَا جَلّٰىهَا ۞

4. By the Night as it conceals it;

وَالَّیۡلِ اِذَا یَغۡشٰىهَا ۞

5. By the Firmament and its (wonderful) structure;

وَالسَّمَآءِ وَمَا بَنٰىهَا ۞

6. By the Earth and its (wide) expanse:

وَالۡاَرۡضِ وَمَا طَحٰىهَا ۞

7. By the Soul, and the proportion and order given to it.

وَنَفۡسٍ وَّمَا سَوّٰىهَا ۞

8. And its enlightenment as to its wrong and its right;-

فَاَلۡهَمَهَا فُجُوۡرَهَا وَتَقۡوٰىهَا ۞

9. Truly he succeeds that purifies it,

قَدۡ اَفۡلَحَ مَنۡ زَكّٰىهَا ۞

10. And he fails that corrupts it!

وَقَدۡ خَابَ مَنۡ دَسّٰىهَا ۞

11. The Thamud (people) rejected (their prophet) through their inordinate wrong-doing,

كَذَّبَتۡ ثَمُوۡدُ بِطَغۡوٰىهَا ۞

12. Behold, the most wicked man among them was deputed (for impiety).

اِذِ انۡۢبَعَثَ اَشۡقٰىهَا ۞

13. But the Apostle of Allah said to them: "It is a She-camel of Allah! And (do not bar her from) having her drink!"

فَقَالَ لَهُمۡ رَسُوۡلُ اللهِ نَاقَةَ اللهِ وَسُقۡیٰهَا ۞

14. Then they rejected him (as a false prophet), and they hamstrung her. So their Lord, on account of their crime, obliterated their traces and made them equal (in destruction, high and low)!

فَكَذَّبُوۡهُ فَعَقَرُوۡهَا ۙ فَدَمۡدَمَ عَلَیۡهِمۡ رَبُّهُمۡ بِذَنۡۢبِهِمۡ فَسَوّٰىهَا ۞

15. And for Him is no fear of its consequences.

وَلَا یَخَافُ عُقۡبٰهَا ۞

SÛRAH-92
AL-LAYL
(INTRODUCTION)

This was one of the first Sûras to be revealed,-within the first ten; and may be placed in date close to S. 89 and S. 93. Note that in all these Sûras the mystery and the contrast as between Night and Day are appealed to for the consolation of man in his spiritual yearning. Here we are told to strive our utmost towards Allah, and he will give us every help and satisfaction.

SÛRAH-93
AD-DHUHÂ
(INTRODUCTION)

This Sûrah is close in date to Sûras 89 and 92, and the imagery drawn from the contrast of Night and Day is common to all three. In this Sûrah the vicissitudes-of human life are referred to, and a massage of hope and consolation is given to man's soul from Allah's past mercies, and he is bidden to pursue the path of goodness and proclaim the botinties of Allah. This is the general meaning. In particular, the Sûrah seems to have been revealed in a dark period in the outer life of the Holy Prophet, when a man of less resolute will might have been discouraged. But the Prophet is told to hold the present of less account that the glorious Hereafter which awaited him like the glorious morning after a night of stillness and gloom. The Hereafter was, not only in the Future Life, but in his later life on this earth, full of victory and satisfaction.

92. The Night

In the name of Allah. Most Gracious, Most Merciful.

سُورَةُ الَّيْلِ مَكِّيَّةٌ (٩) (٩٢)

بِسْمِ اللهِ الرَّحْمٰنِ الرَّحِيمِ

1. By the Night as it conceals (the light);

وَالَّيْلِ إِذَا يَغْشٰى ۞

2. By the Day as it appears in glory;

وَالنَّهَارِ إِذَا تَجَلّٰى ۞

3. By (the mystery of) the creation of male and female;-

وَمَا خَلَقَ الذَّكَرَ وَالْأُنْثٰى ۞

4. Verily, (the ends) you strive for are diverse.

إِنَّ سَعْيَكُمْ لَشَتّٰى ۞

5. So he who gives (in charity) and fears (Allah),

فَأَمَّا مَنْ أَعْطٰى وَاتَّقٰى ۞

6. And (in all sincerity) testifies to the best,-

وَصَدَّقَ بِالْحُسْنٰى ۞

7. We will indeed make smooth for him the path to Bliss.

فَسَنُيَسِّرُهُ لِلْيُسْرٰى ۞

8. But he who is a greedy miser and thinks himself self-sufficient,

وَأَمَّا مَنْ بَخِلَ وَاسْتَغْنٰى ۞

9. And gives the lie to the best,-

وَكَذَّبَ بِالْحُسْنٰى ۞

10. We will indeed make smooth for him the path to Misery;

فَسَنُيَسِّرُهُ لِلْعُسْرٰى ۞

11. Nor will his wealth profit him when he falls headlong (into the Pit).

وَمَا يُغْنِي عَنْهُ مَالُهُ إِذَا تَرَدّٰى ۞

12. Verily We take upon Ourselves to guide,

إِنَّ عَلَيْنَا لَلْهُدٰى ۞

13. And verily to Us (belong) the End and the Beginning.

وَإِنَّ لَنَا لَلْآخِرَةَ وَالْأُولٰى ۞

14. Therefore do I warn you of a Fire blazing fiercely,

فَأَنْذَرْتُكُمْ نَارًا تَلَظّٰى ۞

15. None shall reach it but those most unfortunate ones.

لَا يَصْلَاهَا إِلَّا الْأَشْقَى ۞

16. Who give the lie to Truth and turn their backs.

الَّذِي كَذَّبَ وَتَوَلّٰى ۞

17. But those most devoted to Allah shall be removed far from it,-

وَسَيُجَنَّبُهَا الْأَتْقَى ۞

18. Those who spend their wealth for increase in self-purification,

الَّذِي يُؤْتِي مَالَهُ يَتَزَكّٰى ۞

19. And have in their minds no favour from anyone for which a reward is expected in return,

وَمَا لِأَحَدٍ عِنْدَهُ مِنْ نِعْمَةٍ تُجْزٰى ۞

20. But only the desire to seek for the Countenance of their Lord Most High;

إِلَّا ابْتِغَاءَ وَجْهِ رَبِّهِ الْأَعْلٰى ۞

21. And soon will they attain (complete) satisfaction.

وَلَسَوْفَ يَرْضٰى ۞

93. The Glorious Morning Light

In the name of Allah. Most Gracious, Most Merciful.

سُورَةُ الضُّحٰى مَكِّيَّةٌ (١١) (٩٣)

بِسْمِ اللهِ الرَّحْمٰنِ الرَّحِيمِ

1. By the Glorious Morning Light,

وَالضُّحٰى ۞

SÛRAH-94
AL-INSHIRÂH
(INTRODUCTION)

This short Sûrah gives a message of hope and encouragement in a time of darkness and difficulty. It was revealed to the Holy Prophet soon after the last Sûrah (*Ḍuhâ*), whose argument it supplements.

SÛRAH-95
AT-TÎN
(INTRODUCTION)

This is also a very early Sûrah. It appeals to the most sacred symbols to show that Allah created man in the best of moulds, but that man is capable of the utmost degradation unless he has Faith and leads a good life. In subject-matter this Sûrah closely resembles S. 103.

2. And by the Night when it is still,-

وَالَّيْلِ اِذَا سَجٰى ۙ

3. Your Guardian-Lord has not forsaken you, nor is He displeased.

مَا وَدَّعَكَ رَبُّكَ وَمَا قَلٰى ؕ

4. And verily the Hereafter will be better for you than the present.

وَلَلْاٰخِرَةُ خَيْرٌ لَّكَ مِنَ الْاُوْلٰى ؕ

5. And soon will your Guardian-Lord give you (that wherewith) you shall be well-pleased.

وَلَسَوْفَ يُعْطِيْكَ رَبُّكَ فَتَرْضٰى ؕ

6. Did He not find you an orphan and give you shelter (and care)?

اَلَمْ يَجِدْكَ يَتِيْمًا فَاٰوٰى ۙ

7. And He found you wandering, and He gave you guidance.

وَوَجَدَكَ ضَآلًّا فَهَدٰى ۙ

8. And He found you in need, and made you independent.

وَوَجَدَكَ عَآئِلًا فَاَغْنٰى ؕ

9. Therefore, do not treat the orphan with harshness,

فَاَمَّا الْيَتِيْمَ فَلَا تَقْهَرْ ؕ

10. Nor repulse the petitioner (unheard);

وَاَمَّا السَّآئِلَ فَلَا تَنْهَرْ ؕ

11. But the bounty of your Lord - rehearse and proclaim!

وَاَمَّا بِنِعْمَةِ رَبِّكَ فَحَدِّثْ ۟

94. The Expansion
In the name of Allah. Most Gracious, Most Merciful.

(٩٣) سُوْرَةُ الْاِنْشِرَاحِ مَكِّيَّةٌ (١٢)

بِسْمِ اللّٰهِ الرَّحْمٰنِ الرَّحِيْمِ

1. Have We not expanded you your breast?-

اَلَمْ نَشْرَحْ لَكَ صَدْرَكَ ۙ

2. And removed from you your burden

وَوَضَعْنَا عَنْكَ وِزْرَكَ ۙ

3. Which did gall your back?—

الَّذِيْۤ اَنْقَضَ ظَهْرَكَ ۙ

4. And raised high the esteem (in which) you (are held)?

وَرَفَعْنَا لَكَ ذِكْرَكَ ؕ

5. So, verily, with every difficulty, there is relief:

فَاِنَّ مَعَ الْعُسْرِ يُسْرًا ۙ

6. Verily, with every difficulty there is relief.

اِنَّ مَعَ الْعُسْرِ يُسْرًا ؕ

7. Therefore, when you are free (from your immediate task), still labour hard,

فَاِذَا فَرَغْتَ فَانْصَبْ ۙ

8. And to your Lord turn (all) your attention.

وَاِلٰى رَبِّكَ فَارْغَبْ ۟

95. The Fig
In the name of Allah. Most Gracious, Most Merciful.

(٩٥) سُوْرَةُ التِّيْنِ مَكِّيَّةٌ (٢٨)

بِسْمِ اللّٰهِ الرَّحْمٰنِ الرَّحِيْمِ

1. By the Fig and the Olive,

وَالتِّيْنِ وَالزَّيْتُوْنِ ۙ

2. And the Mount of Sinai,

وَطُوْرِ سِيْنِيْنَ ۙ

3. And this City of security,-

وَهٰذَا الْبَلَدِ الْاَمِيْنِ ۙ

4. We have indeed created man in the best of

لَقَدْ خَلَقْنَا الْاِنْسَانَ فِيْۤ اَحْسَنِ

SÛRAH-96
AL-'ALAQ
(INTRODUCTION)

Verses 1-5 of this Sûrah were the first direct Revelation to the Holy Prophet.

After that there was an interval or break (*Fatra*), extending over some months or perhaps over a year. S. 68 is usually considered to have been the next revelation in point of time. But the remainder of the Sûrah (96: 6-19) came soon after the *Fatra,* and that portion is joined on to the first five verses containing the command to preach, because it explains the chief obstacle to the delivery of the message to man, viz. man's own obstinacy, vanity, and insolence.

moulds,

5. Then do We abase him (to be) the lowest of the low,-

تَقْوِيْمٍ ۞

ثُمَّ رَدَدْنٰهُ اَسْفَلَ سٰفِلِيْنَ ۞

6. Except such as believe and do righteous deeds: for they shall have a reward unfailing.

اِلَّا الَّذِيْنَ اٰمَنُوْا وَعَمِلُوا الصّٰلِحٰتِ

فَلَهُمْ اَجْرٌ غَيْرُ مَمْنُوْنٍ ۞

7. Then what can, after this, contradict you, as to the judgment (to come)?

فَمَا يُكَذِّبُكَ بَعْدُ بِالدِّيْنِ ۞

8. Is not Allah the Greatest of judges?

اَلَيْسَ اللّٰهُ بِاَحْكَمِ الْحٰكِمِيْنَ ۞

96. The Clot of Congealed Blood

(٩٦) سُوْرَةُ الْعَلَقِ مَكِّيَّةٌ (١)

In the name of Allah. Most Gracious, Most Merciful.

بِسْمِ اللّٰهِ الرَّحْمٰنِ الرَّحِيْمِ

1. Read! (or proclaim!) in the name of your Lord and Cherisher, Who created-

اِقْرَاْ بِاسْمِ رَبِّكَ الَّذِيْ خَلَقَ ۞

2. Created man, out of a (mere) clot of congealed blood:

خَلَقَ الْاِنْسَانَ مِنْ عَلَقٍ ۞

3. Proclaim! And your Lord is Most Bountiful,-

اِقْرَاْ وَرَبُّكَ الْاَكْرَمُ ۞

4. He Who taught (the use of) the Pen,-

الَّذِيْ عَلَّمَ بِالْقَلَمِ ۞

5. Taught man that which he did not know.

عَلَّمَ الْاِنْسَانَ مَا لَمْ يَعْلَمْ ۞

6. Nay, but man transgresses all bounds,

كَلَّا اِنَّ الْاِنْسَانَ لَيَطْغٰى ۞

7. In that he looks upon himself as self-sufficient.

اَنْ رَّاٰهُ اسْتَغْنٰى ۞

8. Verily, to your Lord is the return (of all).

اِنَّ اِلٰى رَبِّكَ الرُّجْعٰى ۞

9. Do you see one who forbids-

اَرَءَيْتَ الَّذِيْ يَنْهٰى ۞

10. A votary when he (turns) to pray?

عَبْدًا اِذَا صَلّٰى ۞

11. Do you see if he is on (the road of) Guidance?-

اَرَءَيْتَ اِنْ كَانَ عَلَى الْهُدٰى ۞

12. Or enjoins Righteousness?

اَوْ اَمَرَ بِالتَّقْوٰى ۞

13. Do you see if he denies (Truth) and turns away?

اَرَءَيْتَ اِنْ كَذَّبَ وَتَوَلّٰى ۞

14. Does not he know that Allah sees?

اَلَمْ يَعْلَمْ بِاَنَّ اللّٰهَ يَرٰى ۞

15. Let him beware! If he does not desist We will drag him by the forelock,-

كَلَّا لَئِنْ لَّمْ يَنْتَهِ ۙ لَنَسْفَعًا بِالنَّاصِيَةِ ۞

16. A lying, sinful forelock!

نَاصِيَةٍ كَاذِبَةٍ خَاطِئَةٍ ۞

17. Then, let him call (for help) to his council (of comrades):

فَلْيَدْعُ نَادِيَهُ ۞

18. We will call on the angels of punishment (to deal with him)!

سَنَدْعُ الزَّبَانِيَةَ ۞

SÛRAH-97
AL-QADR
(INTRODUCTION)

The chronology of this Sûrah has no significance. It is probably Makkan, though some hold that it was revealed in Madinah.

The subject-matter as the mystic Night of Power (or Honour), in which Revelation comes down to a benighted world,-it may be to the wonderful Cosmos of an individual-and transforms the conflict of wrong-doing into Peace and Harmony-through the agency of the angelic host, representing the spiritual powers of the Mercy of Allah.

SÛRAH-98
AL-BAYYINAH
(INTRODUCTION)

This Sûrah was probably an early Madinah Sûrah, or possibly a late Makkan Sûrah.

In subject-matter it carries forward the argument of the last Sûrah. The mystic night of revelation is indeed blessed: but those who reject Truth are impervious to Allah's Message, however clear may bef he evidence in support of it.

19. Nay, do not obey him but bow down in adoration, and bring yourself the closer (to Allah)!

97. The Night of Power or Honour
In the name of Allah. Most Gracious, Most Merciful.

1. We have indeed revealed this (Message) in the Night of Power:

2. And what will explain to you what the Night of Power is?

3. The Night of Power is better than a thousand months.

4. Therein come down the angels and the Spirit by Allah's permission, on every errand:

5. Peace!...This until the rise of Morn!

98. The Clear Evidence
In the name of Allah. Most Gracious, Most Merciful.

1. Those who reject (Truth), among the People of the Book and among the Polytheists, were not going to depart (from their ways) until there should come to them Clear Evidence,-

2. An Apostle from Allah, rehearsing scriptures kept pure and holy:

3. Wherein are laws (or decrees) right and straight.

4. Nor did the People of the Book make schisms, until after there came to them Clear Evidence.

5. And they have been commanded no more than this: to worship Allah, offering Him sincere devotion, being true (in faith); to establish regular prayer; and to practise regular charity; and that is the Religion Right and Straight.

6. Those who reject (Truth), among the People of the Book and among the Polytheists, will be in Hell-Fire, to dwell therein (for ever). They are the worst of creatures.

7. Those who have faith and do righteous deeds,- they are the best of creatures.

كَلَّا لَا تُطِعْهُ وَاسْجُدْ وَاقْتَرِبْ ۩

سُوْرَةُ الْقَدْرِ مَكِّيَّةٌ (٩٤) (٢٥)

بِسْمِ اللهِ الرَّحْمٰنِ الرَّحِيْمِ

اِنَّآ اَنْزَلْنٰهُ فِيْ لَيْلَةِ الْقَدْرِ ۚ

وَمَآ اَدْرٰىكَ مَا لَيْلَةُ الْقَدْرِ ۚ

لَيْلَةُ الْقَدْرِ ۙ خَيْرٌ مِّنْ اَلْفِ شَهْرٍ ۛ

تَنَزَّلُ الْمَلٰٓئِكَةُ وَالرُّوْحُ فِيْهَا بِاِذْنِ رَبِّهِمْ مِّنْ كُلِّ اَمْرٍ ۚ

سَلٰمٌ ۛ هِيَ حَتّٰى مَطْلَعِ الْفَجْرِ ۞

سُوْرَةُ الْبَيِّنَةِ مَدَنِيَّةٌ (٩٨) (١٠٠)

بِسْمِ اللهِ الرَّحْمٰنِ الرَّحِيْمِ

لَمْ يَكُنِ الَّذِيْنَ كَفَرُوْا مِنْ اَهْلِ الْكِتٰبِ وَالْمُشْرِكِيْنَ مُنْفَكِّيْنَ حَتّٰى تَأْتِيَهُمُ الْبَيِّنَةُ ۙ

رَسُوْلٌ مِّنَ اللهِ يَتْلُوْا صُحُفًا مُّطَهَّرَةً ۙ

فِيْهَا كُتُبٌ قَيِّمَةٌ ۚ

وَمَا تَفَرَّقَ الَّذِيْنَ اُوْتُوا الْكِتٰبَ اِلَّا مِنْ بَعْدِ مَا جَآءَتْهُمُ الْبَيِّنَةُ ۚ

وَمَآ اُمِرُوْٓا اِلَّا لِيَعْبُدُوا اللهَ مُخْلِصِيْنَ لَهُ الدِّيْنَ ۙ حُنَفَآءَ وَيُقِيْمُوا الصَّلٰوةَ وَيُؤْتُوا الزَّكٰوةَ وَذٰلِكَ دِيْنُ الْقَيِّمَةِ ۚ

اِنَّ الَّذِيْنَ كَفَرُوْا مِنْ اَهْلِ الْكِتٰبِ وَالْمُشْرِكِيْنَ فِيْ نَارِ جَهَنَّمَ خٰلِدِيْنَ فِيْهَا ۚ اُولٰٓئِكَ هُمْ شَرُّ الْبَرِيَّةِ ۚ

اِنَّ الَّذِيْنَ اٰمَنُوْا وَعَمِلُوا الصّٰلِحٰتِ اُولٰٓئِكَ هُمْ خَيْرُ الْبَرِيَّةِ ۞

SÛRAH-99
AZ-ZILZÂL
(INTRODUCTION)

This Sûrah is close in date to the last: it is generally referred to the early Madinah period, though it may possibly be of the late makkan period.

It refers to the tremendous convulsion and uprooting which will take place when the present order of the world is dissolved and the new spiritual world of Justice and Truth takes its place. The symbol used is that of an earthquake which will shake our present material and phenomenal world to its very foundations. The mystic words in which the earthquake is described are remarkable for both power and graphic aptness. With that shaking all hidden mysteries will be brought to light.

SÛRAH-100
AL-'ADIYÂT
(INTRODUCTION)

This is one of the earlier Makkan Sûras. In the depth of its mystery and the rhythm and sublimity of its language and symbolism, it may be compared with S. 79. Its subject-matter is the irresistible nature of spiritual power and knowledge, contrasted with unregenerate man's ingratitude, pettiness, helplessness, and ignorance.

8. Their reward is with their Lord: Gardens of Eternity, beneath which rivers flow; they will dwell therein for ever; Allah well pleased with them, and they with Him: all this for such as fear their Lord and Cherisher.

جَزَآؤُهُمۡ عِنۡدَ رَبِّهِمۡ جَنّٰتُ عَدۡنٍ

تَجۡرِيۡ مِنۡ تَحۡتِهَا الۡأَنۡهٰرُ خٰلِدِيۡنَ

فِيۡهَآ أَبَدًا ۖ رَّضِيَ اللّٰهُ عَنۡهُمۡ وَرَضُوۡا

عَنۡهُ ۖ ذٰلِكَ لِمَنۡ خَشِيَ رَبَّهٗ ۞

99. The Convulsion

In the name of Allah. Most Gracious, Most Merciful.

(٩٩) سُوۡرَةُ الزِّلۡزَالِ مَدَنِيَّةٌ (٩٣)

بِسۡمِ اللّٰهِ الرَّحۡمٰنِ الرَّحِيۡمِ

1. When the earth is shaken to her (utmost) convulsion,

إِذَا زُلۡزِلَتِ الۡأَرۡضُ زِلۡزَالَهَا ۞

2. And the earth throws up her burdens (from within),

وَأَخۡرَجَتِ الۡأَرۡضُ أَثۡقَالَهَا ۞

3. And man cries (distressed): 'What is the matter with her?'-

وَقَالَ الۡإِنۡسَانُ مَالَهَا ۞

4. On that Day she will declare her tidings:

يَوۡمَئِذٍ تُحَدِّثُ أَخۡبَارَهَا ۞

5. For that your Lord will have given her inspiration.

بِأَنَّ رَبَّكَ أَوۡحٰى لَهَا ۞

6. On that Day men will proceed in companies sorted out, to be shown the deeds that they (had done).

يَوۡمَئِذٍ يَّصۡدُرُ النَّاسُ أَشۡتَاتًا ۖ لِّيُرَوۡا أَعۡمَالَهُمۡ ۞

7. Then anyone who has done an atom's weight of good, shall see it!

فَمَنۡ يَّعۡمَلۡ مِثۡقَالَ ذَرَّةٍ خَيۡرًا يَّرَهٗ ۞

8. And anyone who has done an atom's weight of evil, shall see it.

وَمَنۡ يَّعۡمَلۡ مِثۡقَالَ ذَرَّةٍ شَرًّا يَّرَهٗ ۞

100. Those that Run

In the name of Allah. Most Gracious, Most Merciful.

(١٠٠) سُوۡرَةُ الۡعٰدِيٰتِ مَكِّيَّةٌ (١٣)

بِسۡمِ اللّٰهِ الرَّحۡمٰنِ الرَّحِيۡمِ

1. By the (Steeds) that run, with panting (breath),

وَالۡعٰدِيٰتِ ضَبۡحًا ۞

2. And strike sparks of fire,

فَالۡمُوۡرِيٰتِ قَدۡحًا ۞

3. And push home the charge in the morning,

فَالۡمُغِيۡرٰتِ صُبۡحًا ۞

4. And raise the dust in clouds the while,

فَأَثَرۡنَ بِهٖ نَقۡعًا ۞

5. And penetrate forthwith into the midst (of the foe) en masse;-

فَوَسَطۡنَ بِهٖ جَمۡعًا ۞

6. Truly man is, to his Lord, ungrateful;

إِنَّ الۡإِنۡسَانَ لِرَبِّهٖ لَكَنُوۡدٌ ۞

7. And to that (fact) he bears witness (by his deeds);

وَإِنَّهٗ عَلٰى ذٰلِكَ لَشَهِيۡدٌ ۞

8. And he is violent in his love of wealth.

وَإِنَّهٗ لِحُبِّ الۡخَيۡرِ لَشَدِيۡدٌ ۞

9. Does he not know,- when that which is in the

أَفَلَا يَعۡلَمُ إِذَا بُعۡثِرَ مَا فِى

SÛRAH-101
AL-QÂRI'AH
(INTRODUCTION)

This Makkan Sûrah describes the Judgment Day as the Day of Clamour, when men will be distracted and the landmarks of this world will be lost, but every deed will be weighed in a just balance, and find its real value and setting.

SURAH-102
AT-TAKAS
(INTRODUCTION)

This probably early Makkan Sûrah gives a warning against acquisitiveness, i.e., the passion for piling up quantities or numbers, whether in the good things of this world, or in manpower or in other forms of megalomania, which leave no time or opportunity for pursuing the higher things of life.

graves is scattered abroad.

10. And that which is (locked up) in (human) breasts is made manifest-

11. That their Lord had been well-acquainted with them, (even to) that Day.?

الْقُبُورُ ۙ

وَحُصِّلَ مَا فِى الصُّدُورِ ۙ

إِنَّ رَبَّهُم بِهِمْ يَوْمَئِذٍ لَّخَبِيرٌ ۙ

سُورَةُ الْقَارِعَةِ مَكِّيَّةٌ (١٠١) (٣٠)

بِسْمِ اللّٰهِ الرَّحْمٰنِ الرَّحِيمِ

101. The Day of Noise and Clamour

In the name of Allah. Most Gracious, Most Merciful.

1. The (Day) of Noise and Clamor:

الْقَارِعَةُ ۙ

2. What is the (Day) of Noise and Clamor?

مَا الْقَارِعَةُ ۙ

3. And what will explain to you what the (Day) of Noise and Clamour is?

وَمَا أَدْرَاكَ مَا الْقَارِعَةُ ۙ

4. (It is) a Day whereon men will be like moths scattered about,

يَوْمَ يَكُونُ النَّاسُ كَالْفَرَاشِ الْمَبْثُوثِ ۙ

5. And the mountains will be like carded wool.

وَتَكُونُ الْجِبَالُ كَالْعِهْنِ الْمَنفُوشِ ۙ

6. Then, he whose balance (of good deeds) will be (found) heavy,

فَأَمَّا مَن ثَقُلَتْ مَوَازِينُهُ ۙ

7. Will be in a life of good pleasure and satisfaction.

فَهُوَ فِى عِيشَةٍ رَّاضِيَةٍ ۙ

8. But he whose balance (of good deeds) will be (found) light,-

وَأَمَّا مَنْ خَفَّتْ مَوَازِينُهُ ۙ

9. Will have his home in a (bottomless) Pit.

فَأُمُّهُ هَاوِيَةٌ ۙ

10. And what will explain to you what this is?

وَمَا أَدْرَاكَ مَا هِيَهْ ۙ

11. (It is) a Fire blazing fiercely!

نَارٌ حَامِيَةٌ ۙ

102. The Piling Up

In the name of Allah. Most Gracious, Most Merciful.

سُورَةُ التَّكَاثُرِ مَكِّيَّةٌ (١٠٢) (١٢)

بِسْمِ اللّٰهِ الرَّحْمٰنِ الرَّحِيمِ

1.The mutual rivalry for piling up (the good things of this world) diverts you (from the more serious things),

أَلْهَاكُمُ التَّكَاثُرُ ۙ

2. Until you visit the graves.

حَتَّىٰ زُرْتُمُ الْمَقَابِرَ ۙ

3. But nay, you soon shall know (the reality).

كَلَّا سَوْفَ تَعْلَمُونَ ۙ

4. Again, you soon shall know!

ثُمَّ كَلَّا سَوْفَ تَعْلَمُونَ ۙ

5. Nay, were you to know with certainty of mind, (you would beware!)

كَلَّا لَوْ تَعْلَمُونَ عِلْمَ الْيَقِينِ ۙ

6. You shall certainly see Hell-fire!

لَتَرَوُنَّ الْجَحِيمَ ۙ

7. Again, you shall see it with certainty of sight!

ثُمَّ لَتَرَوُنَّهَا عَيْنَ الْيَقِينِ ۙ

SÛRAH-103
AL-'ASR
(INTRODUCTION)

This early Makkan Sûrah refers to the testimony of Time through the Ages. All history shows that Evil came to an evil end. But Time is always in favour of those who have Faith, live clean and pure lives, and know how to wait, in patience and constancy. Cf. the theme of S. 95.

SÛRAH-104
AL-HUMAZAH
(INTRODUCTION)

This Makkan Sûrah condemns all sorts of scandal, backbiting, and selfish hoarding of wealth, as destroying the hearts and affections of men.

SÛRAH-105
AL-FÎL
(INTRODUCTION)

This early Makkan Sûrah refers to an event that happened in the year of the birth of our Holy Prophet, say, about 570 A.D. Yaman was then under the rule of the Abyssinians (Christians), who had driven out the Jewish Himyar rulers. Abraha Ashram was the Abyssinian governor or viceroy. Intoxicated with power and tired by religious fanaticism, he led a big expedition against Makkah, intending to destroy the Ka'ba. He had an elephant or elephants in his train. But his sacrilegious intentions were defeated by a miracle. No defence was offered by the custodians of the Ka'ba as the army was too strong for them, but it was believed that a shower of stones, thrown by flocks of birds, destroyed the invading army almost to a man. The stones produced sores and pustules on the skin, which spread like a pestilence.

8.   Then, you shall be questioned that Day about the joy (you indulged in!).

ثُمَّ لَتُسْئَلُنَّ يَوْمَئِذٍ عَنِ النَّعِيمِ ۝

103. Time Through the Ages
In the name of Allah. Most Gracious, Most Merciful.

(١٠٣) سُوْرَةُ الْعَصْرِ مَكِّيَّةٌ (١٣)

بِسْمِ اللّٰهِ الرَّحْمٰنِ الرَّحِيمِ

1.   By (the Token of) Time (through the ages),

وَالْعَصْرِ ۝

2.   Verily Man is in loss,

إِنَّ الْإِنْسَانَ لَفِيْ خُسْرٍ ۝

3.   Except such as have Faith, and do righteous deeds, and (join together) in the mutual teaching of Truth, and of Patience and Constancy.

إِلَّا الَّذِيْنَ اٰمَنُوْا وَعَمِلُوا الصّٰلِحٰتِ وَتَوَاصَوْا بِالْحَقِّ ۙ وَتَوَاصَوْا بِالصَّبْرِ ۝

104. The Scandal-monger
In the name of Allah. Most Gracious, Most Merciful.

(١٠٤) سُوْرَةُ الْهُمَزَةِ مَكِّيَّةٌ (٣٢)

بِسْمِ اللّٰهِ الرَّحْمٰنِ الرَّحِيمِ

1.   Woe to every (kind of) scandal-monger and backbiter,

وَيْلٌ لِّكُلِّ هُمَزَةٍ لُّمَزَةٍ ۝

2.   Who piles up wealth and lays it by counting (penny by penny).

الَّذِيْ جَمَعَ مَالًا وَّعَدَّدَهٗ ۝

3.   Thinking that his wealth would make him last for ever!

يَحْسَبُ أَنَّ مَالَهٗ أَخْلَدَهٗ ۝

4.   By no means! He will be sure to be thrown into that which breaks to pieces.

كَلَّا لَيُنْبَذَنَّ فِي الْحُطَمَةِ ۝

5.   And what will explain to you that which breaks to pieces?

وَمَا أَدْرٰىكَ مَا الْحُطَمَةُ ۝

6.   (It is) the Fire of (the Wrath of) Allah kindled (to a blaze),

نَارُ اللّٰهِ الْمُوْقَدَةُ ۝

7.   That which mounts (right) up to the Hearts:

الَّتِيْ تَطَّلِعُ عَلَى الْأَفْئِدَةِ ۝

8.   It shall be made into a vault over them,

إِنَّهَا عَلَيْهِمْ مُّؤْصَدَةٌ ۝

9.   In columns outstretched.

فِيْ عَمَدٍ مُّمَدَّدَةٍ ۝

105. The Elephant
In the name of Allah. Most Gracious, Most Merciful.

(١٠٥) سُوْرَةُ الْفِيْلِ مَكِّيَّةٌ (١٩)

بِسْمِ اللّٰهِ الرَّحْمٰنِ الرَّحِيمِ

1.   Don't you see how your Lord dealt with the Companions of the Elephant?

أَلَمْ تَرَ كَيْفَ فَعَلَ رَبُّكَ بِأَصْحٰبِ الْفِيْلِ ۝

2.   Did He not make their treacherous plan go astray?

أَلَمْ يَجْعَلْ كَيْدَهُمْ فِيْ تَضْلِيْلٍ ۝

3.   And He sent against them flights of Birds,

وَأَرْسَلَ عَلَيْهِمْ طَيْرًا أَبَابِيْلَ ۝

4.   Striking them with stones of baked clay.

تَرْمِيْهِمْ بِحِجَارَةٍ مِّنْ سِجِّيْلٍ ۙ

5.   Then He made them like an empty field of stalks and straw, (of which the corn) has been eaten up.

فَجَعَلَهُمْ كَعَصْفٍ مَّأْكُوْلٍ ۝

SÛRAH-106
QURAYSH
(INTRODUCTION)

This Makkan Sûrah may well be considered as a pendant to the last. It the Quraish were fond of Makkah and proud of it, if they profited, by its central position and its guaranteed security, from their caravans of trade and commerce, let them be grateful, adore the One True Allah, and accept His Message.

SÛRAH-107
AL-MÂ'ÛN
(INTRODUCTION)

This Sûrah-at least the first half of it-belongs to the early Makkan period. The subject-matter is the meaning of true worship, which requires Faith, the practical and helpful love of those in need, and sincerity rather than, show in devotion and charity.

SÛRAH-108
AL-KAWSAR
(INTRODUCTION)

This very brief early Makkan Sûrah sums up in the single mystic word *Kawsar* (Abundance) the doctrine of spiritual Riches through devotion and sacrifice. The converse also follows: indulgence in hatred means the cutting off of all hope of this life and the Hereafter.

SÛRAH-109
AL-KÂFIRÛN
(INTRODUCTION)

This is another early Makkan Sûrah. It defines the right attitude to those who reject Faith: in matters of Truth we can make no compromise, but there is no need to persecute or abuse anyone for his faith or belief.

106. The Tribe of Quraish

In the name of Allah. Most Gracious, Most Merciful.

1. For the covenants (of security and safeguard enjoyed) by the Quraish,
2. Their covenants (covering safe) journeys by winter and summer,-
3. Let them adore the Lord of this House,
4. Who provides them with food against hunger, and with security against fear (of danger).

107. The Neighbourly Needs

In the name of Allah. Most Gracious, Most Merciful.

1. Do you see one who denies the Judgment (to come)?
2. Then such is the (man) who repulses the orphan (with harshness),
3. And does not encourage the feeding of the indigent.
4. So woe to the worshippers,
5. Who are neglectful of their prayers,
6. Those who (want but) to be seen (of men),
7. But refuse (to supply) (even) neighbourly needs.

108. The Aundance

In the name of Allah. Most Gracious, Most Merciful.

1. To you We have granted the Fount (of Abundance).
2. Therefore, to your Lord turn in Prayer and Sacrifice.
3. For he who hates you, he will be cut off (from Future Hope)

109. Those who reject Faith

In the name of Allah. Most Gracious, Most Merciful.

1. Say : O you that reject Faith!
2. I do not worship that which you worship,
3. Nor will you worship that which I worship.

SÛRAH-110
AN-NASR
(INTRODUCTION)

This beautiful Sûrah was the last of the Sûras to be revealed *as a whole,* though the portion of the verse v. 4, "This day have I perfected your religion for you," etc., contains probably the last *words* of the Qur'ân to be revealed.

The date of this Sûrah was only a few months before the passing away of the Holy Prophet from this world, Rabi' I, A.H. 11. The place was either the precincts of Makkah at the Farewell Pilgrimage, Zulḥijja, A.H. 10, or Madinah after his return from the Farewell Pilgrimage.

Victory is the crown of service, not an occasion for exultation. All victory comes from the help of Allah.

SURAH-111
AL-MASAD ORAL-LAHAB
(INTRODUCTION)

This very early Makkan Sûrah, though it referred in the first instance to a particular incident in a cruel and relentless persecution, carries the general lesson that cruelty ultimately ruins itself. Then man who rages against holy things is burnt up in his own rage. His hands, which are the instruments of his action, perish, and he perishes himself. No boasted wealth or position will save him. The women, who are made for nobler emotions, may, if they go wrong, feed unholy rage with fiercer fuel-to their own loss. For they may twist the torturing rope round their own neck. It is a common experience that people perish by the very means by which they seek to destroy others.

SÛRAH-112
AL-IKHLÂS
(INTRODUCTION)

This early Makkan Sûrah sums up in a few terse words the Unity of the Godhead often professed, but frequently mixed up in the popular mind with debasing superstitions.

SÛRAH-13
AL-FALAQ
(INTRODUCTION)

This early Makkan Sûrah provides the antidote to superstition and fear by teaching us to seek refuge in Allah from every kind of ill arising from outer nature and from dark and evil plotting and envy on the part of others.

4. And I will not worship that which you have been wont to worship,

5. Nor will you worship that which I worship.

6. To you be your Way, and to me mine.

110. The Help
In the name of Allah. Most Gracious, Most Merciful.

1. When comes the Help of Allah, and Victory,

2. And you see the people enter Allah's Religion in crowds,

3. Celebrate the praises of your Lord, and pray for His Forgiveness: for He is Oft-Returning (in Grace and Mercy).

111. The Father of Flame
In the name of Allah. Most Gracious, Most Merciful.

1. Perish the hands of the Father of Flame! Perish he!

2. No benefit to him from all his wealth, and all his gain!

3. He will be burnt soon in a Fire of Blazing Flame!

4. And his wife, the carrier of the (crackling) wood - as fuel!-

5. A twisted rope of palm-leaf fibre round her (own) neck!

112. Purity (of Faith)
In the name of Allah. Most Gracious, Most Merciful.

1. Say: He is Allah, the One and Only;

2. Allah, the Eternal, Absolute;

3. He begets not, nor is He begotten;

4. And there is none like unto Him.

113. The Dawn
In the name of Allah. Most Gracious, Most Merciful.

1. Say: I seek refuge with the Lord of the Dawn.

SÛRAH-114
AN-NÂS
(INTRODUCTION)

This early Makkan Sûrah is a pendant to the last Sûra, and concludes the Holy Qur'ân with an appeal to us to trust in Allah, rather than man, as our sure shield and protection. It warns us specially against the secret whispers of evil within our own hearts.

2. From the mischief of created things;

3. From the mischief of Darkness as it overspreads;

4. From the mischief of those who blow on knots;

5. And from the mischief of the envious one as he practises envy.

مِنْ شَرِّ مَا خَلَقَ ۞

وَمِنْ شَرِّ غَاسِقٍ إِذَا وَقَبَ ۞

وَمِنْ شَرِّ النَّفّٰثٰتِ فِى الْعُقَدِ ۞

وَمِنْ شَرِّ حَاسِدٍ إِذَا حَسَدَ ۞

---

114. Mankind

In the name of Allah. Most Gracious, Most Merciful.

(١١٤) سُوْرَةُ النَّاسِ مَكِّيَّةٌ (٢١)

بِسْمِ اللّٰهِ الرَّحْمٰنِ الرَّحِيْمِ

1. Say: I seek refuge with the Lord (and Cherisher) of Mankind,

2. The King (or Ruler) of Mankind,

3. The God (Allah) (or Judge) of Mankind,-

4. From the mischief of the whisperer (of Evil), who withdraws (after his whisper),-

5. (The same) who whispers into the hearts of Mankind,-

6. Among Jinns and among Men.

قُلْ أَعُوْذُ بِرَبِّ النَّاسِ ۞

مَلِكِ النَّاسِ ۞

إِلٰهِ النَّاسِ ۞

مِنْ شَرِّ الْوَسْوَاسِ ۙ الْخَنَّاسِ ۞

الَّذِيْ يُوَسْوِسُ فِيْ صُدُوْرِ النَّاسِ ۞

مِنَ الْجِنَّةِ وَالنَّاسِ ۞

Prayer
(To be used after reading the Holy Qur'an)

دُعَاءِ خَتْمِ الْقُرْآن

Allahumma aanis waḥshatee fee qabree! Allahummar-ḥamnee bil-Qur-aanil-'Aẓeemi waj'alhu leee imaamañw-wa noorañw-wa

O Allah! Change my fear in my grave into love! O Allah! Have mercy on me in the name of the Great Qur'an; and make it for me a Guide and Light and

hudañw-wa raḥmah! Allahumma zakkirnee minhu maa naseetu wa 'allimnee minhu maa jahiltu warzuqnee tilaawatahooo aanaaa'al-

Guidance and Mercy! O Allah! Make me remember what of it I have forgotten; and make me know of it that which have become ignorant of; and make me recite it in the hours of

layli wa aanaaa'an-nahaari waj'alhu lee ḥujjatañy-yaa Rabbal-'aalameen.

the night and the day; and make it an argument for me O Thou Sustainer of (all) the worlds! Ameen!

Index

(Bold numerical in the reference numbers denote
Sûrah Nos. while other numerical show the *Ayât* Nos.)

Gardens with everlasting delights, 9:21

Gardens and grapeyards, 78:32

fruits of two gardens, 55:54,62

fruits of all kinds as desired, in plenty, 36:57;
37:42; 43:73; 44:55; 47:15;
55:52,68; 56:20,29,32; 77:42

fruits will be near at hand, 55:54;
69:23

fruit and meat, 52:22

flesh of fowls, 56:21

thornless lote trees and *Talh* (banana trees),
56:28,29

a running spring, 88:12

spring called *Salsabíl,* 76:18

a spring called *Káfúr,* 76:5

a spring *Tasním,* 83:27,28

a river in Paradise, *Kauthar,* 108:1

rivers of wine, milk, clarified honey, 47:15

pure sealed wine, white, delicious,
37:45,46; 56:18; 76:21; 83:25

cup, mixed with, *Zanjabíl,* 76:17;
78:34; water, 76:5

trays of gold and cups, 43:71

vessels of silver and cups of crystal, 76:15,16

green garments of fine and thick silk, 18:31;
22:23; 35:33; 44:53; 76:12,21

adorned with bracelets of gold and pearls,
18:31; 22:23; 35:33; 76:21

coaches lined with silk brocade, 55:54

green cushions and rich beautiful
mattresses, set in row, 55:76; 88:15

thrones woven with gold and precious stones,
raised high 56:15; 88:13

rich carpets spread out, 88:16

beautiful mansions, lofty rooms, one above
another, 9:72; 39:20

abiding therein forever, 3:198; 4:57;
5:119; 9:22,72; 11:108; 43:71;
57:12; 98:8

eternal home, 3:15; 35:35

facing one another on thrones, 15:47; 37:44;
44:53; 56:16

never taste death therein, 44:56

nor they (ever) be asked to leave it,
15:48

hatred or sense of injury removed from their

hearts, 7:43; 15:47

all grief removed, 35:34

no sense of fatigue, toil or weariness, 15:48;
35:35

neither will be any hurt, abdominal
pain, headache nor intoxication,
37:47; 56:19

no vain speaking nor sinful speech, 19:62;
56:25

neither harmful speech nor falsehood, 78:35;
88:11

free from sin, 37:47; 52:23

neither excessive heat nor biter cold,
76:13

there will be a known provision,
37:41; 56:89

in peace and security, 15:46; 44:51,55; 50:34

home of peace, 6:127

greetings in, 7:46; 10:10; 13:24;
14:23; 16:32; 19:62; 36:58; 39:73;
56:26

whoever does righteous deeds will
enter, 4:124; 42:22; 44:51

who kept their duty to their Lord will be led in
groups, 39:73

been made to inherit because of deeds, 43:72

Allâh is pleased with them and they with Him,
5:119

My Paradise, 89:30

the greatest bliss, 9:72

the great success, 57:12; 64:9

the supreme success, 9:72; 44:57

for believers are Gardens as an
entertainment, 32:19

dwellers of Paradise will be busy in
joyful things that Day, 36:35

will be amidst gardens and water
springs, 15:45; 19:63; 44:52; 52:17;
54:54, 55:46

see the angels surrounding the Throne, 39:75

near the Omnipotent King, 54:55

they will have all that they desire,
50:35

Hurs, chaste females with wide and
beautiful eyes, as if preserved eggs.
37:48,49; 44:54; 52:20; 55:58,70;